W44

Presented to Simon
Medical School Library —
With compliments
Nyle Hanz
Oct. 1994.

Medical Negligence

Medical Negligence

Second edition

Michael J Powers BSc MB BS DA
of Lincoln's Inn and the Inner Temple, Barrister

Nigel H Harris MA BA BChir FRCS
Honorary Consultant Orthopaedic Surgeon, St Mary's Hospital, London

Consultant editor
Andrew Lockhart-Mirams
Partner, Hempsons

Butterworths
London, Boston, Dublin, Durban, Edinburgh,
Kuala Lumpur, San Juan, Singapore, Sydney, Toronto,
Wellington
1994

United Kingdom	Butterworth & Co (Publishers) Ltd, 35 Chancery Lane, LONDON WC2A 1EL and 4 Hill Street, EDINBURGH EH2 3JZ
Australia	Butterworths, SYDNEY, MELBOURNE, BRISBANE, ADELAIDE, PERTH, CANBERRA and HOBART
Canada	Butterworths Canada Ltd, TORONTO and VANCOUVER
Ireland	Butterworth (Ireland) Ltd, DUBLIN
Malaysia	Malayan Law Journal Sdn Bhd, KUALA LUMPUR
New Zealand	Butterworths of New Zealand Ltd, WELLINGTON and AUCKLAND
Puerto Rico	Butterworth of Puerto Rico, Inc, SAN JUAN
Singapore	Butterworths Asia, SINGAPORE
South Africa	Butterworth Publishers (Pty) Ltd, DURBAN
USA	Butterworth Legal Publishers, CARLSBAD, California and SALEM, New Hampshire

A CIP Catalogue record for this book is available from the British Library.

First edition 1990
Reprinted 1991

ISBN 0 406 00452 8

Typeset in Palatino by Phoenix Photosetting, Chatham, Kent
Printed in Great Britain by The Bath Press, Avon

Foreword to the second edition

The success which the first edition of this book has deservedly enjoyed bears out the view that it fulfilled a pressing need to bring together in a single volume a comprehensive collection of specialised learning, both legal and medical, addressing the many difficult questions which commonly arise in connection with medical negligence litigation. The second edition now extends the scope of the subject matter treated by the first and will, I confidently expect, be of even greater value to the practitioner as an indispensible work of reference on the subject.

Lord Bridge of Harwich

Foreword to the first edition

Litigation in the field of medical negligence continues regrettably to grow in volume. The growth is probably attributable to two principal causes: first, the greater awareness of patients of their legal rights and a greater willingness to enforce them; secondly, the ever increasing sophistication of medical procedures. It is ironic but perhaps inevitable that the further advances medical science makes in being able to offer potential cures for conditions previously incurable or fatal, the more the medical profession lays itself open to attack in respect of the mistakes which can occur in the highly complex and delicate procedures necessary to make the cures effective. This also has the consequence that many of the issues litigated become more complex. These considerations explain the growing importance of medical negligence as a subject of concern to both the legal and the medical professions. The admirable collection of articles by highly qualified specialists in both professions published in this book makes an important and timely contribution to the literature on the subject. The stereoscopic approach of a publication which offers an overview of the problems as seen through the eyes both of lawyers and doctors will be of great value to both.

Lord Bridge of Harwich

Preface

Four years ago when this book was first published we could not have predicted that a second edition would be required so soon. It comes as no surprise to learn that the growth in medical negligence has continued its upward trend. The principal generator of medical negligence litigation is communication failure. If the medical chapters were more widely read by senior medical students and young doctors in training we believe that standards of practice would improve and the incidence of medical negligence would begin to decline.

The Health Department has kindly given us permission to record the following estimates. In 1990/91, 1,700 cases were settled at a cost of £53m; in 1991/92, 2,000 cases were settled at a cost of £58m. These figures are based on less than 100% returns and exclude ongoing legal costs of cases not yet settled. The present number of cases and the costs are certainly very much higher.

All the chapters in the first edition have been revised and some have been completely rewritten. We have acceded to the pressure to introduce into this edition a chapter on substantive law relating to medical negligence (John Finch and Robert Cowley) and we have corrected a serious omission from the first edition by including a chapter on the position in Scotland (Sheriff Dickson). A new chapter on filing suit in the United States (James Reece) is introduced and particularly worthy of mention are the extensive revisions to the chapters on consent (Sir Henry Brooke and Anthony Barton); group actions (Mark Mildred and Rodger Pannone); pecuniary compensation (Raymond Croxon QC and Colin Nixon); and settlement (Stephen Miller QC and John Frenkel).

In the medical section, changes in practice are reflected in a discussion of the risks of minimally invasive surgery which is bound to generate compensation claims as with any other innovation with inherent risks. Day case surgery has become more common and it is appropriate that the hazards are highlighted.

Claims relating to cerebral palsy continue to rise. These are amongst the most difficult and the most expensive to litigate. Complex issues of causation arise and recent research is reflected in more detailed discussion in the relevant chapters.

Many cases of litigation arise from incidents in accident and emergency departments and this subject has been extensively revised to include new material.

We hope that the additions and other changes have enhanced the value of the book for both lawyers and doctors. It is a pleasure again to record our indebtedness and thanks to Andrew Lockhart-Mirams for his continued wise advice on numerous matters. The publisher's task this time round may have been a little easier, nevertheless we are most grateful for the efficient and prompt assistance we have received in the gestation period of this edition.

May 1994

Michael J Powers
Nigel H Harris

Stop Press

Since the revision of Chapter 3 on medical complaints procedures, the Secretary of State for Health appointed a Review Committee under the Chairmanship of Professor Alan Wilson, Vice Chancellor of Leeds University. The terms of reference of the Review Committee were:

To review the procedures for making and handling of complaints by NHS patients and their families in the United Kingdom, and the costs and benefits of alternatives to current procedures, and to make recommendations to the Secretary of State for Health and other Health Ministers.

The Committee reported in May 1994 in a paper entitled 'Being Heard'. The Secretary of State has established a consultation period of three months and has indicated an intention to create new procedures by introducing legislation at an early opportunity. Any changes in the existing procedures are therefore unlikely to take effect before 1995.

Contents

Contributors

James Badenoch QC MA (Oxon)
of Lincoln's Inn and the Inner Temple

Andrew V B Bartlett QC BA (Oxon) FCIArb
of the Middle Temple

Anthony Barton
Solicitor and medical practitioner

Professor Robert Bluglass MD FRCPsych MRCP DPM
Professor of Forensic Psychiatry, University of Birmingham; Clinical Director and Consultant Forensic Psychiatrist, Reaside Clinic, Birmingham

David Body MA (Oxon)
Solicitor of the Supreme Court; Litigation Partner with Messrs Hall

Mr George Bonney MS FRCS
Honorary Consultant Orthopaedic Surgeon to St Mary's Hospital and Honorary Fellow of the Medical Defence Union

M Briggs MSc FRCS
Consultant Neurosurgeon, Radcliffe Infirmary, Oxford

Sir Henry Brooke
a Justice of the High Court, Queen's Bench Division

Professor A G M Campbell MB FRCP(Ed) DCH
Professor of Child Health, University of Aberdeen; Honorary Consultant Paediatrician, Grampian Health Board; Member of Council and Cases Committee, Medical Protection Society

Roger V Clements FRCS(Ed) FRCOG MBAE
Member, British Academy of Experts;
Consultant Obstetrician and Gynaecologist, Medical Executive Director, North Middlesex Hospital NHS Trust

Mr John R Cobbett MR FRCS
Consultant Plastic Surgeon, Regional Plastic Surgery Unit, Queen Victoria Hospital, East Grinstead

Robert Cowley
of Lincoln's Inn, Barrister

J O M C Craig FRCR FRCS FRCGP MRCP FRCSI FFR RCSI (Hon)
Honorary Consultant, St Mary's Hospital, London;
Honorary Senior Clinical Lecturer, St Mary's Hospital Medical School, London;
Member, President's Advisory Board, Medical Protection Society;
Past President, Royal College of Radiologists

Raymond Croxon QC

Dr A J Davison BA PhD MHSM

Sheriff Robert Dickson LLB WS
Sheriff of South Strathclyde, Dumfries and Galloway at Airdrie

Ian Dodds-Smith MA (Cantab)
Solicitor and Partner with McKenna & Co, London

John Finch BA (Oxon) BCL (Oxon)
Senior Lecturer in Law, Leicester University

Dr Jane Fothergill MRCP FRCS(Ed) FFAEM
Consultant in Accident and Emergency Medicine, St Mary's Hospital, London

John Frenkel BA FCA
Senior Partner, Frenkel Topping & Co, Chartered Accountants and Founding Director, Frenkel Topping Structured Settlements, Manchester

Dr F B Gibberd MA MD FRCP(Lond) FRCP(Ed)
Consultant Physician and Neurologist,
Westminster and Chelsea Hospital, London

Professor John Hankinson MB BS FRCS
Emeritus Professor of Neurosurgery, University of Newcastle upon Tyne; Honorary Consultant Neurosurgeon, Royal Victoria Infirmary and Regional Neurological Centre, Newcastle General Hospital

Mr Nigel H Harris MA MB BChir FRCS FBAE MCIArb
Honorary Consultant Orthopaedic Surgeon,
St Mary's Hospital and St Charles Hospital,
London

Professor Michael Hobsley TD MA MChir PhD DSc (med) FRCS
The David Patey Professor of Surgery, Head of the Department of Surgery, University College and Middlesex School of Medicine,
University College London

Mr Patrick J Holmes Sellors LVO MA BM BCh FRCS FRCOphth
Consultant Ophthalmic Surgeon, Croydon Eye Unit and the Royal Marsden Hospital

Dr J N Horton MB BS DA FRCA
Consultant Anaesthetist, South Glamorgan Health Authority, Honorary Clinical Teacher,
University of Wales College of Medicine

Professor Brian Jarman OBE MA PhD FRCP FRCGP
General Medical Practitioner in Westminster;
Professor of Primary Health Care,
St Mary's Hospital Medical School, London

Dr A M Jelliffe MD FRCP FRCR DCH
North East Thames Regional Cancer Co-ordinator;
Radiotherapist and Oncologist, Cromwell Hospital, London

Paul A Knapman MB BS LRCP MRCS DMJ
Barrister; HM Coroner for Inner West London at Westminster; Honorary Senior Lecturer in Community Medicine, Charing Cross and Westminster Medical School

Sir David Latham
a Justice of the High Court, Queen's Bench Division

E Anthony Machin QC BCL MA
of Lincoln's Inn, the Inner Temple and the South Eastern Circuit

Dr Kenneth D MacRae MA PhD FIS
Reader in Medical Statistics, Charing Cross and Westminster Medical School

A G D Maran MD FRCS FRCS(Ed) FRCP(Ed) FACS
Professor of Otolaryngology, Royal Infirmary, Edinburgh

Mark Mildred BA (Cantab)
Solicitor, Partner with Evans Butler Wade, London

Stephen Miller QC BA (Oxon)

Professor Keith Mortimer BDS PhD LDSRCS
Professor of Conservative Dentistry, University of London; Honorary Consultant Oral Surgeon, South West Surrey District

Robert F Nelson QC MA (Cantab)
of the Middle Temple

Colin Nixon

Rodger J Pannone
Solicitor; President of the Law Society of England and Wales; Member of the Lord Chancellor's Advisory Committee on Civil Justice; Past Member of the Supreme Court Rule Committee

Gillian Parker MA (Oxon)
Solicitor, Department of Health

Michael Powers BSc MB BS DA
of Lincoln's Inn and the Inner Temple, Barrister

James S Reece
Attorney at Law, Minnesota

Mr Peter R Riddle MS FRCS
Consultant Surgeon to St Peter's Group of Hospitals; Senior Lecturer, Institute of Urology, University of London

Professor M Rosen CBE MB ChB FCAnaes FRCOG
Honorary Consultant Anaesthetist, South Glamorgan Health Authority; Honorary Professor in Anaesthetics, University of Wales College of Medicine

Dr Lewis Rosenbloom MB FRCP DCH
Consultant Paediatric Neurologist, Liverpool;
Director of Studies in Child Development and
Handicap, Department of Child Health,
University of Liverpool

Mr John Scurr BSc MB FRCS
Consultant Surgeon, Middlesex and University
College Hospitals; Senior Lecturer in Surgery,
University of London

Arnold Simanowitz
Solicitor, Executive Director of Actions for
Victims of Medical Accidents

Professor G H Smith MB FRCS
Professor of Cardiac Surgery, University of
Sheffield, Northern General Hospital, Sheffield

Michael Spencer QC MA (Oxon)
of the Inner Temple and Midland & Oxford
Circuit

Arthur C Taylor CBE DL MA
Solicitor, Past Chairman of Newcastle Health
Authority

Mr Robin Touquet RD FRCS MRCGP FFAEM DCH
Consultant in Accident and Emergency Medicine to
St Mary's Hospital and St Charles Hospital,
London

Richard Vallance
Partner with Messrs Compton Carr

Anne Winyard MA (Oxon)
Solicitor; Partner, Leigh Day & Co

Table of statutes

References in this Table to *Statutes* are to Halsbury's Statutes of England (Fourth Edition) showing the Volume and page at which the annotated text of an Act may be found.
References in **bold** type indicate where the section of an Act is set out in part or in full.

Table of cases

D

PARA

Department of Health and Social Security v Kinnear (1984) 134 NLJ 886 .... 20.101
Derby & Co Ltd v Weldon (No 9) [1991] 2 All ER 901, [1991] 1 WLR 652 .... 10.29
Devi v West Midlands Regional Health Authority [1981] CA Transcript 491, Kemp & Kemp F5-107 .... 17.8
Devilez v Boots Pure Drug Co Ltd (1962) 106 Sol Jo 552 .... 20.21
Devon and Cornwall Housing Association Ltd v Acland Thorman and Miller-Williams (1986) 6 Con LR 41, CA 13.2
Dews v National Coal Board [1987] QB 81, [1986] 2 All ER 769, [1986] 3 WLR 227, 130 Sol Jo 553, [1986] LS Gaz R 2084, CA; affd [1988] AC 1, [1987] 2 All ER 545, [1987] 3 WLR 38, [1987] ICR 602, [1987] IRLR 330, 131 Sol Jo 840, [1987] NLJ Rep 545, [1987] LS Gaz R 2044, HL 17.30
Dexter v Courtaulds Ltd [1984] 1 All ER 70, [1984] 1 WLR 372, 128 Sol Jo 81, [1984] LS Gaz R 510, CA 17.67
Diaz v Humboldt 722 F 2d 1216 (5th Circ, 1984) 15.18
Dillon v British Gas (1989) Kemp & Kemp F2-027 .... 17.17
Dobbie v Medway Health Authority [1992] 3 Med LR 217 .... 13.13, 13.31
Donnelly v Joyce [1974] QB 454, [1973] 3 All ER 475, [1973] 3 WLR 514, 117 Sol Jo 488, [1973] 2 Lloyd's Rep 130, CA 17.4, 17.39
Donoghue v Stevenson. See M'Alister (or Donoghue) v Stevenson
Donovan v Gwentoys Ltd [1990] 1 All ER 1018, [1990] 1 WLR 472, 134 Sol Jo 910, [1990] 15 LS Gaz R 40, HL 13.30, 13.31, 13.32
Dott v Brown [1936] 1 All ER 543, 154 LT 484, 80 Sol Jo 245, CA 18.66
Doughty v North Staffordshire Health Authority [1992] 3 Med LR 81 .... 13.31
Dove v Banhams Patent Locks Ltd [1983] 2 All ER 833, [1983] 1 WLR 1436, 127 Sol Jo 748 .. 13.6
Dow Chemical Co v Castro Alfaro 786 SW 2d 674 (Tex, 1990); cert den 111 S Ct 671 (1991): 15.49
Dowling v Hyland Therapeutics 767 F Supp 57 (SDNY, 1991) 15.41, 20.104
Dowling v Richardson-Merrell Inc 727 F 2d 608 (6th Circ, 1984) 15.35
Dragon, The. See Daly v General Steam Navigation Co Ltd, The Dragon
Driscoll-Varley v Parkside Health Authority [1991] 2 Med LR 346 .... 13.13, 13.15, 13.34
Dunn v British Coal Corpn [1993] ICR 591, [1993] IRLR 396, 137 Sol Jo LB 81, [1993] 15 LS Gaz R 37, CA 11.47
Dunning v United Liverpool Hospital's Board of Governors [1973] 2 All ER 454, [1973] 1 WLR 586, 117 Sol Jo 167, CA 7.13, 7.14, 8.29

E

EMI Records Ltd v Riley [1981] 2 All ER 838, [1981] 1 WLR 923, 125 Sol Jo 412, [1981] FSR 503 .... 14.13
Eastman v London Country Bus Services Ltd (1985) Times, 23 November, CA 13.31
Eckersley v Binnie (1988) 18 Con LR 1, CA 13.7
Eddy v Inland Bay Drilling & Workover Inc 784 F Supp 370 (1992) 15.50
Edmeades v Thames Board Mills Ltd [1969] 2 QB 67, [1969] 2 All ER 127, [1969] 2 WLR 668, 113 Sol Jo 88, [1969] 1 Lloyd's Rep 221, CA 10.32
Eley v Bedford [1972] 1 QB 155, [1971] 3 All ER 285, [1971] 3 WLR 563, 115 Sol Jo 369 ...... 17.47
Ellis v Wallsend District Hospital (1989) 17 NSWLR 553, [1990] 2 Med LR 103 .... 16.35
Elsroth v Johnson and Johnson 700 F Supp 151 (1988) 20.61
Emeh v Kensington and Chelsea and Westminster Area Health Authority [1985] QB 1012, [1984] 3 All ER 1044, [1985] 2 WLR 233, 128 Sol Jo 705, CA 17.12
Empresa Lineas Maritimas Argentinas SA v Stork-Werkspoor Diesel BV 1991 US Dist LEXIS 1404 (ED La, 5 Feb 1991); affd 955 F 2d 368 (5th Circ, 1992) 15.37
Equitable Debenture Assets Corpn Ltd v William Moss Group Ltd (1984) 2 Con LR 1, 1 Const LJ 131 .... 13.7
Esson v Gloucester Health Authority (1991) unreported 11.46
Everett v Griffiths [1920] 3 KB 163, 89 LJKB 929, 123 LT 280, 84 JP 161, 36 TLR 491, 64 Sol Jo 445, 18 LGR 293, CA; affd [1921] 1 AC 631, 90 LJKB 737, 125 LT 230, 85 JP 149, 37 TLR 481, 65 Sol Jo 395, 19 LGR 283, HL 16.31
Every v Miles [1964] CA Transcript 261 .... 17.6
Eyre v Measday [1986] 1 All ER 488, [1986] NLJ Rep 91, CA 1.23

F

F, Re [1988] Fam 122, [1988] 2 All ER 193, [1988] 2 WLR 1288, [1988] FCR 529, [1988] 2 FLR 307, [1988] Fam Law 337, 132 Sol Jo 820, [1988] NLJR 37, CA 12.65

PARA

M

S

X

Y

Z

CHAPTER 1

The law

John Finch
Robert Cowley *Barrister*

SUMMARY

THE LEGAL CONTEXT OF PROFESSIONAL LIABILITY

1.1 In his book *The Discipline of Law* (1979) Lord Denning wrote that 'an action for negligence against a doctor is for him unto a dagger. His professional reputation is as dear to him as his body, perhaps more so, and an action for negligence can wound his reputation as severely as a dagger can his body.' He was quoting from his own direction to the jury in the case of *Hatcher v Black*.[1] In that case the plaintiff's vocal cords were badly damaged during an operation, carefully performed, on a toxic thyroid gland. The plaintiff's physician (though not her surgeon) had reassured the plaintiff prior to the operation that there was no risk to her voice. There was, and that risk materialised. She was under contract to the BBC as a singer and after the operation she could not broadcast again.

1 (1954, unreported).

1.2 Denning LJ, as he then was, continued to guide the jury's consideration of the doctor's professionai conduct thus:

> You must not, therefore, find him negligent simply because something happens to go wrong; if, for instance, one of the risks inherent in an operation actually takes away the benefits that were hoped for, or if in a matter of opinion he makes an error of judgment. You should only find him guilty of negligence when he falls short of the standard of a reasonably skilful medical man, in short, when he is deserving of censure – for negligence in a medical man is deserving of censure.

1.3 There was much to say, even in 1954, about the picture of professional medical liability so outlined. There is even more to say now, and indeed by 1979, when Lord Denning quoted his own words uttered a quarter of a century earlier, this reassuring picture was ceasing to represent the law.

1.4 This chapter examines the three elements of the tort of negligence: duty of care, breach of that duty by failure to display an acceptable level of professional conduct, and damage or injury in consequence of that breach of duty. These are essential elements of the tort of negligence which may occasionally present difficulty to parties to litigation, both plaintiff and defendant, even in otherwise straightforward road traffic accidents, or 'knocking down' cases. In the context of alleged medical negligence, or 'medical malpractice' as it is sometimes called, each one of these essential elements of negligence may present parties to litigation with formidable obstacles to surmount and complex research to pursue.

THE DUTY OF CARE

The physician

1.5 The issue of whether a physician owes the plaintiff a duty of care rarely (if ever) presents a difficulty in the context of a medical negligence claim. That duty arises, not solely by reason of the concepts of foreseeability and proximity, but by virtue of the doctor–patient relationship itself. Accordingly, a doctor may incur liability in respect of an omission once that relationship has come into being, or put another way he has accepted a responsibility towards the patient.

If a person holds himself out as possessing special skill and knowledge and he is consulted, as possessing such skill and knowledge, by or on behalf of a patient, he owes a duty to the patient to use due caution in undertaking the treatment. If he accepts the responsibility and undertakes the treatment and the patient submits to his direction and treatment accordingly, he owes a duty to the patient to use diligence, care, knowledge, skill and caution in administering the treatment. No contractual relation is necessary, nor is it necessary that the service be rendered for reward.[1]

1 Per Hewitt CJ, in *R v Bateman* (1925) 94 LJKB 791 at 794. Equally that acceptance of responsibility may (arguably) arise by virtue of the physician's contract with the National Health Service.

Institutional health care providers

1.6 Health authorities and National Health Service trust hospitals clearly owe a vicarious duty of care to patients in respect of the acts and omissions of their staff committed in the course of their employment.[1] It is equally well established that institutional health care providers owe to patients a direct duty of care identical to that of their clinicians.

In my opinion authorities who run a hospital, be they local authorities, government boards, or any other corporation, are in law under the self same duty as the humblest doctor; whenever they accept a patient for treatment, they must use reasonable care and skill to cure him of his ailment. The hospital authorities cannot, of course, do it by themselves: they have no ears to listen through the stethoscope, and no hands to hold the surgeon's knife. They must do it by the staff which they employ; and if their staff are negligent in giving the treatment, they are just as liable for that negligence as is anyone else who employs others to do his duties for him. . . . I take it to be clear law, as well as good sense, that, where a person is himself under a duty to use care, he cannot get rid of his responsibility by delegating the performance of it to someone else, no matter whether the delegation be to a servant under a contract of service or to an independent contractor under a contract for services.[2]

1 *Gold v Essex County Council* [1942] 2 All ER 237; *Razzel v Snowball* [1954] 3 All ER 429.
2 Per Denning LJ, in *Cassidy v Ministry of Health* [1951] 2 KB 343 at 356.

1.7 The liability of the health authority or trust hospital, whether vicarious or *Cassidy* direct, is thus dependent upon the breach of duty on the part of an individual health care professional. To that extent the duty, so far as a plaintiff is concerned, is solely concerned with the practicality of who pays and how they approach and defend claims.

1.8 However, it is additionally possible, following the decision of the Court of Appeal in *Wilsher v Essex Area Health Authority*,[1] that a provider unit, be it a health authority, trust hospital or private sector health care provider may be primarily and even exclusively liable for its failure to institute and maintain a safe system of health care provision without there being fault on the part of any health care professional.

1 [1986] 3 All ER 801.

1.9 In this case, a house officer working in an intensive care neonatal unit inserted a catheter into a vein rather than an artery. This caused a misleading blood/oxygen reading to be given with the result that the child was over-oxygenated.

1.10 Whilst no health care practitioner is able in law to shift the burden of liability entirely to another if personal judgment ought to have identified a faulty instruction, the managers of any provider unit cannot shift the blame if they are themselves at fault. As Sir Nicholas Browne-Wilkinson (as he then was), observed:

In my judgment, a health authority which so conducts its hospital that it fails to provide doctors of sufficient skill and experience to give the treatment offered at the hospital may be directly liable in negligence to the patient. Although we were told in argument that no case has ever been decided on this ground and that it is not the practice to formulate claims in this way, I can see no reason why, in principle, the health authority should not be so liable if its organisation is at fault.[1]

1 Ibid at 833 h–j.

1.11 By way of pointing to some of the organisational and legal difficulties which may beset provider units, which are inevitably cash-limited and must act within their budget, Sir Nicholas Browne-Wilkinson continued:

Claims against a health authority that it has itself been directly negligent, as opposed to vicariously liable for the negligence of its doctors, will, of course, raise awkward questions. To what extent should the authority be liable if (e g in the case of a junior houseman) it is only adopting a practice hallowed by tradition? Should the authority be liable if it demonstrates that, due to the financial stringency under which it operates, it cannot afford to fill the posts with those possessing the necessary experience? But, in my judgment, the law should not be distorted by making findings of personal fault against individual doctors who are, in truth, not at fault in order to avoid such questions. To do so would be to cloud the real issues which arise. In the modern world with its technological refinements is it sensible to persist in making compensation for those who suffer from shortcomings in technologically advanced treatment depend on proof of fault, a process which the present case illustrates can consume years in time and huge sums of money in costs? Given limited resources, what balance is to be struck in the allocation of such resources between compensating those whose treatment is not wholly successful and the provision of required treatment for the world at large? These are questions for Parliament, not the courts. But I do not think the courts would do society a favour by distorting the existing law so as to conceal the real social questions which arise.[1]

1 Ibid at 833j–834c.

1.12 The legal implications of such social and financial considerations are indeed complex and challenging. Given the increasing attention being paid in the 1990s to economic aspects of health care provision, with cash-limited budgets, indicative prescribing and the like, it is possible that the courts will shortly be faced with negligence questions of a different order from those which have hitherto been determined.

1.13 However, it is likely that these issues will be approached by drawing a (perhaps artificial) distinction between the exercise of the duty at a policy level and that at operational level.[1]

1 See, for example, Lord Wilberforce in *Anns v Merton Borough Council* [1978] AC 728 at 758.

1.14 A claim at common law based on conduct falling within the policy arena will only lie if, as a prerequisite, the plaintiff can show that the act complained of was not within the limits of a discretion bona fide exercised under the relevant power.[1]

1 *Fellows v Rother District Council* [1983] 1 All ER 513.

1.15 An example of a case falling clearly within the 'policy arena' is provided by *R v Secretary of State for Social Services, ex p Hincks*.[1] The applicants were orthopaedic patients at a hospital in Birmingham who had waited for treatment for periods longer than was medically advisable, because of a shortage of facilities arising, in part, from a decision not to build a new block at the hospital on grounds of cost. The applicants sought declarations that the Secretary of State, the Regional Health Authority and Area Health Authority were in breach of their obligations under section 1 of the National Health Service Act 1977 to continue to promote a comprehensive health service designed to secure improvement in health and the prevention of illness, and under section 3 to provide accommodation, facilities and services for those purposes. It was held by Wien J that it was not the court's function to direct Parliament what funds to make available to the health service and how to allocate them. The Secretary of State's duty under section 3, to provide services 'to such extent as he considers necessary' gave him a broad discretion as to the disposition of financial resources. The court could only interfere if the Secretary had acted so as to frustrate the policy of the Act or had acted as no reasonable Minister could have acted. No such breach had been established and accordingly the applications failed.

1 (1979) 123 Sol Jo 436. See also *R v Central Birmingham Health Authority, ex p Walker* (1987) 3 BMLR 32, CA.

1.16 However, as Lord Wilberforce noted in *Anns v Merton*, 'the more "operational" a power or duty may be, the easier it is to superimpose upon it a common law duty of care'.[1] It may be true that few operational decisions do not include some element of policy. The distinction appears to be one of fact and degree. Within the National Health Service such a distinction is increasingly being made with 'purchasers' and 'providers'. An action against a provider in respect of its institutional failings, be it failure to provide sufficient staff or suitable equipment, is likely to be more easily classified as being within the operational arena as opposed to being one of policy.

1 [1978] AC 728 at 754.

1.17 Whilst Sir Nicholas Browne-Wilkinson said in *Wilsher* that certain questions are for Parliament, and not for the courts, it is likely that the courts will remain unable to escape the burden of determination of negligence when resources even with imposed restrictions have allegedly been incompetently managed.

1.18 Despite the problems involved in distinguishing between policy and operational decisions, a *Wilsher* type claim is important in three respects.

1.19 Firstly, in a given case it may not be possible to identify and establish negligence on the part of an individual physician who may, for example, be faced with more patients who demand attention than he can reasonably be expected to cope with at any one time, or be lacking in the equipment he requires.

1.20 Secondly, once conduct has been classified as falling within the operational arena, the courts may be more willing to find negligence on the part of the institutional provider than they would on the part of the individual physician. Compliance with any recognised and properly accepted procedure would in practice be fatal to a claim against an individual physician.[1] It is far less likely to be so where the claim is being brought against an institution.

1 See paras **1.64–6** below.

1.21 Thirdly, the standard of proof required to establish negligence on the part of the professional man is an onerous one.[1] Again, the courts may be prepared to accept a lower standard of proof where the allegation is being made against an institution.

1 See paras **1.62–3** below.

Liability in contract

1.22 The increasing role of the private sector in the field of health care provision makes it increasingly important for practitioners to consider the possibility of framing a claim both in tort and contract.

1.23 The courts will readily find an implied term that the physician will use reasonable skill and care in his examination, diagnosis and treatment of the patient. However, it is clear that the courts will be very slow to find that the representations of the physician constitute a warranty or guarantee of a certain result, as opposed to mere 'therapeutic reassurance'.[1]

1 *Eyre v Measday* [1986] 1 All ER 488; *Thake v Maurice* [1986] 1 All ER 499. Moreover, if the patient is being treated under a private health insurance plan, it is unlikely that any such representations could be contractual terms, their being likely to have been made post contract.

1.24 Framing such a claim in contract would not materially assist the plaintiff in his claim, the extent of the duty being identical in practical content to that imposed by the law of torts.

1.25 Nevertheless, it is possible for a doctor to give a contractual warranty that he will achieve a certain result.

I accept that there may be cases where, because of the claims made by a surgeon or physician for his method of treatment, the court is driven to the conclusion that the result of the treatment is guaranteed or warranted.[1]

1 Per Neill LJ, *Thake v Maurice* (para **1.23** above) at 510 e–f.

1.26 Whilst each case will of course turn on its own facts, it is likely that the courts will more readily accept the existence of a contractual warranty, the more removed the contract is from therapeutic treatment. An example of this is provided by the Canadian authority of *La Fleur v Cornelis*.[1]

1 (1979) 28 NBR (2d) 569 (NBSC).

1.27 The plaintiff entered into a contract with the defendant, a plastic surgeon, for the reduction of her nose. He drew her a sketch to illustrate the changes he would make and told her that there would be 'no problem' and that she would be 'very happy'. However, the plaintiff was left with scarring and deformity. Barry J, whilst accepting that the courts should be slow to find any representations to constitute contractual terms, was, on the facts of the case, prepared to find that there had been a collateral warranty as to the success of the operation. It is quite clear from his judgment that in doing so he had particular regard to the nature of the service, equating the surgeon more with the businessman providing a product than the physician providing treatment.

1.28 The situation where a parallel claim in contract is likely to be most advantageous is where the contract also involves the supply of goods such as drugs, prosthetics etc. Once it can be established that the product is either of unmerchantable quality or not reasonably fit for its purpose,[1] a claim framed in contract obviates the need to establish fault on the part of the supplier. The 'consumer' may, in the absence of a contractual relationship, have a claim against the supplier under the Consumer Protection Act 1987 where the 'product' is 'defective'. However, a claim in contract has two distinct advantages over a claim under the Consumer Protection Act 1987. Firstly, the contractual duty imposed on a supplier is higher than that imposed on a producer by the Act. A product may therefore not be reasonably fit for its purpose and yet not be 'defective' for the purposes of the Consumer Protection Act 1987.[2] Secondly, the supplier of a product has various statutory defences available to him which are not available when the parties enjoy a contractual relationship.[3]

1 See: Sale of Goods Act 1979, s14; and Supply of Goods and Services Act 1982, s9.
2 A product will only be defective where 'the safety of the product is not such as persons generally are entitled to expect' (s3). An example of a claim that would be likely to succeed in

contract but not under the Consumer Protection Act 1987 is where a patient is provided with ill-fitting dentures: see *Samuels v Davis* [1943] KB 526.

3 See now Consumer Protection Act 1987, s4.

BREACH OF DUTY

1.29 The classic statement of negligence is that laid down by Alderson B in *Blyth v Birmingham Waterworks Co*:[1]

> Negligence is the omission to do something which a reasonable man, guided upon those considerations which ordinarily regulate the conduct of human affairs, would do, or doing something which a prudent and reasonable man would not do.[2]

1 (1856) 11 Ex Ch 781.

2 Ibid at 784.

1.30 Within this test are two requirements. First, the appropriate standard of care must be determined; secondly, the plaintiff must establish that the conduct in question fell below that ascertained standard. Because of the particular characteristics of a medical negligence claim, each of these elements merits separate consideration.

ASCERTAINING THE STANDARD OF CARE

1.31 There can be no doubt that the requisite standard of care must be determined by a legal standard framed by the courts, not by the medical profession. Considerable respect is, however, paid to the practices of the profession, and judicial notice taken of them.

1.32–3 This was recognised in the classic direction of McNair J to a jury in *Bolam v Friern Hospital Management Committee*[1] (now widely referred to as the *Bolam* test):

> A doctor is not guilty of negligence if he has acted in accordance with a practice accepted as proper by a responsible body of medical men skilled in that particular art. . . . Putting it the other way round, a doctor is not negligent, if he is acting in accordance with such a practice, merely because there is a body of opinion which takes a contrary view.[2]

1 [1957] 2 All ER 118.

2 Ibid at 122.

1.34 Despite attempts by Lord Denning to redefine medical negligence as something other than an error of judgment,[1] the *Bolam* test is now uniformly applied to all aspects of the doctor–patient relationship.[2] The only gloss that has been added to the test being that the practice accepted as proper by a responsible body of medical men must be 'rightly' so accepted.[3]

1 See for example *Whitehouse v Jordan* [1980] 1 All ER 650 at 658.

2 '. . . this general duty is not subject to dissection into a number of component parts to which different criteria of what satisfied the duty of care apply, such as diagnosis, treatment and advice', per Lord Diplock in *Sidaway v Board of Governors of the Bethlem Royal and Maudsley Hospital* [1984] QB 493, [1984] 1 All ER 1018. In the context of diagnosis see: *Maynard v West Midlands Regional Health Authority* [1984] 1 WLR 634.

3 *Sidaway v Board of Governors of the Bethlem Royal and Maudsley Hospital* [1984] 2 WLR 778 at 792, CA endorsed by Lord Bridge in the House of Lords [1985] 2 WLR 480 at 505.

1.35 In extreme cases, however, the courts are prepared to reject an established practice shown to be manifestly wrong. One such case is *Clarke v Adams.*[1] The plaintiff was severely burned during a course of heat treatment administered by a physiotherapist. The defendant warned him of the danger in the manner approved by the Chartered Society of Physiotherapists. Nevertheless, the court was prepared to find the warning to be inadequate properly to safeguard the patient.

1 (1950) 94 Sol Jo 599.

1.36 For all practical purposes, compliance by a physician with an accepted practice will be fatal to a medical negligence claim, the legal requirement to display the ordinary skill and competence to be expected of the particular practitioner concerned being a minimalist requirement. Insofar as decided cases on medical liability form a template for future action, their content focuses on incompetence rather than failure to aspire to excellent practice. In this sense, the law sets the lowest level of responsibility below which legal liability for negligence will be imposed.

Particular aspects of the standard of care

The specialist

1.37 It is inherent within the *Bolam* test itself that the specialist is expected to achieve the standard of care of the reasonably competent specialist practising in that field. This was recognised by Lord Bridge in *Sidaway v Governors of the Bethlem Royal Hospital*:

> The language of the *Bolam* test clearly requires a different degree of skill from a specialist in his own special field than from a general practitioner. In the field of neuro-surgery it would be necessary to substitute for the . . . phrase 'no doctor of ordinary skill', the phrase 'no neuro-surgeon of ordinary skill'. All this is elementary, and . . . firmly established law.[1]

1 [1985] 1 All ER 643 at 660 f–g.

1.38 The more skills a person in a specialist field possesses, the higher the standard of skill expected of him. However, he is not required to attain the highest degree of skill and competence, merely a reasonable level of skill within that field. The *Bolam* test will therefore be applied simply by substituting surgeon, dermatologist etc in the place of doctor without gloss either way.[1]

1 Kilner Brown J, in *Ashcroft v Mersey Regional Health Authority* [1983] 2 All ER 245.

Inexperience

1.39 The standard of care expected of the reasonable man is objective, paying no regard to the frailties, idiosyncrasies or weaknesses of the defendant.[1] Accordingly, inexperience will afford no defence to an allegation of negligence.[2] This was recently confirmed by the Court of Appeal in the context of medical negligence in *Wilsher v Essex Area Health Authority.*[3]

1 *Glasgow Corpn v Muir* [1943] AC 448.
2 *Nettleship v Weston* [1971] 2 QB 691.
3 [1988] 1 All ER 871.

1.40 A house officer acquiring training and experience in an intensive care neonatal unit inserted a catheter into a vein rather than an artery. The position of the catheter was checked by means of an X-ray. However, the doctor failed to recognise his mistake (as too did the registrar who was requested to check it had been done correctly). A misleading blood oxygen reading was given, as a result of which the plaintiff was administered excess oxygen.

1.41 The Court of Appeal held that the house officer had, by consulting his superior, discharged the standard of care expected of him. However, the Court went on to state (Sir Nicholas Browne-Wilkinson VC dissenting) that the law requires the trainee or learner to be judged by the same standards as his more experienced colleagues.

> To my mind, this notion of a duty tailored to the actor, rather than to the act which he elects to perform, has no place in the law of tort. Indeed, the defendants did not contend that it could be justified by any reported authority on the general law of tort. Instead, it was suggested that the medical profession is a special case. Public hospital medicine has always been organised so that young doctors and nurses learn on the job. If the hospitals abstained from using inexperienced people, they could not staff their wards and theatres, and the junior staff could never learn. The longer-term interests of patients as a whole are best served by maintaining the present system, even though this may diminish the legal rights of the individual patient for, after all, medicine is about curing, not litigation.
>
> I acknowledge the appeal of this argument, and recognise that a young hospital doctor who must get onto the wards in order to qualify without necessarily being able to decide what kind of patient he is going to meet is not in the same position as another professional man who has a real choice whether or not to practise in a particular field. Nevertheless, I cannot accept that there should be a special rule for doctors in public hospitals; I emphasise public, since presumably those employed in private hospitals would be in a different category. Doctors are not the only people who gain their experience, not only from lectures or from watching others perform, but from tackling live clients or customers, and no case was cited to us which suggested that any such variable duty of care was imposed on others in a similar position. To my mind, it would be a false step to subordinate the legitimate expectation of the patient that he will receive from each person concerned with his care a degree of skill appropriate to the task which he undertakes to an understandable wish to minimise the psychological and financial pressures on hard-pressed young doctors.
>
> For my part, I prefer the third of the propositions which have been canvassed. This relates the duty of care, not to the individual, but to the post which he occupies. I would differentiate 'post' from 'rank' or 'status'. In a case such as the present, the standard is not just that of the averagely competent and well-informed junior houseman (or whatever the position of the doctor) but of such a person who fills a post in a unit offering a highly specialised service. But, even so, it must be recognised that different posts make different demands. If it is borne in mind that the structure of hospital medicine envisages that the lower ranks will be occupied by those of whom it would be wrong to expect too much the risk of abuse by litigious patients can be mitigated, if not entirely eliminated.[1]

1 [1986] 3 All ER 801, per Mustill LJ at 813 d–j.

1.42 His Lordship's reasoning must surely be compelling. The patient's right to complain would be more limited if, by chance, he were treated by a less experienced doctor than the patient in the next bed. Not only would this result in inconsistency, but in inexperience being frequently proffered as a defence.

Prevention of the self-infliction of harm

1.43 A case of liability for self-harm by a patient is *Selfe v Ilford and District Hospital Management Committee*.[1] A 17-year-old patient was admitted to what was in fact a general ward after having taken an overdose of sleeping pills. He was put on the ground floor with an open window at the back of his bed, which was grouped with the beds of three other patients who had demonstrated suicidal tendencies. He absconded through the window and climbed some steps onto a roof from which he threw himself, sustaining serious injuries. The health authority was negligent, and the judge observed that the duty of those in charge of such a patient included the duty to avoid actions by the patient himself which could foreseeably occur and cause self-inflicted harm.

1 (1970) 114 Sol Jo 935.

1.44 The outcome of the *Selfe* case has clear implications also for staffing levels. There had been three nurses on duty in the ward to which Mr Selfe was admitted, and each of them knew that he presented a risk of suicide and had to be kept under constant observation. In addition to the charge nurse there was another nurse who, just before the occurrence which gave rise to this action, had gone to the lavatory without informing the charge nurse. The third on duty, a nursing auxiliary, went into the ward kitchen and was out of vision of the patient. The charge nurse answered a call for assistance by another patient, with the result that none of the staff was observing Mr Selfe. The judge was highly critical of the ward organisation, saying that the incident should never have been allowed to happen, and would not have happened if three or even two nurses had been in the ward keeping Mr Selfe under observation. The case further demonstrates the propositions offered above relating to the management of limited resources, and demonstrates that the management of a provider unit has a legal duty to institute and maintain a safe system of working conditions.

1.45 On the other hand, not all judicial decisions on suicide or self-harm have resulted in the finding of negligence. In *Thorne v Northern Group Hospital Management Committee*[1] the action was brought against the defendant authority by the husband of the deceased who had committed suicide. The deceased was being nursed in a medical ward of a general hospital. Her husband informed the ward sister that she had threatened suicide, and arrangements were instituted to transfer her to a psychiatric unit on account of suspected depression. The deceased somehow managed to leave the hospital unobserved, went home and committed suicide. An allegation of negligence against the hospital and its staff, in particular the nurses, failed. Edmund Davies J, as he then was, stated that the degree of care and supervision required of hospital staff in relation to a patient with known or suspected suicidal tendencies is clearly greater than that called for in relation to patients generally. But, he asked:

> Could it be said that a member of the hospital staff should have remained constantly in sight of the patient until she had departed for the neurosis unit, and ought they to have reasonably foreseen that she might make an unannounced departure from the ward or hospital, or, in some other way, do something harmful to herself?

1 (1964) 108 Sol Jo 484.

1.46 Perhaps surprisingly by modern standards of observation, including that one-to-one observation known in psychiatric practice as 'specialling', the answer was adverse to the plaintiff. His Lordship observed:

As later events showed, the patient was set upon making her escape for the purpose of self-destruction, and it was highly conceivable that she kept a wary eye on the nurses and seized her opportunity immediately their backs were turned and they had absented themselves temporarily.

1.47 That did not, he held, connote negligence on the part of the nurses. The defendant health authority was therefore not liable in negligence.

Disclosure of risks

1.48 The tendency of English courts had been to regard the practitioner's duty of care as an indivisible monolith not susceptible of breakdown into constituent parts. The result has been that the standard of acceptable skill and competence laid down in the case of *Bolam v Friern Hospital Management Committee*[1] has been held to govern all aspects of the practitioner–patient relationship, from initial information, through diagnosis and advice, to treatment and aftercare. In *Bolam*'s case the plaintiff was a psychiatric patient in receipt of electro-convulsive therapy in a psychiatric hospital. There was, it was later held reasonably, disagreement between medical practitioners as to whether ECT should be given 'straight', that is without restraint in any form; or whether it should be given in a 'modified' form, namely following the administration of a mild anaesthetic; or whether, in the absence of anaesthetic, there should be mechanical restraint such as straps round the limbs during the course of administration. McNair J directed the jury thus:

You have to make up your minds whether it has been proved to your satisfaction that when the defendants adopted the practice they did (namely, the practice of saying very little and waiting for questions from the patient), they were falling below a proper standard of competent professional opinion on the question of whether or not it is right to warn.[2]

1 [1957] 2 All ER 118.
2 Ibid at 126.

1.49 While, as is pointed out in a separate chapter of this book, the law has moved on in respect of the question of enquiring or non-enquiring patients, it has been accepted ever since the *Bolam* decision that the practical contents of a practitioner's duty of care to a patient are an indivisible whole. Lord Diplock observed in the case of *Sidaway v Bethlem Royal Hospital Governors*:[1]

In English jurisprudence the doctor's relationship with his patient which gives rise to the normal duty of care to exercise his skill and judgment to improve that patient's health in any particular respect in which the patient has sought aid has hitherto been treated as a single comprehensive duty covering all the ways in which a doctor is called on to exercise his skill and judgment in the improvement of the physical or mental condition of the patient for which his services as a general practitioner or as a specialist have been engaged. This general duty is not subject to dissection into a number of component parts to which different criteria of what satisfied the duty of care apply, such as diagnosis, treatment and advice (including warning of any risks of something going wrong, however skilfully the treatment advised is carried out).

The *Bolam* case itself embraced failure to advise the patient of the risk involved in the electric shock treatment as one of the allegations of negligence against the surgeon as well as negligence in the actual carrying out of treatment in which that risk did result in injury to the patient. The same criteria applied to both these aspects of the surgeon's duty of care. In modern medicine and surgery such a dissection of the various things a doctor has to do in the exercise of his whole duty of care owed to his patient is neither legally meaningful nor medically practical.

1 [1985] 1 All ER 643 at 667h–668b.

1.50 So influential has the *Bolam* approach to accepted practice been on even the initial imparting of information to a patient, that Lord Diplock continued to state that:

No convincing reason has in my view been advanced before your Lordships that would justify treating the *Bolam* test as doing anything less than laying down a principle of English law that is comprehensive and applicable to every aspect of the duty of care owed by a doctor to his patient in the exercise of his healing functions with respect to that patient.[1]

1 Ibid at 668 b–d.

1.51 Nevertheless, the Supreme Court of Canada observed in *Reibl v Hughes*[1] that:

Merely because medical evidence establishes the reasonableness of a recommended operation does not mean that a reasonable person in the patient's position would necessarily agree to it, if proper disclosure had been made of the risks attendant upon it, balanced by those against it.

Laskin CJ observed:

To allow expert medical evidence to determine what risks are material and, hence, should be disclosed and, correlatively, what risks are not material is to hand over to the medical profession the entire question of the scope of the duty of disclosure, including the question whether there has been a breach of that duty.

1 (1981) 114 DLR (3d) 1.

1.52 While expert medical evidence is, of course, relevant to findings as to the risks which reside in or result from recommended surgery or other treatment, what was under consideration in that case, in the view of the court, was 'the patient's right to know what risks are involved in undergoing or foregoing certain surgery or other treatment'.

1.53 The English courts have not adopted this position; and indeed in the *Sidaway* case Lord Bridge observed[1] that he did not see that the *Bolam* test necessarily involved this conclusion. He added that

a decision what degree of disclosure of risks is best calculated to assist a particular patient to make a rational choice whether or not to undergo a particular treatment must primarily be a matter of clinical judgment.

1 [1985] 1 All ER 643 at 673.

1.54 The strength of Laskin CJ's proposition, and the fallacy which is apt to follow from the approach taken by Lord Bridge, is evident from a clear separation of the question of whether a duty of care, or legal connection, exists between practitioner and patient; and the question, given its existence, whether that duty has been broken resulting in injury to the patient. The *Bolam* test was originally intended as, and has always been, a test of professional competence within the confines of a given duty, such as to avoid a negligent failure to measure up to that minimum standard of care. That adopted by Lord Bridge in the *Sidaway* case is apt to result in the *Bolam* test going beyond its proper confines, and becoming constitutive of the practical contents of the duty of care itself. As is evident from the explanation of consent in Chapter 12 of this book, English law proceeds from the principle of self-determination or autonomy, and not from the principle of paternalism, as far as concerns rightful or wrongful intervention with the body of the patient. The facts of the *Bolam* case itself are unrepresentative of the general principle given that it involved a patient whose mental processes were affected by pyschiatric disorder. In the case of a patient of sound mind or ordinary understanding, the question as to what is to be done to the patient's body must at least in part rest with the patient himself. That is to say, while medical choices, including the assessment of clinical risks as established by statistics, are part of the medical practitioner's expertise, the effect which the materialisation of such a risk might produce as a consequence in a patient's life is a matter of patient choice and not clinical expertise.

1.55 Nowhere is this proposition clearer than in the decision in the Supreme Court of New South Wales in *Rogers v Whittaker*.[1] The plaintiff, aged 48 at the time of an operation, had been almost totally blind in her right eye from the age of nine on account of an injury which occurred at that age. Her left eye was normal. The defendant opthalmic surgeon advised her that he could operate on her affected eye to improve its sight. The plaintiff was accustomed to living with her limited vision, and so she made it very clear to the defendant practitioner that she wanted to know exactly what risk the proposed procedure entailed.

1 [1992] 3 Med LR 331 (since upheld by the High Court of Australia).

1.56 Her questioning included a desire to be warned of the possible consequences of the operation, though she did not specifically ask whether the procedure might adversely affect the sight in her good eye. There was in fact a chance of 1 in 14,000, as clinically statistically assessed, of the onset of sympathetic ophthalmia consequent on the operation. The defendant practitioner did not mention the existence of this risk. Had he done so, the plaintiff would not have accepted the risk and would not have consented to the proposed procedure. Following the operation, sympathetic ophthalmia indeed resulted, and the plaintiff lost the sight in her good eye. Within two years of the procedure she had become almost totally blind. The Supreme Court of New South Wales (later upheld by the Australian High Court) upheld the trial judge's finding that the defendant had failed to exercise reasonable skill and care in answering the plaintiff's general question about possible complications by failing to mention the admittedly low risk of sympathetic ophthalmia occurring in her good eye. Mahoney J said:

> For myself, I think it should be clear that if a patient makes it plain to her medical practitioner that she desires to be told or warned of a particular thing, it is in principle a breach of duty by the medical practitioner not to tell her. There are of course

obvious limits and qualifications to this. There may be some questions to which the answer may be 'I do not know'. There may be cases in which the condition of the patient, for example, in the emotional or psychiatric sense, is such that there is a compelling medical reason why the answer should not be given.

1.57 Of the latter case, the particular circumstances of *Bolam* itself are a good example. But his Lordship said that it was not necessary to pursue the circumstances in which such may be the case, in the instance before him.

1.58 In consequence, it may surely be argued that, while the *Bolam* test of a minimum acceptable practice to avoid a finding of negligence begins to operate once the duty of care, or legal relationship, between practitioner and patient has begun to operate, the test of acceptable practice cannot either logically or practically be constitutive of the very relationship itself. It is not the function of a medical practitioner to, so to speak, dictate terms to a patient by way of establishing the legal relationship single-handed, and then to justify the position by saying that ordinary skilled and competent practitioners would have done the same. Any other approach would, in the words of Laskin CJ in *Reibl v Hughes* (above) be to 'hand over to the medical profession the entire question of the scope of the duty of disclosure'.

Negligence and malcommunication

1.59 As many medical accidents are caused by deficiencies in communication as are caused by failure to exercise ordinary skill and competence in diagnosis and treatment. Typical is the discharge from an accident and emergency department of an elderly person who has just received treatment, without making adequate arrangements for safe discharge and return to home or another place of safety.

1.60 Deficiencies in communication may occur as between members of the same, or different, professions involved in an individual patient's treatment and care. Examples include unclear instructions by a surgeon to an anaesthetist or theatre nurse; unclear care plans on the ward; and unclear or illegible prescriptions for medication. Legal liability for injury to a patient resulting from deficiencies in communication may fall on both or all parties concerned, and not just on the shoulders of the person whose instruction is initially unclear. In *Prendergast v Sam and Dee Ltd*[1] a dispensing pharmacist was held 75 per cent to blame for the harmful consequences of an erroneous prescription, the balance of the blame resting with the general medical practitioner who wrote it.

1 (1989) Times, 24 March.

1.61 Deficiencies in communication may amount to 'maladministration' such as may, if it causes 'hardship or injustice' (which includes injury) be investigated by the Ombudsman or Health Service Commissioner pursuant to Part V of the National Health Service Act 1977. The jurisdiction of the Commissioner to investigate is an alternative to, and not concurrent with, legal action for personal injury: National Health Service Act 1977, section 116(1). The investigatory jurisdiction extends to NHS trusts as well as to health authority directly-managed provider units. It also applies to health authorities as purchasers, but such activity is unlikely if ever to figure in the context of a specific complaint alleging medical negligence.

ESTABLISHING BREACH

Proof of negligence

1.62 The legal burden of proof in all medical negligence cases lies on the plaintiff. The standard of proof required to discharge that burden is on the balance of probabilities. However, as Morris LJ has commented:

In some civil cases the issues may involve questions of reputation which can transcend in importance even questions of personal liberty. Good name in a man or woman is 'the immediate jewel of their souls' . . . though no court . . . would give less careful attention to issues lacking gravity than to those marked by it, the very elements of gravity become a part of the whole range of circumstances which have to be weighed in the scale when deciding as to the balance of probabilities.[1]

1 *Hornal v Neuberger Products Ltd* [1957] 1 QB 247 at 266.

1.63 Where the claim involves an allegation of medical negligence and an attack on the competence of the professional man, the nature of this allegation will be reflected in the standard of proof required to discharge the legal burden of establishing negligence on the balance of probabilities. This was clearly demonstrated in *Hucks v Cole*.[1]

A charge of professional negligence against a medical man was a serious charge, on a different footing to a charge of negligence against a motorist or an employer. The reason is because the consequences for the professional man are far more grave. A finding of negligence affects his standing and reputation. It impairs the confidence which his clients have in him. The burden of proof is correspondingly greater. The principle applies that: 'In proportion as the charge is grave, so ought the proof to be clear': see *Hornal v Neuberger Products Ltd* [1957] 1 QB 247.

Another difference lies in the fact that, with the best will in the world, things do sometimes go amiss in surgical operations or medical treatment. A striking illustration was *Roe v Minister of Health* [1954] 2 QB 66. So a doctor is not to be held negligent simply because something goes wrong. It is not right to invoke against him the maxim *res ipsa loquitur* save in an extreme case. He is not liable for mischance or misadventure. Nor is he liable for an error of judgment. He is not liable for choosing one course out of two which may be open to him, or for following one school of thought rather than another. He is liable only if he falls below the standard of a reasonably competent practitioner in his field – so much so that his conduct may fairly be held to be – I will not say deserving of censure, but, at any rate, inexcusable.[2]

1 (1968) 112 Sol Jo 483, CA.
2 Ibid at 484.

Role of the expert

1.64 If compliance with a properly accepted practice will defeat any claim of negligence, it follows that the plaintiff must establish either that the accepted practice was improperly so accepted or that no reasonable doctor could have behaved in the way the defendant did. A graphic example of the evidential consequences of *Bolam* is provided by *Maynard v West Midlands Regional Health Authority*.[1]

1 [1984] 1 WLR 634.

1.65 Mrs Maynard consulted a surgeon and a consultant physician with symptoms indicative of tuberculosis. However, in the opinion of both the physician and the surgeon Hodgkin's Disease, carcinoma and sarcoidosis were also possibilities. Because Hodgkin's Disease was fatal unless remedial steps were taken in its early stages, they decided that, rather than await the result of a sputum test, which would involve some weeks' delay, a mediastinoscopy should be performed to provide them with a biopsy. Such a procedure, even when carefully performed, carries a known risk of damage to the left recurrent laryngeal nerve. Although the operation was carried out properly, that injury in fact ensued. The biopsy subsequently proved negative and the plaintiff was subsequently confirmed to be suffering from tuberculosis. The plaintiff brought an action against the defendant health authority contending, inter alia, that the decision to carry out the mediastinoscopy rather than await the result of the sputum test had been negligent. At trial a distinguished body of expert medical opinion was called, approving of the operation. However, the judge preferred the evidence of an expert witness called for the plaintiff who had stated that the case had almost certainly been one of TB from the outset and should have been so diagnosed. To undertake the mediastinoscopy was unnecessary, dangerous and accordingly negligent, she said.

1.66 The Court of Appeal had no hesitation in upholding the judge on causation but reversed him on negligence. The decision of the Court of Appeal was upheld by the House of Lords.

> I have to say that a judge's 'preference' for one body of distinguished professional opinion to another also professionally distinguished is not sufficient to establish negligence in a practitioner whose actions have received the seal of approval if those opinions, truthfully expressed, honestly held, were not preferred. If this was the real reason for the judge's finding, he erred in law even though elsewhere in his judgment he stated the law correctly. For in the realm of diagnosis and treatment negligence is not established by preferring one respectable body of professional opinion to another. Failure to exercise the ordinary skill of a doctor (in the appropriate speciality, if he be a specialist) is necessary.

1 Per Lord Scarman ibid at page 639.

1.67 Compliance with an accepted practice will satisfy the *Bolam* test and thereby defeat an allegation of negligence. This raises the obvious question: will departure from accepted practice constitute prima facie evidence of negligence? This question was raised in *Clark v MacLennan*.[1]

1 [1983] 1 All ER 416.

1.68 In that case the plaintiff suffered from stress incontinence after the delivery of her first child. Early attempts at conservative treatment failed to bring about any improvement in her condition. An anterior colporrhaphy operation was carried out one month and eleven days after the birth. It was normal practice amongst gynaecologists not to perform such an operation until at least three months after birth so as to ensure its success and to prevent the risk of haemorrhage. The operation was not successful and after it was performed haemorrhage occurred causing the repair to break down. Two further operations were unsuccessful with the result that the stress incontinence from which the plaintiff suffered became a permanent disability.

1.69 The judge held that while it was for the plaintiff to prove negligence, once she had established that the defendants had departed from an accepted practice designed to guard her from the very sort of harm she suffered, the burden shifted to the defendants to justify their departure, which they failed to do.

1.70 In doing so his Lordship sought to rely on *McGhee v National Coal Board*.[1] In that case the plaintiff, who worked at the defendants' brick kilns, contracted dermatitis as the result of exposure to brick dust. The defendants were not at fault in allowing the exposure during working hours, but were at fault for failing to provide adequate washing facilities, thereby increasing the period of time the plaintiff was exposed to the dust before he could return home and wash. It was accepted that the dust had caused the plaintiff's dermatitis. However, such was the state of current medical knowledge that it could not be established whether or not the plaintiff would have contracted dermatitis had he been able to take a shower at work. The plaintiff could not therefore establish that 'but for' the 'guilty' exposure he would not have suffered dermatitis. A majority of the House of Lords, however, were prepared to equate (in the absence of other evidence) a 'material increase in the risk' with a 'material contribution' to the damage.

It is very difficult to draw a distinction between the damage and the duty where the duty arises only because of a need to guard against the damage. In *McGhee*'s case it was accepted that there was a breach of duty. In the present case the question of whether there was a breach remains in issue. It seems to me that it follows from *McGhee* that where there is a situation in which a general duty of care arises and there is a failure to take a precaution, and that very damage occurs against which the precaution is designed to be a protection, then the burden lies on the defendant to show that he was not in breach of duty as well as to show that the damage did not result from his breach of duty.[2]

1 [1972] 3 All ER 1008.
2 *Clark v MacLennan* [1983] 1 All ER 416 at 427f–g.

1.71 However, the Court of Appeal in *Wilsher v Essex Area Health Authority*[1] has more recently been critical of such an approach:

None the less, I would find it impossible, unless impelled by binding authority, to hold that proof of primary facts constituting negligence is in some way dispensed with merely by showing that some step, which is designed to minimise or avert a risk, has not in the particular circumstances been taken.[2]

His Lordship then went on to state:

If I may say so, the summary of the evidence contained in the judgment in *Clark v MacLennan* has certainly persuaded me that, as a decision on the facts, the case is unimpeachable. Moreover, although the judge indicated that he proposed to decide the case on the burden of proof, this could be understood as an example of the forensic commonplace that, where one party has, in the course of a trial, hit the ball into the other's court, it is for that other to return it. But the prominence given in the judgment to *McGhee* and the citation from *Clark* in the present case suggest that the judge may have set out to assert a wider proposition, to the effect that in certain kinds of case of which *Clark* and the present form examples, there is a general burden of proof on the defendant. If this is so, then I must respectfully say that I find nothing in *McGhee* or in general principle to support it.[3]

1 [1986] 3 All ER 801.
2 Per Mustill LJ at 814g.
3 Ibid at 815e–g.

1.72 Nevertheless, Mustill LJ accepted the decision in *Clark v MacLennan* as being impeccable on the facts. If this is to be reconciled with the rest of his Lordship's dicta, the case might alternatively be regarded as one in which the maxim *res ipsa loquitur* applies.

Res ipsa loquitur

1.73 The Latin expression *res ipsa loquitur*, meaning that the matter in hand 'speaks for itself', may be invoked in certain fairly restricted circumstances by an injured person when alleging negligence in diagnosis or treatment. When successful, the plea of *res ipsa loquitur* has the practical effect of shifting the argument on negligence to the defendant's shoulders; and, while it is always for the plaintiff to prove the case of negligence on the balance of probabilities (more likely than not), the defendant is put to an explanation of how the matter in hand (the *res*, or event) could have occurred in the absence of negligence. If the plea is unsuccessful, the plaintiff may still continue with argument as to the defendant's alleged negligence, but without the court's assistance in making the defendant 'explain it away'. The most memorable way of stating this practical effect was that of Denning LJ in *Cassidy v Ministry of Health*[1] in which a patient entered hospital for treatment of Dupuytren's contracture of the hand and left in a worse state. Denning LJ said:

> If the plaintiff had to prove that some particular doctor or nurse is negligent, he would not be able to do it. But he was not put to that impossible task: he says, 'I went into the hospital to be cured of two stiff fingers. I have come out with four stiff fingers, and my hand is useless. That should not have happened if due care had been used. Explain it, if you can.'

1 [1951] 2 KB 343.

1.74 The concurrent requirements for this assistance by way of proof to be granted to an injured plaintiff were set out in the judgment of Scott LJ in *Mahon v Osborne*,[1] a case which involved an allegation that a swab had been negligently left post-operatively in the patient's body. In order to cause the defendant to 'explain it if you can', the court must be satisfied that control over the relevant situation, environment or events rested solely with the defendant, and furthermore, that 'in the ordinary experience of mankind such an event does not happen unless the person in control has failed to exercise due care'.

1 [1939] 2 KB 14.

1.75 That judges can differ over the applicability, and therefore availability to the plaintiff, of the plea of *res ipsa loquitur* in any given case is demonstrated by the result in *Mahon v Osborne* itself, where Scott LJ dissented from his two brethren in the Court of Appeal which held by a majority that the plea was available on the particular facts of that case.

1.76 Not every instance of injury is sufficient in itself to put the defendant to the task of explanation even where the lay person might think that something must certainly have gone wrong as a result of carelessness. In *Fish v Kapur*,[1] the availability of the plea was refused to a plaintiff whose jaw fractured in the course of the extraction of a tooth. The plaintiff had been unable to adduce expert dental evidence that such an event does not occur in the absence of negligence, and the absence of such evidence was fatal to her plea.

1 [1948] 2 All ER 176.

1.77 That even judges may inject uncertainties into a case where an injured plaintiff is experiencing difficulties of proof and seeks, in consequence, to rely on the plea of *res ipsa loquitur* is shown by the somewhat exceptional finding in *Levenkind v Churchill-Davidson*,[1] in which The Lancet reports the judge as having said:

A surgeon is not to be found negligent simply because something has gone wrong at operation in the sense that the patient has suffered some injury which was not a usual hazard of the operation. The reason is not far to seek. The inference of negligence arises, if at all, from the act which causes the injury and not from the injury itself. In non-medical cases for the most part the act is there to be seen as clearly as, if not more clearly than, the injury. In medical cases the opposite often applies. The injury, what has gone wrong, can be determined, but it must be frequently impossible to know what act caused that injury. If the *res* is unknown, how can it be said to speak for itself?

1 (1983) 1 The Lancet 1452.

1.78 It is suggested that this interpretation of the applicability to complex facts of the plea of *res ipsa loquitur* is unduly restrictive. It is likely to be in complex situations of medical treatment that the allegation that the facts speak for themselves, and that the defendant should be put to an explanation, is most likely to be sought by an injured plaintiff. A better approach appears to be that suggested above, whereby even if the *res* does not 'speak for itself', there is cogent medical evidence that such and such a result does not normally occur in the absence of negligence. The raising of the plea is therefore usefully seen as a two-stage process. Firstly, medical evidence is given on behalf of the injured plaintiff, in general terms, as to the known outcome of treatment; and secondly, the two requirements laid down by Scott LJ in *Mahon v Osborne* must then be proved.

DAMAGE

1.79 The burden of establishing that the conduct complained of caused harm or loss rests squarely on the shoulders of the plaintiff, the test most generally accepted by the courts being the 'but for' test: but for the negligence would the harm to the plaintiff have occurred in any event?

1.80 The application of the test is neatly demonstrated by *Barnett v Chelsea and Kensington Hospital Management Committee*.[1] Three night watchmen, one of whom was the plaintiff's husband, presented themselves at the defendant's hospital complaining of vomiting after drinking tea, which unknown at the time had been laced with arsenic. The nurse consulted the duty doctor by telephone who advised that the men should go home and see their own doctors in the morning. Later that day the plaintiff's husband died of arsenical poisoning. It was held that in failing to examine the watchmen, the doctor was in breach of his duty. However, even had the deceased been examined and treated, the probability was that he would have died in any event and the claim therefore failed.

1 [1969] 1 QB 428.

1.81 In the context of medical negligence, however, issues of causation are frequently not so clear cut.[1] The nature of medical negligence is such that the plaintiff will, of course, usually have been suffering from illness in the first place. When the illness is complex it may be difficult to attribute his ultimate prognosis to any negligent act or omission (as opposed to an aspect of the illness) as demonstrated by *Wilsher v Essex Area Health Authority*.[2]

1 See Chapter 16, paras **16.28** et seq.
2 [1986] 3 All ER 801, CA; [1988] 1 All ER 871, HL.

1.82 It will be recalled that Martin Wilsher, who suffered from retrolental fibroplasia, had been administered excessive oxygen. His retinal condition could have been caused by the excess oxygen but also occurred in premature babies who were not given oxygen but who suffered from five other conditions common in premature babies all of which had afflicted him.

1.83 The trial judge (Peter Pain J) found for baby Martin on the basis that in alleging failure to take adequate precautions to ensure that he was not administered excess oxygen, the burden lay on the health authority to show there was no breach of duty and that the damage did not flow from the breach.

1.84 In doing so his Lordship sought to rely on *McGhee v National Coal Board* (the facts of which can be found at para **1.70**) in which the House of Lords were prepared to equate (in the absence of contradictory evidence) a 'material increase in the risk' with a 'material contribution' to the damage.

> But the question remains whether a pursuer must necessarily fail if, after he has shown a breach of duty, involving an increase of risk of disease, he cannot positively prove that this increase of risk caused or materially contributed to the disease while his employers cannot positively prove the contrary. In this intermediate case there is an appearance of logic in the view that the pursuer, on whom the onus lies, should fail – a logic which dictated the judgments below. The question is whether we should be satisfied in factual situations like the present, with this logical approach. In my opinion, there are further considerations of importance. First, it is a sound principle that where a person has, by breach of duty of care, created a risk, and injury occurs within the area of that risk, the loss should be borne by him unless he shows that it had some other cause. Secondly, from the evidential point of view, one may ask, why should a man who is able to show that his employer should have taken certain precautions, because without them there is a risk, or an added risk, of injury or disease, and who in fact sustains exactly that injury or disease, have to assume the burden of proving more: namely, that it was the addition to the risk, caused by the breach of duty, which caused or materially contributed to the injury? In many cases of which the present is typical, this is impossible to prove, just because honest medical opinion cannot segregate the causes of an illness between compound causes. And if one asks which of the parties, the workman or the employers should suffer from this inherent evidential difficulty, the answer as a matter of policy or justice should be that it is the creator of the risk who, *ex hypothesi*, must be taken to have foreseen the possibility of damage, who should bear its consequences.

1.85 The trial judge's approach to establishing causation (but not breach of duty) was followed by the Court of Appeal (Browne-Wilkinson VC dissenting). The House of Lords, however, distinguishing *McGhee*, reversed the decision of the Court of Appeal. Their Lordships did so on the basis that in *McGhee* the defendant's breach of duty had increased the risk that a causal factor (the brick dust) would do harm when a prima facie case had been established in relation to the causal impact of that factor.[1] In *Wilsher*, however, there being several potential factors, the negligence had merely increased the risk of harm. No prima facie case had been established in relation to the impact of that particular factor to the exclusion of the others.

1 An example of where a prima facie case was not made is provided by *Kay v Ayrshire and Arran Health Board* [1987] 2 All ER 417.

1.86 The position is neatly summarised by Andrew Boon:

> *McGhee* saves the court from the impossibility of separating the 'guilty' and the 'innocent' components of a single risk, not from the impossibility of determining the causal impact of distinct risks, even if those risks may have the same consequences on maturity.[1]

1 51 MLR 508 at 513.

1.87 Martin Wilsher would therefore only have been able to invoke *McGhee* if the sole cause of retrolental fibroplasia had been excess oxygen which, although initially administered without negligence, continued to be negligetly administered once it ought to have been apparent that excessive levels were being administered.

1.88 A further peculiarity of medical negligence claims is that the negligence will often be a failure to diagnose or properly treat a pre-existing condition. The nature of such an allegation can be much more difficult to substantiate than in those cases where the harm is initially caused by negligence, particularly where the treatment (properly administered) is by no means certain of success. Nevertheless, the plaintiff must establish that the act or omission in question more likely than not caused the plaintiff identified actual harm. In short he must be able to point to his injury and say 'but for the negligence it is likely that I would not have suffered this injury'. This is clearly illustrated by *Hotson v East Berkshire Area Health Authority*.[1]

1 [1987] 2 All ER 909.

1.89 The defendants negligently failed to diagnose the plaintiff's condition after a fall and he developed a serious disability of the hip joint. On the facts, there was, on the balance of probabilities, a 75 per cent risk that this disability would develop even had the plaintiff been treated properly. The trial judge and the Court of Appeal held that he was entitled to 25 per cent of his full loss but were overruled by the House of Lords. Their Lordships held that the judges' finding of fact amounted to a finding that on the balance of probabilities the negligence had not caused any loss. In short, Stephen Hotson had failed to establish that it was probable that he fell within the 25 per cent of cases where he would have made a recovery had his condition been promptly diagnosed.

CHAPTER 2

Medical negligence – a manager's view

Dr A J Davison

SUMMARY

CULTURAL CHANGE AND PUBLIC EXPECTATION

2.1 The NHS reforms are witnessing a move away from a near monopoly supply of healthcare to a more competitive, response service. These radical changes are against a background of rising public expectation, rising claims and rising costs. The NHS is a large and expensive service with an annual spending in excess of £30 billion, some 5.7 per cent of the gross national product. It is essential therefore that the taxpayer gets value for money. What the NHS reforms have done is to separate the purchasers – District Health Authorities and general practitioner fundholders – from the providers – the hospitals and other organisations responsible for providing services. Contracts between the two parties for a given volume of service at an agreed cost and to a defined quality level mean that there is greater competition between the providers to attract patients and therefore money. It is this competition, within a so-called managed market, that is designed to drive up the quality of services. The individual patient and his or her general practitioner have, in the new system, a greater freedom of choice but within a market which still upholds the principle upon which the NHS was originally based, that of universal access to services largely free at the time of need.

2.2 There are signs that the public are slowly beginning to understand these changes and to exercise their choices. They are clearly assisted in their decisions by an increasing number of GP fundholders keen to exercise their options and using their financial clout. Such consumer empowerment is consistent with rising expectations of all kinds of services from the public at large. The man in the street is becoming more sophisticated in his selection of priorities and choices and more informed. Better education and greater awareness have meant that he is no longer prepared to accept second best and will take remedial action should he be disadvantaged. It is hardly surprising therefore that the numbers of patients ready to complain and to sue have been rising steadily over recent years.

2.3 But why do patients sue? It is probably true to say, but difficult to quantify that there is probably a far greater number of dissatisfied patients who could sue but who do not, than the numbers who actually do take legal action. The vast majority of patients treated in the NHS seem satisfied with the care they receive. Numerous surveys show this to be the case. A typical NHS Trust dealing with around 200,000 in-patients, out-patients, day cases and accidents and emergencies each year might expect to receive something like 3,000–4,000 letters of appreciation against 300 or 400 letters of complaint leading to perhaps only half a dozen new legal actions. More often than not people whom the NHS have failed are seeking not revenge or financial reward but a clear, unambiguous explanation with apology, if that is appropriate, and some indication that the organisation, the hospital or whatever has taken steps to put matters right. The patients or their relatives will feel understandable anger and want some form of redress though not necessarily financial. Their anger will more clearly turn into litigation if satisfactory explanations and apologies are not given clearly at an early stage. We owe our patients a duty of care but above all owe them some explanation of what has happened to them so that they do not feel that someone is trying to pull the wool over their eyes. Often litigation begins because of this continued mistrust and sometimes recourse to the law is seen as a last resort of increasingly desperate patients or relatives.

WHY DO WE FAIL?

2.4 If we had a better understanding of the main reasons for failure of service then at least we would be in a position to do something about them. Clearly with some of the following categories solutions are unfortunately not easy to implement. Some may take a lot of time and money but at the very least hospitals need to be aware of these risks and to have in place a proper means of assessing and managing them.

Staffing levels

2.5 One common cause of things going wrong in the NHS is inadequate staffing levels. Examples of where staffing levels fall well short of some recommendation of a Royal College or other external standard are legion. It is important to be practical, however. It would surely be unreasonable to seek to prevent claims by introducing staffing levels up to a theoretically ideal standard to which no hospital in the country comes anywhere near. What would seem more relevant would be to make sure that compared to other similar organisations or departments the staffing levels seem reasonable. This would surely be a more relevant and practical defence or weakness in a claim. There is enormous pressure on managers and doctors to ensure that maximum numbers of patients are seen, for example in out-patients, in order to reduce the time between GP referral and out-patient clinic. However, this could be in conflict with the need to ensure that patients are not waiting more than half an hour beyond their appointment time and unless very carefully managed there does seem to be some unavoidable trade-off between quantity and quality in so many areas of the NHS. It is against this background and pressure that there may be a tendency to cut corners. A hundred out-patients booked for an out-patient clinic cannot be acceptable in terms of quality. Things are bound to be missed and the explanation to patients will at best be cursory.

Inappropriate skills and training

2.6 Although managers tend to focus on appropriateness of skills, primarily as a means of ensuring that there is some de-skilling in order to reduce costs, there is equally a case for ensuring that more senior people are available to deal with certain problems. Not infrequently we expect junior doctors to carry out surgery at inappropriate times and without adequate supervision. The confidential enquiry into perioperative deaths[1] concluded that too many operations were done at night by junior doctors lacking the necessary expertise and this was a significant risk factor in perioperative deaths. Many operations it was concluded could be, and should be left and that there was no clinical need for such urgency. We know, of course, why such operations are done inappropriately in this way, and that is largely due to the unavailability the following day of appropriate staff and above all theatre time.

1 See Buck et al in Bibliographical References.

Locum/agency staff

2.7 The NHS relies heavily on locum and agency staff to cover doctor and nurse absences. Indeed this may be likely to increase as junior doctors' hours are reduced as part of the 'New Deal'[1] where on wholly laudable grounds of safety junior doctors are required to work no more than 72 hours a week from December 1993. This means that where once in the past junior doctors covered for one another's absences they will in future no longer be able to do so and therefore the hospital will be increasingly reliant on unknown, untested agency staff since it will not usually be able to increase the number of junior doctors because of other manpower restrictions. Locum and agency staff cannot be as familiar with the hospital and its departments as permanent staff. There is therefore considerable risk of things going wrong which could be mitigated by more attention to induction and selection. Many hospitals have a nurse bank which supplies nursing staff available at short notice and these are usually people who are known and trusted.

1 See NHS Management Executive, AL(MD) 192 in Bibliographical References.

Inadequate policies

2.8 Policies and procedures exist within hospitals to improve quality of care. Some appropriate and respected person within the organisation has helped define a policy to which all involved must adhere. For example, a microbiologist would be the major stake-holder in developing and implementing a policy for the handling of glutaraldehyde, no doubt supported by advice from the Health and Safety Executive. The policy therefore describes best practice and a departure from that will leave the hospital vulnerable to claims should something go wrong. It is often the case, however, that a hospital might have not just too few policies and procedures to govern its activities but in some cases too many policies. These may have developed over the years introduced by different individuals in different circumstances and the status of these policies and procedures may be far from clear. This may be just as bad or worse than having no policies at all. It is important therefore that management conduct an audit of their procedures from time to time.

Unclear responsibility

2.9 At all times in a patient's care it must be clear who is responsible for that patient. As patients pass from department to department their care passes through the hands of very many no doubt dedicated professionals, but it is sometimes very unclear who is responsible at any one point in time. A recent well-publicised death of a patient in the private sector was said to be caused by the involvement of too many different consultants, none of whom seemed to have any clear responsibility for the patient or for taking appropriate action when clinical problems started to arise. Whilst this is not so much a problem in the NHS there is at least a potential for confusion and someone saying at an inquest, 'Well I did not think that was my responsibility.'

Communications

2.10 Many problems would be avoided by better communication not only with the patient but between professionals and departments within a hospital. Here we must distinguish between, on the one hand, the genuine breakdown of communication between the surgical department and say X-ray where a delay or missing report had a significant effect on outcome, and on the other hand, failure of communication with the patient to explain exactly why something happened. Very often an unfortunate outcome is not the result of negligence or sub-optimal care but was a wholly natural and unavoidable event. In such a situation the patient or his or her relatives might be forgiven for believing that the care has been negligent and it is critical therefore that full explanations are given to them to correct their misunderstandings and perceptions and hopefully to head off any litigation.

Incompetence

2.11 There will be occasions when a failure of our duty of care is due to the incompetence of a doctor or nurse, in which case remedial action must be taken. This, of course, can range from counselling and further training to restrictions on the types of activity that that particular surgeon or nurse for instance is allowed to do, or through to redeployment or ultimately dismissal. It is important that the hospital has in place some active training programme and the need to access regularly individuals' skills and competences and to check that they are relevant to the task that the staff are expected to perform.

Lack of facilities/equipment

2.12 Often complaints and claims are the result of lack of suitable equipment or facilities. Managers should decide which of those things that are necessary for the adequate performance of good quality care are provided. Such decisions do, of course, have considerable financial implications and the managers need to balance the risks and assess the costs and benefits. However, a report by an external body that suggests that the number of anaesthetic monitoring machines, for instance, needs to be increased will, if ignored by management, mean that any subsequent claim relevant to this will be indefensible.

New technology

2.13 Often the introduction of new technology – lasers are a good example – is down to the committed enthusiasts. They usually go elsewhere for training and import the new skills, but how do we know they have been properly trained? Were the place and the person where they went for training appropriate? How good are they in passing on their newly acquired skills to their colleagues? The Royal Colleges surely should be doing more to establish some form of accredited specialist training of this sort.

Split sites

2.14 It is a common feature of the NHS that services are spread over several geographically distant sites. This often militates against good quality care in a cost-effective manner. Capital investment is the only long-term solution and this is not always easy or within a defined and quick timescale. In the interim, therefore, steps should be taken to ensure that risk is minimised by rationalising services as far as possible and to make sure that staff are available as appropriate. It would be unacceptable to have for instance a surgical registrar on call at one hospital if he is scheduled routinely to do an out-patient clinic at another hospital 20 miles away.

THE NEW ARRANGEMENTS

Changes to the Medical Indemnity Scheme

2.15 Under new arrangements[1] responsibility for medical negligence passes from the medical defence organisations, the Medical Defence Union and Medical Protection Society, to health authorities or NHS Trusts. In April 1991 the introduction of the NHS and Community Care Act brought in further changes shifting financial responsibility quite clearly to directly managed units/NHS Trusts. Transitional arrangements to spread the financial burden were established under which a contingency fund was created on the basis of a threshold of £300,000 as the maximum financial liability for a Trust or directly managed unit with 80 per cent of any excess costs beyond this amount being paid from medical defence organisation reserves. Many regions up to that time had adopted pooling arrangements to mitigate the financial burden of up to £300,000 with risk sharing between districts and regions being commonplace. The basic principle in these changes is to link the costs with responsibility. Those hospitals which have the problem must find ways of spreading the costs. Picking up a large legal bill or indeed the fear of doing so must have an effect on contract prices that a Trust or directly managed unit must set. This would filter through to a hospital's competitiveness and ultimately the survival of a particular service. Most hospitals would try to ensure that the costs of such claims, or the risk of them was devolved to the specialities concerned. It would not be good management or financial practice to try to spread this burden, penalising low risk specialities.

1 See NHS Management Executive, EL(90)195, EL(90)191 and EL(91)19 in Bibliographical References.

The position of NHS Trusts

2.16 With the establishment of NHS Trusts from April 1991 any untoward event or incident occurring before the operational date and resulting in legislation after that date would mean that it was the former District Health Authority that was financially responsible. Whilst this may initially protect Trusts from a sudden catastrophic financial impact, almost certainly any District Health Authority deprived of funds in this way would attempt to mitigate that loss by buying fewer services or the same volume of services at lower cost from the successor Trust responsible. In the end, therefore, the impact would be felt on local services. There can be no hiding place. With the rule of Crown immunity Trusts are encouraged to, and normally do insure against a range of risks, including fire, employer's liability, theft and so on. However, they are unable to insure against medical negligence and therefore must plan sensibly and rationally to minimise that risk and to make appropriate financial arrangements. To ignore such risks may result in a large award theatening the collapse of a local service. Various ways to develop alternative ways of managing the financial risk have been discussed. One suggestion has been the top slicing of a percentage, say 0.25 per cent of revenue centrally, but such top slicing arrangements are not popular within the NHS and do not devolve responsibility to where it matters. An alternative is an NHS self-insurance scheme, whereby some central pool is created, possibly including some kind of no-claims discount. In the absence of such centrally promulgated schemes, NHS Trust and indeed others must ensure that reserves are set aside for the handling of such large claims. In the last analysis, loans with repayment periods up to 10 years can be arranged with the Department of Health.

CUTTING THE COST OF CLAIMS

2.17 The cost of claims in the NHS has been increasing over recent years. In 1983 there were 1.7 claims per hundred doctors rising in 1987 to 4.1. This happily is still far short of the 18 claims per hundred doctors in the United States but the trends are none the less worrying. The total cost to the NHS is said to be £47m per annum. There can be little doubt that a proper system for handling claims can save a lot of time and money. What then are the key issues to check?

Spotting the litigant

2.18 Many but not all cases of litigation start with an innocent complaint or a request for information. It is important to head off the potential threat of litigation by ensuring that patients are given adequate explanations. This cannot be stressed enough. When the more usual series of letters has failed to produce a satisfied customer then it is essential that a face-to-face dialogue be held with the patient or his or her relatives on the one hand, and the hospital consultant and hospital manager on the other. Doctors and managers tend to assume that litigation arises only where they have been negligent. In fact many claims proceed where there is little chance of success. Equally claims which are justifiable are pursued and then dropped either because of mounting costs or because there has been little damage suffered by the patient. All claims must be handled professionally and diligently. Nor should management assume that it is only the articulate well-off who will pursue a claim. Many who do not have the financial resources to sue may be eligible for legal aid and because they are less persistent in seeking explanations may find recourse to the law as the only route to satisfaction.

Incident reporting

2.19 All hospitals must have a good incident reporting system whereby staff are encouraged to bring to the attention of management things that have gone wrong and have the potential for subsequent claims. Timely reports made by staff involved and the responsible consultant whilst incidents are still fresh in their minds are crucial in the subsequent management of claims. Poor, inaccurate and inadequate notes and reports are one of the major stumbling blocks in the successful resistance of claims. There may well be an understandable reluctance on the part of staff to admit to their errors for fear of reprisals such as disciplinary action. However, such measures should be used only as a last resort and have no place in the handling of genuine mishaps committed in good faith. It takes courage to be open and frank about one's errors. From these the organisation and the individuals involved can learn and progress. This constructive culture should be encouraged by managers and senior doctors alike.

Choosing a solicitor

2.20 NHS Trusts and directly managed units will often have a range of lawyers. As in other fields it is horses for courses. It would not be appropriate to engage some high cost London solicitors with an expertise in medical legal work to do routine conveyancing of the lease of the hospital allotments. Similarly much personal injury work and litigation can be handled locally. Indeed it may be felt a good idea to use a range of solicitors for various aspects of legal work since in this way it may keep firms on their toes and prices competitive. However, it is important to use solicitors with a good track record in medical and legal work since this is an increasingly specialist field and access to a comprehensive database of similar cases is critical to the successful management of a case.

Regular reporting and monitoring of claims

2.21 It is important to have in place a good system for reviewing regularly the complaints and litigation against the hospital. Such reports should be disseminated anonymously to clinical directorates or via whatever is the internal organisational structure. In this way obvious trends should be detected and steps taken to minimise a recurrence. Above all individuals should be made accountable for implementing remedial action.

The doctor's contract

2.22 The relationship of doctors to managers is changing with the establishment of Trusts. Doctors can no longer hide behind the oft-used defence of clinical freedom nor escape from the contractual obligations as they sometimes could on occasions when their contracts were held by Regional Health Authorities. Now that NHS Trusts are their employers and are fully accountable for their actions and responsible for the financial burden of any medical negligence, it is clear that managers and doctors must work together to minimise risks. There is, of course, a far wider question than simply the contract of employment for the doctor. There should exist a wider, often unfortunately unwritten, contract between a consultant and management and that relates to the staffing and supporting facilities that a doctor needs to carry out his diagnosis and treatment to a professionally acceptable standard. All too often managers fail doctors badly in this regard. It is essential therefore for doctors to spell out clearly and unambiguously the resources required, even though they cannot be met, so that there can be joint discussion and hopefully agreement as to what progress can be made and how risks can be minimised.

2.23 Within an organisation the failings of a particular individual become known often by word of mouth or by nursing observations or through complaints from patients. It is important that such difficult issues are tackled firmly but sensitively. It may be that some retraining of the doctor is necessary and this should be organised with the advice of the appropriate Royal College. It is important during such a period that peer support is available to him. In other more serious and intractable cases it may be necessary to restrict the duties of a particular doctor by, for instance, ensuring that he does not tackle a particular range of complex procedures and is found other work to do. Increased supervision, for a period, over some of his activities may be necessary. At the end of the day, however, no Trust can afford to carry passengers and if redeployment is not possible then dismissal may be the last resort. The use of short-term contracts of employment has been tried in some places so that there is in effect a probationary period to see how a new consultant performs. However, this seems unnecessary and counter productive. It may well deter many good applicants from applying for a particular job and therefore the Trust might be prevented from getting the highest quality staff which is surely the best way to avoid problems in the future. Such short-term contracts are therefore, in my view, unnecessary and inadvisable.

A proactive approach to the management of risk

2.24 The whole issue of risk management in the NHS is gaining a higher profile. High on everyone's agenda is the need to introduce a systematic and comprehensive programme of risk management, which essentially involves:

(a) identifying, assessing and minimising risks;
(b) better information;
(c) medical audit; and
(d) integrated quality management.

Of these the key is to have in place an effective audit system.

THE NEED FOR EFFECTIVE AUDIT

2.25 The best defence against malpractice claims is to develop an effective clinical audit process.

What is audit?

2.26 Medical audit is usually defined as the systematic, critical analysis of the quality of medical care, including the procedures used for diagnosis and treatment, the use of resources and the resulting outcome for the patient. Audit is very much linked, however, to another key Department of Health initiative, that of resource management. Resource management is primarily an internal hospital management system, which devolves decision-making to clinical heads of departments or directors who are involved, therefore at the heart of hospital management decision-making with associated financial responsibility. It would be too simplistic to say that resource management concentrates on the efficiency of the activities of clinicians, whereas audit focuses on the effectiveness of what they are doing. They are, however, different angles on a common theme, that of improving patient care. Both initiatives must therefore be inextricably linked and planned accordingly.

Organisation of audit

2.27 Since medical audit is about the effectiveness of medical procedures and treatment then it follows that the whole process must be clinically owned and clinically led. The process will not work if it is felt to be imposed from on high and will founder if doctors are not fully involved and committed. The organisation of medical audit, usually through a committee of a wide range of clinicians, must win credibility in a hospital or district. It must be clinically led by a respected clinician who has drive and energy and is able to deliver the goods and commit his colleagues to producing implementation plans for audit in their particular speciality.

2.28 It is important also that junior doctors are at the very least represented in audit arrangements at hospital and departmental level. As part of their learning process, juniors must be involved in audit which is no more than a continuing and wider educational process. Being at the sharp end, junior doctors will also have much to contribute.

2.29 Apart from doctors, there will also be a wide range of professional and technical staff, whose contributions to the overall care of the patient and eventual outcome are critical. This wider, multidisciplinary approach to audit is usually referred to as clinical audit, as opposed to the more narrowly focused unidisciplinary medical audit. Clinical audit is the way forward, but must be introduced in an evolutionary way. It would be unfortunate if the enforced inclusion of nursing staff and professionals allied to medicine in the audit process was felt to be threatening to medical staff, so that they refused to play. Both doctors and nurses can suffer from defensive tribalism which must be broken down.

2.30 Setting up the appropriate organisation for audit is one thing – it is quite another to create the right culture in which open discussion and an honest review of performance can take place. Such a review and the courage to be self-critical must be followed by action. There is no point in investing a lot of time and energy if a change of behaviour or practice does not result.

2.31 All of this, of course, will take time, and thus will have an opportunity cost. The time spent in audit will be time lost to direct care of patients. This has been an oft-voiced criticism of audit, usually by those either unwilling to face the inevitable, or without the courage to analyse the results of their actions critically. The loss of clinical time, however, must be seen in context. It could be argued that any busy clinician must set aside time to stand back from day-to-day commitments and routines to be able to take a more detached view about what he is doing and how well he is doing it. Surely no one can defend the frenetic unthinking treadmill which characterises so much of clinical and indeed managerial practice today. By taking time out, a better sense of proportion and of priorities and practices should be developed. Waiting lists, for example, might be reduced more significantly by auditing what kind of conditions are on a waiting list and what priority, if any, they should be accorded, rather than blindly tackling a remorseless workload, which no sooner is cleared than is replaced by further referrals.

Confidentiality

2.32 One of the critical keys to success in the audit process is in winning and retaining the confidence of medical staff. That can be achieved only where there is absolute confidentiality in the discussions, reports and analyses which medical staff undertake. There are two possible threats, however. First, the new-style District Health Authority in its purchasing role will expect to see at least the aggregated and anonymous results of medical audit in a provider hospital with which it is contracting for service. Such information, the DHA will not unreasonably argue, is essential for it to take an informed decision about the quality of the service provided to its resident population, for which it has a statutory responsibility. Such audit information will be helpful either in comparing the quality of service of two different providers, leading to changes in purchasing decisions or, more likely, resulting in discussions with the home or local provider to ensure improvements in quality.

2.33 The second possible threat to confidentiality concerns patient access to information. The medical profession would, for perfectly understandable reasons, want the Department of Health to ensure that audit data are not accessible to patients under the Data Protection Act. But mere reliance on the confidentiality of the audit process is unlikely to confer an absolute guarantee against legal proceedings. The courts will, at the end of the day, need to balance the rights of the individual against the public interest in maintaining the credibility and integrity of medical audit. No doubt a test case will soon arise, in which the Secretary of State for Health is faced with a decision as to whether to claim Crown privilege or public interest immunity. Such fears, however understandable, should not deflect doctors from the need to commit themselves to medical audit. Indeed, if it can be shown by a patient/plaintiff that no audit process is properly organised by a group of doctors, then a claim against them may be more likely to succeed.

Conclusion

2.34 Times are changing. We cannot simply wring our hands and wish that life were different. We, doctors and managers together, must accept the challenge of a more proactive attitude towards audit, quality strategies and risk management, together with a proper financial plan to protect and improve clinical services locally.

2.35 Much has already been achieved, but there is undoubtedly a long way to go for the successful introduction and development of medical and clinical audit. The commitment and enthusiasm of many clinicians gives encouragement and it is to be hoped that the infection will spread. A more rigorous approach to the evaluation of outcomes, the time and investment undoubtedly needed, together with a corporate, multidisciplinary approach to clinical issues, should in the end improve outcomes and the quality of life of those dependent on the health services of the future.

BIBLIOGRAPHICAL REFERENCES

Buck N, Devlin H B and Lunn J N 'Confidential Enquiry into Perioperative Death' (1987) and a follow up report: Devlin H B, Lunn J N and Campling E A 'Nuffield Provincial Hospitals Trust – The Kings Fund' (June 1990).

NHS Management Executive, AL(MD)192: Working Arrangements and Out of Hours Remuneration for Doctors and Dentists in Training Grades.

NHS Management Executive, EL(90)195: Insurance Arrangements from April 1991.
NHS Management Executive, EL(90)191: Handling Claims for Medical Negligence.
NHS Management Executive, EL(91)19: Clinical Negligence Funding Scheme.

CHAPTER 3

Medical complaints procedures

Arthur C Taylor *Solicitor*

SUMMARY

INTRODUCTION

3.1 It has been estimated that some 5½ million in-patients and 17 million new out-patients and accident and emergency department patients use our hospitals every year. It is also believed that there are some 200 million consultations with general practitioners every year. An average of some 15,000 formal complaints is made by in-patients every year,[1] whereas a much smaller number of formal complaints is made by patients of general practitioners.

1 45,000 complaints about hospital treatment in 1992.

3.2 Obviously, the nature and gravity of complaints vary enormously from the temperature of the soup at one end of the scale to the death of, or serious injury to, the patient at the other. The term 'complaint' is not precisely defined either in the statutes or in the regulations, circulars or directions published in pursuance of such statutes. Accordingly, in considering medical complaints procedures one has to look at the whole spectrum from the serious to the trivial.

3.3 There are many different procedures or avenues for medical complaints depending partly on the location and partly on the seriousness of the complaint. These are as follows:

(a) informal hospital complaints;
(b) formal hospital complaints;
(c) informal community health services complaints;
(d) formal community health services complaints;
(e) informal Family Health Services Authority complaints;
(f) formal Family Health Services Authority complaints;
(g) the Health Service Commissioner;
(h) the courts;
(i) professional bodies;
(j) the Patient's Charter.

This chapter does not deal in detail with claims in the courts or reference to professional bodies in relation to professional conduct or misconduct.

3.4 The National Health Service and Community Care Act 1990 has made radical changes in the manner in which health care services are delivered within the National Health Service. In the vast majority of cases hospitals are now managed either by NHS Trusts or by directly managed Units which provide the necessary services whilst District Health Authorities are responsible for purchasing the services needed for their population from those Trusts and Units. Since health authorities are now distanced from the management of hospitals by the contractual relationship with the Trusts and Units the effect has been to thrust the responsibility for dealing with complaints upon Trusts and Units although, as will be seen, health authorities do retain a residual responsibility. The position is by no means clear in the current transitional state of the NHS.

3.5 The lack of clarity which is referred to in the previous paragraph is partly a function of the incomplete state of the regulations, circulars and guidelines which could be expected to follow the passing of the 1990 Act. For example, the circular issued under the Hospital Complaints Procedure Act 1985, namely HC(88)37, has not yet been replaced or updated except in Scotland.[1] It has therefore to be interpreted in the light of the 1990 Act and this can create some confusion both in terms of nomenclature and responsibilities for implementation of the Act and circular. No doubt this will be clarified as time moves on and the prevalence of NHS Trusts increases. There are other examples which will be referred to later in this chapter.

1 See page 1097.

HOSPITAL COMPLAINTS

3.6 Since NHS Trusts and directly managed Units are the providers of services in the hospitals it is logical that the basic responsibility for dealing with hospital complaints should rest with them. This should be clearly stated in the contract between the Trust or Unit and the purchasing Authority. However the District Health Authority has a responsibility as well. It needs to monitor the performance of the provider under the terms of the contract and ensure that the patients within its population are receiving proper service. It also has with NHS hospitals an obligation under the Patient's Charter to publish details on a regular basis of both the number of complaints received and the time taken to deal with them. Clearly Authorities can only do this if they have access to the information and they must therefore monitor the incidence of complaints for this purpose. The position is also covered in the case of Trusts by a letter issued by the NHS Management Executive, EL(91)107, which places responsibility for complaints about services supplied prior to 1 April 1991 upon the District Health Authority. Where the complaint relates to events after 1 April 1991 the Trust is responsible for handling it and the Annex to EL(91)107 does seek to explain the effect of HC(88)37 in the context of the new situation post the 1990 Act. Finally, EL(91)107 does recommend that the Trust should take the lead where a complaint covers events before and after 1 April 1991 but that it should keep the District Health Authority informed.

Informal complaints

3.7 It is clearly desirable to deal with trivial complaints as speedily and informally as possible both in the interests of the patient and of the staff concerned.[1] In the hospital setting the position is dealt with by paragraph 3 of Annex A to Circular HC(88)37 made under the Hospital Complaints Procedure Act 1985. This requires every District Health Authority or Special Health Authority to make arrangements for staff at every hospital to seek to deal informally to the satisfaction of the complainant with any complaint made at the hospital. This duty will now fall upon managers at the hospital rather than upon the District Health Authority. Such complaints are normally made orally and are best disposed of by open discussion with a senior member of staff in the relevant department. If the complaint cannot be dealt with informally to the satisfaction of the patient then the member of staff must advise the complainant, who may be either the patient or the person acting on behalf of the patient, to make a formal complaint to the designated officer for that hospital.

1 In January 1994 the Health Minister said he would like to see independent conciliators based at hospitals.

3.8 Very many patients seek no more than a full explanation of what has happened or an opportunity to give vent to their feelings and to their perception of the shortcomings in the treatment which they have received whether in clinical or non-clinical areas. The more open and the more sympathetic the attitude of the member of staff dealing with the informal complaint the better the chance of resolving it at that level and avoiding the next step of a formal complaint.

Formal complaints

3.9 The Hospital Complaints Procedure Act 1985 required the Secretary of State to give to each health authority in England and Wales and to each health board in Scotland directions for establishing a complaints procedure in every hospital and for publicising such procedure. The health circular HC(88)37:HN(FP)(88)18[1] was issued in June 1988 and gives directions to every District Health Authority in England and Wales, together with certain Special Health Authorities mentioned in Annex A of the circular, as to the arrangements to be made for dealing with complaints made by or on behalf of persons who are or have been patients at any hospital for the management of which that authority is responsible. Similar directions were issued to Scottish health boards by the Scottish Office in September 1991 and this has now been followed by NHS Circular GEN(1992)27.[2] The essential points in the procedure to be adopted are:

(a) the appointment of a designated officer for each hospital or group of hospitals for which the authority is responsible;
(b) the monitoring by the health authority of the arrangements made for dealing with complaints; and
(c) the publicising of the complaints procedure.

These three issues will now be looked at in further detail to see how they work in practice, and in the context of the 1990 Act.

1 See page 1097.
2 See page 1137.

Designated officer

3.10 This should be a senior officer located in the hospital or one of the group of hospitals for which he is responsible. Normally and perhaps ideally he should be the Chief Executive Officer of the NHS Trust or Unit General Manager but another senior officer may be appointed. Formal complaints should be addressed to him and he is responsible for receiving them and for seeing that action is taken upon them. With the exception of certain categories which are mentioned below the duties of the designated officer must include responsibility for investigating and reporting on the investigation of any formal complaint to the complainant, to any person involved in the complaint and to such other persons as the authority may require. The latter group would normally include the district officers and the chairman and the members of the authority under the monitoring procedure.

3.11 Arrangements for formal complaints should ensure that such complaints are made and recorded in writing. They should normally be made within three months of the matter complained of arising, although the designated officer should have a discretion to allow a longer period for good cause. Clearly, serious illness of the patient or his absence from home for good reason could be reasonable grounds for exercising such discretion. The designated officer should ensure that formal complaints are investigated promptly and some authorities regard one month as the target for completion of the investigation unless there is good reason for extension of that period. The designated officer may delegate the investigation to other officers but retains the responsibility for the outcome. He should ensure that both the complainant and any hospital staff involved have an opportunity to bring relevant information or comments to the designated officer or whoever investigates on his behalf. The designated officer should also be available at the request of a complainant in assisting in dealing with a complaint which is likely to be capable of being dealt with informally.

3.12 There are some categories of complaint in which the duties of the designated officer do not include investigation of the complaint but do require him to bring the matter to the attention of his authority. These categories cover complaints concerning:

(a) the exercise of clinical judgment by a hospital doctor or dentist where the complaint cannot be resolved by discussion with the consultant concerned;
(b) where there has been a serious untoward incident involving harm to a patient;
(c) the conduct of hospital medical or dental staff which the authority considers ought to be the subject of disciplinary proceedings;
(d) the alleged physical abuse of patients; and
(e) a possible criminal offence.

In all the above cases the designated officer must bring the matter to the attention of his senior officers or, if appropriate, the District Health Authority Director of Public Health and the Regional Medical Officer for proper action to be taken in accordance with established procedures. In the case of (a) above the procedure is set out in Annex B to HC(88)37 which appeared originally as part of Circular HC(81)5 and will be described in some detail below. In the case of (b), (c), (d) and (e) above there is a range of options by way of investigation and essentially it is for the senior officers to decide which should be invoked according to the nature and gravity of the complaint. In reaching a decision as to which option to invoke the senior officers must take into account a number of factors. If the complaint is likely to lead to litigation it is important that legal advice should be obtained from a legal adviser at an early stage. This is particularly important because of the effect which the commencement of legal proceedings may have upon the status of documents and statements which may be prepared for the purpose of the investigation of the complaint. In the case of *Waugh v British Railways Board*[1] it was held that material which comes into existence as a result of the authority's own investigation and which cannot be proved to have come into existence predominantly for the purpose of defending legal proceedings is not privileged and may therefore be required to be disclosed in subsequent legal proceedings.[2] Clearly, therefore, the preparation of statements of witnesses, reports and other documents needs to be done carefully so as to ensure their factual accuracy and to avoid admission of liability. For these reasons early legal advice is crucial.

1 [1980] AC 521.
2 See also *Lask v Gloucester Health Authority* (1986) 2 PN 96.

3.13 Again, in deciding how to deal with complaints in categories (b) to (e) above, officers need to have regard to the interests of staff. Management must consider any confusion between the complaints procedure on the one hand and the disciplinary procedure on the other. If there is any question of the interests of staff being in jeopardy the members of staff involved must be advised to seek trade union or staff association advice before interviews proceed. Clearly the investigation into the complaint must proceed and the staff involved must be advised of the status of interviews, i e whether they are in pursuit of the complaints procedure or of disciplinary procedure. The members of staff should be offered the facility of being accompanied by union or other staff during interviews.

3.14 A further problem which can arise is where the complaint does in fact emanate from a member of staff who has observed, for example, physical abuse of a patient by another member of staff or other criminal activity. Here there are many sensitivities which arise, particularly if the member of staff seeks to maintain anonymity, which should be offered to him. This should not, however, impede the progress of the investigation unless the senior officer or officers conclude that the investigation cannot proceed without disclosure of the identity of the complainant. If the complainant insists on anonymity, this should be respected.

3.15 It is recognised that there can be some overlap between the various categories outlined above. The interrelation of the complaints and disciplinary procedures has been discussed above. In all cases under HC(88)37 it is for the senior district officers, where necessary with the chairman and members of the authority, to decide how to proceed in relation to those categories and to involve senior officers from the appropriate disciplines in conducting the investigation. The actual responsibilities as between Trusts or Units and the District Health Authority need to be agreed, pending further direction from government.

3.16 In all cases the outcome of the investigation should be notified to the complainant so that he does receive an answer to his complaint. It should be noted that no appeal as such lies against the authority or its officers against the decision reached under the investigations described above. However, as will be seen below, in many cases the complainant may have recourse to the Health Service Commissioner if he is not satisfied with the conduct or outcome of the Authority's own investigation.

COMPLAINTS INVOLVING CLINICAL JUDGMENT

3.17 As already mentioned the procedure for dealing with complaints concerning the exercise of clinical judgment is contained in Annex B of Circular HC(88)37. It does in fact consist of a memorandum of agreement reached some years ago between the Secretary of State and the medical and dental professions. It is likely that such complaints will be handled by the provider Units but in all cases the Director of Public Health of the purchasing authority must be notified of the complaint. There are three stages to the procedure outlined in the memorandum.

3.18 The first stage is for the complaint to be made or referred to the consultant in charge of the patient. He should seek to resolve the matter with the complainant by open discussion within a matter of a few days from the receipt of the complaint. If another doctor is involved with the patient he should be brought into the handling of the complaint. The consultant should make a factual record in the patient's notes of the outcome of the discussion. If the consultant takes the view that there is a significant risk of legal action being taken he should immediately inform the chief executive or general manager who may wish to take legal advice before responding in detail to the patient. If the complaint also involves non-clinical matters the chief executive or general manager should arrange for these to be considered by the appropriate member of staff. Any response to the complainant on non-clinical matters should be made with the agreement of the consultant.

3.19 At this stage of the procedure the complainant sometimes approaches the consultant through his solicitor to obtain the medical reports relating to treatment given by the consultant or other hospital doctor. This is a premature request and the consultant would be wise through the chief executive or general manager or through his own medical defence organisation to restrict such disclosure at this stage (if it is agreed at all) to an independent medical adviser nominated by the patient and of course subject to the patient's consent.[1]

1 But see later and RSC Ord 24, r7A and Supreme Court Act 1981, s33.

3.20 If the first stage of the clinical judgment procedure does not resolve the complaint the complainant may renew his complaint either to the Trust or Unit or to one of its officers or to the consultant. If he has not already put his complaint in writing the complainant must be asked to put it in writing now and the consultant must then inform the Regional Medical Officer (RMO) and also advise the chief executive or general manager that he has done so. The RMO must discuss the matter with the consultant at this stage. The consultant may wish thereafter to discuss the matter with his own professional colleagues and may feel after such discussions that a further discussion with the complainant will be helpful. If this does not resolve the matter or if the consultant does not feel that such further discussion with the complainant will be helpful, the RMO should discuss with the consultant the implementation of the third stage of the procedure. If the consultant agrees and if the RMO after, where necessary, discussing the proposal with the complainant is satisfied that the third stage is appropriate he should proceed accordingly.

3.21 The third stage of the clinical judgment procedure is for an independent professional review to take place. This should only be carried out in cases of a substantial nature and where the RMO is satisfied that on the evidence before him, and preferably after taking legal advice, it seems unlikely that any formal action will be taken either by the Trust, Unit or health authority or through the courts. It is highly desirable at this stage to seek to obtain from the complainant an undertaking that he will not proceed to taking action in the courts if this third stage of the complaints procedure is implemented. The complainant is not bound to give such an undertaking and if it is refused the RMO must consider whether to proceed with the third stage in any event. A refusal by the RMO could be the subject of an application to the Health Service Commissioner to determine whether such refusal is maladministration. There must be a serious doubt as to whether such an undertaking by a complainant would in any event be enforceable against him even in cases, which have occurred, where a payment is offered to the complainant by way of consideration for the undertaking. Clearly the RMO would be prudent to ask for the undertaking but it would seem to be contrary to the intention of the circular if he refuses to proceed to the third stage because of a refusal by the complainant to give an undertaking. It should be noted that the consultant has no right to prevent the matter proceeding to the third stage.

3.22 Assuming that the RMO is satisfied that the independent professional review should proceed he should arrange for all aspects of the case to be considered by two independent consultants in active practice in the appropriate speciality or specialities. They should be nominated by the Joint Consultants' Committee. At least one of them should be a doctor working in a comparable hospital in another region. Once appointed, the 'Second Opinions', as they are described in the circular, must have access to all the clinical records and then discuss the case with the consultant and any other member of the medical staff involved as well as with the complainant. The meeting between the Second Opinions and the complainant should be in the nature of a medical consultation and the consultant should not be present although he should be available. The complainant should be entitled to have a relative or friend or general practitioner present.

3.23 The Second Opinions should discuss all clinical aspects of the case fully with the complainant. If it is their view that the clinical judgment of the medical staff concerned has been properly exercised they should endeavour to satisfy the complainant's anxieties. They should report their view and the outcome of the discussion with the complainant to the RMO on a confidential basis.

3.24 There may be cases where the Second Opinions may feel that a discussion with medical staff would avoid similar problems in the future. The circular recommends that after such discussion the complainant should be informed and told how it was hoped to overcome the problem which had been identified. The Second Opinions should not give a detailed report to the complainant but they should report the action taken and any recommendations to the RMO. Exceptionally the Second Opinions may feel at any stage of the investigation that the second opinion procedure is not appropriate in which case they should so report to the RMO.

3.25 Finally when the review by the Second Opinions is completed the chief executive or general manager should write to the complainant with a copy to the consultant explaining any action taken by the Trust, Unit or authority as a result of the complaint but any reference to clinical matters should be based on advice from the RMO. The matter should remain confidential so far as the Trust, Unit or authority is concerned unless there has been publicity about the complaint in which case the response of the Trust, Unit or authority should be confined to the terms of the letter from the chief executive or general manager.

3.26 It has to be recognised that the pursuit of the complaint to the third stage in the above procedure does run the risk from the point of view of the Trust, Unit or authority and of the consultant of bringing into existence evidence which may be of assistance to the complainant if he decides to take legal action after completion of the investigation of the complaint.[1] The court may well regard the correspondence and documents relating to the investigation as discoverable in court proceedings, thus improving the information available to the complainant to support his case. It may be possible to maintain a balance and protect confidence attaching to those documents from a defence point of view by including them in an undertaking obtained from the complainant before the commencement of the third stage of the clinical judgment procedure, but as has been indicated above there must be doubt as to the availability and enforceability of such undertakings. Abuse of the clinical judgment procedure with a view to obtaining discovery of additional documents could undermine the availability of medical support for the procedure.

1 See *Lee v South West Thames Regional Health Authority* [1985] 2 All ER 385 at 389, CA and *Naylor v Preston Area Health Authority* [1987] 2 All ER 353 at 360, CA, and Chapter 13 on limitation of actions.

3.27 For completeness it should be noted that complaints relating to clinical judgment are outside the jurisdiction of the Health Service Commissioner except insofar as he can advise complainants whose complaints contain elements of clinical judgment as to the availability of the procedure described above.

Monitoring

3.28 The Circular HC(88)37 at paragraph 5 of Annex A places a clear duty upon health authorities to monitor the arrangements for dealing with complaints at hospitals. The designated officer must prepare quarterly reports, anonymised for patient confidentiality, and ensure that they are produced to the authority or more usually to its Complaints and Incidents Panel. As already discussed, notwithstanding the changes created by the 1990 Act and the transitional uncertainties there remains an obligation upon the District Health Authority as purchaser to monitor the procedure and reports and this duty is reinforced by the Patient's Charter and the guidelines HSG(92)4 issued by the NHS Management Executive dealing with the implementation of the Charter. Accordingly the district general manager should keep the procedures and reports under review.

Publicity

3.29 The circular, but not the directions contained in it, does require authorities to give publicity to the complaints procedure. This requirement is reinforced by the Patient's Charter and the guidelines HSG(92)4. Such publicity should be achieved by including information about making complaints in admission booklets given to patients, including out-patients, on admission to hospital, in leaflets which should be readily available and in notices displayed in Trust, Unit and health authority premises. All such documents should give the name and location of the designated officer.

COMPLAINTS ABOUT COMMUNITY HEALTH SERVICES

3.30 On a strict view complaints about the community health services do not come within the scope of the procedures laid down in the directions made under the Hospital Complaints Procedure Act 1985. This is because section 1 of that Act specifically refers to complaints made by persons who are or have been patients in hospital. However the Circular HC(88)37 – but not the directions contained in it – does suggest that health authorities should consider adopting the procedure directed for hospital complaints in relation also to community health services. There would appear to be no difficulty about appointing a designated officer for community health services and many authorities have done so and also operate similar procedures including quarterly reports to the authority as are required in respect of hospital complaints. In some places community health services are provided by NHS Trusts and otherwise they are provided by Directly Managed Units. The comments about responsibilities made in para **3.10** apply equally to community health services.

COMPLAINTS ABOUT FAMILY HEALTH SERVICES

3.31 There is an important and fundamental difference between hospital complaints and family health services complaints. As has been explained above, complaints about hospital services are substantially addressed to Trusts, Units or health authorities themselves and relate to the services provided by them and to the staff employed by them, which include doctors. The Trust, Unit or health authority itself deals with the complaints in the manner described even though the complaints may be against the Trust, Unit or health authority and its own staff.

3.32 In the case of family health services, however, the situation is quite different. The Family Health Services Authorities have statutory responsibility under the Health and Social Security Act 1984, as amended by subsequent Acts, to administer the general medical services, the general dental services, the general ophthalmic services and pharmaceutical services. The services are provided by independent practitioners working under contract as independent contractors to the FHSAs, and these practitioners are therefore not employees of the FHSAs. The terms of service of these practitioners are now set out in National Health Service (General Medical Services) Regulations 1992, SI 1992/635, which amend and supersede the 1974 Regulations, although the latter are still relevant to events which took place prior to 1 April 1992. The scope of complaints which can be made by patients or persons on their behalf for investigation by an FHSA is limited to questions of whether the practitioner has breached his terms of service. Thus when the FHSA investigates complaints in respect of family health services it does so with a view to determining the narrow point as to whether there has been a breach of the terms of service of the practitioner and not in any way as to the performance of the FHSA itself. The guidance issued by the Department of Health makes it clear that hearings of the service committees established by FHSAs do not exist to remedy patients' personal grievances but to settle disputes about whether or not practitioners have fulfilled the terms of their contracts. It follows from this and from the nature of the FHSA investigation procedures described below that the potential conflicts between statutory complaints procedures and civil litigation which have been discussed in relation to hospital complaints procedures do not generally arise in FHSA complaints procedures.

3.33 In all cases of complaint in relation to the family health services the complaint must be made in writing (except in the case of disability of the patient) to the FHSA stating the substance of the matter which it is desired to have investigated. In relation to complaints against doctors, ophthalmic medical practitioners, chemists or opticians the notice must be given within 13 weeks after the event which gave rise to the complaint. In the case of a dentist, notice of the complaint must be given within six months after completion of the treatment or within 13 weeks after the matter which gave rise to the complaint has come to the complainant's notice, whichever is the sooner. Although the regulations stipulate these time limits there is nevertheless power to investigate a late complaint if there are good reasons and if consent is obtained either from the practitioner concerned or from the Secretary of State.

Informal treatment of complaints

3.34 Although the National Health Service (Service Committees and Tribunal) Regulations 1992 do not specifically refer to informal treatment of complaints, the guidance issued to the former Family Practitioner Committees under the previous regulations does at Chapter 6 set out details of recommended informal procedures for dealing with complaints. These are very helpful procedures and some FHSAs find that over 90 per cent of complaints are disposed of by the informal procedures without reaching the service committees. No guidance has yet been issued under the 1992 Regulations but it is likely that such guidance when issued will also contain recommendations about informal procedures. The key concept of such procedures is that of conciliation and the task is usually allocated to a lay conciliator who is normally a member of the FHSA and who should have the assistance of a professional adviser of the relevant profession. Such informal procedure should be speedy and preferably concluded within a month. If it cannot be speedily resolved or if the complainant is not satisfied then the complaint must proceed as provided in the regulations.

Formal procedure

3.35 The regulations provide for complaints to be dealt with by service committees. There is an obligation upon FHSAs to establish at least one committee for each of the four services for which the FHSA is responsible, that is, medical, dental, ophthalmic and pharmaceutical, and also a joint services committee. In addition it may appoint a denture conciliation committee. The composition of these committees is laid down in Schedule 2 to the 1992 Reguations.

3.36 If a medical complaint cannot be resolved by the informal procedure outlined, then the complaint must be investigated stage by stage in the following manner.

Stage 1

3.37 The FHSA must send to the chairman of the medical service committee a copy of the complainant's statement. If the chairman takes the view that the statement does not disclose any breach of the terms of service of the practitioner the complainant must be so informed and given an opportunity to submit a further statement. If he does not do so or if the chairman takes the view that, even on the basis of the additional statement, no hearing is necessary, the matter should be brought to the service committee who may report to the FHSA without holding a hearing.

Stage 2

3.38 If the chairman of the service committee takes the view that the statement of the complainant, taken with any additional statement which may have been submitted, discloses reasonable grounds for believing that the practitioner has failed to comply with his terms of service, the FHSA shall send a copy of such statement to the practitioner and invite his comments within a period of 30 days. Any such comments should be sent to the complainant who should be given 14 days in which to make any observations on these comments. If the chairman is of the opinion that a hearing of the case is unnecessary the case must be brought before the service committee who may report on the matter to the FHSA without a hearing. If, however, the chairman takes the view that a hearing is necessary in the light of the comments received or if no comments have been received from the practitioner then the chairman must instruct the FHSA to arrange a hearing of the case. If there is a material dispute on the facts it is normal for a hearing to be held. Complainant and practitioner are invited to attend and may be assisted in the presentation of their case by another person who may not address the committee in the capacity of counsel, solicitor or other paid advocate or examine or cross-examine witnesses although he may advise the party concerned. The hearing takes place in private. Each party is invited to give evidence and to call witnesses and parties and witnesses can be cross-examined by the other party and questioned by the committee. The parties are invited to sum up their cases.

Stage 3

3.39 Thereafter the service committee must cause a report to be prepared giving details of the material evidence given to it and stating the relevant facts which they have found to be proved and the inferences in relation to a breach of terms of service or otherwise which they have drawn from the facts. They must also make recommendations as to what action, if any, should be taken in the light of their findings. The action which they can recommend ranges from a warning to the practitioner to observe his terms of service more closely at one end of the scale, to a recommendation that the continued inclusion of the practitioner on the medical list would be prejudicial to the efficiency of the services. The alternatives include the withholding of an amount from the practitioner's remuneration, limiting the number of patients who can be on the list of that practitioner or the payment of expenses reasonably incurred by the patient because of the failure of the practitioner to comply with his terms of service, but such expenses do not include expenses incurred in connection with the investigation by the service committee.

3.40 The report of the service committee goes to the FHSA which is bound by the findings of fact contained in the report but is not bound to accept the recommendations of the service committee as to the action to be taken. If it does not accept the recommendations it must give reasons for rejecting them. The decision of the FHSA must be notified to the parties and to the

Secretary of State with a copy of the report. The decisions of the FHSA are final, subject to the right of appeal, except where it recommends that an amount in excess of £500 should be recovered from the practitioner in which case it is for the Secretary of State to make the decision. It should be noted, however, that in relation to all cases in England (but not Wales), by virtue of SI 1992/660, the functions of the Secretary of State are as from 1 April 1992 exercisable by the Yorkshire Regional Health Authority.

3.41 The parties have a right to appeal to the Secretary of State whose function is exercisable by the Yorkshire RHA, which right must be exercised in writing within 30 days of the date of receipt by the appellant of the notification of the decision by the FHSA. However, no appeal lies to the Secretary of State at this stage against a decision of the FHSA to make representations with regard to the continued inclusion of the practitioner in the medical list since that decision must be pursued by the FHSA in the NHS tribunal from which appeal lies to the Secretary of State after the tribunal has made its decision. The Secretary of State can decide to dismiss the appeal if there are no reasonable grounds of appeal or if it is otherwise frivolous or vexatious but he cannot dismiss the appeal of a practitioner against a recommendation to limit a practitioner's list or impose a financial penalty without an oral hearing unless the appellant does not desire such a hearing. If the Secretary of State does not dismiss the appeal for the above reasons he must send a copy of the notice of appeal and any other papers supplied by the appellant to the FHSA and to the other parties to the service committee hearing and, except in relation to the restriction on dismissal mentioned above, he can decide to determine the appeal without an oral hearing or he can decide to hold an oral hearing.

3.42 If an oral hearing is to be held the Secretary of State appoints three persons of whom one shall be a barrister or solicitor as chairman and in medical cases, two doctors. The parties may be represented by counsel or a solicitor or other paid advocate and the hearing usually takes the form of a re-hearing of the case. The persons holding the inquiry report to the Secretary of State who issues the final decision and the reasons for it. There is power to award costs of the hearing.

COMPARISON OF PROCEDURES

3.43 It will be seen from the description of the two procedures, namely, the hospital complaints procedure and family health services procedure, that there are considerable differences between them as they now stand. Broadly speaking the hospital complaints procedure is reasonably swift and brings a response to the patient without undue pressure and personal involvement for the patient. It may also open up avenues for common law claims as a result of disclosures made in the course of such procedure.

3.44 The family health services procedure, on the other hand, involves the patient in considerable expenditure of time and effort including as it does attendance in many cases at service committees, and even in oral hearings of appeals to the Secretary of State. The duration of these procedures to date has been unsatisfactory. The average case from lodging of complaint to decision by the FHSA takes in the region of six months unless resolved by the informal procedure. As has been seen, where the recommendation has been to recover an amount in excess of £500 from the practitioner the decision has to be made by the Secretary of State which can take a further period of months and past history has shown that appeals to the Secretary of State can take anything up to 18 months to resolve. Thus delays of anything up to two years from start to finish have been taking place and have inevitably discouraged patients from pursuing their complaints. There is the further disadvantage that the procedures do not bring any direct benefit to the patient, limited as they are to questions of whether the practitioner has been in breach of his terms of service. A swifter resolution of such complaints would be to everyone's advantage. It is to be hoped that the increased success of the informal procedure and the shortening of the time scale anticipated by the delegation of the Secretary of State's functions to the Yorkshire Regional Health Authority will achieve considerable improvement.

Voluntary organisations and independent hospitals

3.45 Under section 23 of the NHS Act 1977 District Health Authorities may on behalf of the Secretary of State arrange for services to be provided under the Act by any person or body including a voluntary organisation. The question of complaints which may arise in relation to services provided by a voluntary organisation or independent hospital is covered by EL(90)P/16 and its directions. Such complaints should be dealt with by the procedures explained in HC(88)37 and it is therefore desirable that Health Authorities should ensure when dealing with voluntary and independent organisations that those procedures are referred to and incorporated in their contractual documents.

The Health Service Commissioner

3.46 Within the limits laid down in the NHS Act 1977 the Health Service Commissioner may investigate complaints from members of the public who claim to have suffered injustice or hardship in three main areas. These are a failure in a service provided by a Trust or health authority or FHSA, a failure by one of those bodies to provide a service which it has a duty to provide, or maladministration which has affected any other action taken by or on behalf of one of those bodies. The complaint can be made by any individual or organisation claiming to have suffered injustice or hardship as a result of the failures or maladministration mentioned above. However, local authorities, bodies appointed by the Crown or a minister or government department or whose revenue is funded wholly or in part by Parliament, or nationalised industries cannot ask the Health Service Commissioner to investigate complaints. Although the Commissioner has a wide remit there are restrictions upon the matters which he can investigate. Amongst the matters he cannot investigate are:

(1) grievances for which there is or has been a remedy in the courts or other tribunal, although he can investigate if he thinks it unreasonable for the complainant to have to go to court;

(2) actions taken in connection with the diagnosis of illness or the care or treatment of a patient if in the Commissioner's opinion it was taken solely in consequence of the exercise of clinical judgment;
(3) the actions of family practitioners, dentists, opticians and pharmacists in connection with the services they provide under contract with FHSAs;
(4) actions taken by an FHSA in investigating complaints against their contractors or personnel matters (although he can investigate matters relating to the action taken by FHSA staff before the commencement of formal proceedings);
(5) personnel matters including pay, discipline and superannuation;
(6) contractual or other commercial transactions;
(7) properly taken discretionary decisions which an authority has a right to take (but he can look at whether the authority has followed proper procedures and considered all relevant aspects in reaching its decision);
(8) action which has been or is the subject of an enquiry set up by the Secretary of State;
(9) complaints made more than one year after the date on which the matter first came to the notice of the complainant (although the Commissioner has a right to waive this requirement if he considers the explanation of the delay to be reasonable).

3.47 The Commissioner cannot investigate the complaint unless the complainant has first notified the complaint to the authority concerned and has given that authority an opportunity to investigate and reply to it. The Commissioner will normally arrange a full investigation by his staff and he has power to require information and documents to be produced and also has the powers of the High Court to compel discovery of documents and the attendance and examination of witnesses. When the investigation is complete he sends copies of his draft report to the complainant and the authority and his report may and frequently does make recommendations to the authority to rectify what he regards as wrong. Subject to any comments of the parties he then publishes his final report to them and also to the Secretary of State who lays it before the Houses of Parliament. He publishes two volumes of case reports each year. In addition his work is overseen by a Parliamentary Select Committee and where an authority fails to grant the remedies recommended by the Commissioner or where there is some other feature of the case which attracts the attention of the Select Committee it has power to summon members and officers of the authority to give evidence before it. The Select Committee publishes a report of those proceedings.

3.48 There are offices of the Health Service Commissioner for England, Wales and Scotland so that the posts are separate but the same person may, and in fact does, at the present time hold all three posts.

The Patient's Charter

3.49 The Patient's Charter, published on 30 October 1991, came into effect on 1 April 1992. It is enlarged and explained by guidelines contained in HSG(92)4. Essentially it refers to seven existing rights under the NHS and then creates three new rights and sets in broad terms nine new standards of service to be provided. Of these provisions the point of significance for this chapter is the right of patients to have any complaint about NHS services – whoever provides them – investigated and to receive a full and prompt written reply from the executive or general manager. The Charter also imposes on health authorities and NHS hospitals the duty to publish details regularly of both number of complaints and how long it has taken to deal with them. It also refers to the right to take the matter up with the Health Service Commissioner if the patient is unhappy about the way in which the administration of an NHS service has been handled. The Charter also encourages patients who feel they are denied the National Charter Rights to write to the Chief Executive of the NHS. This would seem to open up a further channel of complaint for patients although it is likely that such complaints will be routed back through the systems already described.

Professional bodies

3.50 If a patient or those advising him feel that a doctor has been guilty of serious professional misconduct they are entitled to make a complaint direct to the General Medical Council. The Council has to investigate such complaints but if formal steps are to be taken the complainant will normally be required to make a statutory declaration setting out details of the complaint. In relation to cases which have been investigated by service committees of FHSAs the result, if adverse to the doctor, is routinely reported to the General Medical Council which will then investigate the matter depending upon the degree of seriousness of the case. If the General Medical Council decides that there is a prima facie case of serious professional misconduct then the matter will be referred to the professional conduct committee for a formal enquiry which will normally involve the patient giving evidence in the proceedings of that committee. If the case is found proved the powers of the committee range from a warning to the doctor to striking him off the Medical Register. In appropriate cases the General Medical Council can refer the matter to the Health Committee of the General Medical Council where the doctor's fitness to practice appears to be impaired by a physical or medical condition. The General Medical Council is presently considering the introduction of a new procedure for dealing with less serious cases falling short of serious professional misconduct but this is still at the consultation stage.

Support for complainants

3.51 It is frequently difficult for patients to make their complaints in the appropriate manner or to the right person or address. It is often advantageous to the would-be complainant to have the support of an advice agency. Those readily available are the community health councils which exist in each District Health Authority district and citizens' advice bureaux. Most leaflets and publicity produced by Trusts, Units or health authorities in pursuit of the directions given in HC(88)37 in fact give the address of the local community health council to assist patients.

3.52 The other agency which is available for would-be complainants, and particularly for would-be plaintiffs, is the organisation known as Action for the Victims of Medical Accidents (AVMA).[1] Whilst AVMA do give help in cases which fall short of formal legal action they in fact specialise in dealing in cases which require the intervention of a lawyer. They provide a range of advice from identifying an appropriate law firm to advising on experts for particular fields of medical advice.

1 See paras **4.71** et seq.

STATE OF THE LAW

3.53 The following points should be noted in relation to the contents of this chapter:

(1) the legal details given reflect the state of the law as at 1 October 1992. As referred to in the text some matters are in fact in the process of being reviewed at the present time;

(2) the hospital complaints procedure act 1985 relates to england, wales and Scotland but not Northern Ireland;

(3) the circular HC(88)37:HN(FP)(88)18 made under the 1985 Act only affects England and Wales. Similar directions were given to Scottish health boards by the Scottish Office in September 1991. The Scottish Office has now issued NHS Circular GEN(1992)27 which applies the September 1991 guidance to NHS Trusts in Scotland and gives guidance on monitoring of complaints to health boards and NHS Trusts (see page 1137).

CHAPTER 4

Agencies

Arnold Simanowitz *Solicitor*

SUMMARY

INTRODUCTION

4.1 A book entitled *Medical Negligence* should be devoted almost entirely to a consideration of the law and how it touches on the mistakes that can occur during medical treatment. As is clearly set out elsewhere in this volume, negligence is a purely legal concept which requires prescribed circumstances to constitute it and which leads to inevitable consequences.

4.2 Long before the law becomes involved, however, long before even the questions of a legal concept arise, the issues thrown up by a mistake made during the course of medical treatment must be identified, faced and dealt with in the best interests of patients and doctors.

4.3 This chapter will look at what the event is that amounts to a medical accident, the relationship between patients and health carers when something has gone wrong during medical care and what help patients and doctors can and do get before the law intrudes into the picture. It will also look at the consequences of the present arrangements for and attitudes towards dealing with medical accidents and the implications for patients and health carers for the future.

4.4 The first major problem facing a patient who has suffered a medical accident is, strangely, knowing that that is in fact what happened.

4.5 It is not easy to define a medical accident. Hospitals in referring to the problem will talk about 'untoward incidents'; lay people are more likely to talk about 'something going wrong'. For the purposes of a consideration of the problem within defined limits and relating what went wrong to what patients and doctors can do about what went wrong, including the legal pursuit of compensation, we can define a medical accident as something which has gone wrong during medical care as a result of an act of commission or omission on the part of one or more health carers.

4.6 If we simply classed as an accident everything that 'went wrong' during such treatment, then that would include in many cases the natural (but unusual) progression of disease, the unavoidable introduction of infection into a wound, or the recuperation which takes longer than it should. Everyone knows (or should know) that 'things go wrong' during medical treatment. What they do not know is when those things are actually caused by someone doing something wrong, or failing to do something which they should have done. Whether what was done or not done was blameworthy or could and should have been avoided is what other chapters in this book will deal with at some length. What I am concerned with at this point is the difficulty for the patient in knowing that such an act of commission or omission has taken place at all.

4.7 This can best be clarified by taking what is a classic example which many people who have had any problems during medical treatment will have come across. A person goes into hospital for a major though common operation; she comes out of the anaesthetic and finds herself in a ward with a number of other people who have undergone the same operation and are at different stages of recovery. One by one, those people get better and are discharged. Only she remains behind – suffering. Even people who have had the operation after her have long since gone home. She repeatedly asks the nurses and the junior doctors whom she sees why she does not seem to be getting better, why the others have gone home before her, when she will go home. Eventually, if she is lucky, she sees the consultant and asks why it is all taking so long. 'Well, my dear' goes the reply, 'don't be in so much of a hurry. You know your body has suffered a major insult and cannot recover in a day.' To the repeated enquiry as to why others have recovered more quickly she will be told that 'we are all different you know, we do not all recover at the same rate'. And this may even be followed, particularly if the patient is a woman and the consultant is a man of a certain age, by a patronising analogy with the situation in the kitchen where sometimes the cakes will take one hour and others, though the same recipe is used, will take one and a half hours!

4.8 A trusting patient – and we are all desperate to trust the medical profession – will accept that explanation. Sometimes it will even be true. Very often, it will not. In the example above it may well have been the case that the surgeon doing, say, an hysterectomy operation, has punctured the bladder. This has led to incontinence, pain, perhaps infection, all of which have delayed the patient's discharge. That puncturing of the bladder may not have been negligent and therefore amenable to an award of compensation – which is something which will be dealt with in another chapter. Nevertheless, it is an accident caused by the surgeon; but the patient does not know that, and may never know. That kind of situation is repeated throughout the Health Service (whether the National Health Service or Private Health Service) day in and day out. Those who have some knowledge of the service, such as people working in the organisations with which I shall deal later in this chapter, know about some of those accidents: we know, for example, that during hip replacement operations, damage is caused to the sciatic nerve; sometimes that is unavoidable, often it is caused by incompetent or at least inferior operating techniques. It is only the curious, articulate and determined patient, however, who will actually know that any 'accident' has happened at all.

4.9 This inability of the patient to ascertain that an accident has taken place has implications not only for the health of the patient and the patient/doctor relationship but also for the right of a victim of an accident to recover damages. That right is lost if no legal action is commenced within three years of an accident taking place or the victim knowing that the accident has taken place (with certain exceptions as explained in Chapter 11). Section 14 of the Limitation Act 1980, which is dealt with in detail elsewhere, defines what 'knowledge' is in this context but it is quite clear that in the circumstances described above doctors may, by not telling patients that something has gone wrong, prevent those patients from seeking compensation in the short term. This means that the possibility of a legal action being brought by patients will hang over the doctors like the sword of Damocles until the end of their days.

FINDING OUT WHAT HAPPENED AND WHY

4.10 Over a period of years there has been a change in the attitudes of patients. Increasing education, increasing confidence and the general attitude of challenge to authority which has developed particularly since the 1990s has meant that more and more patients are taking a greater interest in the way in which they are treated when they are ill. They want to know more about what is being done to them and why. This means that they are more likely to realise (or think, sometimes incorrectly) that all is not as it should be when there are in fact problems with their treatment.

4.11 That is where they come up against the second problem: finding out what has happened and why it has happened when they do want to know. It is my experience, having seen thousands of cases of medical accidents and having talked to people involved with thousands more as well as with health carers who have observed accidents which have gone no further, that when an accident takes place, the most scarce commodity available is information.

4.12 I would like to look now in some detail at the problems that patients face in trying to obtain information about a medical accident or what they believe may have been a medical accident.

4.13 The whole process can seem, to a victim, like nothing less than an obstacle race, each obstacle appearing more formidable than the last.

OBTAINING INFORMATION – OR THE 'TRUTH'

4.14 It is essential that the importance of this particular issue is not underrated by either health carers or patients. It is, in my view, the single most important matter in the whole complex problem of medical accidents not only affecting the relationship between doctors and patients but having implications for the growth in and conduct of legal proceedings. Patients do not want to sue doctors, they do not want to complain about doctors; taking either of those steps undermines their faith in doctors and what patients want above all is to have faith in their doctors. But not blind faith, which it sometimes appears is what *doctors* want patients to have.

4.15 The difficulty is that when a patient begins to seek information about something that appears to have gone wrong the first break in that patient's trust in a doctor has already occurred. The patient invariably believes that he or she is going to be 'cured' by the doctor, or at least is going to be made to feel better. When the consequence of the care is that the patient feels worse, the patient's faith is going to be tested. It is at that point that the health carers hold the key to whether the patient's faith is going to be restored or whether it is going to be destroyed, possibly forever, leaving a bitter patient who is going to believe little the doctor says and is determined to pursue the matter until 'justice' is obtained.

4.16 Before I deal with the response to enquiries made after something appears to have gone wrong, there is another aspect which should be emphasised. I have pointed out that patients invariably believe that they are going to be 'cured' by the doctor. Many of the problems that arise following a less than perfect result that does not involve negligence are the direct results of the doctors failing to warn patients adequately of the risks involved and the possibility of complications.

4.17 The debate on 'informed consent' and its legal implications is an emotive one for both patients and doctors and is only now beginning to gather momentum, notwithstanding the House of Lords attempts in *Sidaway*[1] to close that particular route to compensation. Quite apart from the legal implications however, there are the strongest pragmatic arguments for disclosing real risks to the patient. The reasons advanced by doctors for not giving information are many and varied. There is a suspicion, however, that most doctors think it is not in their interests to give too much information.

1 *Sidaway v Board of Governors of the Bethlem Royal Hospital and the Maudsley Hospital* [1985] AC 871, [1985] 1 All ER 643, HL.

4.18 The most coherent analysis of the situation I have seen appears in the book by Sandra Coney about the government enquiry in New Zealand into the treatment of patients suffering from carcinoma in situ at the Royal National Hospital (*The Unfortunate Experiment*):

The assumption that many patients were simple-minded and in possession of an infantile level of comprehension struck many of us listening at the inquiry, both lay people and lawyers. It was heard from many of the medical witnesses. The information booklets produced by Dr Collison were pitched at the level of an eight-year-old and were, in essence, patronising. If patients said they had not been told certain information, the attitude was that they had not heard or taken it in.

I listened to this view with increasing irritation. I had worked for ten years as a counsellor in a hospital, work which involved the giving of information about contraception, the operative procedure, and gaining consent. We not only explained verbally, we gave written information, we showed the women the operating instruments, models of anatomy, and took them to see the theatre and the recovery room. In addition, as part of Fertility Action work, I had talked to hundreds of women about health problems and given them written information. Our booklet on pelvic inflammatory disease was over thirty pages long. I had never encountered any serious problems about people's understanding. If I did, I took it as my responsibility to ensure I had made myself clear. The tendency at the cancer inquiry was to blame the recipients of information rather than examine the manner in which the information was conveyed. The patients were blamed for not understanding, they were blamed for not asking questions and they were blamed by both Dr Collison and Dr Duncan for having too high an expectation of the health system.

4.19 The fact is, however, that the more information that is given to a patient before treatment, the less likely legal advice is going to be sought when something untoward takes place. It is a pity that doctors cannot be convinced that it is in their own interests to strive for 'informed consent'.

4.20 The patient or a relative will first seek information from the ward staff. If, however, something really has gone wrong and the consultant is implicated in any way, the 'team spirit' or rather the hierarchical nature of the team will invariably mean that junior members of that team will feel bound not to say anything which might reflect badly on the consultant. This leads to their replying in vague terms, trying to gloss over what has happened, trying to deny that anything has gone wrong. At nursing level this may lead to anger and rudeness towards the patient brought about by the nurses' own feelings of guilt.

4.21 The next step is usually to try to obtain information from the consultant. There is no doubt that in many cases consultants will sit down with the patient or relative and explain to the best of their ability exactly what has happened and why the patients find themselves in the state which they are in. There is also no doubt that many patients find the consultants unapproachable, unhelpful and, in many cases, obstructive. It is difficult to know in what percentage of cases these two different attitudes prevail. It is clear that most of the patients who approach organisations like AVMA will have experienced the worst face of the consultant. What is even clearer, however, is that there are enough consultants who behave badly to create the atmosphere of suspicion and antipathy which is beginning to become a serious problem in doctor/patient relationships.

4.22 These problems were, and are, of course not confined to hospital doctors. Attempts by patients to obtain information from their general practitioners often meet with similar responses. Apart from anything else, busy practitioners, with something like five minutes to spend on each of their patients, are not going to have the time or inclination to discuss at any length problems which may touch on their own, or a colleague's wrong behaviour.

4.23 It was precisely because of these difficulties that the procedures for making a formal complaint were developed: the Family Practitioners Committee complaints system under the regulations made under the Health and Social Security Act 1984, and the hospital complaints procedure recommended by HC(81)5 and given statutory force under the Hospital Complaints Procedure Act 1985 and now enshrined in HC(88)37.

4.24 The details of these two procedures and the way they work and their success or otherwise in giving the patients what they want is dealt with in Chapter 3. There is, however, one major obstacle placed in the path of patients' search for information and explanation which is not removed by either of these procedures and which as much as anything else continues to nurture patients' sense of frustration and their lack of trust in the medical profession in the area of medical mishap: I refer to the fact that patients are not shown their medical records. When the first edition of this book was published there was no right for patients to see their medical records. Since then the Access to Health Records Act 1990 was passed and came into effect on 1 November 1992. Although in theory this gives patients the right to see their records, so far it has not greatly affected the position for patients who feel that they are not being told the truth and the paragraphs dealing with this topic still retain their validity. This is partly because access is only allowed to records made after the introduction of the Act but mainly because the attitude of health carers towards the records remains basically the same and there is no voluntary action on their part to explain what has happened by reference to the records actually shown to the patient.

4.25 Among all the words, theories, excuses and interpretations which surround an enquiry into what happened in the course of medical treatment, only one thing stands out as fact: the written case record. This record can be inadequately kept, it may on occasion even be falsified but, by and large, it represents as good a record of what happened as is ever going to be produced. Yet the patient is rarely shown that record other than in the context of legal proceedings.

4.26 The resistance by the medical profession generally to disclosing notes to patients is quite inexplicable save by reference to the issue of power. Francis Bacon writing 'Of Heresys' in his *Religious Meditations* said, 'Knowledge itself is power'. Every request by a patient for information, in every situation, is resisted by the medical profession until that resistance is finally overcome by legislation; and each time that resistance is overcome and the information becomes available, it can be seen that the patient's position improves yet that of a doctor does not suffer. Nevertheless, each new issue on disclosure of information is resisted afresh.

4.27 I have already dealt with the question of giving information before treatment. The situation described in another chapter (Chapter 13) relating to exchange of experts' opinions is another example. The profession and its lawyers resisted such exchange in legal proceedings right up to the Court of

Appeal. Subsequently the defence organisations were heard to say what an improvement for both sides this brought about!

4.28 In the case of medical records, the profession first resisted disclosure of these before legal proceedings had started on the grounds that they would encourage patients to go on a 'fishing expedition' to see if perhaps they could make a claim. The 1972 Administration of Justice Act compelled them to give such disclosure so they then attempted to limit this to disclosure to a medical expert only on the grounds that nobody but a doctor could understand the notes.

4.29 Even when the Supreme Court Act 1981 spelled out that any order for disclosure that was made would be to a plaintiff's legal adviser, the health carers' legal advisers for years (and some of them even today) tried to insist that disclosure by agreement should be to a medical expert only and they placed as many obstacles as possible in the way of disclosure.

4.30 And so it is with making records available in a non-litigious or pre-litigious situation. The profession fights every inch of the way, notwithstanding overwhelming evidence and advice that it is in the doctors' and the patients' interests to let the patients see their records. A more recent example of these obstacles is the case of *Samut v South Lincolnshire HA* (AVMA Medical & Legal Journal Vol 3 No 2 p 9). There the Health Authority resisted a request for disclosure by solicitors who were dealing with an inquest on the grounds that the records were required for that inquest rather than for the litigation which might be initiated. In the event the court ruled that the potential plaintiff was entitled to disclosure. The question arises why the health carers should have resisted disclosure in the first place.

4.31 Where the law has insisted on disclosure then ultimately doctors have to give up their notes. It is interesting, however, to look at their reaction where there is as yet no legal sanction. The position regarding the notes of a general practitioner against whom negligence is alleged provides such an example. Invariably the patient will have changed general practitioners and the notes will be in the possession of the new GP. In order to enable the potential plaintiff to decide on the nature and strength of the case, it is essential that her legal advisers see those notes before proceedings are commenced. However, under section 33 an order for discovery is only available against a person who is 'likely to be a party' to proceedings and clearly the new GP is not. The only way in which the potential plaintiff can see those notes before issuing a writ is by agreement.

4.32 That agreement is often not forthcoming. It has usually been explained to the new GP that by refusing to disclose the notes they may force the patient to issue a writ against a colleague which may turn out to have been unwarranted when the records are eventually disclosed on discovery in the proceedings. The GP may actually be submitting a colleague to the trauma of proceedings unnecessarily. Yet the instinct of the doctor to hold onto the power of possession of knowledge, added to the misguided instinct not to 'let the side down' by giving information which might lead to proceedings against a colleague, often prevails over all reason. There are, however, doctors who have instituted systems for voluntarily showing their patients their medical records. In a number of general practices, the doctors have taken a positive decision actually to give patients their notes to look at on every visit. For example, Dr Brian Fisher in South London was reported in the British Medical Journal (3 February 1988, p 10) as having allowed patients to see their notes for more than three years. He had massive support from his patients. 77 per cent of them read the notes and 12 per cent noticed minor errors whilst one found a serious error. Dr Fisher reported that he encountered considerable opposition and even threats of legal action from consultants who were unhappy about their information being available to patients! Dr Fisher's view was that open access builds trust and encourages patients to pay more attention to their own health.

4.33 Insofar as hospital notes are concerned, Diana Elbourne of the National Perinatal Epidemiology Unit has written extensively on the subject and has reported on a number of experiments. In a letter to the British Medical Journal (1988, vol 296, p 360) she refers inter alia to the experiment at St Thomas' Hospital where pregnant women were given their notes to hold thoughout their antenatal care. No major negative administrative effects were found, the option brought savings in clinical and clerical time and the notes were less likely to go astray! The women allocated their notes felt they could talk more easily to the professionals and it was found that access to their notes did not raise the level of anxiety felt by women under these circumstances. (See also (1987) Br J Obstet Gynaecol 94, 612–619; (1986) British Medical Journal 292, 595–596; (1977) Am Intern Med 86, 474–477.)

HELP FOR VICTIMS FROM THE MEDICAL PROFESSION

4.34 The major problem for victims of medical accidents is that the people who should help and are best placed to help them, the doctors, are least willing to help and in many cases even obstruct them. The question is 'who cares for the patient when something goes wrong?' Up to that point the patient has the benefit of the best care available at the time – from the doctors, from the nurses, from the hospital and from any other service which is appropriate. It is ironic that when something goes wrong, when in most circumstances the patients need more care, not less, that care is withdrawn to a greater or lesser extent. To whom can the patient turn for help?

4.35 I have already discounted the health carers themselves. What about the doctors' organisations? The British Medical Association is, as it always claims, a trade union for the doctors. Its duty is to look after the interests of the doctors, not the patients. The three doctors' defence organisations are what their names imply, organisations to defend (Medical *Defence* Union and Medical and Dental *Defence* Union of Scotland) or protect (Medical *Protection* Society) the doctors, not help patients. The General Medical Council certainly does not help patients – Jean Robinson, a lay member of the GMC for nine years, in her analysis of GMC statistics states that 'the chances of a complaint made direct by a member of the public about the quality of medical care' reaching the Professional Conduct Committee 'is small' (*A Patient Voice at the GMC* – Health Rights Ltd, 1988).

4.36 The hospital administration will not help if there is any question of negligence: 'The procedure [of resolving complaints] at the third stage is intended to deal with complaints . . . which are not prima facie . . . likely to be the subject of more formal action . . . through the courts' [see HC(81)5]. The Ombudsman cannot help with anything which involves 'clinical judgment', i e treatment.

4.37 It is perhaps worthwhile illustrating just what effect that lack of help has on a patient who has suffered a mishap by quoting from the letter received by AVMA from a client in 1988 – her own words perhaps give a more authentic feel to what she went through:

I was employed as head of a home for elderly people and had occasion to lift a little lady from off the floor where she had suffered a fall caused by a blackout.

In the course of doing this, I damaged my back making it necessary to be taken into hospital, where after many tests, was informed that a laminectomy [spinal operation] was the only thing that would help, and relieve the pain in my legs. In December I had this operation, and was extremely ill, and after a week or two, I still could not feel the lower half of my body, no sensation at all and was doubly incontinent.

On questioning the doctors, I was told that this quite often occurred after this type of operation.

However, after several months, I knew something was very wrong and eventually the doctor told me I would have to go into a wheelchair, he *stressed* that the actual operation was successful but also said and I quote – 'unfortunately, it was just one of those hiccoughs'. At that time I had no-one to help or advise me except my brother who did try to take some action but was told that if any negligence could be proved, we might be able to make a claim, but it was also stated however, that as I worked for the Council, and the accident happened during my duties, were they in fact the people to claim from, or the hospital who performed the operation, when something went drastically wrong.

My brother eventually died of cancer and I went into a Cheshire home. My own home was broken up, my mother whom I cared for also went into a home, and my young daughter had to go into care. During these years I have received an industrial injuries benefit at 100 per cent but now I am living an independent life, I am finding it financially hard to cope. I have to have and maintain two electric wheelchairs, and to purchase these I am constantly borrowing from the bank, the repayments on my mobility allowance plus some of my pension. I have never received social security for anything, because my pension is considered above the average allowance.

After listening to a programme about these matters, also being told as well that, even *now* after many years, it may be possible to put in a claim. My health has deteriorated over the years with constant infections resulting now in renal failure.

Surely, something could be done to help in my advancing years as it is really only now I am having great financial difficulties.

4.38 It is possible, of course, that what happened during the laminectomy operation was pure accident and not the failure of the surgeon to come up to the accepted standards of medicine in which case, whoever had tried to help, the result would have been the same. It is, however, at least as possible that the injury was caused by negligence. This would have meant that the woman would have been entitled to substantial compensation and her life would have been made considerably easier – she certainly would not have found herself in the desperate situation in which she now is. If the doctor who had operated, or his colleagues, or any medical person who saw her subsequently, had regarded her future well-being as part of their duty of care, they would have told her what had happened and helped her to receive that compensation.

4.39 There is, therefore, in my view, an obligation on doctors to help victims of medical accidents. That help can take many forms – it may be simply by giving an explanation, it may be by ensuring that the patients receive treatment to relieve them, if possible, of the consequences of the accident, it may, ultimately, even be to help them to obtain compensation so as to enhance their quality of life. Whatever help is required, it is beholden on a doctor to continue to treat the patient *qua* patient and not as an enemy.

4.40 In the absence of or in addition to help from the doctor or his or her colleagues, where can patients obtain help?

4.41 What is remarkable is that there is no medical body available to address the problems for doctors who find themselves in the position where they have, or may have, been involved in a medical accident other than in respect of the financial issues. Doctors in that situation will automatically telephone or write to organisations pledged to 'defend' and 'protect' doctors which will look at the problem from a legal and financial point of view. Whilst the defence organisations do try to 'counsel' doctors who face this problem it is quite clear that as they *are* concerned mainly about the financial and professional implications they are not appropriate bodies to give the kind of counselling that is really required. The time is long since passed when the medical profession should set up an organisation to help and advise doctors on the issue of medical accidents from an ethical, moral, and personal point of view, leaving the defence organisations to deal with what they are best at doing. Such a step will not only help doctors but it will fundamentally change the situation for victims as well.

4.42 As I have said, obtaining information so as to know that an injury, an accident, has actually taken place, is of course the major obstacle. Until a patient actally knows that an accident has taken place, there is no question of even beginning to seek compensation or, indeed, an explanation. It is here that the conspiracy of silence works to such powerful effect.

OBSTACLES TO COMPENSATION

4.43 Once having established that an accident has taken place and that there is a possibility of compensation, the next obstacle is finding a competent solicitor. Medical negligence is a specialised form of litigation and many a good claim has foundered simply because of the lack of expertise of the solicitor. If a victim adopts a hit and miss attitude in selecting a solicitor, the chances are the result will be a miss. I will deal later in this chapter with the way in which attempts are being made and proposed to overcome this problem.

COSTS

4.44 The funding of medical negligence claims has always been a serious problem. As with other litigation, it is often said that a person has to be really poor or really wealthy to be able to litigate. The really wealthy can afford the large sums required to fund a claim and the really poor can do this on legal aid.

Legal aid

4.45 Until recently, the position for people who qualified financially for legal aid appeared to be improving, at least in England and Wales. Over a period of years, the legal aid authorities had come to realise, as the competence of solicitors in the field increased, that medical negligence actions are complex and that save in the most obvious cases, it is not possible to decide whether there is a case worth pursuing until the medical records have been produced and the opinion of an independent medical expert obtained. Accordingly, most legal aid areas had become willing to issue, on the strength of a fairly full statement from the victim showing that there was a need to investigate the reasons for an untoward medical result, a certificate limited to obtaining the records (by a court application if necessary), a medical opinion and counsel's opinion if appropriate.

4.46 Even more recently, however, many solicitors have found, in addition to the increasing problems of delay in issuing certificates, delay in authorising the fees for expert opinions and delay in obtaining payment of their costs, that some legal aid areas are prejudging the medical issues and refusing to issue a limited certificate on the basis simply of their own assessment of the medical situation. This is very much in line with the suggestions made in an article by Dr Clifford Hawkins, author of the history of the Medical Defence Union (*Mishap or Malpractice*, Blackwell Scientific, 1985) that 'the apparent ease for obtaining legal aid is surprising' (British Medical Journal 295, 1535) and suggesting that 'a doctor should sit on the legal aid panel to clarify medical issues arising out of acts or omissions from medical reports supportive of the applicant' (at 1536). Although there is no evidence that legal aid panels have actually adopted this proposal, it does seem that they have adopted the principle thereby implied of deciding the medical issues without allowing the plaintiff to investigate the matter properly.

4.47 The funding of medical negligence, therefore, remains an ever-increasing problem. The obvious solution is, as with all other litigation, to make legal aid available to all with a sliding scale of contribution depending on the resources of the applicant so that, ultimately, those able to finance the litigation themselves will pay the full costs. Instead the government has moved in the opposite direction and the Lord Chancellor's proposals announced in November 1992 have the effect of taking even more people out of eligibility for legal aid. In the absence of any likelihood of an improvement in the legal aid situation the government and the Law Society have looked into contingency fees. Whilst such a scheme might help some individuals I remain unconvinced that it will be in the interests of victims of medical accidents generally. The government's alternative, speculative fees, will help a tiny number of victims only.

EXPERTS

4.48 A medical negligence action stands or falls by the medical evidence. A major problem for victims seeking compensation has always been to find a medical expert who will support the claim. It is not surprising that doctors are not anxious to support someone who alleges that a colleague has been responsible for causing them damage. Given the approach of the medical profession as a whole to the problem of medical accidents in general, it is surprising how many doctors are prepared to help.

4.49 The general attitude of the medical profession towards victims or alleged victims is that they are the doctors' enemies. They it is who will demean them in their colleagues' esteem, they it is who may hold them back in their promotion, they it is who might drag them through the courts and, worst of all, they it is who caused their professional indemnity insurance premiums to rise 'astronomically'. The only counter to these arguments comes from the public and consumer groups such as the Community Health Councils, the Patients Association and Action for Victims of Medical Accidents. The medical establishment, far from trying to educate doctors to see that victims of medical accidents continue to remain patients who require their help, actually fosters the attitude of antagonism. Instead of concentrating on the caring obligations, it concentrates on the financial implications.

4.50 Small wonder that the majority of doctors are reluctant to become involved. For all that, there is a growing band of doctors who are prepared to help. They can be found by solicitors through their own experience, from their colleagues and from counsel. The Law Society maintains a list but has no way of updating that list or verifying the ability or attitude of the doctors on that list.

4.51 The danger of using a doctor who is not known to be helpful is that without the experience in medical litigation to analyse properly a medical report, lawyers will not know whether that report can be relied on. The fact is that many doctors will agree to provide opinions but will remain totally biased against a victim for the reasons I have explained. Simply by changing the emphasis of a report, by not supporting statements made by the plaintiff or by omitting information, negative reports can be produced when, in fact, there has been negligence. Only the experienced solicitors can spot this – others should beware of the experts.

4.52 The only formal way of obtaining the name of a doctor who is likely to be the best for the job is through AVMA which maintains a list of doctors who are 'tried and tested'. It must be realised, however, that with a very limited number of experts about, there can often still be difficulty in obtaining a suitable one.

COMMUNITY HEALTH COUNCILS

4.53 Community Health Councils were set up in 1974 as statutory bodies. They normally have 18 to 24 members of whom one third are nominated by voluntary organisations, half are nominated by the local authorities and the remaining sixth are nominated by the Regional Health Authority. They may also co-opt members to help with particular aspects of their work. The CHC is run by the chief officer, who is a paid employee of the Regional Health Authority but appointed by and accountable to the CHC. The number and role of other staff varies from CHC to CHC, whose methods of work varies according to local priorities.

4.54 The primary job of the CHC is to represent the interests of the local community in the health service, in other words to be, as they describe themselves 'the patient's voice'. They give effect to this in three distinct areas:

As community watchdog

4.55 This means monitoring all developments in the health service which affect the people in their district. Although primarily therefore they will deal with the District Health Authority and Family Health Services Authority, they will also be involved at other levels, such as local hospitals and other providers of health care, the Regional Health Authority, Department of Health etc.

Involvement in decision making

4.56 As CHCs have the right to be consulted about plans to change local health services, they can be involved in reading health authorities' planning documents, suggesting and investigating alternatives, joining in planning discussions and finding out and expressing the views of the public. This last can often involve CHCs in public demonstrations and petitions where the feelings of the public run high. CHCs have no automatic right to take part in meetings of health authorities and Trusts. The National Health Service and Community Care Act 1990 has affected the work of the CHCs. Whilst they retain their rights of visiting with regard to both health authority and Trust hospitals, Trusts are only required to meet formally once a year. Some Trusts and CHCs do meet informally more often. CHCs are in the process of working out their relationships with both commissioners and providers of services.

As the patient's friend

4.57 This involves giving help to members of the public who may have difficulty in finding out how to obtain a service or who want to make a complaint.

4.58 It is with this last service which I am, of course, most concerned. Whilst helping complainants is only one of the roles of CHCs, it is one which is taking an increasing amount of their resources. It is, however, a central role since it gives a service to individuals and provides measures of the quality of the local health services. The priority given to complaints work varies from CHC to CHC. For example some will write letters on headed CHC paper and others will simply draft letters for complainants to sign.

4.59 Most CHCs, however, can be the most accessible and most helpful agency for anyone who has had something go wrong during medical care but who is not seeking compensation. Many people, of course, are either not aware that they are entitled to compensation or are not thinking in those terms when they approach the Community Health Council. In those circumstances, there are some CHC secretaries who consider that they have sufficient expertise to help the patient directly but, in the main, the value of the assistance they can give is that they can usually identify those cases which need further investigation from a compensation point of view and they know where help can be obtained for the patient.

4.60 CHCs are most useful in helping patients to find out more about what went wrong and helping them to make complaints which do not involve seeking compensation. Insofar as hospital care is concerned, the CHC will determine whether the problem involves clinical judgment or an administrative matter. If the latter then it will assist the patient to make a complaint to the Health Services Commissioner (the Ombudsman) and will follow the complaint through, helping the patient to understand and reply to any correspondence received from the Ombudsman.

4.61 If the matter is not an administrative one, the CHC may enter into correspondence with the relevant hospital in an attempt to seek further information and an explanation of what, if anything, has gone wrong. It will also advise the patient whether to make a formal complaint under the provisions of the agreement incorporated in HC(88)37 and many will actually prepare the letter of complaint to be made[1] and give assistance in dealing with any further correspondence.

1 The complaint must be made by the patient personally or by a relative.

4.62 CHCs are able to advise, assist and accompany the complainant throughout the complex procedures. Some will arrange for someone to accompany the complainant to all complaints meetings. Due to lack of resources, however, some may not be able to offer this service.

Complaints about GPs

4.63 The mechanics of a complaint against a general practitioner are dealt with elsewhere (Chapter 2) but it is useful to outline under this topic the important role which can be played and is played by some CHCs. Although the hearing before the Services Committees of the Family Health Services Authority (formerly the FPC) is a formal one akin to that held by many tribunals, the patient cannot be legally represented. This means that input by lawyers into the FHSA complaints system is fairly limited (as was intended by those who set up the procedure). Accordingly, CHC secretaries or members play an important role in advising patients of their rights to make a complaint, helping them to compose their letter of complaint if not actually writing the letter for them and helping them to deal with any correspondence received from the doctor complained against or from the FHSA itself.

4.64 More importantly, they can advise the patients on how to conduct their case at the hearing and can attend the hearing with the patients and speak on their behalf. Once again, because of underfunding which leads to shortage of personnel, some CHCs are unable to involve themselves in every hearing.

THE HEALTH SERVICE COMMISSIONER

4.65 The Health Service Commissioner is severely limited in the help he can give to a patient because of the restriction on investigating matters of clinical judgment. Nevertheless, there are areas where a discretion can be exercised and a robust Commissioner determined to seek justice for patients and not be fobbed off by the bureaucracy of the National Health Service has considerable scope. For example, the way in which a complaint involving clinical judgment is handled by the hospital administration is an administrative matter in which the Ombudsman can and does intervene. The Commissioner in any event has considerable power in dealing with complaints because it is he who decides whether the complaint involves clinical judgment such as to preclude his dealing with it.

THE PATIENTS ASSOCIATION

4.66 The Patients Association was founded in 1963 as a result of concern about reports of medical experiments on patients without their knowledge and consent and in the wake of the thalidomide tragedies. It is an advice service and collective voice for patients. Its aims and activities are general across the whole sphere of issues which affect patients in the public and private sectors.

4.67 More specifically, it describes its aims as to represent and further the interests of patients, give information and advice to individuals, acquire and spread information about patients' interests and promote understanding and goodwill between patients and those in medical practice and related activities.

4.68 It has had some major campaign successes, having contributed to the establishment of the NHS Ombudsman, improved hospital visiting hours and promoted drug safety. With such a wide brief, its resources have been spread thin in the past and a number of its specific interests have been taken up by new bodies such as the Community Health Councils and AVMA. Indeed AVMA's most significant achievement has been to alter the way health professionals regard medical accidents. Anyone working in this field over the past ten years, whether as a health professional or lawyer, recognises that the scene is today a totally different one and that most health professionals now recognise their responsibilities in relation to victims.

4.69 None of these lines of complaint is intended to have anything to do with litigation. Indeed, as I have indicated, one of the objectives of having avenues of complaint of this kind is to try to ensure satisfaction for the patient thereby obviating the necessity of falling into the hands of lawyers at all.

4.70 The reality is, however, that for various reasons these procedures often fail to satisfy patients and they end up looking to legal action to solve their problems. It is perfectly proper for lawyers, whose brief is to seek compensation for those who have been injured by negligence, to use one or more of the complaints systems described above to facilitate the acquisition of compensation in a genuine case of negligence. This will be dealt with in other chapters where the various procedures involved in taking legal action are described.

ACTION FOR VICTIMS OF MEDICAL ACCIDENTS

4.71 There is only one recognised organisation in the United Kingdom whose sole object is to help people who have been injured as a result of a medical accident. Action for Victims of Medical Accidents (AVMA) was established as a charity in September 1982. Like Shelter, which was established following the showing on television of 'Cathy Come Home', AVMA is one of those rare organisations which was inspired by the media. In AVMA's case, it was the showing of 'Minor Complications' in November 1980. Written by Peter Ransley, this portrayed the true story of Stella Burnett who went into hospital for a minor operation, a laparoscopic sterilisation, and suffered a medical accident, the puncturing of her bowel during the operation.

4.72 The play described dramatically and forcefully the problems which Stella had, first with the medical profession which was so determined not to acknowledge that there had been an error that Stella was allowed nearly to die, and then with the legal profession which was so incompetent that it nearly denied her the compensation to which she was so obviously entitled.

4.73 The author received so many letters from viewers who had undergone similar experiences, most, if not all having failed to receive compensation, that he realised that he had stumbled on a substantial social problem which needed addressing urgently. As a result, he set up AVMA to try and do just that.

4.74 As its name implies, AVMA is concerned with medical accidents which include not only occurrences caused by negligence which can and often do involve lawyers, but 'pure' accidents for which there is, under the present legal system, no possibility of compensation. AVMA has a dual role: on the one hand it is concerned to improve the situation generally for victims of medical accidents, ie to ensure that they are treated properly, that their problems are understood, that they receive the appropriate help from every quarter from which it is due and that the systems for ensuring that such victims receive the compensation they need are improved; on the other hand it helps individual victims personally whether to obtain information, explanations, support or compensation. Often these two roles overlap.

4.75 Many people, particularly doctors, see AVMA simply as a body giving legal advice and helping victims to secure compensation. In fact, the non-legal role as described above is seen by AVMA, which is basically a health charity not a legal charity, as by far the most important. Nevertheless it serves as a focal point for agencies dealing with specific issues affecting patients and has been instrumental in setting up the Patients' Forum which is a forum for contact between various agencies and a clearing house for new ideas. It also has close contact with the DOH and therefore the opportunity to convey the opinions of patients to the government. AVMA is involved in both an educative and propaganda role to try to bring about a change in the attitudes of the medical profession in particular and society in general towards the problems of such victims.

4.76 As a result of its experience over the ten years of its existence, and contact directly with some 15,000 victims, it has become clear to AVMA that the only way to effect a significant improvement for victims of medical accidents is to deal with the problem comprehensively rather than in a piecemeal fashion.

4.77 The issues of compensation, standards, complaints and accountability are inextricably bound together and if an attempt is made to improve procedures relating to one aspect others will be ignored or indeed affected detrimentally. This has been the conclusion also of the Community Health Councils who have had even greater experience with the complaints of dissatisfied patients.

4.78 As a result AVMA and ACHCEW have jointly produced proposals for a Health Standards Inspectorate which will deal with all these issues within one body although there will be separate branches of the Inspectorate to deal with the discrete problems. These proposals are now open for discussion and it is hoped that in a modified form to take account of informed comment by all those interested in the problem they will attract the support of the government.

4.79 The main thrust of AVMA's work in the future, whilst maintaining support and assistance for individual victims, will be to seek the implementation of these proposals.

Personal assistance (case work)

4.80 The help that AVMA can give individuals can be divided into two distinct parts, non-legal and legal.

4.81 Once AVMA has assessed a case and decided that legal action for negligence is not a possibility, the help it can give is limited but important. It is a sad fact that the vast majority of people who suspect that something has gone wrong during medical treatment do not seek compensation, indeed that is usually furthest from their minds. What they want is an explanation and, if appropriate, an apology. Above all they want to be believed and treated as rational human beings and not either as recalcitrant school children or as irritants to be pacified. AVMA, with the knowledge that it has built up about the behaviour and attitudes of the medical profession, can often help to obtain such explanations and to reassure victims that what they suffered is not 'all in the mind'. Indeed, it is often a great comfort to victims simply to know that their experience is not unique.

4.82 A startling example of the way patients can come to light is provided by the case of *Ackers v Wigan Health Authority* in June 1985 ([1986] CLY 1048). Mrs Ackers succeeded in a claim for damages arising out of an operation during which she was awake but unable to move in any way to attract the attention of those operating on her. She gave evidence that when she complained subsequently, she was told that she was imagining it all. Through the diligence of her solicitors, she was able to prove that that was not the case. The major significance of the case was that after the judgment received publicity, more than 70 women came forward with similar claims and, without exception, all had been persuaded by their doctors that it was not possible for this to have happened and that it was 'all in the mind'.

4.83 AVMA repeatedly comes across situations where, although they cannot help patients to obtain compensation because there has been no negligence, they are nevertheless able to reassure them that what they are suffering is real and is the consequence of the treatment they have received.

4.84 Often it is necessary, in the quest for an honest explanation which should in the first place have been offered by the doctor treating, or his or her colleagues, for AVMA to refer a client to a solicitor. Although the client is not seeking compensation primarily, the only way in which a satisfactory explanation can be obtained under our present system is for the solicitor to obtain the medical records and then, if necessary, to obtain the opinion of an independent medical expert.

4.85 AVMA can help in other non-legal ways: by referring the victim to a CHC for advice on making a complaint; by putting the victim in touch with others who have shared a similar experience or by referring victims to appropriate self-help bodies who deal with their particular medical problems.

4.86 One area in which AVMA has identified an unmet need of victims is that of counselling. A medical accident can be an especially traumatic event for which victims often need professional help. The first stage is for third parties, including lawyers, to recognise this need but it is then necessary to provide support. AVMA provides what support it can but recognises that at present it cannot provide what is required. It is now endeavouring to raise funds to enable it to improve its service.

OTHER AGENCIES

4.87 Because medical accidents have now become a recognised area of problem for the community, from time to time other well-meaning people set up organisations to try and offer help to victims. Some of these people make contact with AVMA and decide that their efforts can best be channelled into supporting AVMA. Others pursue their own line.

4.88 Of course in an expanding field like that of medical accidents there is ample room and indeed need for more than one organisation. The only requirement is that such organisations, if they are going to divert people from seeking help from AVMA must have the knowledge and professionalism to provide as good a service else they will provide a disservice.

4.89 Solicitors have been asked to support various bodies of this kind. They should be careful to ensure that their support is being requested for something that will genuinely help victims and that the organisation is not simply one which provides well-meaning but amateur support and channels cases to solicitors. Where solicitors pay money to the organisation they should ensure that it has the imprimatur of charitable status and also provides a service to solicitors as well as giving them cases. If not they could find themselves falling foul of their disciplinary rules.

AVMA's legal service

4.90 If it is apparent, once the facts have been assessed and AVMA has researched the medical and legal issues, that negligence is a possibility, a referral will be made to a solicitor.

4.91 In dealing with the obstacles which face victims in their quest for compensation, I referred to the problem of finding a solicitor who will be able to deal competently with the claim. Helping victims to do that forms a large part of AVMA's work.

4.92 The importance of using a solicitor experienced in medical negligence cannot be stressed enough. When AVMA started in 1982 there were few, if any, solicitors able to deal with this branch of the law adequately. The reason was quite clear. A vicious circle existed whereby solicitors were reluctant to take on the work because they did not do enough of it to become proficient; as a result not many claims were made and fewer were successful; therefore few people consulted solicitors because they believed it was impossible to succeed against doctors, and those solicitors who were consulted usually told the clients the same thing; as a result no solicitors did enough medical negligence work to become proficient.

4.93 The two firms acting for the defence organisations, however, acted between them in all the actions against doctors and consequently they were able to build up the expertise required for such work and to run rings around any plaintiff's solicitor who had the temerity to cross swords with them.

4.94 AVMA has made a considerable inroad on that unsatisfactory situation. They have developed a panel of solicitors who do have sufficient work to become experienced in the area. They also run a service to help solicitors who undertake medical negligence work. For a subscription solicitors can receive advice on all aspects of the conduct of medical negligence litigation, details of medical experts most likely to assist, information on recent cases and can consult with other lawyers dealing with similar cases.

4.95 AVMA is not, however, simply a legal referral agency. They monitor the performance of solicitors and persuade them to improve their knowledge and their performance. Solicitors who, in AVMA's view, do not give victims an adequate service are removed from the panel.

4.96 Most importantly, AVMA also requires solicitors to report back regularly. This means not only that they can ensure that the panel solicitors continue to give a good service to victims, but also that they are able to build up their information on performance of experts, responses of health authorities, behaviour of the defence organisations and their solicitors, amounts of judgments and settlements and all the other information which is vital to improving the service solicitors can offer to victims of medical accidents.

4.97 AVMA also works to increase the number of solicitors who are able to deal with medical negligence competently. They do this, apart from helping within their Resource Service, by involving lawyers in discussion on common problems in their Lawyers Support Group, by running training courses and by producing literature.

4.98 The Law Society has recognised the need for specialist solicitors to handle medical negligence cases and at the time of writing this chapter are in the process of setting up a medical negligence panel.

4.99 A specialist panel publicly available would be an ideal solution provided specialist really meant specialist. Medical negligence will never be a large speciality. At present there are probably 6,000 cases in the hands of solicitors. If a specialist panel were to include even 300 solicitors, this would mean an average of only 20 cases per year per solicitor. Many of the best solicitors, however, deal with many more cases than that, which would mean that there were some solicitors on the panel dealing with ten or less cases each year. This would not be enough to make that solicitor a specialist to whom a member of the public could confidently turn.

4.100 AVMA's experience has also disclosed the need for close monitoring. Even solicitors who have undertaken a large caseload have for various reasons, often because litigation, particularly legal aid litigation, is not particularly profitable, allowed their personal attention to cases to lapse and it has been necessary for AVMA to step in smartly and facilitate the transfer of cases to other solicitors.

BIBLIOGRAPHICAL REFERENCES

Bacon F 'Of Heresys' in *Religious Meditations*.
Coney S *The Unfortunate Experiment*.
Elbourne D (1988) British Medical Journal 296, 360.
Hawkins C *Mishap or Malpractice* (Oxford, Blackwell Scientific, 1985). (1988) British Medical Journal 295, 1535.
Robinson J *A Patient Voice at the GMC* (Health Rights Ltd, 1988).

CHAPTER 5

The function of the defence organisations

George Bonney *MS*

SUMMARY

The history of medical defence

5.1 The history of medical defence is one of continuing if intermittent development in response to changing circumstances in medicine, in the law and in society in general. The present and likely future roles of the defence organisations cannot fully be understood without knowledge of these circumstances and of the reactions to them.

5.2 The history begins in the mid-1870s with the formation of the Medical Alliance and the Medical Defence Association. The chief aim of these organisations was the suppression of the practice of medicine and surgery by 'persons not legally qualified'. Doubtless, concern for the welfare of patients influenced doctors to some extent in their attempts to curb the activities of unqualified practitioners. On the other hand, practitioners of orthodox medicine were at that time virtually powerless to arrest or even influence the progress of any malady, and the understanding of disease processes was limited. It is not surprising that then, as now, the successes achieved by 'quacks' and other practitioners of unorthodox medicine should have been perceived as a threat to the livelihood of doctors; hardly surprising that doctors should have taken steps to protect that livelihood. Indeed, as late as the 1960s the prosecution of unqualified practitioners formed part of the work of the defence organisations. The General Medical Council continued into the 1930s to pursue doctors who associated with unqualified practitioners. The threat of such pursuit continued into the 1950s. Even now, the successful osteopath is often regarded with suspicion by the unsuccessful orthopaedic surgeon and rheumatologist, though such suspicion and hostility are not reserved solely for this target.

5.3 Two cases in particular brought home to doctors the peril in which they stood from the operation of the law in the conduct of medical practice. In 1883 Drs Bowers and Keates faced charges of manslaughter following the death of a child patient. The charges were dismissed after a five-day hearing, but later the child's father instituted proceedings alleging medical negligence. At the first trial the jury failed to agree; at the second, judgment was given for the doctors. They had incurred costs of £1,000 – by extrapolation on Hawkins'[1] reckoning, about £60,000 in today's values; by this writer's reckoning, some £200,000. They were saved from ruin by the intervention of Sir William Jenner, then President of the Royal College of Physicians, whose appeal to colleagues for funds was instantly successful.

1 See C Hawkins (1985) in Bibliographical References.

5.4 In the second case, Dr Bradley was accused of criminal assault on a woman patient. In those days, as at present, he who held the longer purse might hold the longer life,[1] and through inadequate representation Dr Bradley was convicted and sentenced to two years' imprisonment with hard labour. He served eight months of the sentence before the Home Secretary was prevailed upon to recognise the inadequacy of the trial procedure and to order his release. Similar events have been re-enacted in our times in different circumstances.

1 See R Kipling (1889) in Bibliographical References.

5.5 The alarm sounded by these two cases probably led to the interest shown in the Medical Defence Union, founded in 1885 on the initiative of five gentlemen and two solicitors. The first Secretary was Charles Rideal, whose conduct of affairs later attracted criticism and eventually led to dismissal. Not all doctors were content to join a Union formed on the initiative of 'lay' persons, even though there was among those persons a preponderance of gentlemen. An attempt was made to induce the British Medical Association to take on the burden of medical defence, but the Association, relying on legal opinion, found itself debarred from accepting this charge. Here, too, similar events have been re-enacted in a later age.

5.6 The firm establishment of the Medical Defence Union and the transfer of its management to doctors was probably due to Lawson Tait, who in 1887 was elected President. Birmingham's great pioneer in abdominal and gynaecological surgery was a man of firm views and decisive character, seemingly never averse to speaking his mind. He appears, thinly veiled as 'Simpson Lyle', in Brett Young's novel *Dr Bradley Remembers*.[1] This story of medical life in and around 'North Bromwich' may have been written in part to counteract the overwhelmingly unfavourable impression of the medical profession provided by A J Cronin's *The Citadel*.[2] Lawson Tait's forceful personality contributed greatly to the early success of the Medical Defence Union, but that personality contained the seeds of destruction: his resignation was enforced in 1893 as a result of his criticism of the conduct of a case by Dr Denholm. The latter sued for libel; the use of Union funds for Lawson Tait's defence was much criticised, just as in a later age the use of public money for purposes predominantly private has been challenged. It is likely that Tait's personality had as much to do with the demand for resignation as did the alleged misuse of funds.

1 See F Brett Young (1938) in Bibliographical References.
2 See A J Cronin (1937) in Bibliographical References.

5.7 Lawson Tait's successor, Victor Horsley, was an outstanding figure in medicine in his time and for all time. Many wise and distinguished Presidents have followed him, but none has matched him in intellectual distinction or in nobility of character.[1] He was the true father of British neurological surgery, a pioneer in the physiology of the nervous system, a severe and persistent critic of an inert General Medical Council, and a reformer in many causes. His death from heat-stroke in Mesopotamia in 1916, in one of the wilder projects of British military strategy, deprived the country, the profession and the world of a man of outstanding character and talent.

1 See D'A Power (1930) in Bibliographical References.

5.8 Dissension over the new constitution of the Medical Defence Union drawn up by Lawson Tait led in 1892 to the schism – to some a matter for regret – that resulted in the formation of the London and Counties Medical Protection Society, later the Medical Protection Society. The new Society flourished greatly, to become almost the equal of the Medical Defence Union in the number of its members, and certainly its equal in the quality of its work and service to members. Other defence organisations arose in other countries: in 1902 the Medical and Dental Defence Union of Scotland; in 1897 Le Sou Médical in France; in 1900 the Canadian Medical Protective Association; in 1925 the Medical Defence Association of Western Australia.

5.9 The firm of Hempson and Elgar, Solicitors, was consulted by the Medical Defence Union in 1892; since 1893 the firm of Hempsons has acted as the Union's legal adviser in the United Kingdom. In recent years a network of advisers has been formed in various countries for the service of members practising overseas. A similar pattern has been followed by the other defence organisations of the United Kingdom, but the length of Hempsons' record of continuing service has not been matched.

THE CHANGING MEDICAL SCENE

The state of medicine in the nineteenth century

5.10 At the time of the formation of the defence organisations, diagnosis in medicine depended largely on clinical acumen; treatment was almost entirely a matter of suggestion. Specific remedies were indeed available in the case of malaria and syphilis, and it was possible with digitalis to alter the action and the output of the heart. In the very best hands, operative surgery was occasionally curative, but anaesthesia was primitive and mortality was high. The rich had access to the best medical advice and treatment of the time; the poor and the working class had restricted access to the lower class of general practitioner and to the public hospitals or workhouses. Members of the middle class might face ruin if confronted with heavy bills for prolonged medical treatment. Because of the risk of infection, hospitals of all sorts were dangerous places, so much so, in fact, that the rich underwent operation, when necessary, in their own homes. This practice persisted into the 1940s.

5.11 The 'voluntary' hospitals ranged in quality from the high standards of ancient institutions, some the inheritors of monastic tradition, to the low standards of some 'cottage' hospitals, the fields of action for general practitioners with aspirations to surgery. Indeed, as late as the 1940s it was said that surgery was a 'sport played in the cottage hospitals of Britain'. The voluntary hospitals were funded by contributions, by income from endowments, by charges levied on patients, by the proceeds of 'flag days' and from other sources such as the rental of advertising space. It has been interesting to observe the revival of some of these sources of revenue following the recent 'reform' of the hospital service. The consultants to the great voluntary hospitals received no pay: they derived their incomes from private practice. The initial appointment was as surgeon or physician to out-patients; in this post the honorary consultant only had access to beds in the teaching hospital through the courtesy of the full surgeon or physician. If there was no great gap between the ages of the two, the junior might continue into his fifties without formal access to beds. Resident medical officers were usually unpaid; registrars might be paid some trifling sum annually. The wages of nurses were similarly low.

5.12 With the rise of the municipal authorities in Victorian times, most hospital activity was transferred to institutions funded and administered by these bodies. Doctors in these institutions were as a rule full-time employees without official access to private practice. In this posture the situation remained until the outbreak of the 1939–45 war. Members of the middle class who could afford to pay entered private 'nursing homes' rather than hospitals. The credentials of many of these were, at least, suspect: in them many tragedies occurred because of inadequate equipment and poor staffing.

5.13 It was necessary in such circumstances for doctors to pretend to knowledge and powers which they did not possess, if they were to sustain their patients' morale and to carry them through the critical phases of their illnesses. The doctor, an almost majestic figure, was often greatly revered; it was hardly possible for a patient of the middle or lower class to contemplate proceedings against such a person. In any case, medical solidarity was in those days so strong that few doctors could be found to give evidence against their colleagues. An indication of the degree of immunity is given by the level of subscription to the Medical Defence Union: for many years until the 1940s it was £1 annually; life membership could be secured for £12. Even so, an observer as acute as Wilfred Trotter wrote 'an occupation for adults should . . . be subject to the tonic of difficulty and the spice of danger', and went on to say that he thought the practice of medicine dangerous 'because it is so meagrely cared for by legal privilege and immunity'.[1] In our day the balance has been shifted decisively in favour of the defendant doctor by the development and application of the *Bolam* principle.[2]

1 See W Trotter (1941) in Bibliographical References.
2 *Bolam v Friern Hospital Management Committee* [1957] 2 All ER 118, [1957] 1 WLR 582.

5.14 It is not surprising that in such circumstances doctors developed habits of authoritarianism which now would bitterly be resented; hardly surprising that such habits persisted even when advances in medicine provided greater facility in diagnosis and greater specificity in treatment. Nowadays the technical part of medicine can be done by doctors in scruffy jeans and T-shirts or in short skirts and blouses quite as well as it can be done by gentlemen in smart suits and clean shirts. However, when it comes to the need for support and advice in cases of deprivation and despair, patients still from time to time turn to the surrogate father or mother represented by the practitioner of former days.

The medical advance

5.15 The Public Health Act 1866 marked the beginning of the process by which, through improvement of sanitation, the provision of an adequate supply of clean water, amelioration of the conditions of life and the development of immunisation, the threat of infectious disease was reduced and in some cases altogether removed. It is only in recent years that we have seen a recurrence of this threat through homelessness, defective living conditions, deprivation of water supply and spread of HIV infection. Tuberculosis, once virtually abolished in the indigenous population, is again on the increase, and 'food-poisoning' is once again a common event. Wright and colleagues[1] have commented on the effects of deprivation.

1 See Wright et al (1992) in Bibliographical References.

5.16 The start of the great advances in diagnosis and therapeutics that have transformed medicine may perhaps be placed in the 1930s, with the development and use of sulphonamides. The advent of availability of penicillin in the 1940s was followed by the development over the years of other antibiotics with greater power and wider fields of activity. Venereal disease was for a time tamed. With advances in anaesthesia, with increased knowledge of body chemistry and with advances in surgical technique, operative surgery became safer and more rational. New fields were opened up in cardiothoracic surgery, in neurosurgery and in transplantation. With the advent of replacement of the hip joint, orthopaedic surgeons at last had an operation of election which actually benefited the patient. The diagnostic advance offered by computed tomography was completed by the development of magnetic resonance imaging, in which accurate images are produced without the use of ionising radiation. Advances in molecular biology and genetic medicine have brought knowledge about the causation of inherited disorders, and have opened up the way for genetic manipulation. Pharmaceutical research has produced a variety of drugs effective in many conditions, though in many cases not yet free from unwanted side-effects. An effective vaccine against poliomyelitis has long been available; work continues on the search for similar protection against HIV infection.

5.17 Dental surgery has seen similar advances in techniques of conservation and repair; in the field of maxillo-facial surgery in particular, very striking changes have taken place.

5.18 The profession of medicine, for long the preserve of men, has since the 1939–45 war progressively been open to women, whose numbers in medical schools now equal those of men. Their penetration of the various branches of medicine has been uneven: although at the time of writing the President of the Royal College of Physicians is a woman, female consultants in any branch of surgery other than obstetrics and gynaecology are still rarities. We still wait to see a female President of the Royal College of Surgeons of England, or for that matter of the Medical Defence Union.

5.19 The increase of medical knowledge and the development of specific treatments signalled the beginning of the decline of the personality cult in medicine. It is no longer necessary for a clinician to pretend to knowledge that he or she does not possess. Indeed, it is often risky for him or her so to act, because in spite of the efforts of successive governments many people are now educated and informed well enough to be able to ask searching questions and to require answers. As has been indicated, the loss of the cult of personality may still be felt in cases in which illness depends on abuse, deprivation and despair. That loss may perhaps be reflected in the rise of the professional counsellor; perhaps the decline of religious belief has played a part here too.

The social advance and decline

5.20 Two of the greatest achievements of the Labour government of 1945 were the introduction of the National Health Service and the implementation of the Beveridge proposals for social security. Both projects had been adumbrated during the war by Winston Churchill's government; indeed, the hospital service was nationalised throughout the war, and together with the medical branches of the armed forces provided in effect a national health service. The poor and the working class had indeed enjoyed some protection since the introduction in 1913 of Lloyd George's National Insurance Act 1911. The provisions of that Act ensured for them a minimum standard of primary treatment; it also gave to many general practitioners a regular income and increased security. The implementation in 1948 of the provisions of the National Health Service Act was seen at the time as a security for the future of the hospital service and for the provision of primary medical care. Payment was now introduced for doctors working in the National Health Service: hospital staff were paid on a full-time or part-time basis; general practitioners were paid on the basis of a capitation fee. Private practice was permitted for part-time consultants.

5.21 From 1948 to 1990 citizens progressively became aware of their entitlement to medical care funded by the state by taxation. Their perception of those giving the service changed from one of gratitude due from the recipient of charity to one of rightful expectation by a customer receiving goods for which he or she had paid. Gratitude often remained, but expectation rightly increased. Doctors have gradually become aware of the change in their status from that of handing out charity to that of providing a service for which they have been paid.

Private practice

5.22 With the introduction of the National Health Service private practice at first declined as members of the middle class availed themselves of 'free' treatment. As the defects of the Service became apparent, and as waiting lists lengthened, private practice began to recover. This revival was aided by the punitive measures adopted by the Labour governments of the 1970s, but it was not until the long period of Conservative government began in 1979 that active encouragement was given to private practice. Stacey rightly comments: 'After 1979 government began to give encouragement to private practice, encouragement renewed in the 1989 NHS Review and the 1990 NHS Act.'[1] Many consultants now derive most of their income from private practice; once again, not a few derive all of it from this source.

1 See M Stacey (1992) in Bibliographical References.

5.23 Between 1948 and 1978 the National Health Service in general and the hospital service in particular strengthened their appeal to the public and established their place in the life of the nation. There were indeed many defects: the level of funding never matched the demand; capital investment was inadequate; management was often ineffective; there was little co-ordination between hospital and community services. The reorganisation of 1974[1] attempted to address the last problem. The project, too complicated and too much dependent on the co-operation of the professional staff in general and of doctors in particular, actually increased the difficulties. Many of the 'reforms' were reversed in the later reorganisation that followed the inquiry headed by Sir Alex Morrison. The central belief of the founders of the Service, that costs would fall as the health of the population improved, was shown to be untrue. Instead, costs rose progressively as more conditions became treatable, as expectation of life increased, as methods of treatment became more expensive, as pay was increased and as more staff were employed. The change in the relation between patient and doctor began in the 1960s and 1970s to influence the readiness of patients to sue doctors. At this time, too, the effects of the availability of Legal Aid started to become apparent. Increasingly during this period the bulk of the work of the defence organisations was provided by claims in respect of alleged medical negligence. As a result, the defence organisations and their legal advisers built up a considerable fund of knowledge concerning risk, damage and associated legal processes. Subscriptions rose steadily in order to fund settlements and legal process and to build up reserves from which claims still not notified could be funded.

1 See 'Management Arrangements' (1992) in Bibliographical References.

The crisis of the National Health Service

5.24 The recurrent crises of funding of the National Health Service came to a head in the 1980s. It was clear to all that the nation could no longer afford 'open-ended' funding of the Service; it was also clear that neither the medical nor the nursing profession could offer sufficient planning or sufficient self-discipline to permit containment of expenditure. The conduct of affairs was therefore removed entirely from the professions. A management inquiry had been conducted in 1983 by Sir Roy Griffiths, then the managing director of a large supermarket chain. The conclusion was reached that 'the machinery of translating policy into action and generally of effecting change was extremely limited'.[1] All who at the time had anything to do with the conduct of affairs in the hospital service will agree that this was a correct conclusion. The management reforms introduced as a result of the implementation of the 1983 report effectively removed executive power from doctors and nurses and placed it in the hands of managers. The power of managers was later extended to effect the suppression of dissent on the part of professional staff.

1 See R Griffiths (1992) in Bibliographical References.

The White Paper

5.25 Next, the government produced in 1989 a White Paper carrying the slightly misleading title 'Working for Patients'. Doctors and nurses thought that they had been doing that for some time. This White Paper was presented by the Secretaries of State for Health, Wales, Northern Ireland and Scotland; it carried a foreword over the signature of the then Prime Minister. Otherwise, there was no direct indication of the identities of those responsible for its compilation. However, the names of those appearing in a later distribution of honours gave some idea of them. The identity of the prime mover was, perhaps inadvertently, revealed by Griffiths: 'at the time of the Thatcher review we had hardly enough management information to run a system of barter let alone a system of costing of medical care'.[1] The White Paper was supplemented by the publication of eight 'Working Papers' on particular aspects of the proposals. There was to be no modification. Provision for care in the community was not to be introduced synchronously with the implementation of the 'reforms', though the 'reforms' certainly meant that heavy burdens would be placed on community services.

1 See R Griffiths (1992) in Bibliographical References.

Community care

5.26 Sir Roy Griffiths' second report 'Community Care – Agenda for Action' was 'written on the basis that when medical services were not required patients were better discharged to nursing homes, residential homes or more generally to the community'. Local authorities were to be responsible for such care and it was recommended that they should be adequately funded. The event was different: discharges from mental hospitals and long-stay institutions began long before the proposals were implemented in April 1993; the funding of councils was barely adequate to sustain the new responsibilities. We have in consequence seen the aged, the infirm and the mentally unstable walking the streets and sleeping in doorways; we have seen large profits made by private contractors offering inadequate residential care; we have seen deranged patients, discharged into an uncaring community, damaging themselves and others.

The mechanism of 'reform'

5.27 The philosophy underlying the 'reform' of the Health Service was simple. Expenditure was to be contained not by planning and rationalisation but by the operation of 'market forces'. An 'internal market' was to be created by:

(1) the separation of 'purchasers' from 'providers';
(2) competition between hospitals; and
(3) the introduction of competition from private organisations.

Financial considerations were to be given priority over clinical need. In addition, the burden of care was to be shifted from expensive hospitals to relatively cheap general practitioners. The latter were to be empowered by 'fund-holding' to determine how much work should be kept in the practice and how much should be delegated to the hospital service. Strict cash limits were to be enforced. Later, funding from private sources was to be sought. Managers were to be encouraged by the introduction of 'performance-related' pay. Responsibility was to be placed at one remove from government by the creation of semi-autonomous 'Trust' hospitals. Each of these was to be administered by a Board, the members of which were appointed by the Secretary of State.

5.28 Most of those who have observed the effects of these 'reforms' have been forced to conclude that their object is the restoration of a system not dissimilar from that in 1938: in this case, an insurance-based privately operated hospital service for the employed; private treatment in private institutions for the rich; a third-rate 'safety net' service for the poor in the remains of the national hospital system. It is evident that a shift from employment of consultants on 'permanent' contract to employment on short-term contract will take place. Consultants will increasingly have to regard themselves as 'free-lances' without attachment to any particular hospital or institution, making a living from private practice and by intermittent hospital employment. General practice may continue to be well-funded, though the old, the mentally disturbed and the chronically sick may find it difficult to obtain 'primary care'. Some have found in the extensive destruction of hospitals a parallel with the Dissolution of the Monasteries of 1535. In both cases, those who worked in the threatened institutions were subject to a campaign of vilification; in both cases the proceeds of the destruction were distributed to supporters of the government in exchange for the assurance of continued support; in both cases the administrative structure introduced to replace the original arrangement was heavily politicised.

The effects of 'reform'

5.29 After three years, expenditure has been contained at the expense of the viability of many hospitals and at the expense of the health and even the lives of many patients. The rationing implicit in the original proposals has taken place, but the odium has been shifted from the Department of Health to the 'providers'. Many consultants have taken early retirement; there has been a large increase of private practice; there has been a very large increase in the costs of management.

5.30 Schemes are in preparation for the enforced reduction in the number of hospital beds available in the metropolis and in other large cities. It may be significant that the Health Service Management Executive has, on the advice of outside consultants, set up a Corporate Affairs Intelligence Unit, with a 'mission' to enable ministers and officials to present a 'positive' account of the health service.[1] Nowadays, the epithet 'positive' implies 'favourable'. The cost of maintaining this Unit has been estimated at £1 million a year. Fund-holding general practitioners are rightly content with their lot, and practitioners are increasingly joining their ranks. The government has certainly succeeded in changing radically the nature and quality of medical practice in the United Kingdom. This change has had a profound effect on the working of the defence organisations.

1 See D Brindle (1993) in Bibliographical References.

NHS indemnity

5.31 At about the time of the introduction of the White Paper the position of the two main defence organisations of the United Kingdom was unsatisfactory:

(1) both were grappling with the problems caused by the rising incidence and cost of negligence claims;

(2) an unseemly schism had soured relations between the Medical Defence Union and the Medical Protection Society and produced at this critical time division and disunity and an appearance of instability;[1] and
(3) the prolongation of proceedings through wrangles over apportionment between the various defence organisations and hospital authorities increasingly gave rise to concern.

The necessary rise of subscriptions evoked protest from junior doctors, which led to subsidisation by employers. The imminence of a further considerable rise in subscription with the consequent necessity of further subsidisation, and the probability that one or both of the defence organisations would introduce differential subscriptions led to drastic action by the Secretary of State. From 1 January 1990 the State assumed responsibility for the indemnification of patients damaged through medical or dental negligence in the hospital and community services.[2] It also took over responsibility for claims still outstanding on the appointed date. In consideration of this last, the organisations made certain payments from their accumulated capital funds. The advantages proposed for NHS indemnity were:

(1) savings of costs through simplification of defence procedure, through administrative savings and through the removal of the need to build up resources;
(2) quicker settlement through removal of the need to argue over apportionment;
(3) benefit to practitioners through the removal of the need for differential subscriptions; and
(4) benefit to part-time consultants by indemnification for work done in the Health Service.

1 See C Dyer (1988) in Bibliographical References.
2 See NHS Circulars in Bibliographical References.

5.32 The change certainly represented one method of solving the difficulties in which the defence organisations and the Health Departments found themselves. The cost to the latter has almost certainly been high: a Health Department Minister, replying on 18 May 1993 to a question in Parliament, indicated that 'the cost of claims *settled* during 1991–92 is *estimated* at around £58 m'. The italics are the author's. Expenditure on indemnity payments and legal costs is almost certain to rise: it may well be running at £100 m a year. The State has, of course, assumed responsibility for the actions of practitioners known to be the most vulnerable to negligence claims – namely, junior hospital doctors and doctors in training in obstetrics and gynaecology, in anaesthesiology and in orthopaedic and accident work. The fragmentation of the hospital service has resulted in the creation of a number of small independent units, each extremely vulnerable to the cost of a large claim. The disadvantages are clear:

(1) the loss of the principle of consultant responsibility;
(2) the loss by individual doctors of any right to a role in determining the course of actions against them;
(3) the removal from those who need it of the incentive to good practice provided by the discipline of a rising annual subscription;
(4) the removal of specialised work from doctors and lawyers specially experienced in that work; and

(5) the loss of the central data bank provided by the defence organisations' records.

A Minister in the Health Department, replying on 18 May 1993 to a question in Parliament on this subject, indicated as follows: 'We require health authorities and National Health Service Trusts to provide annual returns of the *costs* of claims settled each financial year. A working group with representatives of the Department and the NHS is to be set up to look at the *handling* of negligence claims in the NHS, and will consider the adequacy of information collected.' Again, the italics are the author's. The concern, however, is not solely his.

5.33 There is no evidence that claims are being settled any more quickly than was the case under the former system; there is evidence that some hospital authorities at least resist all claims irrespective of their merits. It is unlikely that the responsible Secretaries of State were unaware in introducing NHS indemnity of the certainty that the step would reduce professional independence and that managers would be enabled by it to place restrictions on the type of work being done. Palmer,[1] commenting on the first 18 months of 'NHS indemnity', remarks: 'Early indications suggest that the new scheme is placing a very heavy burden on health authorities which already suffer from under-funding and tight budgetary control.'

1 See R N Palmer (1992) in Bibliographical References.

The regulation of the medical profession

5.34 The regulation of the medical profession was by the Medical Act of 1858 entrusted to the General Medical Council, a body composed largely of medical practitioners. Its remit included, in addition to regulation, the supervision of medical education and the maintenance of the Medical Register. Few regulatory bodies are popular, but the General Medical Council has throughout its life been the object of criticism and even contempt. Stacey[1] comments: 'A number of doctors in general and hospital practice around the country appear somewhat contemptuous of the GMC'; and 'As to the lay public, most hardly know the GMC exists'. Contempt turned to active dislike when in 1969 the GMC, under the sway of an active and determined President, announced its intention of levying an annual subscription as the price of 'self-regulation'. This was, as Stacey says, the trigger for revolt: finally an inquiry headed by then Dr Alec Merrison looked into the operations of the Council. In 1975 the Merrison Committee produced its report;[2] on the basis of this report the Medical Act 1978 was constructed. The size of the Council was increased, elected representation was increased, and functions were extended.

1 See M Stacey (1992) in Bibliographical References.
2 See A W Merrison (1975) in Bibliographical References.

5.35 It is now generally agreed that the Council adequately maintains the Medical Register, although recent events concerning wholly unqualified practitioners have cast doubt on its capabilities even in that respect. Many feel that the Council's role in medical education, and in particular in the education of graduates, could better be undertaken by the Universities and

Royal Colleges. The matter is now raised again in an acute form, with the need to comply with directives of the European Community regarding 'specialist medical training'.[2] In 'Hospital Doctors: Training for the Future',[2] the report of the working group on specialist medical training, recommendations are made concerning the duration of 'specialist training' leading to certification of competence to undertake 'independent specialist practice'. It is recognised that 'doctors will complete specialist training, and hence will be eligible for appointment to consultant posts, earlier than at present'. Unless – which is in the highest degree unlikely – there is a large increase in the number of consultant posts, many doctors qualified for independent specialist practice will remain without permanent appointments. Few doubt that the acceptance of a grade of 'sub-consultant' certificated as having completed specialist training will lead to the abandonment of the concept of the consultant as leader of the hospital team and as the provider of private medical treatment. The dilution of the consultant grade so produced will provide economies for the Health Service and greater availability of private care at lower cost. Further 'casualisation' of medical employment can confidently be predicted.

1 See 'Letter from the Principal Medical Officer' in Bibliographical References.
2 See 'Hospital Doctors: Training for the Future' in Bibliographical References.

5.36 The manner in which the Council exercises its disciplinary function has widely been criticised, though it is right to say that at last powers are being sought for dealing with doctors whose performance, though inadequate, hardly reaches the depths of serious professional misconduct. Unfortunately, even this tardy and hesitant approach to the problem seems now certain to be delayed further by the Labour Party's intervention.[1] The Opposition's spokesman on Health matters has indicated that 'the time has come for a complete overhaul of the disciplinary procedures within the medical profession, with a view to establishing an independent body to investigate and discipline those guilty of professional misconduct. It is no longer good enough for the GMC to have responsibility for these matters given its recent track record.' Although many will agree with Mr Blunkett's characterisation of the GMC, more will regret the loss of the opportunity of dealing with doctors whose performance, though poor and unacceptable, falls short of serious professional misconduct.

1 See 'Letter from Westminster' (1993) in Bibliographical References.

5.37 Although in May 1992 the GMC, at last aware of pressures exerted on doctors by managers, issued 'guidance' on professional responsibility in relation to the clinical needs of patients,[1] its support for doctors forced by managers to place financial before clinical considerations appears, at least, half-hearted. The attitude of the Council to advertising appears to many to be ambivalent.

1 See General Medical Council (1992) in Bibliographical References.

5.38 Mechanisms for dealing humanely with doctors incapacitated by natural process, through use of drugs or abuse of alcohol have been evolved; there are mixed views about the effectiveness of these arrangements. The General Dental Council, formed in 1957 as the successor to the Dental Board of the United Kingdom, appears to enjoy a better relation with dental surgeons than the General Medical Council does with doctors.

The Parliamentary Commissioner

5.39 In creating the post of Parliamentary Commissioner for the Health Service with a departmental staff, the government of the day clearly hoped to help the individual citizen in conflict with departmental power. The operation of the system has proved less than satisfactory: doctors have perceived it as another instance of interference by persons ignorant of conditions of work and of associated difficulties; officials of the civil service have shown themselves adept in foiling the purposes of investigation; managers have found little difficulty in shifting blame and escaping censure. Nevertheless, doctors are still, and probably rightly, required by an organisation possessing large powers of coercion to explain their actions to persons generally ignorant of the processes and practice of medicine. Refinement of the system is required if both claimants and their targets are to be satisfied and if appropriate reforms are to be forthcoming when necessary.

EVOLUTION OF LEGAL PROCESS

The Legal Aid Scheme

5.40 It was, no doubt, the introduction in 1949 of the Legal Aid Scheme that was in a large part responsible for the rise in the number of actions against doctors. Before that time there was one law for the rich and none for the poor. Between 1949 and 1993 there was law for the rich and law for those who could show to the satisfaction of assessors that they were sufficiently poor. Those in between could not afford recourse to law; to this day, the working middle class is effectively debarred from civil litigation.

5.41 The costs of the Legal Aid Scheme rose steadily from the time of its introduction. So much alarmed did the government become that from 1 April 1993 restrictions were placed on the availability of legal aid. The conditions regarding disposable income were made more restrictive, and the liability to contribute to costs was made stricter. Estimates about the number of persons debarred from recourse to legal aid or seriously handicapped in its availability have varied. Some have claimed that as many as 14 million persons will be debarred from recourse to legal aid or will find the attached conditions unacceptable. If this proposal is correct, hard-pressed health authorities may feel some relief from the pressure of negligence claims; further restrictions on the availability of legal aid may be imposed. On the other hand, the reduction in availability of legal aid may lead to the development of a 'conditional fee' system, in which legal advice and representation are provided on the understanding that no fee will be payable if the claim fails. However, if the claim is successful, a doubled fee will be payable. The attractions of such a scheme for potential plaintiffs are diminished by the condition that if the claim fails, the plaintiff will be responsible for the costs of the defendant. It remains to be seen how popular such a system will be once the full effects of the withdrawal of legal aid are felt. Such a scheme differs from the 'contingency fee' system that operates in the United States of America, in which not only an enhanced fee but a proportion of damages goes to the legal advisers of the successful plaintiff. That system too is subject to the disadvantage attaching to the payment of defendants' costs in the event of failure. However, the prospect of receiving a proportion of damages in the event of success may well act as a powerful spur to diligence on the part of the plaintiff's advisers. Less happily, it may lead to exaggeration of the claim and to unnecessary and even harmful litigation. The effect of this system on the practice of medicine in the United States is generally seen as being harmful, but without it many patients injured through medical negligence would have no chance of redress.

5.42 The effect of the Legal Aid Scheme on medical practice was almost certainly beneficial, though many doctors still feel affronted by having their actions criticised, and many are to the end reluctant to admit to error. Medicine is not the only sphere of activity in which such feelings are aroused. Doctors are, however, more ready than they were twenty years ago to explain, to warn, to indicate alternative courses and, occasionally, to admit to error.

Expert witnesses

5.43 With the evolution of the processes of negligence actions, new burdens have been placed on doctors advising as expert witnesses. The rules requiring disclosure of medical records were certainly welcomed, though many hospital authorities have been reluctant to comply and slow in replying and have made charges which sometimes seem excessive. It appears that in the 'reformed' National Health Service inadequate attention is given to the maintenance of good records or to systems for filing and retrieval of records, radiographs and other records of imaging.

5.44 Less happy has been the effect of rules of disclosure on the preparation of experts' reports. The object of the rules was, presumably, the attainment of greater frankness between parties and facilitation of the process of settlement. It is now, unfortunately, the custom for solicitors to require not only a report on circumstances with an analysis of those circumstances, but also a report 'for disclosure', in which any of the expert's views which might be at all helpful to the opposing party are suppressed. Doctors have not been slow to connive with lawyers in these deceptions, designed to subvert the purposes of the rules regarding disclosure. In the author's view, doctors should not allow themselves or their work to be misused in this manner, even for ready money. Hodgkinson[1] speaks and quotes wisely about the duties of the expert witness: '(The) principal and over-riding duty (is) not to the party by whom he is retained, but to the Court.' Again, 'There are particular pressures upon experts, who are frequently in more than one sense professional witnesses, to give evidence which is either intentionally false or, though correct, misleading by omission.' The polarisation encouraged by the new rules and fostered by opposing lawyers has led to the widespread neglect of this important principle. Moreover, medical expert witnesses in active practice in the National Health Service may well be deterred from criticising proceedings in the Service by the well-founded fear that such criticism may lead to hostile action against them by managers. At the least, such action might lead to a bar to advancement; at the most it might involve dismissal.

1 See T Hodgkinson (1990) in Bibliographical References.

5.45 The recommended practice of 'without prejudice' meetings of expert witnesses from opposing parties[1] is in practice almost invariably futile unless the experts are prepared wholly to ignore efforts to influence them. Few nowadays are prepared so to act; all know that failure to comply will result in the loss of any further requests to advise.

1 See RSC Ord 38, r 38.

Doctors and lawyers

5.46 Unless they are being paid by them, most doctors prefer to deal with lawyers through a defence organisation; most prefer altogether to steer clear of the law in their professional work. The reasons are not hard to seek: doctors are commonly treated with contempt by lawyers; they are required to edit, omit and sometimes to distort in clients' interests; often enough when they are involved in court processes they are kept hanging around the corridors apparently at the whim of all-powerful judges and counsel. A system in which a young man can be jailed for 14 days for whistling at a female juror merits neither respect nor confidence; contempt and fear are the emotions aroused. On occasions, scant attention is paid to the calls of doctors' clinical commitments; the ordeal in the witness box is often severe; the excesses of the adversarial process appear ridiculous to men and women whose work is more often done by consensus and co-operation. Yet the discipline afforded by the provision of medical advice to lawyers is often valuable in compelling the clinician to think about what he or she is doing and truly to audit the results obtained. Knowledge of the mistakes of others can lead to a re-examination of one's own work, to the detection in it of unsuspected mistakes and to the correction of those mistakes. Much credit is due to members of the medical secretariats of the defence organisations in mitigating the rigours of relations between doctors and lawyers: credit in this respect also belongs to the legal advisers to the organisations.

Alternatives to litigation

5.47 At the time of the crisis in medical defence, when the number of claims was rising and when awards were steadily increasing, there was much debate about the possibility of replacing litigation as a method of settling claims in respect of medical negligence. In particular, the possibility of the introduction of a scheme of No Fault Compensation was canvassed, and comparisons were made with the systems in operation in Sweden and New Zealand. Certainly, it was time that an equitable and reasonably quick method of resolving claims regarding negligence was developed. The Medical Defence Union, perhaps for a time losing touch with reality, warmly espoused the cause of No Fault compensation. Observers at the time[1] drew attention to the differences between the United Kingdom and the two countries whose systems were adduced in support, and indicated that the concept was 'foreign to the ethos of today's (1990) government'. Things have not changed; the introduction of NHS indemnity surely marks the end of any hope of developing a sensible system for resolution, compensation and reform.

1 See G Bonney (1990) in Bibliographical References.

5.48 More recently, the advantages of professional arbitration have been canvassed. The concept has received the endorsement of the Department of Health,[1] but it appears that there has been little movement towards what might offer a system cheaper and more effective than the present one. It appears to this author unlikely that the entrenched forces supporting continuation of the present system will yield to any but the most determined assault. Such an assault could be made only by a Secretary of State and a government seriously concerned by rising expenditure on NHS indemnity. It is unlikely that this crisis point will be reached: progressive delegation to general practitioners and progressive privatisation and 'casualisation' of the hospital service will before then have shifted much of the burden from the state.

1 See Department of Health (1991) in Bibliographical References.

THE DEFENCE ORGANISATIONS AND THE CHANGING FACE OF MEDICINE AND SOCIETY

5.49 The defence organisations enter the last decade of the twentieth century faced by challenges of a character and a degree of gravity previously unknown to them. They have indeed been freed from the burden of indemnification of patients damaged in the national hospital and community services. However, they face the task of indemnifying patients damaged by general practitioners undertaking increasingly demanding work; they must continue to indemnify patients damaged in private practice; before the end of the century they will, no doubt, be obliged to indemnify patients damaged by private practitioners imperfectly acquainted with their fields of work. Pressure on doctors to subordinate clinical need to financial considerations will doubtless increase; increasingly ruthless action will be taken against clinicians attempting to make public their views about deficiencies in the health service. Despair and disillusion may increasingly affect practitioners who find themselves unable to offer to patients care of an acceptable standard. Legal costs will surely rise, as will awards to damaged patients. The frequency of claims will continue to increase unless there is a sharp reduction in the availability of legal aid, and if that reduction is not followed by the general adoption of a system of 'contingency fees'. Already the Medical Defence Union has adopted a posture in which it may better resist these new pressures. It has moved away from its character as a society whose members offer mutual assistance to that of a business organisation better suited to withstand the rigours of 'the market'. The change is symbolised by the recent appointements to the Board of Management.

The structure of the defence organisations

5.50 The Medical Defence Union has since July 1991 been managed by a Board headed by a Chairman (the former President) and made up of selected members of Council, a Chief Executive (the former Secretary), two General Managers and three members distinguished respectively in the business of insurance, in business and in hospital management and in business studies and practice. The last, a Director of the Bank of England, was one of the chief architects of the purchase of the Rover Car Company by British Aerospace. On 1 April 1993 a fourth such member was added: a Conservative peeress, formerly a minister in various government departments, including that of Health. The post of Deputy Chief Executive has been abolished. Advice is given by a Council, a Dental Committee, and an Irish Affairs Committee, each composed of distinguished practitioners. So far as the writer knows, appointment to the Council is by invitation, after soundings and searches have been made by Council members and the results discussed with the Chairman and officers. The process has been compared with that formerly used in the selection of the Leader of the Conservative party. There is no matter of election here; no question of democratic processes. Although there is a broad representation of the various specialities in medicine and dentistry, there is no question of representation of special interests. The results of the process seem to endorse the perjorative connotation attached by the ancient Greeks to the term 'democracy'. The Medical Defence Union has, in the writer's view correctly, ruled that no person appointed or elected to membership of the General Medical Council can be appointed to or continue in membership of its Council. The Medical Protection Society confines this restriction to membership of the Professional Conduct Committee.

Formerly, the Council, and the 'Elected Members' in particular, exercised a large measure of control over the conduct of affairs in the widest sense. With the present and likely future need for financial stringency and for decisive management, its role has clearly become largely advisory. The Medical and Dental Secretariats provide advice to members, and are assisted by three 'nurse advisers'.[1] In 1992 a radical review of staffing structure was undertaken, as a result of which 40 members of staff retired or were made redundant. The Union's main office is in London; its second office in the United Kingdom is in Manchester. An office is maintained in Sydney, New South Wales, and there are subsidiary offices in Tel Aviv, Budapest and Madrid. It appears that the managers of the Medical Defence Union are now anxious to dissociate the organisation from the titular abbreviation 'Union', with its connotations so objectionable to the present governing party, of association with the trade unions. The implied assumption that the present governing party will continue in office indefinitely does not necessarily have to be accepted. Some would find that too depressing.

1 Since the above was written, the Medical Defence Union has announced the formation of a new legal department, staffed at present by two solicitors, one a former partner in Messrs Hempsons.

5.51 The structure of the Medical Protection Society appears less changed. A President, a Chairman of Council, a Chief Executive and a Secretary and Medical Director are at the head of affairs. Advice is provided by a Council and a President's Advisory Board supplemented by a Medical Secretariat. There is a General Practice Advisory Board. The writer knows little of the process of appointment to the Council and Boards of the Medical Protection Society; it is likely to be similar to that obtaining in the Medical Defence Union. The latter certainly has no monopoly of persons of wisdom and experience to fill the places on its Council. Dental Protection is administered separately by a Board, an Advisory Panel, a Secretary and Dental Director and a Dental Secretariat. Medical Protection (Europe) Limited and Medical Claims Management Services Limited were set up to deal respectively with cases in Continental Europe and with requests from health authorities for expertise in handling claims. The principal office is in London; the second office in the United Kingdom is in Leeds. Offices are maintained in Parkville, Victoria (Australia) and in Frankfurt.

Membership

5.52 Most members of the British defence organisations are medical and dental practitioners in the United Kingdom. Some are members of the professions supplementary to medicine. It is satisfactory to be able to record that the abolition of the requirement of membership of a defence organisation brought about by the introduction of NHS indemnity has had little effect on recruitment. Newly qualified doctors are in fact acting prudently in joining: the cover afforded by NHS indemnity is strictly limited to damage done in the hospital or community service in the process of performing the work for which the authority is responsible. No cover is afforded against claims in respect of work outside this field; even within the field NHS indemnity offers no advice to the practitioner. Members were in 1993 warned by the Chief Executive of the Medical Defence Union that NHS indemnity did not even cover them in work undertaken on contract in private institutions in order to reduce the length of in-patient waiting lists. Clearly, all practitioners must be very cautious in their interpretation of the extent of cover afforded by the government scheme. Evidently, advice and assistance in matters of dispute with employers, in disciplinary matters and in matters concerning the General Medical Council has to be provided by a defence organisation. General practitioners and consultants acting in a private capacity are, of course, dependent on the defence bodies for all cover: in matters involving negligence, the General Medical Council, criminal charges and other difficulties. The cover afforded is almost 'world-wide'. The exceptions are the United States and Canada: members practising there are not covered. This exclusion reflects, of course, the cost of litigation and the size of the awards in North America.

Subscription policies

5.53 The quality of the technical advice available to the managements of the Defence Societies in the setting of subscriptions has improved greatly in recent years. The Medical Protection Society took the lead in grappling with the vexed question of the introduction of 'differential' subscriptions, whose inevitability was adumbrated in 1990.[1] The present policy of the Medical Defence Union in setting subscriptions appears to be to define high and low risk specialities and to combine this factor with one based on declared income from sources outside the National Health Service. This policy and that of the Medical Protection Society seem to have succeeded in combating any challenge posed by insurance companies offering low subscriptions to practitioners in low-risk specialities. Subscriptions for dentists are, as has always been the case, set significantly lower than subscriptions for doctors. In October 1992 the Medical Defence Union offered a new type of membership to doctors and dentists in the United Kingdom. The existing form of membership, now designated 'Classic', entitles the member to apply for assistance if he or she was a member at the time of the incident, even if he or she was not a member when medico-legal problems arose. 'Contemporary' membership, available at a lower rate of subscription, requires membership not only at the time of the incident but also until all medico-legal matters arising from it have been concluded. Cover can be continued after discontinuation of membership if a 'closing payment' estimated not to exceed four times the annual subscription is made.

1 See G Bonney (1990) in Bibliographical References.

5.54 In its Annual Report for 1993, the Medical Defence Union announced the ending of the system by which a member could, having paid 40 consecutive annual subscriptions, be elected to 'honorary' or 'compounded' life membership. At the time of writing, the full effect of the implications of the withdrawal of this system is not known; nor is it known whether the Medical Protection Society, which operated a similar system, will decide similarly to act. The withdrawal of compounded life membership, a valuable privilege for the retired clinician, indicates clearly the Union's concern about future uncertainties. On the other hand, many clinicians continued in active practice for many years after the grant of 'free' membership; all ran the risk of expensive process arising from some act of times past; although death continues to free clinicians from the obligation to subscribe, claims from times past can still be made against their estates. Nevertheless, the prospect of achieving 'honorary membership' through continuity of subscription certainly restrained some aggrieved members from transferring their allegiance to another defence organisation.

5.55 The expectation that overseas recruitment might provide a pool of low-risk members whose subscriptions would in effect subsidise the operation in the United Kingdom appears to have been abandoned. In 1991 the Medical Defence Union took the opportunity of negotiating the transfer of funds and liabilities to Kupat Holim Clalit, the employers of a large group of members in Israel. In return for a payment of £7 m the employer took over responsibility for the entire liabilities of these members.

5.56 The financial position of the Medical Defence Union as declared in its 1992 Annual Report appeared rather to have improved. A reserve fund of £103 m was set against reported liabilities amounting to £113 m at the end of 1991. By 1993 reported liabilities amounted to £146 m and declared reserves to £139 m.[1] It appears still to be the intention of the Board of Management to achieve 'fully funded' status, and this objective is shared by the Medical Protection Society. The financial position of the Scottish organisation appears to continue strong.

1 See 'The Medical Defence Union' (1990) in Bibliographical References.

The work of the defence organisations

5.57 Attention has been shifted from the conduct of negligence claims to methods of reducing their frequency and severity, although the chief financial commitment of the defence organisations is that produced by such claims. The Medical Defence Union in particular was always active in education, producing instructive pamphlets dealing with particular fields and particular risks, organising and subsidising instructional lectures and courses, and producing films and later videotapes illustrating particular aspects of the field of medical negligence. In conjunction with the other defence organisations and with the Royal College of Nursing it produced advisory notes designed to lessen the common dangers produced by incorrect identification and faulty procedures in the operating theatre. This was and remains extremely valuable work, of help to doctors and patients and indirectly of course to the defence organisations. The *Journal of the Medical Defence Union* is now well established as a serious publication in which matters of clinical and medico-legal importance are canvassed. The credentials of the defence organisations as serious bodies capable of making important contributions to the conduct of the medical services in the United Kingdom were well established before the publication of the White Paper. They were frequently consulted by the officers and even by the Ministers of the Department on matters concerned with the safety of patients. It may be that with the fragmentation of the hospital service consequent on the implementation of the 'reforms' and with the associated rise in managerial power, there is less frequent recourse to advice provided by the defence organisations. Certainly, as has been noted, the research function of the organisations has gravely been impaired by the loss to analysis of material arising from hospital practice. It is hardly likely that a providing hospital in competition with other providers would make available for general analysis and publication material potentially so harmful to its prospects in the market.

Risk management

5.58 The concept of risk management was described by Hill.[1] The term was proposed in the 1960s in the insurance industry in the United States to indicate the financing and control of losses on insurance claims. Risk management techniques were applied in the field of healthcare in the early 1970s, with the sharp increase then of the frequency and cost of malpractice claims. Hill records that at the time he wrote: 'more than 70 per cent of hospitals in the USA . . . have to comply with several risk management standards to meet the requirements of the Joint Committee on Accreditation of Healthcare Organisations'.

1 See G Hill (1991) in Bibliographical References.

5.59 'The essential components of a risk management programme are the identification of risks, the prevention of adverse incidents, the minimisation of claims and proper claims management.'[1] Many clinicians may think that they are already doing that, but the discipline imposed by the necessity to think along these lines is almost certain to lead to better and safer clinical practice, to the proper recording of mishaps and their causes and to the more sensible and expeditious handling of claims. The Medical Defence Union has offered to managements in assistance with:

(1) health care risk management;
(2) guidelines for data handling to establish future liabilities;
(3) data handling; and
(4) claims handling.

To what extent hospital managements have chosen to avail themselves of this facility is not clear. Financial stringency is certain to exert an effect on the prospects of this venture; objective evidence seems to indicate that only minimal attention is given even to maintaining good systems of recording, of storage and of retrieval of records. On the other hand, nothing but good could come from instruction of hospital managements in identification, avoidance and management of risks. The handling of claims might well be improved if it were contracted out to the specialists in this field available among the staffs of the defence organisations. In practice, a great deal of 'risk management' is done, and has for many years been done, by means of advice to members over the telephone.

1 See G Hill (1991) in Bibliographical References.

5.60 One of the most valuable and most valued functions of the defence organisations is the provision of a telephonic service by which a member, worried over a course of action to be followed or a decision to be taken, can obtain advice from one of the medical secretariat. This service is used extensively: its provision occupies much of the time of the medical secretariat: doubtless, it is expensive for the organisations.

5.61 A particularly important field, touching on that of risk management, is that of HIV infection in treating doctors or in patients under treatment. Harsh ethical questions arise for the doctor with HIV infection:

(1) the necessity or otherwise of declaring the infection to his or her employing authority;
(2) the necessity or otherwise of declaring the infection to patients; and
(3) the determination of the 'safe' range of work permitted.

Serious problems arise concerning unsuspected infection of doctors; in particular, of doctors whose work could lead to infection of patients. Similar difficulties arise for doctors treating patients known to be infected or known to be at risk of infection.

5.62 The constraints acting on those caring for persons with HIV infection and with declared immune deficiency are well known: it is a fearsome matter for the patient and for the doctor to discover the presence of an untreatable infection which is virtually certain at some stage to cause death. Very serious questions are raised of confidentiality, of duty to the public, of advice to the patient and of the efficacy or otherwise of treatment. The retreat into extreme confidentiality, in which information about infection is withheld from treating doctors and, it seems, from employers and patients of infected doctors, has produced difficulties. Yet it is hard to imagine that open 'screening' would be accepted unless some prospect of effective treatment were offered. Doctors infected by HIV certainly have a duty to reveal their condition in confidence to their employers, though the general disturbance of relations between doctors and administrators has made the process more difficult than it was in former days. It may be thought that patients so infected owe a similar duty to doctors who may in the course of treating them contract the infection. Resolution of these difficulties by wise and informed action is required: until then, the staffs of defence organisations must continue to advise members as best they can in the particular circumstances of each case.

The incident

5.63 Mishaps are certain to occur; doctors do from time to time act with inadequate care and attention; from time to time results do not match patients' expectations; complaints are certain to be made, and claims may result from them. In general practice complaint may be made first to the practitioner or to the Family Health Services Authority. Many complaints can be resolved by the practitioner with explanation and expression of regret. The question of admission of liability is difficult: on the one hand, the patient may seek simply to justify his or her complaint and may allow the matter to rest if liability is admitted. On the other hand, the admission of liability may be a trigger for further action, to be pulled – or perhaps squeezed – at the time or at any time within the next three years. Perhaps the best course is for the practitioner to tell the truth as it appears to him or her, to concede liability but to make no admission as to causation. Indeed, the establishment of causation is often a matter of extreme difficulty. In the case of consultant practice, the complaint will come direct to the responsible consultant or will be intimated to him or to her by solicitors or other agents. It is best to be frank, to express regret if necessary, and to offer if possible, some method of repairing the damage. At these early stages the defence organisations offer advice through their medical and dental secretariats, to such effect that many disputes are resolved without recourse to litigation.

5.64 When a claim is pressed, the defence organisations offer close examination by consultants in the relevant field or fields. The matter may then be further conducted by a member of the medical or dental secretariat, in the hope of resolution without recourse to litigation. Once a writ has been issued, solicitors must of course be involved, but in many cases that involvement is thought advisable at an earlier stage. Some cases clearly fall into one of two categories: defensible and indefensible. Defensible cases are in general defended to the point of the arbitrament of the court and if necessary to the Court of Appeal and the Lords. In plainly indefensible cases, early settlement is sought, though the plaintiff's estimations of value may differ widely from those of the defendant, and negotiation, sometimes prolonged, is always necessary. Regrettably, most cases fall into an intermediate category in which the chances of a successful defence have to be balanced against the moral justification for such defence, the interpretation of the facts of the case, the likely cost of defence in relation to that of settlement, the effect of prolonged action on the life and work of the consultant concerned, its effect upon the patient and other less tangible factors. If some great principle is involved, affecting not only the consultant concerned but the practice of medicine in general, it is usually right to continue to defend. If, on the other hand, the issue is in doubt, the patient has suffered and continues to suffer, and the clinician is uncertain of his or her ground, it is not only more humane but also wiser to explore settlement. To what extent the exercise of humane judgment will remain possible for the defence organisations continues to be a matter of doubt. It may well be that the 'discipline of the market place' will cause all such sentiment to be extruded.

The methods examined

5.65 The critics of the proceedings of the defence organisations name as their principal defects:

(1) defence of the indefensible;
(2) delay and obfuscation in the conduct of the defendants' case;

(3) regular and unjustifiable delay in reaching settlement;
(4) failure to initiate any process of reform on the part of the clinician in cases in which an error has or errors have been made; and
(5) failure to exact any penalty from the responsible clinician in cases in which a gross error has or errors have been made.

The author has viewed proceedings from both sides of the fence and well appreciates the reasons for these criticisms. He considers that – at any rate up to 1990 – the first criticism is unjustifiable. Delay is often due as much to faults in the conduct of the plaintiff's case as it is to faults on the part of the defendant's advisers. It appears inseparable from the process of litigation in an adversarial system, in which the lawyers for each party seek to polarise the issues and to suppress any material which might lead to a meeting of minds. As to reform of the clinician's methods: few clinicians can pass through a process of litigation without reflecting long and closely on their actions in the case under discussion. Few, having had that experience, can fail to seek to reform their methods. Sadly, it has to be admitted that there are still a few who neither reflect nor reform; most of these few are, sadly indeed for patients, in positions of eminence and responsibility.

5.66 The question of penalty for the clinician who has made some catastrophic error has widely been canvassed. It may be that as private practice increases and as doctors' incomes increasingly are derived from this source, the penalty of loss of practice will be sufficient retribution; sufficient stimulus to reform. On the other hand, as consultants know well, success in private practice is not necessarily related to skill or even to competence in the particular field. Availability and an agreeable manner are more often the qualities desired. In those serious cases in which a particular clinician makes frequent errors in a particular field, the defence organisation concerned may well call him or her to order and explore the reasons for the recurrent mistakes. It yet remains the case that there is little or no penalty, save that on the conscience, for gross error. So many and so intractable are the problems attaching to the institution of a 'no claims' system in medical negligence insurance that the defence organisations have now averted their gaze. If the General Medical Council enjoyed the confidence of the medical profession in particular and of the public in general, it might well play a role in the rehabilitation of persistent offenders or in the formulation of policies designed to avoid error. At present such a role is confined to attempts to help and to limit the activities of clinicians whose judgment is impaired by natural process, by use of drugs or by over-use of alcohol. Any extension of this role on the part of the GMC as at present constituted would certainly be resisted by the profession and by the defence organisations.

OTHER WORK OF THE DEFENCE ORGANISATIONS

5.67 Perhaps most of the work of the defence organisations is that concerned with advice to and representation of members in connection with the processes of the General Medical Council, with fraud and crime, with civil offences, with the regulatory mechanisms of the National Health Service, and with processes initiated by the Parliamentary Commissioner.

The General Medical Council

5.68 The practitioner may become involved with the General Medical Council through omitting to notify a change of address, through failure to pay the subscription, through serious professional misconduct, through incapacity in practice from illness or addiction, or through a criminal offence. The penalty for the first two errors is prescribed: it is that of removal of the practitioner's name from the Medical Register. Although in that position of greater freedom and less responsibility the doctor or dentist can continue to function, he or she may not prescribe controlled drugs; may not treat sexually transmitted disease; is debarred from other privileges attached to registration.

5.69 Serious professional misconduct may signify a wide range of offences: neglect or disregard of responsibility in the case of patients; abuse of professional privileges in relations with patients or in the use of drugs; personal behaviour of a nature judged to be derogatory to the reputation of the profession; improper 'advertising' and other offences. The Professional Conduct Committee and the Preliminary Proceedings Committee deal with these matters. It is, sadly, the fact that there are in the medical profession as many desperate rascals, incurable incompetents and persons addicted to drugs, alcohol and sexual overindulgence as there are in other professions, learned or otherwise. The role of the defence organisations in the assistance of members plainly incapacitated by natural or induced causes is difficult and delicate: on the one hand, assistance is clearly due to a member who has paid his or her subscription; on the other hand, the defence organisation no less than the General Medical Council has a duty to protect the public from the activities of addicted incompetents. It is here, perhaps, that the divergence between 'medico-legal' and strictly legal principle is most sharply marked.

5.70 Those who have observed the proceedings of the relevant Committees of the General Medical Council in this wide field are confident enough about the conduct of affairs in fields other than the strictly clinical. Observers have commented that in the field of bad clinical practice the judgment of the GMC is less sure: on the one hand, grotesquely bad practice may earn no more than a rebuke; on the other, a clinician who has made a forgivable mistake in a difficult case may be subjected to a degree of personal humiliation which would not be permitted in open court. The Council's attitude to 'advertising' continues, in the writer's view, to be ambivalent. On the one hand, doctors appear to be subject to disciplinary process for setting out the range of services offered; on the other, consultants appear to be free to extol their own skill in the pages of popular magazines and on the television screen. In the gravest cases of professional misconduct, when a member's name is erased from the Register, the defence organisations may, if it seems appropriate, assist in appeals to the Judicial Committee of the Privy Council. The effect of erasure on membership of the Medical Defence Union is described in article 12 of the Articles of Association adopted in 1991.

Criminal offences

5.71 Many opportunities for and temptations to fraud are offered to practitioners and to general practitioners in particular. False notification and dealing in controlled drugs have for long been among the types of offence committed. The intricate regulations of the National Health Service have provided opportunities for fraudulent claims for expenses and special payments. Doctors with access to controlled drugs have from time to time themselves used such drugs and have become addicted. It has then been necessary to cloak this addiction and over-use of drugs by the issue of false prescriptions. Hospital staff have from time to time misused the designated prescription form in order to obtain controlled and other drugs for themselves. With the introduction of 'fund-holding' practices the large question is raised of the desirability of such a practice contracting with a limited company directed by the fund-holders themselves. Large sums of money are involved in such transactions.

5.72 Fraud and other criminal acts are in the case of the general practitioner likely to be brought to the attention of the Family Health Services Authority; in the case of the hospital practitioner to the attention of management and health authority. Health authorities and management will in serious cases involve the assistance of the police, and criminal proceedings are likely to follow. The involvement of the General Medical Council is certain. Here too the defence organisations steer a difficult course between affording help and safeguarding the public interest.

Manslaughter and murder

5.73 In some cases in which there is a fatal outcome, alleged carelessness or momentary recklessness may appear so great that charges of manslaughter are made. Such cases are fortunately rare. Recently, the subject of such 'involuntary manslaughter' has been raised in connection with the quashing by the Court of Appeal of convictions of two doctors on a charge of manslaughter arising from the intrathecal injection of vincristine. Such process is nowadays initiated by the Crown Prosecution Service, usually after investigation by the police. In the recent case disquiet has been voiced concerning the propriety of the action. Indeed, it appears that the Lord Chief Justice has called for the appointment of a Royal Commission to investigate this subject. If this appeal is heeded, we can be sure that nothing more will be heard of the matter for, at least, the next five years.

5.74 The difficult question of deliberate termination of the life of a patient in intolerable suffering caused by terminal malignant disease is raised regularly and is regularly attended by wide publicity. The ethics and merits of 'euthanasia' have long been debated: it is indeed distressing for the patient, for the doctors and nurses and for the relatives to face the ordeal and the problem of continued suffering unabated by any remedy. Yet methods of control of pain are now so much improved that such cases should certainly be rare. Some patients, of course, request that their lives should be terminated. Yet all doctors know that such requests do not always represent the true wishes of these patients. Certainly, methods of diagnosis are now so good that the diagnosis of terminal illness is more often than not accurate. Yet doctors are sometimes wrong; the results of investigations are sometimes misleading. 'Bethink ye, bethink ye', said Oliver Cromwell, 'in the bowels of Christ that ye may be mistaken.' Certainly there is a gulf between a decision to put a sufferer out of his or her misery and the thought that it would be better not only for the sufferer but also for the public in general if he or she were out of the way. Yet we have seen, and still see, that that gulf can be bridged by persons certain of their wisdom, rectitude and concern for a cause. It may more easily be bridged by persons who have something to gain from the death of a patient, but such persons are still rare in the profession of medicine.

5.75 It may be that the wisest doctor is he or she who thinks deeply, penetrates the patient's mind so far as possible, consults with colleagues and with relatives and acts in such a way that no publicity will be attracted by the death of a patient terminally ill. In the writer's view, no purpose is served by the actions of martyrs in the cause of euthanasia. Doctors do not and should not enter medicine with the object of putting patients to death.

Lesser transgressions

5.76 The defence organisations will assist their members in clashes with the law brought about by alleged misdemeanour so long as the member was at the time of the incident engaged in an activity inseparable from the conduct of his or her medical practice.

Slander and libel

5.77 Doctors find themselves slandered and libelled in connection with the practice of their profession; from time to time it is they who do the slandering and libelling. In recent years the Medical Defence Union has found itself involved in one very prolonged case in which a doctor made allegations of libel against a prominent television personality. In this case the good sense of the presiding judge brought the proceedings to a close when it appeared probable that the length and expense of the hearing would exceed all reason. Rarely, criticism of a colleague's work in a paper in a scientific journal will evoke allegations of libel and may even lead to process in court. The last word on libel law may have been said by Cocklecarrot J: 'The law presumes malice, unless the remark was made on what is called a privileged occasion. Nor need the plaintiff prove damage. The law assumes damage. Thus, the law being what it is, no wonder there are so many plaintiffs.'[1] The defence organisations are ready to assist members in defending such actions; they are, reasonably enough, cautious in advising members to undertake such action and in assisting them in it.

1 See Cocklecarrot J (1944) in Bibliographical References.

Complaints by patients

5.78 Complaints about clinical care and personal behaviour are in the case of general practitioners brought to the attention of Family Health Services Authorities; in the case of hospital practitioners to management and if necessary to the health authority. The Medical Defence Union[1] records that 'allegations of an unprofessional manner or attitude on the part of the doctor or his (sic) staff form the largest single cause of complaints to FHSA's. These are, however, outside the remit of the formal claims procedure. "Failure to visit" is by far the most likely reason for the doctor to be found in breach of his terms of service.' The defence organisations spend much time and money on assisting and representing members in these proceedings.

1 See 'Complaints to FHSA's' (1987) in Bibliographical References.

5.79 In the case of hospital staff and of consultants in particular, regulation of standards of behaviour and clinical competence has been a matter of difficulty. The operation of the procedure prescribed in HM (61) 112 was for long recognised to be expensive and unsatisfactory. Heavy expenses, not recoverable even when a judgment in favour of the 'defendant' clinician was reached, were incurred by the defence organisations. In March 1990 that procedure was superseded by procedures laid down in HC (90) 9, covering disciplinary procedures for hospital and community medical and dental staff.[1] Aggrieved patients have recourse to redress through operation of the procedures described in HC (88) 37. Time will show whether the introduction of these procedures brings improvements in checking bad practice, in safeguarding the public interest and in providing fair treatment for doctors. At present, the practice of suspension from duty appears to be increasing: enough evidently for the Member of Parliament for Hastings and Rye on 19 May 1993 to ask the Secretary of State for Northern Ireland how many NHS hospital doctors and consultants were currently under suspension pending enquiries and disciplinary action. She received the answer that this information was 'not held centrally'.

1 See G Hill (1991) in Bibliographical References.

Suppression of dissent

5.80 Perhaps the most difficult problem confronting the defence organisations is that created by the arbitrary exercise of power by management. Such power may be used to stifle dissent or to discipline a clinician who has voiced publicly concern about the effect of managerial decisions on the care and safety of patients. It is evident that in certain of these cases the British Medical Association is prepared to assist its members. However, not all doctors are members of the Association; the Association can hardly afford to intervene in all cases in which managers appear to have exceeded their authority. In such cases doctors will continue to turn to their defence organisations for help and advice. As the contracts of hospital doctors increasingly come to be held by their employing Trusts on conditions locally evolved and applied, causes for such recourse will become more frequent. It would be wrong to suggest that the presence on the Board of the Medical Defence Union of a Conservative peeress, a former health minister, would lead to any conflict of interest, but some members may see in the appointment a threat to the Union's independence in such matters. Of course, as older members accept the changes, however unwillingly, and as the proportion of younger members who have never known anything different increases, such requests for assistance will die away.

The future of the defence organisations

5.81 The defence organisations face a continuing challenge, with an almost certain increase in the number and cost of negligence claims, with a rising incidence of complaints to Family Health Services Authorities and with other consequences of the attack upon professionalism and upon specialised units providing particularly high standards of care. There is no possibility that any procedure more reasonable or humane than the present one for dealing with claims of negligence will be introduced unless the government becomes seriously alarmed by the cost of providing NHS indemnity. The organisations will be hard put to it to maintain solvency. They may well face a choice. On the one hand they may become financially rigorous insurance companies concerned only with maintenance of solvency, without any thought of a role in the protection of the public, in the education of the medical and dental professions and in the defence of professionalism. On the other hand, they may seek to combine financial rigour with maintenance of the humane approach that has up to now characterised their proceedings and has been a mark of distinction. It appears at present that the will persists to maintain an humane approach, to act in the interests of doctors and patients and to guard professional integrity. Indeed, the defence organisations have only to look at the operations of the major insurance companies to see that financial rigour alone is not enough. All concerned will hope that they will continue to give light in a darkening scene.

THE PATIENT'S CHARTER

5.82 Early in 1992 the Patient's Charter[1] was published over the signature of the then Secretary of State for Health. It was one of a number of Charters promulgated at about that time by the government. Possibly, it and the other Charters owed their existence to a desire to quiet the worries of citizens who saw the conduct of affairs in general and in particular passing from elected bodies to unelected quasi-autonomous non-governmental organisations controlled by retired Government Ministers and other party supporters. The Charter set out seven well-established rights, together with three 'important new rights'. The latter related to rights to:

(1) information about local health services;
(2) admission to hospital within two years of being put on the inpatient waiting list; and
(3) investigation of any complaint about NHS services and to a written reply from 'the chief executive or general manager'.

Charter rights were 'guaranteed' in the sense that a patient who thought that he or she was being denied or likely to be denied one of them could write to the Chief Executive of the National Health Service.

1 See 'the Patient's Charter' in Bibliographical References.

5.83 In addition, nine national and five local 'Charter Standards' were stated, relating to the manner in which patients were to be treated. The extent to which the maintenance of any of these standards was enforceable remains unclear.

5.84 The intention behind the production of the 'Charter' was clearly admirable. In fact, most good clinicians were already practising in accordance with the standards set out; many of those who were not doing so were prevented from compliance by defective provision of facilities. A number of clinicians had no thought of compliance: no amount of such documents was likely to have any effect on these. The extent to which the Charter's provisions can be put into practice remains in doubt. There can, however, be little doubt that the chief targets for the resentment of patients denied their rights or believing themselves to have been denied their rights, will be the doctors and nurses in the front line. Managers and health authorities will find little difficulty in shifting the blame for poor performance caused by inadequacy of staffing or of facilities. It is likely that patients whose rights have been denied will fail to obtain satisfaction through the mechanism described in the Charter, and that they will necessarily turn to litigation in order to secure that satisfaction.

Acknowledgements

I wish to express my deep gratitude to Dr K M Allsopp, formerly Deputy Chief Executive of the Medical Defence Union, and to Dr RN Palmer, Secretary and Medical Director of the Medical Protection Society, for extensive help, without which the preparation of this account would not have been possible. If I have misinterpreted or misrepresented the information provided, the fault is mine. The opinions expressed are mine throughout.

BIBLIOGRAPHICAL REFERENCES

Bonney G in Powers M J and Harris N H (eds), *Medical Negligence* (Butterworths, 1990).
Brett Young F *Dr Bradley Remembers* (William Heinemann Ltd, 1938).
Brindle D in The Guardian (17 May 1993, p 20).
Cocklecarrot J in Morton J B, *Captain Foulenough* (Macmillan & Co, 1944).
'Complaints to FHSA's' (The Medical Defence Union, 1987, revised 1990).
Cronin A J *The Citadel* (1937).
Department of Health 'Arbitration for Medical Negligence in the National Health Service' (October 1991).
'Disciplinary Procedures for Hospital and Community Medical and Dental Staff' (Department of Health Circular HC (90) 9).
Dyer C (1988) 'Defence societies' price war', British Medical Journal 297: 1356.
General Medical Council (1992) 'Contractual arrangements in health care: professional responsibilities in relation to the clinical needs of patients'.
Griffiths R (1992) 'Who cares? Management and the caring services', Journal of the Royal Society of Medicine 85: 663–668.
Hawkins C *Mishap or Malpractice?* (Blackwell Scientific Publications, 1985).
Hill G (1991) 'What is risk management?', International Journal of Risk and Safety in Medicine 2: 83–90.
Hodgkinson T *Expert Evidence: Law and Practice* (Sweet & Maxwell, 1990).
Hospital Doctors: Training for the Future, (Health Publications Unit, April 1993).
Kipling R (1889) 'The Ballad of the King's Mercy' in *Rudyard Kipling's Verse* (Hodder & Stoughton, 1933).
'Letter from the Principal Medical Officer to the Department of Health' (PL/CMO (93) 3).

'Letter from Westminster' (1993) British Medical Journal 306: 1502.
Management Arrangements for the Reorganised National Health Service (HMSO, 1972).
The Medical Defence Union Annual Report (1993).
Merrison A W Report of the Committee of Inquiry into the Regulation of the Medical Profession (HMSO, 1975).
NHS Circular, HC (89) and HC (FP) (89) 22.
Palmer R N (1992) 'United Kingdom "Crown" Indemnity for medical negligence – An overview of the first 18 months of the scheme' International Journal of Medicine and Law 11: 623–627.
The Patient's Charter (HMSO, 1992).
Power D'A in *Plarr's Lives of the Fellows of the Royal College of Surgeons* (John Wright & Sons Ltd, 1930, pp 561–569).
Stacey M *Regulating British Medicine: The General Medical Council* (John Wiley & Sons, 1992).
Trotter W *Collected Papers* (Oxford University Press/H Milford, 1941).
Wright C M, Aynsley-Green A, Tomlinson P, Ahmed L, MacFarlane J A 'A comparison of height, weight and head circumference of primary schoolchildren living in deprived and non-deprived circumstances (1992) Early Human Development 31: 157–162.

CHAPTER 6

Fatal iatrogenic injuries – the inquest

Paul A Knapman *Barrister*

SUMMARY

Introduction

6.1 An inquest is essentially an enquiry presided over by a judicial officer, a coroner to hear how, when and where a person came by their death. The law requires that in England and Wales every unnatural death must be the subject of an inquest. Moreover, every inquest must be held in public (except on grounds of national security) and relatives and their legal representatives must be allowed to ask questions.

6.2 It will be apparent that where there has been a fatal iatrogenic injury there will be an inquest. Although designed as a fact-finding exercise, an inquest has the added advantage for relatives in that the very act of any medical negligence will itself be explored by the coroner. Moreover, the cost of any post mortem, assimilation of evidence, the hearing itself, together with securing attendance of witnesses – all these costs are borne at the public expense.

THE CORONER AND HIS JURISDICTION

The coroner

6.3 A coroner is an independent judicial officer. His office is one of the oldest known to the law and conventionally goes back to at least 1194. He has jurisdiction over deaths reported to him (or treasure found) over that area to which he has been appointed.

6.4 He is appointed by a special committee of the local authority (with the concurrence of the Secretary of State for Home Affairs if it includes a metropolitan district or London borough). A measure of administrative advice and support is given by the Home Office. He may only be removed from office by the Lord Chancellor. It will be seen therefore that once appointed, he may not be removed or disciplined by the local authority or Home Office or any other government department such as the Department of Health, and is therefore unfettered to investigate deaths involving those very departments. Deaths involving local authority nursing homes, or prison and police custody deaths, whose ultimate responsibility may be the Home Office, or deaths in National Health Service hospitals under the Department of Health, all come within his jurisdiction.

6.5 To have jurisdiction he requires contemporaneously a dead body and information about the same. The information may be from doctors, the police, the Registrar of Deaths, or indeed any person. More particularly, a person requiring to remove a body out of England must approach the local coroner.

6.6 There are exceptions from the requirement to have a body within his jurisdiction. These are when the body is destroyed or irrecoverable, but this may only be by direction of the Secretary of State for Home Affairs (Coroners Act 1988, section 15). A coroner may have the investigation of a death transferred to him by another coroner (Coroners Act 1988, section 14). He may also be required to hold an inquest into a death not in his jurisdiction by order of the High Court after a previous inquest has been quashed (Coroners Act 1988, section 13).

6.7 Apart from the above, assuming the coroner has a body within his jurisdiction, the information must go to show that the deceased:

(a) has died a violent or unnatural death; or
(b) has died a sudden death of which the cause is unknown; or
(c) has died in prison or in such circumstances as to require an inquest under any other Act;

then an inquest must be held.

Informing the coroner

6.8 Who is to report the death? It is the duty of every person to give information which may lead to the coroner having notice of circumstances requiring the holding of an inquest.[1] The people who will commonly inform the coroner will be doctors and relatives in respect of iatrogenic death, but also occasionally governors of prisons, police officers, etc. The Registrar of Births, Marriages and Deaths has a duty to report deaths to the coroner under certain circumstances. Before considering this, however, it may be of benefit to consider the process of death certification.

1 *R v Clerk* (1702) 1 Salk 377.

6.9 Where a doctor has attended the deceased 'during his last illness' he is obliged to complete a certificate in the prescribed form, stating to the best of his knowledge and belief the cause of death, and to deliver that certificate to the registrar (Births and Deaths Registration Act 1953, section 22). In practice a doctor will only complete a certificate if he is confident as to the cause of death, and if he has completed a certificate, he will often hand it to a relative or funeral director for ultimate transmission to the registrar.

6.10 Usually the registrar will register the death and issue a certificate for disposal. But the registrar has a duty imposed upon him to report the death to the coroner in certain circumstances set out under the Registration of Births and Deaths Regulations 1987, reg 41(1) and 41(2):

(1) Where the relevant registrar is informed of the death of any person he shall, subject to paragraph (2), report the death to the coroner on an approved form if the death is one—

(a) in respect of which the deceased was not attended during his last illness by a registered medical practitioner; or
(b) in respect of which the registrar—

 (i) has been unable to obtain a duly completed certificate of cause of death; or
 (ii) has received such a certificate with respect to which it appears to him, from the particulars contained in the certificate or otherwise, that the deceased was not seen by the certifying medical practitioner either after death or within 14 days before death; or

(c) the cause of which appears to be unknown; or
(d) which the registrar has reason to believe to have been unnatural or to have been caused by violence or neglect or by abortion or to have been attended by suspicious circumstances; or
(e) which appears to the registrar to have occurred during an operation or before recovery from the effect of an anaesthetic; or
(f) which appears to the registrar from the contents of any medical certificate of cause of death to have been due to industrial disease or industrial poisoning.

(2) Where the registrar has reason to believe, with respect to any death of which he is informed or in respect of which a certificate of cause of death has been delivered to him, that the circumstances of the death were such that it is the duty of some person or authority other than himself to report the death to the coroner, he shall either satisfy himself that it has been reported or report it himself.

6.11 But whether a doctor or a registrar refuses to report a death to the coroner, it is still open to any citizen, not least relatives or legal representatives, to report a death to the coroner.

6.12 It will be apparent that subsection (f) refers to a death 'which occurred during an operation or before recovery from the effect of an anaesthetic'. Similarly the form of the Medical Certificate of Cause of Death has for the benefit of the medical profession the following words:

The Coroner needs to consider all cases where . . . there is reason to believe that the death occurred during an operation or under or prior to complete recovery from an anaesthetic or arising subsequently out of an incident during an operation or an anaesthetic.

6.13 Even if the patient recovers consciousness, if it later transpires that the death was due to unnatural causes (because the surgeon was drunk, for example), then the registrar would refer the case to the coroner under (e) above.

Natural and unnatural death

6.14 Whether a fatal iatrogenic injury is one which the coroner should investigate involves the circular argument whether it was iatrogenic in the first place. However, the requirement of section 18 of the Coroners Act 1988 only needs there to be 'reasonable cause to suspect that the deceased . . . has died an unnatural death'. So, provided the dead body physically lies within that coroner's jurisdiction any person, particularly relatives or legal representatives, may bring to his attention information giving him reasonable cause to suspect the death was unnatural.

6.15 In all cases death will be brought about by the failure of one or more of the organs. The terminal event is not the main consideration, but rather what was the real event which lead inexorably down the path to death. It is suggested that when there is a clear event which began the chain of causation which leads eventually to death, then it is that event of either commission or omission which must be analysed to see whether it was natural or unnatural.

6.16 When an old lady has severe osteoporosis and she has what is medically termed a 'pathological fracture' of her femur which is consequent upon ordinary stress, and the fracture leads to her death, this would be a natural death. When, however, a similarly osteoporotic old lady has a fall and fractures her femur, this is not a natural death. Not all coroners would agree that when the fall precedes the fracture, the death is not a natural one.

6.17 Frequently a death occurs when only one of several simultaneously operating causes could be termed 'unnatural'. When a person is known to be dying from asbestosis, and then has a myocardial infarct caused by atheroma, itself caused by familial hypercholesterolaemia, and then dies from cor pulmonale, is this death natural? The cor pulmonale would not have caused death were it not for the asbestosis but the overriding factor was the myocardial infarction. There is no provision for apportionment between natural and unnatural; it must be one or the other. When a person is fatally injured as a result of violence, the effect of switching off the ventilator (the life support machine) has been judicially considered: see *R v Malcherek*.[1]

1 [1981] 1 WLR 690 at 694, CA.

6.18 The Registrar General does not attempt to define an unnatural death, although he does refer to a death which is 'unnatural or to have been caused by violence or neglect or by abortion or to have been attended by suspicious circumstances'.[1] The *Oxford English Dictionary*[2] says of natural death 'happening in the course of nature, as the result of age or disease as opposed to one brought about by accident, violence, poison, etc'.

1 Registration of Births and Deaths Regulations 1987, reg 41(1)(d).
2 Oxford University Press, 2nd edition, 1989.

6.19 One of the definitions of 'unnatural' given in the *Oxford English Dictionary* is 'at variance with what is natural, usual or to be expected; unusual, strange'. This problematical aspect requires careful consideration. This matter was explored in *R v HM Coroner for Inner North London, ex p Thomas*.[1] In that case, the delay in the arrival of an ambulance essentially turned what had been a natural death into an unnatural death requiring an inquest.

1 (1992) 157 JP 286, DC.

6.20 Although a child may die of peritonitis following appendicitis such a death is not necessarily natural. If there is evidence the child was neglected by its parents, or negligently treated by a doctor or hospital, the death may become unnatural and fall within the coroner's jurisdiction. It is here that we have the nub of the iatrogenic problem: merely because there is interference by a doctor, does that render a natural death unnatural?

6.21 It may be as well here to revert to the definition 'at variance with what is natural, usual or to be expected; unusual, strange'. Most coroners take the view that where, for example, there is a very high likelihood of death following an operation in any event it is not necessary to hold an inquest. Thus a moribund old man of 80 who dies upon the operating table from a ruptured aortic aneurysm would not normally be the subject of an inquest. The coroner, in other words, unless there was evidence to the contrary, would conclude the death was natural, the man dying from the ruptured aneurysm and not 'at variance with what is . . . to be expected'. Compare this, however, with a 20-year-old girl who dies under the anaesthetic for a tonsillectomy operation because the oxygen ran out. This is clearly 'at variance with what is . . . to be expected'. Moreover in the case of *R v HM Coroner for Inner North London, ex p Thomas*,[1] Tudor Evans J in ordering that an inquest be held, considered the public interest advantage of holding an inquest. In *R v HM Coroner for Inner North London, ex p Thomas*[2] their Lordships did however consider that to die from an extremely rare disease (such as typhoid fever or legionnaires' disease) should be considered 'unnatural'. In considering what caused the death the test is that of Lord Salmon in *Alphacell Ltd v Woodward*,[3] namely 'ordinary common sense' per Dillon LJ in *R v HM Coroner for Inner North London, ex p Thomas*.[4] That case involved a girl who died of status asthmaticus but there had been a delay in the ambulance arriving. Dillon LJ did not consider that a natural death (or status asthmaticus) was turned into an unnatural death by the late arrival of the ambulance. Simon Brown LJ in that case considered what view a coroner should take if there were relevant or secondary unnatural causes for an otherwise natural death. He said there might be a natural or an unnatural cause, either of which might prevail over the other, depending upon the facts, to make a death considered natural or unnatural by a coroner. He added 'Cases may well arise in which human fault can and properly should be found to turn what would otherwise be a natural death into an unnatural one, or one into which, therefore, an inquest should be held.'[5]

1 Supra.
2 Supra.
3 [1972] AC 824.
4 (1992) 157 JP 506, CA.
5 Ibid.

6.22 Between these two extremes of examples are the plethora of circumstances where, depending on your view, the death may be considered natural or unnatural. All that relatives or legal representatives may do, is to bring as much information to the attention of the coroner as possible, to show that the death was 'at variance with what is natural, usual or to be expected'. They must do so as expeditiously as possible, while the body still lies within the coroner's jurisdiction, and before the coroner dispenses with the matter. Whether a coroner has power to hold an inquest after the body has been disposed of by means of a notice to the Registrar of Deaths (Pink Form 100, Part A or B) is not clear.

The rights of interested parties

6.23 The coroner has a number of duties which he is required to fulfil in respect of deaths.

The coroner must inquire into deaths reported

6.24 The coroner has a duty to make preliminary inquiries in order to determine if:

(a) he would have jurisdiction;
(b) his statutory duty to hold an inquest arises.

6.25 Though his powers in this respect are limited, he may, where there are reasonable grounds to suspect the deceased died a sudden death of which the cause is unknown, direct a post mortem examination without holding an inquest if he is of the opinion that such examination may prove an inquest unnecessary (Coroners Act 1988, section 19(1)).

6.26 Stephen J in *R v Stephenson*[1] said the coroner has not an absolute right to hold inquests in every case which he choses to do:

> It would be intolerable if he had the power to intrude without adequate cause . . .

1 (1884) 13 QBD 331 at 337.

6.27 In the same case, Williams J, in a unanimous five-strong Divisional Court referring to the coroner's jurisdiction said:

> It is quite clear to me that a bona fide belief in information from reliable sources which if true renders it the Coroner's duty to hold an inquest suffices to give the Coroner jurisdiction.

6.28 If the cause of the 'sudden death' remains unknown following the post mortem examination, the coroner must proceed to hold an inquest. If the coroner, on a death being reported to him, does not have reason to believe his jurisdiction arises having made such preliminary enquiries as he considers to be appropriate, he completes Pink Form 100, Part A and his involvement in the case effectively terminates. This is known as 'Pink Form A Procedure'.

The coroner must hold an inquest

6.29 Provided the coroner has jurisdiction he is obliged by statute to hold an inquest in public into a death where there is reasonable cause to suspect that the deceased has died:

(a) either a violent or an unnatural death;
(b) a sudden death the cause of which is unknown, and remains unknown following a post mortem examination;
(c) in prison;
(d) in such a place or under such circumstances as to require an inquest in pursuance of any Act.

6.30 The only discretion a coroner has is in deciding whether or not there is reasonable cause to suspect one or more of the four criteria above are satisfied. Where there is reasonable cause so to suspect, the coroner must hold an inquest. In an iatrogenic death, if the family are aggrieved, it is at this early stage when the coroner is considering matters that they must bring to his attention their disquiet.

6.31 The autopsy must be made as soon as reasonably practicable after the death (Coroners Rules 1984, rule 5). The pathologist relies a great deal on the information given to him, so relatives must ensure that all their information is available before the autopsy.

The coroner must have regard to certain circumstances in choosing a pathologist

6.32 In considering which legally qualified medical practitioner shall be directed or requested by the coroner to make a post mortem examination the coroner must have regard to certain considerations (Coroners Rules 1984, rule 6). The only provision with which he must comply is that where a person swears on oath before the coroner that in that person's belief the deceased's death was caused partly or entirely by the improper or negligent treatment of a medical practitioner or other person, the coroner must not direct such medical practitioner or other person to perform or assist at the post mortem examination of the deceased (Coroners Act 1988, section 20(3)).

6.33 The considerations are set out in full under subsection (i) of rule 6:

(a) the post mortem examination should be made, whenever practicable, by a pathologist with suitable qualifications and experience and having access to laboratory facilities;
(b) if the coroner is informed by the chief officer of police that a person may be charged with the murder, manslaughter or infanticide of the deceased, the coroner should consult the chief officer of police regarding the legally qualified medical practitioner who is to make the post-mortem examination;

(c) if the deceased died in a hospital, the coroner should not direct or request a pathologist on the staff of, or associated with, that hospital to make a post mortem examination if:
  (i) that pathologist does not desire to make the examination, or
  (ii) the conduct of any member of the hospital staff is likely to be called in question, or
  (iii) any relative of the deceased asks the coroner that the examination be not made by such a pathologist,

  unless the obtaining of another pathologist with suitable qualifications and experience would cause the examination to be unduly delayed;

(d) if the death of the deceased may have been caused by any of the disease or injuries within paragraph (2), the coroner should not direct or request a legally qualified medical practitioner who is a member of a pneumoconiosis medical panel to make the post-mortem examination.

6.34 As a matter of practicality it will of course very often be the case that the pathologist whom the coroner employs for the autopsy is on the staff of the local District General Hospital where the person has died. He would nevertheless ask his usual pathologist to perform the autopsy probably relying on the basis that not to do so would cause the examination 'to be unduly delayed'. Where legal advisers to relatives believe it would be detrimental to have a pathologist on the staff of the same hospital as the alleged negligent doctor to perform an autopsy, they must bear this in mind. At the earliest opportunity they should bring strong representation to bear upon the coroner, bringing rule 6 to his attention if necessary.

The coroner must inform certain persons about arrangements for post mortem examination

6.35 Rule 7 provides:

(1) Where a coroner directs or requests a legally qualified medical practitioner to make a post mortem examination, the coroner shall notify the persons and bodies set out in paragraph (2) of the date, hour and place at which the examination will be made, unless it is impracticable to notify any such persons or bodies or to do so would cause the examination to be unduly delayed.

(2) The persons and bodies to be notified by the coroner are as follows:
  (a) any relative of the deceased who has notified the coroner of his desire to attend, or be represented at, the post mortem examination;
  (b) the deceased's regular medical attendant;
  (c) if the deceased died in a hospital, the hospital;
  (d) if the death of the deceased may have been caused by any of the diseases or injuries within rule 6(2) (other than occupational asthma), the pneumoconiosis medical panel for the area;
  (e) if the death of the deceased may have been caused by any accident or disease notice of which is required by or under any enactment to be given –
    (i) to an enforcing authority, the appropriate inspector appointed by, or representative of, that authority; or
    (ii) to an inspector appointed by an enforcing authority, that inspector;
  (f) any government department which has notified the coroner of its desire to be represented at the examination;
  (g) if the chief officer of police has notified the coroner of his desire to be represented at the examination, the chief officer of police.

(3) Any person or body mentioned in paragraph (2) shall be entitled to be represented at a post-mortem examination by a legally qualified medical practitioner, or if any such person is a legally qualified medical practitioner he shall be

entitled to attend the examination in person; but the chief officer of police may be represented by a member of the police force of which he is chief officer.

(4) Nothing in the foregoing provisions of this rule shall be deemed to limit the discretion of the coroner to notify any person of the date, hour and place at which a post-mortem examination will be made and to permit him to attend the examination.

6.36 It will be apparent that relatives have a right to be represented by a doctor of their choice at the autopsy. The difficulty is that a decision must be made quickly. The coroner will arrange a post mortem as soon as practicable, not least because usually the relatives themselves will be anxious for the body to be released for the funeral.

The coroner must inform certain persons about inquest arrangements

6.37 Rule 19 provides:

The coroner shall notify the date, hour and place of an inquest to:

(a) the spouse or a near relative or personal representative of the deceased whose name and address are known to the coroner; and

(b) any other person who –
  (i) in the opinion of the coroner is within rule 20(2); and
  (ii) has asked the coroner to notify him of the aforesaid particulars of the inquest; and
  (iii) has supplied the coroner with a telephone number or address for the purpose of so notifying him.

6.38 It is essential therefore at the earliest opportunity for legal representatives to make contact with the coroner's office, and usually follow this up with a letter. It is important not only to be informed of inquest arrangements (rule 19) but also to enable a representative to attend the post mortem examination (rule 7).

6.39 Those classes of people with a right to be kept informed are set out under rule 20(2):

(a) a parent, child, spouse and any personal representative of the deceased;
(b) any beneficiary under a policy of insurance issued on the life of the deceased;
(c) the insurer who issued such a policy of insurance;
(d) any person whose act or omission or that of his agent or servant may in the opinion of the coroner have caused, or contributed to, the death of the deceased);
(e) any person appointed by a trade union to which the deceased at the time of his death belonged, if the death of the deceased may have been caused by an injury received in the course of his employment or by an industrial disease;
(f) an inspector appointed by, or a representative of, an enforcing authority, or any person appointed by a government department to attend the inquest;
(g) the chief officer of police;
(h) any other person who, in the opinion of the coroner, is a properly interested person.

The coroner must examine witnesses on oath

6.40 The coroner must examine on oath those persons who tender their evidence respecting the facts and all persons having knowledge of the facts 'whom he thinks it expedient to examine'. Usually it is the coroner who will have made inquiry and received reports from doctors. He will have called the doctors to the inquest. However, where a material witness voluntarily attends court, and has knowledge of the facts, and brings this to the attention of the coroner, it would be difficult for the coroner to exclude him. In a public court, with the press expectant with pencils sharpened, one can imagine the pressure to respond to a question 'Sir, at the rear of this courtroom I have asked to come along a doctor who was present and can assist you on this very point'.

The coroner must adjourn the inquest in event of certain criticism

6.41 The coroner must adjourn the inquest if the conduct of any person is called in question at an inquest on grounds which the coroner thinks substantial and which relate to matters referred to in rule 36. The duty to adjourn only arises when that person is not present at the inquest and has not been duly summoned to attend or otherwise given notice (Coroners Rules 1984, rule 25). It is, of course, not at all uncommon for relatives to voice complaint against the doctor who is not present. The coroner will usually adjourn in such circumstances.

The coroner must give notice of adjournment

6.42 If the date of an adjourned inquest is changed, the coroner, his deputy or assistant deputy (whomsoever's duty it would have been to hold the adjourned inquest) must give reasonable notice of the alteration to any person who has a right to be informed of the inquest arrangements, or any person whose conduct is likely to be called into question, and any other person appearing in person or represented at the inquest (Coroners Rules 1984, rule 33).

The coroner ought to hear applications

6.43 A coroner has a duty to hear any applications that may be made to him at any stage and he must consider each application judicially – *Re Brown and Patterson;*[1] *R v Inner North London Coroner, ex p Greater London Council;*[2] *R v HM Coroner for East Berkshire, ex p Buckley.*[3]

1 (1974) 52 DLR (3d) 64, 6 OR (2d) 441, Can.
2 (1983) 127 Sol Jo 445.
3 (1992) 157 JPR 425.

The coroner must announce publicly that documentary evidence will be admitted

6.44 When the coroner wishes to admit documentary evidence relevant to the purposes of the inquest (Coroners Rules 1984, rule 37) before he admits such evidence he must announce publicly:

(a) that the documentary evidence may be admitted, and
(b) (i) the full name of the maker of the document to be admitted in evidence, and
 (ii) a brief account of such document, and
(c) that any person who in the opinion of the coroner is within rule 20(2) of the Coroners Rules may object to the admission of any such documentary evidence, and
(d) that any person who in the opinion of the coroner is within rule 20(2) of the Coroners Rules is entitled to see a copy of any documentary evidence if he so wishes.

6.45 Unless the coroner otherwise directs, documentary evidence admitted under rule 37 of the Coroners Rules 1984 must be read aloud at the inquest.

6.46 The documentary evidence may well be a medical report concerning the treatment of the deceased. The coroner may only admit such documentary evidence if it is 'in his opinion unlikely to be disputed'. If legal representatives do not object to the admission of the document this is tantamount to saying that they, too, do not wish to dispute the contents of the medical report about the treatment of the deceased.

The coroner must mark exhibits

6.47 The coroner must mark all exhibits produced in evidence at an inquest with consecutive numbers and each number shall be preceded by the letter 'C' (Coroners Rules 1984, rule 38).

The coroner must make notes of evidence

6.48 The obligation upon the coroner to make notes of evidence (Coroners Rules 1984, rule 39) is complied with when he makes a transcript of the proceedings from a tape recording.

The coroner could take a note, or cause another person to take a note for him, or arrange for a tape recording to be made. The method was immaterial.[1]

1 Per Lord Lane LCJ in *R v South London Coroner, ex p Thompson* (1982) 126 Sol Jo 625, DC.

6.49 Moreover, he must be prepared to supply copies by virtue of rule 57, which provides:

(1) A coroner shall, on application and on payment of the prescribed fee (if any), supply to any person who, in the opinion of the coroner, is a properly interested person a copy of any report of a post mortem examination (including one made under section 21 of the Act of 1926) or special examination, or of any notes of evidence, or of any document put in evidence at an inquest.[1]

(2) A coroner may, on application and without charge, permit any person who, in the opinion of the coroner, is a properly interested person to inspect such report, notes of evidence or document.

1 It is a moot point, but arguable that a properly interested party should be entitled to a copy of any post mortem report or special examination *before* the inquest as the 'or' in the Rules is disjunctive (see below).

The coroner has a duty to make a full and proper inquiry

6.50 Subject to the same being necessary or desirable in the interests of justice, the inquisition will be quashed and a new inquest ordered if by reason of fraud, rejection of evidence, irregularity of proceedings, insufficiency of inquiry, or otherwise, the coroner fails in his duty to make a full and proper inquiry (Coroners Act 1988, section 13(1)). But it must be remembered that the proceedings at an inquest should be directed solely to ascertaining the following matters (Coroners Rules 1984, rule 36):

(a) who the deceased was;
(b) how, when and where the deceased came by his death;
(c) the particulars for the time being required by the Registration Acts to be registered concerning the death.

Moreover it cannot be considered an 'insufficient inquiry' merely because other experts would disagree;[1] but where the new evidence is substantial and might alter the verdict a new inquest may be ordered.[2]

1 *R v HM Coroner for Wiltshire, ex p Taylor* (1990) 154 JP 933.
2 *R v HM Coroner for the County of Hampshire, ex p HM A-G* (1990) 155 JP 190.

The coroner must retain exhibits

6.51 Unless a court otherwise directs, every exhibit at an inquest should be retained by the coroner until he is satisfied that the exhibit is not likely to be, or will no longer be, required for the purposes of other legal proceedings, and shall then, if a request for its delivery has been made by a person appearing to the coroner to be entitled to the possession thereof, be delivered to that person or, if no such request has been made, be destroyed or otherwise disposed of as the coroner thinks fit (Coroners Rules 1984, rule 55). 'Legal proceedings' include proceedings for the purpose of obtaining any benefit or other payments under the provisions of the Social Security Act 1975 relating to industrial injuries or under section 5 of the Industrial Injuries and Diseases (Old Cases) Act 1975 (Coroners Rules 1984, rule 2). In most cases the coroner will not be provided with storage facilities, and when one considers some coroners may hold 500 inquests annually, or more, it is understandable that he may wish to dispose of exhibits. If a catheter, or anaesthetic appliance has been produced, it is as well not to delay with any application to have it loaned.

The coroner must retain documents

6.52 Any document (other than an exhibit at an inquest) in the possession of the coroner in connection with an inquest or post mortem examination shall, unless a court otherwise directs, be retained by the coroner for at least 15 years. The coroner may deliver the document to any person who, in the opinion of the coroner, is a proper person to have possession of it (Coroners Rules 1984, rule 56).

The coroner must supply certain documents

6.53 A coroner must supply to any person who, in his opinion, is a properly interested person, a copy of any report of a post mortem examination or special examination, or of any notes of evidence, or of any document put in evidence at an inquest, provided the person applying pays the prescribed fee (if any) (Coroners Rules 1984, rule 57(1)). For this purpose a transcript of a tape recording of the proceedings is deemed to be notes of evidence.[1]

1 *R v South London Coroner, ex p Thompson* (1982) 126 Sol Jo 625, DC.

6.54 When an inquest is adjourned part heard, it would appear from rule 57 that a properly interested party may obtain copies of documents which have already been put in evidence before the adjournment.

The coroner must supply interim certificate of the fact of death

6.55 Upon application, the coroner shall supply to any person, who is in the opinion of the coroner a properly interested person, an interim certificate of the fact of death when an inquest has been adjourned for any reason and section 16(4) of the Coroners Act 1988 does not apply (Coroners Rules 1984, rule 30). These interim certificates of the fact of death are often accepted by life insurance companies.

THE PROCEDURE OF INQUEST

Opening of an inquest

6.56 According to the law it is not necessary to open and adjourn an inquest although it is considered good practice because as mentioned it is a public pronouncement that the coroner is seised of the death. Before a cremation certificate can be issued, the inquest must be opened. It is usual to take formal evidence of identification. It is from the date of the opening of the inquest that there is certainty that proceedings are 'active' for the purposes of the Contempt of Court Act 1981 since a date will usually be set for the hearing (Contempt of Court Act 1981, Schedule 1, sections 12 and 13).

6.57 The act of opening an inquest means the inquest is going on, and all rights regarding representation exist. However, if it is generally known that the inquest opening is merely to take evidence of identification, and a representative tries to introduce other matters, it is likely the coroner will merely adjourn the matter.

Pre-inquest review

6.58 There is no statutory authority for a pre-inquest review. It is, in fact, part of the inquest which all parties know will be adjourned. The coroner may receive applications from legal representatives and, if he thinks it appropriate, indicate which witnesses he has it in mind to call at the resumed inquest.

6.59 Particularly in iatrogenic deaths it would be advantageous because the coroner will know what to expect from the interested parties and what period of time to set aside for the inquest. For their part, the legal representatives may let it be known if they believe a jury should be called, and may bring their witnesses to the attention of the coroner either then or at a later date. Moreover, the whole procedure will have been in open court, before the press and will be part of the record.

Timing of the inquest

6.60 It is essential at an early stage to inform the coroner, preferably in writing, of any particular dates likely to be inconvenient. It is also courteous to inform the coroner of an interest, with perhaps some indication of the anticipated length and line of questioning. Some inquests, upon a death in hospital, proceed with no press, no relatives, a doctor, a nurse, the pathologist and the coroner. These are likely to be dealt with fairly expeditiously in contrast to a packed court with counsel bringing more and more witnesses to the attention of the coroner!

Witnesses and evidence

6.61 It would be perfectly understandable for legal representatives to bring to the attention of the coroner witnesses to bolster their 'side' of the event, but dressed up in terms 'to assist the coroner to get to the truth'. If the order of witnesses has been published, an application may be made upon this. Equally, where the evidence of a previous witness may taint the evidence of following witnesses, an application may be made for their exclusion, particularly in a case of alleged medical negligence, where many coroners believe that everybody should be in court to hear all the evidence.

6.62 It is whilst preparing for the inquest that the legal representatives will be trying to glean as much information as possible. The coroner is not obliged at an inquest to furnish representatives with any information regarding the evidence to be called. It is very often the case that he will allow the relatives to have a copy of the post mortem examination report. If the coroner refuses, he could be prevailed upon by pointing out that since the law gives a relative the right to be represented at the post mortem examination (Coroners Rules 1984, rule 7) this is tantamount to the approbation of the practice of allowing sight of the report. The difference is minimal. By rule 57 of the Coroners Rules, a coroner must supply to a 'properly interested person' (inter alia) a copy of the post mortem examination. It is not clear whether within the list the 'or' is disjunctive or conjunctive but it is submitted that it is disjunctive bearing in mind the wording of rule 39 of the previous Coroners Rules 1953. If this view is correct, a 'properly interested person' has a right to see any report of a post mortem examination.

6.63 The legal representatives may also request sight of the hospital case notes. They could argue that since it is likely that civil proceedings would follow, and that they would in any event be allowed sight of them by order of the High Court, that it would be as well to see them before the inquest. Indeed they might ask for the application to be adjourned until the conclusion of pre-action discovery of medical records pursuant to the Supreme Court Act 1981, section 33 and RSC Order 24, rule 7A. The coroner might not be persuaded by this argument since he may feel it is his enquiry and there is risk of broadening matters to an adversarial situation. A persuasive argument would be that the latter was far from what was contemplated, and that sight of the notes before the inquest was merely to be in a position to assist the coroner in order to bring to his attention evidence designed to get to the truth.

6.64 The coroner would have power to order the hospital notes to be produced by applying to the High Court for the issue of a subpoena duces tecum. Legal representatives may urge him to do this. A coroner received thinly veiled criticism when he disregarded the wishes of the relatives in this respect. See *R v Southwark Coroner, ex p Hicks*.[1]

1 [1987] 2 All ER 140, [1987] 1 WLR 1624, DC; see also *R v Coroner for North Humberside, ex p Jamieson* (1993) 158 JP 1, CA.

Summoning a jury

6.65 There are circumstances when a coroner must summon a jury,[1] but at all times he may do so. He must:

(1) if the death occurred in prison (Coroners Act 1988, section 8(3)(a)). This is so whether or not the death was a perfectly natural death. He must, of course, call sufficient evidence (see *R v Southwark Coroner, ex p Hicks*);[2]
(2) if the death occurred whilst the deceased was in police custody or resulted from an injury caused by a police officer in the purported execution of his duty (Coroners Act 1988, section 8(3)(b));
(3) if the death was caused by an accident, poisoning or disease notice of which is required to be given under any Act to a government department or to an inspector or other officer of a government department or an inspector apppointed under section 19 of the Health and Safety at Work etc Act 1974 (Coroners Act 1988, section 8(3)(c)). This category only comes into force if the coroner will be holding an inquest at all. Where it has been a perfectly natural death then the coroner is not obliged to hold an inquest, as where a person dies of measles, and yet it is still classed as a notifiable disease;
(4) if the death occurred in circumstances, the continuance or possible recurrence of which is prejudicial to the health and safety of the public (Coroners Act 1988, section 8(3)(d)).

1 See *R v Merseyside Coroner, ex p Carr* [1993] 4 All ER 65.
2 [1987] 2 All ER 140, [1987] 1 WLR 1624, DC. See also *R v Inner London North District Coroner, ex p Linnane* [1989] 1 WLR 395, DC, and *R v Inner London North District Coroner, ex p Linnane* (*No 2*) (1990) 155 JP 343.

6.66 The case which examined this in some detail was *R v HM Coroner at Hammersmith, ex p Peach (Nos 1 and 2)*,[1] when the Court of Appeal considered various situations which might be considered as circumstances the 'continuance or possible recurrence of which is prejudicial to the health and safety of the public or any section of the public . . .' It is quite clear from the illustrations of their Lordships in the judgments delivered in *Peach* that 'any section of the public' could be taken to include patients being treated by a system within a health authority:

> For instance in hospitals where the method of prescribing drugs or keeping them might be such that the continuance of such methods might be dangerous to the public . . . it is when the circumstances are such that similar fatalities may possibly recur in the future, and it is reasonable to expect that some action should be taken to prevent their recurrence.[2]
>
> To take an example which was canvassed in the course of the argument, suppose a patient in a hospital dies from a mistaken injection of a drug in a fatal quantity, and suppose that there is reason to suspect that that happened because the system operated in the hospital for the control, issue and handling of dangerous drugs is defective. This, in my judgment, although not a physical circumstance, would quite clearly be a circumstance of the kind contemplated in paragraph (e) . . . 'the continuance or possible recurrence of which is prejudicial to the health or safety of . . . any section of the public', namely those members of the public resorting as patients to that hospital.[3]

1 [1980] QB 211, [1980] 2 All ER 7.
2 Per Lord Denning MR in *R v HM Coroner at Hammersmith, ex p Peach* (*Nos 1 and 2*) [1980] 2 WLR 496 at 508, CA.
3 Per Bridge LJ in *R v HM Coroner at Hammersmith, ex p Peach* (*Nos 1 and 2*) [1980] 2 WLR 496 at 509, CA.

6.67 Circumstances were different at the time of *Peach* because by virtue of rules 27 and 34 of the original 1953 Coroners Rules, now rule 36(2) and rule

42 of the Coroners Rules 1984, the jury or the coroner had power to express an opinion additional to those matters set out in rule 26, now rule 36 of the Coroners Rules 1984, which was designed to prevent the recurrence of fatalities similar to that in respect of which the inquest was being held. Such an opinion was known as a 'rider'.

6.68 At the time of the judgment in *Peach* the jury and the coroner had a right to add such a 'rider':

It is when the circumstances are such that similar fatalities may possibly recur in the future, and it is reasonable to expect that some action should be taken to prevent their recurrence. I use the words prevent recurrence, not only because Bridge LJ used them, but also because they are the very words which were used in the Brodrick Committee's report on Coroners (Cmnd 4810) in para 16.53 and in rr 27 and 34 of the Coroners Rules 1953 whereby juries are entitled to make recommendations designed to 'prevent the recurrence of fatalities similar to that in respect of which the inquest is being held'.[1]

1 Per Lord Denning MR in *Peach*, above at 508.

6.69 Within a few months of the judgment of the Court of Appeal in *Peach*, the power of the jury (and the coroner) to add a 'rider' to the verdict was removed. The original rule 34 provided:

The coroner shall not record any rider unless the rider is, in the opinion of the coroner, designed to prevent the recurrence of fatalities similar to that in respect of which the inquest is being held.

6.70 Rule 11 of the Coroners (Amendment) Rules 1980 substituted a new rule 34 (now rule 43 of the Coroners Rules 1984):

A coroner who believes that action should be taken to prevent the recurrence of fatalities similar to that in respect of which the inquest is being held, may announce at the inquest that he is reporting the matter to the person or authority who may have power to take such action and he may report the matter accordingly.

6.71 Although the jury no longer has any power to add a 'rider' they may continue to express opinion in addition to their findings of fact provided they confine such opinion to the matters referred to in rule 36 (formerly rule 26) and do not frame their verdict in such a way as to appear to determine any question of criminal liability on the part of a named person (rule 42(a)) or civil liability (rule 42(b)).

6.72 Whether or not the coroner summons a jury is in the final analysis a matter for him:

I go on to say this: ultimately it is a matter for the coroner, properly directing himself, to decide whether the circumstances bring the case within para(e) [health and safety of the public].[1]

1 Per Lord Denning MR in *Peach*.

6.73 What the jury may or may not do in respect of expressing an opinion was considered in *R v Shrewsbury Coroner's Court, ex p British Parachute Association*:[1]

Now I have to say that the course taken by the coroner in inviting the jury to make recommendations if they wished, common practice though it may be, was quite wrong in law. It is expressly prohibited, in the clearest terms, by rule 36(2) of the Coroners Rules 1984 . . . (Per Lloyd J.)

1 (1987) 152 JP 123, DC.

Qualifications and constitution of the jury

6.74 A coroner's jury consists of not less than seven and not more than eleven jurors. They are summoned from lists provided to the coroner from the local circuit Courts Administrator. A person is not qualified to serve as a juror at an inquest unless he is qualified to serve as a juror in the crown court. He is not summoned in the same way, however, but a special summons is used.

6.75 The coroner will issue his warrant to his coroner's officer who will normally send a summons to individuals chosen from the list. There are provisions for certain persons who are ineligible or disqualified to be excused and also those who have other reasons to be excused.

6.76 It would seem there is no pre-emptory right of challenge, although this has not been tested in recent times. If a juror were wrongly serving upon a jury, it would seem this would be good grounds to have the inquest quashed.

Advantages of a jury?

6.77 The coroner's jury is traditional, indeed from the inception of the Office of Coroner in 1194 until the Coroners (Amendment) Act 1926, the coroner always sat with a jury. It is the jury who will make the findings of fact based upon the evidence and these will be incorporated in the inquisition. Some advocates consider a jury in a medical negligence case an advantage. It increases the overall sense of 'occasion'. Matters have to be properly explored in more detail 'for the benefit of the jury' rather than for a coroner sitting alone. When sitting alone, of course, he has judicial knowledge of various aspects, and he can indicate a line of questioning will not assist him further. It is rather more difficult for a coroner to overrule a line of questioning designed 'to assist the jury to understand the truth of what went on'.

6.78 A coroner sitting alone is under no duty to sum up, whereas he must when sitting with a jury (Coroners Rules 1984, rule 41). He must also direct them upon the law. If the coroner makes substantial errors in either his summing up or direction upon the law, then the inquest may be set aside. Where he sits alone the summary of events and his direction to himself will be contained within his own head.

6.79 Some believe that a jury is more likely to be swayed by the emotion of the events and might therefore use a form of words in the inquisition rather more critical of a doctor than a coroner who may find the shortcomings of the medical profession of more common occurrence.

6.80 Some coroners are medically qualified and (rightly or wrongly) may feel a measure of sympathy to hear of a doctor taking a decision in a very difficult situation which, in the event, turns out to be a wrong one.

6.81 An inquest held with a jury will take longer and increase the cost both for the coroner in the payment to witnesses and jury (which, of course, comes from public funds), and for the protagonists, who are likely to be the relatives and doctors. Legal aid is not available for appearance in the coroner's court and at the present time there seems little change likely.

Inquest arrangements

6.82 The venue for inquests is very variable. At one end of the scale there may be a purpose built court with all the advantages of facilities. These include amplification and tape recording facilities on the one hand, to toilet facilities on the other. Waiting rooms and side rooms where counsel may talk privately with their clients are helpful. The other end of the scale may be a board room or common room in the very hospital where the event took place! Such insensitivity is to be deprecated, for whereas the National Health Service may boast to look after citizens from the cradle to the grave, to act as host for the inquest also may appear to compromise the independence of the coroner and his inquest.

Tape recorders

6.83 The coroner has a discretion whether to allow the press, or legal representatives, or indeed the public, to bring into court any tape recorder for recording sound. Section 9 of the Contempt of Court Act 1981 provides:

(1) subject to sub-s (4) below, it is a contempt of court:
  - (a) to use in court, or bring into court for use, any tape recorder or other instrument for recording sound, except with the leave of the court;
  - (b) to publish a recording of legal proceedings made by means of any such instrument, or any recording derived directly or indirectly from it, by playing it in the hearing of the public or any section of the public, or to dispose of it or any recording so derived, with a view to such publication;
  - (c) to use any such recording in contravention of any conditions of leave granted under para (a).

(2) Leave under para (a) of sub-s (1) may be granted or refused at the discretion of the court, and if granted may be granted subject to such conditions as the court thinks proper with respect to the use of any recording made pursuant to the leave; and where leave has been granted the court may at the like discretion withdraw or amend it either generally or in relation to any particular part of the proceedings.

(3) Without prejudice to any other power to deal with an act of contempt under para (a) of sub-s (1), the court may order the instrument, or any recording made with it, or both, to be forfeited; and any object so forfeited shall (unless the court otherwise determines on application by the person appearing to be the owner) be sold or otherwise disposed of in such manner as the court may direct.

(4) This section does not apply to the making or use of sound recordings for purposes of official transcripts of proceedings.

Assessors

6.84 There is provision for a coroner to sit with an official assessor under the Regulation of Railways Act 1871. However, some coroners sit from time to time with an informal assessor. Thus where there may be an anaesthetic death with difficult technical aspects, a coroner who is not himself medically qualified may ask an independent anaesthetist to sit with him. The assessor will sit on the bench beside the coroner and may from time to time have an informal word. It is submitted that the assessor may take no part in the proceedings, such as himself ask questions, since he has no locus standi. He certainly may not give evidence, since all evidence has to be given on oath. He may assist a non-medically qualified coroner by indicating to him a useful line of questions. The question of whether such an assessor could be considered a 'properly interested person' within the meaning of rule 20(2)(h) of the Coroners Rules 1984, and so ask questions, has not been judicially tested. He could hardly sit on the bench one minute and then descend to the lawyers and ask questions the next.

The scope of the inquest

6.85 Rule 36(1) of the Coroners Rules 1984 provides:

The proceedings and evidence at an inquest shall be directed solely to ascertaining the following matters, namely:

(a) who the deceased was;
(b) how, when and where the deceased came by his death;
(c) the particulars for the time being required by the Registration Acts to be registered concerning the death.

6.86 The Coroners Act 1988, section 15(1)(b) specifically provides as a reason to the quashing of an inquest 'insufficiency of enquiry'.

6.87 The vexed question is this: how far should a coroners inquest go to satisfy a proper enquiry into *how* the deceased came by his death? This question has not been judicially looked at in recent times.

6.88 Suppose a patient died because an anaesthetist gave pure nitrous oxide by way of anaesthetic instead of a mixture with oxygen. Suppose it is also known to the lawyers acting for the relatives that the anaesthetist has been dismissed from her previous employment for drunkenness. Is that a question which may be put to her? If the answer is affirmative, what if she had been off work with depression two years previously? If that is affirmative, what if her cohabitee had left home one month previously?

6.89 Rule 20(1)(b) of the Coroners Rules 1984 provides:

the coroner shall disallow any question which in his opinion is not relevant, or is otherwise not a proper question.

6.90 What is relevant? It clearly is relevant if it is a question designed to ascertain 'how' the deceased came by his death. How remote may be a question in determining the 'how'? The answer to that question may be answered simply, for example, 'because the nurse gave the wrong drug'. But is the reason why this happened (perhaps because she was not supervised sufficiently) evidence as to 'how' the deceased came by his death?

6.91 Until this aspect of the law is tested in the Divisional Court the spectacle of lawyers for relatives asking questions of questionable relevance to a coroner's enquiry, and lawyers for the medical protection societies urging a restrictive view of rule 36 upon the coroner, will continue.

The evidence

6.92 The 'Best Evidence' rule is that it is desirable that the coroner calls as witnesses those closely connected with the death and that original documents should be produced wherever possible. However, the 'Best Evidence' rule does not enjoy the prominence it did in the mid-eighteenth century following the publication of Chief Baron Gilbert's work on evidence in 1756.

6.93 Against that must be balanced the cost and loss of productive work in calling professional men, such as doctors, to a court. With the advent of photocopying there has been an increase in the admission of documentary evidence. Rule 37 provides:

(1) Subject to the provisions of paragraphs (2) to (4), the coroner may admit at an inquest documentary evidence relevant to the purposes of the inquest from any living person which in his opinion is unlikely to be disputed, unless a person who in the opinion of the coroner is within rule 20(2) objects to the documentary evidence being admitted.

(2) Documentary evidence so objected to may be admitted if in the opinion of the coroner the maker of the document is unable to give oral evidence within a reasonable period.

(3) Subject to paragraph (4) before admitting such documentary evidence the coroner shall at the beginning of the inquest announce publicly:–
  (a) that the documentary evidence may be admitted, and
  (b) (i) the full name of the maker of the document to be admitted in evidence, and
      (ii) a brief account of such document, and
  (c) that any person who in the opinion of the coroner is within rule 20(2) may object to the admission of any such documentary evidence, and
  (d) that any person who in the opinion of the coroner is within rule 20(2) is entitled to see a copy of any such documentary evidence if he so wishes.

6.94 It will be seen there are two separate tests. First the coroner must be of the opinion that the evidence is unlikely to be disputed. Having satisfied that test, a person within rule 20(2), such as a relative, will be entitled to see a copy of such documentary evidence and may object to it being admitted.

6.95 An inquest is an enquiry to hear by means of such evidence as is available, who the deceased was and how, when and where he came by his death. This being so, hearsay evidence is admissible. Care must be taken regarding opinion evidence, but it may help to understand what took place where this is not clear. Thus questions not strictly concerning knowledge of specific events, but nevertheless designed to work out *how* the deceased came by his death, will be admitted. 'Now Mr Smith, whereas nobody apparently knows from which vessel the bleeding occurred, which blood vessels are the most likely?'

Rule against self-incrimination

6.96 No witness is obliged to answer any question if by doing so he would be likely to incriminate himself. He is not privileged from answering any question which might tend to render him liable in civil action, merely that it might tend to show him guilty of a criminal offence.

6.97 In medical negligence cases this is likely to occur in those cases where, for example, the actions of a doctor or nurse might be such as to amount to manslaughter.

Once it appears that a witness is at risk, then great latitude should be allowed to him in judging for himself the effect of any particular question.[1]

1 Per Denning MR in *Re Westinghouse Electric Corpn Uranium Contract Litigation MDL Docket No 235 (No 2)* [1977] 3 All ER 717 at 721.

6.98 A witness cannot refuse to go into the witness box on the grounds that he might incriminate himself. He can only claim the privilege after he is sworn and the question is put.

6.99 A coroner therefore has wide powers to get at the truth. A witness must appear at court or risk fine or imprisonment. He must answer questions or risk fine or imprisonment. If he answers the questions untruthfully, he risks fine or imprisonment. Contrast this with an internal enquiry where all people appear voluntarily, they need not answer questions, and except for disciplinary procedures, may tell lies with impunity.

The verdict

6.100 The verdict of the coroner or his jury are recorded upon an inquisition. Although the few words chosen for the conclusion to the verdict are often referred to as 'the verdict', in fact the whole inquisition is the verdict.

6.101 There was for some time a conflict between what statute provided for the coroner to do and what was required by statutory instrument. By section 11(5) of the Coroners Act 1988 it is now provided:

An inquisition

(a) shall be in writing under the hand of the coroner and in the case of an inquest held with a jury under the hands of the jurors who concur with the verdict;
(b) shall set out, so far as such particulars have been proved
  (i) who the deceased was, and
  (ii) how, when and where the deceased came by his death;
  and
(c) shall be in such form as the Lord Chancellor may by rules made by Statutory Instrument from time to time prescribe.

6.102 Under the Coroners Act 1988, section 32, the Lord Chancellor has power to make rules. Form 22 of Schedule 4 of the Coroners Rules 1984 sets out the form for the inquisition. The matters which are found are under five headings. Parts 1 and 5 are technical in nature, such as the name of the deceased, date of birth etc. Part 2 requires findings on the evidence and is the 'injury or disease causing death'.

6.103 Part 3 is 'Time, place and circumstances at or in which injury was sustained'. Previously there had been conflict as to what was appropriate to include in Part 3. This now appears to be resolved by virtue of the Coroners Act 1988 where it is now quite clear that Part 3 requires an injury to be sustained before further details are required (*Re Inquest into the Death of Adam Bithell*[1] and see also *R v Surrey Coroner, ex p Campbell*[2]).

1 (1986) 150 JP 273.
2 [1982] QB 661, [1982] 2 All ER 545, DC.

6.104 Part 4 is 'conclusion of the coroner/jury as to the death'. In the notes to the Coroners Rules 1984 there are to be found 'suggested' terms to adopt. There are grouped together four verdicts which do not appear to have caused much problem in recent times. These are 'natural causes', 'industrial disease', 'dependence on drugs/non-dependent abuse of drugs' (but see *R v Inner South London Coroner, ex p Kendall*[1]) and 'want of attention at birth'.

1 [1989] 1 All ER 72, [1988] 1 WLR 1186, DC.

6.105 It is the second group that is of particular interest in medical negligence. Included is the 'accident/misadventure' alternative. In *R v HM Coroner for Portsmouth, ex p Anderson*[1] Mann J, on considering the difference between accident and misadventure and deprecating the latter, said: 'The meaning of "misadventure" which is a word I suspect little employed in ordinary speech is in my view indistinguishable from that of "accident" . . . It is a distinction which seems to me to be without purpose or effect and, on any view, it lacks consequence.' Where, therefore, an asthmatic person intends to take a drug but dies as a consequence of unperceived allergy it seems this would be an accident and not a case of misadventure. Three months after that judgment in *R v HM Coroner for Southern District of Greater London*,[2] Henry J said, 'I wonder, in those circumstances . . . the jury would not have been better to express it by the well known verdict of misadventure'. However, in *R v Inner South London Coroner, ex p Kendall*,[3] there was nothing said to encourage the resurrection of misadventure as a verdict.

1 (1989) 152 JP 56.
2 (1988) 152 JP 641.
3 [1989] 1 All ER 72, [1988] 1 WLR 1186, DC.

6.106 Whether 'lack of care' is a free standing verdict, or a verdict which may be added to all or only some other verdicts is a subject for the enthusiast! The leading cases where this has been judicially considered include *R v Surrey Coroner, ex p Campbell*;[1] *R v Walthamstow Coroner, ex p Rubenstein*;[2] *R v Southwark Coroner, ex p Hicks*;[3] *R v HM Coroner for Portsmouth, ex p Anderson*;[4] *R v HM Coroner for Birmingham, ex p Secretary of State for Home Department*.[5] However there has been recent clarification in *R v HM Coroner for East Berkshire, ex p Buckley*.[6]

The expansion of the use of verdicts, including that of 'lack of care' has been reviewed by the Court of Appeal (*R v HM Coroner for South Humberside and Scunthorpe, ex p Jamieson*).[7] Giving the judgment of the court, Bingham MR made a number of statements giving general guidance, including:

(a) that in section 11(5)(b)(ii), Coroners Act 1988 and rule 36(1)(b), Coroners Rules 1984 'How' is to be understood as meaning 'by what means'. The task is not to ascertain how the deceased died but 'how . . . the deceased came by his death', a more limited question;
(b) that any conflict between the statutory duty to enquire how the deceased came by his death must prevail over the prohibition of rule 42, but the scope for conflict is small;
(c) that there can be no objection to a verdict which incorporates a brief, neutral, factual statement, but such a verdict must be factual, expressing no judgment or opinion and it is not the jury's function to prepare detailed factual statements;
(d) that 'lack of care' has been correctly described as the obverse of self-neglect. It is to be hoped that in future the expression 'lack of care' may for practical purposes be deleted from the lexicon of inquests and replaced by 'neglect';
(e) that 'neglect' means a gross failure to provide adequate nourishment or liquid, or provide or procure basic medical attention or shelter or warmth for someone in a dependent position (because of youth, age, illness or incarceration) who cannot provide it for himself. Failure to provide medical attention for a dependent person whose physical condition is such as to show that he obviously needs it may amount to neglect. So would it be if the deceased's mental condition obviously calls for attention;
(f) that neither neglect nor self-neglect should ever form any part of any verdict unless a clear and direct causal connection is established between the conduct so described and the cause of the death;
(g) that the coroner has a duty to ensure the relevant facts are fully, fairly and fearlessly investigated. He fails in his duty if his investigation is superficial, slipshod or perfunctory.

1 [1982] QB 661, [1982] 2 All ER 545, DC.
2 [1982] Crim LR 509.
3 [1987] 2 All ER 140, [1987] 1 WLR 1624, DC.
4 (1988) 152 JP 56.
5 (1990) 155 JP 107.
6 (1992) 157 JP 425.
7 (1994) Times, 28 April.

6.107 If there was any doubt it is now quite clear that a jury may add no rider or recommendation to their verdict (*R v Shrewsbury Coroner's Court, ex p British Parachute Association*[1] and see previously *R v HM Coroner at Hammersmith, ex p Peach (Nos 1 and 2)*[2]).

1 (1987) 152 JP 123.
2 [1980] QB 211, [1980] 2 All ER 7, CA.

6.108 The coroner is now obliged to direct the jury on the standard of proof, which is the balance of probabilities, except those verdicts with a 'criminal element' such as 'unlawfully killed and suicide' (*R v St Pancras*

Coroner's Court, ex p Higgins[1] and reinforcing *R v West London Coroner, ex p Gray*.[2] See also *R v HM Coroner for Wolverhampton, ex p McCurbin*[3]).

1 (1988) 152 JP 637, DC.
2 [1988] QB 467, [1987] 2 All ER 129, DC.
3 [1990] 1 WLR 719.

6.109 Finally it appears from *R v St Pancras Coroner's Court, ex p Higgins*[1] from the judgment of Parker J, that the coroner must allow only certain verdicts to the jury and withdraw the rest. This is best done after consideration of legal argument.

1 (1988) 152 JP 637, DC.

6.110 The whole aspect of the coroner's verdict has taken steps of progressive change throughout the 1980s. For a more informed discussion on this complicated aspect of coroners' law, it might be helpful to refer to the commentaries to be found in *Casebook on Coroners*.[1]

1 See Bibliographical Reference.

BIBLIOGRAPHICAL REFERENCE

Knapman P A and Powers M J *Casebook on Coroners* (Barry Rose, 1989).

CHAPTER 7

Confidentiality – medical records

Gillian Parker *Solicitor*
Michael Spencer *QC*

SUMMARY

CONFIDENTIALITY

7.1 The nature and extent of any duty of confidentiality has been the subject of increasing examination by the English courts, both in relation to the duty owed by an individual confidant to his or her confider and also to the duty owed by government employees to the state. The latter relationship has been the subject of particular focus in the case concerning the disclosures of the former MI5 agent Peter Wright which formed the subject matter of his book *Spycatcher*. This led to a number of decisions of common law courts both here and in the Antipodes of which the most relevant for present purposes was that of the House of Lords in the case of *A-G v Guardian Newspapers Ltd* (*No 2*).[1] The speeches in that case reviewed extensively the law relating to confidentiality both in the private and in the public context. Lord Griffiths provided perhaps the most helpful and relevant elucidation of the law. Speaking of 'the private law of confidence' he stated:

> Although the terms of a contract may impose a duty of confidence the remedy is not dependent on contract and exists as an equitable remedy. Megarry J identified the three essentials to found the duty in *Coco v A N Clark* (*Engineers*) *Ltd*.[2]

> 'Three elements are normally required if, apart from contract, a case of breach of confidence is to succeed. Firstly, the information itself, in the words of Lord Greene MR in the *Saltman* case[3] must "have the necessary quality of confidence about it". Secondly, that information must have been imparted in circumstances importing an obligation of confidence. Thirdly, there must be an unauthorised use of that information to the detriment of the party communicating it.'

The courts have, however, always refused to uphold the right to confidence when to do so would be to cover up wrongdoing. In *Gartside v Outram*,[4] it was said that there could be no confidence in iniquity. This approach has been developed in the modern authorities to include cases in which it is in the public interest that the confidential information should be disclosed: see *Initial Services Ltd v Putterill*,[5] *Beloff v Pressdram Ltd*[6] and *Lion Laboratories Ltd v Evans*.[7] This involves the judge in balancing the public interest in upholding the right to confidence, which is based on the moral principles of loyalty and fair dealing, against some other public interest that will be served by the publication of the confidential material. Even if the balance comes down in favour of publication, it does not follow that publication should be to the world through the media. In certain circumstances the public interest may be better served by a limited form of publication perhaps to the police or some other authority who can follow up a suspicion that wrongdoing may lurk beneath the cloak of confidence. Those authorities will be under a duty not to abuse the confidential information and to use it only for the purposes of their inquiry. If it turns out that the suspicions are without foundation, the confidence can then still be protected: see *Francome v Mirror Group Newspapers Ltd*.[8] On the other hand, the circumstances may be such that the balance will come down in favour of allowing publication by the media, see *Lion Laboratories Ltd v Evans*.[9] Judges are used to carrying out this type of balancing exercise and I doubt if it is wise to try to formulate rules to guide the use of this discretion that will have to be exercised in widely differing and as yet unforeseen circumstances. I have no doubt, however, that in the case of a private claim to confidence, if the three elements of quality of confidence, obligation of confidence and detriment or potential detriment are established, the burden will lie upon the defendant to establish that some other overriding public interest should displace the plaintiff's right to have his confidential information protected.

1 [1990] 1 AC 109, [1988] 3 All ER 545.
2 [1969] RPC 41 at 47.
3 (1948) 65 RPC 203 at 215, CA.
4 (1856) 26 LJ Ch 113.
5 [1968] 1 QB 396, [1967] 3 All ER 145, CA.
6 [1973] 1 All ER 241.
7 [1985] QB 526, [1984] 2 All ER 417, CA.
8 [1984] 2 All ER 408, [1984] 1 WLR 892, CA.
9 [1985] QB 526, [1984] 2 All ER 417, CA.

7.2 The reasons for the need for the protection of medical confidences are obvious. If the patient's right to confidentiality is not protected by law then they will have no encouragement to speak openly to their medical practitioner and without reserve. Such openness is essential in the diagnostic process and the patient must be confident that the consequences of such openness will not enure to his detriment. This is truly in the public interest, for people with undiagnosed conditions should not be deterred from seeking appropriate treatment for fear of consequences beyond those related solely to the proper diagnosis and treatment of the condition itself.

7.3 The existence of the right to confidentiality was widely recognised in the *Spycatcher* case. Thus Lord Keith said:[1]

> The law has long recognised that an obligation of confidence can arise out of particular relationships. Examples are the relationships of doctor and patient, priest and penitent, solicitor and client, banker and customer. The obligation may be imposed by an express or implied term in a contract but it may also exist independently of any contract on the basis of an independent equitable principle of confidence: *Saltman Engineering Co Ltd v Campbell Engineering Co Ltd*.[2] It is worthy of some examination whether or not detriment to the confider of confidential information is an essential ingredient of his cause of action in seeking to restrain by injunction a breach of confidence. Presumably that may be so as regards an action for damages in respect of a past breach of confidence. If the confider has suffered no detriment thereby he can hardly be in a position to recover compensatory damages. However, the true view may be that he would be entitled to nominal damages . . .
>
> . . . Further as a general rule, it is in the public interest that confidences should be respected, and the encouragement of such respect may in itself constitute a sufficient ground for recognising and enforcing the obligation of confidence even where the confider can point to no specific detriment to himself.

1 [1990] 1 AC 109, [1988] 3 All ER 545.
2 (1948) [1963] 3 All ER 413n, 65 RPC 203, CA.

7.4 However, as was observed by Lord Goff of Chieveley in the same case, this area of the law in many respects reflects and often boils down to a conflict between two competing public interests. The public interest expressed above, which favours the maintenance of the confidentiality of information so imparted by one to another, and the public interest in the freedom of speech, in this regard most commonly in the form of the so-called freedom of the press. This same conflict is mirrored in the general statement of principle provided by article 10 of the European Convention on Human Rights which states the fundamental freedom of expression but then qualifies it by providing for an exception 'preventing the disclosure of information received in confidence'. In this respect the common law of England provides fundamentally the same approach.

MEDICAL CONFIDENCES

7.5 The importance of respecting the confidentiality of certain categories and items of information has long been recognised by the law. It is now uncommon to incorporate terms as to secrecy into contracts, particularly in connection with industrial processes, and there has been a developing case law examining the duty of loyalty and confidentiality owed by an employee to his employers. Since the nineteenth century a non-statutory cause of action for breach of confidence developed although the majority of cases concerned the protection of intellectual property rights. Nevertheless, there was a growing recognition of other important categories of information which under certain circumstances should be protected as confidential. Inevitably much of the debate has centred upon the duty to respect the confidentiality of information a doctor owes to his patients.

7.6 The principle of medical confidentiality has a long history. As early as the fourth century BC the Hippocratic oath recognised that 'whatever . . . I see or hear, in the life of men, which ought not to be spoken of abroad, I will not divulge as reckoning that all such should be kept secret'. In 1820 a dictum attributed to Lord Eldon in *Wyatt v Wilson* stated that the court would not have permitted one of the king's physicians to print and publish what he had heard and seen. More recently, the Declaration of Geneva (as amended in 1968) stated 'I will respect the secrets which are confided in me, even after the patient has died'. The BMA *Handbook of Medical Ethics* (1984 edition) confirmed that 'a doctor is responsible to the patient or person with whom he is in a professional relationship for the security and confidentiality of information given to him'. In *Hunter v Mann*[1] the court reaffirmed the importance of confidentiality. Boreham J said, 'Medical practitioners and others in a similar position, such as bankers, accountants, priests and journalists, are bound by a duty which the law respects and enforces, from disclosing without the consent of the patient or client communications or information obtained in a professional capacity, save in certain exceptional situations in the public interest.'

1 [1974] QB 767, [1974] 2 All ER 414, DC.

7.7 Although the common law has sought to protect medical confidentiality there has not been a statutory affirmation of the principle. The medical profession itself has always recognised that there are circumstances in which the disclosure of information will not breach the general duty of confidentiality although interestingly this does not expressly address the case of a patient requesting access to information concerning himself. Thus the BMA's *Handbook of Medical Ethics* envisages five exceptions to the general principle that a doctor must preserve secrecy of all he knows, of which the fifth exception is most relevant:

(1) the patient gives consent;
(2) when it is undesirable on medical grounds to seek a patient's consent, but is in the patient's own interest that confidentiality should be broken;
(3) the doctor's overriding duty to society;
(4) for the purposes of medical research, when approved by a local clinical research ethical committee, or in the case of the National Cancer Registry by the Chairman of the BMA's Central Ethical Committee or his nominee;
(5) when the information is required by due legal process.

A doctor must be able to justify his decision to disclose information. When making such a decision concerning a patient's records and confidences the doctor should always remember that he may, at any time, be required to justify his actions.

7.8 Because the guidelines stress the unusualness of disclosure they focus on when it may be justified – they do not consider to whom it should be given; whether such people should include the patient or be otherwise limited or subject to conditions as to further disclosure. There are two general headings under which disclosure on the grounds of the BMA's fifth exception arises and which are considered later. The first encompasses the statutory provisions requiring disclosure of medical information on the occurrence of specified events and the second arises only in particular cases of litigation and does not impose any duty of disclosure on general categories of information.

NATURE OF THE DUTY

7.9 As is apparent from the passages of their Lordships' speeches in the *Spycatcher* case quoted above the nature of a duty of confidentiality may vary depending on whether it is based upon a contractual relationship or upon a relationship falling short of the contractual but which nonetheless gives rise to a duty in equity. This may be the case equally in the context of medical records. Thus in treatment provided privately there is a contract between the patient and the treating doctor, and in the case of private hospital treatment there is a contract between the patient and the private hospital. In the case of treatment provided pursuant to the National Health Service Acts no such contract exists. However, in the absence of *express* contractual provisions it is unlikely that contractual obligations relating to confidentiality differ in any material respect from those owed by confidant to confider pursuant to the equity of confidence, and the two situations are therefore treated together.

7.10 It must be stressed that the confidentiality which the court will protect is that of the patient. If the confidence is broken then the patient has the recourse against the doctor, either at law in an action for damages and if necessary an injunction, or through the profession's disciplinary body which will be the General Medical Council. In the case of a breach of conditions of service additional recourse may be had to an employing authority. It is appreciated that the doctor may himself have an interest in preserving the confidentiality but this interest is not one which the court will usually protect. Thus in the whooping cough cases of *Kinnear v Wellcome Foundation Ltd* and *Loveday v Renton*[1] the defendants wished to investigate the accuracy of certain data contained in the various reports of the National Childhood Encephalopathy Study. To this end they sought disclosure from the principal author of the study in whose custody the data lay of all the base (or raw) data on which the report had been written. It was common ground that the data had been provided by doctors and hospitals to the study organisers in confidence. Production of the data was opposed on the ground that production would constitute a breach of confidence, the consequence of which (among others) could be the refusal of doctors, hospitals and the public to co-operate in such studies thereafter if they could not be sure that the confidentiality of such material would be preserved. Stuart-Smith J (as he was then) decided that the patients' anonymity could be adequately preserved if they were referred to by number in the course of the trial, and he concluded that the interests of justice in getting at the truth of the factual basis of the study outweighed both the interests of the patients in having the confidentiality of their records preserved and also the general public interest in avoiding damage to the freedom of researchers to conduct such research and the confidence of doctors and the public co-operating with them. It was not suggested either in the course of argument or in the decision of the judge that the authors' concerns were not legitimate concerns to which the court should have regard in balancing the competing interests.

1 [1990] 1 Med LR 117.

7.11 The courts have upheld confidentiality in an increasing number of cases concerning information affecting a broad spectrum of subject matter.

In *Re SL (a minor) (wardship: medical evidence)*[1] Booth J saw fit to ensure that part of her judgment relating to the production of medical reports relating to a witness in wardship proceedings should be published. The court held that where required evidence was available by other means (for example, asking a witness) a writ of subpoena duces tecum for production to the court should not be issued. If a writ is issued and served it is wrong for the recipient (in this case an Area Health Authority was served with respect to a witness's medical records) to send the documents to the applicants. If there are likely to be difficulties in compliance with the writ the court's guidance should be sought. In the case of *Australian Red Cross Society v BC 1992 by her litigation Guardian BD*,[2] a case in which an HIV positive blood transfusion recipient of infected blood sought the identity of the HIV positive blood donor, McGarvie and Gobbo JJ sitting in the Appeal Court of the Australian Victoria Supreme Court acknowledged the confidentiality of the identity of the blood donor but ruled that the public interest in the administration of justice outweighed any public interest (which they discounted) in according anonymity to blood donors.

1 [1987] 2 FLR 412n.
2 [1992] 3 Med LR 273.

7.12 It is not just the nature of the information that has persuaded the courts to protect confidentiality but also the relationship between the giver and the receiver of the information. In *Stephens v Avery*[1] the court upheld the confidentiality of information disclosed in confidence by the plaintiff to a friend who subsequently passed the details of the plaintiff's sexual conduct to a newspaper. The defendants had argued that the relationship between the plaintiff and the defendant could not give rise to a duty of confidence since it was merely a relationship of friendship and had no special characteristics. The court, however, held that the information could be the subject of a legally enforceable duty of confidence if it would be unconscionable for a person who had received information on the express basis that it was confidential subsequently to reveal that information to another.

1 [1988] Ch 449, [1988] 2 All ER 477.

7.13 The interest of the doctor in preserving the confidentiality of the notes is perhaps most starkly revealed in circumstances in which the patient himself desires access to them for the purposes of seeing whether they contain material which may assist in determining whether proceedings should be brought against the doctor or employing authority for damages for negligent treatment. In these circumstances, of course, there can be no question of any breach of confidentiality for the person who seeks disclosure is the very person whose confidentiality is protected. None the less, disclosure of such notes may be legitimately resisted on the grounds that they contain material which it is not in the patient's own best interests to see. In such circumstances a court considering ordering production prior to commencement of proceedings pursuant to the Supreme Court Act 1981, section 33 and Order 24 of the Rules of the Supreme Court is not able to make a conditional order that the documents should be disclosed only to the applicant's legal or, if no legal adviser, to the medical adviser and not to the applicant himself. The 1981 Act thus negatives *McIvor v Southern Health and Social Services Board*[1] and restores *Dunning v Board of Governors of the United*

Liverpool Hospitals.[2] In the Canadian case of *McInerney v MacDonald*[3] the New Brunswick Court of Appeal decided by a majority that a patient had an implied contractual right to all the information in her medical notes which her doctor considered in providing professional services to her, subject only to any regulatory legislation and any superintending role which the court might assume. In this country (England and Wales) patients now have a statutory right to inspect their medical records – see the reference to the Access to Health Records Act 1990 referred to in para **7.40** below.

1 [1978] 2 All ER 625, [1978] 1 WLR 757, HL, and see below.
2 [1973] 2 All ER 454, [1973] 1 WLR 586, CA.
3 [1991] 2 Med LR 267.

7.14 Historically, development of the law of confidentiality has been dominated by arguments derived from paternalistic attitudes rather than an acceptance of the importance of freedom of and access to information. Thus problems arise inevitably in cases which involve a patient requesting release of his own medical records in order to substantiate a claim against the doctor, and these pose most forcefully the question of whose confidence is protected. The provisions under which the courts can order disclosure of documents held by persons (whether or not they be parties to the action in question) were enacted in the Administration of Justice Act 1970 and the reported decisions reflect the importance courts accord to numerous factors other than the question of to whom the documents are confidential, whereas early cases applying these sections tended to grant orders where disclosure was limited to certain persons such as the applicant's medical or legal advisers – see *Dunning v United Liverpool Hospitals Board*.[1] This trend was halted in *McIvor v Southern Health and Social Services Board*[2] when the House of Lords held that the Act clearly provided for disclosure to the applicant for the order himself whether or not he was the patient. This case concerned an application by the defendants against a non-party to the action for discovery of the plaintiff's medical records but the argument had clear relevance to applications made by patients with respect to their own records. Nevertheless, their Lordships' judgments concentrated on the issue of statutory interpretation. Lord Diplock, however, summarised the arguments which had found favour in earlier cases.

1 [1973] 2 All ER 454, [1973] 1 WLR 586, CA.
2 [1978] 2 All ER 625, [1978] 1 WLR 757.

7.15 He said:

> Firstly, that medical notes and records are difficult for laymen to interpret, secondly, that they may include the doctor's fears about the patient's prospects for the future which if disclosed to the patient, might cause him distress or retard his recovery, thirdly, that they may contain statements made by the patient or by relatives which might be embarrassing or distressing if made known and, fourthly, that medical records are of a confidential nature and medical men might be deterred from entering them with the necessary frankness if they feared that they might be disclosed beyond the profession itself.

Lord Diplock went on to say that he did not find these arguments to be of general applicability or convincing although unfortunately there is no discussion of the fourth argument which he dismissed, ie the suggestion that the confidence belongs to the doctor who enters the reports. Their

Lordships did expressly state however that the previous cases such as *Dunning*'s were overruled.

7.16 Nevertheless, the four arguments which were dismissed clearly had some cogency on grounds of public policy and in 1981 sections 33 and 34 of the Supreme Court Act 1981 replaced sections 31 and 32 of the Administration of Justice Act 1970 effectively restoring the law as it stood before the *McIvor* case. The SCA gave the courts a new power to impose conditions upon an order for disclosure by either non-parties or parties to proceedings. In particular, the court could restrict disclosure to the applicant's legal advisers and medical or other professional advisers so effectively preventing the applicant (who in many cases will be the patient whose notes are to be disclosed) from seeing them.

7.17 Furthermore it is interesting and relevant to speculate upon what basis it is that the medical practitioner faced with an allegation of professional negligence justifies the apparent breach of his patient's right to confidentiality by showing the notes to his (the practitioner's) defence organisation, legal advisers etc for the purpose of obtaining their advice and assistance, without having first obtained the patient's express authority. In the Canadian case of *Hay v University of Alberta Hospital*,[1] Picard J considered, if not this precise issue certainly one that is closely allied. The plaintiff who was suing his doctors for medical negligence consented to the release of his medical records to the defence lawyers but refused permission for any discussions between them and his physicians (who were not defendants to the suit). The defendants applied for an order permitting them to interview the physicians treating the plaintiff. In the course of his judgment Picard J stated as follows:[2]

> I find that the right of the patient to confidentiality ceases when he puts his health in issue by claiming damages in a law-suit; the raison d'être for confidentiality is gone. The right to confidentiality is then eclipsed by the right of those who face the action to know the basis and scope of the claim being advanced. The patient cannot use confidentiality to preclude the normal operation of the legal process and the adversary system.
>
> Because of the position of the College of Physicians and Surgeons that a court order or consent of the patient would be required before a physician could ethically consent to an interview, I believe it would be helpful to examine the nature of the waiver. I do not propose here to address the difference between waiver and estoppel or attempt to place 'implied waiver' between the two. Because the act of the patient in putting his health in issue is a clear and unequivocal one and is *his* act, I find it is a case of implied consent by the patient to his treating physician releasing medical information. Should a claim be abandoned, for example, then the right to confidentiality would once again be present but any information released during the tenure of the claim would not be covered by the confidentiality.

In the Benzodiazepine litigation in the High Court Ian Kennedy J in a judgment (unreported) given in April 1983 adopted this reasoning when considering an application by the defendant pharmaceutical manufacturer John Wyeth and Brother for an order requiring the plaintiffs to provide written waiver of confidentiality so as to allow the defendants to have unhindered access to their treating physicians. Ian Kennedy J said:

> any plaintiff in such a case as this inevitably puts in issue his medical history and his manner of life. His GP has, in principle, independent and reasonably reliable knowledge of those facts.

He considered the position of the prescribing physician if the plaintiff were to make him a joint defendant and said:

> if he were to sue the doctor in parallel with the other defendant there could be no objection to the doctor disclosing relevant, and no longer confidential, information. It would be a matter for the doctor.

Thus in this obiter dictum it is clearly the view of Ian Kennedy J that the institution of proceedings (or even the mere threat of proceedings) is sufficient to bring to an end the plaintiff's right to confidentiality. It is submitted that this must be correct. A patient who makes such allegations puts his medical history directly into issue and cannot expect those against whom such allegations are made to resist them with both arms tied behind their backs. However it is doubtful whether such reasoning can be extended to the cases where medical practitioners or health authorities breach confidentiality in circumstances where patients refuse consent to treatment and application to the court for a declaration as to the lawfulness of proposed treatment is made. In such cases (see, for example, *Re T*[3]) the disclosure is to the court and is likely to fall within the category of cases in which disclosure to a responsible body in the patient's and in the public interest is permitted – see para **7.25** below.

1 [1991] 2 Med LR 204.
2 Ibid at 207.
3 [1992] 4 All ER, CA.

MEDICAL RECORDS

Ownership

7.18 Although the ownership of the records themselves is unlikely to be a relevant factor it should be considered. In the case of NHS records true ownership of the notes probably lies in the ownership of the paper upon which they are written. Thus in the case of a GP's notes the owner would be the relevant Family Practitioner Committee, and in the case of hospital notes, records, X-rays etc, the relevant District Health Authority. In the case of private hospital notes they may be the property of either the consultant or the hospital itself. However, X-ray photographs paid for privately are probably the property of the patient himself although they are commonly kept with his other records by the hospital.

7.19 A third category of medical records which has recently assumed relevance with respect to litigation concerns the raw data of research or epidemiological studies. Such records are commonly owned by the academic institutions which employ the research workers who carry out the studies. The information which such studies contain is almost invariably given in confidence, and in certain circumstances orders for production of the base data to parties interested in litigation have been made: see, for example, the whooping cough vaccine cases of *Kinnear v Wellcome Foundation Ltd* and *Loveday v Renton* discussed above.

7.20 Ownership of the notes is of little relevance because it does not affect either the obligation to maintain their confidentiality nor in an appropriate case the obligation to disclose their contents. In neither case will the fact of ownership provide an excuse for refraining from disclosure or for providing disclosure.

Copyright

7.21 Nor is the existence of a copyright in the notes and records a material consideration. If the confider wishes to maintain the confidence in medical records then that will be preserved subject to exceptions determined by the public interest. On the other hand, if the public interest requires disclosure then copyright in the notes or records will not provide an answer to the claim for disclosure of their contents. However, copyright considerations may provide additional remedies, for example injunctions requiring delivery up, where confidential notes have been provided or obtained both in breach of confidence and in breach of copyright.

In what circumstances will the court permit a breach of confidence?

Litigation

7.22 As is apparent from the account given above of the decision to grant disclosure of the NCES base data in the whooping cough vaccine cases the approach of the court must inevitably be to balance the competing interests of the individual on the one hand and of the public's interest in the due administration of justice on the other. A common example is when the defendant to a personal injury claim issues a subpoena duces tecum to the plaintiff's general practitioner so that the plaintiff's notes can be inspected. Their contents may often be very relevant to issues arising in the claim. In these circumstances the court will usually order disclosure if the plaintiff refuses to consent to their production; after all, it would be wrong for a plaintiff who pursues justice to attempt to thwart it by seeking to prevent the defendant from having access to confidential material about him which may very well be highly relevant to the justice of his case. Thus in the course of the litigation concerning the anti-arthritis drug Opren (Benoxaprofen) a number of individual doctors or health authorities resisted production of medical records despite the fact that the patients who were the plaintiffs in the actions had consented to such production and were themselves seeking it. Hirst J observed that where a plaintiff sued a defendant for damages for personal injuries he is entitled to discovery of hospital notes and GP records, even if the health authority or GP is not a party to the action. He stated that health authorities should respond readily and promptly to any requests for disclosure so that unnecessary expense and delay may be avoided: *Walker v Eli Lilly & Co.*[1] See too para **7.17** above and the cases referred to there.

1 [1986] ECC 550.

7.23 Under section 34 of the Supreme Court Act 1981 the court will order disclosure of documents by a non-party to an existing action in which a claim is made in respect of personal injuries or death. This enables the court to avoid unnecessary adjournment at trial brought about by production of documents in the course of a hearing pursuant to a subpoena duces tecum. The subpoena procedure none the less continues. In respect of a production of documents which constitutes a breach of confidentiality the doctor would be wise to adopt the same procedure as he would in respect of his response to a subpoena ad testificandum where his oral evidence similarly involves a breach of confidence. Thus he should attend the hearing and ask the court to excuse him from producing the documents or answering the question on grounds of confidence. Only if the court requires him to produce the documents or to answer the questions should the confidence be broken.

7.24 It should be noted that Order 24, rule 14A of the Rules of the Supreme Court provides that documents once read to or by the court or referred to in open court shall cease to be subject to the implied undertaking given by the parties to the litigation not to use such documents for any purpose other than those of the proceedings. However, the order empowers the court 'on the application of a party or of the person to whom the document belongs' to order otherwise for special reasons. It would seem sensible whenever medical records which are otherwise confidential are ordered to be produced in court, for the health authority or producing doctor to seek an order under Order 24, rule 14A maintaining the parties' undertaking on the grounds that the contents of the documents are confidential to the patient.

The doctor's overriding duty to society

7.25 There are circumstances in which a medical practitioner may be under an overriding duty to society as a whole to breach confidentiality. Thus in the case of *W v Egdell*[1] Scott J dismissed a claim for damages brought by a psychiatric patient against a consultant psychiatrist who had examined the plaintiff and who had disclosed his subsequent report voluntarily and without the plaintiff's consent to the Home Office, the Department of Health and the local health authority. The judge held that given the violent nature of the patient who was endeavouring to obtain his release from detention under the Mental Health Act the extent of the duty of confidentiality owed by the defendant to the plaintiff was 'less extensive' than that ordinarily owed by a doctor to his patient, and that such duty of confidence as existed was overridden by the public interest in disclosure of the report. It would seem that this case is another example of the way in which the court has to balance competing interests; on the one hand that of the individual patient in having his confidence maintained which gives rise to the general public interest in encouraging the public to approach their doctors openly and without inhibition or apprehension of disclosure, and on the other hand that of the public in learning of the danger that such patients can constitute, thereby enabling responsible bodies to take appropriate action. In reality it is doubtful whether it can be said that the duty owed to a violent mental patient is truly 'less extensive'. It is submitted that the better view is that the duty of confidence remains the same but that the public interest in disclosure is proportionately greater. Alternatively this could be regarded as one of the cases in which the court will permit a limited breach of confidentiality by disclosure to responsible bodies or organisations, rather akin to the qualified privilege in defamation where the defamatory information is given by someone acting under a duty of disclosure to someone acting under a duty to receive it.

1 [1990] Ch 359, [1989] 1 All ER 1089 since upheld in the Court of Appeal on the grounds (suggested above) of the balance of competing public interests rather than the overriding of a private interest in confidentiality by the public interest in disclosure – [1990] 2 WLR 471.

7.26 It is worth noting in the context of the current debate over privacy laws that the court does not, in cases of media speculation over a particular person's health, recognise that there is a public interest to override confidentiality with respect to medical care and will impose injunctions to prevent the press having access to physicians treating a patient. In *Re C (a minor) (wardship: medical treatment) (No 2)*[1] the Court of Appeal noted that identifying the patient, her family or her carers would involve pressure which could affect the quality of her care and therefore reinforced the duty of confidentiality owed to C by extending injunctions already in place to previous carers.

1 (1989) Guardian, 27 April.

STATUTORY PROVISION

7.27 This would include the duty to notify the relevant Area Health Authority of cases of certain scheduled infectious diseases.[1] Similarly, any doctor who attends a person whom he has reasonable grounds to suspect is addicted to a drug scheduled in the Misuse of Drugs (Notification of and Supply to Addicts) Regulations 1973 is obliged to furnish information about that person to the Home Office. The information required includes the name and address, sex, date of birth and National Health Service number of the person and is thus sufficient to identify him or her. A doctor or midwife who is present at a birth must inform the Area Health Authority of the birth (or stillbirth) within 36 hours.[2] A medical practitioner who treated a patient in a terminal illness must provide the registrar of deaths with a certificate of death stating, inter alia, the cause of death.[3]

1 Public Health (Infectious Disease) Regulations 1968, SI 1968/1366, reg 2; NHS 'Venereal Diseases' Regulations 1974, SI 1974/29.
2 National Health Service Act 1977, s 124; NHS (Notification of Births and Deaths) Regulations 1974, SI 1974/319.
3 National Health Service Act 1977, s 22.

7.28 There are also a number of provisions wherby persons are required to provide the police with information if requested with respect to criminal offences. In *Hunter v Mann*[1] the court held that a doctor comes within the meaning of 'any other person' in section 168(2)(b) of the Road Traffic Act 1972 who, along with the keeper of the vehicle, is under a duty to provide a police officer with any information which it is within his power to give and which may lead to the identification of the driver of a vehicle alleged to be guilty of an offence. The court held that a doctor acting within his professional capacity and carrying out his professional duty and responsibility came within the words 'any other person' and could therefore be convicted for failing to give the required information on the grounds that this would be a breach of confidence.

1 [1974] QB 767, [1974] 2 All ER 414, DC.

7.29 Where such duties to notify arise they are strictly limited to the terms of the relevant regulation. It would be a breach of the duty of confidentiality to inform any person other than those specified in the relevant regulation that a patient was, for example, the driver of a crashed car or infected with a venereal disease (see *X v Y*).[1]

1 [1988] 2 All ER 648.

7.30 Again, doctors may be required to give police access to medical records containing material which would not otherwise be disclosable. The powers of entry, search and seizure provided for in the Police and Criminal Evidence Act 1984 are wide ranging. While search warrants may not be granted with respect to medical records in the same way as for many classes of documents a circuit judge may, if certain conditions are satisfied, order that the police either be given medical records to take away or be given access to them. The most important conditions are that the documents are likely to be of substantial value to the investigation of a serious arrestable offence. These provisions apply to medical records in their capacity as material (personal records acquired or created in the course of a profession and held in confidence) 'excluded' from the general rules which enable search of premises and seizure of documents. Their special treatment under the Act reflects a recognition of the importance of the principle of confidentiality by protecting this category of confidential material by restricting the methods by which access may be obtained by the police.

HIV POSITIVE PATIENTS

7.31 Other circumstances which have troubled the medical profession concern HIV positive patients. The medical profession has rightly sought the guidance of the General Medical Council as to whether disclosure, e g to a patient's partner or family without the consent of the patient, would amount to professional misconduct. The GMC's view has vacillated. The guidance issued by the GMC on 8 August 1988 permits disclosure without consent to third parties only 'where the doctor judges that the failure to disclose would put the health of any of the health care team at serious risk . . . or to safeguard such persons [sexual partners] from a possibly fatal infection'. In every case of disclosure the doctor concerned must be prepared to justify the decision made, presumably to the General Medical Council, in answering a complaint of professional misconduct. It is likely that the courts would regard such disclosure as one of an overriding duty, provided that the disclosure is strictly limited only to those with a legitimate interest in receiving it.

IMPLIED AUTHORITY TO DISCLOSE

7.32 In a number of well-recognised circumstances it is generally accepted that the patient gives by implication a limited authority to the holder of confidential information to disclose that information to others.

Disclosure to other health professionals

7.33 Plainly it must be accepted that the treating doctor has authority to inform others involved in the patient's care about the patient's condition.

These include the nursing staff, professions supplementary to medicine and other medical staff actively involved in treatment or consulted with regard to it. The burden of confidentiality devolves equally upon them and they are subject to identical duties as the treating doctor himself.

Teaching/medical research

7.34 It is considered to be the better practice to obtain the express consent of patients if it is desired to provide confidential information about them to bona fide medical researchers or to students for teaching purposes. However, if the information were provided in an anonymous form so that the patient could not be identified it is possible that no action would lie for breach of confidence if, for example, an article about a specific patient's condition were to be written and published or if details of the patient's condition were used, for example in an epidemiological study.

Adverse drug reactions

7.35 Doctors recording adverse reactions to drug therapy are encouraged to report such reactions to the Committee of Safety of Medicines (CSM). The drug manufacturers often receive such reports from medical practitioners, and if they do are under a statutory obligation to pass on details of the reactions to the CSM. Such reports frequently identify the patient and the patient's condition.

Given the restricted nature of the disclosure and the duties and responsibilities of those to whom such disclosure is made it is considered unlikely that any court would consider such a breach of confidentiality as actionable and would probably justify it on the basis of implied authority.

NEGLIGENT NON-DISCLOSURE

7.36 It is interesting to consider whether a duty of care is owed by a doctor to third parties who are put at risk by violent or infected patients to warn them of the risk so as to safeguard them from harm. In the Californian case of *Tarasoff v Regents of University of California*[1] the Supreme Court of California held by a majority that a cause of action existed against defendant psychiatrists on the grounds that their patient presented a serious danger of violence to an individual and that they failed to exercise reasonable care to protect her from that danger.

1 Sup 131 Cal Rptr 14 (1976).

7.37 Given the undoubted duty of confidence which the doctor owes to his patient it is unlikely that an English court would hold that such a duty of care exists: it would be unclear precisely to whom the duty is owed, and given the doctor's right (indeed duty) in appropriate circumstances to inform the police or public health authorities about violent or infected patients (see above) it could be argued that the court should not impose another and wider duty of care owed to indeterminate members of the public under the familiar 'neighbour' or proximity principles.

7.38 The public interest exception has, in the absence of statutory intervention, been narrowly defined by the courts. The decision in *Gillick v West Norfolk and Wisbech Area Health Authority and Department of Health and Social Security*[1] did not, for example, support a parent's claim to disclosure of information relating to a child's contraceptive treatment. This was a case primarily concerned with a child's capacity to consent validly to treatment. Nevertheless, by holding that a child does not lack legal capacity on grounds of age alone the court strengthened the duty of confidentiality owed by a doctor to a patient under 16 years of age at least in cases where the child has sufficient understanding to be capable of making decisions. In *X v Y*[2] it was held that the public interest in preserving the confidentiality of hospital records identifying actual or potential AIDS sufferers outweighed the public interest in the freedom of the press to publish such information. The plaintiffs were granted an injunction restraining publication and Rose J noted that there was no necessary precondition to injunctive relief for breach of confidence that the plaintiff has suffered or may suffer detriment in the use of the information.

1 [1986] AC 112, [1985] 3 All ER 402, HL.
2 [1988] 2 All ER 648.

7.39 The current position is complicated further by the rights of patients granted by the Data Protection Act 1984. The Act entitles an individual to be informed, by anyone holding computerised information, whether that information includes his 'personal data' and to be supplied with copies of it.[1] The Act, however, grants the minister power to exempt from the right to access certain categories of information including that relating to the physical or mental health of the data subject (section 29). This power was exercised as follows:[2]

> **4.**(1) The subject access provisions shall not have effect in relation to any personal data to which this Order applies in any case where either of the requirements specified in paragraph (2) below is satisfied with respect to the information constituting the data and the obligations contained in paragraph (5) below are complied with by the data user.
>
> (2) The requirements referred to in paragraph (1) above are that the application of the subject access provisions:
>
> (a) would be likely to cause serious harm to the physical or mental health of the data subject; or
>
> (b) would be likely to disclose to the data subject the identity of another individual (who has not consented to the disclosure of the information) either as a person to whom the information or part of it relates or as the source of the information or enable that identity to be deduced by the data subject either from the information itself or from a combination of that information and other information which the data subject has or is likely to have.

1 Data Protection Act 1984, s 21.
2 The Data Protection (Subject Access Modification) (Health) Order 1987, SI 1987/1903.

7.40 There have not yet been any cases judicially reviewing a refusal to supply information to a patient under these provisions. As more hospitals and general practices computerise it is likely that the requests of patients under the Supreme Court Act for access to their medical records will be influenced by cases examining the Data Protection Act regulation. It appears that while in principle a doctor owes a duty of confidentiality to his patient, the patient will in certain circumstances not be permitted access to the same information on public policy grounds. These by implication at least suggest a recognition that it is important that the medical profession (for analogy see *Gaskin v Liverpool City Council*[1]) can make records and notes on the basis that such information is confidential to members of the profession. The Access to Health Records Act 1990 extended that right of access by patients to (inter alia) their own medical notes and set up a system whereby inaccuracies in these notes could be corrected. Similar exceptions to the Data Protection Act provisions are made together with exemptions where the applicant is not the patient who is the subject of the information. The Act permits applications from a person authorised in writing to apply on the patient's behalf, a dead patient's personal representative, a person appointed by the court to manage the incapable patient's affairs, and in cases of children, those with parental responsibilities. Circumstances such as those in *Gillick* are covered in that access will not be granted when the patient has given the information in the expectation that it would not be disclosed to the applicant.

1 [1980] 1 WLR 1549, CA.

7.41 The law also recognises the need for provision regarding the circumstances in which medical records, even with the patient's consent, should be disclosed to third parties. The Access to Medical Reports Act 1988 provides that insurers and employers may not be shown a report until, in cases where a patient exercises his rights, he has both seen and been able to comment on the contents of the report and has consented to its disclosure both before and after his own inspection of it. If his comments are not accepted by the writer of the report the patient can insist that the report only be shown to the insurer or employer together with a written statement of his comments or he can withdraw his consent to its supply.

BIBLIOGRAPHICAL REFERENCE

BMA *Handbook of Medical Ethics* (1984 edn).

CHAPTER 8

Preliminary legal steps for the patient

Richard Vallance *Solicitor*

SUMMARY

8.1 The good old days have passed when it was rare for professional people to be sued, for social reasons as well as the greater difficulties of taking a case to court. The atmosphere now is quite different and with a greater awareness of legal rights most people are more inclined to institute court proceedings when they feel that they have been wronged. It is therefore not surprising that there has been an increase in claims against the medical profession in the same way as there has been against other professions. This increase has been reflected by the huge escalation in insurance premiums which we all now have to pay, although in the case of NHS hospital treatment doctors have not required insurance cover since the introduction of Crown Indemnity in April 1990. What has happened is unlikely to have been caused by a deterioration of professional standards.

8.2 There are, however, two factors which are peculiar to the medical profession and which have ensured a material increase in the number of medical claims which have been instigated.

LACK OF EXPLANATION OR APOLOGY

8.3 Solicitors undertaking work on behalf of plaintiffs are aware that many claimants (in my experience at least half) would not have consulted them had they been handled sympathetically by the doctors concerned once an adverse event had occurred. In the early stages, patients or their families are often not motivated by the thought of damages but rather by a wish to receive an explanation of what has happened together with expressions of sympathy and regret as appropriate. The absence of these ingredients can cause bitterness in the patient which, if not cured at an early stage, may create an overwhelming desire to pursue a case to trial even if the expert evidence is against negligence having occurred.

8.4 The majority of doctors will deal with these rare situations with openness and sensitivity. However, perhaps because it is not part of a medical student's training to learn how to respond to patients' needs when unexpected difficulties occur, far too many doctors continue to have exaggerated feelings of embarrassment and shame, with the result that they are unable to confront the problem or to deal with its consequences.

8.5 Everyone of course makes mistakes. It is natural to do so. 'It ill becomes anyone to adopt an attitude of superiority.'[1] This premise should be recognised and accepted by the medical profession, without in any way reflecting an acceptance of lower standards of care.

1 Donaldson LJ in *Whitehouse v Jordan* [1981] 1 All ER 267, [1981] 1 WLR 246, HL.

8.6 Lord Donaldson, the Master of the Rolls, has reaffirmed[1] the obvious point that a doctor's duty of care continues after an error has been made, and has thereby highlighted the importance for students to receive training as to how to perform this duty when the need arises, as it almost certainly will. Due to lack of this training, the present reaction of many doctors when confronted by such a problem is to lose the opportunity of performing this continuing duty of care, in order to seek legal advice. In the case of NHS hospital treatment the initiative will be passed over to administrators concerned with the control of hospital budgets whereas general practitioners and doctors providing treatment privately will continue to seek advice from their defence organisations.

1 *Naylor v Preston Area Health Authority* [1987] 2 All ER 353, [1987] 1 WLR 958, CA.

8.7 Naturally the finance committees of District Health Authorities and Trust Hospitals will be deeply concerned to avoid the need to pay compensation to a small group of individuals out of hard pressed NHS hospital budgets. The problem is compounded by the failure of government to make additional funds available to meet such claims following the introduction of Crown Indemnity. Whilst a beneficial effect of this degree of financial accountability will be an improvement of standards generated by an increased determination to avoid expensive claims, there is also the temptation to conceal the circumstances of treatment which might lead to claims being made. The emphasis should of course be on improving standards and ensuring mistakes are not repeated whilst handling those mistakes which are made with integrity and tact.

8.8 Although the main defence organisations, the Medical Defence Union and the Medical Protection Society, who are concerned on behalf of GPs and doctors providing treatment on a private basis, are at pains to point out that they are not insurance companies, they are in fact in the position of insurers. There is therefore a conflict. Their overriding concerns are the legal consequences of any error made and a desire to limit the size of any claim. The treating doctor's concern on the other hand should surely be the welfare of the patient. The doctor does not need insurers' advice. It is sufficient simply to remember not to make an admission of liability for any error made, as this could compromise insurance cover and prejudice the defence of actions which should properly be defended. Care not to admit liability should not prevent full and honest explanations from being given to the patient.

8.9 The code of practice which dictates the behaviour of solicitors requires that a practitioner making a serious error should advise the client to obtain legal advice from an independent solicitor. Unfortunately there is no similar rule so far as the medical profession is concerned. Not only is the doctor who makes a serious mistake not under an obligation to make frank disclosure and to give an honest explanation, but colleagues are also in the embarrassing situation of not being obliged to intervene. A procedure should be introduced under which a serious error is referred to a senior colleague who would be required to meet with the patient or to arrange for this to be done by the most appropriate senior clinician.

8.10 It is true that in some circumstances it may be better for the patient or family to be unaware that an avoidable error has occurred. However, this consideration is outweighed by the greater public confidence which would arise from full and frank disclosure being made in every case.

8.11 Such a code of practice would instil greater public confidence that errors would be admitted by all doctors and honest explanations given. There would then be more willingness on the part of patients to accept that a poor result does not justify an action for damages.

8.12 These views are supported by the fact that many cases which are pursued have very limited monetary value, particularly where the patient has died and there is no dependency claim. The claimant is often motivated by bitterness and by determination to find out what happened, rather than by thought of damages.

8.13 The introduction of such an improved procedure would lead to a reduction in the number of claims, and not an increase as might be expected on first consideration. Whilst there would be claims being made in circumstances which otherwise would have remained undetected, many unmeritorious actions would not see the light of day.

THE INADEQUACY OF THE SYSTEM FOR THE INVESTIGATION OF COMPLAINTS

8.14 The second major factor which has contributed to the increase in medical negligence claims, and which leads on from the profession's failure to perform its duty of aftercare, is the absence of an adequate complaints procedure. Such inadequacy forces the patient to consult a solicitor at a premature stage.

8.15 The Ombudsman can only deal with complaints relating to administrative matters. Otherwise the complaints procedures available to patients (discussed elsewhere in this book) do not provide satisfaction or the assurance that improvements will be investigated or doctors disciplined. A solicitor almost always has to be employed because patients will not normally be given access to their medical records unless they can show that there are prima facie grounds for a medical negligence claim. Those representing the doctors or hospitals concerned will not recognise these grounds unless they are stated by solicitors. This results from section 33(2) of the Supreme Court Act 1981 which provides that a patient is only entitled to the production of medical records if:

(a) the person making this application appears to be likely to be a party to subsequent proceedings in the High Court;
(b) a claim in respect of personal injuries to a person or in respect of a person's death is likely to be made;
(c) the person against whom the order is sought appears to be likely to be a party to such proceedings; and
(d) such person appears to be likely to have or to have had in his possession, custody or power any relevant documents.

8.16 The litigation solicitor whom the patient instructs is by nature aggressive! That solicitor's required task is to set out in a 'Shaw' letter[1] requesting production of records sufficient to show that these four conditions can be met and that allegations of negligence are likely to be pursued. Even if, therefore, it is by no means clear that negligence has been committed it is still necessary to spell out likely allegations in order to justify the entitlement to disclosure.

1 *Shaw v Vauxhall Motors Ltd* [1974] 2 All ER 1185, [1974] 1 WLR 1035, CA.

8.17 Upon receipt of such a letter, the hospital and/or defence organisations of the treating doctors will instruct their own solicitors. An adversarial situation well and truly now exists, with the increased prospect of litigation to follow.

8.18 The obvious improvement to be made here is to provide freer access for patients to all their medical records so that it is not inevitable that solicitors will be instructed on both sides. There is a right of access to health records kept on computer.[1] Since 1 November 1991 it has not been necessary to establish the likelihood of a valid claim for negligence in order to justify a request for access to such records made from that date.[2] However, this new legislation has not yet made it an easy matter for patients to obtain copy records upon request and the assistance of solicitors has continued to be required.

1 The Data Protection Act 1984, s 21.
2 Access to Health Records Act 1990.

8.19 Present procedures therefore dictate that there are very many cases of variable merit to be investigated and pursued by solicitors and they need to be aware of the pitfalls to be avoided and of the specialist requirements of the procedure to be followed.

PARTICULAR DANGERS

8.20 These relate mainly to time problems. The applicable limitation period is dealt with in Chapter 13. Delays which are peculiar to medical negligence proceedings are caused:

(a) by the patient, who may not feel robust enough to instruct solicitors until medical problems and worries have been resolved;
(b) by counsel, who are overworked due to the limited number of true specialists in this field;
(c) by the need to obtain medical records from all sources, which may require preliminary applications to the court;

(d) by the requirement for medical experts' reports, and to have a conference with experts and counsel before a Statement of Claim can be prepared;
(e) by the tactics adopted by the solicitors for the defendants who will take advantage of any inexperience of plaintiffs' solicitors and will encourage delay and limitation problems.

8.21 The first basic precaution is for the solicitor to write the limitation date boldly on the cover of the file and also to make a clear diary note of it. The other major requirement is to act with speed, making early application for a court order for the release of medical records at the first sign of unreasonable delay and taking all procedural steps immediately they are required. Some examples of how to expedite matters are as follows:

(a) in legal aid cases, the first limitation will require an Opinion of counsel following the receipt of a report from a medical expert before authorising the commencement of court proceedings; if, however, the expert's report is clear cut, the Legal Aid Office should be prepared to revoke the requirement for such an Opinion;
(b) shortly after a Defence has been served issue your Summons for Directions. Further procedural matters can be dealt with in the run up to trial, given the long delay to trial caused by the need for a fixed date to be allocated in order to accommodate the attendance of expert witnesses;
(c) never delay procedural steps in order to negotiate.

8.22 The obvious advantages of speed are to reduce the period of worry for the parties concerned, to save costs and to make available damages which may be urgently needed for the provision of nursing care or equipment. There is also the fact that the defendants will often, for various reasons, delay admissions of liability or negotiations until the latest possible time. An increased number of cases have settled as a result of the standard requirement for exchange of experts' reports[1] on liability issues and it is therefore in the interests of the plaintiff to reach the stage of exchange as quickly as possible following the hearing for directions.

1 Following *Naylor v Preston Area Health Authority* [1987] 2 All ER 353, [1987] 1 WLR 958, CA. For a full account of this case, see paras **11.87–11.94**.

8.23 Contrary to the popular view, the overall procedure for medical negligence claims favours the competent plaintiff's solicitor. However, the balance shifts at trial where the burden is on the plaintiff to prove negligence on the balance of probabilities and the defendants can rely on the reputable minority defence, commonly known as the *Bolam* test.[1]

1 *Bolam v Friern Hospital Management Committee* [1957] 2 All ER 118, [1957] 1 WLR 582.

PROCEDURE

Importance of medical records

8.24 It is absolutely vital for the plaintiff's solicitors to obtain release of all medical records to them, and *not* direct to medical advisers save in exceptional circumstances. If they agree otherwise, they should not be undertaking plaintiff medical negligence work. If solicitors for hospitals or doctors state that they will only agree to give disclosure to medical experts, this should be taken as an insult as showing that they suspect the plaintiff's solicitors to be so inexperienced or incompetent as to agree.

8.25 The reasons for requiring disclosure to the plaintiff's solicitors are numerous and include the following:

(a) the records from all sources will be in disarray and it is for the plaintiff's solicitors to reorganise them into sensible chronological bundles which will eventually be used at trial. These should be paginated for circulation between counsel and experts. Solicitors should not be nervous of this task as with experience it becomes easy to differentiate between different categories of forms and other documents. It is a tremendous advantage to have the most important trial bundles prepared before the action is even begun;

(b) during this exercise, the plaintiff's solicitors can ascertain what documents are missing and can make application for their production, if necessary to the court. This is often a crucial task;

(c) it is essential that the solicitor read the records carefully before preparing sensible letters of instruction to experts in the appropriate specialities;

(d) counsel cannot possibly set out an accurate chronological history of events or draft allegations of negligence in a Statement of Claim in the absence of the records, and it is doubtful whether they should be prepared to accept instructions to do so without them being available. Indeed there may be personal liability for solicitor or counsel who fail to obtain disclosure, and make competent analysis, of all relevant records;[1]

(e) it is important to check the plaintiff's statement of events against the medical records in order to avoid problems in cross-examination at trial. The records should be made available to the plaintiff, if desired, but only after they have been checked carefully so that a warning may be given of any information likely to cause upset;

(f) it is disadvantageous for the defendants to be able to monitor the medical experts instructed on the plaintiff's behalf and to be in direct communication with them. At trial the plaintiff may be cross-examined as to why reports of certain experts have not been disclosed, the inference being that those experts did not support the plaintiff's case.

1 *Locke v Camberwell Health Authority* [1990] NLJR 205 (court of first instance).

Letters to obtain release of records from potential defendants

8.26 The first priority is to obtain disclosure of medical records from the hospital or doctors responsible for the treatment about which complaint is made. Precedent A is a suggested form of letter to be adapted to the writer's own style, where records pre-date 1 November 1991. If only records made from that date are required, a simple letter of request should be sufficient. This is because a patient now has a statutory right under the Access to Health Records Act 1990 to copy records made from 1 November 1991 without having to give any reason. They are to be supplied within a maximum of 40 days and for no more than the fixed cost of photocopying, but subject to the limited discretion of the holder defined in section 5.

8.27 In the case of National Health Service hospital treatment, this letter will be addressed to the District General Manager at the District Health Authority responsible for the hospital involved or to the Manager at the Trust hospital. In the case of treatment provided privately or by a GP, it will need to be adapted and addressed to the doctor concerned.

8.28 Insertion of details of the treating doctors will speed up the response, bearing in mind that the health authority or Trust hospital normally feels obliged to obtain consents from them before giving disclosure. It also helps to quote the hospital records number.

8.29 To justify a request for records pre-dating 1 November 1991, it is necessary to set out sufficient facts of what happened, together with an indication of the likely allegations which will be pursued, in order to satisfy the defendants that there is a reasonable basis for a claim and that the application is not just speculative.[1]

1 *Dunning v Board of Governors of the United Liverpool Hospitals* [1973] 2 All ER 454, [1973] 1 WLR 586, CA; *Shaw v Vauxhall Motors Ltd* [1974] 2 All ER 1185, [1974] 1 WLR 1035, CA.

8.30 The plaintiff will not wish to include more detail than is necessary in advance of seeing the medical records and obtaining expert opinions. The more serious the injury, or if an infant is involved, the less information is required as it is an easier task to justify obtaining disclosure if application to the court has to be made.

8.31 Paragraph 14(a) and (b) lays down a timescale within which records are to be produced. Whether or not early application is made to the court is affected by the question of who will have to pay the legal costs involved, a subject dealt with under the next heading.

8.32 In the case of private hospital treatment, only part of the records are likely to be held by the treating doctor and a separate letter will need to be written to the hospital for the remainder, enclosing a copy of the letter to that doctor.

8.33 If the claim is contemplated against a GP, the letter will be shorter and will take account of the fact GPs will only normally hold medical record cards, correspondence and results of tests.

8.34 When a letter in this form is sent to an individual doctor against whom a claim is threatened, rather than to a health authority or hospital, it should be made rather less formal, make the suggestion that it should immediately be passed to a defence organisation and explain that it has been necessary to set out so much information in order to satisfy the defence organisation that the request for disclosure of records is justified.

Application to the court for an order for disclosure by potential defendants

8.35 This is by way of preliminary, separate court proceedings for production of records before a writ is issued. It requires an originating summons under section 33(2) of the Supreme Court Act 1981 and Order 24, rule 7A(1) of the Rules of the Supreme Court Rules 1965 and/or section 8 of the Access to Health Records Act 1990. If and when a writ is later issued, it will commence a completely new action for damages for negligence.

8.36 All that can be achieved by the originating summons procedure is an order in favour of the plaintiff for production of medical records and this question will be considered by a Master or District Judge on the basis of affidavit evidence.[1]

1 See *Harris v Newcastle-upon-Tyne Health Authority* [1989] 2 All ER 273, [1989] 1 WLR 96, CA.

8.37 So long as letters are written along the lines of Precedent A, indicating that there is a proper claim to be investigated, or if records were made on or after 1 November 1991, it should be rare that the defendants will contest an order for records to be disclosed. However, if a plaintiff is forced to issue an originating summons it is sensible to apply for an order that the defendant or a representative of the defendant should swear an affidavit verifying the List of Documents produced to ensure that all relevant documents are included.

8.38 When medical records have been disclosed on a voluntary basis it is still sometimes necessary to obtain an order for a List of Documents to be verified by affidavit if crucial documents are missing.

8.39 Precedents B and C are forms of Originating Summons and Affidavit in Support. The plaintiff's affidavit in support of the Originating Summons need do little more than to exhibit the letter seeking discovery of records.

8.40 The usual order under Order 24, rule 7A/8 of the Rules of the Supreme Court Act 1965 is for the plaintiff to have to pay the defendant's costs of the application, but if the plaintiff is legally aided it is likely to be with the proviso that the order is not to be enforced without leave. A fee-paying plaintiff therefore may not wish to be too hasty in pursuing an application to the court. An order that costs should be 'in the cause', ie that they should be paid by the party losing at trial, would be inappropriate as a writ action may never follow.

8.41 Whilst it is possible that the defendants will be ordered to pay the costs of the Originating Summons this will only be when it can be shown that they have been unreasonably slow in producing records.[1] To get such an order is not something to be aimed for as such delay is to be avoided. However, to obtain an order for costs for a breach of the Access to Health Records Act 1990 should be much simpler.

1 *Hall v Wandsworth Health Authority* (1985) 129 Sol Jo 188.

8.42 It is to be noted that an order for costs against the plaintiff includes the costs of the defendants in complying with an order for discovery under Order 24, rule 7A/8.

8.43 If the plaintiff incurs costs in the Originating Summons proceedings, these should be included as an item of claim for special damages in any subsequent writ action.

Letters to obtain release of records from non-potential defendants

8.44 It is also important to get disclosure from any other hospitals or doctors who have provided treatment which is not the subject of criticism. These records should be for both earlier and later medical care, although where there is a long history of unrelated problems they may be excluded as being of insufficient relevance. Ideally these documents will be included in the paginated bundles prepared before instructions are sent either to experts or counsel.

8.45 For example, a brain-damaged baby may be transferred from the labour ward to an intensive therapy unit or paediatric ward. These further records are essential to establish whether any further crisis occurred, what views are recorded by the paediatricians as to what went wrong and to help assessment of condition and prognosis. There may also be years of follow up treatment, the records of which will also be relevant to damages.

8.46 The GP with whom the plaintiff is currently registered should hold all the relevant notes including those of previous GPs. If there is no current registration, or if the claim is on behalf of a patient who has died, they will be held by the local Family Health Services Authority. They may be relevant to show some other possible cause for the injury in respect of which the plaintiff claims, or to show that he was a frequent visitor to the practice who has tended to exaggerate his symptoms. GPs' notes will invariably be called for by the defendants and form part of the bundles at trial. It is therefore important they they, and all the hospital notes, should be considered by experts and lawyers before proceedings are commenced so that any weaknesses can be taken into account at the outset.

8.47 Precedents D and E are suggested forms of letters to an 'innocent' GP and hospital. Minor adaptation is needed for a letter to a consultant providing private treatment. Less need be said for simple applications under the Access to Health Records Act 1990.

8.48 Hospitals are likely to respond reasonably quickly and to produce photocopy notes on a voluntary basis, as no claim is threatened against them. However GPs are particularly resistant to the idea of giving immediate and full disclosure of records in their possession. This is probably due to the fact that they usually seek the advice of their defence organisations who discourage voluntary compliance and often suggest that an assurance should first be given that no claim is intended against the GP personally. Patience and perseverance are required although delay can seldom be justified for records since 1 November 1991. No assurance can obviously be given that no claim against the GP will follow in advance of seeing the records, although it can be said that the plaintiff presently has no contemplation of a claim.

8.49 It is likely that the GP will have referred the plaintiff to the consultant against whom a complaint has directly or indirectly been made. The GP may therefore have personal reasons for disapproving of a claim and the plaintiff should be warned of the possibility of animosity, which not infrequently occurs.

Application to the court for an order for disclosure by non-potential defendants

8.50 It has been held[1] that health authorities and medical practitioners should respond readily and promptly to any requests for disclosure, so that unnecessary expense and delay may be avoided. It is therefore inexcusable that problems should be put in the way of the plaintiff when good reasons are put forward why the records are needed.

1 *Walker v Eli Lilly & Co* [1986] ECC 550.

8.51 A summons (Precedent F) may only be issued after the main action for medical negligence has been commenced, save for applications only made under the Access to Health Records Act 1990. This summons is a Summons to the Master or District Judge in the action under section 34(2) of the Supreme Court Act 1981 and Order 24, rule 7A(2) in contrast to the section 33 Originating Summons. If therefore it is important to obtain copies of all records from all sources before investigating a claim, it may sometimes be necessary to issue a writ prematurely. This is a technical difficulty and can cause time problems for the plaintiff's solicitor, who may then be put under pressure to serve a Statement of Claim in the writ action.

8.52 It is to be noted that the summons must be served on the defendants as well as on the party against whom disclosure is sought. Although an application for costs is included it is unlikely to be granted in the absence of serious delay.

Action to be taken to obtain disclosure of records pre-dating 1 November 1991 by potential defendants if there is insufficient time for an order for pre-action discovery to be obtained before a writ has to be issued

8.53 The problem is that it is harder to get full discovery of records pre-dating 1 November 1991 once a writ has been issued, and the main action begun. It is then no longer possible to make a section 33 Originating Summons application. Instead it is necessary to issue a summons under Order 24, rule 7 in the form of Precedent G.

8.54 The footnote to Order 24, rule 7(1) provides that in an action the court 'has jurisdiction to order specific discovery under this rule even before service of the Statement of Claim, but the making of such an order generally calls for definition of the issues and should not normally be made'. The court may therefore make a more restrictive order after a writ has been issued.

8.55 The affidavit in support will need to set out why pre-action discovery was not sought and why the medical records are required before the Statement of Claim can be prepared. The most common reason for the premature issue of the writ is of course because the limitation date is about to expire.

8.56 The summons will include paragraph (c) asking for time to serve a Statement of Claim to run from disclosure of the medical records.

Proceedings in the county court

8.57 The Rules require that any action for damages for personal injuries of a value not exceeding £50,000 must be commenced in the county court. Before issue a Writ must therefore be indorsed with a statement as follows:

This Writ includes a claim for personal injury but may be commenced in the High Court because the value of the action for the purposes of article 5 of the High Court Jurisdiction Order 1991 exceeds £50,000.[1]

It may however be appropriate to make application in the county court for the action to be transferred to the High Court even if damages will be materially less than £50,000 on grounds that the claim includes allegations of professional negligence and/or involves a fatal accident.

1 See Practice Direction [1991] 3 All ER 349.

8.58 Procedures in the county court are similar to those in the High Court. An application for pre-action production of medical records is made by notice of application (Precedent B) under section 52 of the County Courts Act 1984.

8.59 If the limitation period is about to expire and it is not yet possible to prepare Particulars of Claim making allegations of negligence, it is possible to ask certain county courts to issue a Summons without Particulars of Claim for service by solicitor within four months. The court may accept an undertaking to file the required medical report substantiating the injuries alleged and Statement of Special Damages to date with an estimate of future losses within the period of time allowed for service of the proceedings but otherwise it may be necessary to apply to the court for such an extension. If your usual court will not issue a Summons without the necessary documents being filed, go to one that will.

Who are the correct defendants?

GPs and private treatment

8.60 There is no alternative but to sue the named doctors if the claim is against a general practitioner or a doctor who provided treatment privately. In these circumstances, the doctors concerned should immediately pass the matter to their defence organisations who will appoint solicitors to represent them and to defend proceedings as appropriate.

NHS treatment

HEALTH AUTHORITIES

8.61 Where hospital treatment is provided under the National Health Service, it is normally sufficient to sue the District Health Authority or Trust hospital as the relevant employer of all clinical and nursing staff involved, and not the Regional Health Authority and the treating doctors as well. The

District Health Authority or Trust hospital will either defend itself through the legal department of its Regional Health Authority or by instructing solicitors in private practice.

8.62 It is important to establish that all documents held by the Regional Health Authority will be deemed to be within the power and control of the District Health Authority or Trust Hospital for the purposes of disclosure of documents in the action against the District Health Authority or Trust hospital. If, for example, an internal investigation has been carried out under the auspices of the Regional Health Authority, it is unlikely that you will otherwise be given voluntary disclosure or even notification of the existence of statements and an investigation enquiry report. You will also not be given disclosure of documents relating to the purchase of drugs carried out at regional level. If therefore the District Health Authority or Trust hospital refuse to give confirmation that they have included disclosure of documents held by the Regional Health Authority, application to the court for an order for disclosure by a non-potential defendant may have to be contemplated.

NAMED DOCTORS

8.63 The plaintiff can choose to sue treating doctors as well as the District Health Authority at his discretion. However, this is usually undesirable. It causes unnecessary stress on the doctor to be named individually, and the plaintiff should appreciate that a judge may feel less inclined to make a finding of negligence against an individual doctor making a serious but isolated error than against an institution. It will also materially add to the costs and difficulty of the conduct of the proceedings because of the involvement on the record of additional solicitors appointed by the defence organisations of the named treating doctors.

8.64 There are two circumstances in which it may be justified to name the doctor as a defendant where the health authority (or Trust hospital) is also to be named as a defendant:

(1) if the limitation date is about to expire, when it may be prudent; for example, if there is doubt whether all treatment was provided under the NHS;
(2) where it would be possible for the defendant to plead a defence without taking into account the description of events of the treating doctor. The health authority or Trust hospital may make half-hearted efforts to obtain a statement from a doctor who is difficult to trace but by making him a party to the proceedings his instructions will have to be taken into account in the preparation of his own defence.

Settlement of claims since introduction of Crown Indemnity

8.65 Since Crown Indemnity, the settlement of claims concerning NHS treatment has become easier. The complication of liability having to be apportioned between the health authority and defence organisations of treating doctors has been removed. The health authority or Trust hospital now having total responsibility for payment of any claims out of their budgets, they have a free hand in deciding which cases should be settled and which should be contested.

8.66 In addition there is the continuing beneficial effect of the *Naylor* decision which has encouraged many more cases to settle than used to happen. This decision made it a standard direction on the hearing for directions for it to be ordered that experts' reports on liability issues of negligence and causation be exchanged well in advance of trial. Whereas in the past the defendants have often contested liability even in the most hopeless cases until near to trial they now either have to admit liability or to negotiate fast if they cannot produce experts' reports which are adequate to continue at least the appearance of disputed liability. On the other hand, plaintiffs too have to reconsider the merits of proceeding to trial after the reports of the defendants' experts have been produced.

8.67 Exchange of statements of witnesses of fact (which will of course include treating doctors and nurses) is also now a Standard Direction.[1] Such an order in relation to witnesses of fact relevant to liability issues of negligence and causation further encourage resolution of proceedings.

1 RSC Order 38, rule 2A.

Role of medical experts

8.68 Although it is for the judge to decide that negligence has occurred or whether such negligence caused the plaintiff's injury, this decision will be based on the opinions expressed by medical experts in the witness box.

Choice of experts

8.69 Evidence and reports will be required on the liability issues of negligence and/or causation, depending upon whether both aspects are in issue; also, separately, on condition and prognosis to establish what damages are appropriate should liability be established. It is necessary to identify the specialities in which allegations of negligence will be appropriate in order to choose the appropriate experts from whom to obtain opinions; similarly with regard to the appropriate experts to deal with causation and condition and prognosis. It may be appropriate for one expert in a particular speciality to deal with all three aspects but separate reports should be prepared (1) for the liability issues of negligence and/or causation, and (2) condition and prognosis, as these may be required to be exchanged at different times and for different purposes.

8.70 Although there is now a greater willingness for experts to act on behalf of plaintiffs, it is important for a plaintiff's solicitors not to send instructions to medical experts whom they do not already know without first checking that they are willing to take matters on and that they do not have a hostile attitude to the idea of medical negligence claims.

8.71 Choice of expert on liability issues should take account of that expert's knowledge of practice at the time that the treatment being criticised was provided; also of the seniority and specialities of the treating doctors concerned.

8.72 It will, of course, be of great assistance to have the supporting evidence of eminent professors in the particular specialities in question. However, it may be risky to rely only on the opinions of those who have not personally treated a patient for many years, or who may be regarded as being too superior or distant from the junior registrar whose actions may be being considered. The evidence of a recently appointed consultant general surgeon might be preferred to that of a world renowned neurologist when judging the treatment provided by a registrar in general surgery.

Preliminary reports

8.73 An expert is first instructed on behalf of a plaintiff to provide a report on liability issues when medical records have been obtained from all sources and usually after detailed statements have been obtained from the plaintiff and any relevant witnesses. Anne Winyard in Chapter 9 gives guidance as to how these instructions should be prepared and as to how the medical records should be presented.

8.74 Reports when received must be considered critically, particularly to decide whether negative views should be accepted. If a first report does not support a claim, consideration has to be given to the question of whether a conference with counsel and expert would be likely to be useful, or to whether a second medical expert opinion should be sought.

8.75 On the other hand it is also in no one's interests for experts to provide reports to plaintiffs which encourage a claim which cannot succeed. It is important for the lawyers acting on behalf of plaintiffs to identify such reports and not to accept them at face value.

8.76 A first report on liability issues having been received supporting the further investigation of a claim, consideration has to be given to what further expert opinions may be required from other specialities, if this has not already been put in hand. At this point a separate report may also be needed on condition and prognosis, as a Statement of Claim will have to set out particulars of injury.

Conference with counsel

8.77 Preliminary reports having been obtained, it is important to have a conference with counsel with experts and client present. The client should be invited even if this may be disruptive or inhibit certain discussions. In most of these cases a major grievance of plaintiffs is that doctors have been secretive and aloof. It is therefore essential that lawyers treat them with candour, involving them fully in every stage of the legal process.

8.78 If the preliminary reports do not support a claim being pursued, the role of counsel and solicitor will be to test the experts' views to satisfy the client that their opinions should be accepted, or to establish whether the expense of obtaining further opinions would be justified.

8.79 If the experts support a claim, the conference is a golden opportunity for counsel to consider what allegations of negligence should properly be included in the Statement of Claim. Subsequently a draft Statement of Claim should be circulated amongst experts before court proceedings are instituted.

Second stage reports

8.80 The Defence served in response to the Statement of Claim will rarely admit liability even if a decision has been made that the case is indefensible. Too often it will contain little more than denials but, if it asserts any kind of positive case, it should be circulated amongst the plaintiff's experts for their comments. At this stage, if not sooner, further experts' opinions should be obtained on liability issues. It is not safe to rely on the evidence of only one expert in each of the specialities in which the allegations of negligence are made.

Second conference with counsel

8.81 This is required after the plaintiff's solicitors have obtained all necessary reports on liability issues. The main purposes are to consider with the experts whether their reports are in a form suitable for exchange, and to review the pleadings. It is important to eradicate inconsistencies from their reports, to ensure that the experts do not stray outside their own specialities and to make certain that they have expressed their views in the way which they intended. It is desirable that this conference should take place after exchange of witness statements, so that these may be taken into account.

Medical literature

8.82 The Order for Directions should provide for exchange of literature lists by a fixed date before trial. As with the requirement for exchange of reports, this will prevent experts from being taken by surprise in the witness box by cross-examination in relation to references of which they are unaware. Experts should therefore be asked to consider what references they wish to rely upon and which should be included for exchange. They should also be invited to produce articles expressing contrary views so that account may be taken of them, even if these are not to be relied upon.

Final conferences with counsel

8.83 A third and possibly fourth conference with counsel will be required following exchange of reports and literature lists in preparation for trial. It is normally most advantageous to have the last conference very close to trial when preparations are almost complete, so that counsel can be certain of understanding all the medical intricacies before describing them in opening to the Judge and embarking upon examination and cross-examination of expert witnesses.

At trial

8.84 The best expert witness is usually the one whose evidence hardens up under cross-examination, not those who overstate their opinion in chief and who have to make concessions in cross-examination. Experts who provide opinions in a large number of legal cases are still unlikely to have given evidence on many occasions, and should not therefore be embarrassed to ask for advice as to how to present themselves. Evidence should not be given as a dissertation but rather by careful answers to the questions put.

8.85 It is desirable that those experts giving evidence on liability issues should hear how the plaintiff's counsel opens the case. The plaintiff's witnesses of fact will usually give their evidence first, and again it is desirable that experts on both sides should hear this if at all possible.

8.86 Traditionally the plaintiff's experts will be called next. However, it may be ordered that the defendant's witnesses of fact should give their evidence at this stage so that this may be taken into account and commented on by the medical experts on both sides when they give evidence subsequently. Consideration should therefore be given in advance of trial as to whether the parties should agree to this change in the normal order of witnesses. Failing agreement on this point, application for a Direction to this effect can be made to the Judge at commencement of trial.

8.87 The plaintiff's experts can expect to be released from remaining at court once cross-examination by the defendants' counsel has concluded. However, counsel on each side will normally hope to have at least one of their experts available in court throughout the evidence of the other side's expert witnesses in order to obtain assistance regarding the questions to be asked during cross-examination.

Experts' fees

8.88 Experts can expect to be very reasonably remunerated, whether they act for the plaintiff or defendants. Even if the plaintiff is legally aided, it should be possible for fees to be paid within six weeks by solicitors obtaining payment on account from the Legal Aid Fund. See paras **9.42** ff.

8.89 A problem sometimes arises concerning the payment of cancellation fees. Either party may find it necessary to agree in advance to pay experts for setting aside time to attend court in the event that an action settles near to trial. Although it has become easier to do so, the winning party may still have difficulty in recovering these fees from the other side upon taxation, i e assessment by the court. In legal aid cases, if cancellation fees cannot be recovered the plaintiff's experts will either go unpaid or the instructing solicitors will have to make payment themselves, as a legally aided person cannot be charged for any part of the work carried out under a civil Legal Aid Certificate.

8.90 Upon taxation, the taxing officers are inclined to take the view that if experts suddenly find themselves with time on their hands, they can usefully spend this in the laboratory, on research or in private treatment. This may not be realistic at short notice and many NHS consultants do not do private work.

8.91 If a locum has to be employed, it should be easy to recover the expense incurred even if in the event the expert does not have to attend court to give evidence. However, the taxing officer may take the view that a locum was not necessary for a full week. Where the expert has cancelled fee-paying patients, it may still be necessary to show that it has not been possible to replace them at short notice and that other fee-paying work was not available.

8.92 One disadvantage for plaintiff's experts is that, whilst Regional Health Authorities may agree to continue to pay NHS salaries to consultants giving evidence on behalf of the defence, they may be required to treat time taken off as unpaid leave.

8.93 It has been held[1] that where experts are unable to replace at short notice by other means earnings which they would have made giving evidence, prima facie the remuneration which they seek should reasonably be recoverable. Clearly the longer the notice of cancellation or the period for which fees are claimed, the harder it will be to obtain payment. Each case must depend on its own facts.

1 *Reynolds v Meston* (24 February 1986, unreported) per Bingham J.

8.94 It is recommended that, at the same time as applying for an Order for costs, the successful party at trial should ask the judge to give approval of specific cancellation fees. If liability is admitted in advance of trial, the plaintiff can insist on a short hearing before the trial judge, even if one is not otherwise necessary, in order to obtain approval of specific cancellation fees if this cannot be agreed with the defendant.

First interview

8.95 The following matters need to be dealt with:

(a) the client needs to be told that it will be an uphill battle with no certainty of success; also to have an explanation of the role of experts and of the test adopted by the court in deciding whether treatment was negligent;

(b) a warning should be given that negotiations and admissions of liability are usually delayed to a late stage and that the assessment of damages, save for financial losses, is ungenerous;

(c) where appropriate, applications for legal aid will need to be completed and the intricacies of legal aid explained;

(d) even if the client will qualify for legal aid, does he wish to incur initial expense to get disclosure of records under way whilst his application is being processed?

(e) where the client will not qualify for legal aid, costs need careful consideration. Very few individuals can afford to pursue an action for medical negligence privately. Many good claims are therefore not pursued as a result. Few contested medical negligence trials are likely to take less than one week and total legal costs in such cases can easily reach £50,000 with the added risk of having to pay the defendants' costs in the event of failure. Even where the client cannot afford the risk of costs of a full-blooded action for negligence, he may well wish to review the case after expert opinions have been obtained on the medical records and then make a final decision. Even if he cannot afford to proceed further, he will at least have an explanation of what went wrong and why, and an understanding of any shortcomings in the treatment provided;

(f) unless the client does not wish to incur the expense pending the grant of legal aid, sufficient factual information should be obtained to enable the solicitor to draft a letter with adequate details to justify disclosure of medical records and to particularise likely allegations of negligence. At this interview, or at least at an early stage, it will be necessary to obtain detailed statements from the client and witnesses as to what happened and what was said, before memories fade. Although the judge will always tend to prefer contemporaneous notes made in the medical records, there are often gaps and the treating doctors and nurses will be unable to recall details of surrounding circumstances relating to one out of thousands of patients whom they will have treated;

(g) the client should be told that he will be asked to approve draft letters to obtain medical records and that on average it takes two or three months after they are sent for the records to be released;

(h) when the records arrive, does the client want copies?

(i) it may be important to advise the client to delay the sending of letters before action until treatment by the doctors who are to be criticised has been completed. It may be sensible for him to ask his GP to refer his treatment to someone else; where the treatment being criticised is given in hospital, it is desirable to seek fresh treatment from a different health authority so that the new doctors involved do not feel inhibited in what they say or do out of misplaced loyalty to colleagues;

(j) it will be necessary to serve a medical report substantiating the personal injuries claimed, and a statement of special damages, at the commencement of proceedings.

Suggestions for change

8.96 Ideally a system would be introduced under which negligence would not be a requisite for compensation and yet patients could still receive substantial compensation together with a proper investigation into what went wrong. However this may be impossible to achieve and, in this event, it is necessary to make the most of the present procedures available. The benefits of improving training of medical students as to how to treat patients when unforeseen medical difficulties occur and of improving the procedure of investigating complaints have been discussed earlier in this chapter. If both these matters could be addressed effectively, there is no doubt that there would be a reduction in the number of claims being pursued through the courts, particularly if patients could be given freer access to their medical records and the need for the involvement of solicitors could be curtailed. However, there would still be a large number of cases requiring litigation and the major, repeated criticisms of the existing system are as follows:

(a) *The incompetence of solicitors* Many of the problems relating to the present system are caused by the lack of expertise of solicitors who act on behalf of plaintiffs in this difficult area of work. Specialist training is required and has become more readily available, largely due to the efforts of Action for the Victims of Medical Accidents. There are, however, still areas of the country where it is difficult to obtain competent legal assistance. The Law Society is at present working on proposals for the introduction of a Panel of Specialist Practitioners.

(b) *Expense* This will always remain a problem. Although legal aid needs to be made more widely available, the opposite has occurred as a result of the reduction in levels for financial qualification with effect from April 1993. There is however the prospect of the introduction of contingency fees, on the basis that lawyers would only be paid if a claim succeeds, and this would help those claimants who do not qualify for legal aid. Whilst it is clearly undesirable and impractical for lawyers here to take a share of damages, there is merit in their being allowed to charge a premium on costs to pay for those cases which do not succeed. A losing defendant should be ordered to pay the plaintiff's actual reasonable costs, not the less generous 'standard' costs as at present, plus a maximum premium of, say, 25 per cent which would be sufficient incentive for lawyers to take cases on a contingency basis.

(c) *Delay* The defendants regard it as advantageous to delay the settlement of claims until as near to trial as possible; if it were otherwise, there would be earlier admissions of liability or attempts to negotiate. Even if it is recognised that a claim will have to be met eventually, the fact of having to pay the legal costs of both sides is outweighed by the following advantages to them:
   (i) the payment of damages will be postponed; this may be fiscally desirable as interest ordered at trial or agreed in settlement will be less than the value of retaining funds for as long as possible. Added to this the health authority or Trust hospital may wish to make payment out of the following year's budget. An admission of liability may be delayed because, once it is made, the plaintiff will be entitled to an interim payment of damages;
   (ii) the plaintiff may die before trial thereby substantially reducing the size of the claim. This may reduce the period of pain and suffering to be compensated, or cancel any claim for future earnings and future nursing care;
   (iii) the plaintiff may lose nerve near to trial and settle for a lesser amount as a result, particularly if he is not legally aided and at risk for costs.

8.97 Where negligence has not occurred, it is of course correct that actions for medical negligence should be defended. Where it is clear that negligence has occurred and damage been done, liability should be admitted at an early stage. Where the merits are borderline because, for example, sub-standard treatment does not necessarily amount to negligence, there should be a greater willingness to negotiate a settlement, particularly if damages claimed are relatively small.

8.98 The changes in court procedure, whereby experts' reports and more recently witness statements have to be exchanged, have forced many earlier negotiated settlements. What is needed is positive encouragement for the defendants to settle claims where there is a material risk of losing at trial. In particular when a defendant makes an early decision that there is no defence to an action he should be encouraged to admit liability at that stage. The advantage of doing so should outweigh any disadvantage.

8.99 An early compromise cannot be achieved unless both sides want one. At present it suits the defendants' purse to delay negotiation until close to trial. The position could be changed by the imposition of penalty interest, or at least interest at a commercial rate on all damages recovered from the date of commencement of proceedings.

Acknowledgment

I gratefully acknowledge the contribution of Peter Latham (barrister) and Anne Winyard (solicitor) in the preparation of these precedents.

PRECEDENT A

Letter before action seeking pre-action disclosure of medical records

8.100

The District General Manager,
(District) Health Authority or The
Manager, [ ] Trust Hospital

Dear Sir,

Mrs Jane Smith (dob 8.9.58)
Hospital Records No:

1. We act for Mrs Jane Smith of who is contemplating a claim against you for damages for personal injuries suffered as a result of negligence in her treatment at Hospital, in May 1992.

2. At about 11.00 a m on 30 April 1992 our client was involved in a motor accident. She was taken to Hospital. At first it was believed that she had simply dislocated her left hip joint. However it was then realised that her hip was fractured and an operation was performed the following afternoon, on 1 May 1992.

3. Our client was admitted under the care of Mr A B Dash, Consultant Orthopaedic Surgeon, and the operation was performed by Mr A B Dot, Orthopaedic Registrar.

4. We understand that the purpose of the operation was, or ought to have been, to achieve by manipulation and/or fixation a satisfactory position of the fracture so as to promote healthy union in good alignment and to optimise our client's chance of regaining normal function in the limb.

5. Three days after the operation, when she first got out of bed, our client realised something had gone wrong. She found that her left leg was pointing inwards. She was told to keep trying to straighten it.

6. At about the beginning of the second week our client pointed out to Mr Dot that her left leg was about two and a half inches longer than her right leg and that her left leg was pointing in the wrong direction. He told her to use her muscles to correct this. Some two days later it seemed that he accepted that something had gone wrong in that he suggested that she accept a built up shoe.

7. On 13 June 1992 our client was discharged. On 26 June 1992, at an out-patient appointment, she was seen by Mr Dash. He examined her, called in Mr Dot, and pointed out to him that her hip had been fixed at 60 per cent internal rotation. He told her that she would require another operation.

8. Our client was readmitted on 1 July 1992 and a second operation was performed on 4 July 1992. She has since required two further remedial operations and is left with a serious disability. She suffers pain, requires two sticks to walk, cannot pursue her pre-accident hobbies and does not now feel able to have children.

9. We anticipate that the allegations which will be made on behalf of our client after we have had access to the hospital records and have obtained expert evidence will include those that the surgical operation was carried out incompetently and incorrectly, with a result which the employment of due care

and skill would have avoided; that there was unreasonable delay in observing the serious surgical mal-position of the fracture following the operation; and that the facts themselves evidence negligence. It may also be alleged that the consultant staff failed to ensure that the operation was performed by someone with the requisite degree of skill and experience.

10. We have set out sufficient particulars to make it clear that our client may well have a claim for negligence arising out of the treatment which she received at the Hospital; also to make it clear that this is a case where medical records should be disclosed to this firm without it being necessary for us to make application to the court under section 33(2) of the Supreme Court Act 1981.

11. We enclose a schedule setting out those documents which should be included.

12. We are not prepared to agree to disclosure being limited to a nominated medical adviser and there is no legal authority for making this requirement. You will appreciate that disclosure to us is essential so that we may advise our client properly as to whether personal injury proceedings brought by her would have reasonable prospect of success, and so that Counsel may draft a precise and well framed Statement of Claim to make it clear precisely what allegations will have to be met by the defence.

13. What we seek from you is, under section 33(2)(a), a list of all those documents which are or at any time have been in your possession, custody or power relating to our client and, under section 33(2)(b), copies of all such documents. The documents within your power do of course include those held by the Regional Health Authority. If any such documents were once but are not now in your possession, custody or power, please itemise them, state when you parted with them and what has become of them.

14. We therefore shall be grateful if you will:

(a) let us have confirmation within 21 days that you will give such disclosure within six weeks of the date of this letter;
(b) let us have within those six weeks either a list of documents or confirmation by reference to the enclosed schedule that the documents are all those which are or ever have been in your possession, custody or power; if you give such confirmation, and the documents are indeed complete, we shall not press for a list;
(c) let us have either the original documents upon our undertaking to copy them and return them to you within five working days (ten working days for the x-rays); or complete copies upon our undertaking to pay the reasonable charges involved;
(d) notify us if you believe that any of the relevant documents are in the possession, custody or power of someone else, identifying that other person;
(e) ensure that the relevant documents will be preserved in their entirety pending production, inspection and trial, notifying us immediately if it is not your intention to do so; and
(f) let us know if you believe that anyone else has responsibility for what has happened to our client, giving us full details now.

15. We emphasise the need for you to include all relevant documents held by the Regional Health Authority in this pre-action discovery. If however you require us to write separately to them in this regard, please let us know.

16. We enclose an authority signed by our client.

Yours faithfully,

Compton Carr

SCHEDULE

Surgical, medical, nursing, drug and other treatment and investigation notes and records, laboratory test reports and contractual documents relating to treatment for surgical, medical and nursing purposes, to include:

1 accident and emergency department record card
2 general practitioner's referral letter
3 admitting doctor's notes on examination
4 patient consent forms
5 ward doctor's clinical notes
6 operating records
7 anaesthetic records
8 intensive therapy records
9 daily nursing notes and book
10 laboratory requests and reports on blood and other bodily samples
11 ultrasound scans, reports, photographs and video tapes
12 electrocardiograms (ECG) and reports
13 echocardiograms and reports
14 electroencephalograms (EEG) and reports
15 temperature, pulse, blood pressure and respiration charts
16 prescription records
17 fluid balance charts
18 blood balance charts
19 blood transfusion records
20 head injury charts
21 X-ray plates, requests and reports
22 theatre registers
23 casualty registers
24 health visitor records
25 CFM records
26 perfusionist records
27 correspondence, including correspondence to and from other hospitals involved in treatment and with the general practitioner
28 internal memoranda
29 directives and circulars
30 doctor's own files relating to treatment of the patient and the type of treatment generally
31 documents relating to any untoward incident or accident investigation by the Hospital, District or Regional Health Authority or DHSS

In maternity cases

32 partogram
33 cardiotacograph (CTG) traces
34 progress of labour chart
35 community midwifery records

PRECEDENT B

In the High Court: originating summons under section 33(2) of the Supreme Court Act 1981 and Order 24, rule 7A of the Supreme Court Rules 1965

8.101

IN THE HIGH COURT OF JUSTICE
QUEEN'S BENCH DIVISION

In the Matter of Section 33 of the Supreme Court Act 1981; and
In the Matter of Order 24, Rule 7A of the Supreme Court Rules 1965

BETWEEN:

Jane Smith *Plaintiff*
and
(District) Health Authority or Trust Hospital *Defendants*

Originating Summons for production of documents before writ issued

LET all parties attend before the Master/District Judge in Chambers in Room No at on the day of 1994 at o'clock in the noon on the hearing of an application by the Plaintiff of an Originating Summons in this action.

LET THE DEFENDANTS within 14 days after service of this Summons on them counting the day of service return the accompanying Acknowledgment of Service to the appropriate Court Office.

BY THIS SUMMONS which is issued on the application of the Plaintiff Jane Smith of

The Plaintiff claims against the Defendants as persons likely to be a party to subsequent proceedings in the High Court in which a claim in respect of personal injuries to the Plaintiff is likely to be made and as persons who are likely to have or to have had in their possession, custody or power documents relevant to issues arising out of the claim and seeks orders:

1 Under Section 33(2)(a) of the Supreme Court Act 1981 and Order 24, Rule 7A of the Rules of the Supreme Court Act 1965 that the Defendants within 14 days do make and serve on the Plaintiff's solicitors a list verified by Affidavit sworn by their Distrist General Manager stating whether any documents included in the Schedule hereto in relation to the Plaintiff's treatment since 30 April 1992 at Hospital , which included a hip operation performed at the said Hospital on 1 May 1992, are or at any time have been in their possession, custody or power and if not then in their possession, custody or power when they parted with them and what has become of them.

2 Under Section 33(2)(b) of the Supreme Court Act 1981 and Order 24, Rule 7A of the Rules of the Supreme Court Act 1965 that the Defendants within 28 days produce such of those documents as are in their possession, custody or power to the Plaintiff and her solicitors with liberty further to disclose them limited to the Plaintiff's legal, medical, and other professional advisers and limited to the purposes of the likely subsequent proceedings in the High Court in respect of personal injuries.

3 And that the Defendants do pay the Plaintiff's costs of and occasioned by and incidental to these proceedings.

SCHEDULE

(As set out in Precedent A)

If the Defendants do not acknowledge service, such judgment may be given or Order made against and/or in relation to them as the Court may think just and expedient.

Dated the day of 1994

Note: This Summons may not be served later than 4 calendar months beginning with the above date unless renewed by order of the Court.

THIS SUMMONS was taken out by

Ref:
Tel:

Solicitors for the said Plaintiff whose address is as stated above.

IMPORTANT

Directions for Acknowledgment of Service are given with the accompanying form.

In the county court: notice of application under section 52 of the County Courts Act 1984 for pre-action discovery

8.102

IN THE COUNTY COURT CASE NO.

In the Matter of Section 52 of the County Courts Act 1984; and
In the Matter of Order 13, Rule 7(1)(g) of the County Court Rules 1981

BETWEEN:

A B *Plaintiff*
and
C D *Defendant*

Originating Application

Mr A B
of
applies to the court for an order in the following terms:

1. Under Section 52(2)(a) of the County Courts Act 1984 and Order 13, Rule 7(1)(g) of the County Courts Rules 1981, that the Defendants within 14 days do (as above in Originating Summons).

2. Under Section 52(2)(b) of the County Courts Act 1984 and Order 13, Rule 7(1)(g) of the County Courts Rules 1981 that the Defendants within 28 days do (as above in Originating Summons).
3. (As above in Originating Summons).

SCHEDULE

(As set out in Precedent A)

The grounds on which the Plaintiff claims to be entitled to the order are:

The Plaintiff claims against the Defendants

(1) as persons likely to be a party to subsequent proceedings in the County Court in which a claim in respect of personal injuries to the Plaintiff is likely to be made; and
(2) as persons who are likely to have or to have had in their possession, custody or power, documents relevant to issues arising or likely to arise out of the claim.

The names and addresses of the persons upon whom it is intended to serve this application are:

The Plaintiff's address for service is:

Dated the day of 19

THIS SECTION TO BE COMPLETED BY THE COURT

PRECEDENT C

Affidavit in support of originating summons

(can be adapted in support of Originating Application in the county court)

8.103

IN THE HIGH COURT OF JUSTICE 1993 J No
QUEEN'S BENCH DIVISION

In the Matter of Section 33 of the Supreme Court Act 1981; and
In the Matter of Order 24, Rule 7A of the Supreme Court Rules 1965

BETWEEN:

Janet Jones (*a minor suing by her father and next friend* MICHAEL JONES) *Plaintiff*

and

[ ] HEALTH AUTHORITY or Trust Hospital *Defendants*

Plaintiff's Affidavit in support of application for production of documents before Writ issued under Section 33 of the Supreme Court Act 1981 and RSC Order 24, Rule 7A

I, MICHAEL JONES of shop keeper,
MAKE OATH and say as follows:

1 I am the father and next friend of Janet Jones, the Plaintiff on this Originating Summons who was born on 26 January 1992.

2 I make this Affidavit in support of the Plaintiff's application under Section 33 of the Supreme Court Act 1981 for disclosure and production of documents before Writ issued in a proposed High Court personal injuries action.

3 There is now produced and shown to me marked *'MJ.1'* a copy of a letter dated 18 September 1992 which I understand the Plaintiff's solicitors sent to the Defendants and of the subsequent correspondence between her solicitors on the one hand and the Defendants and their solicitors on the other. I confirm that the said letter dated 18 September 1992 was approved by me before it was sent and that the information relating to the Plaintiff set out therein is accurate to the best of my knowledge and belief.

4 On 11 September 1992 the Plaintiff was granted a legal aid certificate to take proceedings by me as her father and next friend against the Defendants for damages for medical negligence.

5 For the purposes of Order 24, Rule 7A of the Rules of the Supreme Court:

(i) The Plaintiff is likely to be a party to subsequent proceedings in the High Court as Plaintiff.
(ii) A claim in respect of personal injuries to her is likely to be made in the High Court.
(iii) The Defendants in this Summons appear likely to be a party to the proposed proceedings as Defendants being responsible for the treatment which the Plaintiff received whilst at Redbridge Hospital between March and May 1992.

(iv) I am advised by my solicitors that the Defendants are likely to have or to have had in their possession, custody or power relevant documents for the proposed action as specified in paragraph 1 of the Originating Summons herein and that these documents are relevant to be disclosed and produced under Section 33 of the Supreme Court Act 1981. [I am also advised by them that they may have documents concerning statements, enquiries, clinical correspondence and medical reports on investigations at the time of the Plaintiff's treatment, and subsequently conducted with a view to discovering the most probable cause of the injury done to her at that time. In so far as these documents came into existence primarily with a view to ascertaining the causes therefore, I am advised by them that I am also entitled to disclosure and production of them.]

6 I seek an Order for disclosure and production of the above hospital documents under Section 33 of the Supreme Court Act 1981 with a view to submitting them to expert medical advisers so that I may obtain medical evidence with a view to bringing personal injury proceedings. I also wish my legal advisers to have these documents so that they may advise whether I have a reasonable prospect of success and, if appropriate, Counsel may draft a precise and well framed Statement of Claim on the Plaintiff's behalf to focus the allegations that the Defendants have to meet.

SWORN etc.

PRECEDENT D

Letters seeking disclosure of medical records by non-potential defendant (general practitioner)

8.104

Dear Dr

Jane Smith (*d.o.b. 8.9.58*)
Hospital Records No:

I am acting on behalf of Mrs Jane Smith of in a claim for medical negligence which she is contemplating against Health Authority, in respect of a hip operation which was carried out at Redbridge Hospital on 1 May 1992, and enclose a letter of authority signed by her authorising and requesting you to release any documents and information relating to her condition to my firm.

I have already asked the Health Authority to let me have copies of the Hospital records and anticipate that these will be supplied to me in due course. In the meantime, I shall be grateful if you will let me have copies of any documents in your possession relating to Mrs Smith's medical care and condition, including medical record cards, correspondence with hospitals and results of tests. These are required for the sake of completeness. Those relating to the period before her hospital treatment are also relevant in order to establish the state of her health before her hospital admission.

Alternatively if you prefer to lend me the original documents for photocopying I would return these to you within five working days. Either way, my firm will be responsible for the charges involved.

It is of course important that disclosure be given to me, and not only to the medical expert I shall be instructing, if I am to be able to handle this case properly.

[It would be helpful if at the same time you would supply a report relating to Mrs Smith's operation and her medical condition. If you are prepared to do so my firm will again be responsible for your reasonable fee.]

If there is any problem, please do not hesitate to telephone me.

Yours sincerely,

PRECEDENT E

Letters seeking disclosure of medical records by non-potential defendants (health authority or Trust hospital)

8.105

The Administrator/Manager
[ ] Hospital

Dear Sir

John Smith (*d.o.b. 27.2.41*)
Hospital Records No:

1. We have been instructed by Mr John Smith of who is contemplating a claim for damages for personal injuries suffered as a result of negligence in his treatment at Redbridge Hospital between 26 and 28 May 1992.

2. We enclose a copy of a letter which we have today written to the District General Manager at Health Authority requesting copies of the Hospital notes of Redbridge Hospital so that you may understand the basis of our client's claim.

3. The purpose of this letter to you is to request you to let us have copies of the Hospital notes for the period of our client's stay at Whitebridge Hospital between 28 May 1992 and 2 June 1992. He was readmitted to Redbridge Hospital on 2 June 1992.

4. We do not anticipate that there is any claim to be pursued in relation to the treatment which our client received at Whitebridge Hospital. He was transferred there for specialist life saving treatment following the personal injuries which he had already suffered at Redbridge Hospital. He was admitted to Whitebridge Hospital under the care of Mr A B Green, Consultant Orthopaedic Surgeon.

5. We refer to the Schedule attached to the letter sent to Health Authority and shall be grateful if you will let us have the medical records included in that Schedule relating to our client's treatment at Whitebridge Hospital. We hope that this will be done on a voluntary basis without the need for us to make application under Section 34(2) of the Supreme Court Act 1981.

6. We confirm that we shall be responsible for your reasonable charges in supplying photocopies of the documents and copies of the x-rays. We enclose a letter of authority signed by our client.

Yours faithfully,

____

PRECEDENT F

Summons under section 34(2) of the Supreme Court Act 1981 and Order 24, rule 7A applying for an order for disclosure for medical records by a non-potential defendant

8.106

IN THE HIGH COURT OF JUSTICE 1993 S No
QUEEN'S BENCH DIVISION

BETWEEN:

Jane Smith *Plaintiff*

and

[ ] HEALTH AUTHORITY or TRUST HOSPITAL *Defendants*

Let all parties concerned attend before the Master/District Judge in Chambers at on the day of 1993 at o'clock in the noon on the hearing of an application on the part of the Plaintiff for the following Orders as against Health Authority as persons who are likely to have or have had in their possession, custody or power documents relevant to issues arising or likely to arise in this action.

1 Under Section 34(2)(a) of the Supreme Court Act 1981 and Order 24, Rule 7A(2) of the Rules of the Supreme Court 1965 that Health Authority within 14 days make and serve on the Plaintiff's solicitors a list verified by Affidavit sworn by their District General Manager/Manager stating whether the documents set out in the schedule hereto are or ever have been in their possession, custody or power relating to the treatment of the Plaintiff at Whitebridge Hospital since January 1992; if any such documents were once but are not now in their possession, custody or power, identify those documents and state when they parted with them and what has become of them.

2 Under Section 34(2)(b) of the Supreme Court Act 1981 and Order 24, Rule 7A(2) of the Rules of the Supreme Court 1965 that Health Authority within 28 days produce such of those documents as are or have been in their possession, custody or power to the Plaintiff and her solicitors.

3 And that Health Authority/Trust Hospital do pay the costs of the application.

SCHEDULE

Dated the day of 1993

To: (1) Health Authority/Trust Hospital
(2) The Defendants

This Summons was taken out by

Solicitors for the Plaintiff

PRECEDENT G

Summons under Order 24, rule 7 applying for disclosure for medical records after writ has been issued

8.107

IN THE HIGH COURT OF JUSTICE 1993 S No
QUEEN'S BENCH DIVISION

BETWEEN:

John Smith *Plaintiff*

and

[ ] HEALTH AUTHORITY/TRUST HOSPITAL *Defendants*

Let all parties concerned attend before the Master/Registrar in Chambers at on the day of 1993 at o'clock on the hearing of an application on the part of the Plaintiff.

(a) Under Order 24, Rule 7 of the Rules of the Supreme Court 1965 that the Defendants within 14 days make and serve on the Plaintiff's solicitors a list verified by Affidavit sworn by the Defendants' District General Manager/Manager stating whether the documents set out in the schedule hereto are or have at any time been in their possession, custody or power and if not then in their possession, custody or power when they parted with them and what has become of them.
(b) Under Order 24, Rule 9 of the Rules of the Supreme Court 1965 that the Defendants within 28 days allow the Plaintiff's solicitors to inspect the documents referred to in the said list and said Affidavit (other than any which they object to produce) and to take copies thereof.
(c) That the Plaintiff's time for service of the Statement of Claim be extended for 72 days from service of the said list and Affidavit.
(d) That the Defendants do pay the costs of this application.

SCHEDULE

Dated the day of 1993

To: the Defendants

This Summons was taken out by

Solicitors for the Plaintiff

CHAPTER 9

Preparation of medical evidence on liability

Anne Winyard *Solicitor*

SUMMARY

THE ROLE OF THE SOLICITOR

9.1 The vital role in preparation of medical evidence on liability is that of the expert medical witness. In the UK, whilst the law imposes upon doctors a duty of care, the standard of care is a matter of medical, not legal, judgment. The courts do not determine standards of proper medical practice: these are set by the medical profession. A doctor treating a patient in accordance with approved medical practice (even a practice approved and followed only by a minority of the profession) cannot be found negligent.

9.2 McNair J's classic definition (for the jury) of the test of medical negligence in the case of *Bolam v Friern Hospital Management Committee*,[1] which has been approved by the House of Lords in *Maynard v West Midlands Regional Health Authority*,[2] is that a doctor

> is not guilty of negligence if he has acted in accordance with a practice accepted as proper by a responsible body of medical men skilled in that particular art . . . Putting it the other way round, a man is not negligent, if he has acted in accordance with such a practice, merely because there is a body of opinion who would take a contrary view. At the same time, that does not mean that a medical man can obstinately and pig-headedly carry on with some old technique if it has been proved to be contrary to what is really substantially the whole of informed medical opinion.

1 [1957] 2 All ER 118, [1957] 1 WLR 582.
2 [1985] 1 All ER 635, [1984] 1 WLR 634.

9.3 Hence expert medical evidence is crucial for both plaintiff and defendant as it is upon that medical evidence the judge (juries of course no longer try medical negligence cases) will rely in deciding whether or not the complained of treatment was negligent: that is, whether the conduct of the doctor fell below the standard of the reasonably competent medical practitioner in that field.

9.4 The solicitor's role in obtaining medical evidence on liability (one familiar to all experienced litigation lawyers, successful party-givers and effective interviewers) is that of the facilitator or metteur en scène. You must take the trouble to know the subject, to have your objectives clear, to assemble and set out your materials well and to pick the right people to join you.

9.5 The rest of this chapter examines these steps in more detail. Its writer is only ever instructed by plaintiffs and though much of what follows may be of interest or use to those representing the defendant, it is written from the point of view of a plaintiff's lawyer.

MEDICAL RECORDS

Why they must be released to the plaintiff's lawyer

9.6 A plaintiff's lawyer must obtain release to himself of his client's relevant medical records. This is a cardinal rule. A plaintiff's lawyer who agrees to release of his client's records to a medical expert whom he is proposing to instruct will never be able adequately to conduct the case.

9.7 There is a superficial appeal in the suggestion that only doctors can understand medical records so (the suggestion goes) as the plaintiff's lawyer would not be able to make head nor tail of them, the plaintiff patient's interests are best served by his or her expert medical adviser receiving the records direct. This superficial appeal does not stand up to legal or practical scrutiny and no plaintiff's (or defendant's) lawyer should be seduced by it.

There are a number of reasons why direct disclosure of records to the plaintiff's lawyer is essential, including the following:

(a) there is no legal basis for disclosure to be restricted to medical advisers only, as opposed to both medical and legal advisers. Whilst the court (under section 33(2) of the Supreme Court Act 1981) when ordering disclosure of records does have power to preclude disclosure to the plaintiff, the section gives the court no power to limit disclosure to a medical expert only, when the plaintiff also has a lawyer;
(b) if you have not seen the records, you can neither adequately take your client's instructions on their contents, nor properly and fully instruct your experts;
(c) you have to rely on your experts to tell you whether the records are complete and to quote key passages in their reports;
(d) medical records can be very difficult to photocopy and, apart from margins being cut off, thus obscuring crucial dates and times, your copy set frequently arrives containing a number of illegible pages and having been put through the randomising machine before despatch to you. The same presumably applies to copy sets sent direct to your experts. A busy expert witness, faced with a poorly copied and randomised set of xerox notes is not likely to do justice to his or her forensic skills;
(e) the defendants will know from the outset what expert witnesses you are using and will draw their own conclusions if, when reports on liability issues are exchanged, you fail to exchange a report from one of the experts to whom notes were sent;
(f) sometimes the first expert report you obtain is not satisfactory. It may be insufficiently thorough or insufficiently well argued (it can be difficult to ask pertinent questions of your expert when you have not seen the notes). It may be obviously biased or simply raise points which clearly justify a second opinion. You will then have to go cap in hand to the defendants to seek disclosure to a different expert and perhaps be met with the argument that the initial limited disclosure, to which you agreed, is all you are entitled to;
(g) there will inevitably be discrepancies between the plaintiff's memory of events and what is said in the case notes: that is if the plaintiff has any memory at all of what occurred. Many of these discrepancies are frankly irrelevant to the claim, though others (whether a particular injection was given, whether a consent form was signed) may be vital. If counsel pleads the Statement of Claim without access to the case notes, it may contain a number of details or timings, at variance with the account given in the case notes, which are not key issues for the plaintiff's case but which can then be exploited by the defendants to make the plaintiff appear unreliable or, worse, untruthful and to cast doubt on the validity of the plaintiff's key assertions.

What do medical records look like and contain?

9.8 It can be daunting receiving a set (particularly a photocopied set) of medical records. This section (in the preparation of which I have relied not only upon my own experience but also upon information kindly provided by Dr David Kirby) is intended as a short 'guided tour' and an indication of the documents you can expect to receive on discovery under the Supreme Court Act 1981, section 33. Some illustrations are also included. The subsequent sections contain suggestions on how to deal with medical records.

Hospital records: usually in A4 folder

9.9

(1) Admission record sheet: personal details, date/time of admission, record number, name of consultant, ward. Now often in form of computer print-out.

(2) In-patient medical notes:
 (a) notes made in casualty;
 (b) a first lengthy 'clerking' note (usually by junior doctor) with full history and examination. See para **9.10**;
 (c) daily progress notes;
 (d) typed discharge summary (may be dated months after discharge).

(3) Out-patient medical notes: sometimes typed.

(4) Nursing Kardex (now also known as Nursing Process) (see Figures 9.1–9.4): nurses' notes. Just as valuable to you as medical notes. Nurses are often more forthright and frequently *name* the medical staff whose indecipherable hieroglyphic initials you cannot work out from medical notes. Dates/times usually down right margin and signatures down left margin.

(5) Nurses charts: temperature, pulse, blood pressure, respiration, fluid balance etc (see Figures 9.6–9.8).

(6) Test and investigation results (see Figures 9.9–9.11): usually on small (6″ × 4″) sheets of computer printout stuck sequentially onto one central gummed strip on an A4 'backing sheet' for each category, eg biochemistry, haematology, X-ray report/request forms. These investigation results are the ones you will find hardest to copy and hardest to understand. Don't worry – ask your expert(s) to explain purpose of tests and significance of the results.

(7) Drug sheets (see Figure 9.5): showing what drugs prescribed and administered. Now often in form of computer print-out.

(8) Correspondence: such as GP referral letters, letters to GP after out-patient visit, letters to other hospitals/doctors. Correspondence can sometimes provide interesting insights – not least because it is written in the Queen's English, not sign language.

(9) Ancillary workers' records, eg physiotherapy, social work, psychological assessment. *Not* kept with main records. You should make sure you call for them if they are relevant to the claim and not disclosed with main batch of records.

(10) X-rays themselves: get your own copies (made by the defendant's or an independent X-ray technician).

(11) Anaesthetic record: on a separate sheet. Front looks rather like admission sheet. First part is filled in by anaesthetist when patient seen before operation. Bottom part records drugs given for pre-med and during operation. On back is a chart for blood pressure etc.

(12) Consent forms for operations.

(13) Labour and delivery:

(a) frequently there are separate 'progress of labour' sheets on which entries are made by both midwives and doctors;
(b) cardiotocograph (CTG) traces. These are continuous electronic double trace recordings of fetal heart (top line) and maternal contractions (bottom line). There may be several. Some can be very long (10–20 feet). They look like an old fashioned barometric trace. The more modern machines record real time on the trace. If a belt monitor was used during labour and/or baby had scalp electrode clipped on there should be CTG traces. They are *vital* for your expert obstetrician. They often 'get lost'. *Insist* on having them. It is important that your (and particularly your experts') copies of these traces are on *continuous* paper. Some FAX machines can be adjusted to provide continuous roll copying. Otherwise you must have the traces professionally copied at a copy shop with continuous roll paper copying facilities;
(c) partogram: manual record in chart form of progress of labour;
(d) if mum had a 'co-operation' card during pregnancy, that should be returned to her after the birth. Get hold of it. The card has the usual identifying details of the patient plus details of (blood and other relevant) tests, brief entries for each ante-natal visit and information about the birth.

(14) Neonatal unit charts: typical records used in all neonatal units.

Basic structure of hospital medical notes

9.10 The initial systematic 'clerking note' made by a junior doctor will probably be set out along the following lines (NB nurses keep their notes *separately* – on the nursing Kardex):

C.O.	Complains of
H.P.C.	History of presenting complaint; duration in years, ×/52 (weeks) or ×/7 (days)
P.M.H	Previous medical history (P.O.H. – previous obstetric history)
F.H.	Family history
S.H.	Social history (e g work, smoking, drinking habits, co-residents)

Systematic enquiry:

G.I.T.	Gastro-intestinal tract
G.U.T.	Genito-urinary tract
C.V.S.	Cardiovascular system
R.S.	Respiratory system
C.N.S.	Central nervous system
Neuro	(logical)
Psych	(iatric)
Musculo	(skeletal)
Drugs (current medication)	
Allergies (reaction to drugs in the past)	

O/E	On examination	
General	Appearance, whether anaemic, cyanosed, thyrotoxic, drunk etc	
C.V.S.	(Cardiovascular system) p. . . . . pulse rate; B.P. . . . ./. . . . blood pressure; H.S. heart sounds	
R.S.	(Respiratory system) T...... tracheal position, Expansion R = L, PN: percussion, B.S. breath sounds	
Abdo	(Abdomen) softness, tenderness, masses felt	
	L.S.K.K.	(Liver, spleen and kidneys) – whether these organs palpable (and if so that indicates they are enlarged)
	P.R.	rectal examination (per rectum)
	P.V.	vaginal examination (per vaginam) – uterus, adnexae, cervix, vagina
	B.S.	bowel sounds
C.N.S.	(Central nervous system)	
	Cranial nerves Motor system: power, tone, co-ordination, reflexes Sensory system: pain, touch, temperature, etc.	

9.11 This systematic examination will probably be followed by a summary, a diagnosis (△), a treatment plan, instructions about what observations the nurses are to make, what tests are to be done, drugs given etc. There will then follow subsequent daily/hourly/monthly notes: their frequency depending upon the patient's condition and the doctor's diligence.

General practitioner records

9.12 Usually in cardboard FP5 'envelope' with patient's name, address, NHS number, GP name, date of registration and Family Practitioner (FPC) stamp. Contains:

(a) FP 7 record cards: doctor's notes;
(b) reports, eg from local hospitals of test/investigation results;
(c) letters from, eg hospital out-patient clinics or in-patient discharge summaries.

Structure of GP notes

9.13 Many GPs' notes are highly abbreviated and follow no 'standard' system. Some use the 'SOAP' system, ie:

S subjective (patient's complaint)
O objective (doctor's findings)
A analysis (diagnosis)
P plan (treatment, advice, referral).

How to deal with medical records

9.14 Doctors are reputed to have illegible handwriting. Some do, but so do many lawyers or surveyors or accountants. Doctors and nurses however, unlike lawyers, surveyors or accountants, still write most of their records by hand without recourse to a typewriter or a dictaphone. They also use a confusing (to non-medics) medley of hieroglyphs and abbreviations.

9.15 It is not unusual for a plaintiff's solicitor to be sent the original set of hospital medical records. I do fairly frequently receive original sets of GP records on loan to inspect, copy myself and return.

9.16 Medical records are difficult to copy. Copying is customarily delegated to a relatively lowly employee whose efforts, in my experience, are infrequently checked before the whole horrid and incomplete mess is despatched to me.

9.17 Receipt of that big bundle of indistinct and incomplete photocopies with many edges cut off so you cannot read the dates or times and apparently lacking any logical sequence is the point at which many of us feel tempted to give up or perhaps despatch them quickly in a fresh envelope to our medical expert. Don't! It is imperative you sort them out and do your best to understand the important entries.

Equipment and reference books

9.18 For the task (apart from the whisky in the bottom drawer of the filing cabinet and the wet towel to wrap round your head) you can usefully equip yourself with a heavy duty double hole punch, a supply of folders and treasury tags or lever arch files with dividers. A photocopier with a collator and an efficient copying clerk (who understands the importance of best quality reproductions) is an extra bonus.

9.19 I have included a glossary of some common hieroglyphs and abbreviations under para **9.101**.

9.20 You will find an up-to-date medical dictionary useful, together with a short basic medical text. It is not expensive to acquire a rudimentary medical library. Second-hand medical texts can be acquired reasonably cheaply from medical bookshops or borrowed from medical libraries. If you come by an old edition of a standard text, or are buying the later edition, hang on to the old one. The 1990 edition will come in useful when you are trying to ascertain what standard practice was at the time of your client's complained of treatment in 1991. There are a number of 'pocket guides' intended for house officers or nurses which provide a useful introduction to an area of medicine you are unfamiliar with.

9.21 For the purpose simply of acquiring a basic understanding of the medical background to your client's case, you will probably be able to do without the larger and much more expensive standard medical texts. If these are subsequently required, for example to ascertain what procedures these standard texts recommend or risks they warn of, the texts can be borrowed from or referred to at a library.

9.22 Two of the most useful publications I have are the *Medical Directory* and the *Medical Register*, both published annually. Entry in the latter, which is published by the General Medical Council, is compulsory for all doctors fully or provisionally registered in the Principal List. The entries are, however, brief, consisting of name, registration date, address, qualification and registration number.

9.23 The *Medical Directory* is the medical *Who's Who*. Inclusion is voluntary but the majority of practitioners (particularly those longer qualified) are listed. The entries are more detailed than those in the *Register* and frequently include details of previous posts and publications. In the back of the *Directory* are useful lists of Regional and District Health Authorities, hospitals, consultants at each hospital etc.

9.24 Both the *Directory* and the *Register* can be obtained second-hand and are invaluable to identify practitioners – either those who treated your client or those you wish to instruct. Never throw away your old *Directories* and *Registers*. They are invaluable when trying to identify practitioners who treated your client in past years.

A suggested modus operandi

9.25 This, with variations depending on the nature of the case and the notes, is my system. You probably have or will develop your own method of dealing with medical notes.

(1) Before tackling the notes I re-read my client's proof of evidence to remind myself of the history.

(2) Sort the notes out into logical order, within reason approximating as closely as possible to the way the originals would (or should) have been kept. For GP notes this is simple: record cards in date order followed by correspondence, discharge summaries, test/investigation results also in date order. For hospital records a sensible order is admission sheet, medical notes, nursing Kardex, nurses charts, test/investigation results (if these are very numerous they should be split into separate categories such as 'haematology', 'bio-chemistry' etc), correspondence: each section in date order. If there have been multiple admissions the process is repeated for each. Of course there may well be a number of other sections for other types of document such as consent forms, anaesthetic records etc. As I am doing this sorting process I flag any sheets which require re-copying because they have edges cut off or are indistinct and check as best I can to see if the records appear complete. Sometimes there are obvious pages missing or, in the notes or correspondence, there is reference to items that are not present.

(3) Call for any obviously missing items (have you been sent CTG traces? X-ray request/report forms?) and adequate copies of illegible or partially obscured documents. In the case of the latter (of which there is often a substantial number) there is no reason why you should pay further copying charges.

(4) Arrange for the defendants (or 'your' technician/copy shop) to provide reproductions of X-ray plates, ultrasound scan plates, cardiotocograph traces (which *must* be on continuous paper) and other such items which cannot be routinely photocopied.

(5) At the same time I make an appointment (save in the most straightforward cases, where the notes are limited in volume and appear complete) to inspect the original notes and compare these with 'my' copies. I used to do this much later in the case but now find it saves time to do it early because in nearly all cases (with hospital records) you discover copies of some documents have been omitted from your bundle and if there is one thing worse than having to prepare multiple copy sets of paginated bundles of medical records for your experts and counsel, it is having to do it *twice*!

(6) When satisfied your set is complete and in logical order, flag each of the sections with dividers and punch and file your 'original' copy set in some convenient way – folder with treasury tags (easier to keep with the file) or lever arch file (label the spine clearly with client's name, file number etc so you can spot it at a glance on the shelf). Number the right hand top corners of each copy page of the records (so that you, counsel and your experts can then refer to 'page 69' without having to spend ages identifying the document you are discussing) and prepare an index. I usually label this set of notes clearly 'Original set – not to leave our office'. Then *all* the subsequent copy sets which you will have to produce for experts and counsel can be taken from this 'first generation' set of copies and you will not be left either bereft of any copies at all or with a totally illegible 'third generation' copy set of documents from which it is impossible to produce further legible sets.

(7) Dictate a transcript of the crucial parts of the notes, preferably to be prepared on the word processor for subsequent amendment. It is usually relatively easy to identify which parts of the notes are important for your case e g:

    (a) alleged mismanaged labour causing brain damage to child – the labour and delivery notes together possibly with parts of the ante-natal notes and possibly some neo-natal paediatric notes;
    (b) operation where it is alleged a surgical or anaesthetic error occurred – the operation note and/or the anaesthetic record/notes.

    The difficult part is understanding the handwriting, the hieroglyphs and the abbreviations (see Glossary). You can in due course ask your experts to correct or complete this transcript. It will save you and counsel a great deal of time to have a typed transcript of the relevant case note extracts: which will also be required by the judge if the matter proceeds to trial.

(8) Go through the notes (or transcript) with your client. In all but exceptional cases (or the very rare case where the Order precludes disclosure to the client) I lend 'my' set of notes and provide a copy of my transcript to the client to read in advance of the appointment. It is important to clarify at an early stage where your client's recollections (if any) are at variance with what is recorded in the notes.

YOUR MEDICAL EXPERTS

What speciality?

9.26 In many cases this is fairly obvious. Do remember you will often need more than one expert to cover the liability issues of alleged negligence and causation of disability:

(1) Alleged mismanaged labour resulting in brain damaged baby – *obstetrician* to report on question of negligence (was the labour mismanaged?), *paediatrician* to opine on causation (are the child's handicaps caused by the obstetric mismanagement – for example resulting in fetal anoxia during labour?).
(2) Babies and children – *paediatrician*. As in many disciplines there are specialisms within specialisms: centres like Great Ormond Street in London have a number of refined paediatric specialities such as paediatric surgery, paediatric endocrinology, paediatric cardiology etc. If the advice you require relates to the treatment of a newborn child you should consult a *neonatologist*. If the advice you require is essentially on quantum (long-term prognosis, recommendations for treatment, therapies, special education and so on) you will find a *developmental paediatrician* helpful.
(3) Brain damage or paralysis – *neurologist* or *neuropsychiatrist* (if the brain damage has caused behavioural and personality changes). Depending upon the cause of the brain damage you are likely to need another expert to help you on the question of negligence, e g *anaesthetist* if your client collapsed under general anaesthetic.
(4) Allergic reactions (which come in a wide variety of forms *not* restricted to skin rashes or vomiting: for example alleged anaphylactic reaction to anaesthetic drugs) – *immunologist* may be able to advise (perhaps after further testing) on whether there was an allergic reaction to a particular substance or drug. Depending upon the cause of the allergic reaction you may well need a second expert to advise on negligence – for example an *anaesthetist* if it was an anaesthetic drug reaction.
(5) Spinal surgery – *neurosurgeon* (or possibly orthopaedic surgeon).
(6) Bones/fractures – *orthopaedic consultant*.
(7) Ear, nose and throat – *otorhinolaryngologist* (ENT specialist).
(8) Eyes – *ophthalmologist* or *ophthalmic surgeon*.
(9) Heart – *cardiologist* or *cardiac surgeon*.
(10) Lungs and chest – *chest physician* or *thoracic surgeon*.
(11) Bladder, ureters, prostate and related plumbing (male or female) – *urologist* or *genito-urinary surgeon*.
(12) Gastro-intestinal tract (stomach, bowel, rectum) – *gastro-enterologist* or *gastro-enterological surgeon; colo-rectal surgeon*.
(13) Blood (e g rhesus problems, Sickle Cell Disease) – *haematologist*.
(14) Cancer treatment – *oncologist* (cancer specialist) and/or *radiotherapist* (specialist in *treatment* radiation as opposed to *radiologist* who is a specialist in using diagnostic radiation, e g X-rays to detect bony abnormalities or injuries).
(15) 'Female' surgery (sterilisation, hysterectomy etc) – *gynaecologist* (of course obstetrics and gynaecology are a combined speciality).

9.27 If you find yourself unable to work out the relevant specialism you may get some help by looking up the doctors who treated your client in the *Medical Directory* to ascertain *their* specialist qualifications. Alternatively you can give a brief history to a friendly medical contact or to AVMA and get advice.

Your experts' other qualities

9.28 An eminent expert is of course more likely to impress the judge and, prior to that, the defendants, when medical reports are exchanged under RSC Order 38, rule 37: also, probably, to be less afraid of 'ruining her career' by giving evidence for a plaintiff. Equally you should bear in mind, for example in a GP negligence case, the need for evidence from an appropriate independent (comparator) GP expert witness to advise on accepted standards of general practice. One cannot rely solely on consultant advice about standards of care in general practice. Be alert, when acting for a plaintiff, to the potential downside in having one of the country's leading experts as a liability witness, criticising the standard of diagnosis or treatment in a local general hospital. Your eminent expert's evidence (written and oral) must make plain the standards applied are not those of excellence, but those of ordinary minimum competence.

9.29 An expert with previous medico-legal experience is more likely to set out reports clearly and to understand the way the legal system works.

9.30 Some doctors 'close ranks' and are unwilling to advise a plaintiff. Others – more dangerous from the plaintiff's point of view – evince a willingness to assist and then, because of conscious or subconscious bias, prepare an unjustifiably unfavourable report. Instructing the right expert is vital to avoid this problem.

9.31 It is not wise or appropriate to instruct an expert who works at the same hospital or in the same District Health Authority as those you are suing. Preferably try to avoid experts who work in the same Regional Health Authority.

9.32 If an expert is recommended to you and you are only given the address of his private consulting rooms, it is essential you check his *Medical Directory* entry for details of his NHS appointment. If you do not, sooner or later you will have the same embarrassing experience as I did, some years ago, having written to a recommended expert at his private consulting rooms to ask for help on a case. In my letter I gave brief details of the history and treatment at the complained of hospital and received an understandably tart reply saying the surgeon had been one of those treating my client and he did not feel there was any negligence.

How do you find the right expert?

9.33 If, having identified the appropriate specialism, neither you nor your counsel know of a suitable expert to instruct, you will have to rely on the grapevine.

9.34 Most solicitors and barristers dealing with any volume of medical negligence work keep details of experts they have successfully worked with on previous cases. Alternatively you may be able to obtain a recommendation from a doctor in a different speciality whom you know and trust from a previous medical negligence case: or you can identify and approach plaintiff's experts from medical negligence case reports. You will find the *Medical Register* and *Directory* invaluable for this exercise.

9.35 Be wary, in general, of the local surgeon who has given you able help over the years by providing reports on accident cases. Medical negligence work is very different.

9.36 Fortunately, if your personal grapevine lets you down, you can, upon payment of a modest annual fee, join AVMA's Lawyers Resource Service.

9.37 They (from their own experience and that of their members) will often be able to recommend a suitable expert. Before providing you with a recommendation (which they will do as often as you need) they will wish, quite properly in my view, to be sure you have had the case notes disclosed to yourself.

Treat your experts properly

9.38 There is growing anxiety in the medical profession about professional negligence litigation. Fears are expressed about the effect this is having upon medical practice. The anxiety stems from an increase in the number and the size of claims made against doctors and health authorities. Prior to the introduction on 1 January 1990 of 'Crown Indemnity' arrangements, making health authorities alone responsible for claims against employed doctors, subscriptions to the three defence organisations – Medical Protection Society (MPS), Medical Defence Union (MDU) and Medical and Dental Defence Union of Scotland (MDDUS) – had increased steeply. Doctors, of course, were not alone in facing increases in premia: in fact the rates actually paid by doctors appeared 'to be towards the lower end of the range for professional liability premiums'.[1] Health authorities do not carry insurance for professional negligence claims, which are paid out of budget. Anxieties have been expressed about the proportionate effect a large claim could have upon the budget of an NHS Trust.

1 *Medical Negligence – Compensation and Accountability* (Oxford, Kings Fund Institute and Centre for Socio-legal Studies, 1988).

9.39 Here is not the place to explore the nature or validity of the litigation-related fears of the medical profession. Suffice it to say that we lawyers are generally regarded as being at the root of the problem and as spelling Trouble.

9.40 When approaching and instructing medical experts, particularly to report for a plaintiff, it is therefore important to explain the legal procedures, the time scale and where your experts fit into the legal process. Ill-prepared documentation and poorly drafted instructions (containing no indication of the issues the report should address and no hint as to what you intend to do with the report when you receive it) will make your experts worry about whether they can trust you to handle the legal side of the case properly and will make them chary about helping you.

9.41 Most non-lawyers (doctors are no exception) do not understand that the best run medical negligence case can easily take three to five years from first instructions to trial. You should keep your experts informed of progress of a case and should always notify them of the outcome if the case is settled or discontinued before trial. As a general note this courtesy should also be extended even to those experts whose views you did not, in the end, rely upon. It is essential you liaise closely with your experts when fixing a trial date.

Payment of experts' fees

9.42 It is also advisable to get the question of experts' fees straight from the start. A solicitor is responsible for paying the proper costs of an expert witness instructed on behalf of the client, whether or not the solicitor receives payment by the client. Experts are under no obligation to await the outcome of taxation, unless they have agreed in advance to do so.

9.43 It is wise, unless you know the level of your expert's fees from previous experience, to obtain a fee estimate in advance and have this approved by your client (whether legally aided or not) before firmly instructing the expert to report. A solicitor must always seek the client's authority for any unusual or expensive step (see *Re Solicitors, Re Taxation of Costs*[1]). In Legal Aid cases it is wise (unless you are confident you can justify the fee on taxation) to obtain, in addition, advance authority for the expert's estimated maximum fee under regulation 61 of the Civil Legal Aid (General) Regulations 1989. The current Legal Aid form to use is CLA 31. This authority is *not* the same as an extension of the scope of the Legal Aid Certificate to cover obtaining a medical report (currently applied for on form CLA 30). It is specific approval for that expert's maximum fee and affords protection against ex post facto reduction of experts' fees on taxation.

1 [1982] 2 All ER 683, [1982] 1 WLR 745.

9.44 Under RSC Order 62 both legal aid and inter partes taxations (except in unusual cases so far as inter partes taxations are concerned) are on the 'standard' basis which, per RSC Order 62, rule 12(1), gives 'a reasonable amount for all costs reasonably incurred' with the benefit of any doubt being accorded to the paying party. Taxing masters do nonetheless still appear to accept that certain items which may be disallowed against the paying party on a 'standard' basis taxation, can be allowed against the Legal Aid Fund on that same basis. Such items are often referred to as 'starred' items. In other words this is yet another case of plus ça change, as prior to the introduction of the current RSC Order 62 in 1986 a taxing master might disallow all or part of an expert's fees against the paying party (on the 'party party' basis of taxation) but allow the balance (so long as the client's approval and regulation 61 authority had been obtained) on the more generous 'common fund' basis against the Legal Aid Fund.

9.45 Experts should be paid as promptly as possible. When asking a private client to approve an expert's estimated fee it is wise to seek moneys on account. When acting for a legally aided client seek (under regulation 100 of the Civil Legal Aid (General) Regulations 1989 using form CLA 28) moneys on account from the legal aid office so you may pay your expert without 'drawing' on office account. Unless specifically agreed, your expert is not obliged to wait until you are in funds to be paid himself.

9.46 Some experts, either when booked for a trial or, more frequently, when a case is settled shortly before trial, seek 'Commitment fees' or 'standby payments'. This is a species of fee not favoured by taxing masters nor (unsurprisingly) by paying parties, be these parties your client or the opposition. Why, it is argued, should a medical expert, being a busy and distinguished person with more work available than s/he can fit in, a queue of private patients waiting for cancellations and a mound of medico-legal reports to prepare, be paid for a court attendance that in the end was unnecessary (even though cancelled at the last moment) as no financial loss will have resulted. In the unreported case of *Reynolds v Meston*,[1] a consultant neurologist, an opthalmic surgeon and a clinical psychologist were allowed the commitment fees (£300, £300 and £250) they had claimed when a case was cancelled 24 hours before the hearing. The BMA gave evidence that in Scotland and Northern Ireland it was standard practice for a witness to receive a half fee if a case is cancelled within seven days of the hearing and a full fee if the cancellation is within 48 hours. Bingham J stressed that each case for payment must be judged on its own merits but also said:

> The court is undoubtedly very much assisted by the expert evidence of medical and other witnesses at the peak of their professions. If such men are to respond to invitations to give expert evidence in court and to keep time free for that purpose, it is right that they should not run the risk of a last minute cancellation which would leave them substantially out of pocket. No doubt such witnesses are very conscious of a public duty to assist those finding themselves in the unfortunate position of this plaintiff. But there comes a point at which response to public duty cannot make demands beyond a certain limit on the personal goodwill of any expert, however eminent. It would, therefore, be very unfortunate if witnesses such as these were deterred from making their services available and if the court were dependent on the evidence of those who had no very pressing demands on their time.

1 Bingham J (24 February 1986, unreported).

9.47 I have had difficulty persuading the legal aid office to grant regulation 61 authority for commitment fees (when my experts seek an agreement from me for such fees in advance). I always ask my expert (see Precedent No 1) to provide a supportive letter to back the application. In some cases, where Legal Aid advance authority is none the less refused, I have reluctantly felt obliged, with my client's agreement, to agree, with an expert, commitment fees on a similar basis to those allowed in the *Reynolds v Meston* case. I only do so very rarely when regulation 61 authority is refused as, should the commitment fee be disallowed on taxation, I (or rather my firm) have to pay it from my (our) own pocket. This is a problem peculiar to Legal Aid cases. If, when acting for a private client, an expert's commitment fee is agreed (with the client's approval) but disallowed on taxation against the paying party, the client can't complain about having to reimburse the solicitor. However, regulation 64 of the Civil Legal Aid (General) Regulations 1989 precludes a solicitor from receiving a payment direct from a legally aided client.

9.48 Hence regulation 61 advance authority is the only way a solicitor acting for a legally aided client can be sure that if, on taxation, the commitment fee is disallowed against the paying party, the Taxing Master must none the less order it to be paid by the Legal Aid Fund (ie out of the client's damages in a successful claim). In any event, whenever you agree a commitment fee with an expert, you should notify the opposition of the agreement so they cannot subsequently complain their settlement offer would have been timed differently had they been aware of it. At the end of the day, however, having made such an agreement with an expert, the solicitor must pay the expert as agreed – whether or not the expert's commitment fee is recouped from the legal aid office, the client or on taxation.

OBTAINING THE REPORTS YOU NEED

Instructing your expert

9.49 Before formally instructing your chosen expert it is both courteous and prudent to check whether s/he is willing to accept instructions and if so when, and at what cost, s/he can report. On the question of experts' fees, and having these approved in advance by both client and legal aid office. Precedent No 2 is a specimen letter of approach to a medical expert.

9.50 Your formal letter of instruction (an example is included as Precedent No 3) should make quite plain what you want the expert to do, seek explanations of any specific points you do not understand in the notes, summarise the factual and legal background and the progress of the litigation and enclose all documentation. Your expert should be left in no doubt about what you intend to do with the requested report when you receive it.

9.51 It is worth taking care to send a complete and well organised set of documentation. Depending upon the nature of the case you will need to include:

(a) copies of case notes (as re-ordered and numbered by you: inviting your expert to refer to 'your' page numbers);
(b) reproductions of any X-ray plates, cardiotocograph traces etc;
(c) your client's statement together with any comments your client has on the case notes. Take care you do not send your expert that impressionistic first proof of evidence that might give a false impression of naivete or unreliability on the part of the client;
(d) your typed summary of relevant sections of the records (asking your expert to complete/amend);
(e) in a fatal case – coroner's notes of evidence and post mortem report.

9.52 It is wholly inappropriate to ask your expert simply to tell you whether there has been negligence or not. You are the lawyer and that question is yours to answer. In this context 'negligence' is a term of art which requires proper legal explanation. All the more so as customary English usage of the word connotes dangerous and carefree recklessness implying unfitness ever to practise again. Negligence is an emotive word. If you do not ask the appropriate questions your expert (particularly if s/he has little medico-legal experience) may well think 'there but for the grace of God . . .' and you will get a defensive report containing comments such as 'This is the kind of mistake any doctor could make and cannot in my view be negligent'.

9.53 Remember to point out to your expert the burden of proof for civil cases is 'on the balance of probabilities'. A doctor's previous medico-legal experience may be restricted to criminal work. More importantly you are asking a scientist to deviate from the habits of a professional lifetime by saying 'yes' if 51 per cent convinced of the facts, rather than declining to do so until 99.5 per cent convinced.

Interpreting the report

9.54 There are as many different types of report as there are authors.[1] Some experts write 'mini-theses' quoting relevant passages in extenso from case notes and text books, both to explain the subject or to show how the defendant failed to follow accepted procedures or take well known precautions against inherent risks. Others prepare a couple of terse pages effectively summarising their conclusions without giving background information or explanation of the subject or going into minute detail about the reasons behind the views they have expressed.

1 Guidance is given on the preparation and content of medical reports in Chapter 10.

9.55 Whichever type of report you receive from your experts, a first essential is to translate any word you do not understand with the help of a medical dictionary. If you are still confused ask your expert for an explanation.

9.56 Check that your experts have addressed the matters you feel are important and that they are, as requested by you, dealing with their answers to the issues on the appropriate basis for a civil case: namely answering questions to 'balance of probabilities'.

9.57 If the report supports your client's case, don't just breathe a sigh of relief. Analyse the report carefully and critically. Check that the positive points are closely argued and, where appropriate, supported by references. Does the report explain the points against the writer's conclusions, as well as those in favour? It is a reasonable indication a report is realistic if it does so.

9.58 A negative report also merits careful analysis. Look out for points such as:

(a) 'Nowadays, this condition is relatively easy to treat using . . . but in 1992. . . .' Call for published references. If you can, make your own checks in standard texts to see if you can find a pre-1992 reference to the then 'unavailable' treatment.
(b) 'This condition cannot be diagnosed without special equipment.' What special equipment? Why was it not available? If the equipment is expensive, why was the patient not referred to a specialist centre where such equipment was available?

(c) 'In a proportion of cases the femoral shaft does split when it is being drilled for the prosthesis.' If this is a known risk what are the known precautions? Were these taken? Was the patient warned of the risk? Have you got an informed consent case?

(d) 'Although the treatment given was far from satisfactory I do not think this affected the outcome as . . . [the original condition] . . . frequently results in severe limitation of movement.' In what proportion of cases does severe limitation of movement result? Call for published references. Was your client truly in a 'poor prognosis' category judged, for example, by age or progress/cause of the original condition?

9.59 Be alert for reports which, whilst supporting your client's case on liability issues of alleged negligence and causation of disability, seek to minimise, subtly or otherwise, the true extent of your client's disabilities and will therefore adversely affect quantum.

9.60 If, after analysis, further investigation and consideration (including raising further enquiries with your expert and where necessary cross-checking standard textbooks or papers in the library), your expert's views remain negative, you will have to consider with your client and, where appropriate, counsel, whether you wish to obtain a second expert opinion before deciding whether or not the case is worth pursuing.

9.61 Even in legal aid cases, the legal aid office is normally prepared to allow a second expert opinion if you and counsel can explain why you feel the first report is not entirely satisfactory and fails fairly and adequately to address all relevant issues.

How many reports do you need?

9.62 Depending upon the nature of the case you may well need reports from experts in several specialisms simply to cover both negligence and causation issues.

9.63 For example, in a case where your client was brain damaged following collapse under general anaesthetic in the course of an operation you are likely to need an anaesthetist to advise on the question of negligence, a neurologist to assess disability (quantum) and confirm causation and perhaps a radiologist, as well, to advise on the significance of any X-rays taken in theatre.

9.64 If your client is a handicapped infant whose injuries are alleged to have been caused by mismanagement of the mother's labour, you will at minimum need an obstetrician to advise on negligence and a paediatrician to advise on whether the child's handicaps resulted from the defalcations in obstetric management of the labour. Depending on the nature of the case you may need additional specialist expert advice: for example, if fetal blood sampling was carried out and the results appear dubious, from an obstetrician who specialises in fetal blood sampling procedures. Incidentally, in an obstetric negligence case, where your infant client is brain damaged, obtaining satisfactory paediatric evidence to establish a causal link between the brain injury and the obstetric negligence can require persistence. Causation often turns out to be a more contentious liability issue than negligence.

9.65 In all but the most straightforward cases, or those where quantum is fairly restricted, I favour obtaining corroborative evidence from a second expert in each major specialism. You can be reasonably confident the defendants will do so. You, counsel and the client should make your minds up about this as soon as you can and commission the necessary second reports in advance of close of pleadings, if possible. In a perfect world, the plaintiff assembles all reports at statement of claim stage to ensure the pleaded allegations of negligence and causation are supported by all the expert witnesses, but in most cases this is not, for reasons of time as much as expense, a practical proposition.[1]

1 Even if all the reports are not assembled before the statement of claim is drafted, all the allegations of negligence made must be based upon expert opinion. This is usually provided in conference at an early stage. If this is not done, enormous difficulties may later arise (see *Sayer v Kingston and Esher Health Authority* (1989) Independent, 27 March, CA).

9.66 When instructing a second expert to corroborate the existing positive views you have obtained, you should of course include with his papers copies of the earlier positive reports upon which you will be relying.

9.67 If you are acting for your client under a Legal Aid Certificate you will almost certainly need to get an extension of the Certificate to obtain additional reports. See para **9.43** above.

FROM REPORT TO TRIAL

Prior to service of Statement of Claim

9.68 Now that you have assembled sufficient positive expert evidence you are in position to commence proceedings and instruct counsel to draft a Statement of Claim. If your client has a Legal Aid Certificate beware! You may (particularly on pre-1993 certificates) find the initial limitation on the Certificate reads:

Limited to obtaining the assisted person's medical records (including if necessary an application for pre-action disclosure) obtaining (an) (two) independent medical report(s) and thereafter to the preparation of papers for counsel and obtaining counsel's opinion on merits and quantum.

In other words counsel is *not* covered for drafting a Statement of Claim, *nor* can you issue proceedings. It is of course a monumental waste of time and costs, when your expert evidence is clear, simply to instruct counsel to advise upon the blindingly obvious (namely that your client has a good case) and return the papers without drafting a Statement of Claim. So *before* you instruct counsel, at minimum have the Legal Aid Certificate extended to permit drafting of a Statement of Claim 'if counsel feels proceedings should reasonably be brought' and preferably have the Certificate extended to permit (without a formal written Advice at this stage: the cost of which may not be recoverable inter partes) all steps to close of pleadings, discovery, summons on directions, setting down and exchange of expert reports on liability issues of negligence and causation of disability. If your expert evidence is clear before issue, the appropriate next point for counsel to advise the client and the Legal Aid Fund on merit is when you have seen the other side's evidence after exchange pursuant to RSC Order 38, rule 37.

9.69 The Legal Aid Board have at last seen the sense of these arguments and now say the *first* limitation on a medical negligence certificate will generally be:

Limited to obtaining the appropriate medical records (including if necessary an application for pre-action discovery), obtaining independent medical report(s) (one per specialism) and thereafter to the preparation of papers for counsel and obtaining counsel's opinion [the area office will specify the subject areas to be covered, normally merits and quantum], to include the settling of proceedings if counsel so advises;

and the *second*:

Limited to all steps up to and including setting down, to include mutual exchange of factual witness statements under RSC Order 38, rule 2A and mutual exchange of expert evidence under RSC Order 38, rule 37 and to the preparation of papers for counsel and obtaining counsel's then opinion on merits, quantum and evidence.

9.70 You and counsel must decide whether an expert conference is needed before counsel finalises drafting the Statement of Claim. In general I favour a pre-Statement of Claim conference, though it is, of course, more work for your busy experts (and you).[1] Such conferences can be particularly helpful in multi-disciplinary cases to make sure the views of the experts from each specialism 'mesh' with those of their colleagues specialising in other fields.

1 In most cases, a pre-Statement of Claim conference is essential: see Chapter 10.

9.71 *Prepare well* for a conference. Make sure each expert attending has seen the written views of the others and insist, wherever possible, that counsel prepares a draft Statement of Claim as a discussion document to be circulated in advance. This will optimise the use of the valuable (and expensive) conference time and reduce the risk of spending the first half of the conference having 'talks about talks' rather than the talks themselves.

9.72 *Keep notes* (and/or tape recording, with permission) and take the trouble to dictate, as soon as you can afterwards, a detailed file note of the discussion. If appropriate have this checked and approved by your experts and counsel. At the time one is convinced one will remember salient points for ever (or that one's handwritten notes, often made at great speed, provide easy reference for the future). I have learned that a few conferences, trials, completions or traffic jams later, I cannot even understand my own handwritten notes. To preserve the value of a conference (which is probably more expensive than an expert report) it is essential to have a well set out typed note which you and counsel can refer to later. Taxing masters can be reluctant to allow the time taken in preparation of these conference notes, so I always dictate, at the same time, a short file note explaining why this item of preparation is essential.[1]

1 In legally aided cases, an accurate file note of discussion and advice given by counsel in conference may subsequently be endorsed by counsel and forwarded to the Legal Aid

Committee in lieu of a reiteration in writing of counsel's advice. Costs and counsel's time may be saved by adopting this practice.

9.73 Last but not least, *invite your client* to the conference and let your experts know the client will be there. Most medical negligence plaintiffs feel they have been short-changed in the past on forthright medical explanations. Quite apart from the factual input your client can provide at conference, the opportunity to hear one or more distinguished doctors discussing the case openly will go some way towards restoring faith in the medical profession and allaying fears and suspicions that the process of litigation is simply another expensive bucket of whitewash, concocted this time by lawyers as well as doctors.

9.74 Have the final version of the Statement of Claim checked by your experts prior to service. A specimen letter, explaining why it is so vital your experts support the allegations of negligence (and agree the relevant factual history has been accurately pleaded) is included as Precedent No 4. Counsel, in some instances, may need to be re-instructed to amend the Statement of Claim before service, in the light of your experts' comments.

9.75 RSC Order 18, rule 12(1A) requires a medical report 'substantiating all the personal injuries alleged in the Statement of Claim' to be served with the Statement of Claim. You must therefore obtain an appropriate condition and prognosis report at this stage. A report from your client's current treating doctor is fine, as opposed to one from your independent expert, so long as your expert doesn't take issue with its content and it doesn't contain any hostages to fortune (e g damning liability, asides, over-optimistic prognosis or unduly pessimistic life expectancy). It is normally best not to commission such a report from a doctor employed by the proposed defendant (health authority or Trust), but do bear in mind that the hospital or GP case notes, already disclosed to you, may contain one or more reports on your client which may be perfectly adequate for service with the Statement of Claim. In that case you do not need to commission a further report at this stage.

On service of defence

9.76 It is a sad fact that the defence, that long awaited document, frequently makes boring and uninformative reading. I routinely accede to requests from defendants for relatively substantial voluntary extensions of time to enable them properly to investigate and take instructions on 'the complex issues of the case'. It is rare, in my experience, for the fruits of those investigations to appear in the defence. If you are averagely fortunate your client's date of birth will be admitted (otherwise you must obtain a birth certificate) as well as the details of your client's treatment which have been pleaded from the case notes.

9.77 Defendants, of course, argue that it is uneconomical seriously to investigate the allegations contained in every letter before action as many plaintiffs do not proceed beyond the investigation stage: thus detailed defence investigations only commence on service of writ and Statement of

Claim. It is a strange state of affairs that a person who believes his injuries to be iatrogenic in origin cannot normally hope to have his complaints and queries taken seriously (in legal terms) by his former medical attendants until he has issued and served proceedings, despite the prior despatch of a detailed letter before action. Factory and road traffic accident defendants and their insurers do not generally adopt the 'ignore letter before action: only investigate on service of proceedings' approach.

9.78 The nature of the defence case (as opposed to 'the defence') in a medical negligence action is generally in one of two categories, or a combination of both:

(1) the investigation and treatment of the plaintiff was in accordance with current accepted standards of medical practice and/or;
(2) the plaintiff's injuries were not caused by any negligence on behalf of the defendant(s) but by:
(a) 'unavoidable accident' (some unexpected condition, happening or development which could not reasonably have been foreseen or prevented) or;
(b) the inexorable and unavoidable progress of the plaintiff's original condition and/or unavoidable risk of the treatment of which the plaintiff was warned and decided none the less to go ahead.

9.79 A plaintiff is of course not entitled to Further and Better Particulars of a denial but plaintiffs and their lawyers should note the provisions of RSC Order 18, rule 8 which require a party to plead to any affirmative case likely to take the other party by surprise. This is of particular relevance if the defence is of type (2) above. The defendants should be put on notice of the need to plead any affirmative case and the plaintiff's counsel must be alert at trial to object to any affirmative defence case which has not been pleaded being adduced.

9.80 On service of the defence, apart from instructing counsel, where appropriate, to advise and if necessary draft requests for Further and Better Particulars of Defence and/or interrogatories, you should provide to your experts a copy of the defence (and in due course any Further and Better Particulars, Interrogatories etc) and invite comments. At the same time explain (an example is included as Precedent Letter No 5) that you will shortly, at summons on directions, be seeking an order for simultaneous mutual exchange of expert reports on liability issues of alleged negligence and causation of disability. Factual evidence should be exchanged first, followed by expert evidence. Your experts (who will of course already have seen all your client's evidence) will not wish to finalise their reports for exchange purposes until they have seen the defence factual statements. These (from treating doctors, nurses etc) frequently provide important amplification (or contradiction) of the information in the records. As well as revising their reports for exchange, your experts should be asked to update their references where necessary as your summons for directions should include an application for an order that copies of references are exchanged with the relevant experts' reports. Except in straightforward cases it is usual to have an expert conference to discuss and agree pre-exchange revision of reports.

Summons for directions and orders for exchange of expert evidence

9.81 Medical negligence actions are (usually but not always) personal injury actions. RSC Order 25, rule 8 of course provides automatic directions for personal injury cases but medical negligence actions are specifically excluded from those automatic directions provisions by RSC Order 25, rule 8(5)(b). Therefore in all medical negligence actions it is essential to issue a summons on directions to obtain appropriate interlocutory orders.

9.82 Since the case of *Naylor v Preston Area Health Authority*[1] and the subsequent amendment to RSC Order 38,[2] directions for pre-trial disclosure of the substance of expert liability evidence in the form of written reports should be for simultaneous mutual exchange – not sequential disclosure (plaintiff first). The court has a discretion to order sequential not mutual and simultaneous exchange: for example, where the allegations in the statement of claim are so vague that it would be unfair to the defendants to expect their experts to deal with them until the plaintiff had disclosed either by further particulars or his own experts' reports, what the nature of his case was (see *Kirkup v British Rail Engineering Ltd*[3]).

1 [1987] 2 All ER 353, [1987] 1 WLR 958, CA.
2 For a full account, see Chapter 15.
3 [1983] 3 All ER 147, [1983] 1 WLR 1165, CA; affg [1983] 1 All ER 855, [1983] 1 WLR 190.

9.83 If the medical negligence plaintiff's case has been properly pleaded in the Statement of Claim on the basis of expert medical reports and the case notes it is inconceivable for there to be 'grounds to depart from the norm of simultaneous disclosure' (per Sir John Donaldson MR in *Naylor*).

9.84 For some years the court has had the power, as a term of permitting a party to call oral evidence at trial, to order pre-trial disclosure of the substance of that evidence. Until the *Naylor* case, such interlocutory orders were effectively never made. Now they are required.

9.85 Likewise, orders for exchange of factual witness statements (which should in my view be exchanged before expert evidence) per RSC Order 38, rule 2A are not routine in medical negligence cases.

9.86 The summons on directions is a watershed in preparation of the plaintiff's (and the defendants') case. A timetable will be set for exchange of expert (and possibly non-expert) evidence. You, counsel and your client must agree what 'type' and number of expert witnesses you need. Do not forget non-medical expert witnesses such as midwives, psychologists, speech therapists, occupational therapists, disability experts and so on. Include appropriate provisions for exchange of their reports in the summons and *get your reports ready for exchange*.

9.87 You should also consider the desirability of including in your summons an application for an order that there be (under RSC Order 38, rule 38) a meeting of both parties' experts 'without prejudice' to identify the parts of their evidence which are in issue. Such a meeting should obviously take place after exchange of expert reports and (I suggest) with solicitors for both parties present. After such a meeting the experts 'may prepare a joint statement indicating those parts of their evidence on which they are, and those on which they are not, in agreement'. The purpose of such a meeting is *not* for the experts to 'settle' the case or reach a lowest common denominator of agreement, but to sort out what can genuinely be agreed and enable the true areas of dispute to be clearly defined.

Revision of reports for exchange purposes

9.88 Experts, particularly those who have relatively little medico-legal experience, sometimes ask for guidance about what they should put in their reports for exchange purposes. The expert (by whichever side instructed and paid) has a duty to give independent and unbiased evidence to the court, initially in the form of a report and perhaps, later, in the witness box. The extent to which a lawyer may properly seek to influence form or content of an expert's report is dealt with more fully in Chapter 10.

9.89 The essential point for the lawyer to make to the doctor is obvious – what medical issues are of legal importance for the case. The report should concentrate on these. There may be a mass of interesting medical issues, only a few of which are of *legal* relevance. The importance of experts addressing clearly and to balance of probabilities, not only issues of negligence, but also the issue of causation of your client's disabilities, cannot be over-emphasised.

9.90 Experts' reports which are disclosed on exchange should contain, even if only in short form, an accurate summary of the expert witness' views on the case which each expert would propose to explain to the court when giving his or her evidence *in chief*. If when giving evidence in chief the expert witness endeavours to deal with points not dealt with in his or her report, the judge may rule that evidence to be inadmissible as its substance was not disclosed in advance. It is, of course, not possible to anticipate fully what lines of questioning will be taken by the opposing barrister in cross-examination of the expert witness, therefore in dealing with questions put in cross-examination, the expert witness may well be discussing matters not covered in his or her report. The same applies to references.

Pre-trial preparation: considering the experts

9.91 The plaintiff's solicitor should (in London) take out an application to fix immediately the case has been set down for trial. Fixture provisions differ in district registries. It is vital to liaise closely with expert witnesses when fixing a trial date. Seek their dates to avoid before the application to fix. Notify and book them immediately you have a fixture date. Some practitioners favour issuing and serving a subpoena on their experts 'to preserve priority over other commitments'. Most experts (not unreasonably) regard such a step, unless it has been discussed and agreed in advance, as a hostile and insulting act.

9.92 I have, however, on occasion found myself in difficulties when a (willing) expert paediatric witness whom I had booked and not subpoenaed found herself subpoenaed to the magistrates' court at short notice to give evidence when she was meant to be in the High Court giving evidence for my client.

9.93 Do remember that although the plaintiff's witnesses give their evidence first it will be desirable for some at least of the plaintiff's expert witnesses to remain in court after they have given their evidence to hear the defence expert evidence and give the plaintiff's counsel guidance on cross-examination of defence medical witnesses. If possible, therefore, book your (key) expert witnesses for the duration of the trial.

9.94 Once you have obtained your order on directions you should make diary notes for the due date for exchange, with the defendants, of expert reports. You should try if at all possible, to get your expert witnesses to provide their revised reports, intended for exchange purposes, a couple of weeks prior to the exchange date so that you, counsel and the client can go through the reports and if necessary discuss any appropriate minor amendments with your experts prior to exchange. As mentioned above, not only can an expert conference be useful to discuss pre-exchange revision of reports, but also a forthcoming conference encourages your experts promptly to wield the blue pencil!

9.95 I suggest it is prudent to write to the defendants (when your reports are ready) a week or so before exchange informing them of your readiness to exchange and asking them to confirm their readiness and to agree the 'mechanics' of exchange.

9.96 Exchange is often the point at which defendants admit liability. But if there is no admission of liability and the defendants fail to make reports available for exchange by the due date don't meekly send yours until the defendants have been debarred from adducing expert evidence at trial upon your application by summons to a master.

9.97 If exchange is effective obtain your experts' comments on the defendants' reports and ask counsel to advise on evidence. If you need further expert evidence over and above that provided for in the Order on Directions and exchanged you will have to make a well argued application for leave unless the defendants consent.

9.98 You will need to see your experts again in conference before trial (possibly on more than one occasion). If the matter does proceed to trial it is best to have your last expert conference fairly close to trial so that all last minute developments (which are customarily legion in the immediate pre-trial period) can be considered and important matters are fresh in everyone's mind at trial.

9.99 Have your experts prepare a short CV for use at trial.

9.100 Above all it is vital for the solicitor to keep in close contact with the expert witnesses, to report developments, provide updating information and notify if the case settles.

APPENDIX

9.101

PRECEDENT NO 1

Specimen letter to doctor about trial/commitment fees

Note: see discussion at paras **9.46** and **9.47** of the difficulties commitment fees can cause.

Dear Doctor X,

May I explain the difficulties about commitment fees, from the point of view of my firm and my client, which you may be able to help me resolve.

In civil cases, costs 'follow the event': in other words a successful Plaintiff will get most (not all) of her costs paid by the Defendant, on top of the damages award. If these costs cannot be agreed inter partes, they must be 'taxed' by a Court Official ('Taxing Master'). A detailed bill is drawn and representatives of the Plaintiff's and Defendant's solicitors attend before the Taxing Master to argue what should reasonably and properly be paid.

On taxation, where the successful party has a Legal Aid Certificate, the Taxing Master may:

(a) allow certain items of the successful Plaintiff's bill in whole or in part against the paying party (Defendant) or,
(b) allow certain items of the Plaintiff's bill in whole or in part against the Legal Aid Fund (meaning at the end of the day the Plaintiff pays these items out of her damages) or,
(c) disallow certain items altogether.

Any disbursement items (such as experts fees) which are disallowed altogether have to be paid personally by the solicitor to the expert if the agreement between the solicitor and the expert was that these fees would be paid **irrespective of the result of the taxation**.

The theory, as you will appreciate, is that a solicitor, when acting for a legally aided client, should say to her experts 'your fee seems Okay to me, but I'm not paying it until after taxation and then I will pay you what is allowed on taxation'. However, because the taxation process is so unbelievably long drawn out and the results often are not wholly satisfactory, that theoretical option is not in practice open to solicitors, whose experts will simply say 'well, in that case, I can't help because, unlike you who have no option, I can't accept work on that basis as I would go broke'.

Taxing Masters (and paying party's solicitors) are extremely reluctant to agree commitment fees of any kind: the crude argument being that medical experts are busy and distinguished chaps with more work available than they can fit in and if a trial is cancelled, even a matter of days before fixture, they have a queue of private patients waiting for cancellations and/or medical reports to prepare. Thus, the argument goes, they will not lose money even in the event of a late cancellation.

The purpose of this letter is to ask if you could be good enough to assist me further by writing a letter, which I would intend to show to the Court and the Health Authority's solicitors stating:

1. why you can't undertake work on the basis of waiting for taxation and then only getting paid what is allowed on taxation;
2. the level of your hourly/daily fee for Court attendance and the level of commitment fee you seek, including details of the 'sliding scale' – increasing towards the full level of 'appearance' fee, the shorter the time before the trial that cancellation occurs; and
3. why your particular practice means that in the event of a late cancellation you do not in fact have other remunerative work such as seeing patients or drafting medico-legal reports, which could be 'slotted in' in the event of a late cancellation of the trial fixture.

Yours truly,

Anne Winyard

PRECEDENT NO 2

Specimen letter of approach to obstetric medical expert

Note: see para **9.49**.

(1) I normally do not name my client in this initial letter but identify hospital/doctors so as to allow the expert to 'confess' to any personal or professional difficulties s/he may have in dealing with the matter, e g works at that hospital or has close professional links with the doctor(s).

(2) Before dictating this letter check expert's entry in *Medical Directory* to make sure NHS post is **not at complained of hospital** (or in same Health District). See para **9.32**.

Mr A B Green FRCS, FRCOG
1 High Street
Bristol

Dear Mr Green

I act for a little boy born 22 May 1991 at Welshtown Hospital, Welshtown and his mother born 17 April 1964.

I am investigating on mother's and son's behalf medical negligence claims against Border Health Authority who administer Welshtown Hospital. Your name has been suggested to me by Dr C D Brown with whom I have worked on other medical negligence cases.

I am writing to ask if you would be prepared to assist me with mother's and son's cases. I have already obtained copies of their relevant records from Welshtown Hospital.

Our allegations so far as son is concerned are that mother's labour was mismanaged and indications of fetal distress disregarded. The child has cerebral palsy. On mother's behalf we allege mismanagement of delivery and failure properly to suture her episiotomy. The mother developed vaginal haematoma and the episiotomy had to be re-stitched on two occasions after delivery. There were considerable problems in healing.

If you are able to assist I shall forward all relevant documentation. I would like you at this stage to prepare a report on liability issues, i e negligence and causation. I am acting for both my clients under Legal Aid Certificates. I have authority to obtain reports from you. It would be helpful if you could give me an early indication of your likely maximum fee so that I can get this approved in advance by the legal aid office before you start work on the report.

So long as you are able to do so, I should be able to pay your fee note promptly, as I can then obtain funds on account from the Legal Aid office.

It would also be helpful if you could indicate to me how long it is likely to take you to go through the documentation and prepare the report.

I shall be approaching a consultant paediatrician for help. If you have any suggestions as to whom I should consult, I would welcome these.

Yours truly,

Anne Winyard

PRECEDENT NO 3

Specimen letter of instruction to obstetric medical expert

Note: See paras **9.50–9.53** and **9.42–9.45**.

(1) *Private case* – before dictating this letter check your client has approved the expert's fee and that you have money on account.

(2) *Legal aid case* – before dictating this letter, re-check legal aid position – have you got authority to obtain report? Have you had maximum fee approved in advance under regulation 61 of Civil Legal Aid (General) Regulations 1989? Have you sought a payment on account to cover the expert's fee?

Mr A B Green FRCS, FRCOG
1 High Street
Bristol

Dear Mr Green,

RHIAN JONES born 17 April 1964
Hospital Record no 1234
EMYR JONES born 22 May 1991 at Welshtown Hospital
Hospital Record no 3456
Address: 123 High Street Welshtown Tel:

Thank you for your letter. I am glad you feel able to help me with this case.

Your quoted maximum fee of £650.00 is quite acceptable and has been approved by the Legal Aid office. I am happy to wait until December for your report.

As explained in my opening letter, I am instructed to investigate separate claims on behalf of Ms Rhian Jones and her infant son Emyr Jones.

Documentation

I enclose copies of:

(1) Two replica volumes of medical records, one relating to Emyr and one relating to his mother. I have re-ordered, paginated and indexed these. If you wish to refer in your report to any specific item in the records, could you do so by page number? I have an identical replica set in my possession. You may retain these copy records.
(2) Three separate copy CTG traces. These have some notes of dates and times on them.
(3) Mother's co-operation card.
(4) Mother's statement, checked and signed by her on. . . .
(5) My typed summary of the ante-natal and labour notes (if you could complete/correct these I should be most grateful).

Please tell me if you require any further information or documentation – in particular if you think the records are incomplete.

History

I shall only summarise this briefly as it is made plain in the enclosed documents.

Emyr was born (vaginal delivery no instruments) at Welshtown Hospital at approximately 4.50 a m on 22 May 1991. His mother received her ante-natal care from her GP and Welshtown Hospital. This was the mother's second pregnancy, the first having been terminated at an early stage at Elsewhere Hospital, in approximately February 1983.

Ms Jones arrived at Welshtown Hospital, having telephoned in advance, by ambulance at about 9 p m on 21 May already in established labour. She was accompanied by her friend, Ann Davis, who was with her throughout labour and delivery. After examination by a midwife, who broke her waters, Ms Jones was taken into a delivery room. She says there was no doctor in attendance during her labour or delivery, except for a female paediatrician who came into the room but did not intervene in any way approximately 5/10 minutes before Emyr's actual delivery and a male junior doctor (who stitched the episiotomy) who arrived after the child had been delivered.

As you can see the first CTG machine did not work properly. The second appeared to cause the midwives some concern.

Shortly after 3 a m on 22 May Ms Jones felt the urge to push but was told not to by the midwife. After auscultation some 45 minutes later the midwife told her to push.

Ms Jones states that eventually the trainee midwife performed an episiotomy, prior to doing so having said to the midwife that she did not know where to put the injection and did not know where to cut. The midwife gave the trainee instruction and the trainee apparently administered both injection and episiotomy. Mother says Emyr was delivered approximately 5/10 minutes after the episiotomy was performed, that he was blue when he was born, had to be resuscitated and was admitted to the neonatal intensive care unit (where he was an in-patient for some three weeks after his birth). Fitting started within two hours of birth.

As you will see from Emyr's notes he is severely disabled. You will observe from the notes that late decelerations on the CTG were noted at about 3 a m and subsequent fetal bradycardia was noted on several occasions. Emyr has now been diagnosed as having cerebral palsy.

About two hours after delivery mother was told she had a vaginal haematoma. Her episiotomy stitches were taken out under general anaesthetic, the haematoma was drained and she was re-stitched. Four days after delivery mother had a haemorrhage. She was given a D & C under general anaesthetic and again the episiotomy was re-stitched. When Emyr was about six weeks old she had another haemorrhage and was admitted for a further D & C under general anaesthetic. For at least nine months after delivery the episiotomy scar did not heal properly and intercourse was impossible. The situation has now somewhat improved but the scar remains lumpy and unsightly.

Progress of litigation

My opening letter to the hospital was written in March 1993, shortly after I was instructed. The Defendants prevaricated in disclosing the records. I therefore issued a Summons under section 33 of Supreme Court Act 1981. That Summons was heard by Master Black on 26 July 1993 and he made an Order as sought on the Summons requiring disclosure of all relevant records to me within 28 days. The Defendants did not fully comply with the Order. The records they initially sent were incomplete (mother's records only not child's, no CTG traces and no nursing kardex). I hope I have now been supplied with copies of all relevant records.

A Writ has not yet been issued claiming damages on behalf of Emyr or his mother. I will not be in a position to advise Emyr, his mother or the Legal Aid Fund whether their respective claims have any reasonable prospect of success until I receive your report. For limitation reasons mother's Writ should be issued by May 1994. There is no hurry for Emyr's Writ to be issued – unlike an adult, a child has until his 21st birthday to issue a Writ claiming damages for personal injury inflicted during infancy.

It is upon the views expressed in your report (and upon the views of my expert paediatrician – thank you for the suggestion of Dr White to whom I have written) that a decision will be taken about prospects of success in litigation.

Legal information for preparation of your report

If a plaintiff is to succeed in a claim, she or he has to establish (to balance of probabilities – more likely than not) that there were shortcomings in his or her management (sufficiently serious as to amount to negligence) and that these shortcomings caused or materially contributed to the injuries complained of.

Negligence: We have two potential plaintiffs here: Emyr and his mother. To establish negligence Emyr (the same principles apply to his mother) has to show, through the evidence of his medical experts, that the management of his mother's labour and his delivery fell below the standard to be expected of a reasonably competent practitioner in the relevant field (i e midwife, obstetrician) at that time. It is a defence to an allegation of professional negligence to show that a substantial body of reputable practitioners in that field would have managed the labour and delivery in the way the defendants did. It is possible, of course, that there may have been shortcomings in Emyr's neonatal paediatric management which affected the outcome. I'll be obtaining paediatric advice about that.

Causation: If – on the basis of your views, those of our paediatrician and any other experts instructed – we can establish negligence then, for that to sound in damages, Emyr would have to prove (again on the balance of probabilities and through the evidence of his medical experts) that the negligent acts/omissions:

(i) directly caused his injury or,
(ii) materially contributed to his injuries

'Material' means 'non-negligible'. A plaintiff can succeed in full on this basis even where another (or more than one other) *non*-negligent cause was at work, *provided that* the respective degrees of contribution to the injury of negligent and non-negligent causes cannot accurately be divided up or defined.

So far as Emyr's case is concerned, causation will principally be a matter for our paediatrician.

Exchange of reports: It is now routine in medical negligence cases for the reports of experts for plaintiff and defence to be exchanged prior to trial. There will be ample opportunity for your initial report (if the case proceeds) to be amended prior to exchange with the defence. Further information will almost certainly by then be available in any event. You have my assurance I'm not going to stick a copy of your report in an envelope when I receive it and post it off to the defence. Your initial report is intended *only* to be seen by me and Ms Jones as well as your fellow medical expert and counsel (if and when instructed).

References: If you cite any references in your report, copies would be helpful (not essential – I can get my own copies from a medical library if need be). Any texts in relation to then accepted 'standard practice' should be those current in May 1991.

Your report

The key issues are whether there was negligence and, if so, whether it caused or materially contributed to Emyr's severe handicaps and/or his mother's injuries.

In addition, I have set out below some specific questions which I would like your report to cover. Please do not restrict your report to dealing with the points listed.

All questions should be answered 'to balance of probabilities'. I appreciate it is confusing for a scientist to be asked to answer scientific questions to a non-scientific standard, i e to say 'yes' if 51 per cent convinced, rather than declining to do so until 99.5 per cent convinced.

Emyr

(1) When did fetal distress first become apparent? What were the signs?
(2) Please briefly explain what a CTG trace is, how and what it records and what type I and type II dips are. Please mark any such 'dips' on the three copy traces attached and return them to me.
(3) Ought the midwives to have called for medical assistance? When and why?
(4) Ought earlier delivery to have been attempted? When, why and how? (Forceps? Caesarean?)
(5) Ought an obstetrician to have been present for delivery? Why? What difference would this, on the balance of probabilities, have made?
(6) Please summarise your criticisms of the management of the labour and state what ought to have been done to measure up to minimum standards of reasonable competence. How would this have affected the outcome?
(7) Appreciating this is a question more appropriate for a paediatrician than for you, I would nonetheless be interested to know your views of what, on the balance of probabilities, caused Emyr's handicaps.

Ms Rhian Jones

(1) What is a vaginal haematoma? What do you think caused it in this case? Could this have been avoided?
(2) Why was it necessary to stitch the episiotomy three times?
(3) Did the successive re-stitchings delay/prevent healing and contribute to or cause the scarring?
(4) Can anything now be done to improve matters?
(5) Did the overall standard of care of Ms Jones fall below the minimum standard of reasonable competence and if so, in what specific respects?
(6) What ought to have been done to measure up to minimum standards and, had this been done, in what respects would Ms Jones' condition and prognosis have been improved?

I look forward to receiving your report. Although your estimated fee has been approved, there will be a delay of a few weeks between my receiving your fee note and discharging it whilst I obtain monies on account from the Legal Aid office.

Your truly,

Anne Winyard

PRECEDENT NO 4

Specimen letter to experts to approve Statement of Claim

Note: see para **9.74**.

Mr A B Green FRCS, FRCOG
1 High Street
Bristol

Dear Mr Green,

RHIAN JONES
EMYR JONES

Thank you for your contribution to the very useful conference with counsel. I attach our client account cheque for £300 together with your fee note for the conference which I would be grateful if you would receipt and return.

I also enclose my notes of the detailed discussions at conference, with a summary at the beginning. If there are any errors or inaccuracies, let me know and I will correct and reprint the notes.

Counsel has now revised the Statement of Claim as discussed at conference. I attach a copy of the revised document. Please would you go through it carefully to check firstly that the relevant history has been accurately stated and secondly that you agree with the allegations of negligence. As you know, whilst the law imposes upon doctors a duty of care, the *standard* of care appropriate in a particular case is a matter for the medical, not the legal, profession. Falling below an appropriate 'minimum competence' standard of care amounts to negligence. A plaintiff proves negligence on the basis of the views of his experts about what an appropriate minimum standard of care is. It is therefore very important that you (and our other experts) feel able to support, in the witness box, the allegations of negligence made on behalf of the plaintiff in the statement of claim.

Yours truly,

Anne Winyard

PRECEDENT NO 5

Specimen letter to expert to revise pre-Statement of Claim report for exchange purposes

Mr A B Green FRCS, FRCOG
1 High Street
Bristol

Dear Mr Green,

RHIAN JONES
EMYR JONES

You will recall having prepared on these cases a report dealing with liability issues. You were good enough to attend a conference with Counsel and our expert paediatrician, Dr White, and subsequently to suggest some amendments to the Statement of Claim drafted by Counsel after the conference. The joint (mother and child) Statement of Claim was altered, per your suggestions, prior to service.

A Defence has now been served. I intend shortly issuing a Summons on Directions inter alia seeking orders for exchange of factual evidence, followed by exchange of expert evidence (both on liability issues and to update our existing evidence on condition and prognosis). The factual evidence on our side will be that of Ms Jones and her labour companion, which you have already seen. On the defence side it is likely to include statements from the midwifery, obstetric and perhaps paediatric staff. As soon as factual evidence has been exchanged I will let you have copies of the defence statements.

I am also intending to seek orders for the Defendants to provide some Further and Better Particulars of their Defence and to answer some specific questions on oath ('Interrogatories').

I attach copies of:

(a) (Date) Statement of Claim
(b) (Date) Defence
(c) Draft Request for Further and Better Particulars of Defence.
(d) Draft Interrogatories (questions to be answered in an Affidavit on oath by the 2nd Defendant).

Please can you be kind enough to:
(1) let me have any comments you wish to make on the Defence: and any suggestions for additional points you feel could usefully be raised in our proposed request for further particulars of the Defence or as Interrogatories.
(2) see and examine Ms Jones (please send her an appointment direct: her address and telephone number have not altered) and prepare me a report on her present condition and prognosis for exchange with the Defendants. Your report won't be needed for about four to five months.
(3) amend/edit your original liability report (on issues of negligence and causation) and revise your references in readiness for exchange of reports and references with the Defendants in about five to six months. Ideally I'd like to arrange for us to meet with counsel after you've revised your report, but before we exchange expert evidence with the defence. As soon as factual evidence has been exchanged, I'll see if my secretary can arrange a date for us to meet.

I look forward to hearing from you and confirm that this practice will be responsible for your reasonable fee.

Your truly,

Anne Winyard

Glossary of medical hieroglyphs and abbreviations

Common hieroglyphs

++	Much/many
#	Fracture
▲	Diagnosis
▲▲	Differential diagnosis
℞	Treatment
°	Nil/nothing/no (as in °J = no jaundice)
↑	Up/increasing
→	Constant, normal or lateral shift (e g, of apex of heart)
↓	Decreasing or dropped (e g pulse rate)
⊙	Central as in T ⊙ = trachea central
1/24	One hour
2/7	Two days
3/52	Three weeks
4/12	Four months
$T^{38.6}$	Temperature 38.6 degrees (nowadays mostly centigrade)
T^{+4}	Term (ie date baby due) plus four days
$T^{-2/52}$ (or $T^{-2/40}$)	Term less 2 weeks
37^3	37 weeks and 3 days

Abbreviations

AAL	Anterior axillary line
ABG	Arterial blood gases
ac	Ante cibum (before meals)
ACG	Apex cardiogram
ACh	Acetylcholine
ACTH	Adrenocorticotrophic hormone
ACTH-RH	ACTH releasing hormone
ADH	Antidiuretic hormone
ADI	Acceptable daily intake
AE	Air entry
AEG	Air encephalogram
aet	Aetas (age)
AF	Atrial fibrillation
AFB	Acid fast bacillus (TB)
AFP	Alpha-fetoprotein (maternal serum and occasionally amniotic fluid levels tested in pregnancy to screen for neural tube defect in fetus)

AGL	Acute granulocytic leukaemia
AGN	Acute glomerulonephritis
AI	(i) aortic incompetence (ii) artificial insemination
AJ	Ankle jerk (reflex: see also BJ, KJ, SJ, TJ)
AK	Above knee (as in AK*A* = above knee amputation)
Ala	Alanine
Alk.phos	Alkaline phosphatase
ALL	Acute lymphoblastic leukaemia
ALS	(i) amyotrophic lateral sclerosis (ii) antilymphocytic serum
alt. dieb.	Alternis diebus (every other day)
AMI	Acute myocardial infarction
AML	Acute myelogenous leukaemia
An	Anaemia
ANF	Antinuclear factor
Anti-D	This gamma globulin must be given by injection to Rhesus negative mother who delivers/aborts Rhesus positive child/fetus to prevent mother developing antibodies which could damage a subsequent Rhesus positive baby
A°	Aorta
AP	(i) anteroposterior (ii) artificial pneumothorax
APC	Aspirin, phenacetin and caffeine
Apgar	Apgar score: means of recording baby's condition at and shortly after birth by observing and "scoring" (0, 1 or 2) 5 variables. Apgar score 10 = perfect condition. Apgar 0 = stillbirth.
APH	Ante-partum haemorrhage
APKD	Adult polycystic kidney disease
APR	Abdominal – perineal resection
ARD	Acute respiratory disease
ARDS	Adult respiratory distress syndrome
ARI	Acute respiratory infection or insufficiency
ARM	Artificial rupture of membranes (labour)
AS	(i) aortic stenosis (ii) ankylosing spondylitis
As	Arsenic
ASB	Anencephaly and spina bifida
ASD	Atrial septal defect
ASO	Antistreptolysin
ATN	Acute tubular necrosis
ATP	Adenosine triphosphate
ATPase	Adenosine triphosphatase
Au	Gold
A/V	(i) Anteverted (ii) Arterio-venous (iii) Atrio-ventricular
AVB	Atrioventricular block
AW	Above the waist
A&W	Alive and well
AXR	Abdominal x-ray (plain)

Ba	Barium
BaE	Barium enema
BaM	Barium meal
BBA	Born before arrival
BBB	(i) blood-brain barrier (ii) bundle branch block
BD	To be given/taken twice a day
BDL	Below detectable limits
BID	Brought in dead
bid	bis in die (twice daily)
BJ	Biceps jerk (reflex: see AJ)
BK	Below knee
BMJ	British Medical Journal
BNF (plus date)	British National Formulary (prescriber's bible supplied free to all NHS doctors). New edition each year.
BNO	Bowels not open
BO	Bowels open
BP	(i) (plus date) British Pharmacopoeia (ii) Blood pressure (iii) Boiling point
BPM	Beats per minute
BS	(i) Breath sounds (ii) Bowel sounds (iii) Blood sugar
BSA	Body surface area
BSR	(i) Blood sedimentation rate (ii) British Society of Rheumatology
BT	Bleeding time
BV	(i) blood vessel (ii) blood volume
BW	(i) below the waist (ii) body water (iii) body weight
c̄	with (latin: cum)
cc	(i) Carcinoma (cancer) (ii) Cubic centimetre
C	Carbon
C1, C2 etc	Cervical vertebrae
C_2H_50H	Alcohol
CA	(i) Chronological age (ii) Cardiac arrest
Ca	(i) Carcinoma/cancer (ii) Calcium
Caps	Capsules
CAT scan	Computed axial tomograph
CBD	Common bile duct
CBF	Cerebral blood flow
CBR	Complete bed rest
CCCR	Closed chest cardiac resuscitation
CCF	Congestive cardiac failure
CCU	Coronary care unit

CD	Controlled drug
Cd	Cadmium
CDH	(i) Congenital disease of the heart (ii) Congenital dislocated hip(s)
CF	(i) Complement fixation (ii) Cystic fibrosis
CGL	Chronic granulocytic leukaemia
CHA	Chronic haemolytic anaemia
CHB	Complete heart block
CHD	Coronary heart disease
ChE	Cholinesterase
CHO	Carbohydrate
CI	Contraindications
Cl	(i) Clubbing (of fingers or toe nails) (ii) Chlorine
CLL	Chronic lymphocytic leukaemia
CML	Chronic myeloid leukaemia
CMR	Cerebral metabolic rate
CMV	Cytomegalovirus
CN I-XII	Cranial nerves 1–12
CNS	Central Nervous System
CO	Complaining of
CO_2	Carbon dioxide
COAD	chronic obstructive airways disease
COD	(i) cause of death (ii) chemical oxygen demand
COETT	Cuffed oral endotracheal tube (see COT and ETT)
COLD	Chronic obstructive lung disease
COPD	Chronic obstructive pulmonary disease
CORD	Chronic obstructive respiratory disease
COT	Cuffed oral tube (endotracheal tube used for ventilating a patient who cannot breath unaided)
C&P	Cystoscopy and pyelography
CPAP	Continuous positive airway pressure
CPB	Cardiopulmonary bypass
CPD	Cephalo-pelvic disproportion (baby too big to fit through pelvis)
CPE	Chronic pulmonary emphysema
CPM	Counts per minute
CPP	Cerebral perfusion pressure
CPPB	Constant positive pressure breathing
CPPV	Continuous positive pressure ventilation
CPR	Cardiopulmonary resuscitation
cps	Cycles per second
CR	(i) crown-rump (ii) conditioned reflex
Cr	Chromium
C&R	Convalescence and rehabilitation
CRS	Congenital rubella syndrome
CS	Caesarean section
Cs	Caesium
CSF	Cerebro-spinal fluid

CST	(i) convulsive shock therapy (ii) cavernous sinus thrombosis
CT	(i) computerized (computed) tomography (ii) cerebral (or coronary) thrombosis
CTG	Cardiotocograph (trace during labour of baby's heart and mum's contractions)
CTR	Cardiothoracic ratio
CTS	Carpal tunnel syndrome
Cu	Copper
CV	(i) Cardiovascular (ii) Cerebrovascular
CVA	Cerebro-vascular accident (stroke)
CVP	Central venous pressure
CVR	Cerebrovascular resistance
CVS	Cardio-vascular system
Cx	Cervix
CXR	Chest x-ray
Cy	Cyanosis
DA	Developmental age
D&C	Dilation and curettage
DBP	Diastolic blood pressure
DD	(i) dangerous drug (ii) differential diagnosis
DI	Diabetes insipidus
DIC	Disseminated intravascular coagulopathy
DM	Diabetes mellitus
DNA	(i) Did not attend (ii) Deoxyribonucleic acid
DNR	Do not resuscitate
D&V	Diarrhoea and vomiting
DOA	Dead on arrival
DOB	Date of birth
DOC	11-deoxycorticosterone
DS	(i) disseminated (multiple) sclerosis (ii) Down's Syndrome
D/S	Dextrose saline
DT	Delirium tremens
DTP	(i) distal tingling on percussion (ii) diphtheria, tetanus, pertussis
DVT	Deep vein thrombosis
D/W	(i) discussed with (ii) dextrose in water
Dx	Diagnosis
DXR	Deep x-ray
EAHF	Eczema, asthma, hay fever
EBF	Erythroblastosis fetalis
ECB	Exploration of common bile duct
ECF	Extracelluar fluid
ECG	Electro-cardiogram/graph (electric heart recording)
ECM	External cardiac massage
ECT	Electro-convulsive therapy
ECV	Extracellular volume

EDC	Expected date of confinement
EDD	Expected date of delivery
EDTA	(i) European Dialysis and Transplant Association (ii) ethylenediamine tetraacetic acid (edetic acid)
EFA	Essential fatty acid(s)
EEG	Electroencephalogram/graph (brain recording)
EGDF	Embryonic growth and development factor
EIA	Enzyme immunoassay
EJ	Elbow jerk (see AJ)
ELISA	Enzyme-linked immunosorbent assay
EMF	(i) electromotive force (ii) endomyocardial fibrosis
EOA	Examination, opinion, and advice
EOL	End of life
ERCP	Endoscopic retrograde choledochopancreaticography/scopy
ERPC	Evacuation of retained products of conception
ESN	Educationally subnormal
ESP	(i) end-systolic pressure (ii) extrasensory perception
ESR	(i) erythrocyte sedimentation rate (blood) (ii) electron spin resonance
ETC	(i) Estimated time of conception (ii) Examined through clothes
EtoH	Alcohol
ETT	(i) endotracheal tube (see COT above) (ii) exercise tolerance test
EUA	Examination under anaesthesia
FAS	Fetal alcohol syndrome
FB	(i) finger's breadth (ii) foreign body
FBC	Full blood count
FBS	Fetal blood sampling (carried out during labour to check baby's condition)
FDIU	Fetal death in utero
Fe	Iron
FEUO	For external use only
FFI	Fit and free from infection
FH	(i) family history (ii) familial hypercholesterolaemia
FHH	Fetal heart heard
FHHR	Fetal heart heard regular
FHNH	Fetal heart not heard
FHR	Fetal heart rate
FIUO	For internal use only
FLK	Funny looking kid
FMF	Fetal movements felt
FOB	Faecal occult blood
FP	Freezing point
FRJM	Full range of joint movement
FSE	Fetal scalp electrode
FSH	(i) Family and social history (ii) Follicle-stimulating hormone (produced in pregnancy)

FTBD Full term, born dead
FTND Full term, normal delivery
FTT Failure to thrive
FTVD Full term vaginal delivery
FU Follow up
FVC Forced vital capacity (a resp. function test)
Fx Fracture
GA (i) general anaesthetic
(ii) gestational age
GB Gall bladder
GC Gonococcus
GCS Glasgow Coma Score
GF Growth factor
GFR Glomerular filtration rate
GI Gastro-intestinal
GIT Gastro-intestinal tract
GITT Glucose insulin tolerance test
G6P Glucose 6 phosphate
G6PD Glucose 6 phosphate dehydrogenase
GTT Glucose tolerance test (for diabetes)
GU (i) gastric ulcer
(ii) genito-urinary
GUT Genito-urinary tract
H Hydrogen
Hb Haemoglobin (blood)
HBD Has been drinking
HbF fetal haemoglobin
HbH Haemoglobin H
HbS Sickle cell haemoglobin
HCM Hypertrophic cardiomyopathy
Hct Haemocrit
HDN Haemolytic disease of the new born
HDU High dependency unit
HFPPV High frequency positive pressure ventilation
Hg Mercury
HMD Hyaline membrane disease
HOCM Hypertrophic obstructive cardiomyopathy
HPC History of presenting complaint
HPI History of present(ing) illness
hpRL Prolactin
HR Heart rate
HRT Hormone replacement therapy
HS Heart sounds
HSE (i) Health and Safety Executive
(ii) herpes simplex encephalitis
HTLV Human T cell lymphoma (leukaemia) virus
HVS High vaginal swab
Hx History
IA Intra-arterial
IADHS Inappropriate antidiuretic hormone syndrome
IBS Irritable bowel syndrome
ICF Intracellular fluid

ICP	Intracranial pressure
I & D	Incision and drainage
ICS	Intercostal space (usually as xICS, where x = a number from 1–11)
ICU	Intensive care unit
IDD	Insulin dependent diabetes
IDDM	Insulin dependent diabetes mellitus
IEM	Inborn error or metabolism
IFB	Inflammatory bowel disease
Ig	Immunoglobulin
IgA	Immunoglobulin A
IgD	Immunoglobulin D
IgE	Immunoglobulin E
IgG	Immunoglobulin G
IgM	Immunoglobulin M
IHD	Ischaemic heart disease
IJ	Internal jugular (vein)
IM	(i) intramuscular (ii) infectious mononucleosis
IMV	Intermittent mandatory ventilation
I&O	Intake and output
IOFB	Intra-ocular foreign body
IOP	Intra-ocular pressure
IPPA	Inspection, palpation, percussion, auscultation
IPPR	Intermittent positive pressure respiration
IPPV	Intermittent positive pressure ventilation
Ir	Iridium
ISQ	In status quo (unchanged)
IT	Intrathecal
ITP	Idiopathic thrombocytopenic purpura
ITT	Insulin tolerance test
ITU	Intensive therapy unit
IU	International unit
IUD	(i) intrauterine device (ii) Intrauterine death
IUGR	Intrauterine growth retardation
IUP	Intrauterine pressure
IUT	Intrauterine transfusion
IV	Intravenous
IVC	Inferior vena cava
IVD	Intravertebral disc
IVF	In vitro fertilization
IVGTT	Intravenous glucose tolerance test
IVH	Intraventricular haemorrhage
IVI	Intravenous infusion (drip)
IVP	Intravenous pyelogram
IVT	Intravenous transfusion
IVU	Intraveneous urography
Ix	Investigations
J	Jaundice
JJ	Jaw jerk
°JACCO	No jaundice, anaemia, cyanosis, clubbing or oedema (often seen at start of note of clinical examination)

JND	Just noticeable difference
JV	Jugular vein
JVP	Jugular venous pressure (or pulse)
K	Potassium
KJ	Knee jerk (reflex: see AJ)
KKLS	Kidneys, liver, spleen
kPa	Kilopascal, approximately 7.5 mmHg
KS	Kaposi's sarcoma
L	(i) Litre (ii) Left
L1, L2 etc	Lumbar vertebrae
LA	Local anaesthetic
L&A	Light and accommodation
LBB	Left bundle branch
LBBB	Left bundle branch block
LBF	Liver blood flow
LBH	Length, breadth, height
LBP	Low back pain
LBW	Low birth weight
LE	Lupus erythematosus
LFTs	Liver function tests or lung function tests
LH	Luteinising hormone
LIB	Lump in breast
LIF	Left iliac fossa
LIH	Left inguinal hernia
LKS	Liver, kidney, spleen
LMN	Lower motor neurone
LMP	Last menstrual period
LN	Lymph node
LOA	Left occiput anterior (position of baby's head at delivery: see also LOP, ROA, ROP, LOL, ROL, OA, OP)
LOC	Loss of Consciousness
LOL	Left occipitolateral (see LOA)
LOM	Limitation of movement
LOP	Left occiput posterior (see LOA)
LOPS	Length of patient stay
LP	Lumbar puncture
LRT	Lower respiratory tract
LRTI	Lower respiratory tract infection
LS	Letter sent
LSCS	Lower segment caesarean section (the 'normal' type of caesarean section)
LSKK	Liver, spleen, kidneys
LUQ	Left upper quadrant
LVF	Left ventricular failure
LVH	Left ventricular hypertrophy
L&W	Living and well
M	Menarche – started periods
MAL	Mid axillary line
mane	In the morning
MAP	Mean arterial pressure
MBD	Minimal brain dysfunction

mcg	Microgram
MCL	Mid clavicular line
MCV	Mean cell volume
MGM/F	Maternal grandmother/father
MELAS	Mitochondrial encephalomyopathy, lactic acidosis and stroke
MF	Myelofibrosis
M/F	Male/female
Mg	Magnesium
mg	Milligram
μg	Microgram
MI	(i) myocardial infarction (ii) mitral incompetence (iii) medical inspection
mist	Mixture
mitte 1/12	Supply/give/send/provide (e g, instruction to pharmacist to provide patient with e g, 1 month's supply of drugs)
ml	Millilitres
MM	(i) multiple myeloma (ii) mucous membrane
mmHg	Millimeters of mercury (pressure)
mMol	Millimol
MMR	Measles, mumps, rubella (vaccine)
MRI	Magnetic resonance imaging (= NMRI)
MS	(i) multiple sclerosis (ii) mitral stenosis
MSU	Mid stream urine
N	Nitrogen
Na	Sodium
NAA	No apparent abnormalities
NAD	(i) nothing abnormal detected (ii) nicotinamide adenine dinucleotide
$NaHCO_3$	Sodium bicarbonate (alkaline substance: inter alia given to counteract metabolic acidosis following oxygen deprivation)
NBM	Nil by mouth
ND	Notifiable disease
NET	Naso-endotracheal tube
NFTD	Normal full term delivery
ng	Nanogram
NG	(i) Naso-gastric (ii) Carcinoma/cancer (neoplastic growth) = new growth
NICU	Neonatal intensive care unit
NIDDM	Non insulin dependent diabetes mellitus
NLM	(used by paediatricians) Nice looking mother
NMCS	No malignant cells seen
NMR	Nuclear magnetic resonance
NMRI	Nuclear magnetic resonance imaging
NND	Neonatal death
noct/nocte	At night
NOF	Neck of femur
N/S	Normal size or not significant
NS	Normal saline
NSAID	Non-steroidal anti-inflammatory drugs

NSD	(i) normal spontaneous delivery (ii) nominal standard dose
NSR	Normal sinus rhythm
NSU	Non specific urethritis
NTD	Neural tube defect
NTP	Normal temperature and pressure
N&V	Nausea and vomiting
NWB	Non weight bearing
O_2 (or O)	Oxygen
OA	(i) occipito-anterior (see LOA) (ii) osteo arthritis
OAD	Obstructive airways disease
O&C	Onset and course
OCP	Oral contraceptive pill
OD	Overdose
OE	On examination
ONTRA	Orders not to resuscitate
OP	Occipito-posterior (see LOA)
Orthop.	Orthopnoea (breathlessness on lying flat)
P	Pulse
P or π	Period
PAN	Polyarteritis nodosa
PC	Post cibum (after food)
PD	Peritoneal dialysis
pCO_2	Partial pressure of carbon dioxide
PCV	Packed cell volume
PDA	Patent ductus arteriosus
PERLA	Pupils are equal and react to light and accommodation
PE	(i) Pulmonary embolism (ii) Pre eclampsia
PEFR	Peak expiratory flow rate
PET	(i) pre-eclamptic toxaemia (ii) positron emission tomography
PFT	Pulmonary function test
PGM/F	Paternal grand mother/father
pg	Picogram
PGH	Pituitary growth hormone
pH	Negative log of hydrogen ion activity: 'acidity and alkalinity' scale. Low is acidic. High is alkaline. pH7.4 is normal body level.
PH	Past/previous history
PICU	Paediatric intensive care unit
PID	(i) Pelvic inflammatory disease (ii) Prolapsed intervertebral disc
PIP	Proximal interphalangeal
PKD	Polycystic kidney disease
PKU	Phenylketonuria
PL	Prolactin
PMH	(i) past/previous medical history (ii) previous menstrual history
PN	Percussion note
Pn	Plutonium

PND	Paroxysmal nocturnal dyspnoea
PNH	Paroxysmal nocturnal haemoglobinuria
PN (R)	Percussion note (resonant)
pO_2	Partial pressure of oxygen
POH	Past/previous obstetric history
po	Per os (by mouth)
PoM	Prescription only medicine
POP	Plaster of Paris
PP	(i) placenta previa (ii) private patient
PPB	Positive pressure breathing
PPH	Post partum haemorrhage
ppm	parts per million
PR	(i) per rectum (by the rectum) (ii) pulse rate
prn	As required – of eg pain killers
PROM	Premature rupture of membranes
PRV	Polycythaemia rubra vera
PS	Pulmonary stenosis
P/S	Polyunsaturated/saturated ratio
PTA	Prior to admission
PTD	Permanent total disability
PTH	Parathyroid hormone
PTT	Prothrombin time
PUO	Pryexia of uncertain (or unknown) origin
pv	(i) per vaginam (by the vagina) (ii) polyoma virus
QALY	Quality adjusted life years
QDS	To be given/taken four times a day
qid	quater in die (four times a day)
R	Right
RA	Rheumatoid arthritis
RAP	right atrial pressure
RBB	Right bundle branch
RBBB	Right bundle branch block
RBC	Red blood cell (erythrocyte)
RCT	Randomized clinical trial
RDS	Respiratory distress syndrome
REM	Rapid eye movements
Rh	Rhesus (blood type: can cause problems in pregnancy if mother is Rhesus *negative* and father Rhesus *positive*)
RHD	(i) rheumatic heart disease (ii) rhesus haemolytic disease
RIC	Raised intracranial pressure
RIF	Right iliac fossa
RIH	Right inguinal hernia
RLF	Retrolental fibroplasia
RNA	Ribonucleic acid
ROA	Right occiput anterior (see LOA)
ROL	Right occipito-lateral (see LOA)
ROM	Range of movement
ROP	Right occiput posterior (see LOA)

RS	Respiratory system
RT	Reaction time
RTI	Respiratory tract infection
RUQ	Right upper quadrant
s̃	Without (latin: sine)
S1, 2 etc	Sacral vertebrae
SB	(i) serum bilirubin (ii) stillbirth
S/B	Seen by
Sb	antimony
SBE	Subacute bacterial endocarditis
SBP	Systolic blood pressure
SBR	Strict bed rest
SC	Subcutaneous
SCA	Sickle cell anaemia
SCAN	Suspected child abuse and neglect
SCBU	Special care baby unit
SCI	Spinal cord injury
SCU	Special care unit
S/D	Systolic/diastolic (heart and circulation)
SDHD	Sudden death heart disease
SE	Side effects
SH	Social history
SIDS	Sudden infant death syndrome
SIMV	Synchronised intermittent mandatory ventilation
SJ	Supinator jerk (reflex: see AJ)
SL	Sub lingual (under the tongue)
SLE	Systemic lupus erythematosus
SLR	Straight leg raising
SM	Systolic murmur
Sn	Tin
S/N	Signal to noise ratio
SOA	Swelling of ankles
SOB (OE)	Short of breath (on exertion)
SOL	Space occupying lesion
SOS	(i) si opus sit (if necessary) (ii) see other sheet
SROM	Spontaneous rupture of membranes (labour)
stat	Immediately
STOP	Suction termination of pregnancy
stp	Standard temperature and pressure
Supp	Suppositories
SWD	Short wave diathermy
SVC	Superior vena cava
SVD	Spontaneous vaginal delivery
SVT	Supraventricular tachycardia
SXR	Skull x-ray
T1, T2 etc	Thoracic vertebrae
T&A	Tonsils and adenoids
TAH	Total abdominal hysterectomy
TCI2/52	To come in, in 2 weeks' time
TDS	To be given/taken 3 times a day

TGH	To go home
THR	Total hip replacement
TIA	Transient ischaemic attack
TJ	Triceps jerk (see AJ)
TLC	(i) thin layer chromatography (ii) total lung capacity (iii) tender loving care (ie nursing, no more doctoring)
TLV	(i) total lung volume (ii) threshold limit value
TNS	Transcutaneous nerve stimulation
TPR	Temperature, pulse and respiration count
TOP	Termination of pregnancy
TSH	Thyroid stimulating hormone
TSS	Toxic shock syndrome
TT	(i) tetanus toxoid (ii) tuberculin test
TTA	To take away
TTH	To take home
TVF	Tactile vocal fremitus
UC	Ulcerative colitis
U&E	Urea and electrolytes (biochemical tests)
UMN	Upper motor neurone
UO	Urinary output
URI	Upper respiratory infection
URT	Upper respiratory tract
URTI	Upper respiratory tract infection
USS	Ultra sound scan
UTI	Urinary tract infection
UV	Ultraviolet
UVA	Ultraviolet light, long wave
VA	Visual acuity
VC	Vital capacity (respiratory function test)
VD	Venereal disease
VE	Vaginal examination
VER	Visual evoked response
VF	Ventricular fibrillation
VGH	Very good health
VSIL	'Very sick indeed' list (or 'very seriously ill' list)
VT	Ventricular tachycardia
V/V	(i) Vulva and vagina (ii) Varicose veins
Vx	vertex
V-Z	Varicella-zoster
V-ZV	Varicella-zoster virus
WAIS	Wechsler adult intelligence scale
WBC	White blood corpuscle/white blood cell count
WCC	White cell count
W/O	Wash out
w/o	(i) water in oil (ii) without
WR	Wasserman reaction
XR	X-ray

XRT	X-ray therapy
XS	Cross-section
XX	Sex chromosomes (normal female)
XY	Sex chromosomes (normal male)

FIGURE 9.1 NURSING ASSESSMENT CHART

NURSING ASSESSMENT

GENERAL APPEARANCE (Physical & Emotional)
Pale looking lady in obvious Pain

HEARING (Good) Poor Wears Aid
Remarks:
VISION (Good) Poor (Wears Glasses)
Wears Contact Lenses
Remarks: For Reading only.
ORAL HYGIENE Satisfactory
Condition of Mouth } Satisfactory.
Condition of Teeth }
Dentures Yes No (Full) Partial Crown
DIET Appetite Good
Before illness A/A
Dietary Preferences
Special Diet low fat Diet due to previous cholecystectomy
CONDITION OF SKIN
Satisfactory ✓ Dehydrated
Oedematous Broken Areas
Pressure Areas intact.
Remarks:

Norton Score
Prosthesis/Appliances brought in with Patient: None
Stick Crutches Wheelchair Frame

Property/Appliance Labelled by: N/A

MOBILITY was fully mobile prior to fall
Independent
Help Needed ✓
Appliances and Aids None.

Dressing Independent
Help Needed ✓
ELIMINATION
Micturition No. of Times Day } Normal
Night }
Dysuria None Incontinence NO
Bowel Habit Daily
Before illness A/A

Usual Aperient occasional lactulose
REST, SLEEP AND RECREATION
Sleep Pattern Good
Any Sedation Temazepam but only when in Hospital
Usual Leisure/Hobbies
Reading & knitting.

SOCIAL
Type of Housing Grnd floor flat
Stairs 3 Stairs up to Bathroom.
Living Alone yes
Dependents none
Any problems with e.g. stairs, heating, pets, visiting
will need to do stairs before Discharge.
Patients understanding of illness
Good.
Relatives understanding of illness
very supportive and understanding.
Reason given to patient for Admission if relevant
Neck of femur
Investigations X-RAY

Remarks:

SPECIAL REQUEST BY PATIENT:

History taken and Identiband checked by: 810 @ S/N
History obtained from: Pt + Notes
Date: 30/3/89

GM 94

NURSING RECORD Date Admitted 30/3/89 Time 14⁰⁰ Hospital St Charles Ward B/Bent Age 82 Date of Birth 1/2/07
Surname (Mr, Miss, Mrs) MOORE Forenames Phyllis Folder No: 000001

Address 22a Cambridge Gdns LONDON W10
Next of Kin Daughter Hours of Work 08.30–16.30
MRS Smythe
Relationship Daughter.
Address 72 Barlby Rd. LONDON W10
Tel. No. Home 968-9774 Work 221-5272
Person to Notify Daughter
Address A/A

Tel. No. A/A
Admitted from:– O.P.D. Home List
(A & E) Hospital Other Source
Accompanied by Relative/Friend Daughter
Next of Kin Notified (Yes)/ No
Date and Time 30/3 14⁰⁰hrs
How with pt on admission
Community Services Notified (Yes)/ No
Address c/o Westway Home Care
Tel. No. 402 7886
Care at Home meals on wheels × 5 days
Home Social Worker None
Social Services c/o westway
State Specific Service A/A
Valuables in Custody (Yes)/ No
Receipt No. 139764
Clothing (Stored) Sent Home
Name of G.P. Dr Slade Tel. No. 969-3534
Address 110 Cambridge Gardens W10

Marital Status widow
Occupation Rtd Shop Assistant
Religion C of E
Sacraments of the Sick
Language/Speech Difficulties None
Speaks English.

OBSERVATIONS ON ADMISSION
Temperature 37²°C
Pulse Rate and Rhythm 91 Regular
Respiration 26
Blood Pressure 140/80
Height 5ft 5ins Weight 10 stone 2lbs
Urinalysis NAD

Level of Consciousness fully conscious but in Pain.
Orientated ✓
Confused
Remarks

Any Medication in Current Use (Yes) No
Atenolol 50mg Daily.
Action Taken
Dr Informed To Pharmacy

Provisional Diagnosis
Rt # Neck of femur due to fall in Street.

Confirmed Diagnosis

Operation Date and Procedure

Relevant Past Illness/Admissions

Current Health Problems e.g. Asthma, Diabetes, Epilepsy
Hypertension
cholecystectomy 1974.

Known Allergies/Sensitivities
ELASTOPLAST

FIGURE 9.2 NURSING CARE PLAN

GM81(83)

NAME Phyllis MOORE

NURSING CARE PLAN
ALL ENTRIES MUST BE SIGNED AND DATED

DATE	PATIENTS PROBLEM	OBJECTIVES	NURSING ACTION	Review Date	SIGNATURE
30/3/89	(1) Painful Rt Hip due to recent #	To alleviate Pain	- Analgesia as required & monitor effect - Comfortable positioning of patient with use of bed cradle		
	(2) Pt unprepared for theatre	To prepare pt	- NBM - ECG & X-RAY - Consent + pre-med - Gown & name bands - explain all procedures		
	(3) Potential infection due to invasive surgery.	Prophylactic prevention	- T.E.D Stockings Applied. - pre-op administration of Anti-Biotics - monitor Temperature		[signature]
	(4) Pt has had a General Anaesthetic	To recover patient & observe for signs of shock + haemorrage	- c/o I.V.I - c/o wound site - c/o Redivac Drain - Post op obs - check patient passes urine post-anaesthetic - c/o Blood transfusion		
	(5) Potential Dislocation	To prevent	- use of abduction pillow - careful positioning		P.T.O

NAME Phyllis MOORE HOUSE PHYSICIAN/SURGEON CONSULTANT MR HARRIS

GM81(83)

NAME Phyllis Moore

NURSING CARE PLAN
ALL ENTRIES MUST BE SIGNED AND DATED

DATE	PATIENTS PROBLEM	OBJECTIVES	NURSING ACTION	Review Date	SIGNATURE
			of pt, Roll towards affected side, keeping leg straight. use of bed cradle to relieve pressure of bed clothing		
	Potential Complications of bed rest.	To prevent	- 2 hourly pressure area care, use of Sheepskin & heel booties - chest physio, coughing & deep breathing encouraged. - Active limb excercises and use of ~~DVT~~ TED Stockings to prevent D.V.T.		[signature]

NAME Phyllis Moore HOUSE PHYSICIAN/SURGEON CONSULTANT Mr Harris

FIGURE 9.3 PROGRESS REPORT – EVALUATION OF THE IDENTIFIED PROBLEMS

NAME Phyllis Moore — PROGRESS REPORT-EVALUATION OF THE IDENTIFIED PROBLEMS — GM82 (83)

DATE/TIME		SIGNATURE
30/3/89		
14:00	Pt admitted to ward via casualty with # Rt neck of	
	femur	
①	c/o severe pain in Rt hip 75mg IM Pethidine and 12.5mg IM	
	Stemetil given at 14 15 hrs. c̄ good effect.	
②	Pt is awaiting theatre for (RE) Thomsons Hemi-Arthroplasty	
	this evening. S/B House officer, fully admitted and consent	
	form signed. S/B anaesthetist pt NBM and pre-med is	
	ordered for 17:00 hrs. Pt is fully prepared for theatre	[illegible]
	T.E.D stockings applied.	L Phillips
17:00hrs		
②	pre-med of Pethidine 25mg and Atropine 0.3mg given	
	IV fluclox 500mg to be given on induction.	
	Dentures and jewellery removed. Pt appears	
	comfortable.	[illegible]
30/3 20:30		
④	patient returned to ward at 20:30 hrs following (RE)	
	Thomsons hemi-arthroplasty under G.A.	
	post op observations stable and recorded ½ hourly.	
	currently infusing 2nd unit blood over four hours	
	due at 23:00 hrs Normal saline prescribed to follow.	
	Redivac drain in situ, only 50mls drained at	
	time of report. Dressing in tact and no wound ooze	
	noted.	
	Pt has not ~~[illegible]~~ yet passed urine.	
③	mildly pyrexial post-op. Anti Biotics given as	
	ordered.	PTO.

NAME — HOUSE PHYSICIAN/SURGEON — CONSULTANT

NAME Phyllis Moore — PROGRESS REPORT-EVALUATION OF THE IDENTIFIED PROBLEMS — GM82 (83)

DATE/TIME		SIGNATURE
①	No c/o pain since return to ward.	
⑤	nursed with abduction pillow & bed cradle in situ.	
	tolerating small amounts of oral fluid with no	
	c/o nausea.	[illegible]

NAME — HOUSE PHYSICIAN/SURGEON — CONSULTANT

FIGURE 9.4 REFERRALS/DISCHARGE SUMMARY CHART

DATE	REFERRALS	DISCHARGE SUMMARY
	Physiotherapist	Date of Discharge:
	referred to physio for post-	Time:
	operative mobilisation.	Mode of Transport:
	Occupational Therapist reffered to OT	Follow up Appointment Date:
	to Arrange Home visit &	O.P.D.
	assesment prior to Discharge.	
	Social Worker	
		Referrals
		Community Nurse for:
		Health Visitor for:
		Medications taken home:
		Transport
	Others	Certificates:
		Valuables:
		Relatives Informed:
		Social Services arranged (specify)
		Signature:
		Date:

NAME Phyllis MOORE HOUSE PHYSICIAN/SURGEON CONSULTANT MR HARRIS

DATE	INVESTIGATIONS AND SPECIAL TREATMENTS

GM86(83)

NAME HOUSE PHYSICIAN/SURGEON CONSULTANT

FIGURE 9.5 WARD PRESCRIPTION SHEET AND RECORD

GEN. MED. 122(4R)

WARD PRESCRIPTION SHEET AND RECORD

AFFIX ADDRESSOGRAPH LABEL HERE

NAME: Moore | NUMBER:

FORENAME: Phyllis | D.O.B.: 1.2.07.

HOSPITAL: St charles

WARD: Broadbent | CONSULTANT: MR HARRIS | AGE: 82 | WEIGHT: 10st 2lbs

DATE	NOTES	INITIALS

O.P.D. APPOINTMENT

DISCHARGED TO: CHEPSTOW LODGE ☐ HEREFORD LODGE ☐ HOME ☐ OTHER ☐

DRUGS TO TAKE AWAY	DOSE	FREQUENCY	SUPPLY	PHARM.

DATE SIGNATURE

SENSITIVITY/INTERACTION	AFFIX ADDRESSOGRAPH LABEL HERE
	NAME Phyllis Moore NUMBER
	FORENAME D.O.B. 1/2/07

DATE	TIME	ONCE ONLY DRUGS	ROUTE	DOSE	SIGNATURE	GIVEN	START DATE	DIET	END DATE
30/3/89	17^00	Pethidine	IM	25mg	[signature]	[initials]			
		Atropine	IM	0.3mg	[signature]	[initials]			
30/3/89 on induction)		Flucloxacillin	I.V	500mg	[signature]	TP			
30/3/89	24^00	Flucloxacillin	I.V.	500mg	[signature]	[initials]			
31/3/89	06^00	Flucloxacillin	I.V	500mg	[signature]				

AS REQUIRED PRESCRIPTIONS AND NIGHT SEDATION

DRUG (APPROVED NAME)	ROUTE	DOSE	DATE	SIGNATURE	PHARM	DATE	TIME	DOSE	GIVEN	DATE	TIME	DOSE	GIVEN	DATE	TIME	DOSE	GIVEN
Pethidine	I.M.	50-75mg 3-4 hrly	30/3	[signature]		30.3.89	14^45	75mg	CM								
Stemetil	I.M	12.5mg 6 hrly	30/3	[signature]	31/3	30.3.89	14^45	12.5mg	CM								
Lactulose	O	10-20mls	30/3	[signature]													
Temazepam	O	10-20mg	30/3	[signature]													
Co-Proxamol		1-II 4 hourly	30/3	[signature]													

WARD
Broadbent

AFFIX ADDRESSOGRAPH LABEL HERE
NAME Phyllis Moore
NUMBER 1/2/07

REGULAR PRESCRIPTIONS			FIX CONTINUATION SHEET HERE											
19 89 March/April	DATE/MONTH		30	31	1	2	3	4	5	6	7	8	9	10
DRUG (APPROVED NAME): Atenolol; ROUTE: O														
DOSE: 50mg; DATE: 30/3; PHARM	0800	✓												
	1400													
	1800													
SIGNATURE	2200													
DRUG (APPROVED NAME): Flucloxacillin; ROUTE: O														
DOSE: 500mg; DATE: 30/3; PHARM	0800	✓												
	1400	✓												
	1800	✓												
SIGNATURE	2200	✓												
DRUG (APPROVED NAME); ROUTE														
DOSE; DATE; PHARM	0800													
	1400													
	1800													
SIGNATURE	2200													
DRUG (APPROVED NAME); ROUTE														
DOSE; DATE; PHARM	0800													
	1400													
	1800													
SIGNATURE	2200													
DRUG (APPROVED NAME); ROUTE														
DOSE; DATE; PHARM	0800													
	1400													
	1800													
SIGNATURE	2200													
DRUG (APPROVED NAME); ROUTE														
DOSE; DATE; PHARM	0800													
	1400													
	1800													
SIGNATURE	2200													
DRUG (APPROVED NAME); ROUTE														
DOSE; DATE; PHARM	0800													
	1400													
	1800													
SIGNATURE	2200													

I.V. FLUID THERAPY

Enter drugs given directly by intravenous injection in the Regular or Once Only Section.

NAME

NUMBER

FORENAME

Date	Infusion Fluid Volume and Duration	Start	Drug and Amount to be Added	Presc. Initials	Time Drug Added	Infusion Batch No.	Time Infusion Started	Nurses Initials	Time Discontinued	Nurses Initials	Amount not Infused	
30/3	Whole Blood		one unit over 4 hrs.	RL		881442	19^{00}	PD	23^{00}	PD		
30/3	Whole Blood		one unit over 4 hrs	RL		881544	23^{00}	RL.				
30/3	Normal Saline		1,000 over 10 hrs.	RL								

FIGURE 9.6 BLOOD PRESSURE AND PULSE CHART

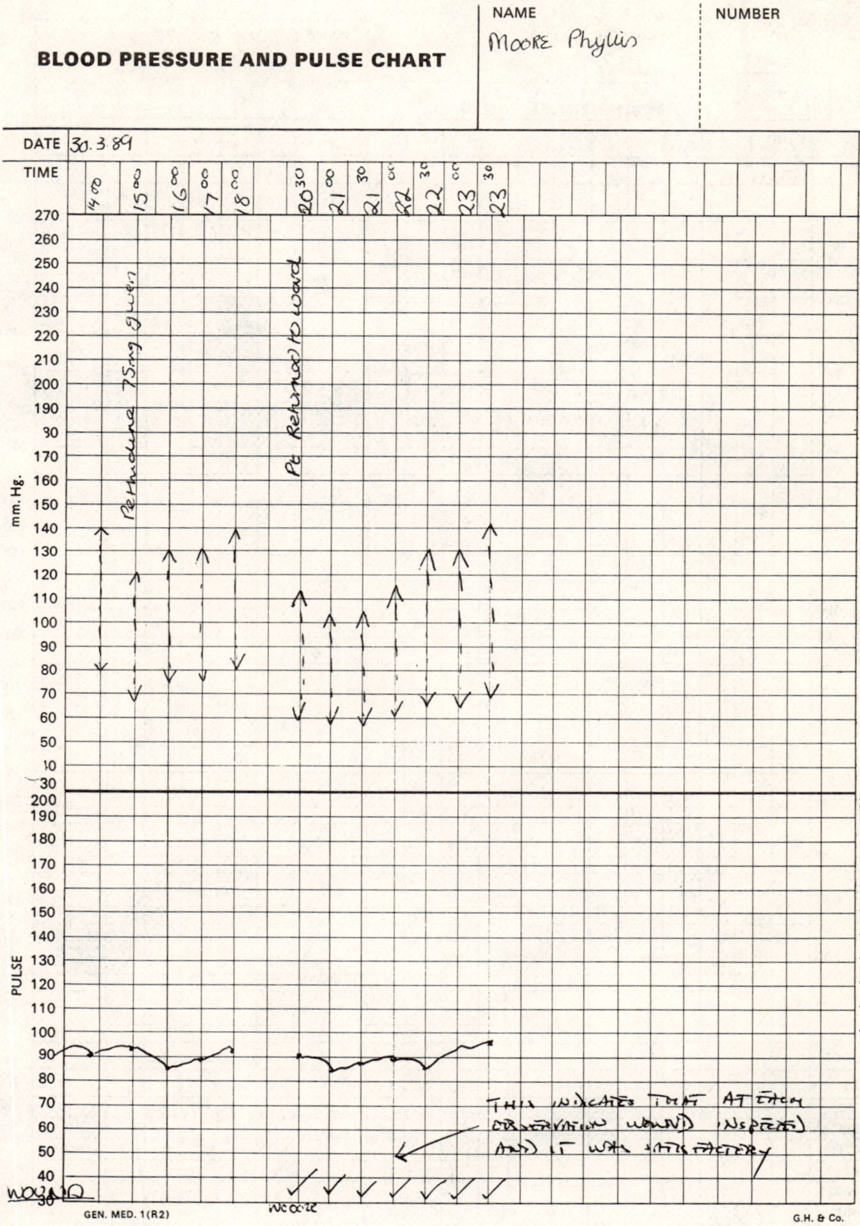

FIGURE 9.7 TEMPERATURE PULSE AND RESPIRATION CHART

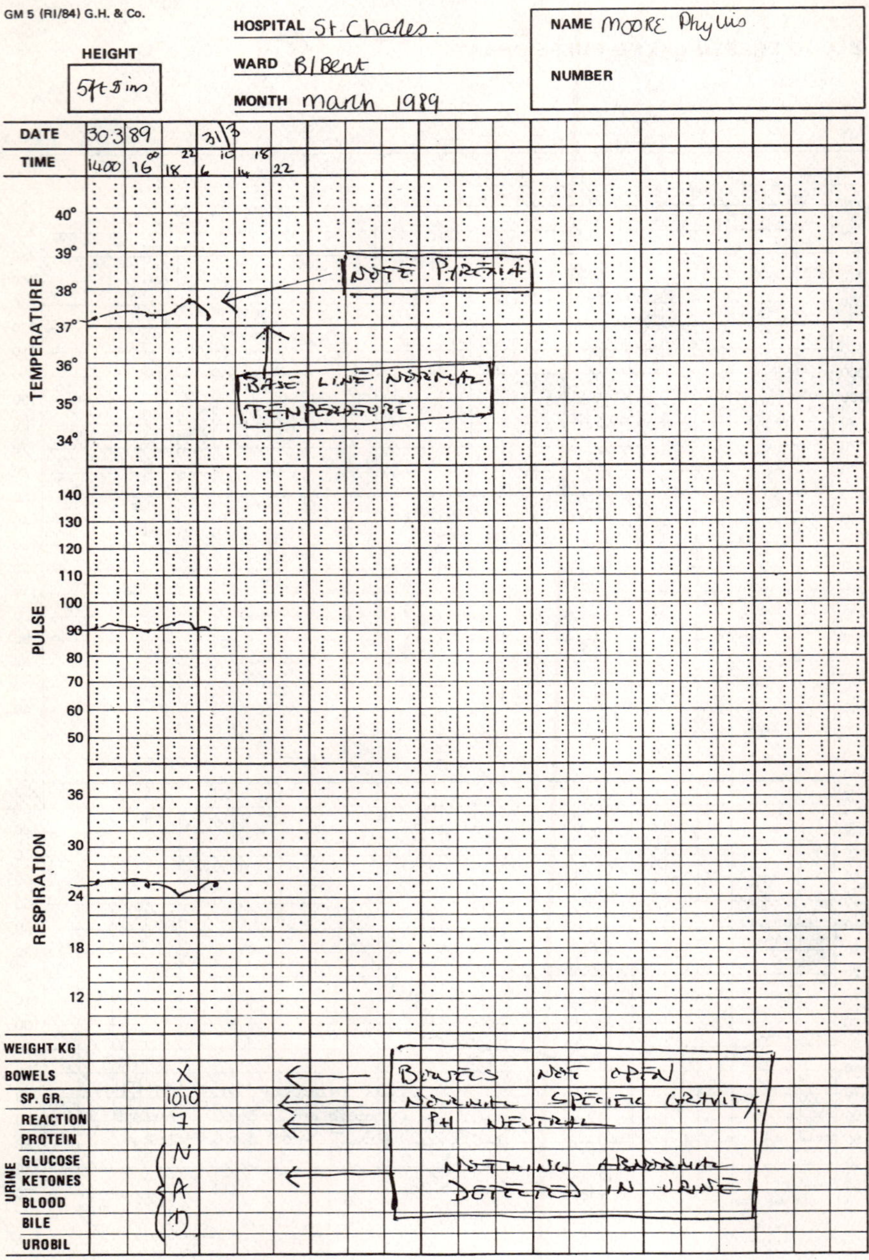

FIGURE 9.8 FLUID BALANCE SHEET

FLUID BALANCE SHEET

WARD Broadbent
Date 30/3/89

SURNAME MOORE
FORENAME Phyllis
HOSPITAL No.
(PLEASE USE ADDRESSOGRAPH LABEL)

	INPUT			OUTPUT			
Hour	Oral/ Enteral	Peripheral IV	Central IV	Urine	Vomit/ Aspirate	Drains	Other
07.00	NBM						
08.00							
09.00	(NIL BY MOUTH)						
10.00							
11.00							
12.00							
13.00							
14.00							
15.00							
16.00							
17.00							
18.00		1 unit whole blood					
19.00							
20.00							
21.00				HNPU			
22.00							
23.00		2° unit whole blood		(HAS NOT PASSED URINE)			
24.00							
01.00							
02.00	Sips of H_2O	Due 03 hrs					
03.00	(WATER)						
04.00							
05.00							
06.00							
Totals							

TOTAL INPUT TOTAL OUTPUT BALANCE

WZW 205 PARKSIDE HEALTH AUTHORITY

FIGURE 9.9 HAEMATOLOGY AND BIOCHEMISTRY RESULT FORM

PATIENT NAME / S99050
28069

JSPS *H

* .

81 Harley Street, W1N 1DE
01-935 7710
& MetPath C.L.S.

Request rec'd 3/2/89 Form dated 2/2/89

HAEMATOLOGY

HAEMOGLOBIN	17.0	g/dL	(M 13.5-18.0 F 12.0-16.4)
Red cells	5.65	x10^12/L	(M 4.5-6.5 F 3.8-5.8)
HCT ratio (PCV)	0.509		(M 0.4-0.54 F 0.37-0.47)
M.C.V.	90.0	fL	(80 - 98)
M.C.H.	30.1	pg	(27 - 32)
M.C.H.C.	33.4	g/dL	(32 - 36)
ESR	3	mm/hour	(up to 10)
WHITE CELLS	7.3	x10^9/L	(4 - 11)

BIOCHEMISTRY

*** Urea**	**7.4**	**mmol/L**	**(2.5 - 7.0)**
Creatinine	109	umol/L	(45 - 120)
*** Uric acid**	**511**	**umol/L**	**(200 - 500)**
Glucose	3.9	mmol/L	(2.8 - 8.9)
Calcium	2.59	mmol/L	(2.1 - 2.6)
Phosphorus	1.23	mmol/L	(0.8 - 1.4)
Total Bilirubin	20.0	umol/L	(3 - 20)
Alkaline Phosphatase	55	IU/L	(30 - 115)
*** Alanine Transferase**	**89**	**IU/L**	**(up to 45)**
*** Aspartate Transferase**	**45**	**IU/L**	**(up to 41)**
Gamma GTP	58	IU/L	(up to 65)
Total Proteins	76	g/L	(60 - 80)
Albumin	48	g/L	(34 - 50)
Globulin	28	g/L	(16 - 37)
*** Cholesterol**	**7.9**	**mmol/L**	**(Optimum < 6.0)**
HDL Cholesterol	1.2	mmol/L	(M 0.8-1.9 F 0.9-2.2)
	15	% of total.	(Optimum > 20)
*** LDL Cholesterol**	**6.1**	**mmol/L**	**(< 4.9)**
Triglycerides	1.37	mmol/L	(0.8 - 2.0)

FIGURE 9.10 BACTERIOLOGY REQUEST/REPORT FORM

Lab. No. | **ST. CHARLES HOSPITAL, W10** | **Tel: 01-969 2488**

Consultant or G.P.	Clinical Details	IF ADDRESSOGRAPH LABEL ALL COPIES	
S. HARWOOD	POST OPERATIVE WOUND INFECTION	Surname: DIXON	Hosp. No.
Doctor's Name for enquiries (BLOCK LETTERS): Dr. S. ROBERTS		Forenames: Robert	
Results to: Ward/Address: Ward 3		Address	
		Date of Birth: 28. 4. 22	Sex: M/~~F~~
Date and time specimen taken: 10. 5. 88	Investigation required: CULTURE AND SENSITIVITY	G.P. Patients only NHS / PRIVATE	Antibiotic therapy: Specify Drug: FLUCLOXACILLIN; ~~to have~~ / is having / ~~has had~~

		FOR LABORATORY USE ONLY	Sensitivity to	1	2	3
White cells/cmm/HPF		Heavy growth of staphylococcus pyogenes.	Penicillin	−		
Red cells /cmm/HPF			Amoxy/Ampicillin	−		
Squames			Flucloxacillin	+		
Trich. vaginalis			Erythromycin	−		
Yeasts			Sulphonamide			
			Trimethoprim			
No growth at 24hrs			Cefazolin/ Cephradine	+		
No growth at 48hrs			Gentamicin			
No growth at			Nalidixic Acid			
No significant growth			Nitrofurantoin			
Normal Flora			Ticarcillin/ Piperacillin			
Faecal Flora		Seen by				
Skin Flora						

BACTERIOLOGY
WZZ 961 | Specimen: WOUND SWAB | Date of report: 13. 5. 88

FIGURE 9.11 X-RAY REQUEST/REPORT FORM

ST. CHARLES HOSPITAL **X-RAY DEPARTMENT** **X-RAY Number**
COMPLETE ENTIRE FORM WITH BALL-POINT PEN **CONSULTANT**

CLINICAL DETAILS
Pain in (R) wrist after a fall ? fracture

SURNAME
SMITH

HOSPITAL NUMBER

FORENAMES
JOE

DATE OF BIRTH
4.3.45

WARD/DEPT.
m A & E

DATE OF PREVIOUS X-RAY

FOETAL RADIATION HAZARD	10 DAY RULE		DATE OF LMP		
	APPLY	IGNORE			

DR.'s SIGNATURE N. Howard.

Ambulant	Chair	Trolley With/Without Drip	Portable

REPORT
RIGHT WRIST 28.3.89:
A recent fracture of the Scaphoid is noted. There has been an old Colles fracture and there is residual displacement.

FG 29.3.89

Result seen by:-

REQUEST (R) wrist.

DATE:
28.3.89.

G.M. 40 (R) ST. C. G.H. & Co. Ltd.

CHAPTER 10

The medical report

Dr Michael Powers *Barrister*
Mr Nigel H Harris *MA MB BChir FRCS*

SUMMARY

10.1 This chapter is written from the plaintiff's viewpoint. However, the format of the reports for exchange is appropriate for whichever side they are prepared.

10.2 'While negligence should be discovered and made answerable if it has taken place, enquiries into cause and effect have to remember that there are accidents which no human agency can foresee or prevent' – 'Regarding an Inquiry into the Cause of a Rail Crash', The Times, 13 December 1988.

10.3 Fundamental to each party's case is the evidence of the medical experts upon whom reliance is placed at trial. The defendant should be able clearly to see the case that he has to meet if the plaintiff's case has been properly pleaded upon the basis of sound and corroborated medical opinions delivered and justified in the early preparation of the case. If there has been no intimation of a willingness on the part of the defendant to settle a claim it is unlikely to follow immediately following the service of the Statement of Claim. Nevertheless, that vital pleading should be full, strong and precise, as it is through this medium that the experts' criticisms of the defendant's conduct are made and it is the allegations of negligence particularised in the Statement of Claim that the experts will be expected to support.

10.4 Paragraphs **11.87–11.94** deal with the *Naylor* and *Kirkup* decisions and the rationale for the simultaneity of exchange of medical evidence. However, in respect of cases where the writ is issued subsequent to 3 June 1990 it is now necessary to serve a medical report with the Statement of Claim (RSC Order 18, rule 12(1A)). To this extent in the county court there is an equivalent procedure under CCR 6, rule 1(5). If the case has been fully and properly pleaded the medical evidence exchanged should cause the respective parties no surprises save perhaps as to the revealed identity of the experts. No new issues of liability or causation should arise and, if indeed they do, amendment to the pleadings will be required.[1]

1 See *Sayer v Kingston and Esher Health Authority*, 9 March 1989 – reported (1989) Independent, 27 March, CA.

10.5 RSC Order 18, rule 12(1C) defines a medical report as a 'report substantiating all the personal injuries alleged in the Statement of Claim which the plaintiff proposes to adduce in evidence as part of his case at the trial'. In the decided cases there is an issue as to whether substantiation includes a requirement to attribute the injuries to an event and, notwithstanding the judgment of the Court of Appeal in *Lort*,[1] it may be that different considerations apply to cases where on the face of the case, the very injuries complained of also pre-dated the event of which complaint is made.[2]

1 *Lort v Thames Water Utilities Ltd* (29 January 1993, unreported, CA).
2 See the judgments of Kennedy J in the benzodiazepine litigation: *L & W v John Wyeth & Brother Ltd* (6 May 1992, unreported) and *Mohammed Nur v John Wyeth & Brother Ltd* (March 1993, unreported). See the application of the principle in a medical negligence case: *Prince v Palmer* (Reading District Registry) (22 June 1993, unreported).

10.6 Often attribution is not necessary. For example in a running down action, the fact that the cuts and fractures referred to in a medical report arise from that event may be obvious. In other cases however it may not reasonably be within the ability of the medical expert to express an opinion on attribution on the information available to him. Indeed such attribution in the generic sense of causation may not be within the ability of a single expert. Clearly if there is any evidence of attribution this must be disclosed under the Rules before trial but it may not be in the plaintiff's interests to disclose this evidence at the time of service of the Statement of Claim.

10.7 'While some degree of consultation between experts and legal advisers is entirely proper, it is necessary that expert evidence presented to the court should be, and should be seen to be, the independent product of the expert, uninfluenced as to form or content by the exigencies of litigation': per Lord Wilberforce in *Whitehouse v Jordan*.[1]

1 [1981] 1 All ER 267 at 276, HL.

10.8 This view was followed by Lord Denning MR shortly after in *Kelly v London Transport Executive*[1] when considering the duties of solicitors acting for legally aided clients:

They must not run up costs by instructing endless medical experts for endless reports or by any unnecessary expenditure. They must not ask a medical expert to change his report, at their own instance, so as to favour their own legally aided client or conceal anything that may be against him. They must not 'settle' the evidence of the medical experts as they did in *Whitehouse v Jordan*, which received the condemnation of this Court and the House of Lords . . .

1 [1982] 2 All ER 842 at 851, CA.

10.9 Lord Denning MR went on to state that counsel was no differently placed in this regard. Clearly there is a duty upon both the solicitor and barrister not to mislead the lay client, legal aid area committee, the court, or indeed anyone, by settling a report which does not represent the validly held and relevant views of the expert concerned. Besides, no self-respecting expert would countenance associating his name with any report which did not accurately and fairly set out *his* opinion. Counsel would find himself in an intolerable position were an expert to be cross-examined successfully upon the basis that his disclosed report (which had been settled by counsel) did not accord with the expert's oral evidence.

10.10 An expert may be asked to amend any preliminary report in the light of the issues which it emerges are central to the case and to make other adjustments to his written opinion so as to reflect more closely the weight and tenor of the opinion he has given in conference. It is commonly the case that a view formed in a first stage report (see below) requires extensive revision if not an about-turn on the opinion expressed once the expert has considered the matter more fully with the client, other experts and the lawyers.[1]

1 *Folkes v Chadd* (1782) 3 Doug KB 157; see generally, Carol Goodwin-Jones 'Role of Expert Witness' in *Men of Science and Men of Law* and *The Expert Witness* by Jean Graham Hall and Gordon Smith (Barry Rose Law Publishers Ltd, 1992); also *Maynard v West Midlands Regional Health Authority* [1985] 1 All ER 635, [1984] 1 WLR 634, HL.

10.11 It should always be remembered that it is for the lawyers and *not* the medical experts to assess the merits of the case. Of course, there will often be a close correlation between the view expressed by counsel and that expressed by the experts. The medical expert has therefore to tread the difficult path between that of witness, lawyer and judge. He should not so express his expert opinion on the medical issues as to amount to a determination of the merits, a fortiori, he should *not* make any conclusions of fact. It is his opinion on the facts, as stated, not his opinion *of* the facts which is required.[1]

1 *Hollington v F Hewthorn & Co Ltd* [1943] KB 587, [1943] 2 All ER 35, CA.

10.12 Finally, the expert has to avoid hyperbole. If he is experienced he will appreciate the danger of using adjectives too loosely. Above all he should endeavour to be objective in his assessment. With these preliminary observations in mind, we seek to give more particular guidance as to the preparation of medical reports which are required in a medical negligence action at different stages.

THE FIRST STAGE REPORT

10.13 It is common, though not invariable, practice that very early in the case, following disclosure of the medical evidence and obtaining all relevant statements that one or more medical experts will be requested to prepare reports on liability and causation to give the client and the lawyers an early opportunity to assess the merits of the matter and make decisions as to the further steps that will have to be taken. In her chapter on 'Preparation of medical evidence on liability', Anne Winyard gives guidance on finding the right expert (para **9.33** et seq). Experienced solicitors and counsel have personal knowledge of experts in different specialities whose opinion is valued. Some experts, like lawyers, are better on paper than in court. This has to be borne in mind. At this stage, forensic ability is not essential: a learned, fair and objective approach is. Regrettably one often has to wait for many months for the best experts who are themselves overworked with clinical and medico-legal case loads. Occasionally, in such circumstances (when those instructing are well known to the expert) a brief and informal opinion may be obtained over the telephone and some idea gained thereby of the likely final opinion.

10.14 It is not always necessary to have a 'first stage' report. Whether or not a report is required will depend in part upon the requirement of the party funding the action. The main purpose is to assist those involved before the assessment of the merits of the case in conference. The preparation of medical negligence cases is essentially team work and each member of the team, be he counsel, solicitor, expert or professional client, comes to know what the others require in order to make an early 'team conference' an effective exercise.

10.15 For example, given a prospective claim in respect of a baby believed to have suffered brain damage associated with birth asphyxia, where there is a history from the parents of poor delivery care and/or delay and the labour ward records are prima facie inadequate and/or consistent with delay in the management of recorded signs of fetal distress, it will be self-evident to solicitor and counsel that there is a case which justifies a full and careful investigation in conference with experts and full written reports. Similarly where a previously fit patient dies or suffers irreversible brain damage under anaesthesia, a prima facie case of negligence is raised and the nature of the pre-conference report (if any) might be quite different from the medical report required to give guidance at a preliminary stage on a prospectively difficult causation point. Each case will have differing requirements for expertise at the pre-conference stage. There was an occasion at the pre-conference stage when a legal aid area committee refused to extend a certificate (which only covered an opinion from counsel on quantum) to allow an advice on liability where a general practitioner had failed on several occasions to make a diagnosis of pregnancy. Initially the committee took the view that the case was so strong on its merits that an opinion was not required from a medical expert or counsel on the issue of liability. In the event, the matter did merit close examination of liability issues.

10.16 Experience has shown that in a significant number of cases the early assessment of the merits, whether by doctor or lawyer, proves unreliable. The early false positive raises hopes only later to be dashed after considerable waste of expenditure on costs. Nevertheless, an optimal consideration of the strength of the cases is ultimately made. Of greater concern is the number of early false negative opinions, for these cases may not be pursued sufficiently for their true merits ever to be ascertained. What then is to go into this first stage report?

10.17 The expert instructed will have been provided with all the relevant primary materials including the statements of plaintiff and other relevant witnesses (see Chapter 9). It is often important for the medical expert instructed to see and examine the proposed plaintiff. This is a matter which should be left to his discretion. He will also have been given some guidance upon the standard of proof required. His opinion will necessarily be dependent upon the facts available to him. As the factual basis later changes or develops, so may his opinion. It is for this latter reason that it is so unsafe in the preliminary stages to give an immutable opinion on the merits. The expert should recognise this and qualify the opinion he expresses in his written report accordingly. This is particularly the case where he is requested to provide a written report before conference.

THE GENERAL STRUCTURE OF THE FIRST STAGE REPORT

10.18 A written report is only necessary where it serves one or more of the following purposes:

(a) to apprise the lay client of the medical issues and the areas where, on the stated facts and the accounts in the medical records, there appears to have been a departure from acceptable practice as it stood at the material time;
(b) to apprise, directly or indirectly, the Legal Aid Committee and/or the 'insurer';
(c) to apprise the solicitors and counsel of the essential medical issues as they appear to the expert and to give such guidance and instruction as may be thought necessary for those issues to be dealt with in an informed way in conference.

10.19 No particular format is essential. However, since most experts use or have access to word processing facilities, the presentation and style of the report later to be exchanged might usefully be employed in generic format for the first stage report. We advise the adoption of the following guidance:

(a) Typescript should be used, 1.5 or double-spaced on A4 paper with 1 inch margins.
(b) The title page should show:
    (i) the name of the plaintiff and his date of birth;
    (ii) a short summary of the report, e g 'Medical Report on the circumstances surrounding the fourth pregnancy of Mrs A B Cee and the delivery of her child, Dee, by Caesarian Section at St Elsewhere's General Hospital, on 1 April 1994';
    (iii) the name, qualifications and appointment of the expert making the report;
    (iv) the date and purpose (e g before first conference with counsel) of the report;
    (v) a statement of on whose behalf the report has been prepared.

(c) A detailed list of all medical records, reports, statements and materials upon which the opinion is based.

(d) A chronological account of the facts – as they appear from the source materials – set out such that random access may be made to any particular date or time.

Frequently there will be discrepancies between the dates/times given by the lay client, his witnesses, and the various entries in the medical records. Most are likely to be of minor significance and ultimately these discrepancies should be reconciled to enable the pleadings to be consistent and to raise as few issues as possible. The lay client should not have his credibility reduced by irrational adherence to unsubstantiated dates and times – particularly where they have no or only minimal importance to the central issues in the case. The expert in this report may usefully draw attention to the chronological discrepancies and, if he so chooses, form and express a view as to the timing of the relevant events, whilst remembering that this part of the report should be reserved for the exposition of fact and not opinion.

(e) The important events in the history should be identified and, where necessary, an account given of the relevant medical principles involved in the plaintiff's management. Where relevant an account of the natural history of the pathological process should be given for it often proves to be of critical importance.

These are perhaps the most difficult tasks for the expert. He has to reduce his great learning and experience into simple quintessential propositions upon which his opinion will be founded. Relevant textbook authorities and learned articles should be cited and copies appended to the report for the pre-conference consideration of all those attending.

(f) Having set out the facts and the relevant fundamental medical principles, the final step is for the expert to express his opinion by formulating a conclusion on the standard and acceptability of all aspects of the care the plaintiff received.

It is important for the expert to cover this ground widely. He should not confine his expression of opinion to those areas upon which the lay client has alighted as being the relevant areas of concern. If he has been provided with the reports from other experts it is useful for him to indicate any areas of disagreement such that these may later be explored in conference.

(g) A brief curriculum vitae, including a list of publications should be included unless the purpose of this report is only for para **10.18**(c) above and there are no publications relevant to the issues concerned which solicitors/counsel should have considered.

10.20 The expert should be aware of the legal dicta. In particular he should know the *Bolam* principle:

> . . . I must tell you what in law we mean by 'negligence'. In the ordinary case which does not involve any special skill, negligence in law means a failure to do some act which a reasonable man in the circumstances would do, or the doing of some act which a reasonable man in the circumstances would not do; and if the failure or the doing of that act results in injury, then there is a cause of action. How do you test whether this act or failure is negligent? In the ordinary case it is generally said that you judge it by the action of the man in the street. He is the ordinary man. In one case

it has been said you judge by the conduct of the man on the top of the Clapham omnibus. He is the ordinary man. But where you get a situation which involves some special skill or competence, then the test as to whether there has been negligence or not is not the test of the man on the top of the Clapham omnibus, because he has not got that special skill. A man need not possess the highest expert skill; it is well established law that it is sufficient if he exercises the ordinary skill of an ordinary competent man exercising that particular art: per McNair J.[1]

In a later passage McNair J cited Lord Clyde, Lord President:[2]

In the realm of diagnosis and treatment there is ample scope for genuine difference of opinion and one man clearly is not negligent merely because his conclusion differs from that of other professional men, nor because he has displayed less skill or knowledge than others would have shown. The true test for establishing negligence in diagnosis or treatment on the part of a doctor is whether he has been proved to be guilty of such failures that no doctor of ordinary skill would be guilty of if acting with ordinary care.

1 Address to the jury in *Bolam v Friern Hospital Management Committee* [1957] 1 WLR 582 at 586. Subsequently approved by the House of Lords in *Whitehouse v Jordan* [1981] 1 All ER 267, [1981] 1 WLR 246 and later in *Maynard v West Midlands Regional Health Authority* [1985] 1 All ER 635, [1984] 1 WLR 634.

2 *Hunter v Hanley* 1955 SLT 213 at 217.

10.21 Unless it is quite clear to the expert that there has been a breach of the duty of professional care, he is best advised to reserve his opinion until he has had the opportunity more fully to consider the matter in conference with the client and the other experts instructed. It is usually wise for the expert to reserve any firm conclusion in the expression of his opinion until the facts upon which it is to be based are agreed or clearly identified to the doctor's professional and lay clients.

THE SECOND STAGE REPORT

10.22 The meeting of the experts in conference with counsel is crucial to the case and has the following objectives:

(a) Collective analysis and interpretation of the medical records. It is frequently the case that it is only when the experts and lawyers are assembled together that the significance of entries in different parts of the notes is fully appreciated.

(b) The identification of all the relevant medical records of which discovery is still to be given.

(c) The resolution of (alternatively, the accounting for) discrepancies of date/time differences between lay client and witnesses' accounts and the dates and times recorded in the medical notes.

(d) The clarification of other matters where lay and recorded medical accounts differ. The lay client may be convinced, for example, that he was not seen by a doctor. The notes may show he was apparently seen by a lady doctor, whom in his distress he had mistaken for a nurse.

(e) The determination of precisely what was done – assuming the medical records to be accurate.

(f) The rationale for action/inaction at the various times in question. In the meritorious cases it is the investigation of the proposed defendants' rationale which throws into relief the negligence which hitherto would only have been suspected. The criteria for the action taken (based upon the pattern of symptoms and signs recorded in the notes and remembered by the plaintiff) may be such that it can be said that more timely intervention would probably have avoided the injury in respect of which complaint is made. An investigation requested may have been reported as abnormal but no notice taken of it, or, its import missed.

(g) The identification/confirmation of the parties to the action.

(h) The identification of the boundaries of contemporary standards of care.

The conference provides the opportunity, often necessary, for the experts to be told or reminded of the *Bolam* principle and the manner in which the principle is to be applied when looking at a particular specialist doctor's actions. For example, the standard by which a general practitioner is to be judged when professing to provide ante-natal care: skilled obstetrician or skilled general practitioner? Particularly in respect of the standard of care to be applied in general practice, the experts may need guidance between the 'common practice' and the minimal standard of practice which (when it comes to court) can be condoned.

(i) The identification of each and every negligent act and omission which the experts are prepared to support and which can be included in the Statement of Claim.

(j) The limitation of the experts' expertise needs to be ascertained and other areas requiring specialist expertise identified.

A decision has to be made upon whether the matter should proceed any further before this assistance is obtained.

(k) The consideration of the issues of causation.

Medical negligence cases, by their very nature, commonly give rise to issues of causation. The experts need to be reminded of the legal principles presently applicable[1] and the extent to which they are willing and able to support the necessary causal nexus between the breach of duty alleged and the injury.

(l) The decision on the merits and the further steps to be taken.

(m) The identification of medical textbooks and learned articles upon which reliance may be placed.

1 See *Bonnington Castings Ltd v Wardlaw* [1956] AC 613, [1956] 1 All ER 615, HL and *Hotson v East Berkshire Area Health Authority* [1987] AC 750, [1987] 2 All ER 909, HL; see also discussion of legal principles in Chapter 16.

10.23 It will be appreciated that by the conclusion of the conference with the experts the ground may have shifted appreciably from that set out in any first stage reports. Where they are acquainted with the legal process, the experts will have no misgivings about making substantial changes for their written (second stage) report. The best time for these changes to be made is immediately after the conference. It is better to persuade those experts who are unaccustomed to the legal process from committing themselves until they have had the benefit of discussing the whole matter in conference. An accurate note of the deliberations in conference may serve the dual purpose of both refreshing the experts (should there be any delay in the provision of their second stage reports) and counsel (should there be any delay in the settling of the Statement of Claim). A good attendance note may also serve as a sufficient advice (particularly if checked and endorsed by counsel) for the purpose of obtaining any requisite extension in the Certificate of Legal Aid. This saves counsel's time, delay and the incurrence of further and unnecessary costs in the provision of a written opinion simply reciting the advice already given in conference. Furthermore such unnecessary costs are not fairly recoverable inter partes.

THE GENERAL STRUCTURE OF THE SECOND STAGE REPORT

10.24 The expert report at this stage serves one or more of the following purposes:

(a) the reduction into writing of the opinions formulated with other experts in conference for the benefit of counsel, solicitor and lay client;
(b) as an aide memoire to the expert who will subsequently be asked to approve the draft Statement of Claim before service;
(c) as a revised and more accurate account for disclosure to other experts who are to be instructed in the case who did not attend the initial conference with counsel; and
(d) as the basis for the report subsequently to be prepared for disclosure.

10.25 In respect of this report we advance the following guidelines, which correspond with those in para **10.19**:

(a) As for the first stage report.
(b) As for the first stage report.
(c) As for the first stage report but including the input from the other experts in conference.
(d) As for the first stage report, save that the chronology should now be the one agreed as the most probable on all the evidence.

This inevitably means that there will be incorporated into the regularised chronology some conclusions on the facts. The expert can best deal with this by a qualification in his report along the lines that: the following chronology has been compiled from the several sources identified and it is upon this presumed factual basis that the opinion had been formulated. This precursor to the final report for exchange overcomes any reticence the expert may have about expressing a favourable view on liability where his own subjective view of the facts differs from that upon which the case is advanced.
(e) The events, the particular management of which falls to be scrutinised, should be specified.
(f) The medical objectives and fundamental principles of management of the relevant events should be set out, illustrated and supported by reference to recognised contemporary textbooks and leading learned articles.

This section of the report is similar to that of the pre-conference report but now better focused upon the issues which have been identified and agreed. In short, the report should define the minimum standard of medical care required in the identified circumstances. This then becomes the benchmark against which that which was actually done may be assessed. The opinion expressed upon that which was done in the light of the particularised deficiencies is the key to the written opinions and should closely correlate with the case to be pleaded – reserving to the other specialists those opinions peculiarly within their separate expertise.

(g) This part of the report is essentially as before with such modifications as are appropriate in the light of the conference and counsel's observations.

THE FINAL REPORT

10.26 A number of steps will have been taken following the previous report:

(a) the plaintiff's case will have been pleaded and approved by the experts;
(b) further and better particulars of the Statement of Claim may have been settled – possibly with the further assistance of the experts;
(c) the defence (it is to be hoped, fully pleaded) and any further and better particulars thereof will have been served;
(d) answers to any interrogatories will have been provided;
(e) further discovery may have been obtained;
(f) other experts may have been instructed and conferences held;
(g) most, if not all of the procedural steps will have been taken;
(h) arrangements will probably have been made for a pre-exchange review of the entire case.

THE PRE-EXCHANGE CONFERENCE

10.27 Armed with all the information referred to above, the team needs to assemble before exchange of expert evidence to ensure that in the light of all the evidence

(i) the merits remain strong;
(ii) the case is fully pleaded;[1] and
(iii) the experts instructed have covered all the relevant ground.

1 See *Sayer v Kingston and Esher Health Authority*, 9 March 1989 – reported (1989) Independent, 27 March, CA.

10.28 This is often the stage (if the nature of the case so requires) at which leading counsel should become involved. The experts dealing with present condition and prognosis (see later) should also attend this conference if possible, for although neither their reports nor their evidence will necessarily deal with issues of liability and causation, those issues may well be within their area of expertise and it is absolutely essential to ensure that their views, if not expressed, accord with those of the experts primarily giving evidence on matters pertaining to liability.

THE GENERAL STRUCTURE OF THE FINAL REPORT

10.29 The only requirement for this report is that the 'substance'[1] has to be disclosed in the form of a written report. There is authority to suggest that the report of an expert will only comply with the rule if the *whole* of the opinion is disclosed and that it is necessary to take the good with the bad if a party proposes to rely upon that expert[2] but the rules require only that the substance of the evidence it is *intended* the expert should give on the pleaded case.[3] An expert should never assume the role of advocate. He should:[4]

(a) make clear the facts and assumptions upon which the opinion was based together with material facts which would detract from the concluded opinion;
(b) make it clear when a question or issue fell outside his expertise;
(c) state if the opinion was not properly researched because it was considered that insufficient data was available: an indication that the opinion was provisional might be necessary. In particular, if he could not assert that the report contained the truth, the whole truth and nothing but the truth then that qualification should be stated on the report; and
(d) in the event of him changing his mind on a material matter (after the exchange of reports) then the change of view should be communicated to the other side through legal representatives without delay and, when appropriate, to the court.

These reports are those which the judge will read and, accordingly, they should be written in a way which is factually accurate, logical and comprehensible. A glance at a selection of expert reports is sufficient to see the range of quality of presentation and care with which they have been prepared. The lawyers' objective must be to ensure that when reference is necessary to the subject matter, the reader chooses to refer to the reports of their experts.

1 RSC Ord 38, r 37.
2 See *Kenning v Eve Construction Ltd* [1989] 1 WLR 1189.
3 See *Derby & Co Ltd v Weldon (No 9)* [1991] 2 All ER 901.
4 Per Cresswell J, *National Justice Compania Naviera SA v Prudential Assurance Co Ltd (Ikarian Reefer)* [1993] 2 Lloyd's Rep 68, (1993) 37 EG 158n.

10.30 In respect of this critical report we propose the following and corresponding guidelines:

(a) As for the second stage report (see para **19.25**).
(b) As for the second stage report, save that it should not be apparent that this report is one of a series.
(c) A list of material relied upon as the basis for the opinion expressed should be included in the final report.

As the parties should have had the benefit of exchanged witness statements pursuant to RSC Order 38, rule 2A (see Chapter 11) before the final report is served, the list should include identification of the relevant statements.

(d) There should be no or only small change to this section from the second stage report. However the detailed chronology should take account of:
  (i) any revisions agreed as a consequence of the pleaded defence, interrogatories, defence witness statements, etc, and
  (ii) any further discovery.

  The substantive change is that by this stage the trial bundle pagination should be on the medical notes. Factual statements in the chronology which arise from the medical notes can be identified by reference to particular page numbers. The principal responsibility for the preparation of the trial bundles falling upon the plaintiff's solicitors places the plaintiff's experts in the position to quote page references. If several experts are involved it is pointless to repeat the chronology in each report. Reference can simply be made to the report in which it has been decided the chronology should be contained. This places upon the expert assuming this responsibility the burden of ensuring that the chronology is accurate.

(e) This should be unchanged from the second stage report.

Every effort should be made to illustrate the principles relied upon to assist in the education of the judge who may be coming to the technicalities of the case for the first time. The report is not written for the benefit of the other side's experts but for the court. It should not be assumed that medical principles and terminology will be understood without explanation or definition. It may be necessary to append a glossary of medical terms.

(f) This may remain as prepared for the second stage report, carefully checking to ensure that following the conference there has been no revision of responsibilities to cover the allegations in the Statement of Claim.

(g) This remains as the second stage report.

THE MEDICAL REPORT ON QUANTUM

10.31 As a general principle it is sensible to avoid instructing as an expert any doctor who has treated the plaintiff. On occasion, by virtue of the particular injuries suffered this may be difficult. In any event, he will have to have expressed views which accord with the plaintiff's experts on liability and causation. He should not be the professional colleague of the alleged tortfeasor. For this reason it is preferable to avoid instructing an expert who practises in the defendants' health district. There is, of course, no reason why one of the experts instructed on issues of liability and causation should not also give an opinion of the present condition and prognosis of the plaintiff for the purpose of quantum.

10.32 No expert can properly give an opinion on the plaintiff's present condition and prognosis without the opportunity of an examination and, occasionally, some further investigation. Whilst the plaintiff usually does not object to an examination by the doctor instructed on his own behalf, it not infrequently happens that an objection is taken to the medical expert nominated by the defendants to examine the plaintiff, or, the further investigation he requires. The plaintiff is, however, under an obligation to afford the defendants' experts reasonable opportunity for examination and should he decline to submit himself for examination the defendants may make an application to the court for an order staying the plaintiff's action until such time as he does submit to examination:[1]

In the exercise of the discretion in this class of case, where a plaintiff has refused a medical examination, I think the court does have to recognise (and here I think *Pickett's* case[2] is helpful) that in the balance there are, amongst many other factors, two fundamental rights which are cherished by the common law and to which attention has to be directed by the court. First, as mentioned in *Pickett's* case by

Wilmer and Donovan LJJ, and by Sachs LJ in *Lane's* case,[3] there is the plaintiff's right to personal liberty. But on the other side there is an equally fundamental right – the defendant's right to defend himself in the litigation as he and his advisers think fit; and this is a right which includes the freedom to choose the witnesses that he will call. It is particularly important that a defendant should be able to choose his own expert witnesses, if the case be one in which expert testimony is significant.

With the initial approach in *Pickett's* case I find I have considerable sympathy; and I do not think it is an approach that has been discarded by these courts. A plaintiff is not to be regarded as acting unreasonably merely because he does not wish, or his advisers do not wish him, to be examined by a doctor chosen by the defendant. But, if a defendant insists on examination of the plaintiff by the doctor he, the defendant, has nominated, then the problem does arise: in what circumstances will the court order a stay unless the plaintiff yields?

First, one has to look to the defendant's request and ask oneself the question: is it a reasonable request? The defendant is not to be regarded as making an unreasonable request merely because he wishes to have the plaintiff examined by a doctor unacceptable to the plaintiff. The decisive factor, therefore, becomes, as I think Lord Denning MR recognised in *Edmeades v Thames Board Mills Ltd*,[4] that of the interests of justice – of the 'just determination' of the particular case. I would add that it can only be the interests of justice that could require one or other of the parties to have to accept an infringement of a fundamental human right cherished by the common law. The plaintiff can only be compelled, albeit indirectly, to an infringement of his personal liberty if justice requires it. Similarly, the defendant can only be compelled to forgo the expert witness of his choice if justice requires it.

And so in every case, as I see it, the particular facts of the case on which the discretion has to be exercised are all important. The discretion cannot be exercised unless each party does expose the reasons of his action. I have already indicated that I do not regard this as a question of proof. There is, in my judgment, a duty for each party in such a situation to provide the court with the necessary material known to him, so that the court, fully informed, can exercise its discretion properly. However, I would add this comment: that at the end of the day it must be for him who seeks the stay to show that, in the discretion of the court, it should be imposed. (Per Scarman LJ in *Starr v National Coal Board*.)[5]

If the defendant has put forward the name of a particular doctor and can show that an examination by a doctor is necessary in his interests and that this particular doctor is apparently well qualified to examine the plaintiff, the plaintiff then has to give reasons for objecting to him. He must at least be able to show that there is some substantial ground on which he or his legal advisers have formed the opinion that the doctor in question lacks the proper qualifications or is likely to conduct his examination and to make his reports unkindly or unfairly. (Per Cairns LJ in *Starr*.)[6]

There is one further principle of general application to be derived from *Starr's* case, where there was no question of risk or discomfort, and that seems to be that where the defendant's request for an examination is reasonable the court can grant a stay if the plaintiff's refusal of that request would be such as to prevent the just determination of the cause, and that the court will normally treat the fact that the defendant would be deprived of the expert of his choice as something which would prevent the just determination of the cause within the meaning of that expression as the Court of Appeal used it. (Per Webster J in *Prescott v Bulldog Tools Ltd*.)[7]

1 See RSC Ord 25, r 6(2).
2 [1961] CLY 7183.
3 [1972] 1 All ER 430 at 435.
4 [1969] 2 QB 67, [1969] 2 All ER 127.
5 [1977] 1 All ER 243 at 249.
6 Ibid at 256.
7 [1981] 3 All ER 869 at 874.

10.33 All the medical records and investigations will be required by the expert. Before writing his opinion he should have seen at least the second stage reports of the experts on breach of duty and causation. It should then only be necessary for him to set out the history in his report very briefly such that the basis upon which he formulates his conclusions on the plaintiff's present condition and prognosis is clear.

10.34 This report is *not* a liability report. Issues of causation[1] should not therefore arise or be considered within it. If they do, then this is a matter to be resolved at the conference with counsel prior to the preparation of reports for exchange.

1 For the meaning of a report substantiating all the personal injuries alleged in the Statement of Claim see para **10.5** above.

THE GENERAL STRUCTURE OF THE QUANTUM REPORT

10.35

(a) Typescript should be used, 1.5 or double-spaced on A4 paper with 1 inch margins.

(b) The title page should show:

 (i) the name of the plaintiff and his date of birth;
 (ii) a short summary of the report;
 (iii) the name, qualifications and appointment of the expert making the report;
 (iv) the date and purpose of the report;
 (v) a statement of on whose behalf the report has been prepared.

(c) A detailed list of all medical records, reports, statements and materials upon which the opinion is based.

(d) *The brief history* Although it is unlikely that by this late stage any new and relevant element of history will emerge it behoves the expert to listen to the plaintiff's story first. Sometimes this is clear and considerable detail is provided. In other cases the story is vague and numerous dates and events are forgotten. Any discrepancies in the history (which have not already been ironed out) should be noted separately and dealt with at the pre-exchange conference with all the members of the team.

(e) *The plaintiff's condition at the time of consultation* The plaintiff's present symptoms and effect of any disability on daily living activities and work must be clearly established. It is not usual for the expert to lead the plaintiff when conducting the interview but it is sometimes necessary to ask specific questions because the plaintiff does not think to mention all relevant facts. Not infrequently when eventually the plaintiff reads the report it is returned because certain vital information has been omitted.

(f) *The medical examination* In addition to obtaining objective evidence of physical disability, the examination offers the expert an opportunity to assess the personality of the patient and form an opinion as to whether he is perhaps to some degree exaggerating symptoms and their effect. A qualitative assessment may be particularly important where date of knowledge and limitation issues arise (see *Davis v City and Hackney Health Authority*[1] on the mixed test on date of knowledge).

(g) *The investigations* X-rays may be relevant and will always be so in orthopaedic cases. An up-to-date X-ray should be obtained if necessary. Consideration should be given to other sophisticated investigations such as CT scan and MRI. The expert should insist on seeing X-rays and must not rely on a radiologist's report. X-rays notoriously have a habit of going astray but it is usually worth persisting with request for early films and this is where good co-operation between expert and solicitor is often useful.

(h) *The opinion* First, it is important to establish the nature of the disability and correlate it with the plaintiff's symptoms. Factual statements should be made as to the likely cause of the disability without apportioning blame. An opinion has now to be given on prognosis and it is likely that this will have to be stated in percentage terms (see generally difficulties of causation in Chapter 16). From a medical expert's point of view this is an inexact science and tends to amount to guesswork. Nevertheless, lawyers need this information when deliberating upon the quantum of damages (e g the increased risk of developing arthritis in a joint in future years) and some sort of estimate should be made with qualifications where necessary. The accuracy of the prognosis should be stated and it should be mentioned if it is considered that a further review at some future date will be necessary.

1 [1989] 2 Med LR 366.

10.36 It is said that one doctor's defensive medicine is another's prudent practice. If a doctor embarks upon a procedure which is done for fear of litigation and which is otherwise not accepted by a competent body of professional opinion as being proper practice, he is, ex hypothesi, negligent. The law has very largely left doctors to set their own standards of acceptable practice and the legal process is only there to see fair play where allegations are made that there has been a departure from those standards which has resulted in harm. We have sought in this chapter to give some guidance to prospective medical experts as to the requirements of the legal practitioner.

CHAPTER 11

The conduct of proceedings

David Body

SUMMARY

INTRODUCTION

11.1 This chapter aims to identify the various differences which exist between the conduct of conventional personal injury litigation and the conduct of a medical negligence action. Further, to comment upon the procedural distinctions that those differences have generated.

11.2 The most immediate difference is that although the claim made is a personal injury claim for compensation, it is nevertheless professional negligence litigation alleging incompetence on the part of the professional man or woman. The refusal of the English courts to adopt an objective test of competence rather than the (medically) subjective test set out in *Bolam v Friern Hospital Management Committee*,[1] means that the plaintiff if he or she is to succeed must persuade a judge to make an adjudication in his or her favour having regard to subjective evidence adduced by both plaintiff and defendant.

1 [1957] 1 WLR 582.

11.3 The complexity of issues in these cases and the amount of expert evidence required to prove the plaintiff's claim, mean that they take a long time to prepare, a relatively long time during pleading, (usually) a long time to list and a long time at trial itself. In the 1970s the Report of the Royal Commission on Personal Injury ('the Pearson Report') (Cmnd 7054) reported that a medical negligence action was then taking 60 months from commencement to completion, compared with 43 months for other personal injury actions.

11.4 Most medical negligence plaintiffs are legally aided. The costs involved and the rule that costs follow the event, inevitably deter all but the wealthiest and most determined private client. The changes to the Legal Aid Scheme which allowed infant plaintiffs to bring claims assessed on their own, rather than their parents' means have been a significant enfranchisement. Unfortunately, the removal of a large proportion of the adult population from eligibility for legal aid is likely to make more widespread the existing public frustration at denial of access to the system of civil justice.

THE PURPOSE OF LITIGATION

11.5 A medical negligence action is a compensation claim and therefore at the end of the case – either by success at trial or by acceptable compromise – the plaintiff's solicitor's achievement on the plaintiff's behalf and the criteria against which performance will be judged, is a sum of money in compensation for avoidable injury. Whilst it is a compensation claim, a medical negligence claim is an action alleging professional negligence from which personal injury results. Strictly therefore it is not a personal injury claim; in *Rahman v Kirklees Area Health Authority*,[1] Ormrod LJ commented:

> it appears to me, from the use of the phrase action for personal injuries in the first line of the rule, that the draftsman contemplated what everyone calls an action for personal injuries, which is a running down case or a factory accident or something similar. I do not think I have ever heard of a medical negligence case spoken about as an action for personal injuries although, of course, in a sense it is.

1 [1980] 3 All ER 610.

11.6 The Court of Appeal in *Naylor v Preston Area Health Authority*[1] reinforced this view. According to Glidewell LJ (at 363):

> An action alleging negligence in the course of medical treatment falls into both categories; obviously it is an action for professional negligence and it is also an action for personal injuries within the definition of RSC Order 1, rule 4.

Lord Donaldson MR wrote (at 363):

> Finally, it was pointed out, quite correctly, that in the context of the proposals to treat medical negligence as personal injury actions, while an action for personal injuries is defined in RSC Order 1, rule 4 in wide terms . . . and would thus often include actions for medical negligence, some would not be included, e g a claim for damages for failing to impair a person's physical condition, where the allegation was that a vasectomy failed to achieve its object.

This difference in definition has no practical advantage in terms of remedy to the plaintiff and the true difference has been deliberately blurred for the practitioner by the revisions to RSC Order 18, rule 12, in June 1990. Despite this the difference between the conventional personal injury action and a medical negligence action (i e that one is more likely to succeed than the other) is one to which potential plaintiffs are very much alive.

1 [1987] 2 All ER 353.

11.7 For this reason at an early stage of any medical negligence claim it is important to make it clear to a potential plaintiff that the sole purpose of proceedings is to achieve adequate financial compensation. Medical negligence cases often have an underlying objective for the plaintiff which goes outside the realm of pure compensation. It is unfortunately commonplace that plaintiffs have not been told the whole truth about the injuries that they have sustained and indeed may often have been misled by those treating them as to the genesis of their injury. This 'breach of trust' by a doctor tends to instil a determination into a plaintiff that the true facts of the situation should be brought to light and any fault discovered in that investigation, duly apportioned. The relationship between doctor and patient reveals the patient at his or her most vulnerable and trusting.

11.8 Contrary to popular medical myth, 'compensationitis' is not endemic among plaintiffs; the failure of a doctor to tell a plaintiff the truth can engender an unwavering, almost obsessional, determination to open the entire matter to a forensic investigation by the courts and is the cause of more medical negligence litigation than anything else. In such cases, the financial aspect of compensation becomes almost a by-product: an unconditional apology and uncensored explanation will be considered a far greater victory. Unfortunately – and a potential plaintiff must be made aware of this – such apologies and explanations do not form an essential part of a successful claim which establishes medical negligence. It is the absence of this investigation and apportionment of fault which makes many plaintiffs wary of a 'no fault' based system.

11.9 As a solicitor acting on behalf of a medical negligence plaintiff, these issues must be in your mind. You also need to explain to your client that whilst the discovery of the true facts of the case is central to the way in which you will conduct it, the tort mechanism is not primarily a forensic investigation into the objective truth of the case. The only aim of the system is to assess the plaintiff's eligibility for compensation and if such eligibility is established, to compensate that plaintiff.

11.10 Sometimes a compromise to achieve compensation for a plaintiff is more important to that plaintiff than the discovery of the 'objective' truth of the case. It may have to be the solicitor's role to point this out.

PLEADINGS

11.11 In all personal injury cases the rules of pleadings set out as a code in RSC Order 18 provide a challenge to the draftsman when preparing the Statement of Claim and the defence to set out the nature of the case without entirely revealing any of the evidence which is to be relied upon at trial. In the introduction to RSC Order 18 the following succinct summary of the intention of pleadings is provided:

> the rules require the pleading to contain and contain only and in summary form the material facts upon which the party relies for his claim or defence, and not the evidence by which they are to be proved (rule 7). The interpretation of these words is a matter of skill and experience. The 'material facts' are such as are sufficient to found the cause of action or ground of defence relied upon, stated with sufficient particularity to give to the other party adequate notice of the case intended to be set up and prevent him being taken by surprise (rule 8). The distinction between the facts relied upon and the evidence to prove them is sometimes a fine one.

The conventional pattern of pleadings is as in any other personal injury action; Statement of Claim followed within fourteen days after the time limit for acknowledging service of the writ by a defence (RSC Order 18, rule 2); if a reply is appropriate it must be served within fourteen days of the service on the plaintiff of the defence (RSC Order 18, rule 3). Other pleadings subsequent to reply exist but can only be served in appropriate circumstances with the leave of the court (RSC Order 14, rule 4).

11.12 Once pleadings are closed a summons for directions is issued and dealt with by a master or district judge. Medical negligence cases differ from conventional personal injury cases in falling outside the scope of the automatic directions set out in RSC Order 25, rule 8 and CCR Order 17, rule 11. The pattern of the case and the considerations to be kept in mind at the summons for directions and afterwards are dealt with below.

ISSUES IN PLEADINGS

11.13 Within the normal scope of the pleading of 'material facts' rather than 'evidence' the plaintiff in a medical negligence action generally has greater scope for the pleading of his or her case as fully as possible, since by the time pleadings are initiated pre-action discovery has taken place within the ambit of the separate originating application required by the Supreme Court Act 1981, section 33, so that basic facts of the case should be undisputed. Further the facts and the inferences to be drawn from them have been subjected to the scrutiny of expert witnesses who have analysed the medical issues in the case and have determined that there is evidence to support the view that the plaintiff's treatment was incompetent and that a cause of action in negligence arises. As a result there are a number of ways in which the pleading of a Statement or Particulars of Claim in a medical negligence action differs from that in a conventional personal injury case.

Parties

Plaintiff

11.14 The plaintiff in the action is the person who sustained the injury *or* a surviving dependant *or* spouse of a deceased whose death was negligently caused. As in conventional personal injury claims, an under age plaintiff acts by his mother or father (or both) as Next Friends. In default of action by a parent, the Official Solicitor may act as Next Friend. A person of full age who is under a disability (within the meaning of the Mental Health Act 1983) may act by the Official Solicitor as Next Friend. Consequences other than direct physical injury may arise from a doctor's breach of duty.

11.15 A patient suing a doctor who has treated him or her on a private basis may have in addition to an action in negligence, an action for breach of contract and for vexation and distress. A similar cause of action arises where a parent has paid for his or her child's medical treatment which has failed in negligent circumstances.

11.16 The parents of an injured child may themselves have an action for damages for nervous shock and for loss of satisfaction in bringing the child up to healthy adulthood, perhaps even for the loss of a prospective dependency upon a child now unable to fulfil that expectation. This claim for nervous shock has not had that widespread an impact because of the difficulty in bringing such a limited claim in cases where the injured child may be legally aided but where the parents are not legal aid eligible and thus may run the risk of an order for costs against them quite disproportionate to the quantum of the claim they bring.

11.17 The court has power to award damages for a negligent failure to warn of material risks. The duty to warn is owed to the injured party and extends further to a parent who gives a consent on behalf of a child to an operation. This parent may have an action (separate from that of the child) for breach of duty since the child is incapable itself of giving an appropriate consent. The difficulty of satisfying the test of causation defined by Hutchison J in *Smith v Barking, Havering & Brentwood Health Authority*[1] may well have reduced such actions to claims for lost opportunity to undertake the complained of procedure on terms and at a time of the plaintiff's choosing.

1 To be reported in the Medical Law Reports.

11.18 Even where this failure to warn is of a nature fundamental to the question of whether there was a true understanding and certainty as to terms between doctor and patient, the judicial attitudes expressed in *Chatterton v Gerson*[1] and *Hills v Potter*[2] suggest that the English courts do not want to develop battery as an alternative to *or* more serious variant of, the failure to warn of risks even where that failure to warn of risk might wholly have vitiated the consent (see Chapter 12 on Consent).

1 [1981] QB 432, [1981] 1 All ER 257.
2 [1983] 3 All ER 716, [1984] 1 WLR 641n.

11.19 Actions for birth of a healthy child, cloaked as claims for a negligent failure to warn of the risks inherent in vasectomy and sterilisation are still brought but the changes in the form of consent used, for example, by the Family Planning Association and increasing judicial scepticism about the inadequacy of warning, may begin to limit the success of these claims.

11.20 A child born suffering from disabilities caused as a result of medical negligence before birth can maintain an action for negligence, since although not a person in law at the time that the injury took place, he or she is deemed (for the purpose of such action) to be born whenever such interests require. See *Burton v Islington Health Authority*;[1] *de Martell v Merton & Sutton Health Authority*.[2] This clarification of the law has opened the way for a number of claims arising from obstetric negligence which took place before the Congenital Disabilities (Civil Liability) Act 1976 had become law.

1 [1993] QB 204, [1993] 4 Med LR 8.
2 [1992] 3 All ER 833.

11.21 The failure to carry out properly or at all an amniocentesis during pregnancy may form the basis for an action for damages, if a mother:

(a) gives birth to a child with the handicap which should have been diagnosed by the test; and
(b) can show that had the test been properly carried out so that she would have been warned of the likelihood of that handicap, she would have had the pregnancy terminated (*Gregory v Pembrokeshire Health Authority*).[1]

1 [1989] 1 Med LR 81.

Defendant

11.22 By the time a Statement of Claim is drafted a decision will have been taken as to which party to join as defendant.

11.23 Where allegations are made against general practitioners, the doctor in question is sued under his or her own name and is indemnified by one of the medical indemnity societies in a manner analogous to that of a driver involved in a motor vehicle claim. A hospital doctor, however, is normally only identified as a servant or agent of the District Health Authority or National Health Service Trust by which he or she is employed and who will be vicariously liable for his or her acts or omissions.

11.24 Occasionally, an individual doctor may be joined as a separate defendant in an action, if it is suggested that his or her act or omission is so far outside the scope of professional behaviour expected of the authority's or Trust's servants or agents as to render that act or omission ultra vires that body. This is a rare occurrence and the normal situation prior to January 1990 was that the authority took responsibility for doctors acts or omissions and then invoked its 'sharing agreement' under HC/3/54 with the medical indemnity societies as to the eventual apportionment of any damages and costs awarded against itself.

11.25 From 1 January 1990 the arrangement changed and the Department of Health instituted the system of National Health Service Indemnity under HC(89)34. This removes the previous sharing agreement in relation to claims brought against doctors employed within the NHS between the Department of Health and the medical defence organisations.

11.26 Naming the doctor separately as a defendant does not always have practical advantage. Provided he is a paid up member, one of the medical defence organisations will undertake to indemnify him or her individually whilst liaising closely with any health authority or National Health Service Trust named as a separate defendant. In this respect, general practitioners, who are not afforded any institutional 'umbrella' by their relationship with a Family Health Services Authority, are in a more exposed position than a junior hospital doctor or consultant whose actions are accepted under the doctrine of vicarious liability as those of the health authority or NHS Trust for which he works.

11.27 The change brought about by HC(89)34 reduces the burden of claims on the medical defence organisations because they will now be required to cover doctors in general or private practice and not, (subject to some transitional arrangements) those working as hospital doctors in the NHS. Hospital doctors still need to maintain medical defence organisation cover if they are to undertake private practice or locum work in general practice. In the days when hospital doctors had to take out indemnity cover with medical defence organisations for which they were reimbursed by the employers, that cover was sufficient to extend to private practice or locum work. NHS indemnity no longer extends that far and it is possible to envisage circumstances (e g where junior doctors are asked by consultants to review private patients either on a private ward or at a private hospital) in which a junior doctor could be exposed to a claim without having indemnity cover. This would pose a problem for both plaintiff and defendant.

11.28 There used to be some advantage in having an individual doctor as a separate defendant when Interrogatories had to be ordered. Provision is made for the answering of Interrogatories for which application had been made under RSC Order 26, rule 2/1, the decision as to who should answer Interrogatories sought, being wholly in the discretion of the master or district judge who hears the application. However, aside from those Interrogatories which may be ordered by the court, parties may now seek Interrogatories without Order (RSC Order 26, rule 1 from February 1990) and any advantage that there may previously have been in naming an individual doctor as defendant for this purpose has been lost.

11.29 In addition, if liability is ultimately found to rest with other defendants than the named doctor, that doctor will have probably experienced a disproportionate and perhaps an unnecessary degree of publicity; this can reinforce determination to contest a claim funded by a medical defence organisation beyond what might be considered the 'commercial judgment' of an insurer in a 'conventional' personal injury action. This can prolong and hinder the progress of the case.

11.30 One issue to have arisen since that alteration in indemnity arrangements had been the question of whether 'inordinate and inexcusable delay' in the conduct of proceedings can effect prejudice to a health authority because it would be required to contribute to a greater extent than it would have done had the delayed case been brought on for trial prior to 1 January 1990. The Court of Appeal has decided that inordinate delay leading to such prejudice is sufficient to support an application that a claim be dismissed for want of prosecution under RSC Order 25, rule 1: *Antcliffe v Gloucester Health Authority*.[1]

1 [1992] 1 WLR 1044.

Liability

11.31 The fine line between 'the facts relied on and the evidence to prove them' is perhaps more difficult to draw in a medical negligence action than in any other personal injury case. Proof of liability will rely upon showing at trial divergence from a well-established clinical practice.

11.32 In order to substantiate such divergence the material facts of the clinical practice relied upon by the plaintiff must be stated. This will often necessitate providing references to current medical text books and learned articles and may include illustrating, by way of diagrams, the facts relied upon in support of a contention. Whilst this may certainly establish 'the facts relied upon', the appropriateness of such clinical practice is most likely to be established only if the court accepts the views of the plaintiff's expert witnesses at trial. Since the test of negligence applied by the court in medical cases is *subjective*, it follows that whilst the draftsman of the pleading must adhere strictly to the facts relied upon, the opinions given by experts in support of the plaintiff must be reflected in the pleading if the defendant is to know the nature of the case to be met.

11.33 The doctrine of 'res ipsa loquitur' may have a place in the pleading of medical negligence claims, particularly in anaesthetic accidents (*Saunders v Leeds Western Health Authority*),[1] but to do this the plaintiff will have to establish facts which if unexplained will give rise to an inference of negligence being drawn by the court: *Ludlow v Swindon Health Authority*.[2]

1 (1984) 129 Sol Jo 225.
2 [1989] 1 Med LR 104.

11.34 This will mean that a Statement or Particulars of Claim will and should be longer and more detailed than in other personal injury cases and may well contain terms, allegations and assertions which are closer to the province of the evidence to be adduced at trial than perhaps originally envisaged by the draftsman of RSC Order 18. The fuller the statement of the case can be, the closer will the plaintiff come to avoiding any suggestion of the 'trial by ambush' approach now condemned by the appellate courts.

11.35 As can be seen from the examples above of consequences other than direct physical injury, medical negligence claims are not necessarily personal injury claims in the 'accident case' sense.

11.36 For example a failure to warn of risk does not in itself cause a *physical* injury, it creates a loss of opportunity. It is important to maintain the distinction in pleading that the negligence alleged is a breach of professional duty of which the injury is an *accidental* consequence. For this reason particulars of breach of duty and causation must be separately pleaded in the Statement or Particulars of Claim.

Causation

11.37 In a collision between motorcars the causation of injury to a driver is rarely in issue, is clear to establish and poses few problems in pleading. However, the causal relationship between e g an anoxic episode at birth and subsequent dysphasia or deafness is far less clear and must be construed and evidenced clearly in a pleading. In particular where there are a number of competing possible causes capable of causing such injury, a plaintiff must be able to prove on the balance of probabilities that the alleged negligence was the cause or that it made a material contribution to the extent of the injury. Further where the basis of the claim is a failure to warn, corroborative evidence of the plaintiff's pre-operation intentions will need to be pleaded; *Smith v Barking, Havering & Brentwood Health Authority*.[1]

1 To be reported in the Medical Law Reports.

11.38 Pressure on judicial time and the significant increases in the number of complex medical negligence cases coming to court, matched to the escalating daily cost of these cases, had led the Court of Appeal to indicate its approval of a 'cards on the table' approach and this approach must be reflected in pleadings, as in all other facets of the case. The more clearly the plaintiff expresses the nature of his or her allegations and gives particulars of breach of duty and causation, the easier it is, or ought to be, for the defendant fully to plead a defence which gives the plaintiff adequate warning of the outline of the case that he or she will have to overcome at trial.

11.39 Until the Court of Appeal's decision in *Naylor*[1] (see below) it was the habit of the defendant's solicitors to rely upon the rule that they need not reveal the nature and extent of their expert opinion evidence before trial and to conduct the defence in a fairly (if not wholly) uncommunicative way. Little, if any, attempt was made in a defence to do other than assert a bare denial of the plaintiff's case and to give the plaintiff no hint of the stance on expert evidence to be adopted by the defendant.

1 *Naylor v Preston Area Health Authority* [1987] 2 All ER 353.

11.40 The *Naylor* decision began a significant shift in the behaviour of defendants' solicitors. The need to disclose expert reports at some distance before trial and the increasing propensity of the plaintiff's solicitors to pressurise such exchange, has meant that independent advice is taken by defendants at an earlier stage. Consequently (and perhaps making a virtue of necessity) defendants' solicitors are using independent experts to consider cases when a Statement of Claim has been received, rather than after close of pleadings as was for so long the case. Defences are much more specific than they were. The corollary of such earlier investigation is a greater propensity to admit negligence and settle indefensible cases at the earliest possible stage. This is a heartening development in a category of compensation claims in which the application for interim payment is much less common than, for example, in road traffic accident claims but where the injury sustained may well be no less susceptible of rehabilitation.

11.41 Continuing pressure by plaintiffs' solicitors in the form of detailed Statements of Claim, searching Requests for Particulars and Interrogatories will continue this trend towards earlier identification of the true issues between plaintiffs and defendants.

11.42 The inherent complexity of medical negligence cases combined with the difficulties in adducing evidence on liability and causation, make it essential from the outset that the plaintiff is enabled to begin the process of pleading with the fullest possible Statement or Particulars of Claim setting out his or her case.

11.43 The tide of judicial times, reflected in the strictures expressed by the Court of Appeal in the case of *Wilsher v Essex Area Health Authority*,[1] indicates that the judiciary expect medical negligence cases in particular to come to court as fully pleaded as possible and with the disputes remaining between the parties clearly identified and presented so that the judge is enabled quickly to grasp the issues and come to a determination.

1 [1986] 3 All ER 801.

THE CHANGES TO RSC ORDER 18, RULE 12

11.44 Obligations to produce a medical report and a statement of special damages as an element of, or adjunct to, the Statement (or Particulars) of Claim were imposed by the following revisions to RSC Order 18, rule 12, which were introduced in June 1990.

(1A) Subject to paragraph (1B), a plaintiff in an action for personal injuries shall serve with his Statement of Claim

(a) a medical report, and
(b) a statement of the special damages claimed

(1B) Where the documents to which paragraph 1A applies are not served with the Statement of Claim, the Court may

(a) specify the time within which they are to be produced, or
(b) make such Order as it thinks fit (including an Order dispensing with the requirements of paragraph (1A) or staying the proceedings)

(1C) For the purposes of this rule:
'Medical report' means a report substantiating all the personal injuries alleged in the Statement of Claim which the Plaintiff proposes to adduce in evidence as part of his case at the Trial;
'a statement of the special damages claimed' means a statement giving full particulars of the special damages claimed for expenses and losses already incurred and an estimate of any future expenses and losses (including loss of earnings and pension rights).

11.45 The problems posed by the requirement to produce a Schedule of Damages at the outset are dealt with below (para **11.212**).

11.46 The problem posed by the obligation to supply a report on condition and prognosis is limited in extent. The major objection is that it offends the principles of mutuality and simultaneity of discovery of expert reports enunciated in *Naylor*. In fact, however, the only difficulty arises where there is insistence upon putting the alleged injury into its causal context. If required by the court to do this, a plaintiff may be unilaterally giving causation opinion evidence to the defendant. There is an authority for this stance

A medical report given in a vacuum merely setting out a Plaintiff's injury and condition and prognosis would be almost valueless and could be misleading . . . a medical report to comply with Rules 12(1A) and (1C) must set out the injuries alleged in this context of the Plaintiff's medical and other relevant history . . . In my judgment in the majority of medical negligence cases these rules should be strictly complied with. If they are not, I would expect that the Court would make an Order under Rule 12(1B)(a) or stay the action under Rule 13(1B)(b). In my judgment, it will only be in exceptional cases right to make an Order dispensing with the requirements under 12(1A).[1]

1 Morland J in *Esson v Gloucester Health Authority* (1991) (unreported).

11.47 This approach, of requiring the plaintiff to put the nature of the injury into context, has been applied by the Court of Appeal in *Dunn v British Coal Corporation*[1] to require disclosure of general medical records. (See Chapter 10 on the Medical Report.)

1 [1993] ICR 591, [1993] IRLR 396.

11.48 The effect of *Esson* would appear to be to require the plaintiff in a condition and prognosis medical report to have the nature of the injury put into the context of his or her general medical history. This must fall some way short of requiring the plaintiff to make a unilateral disclosure of his or her case on causation. This still takes place on a mutual and simultaneous basis as described below.

11.49 Although in general terms the revisions to RSC Order 18, rule 12 do not pose the challenge that once seemed likely, it means having to prepare cases to a greater all round degree before service and certainly enables defendants from the earliest stage to gauge the economics of the case. There is a feeling however that it leads to a higher expenditure on costs at the outset and may cause some duplication of effort in the preparation of the damages schedule.

FORUM

11.50 One of the major changes since the first edition of this book has been the change in forum brought about by the High Court and County Courts Jurisdiction Order 1991, SI 1991/724, which has moved 'personal injury' claims with a value of less than £50,000 from the High Court into the county court.

11.51 This creates an anomaly for doctors who are now the only professional men and women whose professional competence when questioned may be adjudicated in the county court. All other actions for professional negligence have remained in the High Court irrespective of value but the fact that a medical negligence claim is classified with other 'accident cases' as a 'personal injury' claim rather than as a 'professional negligence' claim means that if its value is now £50,000 it is more likely to be heard in the county court than not.

11.52 A writ in a medical negligence action must contain a statement that the action is not one which should be started in the county court (RSC (Amendment No 2) 1991, new RSC Order 6, rule 2(1)(f) and the Practice Direction (Personal Injuries Action: Indorsement on Writ)[1]) requires the following statement:

> This Writ includes a claim for personal injury but may be commenced in the High Court because the value of the action for the purpose of Article 5 of the High Court and County Courts Jurisdiction Order 1991 exceeds £50,000.

1 [1991] 1 WLR 642.

11.53 Unless such indorsement can be made an action must start in the county court (this may be *any* county court, there is no longer a geographical constraint on the issue of county court proceedings (see CCR Order 4, rule 2(1)(c) as amended by CCR (Amendment No 2) 1991)).[1]

1 Any proceedings begun in the High Court which do not satisfy the criterion of such indorsement are subject to the striking out provisions of s 40(1), High Court and County Courts Jurisdiction Order 1991. In *Restick v Crickmore* [1993] NLJR 1712 the Court of Appeal decided that such discretion should only be exercised where the action plainly should have been started in a county court and failure to do so was not a bona fide mistake. No injustice was involved in transferring such a case from the High Court to the county court.

11.54 There are provisions for the transfer to the High Court from the county court of cases where claims do not exceed £50,000 and the High Court retains concurrent jurisdiction with the county court to enable this to happen. However, such a transfer must satisfy the criteria set out in section 7(5) of the High Court and County Courts Jurisdiction Order 1991, SI 1991/724:

(a) the financial substance of the action, including the value of any counterclaim,
(b) whether the action is otherwise important and, in particular, whether it raises questions of importance to persons who are not parties or questions of general public interest,
(c) the complexity of the facts, legal issues, remedies or procedures involved, and
(d) whether transfer is likely to result in a more speedy trial of the action

but no transfer will be made on the ground of sub-paragraph (d) alone.

11.55 As a consequence of those rule changes a number of issues confront those more familiar with High Court than county court procedure.

Issue of protective proceedings

11.56 The County Court Rules do not provide for the issue of protective summonses in the same way that the High Court enables the issue of a protective writ indorsed only in general terms. To be able to issue proceedings in the county court outline Particulars of Claim at least must be provided to the court before a summons will be issued. Furthermore, unless leave to waive the requirement of production of a medical report is given by a district judge no summons can be issued without a medical report on the plaintiff's condition and prognosis and schedule of damages being filed with the court.

11.57 The issue of protective proceedings is not as useful a tool as it was even in the High Court because a writ of summons now only has a validity of four months from its date of issue rather than twelve months but nevertheless this is a significant and unnecessary handicap to litigation in which consistency of approach could be enforced by the Lord Chancellor's Department.

Directions

11.58 The Personal Injury Jurisdiction of the county court is governed by automatic directions (RSC Order 25, rule 8; CCR Order 17, rule 11). Just as above, the High Court has power to make directions which are not automatic directions under the general scope of RSC Order 25, so below in the county court, power to make directions other than automatic directions is given by CCR Order 13, rule 2.

11.59 This needs to be remembered because, few, if any medical negligence cases have been previously conducted in the county court and it is crucial to avoid a situation where the court regards your case as being subject to the 'normal' (ie automatic) directions which are inappropriate to medical negligence cases. Using CCR Order 13, rule 2, a summons for directions in the form set out below should be adopted.

Automatic striking out

11.60 One feature absent from life in the High Court is the provision (enacted by CCR Order 17, rule 11(9)) that if within 15 months of the day on which pleadings are deemed to be closed, no application has been made to set the case down and apply for a hearing date, the action will automatically be struck out.

11.61 Whilst medical negligence cases are not subject to automatic directions and this striking out authority does arise from the county court provisions relating to automatic directions, it is probably safer to assume in the absence of specific rules or authority to the contrary, that this provision can apply to medical negligence as well as to other forms of personal injury action.

Transfer to the High Court

11.62 Assuming that the criteria in section 7(5) of the High Court and County Court Jurisdiction Order 1991 can be met when should you make an application for transfer to the High Court? At the present few have had experience of trying a medical negligence case in the county court but amongst both plaintiffs and defendant representatives there is hesitation about doing so. The difficulty in achieving a fixed date for the convenience of medical witnesses and getting enough sequential dates organised are two reasons cited. In addition, there is the problem that few if any county court judges will have had sufficient experience of medical negligence cases either in practice or on the Bench. Even in the Queen's Bench Division the group of High Court judges with this experience is still fairly small.

11.63 Thus, despite relatively limited quantum it is likely that a good proportion of medical negligence cases begun in the county court will be the subject of applications to transfer to the High Court. Many solicitors representing defendants will also prefer to litigate in the High Court, the question is most likely therefore to be not 'will my opponent contest this application?', but 'is this the right time to approach the court for a transfer?'

11.64 On balance, the court is going to have the best evidence of the likely 'complexity of the facts, legal issues, remedies or procedures involved' when the pleadings are closed and at the giving of directions before setting down for trial.

11.65 Even if the issues have not clarified at this stage, (perhaps because of limited pleading) the possibility of further specific application after discovery of witness statements and then later of expert opinion reports, is still open. Indeed, such an application could still be made up to and including the first day of a trial before a county court judge. But whether such an application should be made at this point seems questionable if the speed at which the matter might be heard is a central consideration. Even if the judge was sympathetic he might enquire why such an application had not previously been made or (if a district judge had previously rejected such an application) why the matter had not previously been considered as an appeal against such a refusal.

SUMMARY JUDGMENT

11.66 Few opportunities arise where a medical accident has taken place to move decisively from institution of proceedings to summary judgment using the procedure outlined in RSC Order 14(1); issues of liability are rarely straightforward enough. For the same reason interim payments are less common in this field than in other, comparably serious, areas of personal injury work.

11.67 However, where the issues are straightforward, there is advantage to be gained by the plaintiff in making such an application because (to a limited extent) the RSC Order 14 procedure upsets the conventional investigation method adopted by defendants.

11.68 A Statement of Claim having been received it has often been the case that a defence is drafted as quickly and as little more than a denial on the basis of evidence given to the defendant's solicitors by the doctor or doctors against whom allegations are made rather than upon the objective independent judgment of a medical expert witness. Where an application for summary judgment is made, the defendant's solicitors must not only take proofs of evidence from the doctors involved but, earlier than normal, seek an independent expert opinion on the competence displayed by the defendant or its employees. Furthermore, in order to satisfy the criterion in RSC Order 14(3)(1) the defendant must establish:

> that there is an issue or question in dispute which ought to be tried or that there ought for some other reason to be a Trial of that claim or part . . .

and in order to do this the defendant must explain the detailed merits of the defence in affidavit evidence to which will have to be exhibited a detailed draft defence. Furthermore, it is desirable that a view on liability from a medical expert be exhibited to that affidavit so that the district judge can be satisfied that the defence is substantive.

11.69 In a case where the plaintiff's case is unanswerable, an application for summary judgment may succeed on its own merits or elicit an admission of liability. In a more marginal case, the effect is to reveal the detailed issues in dispute between the parties at an early stage and perhaps persuade the defendant to consider settlement or payment into court without making any admission of liability.

11.70 At worst, such application will reveal the nature of the defendant's case and the view of one or more of its medical experts and enable the plaintiff's solicitors to prepare the case for trial understanding more about the defendant's strengths and weaknesses.

LIMITATION

11.71 Another chapter in this book[1] is devoted to the particular problem posed by the 'date of knowledge' provisions in the Limitation Act 1980, section 14(1), and the interplay of this section with the Limitation Act 1980, section 33, which confers on the court discretion to disapply sections 11 and 12 of the Act. The only question which needs to be dealt with here is how to confront the issue of limitation from the point of view of (a) pleadings and (b) determination.

1 Chapter 13.

Pleadings

11.72 The notes to RSC Order 18, rule 8(16) seem contradictory in that they assert that in personal injury or Fatal Accident Act 1976 cases the plaintiff must *assume* that the defendant is going to use the defence of limitation before the defendant has actually done so and should give full particulars of the facts and matters relied upon in support of his or her 'date of knowledge' argument. This seems to fly in the face of the idea that a statute bar is a shield available to a defendant rather than a sword.

11.73 This latter view was supported by Bristow J in *Ogunsanya v Lambeth Health Authority*[1] when he indicated that the proper pattern of pleading is for the plaintiff to make no mention of the limitation question in the Statement of Claim but should wait for the defendant to raise this in the defence, then serve a reply to raise the facts and contentions relied upon as to date of knowledge and the power of the court to override the defence of limitation.

1 (3 July 1985, unreported).

11.74 This approach seems to mesh neatly with the idea that the issue of limitation be taken as a preliminary issue (described below) because it does not enable the defendant to defend a meritorious medical negligence claim (which nevertheless requires the preliminary determination of the limitation situation) purely by pleading a statute bar. If this is allowed to happen the court has little if any opportunity to take a view of the merits from the pleadings, when an application is made by the plaintiff under Limitation Act 1980, section 33. The Court of Appeal in *Harris v Newcastle Health Authority*[1] has confirmed that Bristow J's approach to the limitation issue in pleadings is to be preferred.

1 [1989] 2 All ER 273, [1989] 1 WLR 96, CA.

Determination

11.75 Ideally, if in issue, limitation should be considered by the court entirely in isolation from the substantive issues in negligence but at a time which enables the judge to get a comprehensive view of the 'date of knowledge' argument and to consider the evolution of the case from the date of the plaintiff's injury together with the differing merits which arise in the respective parties' favour. A finding of fact as to the plaintiff's date of knowledge within section 14 of the Limitation Act can be straightforward but application for the exercise of the court's unfettered discretion under section 33 of the Limitation Act is governed by six considerations:

(a) the length of and reasons for the delay;
(b) the effect of any delay on the cogency of the evidence;
(c) the conduct of the defendant;
(d) the duration of the disability of the plaintiff;
(e) the conduct of the plaintiff; and
(f) the diligence on the part of the plaintiff in obtaining medical, legal or other expert advice.

11.76 These issues are canvassed together with the overriding question of the balance of prejudice experienced by the respective parties.[1]

1 *Brooks v J & P Coates* [1984] 1 All ER 702.

11.77 Ideally the court should give such consideration after the pleadings have closed and at some distance from the trial so that the judge can see the substantive issues.

11.78 Firstly, because to take such an issue on the first day of a full trial is to risk putting the judge into an impossible situation of seeming to be unfair to the plaintiff if an application is refused and in the defendant's eyes to have been 'blackmailed' by the plaintiff if the application succeeds. Secondly, the risk of such an application being refused on the first day of a full trial in cases which are predominantly legally aided is to waste costs. If the application is heard in isolation shortly after setting the case down for a full trial the costs involved are relatively small because the issue is narrow and full scale preparation for trial has not taken place; if the matter is heard as a preliminary issue on the first day of a full trial and is refused, the costs of preparation of the trial will have been incurred and will be significantly greater. In some cases, however, it will be impossible and even undesirable to separate determination of this issue from the other trial issues of liability, causation and quantum. Paradoxically, cases where the plaintiff has to rely solely on the section 33 discretion may be the ones most likely to be determined in this way. In these instances, limitation has to be taken as a preliminary matter by the trial judge at the trial.

SUMMONS FOR DIRECTIONS

11.79 A summons for directions is issued within one month of close of pleadings (RSC Order 25, rule 1(3)); pleadings are deemed to be closed 14 days after the service of the Defence or Reply, *not* after the completion of requested Further and Better Particulars of pleadings (RSC Order 18, rule 20).

11.80 The automatic directions for personal injury actions (RSC Order 25, rule 8 and CCR Order 17, rule 11) do not apply to medical accident cases, which although concerned with personal injury, are generically professional negligence claims.

11.81 The summons for directions habitually used in medical negligence cases has undergone some evolution from the pattern for conventional personal injury litigation set by RSC Order 25, rule 8. An example of an order following a summons for directions now in use is set out below:

ORDER

1 That the Plaintiff within 14 days do serve on the Defendant a list of what documents are or have been within his possession, custody or power relating to the matters in question in the action.

2 The Defendants do within 14 days serve on the Plaintiff a list of what documents are or have been in their possession, custody or power relating to the matters in question in the action.

3 There be inspection of such documents within seven days of serving such lists of documents.

4 That the issue of Limitation in this case be tried as a preliminary issue before a High Court Judge in London and that the parties file Affidavit evidence on the issue of Limitation for such hearing not later than 14 days before such hearing. If either party wishes to cross-examine a deponent on his affidavit, notice is to be given to the opposite party's solicitors not later than 7 days before the Trial of the issue.

5 **(a)** The Plaintiff and Defendant do mutually disclose by way of simultaneous mutual exchange the substance of all medical and other expert evidence in the form of written reports within four calendar months after the setting down of this action for Trial. Such reports should be agreed if possible. Unless such reports are agreed the parties be at liberty to call expert evidence limited to those witnesses, the substance of whose expert evidence has been so disclosed and to .... witnesses for each party.

(b) In addition to the simultaneous mutual disclosure by way of exchange provided for in sub paragraph (a) above and in respect only of the Plaintiff's present condition and prognosis, each party should be at liberty to serve upon the solicitors for the other party the substance of any updating evidence in the form of written reports no later than two calendar months before the date fixed for Trial. Unless such updating reports are agreed the parties be at liberty to call such updating expert evidence on present condition and prognosis, limited to those witnesses the substance of whose expert evidence has been so served and to .... witnesses for each party.

(c) If any expert witness(es) propose(s) to rely on (a) text book, article or other published item in any other expert or learned journal or (b) other unpublished medical or pharmaceutical research data, a first list and photocopies of such text book, article or research be served by mutual exchange on the other party not less than three months before Trial and any supplemental consequential list and photocopies not less than 28 days before Trial.

6 The Plaintiff and Defendant do mutually disclose, by way of mutual and simultaneous exchange, written statements of the oral evidence on the issues of fact which the parties intend to adduce from the witnesses at Trial not later than fourteen weeks from the date of this Order.

7 The respective parties' medical experts should meet on a date to be fixed but not later than 21 days before Trial with a view to isolating the issues then in dispute between the parties. Following such meeting an agreed note should be prepared by the parties' solicitors and Counsel to be submitted to the Trial Judge at the commencement of the Trial.

8 Special Damages and Future Loss

(a) The Plaintiff do disclose expert reports on Special Damages annexed to a schedule of the Plaintiff's claim for Special Damages and Future Loss, to be served not later than 3 months before the date fixed for Trial. Any counter-schedule in reply on behalf of the Defendant to be served not later than 56 days before Trial.

(b) Such reports and/or schedules to be agreed if possible.

(c) Unless such reports and/or schedules are agreed, the parties be at liberty to call expert witnesses as to Special Damages and Future Loss limited to those expert witnesses whose reports have been so disclosed and to .... witnesses for each party.

9 The parties should agree and prepare for inclusion in the Trial Bundle not later than seven days before the date fixed for Trial

(a) a summary of the issues involved; and

(b) a summary of any propositions of law to be advanced together with a list of authorities to be cited; and

(c) a chronology of events

In default of such agreement, both parties should prepare separate summaries and chronologies for inclusion.

10 There be liberty to apply for further directions.

11 Trial: Place : London
Mode : Judge Alone
Category : B
Estimated Length : (a) Preliminary Issue: ... day
(b) Trial: ... days

12 The main action and the preliminary issue be set down for hearing within 28 days.

13 The costs of the application be in the cause.

RATIONALE FOR DIRECTIONS

Limitation – directions 4 and 12

11.82 These directions enable any limitation issue to be listed before a judge as a preliminary part of the trial. It seems to be conventional in cases habitually listed under category B (see below) to list the consideration of the limitation issues before a judge rather than a master or district judge because of the likely complexity of the issues in these cases and their quantum. Setting down the case in this manner enables *two* fixed dates to be obtained on listing, one of which can be discarded if the application is unsuccessful. On the other hand, if the Limitation Act application is successful the trial date will be much nearer than if the case had to be relisted after determination.

11.83 Defendants' lawyers tend to prefer preliminary issues to be taken earlier rather than at trial because their success at such an application will limit costs exposure. Attempting to list such a hearing *before* exchange of witness statements and expert reports may have the effect of limiting the evidence available to the judge who is asked to exercise his absolute discretion in section 33 of the Limitation Act to disapply the effect of sections 11 and 12. If such an application is to be a true preliminary issue, then it should take place *before* trial but after all witness statements and expert reports have been exchanged.

Exchange of reports – condition and prognosis – direction 5(a) and (b)

11.84 Disclosure four calendar months after setting down of these reports will equip both parties' lawyers and experts with the extent of common ground (or absence of it) on the issues of condition and prognosis. It is desirable to have these reports disclosed simultaneously with reports of liability and causation because differences of view between the respective parties' experts may emerge which need to be investigated to assess their effect on the assumptions made in the plaintiff's Schedule of Damages.

11.85 Updating disclosure only two months before trial enables a plaintiff (whose claim may have taken four to five years to come to trial) to present to the trial judge an up to date view of his or her situation, which will in turn enable the judge to make as accurate as possible an assessment of appropriate damages for pain and suffering and loss of amenity.

11.86 In addition, the trial judge will be equipped with evidence justifying the extent of e g future nursing costs in the Schedule of Special Damages and Future Loss and the views on life expectancy expressed in condition and prognosis reports by the parties' experts which will determine the multiplier to be adopted.

Exchange of reports – liability and causation – direction 5

11.87 Before 1987 the pre-trial disclosure of expert opinion reports on liability and causation did not occur and the practice (approved by the Court of Appeal in *Rahman v Kirklees Area Health Authority*[1] was for both parties to go to trial without knowledge of the evidence on liability and causation to be adduced by their opponent. This practice had gone unquestioned between 1980 and 1986 despite two revisions of RSC Order 38, rule 38, which appeared to alter the situation.

1 [1980] 1 WLR 1244.

11.88 The shortcomings of this approach were identified by the Court of Appeal in the case *Wilsher v Essex Area Health Authority*,[1] Mustill LJ setting out trenchant criticism of the practice of coming to trial 'in the dark' and contrasting the practice in medical negligence cases unfavourably with the rules governing professional negligence and other commercial actions dealt with by the Commercial Court and the Official Referees.

1 [1986] 3 All ER 801.

11.89 It is instructive in considering the developments which have taken place in this area since 1980 to look at the arguments put forward in support of the practice of mutual and simultaneous discovery of expert opinion evidence which culminated in the Court of Appeal's decision in *Naylor v Preston Health Authority*.[1]

1 [1987] 2 All ER 353.

11.90 The Court of Appeal, expressly reversing *Rahman*, held that there was no fetter restricting the court from making orders for mutual and simultaneous pre-trial disclosure of expert opinion evidence in cases of medical professional negligence, since RSC Order 38, rule 38 gave a wide discretion which is to be exercised, taking into account all the circumstances of a particular case, on the basis that in the great majority of cases, the interests of justice would best be served by full pre-trial mutual and simultaneous disclosure.

11.91 In giving his judgment Sir John Donaldson MR (as he then was) referred approvingly to the judgment of Mustill LJ in *Wilsher* and quoted from it as follows:[1]

In the result the parties realised, soon after the case began that they had misunderstood what the case was about. As was stated before us, it was fought 'in the dark'. It lasted four weeks instead of the allotted five days, which not only imposed great pressure of time on all concerned but meant that the scheduling of the expert witnesses was put quite out of joint. The Judge had nothing to read beforehand except some pleadings which told him nothing. The evidence of the Plaintiff's and Defendant's witnesses came forward in no sort of order, sometimes by instalments.

Nearly 150 pages of medical literature were put in without prior exchange or any opportunity for proper scrutiny. All this could have been avoided if there had been adequate clarification of the issues before the Trial. The Master is not to be criticised for making a consent order in the light of *Rahman v Kirklees Area Health Authority* ([1980] 3 All ER 610). But I believe that practitioners do their clients and the interests of justice no service by continuing to pursue this policy of concealment. Certainly, as the very experienced members of the Court pointed out in *Rahman v Kirklees Area Health Authority*, there can be problems in making a Defendant disclose his experts' reports. Nevertheless these and similar problems are faced and solved all the time in cases before the Commercial Court and the Official Referees, where it is now axiomatic on technical issues that all the cards must be on the table before the Trial begins. Those cases are concerned with money. Here, there are also human issues of great importance. To me it seems wrong that in this area of the law, more than in any other, this kind of forensic blind man's buff should continue to be the norm.

1 [1986] 3 All ER 801 at 830.

11.92 The views expressed by the Court of Appeal as to the saving of costs implicit in this 'cards on the table' approach have had the effect of forcing defendants at an earlier stage, to establish the terms of the evidence with which an action will be defended. As the practice is developing it is clear that defences are becoming more thoroughly pleaded in cases in which defendants consider that they have a meritorious defence. As a consequence more cases are being compromised or discontinued because of the clarification of the issues before trial.

11.93 What the *Naylor* decision does reflect is the importance attached by the judiciary to the early clarification of the medical issues in dispute between the parties and the need for those handling these cases to avoid situations such as arose in *Wilsher*. Furthermore, the Court of Appeal in *Naylor* signalled a change in judicial attitudes, towards treating doctors like any other professional men and women and not as the special case for which Lord Denning argued in *Whitehouse v Jordan*.

11.94 Furthermore, the stress laid on the importance of full discovery of expert opinion evidence before trial has impelled the revision of the rules bringing about mandatory mutual and simultaneous discovery of witness statements. *Rahman* has gone but in one respect serves to keep alive a distinction so far lost on the Lord Chancellor and the Rules Committee, that between medical negligence and other personal injury actions. Paras **11.175–11.189** below deal with the timing of such mutual and simultaneous pre-trial disclosure and the steps to be taken to enforce it.

Published and unpublished literature and other data – direction 5(c)

11.95 Necessarily, evidence given by opinion witnesses at trial on questions of liability and causation has greater strength when supported not simply by the word of the expert (however eminent) but also by reference to the standard textbooks and papers on the subject and by any change in the view of the profession wrought by fresh research and/or changing attitudes. The more support an expert can adduce in this way to give perspective to written or oral evidence used at trial, the more credible will be that evidence. The subjective nature of the test of negligence and the availability of the 'responsible body of medical opinion' defence (*Maynard v West Midlands Regional Health Authority*)[1] will make the defendant's task easier if the preparation of this part of the evidence is given priority.

1 [1985] 1 All ER 635.

11.96 Clearly, so that neither party is caught by surprise it is desirable to prepare this evidence sufficiently in advance as to enable both sets of experts to consider the respective lists of medical literature to be relied upon and try to anticipate the opposing parties' in this respect.

11.97 Defining the acceptable practice of the 'responsible' body of opinion has never been easy for judges; possibly because they have rarely, if ever, attempted this task, preferring to allow evidence adduced before them to coagulate into a 'body of opinion' or 'school of thought' but seeking always to deny that any counting of expert heads is going on.

11.98 What is certain is that the need to determine exactly what *objective* evidence an expert for plaintiff or defendant is going to adduce in support of his or her *subjective* opinion is paramount. Once this is established it is possible in the taking of evidence at the trial to discover whether the views being expressed by the expert are wholly those of that expert or whether they are a reporting of views held by others, to which that expert may not in fact him or herself subscribe. It is suggested that if an expert is called in support of a contention either for plaintiff or defendant then that expert should personally espouse his subjective view rather than simply report on the 'I know a man who does' principle.

Exchange of witness statements – direction 6

Pre-1992 exchange of witness statements

11.99 The exchange of witness statements under RSC Order 28, rule 2A has been applied in personal injury/medical negligence actions since 1 October 1988 and extends further the 'cards on the table' approach approved by the Court of Appeal and the Civil Justice Review. This exchange of proofs of evidence taken from the witnesses of fact enables the parties to weigh up the strength of their own expert evidence and isolate the weak points in an opponent's case. Proofs of evidence should be set out in a signed and dated form. This may necessitate alteration in practice on both sides, since the trial judge may be inclined to give greater weight to proofs of evidence prepared closer to the events complained of, even where discovery has widened the issues. From the plaintiff's point of view, discovery of witness statements from the defendant's medical staff enables a distinction to be drawn between the evidence of fact that they can give from strict recollection, the further evidence culled from a reading of the clinical notes and those instances where an element of self-justifying 'expert opinion' has been allowed to creep in.

The 1992 changes

11.100 Through two statutory instruments[1] the principle of exchange of witness statements was widened to all categories of personal injury work. In so doing a wider ranging protocol for production and exchange of proofs of evidence was inaugurated which to a certain extent built upon the perceived success of the pre-1992 application of the rules to medical negligence cases. The changes in the rules are effective in both the High Court and the county court, the changes in the High Court being chiefly to RSC Order 38, rule 2A and in the county court to CCR Order 20, rule 12A.

1 RSC (Amendment No 2) 1992, SI 1992/1907 and CCR (Amendment No 2) 1992, SI 1992/1965.

INSPECTION OF DOCUMENTS REFERRED TO IN PLEADINGS AND AFFIDAVITS (RSC ORDER 24, RULE 10)

11.101 This provision is amended to cover witness statements as well as pleadings and affidavits. Under this rule, the court has jurisdiction under RSC Order 24, rule 11(1) to order the production for inspection of any document referred to in a pleading or affidavit *or witness statement* whether or not the document is in the possession, custody or power of the party in whose pleading, affidavit or witness statement the reference is made.

EXCHANGE OF WITNESS STATEMENTS AMENDMENTS TO RSC ORDER 38, RULE 2A

11.102 The existing provisions of RSC Order 38, rule 2A (and CCR Order 20, rule 12A) are wholly replaced by a new set of provisions:

(1) The powers of the Court under this Rule shall be exercised for the purpose of disposing fairly and expeditiously of the cause or matter before it, and saving costs, having regard to all the circumstances of the case, including (but not limited to) –
  (a) The extent to which the facts are in dispute or have been admitted;
  (b) The extent to which the issues of fact are defined by the Pleadings;
  (c) The extent to which the information has been or is likely to be provided by Further and Better Particulars, Answers to Interrogatories or otherwise.

(2) At the Summons for Directions in an action commenced by a Writ, the Court shall direct every party to serve on the other parties, within fourteen weeks [ten weeks in the County Court] (or such other period as the Court may specify) of the hearing of the Summons and on such terms as the Court may specify, written statements of the oral evidence which the party intends to adduce on any issues of fact to be decided at the Trial.
  The Court may give a direction to any party under this paragraph at any other stage of such an action and at any stage of any other cause or matter.
  Order 3, rule 5(3) shall not apply to any period specified by the Court under this paragraph.

11.103 This rule is intended to empower the High Court to direct any of the parties to an action at any stage of the proceedings, to serve on other parties the written statements of the oral evidence which that party intends to lead on any issues of fact to be decided at the trial. The objectives of this provision are ostensibly:

(1) the fair and expeditious disposal of proceedings and the saving of costs, ie the acceleration of process and the reduction of costs in contested litigation;
(2) the elimination of any element of 'surprise' before or at the trial. The parties are intended no longer to be able to spring or to be exposed to surprises as to the trial witnesses or their evidence but will be required to 'place their cards on the table';

(3) the promotion of a fair settlement between the parties. With all or substantially all the factual evidence before them, subject to cross-examination, the parties will be able to make a more realistic appraisal of the strengths and weaknesses of their own and each other's cases which should contribute towards the fair and expeditious disposal of the proceedings by settlement or otherwise;
(4) the avoidance of a trial, saving time, effort and cost on the part of practitioners, the judiciary and the court staff as well as the parties and their witnesses;
(5) the identification of the real issues and the elimination of unnecessary matters;
(6) encouraging the parties to make admission of facts in the process of identifying the real issues;
(7) the reduction in the number of pre-trial applications;
(8) the provision of a framework enabling evidence-in-chief to be given in summary form;
(9) the improvement of the process of cross-examination;
(10) the concentration of both the parties and the trial judge on the real matters in controversy between the parties.

The exclusion of the effect of RSC Order 3, rule 5(3), which enables an extension of time to be agreed by consent between the parties without any court order, implies that the court expects to govern time in relation to the service of witness statements strictly and, in default of compliance with such time provisions, debar a party's evidence at the trial. It may also be that this provision will be used to enable judicial management of the speed at which an action progresses.

11.104

(3) Directions under paragraph (2) or (17) may make a different provision with regard to different issues of fact or different witnesses.
(4) Statements served under this rule shall
  (a) Be dated and except for good reason (which should be specified by letter accompanying the statement) be signed by the intended witness and shall include a statement by him that the contents are true to the best of his knowledge and belief.
  (b) Sufficiently identify any documents referred to therein; and
  (c) Where they are to be served by more than one party, be exchanged simultaneously.

The principle of mutuality and simultaneity of expert evidence is carried over into the pre-trial service of witness statements, the intention being that neither party shall be allowed to operate the machinery of exchange to obtain an unfair or undue advantage. Mutuality and simultaneity of exchange is intended to give to the other party, a 'true and fair' view of the party serving the statement; sequential discovery may tend to make the statements of the party going second a commentary upon the statement of the party going first. Nevertheless, the court retains the discretion to order sequential discovery.

The trial judge's discretion to require a witness to give evidence orally, irrespective of the fact that pre-trial exchange of witness statements has taken place, remains unfettered.

11.105

(5) Where a party is unable to obtain a written statement from an intended witness in accordance with paragraph 4A, the Court may direct the party wishing to adduce that witness's evidence to provide the other party with the name of the witness and (unless the Court otherwise orders), a statement of the nature of the evidence intended to be adduced.

Under this rule, the prior consent of the parties is not required to empower the court to give a direction under paragraph 2 for the service of witnesses' statements. The notes to the rules envisage a situation where a party cannot obtain the statement from a witness, perhaps a government servant who will not give a statement except under subpoena and thus, the party may find itself being required to give the name of this potentially useful witness and the gist of the evidence which he may give.

Again, the court is reserving its power to avoid the other party to the proceedings being taken by surprise by the calling at the last minute of a witness in respect of whom no statement has been served.

11.106

(6) Subject to paragraph (9) where the party serving a statement under this rule does not call the witness to whose evidence it relates, no other party may put the statement in evidence at the Trial.

This rule does not apply to cases covered by the Civil Evidence Act 1968 (see below). This rule highlights the fact that evidence in witness statements will not stand as evidence-in-chief unless it is 'proved' by calling the witness who made the statement to give that evidence-in-chief at trial.

Whilst no other party may put the statement in evidence at the trial, this presumably does not stop another party to the proceedings calling the maker of the witness statement (with the leave of the court) to give evidence.

11.107

(7) Subject to paragraph (9) where the party serving the statement does call such a witness at the Trial

- (a) Except where the Trial is with a jury, the Court may, on such terms as it thinks fit, direct the statement served or part of it shall stand as the evidence in chief of a witness or part of such evidence;
- (b) The party may not without the consent of the other party or the leave of the Court, adduce evidence from that witness the substance of which is not included in the statement served, except
  - (i) Where the Courts directions are under paragraph 2 or 17 specify that statements should be exchanged in relation to only some issues of fact, in relation to any other issues;
  - (ii) In relation to new matters which have arisen since the statement was served on the other party; and
- (c) Whether or not the statement or any part of it is referred to during the evidence in chief of the witness, any party may put the statement or any part of it, in cross examination of that witness.

This rule highlights the fact that statements which have been served:

(a) are intended for use at the trial itself; and
(b) are intended to relate to issues of fact in dispute at trial.

Thus, the written statement of a witness must contain only such material facts as the witness is able to prove *from his own knowledge*. This is in its effect, the same requirement as governs the contents of affidavit evidence which is explicitly equated to the oral evidence given in court by the provisions of RSC Order 41, rule 5.

Because of this equivalent status, the trial judge may direct that the statement served or part of it, should stand as the evidence-in-chief of that witness.

The written statement must not contain any expressions of opinion but be confined only to matters of fact, nor should it seek to anticipate the evidence of a witness of the opposite party and seek to contradict it or otherwise deal with it. Whilst the witness statement may be put in as that witness's evidence-in-chief, it is not intended to anticipate cross-examination. The giving of evidence is limited to the facts deposed to in the statement subject to novel issues which have arisen since the statement was drafted.

11.108

(8) Nothing in this rule shall make admissible evidence which is otherwise inadmissible.

(9) Where any statements served to which the Civil Evidence Acts 1968 and 1972 apply, paragraphs 6 and 7 shall take effect subject to the provisions of the Acts and Parts III and IV of this Order. The service of a witness statement under this rule shall not, unless expressly so stated by the party serving the same, be treated as a notice under the said Acts of 1968 and 1972 and where a statement or any part thereof would be admissible in evidence by virtue only of the said Acts of 1968 or 1972 the appropriate notice under Part III or Part IV of this Order shall be served with the statement notwithstanding any provision of those Parts as to the time for serving such a notice. Where such a notice is served, a counter notice should be deemed to have been served under Order 38 Rule 26(1).

Just like the oral evidence of the trial witness, a written statement must not contain any inadmissible evidence, therefore it should not contain any hearsay evidence or any statement of any information or belief even if the grounds and reasons for that belief are reasonable.

This provides a contrast between the witness statement and an affidavit which at least in interlocutory proceedings, may contain statements of information or belief. Unless specifically stated, a witness statement will not be regarded as giving sufficient notice under the Civil Evidence Act 1968 to come within Part III of RSC Order 38 for the admission of hearsay evidence.

Thus, if it is intended to use the witness statement as a means of bringing in hearsay evidence, the provisions of RSC Order 38, rules 20–34 will have to be complied with.

The note in the White Book to RSC Order 38, rule 2A(8) (p 646) also identifies the form that a witness statement should take.

The statement should be expressed in the first person and it should state:

1. The full name of the witness
2. His place of residence or if he is making the statement in his professional business or other occupational capacity, the address at which he works, the position he holds and the name of his firm or employer
3. His occupation or if he has none, his description
4. The fact that he is a party to the proceedings or is the employee of such a party.

The statement of the witness should represent his evidence-in-chief and should be treated as if he were giving evidence in the witness box. It should be stated in a clear straightforward narrative form and should use the language of the witness ipsissimma verba. For the sake of clarity, it should follow the chronological sequence of the events or matter dealt with. For the sake of easy and ready reference, it should be divided into paragraphs numbered consecutively, each paragraph being as far as possible confined to a distinct portion of his evidence. If the evidence contains dates, sums or numbers, they should be expressed as figures and not in words.

The statement should be on paper complying with the requirements of RSC Order 66, rule 1 (ie A4, not foolscap) and should be fully legible. It should normally be typed double spaced, on one side of the paper only. Before it is used at the trial it should be paginated either individually or as a separate statement or as one of several statements contained in a file. If it mentions any document or documents, the reference to each of them should, where possible, be given in the margin.

The statement must be signed by the witness except for good reason which much be supplied in a letter accompanying the statement (paragraph 4A). The witness must state in the statement that the contents are true to the best of his knowledge and belief.

With the introduction of RSC Order 34, rule 10 the normal practice would be for the parties to exchange witness statements and for these to be included in the 'Court Bundle' which must now be lodged with the Clerk of the Lists a few days before the trial. The statement should therefore not be bound with thick plastic strips or anything else which would 'hamper filing'.

Once drafted, the witness statement becomes a document for which leave to amend will become necessary once it has been served. Practice in the Official Referee's Court, where exchange of witness statements has been mandatory for some time, suggests that arguments as to inadmissible evidence or other objectionable material should be left to be heard until the witness has produced his statement at the trial and sworn to its truth.

11.109

(10) Where a party fails to comply with a direction for the exchange of witness statements, he shall not be entitled to adduce evidence to which the direction related without the leave of the Court.

The whole tenor of the new rules seems to suggest that this leave will be given only where there are very good reasons for failing to comply with the direction and it appears to be implicit that in default of such compliance, the court will debar a party which does not comply with the direction for exchange of witness statements from adducing that evidence at the trial, in the same way that expert opinion evidence can be debarred in default of compliance with an order for mutual and simultaneous discovery.

11.110

(11) Where a party serves a witness statement under this rule, no other person may make use of that statement for any purpose other than the purpose of the proceedings in which it was served
  (a) Unless to an extent, that the party serving it gives his consent in writing or the Court gives leave; or
  (b) Unless to an extent that it has been put in evidence (whether pursuant to a direction under paragraph 7A) or otherwise.

(12) Subject to paragraph (13) the Judge shall if any person so requests during the

course of the Trial, direct the Associate to certify, as open to inspection, any witness statement which is ordered to stand as evidence in chief under paragraph 7(A).

A request under this paragraph may be made orally or in writing.

(13) The Judge may refuse to give a direction under paragraph (12) in relation to a witness statement or may exclude from such a direction, any words or passages in the statement, if he considers that inspection should not be available
(a) In the interests of justice or national security; or
(b) Because of the nature of any expert medical evidence in the statement; or
(c) For any other sufficient reason.

Witness statements which have been exchanged under RSC Order 38, rule 2A are not put in evidence by the fact of exchange but remain confidential until the witness makes the statement public by verifying it on oath in the witness box, or, the party who served the statement waives the privilege. Rules 11, 12 and 13 identify the circumstances in which the judge may put evidence into the public domain despite the fact that the witness has not given that evidence on oath and it is only contained in a witness statement *either* by ruling that the witness statement should stand as evidence-in-chief (under paragraph 7A), *or* through the consent in writing of the party who made the statement *or* the court exercising its general discretion to enable use of the witness statement to be made for other purposes.

Under paragraph 12, the judge is given power to certify as open to inspection the witness statement ordered to stand as evidence-in-chief under paragraph 7A, but this period of inspection will only run until seven days after the conclusion of the trial.

Rule 13 indicates the ambit of the judge's discretion in relation to witness statements becoming public knowledge. Under the provisions of RSC Order 38, rule 2A, which are replaced by these rules, there was a specific limitation that:

Nothing in this rule should deprive any party of his right to treat any communication as privileged or make admissible evidence otherwise inadmissible.

The notes to these rules in the supplement simply state:

The form of provisions of the rules saving the right to privilege has not been preserved in the new rule.

11.111

(14) Where the Associate has been directed under paragraph 12 to certify a witness statement as open to inspection, he shall
(a) Prepare a certificate which will be attached to a copy (the certified copy) of that witness statement; and
(b) Make the certified copy available for inspection.

(15) Subject to any conditions which the Court may, by special or general direction impose, any person may inspect and (subject to payment of the prescribed fee), take a copy of the certified copy of a witness statement from the time when the Certificate is given until the end of seven days after the conclusion of the Trial.

This is going to make it considerably easier for anyone interested to establish the substance of the issues in the case which have formed a part of the evidence. This provision of certified copies will make such evidence much more accessible than awaiting the transcript of tape recorded evidence.

11.112

(16) In this rule
- (a) Any reference in paragraphs 12 to 15 to a witness statement shall in relation to a witness statement to which only part has been ordered to stand as evidence in chief under paragraph 7A, be construed as a reference to that part;
- (b) Any reference to inspecting or copying of a certified copy of a witness statement shall be construed as including a reference to inspecting or copying a copy of that certified copy.

This is the sanity clause.

11.113

(17) The Court shall have power to vary or override any of the provisions of this rule (except paragraphs 1, 8 and 12 to 16) and to give such alternative directions as it thinks fit.

The courts discretion to impose or alter directions as to the exchange of witness statements is limited only by:

(a) the overriding need to deal with the matter fairly and expeditiously; and
(b) maintaining a clear distinction between admissible and inadmissible evidence; and
(c) limiting the courts ability (save in respect of the specific provision to do so given by the rules) to maintain the privacy of witness statements which have become evidence at the trial.

Separation at trial of issues of fact and opinion

11.114 Judicial approval has been given to the separation at trial of evidence of fact and evidence of opinion (*Bayer v Clarkson Puckle Overseas Ltd*).[1] Both parties call witnesses of fact, the defendant's witnesses being called directly after the plaintiff's without the plaintiff having closed his or her case. The nature of any factual disagreement is then apparent to the trial judge. Next, the opinion witnesses for the parties are called in sequence, able to give their expert evidence taking into account the factual disagreements revealed.

1 [1989] NLJR 256, (1989) Times, 23 January.

11.115 In contested medical negligence cases this method of trial has become commonplace and has had some effect in shortening the time taken over expert opinion evidence. Application to use this procedure should be made to the trial judge on the first day of the trial, because the decision to hear factual evidence in this way is wholly a matter for the judge's discretion.

Meeting of experts – direction 7

11.116 If the timetable of the summons for directions has been adhered to, by a date 21 days before trial, the parties should have exchanged:

(a) reports on condition and prognosis;
(b) reports on liability and causation;
(c) witness statements;
(d) schedules of special damages and future loss;

and by this stage the general scheme of the case should be clear to the respective solicitors and those residual (perhaps irreconcilable) issues which will form the basis for the trial of the action will have emerged. It is sometimes the case that both parties will benefit from a 'without prejudice' meeting between experts to narrow the issues as far as practicable. From 1 October 1987, RSC Order 38, rule 38 has contained provision for such a meeting to take place and it appears that there is a role for such a meeting to limit the issues to be put before the judge and thus contribute to the saving of costs.

11.117 There is some judicial support for the use of such a meeting to narrow issues and diminish the use of court time (*McIvor v Southern Health and Social Services Board*)[1] and such meetings between expert witnesses are regularly ordered in the Official Referees jurisdiction.

1 [1978] 2 All ER 625, [1978] 1 WLR 757, HL.

11.118 It seems doubtful that such a meeting of experts can be compelled; no case law exists on this point but plainly if one party's experts are agreeable to such a meeting taking place and the other side's are not and this refusal to attend a meeting materially contributes to the time taken in the hearing of the action, then the judge may make such order in costs at the end of the trial as may seem appropriate.

Schedule of damages – direction 8

11.119 The amended provisions of RSC Order 18, rule 12 (see para **11.44** above) provide for service with the Statement of Claim of a Schedule of Special Damages. The notes to RSC Order 18, rule 12(9) indicate that this obligation to provide particulars extends to 'special' but not 'general' damages. However, it also indicates that such 'special damages' includes future losses as well as past damages. Thus the obligation at the beginning of the case is to serve a Schedule of Damages which is as full as possible with the implicit indication that such schedules will be amended (by extension or updating) as the case proceeds to trial.

11.120 The objection to this at first was that the long period between the instigation of proceedings meant that the schedule would have to be prepared twice, once at the outset and again before trial. This argument still has force despite the radical difference in speed of listing in the High Court since the transfer to the county court of cases with a value up to £50,000.

11.121 The better argument from the point of view of medical negligence cases seems to be this. Whilst liability may be arguable, it is rarely certain and the burden imposed on a plaintiff's Legal Aid Certificate (which may eventually produce a bill to be taxed against the Legal Aid Fund if liability though arguable is ultimately unsuccessful) is unnecessarily increased at the outset by having to undertake an expensive investigation of the quantum side of the case. This is particularly so in high quantum cases where liability and causation will necessarily be fully contested.

11.122 In such cases it is open to the court, on application, to make an order providing for service of the schedule at a later stage in the action, though almost inevitably earlier than the timetable envisaged by the 1984 practice direction dealt with below.

11.123 Under the practice direction relating to Schedules of Special Damages and Future Losses claimed in a personal injury action,[1] a plaintiff is under an obligation to serve such a full schedule not later than 28 days before a fixed date hearing. This will be an amended (or at least updated) version of the schedule served earlier in the case and should have all its calculations drawn to the date of trial.

1 [1984] 3 All ER 165.

11.124 This is an acceptable approach where a Schedule of Special Damages is straightforward but less desirable where a complex document has been prepared and the defendant is required to assess it, prepare a critique and then make a decision about the merits of an effective payment into court (if the defendant is to comply with RSC Order 22, rule 1 and allow to the plaintiff the full 21 day period allowed by RSC Order 22, rule 1(3)[1] within seven days of service of the schedule.

1 *Bowen v Mills & Knight* [1973] 1 Lloyd's Rep 580.

11.125 Conventionally therefore the terms of the practice direction are varied as shown to provide for the service of a schedule and counter schedule sufficiently early to provide ample time for full analysis of strengths and weaknesses in the schedule and sufficiently short a time before trial that calculations can readily be drawn to the trial date on the basis of the most up to date evidence on condition and prognosis.

Trial bundle – direction 9

The trial bundle

11.126 An enormous variation in practice regarding trial bundles has led the Rules Committee to set out in RSC Order 34, rule 10 what it regards as the critical documents which need to be before the trial judge:

Rule 10(2)(a) Witness statements which have been exchanged, and expert reports which have been disclosed, together with an indication of whether the contents of such documents are agreed,

(b) those documents which the Defendant wishes to have included in the bundle and those central to the Plaintiff's case; and

(c) where a direction has been given under O25 r3(2) RSC, a note agreed by the parties or, failing agreement, a note by each party giving

(i) a summary of the issues involved

(ii) a summary of any propositions of law to be advanced together with a list of authorities to be cited; and

(iii) a chronology of relevant events

(3) Nothing in this rule shall

(a) prevent the Court from giving, whether before or after the documents have been lodged, such further or different directions as to the documents to be lodged as may, in the circumstances, be appropriate . . .

11.127 These bundles (at least two in number for the court) must be filed at least *two clear days* before a date *fixed* for trial (or two days before a case not fixed enters a warned list). These bundles will be filed with the Queen's Bench Division clerk of the lists and in the District Registries with the chief clerk or the clerk to the trial judge.

Trial – direction 10

Place of trial

11.128 The place of trial should obviously be at the trial centre in which the Writ has been issued. However the court has power (RSC Order 4, rule 5) to transfer a case from London to a District Registry and/or between such registries. The discretion in RSC Order 4, rule 5(4) is such that transfer can be ordered '. . . on such terms, if any, as may be just' and this includes a situation where the ground for transfer is that an earlier listing date for the case can be achieved at another court centre than in the court in which proceedings were initiated. In considering such a transfer, the court will consider the convenience of the parties to the action and of the expert and other witnesses to be called to give evidence.

Mode of trial

11.129 This is conventionally 'judge alone' but it is clear from RSC Order 33, rule 5 (referring in turn to section 69 of the Supreme Court Act 1981), that the court can order a jury trial in a suitable case: *Ward v James*[1] established that a personal injury plaintiff must show exceptional circumstances before the court will order such a mode of trial.

1 [1965] 1 All ER 563.

11.130 The reasoning used by Lord Denning MR in coming to this view, was the desirability for plaintiff and defendants alike, of uniformity, predictability and assessability of damages awards and he expressed at some length his view that a judge sitting alone was best placed to bring knowledge of conventional awards and predictability to bear on individual cases. The Court of Appeal reconsidered this approach in *H v Ministry of Defence*[1] and having reconsidered the issues found that a jury trial was inappropriate for personal injury actions 'in so far as the jury was required to assess compensatory damages'. They drew comfort in this conclusion from the fact that no jury trial for personal injuries had taken place for over 25 years; this finding was somewhat self-fulfilling in that each time such an application had come before the High Court during that time it had been rejected.

1 [1991] 2 QB 103, CA.

11.131 However, the Court of Appeal left open the possibility that jury trial might be appropriate in cases where other than compensatory damages were being sought in respect of personal injuries arising from conduct in which deliberate abuse of authority was being alleged. The limits on claims for exemplary and aggravated damages set out by the Court of Appeal in *AB v South West Water Services Ltd*[1] would appear to have closed off even this possibility for jury trial.

1 [1993] 1 All ER 609.

Category

11.132 All medical negligence cases fall into Category B, ie cases of substance or difficulty; conceivably an exceptional case might fall into Category A as a case of 'great substance or great difficulty . . .' RSC Order 25, rule 3(7).

Speedy trial

11.133 In a suitable case, it is open to the master or registrar to order a 'speedy trial'. This works as an instruction to the Clerk of the Lists or Listing Officer to fix as early a date for the trial as is 'practicable' given the state of the court lists. In the case of a very elderly or infirm plaintiff this provision should be employed.[1]

1 RSC Ord 34, r 4 'Directions for London' [1981] 3 All ER 61 and 'Directions for Trial out of London' [1972] 1 All ER 287.

Split trial

11.134 Circumstances arise where the trial of sufficiently distinct issues of liability and quantum within the terms envisaged by RSC Order 33, rule 4(5), is desirable in medical negligence actions. For example, a brain damaged infant plaintiff's entitlement in damages changes as he or she gets older and the impact of the injury can be better assessed at a later stage. However, the liability and immediate causation issues are distinct enough to be tried separately from quantum and the earlier such trial takes place, the more accurate will be the recollections of the respective parties on issues of fact. Theoretically, such split trial is shorter and thus likely to be listed more quickly than a trial on both issues. Similarly, the effect of a finding in the plaintiff's favour ought to operate to make the quantum issues susceptible of negotiation and agreement and thus obviate the necessity for the second part of the trial. Where a split trial is ordered, the plaintiff is always vulnerable to a payment in, particularly where liability is strongly contested. In *Pollitt v Trustees of the National Heart Hospital*[1] it was ordered that the plaintiff's position be protected by providing an extension of time of six months, from the date of payment in within which time to accept or reject such offer, such extension of time to operate up to the date of the trial on liability and causation; thus the plaintiff is not put into a position of having to assemble quantum evidence within 21 days having been taken by surprise by a speculative payment in by a defendant. Such protection only continues until six months after the trial on liability and causation and (provided the quantum trial does not come too quickly) does not give the plaintiff undue advantage when the second part of the trial takes place.

1 Unreported.

Setting down for trial – direction 12

11.135 In setting down the action for trial, the rules as to time and lodging documents set out in RSC Order 34 must be adhered to. In setting down a medical negligence case for trial, the plaintiff's solicitor is looking to fix a date rather than to have the case come on at too short notice for the convenience of his expert witnesses. A fixed date for hearing is essential and this may unfortunately cause its own delay. The London system of listing fixtures is not reflected all over the country; different district registries have different policies about giving fixed dates to civil cases whether in the High Court or county court. This may be argument for commencing proceedings in London or at least for getting the listing office of your district registry to appreciate your problem with experts and offer you an effective fixed date.

11.136 Once a fixed date is established to the convenience of the expert witnesses it is important to ask those witnesses to set aside the whole or as much of the trial as possible. Until exchange of reports has taken place it will not be possible to tell those experts whether they will or will not be needed to give evidence and if they are required to give evidence it will not be possible until perhaps a week before trial (which may be much too late for them) to set a timetable for their attendance. Having to cancel clinics or delegate operation lists tends to antagonise experts.

11.137 Provisions differ in this respect between London and the district registries and the different provisions on setting down are set out in RSC Order 34, rule 4. The most immediate difference is in the certificate required by the Practice Note of 31 July 1987.[1] The obligation in the district registries is thus to set down when all elements of the Order following summons for directions have been complied with; in London it is possible to set down and fix a date for trial and to use the period between setting down and trial to comply with directions. The underlying assumption is that the longer list in London will result in a longer wait for a fixture; it seems also to imply that any regular notion of fixed dates in the district registries is unknown. A move to consistency of practice throughout the country would benefit practitioners in this field.

1 [1987] 2 All ER 1039.

Generally

11.138 The summons for directions aims to set out a timetable to take the case up to trial. The key to success is to adhere to the slightly more elaborate timetable dictated by a medical negligence action and to keep the initiative within the framework of that timetable.

DISCOVERY

11.139 Discovery happens twice in a medical negligence action. Pre-action discovery of the medical case notes and x-rays and other documents is the starting point for investigation of the case and discovery following the summons for directions is largely of the same documents.

11.140 Pre-action discovery of medical records obtained in this way is to enable all appropriate inquiries into the salient facts upon which an action would be based and for this reason the determination of a cause of death at a coroner's inquest is well within the proper ambit of such discovery and is a good reason in itself for seeking such discovery.[1] The plaintiff's List of Documents is standard form in its nature, listing correspondence before the issue of proceedings with the defendant and in Schedule 1, Part 2 those documents privileged from discovery. The plaintiff's solicitor may choose at this stage to list in Schedule 1, Part 2 any medical reports that have been prepared on the plaintiff's behalf and which are later to be disclosed but this is not a good idea because those reports at this time will not be finalised and should only be disclosed when the plaintiff's experts have agreed that the reports are in final form and ready for disclosure. From the plaintiff's point of view this is the time to ask the defendant for a further set of photocopies of medical notes other than those which have been disclosed at pre-action discovery.

1 *Stobart v Nottingham Health Authority; Sammut v South Lincolnshire Health Authority* and *Yafi v North Lincolnshire Health Authority* [1992] 3 Med LR 284.

11.141 The set first disclosed, having gone from solicitor to counsel to medical expert(s), will by now have become dog-eared and rather battered and probably scribbled all over. More importantly, it is critical to check that the notes received at pre-action discovery are a complete set. If this has already been checked, then check again. Obviously, at pre-action discovery, the plaintiff's solicitor may have seen the original medical notes and checked the copies against those originals but it is often the case that as the litigation progresses medical notes which have been missing or which have been thought not to be in existence, emerge into the light. There will also be the need to update this set with copies of the plaintiff's medical records which have come into existence since pre-action discovery because of further treatment.

11.142 Furthermore the defendant may list in Schedule 1, Part 2 of the List of Documents an accident report as being privileged from production and disclosure to the plaintiff. Such an accident report, the preparation of which is required by a National Health Service Circular, is not subject to legal professional privilege where the 'dominant purpose' of its preparation is not submission to solicitors in anticipation of litigation even though one of the purposes of such reports mentioned in the circular is use by solicitors if litigation should be commenced in respect of the accident.[1] Thus where the dominant purpose in the preparation of an accident report is the avoidance of similar accidents in the future the report will not be privileged even though a subsidiary purpose in its preparation is its use in the conduct of anticipated litigation.

1 *Lask v Gloucester Health Authority* (1986) 2 PN 96.

11.143 In the event that such an accident report appears in Schedule 1, Part 2, an application to court for its disclosure must be made and the court asked to assess whether or not it was prepared wholly in contemplation of litigation. At worst such an accident report, if disclosed, will give you further information about the circumstances in which the injury to the plaintiff occurred; at best it may give you critical information which may lead to the settlement of the action.

11.144 This phase of discovery is distinct from the pre-trial phase of discovery of reports on liability and causation, condition and prognosis and schedules of damages. However, so critical is this phase of discovery that because of the length of time taken to list interlocutory applications it may well spread over the period of time between setting down and trial and may overlap with the timing of discovery of opinion reports. As and when discovery of vital information is achieved, the results of that discovery need to be communicated quickly to all experts.

THE PERIOD BETWEEN DISCOVERY AND TRIAL

11.145 In some district registries, this period between setting down and trial can be as short as six months; in London it can be anything up to two years. The London experience tends to bring about the unfortunate consequence that the case can be broken 'in half'. The plaintiff's case is investigated after pre-action discovery and pleadings completed and then before the trial phase of the action is begun there is a long hiatus which allows the case to go to sleep.

11.146 The removal from the London list of large quantities of conventional personal injury work means that waiting lists are shorter than when this text was in its first edition. Even so the speed of listing could be improved both in London and in the district registries by adopting everywhere the same mechanism for listing fixed date trials.

11.147 Before considering the preparation of the case at the different stages before trial, three particular issues must be considered:

Relationship with counsel

11.148 In most personal injury litigation the role of the solicitor is clear cut; it is to liaise with the client and to ensure that the liaison with counsel has the effect of speeding up the pace at which pleadings are produced, advices prepared and the case resolved.

11.149 The complexity of medical negligence cases and the many different facets of liability, causation and quantum ensure that these cases benefit from a two-way (or if leading counsel is instructed, three-way) decision-making debate. Since the solicitor has the everyday conduct of the action he or she is entitled to have considerable say about the direction and manner in which the case proceeds. Furthermore, it is to the solicitor that the client will communicate any dissatisfaction with the way in which the case is being conducted.

11.150 Therefore the solicitor has to be seen to be taking a lead and determining the progress of the action. More is expected from a solicitor in the conduct of litigation than ever before; failure to take the initiative is now unacceptable.

11.151 Certainly if anything goes badly wrong in court, for example if witnesses are less impressive than expected or if a judge seems unreceptive, responsibility for all of this falls upon the solicitor who decided on the counsel to instruct and who found and instructed the expert witnesses.

11.152 The overwhelming importance of a medical negligence action to the plaintiff and the emotional as well as financial quantum involved, means that the solicitor must not fear to conduct the case positively rather than allowing counsel to do the lion's share of work; especially if 'care and conduct' is to be commensurately rewarded at taxation.

11.153 Conversely, a failure to conduct the case promptly and expeditiously may result in a more limited achievement at taxation. In extreme cases a failure competently to act can result in an award of the defendant's costs *personally* against the plaintiff's solicitor.[1]

1 *Locke v Camberwell Health Authority* [1991] 2 Med LR 249.

11.154 The ideal relationship should be one in which both counsel and solicitor co-operate fully at every step in the action from the investigation of the case with the first medical expert to the submission to be made on costs to the judge at the end of the trial. There is, or should be, an equality of responsibility emerging between solicitor and counsel; the days of leaving the initiative in counsel's hands and/or those of the medical experts are gone and should be forgotten.

The team

11.155 The fact that from the mid-1980s onwards, plaintiffs have begun in greater numbers to succeed in claims of medical negligence has much to do with the increasing preparedness of solicitors and counsel to take on cases and also with the fact that there is an increasing preparedness amongst the judiciary to find for plaintiffs in claims. However the principal reason why such claims have succeeded is that eminent doctors and surgeons have been prepared to write reports and give evidence on behalf of plaintiffs. This has happened because those doctors and surgeons at the top of the medical profession see the need to maintain standards as paramount and are prepared to risk criticism by their more cautious professional colleagues to maintain those standards.

11.156 The position of a medical opinion witness in a medical negligence case is potentially a very exposed one and in an effort to diminish this exposure it is a good idea to let your medical experts know at an early stage that they are part of a team of experts each prepared to contribute their individual skills to help the plaintiff.

11.157 It is important in the period between discovery, the various pre-trial phases and trial itself to have a series of conferences with counsel at which as many of the experts as possible are present with the client to allow them to explore each other's views and to debate the material issues.

11.158 It is not only important that counsel should be aware of the views of the respective medical opinion witnesses but also that the medical witnesses should know each other's views to establish whether they agree and/or disagree between themselves. This ought to be a valuable contribution to establish the 'hard core' of the plaintiff's case which everyone supports and the lacunae (if any) in the available evidence. The experts also have to be aware of the obligations that they owe the court, in their capacity as experts.

11.159 In *National Justice Compania Naviera SA v Prudential Assurance Co Ltd, The Ikarian Reefer*,[1] Cresswell J set out a list of the responsibilities of expert opinion witnesses in civil cases:

(1) expert evidence presented to the court should be, and should be seen to be, the independent product of the expert uninfluenced as to form or content by the exigencies of litigation;
(2) independent assistance should be provided to the court by way of objective unbiased opinion regarding matters within the expertise of the expert witness. An expert witness should never assume the role of advocate;
(3) facts or assumptions upon which the opinion was based should be stated together with material facts which could detract from the concluded opinion;
(4) an expert witness should make it clear when a question or issue fell outside his expertise;
(5) if the opinion was not properly researched because it was considered that insufficient data was available then that had to be stated with an indication that the opinion was provisional. If the witness could not assert that the report contained the truth, the whole truth and nothing but the truth then that qualification should be stated in the report;
(6) if after exchange of reports an expert witness changed his mind on a material matter then the change of view should be communicated to the other side through legal representatives without delay and, when appropriate, to the court;
(7) photographs, plans, survey reports and other documents referred to in the expert evidence had to be produced to the other side at the same time as the exchange of reports.

1 [1993] 2 Lloyd's Rep 68, [1993] 37 EG 158n.

11.160 This code, promulgated in the Commerical Court, is partly drawn from the practical application of 'cards on the table' litigation in the field of medical negligence. It is perhaps indicative of the extent to which the standards required by medical opinion experts in medical negligence cases have professionalised the giving of evidence by experts generally in civil litigation.

11.161 Clearly, the size of the 'team' varies from case to case but recent neurosurgical cases have involved three neurosurgeons to evaluate competence and to give evidence on liability; two neurologists, one to assess condition and future prognosis and another to comment exclusively on the causation of condition, a rehabilitation expert, occupational therapist, nursing adviser, architect, electronic aids adviser and a firm of forensic accountants. Adding to the solicitor and junior and leading counsel, the total membership of the plaintiff's team in such cases can be as many as 13. The key members of the team are those dealing with fault and causation and it is upon them that most will depend. Nevertheless in a large quantum case it is not unusual to have one expert upon whom substantiation of a figure of say, £400,000 in the schedule may depend. Not an expert to be lightly ignored.

11.162 The solicitor's role at all times is to ensure that everybody is aware of all of the developments in the case. Perhaps more importantly, he or she interprets for the plaintiff the way in which the various experts' views affect the case and the practical likelihood of the plaintiff succeeding in his or her claim and being awarded damages.

Acting for the legally aided plaintiff

11.163 This section assumes that a contested medical negligence case almost inevitably implies the support of a legal aid certificate. Many of these cases once identified as contested, move beyond the means of an individual private client; few trade unions support such cases and legal expenses insurance policies often specifically exempt 'professional negligence' litigation whilst supporting 'personal injury' litigation generally. The likely funding source is therefore the Legal Aid Board.

Scope of certificate

11.164 In the first instance a typical initial certificate in a medical negligence case will have a limitation that reads as follows:

> Limited to obtaining the appropriate medical records (including, if necessary, an application for pre-action discovery), obtaining independent medical expert reports, (one per speciality) and thereafter to the preparation of papers for Counsel, and obtaining Counsel's opinion. Authority is included for Counsel to settle the letter of instruction to the medical expert if the Solicitor considers this desirable.
>
> It is a condition that the solicitor shall report to the area office on Form CLA 30 if profit costs, disbursements and Counsel's fees exceed £7,500. If an extension is not obtained, subsequent profit costs may be deferred.

11.165 This envisages the completion of the pre-action phase of the case including an originating application under section 33 of the Supreme Court Act 1981 and to legislate for the need to instruct e g an obstetrician, paediatric neurologist, neonatologist and developmental paediatrician.

Amendment to limitation

11.166 An initial advice on merits having been given by counsel, often in the form of an agreed conference note prepared by the solicitor, the limitation on the certificate will need to be partly removed. This is also the point where any specific definition of the defendant may need to take place; for example proceedings might have been contemplated against only one hospital at the outset but investigation has implicated another. To protect the plaintiff's position an amendment should be sought to the Legal Aid Certificate.

11.167 The limitation will normally be removed in such a way as to empower you to take further steps to prosecute the action whilst imposing an obligation upon you to report before the case proceeds inevitably to trial. Thus

> Limited to all steps up to close of pleadings, summons for directions and discovery of documents and setting down to include mutual and simultaneous exchange of witness statements under RSC Order 28, rule 2A and of expert evidence under RSC Order 38, rule 37 and to the preparation of papers for counsel and then obtaining counsel's Advice on evidence, merits and quantum.

The removal of such limitation is requested by the completion of Form CLA 30.

Prior authority

11.168 Regulations 59 and 61 Civil Legal Aid (General) Regulations 1989 cover the seeking by a solicitor of specific prior authority to instruct counsel and specific experts *additional* to those for whom general authority is given in the limitation on the Legal Aid Certificate.

11.169 Such prior authority is sought on Form CLA 31 and must be prospective and not retrospective. On the face of it, such authority, if granted will render untouchable the costs involved if the claim is unsuccessful and the Bill of Costs has to be taxed against the Legal Aid Fund (or if inter partes items are transferred to the Legal Aid side of the Bill) provided that this extension has been notified to the client who is content that such a step should be taken and is prepared to run the risk of a knock-on effect in the shape of an increase in the statutory charge.

11.170 It is *essential* to obtain such prior authority in any case where you wish to instruct leading counsel. The taxing master or district judge has discretion under regulation 64(5) of the Civil Legal Aid (General) Regulations 1980 to allow counsel's fees for which prior authority has not been sought, but the wording of regulation 60 (now regulation section 9(i)(b)) specifically states that without prior authority, 'a Queen's Counsel or more than one Counsel *shall not* be instructed'.[1] In these circumstances, the obligation to pay counsel's fees will fall directly upon the instructing solicitor.

1 *Hunt v East Dorset Health Authority* [1992] 2 All ER 539.

Payment of disbursements and profit costs on account

11.171 A claim for a disbursement over £30 can be made to the Legal Aid Fund at any time during the conduct of proceedings in respect of e g court fees, medical reports, taxing fee.

11.172 This sum will be paid, generally, within 28 days if a claim is made on Form CLA 28. Prompt use of this form will aid cash flow and gratify medical experts who are unused to the (historically) uncommercial attitude to the payment of experts' fees by solicitors.

11.173 Claims for payment on account may be made on this form where retainer has been determined and it is unlikely that the taxation of costs will take place within the next six months. Similarly in cases of demonstrable hardship it may be appropriate to seek a payment of profit costs if the certificate has been in force for more than 12 months and taxation of costs is unlikely within the next 12 months. These cases are distinct from the circumstances which prevail where an annual report is sought from a solicitor and an invitation to apply for payment on account is made. This authority arises from Civil Legal Aid (General) Regulations 1989, regulation 100(6) and 100(1). In either case a proportionate payment inclusive of VAT will be made by the Legal Aid Board, on a scale calculated in accordance with a formula in regulation 100(5).

Final order/taxing authority

11.174 In a successful case, the final order whether it be judgment or a Tomlin Order should contain a provision for taxation and also for Legal Aid taxation. Such a Legal Aid taxation authority will also be required where the plaintiff's claims have been unsuccessful. This taxing authority arises from Civil Legal Aid (General) Regulations 1989, regulation 107 and should be specifically recited in such judgment or order by consent.

COUNTDOWN TO TRIAL

Four months after setting down – exchange of witness statements and medical reports

11.175 Exchange of witness statements 14 weeks (ten weeks in the county court) after the giving of directions is the second stage in the determining of the facts in the case (the first being the factual context revealed by the pleadings). The trade in such exchange is almost inevitably one-sided. The plaintiff may have only a limited recollection of what was said before an operation was carried out and may be disabled from much post-operative recollection. The medical staff on the other hand were there and will have had their memories jogged by their study of the contemporaneous medical record. There may be conflicts of recollection between different medical or nursing staff.

11.176 On both sides exchange of witness statements may provide an opportunity for sharpening up the case by either extending the pleadings or seeking by Interrogatories to limit the issues in dispute between the parties. Once witness statements have been disclosed they *must* be circulated to all of your medical experts who will then be able to consider whether any inferences that they have drawn from the medical records in their reports have been supported, negated or distorted by the views of the opposing witness(es) of fact.

11.177 On the plaintiff's side before such exchange of medical reports can take place, counsel and solicitor have to decide which experts are going to be called to give evidence at trial and on what aspects of the case their expertise will be required. It is usual to have a conference with the opinion experts before this disclosure takes place to see whether their views have varied from the time when the reports were first written and in the light of the defence which has been served and the exchange of witness statements which has taken place.

11.178 This conference should take place some time before disclosure is due so that the experts are given as much time as they need to complete their reports or carry out any further research into the medical literature to support the conclusions that they have drawn in their reports.

11.179 It is not open to counsel or solicitor at this conference to dictate to the medical expert the opinion that will be expressed in that report; the opinion must be the honest view of the expert, expressed in the expert's own words. Nevertheless it is often the case that the reports prepared before pleadings have been written on a question and answer basis and at this stage reports for disclosure may be of more value if written on a narrative basis. In this situation the experts should therefore be invited to change their reports from question and answer format into narrative to make them more succinct. It is also desirable to ask experts who have commented on condition and prognosis as well as liability and causation to separate their reports into these two differing categories so that if they wish to update their reports on condition and prognosis before trial, it is open to them to do so. It is important that they should do so because the initial report on condition and prognosis which was served with the Statement or Particulars of Claim may, by this time be 18 months to two years old.

11.180 It is critical that *no* report is ever disclosed without first having been checked and its form agreed for disclosure by that expert. Disclosure without making such a check will only lead to an alienated and irascible expert who may refuse to give evidence at trial and who may become, if subpoenaed, almost a hostile witness.

11.181 Once the form of the report is agreed with all experts, the plaintiff's and defendant's solicitors can effect exchange. This can either be done by a meeting and actually exchanging the reports on a simultaneous basis or agreeing to put the reports into the post or the Document Exchange (DX) at the same time. Because of the importance of simultaneity in such exchange it is perhaps appropriate to consider this problem as analogous to that facing the conveyancer in effecting exchange of contracts. Exactly the same mechanism holds good for the exchange (and enforcement of exchange) of witness statements.

11.182 It is important not to proffer a witness statement or an expert's report unilaterally but to show oneself *ready and willing* to effect exchange with the defendant. In the event that the defendant has no statement or report to exchange or is unwilling to exchange the report in its solicitor's possession then it is important to seek from the master or district judge an order debarring the defendant from adducing expert evidence at trial. Such order (following on from the order for exchange in the form sought by directions 5(a) and 6 of the summons for directions) is usually sought by an application in the following form:

The Plaintiff having (today) made available for exchange pursuant to the Order of Master made on such expert medical reports as s/he will seek to rely upon at Trial and the Defendant not having made any such reports available, the Defendant be debarred from adducing, by cross-examination or otherwise any expert medical opinion evidence on liability and causation issues at Trial.

11.183 Clearly, the defendant will be in some difficulty at trial if unable to adduce expert opinion evidence on its behalf. This cannot fetter the discretion of the trial judge to admit expert evidence of the party in default. It is submitted however that the circumstances would be exceptional in which the proper exercise of discretion would permit expert evidence to be admitted in the face of such a 'debarring' order, if, (as occasionally happens) the order is made with the consent of the parties.

11.184 The changes to RSC Order 38, rule 2A which widen to all forms of personal injury litigation the principle of mutual and simultaneous discovery of witness statements, confirm that in the absence of suitable discovery in compliance with RSC Order 38, rule 2A(2), a party shall not be entitled to adduce evidence without leave of the court.

11.185 It is important to consider the use of such summons in appropriate circumstances because a defendant without expert evidence to adduce may occasionally take the view (particularly if confronted with a private client plaintiff) that delay adds to the psychological pressure on such plaintiff, even if the utlimate aim is to compromise the claim and avoid trial.

11.186 The importance of simultaneity of disclosure which was argued so long and hard in the *Naylor* appeals rests on the suspicion that if sequential disclosure is made in a case of this sort, with the plaintiff going first, then the witness statement or report prepared by the defendant will not be an objective assessment of the defendant's position regarding liability and causation but will be principally a critique by the defendant's expert(s) of the plaintiff's expert's report. Simultaneous disclosure aims to reveal to both parties the objective attitudes to the alleged negligence taken by the respective experts. Similar considerations apply in exchange of witness statements.

11.187 Obviously, the plaintiff's experts must see the defendant's experts' report(s) as soon as possible after exchange and must comment upon them in detail; in particular comment should be made upon the perceived strengths and weaknesses of those reports. In the event that a novel point is identified which has not previously been considered, then the experts must subject it to immediate and detailed scrutiny.

11.188 It may be appropriate at this stage to have a further conference with the medical experts in order to ensure that both solicitor and counsel understand the nature of the points raised.

11.189 If the plaintiff is legally aided this is the moment for counsel to be asked to write a further advice on merits for submission to the Legal Aid Board.

Five months after setting down for trial – the schedule of special damages and future loss

11.190 By this stage the schedule should need little more than updating. The effect of the changes to RSC Order 28, rule 12 in June 1990 moved forward the investigation of quantum in all personal injury cases so that details of 'special damages' at least become a required particular of pleading as an element of the Statement of Claim. 'Special damages' is taken by the notes to RSC Order 18, rule 12 to include future losses of earnings, of pension rights and of anticipated care costs.

11.191 Thus on the face of it the plaintiff has an obligation at the beginning of a medical negligence action to provide a full schedule of damages claimed (save for general damages) so that the defendant can understand the nature of the claim to be met and the general quantum of the injury to be compensated, so that, if appropriate, a payment into court may be made immediately.

11.192 This provision whilst appropriate for a 'conventional' personal injury action causes problems in many medical negligence actions, particularly where the solicitor is acting under a Legal Aid Certificate and is under a duty to the Legal Aid Board not to spend more in costs than is necessary. For example a cerebral palsy claim, even if strongly supported by all experts will inevitably be uncertain at least until discovery of witness statements and medical opinion reports has taken place. Assuming the operation of the summons for directions set out above, this would fully equip the plaintiff's lawyers to take a view on the overall merits.

11.193 But the provisions of RSC Order 18, rule 12 envisage the giving of such information by schedule at the time of the service of the Statement of Claim. This requires the expenditure of a considerable extra sum of the Legal Aid Board's money to ensure compliance.

11.194 The experience since 1990 has been of defendants prepared to agree to the service of a Schedule of Damages after the close of pleadings but earlier than the timetable envisaged by the 1984 Practice Direction.

11.195 A Schedule of Special Damages and Future Loss is required by the 1984 Practice Direction to set out any claim for:

(a) loss of earnings;
(b) loss of future earning capacity;
(c) medical or other expenses relating to or including the cost of care, attention, accommodation or appliances;
(d) loss of pension rights.

The Practice Direction envisages the service of these details 28 days before trial but in view of the increasing complexity of these schedules and the provisions of RSC Order 22 relating to payments into court, it is desirable that this should be sooner.

11.196 Failure to give the defendant's solicitors sufficient notice of the schedule will antagonise them just at the moment when a friendly channel of communication may be needed and may also open the door for a justifiable application to adjourn the trial in order to give the defendant a chance to consider an elaborate schedule. An adjournment brought about in this way would be a considerable disappointment to the plaintiff and a possible burden in costs personally for the solicitor if it can be shown that such delay in serving a schedule was an incompetent one. (Supreme Court Act 1981, section 51(6)).

11.197 Thus service of a schedule either with the Statement of Claim or by agreement after the close of pleadings should ensure that it can be updated in plenty of time before trial if necessary and should ensure that the schedule is sufficiently up to date to ensure that a harassed defendant's solicitor actually pays some attention to the schedule and takes some immediate steps to assess its merit and accuracy.

11.198 Schedules of special damages and future loss can take any reasonably logical form. There has not yet emerged any recognisably standard document which should be used but the increasing tendency to use forensic accountants in larger claims has meant that the schedules have become much more detailed than when they were prepared exclusively by solicitors or counsel. The form itself is to some extent immaterial provided that the information required by the Practice Direction is given and that the information is reduced to historic and prospective annualised figures of consequential loss to which (in respect of future losses) a multiplier based on the condition and prognosis evidence can be attached. The simpler the form to which a schedule can be reduced, the better.

11.199 Before this schedule is served the solicitor and counsel must examine the assumptions contained in it and reject all but those which can be sustained from credible corroborative evidence. If the schedule of special damages is as accurate and cautious as it can be made, it will be a good basis from which to consider any payment into court made by the defendant before trial. It is easy in a large damages claim, particularly when forensic accountants are instructed, to allow fanciful figures to be calculated. At the risk of disappointing the plaintiff these figures must be examined on several occasions until such time as everyone is satisfied that they can be accurately evidenced.

11.200 The best measure of the success of a schedule of special damages is not how much the plaintiff receives in damages but what percentage those damages represent of the schedule first served on the defendant: however cautious the plaintiff's assumptions may be, a note of optimism is bound to obtrude.

Six months after setting down

11.201 Following the timetable set out by the summons for directions this is the point at which two things happen: firstly, the updated medical reports relating to the plaintiff's condition and prognosis are served and secondly, the counter-schedule of special damages prepared by the defendant is served.

Service of reports on condition and prognosis

11.202 The length of the average medical negligence case means that the plaintiff's condition and prognosis may well have changed during the period of the litigation. This is particularly true in the case of infant plaintiffs and it is an important consideration for the solicitor running the case to ensure that his or her evidence on condition and prognosis is updated regularly throughout. This not only has significant bearing on the damages for pain and suffering and loss of amenity likely to be awarded by the court but also on the reasonableness of assumptions underlying the schedule of special damages. For example, trends in the evidence of educational psychologists in relation to infant plaintiffs can have a profound influence on assumptions as to ultimate educational achievement and thus eventual employability of an infant plaintiff.

11.203 Since there is much overlap between the condition and prognosis evidence and the information needed to prepare the schedule of special damages it is important at one of the pre-trial conferences to test the assumptions used in the schedule of special damages. In addition there may be a need to bring along to this conference any other experts whose role is to give future costs assessments based on the condition and prognosis evidence.

Defendant's counter-schedule

11.204 Whilst the receipt of the defendant's counter-schedule may not give a hint of the true reception given to the plaintiff's schedule and is most likely to be merely a critique of that schedule showing the defendant's most pessimistic view of the plaintiff's likely recovery, it is nevertheless a moment when both solicitors are finally equipped with an idea of the range across which the dispute as to compensation and consequently as to settlement is likely to be transacted.

11.205 Such counter-schedule may well form the basis for the defendant's payment into court but often before such payment into court is made, it may form the basis for 'without prejudice' discussions about the quantum of the claim and about the defendant's intentions generally.

11.206 Medical negligence litigation at this point is almost identical to any other sort of personal injury litigation so far as the protocol of such negotiations is concerned and the conventions of settlement and compromise are almost too well known to comment upon. With one exception; the cathartic importance of a concession of liability to a plaintiff can be underestimated by his or her solicitor rightly concerned with the getting of compensation. Before *any* settlement is advocated by the solicitor to the plaintiff this issue should be canvassed with the plaintiff and his or her view made clear.

11.207 It is worth restating the definition of the tort of negligence offered in *Charlesworth on Negligence* (9th edn):

1. The existence of a duty to take care which is owed by the Defendant to the Plaintiff; and
2. The failure to attain the standard of care, prescribed by the law, thereby committing *a breach* of such duty; and

3. Damage which is both *causally connected* with such a breach and recognised by the law, has been occasioned to the Plaintiff.

11.208 Thus an admission of 'negligence' clearly connotes the concession by the defendant of a 'breach of duty' and 'causation of injury' by such breach; an admission of 'breach of duty' or 'liability' alone leaves it open to the defendant to defend the claim at trial by adducing expert evidence to show that whilst 'breach of duty' or 'liability' has been established the plaintiff's injury is unconnected with it or only partly related to it and that 'causation' has not been proved.

11.209 These slightly differing forms of admission may disguise a quite different approach to the damages to be offered by the defendant and the terms of any admission made before trial must be scrutinised closely.

11.210 If negligence is admitted it is conventional to ask the defendant's solicitors to consent to the entry of judgment so that the admission made is on the court record rather than simply in correspondence between solicitors.

11.211 A more limited gesture which will not rank as an admission will be an apology. Often sought and rarely conceded, the importance of an apology; especially in a fatal accident claim can scarcely be underestimated. The concession of an apology is in no way a concession of liability nor is there any case law to support the proposition that an apology may form the basis, in medical negligence litigation, of an application for summary judgment. It involves humanity rather than liability.

Twenty-eight days before trial

11.212 Ideally at 28 days before trial, any consequential medical reports will have been served, lists of textbooks and other medical literature will have been forthcoming and the common ground (if any) between the parties will have emerged from the Schedule and Counter-Schedule of Special Damages and Future loss.

By this time therefore plaintiff and defendant have an opportunity to take stock.

11.213 (a) The plaintiff:

(a) knows the defendant's position on liability and causation and can test the issues raised in the witness statements, liability and causation reports and condition and prognosis reports with the plaintiff's experts;
(b) the agreed facts and those in dispute will have emerged from exchange of witness statements;
(c) at an evidential level, counsel and the solicitor for the plaintiff can assess the strengths and weaknesses of their own experts' position and consider whether the experts are sufficient in quality and number. If they are insufficient in number or if there is any remaining point which needs to be canvassed a late medical report may need to be sought at this stage and the leave of the trial judge obtained to admit such evidence. The strengths and weaknesses of the factual evidence will also have emerged by exchange of witness statements;

(d) if the plaintiff is legally aided the Legal Aid Board can be advised on merits, liability and evidence. Continuing with a medical negligence case when evidence to substantiate the claim is insufficient can result in an application by a successful defendant in an application for costs against the plaintiff's solicitor personally under RSC Order 62, rule 11.[1] Whilst the Court of Appeal reversed Morland J's decision on its facts after the admission of fresh evidence, the principles underlying that decision are undisturbed:

(1) that a solicitor conducting litigation competently has to consider the appropriateness of his own instructions that he gives to counsel and at least the prima facie validity of counsel's advice;

(2) that comments on the defence made by the plaintiff's medical expert may alert solicitor and counsel to the insubstantial state of the plaintiff's case;

(3) not having sufficiently examined the medical case notes, counsel was not justified in stating that there was a good arguable case as pleaded;

(4) knowing that counsel had not examined the medical records and knowing that the medical experts' reports had shown inconsistencies a complete assessment of the medical records had to be undertaken; and

(5) that it was the *primary responsibility* of the plaintiff's solicitor to ensure that the hospital records were examined carefully by someone with the appropriate legal expertise so that the strength of the plaintiff's claim could be evaluated properly;

(e) the plaintiff can now be advised by his or her lawyers of the realistic prospects of success in the light of the mutual discovery of evidence which has taken place.

1 *Locke v Camberwell Health Authority* [1991] 2 Med LR 249.

11.214 (b) The defendant:

(i) can assess the strength of its case on liability and causation and the prospect of successfully defending the action. If the likelihood of a successful defence seems limited the defendant's solicitors can make overtures for compromise and consider an admission of liability but in any event pay into court with a view to making it more difficult for the plaintiff to decide whether or not to fight or settle the case;

(ii) if the case on one or other aspect is weak but on the balance of probabilities might succeed or, if the plaintiff is privately funded, makes a 'no admissions' payment into court, thus posing to the plaintiff's solicitors and counsel the dilemma of having to judge the merits of a payment into court against the obvious risks and pitfalls of continuing to trial;

(iii) if the plaintiff's case is 'frivolous', write a Calderbank letter offering a discontinuance on terms to the plaintiff but making it clear that in the event that the offer of discontinuance is not accepted, an order for indemnity costs will be sought by a successful defendant and/or against the plaintiff's legal adviser. This may have more effect on a privately funded plaintiff than on a legally aided plaintiff who is unlikely to have progressed this far if the case is frivolous.

11.215 At this stage a privately funded plaintiff is in a very difficult position, whether or not his or her claim is a strong one. It may be a very important part of the catharsis involved in the claim from the plaintiff's point of view that an admission of liability is made or a finding is made by the court. However, the mechanism of payment into court places a privately funded plaintiff in a more vulnerable position than a legally aided litigant. A suitable lodgment enables a defendant to make it difficult for a plaintiff to continue to trial in order to obtain an admission or a finding of negligence. In this respect a legally aided plaintiff is in a strong position to take a risk to get a judgment but is still in some difficulty because he or she may be ordered to pay the defendant's costs, from the date of the payment in, out of any damages awarded eventually made at trial. This highlights the advantage given to the defendant of a payment into court without admission of liability.

11.216 It also highlights the fact our tort system, although partly adapted to the task of investigating and attributing fault, is actually a mechanism for establishing whether or not a plaintiff is eligible for compensation.

PAYMENT INTO COURT

11.217 Payment into court of sums in satisfaction of a cause of action of a plaintiff is governed by RSC Order 22. A payment into court may be made at any time after the service of the writ but to be effective on the question of costs the payment or last payment in must be made not less than 21 days before the trial or hearing of the action to enable the plaintiff to have the full time allowed to him or her by RSC Order 22, rule 3 to accept the sum paid in. The trial judge has no knowledge of the payment into court at the time when the trial takes place and the payment into court only has significance in the issue of costs at the point when an award has been made and that award is found to be equal to or less than the sum paid into court.

11.218 The general rule on entitlement to costs is set out in RSC Order 62, rule 3 in the form of a general discretion. RSC Order 62, rule 9 sets out matters which the court must take into account in exercising discretion and RSC Order 62, rule 9(1)(b) identifies 'any payment of money into court and the amount of any such payment' as an issue to be taken into account. The effective position is that the trial judge must consider every case on its particular merits and can make such award of costs as he thinks fit. However the most likely order for costs which will be made if a plaintiff fails to beat a payment into court will be that the plaintiff will be required to pay the defendant's costs on a standard basis from the date of the payment until date of judgment.

11.219 Since a proportion of costs in any medical negligence action are incurred at the trial, failure to beat a payment into court has a significant effect on the value of the award made to the plaintiff which will effectively be reduced, not only by having to meet his or her own costs, but also by having to meet the defendant's costs of the trial on a standard basis.

11.220 In considering a payment into court the most difficult task for the solicitor in this sort of case is to persuade his client that the purpose of the whole action is to achieve damages rather than to go to court and pursue a finding of negligence against the defendant. There is no doubt that if the solicitor and counsel believe that a payment into court at this stage is acceptable they must make it clear to even the most bullish privately funded litigant that the purpose of the payment-in system is to exclude from court those cases in which reasonable sums have been offered in settlement and in which, as a consequence, the court will regard the plaintiff as having achieved adequate compensation.

11.221 A legally aided client is in a less independent position at this stage since the view taken by counsel and the solicitor in the case is subject to two potentially distinct duties. The first is owed to the client to take instructions and to prosecute the case as successfully as possible, but in an instance where a payment into court is made and counsel and the solicitor are of the view that that payment into court is acceptable, they must exercise their second duty which is owed to the Legal Aid Fund to recommend to the Law Society that a payment into court is satisfactory and appropriate to the claim. Such a recommendation must necessarily influence the Legal Aid Board in its decision to continue or discharge a Legal Aid Certificate.

11.222 The effect on a legally aided plaintiff of failing to beat a payment into court is the same as that for a privately funded plaintiff since the defendant is entitled to his costs after the date of payment in and those costs are set off against the damages and the plaintiff's costs before a payment out of court.[1]

1 *Cook v S* [1967] 1 All ER 299.

ACCEPTANCE OR REFUSAL OF PAYMENT INTO COURT

11.223 The decision to refuse a payment into court is perhaps the most difficult judgment for any solicitor or counsel to make in the whole progress of any personal injury claim and particularly so in a medical negligence action.

11.224 A simple claim with limited special damages and a clear cut injury in which the conventional award is readily assessable may enable a straightforward judgment to be made as to whether to reject the payment-in. A nominal payment in, in a case where the quantum of damages is substantial, is also easy to reject. However, in medical negligence cases it is possible for injuries to be more complex than in other areas and for the various heads of special damages including lost earnings and future medical expenses to cover wide and extremely variable ranges dependent on the view taken of life expectancy. An accurately judged payment into court is extremely difficult for a plaintiff to reject.

11.225 It is at this point that the amount of common ground between the respective parties' experts in the condition and prognosis reports and the reasonableness of the assumptions made at the time of the compilation of the Schedule of Special Damages, become critical: it is on this information that a judgment will be made as to whether or not a payment into court is to be accepted. The only ground on which to reject a payment into court is a well-founded belief that the payment is inadequate and that it can be beaten with the available evidence. This argument will have to be rehearsed on paper by counsel in the form of an advice on quantum if a plaintiff is legally aided; such an advice which will be a condition precedent to the removal of the limitation on the Legal Aid Certificate.

TWENTY-ONE DAYS BEFORE TRIAL

11.226 By this time it will be possible to see whether a payment into court has been made and whether the plaintiff's lawyers are required to exercise the fine judgment required to assess the acceptability of a payment into court. If no such payment into court has been received it will be a hint from the defendant's solicitors that not only is the claim regarded as defensible but that so confident are they of succeeding that a payment in is unnecessary.

11.227 Another way of assessing the defendant's attitude is to see whether their experts are prepared to attend a meeting on a 'without prejudice' basis to narrow the issues likely to be in dispute at trial. If, as is often the case, the defendant's experts are sceptical about attending this meeting then it may be that this matter should be raised in a submission upon costs at the end of the trial.

PREPARATION BY THE SOLICITOR FOR TRIAL

11.228 If no payment in is made or if such a payment is unacceptable, the solicitor must brief counsel and prepare the case for trial.

11.229 As long before trial as possible, the solicitor and counsel must decide on the sequence in which experts will be called to give their evidence. This sequence can then, as far as possible, be arranged and thought given to presentation of the evidence. Whilst oral submission and examination is still at the heart of the presentation of the case, counsel is likely to have more paper to refer to and more developed means of illustrating the plaintiff's condition and prognosis or putting into context a particular surgical technique. The paper will be in the trial bundle, the illustrations in the visual aids.

The trial bundle

11.230 The terms of RSC Order 34, rule 10 define in a minimal fashion the required contents. In practice the bundle in a medical negligence action is likely to contain:

(a) the pleadings in chronological order (these should include copies of any Legal Aid Certificate and amendments);
(b) the witness statements in chronological order;

(c) the expert opinion reports on liability and causation as exchanged and in chronological order together with articles from the medical literature referred to in those reports;
(d) the expert opinion reports on condition and prognosis as exchanged and in chronological order;
(e) the curricula vitae of the experts whose reports are contained in sections (c) and (d);
(f) the Schedule of Damages, which will contain as appendices the expert opinion reports on quantum; and
(g) the medical records in a format agreed with the defendant.

11.231 All of these separate parts of the bundle should be paginated and should be readily referable from an index front sheet at the beginning of each section. This will promote ease of reference within each section. The bundle should have an overall front sheet describing the different sections.

11.232 The medical records *must* have been agreed to be a complete set and must have been properly ordered. This should be an order that will be clinically recognisable to the doctors present giving evidence and should be organised, so far as possible, to ensure that the material records from which facts or inferences are to emerge are instantly referable.

11.233 The set of medical records should be sequentially paginated but will obviously be divided in places to reflect the separation between for example, obstetric records relating to delivery and neonatal records relating to ITU care. Where there are X-rays or scans which are material these must be individually tagged and identified so as to eliminate confusion and an index to them provided as a part of the trial bundle.

11.234 If, as sometime happens at trial, a fresh document emerges which has not previously been disclosed or whose relevance has not previously been highlighted, a copy must be added to each bundle and paginated. This tends to happen particularly in the case of items from medical literature.

11.235 Trial bundles will be needed for:

(1) the trial judge;
(2) your counsel;
(3) yourself;
(4) the plaintiff's expert;
(5) the defendant's counsel;
(6) the defendant's solicitor;
(7) the witness box (both plaintiff's and defendant's witnesses can often forget their copies and thus will inevitably be asked to refer to the bundle, whilst giving evidence).

It is axiomatic that you should have one other copy made for no better reason than that you may need it. Ideally, the trial judge should be able to read the bundle beforehand and grasp the true issues in the case, thus enabling him or her to speed the action.

11.236 Allied to the power in RSC Order 35, rule 7(1) to dispense altogether with opening speeches, this rule about trial bundles may be seen as some limit on the oral/adversarial nature of medical negligence trials and the beginning of the trial 'on paper' with the possibility of the judge taking a more inquisitorial role.

Visual aids

11.237 Historically, these have been seldom used in any sort of personal injury litigation but they are increasingly useful in demonstrating the plaintiff's condition and prognosis and/or demonstrating some facet of the plaintiff's case on liability and causation. Illustration of the plaintiff's condition and prognosis to a large extent speaks for itself; video evidence is now commonplace and can give a much more developed impression to the judge of the reality of the plaintiff's condition than any number of written reports. Furthermore, the judge can consider such evidence as often as necessary for the whole nature of the plaintiff's injuries to become apparent.

11.238 Illustration of the plaintiff's case on liability is a less developed area of presentation. Medical experts themselves can often provide anatomical illustrations, and will always bring along surgical instruments alleged to have been employed inappropriately. Nevertheless what the trial judge needs (and what the trial judge most often lacks) is a guide to the exact nature of the alleged negligence. The use of a medical artist to prepare a series of drawings which the medical expert can use to make a point to the trial judge, is often helpful. However experienced in personal injury litigation whilst in practice, few judges have the comprehensive medical knowledge necessary to grasp the usually esoteric demands of medical negligence litigation and great pains should be taken visually to simplify anatomy involved and the nature of the failings alleged.

11.239 The job of the plaintiff's solicitor in this aspect (as in all other aspects of the case) is to keep the issues as simple as possible and not to allow the defendant by its solicitors or experts to confuse those simple issues with extraneous detail. Apart from anything else, successful illustrations of the liability issues can result in a marked shortening of the time taken to hear expert witnesses for the parties.

Arrangements for expert witnesses

11.240 The case will fail if your expert witnesses are not at court. Whilst you have doubtless booked them since the moment that the case was set down and given a fixture, now is the time to ensure their availability for the exact time when you and counsel wish them to give evidence and to sit in court whilst the defendant's expert gives opposing evidence. Most trial judges are tolerant of an elastic order of giving evidence and will work hard to accommodate the vagaries of clinics and operating lists but it is important that you let your witnesses know when and if they are needed. Try not to achieve a situation where your expert is told only at the last minute that he is not needed because his evidence has been agreed by the defendant. Agree if you can (if possible with specific authority under Legal Aid (General) Regulations 1980, regulation 62) any fee for late cancellation if you put your expert into this position.

11.241 You must establish your expert's bona fides as an expert. The trial judge may be content to rely upon your expert's entry in the Medical Directory but it is a courtesy to your expert and to the court to have him or her supply you with a curriculum vitae which can be shown to the trial judge. Medical CVs are lengthy and voluminous and you should ask your expert to provide only a synopsis of his or her professional career.

11.242 Lastly, whilst solicitors and counsel are familiar with the tradition of remaining unpaid until a year after the trial, expert witnesses are not and are likely to regard this quaint legal custom with scepticism. If your client is legally aided, apply for payment of their fees on account of disbursements (Legal Aid Form: CLA 28) immediately a fee note is rendered. Similarly if you are acting for a private client ensure you hold enough money on account to meet experts' fees immediately after trial.

CONCLUSION

11.243 The Civil Justice Review, reporting on Personal Injury litigation to the Lord Chancellor in 1986, criticised present personal injury litigation as too slow and too costly and concluded that it 'cannot be defended'.

11.244 The developments of both law and practice in the field of medical negligence litigation serve as an example of the way in which practitioners can drive the Rules Committee and the appellate courts into changes which benefit all parties to litigation and limit costs.

11.245 A fault-based system of compensation assessment has many imperfections but it contains within it the elements that all plaintiffs want if they are to achieve a coming to terms with an injury caused by a medical accident. In changing or adapting this system it will be crucial to avoid the English reform habit of aiming for the best but allowing it to be the enemy of the good.

11.246 Practitioners must be adept in use of the system we have and quick to press for changes where they see it to be inadequate. If this concern is not to be dissipated, the administration must be more sensitive to the demands of practitioners and their clients. Practitioners and the courts administration must work to keep the present system sensitive to changing needs if the arguments for the replacement of our fault-based system are not to become unanswerable.

CHAPTER 12

Consent to treatment

Sir Henry Brooke
Anthony Barton

INTRODUCTION

12.1 'Every human being of adult years and sound mind has a right to determine what should be done with his body, and a surgeon who performs an operation without his patient's consent commits an assault for which he is liable in damages'.[1]

1 *Schloendorff v Society of New York Hospital* 103 NE 92 (1914) at 93–94, per Cardozo J.

12.2 Treatment of a patient requires his consent. This consent can in certain circumstances be granted by a third party who has lawful authority to grant such consent. In other, exceptional, circumstances, consent can be dispensed with. The rule of law which requires the giving of consent is a basic rule of the civil law, and good standards of medical and surgical care have been developed round that rule.

12.3 This chapter will explain what the law requires in the case of conscious adult patients of sound mind (who will be referred to as 'patients'). It will then discuss some of the exceptions to the general rule; how it is to be applied in the case of children, or the mentally disordered, or the unconscious. It will end with some thoughts about the underlying jurisprudence of the law of consent, the different elements of consent, and the different consequences which may flow from the absence of one or more of these elements.

12.4 In addition to judicial expositions of the law relating to consent, some leading writers have provided helpful accounts of the nature of consent. Michael Jones, writing in *Medical Negligence* (1990),[1] states:

The patient's consent must be a 'valid' consent, which means that it must be voluntary, the patient must have the mental capacity to understand the nature of the procedure to which he is consenting, and he must have a certain minimal amount of information about the nature of the procedure.

Professor Ian Kennedy, writing in *Doctors, Patients and the Law* (1992),[2] states:

In essence consent is legally valid only if certain conditions are satisfied. This means that in any particular case a doctor or dentist must satisfy himself that any consent obtained from his patient meets these conditions. At their most general, they are:

(i) the patient must be legally competent (ie capable of consenting);
(ii) the consent must be freely given;
(iii) the person consenting must be suitably informed.

Dieter Giesen, writing in *International Medical Malpractice Law* (1988),[3] states:

Consent is legally valid only where it is freely given by the patient with the capacity to consent on the basis of adequate information as to the nature and consequences of the proposed treatment and its alternatives including that of non-treatment.

1 At 200–201.
2 At 52.
3 At 252–253.

THE NECESSITY FOR CONSENT

12.5 The well-known quotation from a judgment of the American judge, Cardozo J, at the beginning of this chapter sets out the basic rule in clear and simple terms. The rule applies to all kinds of medical and surgical treatment which involves interference with the human body or the application of substances, such as drugs and other medicine or X-rays, for instance, to the human body. If the doctor or surgeon does not obtain his patient's consent to treatment and does not have any other lawful authority to treat him without his consent, he will be committing an unlawful battery on him: the traditional definition of an unlawful battery is an act that directly and either intentionally or negligently causes some physical contact with the person of another without that person's consent.[1]

1 45 *Halsbury's Laws* (4th edn) para 1311.

12.6 In addition to the need to obtain consent to treatment, it is also necessary to obtain the patient's consent for his detention for treatment, because detention of a patient against his will, for however short a period, will amount to the civil wrong of false imprisonment, unless there is some lawful authority for the compulsory detention. This rule will not, however, be mentioned again in this chapter. It is mainly of relevance in the case of the treatment of those with mental disorders and a statutory code, now set out in the Mental Health Act 1983, has been developed to set out the conditions in which the compulsory detention of such patients can lawfully take place.

12.7 In order to constitute a valid consent, the courts have said that the consent must be 'real'. This rule has been explained in recent years in the following terms: 'Once the patient is informed in broad terms of the nature of the procedure which is intended, and gives her consent, that consent is real'.[1] Consent is not real if it is procured by fraud or misrepresentation, but subject to the patient having been informed in broad terms of the nature of the proposed treatment, consent in fact amounts to consent in law.[2] If a person who is compulsorily detained, like a prisoner, claims that his consent is invalid because the responsible medical officer treating him had influence over his life and his prospects of release on licence, a court must be alive to the risk that what may appear on the face of it to be a real consent was not in fact valid.[3]

1 *Chatterton v Gerson* [1981] QB 432 at 443, per Bristow J.
2 *Freeman v Home Office (No 2)* [1984] QB 524 at 556, per Sir John Donaldson MR.
3 Ibid at 555, impliedly approving a dictum of McCowan J in the case at first instance, ibid at 542.

12.8 In order to constitute a valid consent, the consent must be given to the procedure which is intended. Consent to the amputation of the left leg does not constitute lawful consent to the amputation of the right leg. The common law does not require the consent to be given in any particular form, but good practice dictates that the patient should give a written consent for any treatment which is out of the ordinary, such as surgery, and one of the standard consent forms for surgery contains a space for a patient's signature after an acknowledgment that the nature and purpose of the operation has been fully explained to him.

12.9 Two civil remedies may be available to a patient who complains that he did not give a valid consent to what was done to his body. The first is an action in battery, which is a form of trespass to the person. The second is an action in negligence, which means a failure to take reasonable care, which results in injury to another. For reasons which will be explained in this chapter, it is the remedy in negligence which will be relevant in most doctor–patient situations, but it is important to make the distinction between the two causes of action clear at the outset. Some of the differences between them will be discussed at the end of the chapter.

12.10 Both battery and negligence are known as torts, or civil wrongs. In tort the purpose of the remedy is compensatory; that is, the damages awarded are intended to put the injured party back, so far as an award of money can achieve this, in the position he would have been in had the tort not been committed.

12.11 In the 1970s and early 1980s there were suggestions that a consent which is not properly informed is not a 'real' consent. It is now firmly settled as a matter of English law[1] that when a doctor decides what he ought or ought not to tell his patient about the risks of the proposed procedure, the lawfulness of what he does will be principally judged by tests founded on evidence of appropriate contemporary standards of professional care. It will not be held against him that he has committed an unlawful battery because he did not make adequate disclosure of the possible risks.[2] He may, however, be found to have been in breach of his duty of care to his patient and liable to pay damages for negligence if he did not make adequate disclosure and his patient satisfies a court that he has suffered harm as a consequence of the non-disclosure.

1 *Sidaway v Board of Governors of the Bethlem Royal Hospital and the Maudsley Hospital* [1985] AC 871 ('the *Sidaway* case').
2 The *Sidaway* case (see n 1 above) per Lord Scarman at 883 and per Lord Diplock at 894. Lord Scarman, who gave a dissenting speech on the issue of informed consent, nevertheless approved a dictum of Hirst J in *Hills v Potter* [1983] 3 All ER 716, [1984] 1 WLR 641n, that it would be deplorable to base the law in medical cases of this kind on the torts of assault and battery.

12.12 In the Canadian case of *Reibl v Hughes*[1] Laskin CJC gave a helpful list of examples from earlier Canadian cases where the consent might not have been held to be a 'real' consent:

> In my opinion, actions of battery in respect of surgical or other medical treatment should be confined to cases where surgery or treatment has been performed or given to which there has been no consent at all or where, emergency cases apart, surgery or treatment has been performed or given beyond that to which there was consent . . .
>
> This standard would comprehend cases where there was misrepresentation of the surgery or treatment for which consent was elicited and a different surgical procedure or treatment was carried out. See, for example, *Marshall v Curry*[2] (consent given to operation to cure hernia; doctor removes left testicle: action in battery); *Murray v McMurchy*[3] (consent given to a Caesarian operation, doctor goes on and sterilises the patient; doctor liable for trespass to the person) . . . *Schweitzer v Central Hospital*[4] (patient consented to operation on left toe; doctor operated on the back instead (spinal fusion); doctor liable for trespass to the person).

1 (1980) 114 DLR (3d) 1 at 10.
2 [1933] 3 DLR 260.
3 [1949] 2 DLR 442.
4 (1974) 53 DLR (3d) 494.

12.13 Some of these cases reached the Canadian courts because a surgeon, acting in good faith, took his operation further than the patient's original consent permitted when he discovered a further condition for which surgery was necessary or desirable. It is for this reason that standard English consent forms generally authorise 'such further or alternative operative measures as may be found to be necessary' so that the patient's express consent will have been obtained by the surgeon before the operation starts. Emergency treatment is discussed in paras **12.56–12.60**.

12.14 Because the English courts will judge the lawfulness of the doctor's conduct by reference to the standards practised by competent and caring practitioners in the same field, it is unlikely that when determining whether he has given a 'real' consent they will apply any particularly rigorous test of the patient's capacity to understand what he was being told before deciding whether he in fact gave consent, at all events in any case where the proposed treatment is necessary on medical grounds and is not irreversible and of major significance (for example, sterilisation). English law imposes different tests of capacity to understand in different circumstances (capacity to consent to sexual intercourse or capacity to understand when making a testamentary disposition or a gift inter vivos or a contract, for example).[1] If the patient's mind is confused or muddled he will not readily be deprived of his legal right to decide for himself what should be done to his body for his benefit by his doctors,[2] although the doctor may be liable in negligence if he fails to follow proper professional standards of care when obtaining his patient's consent.

1 For the standard required for consent to sexual intercourse see *R v Lang* (1975) 62 Cr App Rep 50 at 52 ('the crucial question is whether she understood her situation and was capable of making up her mind') and compare the Australian case of *R v Morgan* [1970] VR 337 at 341–342. For the degrees of understanding which may be required for making dispositions of property, see *Re Beaney* [1978] 2 All ER 595, [1978] 1 WLR 770, where Nourse QC, sitting as a deputy high court judge, said that in the case of a will the degree of understanding required is always high, but in other cases the degree required varies with the circumstances of the transaction.

2 In his *Textbook on Criminal Law* (2nd edn, Stevens & Sons, 1983, at 572), Professor Glanville Williams cites with approval an American academic writer who pointed out in an article in 84 Yale LJ 691 that a finding of incompetence which deprives a patient of authority to decide for himself constitutes the ultimate disregard of his human dignity. In Part II of its Consultation Paper No 119, 'Mentally Handicapped Adults and Decision-Making: An Overview', where these issues are discussed, the Law Commission suggests at para 2.20 that the test of capacity to consent to medical treatment is based on the usual common law criterion of understanding in broad terms the nature and likely effects of what is to take place.

WHAT A DOCTOR SHOULD TELL HIS PATIENT

12.15 A doctor or surgeon following the principles of good medical and surgical practice will do his best to inform his patient fully of the advantages and disadvantages, the risks and the benefits of any proposed course of treatment. In the *Sidaway* case[1] in 1985 the House of Lords had to determine, for the first time in an English court, a case in which it was being contended that the doctor owed a legal duty to his patient to inform him of all material risks in a course of treatment and that if he failed to do so, the doctor would have been guilty of a breach of his duty of care to his patient.

1 See para **12.11**, supra, n 1.

12.16 The majority of the House of Lords in the *Sidaway* case gave the following guidance on the law and practice in such cases:

(1) The standard by which English law measures the doctor's duty of care to his patient when advising him about a particular course of treatment is the standard of the ordinary skilled man exercising and professing to have the special skill which that doctor is exercising and professing to have.
(2) The decision what degree of disclosure of risks is best calculated to assist a particular patient to make a rational choice as to whether or not to undergo a particular treatment must primarily be a matter of clinical judgment.
(3) An issue whether non-disclosure of a particular risk or cluster of risks in a particular case should be condemned as a breach of the doctor's duty of care is an issue to be decided primarily on the basis of expert medical evidence. In the event of a conflict of evidence the judge will have to

decide whether a responsible body of medical opinion would have approved of non-disclosures in the case before him.

(4) A judge might in certain circumstances come to the conclusion that disclosure of a particular risk was so obviously necessary to an informed choice on the part of the patient that no reasonably prudent medical man would fail to make it, even in a case where no expert witness in the relevant medical field condemned the non-disclosure as being in conflict with accepted and responsible medical practice.

12.17 The significance of tying the standard of care required by the law to the standard adopted by reasonably careful and prudent practitioners is that the law is enabled to keep pace with changing standards as medical and surgical practice changes over the years. Accordingly, it must not be assumed that standards of patient care which were considered appropriate ten or fifteen years ago will necessarily be endorsed as appropriate by a judge today. He will determine any disputed issue principally on the evidence of practitioners practising in the same field as the doctor whose standard of professional care has been called in question, and he will be concerned only with evidence of the standard which was appropriate at the time of the incident complained of.

12.18 The reason why the House of Lords decided the *Sidaway* case as it did throws light on the willingness of the courts to allow doctors and surgeons to develop appropriate standards of care without being put in a straitjacket by the uncertainty of not knowing what a court, judging with the benefit of hindsight, might consider to be material in any given case. Lord Bridge observed that a very wide variety of factors must enter into a doctor's clinical judgment not only as to what treatment is appropriate for a particular patient but also as to how best to communicate to the patient the significant factors necessary to enable the patient to make an informed decision whether to undergo the treatment:[1]

The doctor cannot set out to educate the patient to his own standard of medical knowledge of all the relevant factors involved. He may take the view, certainly with some patients, that the very fact of his volunteering, without being asked, information of some remote risk involved in the treatment proposed, even though he describes it as remote, may lead to that risk assuming an undue significance in the patient's calculations.

1 At 899.

12.19 Lord Diplock said that some patients, though not necessarily all, have a vague knowledge that there may be some risk in any form of medical treatment:[1]

To decide what risks the existence of which a patient should be voluntarily warned and the terms in which such warning, if any, should be given, having regard to the effect that the warning may have, is as much an exercise of professional skill and judgment as any other part of the doctor's comprehensive duty of care to the individual patient.

1 At 895.

12.20 The House of Lords made it clear that if there was an operation involving a substantial risk of grave adverse consequences, such as a 10 per cent risk of a stroke from an operation, a judge would be entitled to conclude on his own that in the absence of some cogent clinical reason why the patient should not be informed, a doctor, recognising and respecting his patient's right of decision, could hardly fail to appreciate the necessity for an appropriate warning. Lord Templeman said that there was no doubt that a doctor ought to draw the attention of a patient to a danger which might be special in kind or magnitude or special to the patient.

12.21 It is therefore clear that English law has refused to follow Canadian law[1] or the law in some American states[2] in developing a doctrine of informed consent which leaves it to the court to judge, according to different tests suggested in different jurisdictions, whether the risk of which the doctor failed to warn his patient was a material matter which the patient was entitled to know before he gave his consent to the treatment proposed. On the other hand, the growing emphasis on the patient's right of self-determination is going to lead inevitably to a greater emphasis by the professional bodies on the desirability of warning a patient about the risks of treatment when they give guidance on good practice.

1 See *Reibl v Hughes* (1980) 114 DLR (3d) 1; *Hopp v Lepp* (1980) 112 DLR (3d) 67.
2 See *Canterbury v Spence* 464 F 2d 772 (1972); and the discussion in an article by Gerald Robertson entitled 'Informed Consent to Medical Treatment' in (1981) LQR 102.

12.22 In the *Sidaway* case the House of Lords was concerned with the nature and extent of a doctor's duty to volunteer information about the risks of treatment. It was common ground that if a patient asked questions, it was in principle the doctor's duty to answer them truthfully. Lord Bridge said, obiter, that in his opinion when questioned specifically by a patient of apparently sound mind about risks involved in a particular treatment which is proposed, the doctor's duty must be to answer both truthfully and as fully as the questioner requires.[1] The doctor's duty to volunteer information about the risks of treatment was recently examined in an Australian case.[2]

1 Lord Templeman said (at 902): 'Mrs Sidaway could have asked questions. If she had done so, she could and should have been informed that there was an aggregate risk of between one per cent and two per cent of some damage either to the spinal cord or to a nerve root resulting in injury which might vary from irritation to paralysis'.
2 See *Rogers v Whittaker* [1992] 3 Med LR 331. Where a patient, almost blind in one eye, consulted an ophthalmic surgeon and asked about possible complications if an operation was performed on it, but did not expressly ask whether sympathetic ophthalmia (ie damage to other eye) might result, the surgeon was under a duty to inform the patient of a slight risk. Failure so to inform the patient was the cause of sympathetic ophthalmia which followed the operation.

12.23 The Court of Appeal[1] has held that for the purposes of ascertaining the test as to the duty of care owed by a doctor to a patient there was no distinction to be made between advice given in a therapeutic context and advice given in a non-therapeutic context. In that case a plaintiff had become pregnant with a fourth child after saying that she did not want to have any more children and undergoing a sterilisation operation. She complained that she had not been warned of the failure rates in such operations, but the Court of Appeal held that because at the time of the incident complained of there was a substantial body of responsible doctors who would not have warned the plaintiff of the failure rate of female sterilisation operations, her claim for damages for negligence failed.

1 *Gold v Haringey Health Authority* [1988] QB 481, [1987] 2 All ER 888, CA.

CASES INVOLVING CHILDREN

12.24 At common law the parent of a child has the legal power to give consent for medical or surgical treatment on behalf of his child. This rule was derived from the principle, which is now obsolete, that the father had the control over the person, education and conduct of his children until they were 21.[1]

1 In *Re Agar-Ellis* (1883) 24 Ch D 317 at 326, per Sir William Brett MR disapproved as a correct statement of contemporary law a hundred years later by the House of Lords in the *Sidaway* case.

12.25 The Family Law Reform Act 1969, which reduced the legal age of majority to 18, provided by section 8(1) that:

The consent of a minor who has attained the age of 16 years to any medical, surgical or dental treatment which, in the absence of consent, would constitute a trespass to his person, shall be as effective as it would be if he was of full age, and where a minor has by virtue of this section given an effective consent to any treatment it shall not be necessary to obtain any consent for it from his parent or guardian.

12.26 Sub-section (2) extends the protection of this section to include any procedure undertaken for the purposes of diagnosis and also to any procedure (including, in particular, the administration of an anaesthetic) which is ancillary to any medical, surgical or dental treatment. Sub-section (3) provides that nothing in the section is to be construed as making ineffective any consent which would have been effective if the section had not been enacted.

12.27 In *Gillick v West Norfolk and Wisbech Area Health Authority and Department of Health and Social Security* ('the *Gillick* case')[1] the House of Lords held that although this provision, and a comparable provision in section 131(2) of the Mental Health Act 1983, may clarify the powers of minors to give effective consents in certain cases, they do not alter the governing common law rule that there is no fixed age at which a child may or may not himself give a valid consent.

1 [1986] AC 112.

12.28 In the *Gillick* case the House of Lords said that in appropriate circumstances a child under the age of 16 might give an effective legal consent to medical treatment, including contraceptive treatment, notwithstanding that his or her parents had not been consulted and would be likely, if consulted, to refuse consent. The extent and duration of the parental right to control a minor child could not be ascertained by reference to a fixed age, but depended on the degree of intelligence and understanding of that particular child. The parents' right to determine whether a child under 16 should have medical treatment terminated when the child achieved sufficient intelligence and understanding to make that decision itself.

12.29 It was therefore held in that case that a doctor will be entitled to give contraceptive advice and treatment to a girl under 16 without her parents' knowledge and consent if he is satisfied that the girl will understand the advice; that he cannot persuade her to inform her parents or to allow him to inform her parents that she is seeking contraceptive advice; that she is very likely to begin or to continue having sexual intercourse with or without contraceptive treatment; that unless she receives contraceptive advice or treatment her physical or mental health or both are likely to suffer; and that her best interests require him to give her contraceptive advice, treatment or both without the parental consent.

12.30 The common law right of a parent to make the relevant decisions may be supplanted by the statutory right of a local authority to make such decisions in cases where a child has been committed to the care of a local authority by a care order or received into care by a local authority and the local authority has assumed parental rights and duties over the child. Alternatively, it may be supplanted by the court in cases where the wardship jurisdiction of the court has been invoked. In these cases the relevant authority or the court may exercise rights equivalent to the common law rights of the natural parent. Since the enactment of the Children Act 1989 has limited the availability of wardship proceedings to local authorities, it is now more appropriate for such authorities to seek other remedies specifically available to them.

12.31 The concept of '*Gillick* competence' has been given statutory effect in England and Wales to a limited extent in the Children Act 1989.[1]

1 See in particular sections 1, 38(6), 43(8), 44(7) and Schedule 3, paragraphs 4(4)(a) and 5(5)(a).

12.32 Until recently the legal position of children in Scotland was different from that in England, Wales and Northern Ireland. The Age of Legal Capacity (Scotland) Act 1991, however, has abolished the old Scottish legal concepts of pupillarity (girls under 12, boys under 14) and minority (persons under 18, not being pupils), and the two tier system has been replaced by a single tier of children under the age of 16. Section 2 of the Act puts the concept of '*Gillick* competence' on a statutory basis in Scotland:

> A person under the age of 16 years shall have legal capacity to consent on his own behalf to any surgical, medical or dental procedure or treatment where, in the opinion of a qualified medical practitioner attending him, he is capable of understanding the nature and possible consequences of the procedure or treatment.

12.33 A court exercising wardship jurisdiction may in exceptional circumstances authorise an operation for the sterilisation of a ward under the age of 18. In deciding whether to do so, the court will be concerned only with one primary and paramount consideration, namely the welfare and best interests of the ward. In the leading case[1] Lord Oliver of Aylmerton said that the jurisdiction in wardship proceedings to authorise such an operation was one which should be exercised only in the last resort, and Lord Templeman said that sterilisation of a girl under 18 should only be carried out with the leave of a High Court judge; a doctor performing a sterilisation operation with the consent of the parents alone might still be liable in criminal, civil or disciplinary proceedings.

1 *Re B (a minor) (wardship: sterilisation)* [1988] AC 199.

12.34 In that case, which was concerned with a girl of 17 who had a very limited intellectual development, the House of Lords was satisfied that a sterilisation operation would be in the girl's best interests on the evidence which had been adduced concerning the risk of the girl becoming pregnant, the lack of any effective contraceptive regime being formulated for her, the trauma which childbirth would present to her and the risk of injury to her and her child and her inability ever to desire or care for a child.

12.35 In the earlier case of *Re D (a minor) (wardship: sterilisation)*[1] a judge had refused to give authority for the sterilisation of a girl of 11, where the operation was neither medically indicated or necessary. The judge said that the operation would violate the basic human right of a woman to reproduce and said that the girl would almost certainly understand the implications of such an operation by the time she reached 18. The judge applied the principle that it was the function of the court in its wardship jurisdiction not to risk the incurring of damage to children which it could not repair, but rather to prevent the damage being done.[2]

1 [1976] Fam 185, [1976] 1 All ER 326, per Heilbron J.
2 *Wellesley v Duke of Beaufort* (1827) 2 Russ 1 at 18, per Lord Eldon LC.

12.36 In *Re P (a minor)*[1] a judge, exercising the wardship jurisdiction of the court, decided that it was in a 15-year-old girl's best interests to direct that a pregnancy be terminated notwithstanding the wishes of the girl's parents that she should bear her child. The judge also directed that the girl be fitted with a suitable internal contraceptive device. The girl, who wished her pregnancy to be terminated, was in the care of a local authority and had already given birth to one child.

1 (1982) 80 LGR 301, per Butler-Sloss J.

12.37 The power of a court, exercising its wardship jurisdiction, to overrule a 15-year-old girl's refusal to consent to medical treatment was explained in the case of *Re R (a minor) (wardship: consent to treatment)*.[1] The court was then concerned with a 15-year-old girl in the care of a local authority who suffered from increasingly serious episodes of mental illness characterised by violent and suicidal behaviour. After one such episode, which had led to her being compulsorily detained in a mental hospital for a period, she was admitted to an adolescent psychiatric unit where the proposed programme of treatment included the compulsory administration of certain anti-psychotic drugs. The local authority initially consented to these proposals, but after R, in a lucid interval, had indicated that she would refuse such treatment, consent was withdrawn, and the authority applied to the court for directions.

1 [1992] Fam 11.

12.38 The Court of Appeal held that in the exercise of its wardship jurisdiction the court was entitled to override a minor's decision, whether it was consenting to or refusing treatment, and irrespective of his or her 'competence', in the sense of that word as explained by the House of Lords in the *Gillick* case. In any event the court held that having regard to the fluctuating nature of her illness, R was not 'competent' to give or withhold her consent, and that since the proposed treatment was in her best interests it was right to authorise it.

12.39 An issue arose about the effect of section 8 of the Family Law Reform Act 1969 in the case of *Re W (a minor) (medical treatment: court's jurisdiction)*.[1] The court was concerned with an adolescent girl suffering from anorexia nervosa who had been admitted to an adolescent residential unit for treatment. When her condition deteriorated the local authority sought directions to the effect that, contrary to W's wishes and the views of the consultant treating her, she should be transferred to a unit specialising in the treatment of eating disorders. By the time of the court hearing she was 16.

1 [1993] Fam 64, [1992] 4 All ER 627.

12.40 The Court of Appeal held that that section did not confer on a 16-year-old minor an absolute right to determine whether or not she received medical treatment. It simply enabled her to give consent to treatment as effectively as if she were an adult so that her medical practitioners would be protected from civil or criminal liability if they treated her with her consent. As the law now stood, a minor of any age who had sufficient maturity might consent to treatment. However, if she refused to give consent, her refusal could not override any consent given by the court. In the exercise of its inherent jurisdiction the court would take particular account of the minor's wishes, the importance of which increased with age and maturity, but would override them where her best interests so required. The court held that having regard to W's illness and the serious deterioration in her condition, her best interests required a direction that she should be transferred immediately to the new unit to receive treatment there without her consent.

12.41 Two recent cases have illustrated the way in which the courts are now exercising their powers in sanctioning aspects of the treatment of very handicapped children. In the case of *Re C (a minor) (wardship: medical treatment)*[1] the court was concerned with a baby suffering from congenital hydrocephalus. She was assessed to be severely and irreversibly brain-damaged, and the prognosis was said to be hopeless. When the local authority applied to the court for directions, the Court of Appeal said that she was to be treated in a manner appropriate to her condition. The court accepted the medical assessment that the child was terminally ill, and held that it was entitled to approve recommendations designed to ease her suffering rather than prolong her life.

1 [1990] Fam 26, [1989] 2 All ER 782.

12.42 In the later case of *Re J (a minor) (child in care: medical treatment)*[1] the court was concerned with a one-year-old child who had sustained serious head injuries at the age of one month. He was profoundly mentally and physically handicapped. He suffered from microcephaly, cerebral palsy, cortical blindness and severe epilepsy and had to be fed by a nasogastric tube. He was considered unlikely to develop greatly beyond his present state and had an uncertain but shortened life expectancy. His intermittent convulsive attacks required resuscitative treatment in hospital, and when he was nearly a year old it was considered by responsible medical opinion that it was medically inappropriate to use mechanical ventilation procedures in any future resuscitation, a view which was challenged by the child's natural mother.

1 [1993] Fam 15, [1992] 4 All ER 614.

12.43 The Court of Appeal held that in the exercise of its inherent jurisdiction it would not order a medical practitioner to treat his patient in a manner contrary to his clinical judgment and professional duty. Pending any final decision, the proper approach was for the court to consider the options available to it in exercising its inherent powers and to make such order as served the child's best interests.

CASES INVOLVING TREATMENT FOR MENTAL DISORDER

12.44 There is no general principle of English common law that because a patient is suffering from some form of mental disorder a doctor is entitled to treat him without his consent. In practice such treatment, when necessary, has been carried out during the last hundred years under the statutory protection of the Lunacy Acts or their modern successors the Mental Health Acts, and before those Acts were passed the judges were willing to hold that doctors were entitled to a certain power and protection in the honest exercise of their professional functions when taking necessary measures for the benefit of their patients or for the protection of the public.[1]

1 Per Cockburn CJ in *Symm v Fraser* (1863) 3 F & F 859. Compare *Scott v Wakem* (1862) 3 F & F 328, and *Bradshaw v Hopkins* (1773) Lofft 243.

12.45 Under the scheme of this legislation Parliament has created statutory powers whereby the mentally disordered might be detained for treatment under compulsion[1] and actions might not be brought against any person exercising such powers unless it were shown that that person had failed to act in good faith or with reasonable care.

1 It is of course good practice, notwithstanding the existence of these statutory powers, for the patient's consent to be obtained whenever possible before he is detained.

12.46 Section 34(1) of the Mental Health Act 1959 (now repealed) gave to guardians of patients suffering from mental disorders all the powers of a father of a child under 14 years of age. The Act did not, however, make it clear beyond doubt that in cases where there was no readily available guardian and the patient was lawfully detained for treatment without his consent a doctor was in fact entitled to treat him without his consent, although practitioners assumed that this was the case and acted accordingly. In the Mental Health Act 1983 Parliament set out unequivocally for the first time the extent of a doctor's powers to give medical treatment to a mentally disordered patient for his mental disorder[1] (but not other medical conditions) without his consent. Most of these powers, which are contained in Part IV of the Act, are limited to the cases of patients who are liable to be detained compulsorily under other provisions of the Act.[2]

1 The Act defines 'mental disorder' as 'mental illness, arrested or incomplete development of mind, psychopathic disorder or disability of mind'. Severe mental impairment, mental impairment and psychopathic disorder are defined to include 'abnormally aggressive or seriously irresponsible conduct on the part of the person concerned'.
2 The relevant statutory provisions are fully set out in the chapter on Mental Health, and are not, therefore, reproduced here.

12.47 The effect of these new provisions was explained by McCullough J in *R v Hallstrom, ex p W*,[1] a case in which the judge declared unlawful the treatment given by consultant psychiatrists in good faith but without consent to two patients suffering from chronic schizophrenia. They were not in a condition in which they were liable to be detained compulsorily and their treatment was therefore not sanctioned by Part IV of the Act. The judge said that it went without saying that unless clear statutory authority to the contrary existed no one was to be detained in a hospital or to undergo medical treatment or even to be submitted to a medical examination without his consent and that this was as true of a mentally disordered person as anyone else.

1 [1986] QB 1090, [1986] 2 All ER 306.

12.48 The 1983 Act abolished the power of a guardian to consent to treatment on a patient's behalf.[1] It follows that unless a case can be brought within Part IV of the Act (and any ambiguity will be construed in favour of the patient) or unless it can be brought within one of the other exceptions to the general rule (e g a parent consenting for a minor child) a doctor may not lawfully give medical treatment to a mentally disordered patient for his mental disorder without his consent, however disturbed and ill the patient may be and however much everybody concerned with the patient's care may wish the patient to have the treatment in his own best interests.

1 The guardian is granted the more restricted power to require the patient to attend at places and times so specified for the purposes of medical treatment (Mental Health Act 1983, s 8(1)(b)).

ADULT PERSONS INCAPABLE OF GIVING CONSENT

12.49 This Act has now given certainty to the law in the cases of persons suffering from mental disorder in a comparatively limited class of cases where they are liable to be detained under the provisions of that Act. It has also had the effect of making it clear that it is not lawful to treat such persons for their mental disorders without their consent except so far as the Act permits, but it does not explain what the law is when the patient is incapable of understanding what is being said to him but compulsory detention under the Mental Health Act is neither necessary nor desirable.

12.50 Parliament has provided no guidance at all, except in the Mental Health Act, about the circumstances in which an adult person who is incapable of giving consent may be treated. Before 1960 the Crown had had the power and the duty to protect the persons and property of those unable to do so for themselves, but this prerogative jurisdiction was revoked when the Mental Health Act 1959 came into force and nothing was put in its place.[1] Adult mentally handicapped patients cannot, therefore, be made the subject of wardship proceedings.

1 See *Re F (mental patient: sterilisation)* [1990] 2 AC 1, per Lord Brandon at 58.

12.51 In *Re F (mental patient: sterilisation)*[1] the House of Lords was concerned for the first time with a case in which the power of the court to authorise the sterilisation of a mentally incompetent adult woman was in issue. F was a voluntary patient at a mental hospital. She was 36 years old with a general mental capacity of a child of four. She had formed a relationship with a male patient which was thought to involve sex. There was evidence that this relationship was pleasurable to her but that a pregnancy would be 'disastrous' from a 'psychiatric point of view'. The House of Lords held that in these circumstances such an operation was permissible and lawful since it was within the patient's 'best interests'. 'Best interests' was to be taken in a sense wide enough to include the public interest but in the area of non-therapeutic sterilisation was not to include the convenience of those charged with the patient's care.[2]

1 [1990] 2 AC 1, HL.

2 There is a critical examination of this controversial decision by the Law Commission in its Consultation Paper No 119, 'Mentally Incapacitated Adults and Decision-Making: An Overview' at paras 2.20 to 2.24.

12.52 The House of Lords held that the test to be applied to the lawfulness of such an operation, and of any other operation or treatment carried out for adult persons who are incapable of consent, is to be that laid down in *Bolam v Friern Hospital Management Committee*,[1] namely that a doctor will not be negligent if he acts in accordance with responsible medical practice current at the time.

1 [1957] 2 All ER 118, [1957] 1 WLR 582.

12.53 The House of Lords also held that the High Court had the power, in its inherent jurisdiction, to make a declaration as to the lawfulness of an operation upon an adult unable to give a valid consent. It said that as a matter of practice, though not of law, the opinion of the court should be sought as to the lawfulness of a sterilisation operation on an adult woman of child-bearing age who is incapable of giving or refusing her consent herself.

12.54 Different opinions were expressed in the House as to whether the doctor's powers in such cases were derived from a so-called 'agency of necessity' or because it was in the public interest that the doctor should have such powers. Lord Goff, who favoured 'agency of necessity', said that the governing principles were that there must not only be a necessity to act when it is not practicable to communicate with the person who is being assisted, but also that the action which is taken must be such as a reasonable person would take in all the circumstances, acting in the best interests of the assisted person. He suggested that there should be little difficulty in applying this principle in the case of routine treatment of mentally disordered patients. In the case of more serious treatment, it was likely that good medical practice would involve discussions with others before a decision was taken. These could include relatives and others who were concerned with the care of the patient, or a specialist or specialists, or, in an appropriate case, an inter-disciplinary team. 'The overriding consideration is that they should act in the best interests of the person who suffers from the misfortune of being prevented by incapacity from deciding for himself what should be done to his own body, in his own best interests'.

12.55 The doctrine of 'best interests' was examined by the House of Lords in the case of a young man who was suffering from a condition known as persistent vegetative state as a result of injuries sustained in the Hillsborough tragedy.[1] It was held that the object of medical treatment and care was to benefit the patient; since a large body of informed and responsible medical opinion considered that the persistent vegetative state was not a benefit to the patient, the principle of the sanctity of life, which was not absolute, was not violated by ceasing to give medical treatment to which the patient had not consented and which conferred no benefit upon him. Furthermore, it was held that the doctors responsible for the patient were neither under a duty, nor entitled to continue such medical care since the patient had no further interest in being kept alive. It was stated also that until a body of experience and practice had been built up it was desirable that application should be made to the Family Division in any case where medical staff considered that continued treatment of a patient in the persistent vegetative state no longer conferred benefit upon him; this was in the interests of the protection of patients and doctors, the reassurance of patients' families and that of the public. The court stated that the moral, social and legal issues of the case should be considered by Parliament. Lord Mustill considered that in such cases the 'best interests' test was really an ethical question rather than a matter of medical practice; his Lordship questioned the appropriateness of determining the best interests in such cases in accordance with the *Bolam* test.

1 *Airedale NHS Trust v Bland* [1993] 1 All ER 821, HL. In its Consultation Paper No 129, 'Mentally Incapacitated Adults and Decision-Making: Medical Treatment and Research', published in April 1993, the Law Commission ventilated some of the issues raised by this case and sought views on the way in which those concerned with the care of such patients may receive authority for the way they treat such patients.

EMERGENCY TREATMENT

12.56 Occasions may arise when there are medical indications requiring rapid intervention when the patient is unconscious or otherwise incapable of giving consent. Until recently the doctor's right to take emergency action in what he regarded as the best interests of his patient was taken for granted. In the *Gillick* case,[1] for example, Lord Templeman said:[2]

> A doctor may safely carry out treatment in an emergency if the doctor believes the treatment to be vital to the survival or health of an infant. In such a case the doctor must have the courage of his convictions that the treatment is necessary and urgent in the interests of the patient and the court will, if necessary, approve after the event treatment which the court would have authorised in advance even if the treatment proves to be unsuccessful.

1 See para **12.27**, supra.
2 Ibid, at 200.

12.57 In *Re F*[1] Lord Goff took the matter a little further. Developing his thinking on the common law doctrine of 'agency of necessity', he said that in emergency treatment a conservative approach should be adopted:[2]

> Where, for example, a surgeon performs an operation without his consent on a patient rendered temporarily unconscious in an accident, he should do no more than is reasonably required, in the best interests of the patient, before he recovers consciousness. I can see no practical difficulty arising from this requirement, which derives from the fact that the patient is expected before long to regain consciousness and can then be consulted about longer term measures. The point has however arisen in a more acute form where a surgeon, in the course of an operation, discovers some other condition which, in his opinion, requires operative treatment for which

he has not received the patient's consent. In what circumstances he should operate forthwith, and in what circumstances he should postpone the further treatment until he has received the patient's consent, is a difficult matter which has troubled the Canadian Courts[3] . . . but which it is not necessary for your Lordships to consider in the present case.

1 See para **12.51**, supra.
2 Ibid, at 77.
3 See paras **12.12** and **12.13**, supra, for examples.

12.58 This statement of the law accords with prudent clinical practice of limiting the extent of emergency procedures and of confining medical treatment to elective procedures where possible.

12.59 The House of Lords has now made it clear[1] that doctors and other professionals may lawfully administer curative or prophylactic treatment to unconscious or incompetent patients without their consent provided that in doing so they administer treatment which would be accepted as appropriate treatment at the time by a reasonable body of skilled professional opinion. In the later case of *Re R*[2] Lord Donaldson MR summarised the legal position in these words:

[The general rule] is subject to the necessary exception that in cases of emergency a doctor may treat the patient notwithstanding the absence of consent, if the patient is unconscious or otherwise incapable of giving or refusing consent and there is no one else sufficiently immediately available with authority to consent on behalf of the patient.

1 *Re F*, see para **12.51**, supra.
2 See para **12.37**, supra.

12.60 Except in the case of incompetent minors, the consent of a third party generally has no legal effect. It is common medical practice, however, to seek consent from relatives when an adult is unable to give consent for treatment, and Lord Goff applauded such practice in his speech in *Re F*. What is lawful in the management of such patients is, however, to be determined in accordance with the 'best interests' doctrine.

REFUSAL OF CONSENT BY AN ADULT

12.61 There have been two recent cases in which the courts have shown themselves ready to intervene notwithstanding the fact that the relevant adult has refused consent for the medical intervention which the court subsequently sanctioned on the 'best interests' principle.

12.62 In the case of *Re T (adult: refusal of treatment)*[1] the court was concerned with a 20-year-old woman who had been brought up by her mother in accordance with the tenets of Jehovah's Witnesses. An issue arose concerning the validity of a form she had signed in which she had refused to consent to a blood transfusion following a road traffic accident. Her mother had been with her at important moments following the accident before her condition deteriorated. Her condition then became critical and she was sedated and placed on a ventilator. The Court of Appeal held that although an adult patient was entitled to refuse consent to treatment irrespective of the wisdom of her decision, for such a refusal to be effective her doctors had to be satisfied that at the time of her refusal her capacity to decide had not been diminished by illness or medication or by false assumptions or misinformation, that her will had not been overborne by another's influence and that her decision had been directed to the situation in which it had become relevant.

1 [1993] Fam 95, [1992] 4 All ER 649 and see *Re C* [1994] 1 All ER 819 where the principle of competent refusal was upheld.

12.63 The court held on the facts of that case that the patient's refusal was not effective for these reasons. It went on to hold that her doctors were free to treat her in accordance with their clinical judgment of her best interests. Lord Donaldson MR added that in cases of doubt as to the effect of a purported refusal of treatment, where a failure to treat would threaten the patient's life or cause irreparable damage to her health, doctors and health authorities should not hesitate to apply to the courts for assistance. He also suggested that forms of refusal should be redesigned to bring the consequences of a refusal forcibly to the attention of patients.

12.64 In that case the judge and the Court of Appeal found a means of determining that what appeared to be a valid refusal of treatment was not valid at law. This was not the situation in a case which came at very short notice before Sir Stephen Brown, the President of the Family Division, in October 1992.[1] He had to decide, literally within minutes and with no time for proper argument, a case in which a health authority sought a declaration that an operation for a Caesarian section might be performed on a pregnant woman, notwithstanding the fact that both she and her husband had refused consent for such an operation on religious grounds. The judge was told that the mother's situation was desperately serious, as also was the situation of the as yet unborn child, which could not be born alive unless the operation was carried out. In those circumstances he granted the declaration sought, while being aware that there was no English authority directly in point.

1 *Re S (adult: refusal of treatment)* [1993] Fam 123, [1992] 4 All ER 671. Sir Stephen Brown P said that there was some American authority which suggested that if the case were being heard in the American courts the answer would be likely to be in favour of granting a declaration in these circumstances. See *Re AC* 573 A2d 1235 (1990).

12.65 A decision taken in such circumstances does not have the persuasive effect of a decision taken by a judge after hearing full argument, and the case raised issues fit for consideration in due course by the House of Lords about the way in which the courts should balance the interests of the unborn fetus against the right of her mother to self-determination, so far as invasions of her body are concerned. In *Re F (in utero)*[1] Balcombe LJ said:[2]

> the court might be asked to order that the baby be delivered by Caesarian section . . . it would be intolerable to place a judge in the position of having to make such a decision without any guidance as to the principles on which his decision should be based. If the law is to be extended in this manner, so as to impose control over the mother of an unborn child, where such control may be necessary for the benefit of the child, then under our system of parliamentary democracy it is for Parliament to decide . . . In such a sensitive field, affecting as it does the liberty of the individual, it is not for the judiciary to extend the law.

1 [1988] Fam 122, [1988] 2 All ER 193.
2 At 143.

RESEARCH

12.66 There is now a growing interest in the legality of certain types of research, but the courts have not yet been given the opportunity of having to decide on these issues. Research may be therapeutic (in patients) or non-therapeutic (in healthy volunteers). There seems to be no good reason why the principles of consent which apply to ordinary therapeutic relationships should not also apply to both therapeutic and non-therapeutic research which is not of an exceptional nature.

12.67 Therapeutic research in all patients and non-therapeutic research in adults of sound mind should, therefore, present no new problems. On the other hand, non-therapeutic research in children and adults with mental incapacity presents very great legal and ethical difficulties. Non-therapeutic procedures can rarely be said to be in the best interest of the individual concerned, irrespective of the benefits such research may bring to society at large, and it is the best interests of the individual which are paramount in matters of consent.

12.68 Some commentators have suggested that parental consent is valid in certain cases of non-therapeutic research in children, being those where the risks are minimal, pain and discomfort are negligible, and the procedure is not against the interests of the child. The validity of their views has not yet, however, been tested in the courts. Nobody, on the other hand, can give consent on behalf of a mentally incompetent adult, and there is nothing in the decision of the House of Lords in *Re F* which suggests that such research would be lawful if it could not be shown to be in the patient's own best interests. This creates a dilemma because in certain circumstances it is only through such research that man's understanding of certain conditions which affect incompetent adults can be advanced.[1]

1 Publications from Royal College of Physicians of London: *Guidelines on the practice of ethics committees involved in medical research involving human subjects* (2nd edn, 1990), *Research involving patients* (1990), *Research on healthy volunteers* (1986), *Relationship between physicians and the pharmaceutical industry* (1986) and *ABPI Code of Practice for the Pharmaceutical Industry* (7th edn, 1991).

CONSENT AND REFUSAL FORMS

12.69 The use of consent forms for surgical procedures and for certain invasive investigations is universal in medical practice. Standard forms of refusal are now being used increasingly, for example, where a patient declines to accept a blood transfusion. The consent form must not be equated with consent itself, but it is evidence of consent. Procedures may be carried out without true consent even where there is a completed consent form, and on the other hand procedures may be carried out with true consent where there is not a completed consent form. Consent forms are usually only evidence of the voluntariness of the procedure:[1] they are not usually evidence of the discharge of the duty to inform, although increasingly elaborate consent forms are now being devised.

1 See para **12.73** below. In its Consultation Paper No 129, 'Mentally Incapacitated Adults and Decision-Making: Medical Treatment and Research', the Law Commission has sought views

on the effect of the dicta of Lord Keith and Lord Goff in *Airedale NHS Trust v Bland* [1993] 1 All ER 821 that adults may lawfully give advance directions concerning their future treatment if and when they lose capacity to give such instructions (see pp 360–361, 367).

12.70 Most consent forms are not limited to any named procedure but contain expressions which extend the procedure to what may be necessary and in the best interests of the patient if unforeseen circumstances should arise.[1] Conservative principles should be adhered to: it is inappropriate to perform procedures without consent under emergency conditions if these can be performed electively with consent.[2]

1 See para **12.13**, supra.
2 See paras **12.57–12.58**, supra.

12.71 The limitations of consent forms are best demonstrated by the success of some plaintiffs in 'failure to warn' cases founded on allegations of medical negligence. In such cases the existence of a completed consent form does not necessarily prove conclusively that warnings and adequate information were in fact given, and the court is not normally willing to infer that this occurred simply because a signed consent form is produced. The limitations of refusal forms were illustrated in *Re T*[1] where the purported refusal was held not to be a true refusal. Prudent practice suggests that a separate note should be made in the patient's clinical records of the information which was disclosed. For illustrative purposes a selection of model consent forms prepared by the NHS Management Executive is contained in the Appendix.

1 See paras **12.62–12.63**, supra.

THE JURISPRUDENCE OF CONSENT

12.72 In this chapter we have been concerned to set out relevant principles of English law as they have been explained by the higher courts, particularly during the last decade when much greater attention has been paid to identifying the principles which should govern the way in which patients should be treated while respecting their autonomy and their right in most circumstances to refuse treatment if they do not wish to receive it. The issues which courts are going to have to decide are not going to become any easier, and this section contains an attempt to analyse in jurisprudential terms some of the issues with which the courts have been grappling.

12.73 It is difficult to provide a succinct definition of 'consent'. It is easier to identify its essential characteristics. 'Consent' consists of three separate but related elements: voluntariness, capacity and knowledge. By 'voluntariness' we mean the willingness of the patient to undergo treatment. By 'capacity' we mean a sufficient degree of ability of the patient to understand the nature and consequences of the treatment offered. By 'knowledge' we mean that a sufficient amount of information as to the nature and consequences of the treatment has been disclosed to the patient. These three elements are interdependent, and for a consent to be legally valid, all three must be present: a failure of any one of them means the failure of consent. However, because of the approach adopted by the English courts, the way in which the court tests whether each element is present differs and the consequences of the absence of different elements are also different. On some occasions the court leaves the matter to be tested in accordance with the standards of care currently adopted by those practising in the relevant field, and a breach of those standards (in the provision of information, for example) may leave a defendant liable to pay damages for negligence: on others the court itself decides the matter as an issue of fact without any reference to contemporary standards of care, and the absence of the element of voluntariness may leave the defendant liable to pay damages for an unlawful battery.

12.74 Thus, when the courts have been examining whether what they call a 'real consent' exists, they are examining the first of the three elements, the element of voluntariness. This is illustrated by Bristow J in *Chatterton v Gerson*:[1]

> It is clear law that in any context in which consent of the injured party is a defence to what would otherwise be a crime or civil wrong, the consent must be real . . . In my judgment what the court has to do in each case is to look at all the circumstances and say, 'Was there a real consent?' I think justice requires that in order to vitiate the reality of consent there must be a greater failure of communication between doctor and patient than that involved in a breach of duty if the claim is based on negligence . . .
>
> In my judgment once the patient is informed in broad terms of the nature of the procedure which is intended and gives her consent, that consent is real, and the cause of action on which to base a claim for failure to go into risks and implications is negligence, not trespass. Of course, if information is withheld in bad faith, the consent will be vitiated by fraud. Of course, if by some accident, as in a case in the 1940s in the Salford Hundred Court, where a boy was admitted to hospital for tonsillectomy and due to administrative error was circumcised instead, trespass would be the appropriate cause of action against the doctor, though he was as much a victim of error as the boy. But in my judgment it would be very much against the interests of justice if actions which are really based on a failure by the doctor to perform his duty adequately to inform were pleaded in trespass.

1 [1981] QB 432 at 442.

12.75 Because the components which make up consent are not independent but interdependent (for example, whether voluntariness exists depends to some extent on both the information imparted to the patient and upon the patient's capacity to understand) it is not safe to draw too rigid a line between those cases which can properly be identified as being founded on an unlawful battery and those which give rise to an action founded in negligence.

12.76 The jurisprudential differences between battery and negligence may have considerable practical consequences, so that the distinction is not purely of academic interest. For example, in the first place anyone may bring an action in battery, and he does not have to prove the existence of a duty of care. In contrast, for a cause of action in negligence to lie, there must be a legal duty of care owed to the injured party, a breach of that duty, a causal link between the breach of duty and the damage which is suffered, and a loss of a type recoverable in law. Next, in battery, the plaintiff must prove that the defendant intended to cause the act which comprises the battery: there is no such requirement in negligence. Furthermore, battery is actionable without proof of damage, since the very fact of the use of unlawful force gives rise to a cause of action regardless of damage. In negligence, on the other hand, the plaintiff must prove that he has suffered material damage which is not so small as to fall within the maxim *de minimis non curat lex*. The rules concerning limitation are also different for actions in trespass and negligence.[1]

1 *Stubbings v Webb* [1993] AC 498, [1993] 1 All ER 322, HL.

12.77 The main defence to an action in battery is consent (that is, voluntariness). An action in negligence is more complex and there are several defences available, the principal defence being that the act complained of was not negligent and that a breach of reasonable care has not been proved. Other defences include the willing assumption of a known risk of injury by the injured person (*volenti non fit injuria*) and contributory negligence on his part, which may form a complete or, more usually, a partial defence. The absence of any loss caused by the alleged negligence may also be a defence.

12.78 Although the test of causation in battery and negligence is the same (would the injury have occurred 'but for' the tort complained of?) it will be applied, on the same set of facts, to different aspects of a case. In battery, where voluntariness is absent, the test of causation is applied to the medical intervention itself. In negligence, on the other hand, the test is applied to the circumstances giving rise to the medical intervention. Thus, in battery the relevant question will be whether the procedure caused the injury: in negligence (if 'knowledge' is in issue) it will be whether the patient would have elected to undergo the procedure if he had been properly informed. It could be said that in battery the test of causation is based on historical fact, whereas in negligence it is based on hypothetical fact.

12.79 The rules by which damages are recoverable in battery or negligence are different, too. In battery the general rule is that all damage directly caused can be recovered. In negligence the general rule is that loss must be reasonably foreseeable to be recoverable. In battery, there is a willingness in the courts to award aggravated (and in exceptional cases, exemplary, damages) because of the circumstances in which the tortious act is committed, in addition to purely compensatory damages, which are usual in negligence. It is for this reason the courts may award significant sums as damages when the actual degree of hurt inflicted or the actual length of a period of unlawful detention may, in objective terms, seem comparatively small.

12.80 Recent case law on issues of consent in cases involving adults of full capacity has generally been concerned with issues of 'knowledge': in other words, an alleged failure to inform. The courts have determined that the duty to inform is part of a bundle of duties which are owed by a doctor to his patient arising out of the therapeutic relationship, and whether the doctor has acted in breach of his duty is to be tested by what has been described as the '*Bolam* test',[1] by which a doctor is not to be found guilty of negligence if he has acted in accordance with a practice accepted as proper by a responsible body of medical men skilled in that particular art.

1 This test is taken from the address of McNair J to the jury in *Bolam v Friern Hospital Management Committee* [1957] 1 WLR 582 at 586, which has received the approval of the House of Lords.

12.81 There has been considerable controversy about the *Bolam* test. It has been suggested, for example in the context of the *Sidaway* case, that the approaches favoured by the majority of the House of Lords[1] and that favoured by Lord Scarman, in a dissenting minority of one (by which the materiality of a risk was to be determined by what would be so considered by a hypothetical prudent patient, although Lord Scarman recognised that information need not be disclosed if its disclosure would be detrimental to the health of the patient), reflected different perceptions and expectations of the therapeutic relationship: medical paternalism or a consumer commodity. However this may be, the House of Lords has settled the law for the time being in favour of the *Bolam* test in those areas in which it is properly applicable.

1 See para **12.16**, supra.

12.82 There is bound to be a continuing tension between those who place paramount emphasis on the right to self-determination, both in mentally competent adults and in '*Gillick* competent' children, and those who favour a modicum of 'medical paternalism', where they consider it necessary, but for the time being, at any rate, the most difficult issues have been resolved by the decisions of the House of Lords which are described in this chapter which allow the courts to operate the 'best interests' test in all cases where it is legally open to them to do so. The difficulties of these issues will not, however, go away, and the growing influence of both the Children Act 1989 and the European Convention of Human Rights and a widely felt contemporary desire to set the general law relating to the mentally disordered and mentally incapacitated on a much clearer footing[1] accentuate the need for clarity in determining what are the underlying jurisprudential principles which should be applied to decision-making in this controversial field.

1 Following the publication of its consultation paper in 1991 (see para **12.51**, supra), the Law Commission is now preparing proposals which, if accepted, are bound to lead to greater precision about the way in which the mentally disordered and mentally incapacitated may be lawfully treated, and about the sources of the powers to treat them.

12.83 Ethical principles provide the basis of an enforceable code protecting the individual's right to self-determination. Recent decided cases in the courts provide examples of the way in which ethical issues may be resolved. The House of Lords has recognised the limitations of the courts and the potential strength of the development and dissemination of ethical principles in decision-making in medical practice. This is a responsibility which the medical profession must assume. It appears that increasingly some knowledge of the legal aspects of consent is being regarded as part of clinical competence.

BIBLIOGRAPHICAL REFERENCES

Gaskell, 'Consent and the Incompetent Patient: Ethics, Law and Medicine', proceedings of meeting held at the Royal Society of Medicine, 9 December 1986 (Royal College of Psychiatrists, 1988).

Glanville Williams *Textbook on Criminal Law* (2nd edn, Stevens & Sons, 1983) p 572. [1978] Crim LR 128 at 132.

Green Paper on the Codification of the Criminal Law, March 1985 (HC 270), pp 119–121, 195 and 197.

Speller J *Law Relating to Hospital and Kindred Institutions* (6th edn) p 772.
Latey Report on the Age of Majority (Cmnd 3342, 1967) para 475.
Devlin Lord *Samples of Lawmaking, Medicine and the Law* (Oxford University Press, 1962) pp 91–92.
Powers M J and Harris N H *Medical Negligence* (Butterworths, 1st edn, 1990).
Skegg P D G 'A Justification for Medical Procedures Performed without Consent' [1974] LQR 512.
Law, Ethics and Medicine: Studies in Medical Law (Clarendon Press, 1984).
Robertson G 'Informed Consent to Medical Treatment' [1981] LQR 102.

CHAPTER 13

Limitation of actions

Robert F Nelson *QC*
Andrew V B Bartlett *QC*

SUMMARY

OVERVIEW

13.1 Since the time of King Henry VIII, if not before, Parliament has enacted a variety of statutes setting limits to the period within which a plaintiff is entitled to commence a legal action. Different periods have been set for different kinds of claim. In 1623 a six year limit was introduced for claims founded on what would now be termed tort or contract.[1] The purpose of statutes of limitation is threefold:

(1) to protect defendants from being vexed by stale claims relating to long past incidents about which their records may no longer be in existence and as to which their witnesses, even if they are still available, may well have no accurate recollection;
(2) to encourage plaintiffs to institute proceedings as soon as it is reasonably possible for them to do so;
(3) to ensure that a person may with confidence feel that after a given time he may regard as finally closed an incident which might have led to a claim against him.[2]

1 By s 2 of the Statute of James I, 21 Jac 1, c 16.
2 *Birkett v James* [1978] AC 297 at 331, HL, per Lord Edmund-Davies.

13.2 A defendant is entitled to the protection of the statutes of limitation where the claim against him is commenced after the expiry of the limitation period. For this purpose the commencement of a claim means in practice the issue of a writ in the High Court or the issue of a summons in the county court. In the general run of medical negligence cases the plaintiff must begin his claim within a period of three years from the date of the mishap, but there are numerous exceptions to this, which are considered in detail below. In order to take advantage of the protection afforded by the expiry of the limitation period the defendant must expressly plead the statute in his defence[1] or, in a very clear case, apply to strike out the claim as being vexatious.[2] A defendant is under no obligation to raise a limitation defence, and if he does not do so, the court will not take the point of its own motion. The parties are free to agree that a limitation point will not be relied upon, and in certain circumstances a defendant might be held to be estopped by his conduct from relying upon a limitation defence, as where, for example, he misled the plaintiff into not starting his action in time.[3]

1 RSC Ord 18, r 8(1).

2 *Ronex Properties Ltd v John Laing Construction Ltd* [1983] QB 398, [1982] 3 All ER 961, CA. The determination of an issue as to limitation on an application before trial is a final order within the meaning of RSC Order 59 rule 1A(3) by virtue of rule 1A(4) and accordingly a defendant does not require leave to appeal against the Order: *Dale v British Coal Corpn* [1992] 1 WLR 964, CA.

3 *Kaliszewska v John Clague & Partners* (1984) 5 Con LR 62; *Westlake v Bracknell District Council* [1987] 1 EGLR 161; cf *Wright v John Bagnall & Sons Ltd* [1901] 2 QB 240, CA; *The Sauria and The Trent* [1957] 1 Lloyd's Rep 396 at 402, CA; *Bryan v Ferranti Ltd* (2 November 1979, unreported) QB, Birmingham (referred to in S Todd *Limitation Periods in Personal Injury Claims* (1982) p 31); *Billam and Billam v Cheltenham Borough Council* (1984) 3 Con LR 99 at 122–123; *K Lokumal & Sons (London) Ltd v Lotte Shipping Co Pte Ltd* [1985] 2 Lloyd's Rep 28, CA; *Devon and Cornwall Housing Association Ltd v Acland Thorman and Miller-Williams* (1986) 6 Con LR 41, CA, and see 28 *Halsbury's Laws* (4th edn) paras 608, 644, 916. To the contrary effect it may be argued that to allow estoppel to defeat a limitation defence could in certain circumstances run contrary to the reasoning of *Cartledge v E Jopling & Sons Ltd* [1963] AC 758, [1963] 1 All ER 341, HL, as cited again by the House of Lords in *Pirelli General Cable Works Ltd v Oscar Faber & Partners* [1983] 2 AC 1 at 13, viz, that Parliament expressly provided for fraud and mistake in the Limitation Act 1939 (now 1980), so must have intended that there should be no other exceptions based on any difficulty of discovering the facts giving rise to the cause of action.

13.3 The current principal statute of limitations is the Limitation Act 1980. This contains no provisions specific to actions for medical negligence. The relevant provisions are those governing actions founded on tort or contract, together with special rules applicable in cases of personal injuries or death, and rules which postpone the running of the period in cases of legal disability (ie where the plaintiff is under 18 or of unsound mind) and cases of concealment. A simplied overview of the relevant provisions is given in Table 13.1 after para **13.4**. The imposition of a cut-off date in large group actions is essential for efficiency and the proper conduct of such substantial litigation. It does not however destroy any claim and hence does not operate as a limitation period for those who fail to meet the deadline.[1]

1 *AB v John Wyeth & Brother Ltd* [1993] 4 Med LR 1, CA.

WHEN A CAUSE OF ACTION ACCRUES

13.4 The general rule is that time begins to run against a plaintiff from the date when his cause of action accrues to him. A 'cause of action' is simply a factual situation the existence of which entitles one person to obtain from the court a remedy against another person.[1] The first date on which that factual situation comes into existence is the date of accrual of the cause of action. (In computing the relevant period of years the day during which the cause of action arose is excluded;[2] and when on the last day of the period the court office is closed, the time is extended to the first day on which the office reopens.[3])

1 *Letang v Cooper* [1965] 1 QB 232, [1964] 2 All ER 929, CA, per Diplock LJ.
2 *Marren v Dawson Bentley & Co Ltd* [1961] 2 QB 135, [1961] 2 All ER 270.
3 *Pritam Kaur v S Russell & Sons Ltd* [1973] QB 336, [1973] 1 All ER 617, CA.

TABLE 13.1

Personal injury claims

Primary period
3 years from accrual of cause of action, or, if later, from 'date of knowledge'.

Extensions
1 Legal disability: 3 years from end of disability.
2 Concealment: 3 years from discovery of concealment, or from when plaintiff could with reasonable diligence have discovered it.
3 Discretion: court has power to override time limit where equitable to do so.

Claims not involving personal injury

Primary period
6 years from accrual of cause of action: or, in negligence claims only, 3 years from 'starting date'* if that period expires later than the 6 years, but subject to overall limit of 15 years from last act of negligence.

Extensions
1 Legal disability: 6 years from end of disability.
2 Concealment: 6 years from discovery of concealment, or from when plaintiff could with reasonable diligence have discovered it.

*Explained in paras **13.20–13.24** below.

13.5 A cause of action founded on tort is not complete until the plaintiff suffers damage.[1] Thus in a case of medical negligence the date of accrual of the cause of action is normally the date when the plaintiff suffers injury. Difficult factual questions can arise where the injury is at first imperceptible so that the date of the injury cannot readily be ascertained. In such cases it is a question of fact and degree at what point the plaintiff has suffered material damage by reason of physical changes in his body. Changes within the principle *de minimis non curat lex* ('the law is not concerned with trifles') are ignored, but anything greater than this is regarded as substantial damage.[2]

1 Except in the case of torts actionable per se, i e without proof of damage, such as trespass to the person.
2 *Cartledge v E Jopling & Sons Ltd* [1963] AC 758 at 779, per Lord Pearce, cf at 772 damage 'beyond what can be regarded as negligible' (per Lord Reid) and at 774 'real damage as distinct from purely minimal damage' (per Lord Evershed).

13.6 In practice the bulk of medical negligence cases are claims for damages for personal injuries. However, such cases are not the only possible instances of negligence liability in the medical profession. Damages may be sought for loss of a solely financial nature (usually termed 'economic loss') where the negligent report or statement complained of and relied upon was given to a known recipient for a specific purpose of which the maker was aware.[1] Where a doctor makes a report on a patient to a prospective employer a negligent misstatement may cause such loss. If the misstatement is unduly optimistic as to the patient's state of health, loss may be suffered by the employer. If it is too negative, the patient may be the loser.[2] An insurance company may suffer loss by relying on a negligent report by a doctor who examines a person proposing for life assurance. Where the damage is in the nature of economic loss,[3] difficulties of a conceptual nature can arise in ascertaining the date of occurrence of the damage. If, for example, an insurer issues a policy on the life of a person who is in poorer health than was reported, it might be thought that the economic loss occurs only when the patient dies, so giving rise to a claim under the policy (indeed in the case of a term assurance there may be no loss at all if the patient, though ailing, outlives the term).[4] But it may be a more accurate analysis to state that the economic loss occurs when the policy is issued, since at that time the insurers have taken on an obligation more onerous than expected.[5]

1 *Caparo Industries Plc v Dickman* [1990] 2 AC 605, HL.
2 Depending on the circumstances, the patient may have no remedy based on negligence but only by way of an action for defamation. In general, the giver of a reference owes no duty of care in the tort of negligence to the subject of the reference: *Spring v Guardian Assurance Plc* [1993] 2 All ER 273, [1993] ICR 412, CA.
3 See para **13.24** for a further example.
4 This class of case might be regarded as analogous to the case of the negligently installed security gate which yielded to the attack of a burglar: the damage was held to have occurred at the date of the burglary, not the date of installation of the gate: *Dove v Banhams Patent Locks Ltd* [1983] 2 All ER 833, [1983] 1 WLR 1436. See also *UBAF Ltd v European American Banking Corpn* [1984] QB 713, [1984] 2 All ER 226, CA.
5 Cf *Forster v Outred & Co* [1982] 2 All ER 753, [1982] 1 WLR 86, CA and *D W Moore & Co Ltd v Ferrier* [1988] 1 All ER 400, [1988] WLR 267, CA, where solicitors had advised on a transaction which was disadvantageous, and the cause of action was held to accrue at the date of the transaction, not at the later time when the disadvantage materialised.

13.7 Where a claim is based on breach of contract the cause of action is complete when the contract is broken, irrespective of the date when damage results to the plaintiff.[1] Where, therefore, a doctor acts in contravention of his contractual duty to his patient, time runs from the date of the breach. Most such duties relate to the mode of performance of a particular act at a particular time. However, where the contractual duty in question is of a continuing nature, the plaintiff can rely on the breach latest in time. This is most likely to arise in the context of an omission to act, when the duty to rectify the omission may continue until the act becomes impossible to carry out or until the contractual relationship is terminated.[2] For example, if a general practitioner fails to advise a private patient, whom he puts on a course of drugs, of the risks of drinking alcohol while taking the drugs, he would be under a continuing duty to rectify his failure by giving the correct advice. This duty would continue until fulfilled or until the course of treatment ends.

1 *Howell v Young* (1826) 5 B & C 259.

2 The relevant legal reasoning was considered at some length in a solicitor's negligence case, *Midland Bank Trust Co Ltd v Hett, Stubbs & Kemp* [1979] Ch 384, [1978] 3 All ER 571. Further discussion of this kind of issue is to be found in the cases on the duty of architects to keep their design of a building under review: *Brickfield Properties Ltd v Newton* [1971] 3 All ER 328, [1971] 1 WLR 862, CA; *Merton London Borough Council v Lowe* (1981) 18 BLR 130, CA; *Chelmsford District Council v Evers* (1983) 25 BLR 99; *Equitable Debenture Assets Corpn Ltd v William Moss Group Ltd* (1984) 2 Con LR I; *Victoria University of Manchester v Hugh Wilson & Lewis Womersley (a firm) and Pochin (Contractors) Ltd* (1984) 2 Con LR 43; *University of Glasgow v Whitfield* (1988) 42 BLR 66, 19 Con LR 111. See also the cautionary remarks of Bingham LJ in *Eckersley v Binnie* (1988) 18 Con LR 1, 146–147.

13.8 Interesting questions arise as to a doctor's duty to inform his patient that he has broken his contract. There is some authority that a contracting party who knows he has made an error which may have dangerous consequences is under an implied duty to inform the other party.[1] A doctor who has made a mistake such that further treatment ought to be sought might be held to be under a duty to inform his patient. Such a duty might be held to continue in some circumstances beyond the duration of the contractual relationship.[2]

1 *Stag Line Ltd v Tyne Shiprepair Group Ltd, The Zinnia* [1984] 2 Lloyd's Rep 211. Staughton J, who held that there was such a duty nevertheless described it as 'a novel concept'. Contrast *Wood v Jones* (1889) 61 LT 551.

2 See the vigorous obiter dicta of Sir John Donaldson MR in *Naylor v Preston Area Health Authority* [1987] 2 All ER 353 at 360, CA. Cf *Lee v South West Thames Regional Health Authority* [1985] 2 All ER 385 at 389–390, CA.

13.9 Injuries caused to a child by acts done before his birth (and even before his conception) are the subject of special provisions in the Congenital Disabilities (Civil Liability) Act 1976. Liability under the Act is regarded as liability for personal injuries sustained by the child immediately after his birth.[1] This means that the ordinary limitation provisions apply as from the date of birth. The practical effect is that the period of limitation runs during the child's minority and then for three years, ie until the child's 21st birthday.[2]

1 Section 4(3) of the Act.

2 See para **13.27** as to the extension of the limitation period while the child is a minor.

PERSONAL INJURY CASES[1]

13.10 A three year period applies to actions for damages for negligence or other breach of duty[2] where the damages claimed consist of or include damages in respect of personal injuries.[3] In *Ackbar v CF Green & Co Ltd*[4] the plaintiff was injured when travelling in his own lorry as a passenger. He was unable to recover compensation from the driver because the insurance did not extend to passenger liability. Although the plaintiff suffered loss by reason of his injuries, his claim against his insurance brokers for failing to obtain proper insurance was held not to be a claim where the damages consisted of or included 'damages in respect of personal injuries'. It was therefore not subject to the three year limit. Thus if, for example,[5] a doctor omits relevant material from a report made for the purposes of litigation, and the injured plaintiff recovers reduced damage as a result, the plaintiff's subsequent claim against the doctor to recover the shortfall would not be an action 'in respect of' personal injuries.

1 Limitation Act 1980, ss 11–14.
2 Whether the duty exists by virtue of a contract or of provisions made by or under a statute or independently of any contract or any such provision, and including a duty in the law of nuisance: Limitation Act 1980, s 11(1).
3 1980 Act, s 11. The time limits when the injuries are fatal are dealt with in para **13.17**, below. Section 11 is limited to actions for personal injury arising from accidents caused by negligence, nuisance or breach of duty of care. It does not apply to injury arising from assaults: *Stubbings v Webb* [1993] AC 498, [1993] 1 All ER 322.
4 [1975] QB 582, [1975] 2 All ER 65. But see *Howe v David Brown Tractors (Retail) Ltd* [1991] 4 All ER 30, CA, where the three year limit was held to apply to a claim for loss of profits by a firm owned by the injured plaintiff.
5 As illustrated by *McGrath v Kiely and Powell* [1965] IR 497.

13.11 'Personal injuries' is defined as including any disease and any impairment of a person's physical or mental condition.[1] A claim which is essentially economic but which includes an allegation of anxiety and distress must be tested against this definition. It would seem that the damages claimed by a male plaintiff in respect of a failed vasectomy[2] would not include damages in respect of personal injuries, but the damages claimed by a female plaintiff in respect of her husband's failed vasectomy or her own failed sterilisation would include such damages if (for example) she underwent the pain and suffering of pregnancy. Assuming separate actions were brought, only the female plaintiff would be subject to the three year limitation period.

1 1980 Act, s 38(1).
2 As in *Thake v Maurice* [1986] QB 644, [1986] 1 All ER 497, CA.

13.12 The three year period runs from the date on which the cause of action accrued,[1] or the 'date of knowledge' (if later) of the person injured. The 'knowledge' referred to is, broadly, knowledge of facts sufficient to bring an action against the wrongdoer. The policy of this provision is to alleviate the hardship that would be suffered by a plaintiff who failed to start his action in time because he was unaware that he had been injured by someone's negligence.

1 As to accrual of a cause of action see paras **13.4–13.5** and **13.7**, above.

13.13 The extent of the knowledge necessary to start time running against the plaintiff is closely defined in the 1980 Act.[1] There must be knowledge[2] of the following facts:

(a) that the injury in question is significant;[3] and
(b) that the injury was attributable[4] in whole or in part to the act or omission which is alleged to constitute negligence or other breach of duty; and
(c) the identity of the defendant.[5]

The period of limitation begins to run when the plaintiff can first be said to have knowledge of the nature of his injury to justify that particular plaintiff taking the preliminary steps for the institution of proceedings against the person or persons whose act or omission caused the significant injury concerned.[6] In *Scuriaga v Powell*[7] the plaintiff had an operation to terminate her pregnancy, but the operation was unsuccessful and she subsequently gave birth. The defendant doctor falsely told her that the lack of success was due to a physical defect in her. More than three years later she discovered, as a result of further medical advice, that the lack of success of the operation was attributable to the manner in which the doctor had performed the operation. The court held that her date of knowledge, from which time ran, was the date on which she received the further advice. While the plaintiff must have knowledge of the essence of the act or omission to which the injury is attributable, it is not necessary for him to know the precise terms in which negligence or breach of duty would be alleged.[8]

1 The relevant provisions are discussed in detail in *Nash v Eli Lilly & Co* [1992] 3 Med LR 353, CA. See also 28 *Halsbury's Laws* (4th edn) para 692.
2 'Knowledge' is to be given its ordinary English meaning and is not to be equated with 'reasonable belief' or 'suspicion': *Davis v Ministry of Defence* (26 July 1985, CA Transcript 413). But see further para **13.15** below.
3 An injury is significant if the person whose date of knowledge is in question would reasonably have considered it sufficiently serious to justify his instituting proceedings for damages against a defendant who did not dispute liability and was able to satisfy a judgment: 1980 Act, s 14(2). This is an entirely different test from the test of what is a material injury for the purposes of ascertaining the date of accrual of a cause of action: see para **13.5**, above.
4 I e 'capable of being attributed' (not 'caused by'): *Davis v Ministry of Defence* (26 July 1985, CA Transcript 413); *Wilkinson v Ancliff (BLT) Ltd* [1986] 1 WLR 1352, CA; *Nash v Eli Lilly & Co* [1992] 3 Med LR 353, 367.
5 1980 Act, s 14(1).
6 *Nash v Eli Lilly & Co* [1992] 3 Med LR 353, 367. See also *Halford v Brookes* [1991] 1 WLR 428, CA.
7 (1979) 123 Sol Jo 406.
8 *Nash v Eli Lilly & Co* [1992] 3 Med LR 353, 368; *Wilkinson v Ancliff (BLT) Ltd* [1986] 1 WLR 1352, CA; *Driscoll-Varley v Parkside Health Authority* [1991] 2 Med LR 346; *Dobbie v Medway Health Authority* [1992] 3 Med LR 217; *Broadley v Guy Clapham & Co* (1993) Times, 6 July, CA.

13.14 In a case where it is alleged that the act or omission was that of a person other than the defendant, the necessary knowledge includes the identity of that other person and the additional facts supporting the bringing of an action against the defendant.[1] This provision may be of assistance to a plaintiff wishing to sue a private hospital but unaware of the identity of the treating doctor and his relationship with the hospital.

1 1980 Act, s 14(1)(d).

13.15 If the criteria defining the date of knowledge were applied by reference only to the actual knowledge of the particular plaintiff under consideration, the time limit would operate in favour of plaintiffs with a high degree of ignorance and against those of a more inquiring disposition. The Act therefore attributes to the plaintiff such knowledge as he might reasonably have been expected to acquire from facts ascertainable by him, whether on his own or with such medical or other expert advice as it is reasonable for him to seek.[1] But the court has to determine what the particular plaintiff should reasonably have observed or ascertained. Whether the steps taken or the enquiry made were reasonable is to be considered in the light of the age, circumstances, character and intelligence of the plaintiff.[2] Once a firm belief amounting to knowledge is held, a subsequent report from an expert saying that the injury is not attributable does not stop time running. If a plaintiff has the requisite knowledge he cannot subsequently lose it[3] but, if the plaintiff felt he needed confirmation from experts before he was sufficiently certain, time would not run until the result of that enquiry was known or – if he delayed in obtaining that confirmation – until the time at which it was reasonable for him to have got it.[4]

1 1980 Act, s 14(3). It should be noted that a person is not fixed with knowledge of a fact ascertainable only with the help of expert advice so long as he has taken all reasonable steps to

obtain (and, where appropriate, to act on) that advice: ibid, s 14(3). This provision protects him in the event of a blunder by his expert adviser.

2 *Davis v City & Hackney Health Authority* [1991] 2 Med LR 366; *Nash v Eli Lilly & Co* [1992] 3 Med LR 353, 368; *Atkinson v Oxfordshire Health Authority* [1993] 4 Med LR 18 (acceptance of legal advice that no cause of action existed was reasonable); *Driscoll-Varley v Parkside Health Authority* [1991] 2 Med LR 346 (reluctance to take steps which might discourage the doctor in whom the plaintiff had confidence from continuing to treat her was held reasonable).

3 *Nash v Eli Lilly & Co* [1992] 3 Med LR 353, 366.

4 Ibid at 367. The case of *Nash* also deals in detail with the circumstances in which a firm belief may constitute knowledge.

13.16 These provisions are directed to the plaintiff's knowledge of the relevant facts, not of the law relating to his right to sue. Knowledge that any acts or omissions did or did not, as a matter of law, involve negligence or breach of duty is irrelevant.[1] In line with this, the expert knowledge which may be attributed to a plaintiff is the knowledge derivable from those who are experts as regards matters of fact: a lawyer is not an expert for this purpose.[2]

1 1980 Act, s 14(1).

2 *Fowell v National Coal Board* [1986] CILL 294, (1986) Times, 28 May, CA.

13.17 If the injured person dies before the expiry of the three year period applicable to an action by him, the limitation period applicable to an action on behalf of his estate[1] is three years from the date of death or from the date of the personal representative's knowledge, whichever is later.[2] The time limit for bringing an action on behalf of dependants under the Fatal Accidents Act 1976 is three years from the date of death or from the date of knowledge of the person for whose benefit the action is brought, whichever is later.[3] Dependants who acquired the necessary knowledge on different dates are therefore subject to different time limits.[4]

1 By virtue of the Law Reform (Miscellaneous Provisions) Act 1934.

2 See 1980 Act, s 11(5)–(7).

3 Ibid, s 12(2). But no action under the Fatal Accidents Act 1976 may be brought if the death occurred at a time when the person injured had already lost his right of action: ibid, s 12(1).

4 Ibid, s 13.

13.18 The possible extensions of time available in cases of disability or concealment, and the court's discretion to override the normal time limits, are dealt with below.[1]

1 At paras **13.27–13.28**, **13.29** and **13.30–13.33** respectively.

CLAIMS NOT INVOLVING PERSONAL INJURY

13.19 In general the limitation period for a claim where the damages do not consist of or include damages for personal injury is six years from the date on which the cause of action accrued.[1] This is so whether the action is founded in tort or in contract.[2] The date of accrual of causes of action in tort and in contract has been discussed in paras **13.4–13.8** above.

1 See paras **13.10–13.11**, above for the precise distinction between personal injury cases and other cases.

2 1980 Act, ss 2 and 5.

13.20 Where an action (not being a personal injury action) is for damages for negligence, an alternative limitation period is available where facts relevant to the cause of action are not known to the plaintiff at the date when the cause of action accrues.[1] The plaintiff can take advantage of this period if it expires later than the ordinary six year period from the date of accrual of the cause of action. This applies only to claims founded on tortious negligence and not to claims for breach of a contractual duty of care.[2] Where the plaintiff does not have the necessary knowledge at the date of accrual of the cause of action the alternative period is three years from (broadly) the date when he acquires that knowledge ('the starting date').[3]

1 1980 Act, s 14A (inserted by the Latent Damage Act 1986).
2 *Irontrades Mutual Insurance Company v J K Buckenham* [1989] 2 Lloyd's Rep 85, [1990] 1 All ER 808; *Société Commerciale de Réassurance v ERAS (International) Ltd* [1992] 2 All ER 82 (Note), [1992] 1 Lloyd's Rep 570.
3 The 'starting date' is the earliest date on which the plaintiff or any person in whom the cause of action was vested before him first had both the knowledge required for bringing an action for damages in respect of the relevant damage and a right to bring such an action: 1980 Act, s 14A(5).

13.21 The knowledge that the plaintiff needs to have at the 'starting date' is:

(a) the material facts about the damage in respect of which damages are claimed;[1] and
(b) that the damage was attributable in whole or in part to the act or omission which is alleged to constitute negligence; and
(c) the identity of the defendant.[2]

1 That is, such facts about the damage as would lead a reasonable person who had suffered such damage to consider it sufficiently serious to justify his instituting proceedings for damages against a defendant who did not dispute liability and was able to satisfy a judgment: 1980 Act, s 14A(7).
2 1980 Act, s 14A(8).

13.22 Further, in a case where it is alleged that the act or omission was that of a person other than the defendant, the necessary knowledge includes the identity of that other person and the additional facts supporting the bringing of an action against the defendant.[1]

1 1980 Act, s 14A(8)(c).

13.23 As in the case of the date of knowledge provisions applicable to personal injury cases,[1] the Act attributes to the plaintiff such knowledge as he might reasonably have been expected to acquire from facts ascertainable by him, whether on his own or with such expert advice as it is reasonable for him to seek.[2] These provisions are likewise directed to the plaintiff's knowledge of the relevant facts, not of the law relating to his right to sue. Knowledge that any acts or omissions did or did not, as a matter of law, involve negligence is irrelevant.[3]

1 See paras **13.12–13.17**, above.
2 1980 Act, s 14A(10). However, a person is not fixed with knowledge of a fact ascertainable only with the help of expert advice so long as he has taken all reasonable steps to obtain (and, where appropriate, to act on) that advice: ibid. This provision protects him in the event of a blunder by his expert adviser. Presumably the expert knowledge which may be attributed to a plaintiff is the knowledge derivable from those who are experts as regards matters of fact, so that a lawyer would not be regarded as an expert for the purpose of a medical claim. Cf *Fowell v National Coal Board* [1986] CILL 294, (1986) Times, 28 May, CA.
3 1980 Act, s 14A(9).

13.24 These provisions assist a plaintiff who does not know of the facts justifying a claim until the normal six year period of limitation has expired. Suppose a man is offered a financially rewarding job. His general practitioner negligently advises him that he should not take it because of some chronic condition which would affect his ability to carry out the work. He therefore suffers financial loss. Seven years later he discovers that the condition was easily remediable and that he could have performed the work. The 'starting date' would be the date when he discovered the truth about his condition.

13.25 Since the alternative three year period runs from the time when the plaintiff gains the necessary knowledge, in extreme cases the cut-off date for the bringing of an action would be postponed indefinitely. This would be contrary to the policy of the Limitation Act. To meet this situation there is an overriding limitation period of fifteen years for negligence actions not involving personal injuries. The fifteen years runs from the last date on which there occurred any act or omission which is alleged to constitute negligence and to which the damage is alleged to be attributable.[1] This provides a 'long stop' which restricts the right of a plaintiff to rely on the alternative three year period where more than twelve years elapse before he gains the necessary knowledge.[2] The long stop also bars claims which would otherwise be within the ordinary six year period from the accrual of the cause of action if they are not commenced within fifteen years from the last breach of duty. This is so even if the damage has not occurred within the fifteen years, so that the cause of action has not even accrued within that period.[3] The long stop does not apply, however, to concealment cases.[4] The effect of the long stop on disability cases is considered below.[5]

1 1980 Act, s 14B(1).
2 Ibid, s 14B(2).
3 Ibid, s 14B(1), (2).
4 Ibid, s 32(5). As to concealment, see para **13.29**, below.
5 See paras **13.27–13.28**.

13.26 The three year and fifteen year periods do not apply to any action commenced before 18 September 1986.[1] Nor can a plaintiff whose claim was already barred before that date under the previous law rely on the three year period in order to bring an action.[2] Aside from these restrictions, the three year and fifteen year periods apply to any cause of action accruing before, as well as after, that date.[3]

1 Latent Damage Act 1986, s 4(1)(b).
2 Ibid, s 4(1)(a).
3 Ibid, s 4(2).

PLAINTIFF UNDER A LEGAL DISABILITY

13.27 A person is under a disability if he is an infant, i e under the age of 18 years,[1] or of unsound mind,[2] i e incapable of managing and administering his property and affairs by reason of mental disorder within the meaning of the Mental Health Act 1983.[3] If on the date when a right of action accrued the person to whom it accrued was under a disability, the action may be brought at any time before the expiry of six years or, for personal injury cases, three years from the date when he ceased to be under a disability or died (whichever first occurred).[4] This extension for disability takes effect notwithstanding the expiry of the fifteen year long stop period referred to in para **13.25** above. If a person is of sound mind at the time when the right of action accrues, but subsequently becomes of unsound mind, the supervening incapacity does not prevent the ordinary limitation period running against him.[5]

1 Family Law Reform Act 1969, s 1.
2 1980 Act, s 38(2).
3 Ibid, s 38(2), (3). Whether a person is of unsound mind will normally be a question of fact, but a person is conclusively presumed to be of unsound mind (a) while he is liable to be detained or subject to guardianship under the Mental Health Act 1983 (otherwise than by virtue of s 35 or 89); and (b) while he is receiving treatment as an in-patient in any hospital within the meaning of the Act of 1983 or mental nursing home within the meaning of the Registered Homes Act 1984, s 22 without being liable to be detained under the Act of 1983 (otherwise than by virtue of s 35 or 89), being treatment which follows without any interval a period during which he was liable to be detained or subject to guardianship under the Mental Health Act of 1959, or the Act of 1983 (otherwise than by virtue of s 35 or 89) or by virtue of any enactment repealed or excluded by the Mental Health Act 1959.
4 1980 Act, s 28(1), (6). However, when a right of action which has accrued to a person under a disability accrues, on the death of that person while still under a disability, to another person under a disability, no further extension of time is allowed by reason of the disability of the second person: s 28(3).
5 See 28 *Halsbury's Laws* (4th edn) para 868.

13.28 In personal injury cases the extension on the ground of disability only applies when the disability exists at the date when the right of action accrues. There is no such extension for an injured plaintiff who is under a disability at his date of knowledge (in the sense explained in paras **13.12–13.16** above).[1] However, where a claim is for damages for tortious negligence, not including damages for personal injuries, there is an extension for disability if all the following conditions are fulfilled:

(a) the action is commenced before the expiry of fifteen years from the last act of negligence;[2]
(b) the period of three years from the 'starting date'[3] expires later than the period of six years from the accrual of the cause of action;
(c) on the starting date the plaintiff[4] was under a disability;
(d) on the date when the cause of action accrued the plaintiff[5] was not under a disability.

In this event the extension is for three years from the date when the plaintiff[6] ceased to be under a disability or died, whichever first occurred.

1 But see paras **13.30–13.33** as to the court's discretionary power to extend the limitation period.
2 As further explained at para **13.25**, above. Note that, in contrast with the position under s 28 of the 1980 Act, the fifteen year long stop limits this disability extension.
3 As defined in the 1980 Act: see paras **13.20–13.24**, above.
4 Or any person in whom the cause of action was vested before him: 1980 Act, s 14A(5), s 28A(1)(b).
5 Or other person to whom it accrued: 1980 Act, s 28(1), s 28A(1)(c).
6 Or any person in whom the cause of action was vested before him: see n 4, above.

CONCEALMENT

13.29 Where any fact relevant to the plaintiff's right of action has been deliberately concealed from him by the defendant,[1] the period of limitation does not begin to run until the plaintiff has discovered the concealment or could with reasonable diligence have discovered it.[2] For this purpose, deliberate commission of a breach of duty in circumstances in which it is unlikely to be discovered for some time amounts to deliberate concealment of the facts involved in that breach of duty.[3] These provisions were intended to give effect, subject to some modifications, to a recommendation of the Law Reform Committee[4] that the relevant provision of the Limitation Act 1939[5] should be reformulated so as to express its true legal purport as decided by the courts.[6] Whether they do so is open to question. It should be noted that concealment does not postpone the running of the limitation period for claims under the Fatal Accidents Act 1976.[7]

1 Or the defendant's agent, or any person through whom the defendant claims or such a person's agent: 1980 Act, s 32(1).
2 Ibid, s 32(1). A similar extension applies (inter alia) where the action is based on the fraud of the defendant. In *Tito v Waddell (No 2)* [1977] Ch 106, 245, Megarry J held that the words 'shall not begin to run' indicated a concealment at the time of the accrual of the cause of action, so that the postponement of the limitation period would not operate in a case where the concealment took place only at a later time. But in *Sheldon v RHM Outhwaite (Underwriting Agencies) Ltd* [1993] TLR 632 Saville J decided to the contrary.
3 Ibid, s 32(2).
4 In paras 2.24 and 2.35 of its 21st Report (Final Report on Limitation of Actions) (Cmnd 6923).
5 I e s 26 of that Act.
6 The main cases were *Kitchen v Royal Air Force Association* [1958] 2 All ER 241, [1958] 1 WLR 563, CA; *Clark v Woor* [1965] 2 All ER 353, [1965] 1 WLR 650; *Applegate v Moss* [1971] 1 QB 406, [1971] 1 All ER 747, CA; *King v Victor Parsons & Co (a firm)* [1973] 1 All ER 206, [1973] 1 WLR 29, CA.
7 This is the effect of the 1980 Act, s 12(3).

DISCRETION TO OVERRIDE TIME LIMITS

13.30 The court has a discretionary power to disapply the time limits set by sections 11 and 12 of the Limitation Act 1980, which apply in cases of personal injury or death.[1] The power is exercisable where[2] it appears to the court that it would be equitable to allow a claim to proceed having regard to the degree to which:

(a) the provisions of section 11[3] or 12 prejudice the plaintiff;[4] and
(b) any decision of the court on the application to disapply would prejudice the defendant.[5]

If a plaintiff starts an action in time but fails for some reason to proceed with it, he is unlikely to be allowed after the expiry of the three years to pursue a second action by virtue of the court's power to disapply the limit, for in such circumstances he has been prejudiced not by the provisions of section 11 but by his failure to proceed with the first action.[6] Where the claim is first commenced outside the three year period, the court has a wide and unfettered discretion to disapply the time limit.[7] Even if the plaintiff has an unanswerable claim against his own solicitors, he may nevertheless be regarded as prejudiced, since (inter alia) if the action is not allowed to proceed he may be personally liable for the costs and may suffer further delay in finding new solicitors and suing those at fault.[8] But if that prejudice is slight compared with the prejudice the defendants would suffer in having to meet a stale claim, then the existence of such a claim against the plaintiff's solicitors may be decisive in causing the court to refuse to disapply the time limit.[9]

1 See paras **13.10–13.17**, above. Note also that the existence of this discretionary power is relevant in support of an application for pre-action discovery under s 33(2) of the Supreme

Court Act 1981 and RSC Ord 24, r 7A: *Harris v Newcastle Health Authority* [1989] 2 All ER 273, [1989] 1 WLR 96, CA.

2 1980 Act, s 33(1).

3 Ie the three year period from the date of accrual of the cause of action or from the date of knowledge if later, as extended where appropriate in cases of disability or concealment: see s 33(8).

4 Or any person whom he represents: 1980 Act, s 33(1)(a).

5 Or any person whom he represents: ibid, s 33(1)(b).

6 *Walkley v Precision Forgings Ltd* [1979] 2 All ER 548, [1979] 1 WLR 606, HL; *Chappell v Cooper* [1980] 2 All ER 463, [1980] 1 WLR 958, CA. This is so even where the defendant has made an interim payment in respect of the plaintiff's claim: *Deerness v John R Keeble & Son (Brantham) Ltd* [1983] 2 Lloyd's Rep 260, HL.

7 *Thompson v Brown Construction (Ebbw Vale) Ltd* [1981] 2 All ER 296, [1981] 1 WLR 744, HL.

8 Ibid. See also *Ramsden v Lee* [1992] 2 All ER 204, CA. There may be further prejudice in that the plaintiff's solicitors will know the weaknesses in his case against the original tortfeasor whereas that tortfeasor may not know of them: *Hartley v Birmingham City Council* [1992] 1 WLR 968, CA.

9 *Donovan v Gwentoys Ltd* [1990] 1 WLR 472, HL.

13.31 The Act directs the court to have regard to all the circumstances of the case and in particular to:

(a) the length of, and the reasons for, the delay on the part of the plaintiff;[1]

(b) the extent to which, having regard to the delay, the evidence adduced or likely to be adduced by the plaintiff or the defendant is or is likely to be less cogent than if the action had been brought within the time allowed by section 11 or 12;

(c) the conduct of the defendant after the cause of action arose, including the extent (if any) to which he responded to requests reasonably made by the plaintiff for information or inspection for the purpose of ascertaining facts which were or might be relevant to the plaintiff's cause of action against the defendant;

(d) the duration of any disability of the plaintiff arising after the date of the accrual of the cause of action;

(e) the extent to which the plaintiff acted promptly and reasonably once he knew whether or not the act or omission of the defendant, to which the injury was attributable, might be capable at that time of giving rise to an action for damages;[2]

(f) the steps, if any, taken by the plaintiff to obtain medical, legal or other expert advice and the nature of any such advice he may have received.[3]

1 Ie the delay which occurred between the expiry of the limitation period and the issue of the writ, not the period between the beginning of the limitation period and the issue of the writ: *Eastman v London County Bus Services* (1985) Times, 23 November, CA, applying *Thompson v Brown Construction (Ebbw Vale) Ltd* [1981] 2 All ER 296, [1981] 1 WLR 744, HL. Nevertheless in considering the exercise of the discretion generally under section 33(1) the Court should also have regard to conduct before the expiry of the limitation period: *Donovan v Gwentoys Ltd* [1990] 1 WLR 472, HL; *Nash v Eli Lilly & Co* [1992] 3 Med LR 353, 370.

2 See *Dobbie v Medway Health Authority* [1992] 3 Med LR 217; *Doughty v North Staffordshire Health Authority* [1992] 3 Med LR 81.

3 1980 Act, s 33(3). The various factors are discussed in the speech of Lord Diplock in *Thompson v Brown* [1981] 1 WLR 744 at 751–752. The court will need to know whether legal advice received was favourable to the plaintiff's alleged cause of action: *Jones v G D Searle & Co Ltd* [1978] 3 All ER 654, [1979] 1 WLR 101, CA. Further specific provisions of s 33 relate to fatal cases: see s 33(2)(4)(6).

13.32 The consideration under section 33 has to be broadly based. The primary purpose of the limitation period is to protect the defendant against the injustice of having to face a stale claim. Once a plaintiff has allowed the permitted time to elapse, the defendant is no longer subject to the disability of accepting without protest the limitation period itself. In such a situation the court is directed to consider all the circumstances of the case including conduct before the expiry of the limitation period and to balance the prejudice to the parties.[1] The overall prospects of success of the plaintiff's claim should be taken into account in considering the exercise of discretion.[2] If the claim is a poor case lacking in merit there may be significant and relevant prejudice to the defendant if the limitation period is disapplied.[3] Since it is legitimate to take into account that the plaintiff may have a claim against his own solicitor, it follows that it is legitimate to take into account that the defendant is insured, for, if the defendant is deprived of his limitation defence, he will have a claim upon his insurers.[4] It has also been stated that the court may have regard to the insurance position of other defendants who have been sued in time.[5]

1 *Nash v Eli Lilly & Co* [1992] 3 Med LR 353, 370; *Donovan v Gwentoys Limited* [1990] 1 WLR 472.
2 *Dale v British Coal Corpn (No 2)* (1992) 136 Sol Jo LB 199, (1992) TLR 328, CA.
3 *Nash v Eli Lilly & Co* [1992] 3 Med LR 353, 371, though their Lordships did not share the view of the Court of Appeal in *Hartley v Birmingham City Council* [1992] 1 WLR 968 that the benefit of the Limitation Act defence should necessarily be described as a windfall where a defendant's ability to defend was unaffected by the delay.
4 *Hartley v Birmingham City Council* [1992] 1 WLR 968, CA.
5 *Liff v Peasley* [1980] 1 WLR 781 at 789, cf *Firman v Ellis* [1978] QB 886 at 912, 916, CA. (The decision in *Firman v Ellis* was overruled by the House of Lords in *Walkley v Precision Forgings Ltd* [1979] 2 All ER 548, [1979] 1 WLR 606 on another point.)

13.33 In *Hills v Potter*[1] these provisions were applied in favour of a plaintiff whose action had been begun more than six years after her unsuccessful operation, but her claim failed on the issue of liability. The court, in exercising its discretion, will give weight to the consideration that a professional negligence action is a serious matter for a medical practitioner and that such actions ought to be dealt with expeditiously.[2]

1 [1983] 3 All ER 716, [1984] 1 WLR 641n.
2 See *Professional Negligence* by R M Jackson and J L Powell (3rd edn) para 1–131 and cases there cited.

BURDEN OF PROOF

13.34 Since the expiry of a relevant limitation period is a statutory defence which the defendant must plead if he desires to rely upon it,[1] it might be expected that the burden of proving that the claim was commenced outside the period would lie upon the defendant. This view has been expressed in the Court of Appeal.[2] However, the Court of Appeal has twice decided the contrary, ie that where a defendant raises a limitation defence it is incumbent on the plaintiff to show that the cause of action accrued within the limitation period.[3] Presumably this approach would be extended to cases where the plaintiff contends that the relevant limitation period runs not from the accrual of the cause of action but from his 'date of knowledge'[4] or 'the starting date',[5] so that it would be for the plaintiff to show that he did not have the necessary knowledge until a date within the limitation period.[6] Further, in cases where a plaintiff seeks to have the limitation period disapplied under section 33 of the Act of 1980, it is clear that the onus lies upon him to show that in the particular circumstances of the case it would be equitable to make an exception.[7]

1 See para **13.2**, above.
2 *Fowell v National Coal Board* [1986] CILL 294, (1986) Times, 28 May, CA.
3 *Cartledge v E Jopling & Sons Ltd* [1962] 1 QB 189, [1961] 3 All ER 482, CA; *London Congregational Union Inc v Harriss & Harriss (a firm)* [1988] 1 All ER 15, CA; cf *Darley Main Colliery Co v Mitchell* (1886) 11 App Cas 127 at 135; *O'Connor v Isaacs* [1956] 2 QB 288 at 364, CA; *The Pendrecht* [1980] 2 Lloyd's Rep 56 at 60; *Bromley London Borough v Rush & Tompkins Ltd* (1985) 35 BLR 94.
4 See paras **13.12–13.17**, above.
5 See paras **13.20–13.24**, above.
6 This question is discussed in the *Supreme Court Practice 1992* vol 2, para 6152. In *Fowell v National Coal Board* [1986] CILL 294, (1986) Times, 28 May, CA, Parker LJ stated that where the limitation period running from the accrual of the cause of action had elapsed it was for the plaintiff in the first instance to assert and give evidence that he first had knowledge of the relevant facts on a date later than the accrual of the cause of action. If, however, the defendant wished to displace this by asserting earlier knowledge, it must be for him to prove such earlier knowledge. This was the approach adopted by Hidden J in *Driscoll-Varley v Parkside Health Authority* [1991] 2 Med LR 346, 358 and approved by the Court of Appeal in *Nash v Eli Lilly & Co* [1992] 3 Med LR 353, 367.
7 *Thompson v Brown* [1981] 1 WLR 744 at 752.

BIBLIOGRAPHICAL REFERENCE

Jackson R M and Powell J L *Professional Negligence* (3rd edn, London, Sweet & Maxwell, 1992).

CROSS-REFERENCES

For information related to topics in this chapter see Chapters 8, 14 and 20.

CHAPTER 14

Group actions

Mark Mildred *Solicitor*
Rodger J Pannone *Solicitor*

SUMMARY

INTRODUCTION

14.1 'The concept of the "class action" is as yet unknown to the English courts. In some jurisdictions, notably in the United States, where large numbers of plaintiffs are making related claims against the same defendants, there are special procedures laid down enabling all the claims to be disposed of in a single action. Clearly this is something which should be looked at by the appropriate authorities with a view to seeing whether it has anything to offer and, if so, introducing the necessary procedural rules. Meanwhile the courts must be as flexible and adaptable as possible in the application of existing procedures with a view to reaching decisions quickly and economically. . .'[1]

This passage appeared in a judgment of the Court of Appeal after it and Hirst J had been obliged to consider in the context of the first *Opren* litigation the two principal issues which affect multi-plaintiff actions: procedure and funding.

1 Lord Donaldson MR in *Davies v Eli Lilly & Co* [1987] 3 All ER 94.

14.2 Those two issues, in the context of multi-plaintiff actions and of a period of rapid change, are the matters to be discussed in this chapter.

14.3 In the popular mind, and apparently also in the judicial mind, the term 'class action' is used generically. The class action itself is a particular form of approach to the resolution of these two issues but one which has seldom been used, even in the United States, in multiple actions relating to alleged injuries either by defective products or by medical negligence. Whilst there are exceptions to this assertion, the more common approach is for cases of this sort to be taken on individually by trial lawyers and processed individually to trial or settlement. Part of the reason is that cases where there is wide diversion between members of the class both in terms of susceptibility to damage and the nature of the damage caused do not happily lend themselves to a process predicated on the commonality of all issues. Another more venal reason is that there is a considerable financial incentive to plaintiffs' attornies working on a contingency fee basis to harness the enthusiasm of juries for awarding punitive damages in individual cases. It is frequently only when there is a sense that the defendant has been punished enough that a class action may be filed, if possible, to mop up the claimants who are left.

14.4 We shall give a relatively brief description of the present alternatives in different jurisdictions, including England and Wales, for coping with multiple claims. We shall then go on to examine the issues raised in such claims both relating to procedure and to funding, how they arise and how they have been dealt with to date, including official reforms and proposals.

14.5 Finally, we shall propose a framework which we, as practising plaintiffs' lawyers, feel would be apt to do justice for all the parties.

ENGLAND AND WALES

14.6 The only formal procedure contained in the Rules of the Supreme Court for dealing with multiple claims is Order 15, rule 12 – the representative action. This states: 'Where numerous persons have the same interest in any proceedings. . . the proceedings may be begun and, unless the court otherwise orders, continued, by or against any one or more of them as representing all or as representing all except one or more of them.'

14.7 In the leading case of *Duke of Bedford v Ellis*[1] the House of Lords said, 'considering whether a representative action is maintained you have to consider what is common to the class and what differentiates the cases of individual members. Given a common interest and common grievance, a representative suit was in order, if the relief sought was in its nature benefit to all whom the plaintiff proposed to represent.'

1 [1901] AC 1.

14.8 The requirement to show that the relief sought was in its nature beneficial to all the class has been interpreted to mean that the relief must be equally beneficial to all. This in turn would mean that the action could only be used in cases where damages are recovered for a collective fund rather than for individuals, as no individual would have an interest in damages recovered by any other individual.

14.9 In the subsequent Court of Appeal case of *Markt & Co Ltd v Knight Steamship Co Ltd*,[1] Fletcher Moulton LJ interpreted *Duke of Bedford v Ellis* in the following way: 'Where the claim is for damages the machinery of a representative suit is absolutely inapplicable. The relief which he is seeking is not a personal relief applicable to him alone, and does not benefit in any way the class with whom he purports to be bringing action.' Whilst this was in a sense a minority view it is enshrined in the Supreme Court Practice as follows: 'No representative action will arise to establish the right of numerous persons to recover damages each in his own right, where the only relief claimed is to recover damages, for none of the parties sought to be represented have any interest in the damages recoverable by the particular plaintiff claiming to represent them.' In recent years there have been attempts to undermine this principle with some success.

1 [1910] 2 KB 1021.

14.10 In *Prudential Assurance Co Ltd v Newman Industries Ltd*[1] Vinelott J rejected the proposition of law contained in the White Book note referred to above and decided that the representative action could be utilised in a damages claim provided two conditions apply.

1 [1981] Ch 229, [1979] 3 All ER 507.

14.11 The first is that an order could not be made in favour of a representative plaintiff if that order could potentially confer upon a member of the represented class a right which he or she would not have been able to exercise in a separate action, or deprived the defendant of a defence upon which that defendant could otherwise successfully rely (for example, a Limitation Act defence) in a separate action.

14.12 The second is that no order would be made in favour of their representative plaintiff without there being an element common to the claim of all members of the class which the representative plaintiff holds himself out as representing.

14.13 This authority was followed in *EMI Records Ltd v Riley*[1] and *M Michaels Furriers Ltd v Askew*[2] but not in *News Group Newspapers Ltd v Society of Graphical and Allied Trades '82* (*No* 2).[3]

1 [1981] 2 All ER 838, [1981] 1 WLR 923.
2 (1983) 127 Sol Jo 597, CA.
3 [1987] ICR 181.

14.14 Megarry J in *John v Rees*[1] decided that the rule should be treated as not being a rigid matter of principle but a flexible tool of convenience in the administration of justice.

1 [1970] Ch 345, [1969] 2 All ER 274.

14.15 In passing it should be noted that the Ontario Court of Appeal decided in 1979 in the case of *Naken v General Motors of Canada Ltd*[1] that the view of Fletcher Moulton LJ in the *Markt* case was not the judgment of the Court of Appeal but only of one judge and allowed a claim for damages for each member of a class to proceed and this has been followed in subsequent Canadian cases.

1 (1979) 92 DLR (3d) 100.

14.16 *Irish Shipping Ltd v Commercial Union Assurance Co Ltd, The Irish Rowan*[1] is a recent authority which may have settled the question in favour of the representative action being able to include a claim for damages in appropriate circumstances.

1 [1991] 2 QB 206, [1989] 3 All ER 853, CA.

THE USA

14.17 A class action exists here both in the federal court and in all the state courts. The rule is merely procedural and does not affect substantive rights at all: the burden and standard of proof, limitation provisions and the law of liability itself are unchanged. It is possible in a class action to award damages either individually or as a global sum. For this reason the class action has most often been used where a large number of people have suffered a comparatively small loss in the same manner. Examples would include overcharging by statutory authorities or utility companies, environmental pollution or other nuisance and the like.

14.18 In the Federal Rule the essential elements are:

(1) the class is so numerous that joinder of all members is impracticable;
(2) there are questions of law or fact common to the class;
(3) the claims or defences of the representative parties are typical of the claims or defences of the class; and
(4) the representative parties will fairly and adequately protect the interest of the class.

14.19 If these primary conditions are satisfied, one of the following additional criteria must also be satisfied:

(1) the prosecution of separate actions would create a risk (a) of inconsistent adjudications which would establish incompatible standards of conduct for the party opposing the class, or (b) of adjudications with respect to individual members of the class which could as a practical matter dispose of the interest of the other members who were not party to adjudications or might substantially impair their ability to protect their interests; or
(2) the party opposing the class has acted or refused to act on grounds generally applicable to the class, thereby making appropriate final injunctive relief or corresponding declaratory relief with respect to the class as a whole; or
(3) the court finds that the questions of law or fact common to the members of the class predominate over any questions affecting only individual members and that the class action is superior to other available methods for the fair and efficient adjudication of the controversy.

14.20 The rule provides as soon as possible after the action is commenced that the court must order whether it should proceed as a class action. If so, the court shall direct that the members of the class be given the best notice practicable under the circumstances giving each member the option to opt out of the action.

14.21 The court may divide the class into sub-classes and may make conditions and procedural directions for the conduct of the action. The class action may not be dismissed or settled without the approval of the court and notice of the proposed dismissal or settlement must be given to all class members in accordance with the court's direction.

14.22 A further problem was a decision of the Supreme Court in 1978 in *Coopers & Lybrand v Livesay*[1] to the effect that no interlocutory appeal against certification decisions was possible. This would have prevented any class of plaintiffs who were the victims of a wayward certification decision from being allowed to proceed with their action.

1 437 US 463 (1978).

14.23 There are proposals to reverse this decision by allowing appeals against such interlocutory decisions but this in turn raises the question whether only the plaintiff is to have the right of appeal. If so there is an argument that the defendant can then be said to be denied equal rights under the law but, if the defendant also has the right of appeal, there is the prospect of serious delay as a spoiling tactic.

14.24 The US procedure requires no preliminary examination of the merits of the case at the certification stage but only of the existence of common questions rather than the merits of those questions. On the other hand, the United States rule 23 requires that common questions of law and fact predominate over questions affecting only individual members. This test, however, encourages minute dissection of what exactly is common between individual members of the class and is again a weapon for delay in the defendants' armoury. There have over the last few years been constant calls, mostly from the side of industry, for reform of the procedures. At the time of writing, however, there have been no official proposals for reform.

CANADA

14.25 We have seen that Ontario has a representative action similar to the English form and interprets it more liberally to include claims for damages.

14.26 In 1982 the Ontario Law Reform Commission recommended the introduction of procedure similar to that of rule 23 in the US Federal Rules of Civil procedure. It was proposed that notice in each class action had to be given to the Attorney General who would have the right to intervene in any matter of public interest and also to act in appropriate cases as representative plaintiff.

14.27 The report proposed a three-stage procedure involving judicial certification of a class action, which was followed by proceedings to resolve the issues common to the class and, where the plaintiffs were successful, by proceedings to determine individual issues, principally in relation to damages.

14.28 The Commission recommended a first certification test on the preliminary merits. Only those class actions brought in good faith with a reasonable *possibility* that material questions of fact and law common to the class would be resolved at trial in favour of the class would be certified. The mere fact that the action as pleaded discloses a reasonable cause of action would not be sufficient to satisfy this test.

14.29 Two further conditions recommended were that the class on whose behalf the action was to be brought should be numerous and that the class action should raise questions of fact or law common to members of the class. 'Common questions' is a considerably less stringent test than the 'same interest' test applied in the representative action in both Ontario and England and Wales. It was not thought to be necessary that the class be so large as to make joinder impracticable or that questions common to the class should predominate over issues affecting individual members of the class (both of which conditions were imposed by rule 23 of the US procedure).

14.30 In order that the interests of absent members of the class should be adequately protected it was recommended that an action should be allowed to be maintained in class form only if the court were satisfied that the representative plaintiff would fairly and adequately protect the interests of the whole class. This would include consideration of the question whether competent legal representation was available for the protection of the interests of the whole class and the power in the court to substitute another class member as representative plaintiff.

14.31 Additional criteria would ensure that class actions are employed only where the court is satisfied that a class action is superior to other available methods for the fair and efficient resolution of the underlying controversy. In making this determination the court would be required to consider amongst others the following factors, none of which by itself would necessarily be conclusive: whether the questions of fact or law common to the members of the class predominate over any questions affecting only individual class members; whether a significant number of members of the class have a valid interest in individually controlling the prosecution of separate actions; whether the class action would involve claims that are or have been subject to any other proceedings; whether other means of resolving the claims are less practicable or less efficient; and whether the administration of the class would create greater difficulties than those likely to be experienced if relief was sought by other means.

14.32 The court would be entitled to refuse to certify a class action, despite its satisfying all the other tests for certification, if the court was satisfied that the adverse effects of the proceedings upon the class, the courts or the public would outweigh its benefits.

14.33 It was recommended that a particular judge would preside over all pre-trial motions and interlocutory proceedings until trial and another judge would then preside over the trial of the common questions and would also be responsible for supervising any subsequent proceedings. The trial judge should have a broad discretion to fashion proceedings for the resolution of individual issues and a duty to order the simplest, least expensive, and most expeditious method of determining these issues consistent with fairness to the class members, the defendants and the representative plaintiff.

14.34 The Report proposed that the costs of the successful plaintiff should not normally be recoverable from the defendants but that a contingent fee in the case of a successful plaintiff should be fixed by the court and should be a first charge on the damages recovered by the class.

14.35 Quebec since 1979 has had a procedure for class actions.

14.36 The class action is defined as a procedure which enables one member to sue without a mandate on behalf of all the members. The court is entitled to sanction a class action if it is of the opinion that:

(a) the *resources* of the members of the class raise identical, similar or related questions of law and fact;
(b) the facts alleged seem to justify the conclusions sought;
(c) the composition of the group makes various other, otherwise relevant rules of procedure, inapplicable; and
(d) the prospective class representative can adequately represent the interest of the class members.

14.37 Initially interlocutory appeals were available to both parties as of right but in 1982 the right of the defendant to appeal (as opposed to the defendant's right to apply for leave to appeal) was removed for fear of the overuse or abuse of interlocutory appeals which it was felt could diminish the efficacy of the procedure.

14.38 Condition (c) has been interpreted by the Supreme Court of Canada to mean that there must be prima facie substance to the case advanced by the plaintiffs but that a firm determination of the merits should not take place at this early interlocutory stage. Even this test apparently provokes determined efforts by defendants to have the class action dismissed at the certification stage.

14.39 The 'commonality' criterion is comparatively liberal, there being no necessity to show a predominance of common facts over individual facts.

14.40 It is, however, the custom of defendants to interrogate the plaintiffs at the preliminary hearing stage on matters of detail concerning characteristics which are said to be or should be common to class members and even those who are yet to be identified. Some have proposed that it should be for the plaintiff only to make a prima facie case of similar facts and that the defendant should not be entitled at the preliminary hearing stage to attempt to undermine the plaintiff's case. The protagonists of class actions argue that experience shows that consumers do not utilise private remedies sufficiently frequently to give corporate defendants any incentive for compliance with consumer protection legislation and further that 'little injustices' are important to those who suffer them. If in practice the law does not provide a remedy, confidence in the law may be diminished.

AUSTRALIA

14.41 At the time of writing Australia provides an extremely interesting example of the development of proposals of both aspects – procedure and funding – in a common law jurisdiction with close links to the English system.

14.42 The Federal Court of Australia Amendment Act 1992 will entitle a person to bring proceedings on behalf of a group of persons where the claims of those persons arise out of the same, similar or related circumstances and a common question of law or fact arises with respect to all of their claims. The stated intention is to provide a real remedy where, although many are affected, the individual loss of any is so small as not to be economically viable and thus to open up access to courts. The other object is to deal efficiently with cases where, whilst each claim might be viable by itself, the weight of numbers requires an efficient and streamlined procedure for saving time and costs.

14.43 The minimum number of claimants is seven for each defendant. The Act provides that a person who has a sufficient interest to commence a proceeding on his or her own behalf has a sufficient interest to commence a representative proceeding against the same defendant on behalf of others who have a similar claim against the same defendant, to continue that proceeding on their behalf and to appeal any judgment in the proceedings even if the representative plaintiff ceases to have a claim against the defendant.

14.44 Interestingly, the procedure adopted is an 'opt-out' so that the consent of any individual member is not required. Persons under disability do not need a next friend to be a group member. The application beginning a representative proceeding must describe or identify the group members to whom the proceeding relates and specify the nature of the claims made on behalf of the group members and of the relief claimed and specify the questions of law or fact under the claims of all. It is not necessary to identify or list individual group members.

14.45 The court must then fix an opt-out date before which any group member may opt out of the proceedings. The date may be extended and the case cannot be heard until after the opt-out date. A defendant can obtain an Order disqualifying the representative proceeding, if it can convince the court that the cost of identifying group members and distributing damages to them would be excessive in relation to the total amount of the damages at stake. The court can also disqualify representative proceedings, if satisfied that the costs to be incurred would exceed the costs which would have been incurred, if each group member had conducted the proceedings separately, or if the relief sought could be obtained by other means, or if the representative proceedings would not provide an efficient and effective means of dealing with the claims of other members, or if it is otherwise inappropriate.

14.46 The court has power to establish sub-groups of group members and to appoint a sub-group representative party where there are issues common to some but not all the group members. The court has power to allow an individual group member to appear in the proceedings for the purpose of determining an issue which relates only to the claims of that member.

14.47 The court may, on the application of a group member, substitute another group member as a representative party if convinced that the existing representative party is not able adequately to represent the interest of the group members. The same applies in relation to sub-group representative parties. A representative proceeding cannot be settled or discontinued without the approval of the court and the court, in giving its approval, may make orders in respect of the distribution of any money paid under a settlement or paid into court. This is a vital safeguard against a defendant undermining a group action by offers of payment to individuals or against conflicts arising within the plaintiff cohort where some, but not others, wish to settle an action. For the first reason, a representative party needs leave of the court to settle his or her individual claim.

14.48 There are wide provisions for notice to be given to group members of significant events in the representative proceedings including requirements that notice be given by means of press, radio or television announcement. Personal notice is only required when it is reasonably practicable and not unduly expensive.

14.49 The court has power to determine an issue of law or fact and to make a declaration of liability and to make an award of damages for group members, sub-group members or individual group members. The court also has power to award damages in an aggregate amount without specifying amounts ordered in respect of individual group members but must make provision for the payment or distribution of the money to the group members entitled. An aggregate award can only be made when a reasonably accurate assessment of the total amount to which group members will be entitled is possible.

14.50 On the commencement of a representative proceeding the running of any limitation period against a group member is suspended until the member opts out or the proceeding is determined without finally disposing of his or her claim.

14.51 The major difference between this solution and the cost-sharing informal solutions seen in recent English cases is that the representative party is, as against the other party, solely responsible for costs. It had been thought that this simply reflected the common law position but a judgment of the Victoria Supreme Court[1] to the effect that all represented persons bore a responsibility for the costs of the defendant and the representative plaintiff led to amendment of the Federal Court of Australia Act 1976 at the end of 1992 to restore liability for costs to the representative plaintiff alone. It may be, of course, that the representative party will make arrangements within the group to share liability for costs of both sides although it might be thought preferable for this to be made explicit in the Act. The court has power to award a representative plaintiff out of the damages recovered any shortfall of the costs recovered from the defendant as against those reasonably incurred in fighting the representative proceedings.

1 *R N Burns Philp & Co Ltd v Bhagal* (31 January 1992).

14.52 The other major event in Australia is the passing of the Trade Practices Amendment Act 1992 which reforms the law on product liability. It is based on the 1985 EC Product Liability Directive incorporating a development risk defence on the narrow Directive wording. The original proposal was that there should be liability if a consumer proved loss or damage caused by a product and that loss or damage suffered did not result solely from the product being used unreasonably. As a result of lobbying by the manufacturing and insurance industries, the test will be whether a defect in a product has caused injury or loss. A product is defective if it is not as safe as persons are generally entitled to expect, following very closely the EC definition of defect. The initial proposal itself represented a compromise which watered down the recommendation of the Australian Law Reform Commission that there should be liability on proof of causation only.

14.53 A defendant is obliged to compensate another person for loss caused to the first person, provided the relationship between the two people is not a business relationship. The defendant is also liable for damage to property, provided the goods are of a kind ordinarily acquired for personal, domestic or household use. There is no liability for damage to the product itself.

ISSUES ARISING IN MULTIPLE CLAIMS

Negligence

14.54 Before the implementation of the Consumer Protection Act 1987 on 1 April 1988 it was necessary in a product liability action to prove negligence. In medical negligence actions it is of course still necessary.

14.55 If the alleged act or acts of negligence all occurred at the same time, then they could be tested fully in one plaintiff's action even where there were hundreds or thousands of plaintiffs. In a product liability action however, and for our purposes an action for damage caused by pharmaceutical products is the best example, it is inconceivable that all potential plaintiffs would have consumed the pill at the same moment. It is equally obvious, moreover, that the corpus of knowledge of the manufacturer relating to his potential negligence in putting or keeping the product on the market must have increased over time and thus different issues arise for different plaintiffs.

14.56 Further, the risk/benefit doctrine must have effect on different plaintiffs in different ways. To take again an example from the pharmaceutical field, it might be negligent to promote a product with known side effects to a patient with a mild condition but for the same promotion not to be the least negligent to a plaintiff with the same condition to a life-threatening degree. Again in the pharmaceutical field, the genetic and environmental differences between the plaintiffs are almost certain to render the question of negligence as well as causation at large in every individual case.

14.57 After 1 April 1988 in product liability actions the question will turn from negligence to whether the product in question was defective, that is 'less safe than persons generally are entitled to expect'. This is very far from absolute liability and may not even amount to strict liability for damage caused by a product.

Causation

14.58 If 400 individuals are killed in a plane crash, it is reasonable to assume that causation is identical in every case. The issue of causation can therefore be decided once and for all by a representative plaintiff, as indeed could the question whether the conduct of the carrier had been reckless so as to deprive the carrier of limitation of damages conferred upon it by Convention.

14.59 The same identity of causation might be available for the victims of, for example, Legionnaires Disease acknowledged to emanate from the same source: likewise an epidemic poisoning traceable to a single source or a consignment of exploding children's toys causing injury to all children receiving them.

14.60 The fact, however, that no pharmaceutical or other product causes a unique adverse medical condition means that causation is likely to be a live issue in every individual case so that the search can be made for other potential causes and evidence can be given by experts in basic research, animal research and epidemiology and, indeed, clinical medicine as to the likelihood that the product in question has been the cause of the damage suffered. This is likely to be an even more live issue than before following the speech of Lord Bridge in *Wilsher v Essex Area Health Authority*[1] where he held that, contrary to the impression to be gained from the earlier House of Lords case of *McGhee v National Coal Board*,[2] it is first necessary to prove on the balance of probabilities that a plaintiff's damage had been caused by a particular cause before going on to give the defendant the opportunity to rebut causation for reasons particular to the plaintiff.

1 [1988] AC 1074, [1988] 1 All ER 871, HL.
2 [1972] 3 All ER 1008, [1973] 1 WLR 1, HL.

14.61 All pharmaceutical products which have been alleged to cause serious side effects are alleged to cause a number of different side effects. Whilst Thalidomide is best known as a potent cause of phocomelia, it also causes very many other injuries.

14.62 Not only will there be the necessity of calling evidence in respect of each, the issues of alternative potential causes and, indeed, negligence in the administration of the product in relation to each potential injury are likely to be very different.

14.63 It is important to bear in mind that proof of causation is not in itself enough to found liability. In the *HIV haemophilia* litigation, for example, the causative agent of infection was clear. The question remained, however, whether the provision of the product or the prescription of it by a treating doctor *at the time the infection was caused* was negligent. Many suffering from haemophilia had been treated almost daily over a period of ten years. It was often impossible to say for certain when the infection had occurred. A later supply of the product may well have been negligent, earlier supply may well not.

14.64 In failure to warn cases defendants are becoming much more astute to put the plaintiff to strict proof of the difference which the warning would have made. This is equally true in conventional medical negligence litigation (risks of treatment) and product liability litigation (whether the doctor, let alone the patient would have chosen any differently if the data sheet had been as the plaintiff says it should have been). In the latter case there may be difficulties in calling first hand evidence as well as difficulties of credibility. In a Canadian case[1] the court decided that generic evidence of the effect of a different warning on a reasonable practitioner might be given. In a recent judgment in the Benzodiazepine litigation Ian Kennedy J decided that, whilst such evidence might not be inadmissible in strict terms, it was of far less weight than evidence addressed directly to the circumstances of the case.

1 *Buchan v Ortho Pharmaceuticals (Canada) Ltd* (1984) 8 DLR (4th) 373, affd 25 DLR (4th) 658 (1986).

Limitation

14.65 It is clear from the words of the Limitation Acts and the decided cases upon them that limitation is an individual and subjective issue. It is equally clear that it is sensible and desirable that, in a case involving many plaintiffs, all those plaintiffs should be placed procedurally into one basket.

14.66 This immediately creates a tension: there has to be a trade-off between the convenience of dealing with all cases together and the dangers of depriving a plaintiff who arrives once the basket lid is closed of the means of pursuing his rights which for individual reasons still subsist.

14.67 In a recent trial of a limitation issue, in a sample of cases in the group of *Opren* cases who were not party to the first group proceedings, Hidden J held that there were no special limitation rules or considerations for group cases and each plaintiff's limitation case should be dealt with on its merits.[1]

1 *Nash v Eli Lilly & Co* [1991] 2 Med LR 169.

14.68 After this decision, a further group of cases thought to satisfy his criteria were tried on limitation and failed. Both decisions of Hidden J were appealed and judgment was given in the Court of Appeal.[1] This is the first judgment on limitation issues in multi-party proceedings and therefore of considerable interest.

1 [1993] 1 WLR 782.

14.69 The points which emerged were:

(a) there is no true antithesis between knowledge and belief;
(b) for the purpose of section 14 of the Limitation Act 1980 a plaintiff must have actual knowledge: the only relevant constructive knowledge is that which the plaintiff should reasonably have acquired with or without the help of medical or other appropriate experts;
(c) the limitation period begins to run when the plaintiff first has knowledge of the nature of his injury justifying him taking preliminary steps for the institution of proceedings against the person who has caused the injury;
(d) if the plaintiff has belief which requires confirmation from experts, that belief will not turn into knowledge until confirmation from the expert is obtained;

(e) in a pharmaceutical case the act or omission for the purpose of section 14(1)(b) can best be expressed as 'providing for the use of patients a drug which was unsafe in that it was capable of causing the damage complained of in those patients and/or failing to discover that such was the case so as properly to protect such patients'. No further specificity is required;
(f) on the question of constructive knowledge, the burden of proof is on the defendant. The defendant must establish that the plaintiff should have consulted a solicitor and that the solicitor would have had the necessary knowledge.

14.70 The Court of Appeal went on to consider the question of discretion under section 33 of the Limitation Act 1980:

(a) the cogency of a plaintiff's case is a matter for the trial judge, not for the judge trying a limitation issue;
(b) the judge trying a limitation issue may take into account the inherent weakness (by way of lack of evidence) in a plaintiff's case;
(c) there is no public policy requiring a different approach to the exercise of discretion in group actions: a change may be desirable but this must be achieved by legislation;
(d) the fact that a defendant has already settled a group of cases in relation to the same cause of action is not a reason for refusing to exercise discretion on a limitation issue.

14.71 It is also interesting to consider the relationship between a cut-off date imposed by a judge in control of a multiparty case and the formal Limitation Act position. It is becoming commonplace for a cut-off date to be imposed and it is obviously sensible that this should be so. From the plaintiffs' point of view, there is a reasonable prospect of getting on with the case without waiting for anyone who has ever bought a product or swallowed a pill to come forward. Further, the plaintiffs know how many of them there are to share the costs risk so that they (and indeed the Legal Aid Board) may make a judgment about the cost-benefit ratio which the action will support. From the defendant's point of view, there is some finality of numbers, examination of medical records and pleadings should throw up suitable cases to be tried as lead cases and they can consider their position on the likely damages if they fail as against the likely cost of a settlement.

14.72 In the *Benzodiazepine* litigation, Ian Kennedy J set a cut-off date by reference to application for Legal Aid for those who wished to apply for it and service of proceedings for those who did not. Despite the overwhelming weight of numbers (apparently 18,000 applied for Legal Aid) only a very short extension to the cut-off date was allowed and further attempts to extend it were rejected. Further, he refused to extend the cut-off date in respect of those complaining of the effects of Halcion whose product licence had been withdrawn by the licensing authority very shortly before that date. The decision was upheld by the Court of Appeal mainly on the ground that a judge assigned to a group action of this nature should be allowed to exercise his discretion freely in the light of his intimate knowledge of the case and on the ground that the availability of Legal Aid was not a factor to determine time limits.[1]

1 *AB v John Wyeth and Brother Ltd* (1992) 12 BMLR 50, CA.

14.73 Balcombe LJ said:

The Halcion claimants' complaint was that a group of 40 was unlikely to be large enough to select suitable lead cases and hence to persuade the Legal Aid Board to grant financial support to their actions. In addition they spoke for the 563 claimants who had not applied for legal aid before the cut-off date of 24 September imposed by Mr Justice Ian Kennedy and whose subsequent applications had been refused.

Multiple claims arising out of some drug alleged to be defective or from some disaster, have become a well established feature of litigation in this and other countries in recent decades. The Rules of the Supreme Court made no specific provision for group litigation but a procedure had gradually evolved and in May 1991 the Supreme Court Procedure Committee produced a most helpful Guide for Use in Group Actions.

Experience showed and the Guide recommended that each substantial group of actions should be assigned to one judge who would supervise the interlocutory conduct of the proceedings as well as hear the trial. When it became apparent that there was a large number of claims arising from the use of Benzodiazepine drugs, on 20 June 1990, Mr Justice Ian Kennedy was appointed as the judge to whom any actions were to be assigned.

At an early stage Mr Justice Ian Kennedy imposed cut-off dates to determine who should be eligible to join in the group litigation. On 28 June 1991 he ordered that for claimants in respect of Benzodiazepine drugs to be eligible to participate in the group litigation they must have made an application for legal aid, if so desired and they must have served a Writ and Statement of Claim, or in the county court, a summons and Particulars of Claim before 15 April, subsequently extended to 31 August 1992.

Those cut-off dates were given wide publicity and no complaint at the time was made about the imposition of the cut-off dates. By their amended notice of appeal the Halcion claimants asked that a new cut-off date be imposed.

There was a fatal flaw in the claimants' arguments for they had confused what the judge had done with its effect both in relation to legal aid and in relation to subsequent steps of proceedings by any late-comers.

What Mr Justice Ian Kennedy did was to decide that the Halcion claimants who had not made their applications for legal aid by the cut-off date should not be entitled to join the existing group litigation. He did not, indeed he could not, say that they would forever be precluded from presenting their claims.

There was no substance in the matters on which the claimants relied as justification for their failure to make their claims earlier, as to which his Lordship made no opinion. Those were matters which could be put to the Legal Aid Board.

There was no basis upon which the Court of Appeal could interfere with the proper exercise of discretion by Mr Justice Ian Kennedy. As the Guide made clear, group litigation would become impossible if it was open-ended. Late additions of additional Halcion claimants would place intolerable delays and burdens not only upon defendants but also on the 500 existing Ativan and Valium plaintiffs.

14.74 Steyn LJ added:

The Court of Appeal ought to be particularly reluctant in group actions to interfere with a trial judge's procedural directions. The judge had a much better perspective of the interests of all the parties and of the needs of efficient case management than the Court of Appeal could ever achieve. Interference by the Court of Appeal with the trial judge's directions on one aspect would often upset the coherence of the entire structure of the litigation.

Pleadings

14.75 In litigation with 1,000 plaintiffs, it is formally necessary to serve 1,000 individual pleadings common as to general matters, unique as to individual matters. This must involve a colossal waste of time, physical resources and costs. At present, however, there is no formal alterative to be found in the Rules to circumvent this.

Discovery

14.76 The same applies: to take again the example of claims in respect of a pharmaceutical product, the issues are bound to be separate both on the risk/benefit question and the nature of the individual damage in every case and consequently it is formally necessary for all parties (and here the burden falls disproportionately upon the defendants) to make discovery individually in each case. In such cases the defendants have disclosed anything from 30,000 to 1.2 million pages from which the enormity and impracticability of the exercise may be clear.

14.77 The defendants may wish to consider whether discovery should be given in relation to every issue on the generic pleadings or whether they are entitled to be convinced that the allegations made in the Main Statement of Claim are in fact relevant to at least one individual plaintiff.

Expert evidence

14.78 Exactly the same applies. Without an informal and sensible solution, the plaintiffs' experts would have to come to testify in 1,000 trials and before that write 1,000 expert reports and 1,000 supplementary reports, once having seen the evidence of the defendants' experts. Whatever may be the availability of expertise to the defendants (and it is for obvious reasons likely to be greater than that available to the plaintiffs), those experts who are prepared to assist plaintiffs fit their assistance into an already overcrowded curriculum of teaching, research and clinical commitments.

Payment into court

14.79 At present a defendant faced with 100 or 1,000 claims may wish to protect the position by paying a reasonable sum into court in satisfaction of the claim of a plaintiff who appears most likely to succeed or most vocal in his or her criticism of the defendant's conduct. Plaintiffs' advisers must advise such a plaintiff in that plaintiff's individual interest rather than in the interest of the group of plaintiffs together.[1]

1 *Davies v Eli Lilly & Co* [1987] 1 WLR 1136.

14.80 At present there is nothing to stop a defendant undermining the strength of the cohort of the plaintiffs in a very effective manner by means of strategic payments into court in carefully chosen actions. In the *Myodil* litigation an application was made by the plaintiffs to obtain a Direction from Steyn J (as he then was) requiring leave of the court for any settlement or the acceptance of any payment in. Objection was taken to this proposed Direction by the manufacturer defendants on the ground that it would preclude a global offer of settlement and the judge held that he had no power to fetter offer and acceptance on a normal contractual basis between any plaintiff and the manufacturer defendant.

14.81 In a representative action, the representative plaintiff is the sole plaintiff and in charge of the suit until judgment. He or she can discontinue or settle proceedings or agree to their dismissal without the consent of those represented.

14.82 Bankruptcy of the representative plaintiff will put an end to the action. It should be added, however, that if the representative plaintiff should fall out of the action for any reason, the court has power to add or substitute any person represented (although unnamed) in the representative action and to make this change effective as from the date of the original writ so as to prevent Limitation Act difficulties.

Settlement

14.83 If a defendant announces the will to settle all cases on an individual basis, great is the rejoicing all round. Recently, a two-fold variation on this theme, far more painful to the plaintiff cohort, has been observed.

14.84 Firstly, the defendants may say that they will settle claims on an individual basis but only if all plaintiffs agree to settlement. If all plaintiffs agree, rejoicing is still the order of the day. If not, resentment is bound to intrude and those hitherto advising the plaintiffs as a group on general issues are faced with a potential conflict between the interests of those of their clients who wish to settle and those who do not.

14.85 The second recent practice is to offer all the plaintiffs in the basket a global sum of damages to be shared between them or, alternatively, individual sums of damages capped at a global total. If the global sum is sufficient properly to compensate all plaintiffs, no problem and no conflict will arise. If not, problems and conflicts may well arise since in litigation with large numbers of plaintiffs it is not always possible to quantify each plaintiff's claim with the sophistication which would be possible if there were only one or two plaintiffs to be considered. These problems are exacerbated when the number of the plaintiffs together makes their comparatively modest claims for damages collectively worthwhile.

14.86 The Law Commission has announced a review of the law of damages in its new programme. Amongst items for consideration will be whether it is appropriate for global awards of damages to be made in group actions and how a court should arrange for division of such damages between the plaintiffs.

Trial and after

14.87 The trial with 1,000 plaintiffs with individual causes of action would certainly be unmanageable. If at the limited trial issues are resolved in the plaintiffs' favour, the expectation is that all other plaintiffs whose actions raise the same issues will be compensated by agreement by trials on quantum only or by a form of arbitration or enquiry as to damages.

14.88 If all issues at trial are resolved in the defendant's favour, it is unlikely that they will be troubled with any further plaintiff's claim.

14.89 The outcome is likely, given the traditional reluctance of the court to decide hypothetical issues and the likelihood that the complexity and variation within the plaintiff cohort may lead to one or more plaintiffs slipping through the net, to be somewhere in between. The less the uncertainty, the easier it will be resolved.

Practical solutions to date

14.90 The large-scale industrial diseases litigation has been a conspicuous success. Tens of thousands of workers exposed to the risk of contracting, and then contracting pneumoconiosis, asbestosis, mesothelioma, industrial deafness, or industrial white finger are now compensated as a matter of routine following successful litigation undertaken in specimen cases by lawyers instructed by the relevant trades unions. In those cases causation was identical apart from potential confounding factors and negligence varied only with the date and amount of exposure. The purse strings were held by the trades unions who were able to dictate how many and which cases should proceed at any one time.

14.91 In product liability cases, and particularly in the pharmaceutical field, the picture has been much less clear.

14.92 In the *Thalidomide* cases causation was never an issue. The action was fought on the question of negligence. It was obvious from early on that a settlement was there to be achieved and the questions for discussion were the discount for the risks of litigation and the proper approach to quantum. The whole matter was resolved with very little recourse to the court and the problems mentioned above.

14.93 In the *Eraldin* case ICI pre-empted the issue of proceedings by announcing a voluntary settlement for which they obtained a great deal of credit. It was only necessary to prove causation (and this was relatively straightforward, there being a highly typical and otherwise unusual constellation of side effects).

14.94 The *Primodos* litigation with two legally aided lead plaintiffs was discontinued in 1982 because of the perceived problem of proving causation of damage.

14.95 The litigation in relation to Debendox, another drug used in pregnancy, is still continuing and has at the time of publication not reached the stage where the issues raised above have been decided.

14.96 The catalyst for the examination of these issues, and particularly the manner in which multiple actions are to be funded, was the *Opren* litigation which began in 1983 after the withdrawal of the anti-arthritic drug Opren manufactured by Eli Lilly.

14.97 After unsuccessful proceedings to obtain forum in the United States the English litigations began in earnest in 1985. In 1986 the assigned judge Hirst J made a series of Master Directions in an attempt to avoid the duplication and waste in relation to pleadings, discovery and ultimately trial mentioned above. Thus, a Master Statement of Claim and a Master Defence from each of the defendants was served for the benefit of actions within the Co-ordinated Arrangements, entry to which was determined by the issue and service of a writ and service of a Schedule of Claim by a certain date. All interlocutory proceedings took place in the name of a particular token plaintiff and it was intended that after the general discovery given for the benefit of all actions in the Co-ordinated Arrangements, issues would be identified for decision at trial and individual plaintiffs' actions chosen to illustrate all those issues in practice were to be nominated as lead actions to be tried together with a view to giving answers to all the live questions outstanding between the parties.

14.98 The strength of these arrangements was the saving of time and costs. The weakness was that they were voluntary and it was assumed on both sides, but particularly by the defendants that, since the arrangements were voluntary, additions or amendments to them could only be made within the court's discretion, if the parties agreed to their being made. Although the precise extent of the jurisdiction outside the formalities of the White Book was never decided, the risk of a successful challenge to this procedure was no doubt an inhibiting factor on the ability of the parties to fashion the litigation in the most effective manner.

14.99 At this point the question of costs, to which we have so far very little referred, became an issue. As mentioned above, in the past actions have either been financed by trades unions or the Legal Aid Fund has accepted that one or two legally aided plaintiffs should proceed in the forefront on behalf of all other plaintiffs. The defendants acquiesced in this (examples are the *Thalidomide* and *Primodos* litigation) and the Law Society took no point upon it.

14.100 In the spring of 1987 the government defendants in the *Opren* litigation issued a summons asking how the costs incurred by the plaintiffs and any costs ordered to be borne by the plaintiffs should be paid.

14.101 The problems arose in two ways. Firstly, in respect of interlocutory issues (for disclosure of evidence, for more specific allegations etc) of which there were several, many being argued before the judge for days rather than hours, it was necessary to issue the summons in a particular name. On the face of it, therefore, the individual plaintiff named in that action was personally liable for any costs awarded to successful defendants notwithstanding the fact that the summons had been issued for the benefit of the plaintiff group as a whole. Similarly, since that plaintiff was in receipt of a Legal Aid Certificate, any of those costs which were not recoverable from the defendants (for example if the judge made no order for costs) would be deducted from any compensation that that plaintiff might receive at the end of the case.

14.102 Clearly, the large amount of costs incurred or at least put at risk on each application would, on a strict interpretation of the legal aid regulations, have raised progressively the amount which that particular plaintiff would have to recover by way of damages before he would actually see a penny of those damages after the deduction of those costs which were secured upon the damages by the statutory charge. Further, immense costs were being built up going through the discovery process examining more than a million documents disclosed by the defendants. If only part of those costs were recoverable, the rest would on the face of it be sufficient to extinguish the damages expected to be recovered on one individual plaintiff's behalf many times over. It has been estimated that the costs of the *Opren* litigation exceeded the amounts which the claimants received.

14.103 The second way in which the problem manifested itself was in relation to the necessity of selecting lead actions to determine the key issues in the trial. Issues which required decisions on behalf of the whole group of plaintiffs and the defendants were raised by reference to some 20 lead actions. This was necessary because of the variety of side effects and the time at which the drug manufacturers should have been aware of any particular risk. It was decided that the most appropriate means of selecting these cases was by making sure that all the lead plaintiffs were in receipt of Legal Aid Certificates so that their own costs would be met out of the Legal Aid Fund if they were unsuccessful, and so that it would not be possible for the trial judge to order the costs of successful defendants to be paid by those plaintiffs.

14.104 The defendants argued that that would be an unfair result since approximately one third of the total of 1,500 plaintiffs were not legally aided. They said it would be wrong in principle for the plaintiffs in all the lead actions to be legally aided. The effect would be to give 500 private plaintiffs a free ride on the backs of those who had legal aid. Their argument was supported by section 7(6)(b) of the Legal Aid Act 1974 (now section 31 of the Legal Aid Act 1988) which provides that: 'the rights conferred by this part of the Act on a person receiving legal aid shall not affect the rights or liabilities of other parties to the proceedings or the principles on which the discretion of any court . . . is normally exercised'. The fact that none of the 500 private plaintiffs would be able to afford to finance such a complex case could not affect the application of this section.

14.105 The relevance of this to the defendants was that the costs of a successful defendant are not awarded against a legally aided plaintiff, and therefore the court would be unable to award the defendants their costs irrespective of the merits of the matter.

14.106 The judge, Hirst J, decided that the only proper order was that any costs to be borne by the plaintiffs should be borne or paid by them equally. He acknowledged that this would create somewhat rough justice since a perfectly possible scenario was that a large amount of costs would be expended on an issue which might only affect 100 out of 1,500 plaintiffs (ie if 100 claimants alleged the drug had affected them in a particular way) but was sufficiently important to need decision in a lead action. If the court later decided that the drug had not caused that particular symptom, then those of the remaining 1,400 claimants who received compensation for their injuries would be obliged to bear some of the costs of an issue that could not have benefited them.

14.107 The *Opren* claimants appealed. The judgment of the Master of the Rolls[1] forcibly expressed the problems and the need for some review. We set out extracts from his judgment:

Very naturally no individual plaintiff wanted to undertake the burden, including the costs, of a lead action. So unfair would this burden be, that consideration was given to how, within the powers and procedures of the court, the costs of the lead actions could be taken off the shoulders of the plaintiffs in whose names they were being brought.

In this way, it was thought, the whole cost of the lead actions, which might well be a very significant part of the cost of the whole proceedings, could be transferred to the broad shoulders of the state in the shape of the legal aid fund. Such an approach has very considerable merit, at least from the point of view of the plaintiffs, and I do not criticise those who have espoused it. Unfortunately it betrays a woeful misunderstanding of how the legal aid scheme works. This is a point of general importance and the basis of the scheme deserves to be better known.

Put simply, but for present purposes wholly accurately, legal aid helps those who lose cases, not those who win them. Legal aid makes 'out and out' grants to those who lose cases. It only makes loans to those who win them.

But suppose the plaintiff wins, as the legal aid fund claims that he does more often than not. Then a very different picture emerges. As the successful party, he does not have to pay the defendant's costs and usually the defendant will be ordered to pay his. Let him not celebrate too soon. He may find that the defendant has no money or the legal aid fund may have to incur further expense in making the defendant pay. Furthermore, and this is very important, the defendant will, at best, only be ordered to pay the plaintiff's 'taxed costs' and this is almost always less than the costs which have been incurred by the plaintiff in prosecuting his case to a successful conclusion. So there will always be a shortfall which may be very large if the defendant cannot meet the order for costs or if the plaintiff failed on some subsidiary issue and has been ordered to pay the defendants' costs in fighting that issue.

'Why worry?' says the successful plaintiff to himself, 'I have my damages, I have paid my contribution to the legal aid fund and that fund has met all the costs which I have incurred.' Unfortunately for the temporarily happy plaintiff, Parliament has required the defendant to pay the damages not to him but to the legal aid fund. That fund is required to use his damages to pay itself back every penny of costs which it has incurred in assisting him to fight his case. It is only if, after this has been done, that anything which is left will be paid to him. It may be that nothing will be left or it may only be relatively small change. In other words, for the successful plaintiff the legal aid fund provides a loan, not a grant, at least to the extent that his damages are sufficient to repay the loan. Put slightly differently, every legally aided plaintiff should realise that if he succeeds in recovering more by the way of damages, costs and interest than it has cost to recover them – if the money actually paid by the defendant in respect of damages, costs and interest exceeds his own costs, which after all is what he expected – he will be in no better position than an unassisted litigant.

1 [1987] 1 WLR 1136 at 1139/1140.

14.108 The decision of the Court of Appeal in favour of the costs sharing order had provoked the inevitable response that all but a tiny handful of the 500 non-legally aided plaintiffs in the *Opren* case were on the point of discontinuing their actions. Then an offer was received from a millionaire Mr Godfrey Bradman to underwrite the costs of their claims. No doubt partly due to his intervention, encouragement from the judge and the prospect of interminable and vastly expensive litigation, the parties came to terms and all but a handful of the 1,500 plaintiffs accepted a scheme of settlement in February 1988.

14.109 Since then there have been new hitherto unsuccessful attempts to run new group actions.[1] There has also been the *HIV haemophilia* litigation where causation of damage could not have been more apparent and, unusually for a product liability action, the question at issue was the proper test in relation to breach of duty to be applied to a government department allocating scarce resources.

1 Including the *Benzodiazepine* litigation.

14.110 It has long been proposed by textbook writers that the appropriate test may be that of *Wednesbury* unreasonableness but obiter dicta in a Privy Council case *Rowling v Takaro Properties Ltd*[1] suggest that not even this may be enough. This litigation was settled in early 1991 probably due to political pressure. The problem endures, however, for example in relation to transmission of the hepatitis C virus through blood transfusions in the period after the hepatitis C virus had been identified.

1 [1988] AC 473, [1988] 1 All ER 163.

14.111 The Legal Aid Board has withdrawn support for claims in relation to all but the Halcion part of the *Benzodiazepine* litigation principally because of perceived difficulties in relation to proof of causation of damage in the individual case. Ian Kennedy J has taken upon himself the role of arbiter of the financial viability of the litigation, thus urging upon those representing individual plaintiffs the need more rigorously to examine the strength of an individual claim at the earliest possible moment and possibly presaging the future constriction of Legal Aid availability. There is also litigation in respect of the oil-based contrast medium, Myodil, fixed for trial in October 1994 where the principal issues may well be the risk-benefit ratio of the product in relation to a therapeutic need and available alternatives and individual causation. This is the first group action where the date for the generic trial has been put back because of the delay in slipping individual plaintiffs through a very complex individual causation gate. Claims which have been advanced in relation to lack of warning of hypoglycaemia allegedly induced by transfer from animal to human insulin for insulin-dependent diabetics have also run aground for once on the basis of no generally convincing grounds for proof of negligence. There persist claims in relation to other pharmaceutical products used in psychiatry, geriatrics, urinary incontinence and child growth development, albeit in much smaller numbers.

14.112 The question of the nature of the duty of care owed by the Department of Health, the Medicines Act Licensing Authority and the Committee on Safety of Medicines to members of the public has not been resolved. The health authorities, for example, in the *HIV haemophilia* and the *Myodil* litigation, grouped together and instructed legal advisers to co-ordinate the generic aspects of the defence to claim against all the different authorities. In the former case it was alleged that the authorities had duties in relation to research, obtaining of better medicinal products, promotion of different sources of supply etc. Although the point was never tried to judgment, the better view must be that the duty of the health authorities is substantially that of affording treatment which is not *Bolam* negligent. In the latter case, again for *Bolam* reasons, no argument could sensibly be advanced that doctors or health authorities were negligent in using an accepted product, particularly in the absence of any preferable alternative.

OFFICIAL PROPOSALS FOR THE FUTURE

14.113 It now appears inevitable that in future multi-plaintiff litigation a similar cost sharing order will be made. The effect of this is likely to be that few who do not qualify for legal aid will ever take on the risk inherent in participation in a multiple action unless they are very rich indeed or the number of claimants sharing the generic costs is large enough to make the financial exposure of the individual very small indeed. Since the latest estimates conclude that approximately 50 per cent of the adult population is out of financial scope for legal aid this may be thought to be a serious social problem.

The user's guide for multi-party actions

14.114 This is a summary aimed at lawyers with little experience of this type of litigation giving essentially practical advice about the law and procedure as it stands. It expressly disclaims any intention to make new law or even new practice but aims simply to point to the procedural devices available under the Rules of the Supreme Court and to informal sources of assistance. The Guide discusses with practical pleading examples the concepts of joinder and the procedure of the representative action contrasted with the joining of several plaintiffs in one Writ under Order 15. It is heavily in favour of the latter on a case where liability is likely to be similar for all plaintiffs e g the transport accident.

14.115 The Guide identifies the procedure in RSC Order 4 to allow other actions to be stayed so that a lead case may proceed and points to the possibility of the other parties binding themselves to accept the judgment of the lead case on the facts.

14.116 The Guide sets out for the inexperienced the existence of the Law Society's co-ordinating function, the customary form of cost-sharing Order and the availability of assigned judges to take control of the procedure and timing of a multi-party case with early and far-reaching orders for Directions and a fixed date for trial. It further sets out the necessity for defences to be particular (Order 14 rule 12), the availability of split trials under Order 33 rule 3 and Order 33 rule 4 and for liability to be decided before damages in personal injury cases. Discovery under Order 24 can be limited under rule 2(5) to that necessary for disposing of the action or for saving costs. Attention is also drawn, perhaps unnecessarily, to the availability of exchange of witness statements of fact.

14.117 Interestingly, there is a suggestion that experts should be shared. This presumably owes something to the fact that the judge who was a member of the Working Party which produced the Guide was an Official Referee. That is also presumably the reason for the call for a computer database for clients and documents with only core bundles of documents in court. It is certainly desirable to restrict the documents of crucial importance to liability and to expert testimony as far as possible and to an agreed bundle but, in a product liability action, this may well be a core bundle of very considerable volume. The call to share experts may be more appropriate to the building contract field where there are many experts all of a discipline involving less controversy and all in private practice. In pharmaceutical product liability actions, on the other hand, there are relatively few experts and most of those are in academic life often with a personal stake in the interpretation of results of basic research and in many cases with defendants sponsoring research in those academic institutions in which they work. In building contract litigation, there is almost certainly less area for dispute on qualitative matters than in product liability litigation. Whilst the Guide has achieved its limited aim of setting out what exists, the question of what ought to be is left wholly unexplored by it.

The Legal Aid Board arrangements for multi-party actions

14.118 The report on the above by the Board to the Lord Chancellor's Department was published in September 1991 with a view to Regulations being made under the Legal Aid Act 1988 to take effect in April 1992. The timetable was kept and Regulations and Multi-Party Arrangements have been in force since 1 April 1992. The catalyst for these proposals was the acceptance that cost-sharing orders to provide generic costs have no foundation under the Legal Aid Regulations. The Legal Aid Board has dealt with the position informally by dividing all generic costs incurred in a particular litigation between all certificates granted for it. However, there have been various ways of interpreting and implementing this situation and, where a steering committee exists, costs have been debited to certificates of individuals who have no relationship of their own with any firms on a steering committee. Further, liability for costs inter partes can only bite on those who have issued and served proceedings whereas liability as between plaintiffs can be and is regularly apportioned by the Board between all those currently in receipt of a Legal Aid Certificate.

14.119 The Board states its object as that of building upon and formalising the de facto arrangements already in existence and making special arrangements for generic work. The statutory basis for the proposals is in sections 4(2)(a) and 15(6) of the Legal Aid Act 1988 which permits the Board to enter into a contractual arrangement with one or more firms. The Board in its proposals reserves the right to implement or not to implement (in its discretion) particular arrangements confined in the first instance to those in personal injury litigation involving many claimants. Ten certificates will be necessary to trigger the arrangements but even then the Board retains a discretion not to invoke the special procedure.

14.120 The firm or firms involved in those first ten certificates and outstanding applications will be invited to submit proposals for co-ordinating the litigation and progressing it. It is intended that groups of those involved should get together to make a proposal to the Board. There are complex proposals for the Board to frank or refuse the proposals, having visited the firm and taken stock of the resources offered for the conduct of the litigation. If none of those firms involved who have offered to co-ordinate the litigation are acceptable, the Board will invite offers from other firms. The successful firm or firms will be obliged to make six-monthly reports on the legal and financial and the management aspects of the litigation to the Board and three monthly (at least) reports to the other firms not co-ordinating the litigation and to their clients. The reports to the Board will have to include estimates of cost and of the prospects of success and a cost-benefit analysis. Given the colossal uncertainties in relation to the first two, the third seems a remarkably tall order on anything but a trite level.

14.121 The Board will retain the power to terminate the arrangements and to substitute new solicitors, if need be. Individual clients will have a general choice of solicitors who can only act on the non-generic aspects of the claim. In localised cases, the choice of solicitor may be restricted. Lead firms will be obliged to comply with a general policy. Each certificate will contain a confidentiality waiver clause so that information may be disseminated widely by the co-ordinating firms to the lead firms. There will be an express or implied authority by clients to the generic solicitors to act in accordance with the claimants' instructions. The Board has set up a new Multi-Party Actions Committee with outside representatives on it.

14.122 There are provisions for the lead firms to receive regular payments under the contract at 75 per cent of a reasonable charge for the generic work carried out. The contracts will not specify fixed hourly rates because these are thought to be incompatible with the taxation process. The Board will publish the arrangements it has made in any individual case. It anticipates that the general rule in any multi-party action will be equal sharing of costs in the first instance. The normal rules for the statutory first charge in favour of the Board will remain in multi-party litigation. Forum advice will not be subject to remuneration under the contract. The general putting in touch of prospective litigants with solicitors is deemed by the Board to be part of normal office overheads on the part of the lead firms although it may exercise its grant-making powers in exceptional cases.

14.123 The report of the Board and subsequent Regulations and Arrangements comes in the middle of a wide ranging eligibility review by the Lord Chancellor's Department on legal aid generally. It has apparently been conceded that eligibility for multi-plaintiff actions needs to be considered separately and separate Regulations made. It is a matter for debate whether a person not normally qualifying for legal aid is in a worse position suing a multi-national pharamaceutical company, but having the benefit of a cost-sharing Order, compared with the position of an individual with the same means suing an individual health authority in a medical negligence action on his or her own behalf only.

14.124 The Arrangements set out the procedure in case of conflict. It distinguishes cases where the conflict relates to the subject matter of the litigation itself in which case the conflict is capable of resolution by the establishment of different sub groups of litigants. If, however, the conflict relates to the conduct of the action, the Board recommends that it is possible for those dissatisfied with the conduct of the lead firms to ask for their certificates to be amended. The request for amendment will be decided on normal principles but taking into account the special arrangements and their purpose. In questions relating to settlement of the actions the Board is against a compulsory valuation machinery being introduced. However, if claimants are not willing to have their claims valued, that is a matter which the lead firms should report to the Board with a view either to the operation of the 'show cause why the certificate should not be discharged' procedure or to amendment of certificates to give special provision to these litigants.

14.125 The Board reserves the power to terminate the contractual arrangements if the lead firms have broken their obligations in a way likely to cause substantial prejudice to the claimants or to the Board. The Arrangements contain a list of reasons for termination of the contract. These reasons include poor quality work, excessive claims for payment on account, material alteration to the team undertaking the work and complaints or loss of confidence by claimants. The list is worth reading in full. Termination only applies to generic work. The Board is concerned that a lead firm should not be permitted to withdraw from the contract by reason of marginal profitability and believe that the safeguards built into the selection procedure will make this a rare occurrence. The report ends by recording the Board's view that it is desirable a review of the procedures by which multi-party action cases are handled in the High Court should take place. The Board thus adds its weight to the wide-ranging call for formalisation of the procedural rules of court governing these actions. If has often been rumoured that such reforming rules might be made or that the Law Commission might be asked to report but there is as yet no sign of this.

14.126 The advantages of these Regulations will accrue to both sides. It will give the advisers to the claimants who undertake generic work the authority to progress the case as quickly as possible towards trial or settlement and will define the relationship between all the claimants and all lawyers involved on their behalf. From the defendants' point of view the risk of having to deal with groups of claimants and their advisers with different tactics or, indeed, goals will be vastly diminished and the defendants will have a focus for their attempts to evaluate the risks of the litigation and the total damages involved, if they are unsuccessful. This will allow them to take an earlier and more informed decision on settlement. Since the Regulations and Arrangements came into effect no contracts have in fact been awarded. There was an attempt, by way of trial run, to enter into a contract in the human insulin case but this failed on liability grounds before the contract could be concluded. To those involved, the tendering requirements appeared onerous in the extreme. In other multiple cases the Legal Aid Board did not to wish to grant contracts. The accidental result of this may have been that elected Steering Committees incurred generic costs greater than would have been incurred by a smaller number of firms acting under a contract.

Law Commission's review of the law of damages

14.127 In June 1991 the Law Commission introduced its Fifth Programme of Law Reform including as a major topic the remedy of damages. The Law Commission is to give specific consideration to the use of structured settlements, deduction and set-offs against monetary loss, awards to cover medical and nursing expenses, bereavement damages, the principle relevant to awards of punitive or exemplary damages and, for our purpose, the effectiveness of the present remedy of damages in multi-party litigation, examining in particular whether awards of damages should be assessed for the class as a whole and the means for determining their application between individual parties. The Commission referred to the suggestion that new powers are needed by courts in multi-party litigation to make global awards of damages.

14.128 The advantage of the 'global award' system or any court power to invoke it are only two:

(a) it may encourage settlement; and
(b) money will be available sooner rather than later.

A power given to a court to impose such a solution would at least resolve the presently almost untenable position in which plaintiffs' advisers find themselves when confronted with a global offer by the defendants.

14.129 In pharmaceutical-type cases, the plaintiffs are likely to be pulled different ways. In these cases where liability is usually far from straightforward, the need to obtain expert evidence and the weight of documentary evidence may result in a delay of at least five years between damage and trial. Causation is proverbially difficult: certain types of injury may be reasonably capable of proof while in respect of other types it may be hopeless. Questions of breach of duty differ within the plaintiff cohort with those earliest exposed to the product least likely to establish breach of duty and vice versa.

14.130 Thus, the pressure for settlement to avoid the difficulties of the litigation will be strong. The defendants, considerations of adverse publicity apart, will wish to achieve a settlement which brings the whole litigation to an end and avoids subsequent proceedings by a few plaintiffs which would involve them, the defendants, in the same effort as would have been involved in fighting the whole plaintiff cohort. The defendants will know that the costs of both sides in fighting the case including the management and professional time required within the defendant corporation will be astronomical and irrecoverable. They will also wish to cap their liability for costs as at the date of settlement rather than incur the costs of a serial evaluation of all individual cases. They will wish to pass the responsibility for this to the plaintiffs' advisers who will in turn then bear the brunt of accusations of inequality.

14.131 The present problem in practice is that settlements of this nature can only be arrived at consensually. Whilst the court may be relieved to give an informal blessing to the arrangements, it has no power (absent minor plaintiffs) to enforce it. It is thus entirely the responsibility of the lawyers acting for both sides. But how are the plaintiffs' lawyers to resolve the conflicts between their various clients? In a pharmaceutical case, the age of the plaintiff, the indication for which the product was prescribed, the pre-existing health of the plaintiff, the date of prescription and the nature of damage sustained, will all affect the prospects of success and in different ways. Prognosis may be uncertain and, the greater the number of plaintiffs, the less likely it is that quantum can be worked up (since it is no priority in a lead case system) in advance of a global offer. The plaintiffs' advisers can only produce an educated gut response to any such offer.

14.132 Whilst many, if not most plaintiffs will be relieved at settlement on any reasonable terms approved by leading counsel and the court, there is certainly a number of plaintiffs likely to be disaffected by the outcome. What powers of coercion should be exercised upon them particularly if the advice to settle is necessarily based on an incomplete analysis? What if the court is to be involved? Ex hypothesi the court cannot make a full finding on the prospects of success (liability) or causation of damage without a full trial. Such a trial would remove the advantages of saving of time and costs. Without it, the system will be no better than the informal blessing referred to above.

14.133 If this obstacle could be overcome, how would the court approach division of the global award between plaintiffs? Presumably, the same would apply: it would either embark upon a lengthy and expensive examination of a large sample of individual cases to produce some form of 'points system' indication or it would simply endorse such a system produced by the lawyers thus raising the same problem in relation to division of the award as those raised in relation to the size of the award. Ironically, the only beneficiaries of such an investigation would be the plaintiffs' lawyers who would have the authority of a judgment of the court to deflect criticism of them and they would probably stand to gain by extended work on the settlement at the defendant's expense.

14.134 It is unlikely that those advising defendants would allow their clients to be pitched into a system out of which would come a mandatory global award without any indication in advance what that award would be. If, however, the matter had to go to a trial for a rational award to be made, there would be little saving in time or expense. The advantage of the present lead case system is that it should be possible after a lead trial to identify winners and losers amongst the plaintiff cohort and then to settle the winners' claims on a conventional basis without further recourse to the court. Making a global award would not in itself help unless it could identify the winners and the losers or give very precise weighting factors to be applied in relation to the variables (age etc) mentioned above.

14.135 Without such a weighting system, the same unquantifiable cross-subsidies as at present would continue producing the same conflicts between plaintiffs represented by the same lawyers along the way.

14.136 In a further innovation in respect of funding the Courts and Legal Services Act 1990 enabled the Lord Chancellor to make regulations to permit speculative funding of litigation in certain cases. It is widely believed that the first type of cases where this will be permitted will be personal injury litigation. A plaintiff's solicitor will be at liberty to make an arrangement that, in the event of no recovery by the plaintiff, there will be no fee charged by the solicitor. If there is a recovery, the plaintiff's solicitors will still be able to recover costs from the unsuccessful party in the normal way but will be allowed to charge the plaintiff an additional sum being a proportion of the costs recovered from the defendant which the plaintiff will have to pay out of his or her own pocket. The rationale is to reward the lawyer for taking the risk. Whilst this may become a common occurrence in, for example transport accidents, it is hard to see that any plaintiff's solicitor in England would have the financial resources to take on a large product liability action which was not entirely straightforward on such a basis since the delay and risk relating to recovery would be prohibitive. If the case is, on the other hand, entirely straightforward, why should the plaintiff's solicitor have a bonus at all? The question remains academic because Regulations to authorise and set levels for speculative funding have not yet been made.

OUR OWN PROPOSALS

14.137 At the beginning of 1989 the National Consumer Council published a report entitled 'Group Actions – Learning from *Opren*' which suggested by way of reform a new Rule for Group Actions and a new Regulation for Legal Aid for Group Actions to support it. The report deals in detail with the procedure available in different jurisdictions and with alternative approaches to the procedural choices available in the conduct of multi-plaintiff actions.

14.138 Despite the massive progress in the area of legal aid regulations, there is still no formal basis in the Rules of the Supreme Court for the administration of group actions. Steyn J (as he then was) said in the *Myodil* litigation:

> At present English law does not permit a class action in the sense in which that expression is used in the United States. Admittedly, our law does recognise, by virtue of Order 15, rule 12, the notion of a representative action, the objective of which is one binding judgment on common questions instead of a multiplicity of separate determinations. That procedure is no doubt capable of development but its present limitations are such that it cannot be used where damages have to be separately assessed in respect of different cases. It seems that representative actions for damages are not permitted. In England the parties must use the ordinary procedures, devised for the trial of single actions, to cope with the exigencies of group litigation. Moreover, there is in England nothing like the Manual for Complex Litigation, 1985, which gives guidance to practitioners in the United States as to the procedures to be adopted in multi-party litigation. In the *Myodil* litigation practitioners, and the courts, will have the benefit of the experience gained in recent examples of group litigation, and notably of the procedures devised by Mr Justice Hirst in the *Opren* litigation. If the courts did not have the power to devise entirely new procedures to deal with such cases the system would break down entirely. That is no doubt why the Master of the Rolls recently emphasised in *Horrocks v Ford Motor Co Ltd*[1] that in such cases the courts are entitled to devise new procedures adapted to the circumstances of the particular group litigation. Subject to the need to bear in mind the essential protections of the adversarial system, I must proceed on the basis

that our courts have a broad and flexible power to adopt new procedures which will promote the ends of justice.

This is not a satisfactory state of affairs. Our system of civil justice ought, for the benefit of parties involved in group litigation, to prescribe at least in outline the procedures to be adopted. The nineties may well witness an increase in group litigation. It is to be hoped, therefore, that this problem will be investigated and addressed.

Possibly, a gradualist approach is the best way forward in this complex area; instead of promoting very complex primary or subordinate legislation a short Guide to Group Litigation, backed by a Practice Direction issued by the Lord Chief Justice, could be published. The aim of such a guide would not be to produce a procedural straitjacket but to set out in outline the alternative procedures which are available, and the range of the court's powers. Prima facie, and subject to further argument, I have in mind that in the *Myodil* litigation the procedures to be adopted will involve, amongst others, directions along the following lines:

(a) as to the simplification of pleadings with reference to a master statement of claim and defence;
(b) as to the restriction of the discovery process pending the determination of common questions;
(c) the selection from the category of duly constituted actions of suitable lead cases for the trial of common issues in the group litigation; and
(d) a stay of all other proceedings until the determination of those lead cases.

Of course, on all these matters, interested parties who have issued writs will be entitled to be heard.[2]

1 (1990) Times, 15 February, CA.
2 *Chrzanowska v Glaxo Laboratories Ltd* (1990) Times, 16 March.

14.139 Moreover, where a case involves complex multi-party litigation, the 'sporting theory of justice' has no place but on the contrary, the concept of a party being in control of the litigation ought, as far as possible to be subordinated to case management techniques controlled by the court.[1]

1 *Chapman v Chief Constable of South Yorkshire* (1990) 134 Sol Jo 726.

14.140 The draft legal aid regulation propounds the view that in such actions legal aid should be available to all, but in order to restrict the impact of the conventional contribution rules suggests an upper limit of £1,000 (with power to revise this) by way of contribution payable for the grant of a certificate. Such a figure is arbitrary: some plaintiffs will think it too high, many defendants too low. Our view is that it may be a suitably pitched figure to ensure that no citizen is for financial reasons denied his or her right to ask a judge to decide whether the complaints he or she wishes to make justify a claim for damages. The draft legal aid regulation is of interest now simply in comparison with the result of the forthcoming eligibility review whilst the draft rule of court may serve as a reminder of the still unfulfilled need for reform. It may be a matter for amusement that this liberal approach has been overtaken by initiatives by the Lord Chancellor which will certainly very seriously detract from the position of the existing plaintiff.

Draft amended rule for group claims

14.141

1 This Rule shall apply to proceedings in which the following conditions are satisfied:

(a) the matter or thing giving rise to the cause of action has given or will give rise to a similar cause of action in numerous other proceedings issued or to be issued by other plaintiffs or potential plaintiffs, as the case may be; and
(b) the number of such plaintiffs or potential plaintiffs is so great as to make joinder of all such proceedings impracticable *or* that proceeding under this Rule would lead to a substantial saving of time or costs; and
(c) the claims of all such plaintiffs or potential plaintiffs can fairly be represented by one or more such plaintiff (save as to individual questions of loss or damage); and
(d) the interests and administration of justice are served by proceeding under this Rule.

2 Any party to any proceedings may apply by summons to a Judge of the Queen's Bench Division for a declaration whether or not the conditions set out in paragraph 1 above apply.

3 If on the hearing of a summons under paragraph 2 above the Judge shall consider that the conditions set out in paragraph 1 above are fulfilled, he shall so certify and shall give directions.

4 The Directions referred to in paragraph 3 above shall include but not be limited to the following:

(a) definition of the extent of, parties to, subject matter of and issues in the actions to which the certificate is intended to apply (hereinafter referred to as 'the certified actions');
(b) notice by the Central Office of the High Court to all parties to all the certified actions of the fact of the certificate and the definitions comprised in sub-paragraph (a) hereof, and the manner of such further notice to other persons as may be desirable;
(c) that all proceedings within sub-paragraph (a) hereof issued before or after the giving of such certificate shall, subject to an application by any party in any such proceedings for an Order to the contrary, be subject to the provisions of this Rule and setting out, subject to the provisions of the Limitation Acts, a date or dates before which all proceedings falling with the definition referred to in sub-paragraph (a) hereof should be issued;
(d) identifying an action or actions in which all interlocutory applications in respect of the certified actions shall be made and directing that the costs of such applications be reserved until the conclusion of the trial of the certified actions, unless the interests of justice require otherwise;
(e) for service of pleadings, particulars thereof and for discovery;
(f) for providing for the sharing of costs of and incurred in the certified actions;
(g) appointing solicitors to act for the plaintiffs within the certified actions and defining the responsibilities of those solicitors.

5 Application shall be made by any plaintiff in an action falling within the provisions of sub-paragraph (d) of paragraph 4 of this Rule within 84 days of compliance with the directions set out in paragraph 4 of this Rule for further directions which shall include but not be limited to the following:

(a) definition by Schedule of all actions falling within the terms of the certificate in paragraph 3 of this Rule;
(b) definition of the issues arising between the parties of the certified actions;
(c) identification of individual actions in which the issues referred to in sub-paragraph (b) of this paragraph shall be tried for the benefit of the certified actions;
(d) directions as to the exchange and giving of expert and other oral evidence and the use of documentary evidence at trial;

(e) giving a timetable for preparation for and conduct of the trial;
(f) providing as between the plaintiffs in the certified action for the costs of the trial.

6 A judgment or order given in proceedings to which this Rule applies shall subject to paragraph 8 of this Rule be binding on all parties to the certified actions.

7 After determination of the issues defined by the Judge under sub-paragraph 5(b) of this Rule the Judge shall give such directions as are necessary for the disposal of questions of individual loss or damage in the certified actions.

8 If a party to an action falling within the terms of a certificate given under paragraph 3 of this Rule considers that that action should not properly be dealt with under the provisions of this Rule he shall make application by Summons to a Judge of the High Court for an Order that that action shall not be subject to the provisions of this Rule and it shall be for him to show:

(a) that by reason of the particular facts or matters of the case his action does not properly fall within the definition given under sub-paragraph 4(a) of this Rule *or*
(b) that the inclusion of his action in the certified actions would result in an injustice to himself or to any party within the certified actions.

9 No party to any certified action may withdraw, discontinue or compromise the action or any part thereof without having first obtained leave from a Judge of the High Court, upon notice of the application to the solicitors appointed under sub-paragraph 4(g).

Draft legal aid regulation

Explanatory note

14.142 This regulation deals only with the financial provisions that should apply to grants of legal aid in group actions – it does not alter the application of any other part of the legal aid scheme (eg the merits test in individual cases).

The regulation provides that in an action certified by a High Court Judge under the proposed Order 15, rule 12 no applicant will be refused legal aid on income or capital grounds. Further the maximum contribution that any applicant can be required to make towards the cost of the case is £1,000, such sum being variable by regulation. As regards the statutory charge this will be limited to £1,000 and any contributions made shall be discounted from the amount of any statutory charge due. However the charge will be spread amongst all assisted persons.

The justification for such special treatment for group actions is twofold. Firstly, it is only in such actions that a costs sharing order will be made and therefore a successful plaintiff will be at risk of meeting some of the legal costs of an unsuccessful fellow plaintiff. Secondly, public funds can be better expended if not saved (as regards court time and legal aid moneys) by encouraging group actions.

In the proposed Order 15, rule 12 there is a provision designed to fetter a defendant's discretion to buy off the leading claims, by requiring leave of the court for any settlement or compromise and by giving the solicitors representing the group as a whole the right to be heard. A further provision in the rule bites on the costs of the case – we propose that the costs of all interlocutory matters should generally be reserved to the trial judge and that they should follow the event except where any such costs were incurred unreasonably.

(1) this Regulation shall apply in any case in which either:

(a) the Board has entered into a contract with a firm or firms of solicitors pursuant to Part IV of the Legal Aid Act 1988, or

(b) a Judge of the High Court has given a Certificate under the provisions of Order 15, rule 12 of the Rules of the Supreme Court.

(2) In respect of any person involved as a plaintiff in an action in relation to which paragraph 1 of this Regulation applies, the Board shall:

(a) grant a certificate:

 (i) to a person who would otherwise be ineligible for Legal Aid on the ground of his income alone or on the grounds of his income and his capital on payment by that person of a sum of £1,000 or such sum as the Lord Chancellor may from time to time by regulation substitute therefor;
 (ii) to a person who would otherwise be ineligible for Legal Aid on the ground of his capital alone on payment by that person by way of contribution of the sum of £1,000 or such sum as the Lord Chancellor may from time to time by regulation substitute therefor; *and*

(b) not enforce any charge under section 16(6) of the Legal Aid Act 1988 save up to the sum of £1,000 and any contribution made under a(i) or (ii) above shall be discounted from any statutory charge payable; and
(c) in considering whether it is reasonable to grant a certificate to any applicant to disregard the fact that the damages recoverable by that applicant would not justify the prosecution of proceedings, if the amount of damages recoverable by other plaintiffs in similar actions together is likely to be such as to justify the taking of all those proceedings.

BIBLIOGRAPHICAL REFERENCE

Report of the National Consumer Council 'Group Actions – Learning from *Opren*' (1989).

CROSS-REFERENCES

For information related to topics in this chapter see Chapters 18 and 20.

CHAPTER 15

Filing suit in the United States

James S Reece

SUMMARY

INTRODUCTION

15.1 Larger damage awards and other procedural and substantive advantages have interested lawyers representing injured persons who live in other countries to consider filing suit in the United States. Success in keeping these cases in the United States will depend on the doctrine of *forum non conveniens*.

15.2 *Forum non conveniens* is a common law doctrine recognised in both the United States and England[1] that allows a court in its discretion to decline jurisdiction and dismiss a case on the ground that the case can be tried more conveniently in an alternative forum. It is an exception to the requirement that a court hear an action where jurisdiction is properly laid.[2] In 1821, Chief Justice Marshall of the United States Supreme Court stated in a dictum that the judiciary has 'no more right to decline the exercise of jurisdiction which is given, than to usurp that which is not given' (*Cohens v Virginia*).[3] However, as personal jurisdiction expanded (see *International Shoe Co v Washington*,[4] and its progeny), courts began to recognise the utility of a discretionary doctrine to decline jurisdiction. Currently in both England and the United States there has been increasing dependence on the courts' discretion to decline jurisdiction as the 'chief weapon against transnational forum shopping', because the rules determining the existence of jurisdiction are liberal in both countries.[5]

1 David Robertson, 'Forum Non Conveniens in America and England: "a Rather Fantastic Fiction"', 103 LQ Rev 398, 426 n 197 (1987) (citing Fawcett, 'Forum Shopping: Some Questions Answered', 35 NILQ 141, 147 (1984)).
2 See *Canada Malting Co v Paterson Steamships Ltd*, 285 US 413, 423 (1932); see also Note, 'Considerations of Choice of Law in the Doctrine of Forum Non Conveniens', 74 Cal L Rev 565, 567 (1986).
3 19 US (6 Wheat) 264, 404 (1821).
4 326 US 310 (1945).
5 Robertson, at 398–399; see also Note, at 567. The English courts and the courts of other countries have been said to have a more accommodating attitude towards forum shoppers than the United States. See Friedrich K Juenger, 'Forum Shopping, Domestic And International' 63 Tul L Rev 553, 564–574 (1989).

15.3 The forum in which a case is tried can have a significant effect on its outcome.[1] For example, there are a number of features of American law which might benefit an international plaintiff. The compensation paid to medical malpractice claimants in the United States has been reported to have exceeded $1.5 billion in 1985,[2] while the annual rate of growth in total compensation paid from 1979 to 1985 averaged 25.0 per cent. Per claim, medical malpractice compensation paid by insurers averaged $50,289 in 1985,[3] up 35 per cent from 1982.[4]

1 David W Robertson and Paula K Speck, 'Access to State Courts in Transnational Personal Injury Cases: Forum Non Conveniens and Antisuit Injunctions', 68 Tex L Rev 937 (1990); Laurel Miller, 'Forum Non Conveniens and State Control of Foreign Plaintiff Access to US Courts in International Tort Actions', 58 U Chi L Rev 1369 (1991); Robertson (see para **15.2**), at 413.
2 See James S Kakalik, Nicholas M Pace, 'Costs of Compensation Paid in Tort Litigation' at 30 (Rand, 1986); see also P S Atiyah, 'Tort Law and the Alternatives: Some Anglo-American Comparisons', Duke LJ 1002, 1014–1015 n 58 (1987) (citing study performed by The Institute for Civil Justice, as published in 'General Liability and Medical Malpractice Insurance Marketing', Best's Rev, Sept 1985 at 108.)
3 Kakalik and Pace, at 142.
4 Ibid.

15.4 American law also provides plaintiffs with the availability of contingent fee representation; extensive discovery; more favourable substantive law in certain areas; relatively prompt trial settings; the possibility of class actions; liberal joinder rules; and the minimal likelihood of having to pay the other party's expenses, including attorney fees, in the event of a loss.[1]

1 See Note, 'The Southern District Reexamines the Doctrine of Forum Non Conveniens', 54 Brook L Rev 379 (1988); Juenger (see para **15.2**), at 560–562.

15.5 Because forum can affect liability and damage outcomes dramatically, a plaintiff can expect a forum battle in significant cases. The factual and legal preparation necessary to present persuasive forum evidence and arguments makes the typical forum battle a costly and time-consuming process.[1] Thus, it is advisable thoroughly to assess the potential chances of winning the *forum non conveniens* issue, before initiating suit in the United States.

1 Robertson (see para **15.2**), at 413–414 (citing, e g *McClelland Engineers Inc v Munusamy* 784 F 2d 1313 (5th Circ 1986) wherein suit was filed in October of 1981 and *forum non conveniens* proceedings continued into March of 1986).

FORUM NON CONVENIENS IN FEDERAL COURTS – THE ANALYTICAL FRAMEWORK

15.6 As applied to international plaintiffs in the federal courts, the *forum non conveniens* doctrine becomes an issue when defendants seek an alternative forum in a foreign country.[1]

1 See Miller (para **15.3**).

15.7 Jurisdictional questions are generally resolved first, but *forum non conveniens* issues are also considered in the early stages of litigation so that the parties do not waste resources on discovery and trial preparation in a forum that will later decline to exercise its jurisdiction over the case.[1] The basic analytical framework for considering a motion for dismissal based upon *forum non conveniens* is derived from *Gulf Oil Corpn v Gilbert*,[2] as refined by *Piper Aircraft Co v Reyno*.[3] The only party who can utilise the doctrine is the defendant, who also has the burden of proof with regard to it.[4] If the court finds the defendant has failed to meet his burden of proof, appeal is not available until final judgment is rendered in the case.[5]

1 *Lony v E I du Pont de Nemours & Co*, 935 F 2d 604 (3d Circ 1991).
2 330 US 501, 508–509 (1947).
3 454 US 235, 257 (1981).
4 See, e g *Reid-Walen v Hansen*, 933 F 2d 1390, 1393 (8th Circ, 1991) (citing *Lacey v Cessna Aircraft Co*, 862 F 2d 38, 43–44 (3d Circ, 1988)).
3 *Van Cauwenberghe v Biard*, 486 US 517 (1988).

15.8 A party moving to dismiss on grounds of *forum non conveniens* must show: (1) the existence of an adequate alternative forum and (2) that the balance of private and public interest factors favours dismissal.[1]

1 *Gulf Oil* (see para **15.7**), at 507–508.

15.9 The 'private interest factors' are those affecting the litigants themselves and include: the relative ease of access to sources of proof;[1] the availability of compulsory process for attendance of unwilling witnesses; the cost of obtaining attendance of willing witnesses; and all other practical concerns that lead to an easy, expeditious and inexpensive trial of the case.[2]

1 *Van Cauwenberghe* (see para **15.7**), at 517.
2 *Gulf Oil* (see para **15.7**), at 508.

15.10 The 'public interest factors' affect the court and the community and include: the benefit of having cases affecting a particular forum adjudicated in that forum; the avoidance of choice of law issues; the benefit of having a court familiar with the substantive law adjudicate the suit; and docket congestion and the burden of jury duty on a community that has no relation to the lawsuit.[1]

1 *Gulf Oil* (see para **15.7**), at 508–509.

15.11 The private interest factors are generally considered before the public interest factors,[1] but the Supreme Court has not indicated the amount of weight to be given to any given factor in either category. The inquiry with regard to the private interest factors is whether the defendant has established 'oppressiveness and vexation to a defendant . . . out of all proportion to a plaintiff's convenience'.[2] If the private interest factors are at or near 'equipoise', it is inappropriate for a court to grant a defendant's *forum non conveniens* motion unless the public interest factors weigh in favour of dismissal.[3] *Gulf Oil* provides that the overall balance should be 'strongly in favour of the defendant' before a court grants a *forum non conveniens* motion.[4]

1 See *Piper* (para **15.7**), at 257; see also *Baris v Sulpicio Lines Inc* 932 F 2d 1540, 1551 (5th Circ, 1991); cert denied 112 S Ct 430 (1991).
2 *Piper* (para **15.7**), at 241.
3 See, e g *Lony v E I du Pont de Nemours & Co* 886 F 2d 628, 635 (3d Circ, 1989); *American Cyanamid Co v Picaso-Anstalt* 741 F Supp 1150, 1156–1157 (DNJ 1990).
4 *Gulf Oil* (para **15.7**), at 508.

15.12 A *forum non conveniens* determination is left to the 'structured discretion' of the trial judge. The analytical framework set out in *Gulf Oil* provides the structure.[1] And at least one court has held that the failure to follow that framework constituted reversible error.[2] In applying the *Gulf Oil* test a court must not merely describe the underlying facts of a case as they relate to the *Gulf Oil* factors, it must actually balance the factors to determine which forum is the most appropriate. Failing to balance the factors properly is an abuse of discretion.[3]

1 See *Cliffs-Neddrill v M/T Rich Duke*, 734 F Supp 142, 145 (D Del; 1990) ('the Supreme Court's decision in *Gulf Oil Corpn v Gilbert* 330 US 501 (1947) provides the analytical framework for all *forum non conveniens* analyses') (citing *Lacey* (para **15.7**), at 42).
2 See, e g *Baris* (para **15.11**), at 1552.
3 *Reid-Walen* (para **15.7**), at 1393.

Adequacy of alternative forum

15.13 The 'alternative forum' requirement is a threshold requirement.[1] The Supreme Court has stated that the requirement usually will be satisfied when the defendant is 'amenable to process' in the other jurisdiction.[2] However, most federal courts have expanded the defendant's burden of proof, requiring him to show in addition that the alternative forum is 'adequate'.[3]

1 See *Gulf Oil* (para **15.7**), at 506–507.
2 *Piper* (see para **15.7**) indicated that amenability to process will not be sufficient in 'rare circumstances' where 'the remedy offered by the other forum is clearly unsatisfactory' (at 254–255 n 22, citing *Gulf Oil* see para **15.7** at 506–507). Under the facts in *Piper*, the District Court found an alternative forum existed in Scotland since the defendants agreed to submit to jurisdiction there and to waive any statute of limitations defences (ibid at 242). Most courts have followed *Piper's* lead in this regard. See, e g *Re Union Carbide Corpn Gas Plant Disaster at Bhopal, India* 634 F Supp 842, 866–867 (SDNY, 1986); affd in part, modified in part 809 F 2d 195 (2d Circ, 1987), cert denied, 484 US 871 (1987) (defendant was amenable to process in India because it had unequivocally accepted the jurisdiction of the Indian courts).
3 See, e g *Reid-Walen* (para **15.7**), at 1393 n 2 (determining whether an alternative forum exists is 'a two part inquiry' focusing on 'availability and adequacy'). *Kontoulas v A H Robins Co Inc* 745 F 2d 312 (4th Circ, 1984) (domestic defendants lost motion for dismissal based on doctrine of *forum non conveniens* in products liability action against inventor and manufacturer of intra-uterine device. Defendants failed to show that Maryland was not the best forum or that a different forum was more appropriate).

15.14 As a general matter, 'adequacy' means that the parties not only are amenable to process in that forum, but also that some form of 'justice' will be available in the foreign courtroom.[1] The most typical factors analysed in making the 'adequacy' determination are: whether the plaintiff's cause of action will exist in the alternative forum; whether the plaintiff will be able to enforce a judgment there; and whether there are procedural bars to suit in the alternative forum, such as a statute of limitations.[2] The burden is on the defendant, as it is with all other aspects of the *forum non conveniens* analysis, to show that the alternative forum is adequate.[3]

1 *Reid-Walen* (see para **15.7**), at 1393 ('an alternative forum is adequate when the parties will not be deprived of all remedies or treated unfairly.')
2 See, eg *Weltover Inc v Republic of Argentina* 753 F Supp 1201, 1209 (SDNY, 1991).
3 Cf *Lony* (para **15.11**), at 633.

15.15 Differences in substantive law between the US forum and the alternative forum will bear on adequacy. However, *Piper* discouraged an extended substantive analysis of the adequacy of the law of the alternative forum,[1] and narrowed the bases for dismissal on that ground.[2] Some courts, interpreting *Piper* strictly, have dismissed without performing an in-depth analysis of the relief available in the alternative forum[3] or even when the law in the alternative forum is much less favourable to the plaintiff.[4] Other courts have been more willing to consider and weigh an unfavourable change in the scope and extent of recovery for a plaintiff in the alternative forum.[5]

1 *Piper* (see para **15.7**), at 251 (*forum non conveniens* doctrine was intended to help courts avoid 'complex exercises in comparative law').
2 Ibid at 249–251, 254 n 22.
3 See, eg *Forsythe v Saudi Arabian Airlines Corpn* 885 F 2d 285, 290 (5th Circ, 1989) (upholding the District Court's determination that a forum in Saudi Arabia was adequate because, '[t]here is no indication that a Saudi Arabian forum would treat [the plaintiff] unfairly or deprive him of all remedies').
4 See, eg *Needham v Phillips Petroleum Co of Norway* 719 F 2d 1481, 1485 (11th Circ, 1983) (lack of wrongful death or pain and suffering awards insufficient to disqualify foreign forum); *Borden Inc v Meiji Milk Products Co* 919 F 2d 822, 829 (2d Circ, 1990); cert denied 111 S Ct 2259 (1991) ('the prospect of a lesser recovery does not justify refusing to dismiss on the ground of *forum non conveniens*') (quoting *Alcoa S S Co v M/V Nordic Regent*, 654 F 2d 147, 159 (2d Circ, 1980) (*en banc*); cert denied 449 US 890 (1980)) (maximum recovery of $570,000 in foreign forum versus $8,000,000 in United States does not render foreign forum inadequate).
5 See, eg *Lake v Richardson Merrell Inc* 538 F Supp 262, 274 (ND Ohio, 1982).

15.16 The adequacy of the alternative forum has not been limited to the availability of a substantive remedy. Courts have assessed the procedural adequacy of the foreign forum as well.[1] In extreme cases, where a fair and impartial trial did not appear likely because of the structure or makeup of the judiciary, American courts have refused dismissal. For example, in *Canadian Overseas Ores Ltd v Compania de Acero del Pacifico SA*,[2] the court denied dismissal where the defendants failed to prove that the Chilean judiciary was independent of the ruling junta and capable of conducting a fair trial. Similarly, in *Rasoulzadeh v Associated Press*,[3] the court denied dismissal where it was not convinced of the impartiality of the Iranian Mullahs and feared the plaintiff would be shot should he return to Iran. In other cases, an American court refused to dismiss because of extensive trial delays in the alternative forum[4] and because the plaintiff could not afford representation in the alternative forum because of the unavailability of contingent fee agreements.[5]

1 See, eg *Macedo v Boeing Co* 693 F 2d 683, 690–691 (7th Circ, 1982) (substantial filing fees and the illegality of contingent fees were relevant to the adequacy of Portugal as an alternative forum); *Nai-Chao v Boeing Co* 555 F Supp 9, 15 (ND Cal 1982) (fact that Taiwanese courts required significant filing fee did not bar dismissal); affd sub nom, *Cheng v Boeing Co* 708 F 2d 1406 (9th Circ, 1983); cert denied 104 S Ct 549 (1983).

2 528 F Supp 1337, 1342 (SDNY); order affd 727 F 2d 274 (2nd Circ, 1984).
3 574 F Supp 854, 861 (SDNY); affd 767 F 2d 908 (2nd Circ, 1985).
4 *Re Aircrash Disaster near Bombay, India* 531 F Supp 1175, 1181 n 7 (W D Wash 1982) (motion denied due to extensive delays in the Indian judicial system and lack of procedure for speedy disposal of matters of public importance by the Indian Supreme Court).
5 See, eg *Odita v Elder Dempster Lines Ltd* 286 F Supp 547, 550–551 (SDNY, 1968) (defendant denied dismissal because destitute plaintiff would have difficulty suing in Great Britain, where contingent fees are unlawful: 'To require this impecunious plaintiff to try the present lawsuit in Great Britain might effectively deny him any remedy at all'); *Reid-Walen* (see para **15.7**) at 1399 (American plaintiff's inability to retain counsel in Jamaica because system lacked contingent fee system for attorneys and plaintiff could not otherwise afford counsel was 'an important factor counseling against dismissal,' along with failure of Jamaican system to provide jury trials).

15.17 Absent fundamental challenges to the alternative forum's judicial system or plaintiffs' access to it, plaintiffs' arguments that no adequate alternative forum was available have generally not prevailed.[1]

1 See, eg *Lockman Foundation v Evangelical Alliance Mission* 930 F 2d 764, 768 (9th Circ, 1991) (difference in discovery standards and appellate standard of review in Japan insufficient basis for dismissal); *Borden Inc* (see para **15.15**) at 829 (dismissing suit for adjudication in Japan; 'some inconvenience or the unavailability of beneficial litigation procedures similar to those available in the federal district courts does not render an alternative forum inadequate') (citing *Shields v Mi Ryung Constr Co* 508 F Supp 891, 895 (SDNY, 1981)); *Alcoa* (see para **15.15**), at 159 ('the prospect of a lesser recovery does not justify refusing to dismiss on the ground of *forum non conveniens*').

15.18 However, while the tendency has been to dismiss these cases, courts very often condition dismissal in such a way as to address the plaintiff's principle concerns.[1] Examples of conditional dismissals include requiring the defendant: to submit to the jurisdiction of the foreign court and to waive any procedural obstacles barring the plaintiff's suit;[2] to agree to abide by the judgment of the foreign court;[3] and to stipulate that it would not contest liability.[4] At least one federal appellate court has found that foreign as well as US plaintiffs are entitled to receive the benefits of conditional dismissals.[5]

1 See Note, 'Forum Non Conveniens in the Absence of an Alternative Forum', 86 Colum L Rev 1000, 1005 n 31 (1986).
2 See Robertson (para **15.2**), at 408, n 72. (('By the mid-1970s, almost all *forum non conveniens* dismissals had come to be conditioned rather than outright.' 'Courts of appeal today routinely remand cases for the imposition of conditions') citing *Diaz v Humboldt* 722 F 2d 1216, 1219 (5th Circ, 1984)).
3 *Nai-Chao* (see para **15.16**), at 11.
4 *Pain v United Technologies Corpn* 637 F 2d 775, 785 (DC Circ, 1980); cert denied, 454 US 1128 (1981) (suit dismissed in favour of Norway where damages issue alone was litigated).
5 See *Baris* (para **15.11**), at 1551.

15.19 There are a number of decisions holding that the legal systems of certain other countries generally provide an adequate alternative in particular cases.[1] Legal systems dissimilar to that of the United States have not been discriminated against simply because they employ radically different procedures, as long as they provide an 'adequate' remedy.

1 See, eg *Lockman Foundation* (para **15.17**), at 769 n 3 ('federal courts have consistently found that Japan provides an adequate alternative forum to litigation in the United States. We have found no reported cases holding Japan to be an *in*adequate forum.' [citations omitted]); *Murty v S A Prince Aga Khan* 92 FRD 478, 482 (EDNY, 1981) ('the French courts can be expected to protect American litigants').

15.20 In *Brazilian Investment Advisory Services Ltda v United Merchants & Mfg Inc*,[1] the court refused to find that the Brazilian civil code procedures were 'entirely unable to deal with the issues' involved in the plaintiff's lawsuit, and dismissed in favour of Brazil, stating:

> There appears to be no question that Brazil, one of the many countries in the world whose legal system is structured by a civil code, would resolve this dispute by means of different procedures. 'A Brazilian civil trial is "inquisitorial" rather than "adversarial", with the judge acting as fact-finder, and the presentation of proof relying heavily upon documents, although witnesses appear in court for examination by the judge. It also appears that pre-trial discovery of an opponent's documents or employees, or of third party witnesses, is not provided for by the Brazilian Procedure Civil Code.' Although these procedural infirmities seem to favour a plaintiff's choice of forum, 'the Second Circuit, in the *forum non conveniens* context, is apparently prepared to accept procedural differences in the law of the proposed transferee forum, so long as those differences do not rise to the level of a complete denial of due process.'[2]

1 667 F Supp 136, 139 (SDNY, 1987).
2 Ibid at 138–139 (quoting *Panama Processes SA v Cities Service Co* 500 F Supp 787, 800 (SDNY, 1980); affd 650 F 2d 408 (2d Circ, 1981)).

Private interest factors

15.21 The focus of the private interest factors is on the convenience of the witnesses.

The citizenship or residence of the parties

15.22 Although citizenship or residence are merely 'proxies for convenience', and not dispositive of the *forum non conveniens* issue,[1] 'courts have continued to treat the residence of the suitor as "a fact of high significance"',[2] and trends in the case law reveal that where the parties live will play a prominent role in the *forum non conveniens* analysis in almost every case. Ordinarily, the courts start with a 'strong presumption in favour of the plaintiff's choice of forum'.[3] 'Where the decision to exercise jurisdiction turns solely on the balance of convenience between the parties, federal courts are reluctant to force an American plaintiff to litigate in a foreign court.'[4] They are likely to deny a US forum to an American plaintiff only where the suit's connection with the United States is negligible[5] or where the foreign sovereign has a primary interest in resolving the dispute.[6] They almost always retain jurisdiction where both the plaintiff and defendant are US citizens.[7]

1 *Piper* (see para **15.7**), at 255 n 23, 256 n 24; see also *Alcoa* (para **15.15**), at 157.
2 *Rudetsky v O'Dowd* 660 F Supp 341, 345 (EDNY, 1987) (quoting *Koster v Lumbermens Mut Cas Co* 330 US 518, 525 (1947)).
3 *Wilson v Humphreys (Cayman) Ltd* 916 F 2d 1239, 1245 (7th Circ, 1990); cert denied 111 S Ct 1415 (1991) (quoting *Macedo* (para **15.16**), at 688).
4 See, e g *Murty* (para **15.19**), at 480 (citing *Leasco Data Processing Equipment Corpn v Maxwell* 468 F 2d 1326, 1344 (2d Circ, 1972)).
5 See, e g *Poole v Brown*, 706 F Supp 74, 77 (DDC, 1989) (where trained attack dog injured the child of American citizen stationed in Zaire, defendant's *forum non conveniens* motion was granted since lawsuit seeking damages had no connection with United States district where it was filed).
6 See *Gulf Oil* (para **15.7**), at 509 ('there is a local interest in having localised controversies decided at home').

7 See, eg *Founding Church of Scientology v Verlag*, 536 F 2d 429, 435 (DC Circ, 1976) (fact that both plaintiff and defendant were US citizens was of 'great significance').

15.23 A corporate plaintiff's citizenship or residence, however, may not play as great a role, since it does not correlate as often with convenience.[1] Also, where neither party is a US citizen, the courts have more readily dismissed cases on *forum non conveniens* grounds.[2]

1 See *Reid-Walen* (para **15.7**), at 1395 n 8.
2 See, eg *Lauritzen v Larsen*, 345 US 571, 592 (1953); *Quintero v Klaveness Ship Lines*, 914 F 2d 717, 729 (5th Circ, 1990); rehg denied, 920 F 2d 931 (5th Circ, 1990); cert denied 111 S Ct 1322 (1991).

15.24 Most often, *forum non conveniens* as applied in the federal courts is now limited to suits brought by foreign plaintiffs against United States-based corporations. Courts have declined jurisdiction in most of these cases,[1] but there are exceptions,[2] and the decisions are not always uniform so outcomes are not always easy to predict. As a general matter, the foreign plaintiff's choice of forum is accorded less deference than the American plaintiff's choice under *Piper*, but the degree of deference will vary.[3] In *Lony v E I du Pont de Nemours & Co*,[4] the Third Circuit reversed the outcome in a case where the district court failed to indicate properly how much deference it gave to the foreign plaintiff's choice of forum. It stated:

> It (the district court) must decide how much less deference is due this plaintiff's choice of forum, if, indeed, it is due any less than that of a domestic plaintiff. The district court's failure to give adequate consideration to these questions and to make a determination based on the facts of this case was an abuse of discretion and constitutes reversible error.[5]

1 See, eg *Stewart v Dow Chem Co* 865 F 2d 103 (6th Circ, 1989) (products liability suit by Canadian plaintiffs against Michigan manufacturer of herbicide); *DeMelo v Lederle Lab* 801 F 2d 1058 (8th Circ, 1986) (Brazilian plaintiff suing US producer of drugs on products liability basis); *Oxley v Wyeth Laboratories Inc* No Civ A 91–1285, 1992 US Dist LEXIS 6858 (ED Pa 19 May, 1992) (suit by Irish nationals and residents of the Republic of Ireland seeking to recover against American corporations for injuries resulting from pharmaceutical product use).
2 See, eg *Carlenstolpe v Merck & Co Inc* 638 F Supp 901 (SDNY, 1986), mandamus denied, appeal dismissed, 819 F 2d 33 (2nd Circ, 1987) (retaining jurisdiction in an action brought by Swedish plaintiff against New Jersey producer of hepatitis vaccine for negligent or tortious activity).
3 In *Oxley* (supra), the foreign plaintiff's forum choice was given full deference where the weight accorded it was governed by an international treaty between the US and Ireland.
4 886 F 2nd 628, 634 (3rd Circ, 1989).
5 Ibid at 634.

Other private interest factors

15.25 In general, when considering private interest factors, courts will critically assess the need for the sources of proof sought by either party.[1] Some courts will assess not only the location of the pertinent evidence, but its availability.[2] Most courts will pay particular attention to the evidence needed by the defendant to present its defence. An example is *Nolan v Boeing Co*,[3] which involved a controversy arising from an aeroplane crash in England. The court dismissed suit for adjudication in England even though evidence necessary to the plaintiffs' case in chief regarding the design, assembly, manufacture and testing of the subject aircraft was in the United States, in part because evidence necessary to the defence regarding the crash and the actions of the British airlines that owned and operated the plane was in the United Kingdom (the American defendants were claiming pilot error).

In *Banco Nominees Ltd v Iroquois Brands Ltd*,[4] the court dismissed the case to London because litigating the case in Delaware risked depriving the defendant of key witnesses necessary to establish its affirmative defences.

1 See, eg *Volkswagen De Mexico, SA v Germanischer Lloyd* Nos 90 Civ 1248, 1298, 1991 US Dist LEXIS 15572 (SDNY, 28 Oct, 1991).
2 See, eg *Bank of Crete SA v Koskotas* No 88 Civ 8412, 1991 US Dist LEXIS 18586 (SDNY, 19 Dec, 1991) ('because discovery rules are more liberal in the United States than in Greece, . . . it will be easier to gain access to documents, even Greek documents, in this country').
3 919 F 2d 1058, 1068 (5th Circ, 1990).
4 748 F Supp 1070, 1075 (D Del, 1990).

15.26 A key factor in the *forum non conveniens* analysis often will be where the incident occurred that gave rise to the lawsuit, as most of the evidence is likely to be located there. A tremendous number of cases turn on this factor.[1]

1 See, eg *Howe v Goldcorpn Investments Ltd* 946 F 2d 944, 951 (1st Circ, 1991); cert denied 432 US 1052 (1976), where the court found the balance of conveniences to favour 'with unusual strength' the Canadian defendants because all relevant events to plaintiff/shareholder's misrepresentation and breach of fiduciary duty claims against them took place in Canada, not in the United States.

15.27 With regard to witnesses or parties, courts typically prefer to dismiss in favour of the foreign forum if it will allow the defendant to implead third parties that are not subject to the jurisdiction of the US courts.[1] Similarly, compulsory process over witnesses has been considered to be an important factor in the *forum non conveniens* analysis,[2] but often the problem of compelling witness testimony may be problematic in either forum.[3] Requiring the parties to sue in certain foreign countries may prejudice the parties if those countries have no compulsory process to compel witnesses to appear to testify.[4] On the other hand, transporting witnesses to the United States for trial can be costly, and substituting depositions for live testimony to decrease the cost is not considered to be 'the optimal way for a jury to decide a case.'[5]

1 See, eg *Fitzgerald v Texaco Inc* 521 F 2d 448, 453 (2d Circ, 1975); cert denied 423 US 1052 (1976).
2 See, eg *Nai-Chao* (para **15.16**), at 11; *Howe* (para **15.26**), at 952 (finding compulsory process to be 'especially important' where fraud and subjective intent were elements of plaintiffs' claim, 'making the live testimony of witnesses for the purposes of presenting demeanour evidence essential to a fair trial').
3 See, eg *Reid-Walen* (para **15.7**), at 1397 (acknowledging compulsory process problems regardless of whether suit is brought in United States or Jamaica).
4 See, eg *Bank of Crete SA v Koskotas* (para **15.25**).
5 See, eg *Gazis v John S Latsis Inc* 729 F Supp 979, 989 (SDNY, 1990).

15.28 A court may find that certain witnesses sought by the parties are not key to the case, and accord less significance to the fact that they are unavailable or not subject to compulsory process in the alternative forum.[1] The location of expert witnesses in the United States, for example, will not be sufficient to tip the balance in favour of the US forum where other witnesses and documentary evidence are available in the alternative forum.[2]

1 See, eg *Walpex Trading v Yacimientos Petroliferos* 712 F Supp 383, 393 (SDNY, 1989).
2 See, eg *Vargas v M/V Mini Lama* 709 F Supp 117, 119 (ED La, 1989).

15.29 Some courts have recently taken the position that modern technology has decreased the importance of the location of documents;[1] however, in most cases courts still find this factor significant.[2]

1 See, eg *Jayaraman v Salomon Inc* No 87 Civ 2781, 1991 US Dist LEXIS 4205 (SDNY, 29 Mar, 1991).
2 See, eg *Interpane Coatings v Australia and New Zealand* 732 F Supp 909, 916 (ND Ill 1990).

15.30 As part of the private interest analysis, courts will also consider matters having practical implications for the efficiency of the litigation, such as the existence of pending suits in the alternative forum,[1] and language barriers relating to the witnesses.[2] Although financial obstacles to suit generally will be considered in determining whether the alternative forum is 'adequate', some courts also consider pecuniary barriers to suit in the private interest analysis.[3]

1 See, eg *Banco Nominees Ltd v Iroquois Brands Ltd* 748 F Supp 1070, 1073 (D Del, 1990) (where High Court of Justice in England had two related actions pending, which plaintiff's action potentially could be consolidated with, retaining jurisdiction would be a waste of judicial time and resources).
2 See, eg *Bank of Crete* (para **15.25**) (factor in favour of US forum was that Greek witnesses spoke English, whereas US witnesses did not speak Greek).
3 See, eg *Rudetsky* (para **15.22**), at 346–347.

15.31 *Piper* (see para **15.7**), illustrates the court's balancing of private interest factors. *Piper* arose out of an aeroplane crash in Scotland. The plane was manufactured by a US company, but owned and maintained by a British company and operated by a Scottish company subject to Scottish air traffic controllers. Wrongful death actions were brought in California by Reyno, the personal representative of the estates of Scottish subjects who were killed in the crash, against the American manufacturers of the aircraft and the propeller. The case was transferred to the federal court in Pennsylvania where Piper had manufactured the aeroplane pursuant to 28 USC §1404(a). That court granted the defendant's *forum non conveniens* motion. The intermediate appellate court reversed, but the United States Supreme Court ultimately affirmed the district court's decision.

15.32 The *Piper* decision turned on the following four private interest factors:

(1) the plaintiffs were representatives of decedents, who were all citizens of Scotland;
(2) all witnesses to the aircraft's maintenance, pilot training, and accident investigation were in Great Britain;
(3) all the witnesses for the damages issue were in Scotland; and
(4) the witnesses were beyond compulsory process in the United States, and the defendants would be unable to implead third party defendants, making it unfair to the parties to proceed in an American court.

The court also concluded that Scotland had a greater interest than the United States in deciding the controversy because the accident occurred in Scottish airspace, all of the decedents were Scottish, and all potential parties were Scottish or English (apart from Piper and Hartzell, the aeroplane propeller manufacturer) ('there is a local interest in having localised controversies decided at home').[1]

1 *Piper* (see para **15.7**), at 260–261, quoting *Gulf Oil* (see para **15.7**), at 509.

Public interest factors

15.33 The public interest factors focus on the relative interests of the sovereigns hosting the alternative forums, and administrative burdens on the court and the community that would arise from an adjudication of the case.[1]

1 See, eg *Gulf Oil* (para **15.7**), at 508–509.

15.34 The relative interests of the sovereign will be determined, in part, by the applicable law. Because United States courts generally try to avoid having to apply another country's law, they are more likely to dismiss a case when the choice of law rules require application of foreign law. In *Piper*, the Supreme Court stated:

> [T]he public interest factors [in *Gulf Oil*] point towards dismissal where the court would be required to 'untangle problems in conflict of laws, and in law foreign to itself'.[1]

Likewise, the courts have found the application of American law constitutes a strong reason for retaining jurisdiction.[2] In sum, 'usually if forum law is applicable, the suit is retained';[3] however, the fact that a court must apply foreign law will not by itself necessarily require dismissal.[4]

1 *Piper* (see para **15.7**), at 251 (quoting *Gulf Oil* (para **15.7**), at 509).
2 See, eg *Gates Learjet Corpn v Jensen* 743 F 2d 1325, 1336–1337 (9th Circ, 1984); cert denied 105 S Ct 2143 (1985).
3 Margaret G Stewart, 'Forum Non Conveniens: a Doctrine in Search of a Role', 74 Cal L Rev 1259, 1321 n 205 (1986).
4 See, eg *Cliffs-Neddrill* (para **15.12**), at 150 (refusing to grant *forum non conveniens* motion where private interest factors were at equipoise and applicability of foreign law was only public interest factor pointing in favour of dismissal).

15.35 Courts in the United States have shown little interest in adjudicating cases that are 'purely foreign'.[1] For example, in *Quintero*,[2] a federal appellate court held that the United States has 'virtually no interest' in deciding a dispute under the law of the Philippines arising out of injury to a Filipino plaintiff by a Norwegian defendant that occurred in New Orleans aboard a vessel owned by Norwegian interests. These decisions are sometimes based on considerations of comity, wherein, for instance, the foreign sovereign has been found to have an interest in regulating the conduct of business enterprises engaged in business within their territory.[3] This is especially true when the defendant corporation is owned by the foreign government,[4] or the issues in the case involve the internal affairs of a foreign corporation.[5] Moreover, where the foreign government already has a regulatory scheme in place, this will be considered evidence of that country's 'local interest' in resolving the dispute.[6]

1 *Pain* (see para **15.18**), at 798.
2 See para **15.23**, at 729.
3 See, eg *Dowling v Richardson-Merrell Inc* 727 F 2d 608 (6th Circ, 1984) (United Kingdom had interest in regulating the safety of drugs manufactured and marketed within that country).
4 See *Forsythe* (para **15.15**), at 291 (suit dismissed where defendant corporation was 'wholly owned by the Saudi Arabian government' and employment contract at issue contained choice of law and choice of forum provisions tying the dispute to Saudi Arabia).
5 *Scottish Air Int'l v British Caledonian Group* 751 F Supp 1129, 1135 (SDNY 1990); revd, 945 F 2d 53 (2d Circ, 1991) (New York had 'little interest' in dispute over legal right to seats on the board of directors of a Scottish corporation).

6 Most of the reported cases deferring to foreign nations' regulatory interests have involved chemicals, aviation and drugs. See, eg *Re Union Carbide Corpn* (para **15.13**), (emphasising Indian government's extensive regulation of chemical industry as evidence of India's strong interest in suit arising out of chemical disaster brought against Indian subsidiary company and American parent); *Jennings v Boeing Co* 660 F Supp 796, 808 (ED Pa 1987); affd 838 F 2d 1206 (3d Circ, 1988) (litigation arising from helicopter crash filed by Irish plaintiff in Pennsylvania against Pennsylvanian manufacturer of aircraft was dismissed in favour of English or Scottish courts: '[t]he sale and operation of commercial aircraft is a highly regulated activity in Scotland and England'); *Oxley* (see para **15.24**) (fact that Irish administrative agency regulated content of warning label on pharmaceutical product that was subject of suit provided support for dismissal).

15.36 Cases are not considered to be 'purely foreign' where US citizens are involved, as it is well entrenched in the law that there is a public interest in providing US citizens with access to US courts to adjudicate their disputes.[1] Cases also are not 'purely foreign' where the incident that gave rise to the suit occurred in the United States, and uniformly, the courts will consider 'the locus of the alleged culpable conduct' and the 'connection of that conduct to the chosen forum' when evaluating the public interest factors.[2]

1 *Pain* (see para **15.18**), at 798.
2 See, eg *Van Cauwenberghe* (para **15.7**), at 528.

15.37 In cases where both nations have a significant interest in the suit, the balance of interests has been found to tip in favour of adjudication in the United States in diverse types of cases. Examples include those in which the health of US nationals may be affected;[1] in which there will be an impact on the US financial community;[2] or where retaining jurisdiction is mandated by considerations of judicial economy.[3] However, US courts generally have not been persuaded that the United States has an automatic interest in cases described as 'international' in character, or that involve defendant corporations conducting business 'worldwide', if the suits otherwise have no connection to the United States.[4] Courts have also not been overly concerned about the practical problems associated with enforcing foreign judgments in the United States.[5]

1 See, eg *Carlenstolpe* (para **15.24**) at 35 (United States had interest in regulation of New Jersey producer of hepatitis vaccine that injured Swedish plaintiff); *Hodson v A H Robins Co* 528 F Supp 809, 823 (ED Va, 1981); affd 715 F 2d 142 (4th Circ, 1983) (refusing to dismiss even though plaintiff was British, British law would apply, and the injury was incurred in England; United States had strong interest in regulating the safety of intra-uterine contraceptive manufactured by American defendant).
2 *CL-Alexanders Laing & Cruickshank v Goldfedl* 709 F Supp 472, 481 (SDNY, 1989) (refusing to dismiss securities fraud case in favour of British forum where securities were those of a United States corporation, and a United States auditing firm and New York law firm were intimately involved: 'although Britain obviously has a strong public interest in protecting British citizens from alleged fraud perpetrated by British auditors, the United States has an equally strong interest in preventing alleged securities frauds planned and executed in the United States').
3 See, eg *Jose v M/V Fir Grove* 765 F Supp 1024, 1035–1036 (D Or 1991) ('interest of the Philippines in protecting its workers and regulating claims that arise out of the employment relationship [was] substantial' but outweighed by economies in combining it for adjudication with related claim in US court).
4 See, eg *Empresa Lineas Maritimas Argentinas SA v Stork-Werkspoor Diesel BV* No Civ A 90–1294, 1991 US Dist LEXIS 1404 (ED La, 5 Feb, 1991); affd, 955 F 2d 368 (5th Circ, 1992) (although defendant was 'worldwide manufacturer', court found there was 'no benefit to be gained by having a court in Louisiana decide this foreign controversy which revolves around a foreign contract in a foreign language, and involves foreign parties, engines manufactured in a foreign country, installed in a foreign ship in a foreign country, and said to be involved in an accident on the high seas').

5 See, e g *Poole* (para **15.22**), at 77 (rejecting plaintiff's argument that judgment obtained in Zaire would not be easily enforced in the United States).

15.38 Although the interests of the courts and the community are usually least significant to the public interest analysis in a *forum non conveniens* determination, courts have not ignored the administrative burdens on the courts and the expense to the community that arises from adjudication of complex international lawsuits: 'There is a strong policy in favour of not subjecting "other litigants and the community at large [to] unwarranted imposition upon the local courts' jurisdiction."'[1] Court congestion and the burdens imposed on US citizens required to sit on the jury and absorb the costs of the lawsuit are typical considerations relating to the appropriateness of dismissing to the alternative forum.[2]

1 *Gazis* (see para **15.27**), at 989.
2 See, e g *Murty* (para **15.19**), at 481 ('*forum non conveniens* . . . may be invoked in response not only to the prospect of prejudice to the defendant, but also where "facts . . . make trial in the chosen forum inappropriate because of considerations affecting the court's own administrative and legal problems." Administrative difficulties follow for the courts when litigation piles up in congested centres instead of being handled at its origin') (quoting *Koster* (see para **15.22**), at 524).

FORUM NON CONVENIENS IN STATE COURTS

15.39 Transnational personal injury actions are increasingly being brought in certain state courts where a more liberal standard is being applied to retain such cases.[1]

1 Robertson and Speck (see para **15.3**), at 940.

15.40 Traditionally, states have been free to develop their own *forum non conveniens* doctrine as opposed to following the federal rules. Although some commentators have suggested that state courts should be bound by the federal formulation of the doctrine because its application implicates foreign policy concerns,[1] the degree of adherence to the federal *forum non conveniens* standard presently varies among states. Some state legislatures have enacted codifications of their *forum non conveniens* rule; others have developed it exclusively through the courts.

1 See, e g Mark D Greenberg, 'The Appropriate Source of Law for Forum Non Conveniens Decisions in International Cases: a Proposal for the Development of Federal Common Law', 4 Int'l Tax and Bus Law 155, 187 (1986).

15.41 According to a survey done by Robertson and Speck, published in 1990,[1] approximately 32 states and the District of Columbia have likely adopted the federal doctrine or something that resembles it.[2] Three other states, according to Robertson and Speck, have given some indication that they intend to follow the federal doctrine.[3] Since the Robertson and Speck survey, West Virginia has adopted the federal doctrine, overruling its earlier rejection of the doctrine in cases brought under a US law establishing employers' liability.[4] Mississippi has firmly embraced the federal doctrine.[5] As illustrated in *Shewbrooks v A C & S Inc*,[6] Mississippi along with many other states[7] that employ the federal doctrine will not dismiss an action on *forum non conveniens* ground if no alternative forum is available to a plaintiff because the statute of limitations has run elsewhere. Virginia has adopted a *forum non conveniens* statute which has been interpreted by the Virginia courts as a codification of the federal doctrine.[8]

1 Robertson and Speck (see para **15.3**).
2 See, eg *Ledingham v Parke-Davis Div of Warner-Lambert Co* 628 F Supp 1447 (EDNY, 1986) (foreign plaintiff loses dismissal on basis of *forum non conveniens* to domestic defendants in a negligence, strict liability and breach of warranty action arising out of plaintiff's mother's ingestion of Dilantin during her pregnancy. Court finds alternative forum suitable and balances public and private factors against plaintiff); *Frazier v St Jude Medical Inc* 609 F Supp 1129 (D Minn, 1985) (foreign plaintiff loses on *forum non conveniens* motion against domestic defendant in products liability action over allegedly defective heart valve); *Dowling v Hyland Therapeutics* 767 F Supp 57 (SDNY, 1991) (action brought by foreign plaintiff who contracted AIDS after injection of blood clotting product manufactured by domestic defendants dismissed on basis of *forum non conveniens*); *Bergquist v Medtronic* 379 NW 2d 508 (Minn, 1986) (court dismisses foreign plaintiff's action against domestic defendant on basis of *forum non conveniens* after balancing private and public factors in a wrongful death action arising out of an allegedly defective heart valve); *Chambers v Merrill-Dow Pharmaceuticals Inc* 519 NE 2d 370 (Ohio, 1988) (court dismisses action by foreign plaintiffs against domestic defendant arising out of sale of pregnancy nausea drug on basis of *forum non conveniens*).
3 Robertson and Speck (see para **15.3**), at 950–951.
4 *Norfolk and Western Ry Co v Tsapis* 400 SE 2d 239 (W Va, 1990).
5 *Missouri Pacific Rly Co v Tircuit* 554 So 2d 878 (Miss, 1989).
6 529 So 2d 557 (Miss, 1988).
7 See, eg *Johnson v Searle* 552 A 2d 29 (Ct App Md 1989) (lower court abused its discretion in dismissing action by plaintiffs injured from use of intra-uterine device that is barred elsewhere by statute of limitations).
8 *Norfolk & Western Rly Co v Williams* 239 Va 390 (Va, 1990).

15.42 In Colorado and South Carolina, a suit brought by a resident plaintiff generally will not be dismissed on *forum non conveniens* grounds.[1] In Florida, a non-resident plaintiff has a better chance of avoiding dismissal on the grounds of *forum non conveniens* because a case will only be dismissed for *forum non conveniens* if both the plaintiff and the defendant are non-residents and the cause of action arose outside of Florida.[2] Similarly, in Vermont, a plaintiff's case will be dismissed on grounds of *forum non conveniens* only when the court finds that the plaintiff is 'seeking to vex, harass or oppress the defendant' or abuse the defendant's rights.[3]

1 *McDonnell-Douglas Corpn v Lohn* 557 P 2d 373 (Colo, 1976) (*en banc*); *Santa Fe Engineers Inc v Carolina Door Products Inc* 259 SE 2d 110 (SC, 1979).
2 *Seaboard Coast Line RR v Swain* 362 So 2d 17 (Fla, 1978).
3 *Burrington v Ashland Oil Co* 356 A 2d 506, 510 (Vt, 1976).

15.43 In four states the existence of the doctrine is still undetermined.[1] Montana rejects the doctrine in actions under a federal employers' liability statute.[2]

1 Robertson and Speck (see para **15.3**), at 951.
2 *Labella v Burlington N Inc* 595 P 2d 1184 (Mont, 1979).

15.44 Louisiana has adopted a *forum non conveniens* doctrine that precludes dismissal except under very narrow circumstances.[1] Georgia seems to have rejected the doctrine completely.[2]

1 *Kassapas v Arkon Shipping Agency Inc* 485 So 2d 565, 566–567 (La Ct App, 1986); writ denied 488 So 2d 203 (La, 1986); cert denied 479 US 940 (1986). After *Kassapas*, the legislature amended the state's procedure code to provide for *forum non conveniens* dismissal of cases in which 'a claim [is] predicated solely on a federal statute' and is not 'brought under [the Jones Act] or federal

maritime law'. *Markzannes v Bermuda Star Line Inc* 545 So 2d 537 (La 1989) (per curiam); cert denied 493 US 1043 (1990), relying on La Code Civ Proc Ann art 123 (West Supp 1989).
2 See *Smith v Bd of Regents*, 302 SE 2d 124, 125–126 (Ga Ct App 1983).

15.45 During the 1980s, the California Appellate Courts deviated from the federal interpretation of the doctrine of *forum non conveniens*.[1] This brief deviation from the federal standard, however, came to an end in 1991 with *Stangvik v Shiley Inc*.[2]

1 See, e g *Holmes v Syntex Laboratories* 156 Cal App 3d 372 (Ct App, 1984); *Corrigan v Bjork Shiley* 182 Cal App 3d 166 (Ct App, 1986); cert denied; *Shiley Inc v Corrigan* 479 US 1049 (1987).
2 54 Cal 3d 744 (1991).

15.46 In *Holmes v Syntex Laboratories*,[1] the court afforded great weight to '[t]he difference in conflict of law rules applicable in this state and in [the] alternative forum and [w]hether any party would be substantially disadvantaged in having to try the action (a) in this state; or (b) in the forum in which the moving party asserts it ought to be tried'.[2] The plaintiffs in *Holmes* were British citizens suing a California corporation for disabling or fatal injuries allegedly sustained after ingestion of oral contraceptives. Under British law, the 'appellants would lose any cause of action for strict liability'.[3] The court concluded that loss of a strict liability cause of action 'would result in "substantial disadvantage" under California law'.[4] The *Holmes* court also deviated from *Piper* by deferring to the plaintiffs' choice of forum, even though the plaintiffs were foreign.[5]

1 156 Cal App 3d 372 (Ct App 1984).
2 Ibid at 381.
3 Ibid at 384.
4 Ibid.
5 Ibid at 382. See *Piper* (para **15.7**).

15.47 A different California appellate court declined to follow the *Holmes* holding that a foreign plaintiff's choice of forum should be given substantial deference in *Corrigan v Bjork Shiley Corpn*,[1] which involved a wrongful death action by Australian citizens against a California corporation. Instead, the court held:

> [a]lthough the rule of substantial deference is not eliminated when plaintiff is foreign (either non-citizen or non-resident), the deference accorded his choice is less than that accorded the choice of a California resident.[2]

The *Corrigan* court also declined to give the 'suitability of the alternative forum issue' the same weight as the *Holmes* court gave it. While the *Holmes* court found the issue to be very significant,[3] the *Corrigan* court found that the issue was only entitled to some weight.[4]

1 See para **15.45**.
2 Ibid at 252.
3 *Holmes* (see para **15.45**), at 381.
4 *Corrigan* (see para **15.45**), at 253.

15.48 In 1991, the Supreme Court of California in *Stangvik v Shiley*,[1] rejected both the *Holmes* and the *Corrigan* decisions. The *Shiley* decision held that the suitability of alternative forums is merely a threshold inquiry, not a discretionary determination.[2] In making this determination, the *Shiley* court returned to the federal rule as enunciated in *Piper* and rejected the substantial disadvantage test in *Holmes*.[3] Similarly, the *Shiley* court adopted the federal rule which gives less deference to a foreign plaintiff's choice of forum.[4] Thus, the *Shiley* court overruled both *Holmes* and *Corrigan* and brought California law full circle, realigning it with the federal doctrine.

1 See para **15.45**.
2 Ibid at 752, fn 3.
3 *Holmes* (see para **15.45**), at 384.
4 *Shiley* at 755.

15.49 Texas' position on *forum non conveniens* is also noteworthy to those involved in transnational suits because of the 1990 decision of the Texas Supreme Court in *Dow Chemical Co v Castro Alfaro*.[1] In *Dow*, Costa Rican banana plantation workers sued Dow Chemical Company in Texas, claiming serious personal injuries as a result of exposure to a pesticide manufactured by Dow. Dow was incorporated in Delaware and did business in Texas. The plaintiffs were suing under the Wrongful Death Act of Texas (1860) which provided for a cause of action for personal injury or death regardless of where the death or injury took place.[2] The trial court had dismissed the action on the grounds of *forum non conveniens*. The issue before the Supreme Court was whether the Wrongful Death Act, giving foreign parties a right to sue for wrongful death and personal injury, permitted a trial court to relinquish jurisdiction based on *forum non conveniens*. The court answered in the negative, basing its argument on statutory interpretation, rather than public policy grounds.[3] The court reviewed the history of *forum non conveniens* in Texas and held that the legislature had statutorily abolished the doctrine through its passage of the Wrongful Death Act.[4] Texas' open court position has received considerable attention and criticism from some sectors and will likely continue to be challenged as the make-up of the court or other relevant factors change.[5]

1 786 SW 2d, 674 (Tex 1990); cert denied 111 S Ct 671 (1991).
2 Ibid at 679.
3 Ibid at 675.
4 Ibid at 679.
5 *Wall Street Journal*, 19 August 1992, at A11. The Texas Supreme Court has recently decided to hear a case involving a shipping accident in Singapore which will provide an opportunity to reconsider *Dow*.

15.50 Even if a case in a state court is not dismissed on the basis of *forum non conveniens*, a defendant can still move to transfer or 'remove' the case to federal court.[1] In order successfully to remove a case from a state to a federal court, two requirements must be met. First, there must be diversity of citizenship, meaning all of the defendants must be domiciled in states different from the plaintiffs' domicilary states. Second, none of the defendants can be citizens of the state where the action is originally brought. Only a defendant can bring such a motion. Once a case is in federal court, the federal doctrine of *forum non conveniens* can be used to dismiss the suit.[2]

1 28 USC §1441.
2 See, e g *Sibaja v Dow Chemical Co* 757 F 2d 1215 (11th Circ, 1985); cert denied 474 US 948, 106 S Ct 347, 88 L Ed 2d 294 (1985); but see *Eddy v Inland Bay Drilling & Workover Inc* 784 F Supp 370 (SD Tex, 1992) (defendant's motion to remove denied because Texas does not recognise doctrine of *forum non conveniens*).

CHAPTER 16

Preparation for trial: leading counsel and causation

E Anthony Machin QC

16.1 The purpose of this chapter is to examine and define the role of counsel, and in particular of leading counsel, in the preparation for trial of a medical negligence action. The matter of primary concern is that of liability (including causation); preparation on the issue of quantum differs little as between a medical negligence action and an ordinary action for personal injury.

STEPS TO BE TAKEN

16.2 The function of leading counsel is of course of importance, whether he is instructed for a plaintiff or for a defendant. He will normally have been selected because of his expertise in this class of work; in recent years there has evolved a medical negligence Bar, comprised of those having special familiarity with medical negligence issues. His function is, however, particularly crucial when he appears for a plaintiff, for then his is the responsibility for deciding upon the overall strategy of the attack to be made upon the defendant, and upon the forensic weapons most apt to translate that strategy into victory. The function of leading counsel for a defendant is more circumscribed; he cannot decide what case he has to meet but has to meet that presented by the plaintiff. His strategy is in most cases limited to advising which of the issues advanced by the plaintiff should be contested, with what vigour they should be contested, and with what material. He has the choice, which plaintiff's counsel does not, of relying upon cross-examination alone to defeat his opponent's witnesses, mindful of the potential peril which the calling of any witness harbours for the case of the party calling him. Considerations such as the foregoing, which are illustrative rather than exhaustive, make it appropriate to deal separately with the role of counsel when acting for a plaintiff and his role when acting for a defendant.

THE ROLE OF COUNSEL FOR THE PLAINTIFF

16.3 This section begins at the point of time when leading counsel is first involved. When should this be?

16.4 Much, plainly, will depend upon the complexity of the particular case; this chapter assumes litigation of weight and complexity involving a substantial issue of liability. Injuries stemming from medical negligence often unhappily lead to grave and permanent incapacity, and current awards in the most serious cases commonly exceed £1,000,000. Litigation where compensation of this order is at stake is usually, and properly, the responsibility of leading counsel. Added to this purely monetary consideration is the need for the expertise and experience required effectively to cross-examine expert medical witnesses of the highest calibre, a function which presupposes an ability to grasp the medical issues involved and to study with comprehension and profit the literary effusions of an alien discipline.

16.5 In medical negligence litigation of the foregoing character it is preferable that either experienced junior counsel or leading counsel be instructed at an early stage, that is to say, when the medical records have been obtained and the plaintiff's medical experts have given their preliminary views in writing. It is at this stage that the allegations of fault must be formulated and the broad strategy of the attack upon the defendant (and often the choice of whom to sue) decided. Embarrassment and difficulty may be caused if leading counsel, brought in much later, feels compelled to disagree with the strategy employed before his instruction. Furthermore if (as is usually the case) the plaintiff is legally aided, in any case of substance the authorities may well require the opinion of leading counsel at least within a short time after close of pleadings.

16.6 It is therefore suggested that when that material has been assembled which is essential to at least a preliminary assessment of the prospects of success and of the best means of achieving it there should take place a consultation at which should attend the plaintiff (or the next friend), the experts who have given reports and solicitors and counsel. This consultation has important functions. Foremost among them is the fostering of a team spirit. Complicated litigation such as that under discussion demands a team composed of lawyers, doctors and on occasions members of other disciplines, such as biologists, pharmacologists and statisticians. It is important that all members of the team know or become known to each other and that channels of communication are freely open between them, with the instructing solicitor being kept fully informed at all times. Never should it be forgotten that it is for the benefit of the plaintiff, who may have little or nothing to contribute evidentially, that the litigation will have been initiated, and he or she should be kept fully involved, and invited to attend consultations, even those of a purely technical character, if he or she so desires. Regrettably often the plaintiff, rightly or wrongly, feels that the treating doctors have not been forthcoming; the legal profession must not run the risk of deserving a similar response.

16.7 The team having been assembled, decisions should be taken upon (at least) the following matters:

(1) what allegations to pursue, and what not to pursue;
(2) whether there appear to be further medical records, not yet disclosed (if so, they must be asked for);
(3) whether there is a need for evidence of fact on the issue of liability and, if so, from what source;
(4) whether there is need for other or further medical evidence;
(5) whether the opinions of the experts should be fortified by the production of medical literature;
(6) the broad timetable to be followed.

16.8 The detailed preparation for trial, including the conduct of the interlocutory stages, is dealt with in Chapter 11. The detailed steps there discussed will be shaped by early decisions upon the foregoing matters, bearing always in mind the need for flexibility of approach in the light of future developments including, most importantly, the contents of the defence where this is (as it should be) fully pleaded.

16.9 Such is the importance of the early consultation referred to that it is desirable to deal particularly with at least some of the matters set out above as meriting early decision.

What allegations to pursue

16.10 It must throughout be borne in mind that an allegation of negligence against a professional person concerning his professional conduct is a serious matter. It may cause him distress and harm, even if later it is held to have been unfounded. It goes without saying that the most careful consideration should be devoted to ensuring that only such allegations are made as are relevant and can be supported by the evidence. The lamentable approach, sometimes adopted, of discharging every available arrow, however unpromising its flight, in the hope that one will hit the target must be eschewed. It should be one of the important functions of the preliminary consultation to assess which allegations can be fairly supported, so that others not falling within that category can be put aside, at least unless or until further evidence justifies them. Ex hypothesi the preliminary consultation takes place before the Statement of Claim is drafted; if leading counsel is instructed at this stage he should be invited to approve the pleading when it is in draft. If this is done, it will escape the disdain sometimes cast upon such a document by a leader later instructed and who would, of course, himself have drafted it so much more elegantly.

Further records

16.11 The importance of ensuring that all the medical records have been disclosed, and the procedure for compelling disclosure, is discussed earlier (see Chapter 11). Never must it be forgotten that a case may be decided upon the contents of a single document. Medical experts usually know what to look for and can advise on the question, whether there is an obvious lacuna in the records, suggestive of incomplete disclosure. Of course, a lacuna may be truly such; in other words, the record may never have existed, in which case if a competent practitioner should have made it, its absence may present the defendant with difficulty.

Evidence of fact

16.12 Whether evidence of fact (apart from the contents of the records) is required must depend upon the particular case; the possible need for it should be discussed. There may be circumstances (for example, the deteriorating condition of the plaintiff) which may make it advisable for a signed statement to be taken which may later be served under the Civil Evidence Act 1968.

Other or further medical evidence

16.13 It must not be assumed that the medical experts assembled for the preliminary consultation are necessarily those appropriate to the successful advancement of the plaintiff's case. Their expertise may not be that which precisely is required; they may have professional commitments or hold offices which make them reluctant to give evidence; they may simply be poor witnesses, however skilled as practitioners. Counsel should be alert to detect such weaknesses so that guidance can be given to instructing solicitors concerning the need for reinforcements or substitutes. Usually the existing experts will be found most helpful in suggesting the names of suitable colleagues.

16.14 Many advocates consider it desirable to call two witnesses at least whose expertise lies within each area of contest, in order to avoid judicial suspicion that one witness alone in support of the plaintiff's case could be engaged. On the other hand, calling more in number affords greater opportunity for damaging cross-examination and for contradictions to emerge in the evidence called on the plaintiff's behalf. The decision as to what expert witnesses to have at court is made at a later stage, but the opportunity for that decision to be made in the light of the best possible options is laid at the stage now under discussion.

Medical literature

16.15 The value of carefully researched studies by acknowledged medical experts, some of whom may hold academic posts which permit greater opportunity for reflection than that afforded to the busy consultant practitioner, cannot be over-emphasised. If a medical expert witness puts forward a thesis which cannot be supported from the corpus of extant studies it runs the risk of being belittled as idiosyncratic. Thus, the medical experts forming part of the team should be asked at an early stage to research the literature in support of views advanced by them which are likely to prove controversial. This procedure should be repeated at the later stage, when reports from the defendant's experts have become available.

16.16 Medical literature, such as standard textbooks and articles in learned journals, is not of itself evidence but may be used by experts in support of their views, or in cross-examination of opposing experts to destroy their opinions. The relevance of such material is discussed in *H v Schering Chemicals Ltd.*[1]

1 [1983] 1 All ER 849, [1983] 1 WLR 143.

Interrogatories

16.17 It is not within the compass of this chapter to deal with the circumstances in which leave to administer interrogatories may be obtained; for this topic, see the Annual Practice. The observation may, however, be permitted that interrogatories are too neglected a weapon, particularly in the context of an action for medical negligence, where so often the vital facts are wholly outside the knowledge of the plaintiff and are not fully revealed by the records. The subject is referred to here since, if interrogatories may at the appropriate stage be required, it is necessary at the outset to consider, where the defendant is not a single medical practitioner, whether a particular member of the defendant's staff should be joined as a defendant so that he can be interrogated. An answer to an interrogatory made on oath by a personal defendant is far more useful, particularly in cross-examination, than is an answer given by an officer of a health authority after enquiry from employees, none of whom can be specifically identified with the answer and who may therefore escape effective cross-examination upon it.

The timetable

16.18 The mental suffering caused to patients and relatives by the current indefensible delays in the trial of medical negligence actions is referred to earlier (see Chapter 11). It follows that from the earliest moment a strategy should be evolved to reduce such delays. Some causes of delay are outside the control of the plaintiff and his advisers, but others are not, and it is a useful discipline to establish at, or about the time of, the preliminary consultation a broad timetable which has the assent of all affected members of the team and to the fulfilment of which the efforts of all can be bent. The authorities (judges, masters and district judges and listing officers) are well aware of the current difficulties and are the more likely to assist to overcome them if the plaintiff's solicitors can demonstrate that they have done everything within their power to progress the case of their client; in particular, by taking procedural steps well within the time-limits prescribed by rules of court and by ensuring (if necessary by summons) that their opponents do likewise.

16.19 By the time that pleadings are closed instructing solicitors and junior counsel will have dealt with necessary interlocutory matters, if need be after consulting leading counsel. At this stage the issues will have been crystallised. If the defence has not raised any positive allegation, and has not blamed any third party, a further consultation may be delayed until mutual exchange of medical reports has taken place, although leading counsel should always be sent the Defence and asked if it calls for any particular step to be taken. Where, however, the Defence is informative and deals with particularity with the plaintiff's allegations (as Defences in this class of case increasingly, and properly, do) a further consultation will be appropriate at which the experts should attend, in order to assess the strength of the opposing contentions and to determine what should be done to rebut the assertions made on behalf of the defendant. Leading counsel's opinion may in any event be required at this time for the purpose of a review by the legal aid authorities. If the defendant blames a third party it will be necessary to consider whether he should be joined as a defendant. The cast of the Defence may be such as to demand the instruction of experts in a fresh field. Decisions on such matters must be considered at this stage, so that the forthcoming Summons for Directions may deal with every necessary matter and so that the ambit of the expert evidence required at the trial can be reviewed. (See paras **11.79** et seq.)

16.20 Once the Summons for Directions has been heard, and directions for trial have been given, counsel should be asked to advise on evidence. This important step is often omitted, or left until too late; solicitors who fail to ask for such advice run an unnecessary risk. In most cases advice on evidence can be given by experienced junior counsel, but in a weighty or unusually difficult case it is best for leading and junior counsel to advise jointly and, according to the circumstances, such advice may usefully be preceded by a consultation with instructing solicitors. The advice should always be written, or confirmed in writing. Among the matters to be dealt with will figure predominantly the adequacy of the expert medical evidence, both as to its scope and its authority. Now is the time to decide whether further medical evidence is required, so that if it is, the expert who comes afresh to the litigation will have adequate time in which to familiarise himself with the case, and with the opinions of his co-experts, and possibly to suggest still further lines of enquiry. Factual witness statements should be considered and approved before mutual exchange. (See para **11.102**.)

16.21 Certainly not later than one month before trial there should be held a final pre-trial consultation at which all experts should attend; it may be convenient to hold two such consultations, one dealing with the issue of liability, and the other with the issue of quantum, in order to avoid waste of expert time. If there has been a payment into court the consultation or consultations may have to be advanced in order that the plaintiff may be properly advised on the merits and on quantum and hence enabled to make an informed decision, whether to accept what has been paid in, or to negotiate, or to fight.

16.22 The purposes of the final pre-trial consultation are primarily:

(1) to assess or reassess the merits of the case on liability;
(2) to assess or reassess quantum;
(3) to decide whether to accept any money paid into court, or which may have been otherwise offered;
(4) to decide finally which expert witnesses are to be asked to attend court in connection with the issues of liability;

(5) to decide finally which expert witnesses are to be asked to attend court in connection with the issue of quantum;
(6) to decide finally which witnesses as to fact should attend court;
(7) to ensure that all necessary documentary evidence has been obtained and that it is or will be properly bundled (as to bundles, see para **11.229**);
(8) to check finally that every fact requiring proof can be established by properly admissible evidence and if necessary to initiate the service of appropriate Civil Evidence Act notices even though their time for service may strictly have expired (see RSC Order 38, rules 21(1), 29(1)).

16.23 After the final pre-trial consultation it will be for instructing solicitors to ensure that any loose ends are properly dealt with. Subject to this, the plaintiff's team of advisers may now await the date of trial (which will usually be a fixed date) unless negotiations for settlement continue or begin, when the advice and assistance of counsel is invariably sought. The conduct of the trial itself lies within the scope of another chapter (Chapter 19).

THE ROLE OF COUNSEL FOR THE DEFENDANT

16.24 The involvement of counsel for the defendant, and particularly of leading counsel, differs from that of counsel instructed on behalf of a plaintiff principally by reason of the following:

(1) the client is a professional, being in most cases a hospital, a doctor or a drug company;
(2) if the client is a doctor, he may be supported by the Medical Defence Union or the Medical Protection Society, both extremely well versed in medical negligence litigation;
(3) cases where there is no defence on liability are usually recognised as such at least by the time solicitors are instructed on behalf of the defendant and in these circumstances in straightforward cases counsel is not instructed on the issue of liability and may not be instructed on the issue of quantum;
(4) solicitors acting for health authorities or defence organisations are highly experienced and require little or no guidance on matters of preparation and procedure; save for interlocutory matters counsel's pre-trial involvement is likely only in the weightier and more complex cases and he may well be instructed at a far later stage than his counterpart who acts for the plaintiff;
(5) counsel has not to frame an attack, but to repel one. There is little scope for heroism and panache in the ordering of the lines of battle.

16.25 It is appropriate here to comment upon the nature of the pleaded Defence in medical negligence actions. The rule that a defendant should not plead to particulars is out of place in a case involving complex medical issues, and should be discarded, just as it has been discarded in other fields of like complexity (for example, in construction actions). If plaintiff's counsel has framed a properly particularised Statement of Claim setting out in numbered sub-paragraphs precisely what it is alleged that the defendant did or failed to do which connotes fault, then the defendant should plead to each. In this way the medical issues will be defined, and usually narrowed, and the medical evidence can be directed aright. A Defence which admits facts which are never likely to be in dispute, and which then proceeds to put forward a blanket denial only, fails to inform the plaintiff of the case which he has to meet and should be regarded as a creature of the past. If the prehistoric head should reappear, it should be struck down by the use of the interlocutory processes.

16.26 For the reasons enumerated above, although junior counsel will of course have been instructed at the pleading stage, leading counsel may only receive his papers a relatively short time before trial, simply because experienced junior counsel and instructing solicitors between them will properly and adequately have prepared the case up to that point. There are, naturally, exceptional cases involving complex issues of medical expertise, or difficult points of law, which fall outside the general pattern.

16.27 When leading counsel receives his instructions he is afforded the opportunity delicately to comment upon his junior's pleadings and the preparation of the case generally, if so emboldened. He comes to the scene with all the benefit of freshness, and if he feels that a further or different approach should be taken he must of course so express himself. This is in part why he is instructed, and no offence should, or will, be taken. His function when first instructed will depend upon his instructions; he may be asked to advise on liability, or on quantum, or both; he may be asked to advise on evidence; he certainly should at some stage not later than one month before trial be asked to see the defence experts in consultation. At or as a result of this consultation he will be able to advise the defendant in the same way, *mutatis mutandis*, as earlier in this chapter it is suggested that counsel for a plaintiff should advise his client; as regards payment into court he will (if so asked) advise whether money should be paid in and, if so, how much, or whether an offer should be made outside the formal procedure. Here it may be observed that a payment into court should be on the generous, rather than on the mean, side, since even if it is not accepted it will if sufficiently ample exert an influence in later negotiation.

CAUSATION

16.28 This chapter closes with a discussion of some of the problems which may arise in connection with the issue of causation in medical negligence actions, including actions against drug manufacturers and suppliers. This type of litigation is peculiarly apt to generate difficulties in this area. The functioning of the human body is such that the link between the negligence of a defendant in treating a patient, or in manufacturing or supplying a drug, is often secretive, and has to be established, if established it can be, by indirect evidence (for example, epidemiological evidence or evidence pointing to a biologically plausible connection between the treatment or drug and the harmful consequence). Frequently a pathology is multifactorial (for example, retrolental fibroplasia); problems arise if not all factors can be ascribed to the negligence of a single defendant. The pathology may be insidious in onset and slow in development (for example, pneumoconiosis); part of that development may be referable to fault on the part of the defendant, part may not be. There may be a pathology pre-existing any culpable activity by the defendant, and questions may then arise as to whether the defendant's fault worsened the plaintiff's condition. Problems may also arise as to the proper burden of proof in such cases.

16.29 It is thus of special importance that in preparing for trial counsel should correctly advise the expert medical witnesses concerning the criteria to which they should direct their minds when considering whether the plaintiff's condition, or any particular aspect of it, was in contemplation of law caused by the alleged fault of the defendant. It is also of importance that the medical experts should be properly advised upon what constitutes proof for legal purposes; this is by no means the same as medical or scientific proof, which imports a higher degree of certainty (rarely precisely defined) than is required by law. A doctor is unlikely to ascribe a sequel to a pathology if it is only just more likely than not to have been caused by that pathology, whereas such a likelihood would establish causation to the satisfaction of a court.

16.30 Given the complexities of physiopathology it is not surprising that several medical negligence cases have been the subject of decision at the highest level with reference to the issue of causation. This section of the chapter does not purport to constitute a monograph upon the topic of causation. For such a treatment, the reader is referred to Hart and Honoré *Causation in the Law* and to the standard textbooks on tort and negligence. What it is hoped will be helpful to the practitioner is to isolate and expose some of the problems which have emerged, and to indicate how the courts have thus far solved them.

Causation: probability and chance

16.31 Medical negligence cases are commonly framed in tort, since usually the plaintiff will have provided no monetary consideration for the doctor's services. It may be that even in such cases the action can be framed in contract; submission to the treatment may be good consideration to found an undertaking by the doctor to use reasonable care.[1] Where the patient is fee-paying there is undoubtedly a contractual relationship between him and the doctor. Whether the action be brought in contract or in tort the problems here considered will be the same, the nature of the cause of action being in the present context of no materiality.

1 Per Scrutton LJ in *Everett v Griffiths* [1920] 3 KB 163 at 193.

16.32 In all cases the onus of proving a causal nexus between the negligence complained of and the damage suffered lies on the plaintiff,[1] although he may of course be assisted by inferences to be drawn from the unlikelihood of the occurrence of the harm complained of in the absence of fault. An admission of 'liability' by a defendant is generally understood to include an admission that the harmful consequences pleaded (though not their pecuniary evaluation) were caused by fault on the part of the defendant, but for the avoidance of doubt a written and open admission that such consequences were in fact so caused must always be expressly obtained before a plaintiff may safely proceed to trial on the issue of quantum alone.

1 *Bonnington Castings v Wardlaw* [1956] AC 613, [1956] 1 All ER 615, HL; *Wigley v British Vinegars Ltd* [1964] AC 307, [1962] 3 All ER 161, HL; *Wilsher v Essex Area Health Authority* [1988] AC 1074, [1988] 1 All ER 871, HL.

16.33 The rule that the onus of proof lies on the plaintiff has particular application in two categories of medical case. The first is where a plaintiff alleges that he would not have consented to undergo the treatment prescribed had he been given different and more appropriate advice as to its possible consequences. The second is where the conduct of a third party intervenes between that of a defendant and the injury of which the plaintiff complains. This latter situation may arise in a pharmaceutical case involving a prescription-only drug where, for example, the plaintiff alleges that a failure by the manufacturer to warn of an allegedly harmful propensity was causative of his injury.

16.34 In both these categories of case the onus lies on the plaintiff to allege and prove causation, that is to say (in the first case) that he would not have consented to undergo the treatment had he been given different advice and (in the second) that if the alleged warning had been given the treating physician would have prescribed differently, and that the injury complained of would thereby have been avoided or lessened. That the onus is so disposed follows from the authorities referred to in para **16.32**. There is no presumption that once it is proved that the manufacturer, by lack of due care, failed to give the warning, then causation is established unless he proves the contrary; to erect such a presumption would be to run counter to those authorities. The dictum to the contrary of the Ontario Court of Appeal in *Buchan v Ortho Pharmaceutical (Canada) Ltd*[1] would not, it is submitted, be followed here, precariously founded as it is upon a slim catena of American authority without support from any other source.

1 (1986) 54 OR (2d) 92 at 116.

16.35 Furthermore, what is material is whether the particular plaintiff or (as the case may be) the particular treating physician would in the postulated circumstances have taken a different course, and not whether a reasonable plaintiff or treating physician standing in their shoes would have done so; see *Wigley v British Vinegars Ltd*.[1] This subjective approach was applied by the NSW Court of Appeal in *Ellis v Wallsend District Hospital*.[2] The law of Canada, on the other hand, favours an objective test[3] but these decisions are contrary to those of the House of Lords cited in para **16.32**, note 1, and would not, it is submitted, be followed here.

1 [1964] AC 307, HL per Viscount Kilmuir at 325.
2 [1990] 2 Med LR 103 (see per Kirby J at 108, Samuels JA at 118–119 and Meagher JA at 131).
3 *Reibl v Hughes* (1980) 114 DLR (3rd) 1 (Supreme Court of Canada); *Kitchen v McMullen* [1990] 1 Med LR 352 (New Brunswick Court of Appeal).

16.36 The recent case of *Bolitho v City & Hackney Health Authority*[1] requires consideration in this context. When the infant plaintiff ('P') was two years old, he suffered a number of fits as a result of which he was taken to a hospital for which the defendants were responsible. There he had an operation to correct a patent ductus arteriosus. Shortly thereafter he was readmitted suffering from croup. After a few days he was discharged but at home he experienced breathing difficulty and was re-admitted. On the following day at about 12.40 the duty sister became concerned about his condition and bleeped the Senior Paediatric Registrar ('SPR'), asking her to come straight away. She failed to do so. At about 14.00 the sister observed that P still had breathing difficulties and telephoned the SPR, who said that she had asked Dr R (a SHO) to come in her place. Dr R did not receive that message because her bleep was not working. At about 14.30 P collapsed due to a cardiac arrest. Before he could be resuscitated he suffered brain damage in consequence.

1 [1994] Med LR 381, CA. It is understood that this case may be considered by the House of Lords.

16.37 P alleged that the failure of any doctor to attend on either of the two occasions upon which the sister asked for medical help was negligent and in the course of the trial the defendants conceded that the SPR had been negligent not to have attended P when called. There was a conflict of evidence as to what treatment should have been given to P had the SPR attended. On his behalf it was contended that he should have been intubated. Experts called for the defendants rejected that suggestion. It was conceded by the defendants that if intubation had taken place at any time prior to the cardiac arrest this would probably have averted the collapse and any serious consequences. The question for the court was thus one of causation.

16.38 The trial judge, having considered the conflicting evidence of the medical witnesses, and applying the *Bolam*[1] test, held that it had not been proved that a competent doctor would have intubated P before his collapse. He made no finding as to whether the SPR would have procured an intubation, had she attended when she ought to have done. Therefore, P's case failed.

1 *Bolam v Friern Hospital Management Committee* [1957] 1 WLR 582 (see Chapter 1).

16.39 In the Court of Appeal, the issue arose, whether the trial judge should have applied the *Bolam* test to the issue of causation. P, now the appellant, contended that the *Bolam* test was not relevant to the issue of causation, and that on the evidence the SPR, had she attended, would probably have procured his intubation. Therefore, on a balance of probabilities, the failure to attend was causative of the disaster.

16.40 The majority of the Court of Appeal rejected this submission. Farquharson LJ held that it was necessary for the trial judge to decide what course of events would have followed had the duty been discharged. In those circumstances, he was bound to rely on the expert evidence; it was for P to prove that if she did not do so her 'failure was contrary to accepted medical practice'. The judge having found that non-intubation accorded with accepted medical practice, P failed on the issue of causation.

16.41 Dillon LJ pointed to the evidence of the SPR, that had she attended she would not have intubated, and said that this evidence could only be displaced by showing that if she had done that she would have been negligent. However, that she would not have been negligent was supported by a body of medical opinion. Alternatively, if the evidence of the SPR were ignored, there was medical opinion both for and against intubation. It could not in the present case be said that the opinion of those doctors who contra-indicated intubation was such that no reasonable body of doctors could have held it. Therefore, it followed that causation had not been proved. On the state of the medical evidence there was no material entitling the appellate court to say that on the balance of probabilities P would have been intubated if a doctor had attended promptly in response to the 14.00 call.

16.42 Simon Brown LJ dissented. He thought that it was obviously right that the issue of causation should be decided by a test of probability, rather than by an application of the test in *Bolam*. The issue was: had the SPR or a suitable substitute attended when called, would P on the balance of probabilities have been intubated? In the event the trial judge did not address this question. Although he found that had the SPR attended, she would probably not have intubated, it was far from clear that the SPR would have been the attending doctor; further it would be unsatisfactory to place much reliance on the evidence of a doctor as to what he or she would have done. The question was: what would an attending doctor probably have done? He or she would probably have done that which he or she should have done, so that the question became, what should a doctor do in such circumstances? Having considered the authorities, Simon Brown LJ addressed the question, whether the material before the court was sufficient to enable it to decide the matter finally, or whether a retrial should be ordered. He held that there was sufficient material to conclude the case, and to conclude it in favour of P. The ultimate question was not, would it have been unreasonable and thus negligent for an attending doctor not to intubate P (to which the answer was clearly No). It was rather, should and therefore would an attending doctor probably have intubated P, to which the answer was an equally clear Yes. The trial judge's conclusion that the views of the defendants' principal consultant witnesses represented those of a respectable body of medical opinion was irrelevant, unless they sufficed to rebut the assumptions otherwise arising in P's favour and to defeat the inferences that a doctor's attendance would probably have benefited him. In the view of Simon Brown LJ those views were unpersuasive that attendance in response to the sister's calls would have been useless.

16.43 Despite the difference of opinion between the Lords Justices, each of them agreed that the issue of causation fell to be decided by asking the question: 'what course of events would have followed had the duty been discharged?' (Farquharson LJ); 'The question surely is: what would an attending doctor probably have done?' (Simon Brown LJ); Dillon LJ did not directly formulate the question but it is clear from his judgment as a whole, and his express agreement with that of Farquharson LJ, that he took the same view. The difference of opinion related, not to this basic principle, but to whether in deciding the issue, it was relevant to take into account the quality of the conduct of the hypothetically attending doctor. The majority held that it was, so that not only had P to prove that the SPR would probably have intubated but, further, that if she had not done so her failure would have been contrary to accepted medical practice. This involved a consideration of the expert evidence, which demonstrated that there was a responsible body of medical opinion in favour of non-intubation. Therefore, P failed on the issue of causation. On the other hand, Simon Brown LJ held that consideration of the *Bolam* test was irrelevant, being a test of liability and not of causation. On the facts of the case, he was prepared to hold, putting on one side the expert medical evidence, that there was sufficient material before the court to conclude the case in favour of P.

16.44 It is submitted that the judgment of Simon Brown LJ is to be preferred in its rejection of the materiality of the *Bolam* test. Although evidentially the question, what would the attending doctor have done, might depend wholly or in part upon a prior consideration of what she should have done, the fact that had she not procured intubation this would have accorded with a responsible body of medical opinion is not decisive. In the present case, a responsible body of medical opinion supported both intubation and non-intubation. Medical opinion was, therefore, neutral. If the SPR had said in evidence that she would have procured intubation it is inconceivable that a court would have found that she would not have done so, merely because one body of doctors would have considered this procedure contra-indicated. In truth, causation in the present case was a question of hypothetical fact – what events would have occurred on a particular premise? – and the quality of the acts or omissions forming part of the chain of causation is immaterial. What is material is, simply, what in fact would on a balance of probability have occurred?

16.45 The burden of proof is the civil burden of proof – a balance of probability. Medical cases may involve the ascertainment of present or past fact, or the prognostication of future events, or both. Where what is in issue is the ascertainment of a present or past fact, then the ordinary rule applies: the present or past fact is established for legal purposes if upon the evidence its existence is, or was, more probable than its non-existence. Thus, in *Hotson v East Berkshire Area Health Authority*[1] the infant plaintiff fell from a tree, sustaining a fracture of the left femoral epiphysis. He was taken to hospital where staff negligently failed to diagnose the injury and sent him home. After five days he was taken to hospital again and the correct diagnosis was made. He was operated upon, but suffered an avascular necrosis of the epiphysis, involving immediate disability and the almost certain consequence that in later years he would develop osteoarthritis. The trial judge found that even had the defendants correctly diagnosed and treated the plaintiff on his first admission there was a 75 per cent risk that the plaintiff's injury would have followed the same course as in fact it did; what the defendants' negligence did was to transform that risk into a certainty. Had avascular necrosis not occurred, the plaintiff would have made a nearly full recovery. Hence, he held that the plaintiff was entitled to damages for the loss of the 25 per cent chance that, if the injury had been promptly diagnosed and treated, there would have been no avascular necrosis.

1 [1987] AC 750, [1987] 2 All ER 909, HL.

16.46 This aspect of the judgment having been upheld by the Court of Appeal, the defendants appealed to the House of Lords. Their Lordships allowed the appeal. On the judge's findings, on a balance of probability the injury caused by the fall left insufficient blood vessels intact to keep the epiphysis alive. There was no question of evaluating the loss of a chance. The relevant facts lay in the past. Either the fall had already (on a balance of probability) caused the necrosis, or it had not. If it had, as the trial judge in effect found, then the defendants could not be responsible for that necrosis. The fundamental question of fact related to a point of time before the negligent failure to treat began; that fundamental question related to a past fact and no question was raised as to what might have been the situation in a hypothetical or future state of facts.

16.47 Their Lordships left open the question whether, where the cause of injury is unascertainable and all that the plaintiff can show is a less than even statistical chance that, but for the defendant's fault, he would not have suffered the injury, it could ever be appropriate to award a proportionate fraction of the full damages as the measure of damages for the lost chance.[1] This question was kept open in deference to the decision of the House of Lords in *McGhee v National Coal Board*[2] (discussed below) and in the knowledge that *Wilsher v Essex Area Health Authority*[3] was shortly to be considered by their Lordships' House. Since the decision of their Lordships in *Wilsher v Essex Area Health Authority*[4] (also discussed below) it is submitted that there is no longer room for argument that in a case where the material facts lie in the past anything less than proof of causation on a balance of probability suffices to discharge the necessary burden.

1 See per Lord Bridge at [1987] AC 750, 782–783 and per Lord Mackay at 786.
2 [1972] 3 All ER 1008, [1973] 1 WLR 1, HL.
3 [1987] QB 730, [1986] 3 All ER 801, CA.
4 [1988] AC 1074, [1988] 1 All ER 871, HL.

16.48 With *Hotson v East Berkshire Area Health Authority* may be contrasted *Davies v Taylor*,[1] a Fatal Accidents Act case where it was sought to establish a potential dependency on behalf of a widow whose husband had been killed due to the defendant's negligence, and who had deserted him five weeks before his death, on the basis that she would have been reconciled with him had he lived. The trial judge held that there was an onus on the widow to prove that on a balance of probability she had an expectation of continued dependency – that it was more probable than not that there would have been a reconciliation. The House of Lords held that this approach was erroneous. Where the issue is whether a certain thing is or is not true, or whether a certain event did or did not happen, then the court must decide that issue one way or the other. If there is a balance of probability in favour of it having happened, then for legal purposes it is proved that it did happen. In the instant case, however, whether the widow would or would not have returned to her husband was not a past fact – it lay in the future at the material time (the time of the husband's death). Therefore, the chance of a reconciliation had to be evaluated. On the facts of the case, however, their Lordships held that there was no significant chance that the husband and wife would have become reconciled, so that the claim failed.

1 [1974] AC 225.

16.49 Merely because at the time of the tort facts relevant to the assessment of damages lie in the future it does not follow that the proper approach is to evaluate the chance of their occurrence, if in the period between the commission of the tort and the trial the relevant facts have become past facts. The court should never speculate where it knows (see, for example, *Curwen v James*[1]). Thus, if as a result of negligence a joint is injured, giving rise to a risk of osteoarthritis, and at the date of trial osteoarthritis has on a balance of probability supervened, then the court must evaluate damages on the basis that osteoarthritis is an established fact, even though at the date of the tort it might only have been prognosticated as a chance sequel. Whether or not the osteoarthritis will get better or worse after trial and, if so, to what extent, are however matters lying in the future and which must be evaluated on the basis of the chance of their occurrence.

1 [1963] 2 All ER 619, [1963] 1 WLR 748, CA.

16.50 It is clear from *Davies v Taylor*, above, that the principle of the evaluation of a chance applies, not only where events lie in the future at the trial date, but also where they lay in the future at the date of commission of the tort, but cannot at the trial date be established as past or present facts because the circumstances make this impossible. Such indeed was the case on the facts of *Davies v Taylor* itself: the death of the husband which gave rise to the cause of action itself prevented a reconciliation from ever occurring. On the other hand, merely because the absence of evidence makes it impossible to decide, on a balance of probability, whether a given sequel has occurred by the date of trial, the sequel is not to be classified as a future fact, and evaluated as a chance. Suppose that the plaintiff's knee-joint is injured by the defendant's negligence. The medical evidence is that osteoarthritis may occur. If at the date of trial there is no evidence that by that time osteoarthritis has actually supervened, damages must be assessed on the basis that it has not done so, even though the medical evidence may be that by the trial date there was a possibility that it might have done so. Of course, if that evidence were also that after the trial it might present a continuing risk, then that risk would have to be evaluated, in the usual way, according to the chance of its coming to pass.

16.51 An area in which, it is suggested, the courts have erred with regard to the proof of events which lie in the future is that of the evaluation of the consequences of a reduction in expectation of life. In many cases involving damages for personal injury it becomes necessary for the court to estimate for how long a person is likely to live, given the injuries sustained. The practice is for the court, upon receiving medical evidence as to expectation of life, to decide the future date of death upon a balance of probability, and having established that date, to treat it as virtually certain, or at least extremely probable, for the purpose of assessing damages (for example) for loss of future earnings, or the value of future care, and to treat it as the only relevant date for that purpose.

It is submitted that this approach is flawed. A person living today has a chance, capable of expression as a percentage, that he will live to the age of x years. As x varies, so does the percentage chance of achieving it vary. Obviously, the closer x lies to his present age, the greater is the percentage chance that he will in fact live to the age of x years; the further away that x lies, the less is that percentage chance. There is of course an age which lies at the median of the spectrum of chances, that is to say, an age to which it is equally probable that he will survive as that he will not. It cannot however be right to treat that age as the only relevant age of presumed death for the purpose of calculating losses which will cease at death. Such an approach assumes that survival to that age is virtually certain and that there is no chance of further survival, whereas ex hypothesi there is but a 50 per cent chance of survival to that age, followed by a substantial chance of further survival thereafter. The only merit of the present practice is its simplicity, recognising as it does the extreme difficulties of prognostication.

In theory, the court could assess the relevant head of damage by taking separately each future year up to a date when the chance of survival is too small to play any significant part in the calculation, and then evaluating the loss for each such year by discounting (i) for the chance that survival to that year will not be achieved and (ii) for futurity. The damages in respect of the type of loss under consideration would be the aggregate of the yearly losses so ascertained.

Such an approach would of course be quite impracticable and it would assume an accuracy in the estimation of expectation of life which is quite unrealistic. On the other hand, it is suggested that there is room for a compromise between the present practice and the theoretical ideal, whereby the court would look broadly at the percentage chances of survival to relatively few chosen ages and would assess damages accordingly. This would palliate the anomaly of the existing system, by which a man whose probable date of death represents in fact a chance probability of 90 per cent that he will die at that date receives the same relevant damages as a man whose probable date of death represents a chance probability of only 60 per cent. In the first case, only a 10 per cent chance of further survival is ignored, whereas in the second the neglect is of a chance of 40 per cent. Since damages for future loss in personal injury cases of the more serious kind are very largely influenced by the elements of loss of earnings and cost of future care, the difference between the two cases postulated is highly significant in monetary terms.

Causation: material contribution

16.52 It has for many years been well settled that if the fault of the defendant makes a material contribution to the plaintiff's injury, even though it was not the sole cause of it, then the injury is for legal purposes regarded as having been caused by the fault (*Bonnington Castings Ltd v Wardlaw*[1]). In *McGhee v National Coal Board*[2] the House of Lords was faced with a problem resulting from the paucity of evidence relating to causation. A worker employed at a brick kiln contracted dermatitis. There was no doubt that this condition was caused by brick dust emanating from the kiln. His employers admitted a breach of duty in failing to provide showers to wash away the dust after work ceased, but denied causation. The medical evidence was that when the plaintiff cycled home the brick dust attaching to his skin injured the cells, whereafter dermatitis might result. Washing immediately after work was the only practicable way of removing the danger. The question therefore was, whether the failure to provide showers caused or materially contributed to the dermatitis. The evidence did not show how the dermatitis began, but was in their Lordships' view sufficient to justify a conclusion that culpably to allow the plaintiff to cycle home unwashed was fault on the employers' part which made a material contribution to the onset of dermatitis, although it may not have been the sole cause.

1 [1956] AC 613, [1956] 1 All ER 615, HL.
2 [1973] 3 All ER 1008, [1973] 1 WLR 1, HL.

16.53 Thus far there is nothing particularly remarkable about this decision, which may be regarded as one of fact assisted by the considerations that the employers were the cause of the whole of the plaintiff's exposure to brick dust (although not culpably so with respect to contact with brick dust within the kiln), that they were culpably responsible for the continuing exposure to brick dust after the plaintiff left work, and that it would be unfair to expect an injured workman to prove more. However, passages in some of their Lordships' speeches could be read as establishing a general proposition, that if a defendant by his fault increases the risk of injury, and injury comes to pass, that is equivalent to the fault having made a material contribution to the injury.[1]

1 See per Lord Reid [1973] 1 WLR at 5, per Lord Wilberforce at 6, 7, per Lord Simon at 8, per Lord Salmon at 12.

16.54 There, so far at least as medical negligence cases are concerned, the topic might have rested had it not been for the enthusiasm of counsel for the plaintiff in *Clark v MacLennan*,[1] who persuaded Peter Pain J to apply *McGhee v National Coal Board* to a medical negligence situation and to hold on the issue of damages that where there was a negligent failure to take a precaution and the very damage against which the precaution was designed to be a protection occurred, the onus shifted to the defendant to show that his negligence did not cause the damage. It is now clear that this aspect of the decision was wrong (see the succeeding paragraph).

1 [1983] 1 All ER 416.

16.55 *Wilsher v Essex Area Health Authority*[1] was also tried at first instance by Peter Pain J. This was a case of retrolental fibroplasia ('RLF') of particular complexity and difficulty. RLF is a retinopathy of prematurity in which the eyes of a new-born baby who is premature suffer damage due to a pathology which may have a number of causes, among them being the administration of oxygen in excessive quantities, the administration having been necessary to preserve the life of the child. The trial judge held that the negligent misplacement of a sensing catheter by the hospital staff had led to excessive oxygen being administered until the misplacement was discovered and corrected. He held further that on five later periods oxygen was also excessively administered, due to staff negligence. He applied his earlier decision in *Clark v MacLennan* and held (in relation to causation) that the onus shifted to the defendants to show that they had not caused the RLF, since excessive oxygen administration increased the risk of that condition. On appeal, the Court of Appeal[2] reversed the trial judge's findings of negligence in relation to the five later periods, so that that court, and later the House of Lords, had to consider an issue of causation arising only in relation to the first episode (the misplaced catheter). There was no doubt that the excessive administration of oxygen during that period could have caused the RLF. There were, however, other credible causative agents also present in the case (hypercarbia, intra-ventricular haemorrhage, apnoea, patent ductus arteriosus) none of which could be ascribed to fault on the part of the defendants. The majority of the Court of Appeal (Mustill and Glidewell LJJ) held that the fact that in the case before them there were a number of risk factors, any one of which might have caused the injury, but only one of which was referable to negligence on the part of the defendants, did not take the case out of the principle of *McGhee v National Coal Board* as they interpreted it, that is to say, that if conduct of a particular kind creates a risk that injury will be caused to another or increases an existing risk that injury will ensue and if the two parties stand in such a relationship that the one party owes a duty not to conduct himself in that way; and if the first party does conduct himself in that way; and if the other party does suffer injury of the kind to which the risk related; then the first party is taken to have caused the injury by his breach of duty, even though the existence and extent of the contribution made by the breach cannot be ascertained.[3] Sir Nicolas Browne-Wilkinson V-C, in a judgment later approved on this point by the House of Lords, dissented, distinguishing *McGhee v National Coal Board*.[4] In that case there was only one possible agent which could have caused the dermatitis, whereas in *Wilsher v Essex Area Health Authority* there were a number, there being no satisfactory evidence that excessive oxygen was more likely than any of the others to have caused the plaintiff's RLF.

1 (21 December 1984, unreported) QB.
2 [1987] QB 730, [1986] 3 All ER 801.
3 See per Mustill LJ [1987] QB 730 at 771, 772 and per Glidewell LJ at 776.
4 [1987] QB 730 at 779.

16.56 The equiparation, for legal purposes, of increase of risk of injury with the making of a material contribution to it is plainly a fiction, as Lord Wilberforce in *McGhee v National Coal Board*[1] and Mustill LJ in *Wilsher v Essex Area Health Authority*[2] recognised. They are different concepts. A statement as to risk is a statement as to a future chance based, usually, on experience of earlier similar cases. A statement that a material contribution has been made is a statement as to past fact based upon evidence relating to the plaintiff's particular circumstances. The leap from the first to the second is the triumph of policy over logic.

1 [1973] 1 WLR at 6.
2 [1987] QB at 752.

16.57 When *Wilsher v Essex Area Health Authority* came before their Lordships' House they overturned the decision of the Court of Appeal on the issue of causation. Only one full speech was delivered, that of Lord Bridge, in which the remainder of their Lordships concurred. *McGhee v National Coal Board* was subjected to a searching analysis and passages in the speech of Lord Wilberforce stating that in the circumstances the burden of proof of causation was reversed were disapproved.[1] In the event, *McGhee v National Coal Board* was held to have laid down no new principle of law whatever; on the contrary, said Lord Bridge,[2] it affirmed the principle that the onus of proving causation lies on the plaintiff: 'to attempt to extract from it some esoteric principle which in some way modifies, as a matter of law, the nature of the burden of proof of causation which a plaintiff or pursuer must discharge once he has established a relevant breach of duty is a fruitless one'. The dissenting judgment of Sir Nicolas Browne-Wilkinson V-C in the Court of Appeal, so far as it dealt with the matter of causation, was approved.[3]

1 [1988] AC at 1087.
2 At 1090.
3 At 1090–1091.

16.58 The law therefore now stands where it had always been thought to stand before *McGhee v National Coal Board*. The onus of proving causation, on a balance of probability, lies on the plaintiff, and that onus is satisfied if the plaintiff proves that the defendant's breach of duty made a material contribution to his injury. Mere proof that the defendant's breach increased the risk of injury is not of itself sufficient to discharge that onus; in particular, where a pathology may in the instant case have been caused by any one or more of a number of factors it is necessary for the plaintiff to prove affirmatively that at least one factor for which the defendant is in law responsible caused or made a material contribution to that pathology.

Causation: drug cases

16.59 Cases in which it is alleged that a therapeutic drug has caused injury to the recipient pose special problems in the field of causation. One aspect (the interposition of a prescribing intermediary) has already been touched upon (see paras **16.33** ff). Although in some cases within this class the nature of the harmful consequence complained of coupled with its repeated temporal relationship to the administration of the drug amply demonstrates a causal link (as in the phocomelia, or 'Thalidomide', cases) this is by no means always the case. In less obvious circumstances it may be necessary to assess many different classes of evidence in order to decide whether causation has been proved, and the preparation for trial of such litigation demands the most meticulous and skilled attention.

16.60 In England there appears to have been only one case in which such issues have been litigated to a decision: *Loveday v Renton and Wellcome Foundation Ltd*[1] in which on 29 and 30 March 1988 the trial judge, Stuart-Smith LJ, delivered a judgment running to some 204 pages following a trial lasting several months in the course of which 18 expert witnesses were called whose evidence ranged over many disparate specialities. The trial was one of a preliminary issue ordered by the judge: 'Can or could pertussis [whooping cough] vaccine cause permanent brain damage in young children?' To this preliminary issue there were effectively but two parties – the infant plaintiff, who had suffered brain damage after the administration of pertussis vaccine of unknown manufacture, and Wellcome Foundation Ltd ('Wellcome'), manufacturers of 'Trivax', a triple vaccine containing a pertussis component. No allegation of negligence was made against Wellcome, who were at their own request joined in the litigation under RSC Order 15, since they were, at the time of that litigation, the sole manufacturers in the United Kingdom of pertussis vaccine. Many other actions involving the same issue were stayed pending the trial of *Loveday*; in the event the court decided that the preliminary issue had not been proved, thereby making it extremely unlikely that any further such case will be pursued in this country.

1 [1990] 1 Med LR 117.

16.61 The interest of the case for the present purpose resides in the fact that an English court was called upon to decide what was almost wholly a scientific question, although of course it applied to the resolution of that question the standard forensic equipment of oral expert evidence tested by cross-examination and assisted by abundant references to the corpus of medical literature. In resolving the question the court, having considered both *McGhee v National Coal Board* and *Wilsher v Essex Area Health Authority* (which by this time had been decided in the House of Lords) approached the matter on the basis that it had to decide as a question of fact whether the vaccine could cause permanent brain damage in young children and that the onus of proving that it could rested on the plaintiff, the standard of proof being the balance of probability.[1]

1 At 123.

16.62 Medical opinion is agreed that in evaluating cause and effect in cases of the type under discussion the approach to be followed is that set out by Sir Austin Bradford Hill, Professor Emeritus of Medical Statistics in the University of London, in his classic work *Principles of Medical Statistics* (1971). In chapter XXIV of his book Bradford Hill enumerated those matters which should be considered in deciding whether the relationship of a risk factor to an effect of interest is merely an association, or whether it is truly causal. The matters are these:

(1) The strength of the association (what is the relative incidence of the condition under study in the various contrasted groups of patients studied?)
(2) The consistency of the association: has it been repeatedly observed by different persons, in different places, different circumstances and times?
(3) The specificity of the association: is it limited to specific workers or to specific sites and types of disease?
(4) The temporal relationship: does the alleged cause precede the effect?
(5) The biological gradient: is there a dose–response curve (the more the exposure, the greater the effect)?
(6) Biological plausibility: is there a plausible biological mechanism to explain the supposed causal link? (Note that the absence of such a demonstrable mechanism is not fatal to the hypothesis; what is biologically plausible depends upon the state of medical knowledge.)
(7) Coherence of the evidence: the interpretation of an association as causal should not seriously conflict with the generally known facts of the natural history and biology of the disease.
(8) Experimental evidence: may it be possible to alter or eliminate the risk factor so that the effect of interest is lessened, or disappears?
(9) Analogy: in some circumstances it is fair to judge by analogy; with the known effects of thalidomide and rubella we would be ready to accept slighter but similar evidence with another drug or another viral disease in pregnancy.

To these nine points may be added a tenth:

(10) Animal experimentation: the administration of the drug to animals having in relevant respects similar biological mechanisms to man may under controlled conditions produce similar results to those observed after administration to humans. Extrapolation from animal to man must be done with caution; it cannot be postulated with certainty that effects in animals mirror those in man.

Bradford Hill was careful to point out (at 320):

> Clearly none of these nine viewpoints can bring indisputable evidence for or against a cause-and-effect hypothesis and equally none can be required as a sine qua non.

What they can do, with greater or less strength, is to help us to answer the fundamental question – is there any other way of explaining the set of facts before us, is there any other answer more likely than cause and effect?

16.63 It is beyond the scope of this chapter to expand upon the factors set out above, and the reader is referred to *Principles of Medical Statistics* pp 313–320 for a full discussion. It is, however, appropriate to comment upon epidemiological evidence generally, since in preparing for trial in a case where such evidence is likely to be relevant (as it most often is in drug cases) particular care is required.

16.64 Epidemiology is the study of the determinants of disease in groups or populations (see Chapter 21). By definition it is not concerned with the question of association, far less of causation, in an individual subject. It is a method of study which, correctly performed and properly interpreted, may yield results which are fit to be considered along with other relevant evidence in deciding the issue of causation; on occasions, epidemiological evidence is the only relevant evidence available.

16.65 It is not the purpose of an epidemiological study either to establish or to disprove causation. Its purpose is simply to assess whether there is an association between a risk factor and an effect of interest and, if so, whether that association occurs more frequently than it would be expected to occur by chance. If it does so, then the strength of the association may be assessed by statistical methods.

16.66 An apparent association may indeed be due to chance alone. It may also be due, in whole or in part, to the bias inherent, in varying degrees, in all epidemiological studies. It may be due to the operation of confounding factors. Epidemiology, including medical statistics, cannot eliminate, but should as far as possible reduce, the incidence of such aberrations or, at least, assess and express their existence and probable effect. Hence, the design of epidemiological studies (such as randomised clinical trials, cohort studies and case-control studies) requires the greatest skill if their results are to command respect; one means of impugning the validity of such studies is to demonstrate a faulty methodology in the design of the study. Quite apart from study design, questions deserving close examination may arise as to the manner in which the study was operated in the field. How were the data collected? Was it a blind, or double blind, study? Were there other opportunities for bias to creep in? Were the data correctly presented for analysis? Then, at the analytical stage, there may be criticism of the way in which the data were assessed, and conclusions drawn from the analysis. Was the analysis performed in accordance with established principles and, if so, did it yield a statistically significant result? Only if a critical examination of the study permits confidence to be reposed in its conclusions is it fit to take its place, together with other relevant evidence, in the corpus of evidence from which inferences as to causation may be drawn.

16.67 It is obvious that the proper preparation for trial of a case involving such issues requires the assistance of epidemiological or medical statistical expertise or of both. Neither counsel nor the court can be expected to grapple with such arcane complexities unless they are fully informed. Even with such assistance, critical assessment of a published study is usually inhibited by the fact that although its methodology and results may be expounded in a reputable medical journal, the raw data alleged to support the results are not customarily made available, both for practical reasons and for fear of breaching medical confidentiality. In the absence of the raw data the conclusions of the study cannot be confirmed. How then is the problem to be approached?

16.68 When many studies have been published on a given topic considerations of time and money are likely to make an examination and analysis of the raw data appertaining to each an impracticable task, even if the raw data are extant and available. However, if there are few studies, and particularly if there is one only, bearing upon the issue, then it may well be feasible to obtain the raw data and to examine the methodology and analysis of the study afresh in the light of them. In such a case, if the raw data exist, but those in possession of them are unwilling to make them available, the court may well order third party discovery of them, the order containing provisions to safeguard confidentiality. Such a procedure in fact took place in *Loveday v Renton*, above. There was in that case only one study which purported to answer the question, whether whooping cough vaccine caused brain damage in children. This was the National Childhood Encephalopathy Study ('NCES') published by the Department of Health and Social Security in *Whooping Cough* (1981) but conducted by a team from the Department of Community Medicine of the Middlesex Hospital Medical School, London. This mammoth study, set up in 1976 because of widespread public and professional concern over the safety of whooping cough vaccination, took the form of a case-control study of children aged between 2 and 36 months admitted to hospital with defined neurological illnesses during a three-year period from the middle of 1976 to the middle of 1979. In *Whooping Cough* the study team published its preliminary results, relating to children with illness onset dates in 1977 and 1978 (Appendix VE). Children who (it was said) had persisting neurological damage at final follow-up a year or more after admission to hospital and who had (it was said) been immunised with DTP (diphtheria, tetanus and pertussis vaccine) within 7 days of onset of illness numbered 7; the controls numbered 3 (see p 167 of *Whooping Cough*). Since there were two controls to each case the relative risk of serious neurological illness persisting at final follow-up was 4.67 (7 divided by $^3/_2$). From this the authors calculated an attributable risk of 1 in 310,000 immunisations, this being an estimate of the attributable risk of onset of a serious neurological illness within 7 days after DTP vaccination in previously normal children with evidence of permanent neurological damage one year later.

16.69 These results were later extended to all children admitted to the study (not merely those within restricted onset dates) with the exception of cases of infantile spasms, since the study itself had shown that this pathology could not be referred to whooping cough vaccination. The later results were made public in a paper delivered at a Symposium in Geneva in 1984. They differed only marginally from those earlier arrived at in *Whooping Cough*.

16.70 The methodology, analysis and conclusions of the NCES were internationally accepted. The doctrine that whooping cough vaccine could cause permanent brain damage in young children became common medical currency. Faith in the safety of the vaccine, which had waned since the public concern earlier referred to, was not restored, and uptake rates remained low.

16.71 It would be out of place to deal in any detail with the data of the study or with the criticisms of it made in court by Wellcome on the basis of the examination of that data by their paediatric neurological, epidemiological and statistical experts. For a critical analysis see 'Permanent Brain Damage and Pertussis Vaccination: Is the End of the Saga in Sight?' (A H Griffith in Vaccine vol 7, June 1989). In the course of his judgment Stuart-Smith LJ undertook (in Chapter 12 of his judgment) an extensive analysis of the NCES. He concluded:

(1) That the study was intentionally biased against the vaccine in that steps were taken at every stage to ensure that the results would over-estimate rather than underestimate the risk (p 178).
(2) That the study was unintentionally biased by the presence of admission bias (p 172), detection signal bias (p 172), selective notification bias (p 172) and control selection bias (p 174). All these biases operated in the directions of overstating the risk of the vaccine; the study report played down the problems created by bias (p 174).
(3) That the study protocol was unjustifiably changed during the course of the study, constituting a flaw in the methodology the effect of which was almost impossible to gauge (p 175).
(4) That of the cases admitted to the study, 6 should not have been included as they failed to meet the study guidelines for inclusion and a further two were doubtfully included (p 176).
(5) That the analysis of the cases for the purpose of deciding whether it was appropriate to include them in the table from which the relative risk of permanent brain damage was calculated was flawed. There should not have been 7 exposed cases in the table at p 167 of *Whooping Cough*, but only 5; in the cognate table presented at Geneva there should only have been 4 (p 184). As to the controls, their number should be increased by one in the *Whooping Cough* table and by two in the Geneva table (p 184). Thus revised, neither table yielded a statistically significant relative risk that whooping cough vaccine was associated with permanent brain damage.

16.72 Stuart-Smith LJ accordingly concluded (p 184):

In my judgment the results of the NCES do not support the plaintiff's case on the preliminary issue

and:

An examination of the data in relation to the follow-up tables has led me to the conclusion that the results cannot be justified and cannot be relied upon as a measure of brain damage . . . No meaningful attributable risk can be derived from these results.

16.73 *Loveday v Renton* teaches important lessons both to the epidemiologist and to the lawyer who has to prepare a case in which epidemiological evidence is prominent. So far as epidemiology is concerned, the only comment which may be permitted to a non-medical author is that those conducting such a study should carefully preserve the raw data and working papers, so as to permit of later peer review. Had the raw data of the NCES not ultimately been obtained and scrutinised, that study might still retain credibility in relation to permanent brain damage. In the event, its pronouncements on this topic lie devastated. Not only, it is suggested, should the raw data and working papers be preserved but they should for proper reason and under controlled conditions be voluntarily released for peer scrutiny, since otherwise the validity of the results cannot be independently assessed.[1]

1 The judgment of Stuart-Smith LJ has recently been vindicated by the analysis of a further follow up of 754 of the NCES cases, carried out when most of the children were 10–12 years older ('Pertussis immunisation and serious acute neurological illnesses in children' (Miller et al (1993) British Medical Journal, vol 307, 1171)). The authors concluded (p 1175) '. . . although children with severe acute neurological illnesses resulting in death or later dysfunction had a significant excess risk of recent diphtheria, tetanus, and pertussis immunisation when compared with controls, this does not prove that the vaccine was the sole or even the prime cause of either the illnesses or the adverse outcomes in these cases. It remains an open question as to whether or not such illnesses occur related to diphtheria, tetanus, and pertussis vaccine in children whose brains are structurally and functionally normal and in the absence of concomitant factors. Certainly, attribution of a cause in individual cases must be speculative'.

16.74 For the lawyer preparing for a trial in which epidemiological studies are relied upon the lesson is to seek to obtain the raw data and working papers by agreement, and if agreement is not forthcoming, then by order of the court. Once the data have been obtained, a team should be assembled, to include epidemiological and statistical experts, together with experts in the field of medicine to which the study relates, in order that they may prepare a detailed critique. The history of the NCES has shown that only by such means, steadfastly pursued, can the conclusions of such studies be truly evaluated.

BIBLIOGRAPHICAL REFERENCES

Bradford Hill Sir A *Principles of Medical Statistics* (1971).

Department of Community Medicine, Middlesex Hospital Medical School, London, National Childhood Encephalopathy Study ('NCES') in *Whooping Cough* (London, DHSS, HMSO, 1981).

Griffith A H 'Permanent Brain Damage and Pertussis Vaccination: Is the End of the Saga in Sight?' Vaccine (1989) vol 7, June.

Hart H and Honoré A M *Causation in the Law*.

Miller et al 'Pertussis immunisation and serious acute neurological illnesses in children' (1993) British Medical Journal, vol 307, 1171.

CROSS-REFERENCES

For information related to topics in this chapter see Chapters 9, 10, 11, 19 and 21.

CHAPTER 17

Pecuniary compensation

Raymond Croxon *QC*
Colin Nixon

SUMMARY

INTRODUCTION

17.1 The remedy which the law affords a person injured by the tort of another is the right to recover damages in the form of monetary compensation. The objective of the courts in assessing the appropriate award of damages is to place the plaintiff in the same position, so far as can be done by an award of money, as he would have occupied had the injury not occurred. In *Livingston v Rawyards Coal Co*[1] Lord Blackburn held:

> where any injury is to be compensated by damages, in settling the sum of money to be given for reparation of damages you should as nearly as possible get at that sum of money which will put the person injured, or who has suffered, in the same position as he would have been in if he had not sustained the wrong for which he is now getting his compensation or reparation.

In *Admiralty Comrs v Valeria*[2] Viscount Dunedin held:

> The true method of expression, I think, is that in calculating damages you are to consider what is the pecuniary consideration which will make good to the sufferer, as

far as money can do so, the loss which he has suffered as the natural result of the wrong done to him.

1 (1880) 5 App Cas 25 at 39, HL.
2 [1922] 2 AC 242 at 248.

17.2 A plaintiff will usually suffer two distinct types of loss, namely non-pecuniary and pecuniary loss. The pecuniary loss is that which is capable of being directly calculated in monetary values, whether this be past or prospective loss, such as loss of earnings and medical expenses. Since the decision in *Jefford v Gee*[1] the courts are required to assess the damages under three broad heads, so the parties may understand the basis of award and for the purpose of awarding interest. These heads are the non-pecuniary damages, the pecuniary loss to the date of assessment and prospective pecuniary loss. In practice these heads of loss themselves are particularised in detail, since many separate items of claim may be involved. It is a matter of convention that the pecuniary loss to the date of assessment is described as special damage and the other heads as general damages.

1 [1970] 2 QB 130.

Non-pecuniary loss

17.3 The application of the basic rule of assessment is problematic in respect of the loss suffered by the plaintiff which is not pecuniary, namely the physical injury. It is not possible to assess an award for his pain, suffering and loss of amenity on any logical basis, and the practice of the courts is to award conventional sums. In *Wright v British Railways Board,*[1] Lord Diplock said of this head of loss:

> Such loss is not susceptible of measurement in money. Any figure at which the assessment of damages arrives cannot be other than artificial and, if the aim is that justice meted out to all litigants should be even-handed instead of depending on the idiosyncrasies of the assessor . . . the figure must be 'basically a conventional figure derived from experience and from awards in comparable cases'.

Hence, the awards for such non-pecuniary loss are based on the levels of award in previous cases in which the injuries were comparable, making allowance for the fall in the value of money since the comparable awards were made. The court will take judicial notice of the levels of damages awarded in such previous cases. In 1992 the Judicial Studies Board published 'Guidelines for the Assessment of General Damages in Personal Injuries Cases'. This provides guidelines by indicating the brackets within which damages for particular injuries should fall.

1 [1983] 2 AC 773, [1983] 2 All ER 698, HL.

Pecuniary loss

17.4 The application of the basic rule of assessment presents no difficulty in principle in the case of pecuniary loss, although in practice the assessment can give rise to difficulties. The award of damages is on an indemnity basis, to provide monetary compensation for actual or prospective pecuniary loss so as to place the plaintiff in the same position he would have occupied had the injury not occurred. The test applied when deciding the amount of an award for any particular item claimed is that the award should be reasonable and strike a fair balance between the parties. The word 'compensation' is derived from the latin 'compensare' (weigh together) and denotes a careful balancing, doing justice to each of the parties to the dispute. The test applied when deciding claims for past or prospective expenditure, is that if the plaintiff's injury has created needs which are or are likely to be productive of pecuniary loss then damages will be awarded, the measure of which is the sum required to meet those needs.[1]

1 *Donnelly v Joyce* [1974] QB 454, [1973] 3 All ER 475, CA.

Future pecuniary loss

17.5 The assessment of the award for future pecuniary loss often involves coming to terms with great uncertainty. In *Lim*'s case[1] Lord Scarman commented that 'there is really only one certainty: the future will prove the award to be either too high or too low.' The court has to award the present value of prospective loss, and make a broad estimate in so doing, taking into account the proven facts and the probabilities of the case.

> In determining what did happen in the past the court decides on the balance of probabilities. Anything that is more probable than not it treats as certain. But in assessing damages which depend upon its view as to what will happen in the future or would have happened in the future if something had not happened in the past, the court must make an estimate as to what are the chances that a particular thing will or would have happened and reflect those chances, whether they are more or less than even, in the amount of damages which it awards.[2]

1 *Lim Poh Choo v Camden and Islington AHA* [1980] AC 174, [1979] 2 All ER 910, HL.
2 Per Lord Diplock in *Mallett v McMonagle* [1970] AC 166 at 176; see also *Davies v Taylor* [1974] AC 207, [1972] 3 All ER 836 in which Lord Reid drew a dividing line between a chance which was a mere possibility or speculative, which was to be ignored, and a chance which was substantial. 'It must be left to the good sense of the tribunal to decide on broad lines, without regard to legal niceties, but on a consideration of all the facts in proper prospective.'

17.6 A preliminary question is whether the award for future pecuniary loss should take into account future inflation. The concern is that in times of high inflation an award of damages may become inadequate to meet the plaintiff's needs, and may become depleted before the end of the anticipated period of loss. The question of whether inflation should be taken into account was posed in different ways in a number of cases.[1] The answer was given in *Mallett v McMonagle* by Lord Diplock. This was a Fatal Accidents Act claim, but the principle applies equally to personal injury claims:

> In my view the only practical course for courts to adopt in assessing damages awarded under the Fatal Accidents Acts is to leave out of account the risk of further inflation, on the one hand, and the high interest rates which reflect the fear of it, on the other hand . . . money should be treated as retaining its value at the date of the judgment, and in calculation of present value of annual payments which have been received in future years, interest rates appropriate to times of stable currency such as 4 per cent to 5 per cent should be adopted.

Further, in *Taylor v O'Connor*[2] Lord Pearson said:

> I think protection against inflation is to be sought by investment, and the lump sum of damages should be assessed on the basis that it will be invested with the aim of obtaining some capital appreciation to offset the probable rise in the cost of living.

1 *Every v Miles* [1964] CA Transcript No 261; *Mallett v McMonagle* [1970] AC 166, [1969] 2 All ER 178, HL; *Taylor v O'Connor* [1971] AC 115, [1970] 1 All ER 365, HL; *Walker v John McLean & Sons* [1979] 2 All ER 965, [1979] 1 WLR 760, CA; *Housecroft v Burnett* [1986] 1 All ER 332, CA.
2 [1971] AC 115 at 143.

17.7 The present value of the prospective loss is awarded as a lump sum. A further preliminary question is how the assessment should take into account the fact that the lump sum award for future loss will be available to the plaintiff for investment in advance of the time when the loss will be suffered. The solution adopted by the courts is to apply a discount rate, when assessing the lump sum award, which is equivalent to the net return to be derived from investing the award. The assumption is that the lump sum and investment income will be sufficient to cover the future loss and inflation. The current practice is to apply a rate of between 4 per cent and 5 per cent, regardless of the real net rate of return. This discount is applied whether the prospective loss is a recurring annual loss, or one which may not arise for many years. The annual loss usually will be capitalised on the familiar multiplier/multiplicand basis.

PAIN AND SUFFERING

17.8 The same principles and tariffs apply to the assessment of general damages for pain suffering and loss of amenity as in ordinary personal injury claims. There are relatively few reported awards of general damages for pain and suffering in medical negligence cases, and those reported are nowhere conveniently indexed. The position has improved with the advent of the Medical Law Reports. The nature and range of injury suffered by claimants is so varied it is not possible to categorise them and identify specific tariffs adopted by the courts for specific injuries. In some areas there may be a sufficient number of comparable awards to identify a tariff, such as awareness during surgery[1] and the birth of a child following an unsuccessful sterilisation.[2] In other areas there may be the occasional useful report on its facts, as in cases of unauthorised or unnecessary[3] and unsuccessful procedures.[4] In most cases the practitioner will be fortunate to find a really useful comparable, and in the main must be guided by the tariffs which apply to the ordinary personal injury cases which most closely equate with the medical injury in question.

1 *Phelan v East Cumbria HA* [1991] 2 Med LR 419; *Taylor v Worcester and District HA* [1991] 2 Med LR 215; *Ackers v Wigan HA* [1991] 2 Med LR 232.
2 *Allen v Bloomsbury HA* [1993] 1 All ER 651, 13 BMLR 47; *Robinson v Salford HA* [1992] 3 Med LR 270.
3 *Malette v Shulman* [1991] 2 Med LR 162 (unauthorised blood transfusion); *Biles v North East Thames Regional HA* (1987) Kemp & Kemp F5–112 and *Devi v West Midlands Regional HA* (1981) Kemp & Kemp F5–107 (non-consensual sterilisation); *Harling v Huddersfield HA* (1992) Kemp Casewatch 2/1992 (unnecessary mastectomy); *Grayson-Crowe v Ministry of Defence* [1992] CLY 1663 (unauthorised hysterectomy).
4 *Bovenzi v Kettering HA* [1991] 2 Med LR 293 (damage to small bowel during D and C); *Grieve v Salford HA* [1991] 2 Med LR 295 (prolongation of labour); *Heath v West Berkshire HA* [1992] 3 Med LR 57 (injury to nerve during dental surgery); *Moore v Worthing District HA* [1992] 3 Med LR 431 (peri-operative ulnar nerve palsy); *Morgan v Gwent HA* (1987) Kemp & Kemp F5–015 (blood transfusion causing raised level of rhesus incompatibility); *Urry v Bieber and Harley Street Nursing Home* (1955) Kemp & Kemp F5–013 (surgical pack left in abdomen); *Gallagher v Ministry of Defence* (1981) Kemp & Kemp F4–013 (paralysis of urinary system and bowels after injection); *Hendy v Milton Keynes HA* [1992] 3 Med LR 114 (uretero-vaginal fistula and kidney damage during hysterectomy); *Marram v North Tees HA* [1992] CLY 1665 (vesico-vaginal fistula during hysterectomy).

17.9 The court may take into account the manner in which the tort was committed when assessing damages, and if it was such as to injure the plaintiff's proper feelings of dignity and pride, or was committed in a malicious, insulting or oppressive manner, may award aggravated damages.[1] However, in *Kralj v McGrath*[2] Woolf J rejected such claim based on the outrageous conduct of an obstetrician as inappropriate. In principle it is difficult to understand why a doctor should be immune from an award of aggravated damages, the purpose of which remains compensatory. Nonetheless, even if a separate award of aggravated damages cannot be maintained, the manner of treatment may increase the award of general damages. The restricted availability of exemplary damages makes it unlikely that such an award would be made in a medical negligence action.[3]

1 *Broome v Cassell & Co Ltd* [1972] AC 1027.
2 [1986] 1 All ER 54.
3 *Rookes v Barnard* [1964] AC 1129; *AB v South West Water Services Ltd* [1993] 1 All ER 609, [1993] PIQR P167, CA.

17.10 It was formerly the practice to award a specific sum of damages for loss of expectation of life, that is for the shortening of life by a number of years.[1] The awards were made for living plaintiffs and the estates of deceased persons. The award of modest and conventional sums became the norm,[2] and latterly the bracket was £1,250–£1,500. This head of claim was abolished by section 1(1)(a), Administration of Justice Act 1982, but loss of expectation of life remains a relevant factor in respect of living plaintiffs. If life has been shortened, and the injured person is aware of that fact, it must be taken into account when assessing the award of general damages for pain, suffering and loss of amenity. Section 1(1)(b) provides that the court 'shall take account of any suffering caused or likely to be caused to him by awareness that his expectation of life has been so reduced'. The section does not extend to a plaintiff who is unaware that his life expectancy has been reduced.

1 *Rose v Ford* [1937] AC 826, [1937] 3 All ER 359, HL.
2 *West v Shephard* [1964] AC 326, [1963] 2 All ER 625, HL.

THE LOST YEARS

17.11 Where a plaintiff's life expectancy has been reduced by reason of his injuries, this may have reduced the number of years during which he would have been working and earning. A claim for loss of earnings during these 'lost years' was approved by the House of Lords in *Pickett v British Rail Engineering Ltd*.[1] The scope of the claim was extended in *Gammell v Wilson*,[2] in which it was held that this right survived for the benefit of the estate of a deceased person, under section 1 of the Law Reform (Miscellaneous Provisions) Act 1934. The legislature intervened with the Administration of Justice Act 1982, which applies to deaths which occurred after the end of 1982. Section 4(2) of the Act amended section 1 of the 1934 Act by providing that where a cause of action survives for the benefit of the estate of a deceased person, the damages recoverable for the benefit of the estate shall not include any damages for loss of income in respect of any period after that person's death. The result is that a 'lost years' claim is limited to the case of a living plaintiff with an impaired life expectancy.[3]

1 [1980] AC 136, [1979] 1 All ER 774.
2 [1982] AC 27, [1981] 1 All ER 578, HL.
3 For assessment of such claims see para **17.28** below.

WRONGFUL BIRTH CLAIMS

17.12 The claims for 'wrongful birth' are cases in which a child is born, healthy or handicapped, as a result of a failed sterilisation or vasectomy, or following an omission to warn about the risks of a sterilisation operation failing to achieve its purpose, or a failure to terminate a pregnancy, or a failure to diagnose a pregnancy in time for a termination, or a failure to advise that a fetus was likely to be born deformed, thereby denying the mother the chance of a termination. The essence of the complaint is that the child would not have been born but for the medical negligence of which complaint is made. The basis of assessment of damages will vary according to whether the child was unplanned and unwanted, or whether it was planned and wanted, but was born deformed and the pregnancy would otherwise lawfully have been terminated. It may be material also if a child was planned for some future date, but the conception and birth took place prematurely by reason of the medical negligence of which complaint is made. In *Emeh v Kensington and Chelsea and Westminster AHA*[1] it was held at first instance that a failure to terminate a pregnancy was also an unreasonable failure to mitigate loss. On appeal Slade LJ commented that 'save in the most exceptional circumstances, I cannot think it right that the court should ever declare it unreasonable for a woman to decline to have an abortion in a case where there is no evidence that there were any medical or psychiatric grounds for terminating the particular pregnancy'.

1 [1985] QB 1012, CA.

17.13 The principles on which damages are to be awarded in the case of the unwanted child have been considered by the Court of Appeal a number of times. In *Allen v Bloomsbury HA*[1] Brooke J summarised the principles as follows:

(a) if a child is born whose potential for life would have been lawfully terminated but for the doctor's negligence, a plaintiff mother is entitled to recover damages for the foreseeable loss and damage she suffers in consequence of the doctor's negligence;[2]

(b) a plaintiff mother is entitled to recover general damages (and any associated financial special damage) for the discomfort and pain associated with the continuation of her pregnancy and the delivery of her child. On the facts of *Allen* (failure to diagnose a pregnancy), she must set off against this claim a sum in respect of the benefit of avoiding the pain and suffering and associated financial loss which would have resulted from the termination of her pregnancy under general anaesthetic, since in the events which have happened she has not had to undergo that operation;[3]

(c) a plaintiff mother is also entitled to damages for economic loss quite unassociated with her own physical injury which falls into two main categories:
   (i) the financial loss she suffers because when the unwanted baby is born she has a growing child to feed, clothe, house, educate and care for until the child becomes an adult;
   (ii) the financial loss she suffers because she has lost or may lose earnings or incur other expenses because of her obligation toward her child which she would have sought to avoid;[4]

(d) although it is foreseeable that if an unwanted child is born a mother may suffer wear and tear and tiredness in bringing up a healthy child, the claim for general damages she might otherwise have had on this account is generally set off against and extinguished by the benefit of bringing a healthy child into the world and seeing one's child grow to maturity;[5]

(e) however, the law is willing to recognise a claim for general damages in respect of the foreseeable additional anxiety, stress and burden in bringing up a handicapped child, which is not treated as being extinguished by any countervailing benefit, although this head of damages is different in kind from the typical claim for anxiety and stress flowing from an injured plaintiff's own personal injuries.[6]

1 [1993] 1 All ER 651, 13 BMLR 47; see also damages for wrongful birth, *Tribe v Korgaonkar* (1992) 136 Sol Jo 1141.
2 *Emeh*'s case, supra. The father could claim for the financial consequences of the birth; the child itself has no right of action.
3 *Emeh*'s case, supra, per Purchas LJ at 1028; *Thake v Maurice* [1986] QB 644 per Kerr LJ at 682; *Gardiner v Mounfield and Lincolnshire Area HA* [1990] 1 Med LR 205, per Scott Baker J at 207–208.
4 *Emeh*'s, case, supra, per Slade LJ at 1025; and per Purchas LJ at 1028; adopted and applied by the Court of Appeal in *Thake v Maurice*, supra.
5 *Thake v Maurice*, supra, per Kerr LJ at 682.
6 *Emeh*'s case, supra, per Waller LJ at 1022.

17.14 The Court of Appeal has not provided clear guidance as to the basis on which the future cost of maintaining the unplanned child should be assessed. In *Allen*, supra, Brooke J held:

> In my judgment in this type of case defendants are liable to pay for all such expenses as may be reasonably incurred for the education and upkeep for the unplanned child, having regard to all the circumstances of the case and, in particular, to his condition in life and his reasonable requirements at the time when the expenditure is incurred.

The cost of maintenance to the date of trial is based on the actual expenses incurred.[1] One means of approaching future loss is to assess the cost of upkeep on the basis of the National Foster Care Association rates of payment to foster parents. In *Allen*, Brooke J analysed this basis in detail, and concluded that it was 'a reasonable basis on which to make an award for the cost of maintaining (the child) until she is 18'. However, it is important to bear in mind the lifestyle the child should expect. This factor explains the wide divergence in the reported awards. In *Thake v Maurice* (supra) the cost of upkeep was agreed on the basis of supplementary benefit scales. Pain J commented that this was right, since the child 'had been born into a humble household and the defendant should not be expected to do more than provide her with necessaries'. By comparison, in *Benarr v Kettering Health Authority*[2] Hodgson J awarded, inter alia, £20,000 to pay for the child's private schooling.

1 See *Allen*, supra, per Brooke J at 264 and *Robinson v Salford HA* [1992] 3 Med LR 270 per Morland J at 271.
2 [1988] NLJR 179, Kemp & Kemp F5–116.

17.15 In the case of a failed sterilisation a plaintiff mother is entitled not only to an award of general damages for the pain and suffering involved in the pregnancy and birth, but also the pain and suffering involved in a second sterilisation operation and the costs of that operation. If the parents decide not to have further children because of the problems of having to raise a handicapped child, this will result in a saving in expenditure which would otherwise have been incurred, which must be brought into account in assessing the cost of maintaining the handicapped child. The justice of having to give such credit may be in doubt, but the requirement to do so is supported by high authority.[1] In all cases full credit must be given for child benefit, which is not a 'relevant benefit' for the purpose of the recoupment provisions introduced by the Social Security Act 1989.

1 See *Salih*, supra.

PROVISIONAL DAMAGES

17.16 Until 1981 damages in personal injury cases were assessed at the date of trial on a 'once and for all' basis. If there was a chance of an adverse development in the plaintiff's condition at some time in the future, the judge was obliged to assess the chance as best he could on the evidence, and reflect it in the quantum of the award. By the Supreme Court Act 1981, section 32A the court was given powers to award provisional damages where:

> there is proved or admitted to be a chance that at some definite or indefinite time in the future the injured person will as a result of the act or omission which gave rise to the cause of action, develop some serious disease or suffer some serious deterioration in his physical or mental condition.

17.17 In cases to which the section is admitted or held to apply the award of damages is assessed without reference to the chance of the serious disease or serious deterioration, and the order permits the plaintiff to claim further damages if the disease or deterioration occurs.[1] The power to award provisional damages is used frequently in cases where there is a clearly defined risk, such as epilepsy or cancer, but its application to progressive conditions, such as existing or anticipated arthritis and respiratory conditions, often is restricted.[2] The difficulty in these cases lies in satisfactorily defining or identifying the degree of decline required before the deterioration can properly be defined as 'serious', when the plaintiff becomes entitled to make a further claim for damages. There are several reported cases in which progressive conditions have been made the subject of provisional awards,[3] but the wording of the orders often is so vague that future litigation to determine whether entitlement to make a further claim has arisen may be required.

1 RSC Order 37, rule 7; Practice Direction (Provisional Damages, Procedure) [1985] 2 All ER 895; Practice Direction [1988] 2 All ER 102.
2 *Willson v Ministry of Defence* [1991] 1 All ER 638; *White v Inveresk Paper Co Ltd* 1987 SC 143, 1987 SLT 586.
3 *Mears v Kitson* [1991] CLY 1415; *Dillon v British Gas* (1989) Kemp & Kemp F2–027.

17.18 An interesting variation of the principle of provisional damages has been developed in some recent medical negligence cases, by which the parties agree, with the consent of the court, that the plaintiff shall have liberty to apply for a further trial of an issue in respect of damages if a certain event does or does not occur. For example, in the case of a young plaintiff the local education authority may have a policy of funding specialist school fees, but there may be doubt that the policy will continue in the long term. The parties may agree that if the policy does change the plaintiff may apply for a further trial of the issue of whether damages should be awarded in respect of such cost and quantum. This approach could be applied to solve many difficult problems not related directly to a change in the plaintiff's medical condition. It may be prudent to keep the terms of the agreement private by means of a Tomlin Order.

DAMAGES FOR PECUNIARY LOSS

17.19 There are few aspects of claims for pecuniary loss which are peculiar to medical negligence actions, and no more than a general review and some practical advice will be provided. For a more detailed exposition reference should be made to textbooks such as *Butterworths Personal Injury Litigation Service*; Kemp & Kemp, *The Quantum of Damages*; *McGregor on Damages*; Munkman, *Damages for Personal Injury and Death*.

17.20 The following areas require consideration:

(i) future loss assessment;
(ii) loss of earnings and pension;
(iii) medical and related expenses;
(iv) accommodation;
(v) care and attendance;
(vi) aids and equipment;
(vii) transport;
(viii) loss of services;
(ix) benefits;
(x) Court of Protection.

Future loss assessment

17.21 As has been discussed above, the award for pecuniary loss is on an indemnity basis, to provide monetary compensation for actual or prospective loss so as to place the plaintiff in the same position he would have occupied had the injury not occurred. The present value of the prospective loss is awarded as a lump sum, making a broad estimate and taking into account the proven facts and the probabilities of the case. The accelerated receipt of damages is dealt with by applying a discount rate equivalent to the net return to be derived from investing the award.

17.22 A recurring annual loss may be capitalised by means of the multiplier/multiplicand method, which is applied as follows:

(a) the first stage is to identify the amount of the recurring annual loss (the multiplicand) on the basis of present value and ignoring future inflation. This figure may be adjusted to allow for any likely decrease or real increase in the loss in the long term, which may be achieved by some averaging of the figures, or by identifying more than one multiplicand and apportioning the multiplier between those figures;
(b) the second is to identify a multiplier to convert the annual loss into a lump sum. The multiplier is based on the anticipated period of loss,[1] discounted for accelerated receipt of damages and the contingencies of life. The former discount will depend on the rate of interest it is assumed the lump sum will earn. The higher the rate the lower the

multiplier. The discounts applied by the courts at present assume a rate of return on investment after tax of 4 per cent to 5 per cent.[2] A precise means of discounting the multiplier for accelerated receipt is by reference to an annuity table based on interest rates of between 4 per cent and 5 per cent; this will show what number of years purchase is required to purchase an annuity for the estimated period of loss;

(c) the multiplier is further discounted to allow for the contingencies of life. The factors which will be taken into account and the extent of the discount will depend on the 'proven facts and the probabilities of the case'. In the case of life long expenses the discount may take into account the risk of premature death, or the chance that some of the expenses may have been incurred in old age in any event. In the case of loss of earnings to retirement, the discount may encompass the risk that the plaintiff might have ceased to earn due to ill health, injury or loss of employment for periods in any event; a significant discount may be made in the case of a man in hazardous work, or with a poor work record, or in insecure employment. On the other hand, the multiplier may be increased if the plaintiff had the opportunity and intention to work beyond normal retirement age;

(d) apart from the application of these broad principles the multiplier cannot be said to be assessed on any truly analytical basis, as Mustill LJ has observed:[3]

> the process seems to have no clear intellectual basis . . . in practice . . . the judge adopts an intuitive process buttressed by reference to previously decided cases. These cases partly operate as reference points whose features are compared with those of the case under consideration and partly from the basis of a general climate of opinion on the proper multiplier in a particular class of case with which a judge of long experience in the field will be entirely familiar. But it must be observed that these previous cases themselves must ultimately be intuitive in origin. Now this may be a rough and ready approach but it operates in an economical way and it enables the court to achieve a consistency of award which is at least the start of a just system for computing damages.

A useful table of multipliers awarded in previous cases is to be found in *Kemp & Kemp*,[4] although it must be borne in mind that the personal circumstances of the plaintiff played a part in the selection of these multipliers. In practice it is rare to find a multiplier of more than 16 for loss of earnings and more than 18 for a life-long loss;[5]

(e) the courts have never been particularly receptive to actuarial methods of assessing future loss. However, in 1984 a Joint Working Party of Actuaries and Lawyers produced a Report which contained actuarial Tables prepared by the Government Actuary, which have begun to play a part in the selection of multipliers.[6] These Tables contain multipliers at rates of interest between 1.5 per cent and 5 per cent, although the rate of 4–5 per cent continues to be used. There are separate Tables for men and women in respect of pecuniary loss for life, loss of earnings to pension age and loss of pension from retirement, and detailed explanatory notes. The Tables allow for accelerated receipt of damages and have been calculated to take into account the chances that the plaintiff will die young or live to be very old, based on population mortality. The Tables for loss of earnings to pension age do not allow for the risks that he might have ceased to earn due to ill health or loss of employment for periods in any event; in practice a 10 per cent discount often is used to allow for these factors, but the rate must vary from case to case. In *Spiers v Halliday*[7] the Tables were held to be inadmissible, but the courts generally take judicial notice of them[8] and they are regularly used, at least as a cross reference to check the accuracy of the multiplier selected by the traditional method.

1 This will depend on the evidence of the duration of loss, and may be a fixed period, for example to retirement, or for life. If the latter, a life expectancy table or the medical evidence will define the period.
2 This level of rate has been the subject of criticism, on the basis that it is appropriate only in times of stable currency, does not represent the real rate of return and undercompensates plaintiffs; see *Kemp & Kemp*, chapters 6 and 7 and The Law Commission's Consultation Paper (No 125) 'Structured Settlements and Interim and Provisional Damages'.
3 *Cunningham v Camberwell* HA [1990] 2 Med LR 49.
4 *Kemp & Kemp* 6–320.
5 A rough means of assessment used in practice, where the period of loss is more than 10 years, is to divide the period by 2 and add 1. In the case of a 45-year-old man with 20 years to retirement this would produce a multiplier of 11, which accords with the comparables.
6 *Kemp & Kemp* 6–320.
7 (1984) Times, 30 June.
8 See *Mills v BR Engineering Ltd* [1992] 1 PIQR Q130, CA; *Woodrup v Nichol* [1993] PIQR Q104, CA.

17.23 The prospective loss may not arise for some time. For example, the evidence may be that the plaintiff will probably require a hip replacement operation in about 15 years' time. The present payment of the full cost of surgery would give him an unwarranted advantage, allowing him to increase the real value of the award by investment until the expenditure is required. The solution is to discount the full amount by a rate of 4 per cent to 5 per cent for each year between the probable date of expenditure and the date of assessment, to produce a lump sum which, with investment, will produce an amount sufficient to cover the cost of the expenditure (and inflation) when it is needed. There may have to be some further discount of the figure if there is uncertainty as to whether the treatment will be required.

Loss of earnings and pension

Loss of earnings

17.24 In calculating loss of earnings to the date of assessment the court must determine what the plaintiff would have earned but for the injury. The starting point usually will be the level of earnings and the value of lost benefits (such as housing or a motor car) at the date of the injury, which may be uplifted to the date of assessment to allow for probable real increases in earnings and benefits as a result of promotion, better paid employment or otherwise, and inflationary increases. From the gross loss so assessed must be deducted income tax,[1] national insurance contributions,[2] trade union and other dues, any actual earnings and expenses which would have been incurred in the course of employment, such as the cost of travel to work. The plaintiff must give credit for any refund of tax which results from the cessation of work. The net loss so assessed may have to be reduced to take account of periods of unemployment the plaintiff may have encountered. The damages recovered for loss of earnings are not themselves subject to tax.[3]

1 *British Transport Commission v Gourley* [1956] AC 185, [1955] 3 All ER 796.
2 *Cooper v Firth Brown* [1963] 1 WLR 418.
3 Income and Corporation Taxes Act 1988 and the Finance Act 1971.

17.25 In many cases there is considerable uncertainty as regards prospective loss. The starting point will be the findings made in valuing the loss to the date of assessment. The court has to continue this process of assessment and determine in the long term what the plaintiff is likely to have done and earned had he not been injured, and prophesy what he is likely to do and earn in his injured state. No allowance will be made on either side of the formula for the prospect of inflationary increases in earnings, but the potential for real increases by promotion or otherwise will be taken into account. If the loss is likely to increase or decrease in real terms in the future it may be necessary to adjust the multiplicand, or to determine more than one multiplicand and apportion the multiplier between those figures. If a continuing loss can be established it must be net of all relevant deductions, such as income tax, and the future loss will be capitalised on a multiplier-multiplicand basis.[1] The extent to which the multiplier falls to be discounted for contingencies will depend on the facts of the case.

1 See para **17.22** above.

17.26 The court must be provided with evidence on which to base the assessment of loss. The plaintiff and the medical experts are obvious sources of evidence, as are actual or prospective employers, comparable employees, trade and professional bodies, and trade union representatives. It is increasingly the practice to obtain evidence from employment consultants. If the consultant is appropriately qualified, the court may be prepared to consider his opinion on the type of work for which the plaintiff is fit in his injured state.[1] The consultant's main function is to gather information as to the availability of work and the level of earnings the plaintiff might earn in the work for which he remains fit, or might have earned in the work for which he would have been fit but for the injury. He might also provide useful information as to the prospects of retraining and assistance available to disabled persons. Other helpful sources of evidence are the annual New Earnings Survey, published by HMSO, which contains an analysis by occupation of the earnings of employed persons,[2] the retail prices index and average earnings index.

1 However, in *Larby v Thurgood* [1993] ICR 66, 136 Sol Jo LB 275 the court refused a stay to compel the plaintiff to submit to an interview by a consultant to determine his motivation and willingness to seek better paid employment, these being matters for the court.
2 *Kemp & Kemp* 6–332.

Lump sum awards

17.27 The evidence may demonstrate the probability of a future loss of earnings, but there may be so many imponderables that no satisfactory arithmetical means of calculating the compensation can be found. The court may reject the conventional multiplier/multiplicand approach in favour of a broad brush assessment of the present value of the risk of future financial loss, and award a lump sum.[1] The imponderables tend to be most acute in the case of young children and it here that the lump sum approach most often is adopted.[2] However, if the child is permanently disabled from work the conventional approach remains appropriate, with reliance usually placed on family background to provide a guide to the child's probable career and earnings.[3]

1 For example, see *Blamire v South Cumbria HA* [1993] PIQR Q1, CA.
2 *Connolly v Camden & Islington Area HA* [1981] 3 All ER 250; *Croke v Wiseman* [1981] 3 All ER 852,

[1982] 1 WLR 71, CA; *Joyce v Yeomans* [1981] 2 All ER 21, [1981] 1 WLR 549, CA; *Mitchell v Liverpool Area HA* (1985) Times, 17 June; *Cronin v Redbridge LBC* (1987) Times, 20 May.

3 *Taylor v Bristol Omnibus Co Ltd* [1975] 2 All ER 1107, [1975] 1 WLR 1054, CA; *Cassel v Riverside HA* [1991] PIQR Q168; see also Denyer, *Children and Personal Injury Litigation* (Butterworths, 1993).

17.28 An award of damages for future partial loss of earnings on a multiplier/multiplicand basis may not adequately guard the plaintiff against all reasonable foreseeable future loss. For example, if he has to go in search of employment he may be at a disadvantage, because his injuries may limit the work he can perform and the posts for which he can apply, or may make him a less attractive worker and reduce his chances of finding and keeping employment. He may face the risk of greater periods of unemployment as a result. The main feature of such cases is that there is no present loss, subject to compensation for partial continuing loss, and future loss is uncertain. The awards of damages in such circumstances are described as being for disadvantage on the labour market, or diminution of earning capacity, or as a *Smith v Manchester City Corpn*[1] award. The correct approach to the assessment was considered by the Court of Appeal in *Moeliker v Reyrolle & Co Ltd*.[2] The preliminary question is whether there is a 'substantial' or 'real' risk that the plaintiff will lose his employment before the end of his working life. If there is such a risk,[3] the court must assess and quantify the present value of the risk of the financial damage he will suffer if he loses his employment, having regard to the degree of the risk, the time when it may materialise and the factors, both favourable and unfavourable, which will or may affect his chances of finding further employment, or equally well paid employment. The court will take into account matters such as the plaintiff's age, skills and adaptability, the effects of his injury, his personal drive, the prospects of his retraining, the state of the employment market and the chance he may have become unemployed in any event. The court must apply its judgment to all relevant factors and assess a lump sum award. An award may be made for reasons other than the risk of loss of employment and may be warranted, for example, if there is a long-term risk that the plaintiff's condition may deteriorate and limit the hours he can work, or require him to take time off work, or cause him to retire prematurely. There is no such thing as a conventional award, and awards in other cases are seldom any useful guide. An approach often adopted is to quantify the award on the basis of a multiple of the plaintiff's current net annual earnings.

1 [1974] 118 Sol Jo 597, 17 KIR 1, CA; in *Frost v Palmer* [1993] PIQR Q14, CA it was held that it is not wrong in principle to award damages for loss of earning capacity as well as damages for future loss of earnings.

2 [1977] 1 WLR 132, CA.

3 In *Watson v Mitcham Cardboards* [1982] CLY 78, Kemp & Kemp 5–009/7/6/6 the Court of Appeal held that the *Moeliker* test, requiring a 'real' or 'substantial' risk, must not be applied too narrowly. See also *Robson v Liverpool City Council* [1993] PIQR Q78 and *Forey v London Buses Ltd* [1992] PIQR P48, CA.

The lost years

17.29 If the plaintiff's life expectancy has been reduced there may be a claim for loss of earnings in the 'lost years'. The assessment of the loss is based on the surplus of earnings available to the plaintiff after deduction of the reasonable living expenses which would have been expended to maintain him at the standard of life appropriate to his case.[1] The value of the award will depend on his age and expectation of life at the date of assessment, and how far into the future the loss will be suffered. In the case of a young child the loss may be so distant and speculative that no award will be made. In *Housecroft v Burnett*,[2] O'Connor LJ commented on the basis of assessment in the case of a 16-year-old paraplegic with a life expectancy of 27 years, for whom a multiplier of 10 was applied by the trial judge, as follows:

> The lost years, because of their remoteness in time, are highly speculative and I think are better dealt with by some small adjustment in the multiplier, such as a factor of one, or even half, as applied to the full multiplicand, rather than trying to speculate what proportion of notional earnings 30 years hence would not form part of the plaintiff's then living expenses.[3]

1 *White v London Transport Executive* [1982] 2 QB 489; *Harris v Empress Motors* [1984] 1 WLR 212.
2 [1986] 1 All ER 332 at 345F.
3 For a full analysis of the basis of assessment see *Kemp & Kemp*, 6–065.

Loss of pension benefits

17.30 Except where the plaintiff has already reached pensionable age at the date of assessment, loss of pension claims will be claims for prospective loss. It may be that a pension will be lost or reduced because employment is lost, or the length of employment service will be shortened, or because the plaintiff will be unable to maintain the level of financial contribution he would otherwise have made. The right to recover exists whether or not actual contributions were made. The leading case on the assessment of loss is *Auty v National Coal Board*.[1] The loss is assessed in two stages:

(a) the first stage is to value the loss at the date of future retirement. It is necessary to determine, on the basis of the relevant pension fund rules, how much the annual pension would have been at that date had the plaintiff served his full term or made his full contributions, and how much it will be on the basis of the reduced service or contributions, to produce an annual loss. The earnings used for this purpose should be at present day values, making allowance if needs be for the prospect of real increases in future. The plaintiff's life expectancy at the date of retirement is assessed on the basis of life tables, and an appropriate number of years' purchase, or multiplier, is determined.[2] The multiplier is applied to the annual loss to produce a capital value at the date of retirement. There may be loss of a lump sum payment to add to that value;

(b) the second stage is to reduce the capital value to its value at the date of assessment for accelerated receipt, by applying an annual discount rate of 4 per cent to 5 per cent to the number of years between the dates of assessment and retirement. In *Auty* a further discount was applied for adverse contingencies,[3] to take account of the possibility that the plaintiff may not live or work to normal retirement age.[4]

1 [1985] 1 WLR 784; an attempt to recover 'lost' pension contributions failed in *Dews v NCB* [1987] QB 81, CA.
2 The life expectancy is determined at the date of trial, and reduced by the number of years to retirement; the multiplier is based on the balance.
3 In *Auty* a discount of 27% was applied, but see *Anderson v Davies* [1993] 5 PIQR Q87 for discussion of the factors relevant to the discount.
4 An alternative to the *Auty* method is to select a multiplier from the Government Actuary's Tables and apply it to the annual loss of pension.

Medical and related expenses

17.31 The claims typically which arise are for expenditure incurred as a result of admission to hospital and in the course of recuperation, travelling expenses incurred by the plaintiff when undergoing treatment or as a result of being unable to use public transport, and expenditure incurred by members of his family when visiting him in hospital or at home. Expenses incurred by family are recoverable, provided the visits were reasonable and of benefit to the plaintiff. The family visits can be said to be an aid to his recovery and be justifiable on that basis.[1] The plaintiff should be advised to keep a careful log of expenditure and of the date, destination, distance and purpose of each journey. The mileage claim may be assessed on the basis of the table of running costs produced by the RAC and AA. These apparently small items of claim can amount to a substantial sum, especially when interest is added.

1 *Kirkham v Boughey* [1958] 2 QB 338, per Devlin J.

17.32 A plaintiff is entitled to recover all expenses reasonably incurred in the medical treatment of his injuries. These may range from the cost of prescriptions, to the cost of medical advice, surgical and other medical treatment and hospital care. The cost of transport to and from the place where treatment is received usually is allowed. The cost of a recuperative holiday, if reasonably taken on medical advice, may be recoverable. If the cost of treatment in hospital, or the cost of the recuperative holiday, includes the cost of food, credit may have to be given in that amount. If the plaintiff is so severely injured that he becomes resident in an institution, and claims the cost of care and a full loss of earnings, he will be required to give credit for the living expenses he is longer required to incur.[1]

1 *Lim Poh Choo v Camden and Islington Area HA* [1980] AC 174, [1979] 2 All ER 910, HL. See also Adminstration of Justice Act 1982, sections 5 and 11.

17.33 A plaintiff is not obliged to avail himself of free hospital treatment, and may elect to be treated as a private patient even if the treatment will not differ in substance from the care he would receive under the National Health scheme; Section 2(4) of the Law Reform (Personal Injuries) Act 1948. However, if there are no private facilities available, the court will not award the cost of such treatment since the plaintiff will incur no loss.[1] If a plaintiff incurs medical expense on a course of treatment recommended by his medical adviser, he may recover such expenditure as reasonably incurred, even if it is subsequently discovered that the treatment was incorrect. The defendant may avoid such a claim if it can be shown that the medical adviser, to the knowlege of the plaintiff, was unqualified to give any such recommendation.[2]

1 Slade J considered this section in *Harris v Bright Asphalt Contractors Ltd* [1953] 1 QB 617 at 635: 'I do not understand section 2(4) to enact that a plaintiff shall be deemed to be entitled to recover expenses which he will never incur.' See also *Woodrup v Nichol* [1993] PIQR Q104, CA.
2 *Rubens v Walker* 1946 SC 215 at 216.

17.34 There are seldom real difficulties in respect of medical expenditure incurred to the date of assessment, but prospective expense may be problematic. The plaintiff may require regular and continuing treatment, perhaps in the form of physiotherapy or counselling, in which case the annual long-term cost may be awarded on a multiplier/multiplicand basis. The multiplier will be based on the medical evidence of the period for which the treatment will be required. There may be a risk that treatment will be required at some uncertain time in the future. An example given above[1] is that of the man who will probably require an operation in about 15 years' time, where the cost of the surgery is discounted for accelerated receipt, and possibly also for uncertainty if there is reasonable doubt that the treatment will be required.

1 See para **17.23**.

Accommodation

17.35 The injury may have a substantial and expensive impact on the plaintiff's accommodation needs. It may be necessary to purchase new housing if his existing home is inadequate for his needs, for example because he is restricted to a wheelchair and his home cannot sensibly be adapted, or because his home is too small for him, his family and his carers. It may be necessary to adapt the existing or new accommodation to meet his needs, and such accommodation may be more expensive to run. A variety of capital and annual costs may be incurred. This head of claim may have to be considered in consultation with an architect[1] and the other experts in the case, such as the medical, care and aids and equipment advisers. There are many associations which can provide useful advice and guidance.[2]

1 The Royal Institute of British Architects, 66 Portland Place, London W9 2HU (tel 071–289 6111) has a list of architects specialising in design for the disabled.
2 Disabled Living Foundation, International Paraplegic Claims Service, Spinal Injuries Association, Centre on Environment for the Handicapped.

17.36 In *Roberts v Johnstone*[1] the Court of Appeal held that:

(a) the damages to be awarded in respect of the cost of purchase of accommodation should not be the net capital cost of the purchase, but the additional annual cost over the plaintiff's lifetime of providing that accommodation. The annual cost should be taken at 2 per cent of the net capital cost which, if necessarily expended, was not to be reduced by reason of any element of betterment not required to meet the plaintiff's needs;
(b) in addition, damages amounting to the full capital cost of any conversion works necessary to adapt a property for the plaintiff's needs are recoverable, save in so far as such costs enhance the value of the property.

1 [1989] QB 878, CA; see also *George v Pinnock* [1973] 1 All ER 926, [1973] 1 WLR 118.

17.37 By way of illustration, a plaintiff may sell his existing property for £150,000 and purchase another for £200,000. He may incur incidental costs in the form of surveyor's and solicitor's fees, stamp duties and removal costs of £10,000. He may have to expend £50,000 on conversion works to widen doorways, instal ramps and construct an extension for a resident carer:

(a) the capital cost of £200,000 − £150,000 = £50,000 will be assessed on the basis of a multiplicand of £50,000 × 2 per cent = £1,000 per annum, and a multiplier appropriate to the plaintiff's life expectancy. The logic of this basis is to compensate him for loss of investment income on the capital sum, whilst recognising that the investment in the better housing will provide financial benefit in the long term. It is debatable whether the rate of 2 per cent remains appropriate, in the light of the fall in house prices in recent years. The capital sum used as the basis of the assessment may be reduced if the new house is unreasonably large or grand for the plaintiff's actual needs;

(b) the incidental costs are recoverable in full, unless there is reason to believe that the plaintiff would have moved house in the short or medium term regardless of the injury. There may be reason for a discount, geared to the quantum of the chance that he would have moved in any event;

(c) there will be aspects of the conversion works which are necessitated by the plaintiff's condition and do not enhance the value of the property, such as works to widen doorways and instal ramps. The costs of these works are recoverable in full, together with incidental expenses such as architect's fees. Conversely, there may be other works which do add to property value, such as construction of an extension, which generally are irrecoverable.

17.38 Whether the plaintiff remains in his existing property or purchases another there may be additional household costs. If he has become largely or entirely housebound there may be an increase in household accounts for gas and electricity, since he would otherwise have been out and about. The multiplier may be limited to the notional date of retirement from work, or the multiplicand may be reduced at that date. If a larger property is purchased the bills for rates, gas, electricity, insurance, maintenance, gardening may be correspondingly greater. Here the multiplier is likely to be for life. If an architect is involved in respect of conversion works it is often convenient to have him deal with some or all of these additional costs.

Care and attendance

17.39 The injury may have rendered the plaintiff dependent on others for aspects of his daily living. This dependency may range from the need for a few hours' assistance a week with housework, to the need for a full-time residential nurse. Such assistance often is provided by members of the plaintiff's family. Prior to 1973, a claim for 'voluntary' services so rendered could succeed only if there was an agreement for remuneration and the plaintiff was legally liable to pay the volunteer. In *Cunningham v Harrison*[1] and *Donnelly v Joyce*[2] the Court of Appeal overruled the old cases and held that if an injury has created the need for nursing services, there is a proper claim for the reasonable cost of such services, the value of which may be measured by a sum which will allow the plaintiff to make reasonable recompense to his helper, or reimbursement of lost wages. The claim remains that of the plaintiff, since the helper has no cause of action.

1 [1973] QB 942, [1973] 3 All ER 463, CA.
2 [1974] QB 454, [1973] 3 All ER 475, CA.

17.40 The past care provided by members of the family may be assessed on the basis of the hours devoted and at commercial rates,[1] although the award is usually for less than that rate,[2] or on the basis of the value of lost earnings.[3] The past care may also include expenditure for domestic or nursing assistance. In the case of serious injury the involvement of a nursing care expert will be required, who will assess the plaintiff's needs, and the skills, amount of time and cost required to satisfy those needs. The care regime may involve employed assistance, ranging from 'home help' and unskilled care attendants, to resident nursing auxiliaries. The basis of assessment may be on hourly rates or an annual salary, and may include agency fees, VAT, employers' national insurance contributions and travelling expenses. If it is likely that all or some of the care will be provided by members of the family the award is usually for less than the commercial rate. In *Mills v British Rail Engineering*,[4] the Court of Appeal held that if the care has been or will be provided by a wife or some other close relative the services must involve care well beyond the ordinary call of duty. In a serious case the costs of a 'case manager' to administer the regime may be claimed.[5] The claim may extend to the additional costs of going on holiday, in terms of a companion, motor car hire and the extra cost of hotels with appropriate facilities. The annual costs of the care regime may be assessed at increasing levels, if it is anticipated that the plaintiff's condition will deteriorate and his needs will increase in the long term. It is prudent to have the medical experts consider and comment upon the reasonableness of the care regime proposed.

The multiplier will be based on the probable duration of the incapacity, usually for life, and may be apportioned between the increasing levels of multiplicand. The fact that the proposed care is to be carried out in the plaintiff's home and will cost more than institutional care is not a sufficient reason to deprive him of his damages,[6] but the burden of establishing that home care is reasonable is on the plaintiff.

1 The rates commonly used are those of the Crossroads Care Attendant Scheme, Local Authority Home Care and British Nursing Association.
2 In *Maylen v Morris* [1988] Kemp & Kemp A3–105 the commercial cost was reduced by 25%; and in *Nash v Southend HA* [1993] PIQR Q156 by one third.
3 In *Bell v Gateshead HA* [1986] Kemp & Kemp A4–101 an award was made for the mother's loss of earnings, together with a further sum to reflect the value of her care.
4 [1992] PIQR Q130; see also *Housecroft v Burnett* [1986] 1 All ER 332.
5 *Goldfinch v Scannell* [1993] PIQR Q143, CA.
6 See *Lim*'s case [1980] AC 174; *Rialas v Mitchell* [1984] 128 Sol Jo 704, CA and see *Kemp & Kemp* (Vol II), para 1–012.

Aids and equipment

17.41 The injury may have rendered the plaintiff reliant on a variety of aids and equipment, ranging from a simple walking stick to expensive wheelchairs and complicated hoists. In cases of more serious injury it will be necessary to obtain expert assistance to assess the plaintiff's needs and the costs. There are many associations which can provide useful advice and guidance.[1] It is prudent to have the medical experts consider and comment upon the reasonableness of the aids and equipment proposed. The past loss will be based on actual expenditure and usually presents no difficulty, provided it was reasonably required. As for the future, if certain equipment is required and has not been purchased, the full capital cost is claimed. Thereafter, it may need to be replaced every few years; the multiplicand is determined by dividing the capital cost by the number of years service life the equipment will provide, and adding any annual costs such as maintenance and insurance. The multiplier will be based on the probable duration of the need, usually for life. If certain equipment may not be required for several years the cost must be capitalised at some future date and discounted for accelerated receipt, if needs be with a further discount for the possibility that it may not be required.

1 Disabled Living Foundation, International Paraplegic Claims Service, Spinal Injuries Association, Centre on Environment for the Handicapped.

Transport

17.42 It may be that the plaintiff requires a motor car, which he would not otherwise have purchased, or has lost the benefit of a company car. The past loss will be based on actual expenditure. As for the future, the most convenient means of determining the multiplicand is by reference to the AA and RAC Tables of standing and running costs, or by reference to the annual cost of the provision of a motor car on lease or hire purchase under the Motability Scheme. If the plaintiff has lost the benefit of a company car the income tax implications must be taken into account in the assessment. There may be claims for the cost of items such as a special conversion and a mobile telephone; the multiplicand is determined by dividing the capital cost by the number of years service life the equipment will provide, and adding any annual costs such as maintenance and rental. A discount may be required to account for the saving in the use of public transport. If the plaintiff would have owned a motor car in any event, he may need a larger and more expensive car, or may need to replace it more frequently.[1] The insurance premium is likely to be greater and the plaintiff may travel more mileage than he would otherwise have done.

1 *Goldfinch v Scannell* [1993] PIQR Q143, CA; *Woodrup v Nichol* [1993] PIQR Q104, CA.

Loss of services

17.43 The injury may have deprived the plaintiff of the ability to perform household tasks, such as housekeeping, decorating and maintaining the family home, garden and motor car. He may have to pay others to do work he would otherwise have done. In *Daly v General Steam Navigation Co Ltd*[1] the plaintiff lost her housekeeping capacity; the cost of home help was considered to be a reasonable measure of her future loss, even if she did not intend to employ such help. It was held also that no such claim could succeed in respect of the pre-trial period in the absence of actual expenditure, although general damages could be increased to account for the additional effort and stress in coping without outside help. Hence, past loss is based on actual expenditure. As for the future, the multiplicand can properly be based on the commercial rate to replace the services or, in the case of decorating, by obtaining tradesmen's estimates of the labour cost of doing the work and dividing the cost by the number of years which will elapse before the work has to be repeated.

1 [1980] 3 All ER 696, [1981] 1 WLR 120, CA.

Benefits

17.44 Financial gains or benefits accruing to the plaintiff which he would not have received but for the event which constitutes his cause of action prima facie are to be taken into account in mitigation of losses which that event causes.[1] There are two well-established exceptions to that rule, namely charitable payments and pension money:

(a) if the plaintiff receives money or benefits from the benevolence of others prompted by sympathy for his misfortune, for example from a disaster fund, such charitable receipts are disregarded.[2] A particular application of this principle is to be found in *McCamley v Cammell Laird Shipbuilders Ltd*.[3] The plaintiff was the beneficiary of an insurance policy taken out by his employers, to which he had not contributed; benefits were paid in the form of a lump sum, which was not in substitution for loss of earnings. It was held that the payment was made as an act of benevolence and was not deductible;

(b) if the plaintiff receives money from a pension from his employers, or from an insurance policy, these usually are not deductible. Money received under an accident insurance policy is not taken into account, whether the payment takes the form of a lump sum or weekly payments to replace earnings lost during a period of incapacity.[4] In *Parry v Cleaver*[5] it was held that a disability pension is not to be set off against loss of earnings, although if the claim is for loss of pension then a disability pension may be set off against such loss in respect of the period following retirement.[6] The fact that insurance money is the source of the benefit is not conclusive. In *Hussain v New Taplow Mills*[7] the plaintiff was entitled to long-term sickness benefit under his contract of employment, against which liability his employers had insured themselves, with no contribution from the plaintiff. The benefit he received was a partial substitute for earnings and was held to be deductible;

(c) the benefits received may not fall neatly on one side of the line or the other. As Lord Bridge commented in *Hussain v New Taplow Mills*,[8] there are a variety of borderline cases in which there is no obvious answer, in respect of which Lord Reid aptly summed the matter up in *Parry v Cleaver* when he said: 'The common law has treated the matter as one depending on justice, reasonableness and public policy.'

1 *Hussain v New Taplow Mills* [1988] 1 All ER 541 per Lord Bridge at 544.
2 *Peacock v Amusement Equipment Co Ltd* [1954] 2 QB 347, [1954] 2 All ER 689; *Hodgson v Trapp* [1988] 3 All ER 870, [1988] 3 WLR 1281, HL.
3 [1990] 1 All ER 854.
4 *Bradburn v Great Western Rly Co* [1874] LR 10 Exch 1.
5 [1970] AC 1, [1969] All ER 555.
6 See also *Smoker v LFCDA* [1991] 2 All ER 449.
7 [1988] 1 All ER 541 at 544.
8 Supra.

17.45 The law relating to the deduction of state benefits was altered radically by the Social Security Act 1989, which applies to any cause of action which arose on or after 1 January 1989. The law before that date may be summarised as follows:

(a) the Law Reform (Personal Injuries) Act 1948 provides that 50 per cent of specified benefits received by the plaintiff shall be deducted from the loss of earnings or profits claim for the five years commencing when the cause of action accrued. These are sickness benefits, invalidity benefit, non-contributory invalidity pension, injury benefit and disablement benefit. The Act provides a complete code and no deduction at all is required after the five-year period;

(b) there are other health and social security benefits which may be paid which do not come within the Act. The courts have held that benefits which replace earnings must be set off in full against the loss of earnings claim. Hence, unemployment benefit,[1] supplementary benefit (income support),[2] family income supplement (family credit),[3] reduced earnings allowance[4] and Job Release Scheme allowances[5] are to be set off in full against any claim for loss of earnings or profit.[6] In *Hodgson v Trapp*[7] it was held that mobility and attendance allowances must be set off against similar categories of pecuniary damage; if it is probable payment of such benefits will continue after trial, a set off against future loss also must be made. In *Lay v South West Surrey HA* Phillips J accounted for the risk that payment of the benefit would not continue by applying a reduced multiplier to the multiplicand representing the future allowance for attendance.[8] The benefits which replace earnings are rarely relevant to future loss, since almost all are means related and will cease on receipt of the damages award.

1 *Nabi v British Leyland (UK) Ltd* [1980] 1 All ER 667, [1980] 1 WLR 529; *Hussain v New Taplow Mills Ltd* [1988] 1 All ER 541.
2 *Plummer v P W Wilkins & Son Ltd* [1981] 1 All ER 91, [1981] 1 WLR 831; *Lincoln v Hayman* [1982] 2 All ER 819, [1982] 1 WLR 488.
3 *Gaskill v Preston* [1981] 3 All ER 427.
4 *Flanagan v Watts Blake Bearne & Co plc* [1992] PIQR Q144.
5 *Liney v Tarsen Lal* [1984] CLY 1031; *Crawley v Mercer* [1984] CLYB 1043, Times, 9 March.
6 Per Lord Reid in *British Transport Commission v Gourley* [1956] AC 185, [1956] 3 All ER 796.
7 [1989] AC 807.
8 *Kemp & Kemp* 10–074.

17.46 The new legislation[1] governs the deduction of state benefits in respect of causes of action which arose on or after 1 January 1989. The legislation provides that a person making a compensation payment (the compensator), whether on behalf of himself or another, in consequence of an accident, injury or disease suffered by any other person (the claimant), shall not do so until the Secretary of State has furnished him with a certificate of total benefit. The compensator is bound to deduct from the compensation payment and pay to the Compensation Recovery Unit of the Department of Social Security an amount equal to all the relevant benefits received or likely to be received in respect of the injury or disease during the relevant period. In effect, the benefits are treated as a loan to the plaintiff which are to be repaid from damages recovered:[2]

(a) the range of 'relevant benefit'[3] is far wider than under the 1948 Act. The benefits are attendance allowance, disability benefit, family credit, income support, invalidity pension and allowance, mobility allowance, benefits payable under schemes made under the Old Cases Act, reduced earnings allowance, retirement allowance, severe disablement allowance, sickness benefit, statutory sick pay, unemployment benefit and increases of any of these benefits;
(b) the 'relevant period'[4] in the case of disease is the period of five years beginning with the date on which the claimant first claims a relevant benefit in consequence of the disease. In any other case, the period of five years is that immediately following the day on which the accident or injury in question occurred. However, if the compensator makes a compensation payment in final discharge of any claim made by the victim and arising out of the accident, injury or disease, before the end of that five-year period, the relevant period ends on the date when the

payment is made. Hence, the period ends when damages are paid following a settlement or trial;

(c) the deductions must be made in full and against all heads of damage, including non-pecuniary damages. These are distinct changes from the 1948 Act, which required that the specified benefits be deducted to the extent of 50 per cent and from the loss of earnings or profits claim alone. Further, there is no provision in the scheme for a reduction in the benefits to be recouped and repaid where the plaintiff's damages have been reduced for contributory negligence. The full value of the benefits received must be recouped regardless of the degree of contributory negligence. The disadvantage to the plaintiff may be offset to some extent by not having to deduct any benefits after the end of the relevant period. This avoids the effect of the decision in *Hodgson v Trapp*, that some prospective benefits should be deducted, and means that the earlier the plaintiff settles his case the more advantageous it is for him. However, the net result of the scheme is that plaintiffs receive less in compensation and defendants pay out more in damages. It has also become more difficult to dispose of cases by 'nuisance payments';

(d) a number of compensation payments are exempt from recovery, few of which are likely to be relevant to medical negligence litigation, except perhaps for those in respect of claims brought under the Fatal Accidents Act 1976, payments made under the Vaccine Damage Payments Act 1979 and payments made out of the MacFarlane Trust (for families of haemophiliacs affected by possible HIV infection through blood transfusion);

(e) the administrative details of the scheme are beyond the ambit of this chapter, as are the various provisions for multiple compensation payments, payments by more than one defendant, structured settlements, insolvency of a recipient, legal aid charges, overpaid benefits and foreign defendants;[5]

(f) a payment into court is treated as a compensation payment.[6] If a certificate of total benefit has been obtained the defendant may withhold from the payment an amount equal to the total deduction and furnish the court with a certificate of the amount so withheld. The amount paid into court is regarded as increased by the amount so certified, although the plaintiff is not allowed to take out of court more than the amount actually paid in. The defendant is not required to make the relevant repayment until he receives notice of payment out. If a certificate of total benefit has not been obtained a provisional reserve must be deducted and the defendant must apply for a certificate on the day when the payment into court is made. If the money is not accepted by the plaintiff within the required 21 days, further benefit will be deductible until the actual date of payment out. In such cases the court should be asked to authorise a further deduction when ordering the payment out.

1 Social Security Act 1989 (s 22 and Sch 4), as amended by the Social Security Act 1990 (s 7 and Sch 1), and the Social Security (Recoupment) Regulations 1990 and 1991. The 1989 Act, as amended, is consolidated in Part IV of the Social Security Administration Act 1992.
2 See *Rees v West Glamorgan County Council* [1994] PIQR P37, CA in which the claim was settled without reference to the benefits.
3 Social Security (Recoupment) Regulations 1990 and 1991.
4 Social Security Administration Act 1992, s 81(1).
5 See *Kemp & Kemp* 10–030–10–054/6.
6 Social Security Administration Act 1992, s 93.

17.47 The old and new benefits regimes provide for deduction of sickness benefits and statutory sick pay. If the plaintiff is entitled as of right to sick pay under the terms of his contract of employment this must be deducted in full from his loss of earnings claim. If his contract requires such payments to be treated as a temporary loan and repaid out of the damages recovered by him, or are paid subject to such an agreement, then they are disregarded.[1] If the employer makes payments voluntarily they are not deducted if the defendant is a third party, since they are due to the benevolence of the employer and qualify as charitable payments.

In *Colledge v Bass Mitchells & Butlers Ltd*[2] the plaintiff was selected for redundancy because of a relevant injury. The Court of Appeal held that his redundancy payment should be set off against his loss of earnings claim, as its purpose was to compensate for loss of earnings. In *Mills v Hassall*[3] the court held there should be no deduction if the redundancy was not caused by the injury. In *Sully v Doggett*[4] a student maintenance grant was set off against a loss of earnings claim.

In *Eley v Bedford*[5] it was held, under the 1948 Act, that benefits which had been lost by failure to claim them in time were of no value and were to be ignored, and that a failure to exercise a right to claim a benefit of which the plaintiff was ignorant was not an unreasonable failure to mitigate. In *Moriarty v McCarthy*[6] it was held that no deduction should be made for Irish non-contributory state benefits. In *Berriello v Felixstowe Dock & Rly Co*[7] there was a similar decision in respect of Italian state benefits recoverable from the plaintiff's damages.

1 In *Franklin v British Railways Board* [1994] PIQR P1, CA it was held that the plaintiff was obliged to repay only the net amounts he received, and not statutory deductions paid by his employer.
2 [1988] 1 All ER 536 CA; see also *Mills v Hassell* [1983] ICR 330.
3 [1983] ICR 330.
4 (5 December 1984, unreported) CA.
5 [1971] 3 All ER 285.
6 [1978] 2 All ER 213.
7 [1989] 1 WLR 695.

Court of Protection

17.48 If the injury has rendered the plaintiff incapable of managing and administering his property and affairs so as to render him a patient within the meaning of the Mental Health Act 1983, and the damages are worth more than £5,000, the damages will be administered by the Court of Protection.[1] The court's administration expenses and the fees of a professional receiver are recoverable as damages,[2] and should be pleaded. The expenses and fees are damages and are not akin to the costs of the action, so if the plaintiff is found guilty of contributory negligence or if liability is agreed at a reduced percentage to reflect litigation risk, the award is reduced accordingly.[3] This right of recovery should apply to the costs of setting up a trust.[4] The Court of Protection fees can be quantified only when the award of damages has been determined, since the fees are based on income.[5] The court will provide assistance to enable the fees to be projected. The multiplier will be based on the probable duration of the plaintiff's incapacity, but may be discounted to allow for the reduction of the capital sum, and consequently the administration expenses, with the passage of time.[6]

1 RSC Ord 80/12/5.

2 *Rialas v Mitchell* (1984) 128 Sol Jo 704, CA: see *Thomas v North West Surrey HA* (9 November 1989, unreported) per Tucker J, and *Cassel v Riverside HA* [1991] PIQR Q1 and Q168.
3 *Cassel v Riverside HA*, supra.
4 RSC Ord 80/12/11.
5 Court of Protection Rules 1984, r 7; RSC 9–271; *Kemp & Kemp* 5–008/11. See *Cassel v Riverside HA*, supra, for the meaning of 'clear annual income', on which the fees are levied.
6 *Roberts v Johnstone*, supra; *Cassel v Riverside HA*, supra.

MITIGATION OF LOSS

17.49 The onus of proof on the issue of mitigation is on the defendant. This has long been settled, since the decision in *Roper v Johnson*,[1] confirmed by the House of Lords in *Garnac Grain Co v Faure & Fairclough*.[2] There is no support for the apparent contrary dicta in *Selvanayagam v University of the West Indies*,[3] a decision of the Privy Council. It is the duty of the plaintiff to mitigate his loss. He cannot recover damages for a worsening of his injury or loss caused by any wilful act or neglect or unreasonable conduct on his part. Such conduct may amount to a novus actus interveniens and break the chain of causation. This may occur, for example, where the plaintiff's disability has continued or been aggravated by his unreasonable failure to undergo a surgical operation,[4] or his refusal to submit to hospital treatment for an anxiety neurosis,[5] or where the aggravation and prolongation of a neurosis were due to the delay in bringing an action to trial.[6] This may occur also where the plaintiff has delayed unreasonably in returning to work, failed to seek employment within his reduced capabilities, or has behaved unreasonably in his injured state, suffered a further accident and aggravated his injury and increased his loss.[7]

1 *Roper v Johnson* (1873) LR 8 CP 167, 42 LJC P65.
2 [1968] AC 1130, [1967] 2 All ER 353, HL.
3 [1983] 1 All ER 824.
4 *Steele v Robert George & Co Ltd* (1937) [1942] AC 497, [1942] 1 All ER 447; *Janiak v Ippolito* [1985] 16 DLR (4th) 1 (Supreme Court of Canada), *Halsbury's Laws of England* Annual Abridgment [1983] 720.
5 *Marcroft v Scruttons Ltd* [1954] 1 Lloyd's Rep 395.
6 *James v Woodall Duckham Construction Co Ltd* [1969] 2 All ER 794, [1969] 1 WLR 903.
7 *McKew v Holland & Hannen & Cubitts (Scotland) Ltd* [1969] 3 All ER 1621; *Wieland v Cyril Lord Carpets* [1969] 3 All ER 1006.

DUPLICATION

17.50 When assessing the claim it is necessary to ensure that there is no duplication or overlapping between the various heads, which can occur in the awards of special damage and future pecuniary loss. In *Fletcher v Autocar*[1] it was held that 'in assessing additional expenses all economies consequent on the action taken that involved the expenses claim should be brought into consideration'. In *Lim Poh Choo v Camden and Islington Area HA*[2] Lord Scarman said:

> The separate items, which together constitute a total award of damages, are interrelated. They are parts of a whole, which must be fair and reasonable. 'At the end', as Lord Denning said in *Taylor v Bristol Omnibus Co Ltd*, 'the judges should look at the total figure in the round, so as to be able to cure any overlapping or other source of error.' In most cases the risk is not great nor, where it occurs, is it substantial.

Lord Scarman held that overlap does occur where the plaintiff is being maintained in an institution and is compensated for loss of earnings without having to incur living expenses, which expenses were deducted from the award.[3] 'Economies' of this sort can indeed amount to substantial sums, examples of which have arisen from time to time in the text. A further example arose in the case of *Cassel v Riverside HA*,[4] in which the handicapped infant would have been privately educated; the sum of £65,000 was deducted as a saving in school fees. In *Fish v Wilcox*[5] the Court of Appeal held that an award of damages to a mother in respect of the birth of her handicapped child could not include an amount in respect of the mother's loss of earnings in addition to the compensation to which she was entitled for the services she was rendering in caring for the child.

1 [1968] 2 QB 322, [1968] 1 All ER 726.
2 Supra.
3 A useful source of information to assess living expenses in the annual Family Expenditure Survey published by HMSO.
4 Supra.
5 (1993) 13 BMLR 134, CA.

FATAL ACCIDENTS ACT CLAIMS

17.51 The Fatal Accidents Act 1976 confers on dependents of the deceased an independent right to recover damages, which is related to the deceased's cause of action, but is not a continuation of that cause. Section 1(1) provides:

> If death is caused by any wrongful act, neglect or default which is such as would (if death had not ensued) have entitled the person injured to maintain an action and recover damages in respect thereof, the person who would have been liable if death had not ensued shall be liable to an action for damages, notwithstanding the death of the person injured.

The dependents entitled to claim under the Act are:

(a) the wife or husband, or former wife or husband of the deceased, including a person whose marriage to the deceased has been annulled, declared void or dissolved;
(b) a person who was living with the deceased in the same household immediately before the date of the death, and who had been so living for at least two years before that date, and was living during the whole of that period as the husband or wife of the deceased;
(c) a parent or grandparent of the deceased, or any person who was treated by him as his parent;
(d) a child or grandchild of the deceased, or any person (not being an actual child of the deceased) who in the case of any marriage to which the deceased was at any time a party, was treated by the deceased as a child of the family in relation to that marriage;
(e) a brother, sister, uncle or aunt of the deceased, and the issue of any of them.[1]

1 For the purpose of deducing these relationships, any relationship by affinity (marriage) shall be treated as one of consanguinity, a relationship of the half blood is treated as one of the whole blood, a stepchild is treated as a child, and an illegitimate child is treated as the legitimate child of his mother and reputed father (s 1(5)).

17.52 The action usually is brought by and in the name of the executor or administrator of the deceased. If there is no executor or administrator, or if no action is brought by him within six months after the death, the action may be brought in the name of all or any of the dependents. There can be only one action, which must be brought on behalf of all persons entitled to claim, and the defendant must be provided with particulars of the dependents and the nature of their claims. If a payment into court is made the defendant is not obliged to specify the share of any particular claimant. If the money paid into court is acceptable, the approval of the court will be required if any of the claimants is a minor.[1] In any event, the damages recovered, after deducting the costs not recovered from the defendants, must be apportioned among the dependents by the court.[2] The money apportioned to the minor will be administered by the court.[3]

1 RSC Ord 80.
2 See RSC Ord 80/12/6 for apportionment, and the table in *Kemp & Kemp* 23–004 and 23–005.
3 RSC Ord 80, r 12.

17.53 The following matters require further consideration:

(a) bereavement award;
(b) basis of assessment;
(c) financial dependency;
(d) services dependency;
(e) benefits.

Bereavement award

17.54 This award was introduced by the Administration of Justice Act 1982, and provides damages in a fixed sum for the distress suffered as a result of the death by defined close relatives. The award initially was for £3,500, and was increased to £7,500 in respect of causes of action arising after 1 April 1991.[1] The award is limited to the wife or husband of the deceased, and to the case of a person who was a minor at the date of his death and who was never married; in such a case the award is made to his parents (who share the award equally) if he was legitimate and to his mother if he was illegitimate.

1 Damages for Bereavement (Variation of Sum) (England and Wales) Order 1990, SI 1990/2775.

Basis of assessment

17.55 Section 3(1) of the Act provides that 'such damages, other than damages for bereavement, may be awarded as are proportioned to the injury resulting from the death to the dependents respectively'. In the case of the death of a husband and father it has been held that 'the purpose of an award of damages under the Act is to provide the widow and dependents of the deceased with a capital sum which, with prudent management, will be sufficient to supply them with material benefits of the same standards and duration as would have been provided for them out of the earnings of the deceased had he not been killed by the tortious act of the defendant.'[1] In *Davies v Powell Duffryn Associated Collieries Ltd*[2] Lord Wright observed that:

> There is no question here of what may be called sentimental damage, bereavement pain or suffering. It is a hard matter of pounds, shillings and pence, subject to the element of reasonable future probabilities. The starting point is the amount of wages which the deceased was earning, the ascertainment of which to some extent may

depend on the regularity of his employment. Then there is an estimate of how much was required or expended for his own personal and living expenses. The balance will give a datum or basic figure which will generally be turned into a lump sum by taking a certain number of years' purchase.

The basis of quantification in most fatal accident cases is similar to that used to assess past and future loss of earnings in the case of a living plaintiff, but there are differences as to deduction of the deceased's 'personal and living expenses', and the multiplier. The loss need not be purely pecuniary, since services gratuitously provided by the deceased are a loss which may be converted into a money claim.

1 Per Lord Diplock in *Mallett v McMonagle* [1970] AC 166 at 174.
2 [1942] AC 601, [1942] 1 All ER 657.

Financial dependency

17.56 A dependency may arise is many different circumstances, and the quantification must be tailored accordingly. The following is the approach taken in a typical claim involving a family unit of a husband and wife, with or without children.

The loss to the date of assessment

17.57 The first stage is to estimate the value of the loss to the date of assessment. The value of the deceased's net income and benefits in kind for each of the years from the date of death must be determined, making due allowance for probable past real and inflationary increases. The income may be earned, investment or pension. The benefits may include the provision of a company motor car and housing. If part of the income is not spent for the benefit of the family, for example because it is contributed to charity, such expenditure is left out of account.

17.58 Thereafter, the value of the loss of dependency must be determined. The modern practice is to deduct from the net income figure a percentage to reflect what the deceased would have spent on maintenance of himself. These percentage deductions have become conventional and tend to be applied unless there is evidence that they are inappropriate. If the family unit is a husband and wife the deduction is 33 per cent, the logic being that the net income was spent as to one third for the benefit of each spouse and as to one third for their joint benefit. If the family includes children the deduction is 25 per cent for as long as the children remain dependent, and 33 per cent thereafter.[1]

The simple application of these rates to the income of the deceased as a means of quantification does not necessarily apply where husband and wife were earning significant sums prior to the death and were contributing to household expenditure; the assessment usually is performed on the basis of pooling their income, applying the conventional rates to the total and deducting the income of the survivor.[2] In these cases it does not necessarily follow that there is any loss of dependency.[3]

The loss of dependency to the date of assessment is calculated as special damage, based on the value of the deceased's net income and benefits for each of the years from the date of death, less the appropriate rate of dependency.

1 *Harris v Empress Motors Ltd* [1983] 3 All ER 561.
2 *Coward v Comex Houlder Diving Ltd* [1988] (unreported) CA Kemp & Kemp M 27–322; *Davies v Hawes* [1990] (unreported) Kemp & Kemp M 27–323; *Crabtree v Wilson* [1993] PIQR Q24, CA.
3 *Ridgen v Beard* [1988] (unreported) CA.

The future loss of dependency

17.59 The multiplicand is based on the probable value of the deceased's net income and benefits in kind at the date of assessment, making due allowance for probable future real increases, but ignoring inflationary increases, less the appropriate percentage rate of dependency. The multiplier is set at the date of death,[1] unlike cases involving living plaintiffs where it is set at the date of assessment. However, the same principles apply to determining the multiplier as in the case of a living plaintiff.[2] The years from the date of death to the date of assessment, in respect of which special damages have been awarded, are deducted from the multiplier. If the dependents include children, so that there are different percentage rates of dependency (25 per cent and 33 per cent deductions), the multiplier will have to be apportioned between those rates.

1 *Graham v Dodds* [1983] 2 All ER 953, HL.
2 See para **17.22** above.

17.60 In dependency claims a multiplier of 16 generally is regarded as the maximum, but this is only appropriate in the case of a well established marriage, probably cemented by the presence of children, and where there is no more than a speculative chance of separation and divorce.[1] The risks of divorce may be considered and the multiplier discounted appropriately.[2] In the case of an unmarried partner, the court must take into account the fact that the partner had no enforceable right to financial support by the deceased;[3] whether a discount of the multiplier is required will depend on the facts of the case. Conversely, the multiplier may be extended if the deceased had the opportunity and intention to work beyond the normal retirement age, or if the loss of dependency includes pension income after retirement.

If the husband and wife were separated at the date of death the court will have to estimate the chance that they would have become reconciled, determine the value of the award had they been living together and discount the award to take account of the probability of their not becoming reconciled.[4]

The Act provides[5] that when assessing damages payable to a widow her remarriage or the prospects of remarriage shall not be taken into account. The Act is silent as regards a husband, but the effect of the Court of Appeal decision in *Stanley v Saddique*[6] appears to be that his remarriage or the prospects of remarriage should be disregarded as a benefit within section 4 of the Act. If this is right, it may be that the marriage or prospects of marriage of an unmarried partner similarly should be disregarded.

If the dependents are or include children the multiplier in respect of their dependency (or the apportionment of the full multiplier between the 25 per cent and 33 per cent rates of dependency) is based on the period during which they will remain dependent, which may extend past their majority if tertiary education is likely. In *Corbett v Barking Havering and Brentwood HA*[7] the Court of Appeal held that in determining the multiplier in an infant's claim for loss of dependency of his mother, where there was prolonged delay in bringing the claim, the known fact of his survival to the date of trial could be taken into account to increase the multiplier.

1 *Owen v Martin* [1992] PIQR Q151, CA.
2 Ibid; *Wheatley v Cunningham* [1992] PIQR Q100.
3 Section 3(4).
4 *Gray v Barr* [1971] 2 All ER 949; *Davies v Taylor* [1972] 3 All ER 836, HL.
5 Section 3(2).
6 [1992] QB 1.
7 [1991] 1 All ER 498.

17.61 If the widow was not working prior to the death she will not be expected to find work to mitigate her loss, nor will her earnings be taken into account if she does go out to work to support herself and her children;[1] if she would have resumed work in future in any event, perhaps when her children had reached a certain age, her prospective earnings may be taken into account in determining her dependency. A widow is not entitled to an increased dependency merely because she and her husband, prior to his death, had decided to have a family, which would have increased the amount of her dependency.[2]

1 *Howitt v Heads* [1973] QB 64, [1972] 1 All ER 491.
2 *Malone v Rowan* [1984] 3 All ER 402.

17.62 The Act provides for a wide range of claimant, whose claims will be assessed on their own facts. The essential question in each case is whether there was an actual dependency at the date of death, or a reasonable expectation of benefit in future. A category of claim frequently made is by parents for the loss of financial support of a child. In the case of an adult child paying a regular sum the multiplicand will not be difficult to assess. If the child was living at home and the payments were for board and lodging, only the surplus after deduction of expenses will be allowed.[1] If there was no dependency at the date of death an award might still be justified if there was a reasonable prospect of support in future.[2] If the child was unmarried the prospect of marriage may substantially limit the multiplier, as may the age of the dependant parent.

1 As an example, see *Riley v AC Products* [1992] CLY 1785.
2 *Bishop v Cunard White Star Co Ltd* [1950] 2 All ER 22; *Wathen v Vernon* [1970] RTR 471.

Services dependency

17.63 The loss required to found a dependency claim need not be purely pecuniary. The services gratuitously rendered, for example by a wife and mother or husband and father in the home, are a loss which may be converted into a money claim.

The loss of a mother's services often is assessed by reference to the annual cost of employing a housekeeper or nanny. The past loss is recovered as special damage and the future loss is capitalised on a multiplier/multiplicand basis. The commercial cost of providing the substitute services is not the invariable basis of assessment,[1] although it is commonly adopted at least as a starting point. There is a useful discussion of the relevance of the commercial cost in the Australian case of *Nguyen v Nguyen*.[2] In *Hayden v Hayden*[3] it was held wrong to use the cost of a substitute if such employment would never have taken place. If the loss of a mother's services is based on the cost of a substitute, the long term cost must be adjusted to allow for the fact that the child will need less care as he grows older.[4] The multiplier will be set at death and will be based on the period during which the child will remain dependent. In *Stanley v Saddique* it was held that if the mother's care was unreliable, and there was a real possibility she would not have been available to provide steady parental support had she lived, the multiplier/ multiplicand approach support may be inappropriate.

In *Mehmet v Perry*[5] the father had given up work to care for the children; it was held the loss of housekeeping services should be assessed by reference to his loss of earnings, and not on the basis of the cost of providing a housekeeper. It is a matter of fact whether it is reasonable for a parent to give up work and claim lost earnings, which can be greater than the cost of a housekeeper. In *Mehmet v Perry* the decision was reasonable because the children had a blood disorder.[6] In *Cresswell v Eaton*[7] the children's aunt gave up work to care for them, and the claim was valued on the basis of her lost earnings, although a discount was applied because the mother had worked and cared for the children part-time.

A husband can no longer sue for loss of consortium in respect of the death of his wife, but can claim damages for loss of her housekeeping services. A wife may claim damages for loss of her husband's services, in terms of decorating and maintaining the family home, garden and motor car. These claims in respect of the period to date of assessment usually are limited to the recovery of actual expenditure as special damage, and thereafter are capitalised on the usual basis, on a life multiplier.

In the case of claims by parents for the death of an infant or adult child a claim for loss of services may be made if, for example, the child assisted an elderly parent with home, garden and motor car maintenance. There are even examples of claims of this sort, and for loss of babysitting services, by adult children in respect of the death of a parent.[8]

1 In *Spittle v Bunney* [1988] 3 All ER 1031, CA an attempt to assess on the basis of payments by a local authority to foster parents was rejected (at 1038J).
2 91 ALR 161; Kemp & Kemp 28–000/3.
3 [1992] 4 All ER 681, CA.
4 *Spittle v Bunney* [1988] 3 All ER 1031, CA.
5 [1977] 2 All ER 529.
6 See also *Regan v Williamson* [1976] 2 All ER 241; *Bailey v Barking and Havering HA* [1979] Law Society Gazette, 2 August p 793 and *Watkins v Lovegrove* [1982] Kemp & Kemp 28–105 (father was in the Navy).
7 [1991] 1 All ER 484.
8 See *Betney v Rowlands and Mallard* [1992] CLY 1786.

17.64 In *Regan v Williamson* it was held that in assessing the pecuniary value of a mother's services the court should not construe 'services' too narrowly by limiting it to the services of a housekeeper. Account should be taken of the fact that she does not work set hours, but is in constant attendance on the family and is able to give instruction to the children on matters essential to their upbringing. The multiplicand was increased by some £400 per annum to allow for this factor, which added some £5,000 to the award of the four young children at present day values. A similar award was made in *Mehmet v Perry*, in which a total of £1,500 was awarded to two young children, covering a period of eight years, which would now also be worth some £5,000. This additional level of award was approved, at least by implication, by the Court of Appeal in *Spittle v Bunney*.[1]

1 Supra, at 1037H.

Benefits

17.65 The new benefits regime introduced by the Social Security Act 1989 does not affect claims under the 1976 Act, since amongst the exempt payments are 'any payment to the extent that it is made (i) in consequence of an action under the Fatal Accidents Act 1976, or (ii) in circumstances where, had an action been brought, it would have been brought under the Act'.

Section 4 of the 1976 Act provides:

> In assessing damages in respect of a person's death in an action under this Act, benefits which have accrued or will or may accrue to any person from his estate or otherwise as a result shall be disregarded.

This section has been strictly construed. In *Pidduck v Eastern Scottish Omnibuses Ltd*[1] the widow was dependent on her husband's pension. After his death she received a widow's allowance from the same pension fund; it was held that this was not a continuation of the pension but a new benefit, which was to be disregarded. In *Wood v Bentall Simplex Ltd*[2] the father's income was derived from a farm, which his family inherited on his death. It was held that the family had lost support from his earnings and that the capital value of the farm was to be ignored. Section 4 is not limited to financial benefit. In *Stanley v Saddique*[3] the Court of Appeal considered the meaning of 'or otherwise' and held that the replacement of an unsatisfactory mother by a stepmother who provided a higher standard of services was to be disregarded in assessing damages for loss of the mother's services. If carried to its logical conclusion, this decision appears to have excluded from consideration the remarriage or prospects of remarriage of a widower, in respect of which the Act is silent.[4] It is apparent that the effect of section 4 is that the assessment of damages in these claims has become an artificial exercise; the purpose of the exercise is no longer to put the dependents in the same position they would have occupied but for the death.

1 [1990] 2 All ER 69.
2 (1992) Times, 3 March; Kemp & Kemp 22–006.
3 Supra.
4 In *Hayden v Hayden* [1992] 4 All ER 681, [1992] 1 WLR 986, CA it was held that *Stanley* is binding on the Court of Appeal.

LAW REFORM ACT CLAIMS

17.66 Under Law Reform (Miscellaneous Provisions) Act 1934 the right of action which vested in the deceased in respect of the tort which caused his death passes to his estate. This was of importance and value for so long as claims in respect of 'loss of expectation of life' and 'lost years' were permitted. Since their abolition by the Administration of Justice Act 1982 the estate claims have been limited to those for general damages for pain and suffering and consequential loss, if the deceased survived for a time after the injury, funeral expenses[1] and interest. If any relevant benefits were paid between date of injury and date of death these are subject to the recoupment provisions in the usual way.

1 Funeral expenses can be claimed under the Fatal Accidents Act 1976, s 3(5); these must be reasonable and may include the cost of embalming and a tombstone, but not an expensive tombstone or monument; *Hart v Griffiths-Jones* [1948] 2 All ER 729; *Stanton v Ewart F Youlden Ltd* [1960] 1 All ER 429, [1960] 1 WLR 543.

INTEREST

17.67 The power of the courts to award interest on damages is derived from section 35A of the Supreme Court Act 1981. The present regime for the award of interest may be summarised thus:

(a) general damages for pain suffering and loss of amenity attract interest at the rate of 2 per cent per annum from the date of service of the writ of summons;[1]

(b) special damage usually attracts interest at half the prevailing special account rate from the date when the cause of action arose. There may be special reasons which justify a claim for interest at the full rate, as where substantial expenditure was incurred at an early stage. If such a claim is to be made it should be fully pleaded in the Statement of Claim.[2] Interest is calculated on net damages, after deduction of statutory benefits. Under the new benefits regime, benefits should be deducted first from the loss of earnings claim and any surplus from the other special damage.[3] If an interim payment has been made it should be set off against special damage for the purpose of calculation of interest;[4]

(c) in Fatal Accidents Act claims interest is awarded on the loss of dependency to the date of assessment on the same basis as special damage in the case of a living plaintiff. Interest on the bereavement award and funeral expenses is awarded at the full rate.[5] In Law Reform Act claims interest on general damages for pain and suffering is awarded on the same basis as in the case of a living plaintiff and on funeral expenses as above;

(d) where there has been unjustifiable delay in bringing an action to trial interest may be disallowed for the period of delay.[6] When money is paid into court under Order 22 it is placed in the basic account and attracts interest. When an order for payment out is made the usual order is that interest accrued between the date of the payment into court and the order for payment out goes to the party who made the payment.[7] Under section 17 of the Judgments Act 1838 interest runs from the date when damages are assessed or agreed and not when judgment on liability is given.[8] Interest awarded on damages for personal injury or death is not taxable as income.[9]

1 *Wright v British Railways Board* [1983] 2 AC 773, [1983] 2 All ER 698, HL.
2 *Jefford v Gee* [1970] 1 All ER 1202, CA; *Dexter v Courtaulds Ltd* [1984] 1 All ER 70.
3 Social Security Administration Act, s 103.
4 A portion of the interim payment may even be set off against general damages; see *Bristow v Judd* [1993] PIQR Q117, CA.
5 *Prior v Hastie* [1987] CLY 1219; *Sharman v Sheppard* [1989] CLY 1190.
6 *Spittle v Bunney* [1988] 3 All ER 1031, CA.
7 RSC Ord 23/13/1; Practice Direction [1988] 3 All ER 896.
8 *Thomas v Bunn* [1991] 2 WLR 27.
9 Income and Corporation Taxes Act 1988, s 329(1).

INTERIM PAYMENTS

17.68 A plaintiff may apply for an interim payment of damages under Order 29, rule 11 at any time after expiry of the time limited for acknowledgment of service of the writ, provided the defendant is insured, a public authority or has sufficient means. The award will be made if the court is satisfied the defendant has admitted liability, or the plaintiff has obtained judgment, or the plaintiff would obtain judgment for substantial damages were the action to proceed to trial. In the absence of an admission or judgment, it is for the plaintiff to adduce affidavit evidence to discharge the burden of showing he would succeed at trial. The burden of proof is high, but it remains a civil burden on the balance of probabilities.[1] There are often problems where there are two defendants, since the plaintiff must prove his case against the particular defendant from which he seeks an interim award.[2] In difficult medical negligence litigation, where liability turns on the opinions of medical experts, the plaintiff often is unable to discharge the burden. In a doubtful case it will not necessarily benefit him to have an interim payment; if he discontinues or fails on liability at trial he may be ordered to repay with interest.[3] In such cases the better course may be to seek summary judgment under Order 14 or a split trial under Order 33, rule 3, so as to resolve the issue of liability as soon as possible.

1 *Shearson Lehman Bros Inc v McLaine Watson & Co Ltd* [1987] 2 All ER 181.
2 RSC Ord 29/11/1; *Breeze v R McKennon & Sons Ltd* (1985) 130 Sol Jo 16, 32 BLR 41, CA; *Ricci Burns Ltd v Toole* [1989] 3 All ER 478, CA.
3 RSC Ord 29, r 17; *Wardens & Commanlty of Mercers v New Hampshire Insurance Co* [1991] 4 All ER 542, [1991] 1 WLR 1173.

17.69 The affidavit in support of the application must verify the amount of the loss to which the application relates, and exhibit any documentary evidence relied upon by the plaintiff in support of the application. If the claim is in respect of past loss this will usually present no difficulty, but problems often arise when the payment is sought to meet future expenditure for medical treatment or equipment, or accommodation. It is usually necessary to exhibit reports from experts in these fields in support of the application. It is customary in personal injury actions for the interim payment to be limited to past loss and sums for which the plaintiff can show a need, to avoid the risk of overpayment. However, the payment is in the discretion of the court and there is nothing in the rules which requires the plaintiff to show need to found jurisdiction. Further, if the full value of the claim can be reasonably well assessed when the application is heard the courts are much more willing to award a reasonable proportion of that value, which does not run the risk of overpayment.[1] The payment usually is ordered to be in respect of special damage, to simplify the interest calculation at the end of the day.

1 RSC Ord 29/11/2; *Schott Kem Ltd v Bentley* [1990] 3 All ER 850; *Paul Monroe Smith v Glennon* (1990) Times, 26 June, CA; see also *Stringman v McArdle* (1993) Times, 19 November, CA for the relevance of the use to which it is intended to apply the award.

17.70 When claiming an interim payment care should be taken to make allowance for the defendant's duty, in respect of claims arising after January 1989, to deduct from the payment and pay to the Compensation Recovery Unit an amount equal to all the relevant benefits paid in respect of the relevant injury or disease during the relevant period. This duty arises in respect of each interim payment. If the plaintiff is a patient, the Court of Protection should be involved since issues of management and investment of the interim payment will arise.[1]

1 RSC Ord 80.

PRESENTATION

17.71 In a complex case there will be many heads of claim, in respect of which the parties should present their positions in as coherent a fashion as possible. Under Order 18, rule 12(1A) a plaintiff is required to serve with his Statement of Claim a 'statement of the special damages claimed', which must include full particulars of expenses and losses already incurred and an estimate of any future losses and expenses (including loss of earnings and pension rights). It has become common practice that this statement takes the form of a Schedule. It is often not possible to particularise the claim fully at the outset, but a full Schedule should be prepared when the evidence is complete, and an updated Schedule for use at trial must be served within strict time limits prior to the hearing.[1]

1 Practice Direction [1984] 3 All ER 165.

17.72 The Schedule should ideally be in narrative form, and contain a brief chronology and recitation of whatever information and discussion is required to identify, explain and justify each head of claim. Most of the information will be in the expert reports and witness statements, but a summary is a useful means of providing a framework within which to advance the claims. The object of the exercise is not only to comply with the Rules, but to inform and persuade the opposition and the court. Where there are many items of claim it is often convenient to set them out in the form of a Scott Schedule, as is the practice in Official Referee's business.[1] The Schedule should contain detailed calculations of past loss, and the capital sums and multiplicands claimed for future loss. The Schedule produced for trial should contain interest calculations, discounts for accelerated receipt, multipliers and a summary of all the heads of claim. It is now common practice for the damages at large to be particularised.

1 RSC Ord 18/12/29.

17.73 Under Order 18, rule 12(1)(c) the defendant is required in his defence to plead particulars of any facts relied on in mitigation of or otherwise in relation to the amount of damages. If the plaintiff's claim has not been fully particularised, or the defendant's own enquiries and evidence are not complete, it may not be possible to say much about the damages claim at that stage. However, when the claim has been particularised and his enquiries and evidence are complete he should serve a Counter-Schedule, responding to each item of claim and putting forward his arguments on mitigation, alternative bases of quantification and the like. When served with the plaintiff's updated Schedule prior to the hearing he is required to serve a Counter-Schedule within strict time limits.[1]

1 See *Coombs v BREL* [1993] PIQR Q131 for late amendment of a Counter-Schedule.

BIBLIOGRAPHICAL REFERENCES

Butterworths Personal Injury Litigation Service.
Charlesworth and Percy on Negligence (7th edn, 1983).
Heywood and Massey, *Court of Protection Practice* (11th edn, 1985).
Kemp and Kemp on Damages (1986).
McGregor on Damages (15th edn, 1988).
Mayne on Damages (11th edn).
Munkman, *Damages for Personal Injury and Death* (9th edn, 1993).

CHAPTER 18

Settlement

Stephen Miller *QC*
John Frenkel *FCA*

INTRODUCTION

18.1 Only a small proportion of claims based on allegations of medical negligence reach trial. Some are abandoned, but most, the vast majority, are compromised. This is not unusual. Our legal system operates on the premise that most legal disputes would be settled more or less amicably by the parties themselves. If the premise were incorrect, not only would trial dates disappear over the horizon, but there would be an enormous waste of money on lawyers and other trial expenses with no sure prospect of a just result at the end of the day. This is not intended as a criticism of the judges, nor of our legal processes. But litigation is fraught with uncertainty; and the ability to create and take advantage of the right moment to reach a fair compromise is one of the most valuable skills a lawyer can bring to the service of his client.

18.2 This chapter cannot, however, deal with the question of how to create or take advantage of such a moment; this depends entirely on the circumstances of each case. The first part of the chapter deals with the way in which a settlement can be reached, and the legal and procedural steps required in any particular case in order to give effect to a settlement. In the second part of the chapter the benefits and the practical effects of Structured Settlements are discussed.

GENERALLY

Nature

18.3 Essentially the settlement of any dispute is a contract. It may be complete in itself in that all pre-existing rights and liabilities are replaced by the obligations under the contract; it may involve one or both of the parties to the dispute agreeing to subject themselves to an order of the court. Likewise the effects of a settlement depend on the terms of that contract. Whatever the structure of the settlement, it is always underpinned by a contract. It may replace all pre-existing rights and liabilities; it may redefine them; it may suspend them.

18.4 The important point is that because a settlement is a contract, it requires as much care on the part of legal advisers as any contract. They must ensure that the parties are truly ad idem; and the terms must be properly thought through to ensure that there are no opportunities for further disputes to emerge.

Formalities

18.5 With two exceptions, there are no formalities required to effect a valid settlement other than those required to create a valid contract. It can, therefore, be concluded by an oral agreement, in correspondence, by a formal signed agreement, by fax or telex, or by an agreed form of order. The exceptions are settlements involving persons under a disability (minors or patients) and those effected using the payment into court machinery. These are dealt with separately below.

Authority to compromise

18.6 The general principle is that a solicitor has an implied actual authority to compromise a claim by his client if proceedings have been commenced: see *Macaulay v Polley*[1] and 44 *Halsbury's Laws* (4th edn) para 116. A barrister's implied authority is less extensive; the only certainty is that such implied authority arises when the barrister is present at court, conducting or about to conduct the case: see *Green v Crockett*.[2]

1 [1897] 2 QB 122, CA.
2 (1865) 6 New Rep 368, 34 LJ Ch 606.

18.7 However, it goes without saying that the lawyers advising settlement should ensure that the client (plaintiff or defendant) has given actual and express authority to compromise a claim before the lawyer makes any unconditional agreement. This is particularly so in medical negligence actions. From the plaintiff's point of view, he has transferred his trust from one group of professionals (the doctors) to another (the lawyers), the former having, so he believes, let him down; it is only right that he is given the benefit of full and comprehensible advice before he agrees to compromise his claim.

Benefits

18.8 There are obvious benefits from compromise: certainty, a saving in overall costs, the avoidance of acrimonious argument in court. There are also less obvious benefits. A judgment can only provide a sum of money. Apart from the relatively limited power to award provisional damages (pursuant to section 32A of the Supreme Court Act 1981, and RSC Order 37, rules 7 to 10), the judge has no alternative but to award damages once and for all: see *Burke v Tower Hamlets Health Authority*.[1]

1 [1989] CLY 1201.

18.9 Compromise gives the opportunity for more flexible arrangements to be made. One example is that of Structured Settlements which are discussed in greater detail later in this chapter. They are essentially agreements to provide annuities of regular or defined sums combined with periodic capital payments. Structured Settlements have the great advantage that payments can be guaranteed for life whereas experience has shown that even very substantial lump sums will be exhausted within 20 to 30 years of the settlement.

The machinery of compromise

18.10 Save where a plaintiff is a minor or a patient, or wishes to accept money paid into court, the parties have a choice as to how to give effect to their agreement. If no proceedings have been commenced, settlement would be by simple contract. After the issue of the writ, it may be by simple contract, or by means of an agreement which involves an order related to the action. Where there is no order of the court, the effect of the settlement will entirely depend on the terms of the contract which will be one of accord and satisfaction, i e it would usually require the parties to implement it before the claim by the plaintiff is satisfied.

18.11 Where an order of the court is involved, there may be consequences which arise from the form of that order. If, by agreement, an action is withdrawn or dismissed, there is no complication. If by agreement there is a judgment of a sum of money, this will have the advantage from the plaintiff's point of view of enabling him to invoke the machinery of enforcement, and the judgment debt will carry with it interest in accordance with the Judgments Act 1838. Many settlements are, however, effected by a 'Tomlin' order. This is an order of the court by which the action is stayed on terms (usually endorsed on counsels' briefs) save that there is liberty to apply to court to give effect to those terms. This form of agreement is common in actions which are settled on or near the date of trial, and has the advantage that it gives privacy to both parties as to the basis of the compromise, whilst giving the plaintiff the opportunity to return to the court if there is any difficulty in resolving the details of the agreement (see generally the notes in *Supreme Court Practice*, vol 2 at para 4616).

18.12 A recent example of the way in which a 'Tomlin' order works is the case of *Hollingsworth v Humphrey*.[1] The defendant had failed to carry out the terms of the compromise. The plaintiff therefore applied to the court to lift the stay on the action and permit the matter to proceed to trial, alternatively for an order enforcing the terms of the compromise, and an enquiry as to the loss or damage suffered. The Court of Appeal held that the judge was right not to lift the stay; the appropriate order, which is the order which he made, was for specific performance of the relevant terms of the compromise. It held, on the other hand, that the judge was wrong to award damages for the breach of the terms of the compromise; the court's jurisdiction was simply to give effect to its terms. Any damage sustained by reason of the breach would be damage resulting from a breach of contract, necessitating a separate action.

1 [1988] CLY 2931, CA, (1987) CA Transcript 1244.

18.13 It should be noted, however, that under the usual form of 'Tomlin' order, where an action is stayed upon terms agreed between the parties and the terms provide for the payment of a sum of money and costs by one party to the other, the statutory interest on the sum and costs, which would normally run from judgment (see *Hunt v R M Douglas (Roofing) Ltd*[1]) does not become payable unless and until a judgment or order for the payment is entered pursuant to a further order made under the liberty to apply.

1 [1990] 1 AC 398, [1988] 3 All ER 823.

Minors and patients

18.14 Persons under a disability cannot effectively conclude contracts of settlement, any more than they can conclude contracts of any other kind, unless they are contracts which are in the interests and for the benefit of the minor or patient. Equally, no contract can be made on their behalf by a next friend or guardian ad litem, unless it is in the interest and for the benefit of the minor or patient. A minor is a person under the age of 18 years; a patient is a person who falls within the definition of 'patient' in section 94(2) of the Mental Health Act 1983. Rules of Court, however, provide machinery by which the court can approve any settlement reached on behalf of a minor or a patient so as to bind the plaintiff and provide protection for the defendant. The method by which the court's approval is obtained is governed in the High Court by RSC Order 80 and in the county court by CCR Order 10.

18.15 The mode of application differs, depending on whether or not proceedings have been commenced. If approval is required before proceedings have been commenced, it will be necessary to issue an originating summons, if the case is one which would obviously have been commenced in the High Court, or particulars of claim if it would have been a county court claim (RSC Order 80, rule 11 and CCR Order 10, rule 10(2)). The appropriate forms for High Court proceedings can be found as Practice Forms Nos 170–175 in the *Supreme Court Practice*, vol 2, paras 370–375. In the county court, apart from the ordinary form of the particulars of claim, the only special form is the order approving settlement which is Form N292. Approval in such cases would usually be given by a master or district judge in High Court actions, and the district judge in the county court, unless it is apparent that there are special problems in which case the matter may be dealt with by a judge.

18.16 After commencement of proceedings, a summons in the action will be the appropriate procedural step to take, unless the action has been listed for trial. The summons will be heard by the master or the district judge in the district registry or county court (or by the judge as above). If the case has been listed for trial, the matter will usually be dealt with by the judge.

18.17 Where an appeal is pending after a trial, any compromise of the appeal will require approval for the same reasons. If an appeal is pending to the Court of Appeal, the approval of the Court of Appeal must be obtained: *Walsh v George Kemp Ltd*.[1] Correspondingly, if the appeal is to the House of Lords, the approval is required by the judicial committee of the House: *Leather v Kirby*.[2]

1 [1938] 2 All ER 266, CA.
2 [1965] 3 All ER 927n, [1965] 1 WLR 1489, HL.

18.18 The purpose of the hearing of any application for the approval of a settlement made on behalf of a person under a disability is to ensure that the terms of the settlement are indeed in the interests and for the benefit of that person. The court must therefore be provided with all relevant information in relation to liability (if, for example, the settlement is intended to take into account some reduction in what would otherwise be the appropriate full award on the grounds of contributory negligence, the risk of failure, or the general risks of litigation). It must also be provided with all the necessary information on quantum of damages, such as medical reports, other expert reports relating to any future care, or to life expectancy, or to earning capacity. If any element of the settlement figure is for special damages, or for future costs, the necessary evidence must also be made available.

18.19 By the time a case reaches the stage where approval is sought from a judge, a Schedule of Special Damages and a Counter-Schedule will have been served either in accordance with the Practice Note (Personal Injury Action Special Damages) [1984] 1 WLR 1127; (see vol 1 of the *Supreme Court Practice* at RSC Order 18, rule 12/32), or pursuant to an order on summons for directions. It will be helpful, however, in a complex case, to provide the court with the summary of the elements which go to make up the overall claim. The court's task is to come to some sort of conclusion as to whether or not the figure arrived at for settlement is a sensible and fair compromise figure. In theory this can only be done by the court trying the action and reaching its own conclusion. In practice, it is usual in a complicated case to explain to the judge the basis upon which the plaintiff is being advised to accept a certain figure for each component of the damages claim. Time may be saved in an appropriate case by the plaintiff's counsel preparing a detailed written Advice on the proposed compromise which can be submitted to the judge in advance of the hearing.

18.20 In the case of minors, any sum to be paid by reason of the settlement must either be paid into court to be invested until the age of majority subject to the court's control, in accordance with the forms already referred to, or into a trust fund set up for the benefit of the minor, the terms of which have been approved by the court. The latter is a popular and sensible alternative, providing as it does considerably greater flexibility in terms both of investment and in terms of disbursement. As far as patients are concerned, no such alternative, in practice, exists. The patient's affairs are subject to the control of the Court of Protection. It follows that any sums of money recovered by way of settlement must be paid to the Court of Protection. It is, however, possible for those advising a patient to obtain some control over the way in which the funds are dealt with if the Court of Protection is persuaded to appoint one or more such advisers as the Receiver controlling the patient's funds. The costs of administering the funds in the Court of Protection may run into tens of thousands of pounds and form a legitimate and necessary part of any overall settlement figure.

18.21 The Court of Protection Rules 1984 govern the administration of the affairs of a patient. They are to be found in the *Supreme Court Practice* vol 2 at 1043 ff. The fee scales for the time being are set out in the Appendix to these Rules, to be found at pages 1070–1071 and updated from time to time in the supplement. It is not easy to determine in any given case precisely how much the fees are likely to be. Much will depend upon the proportion of the fund which is to be applied to capital expenditure, and the proportion remaining in the fund for investment. Two different fee structures apply and a judgment has to be made as to the likely overall consequence, bearing in mind the fact that the fund is intended to be exhausted at the end of a patient's life. However, a provisional calculation will have to be made before settlement, since it will need to form part of the total sum for damages.

18.22 Different rules for calculation apply in the case of structured settlements. Under the newly introduced Rule 82A only one half of the recurring payments are treated as income for the purposes of calculating any fee payable under the Rules.

18.23 As for the costs of the proceedings, the usual order will be the costs to be taxed on the standard basis. There may be exceptional circumstances in which costs should be asked for on an indemnity basis but those advising a minor or a patient must be prepared to justify this. It is not for the defendant to justify an award on the standard basis. The mere fact that the minor or patient is appearing by a next friend, who must, of necessity, make decisions on the patient's behalf, would not be an exceptional circumstance.

Payment into court

18.24 A defendant who wishes to settle a case in which the claim is merely for a money judgment and costs and is unable to agree informally with the plaintiff as to quantum, can make his offer formally by paying the money into court. Payments into court are governed in the High Court by RSC Order 22 and in the county court by CCR Order 11. Before trial, the plaintiff has 21 days from receipt of the notice of payment into the High Court within which to determine whether or not to accept the sum in court and 14 days in the county court. If he accepts the sum, the action is stayed and he is entitled, as of right, to his costs to the date of acceptance of the payment into court, to be taxed on a standard basis. If he does not, and at trial he recovers less than the sum paid into court, then, although strictly costs remain at the judge's discretion, the usual practice will be to order that the plaintiff have his costs to the date of the payment into court and the defendant have his costs thereafter.

18.25 If the payment into court is made close to the date of trial, the defendant should remember two things as to costs. First, the plaintiff has the full period (be it 21 days or 14 days) in which to determine whether or not to accept and he is not obliged during that time to suspend his preparation of the case. It follows that if the plaintiff, during that period, delivers a brief to counsel or otherwise takes some expensive step, there would be no justification for depriving him of his right to include such elements of cost in the bill he lodges for taxation. Secondly, since the plaintiff is entitled to the full period in which to make up his mind, if the payment into court is made less than 21 days or 14 days before trial, the defendant will have no protection as to costs in relation to that payment in: *Bowen v Mills & Knight Ltd.*[1] On the other hand, if the defendant is prevented from paying into court through some default upon the part of the plaintiff or his advisers, e g not serving a proper Schedule of Damages, a payment in made less than 21 days before trial may still give the defendant a prima facie entitlement to costs if it is not exceeded: *King v Weston-Howell.*[2]

1 [1973] 1 Lloyd's Rep 580.
2 [1989] 2 All ER 375, [1989] 1 WLR 579, CA.

18.26 In the High Court there is special provision for payment into court after the trial or hearing of the action has begun. By RSC Order 22, rule 3(2) the plaintiff may accept any money paid into court after the trial or hearing of the action has begun within two days after receipt of notice of the payment in, or the receipt of the notice of any further payment in if the defendant has taken the step of increasing an earlier payment into court. This enables the defendant to attempt to bring to an end a costly trial, but obviously at the expense of any costs already incurred. If the total sum thereby made available to the plaintiff by way of payments into court is more than that which the judge eventually awards, then again the usual order will be for the plaintiff to pay the costs incurred by the defendant after the date of the payment into court.

18.27 Though a payment into court has not been accepted, it will usually remain in court after the expiry of the 21 or 14 day period until judgment or other disposal of the action. Once in court, the money can only be paid out pursuant to an order of the court itself. This is so even after judgment, when the usual order, if the plaintiff is successful, is for the sum in court to be applied in part or full satisfaction of the plaintiff's claim, with the interest that has accumulated going to the defendant. If before judgment there has been a settlement of the action then an application will have to be made to the court for an order dealing in whatever way has been agreed with the sum in court. By RSC Order 22, rule 1(3), a court can give leave to a defendant to withdraw any sum in court on such condition as it considers appropriate. Such an order is only likely to be made where there has been a significant change of circumstances since the payment into court was made.

SETTLEMENTS IN MEDICAL NEGLIGENCE ACTIONS

18.28 Generally speaking, medical negligence actions raise no special difficulties as to settlement, except for the fact that a significant proportion involve minors and patients, with the need to consider carefully the justification for settlement at a particular figure, and the procedural requirements dealt with above. Otherwise, settlement is likely to be straightforward, in the sense that it will involve payment of a lump sum, or an agreement for a Structured Settlement, in circumstances where the defendant is either a health authority or the defendant's insurers (or a combination of the two), as a result of which the need for special care to ensure enforcement of the settlement is unlikely to be a problem. However, even if payment is probably going to be prompt, it will still be necessary to insert a term into the settlement contract to provide for interest to accrue in the same way on the settlement sum as it would on a judgment debt, given the size of the awards in many medical negligence actions and the preferential rate of interest on judgment debts.

18.29 However, before agreeing to a straightforward financial settlement, those advising plaintiffs should at least give consideration to two matters: first, the extent to which the plaintiff may need advice and help in relation to the sensible administration of the fund which would be made available; second, thought must be given to the real possibility that some other form of award rather than a straightforward lump sum, may be appropriate.

18.30 As to the first, there is some evidence to suggest that most plaintiffs spend either all or the majority of the award within a relatively short time of its receipt. There is no doubt that those who receive large sums of money are placed under great pressure from family and 'friends' who make demands upon them – large numbers of organisations immediately target those identified as having received such sums in order to provide 'advice' or other more direct services in relation to the use of the money. Since many plaintiffs are unsophisticated, the pressures and demands produced as a result are often difficult to resist. On a number of occasions it has proved sensible to persuade the plaintiff to permit the sum to be placed in a trust (albeit as sole beneficiary he is in law entitled to the whole sum immediately) in order to provide some sort of structure for the professional advice which may be necessary for prudent management. Obviously, this aspect of the matter will have to be handled with some delicacy so as to ensure that the lawyers or other advisers involved are not themselves accused of being parasites. None the less, plaintiffs have frequently been very pleased to use such a device as a means of protecting them from those whom they might otherwise have difficulty in resisting. Of course, in many medical negligence actions, a claim will be made by a plaintiff to reimburse the legitimate cost of the care that has been provided by a parent or relative between the date of the injury and the date of the trial or settlement; see *Cunningham v Harrison*.[1] Even if the settlement requires that the damages for the plaintiff are paid into the Court of Protection, the judge will usually be invited to order that the damages referable to the past care be paid over to the relative who has provided that care.

1 [1973] QB 942.

18.31 As to the second, in cases where the need for future nursing care, therapies and sophisticated equipment require regular annual payments for the rest of the plaintiff's life, multipliers and multiplicands assessed at the time of settlement may well lead to a shortfall towards the end of the predicted period. Although experience of Structured Settlements in this country is relatively short they do appear to provide a degree of certainty that future provision will endure to the end of the plaintiff's life.

18.32 The court's approach to Structured Settlements is still developing. From a procedural point of view, the current practice is that provisional settlement is reached on a conventional lump sum basis employing multipliers and multiplicands to allow for future expenditure. The judge is initially asked to give approval for settlement arrived at on a conventional basis and once that approval is given enquiries can be made as to whether or not a Structured Settlement would provide a better return for the plaintiff. However, to all intents and purposes the case is settled at that point because, if a Structured Settlement cannot be achieved, it is not open to the plaintiff to go back to the court and argue for more money. He is compensated if there is any delay caused by the enquiries proving abortive, by the fact that the whole of the fund of damages will bear interest at judgment rate from the date of the initial approval by the judge.

18.33 Finally, there are two respects in which the potential involvement of the Health Service may make a difference to the award which a plaintiff may recover. First, although damages for the cost of future care are frequently calculated on the basis that professional care will be 'bought in' to look after the plaintiff in his own home, there may well be cases where this will not be feasible. If the plaintiff can only properly be looked after in a National Health Service institution, then of course no damages will be recoverable for that element of his future care.

18.34 Secondly, many claims for medical negligence arise as a result of negligently performed operations. If a remedial operation is considered necessary or desirable then the cost of that operation being performed privately will be a recoverable head of damages in the plaintiff's claim. If the need for such an operation has only been necessary as a result of the defendant's negligence, it is not open to the defendant to argue that the plaintiff should have it as a National Health Service patient.

STRUCTURED SETTLEMENTS

Overall introduction

18.35 Medical negligence is a vast area of litigation. By the very nature of the action it seems that if, unfortunately, something goes wrong it tends to go wrong in a big way which can result in substantial injury and substantial damages. The source of the compensation is different to the normal insurance company road traffic accident claim as there it is only the insurance company's money involved (although higher claims do ultimately make their way into higher premiums generally and thus affect us all eventually). Medical negligence cases are, on the other hand, quite different. From the plaintiff's point of view, the injured party was actually a customer of the hospital (as compared to a third party) and arguably therefore should be accorded a more sympathetic approach in relation to liability, causation and quantum. From the defendant's perspective, and from that of society in general, the situation is quite different. Every pound spent on a successful claim cannot be spent on care and either results in a loss to the public purse or a reduction in service – all this at a time when there are enormous pressures on public expenditure.

18.36 The situation becomes even more fraught given the fact that we live in a far more litigious society and the impact of the media sharing information around the world. The change in the Legal Aid rules resulting in plaintiffs under the age of 18 qualifying for assistance, based upon their own financial circumstances and not that of their parents, has opened the way for the brain-damaged baby cases – which, naturally, tend to be high in damages – to be litigated far more earnestly than was previously the case.

18.37 Given the above growth in the potential for large damages cases, there are enormous opportunities for the Health Service to save money by means of a Structured Settlement and for plaintiffs to receive damages in a far more appropriate manner to what they have actually lost. These opportunities should not be wasted as, at the end of the day, we will all pay for it one way or another.

18.38 It is five years since the first Structured Settlement involving Catherine Kelly (July 1989) was implemented. The concept has moved on tremendously since then, so much so that in November 1992 there was a publication issued by the Law Commission of a Consultation Paper on Structured Settlements (as well as on Interim and Provisional Damages). This document emphasises the way this relatively new method of paying damages is becoming part of the fabric of the personal injury field.

18.39 Practitioners are falling into two categories – firstly, those who have had some direct experience of Structured Settlements and would wish to share in some of the practical experiences that specialist firms have had and, secondly, those who have not yet been involved in a suitable case and would wish to be apprised of the basics of the concept. With this distinction in mind these notes reflect the different levels of experience and the remainder of this chapter is divided into 'Introduction to Structured Settlements' (paras **18.42–18.84**) and 'Practical aspects to Structured Settlements' (paras **18.85–18.172**).

18.40 In recent years Structured Settlements have been introduced to medical negligence actions. Frenkel Topping & Co have been holding many meetings and discussions with the Department of Health as they recognise that structures do offer a tangible method of saving money. To date, this firm has implemented well over 150 Structured Settlements covering all types of personal injury and fatal accident litigation.

18.41 The growth of Structured Settlements has intensified the debate regarding practitioners being negligent for failing to consider them. The point has been raised by a number of leading counsel and in the Law Society Guidance Notes on Structured Settlements (issued October 1992) caution is noted against failing to advise a client that a structure might be appropriate and they conclude that 'Numerous commentators have suggested that such a failure might amount to negligence.'

Introduction to Structured Settlements

18.42 Structured Settlements arise as a result of a facility set up around mid-1987 by the Inland Revenue and the Association of British Insurers (ABI), following which damages can be paid wholly or in part by means of instalments for the life of the plaintiff.

18.43 A Structured Settlement is the means for a defendant to pay damages in the form of a stream of future annual payments rather than in the traditional lump sum. Such payments are guaranteed for the lifetime of the plaintiff and there is complete flexibility at the outset as to the proportion of the total damages which are paid by means of these instalment payments. This is because, unless there are special reasons to justify the contrary, all Structured Settlement programmes will involve plaintiffs receiving *part* of their damages in the conventional lump sum and *part* by means of the future annual payments. If the form of such a settlement abides by the agreement made between the Inland Revenue and the ABI, then such future payments will be non-taxable.

18.44 As a result of these arrangements, plaintiffs have the opportunity to save tax and costs that would otherwise have arisen on the investment of the traditional lump sum. They also have the option of receiving their damages in a manner which is linked to their own life expectancy and can also have the certainty of an increasing income guaranteed for their life.

18.45 Because plaintiffs receive their damages in a much more efficient manner and because such settlements can only be implemented by *consent* between the parties, this additional option will provide insurance companies with the possibility of settling the large personal injury and fatal accident cases at sums appreciably lower than might otherwise have been the case. The point of consent was confirmed in the case of *Burke v Tower Hamlets Health Authority*[1] in which the court of first instance held that an award for periodic payments could not be made unless both parties consented.

1 [1989] CLY 1201.

18.46 It should be borne in mind at an early stage that plaintiffs cannot go into the marketplace and acquire a return which is paid for life and *tax-free* in any alternative investment medium. Thus, they cannot accept the conventional lump sum and achieve the tax-free status of the structure without the co-operation of the defendant.

Comparison of the Structured Settlement with the conventional lump sum

18.47 In the next two sections a comparison of the effects on the net income of a plaintiff adopting the conventional lump sum as compared to the Structured Settlement will be carried out.

18.48 The comparison is based on the facts of the case involving Catherine Kelly, which was the first case in the UK to be settled by means of a Structured Settlement. A full case synopsis is provided later; suffice it to say here that she was aged in her mid-twenties at the time and her husband died in the same accident. There were no dependants and, as she was left in a comatose state, there was very great uncertainty regarding her future life expectancy.

Investment of the conventional lump sum

18.49 The theory of damages is that a lump sum for future loss should enable the plaintiff to live off the interest which the damages generate as well as every year drawing on the capital sum such that, at the end of his life, the lump sum is fully exhausted. However, unless an investment is made which links the future payments to the life of the plaintiff, this would be an impossible task to achieve as there are too many unknowns and variables.

18.50 The only type of investment available which guarantees cash for as long as the investor is alive is an annuity. The annual cash received under the annuity is *partly* return of the cost of the investment which is non-taxable and *partly* income which is subject to income tax in the normal way of any investment income. Thus, if a plaintiff were to use the conventional lump sum award to purchase an annuity from a life office then he would be guaranteed to achieve the certainty of the cash stream for as long as he were to live. There would, however, be no income tax advantage as all the income arising under the annuity is taxable as investment income.

18.51 Appendix 1 includes a diagrammatic presentation of the sequence of events of such an investment which highlights the fact that the income element of the annuity is taxable. The sample is based on the numbers in the *Kelly* case and assumes that the £300,000 used to purchase the structure would have been available to buy an annuity. The effects of this course of action are as follows:

(a) the plaintiff does not have to worry about life expectation as the annuity will pay for life;
(b) the plaintiff does not have to worry about changes in investment conditions as the return is guaranteed to increase in line with the Index of Retail Prices irrespective as to what happens to investment returns generally;
(c) the plaintiff will receive the initial annual sum of £17,700 after all taxes *and* will carry the risk of a reduced income in the event of income tax rates increasing over the life of the plaintiff. As the rates used in the analysis are based on the current rates (as at April 1993) and these are the lowest rates this century then there is only likely to be upward pressure on income tax rates which would further reduce this sum of £17,700.

18.52 It is clear that the tax consequences of such an investment are unfavourable, notwithstanding that the investment programme does go a long way towards achieving the rationale of damages, i e the certainty of an income stream for life.

What exactly is an insurance company Structured Settlement?

18.53 The concept of Structured Settlements allows plaintiffs to receive whatever proportion of their damages they so wish in the form of a series of future annual payments, linked to their own life and individual projected future cash requirements. The balance of the damages is paid in the manner of the traditional lump sum.

18.54 The general philosophy behind the structure is that once a plaintiff in a large personal injury or fatal accident case has been provided with his/her set-up costs, eg home, equipment and car, and, also, has a reasonable contingency cash fund, then the balance of the lump sum is normally required as a means to provide an annual income for life.

18.55 What happens in fact is that the amount of money that is used to provide a structure is applied by the general insurer (or health authority in a medical negligence case) to purchase an annuity in order to fund the regular payments that it has to make to the plaintiff as damages by instalments. Effectively, the arrangements are back-to-back.

18.56 Appendix 2 is a diagrammatic representation of what happens in a structure keeping the same format as for Appendix 1 in order to contrast the differences. The important point is that there are two very distinct contractual relationships:

(1) firstly, the general insurer (or health authority) has an obligation to pay damages by instalments to the plaintiff. This is considered in further detail at Appendix 3;
(2) secondly, by the purchase of an annuity, the general insurer (or health authority) has a right to receive a series of future payments which are linked to the life of the plaintiff. This is considered in further detail at Appendix 4.

18.57 The effects of the above contractual relationships are summarised below and are compared to the position of the investment of the conventional lump sum award directly into the annuity as per above:

(a) the plaintiff does not have to worry about life expectation as the annuity will pay for life – *exactly the same as for the conventional award;*
(b) the plaintiff does not have to worry about changes in investment conditions as the return is guaranteed to increase in line with the Index of Retail Prices, irrespective as to what happens to investment returns generally – *exactly the same as for the conventional award;*
(c) the plaintiff will receive the initial annual sum of £25,700 which is not subject to any taxes *and* carries no risk of a reduction in income in the event of income tax rates increasing over the life of the plaintiff – *this figure is to be directly contrasted to the net income of £17,700 which is subject to erosion from changes in future tax rates.*

18.58 The effect of the structure is to make available some 45 per cent more under the structure than would otherwise have been available under the conventional lump sum approach and offers both parties the opportunity to save money. Put simply, the plaintiff can receive more under the structure at a lower cost to the defendant.

Administrative aspects to the insurance company Structured Settlement

18.59 The mechanics are that the general insurer will pay out to the plaintiff damages by instalments which may be index-linked and last for the life of the plaintiff or for a specified number of years, if longer. In turn, the general insurer purchases an annuity from a life office in order to fund the series of payments. Under current tax legislation, the life office have to pay to the general insurer the required annuity after deduction of income tax. The general insurer in effect has to pay to the plaintiff the gross equivalent of the annuity. There will thus be a loss in cash flow to the general insurer but, as discussed below, the whole arrangement is fiscally neutral.

18.60 It should be pointed out that, under current legislation in Canada and the United States, there is provision for annuities which relate to personal injury or fatal accident cases to be paid directly by the life office as agent of the insurer to the claimant, *without* deduction of tax, on the condition that such an annuity is non-transferable, non-commutable and non-assignable (see Appendix 5). In the UK such a method of payment is not possible under existing tax legislation and, until it is, it is expected that a high degree of co-operation is going to be needed by the general insurer in order to facilitate the administration required. The costs of the general insurer in funding the tax withheld are part of the reason for their negotiating a discount with the plaintiff at point of settlement.

18.61 Despite lengthy meetings with the Investment Division of the Inland Revenue and direct representations to the Chancellor of the Exchequer, there is, as yet, little prospect of a change in legislation in order to facilitate gross rather than net payments. Thus, while the insurers will have to meet the costs of the loss of cash flow and some administration, this is to be set against the advantages of a reduced cost to the insurer in the overall settlement of the case. Also, the insurance industry is not unfamiliar with the receipt of income after deduction of income tax and the annuity merely provides a further source of such income. It is to be hoped that there will be sufficient strength of representation to the Law Commission which will result in some political initiative to facilitate this aspect of the structuring process such that, ultimately, the life office will be able to pay directly to the plaintiff, as agent of the general insurer, the gross amount of the annuity.

18.62 Once the matter has been agreed to be structured then the file is no longer considered a live claim by general insurers and it moves to the accounts and administrative departments for them to arrange for the payments to be made to the plaintiff and for the monitoring of receipts from the life offices.

Tax consequences of the insurance company Structured Settlement

18.63 The fiscal consequences of the above transactions are as follows:

(a) the purchase of the annuity can be treated as a reinsurance premium and, accordingly, treated as a write-off by the general insurer as the damages would have been in any event;
(b) the receipt of the regular annuity is wholly taxable in the hands of the general insurer;

(c) the payment of the gross amount of the debt to the plaintiff can be fully written off as a tax-deductible item by the general insurer;
(d) the general insurer can obtain relief for the withholding tax that it has effectively had to fund until its normal due date for corporation tax;
(e) the regular receipts by the plaintiff are not subject to taxation as they are effectively capital receipts by instalments. Provided that all of the regulations are adhered to and the Model Agreement is the *overriding* agreement which gives the discharge from the plaintiff to the defendant, then the regular receipts by the plaintiff do not need to be included on the plaintiff's income tax return.

18.64 In order that the full advantages of a Structured Settlement can be realised, insurers must fully appreciate the overall net benefit to themselves. Thus, while a claims manager may see a benefit in the lower cost of settling the larger personal injury cases he may not be able to have any input in the control of the administration and cash-flow costs of the exercise.

18.65 Over the last four years Frenkel Topping & Co have spoken to a large number of the major insurers and reinsurers as well as speaking to a joint gathering of Lloyd's and the Association of British Insurers. It has found that it is only when a decision has been taken at a sufficiently high corporate level, perhaps by the corporate tax manager (in view of the corporation tax consequences) and head office claims' managers, that insurers have actively promoted the concept. A broad corporate view has been required to ensure that the tax, cash-flow and administrative implications of a structure are costed and weighed against the savings. A number of insurance companies have indicated that the administrative on-going requirements of Structured Settlements are not as extensive as had originally been anticipated.

18.66 It is the judgment in the case of *Dott v Brown*[1] which is the legal basis for the Inland Revenue allowing instalment payments of a debt to be treated as capital and not income and, therefore, achieve the tax-free status.

1 (1936) 154 LT 484.

18.67 Appendix 6 is a copy of the final Model Agreement and related Schedule which was approved by the Inland Revenue in the *Kelly* case. The actual agreement was based on the pro-forma Model Agreement but had to be modified to reflect the involvement of the Court of Protection. The Schedule is a modified version of the standard Model Agreement which allows for payments to be fully index-linked both upwards and downwards. The original documentation only allowed for indexation upwards. This was found to be prohibitively expensive but the Inland Revenue indicated that there was no tax reason why the payments should not be fully linked to the Retail Price Index.

18.68 Appendix 7 is a copy of the basic Model Agreement agreed between the Inland Revenue and the ABI.

Health authority Structured Settlements

18.69 Health authority structures have a number of unique features when compared to those of insurance companies although, from the plaintiff's point of view, there is really no difference at all.

18.70 The *Rebecca Field* case referred to below was the first case involving a health authority which settled by means of a Structured Settlement. Since that time dozens have been implemented. Some cases are not completed with Structured Settlements as either the Treasury do not consider them to be value for money or the plaintiffs consider the same in that defendants seek too high a discount.

18.71 The possibility of structuring medical negligence cases arose after January 1990, when the rules regarding Crown Indemnity changed such that, ultimately, it is now the Crown which is responsible for the major proportion of the damages to be paid in the larger cases.

18.72 From the defendant's point of view these cases have to be costed out somewhat differently to normal insured losses as the cash flows are affected by the implementation of a Structured Settlement in the following areas:

(1) there is an immediate saving in the 'discount' that is normally available in an insured case;
(2) the Crown suffers a loss of income tax and capital gains tax on the investment of the lump sum which would have been generated on a conventional award;
(3) it is typically assumed that, under the lump sum, the damages are in danger of expiring and from this point in time the Crown (through the Health Service) would be required to provide the care which would otherwise be available under the Structured Settlement;
(4) all the cash flows are brought to values in terms as at the date of trial under alternative scenarios of investment returns, life expectancies and rates of inflation;
(5) the Treasury will also want to know whether it is worthwhile to annuity-back the agreement (which will involve the health authority buying an annuity – this is Contract 2 as referred to at Appendix 4) or to go self-funded with the obligations of the structure being met out of future annual budgets (in which case some form of cost sharing arrangements with the Department of Health will take place and there will be no Contract 2). Suffice it to say that the Treasury have expressed a strong preference for self-funded Structured Settlements as they do leave the cash within the Health Service and do not result in large amounts of money either going to the plaintiff in the form of damages or to life offices in the form of annuities.

18.73 The first five cases which Frenkel Topping completed were all annuity-backed. The health authorities all received their annuities after income tax was deducted. However, as non-tax-paying bodies, they have been able to reclaim the tax on a monthly basis and they were helped to establish a relatively simple claims' procedure. All the subsequent cases with the exception of one have been self-funded and, obviously, here there are no tax implications for the defendants as they are not in receipt of an annuity but merely pay out every year from their budgets.

18.74 In considering financial decisions generally, the Department of Health is obligated to bear in mind that they should represent value for money. At present, these cases are being referred by the Department of

Health to the Treasury for their view on value for money. At first, value for money was taken as meaning that the expected changes in cash-flow, as referred to above, should result in a positive cash gain to the Crown as at the time of settlement.

18.75 As the concept has developed, there has been some political initiative to recognise the non-financial benefits to structures and the feedback from the Department of Health and the Treasury is that they consider structures to be a significant improvement on the conventional lump sum award basis and they are actively assisting in trying to get structures more widely recognised and implemented. However, while cases which show an expected cost to the Treasury have been approved, there are at present no distinct guidelines which set out exactly how much tolerance the Treasury will allow. Given the relatively novel aspect to the whole question of Structured Settlements, it is not surprising that the position is not yet finalised. However, with the present rate of progress, major changes to facilitate medical negligence cases settling by means of a Structured Settlement will be very far away.

18.76 As regards Trusts, it is still relatively early days as they are only responsible for their claims for *incidents* after the date of taking Trust status, so the earliest incident date is 1 April 1991. Given the normal course of the litigation process, it is unlikely that any incident involving a large amount of damages would be ready for settlement much before 1995.

Different types of Structured Settlements

18.77 While there is maximum flexibility as to how the annuity can be established at the outset, it should be pointed out that, once the structure is in place, it cannot be varied. Hence the need for an adequate contingency cash fund and expert financial advice prior to implementation.

18.78 The types of annuity that are of interest to a plaintiff are as follows:

(a) index-linked or increasing at a fixed compound rate;
(b) guaranteed for a minimum number of years or for the duration of the plaintiff's life, whichever is longer;
(c) immediate annual sums or deferred for a number of years to match changing requirements (similar to the concept of splitting the multiplier);
(d) can allow for streamed lump sum payments in the future in anticipation of replacing the vehicles/equipment etc, required by the plaintiff.

General benefits of Structured Settlements to defendants and plaintiffs

18.79 It is often considered socially desirable that plaintiffs in severe personal injury cases should have a guaranteed income for the duration of their lives. Indeed, this strikes at the very heart of the rationale of the annual loss and multiplier approach to the traditional assessment of damages whereby the lump sum is intended to be fully exhausted at the end of the plaintiff's life. As there are so many uncertainties and difficulties for plaintiffs to face, there will either be too much damages left over at the end of the plaintiff's life which might mean that, as a result of being excessively prudent, the plaintiff has gone without certain care. Alternatively, the damages will be extinguished before the plaintiff has died in which case the plaintiff will become a burden to the family and, more likely, to the Social Services system. Both of these scenarios are far from ideal. The advantage of an income secured for life is of particular benefit in impaired life cases where the projected life expectancy is uncertain. However, as is apparent from the cases considered below, structures should not merely be confined to these cases since they do have a far wider application for most types of personal injury and fatal accident cases.

18.80 Plaintiffs are protected from any temptation to dissipate the lump sum and are spared some of the financial pressures which can arise with the management of large sums of money. In particular, plaintiffs can be vulnerable to approaches from family and friends for doomed business ventures.

18.81 There can be significant savings in the costs of administration of the fund, not all of which can be recovered in the action but which would nevertheless actually be incurred by the plaintiff.

18.82 Against the background of the tangible and intangible savings and benefits accruing to the plaintiff, the defendant can see substantial cash savings in the payment of damages arising as a result of savings for the plaintiff in the taxation on the income and in the costs of administering the fund which would otherwise have been generated by the lump sum.

18.83 While there are some disadvantages to the plaintiff, principally in a potential loss of flexibility once the structure is established, this problem can be overcome by the careful planning of the plaintiff's changing requirements at an early stage and, also, in allowing for an appropriate contingency fund at the outset. Indeed, it has been pointed out that the plaintiff, prior to the accident, probably had very little flexibility in the way he conducted his lifestyle in that he would have had to work to pay for his regular outgoings and he did not have the opportunities available to people with capital. Why therefore, just because he has suffered personal injury, should he have the greater degree of flexibility that a large lump sum can afford?

18.84 Maximum benefit can only be obtained by the careful assessment and planning of the plaintiff's needs at the outset. The concept will not work if advisers merely consider that they only need to arrange for an index-linked annuity. The fact is that the arrangements must be 'structured' and thus allow for anticipated changes in circumstances. These could be catered for by, for example, the inclusion of periodic lump sums at key stages in the plaintiff's life.

Practical aspects to Structured Settlements

18.85 The matters considered here are as follows:

(1) review of four sample cases;
(2) some common questions answered;
(3) implications for plaintiffs and defendants;

(4) the Law Commission Consultation Paper; and
(5) conclusions.

Review of sample cases settled by a Structured Settlement

CASE 1 – NJO

18.86 Plaintiff was aged seven at the time of the accident and there were significant issues on liability.

18.87 She is quadriplegic from below the mid-neck and is dependant on a ventilator for breathing.

18.88 There was wide divergence on her life expectancy which ranged from 20 years from the date of the accident to 30 years from the date of trial with the risk of earlier death if there were problems with access to a ventilator.

18.89 On the basis of full liability and for the plaintiff to be compensated for the possibility of living longer, the claim was in the order of over £600,000.

18.90 The matter settled for £315,000 on the basis that £165,000 was used to set up the family home with adaptations and the balance was used to fund an annuity providing some £16,800 per annum indexing at 5 per cent per annum compound and payments being guaranteed for five years or life, whichever was longer.

18.91 The matter was approved by the courts and, in passing comment, the judge indicated that he thought such settlements should be far more widely deployed. The certainty of income for life in cases such as this provided great comfort to the family and the tax-free nature of the payments was an additional advantage.

18.92 This had been a particularly difficult case to handle and had remained unresolved for a number of years. Frenkel Topping were retained by the insurers, General Accident, and the option of being able to offer the plaintiff this type of settlement enabled a long-standing contentious case to be resolved relatively quickly.

18.93 As a rider to the above it should be pointed out that, sadly, NJO died in January 1993. Notwithstanding that the defendants had sought to implement the structure, the plaintiff's advisers were persuaded they should take an annuity with a five-year guarantee. There was only a £25 reduction in the annual income to provide a five-year rather than a nil guarantee. The effect of the above has been that there is over £40,000 due to her estate which might well be commuted rather than have to wait for the balance of the monthly payments for the residual part of the five-year period. This highlights the point regarding optimum broking to ensure that maximum value for money is obtained when settling the case.

CASE 2 – LOM

18.94 The action arose at a cross-country event when two horse riders collided.

18.95 The plaintiff suffered a broken back and quadriplegia and sued the other rider for negligence. There were great issues on liability.

18.96 Without admitting liability, the defendants offered the plaintiff the lump sum of £130,000 but this amount was not accepted.

18.97 The defendants then offered the plaintiff the lump sum of £30,000 plus £8,000 per annum for life increasing every year at the rate of 5 per cent per annum compound. This was accepted by the plaintiff and in fact cost the defendants the same figure of £130,000 which had previously been rejected.

18.98 The structure therefore assisted in disposing of a very difficult case without the apportionment of liability ever being resolved.

CASE 3 – RF

18.99 The action arose as a result of the negligent use of forceps during birth.

18.100 The plaintiff is left with severe brain damage and she is dependent on a ventilator for breathing.

18.101 Life expectancy had been impaired and it was projected as being likely that she would not live much beyond her thirties.

18.102 A conventional award had been provisionally indicated at the level of £1,700,000 in June 1991. Eventually, the case settled on the following basis:

(a) £59,000 per annum payable immediately, guaranteed for ten years and indexed at 5 per cent per annum compound;
(b) £15,315 per annum payable commencing in five years' time, guaranteed for ten years and indexed at 5 per cent per annum compound;
(c) £32,578 per annum payable commencing in ten years' time, guaranteed for five years and indexed at 5 per cent per annum compound;
(d) lump sums payable at the end of every five years. The lump sum is based on the present cash figure of £50,000 and will be indexed in line with the Retail Price Index when each payment is made. There are no minimum number of payments and payment will be made for as long as she is alive.

18.103 Appendix 8 sets out the above financial programme. At Appendix 9, a Schedule shows that a conventional award would only last some 23 years until RF is aged in her late twenties.

18.104 Additionally, the family received the sum of about £550,000, part of which was paid to the Court of Protection for them to retain in the normal way.

18.105 The total cost to the defendants was some £1,600,000 and this was paid at the end of October 1991. In other words, the defendants paid the sum of £100,000 less than the conventional figure which might otherwise have been agreed and paid it over four months later, representing a total saving of some £200,000.

18.106 This was the first medical negligence case to be structured.

CASE 4 – DM

18.107 The case arose as a result of negligent procedures resulting in the boy having spastic quadriplegia and an agreed reduced life expectancy at 30–35 years.

18.108 The case was compromised in July 1992 when it was agreed that the conventional award would have been £1,150,000. The case was adjourned for a structure to be considered and the case eventually settled on the basis of a self-funded Structured Settlement.

18.109 The plaintiff received the following:

(1) £450,000 in interims and cash sums;
(2) £25,000 per annum as an immediate annuity, fully Retail Price Index-linked and guaranteed for lifetime with a minimum payment period of five years;
(3) £26,490 per annum in today's terms, fully Retail Price Index-linked, deferred for a period of seven years, payable for life with no minimum payment period;
(4) £21,560 lump sum, in today's terms, fully Retail Price Index-linked, payable every five years for life with no minimum payment period;
(5) the notional cost of the structure was taken as £625,000 so the plaintiffs agreed to a £75,000 discount – equivalent to 12 per cent of the purchase price of the structure.

18.110 The defendants also saw considerable savings in this case. In view of their particular methodology of costing and the fact that they are taking an open-ended risk, there were savings for both the health authority and the Department of Health which were of a sufficiently satisfactory level to induce them both to enter into the Structured Settlement.

Common questions answered

UP UNTIL WHAT TIME CAN A STRUCTURE BE CONSIDERED?

18.111 A structure can be considered at any point in time until the parties have entered into a binding contract for the settlement of the case. Thus, assuming some conditional element still applies or an approval from the judge is still to be obtained then, in my opinion, it is not too late.

18.112 However, where formal notice of acceptance of a payment into court has been accepted, it is too late to structure the case as the parties have entered into a binding contract to compromise the matter.

18.113 Payments into court per se do *not* automatically preclude the possibility of a Structured Settlement. However, they can be open to different interpretations as to whose money it is in court and, generally speaking, they should be discouraged if a structure is a genuine possibility. This is because the ownership of the funds may unwittingly be transferred from the defendant to the plaintiff thus preventing the instalment payments being tax-free in the hands of the plaintiff.

18.114 The greatest benefits of structuring will, in my opinion, not be realised until both sides to the litigation process start to talk as early as possible about structuring, thus avoiding last minute panics and enabling maximum savings to be made.

WHAT IS THE MINIMUM SIZE OF CASE THAT COULD BE CONSIDERED FOR STRUCTURING?

18.115 A small case structured involved a purchase price of the annuity of just over £53,000 out of a total claim value of £65,000. The smallest amount that Frenkel Topping have structured is £50,000 out of a £99,000 fatal accident claim.

18.116 A number of insurers have indicated that their threshold involves a total claim value of £100,000. As regards medical negligence cases, the threshold has tended to be higher but, as familiarity and the speed of approvals process quickens, this is expected to be the same as for the insurance company market.

18.117 There clearly has been downward pressure on the size of case to be structured. On a recent fact-finding trip to the United States, Frenkel Topping were advised by a Structured Settlement company that their *average* case size is $70,000. Their early experience did mirror ours as they started out with a much higher average.

DOES THERE HAVE TO BE 100 PER CENT LIABILITY BEFORE YOU CAN STRUCTURE?

18.118 The apportionment of liability is irrelevant. All that matters is that there is a debt due from the defendant to the plaintiff which is being discharged by instalment payments. The NJO case referred to at Case 1 above was complicated by great issues on liability as well as life expectancy.

18.119 The parties never actually resolved the liability apportionment nor did they ever determine the exact life expectancy position. They merely agreed that, at a total cost acceptable to the defendant, a package acceptable to the plaintiff was agreed upon. Both sides carried significant risks on the case and the structure bought out their respective risks at a satisfactory compromise with the major benefit for the plaintiff being that she had the certainty of the damages for as long as she lived.

18.120 A far more risk-management approach should be taken with regard to health authority litigation of this nature. The opportunity to offer the plaintiff a structure, at a figure which reflects the risks of the litigation to both sides, could reduce costs overall for the Health Service, give plaintiffs more appropriate damages and move away from the concept of 'winners' and 'losers' in what are very tragic individual circumstances.

CAN YOU STRUCTURE A FATAL ACCIDENT CASE?

18.121 The answer to this question is an undoubted 'yes'. Practitioners should look out for these cases, especially where there is likely to be a large award.

18.122 One fatal case involved a dependency claim following the death of a leading surgeon in a road traffic accident. Despite liability only being 50 per cent there was still sufficient benefit for the widow who was already a higher rate taxpayer as a result of the high level of widow's pension that she was receiving.

EXACTLY WHAT STEPS HAVE TO BE TAKEN TO IMPLEMENT THE STRUCTURE?

18.123 From the experience of the large number of cases in which we have been involved, the following is a brief résumé of all of the steps which need to be taken to implement the structure and to make sure that it operates properly. The extent and requirement of each item will depend on the nature of the case involved. It is usually the case that such work should be undertaken by the accountants/financial intermediary (with the exception of item (5), which tends to be a joint effort between solicitors, counsel and the intermediary). It is certainly Frenkel Topping's normal practice to deal with all these items for each case in which we are instructed.

18.124 The steps are as follows:

(1) detailed appraisal of the plaintiff's current and future needs;
(2) within the level of damages available, formulating the financial package best suited to meet those needs;
(3) broking of the markets to identify the most appropriate and cost-effective annuity and assurance products;
(4) meeting and/or liaising with the parties to assist in reaching agreement as to the form of the structure;
(5) drafting the various orders and agreements for agreement by the lawyers and taking into account the tax implications of such documents;
(6) preparation of forensic accountancy reports and other reports required as may be necessary to obtain the approval of the Inland Revenue, the Court of Protection, the courts, the Department of Health, the Treasury etc, and being available to deal with any matters that may arise, eg court attendance to deal with questions raised by the judge;
(7) preparation of all the documentation required by the defendant for the purchase of the annuity package;
(8) monitoring, post-implementation, the actual working of the structure and ensuring that all payments flow to and from the correct parties and advising on annual changes.

18.125 It is good practice for the parties to be ad idem, before any such work is undertaken, regarding who should be carrying out the respective functions.

WHAT EXACTLY IS INVOLVED IN BROKING THE ANNUITY MARKETS?

18.126 It is the role of the broker to ensure that the requirements of the plaintiff are fully realised within the concept and implementation of the structure. In other words, a Structured Settlement is far more than the mere purchase of an annuity. It is the careful drawing up of a future financial plan for the lifetime of the plaintiff and, since once in force it cannot be altered, it is vital that the needs of the plaintiff are catered for in their entirety at the outset.

18.127 It is important to realise that, as with any annuity, the initial sum determines the level at which payments will be made for the guaranteed period. This initial level is determined by the life office with reference both to the investment return anticipated and the life expectancy of the plaintiff. There are specific life offices which are well known for their more favourable treatment of impairments but different life offices specialise in different types of annuity. Contrary to normal life assurance practice, where an impairment in life will normally bring a loading on a life assurance premium or, in severe cases, a declinature, the impairment works in favour of the plaintiff on an annuity and, the shorter the life expectancy, the larger the initial annuity which is to be paid out.

18.128 In view of the fact that annuity underwriters at present do not have a great deal of experience in the underwriting of impaired lives, quite a few of the life offices are wary of quoting other than normal rates on impaired life situations. Again, this situation is likely to change dramatically once the concept of Structured Settlements is accepted within the life assurance industry.

18.129 What is required is that everybody concerned fully realises the benefits to be derived from Structured Settlements. Solicitors and barristers must be aware that it is not merely the lump sum which determines the success of their case but the application of the monies to provide the best possible benefits for the plaintiff. From the defence point of view, it is preferable that the monies expended on an award are not dissipated at an early stage but are utilised to meet the annual losses for which they were originally intended.

18.130 From the schedules in the examples, it is evident that there is a great deal of flexibility in what the structure can provide but it is essential that the adviser on the structure is fully aware of the position of the plaintiff and what his/her future requirements may be. Only by careful examination of the plaintiff's situation can a settlement be properly structured to ensure that all of the necessary requirements are met and to cope with the likely eventualities necessary for future care.

18.131 The experienced broker should be able to bring all of the above into play.

WHAT DO THE LAW SOCIETY'S GUIDANCE NOTES SAY IN RELATION TO THE BROKER?

18.132 Litigation involves each side's advisers taking a partisan view in relation to the case and, subsequently, either compromising the matter or going to court for a ruling. Structured Settlements have thrown up new issues as they can only be implemented by consent between the parties and they do require a relatively high degree of co-operation between the parties, a concept which is often in short supply in large contentious litigation.

18.133 There are two methods of reaching agreement on a structure:

(a) *Bottom up* This is where either the defendants offer, or the plaintiff requests, an overall financial package including the Structured Settlement programme. No conventional figure is ever formally determined. The plaintiff receives an acceptable package at a total cost acceptable to the defendant. This is in fact how we structured the case of NJO above. In that case, the plaintiffs were aware of the total cost of the annuity package to the defendant.

In one case there were great difficulties on life expectation. The defendants put a Structured Settlement proposal to the plaintiffs without disclosing the cost to the plaintiffs. The plaintiffs took issue with this and the matter was considered by the Master of the Court of Protection who considered that the offer was in the plaintiff's best interest and was prepared to defer to the courts the question of the plaintiff's *having* to know the annuity cost. In fact, this specific point was heard in chambers and the judge ruled that the plaintiff did not need to know the cost. The trial judge subsequently approved the case on the same basis. The case demonstrates the possible different approaches.

(b) *Top down* Virtually all of the cases in which Frenkel Topping have been involved have settled on the basis of the legal advisers determining the conventional award and then negotiating a discount therefrom and, subsequently, structuring. The solicitors, barristers and insurance claims' managers have *always* done the contentious part, i e the calculation of the lump sum and the agreement to the discount.

18.134 The Law Society's Guidance Notes include the following:

(a) the plaintiff should have independent advice in relation to comparing a structure with a conventional lump sum;
(b) the plaintiff should have independent advice in relation to the cost of the annuity;
(c) the plaintiff should have independent advice in relation to the discount;
(d) the plaintiff should have independent advice in relation to the costs of the broker.

18.135 In relation to the above Notes:

(1) from the defendants' perspective, they are only concerned with the defined amount of cash net of discount (all calculated by the legal advisers). They tend not to be concerned with how the plaintiff would wish that cash to be applied. They want the appropriate tax neutrality of the structure (which, if drafted properly within the Model Agreement, is achievable while still giving the plaintiff the tax-free nature of the structure). They also want no further costs in relation to monitoring the structure;

(2) from the plaintiffs' perspective, they are only concerned with how the defined amount of cash, net of discount (all calculated by the legal advisers), can best be packaged to meet their future requirements. They want the tax-free income of the structure which is achievable under the Model Agreement without prejudicing the position of the defendants. They want advice as to how to compare the performance of the structure with that of the lump sum alternative;

(3) it is in regard to this final point that some plaintiffs have sought an element of independent advice. If plaintiffs want this, they should put the defendants on notice and try to agree costs for this in advance;

(4) many firms of plaintiffs' solicitors have been satisfied with joint instructions and here are some of the reasons why:
    (a) quicker;
    (b) saves costs;
    (c) plaintiff solicitors are concerned that if it proves more costly then defendants will seek higher discount; and
    (d) it provides one focal point for problems pre- and post-implementation;

(5) the Notes do not advise that defendants need independent advice. Thus, presumably, if the plaintiff approaches the intermediary and the defendant decides not to take separate advice it would appear that the Notes have been complied with in this respect;

(6) whichever way you consider approaching your structure, whether plaintiff or defendant, whether fees or commissions, whether one or two firms of intermediaries, *before* any work in relation to the structure is undertaken it is strongly advised that it be determined:
    (a) what has to be done pre- and post-settlement;
    (b) who will do what has to be done;
    (c) who will pay for what has to be done if it structures; and
    (d) who will pay for what has to be done if it does not structure.

    The Notes summarise the position with regard to costs in the following way:

> Costs incurred in exploring a Structured Settlement before confirming that the parties wish to consider resolving the claim in this manner might prove to be irrecoverable. In a Legal Aid case, consider obtaining authority from the Legal Aid Board before proceeding.

WHAT ARE THE BENEFITS TO THE HEALTH AUTHORITY FROM STRUCTURING?

18.136 Aside from the points already made, there are a number of points that the health authorities should bear in mind when considering a structure.

18.137 Apart from the obvious immediate costs savings there is a greatly reduced risk of the plaintiff coming back on to the Health Service for care.

18.138 If a régime is established and is guaranteed to continue for lifetime irrespective of changes in investment conditions, variations in the tax environment and movements in inflation, then it is far less likely that the plaintiff will need to seek further assistance from the public purse.

18.139 The opportunity for health authorities to spread the cost of their litigation over a number of years is also seen as being of great benefit as cash thereby stays in the system longer.

HOW CAN THE PLAINTIFF BE SATISFIED REGARDING THE SECURITY OF THE ARRANGEMENTS?

18.140 There have been two security issues from the point of view of the plaintiffs' advisers. These issues arise as a result of the layman's perception of the information that hospitals are regularly cutting back on services because of a lack of funding. The advisers therefore want to be sure to be able to recommend that their clients can happily enter into long-term contractual arrangements with these bodies. The Department of Health on the other hand point out, quite rightly, that no public body has ever reneged on a valid debt. But therein lies the power of perception.

18.141 *Annuity Structured Settlements*:

(1) in these cases the health authority parts with all the cash at the point of settlement in order to buy the annuity;
(2) such cases have generally not caused plaintiffs much concern as they know that all of the future cash obligations which the health authority has to the plaintiff will be fully matched by the cash it receives from the annuity and, accordingly, there is no concern regarding the financial security of the authority.

18.142 *Self-funded Structured Settlements*:

(1) in the early stages of medical negligence structure the security issue on self-funded cases was proving to be the 'deal buster'. Plaintiffs were not satisfied that, long term, their money would be safe;
(2) the perception point was recognised by the Department of Health and the first few cases were got through the courts by means of an official from the Department of Health giving evidence in camera regarding the mechanism by which plaintiffs could obtain security;
(3) latterly, and from a forward looking basis, the point has been resolved by confirmation via the Secretary of State for Health that there will, at some stage during the life of this Parliament, be legislation which will empower the Secretary of State to give guarantees of the contracts entered into by the health authorities. The presence of this intent has resolved the issue with regard to security.

CAN A HEALTH AUTHORITY STRUCTURE A CASE UNDER £300,000?

18.143 The significance of the £300,000 figure is that this is the level of claim up to which the Regional Health Authority is fully responsible. For claims in excess of that figure the Regional Health Authority can call on the 'pool of funds' held by the Department of Health. The reimbursement by the Department of Health is 80 per cent of the excess amount over £300,000 including costs. The Department of Health will be subsequently involved in the costing analysis to determine the value for money qualities of the Structured Settlement proposal.

18.144 The Department of Health have confirmed that, while the Regional Health Authority will not be able to call on the fund for cases under the threshold of £300,000, they will nevertheless have to cost out the cases in the same manner and the Department of Health will make their resources available to assist in the costing process.

18.145 A Regional Health Authority cannot enter into a Structured Settlement without obtaining the prior approval of the Department of Health.

18.146 It is perhaps worth mentioning that the same position applies to non-medical negligence litigation that the health authority might get involved in, e g employer's liability and third party claims.

WHAT IS THE PRESENT POSITION OF THE COURT OF PROTECTION?

18.147 The Court of Protection will be involved in those cases where the plaintiff is a patient and incapable of looking after his own affairs. As many of the larger cases concern catastrophic injuries in which the Court of Protection are involved they have already approved a substantial number of Structured Settlements. In all the cases that Frenkel Topping have put to them we have prepared schedules which compare the performance of the Structured Settlement programme with a conventional award, typically invested in a combination of gilts and equities but the income and capital growth thereon being subject to income tax and capital gains tax respectively.

18.148 The overriding benefit of the structure is the certainty that the funds can never run out and the Master of the Court of Protection has been willing to acknowledge this fact and, provided that a carefully thought out financial programme is submitted to the Master, then the structure should be approved.

18.149 As a demonstration of the fact that structures have very much become accepted by the Court of Protection, on 12 February 1992, a Practice Note [1992] 1 WLR 328 was issued. This document sets out a very useful sequence of events that needs to take place when a Structured Settlement involving the Court of Protection is to be implemented. It is particularly necessary to adhere to a known short timetable in view of the relatively short lives of annuity quotes, the exact details of which are required before all the documentation can be finalised.

18.150 One question that needed answering was the level of Court of Protection fees in cases which structured. In August 1992, the Court of Protection issued a press release to the effect that 50 per cent of the moneys which arise under the structure should be defined as 'clear annual income' for fee purposes. This should have the effect of reducing the costs of these fees in cases which structure. Defendants should particularly see this as a further saving as their obligation is to pay these costs on top of the damages figures which have been calculated. This saving should be in addition to any discount achieved.

WHAT IS THE POSITION WITH MUTUAL INSURERS?

18.151 Such insurance companies do not pay tax on any of the trading profits that they make because trading effectively takes place with their own members and it is not possible to make a profit on dealing with oneself. Thus, the insurance company would have to pay tax on the annuity it receives from the life office as it is treated as investment income. However, it would not get the corresponding write-off for the payments that it makes to the plaintiff as this could *not* be set against the investment income of the company. This means that the insurer would have to bear the cost of the taxation and therefore would need to appraise a structured settlement differently as compared to a normal trading (ie Schedule D, Case I) insurer.

18.152 It is interesting to note that a number of mutual insurers have recently demutualised as a result of which they can benefit in full from a structure. The point here is to make sure that the position has not changed before the case is settled. It can do no harm to ask again. An authoritative answer should be given as the cost of an incorrect answer could be quite significant.

18.153 Frenkel Topping have managed to find a way to structure a case in which a mutual insurer was involved but in that case there were special, although not such rare, circumstances.

CAN YOU STRUCTURE A CASE INVOLVING ONE OF THE MEDICAL DEFENCE ORGANISATIONS?

18.154 The MDOs are mutual organisations as defined above and are therefore subject to the same limitations in that, while they can technically structure, they will not be able to reclaim their tax and, therefore, one of the major benefits of structuring will have disappeared.

18.155 There is a further issue with regard to the security position in that the MDOs are not defined as insurance companies and are therefore not subject to the same financial strength criteria. Their future form and role are uncertain and so plaintiffs have not been willing to enter into long-term contractual arrangements with them.

Implications for plaintiffs and defendants

PLAINTIFFS

18.156 This new concept should be viewed as an alternative means of settling certain types of cases. It should not be automatically assumed to be the solution to all cases nor only as a means to settle a very narrow range of case types. It should be considered in the context of the particular case under consideration. It should be added to the armoury of all those involved in large personal injury/fatal accident cases.

18.157 Advisers will be encouraged to think about the concerns of their clients in the post-settlement position. It is often the case that the pressures and problems of the plaintiffs and their families are greater after, rather than before, settlement. The advisers must be aware of these difficulties and the option of being able to achieve a satisfactory settlement and solve some of the major concerns of clients all at the same time is to be commended.

18.158 Consideration of the structure must be brought into the negotiations early so that it can be fully explored. Families may be mentally preparing themselves for large sums of money but this may not be in the best interests of the plaintiff. If the option is introduced too late then expectations may not allow it to be fully investigated.

DEFENDANTS

18.159 Substantial interest has been shown by a large number of insurers, by the Department of Health and by health authorities generally. The education process must continue. Now that hundreds of structures have already been established, there will be a large number of other such cases which could be similarly settled.

18.160 The potential size of the annuity market arising out of structured settlements could provide a very significant source of new business for the life insurance industry.

18.161 There may yet need to be further pressure to be brought to bear on current legislation as it is desirable that the mechanics for the payment of the structure be simplified, so that payments could be made directly by the life office as agents to the plaintiff, without having to deduct tax. This would ease administration and would mirror the way the concept was developed in North America. However, only after the concept has been running for some time and far greater experience developed on the problems yet to be encountered can any amendments to legislation be effectively approached. To do so too early might merely result in a compounding of the difficulties in achieving widespread implementation of the concept.

18.162 Financial benefits must be appreciated at a high level within the industry. This should be communicated, preferably from head office level, to the claims managers whose responsibility it is to settle these cases. This is because only head offices can ensure that the tax, cash-flow and administrative consequences are all understood and costed and are calculated as being of overall benefit to the insurer.

18.163 The same considerations apply to medical negligence litigation in that the overall benefits must be viewed from the Department of Health level and political level as well. When the appropriate streamlining of this litigation comes in, as it surely will soon, then the full benefits of the structure will be able to be felt by all those parties involved in the process.

Law Commission Consultation Paper

18.164 This HMSO publication takes the reader through all of the issues in relation to structures and debates the way forward. In particular, the Paper discusses and wants answers to the following major issues:

(1) should there be a right of judicial imposition on either or both sides?
(2) how can arrangements be made to further strengthen the security of both contracts – for the plaintiff (with the defendant) and for the defendant (with the life office)?
(3) how can the whole process be streamlined to avoid the administrative requirements that the present system places on insurers?
(4) the role of the intermediary and the basis of remuneration and instruction is debated with replies invited;
(5) should the tax régime be amended so that structures no longer rely on the Inland Revenue's interpretation of the 1936 case of *Dott v Brown* but instead that structures should derive their tax-free status from statute as now happens in North America?

Conclusions

18.165 Structures provide a means for paying a debt due in a personal injury/fatal accident case by means of a series of future tax free annual payments which are linked to the life of the plaintiff.

18.166 Such annual payments must be tailored according to the needs of each individual plaintiff and substantial consideration is to be given in advance as to the ongoing needs of the plaintiff in relation to his/her personal circumstances.

18.167 The experience of North America has indicated this to be a very popular form of settlement with both plaintiffs and defendants. They should be perceived as another piece of armoury capable of settling a wide range of cases.

18.168 In the nature of our inherently adversarial legal system, there is an opportunity to set up a 'win-win' position. Health authorities can demonstrate their concern for their customers by offering damages which are far more suited to the losses suffered by the plaintiffs. By judicious use of the whole process, difficult cases on liability and causation could be bought out by the offering of an appropriate instalment financial programme.

18.169 Careful steps must be taken to ensure that all the requirements of the Inland Revenue, as regards paperwork, are agreed in advance before a structure is established.

18.170 For a structure to be implemented there will have to be substantial co-operation between all parties involved in the litigation process.

18.171 There is widespread belief that a Structured Settlement is merely the placing of an annuity. This is not the case. Knowledge of the plaintiff's specific situation is vital, as is the expertise to translate this knowledge into the specific financial programme.

18.172 It cannot be stressed enough that, given the novelty of the concept, appropriate advice must be taken before attempting to implement a structure as there are many potential problems to be overcome. Each specific potential case must be considered and progressed on its own merits.

CROSS-REFERENCES

For information related to topics in this chapter see Chapters 8, 10, 11 and 16.

APPENDIX

18.173

No 1: conventional award

Investing to provide income for life (based on figures in **Kelly***)*

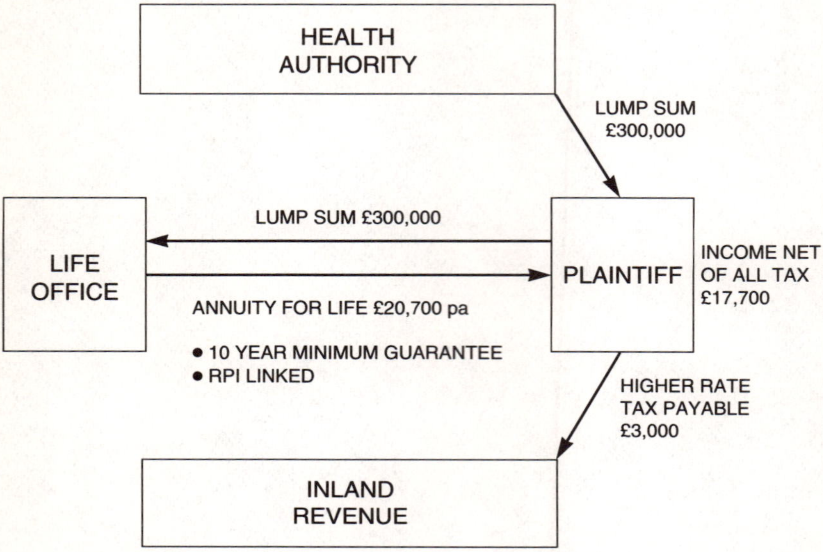

No 2: Structured Settlements

Double contractual position (based on figures in **Kelly***)*

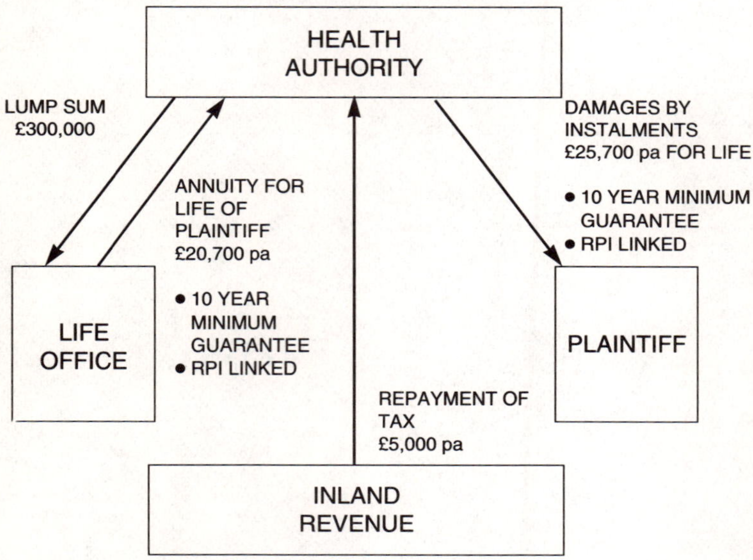

No 3: double contractual position

Contract 1

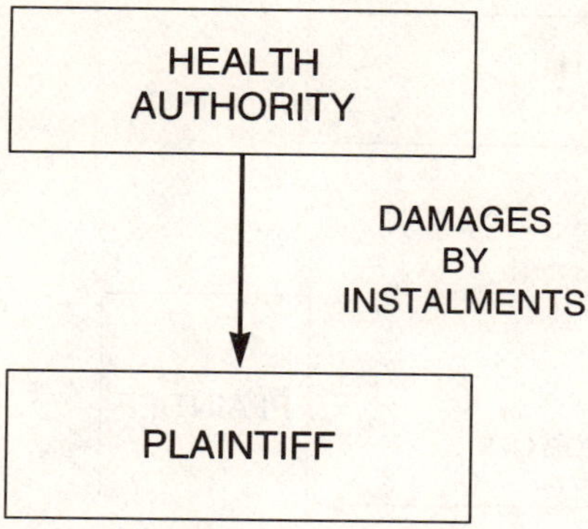

- INSTALMENT DAMAGES FUNDED BY ANNUITY PURCHASED BY HEALTH AUTHORITY (CONTRACT 2)
- RECEIPT BY PLAINTIFF TREATED AS CAPITAL
- PLAINTIFF NO NEED TO INCLUDE ON INCOME TAX RETURN

No 4: double contractual position

Contract 2

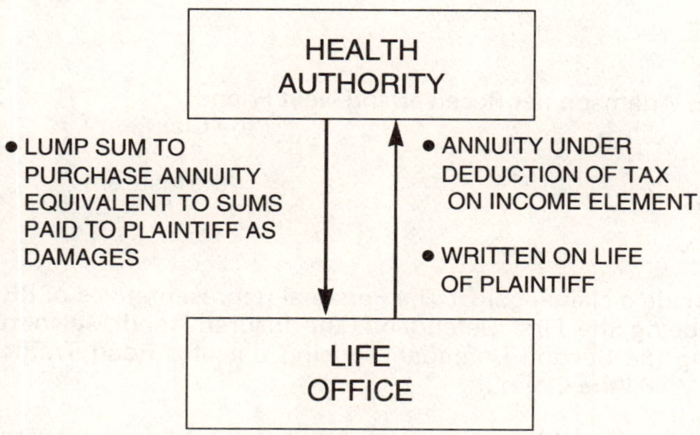

HEALTH AUTHORITY ALSO DOES THE FOLLOWING

- RECLAIMS WITHHOLDING TAX MONTHLY OR QUARTERLY
- HAS TO ADMINISTER DURING LIFE OF PLAINTIFF

No 5: Structured Settlements

Ideal position based on North American model (based on figures in **Kelly***)*

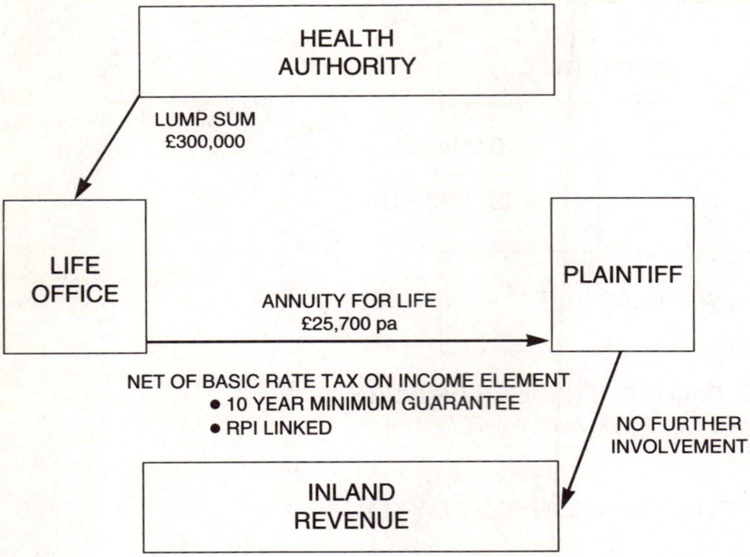

No 6: Catherine Kelly model agreement

Catherine Kelly – Agreement

PARTIES:

(1) CATHERINE KELLY
(A patient by James Adamson her Receiver and Next Friend)
('the Claimant')

(2) ('the Insurer')

WHEREAS

1 The Claimant has made a claim against The Personal Representatives of BB Dawes Deceased, being the First Defendant ('the Insured') and Malcolm George Gault, being the Second Defendant, arising out of a Road Traffic Accident on 5 July 1986 ('the Claim').

2 The Claimant is a patient, and brings the claim by her Next Friend, James Adamson.

3 James Adamson has been appointed by the Court of Protection as the Receiver of the Claimant.

4 It has been agreed, subject to the approval of the High Court of Justice, that the claim shall be settled for £410,000 (Four hundred and ten thousand pounds).

5 The High Court of Justice has approved the Agreement recited at (4) above.

6 The Court of Protection has authorised the Receiver to sign this Agreement for and on behalf of the Claimant.

AGREED

1 The Insurer shall be substituted for the Insured to the extent that any liability of the Insured to the Claimant in respect of the Claim shall attach to and be the sole responsibility of the Insurer and that the Insured shall be discharged from any such liability.

2 By way of settlement of the Claim, the Insurer shall pay or procure to be paid to or for the benefit of the Claimant, the sum of £410,000 (four hundred and ten thousand pounds), and the Claimant shall accept such sum in full and final settlement of the claim, which is discharged.

3 Subject to the compliance by the Next Friend with Clause 4 to the satisfaction of the Insurer, the debt of £410,000 (four hundred and ten thousand pounds) arising under Clause 2 shall be discharged by payments by the Insurer to or for the benefit of the Claimant as follows:

(a) The sum of £60,000 (sixty thousand pounds) which has already been paid directly to the Receiver on behalf of the Claimant, receipt whereof is hereby acknowledged by the Receiver.
(b) the further sum of £50,000 (fifty thousand pounds) . . . . .
(c) . . . . . the further sums as specified in the attached schedule.

4.1 The Next Friend, acting on behalf of the Claimant, shall forthwith take all necessary steps to discontinue any proceedings which have been begun or threatened against the Insurer or the Insured or the Second Defendant in connection with the claim.

4.2 Neither the Claimant nor the next Friend shall institute any proceedings against the Insurer or the Insured or the Second Defendant in connection with the claim.

Dated:

Signed (1) (the Claimant, acting by the Receiver)

(2) (for the Insurer)

Indexed terms for life

The Schedule

Amount	*Date for Payment*
£2,146.99 (Two thousand, one hundred and forty six pounds and ninety nine pence)	At the end of each calendar month the first payment to be made on or before the day of August 1989

Amounts payable under this Schedule shall be made as follows:

(a) After one year's payments have been made and at the end of every 12(twelve) months thereafter up to and including the end of the twelve month period ceasing in the year 2023, the amount will be increased (or decreased) in proportion to the Increase (or Decrease) in the General Index of Retail Prices (all items) for the year ending 3(three) months prior to the date of the alteration. From the anniversary of the policy in the year 2024, and in subsequent years, payments will continue to Increase (or Decrease) similarly, provided that at the time in the opinion of the Insurer suitable British Government Index Linked Stocks still exist to support the continuation of such Increases (or Decreases). Should the Insurer deem on any subsequent anniversary that suitable Stocks no longer exist the increase due then and in each subsequent year would be 7 per cent of the amount payable immediately prior to the date of increase.

(b) A minimum of 120 (one hundred and twenty) payments shall be made under this Schedule, regardless of the date of death of the Claimant, but subject to this no amounts shall be payable after the date of death of the Claimant.

No 7: standard model agreement

DRAFT

Structured Settlement

Model Agreement

PARTIES: (1)

('the Claimant')

(2)

('the Insurer')

WHEREAS:

(1) The Claimant has made a claim against .... ('the Insured') arising out of the .... ('the Claim').

(2) It is agreed that the Claim shall be settled for £...........

AGREED:

1 The Insurer shall be substituted for the Insured to the intent that any liability of the Insured to the Claimant in respect of the claim shall attach to and be the sole responsibility of the Insurer and that the Insured shall be discharged from any such liability.

2 By way of settlement of the Claim the Insurer shall pay or procure to be paid to the Claimant the sum of £ .... and the Claimant shall accept such sum in full and final settlement of the Claim, which is discharged.

3 Subject to the Claimant complying with Clause 4 to the satisfaction of the Insurer, the debt of £........... arising under Clause 2 shall be discharged by payments by the Insurer to the Claimant in accordance with the Schedule.

4.1 The Claimant shall forthwith take all necessary steps to discontinue any proceedings which have been begun or threatened against the Insurer or the Insured in connection with the Claim.

4.2 The Claimant shall not institute any proceedings against the Insurer or the Insured in connection with the Claim.

DATED: ______________________________

SIGNED: (1) ____ (the Claimant)
(2) ____ (for the Insurer)

No 8: RF Structured Settlement programme

RF Net Damages for Plaintiff Based on Structured Settlement
Indexation Annuities 1 & 2 5.00%   Indexation Lump Sum 7.00%

Years from Settlement	*Age of Plaintiff*	*Annuity 1 Annual Sum* £	*Annuity 2 Annual Sum* £	*Annuity 3 Annual Sum* £	*Total Annual Sum* £	*Monthly Equivalent* £	*Lump Sums* £	*Total Cash* £
1	6	59,000			59,000	4,917		59,000
2	7	61,950			61,950	5,163		61,950
3	8	65,048			65,048	5,421		65,048
4	9	68,300			68,300	5,692		68,300
5	10	71,715			71,715	5,976		71,715
6	11	75,301	15,315		90,616	7,551	70,127	160,743
7	12	79,066	16,081		95,147	7,929		95,147
8	13	83,019	16,885		99,904	8,325		99,904
9	14	87,170	17,729		104,899	8,742		104,899
10	15	91,529	18,615		110,144	9,179		110,144
11	16	96,105	19,546	32,578	148,229	12,352	98,357	246,586
12	17	100,910	20,523	34,207	155,640	12,970		155,640
13	18	105,956	21,549	35,917	163,422	13,619		163,422
14	19	111,254	22,626	37,713	171,593	14,299		171,593
15	20	116,817	23,757	39,599	180,173	15,014		180,173
16	21	122,658	24,945	41,579	189,182	15,765	137,951	327,133
17	22	128,791	26,192	43,658	198,641	16,553		198,641
18	23	135,231	27,502	45,841	208,574	17,381		208,574
19	24	141,993	28,877	48,133	219,003	18,250		219,003
20	25	149,093	30,321	50,540	229,954	19,163		229,954
21	26	156,548	31,837	53,067	241,452	20,121	193,483	434,935
22	27	164,375	33,429	55,720	253,524	21,127		253,524
23	28	172,594	35,100	58,506	266,200	22,183		266,200
24	29	181,224	36,855	61,431	279,510	23,293		279,510
25	30	190,285	38,698	64,503	293,486	24,457		293,486
26	31	199,799	40,633	67,728	308,160	25,680	271,370	579,530
27	32	209,789	42,665	71,114	323,568	26,964		323,568
28	33	220,278	44,798	74,670	339,746	28,312		339,746
29	34	231,292	47,038	78,404	356,734	29,728		356,734
30	35	242,857	49,390	82,324	374,571	31,214		374,571

31	36	255,000	51,860	86,440	393,300	32,775	380,610	773,910
32	37	267,750	54,453	90,762	412,965	34,414		412,965
33	38	281,138	57,176	95,300	433,614	36,135		433,614
34	39	295,195	60,035	100,065	455,295	37,941		455,295
35	40	309,955	63,037	105,068	478,060	39,838		478,060
36	41	325,453	66,189	110,321	501,963	41,830	533,825	1,035,788
37	42	341,726	69,498	115,837	527,061	43,922		527,061
38	43	358,812	72,973	121,629	553,414	46,118		553,414
39	44	376,753	76,622	127,710	581,085	48,424		581,085
40	45	395,591	80,453	134,096	610,140	50,845		610,140
41	46	415,371	84,476	140,801	640,648	53,387	748,717	1,389,365
42	47	436,140	88,700	147,841	672,681	56,057		572,681
43	48	457,947	93,135	155,233	706,315	58,860		706,315
44	49	480,844	97,792	162,995	741,631	61,803		741,631
45	50	504,886	102,682	171,145	778,713	64,893		778,713
46	51	530,130	107,816	179,702	817,648	68,137	1,050,114	1,867,762
47	52	556,637	113,207	188,687	858,531	71,544		858,531
48	53	584,469	118,867	198,121	901,457	75,121		901,457
49	54	613,692	124,810	208,027	946,529	78,877		946,529
50	55	644,377	131,051	218,428	993,856	82,821		993,856
51	56	676,596	137,604	229,349	1,043,549	86,962	1,472,839	2,516,388
52	57	710,426	144,484	240,816	1,095,726	91,311		1,095,726
53	58	745,947	151,708	252,857	1,150,512	95,876		1,150,512
54	59	783,244	159,293	265,500	1,208,037	100,670		1,208,037
55	60	822,406	167,258	278,775	1,268,439	105,703		1,268,439
56	61	863,526	175,621	292,714	1,331,861	110,988	2,065,733	3,397,594
57	62	906,702	184,402	307,350	1,398,454	116,538		1,398,454
58	63	952,037	193,622	322,718	1,468,377	122,365		1,468,377
59	64	999,639	203,303	338,854	1,541,796	128,483		1,541,796
60	65	1,049,621	213,468	355,797	1,618,886	134,907		1,618,886

NOTES ON PAYMENT

1 Payments to plaintiff increase every year and will need changing accordingly

2 Receipts will change every year and may change after each Budget if the Basic Rate of Income Tax changes

3 Amount of Lump Sum to be paid cannot be determined as the programme is Index-Linked

4 Payments after the Guarantee period only to be made if Rebecca is still alive

No 9: conventional investment of the lump sum

RF Net Damages for Plaintiff Based on Traditional Lump Sum-Equities/Gilts Indexation 5%

A	*B*	*C*	*D*	*E*	*F*	*G*	*H*	*I*
Years from Settlement	*Age of Plaintiff*	*Lump Sum* £	*Gilts Annual Interest @ 10.00%* £	*Equities Annual Interest @ 5.00%* £	*Total Interest* £	*Income Tax 25%* £	*Income Tax 40%* £	*Total Income Tax* £
1	6	1,350,000	40,500	47,250	87,750	5,499	26,302	31,801
2	7	1,402,582	42,077	49,090	91,167	5,499	27,669	33,168
3	8	1,456,431	43,693	50,975	94,668	5,499	29,069	34,568
4	9	1,511,502	45,345	52,903	98,248	5,499	30,501	36,000
5	10	1,567,740	47,032	54,871	101,903	5,499	31,963	37,462
6	11	1,625,072	48,752	56,878	105,630	5,499	33,454	38,953
7	12	1,597,975	47,939	55,929	103,868	5,499	32,749	38,248
8	13	1,634,301	49,029	57,201	106,230	5,499	33,694	39,193
9	14	1,668,784	50,064	58,407	108,471	5,499	34,590	40,089
10	15	1,701,038	51,031	59,536	110,567	5,499	35,429	40,928
11	16	1,730,633	51,919	60,572	112,491	5,499	36,198	41,697
12	17	1,626,160	48,785	56,916	105,701	5,499	33,482	38,981
13	18	1,604,254	48,128	56,149	104,277	5,499	32,913	38,412
14	19	1,572,808	47,184	55,048	102,232	5,499	32,095	37,594
15	20	1,530,669	45,920	53,573	99,493	5,499	30,999	36,498
16	21	1,476,570	44,297	51,680	95,977	5,499	29,593	35,092
17	22	1,271,172	38,135	44,491	82,626	5,499	24,252	29,751
18	23	1,177,790	35,334	41,223	76,557	5,499	21,825	27,324
19	24	1,066,986	32,010	37,345	69,355	5,499	18,944	24,443
20	25	936,866	28,106	32,790	60,896	5,499	15,560	21,059
21	26	785,356	23,561	27,487	51,048	5,499	11,621	17,120
22	27	416,714	12,501	14,585	27,086	5,499	2,036	7,535
23	28	199,914	5,997	6,997	12,994	3,249	0	3,249

NOTES
1 30% of fund invested in gilts
2 70% of fund invested in equities
3 Other taxable income estimated at £5,000
4 Dealing costs taken as 0.25% of capital sum
5 Capital growth of 7% assumed on the equity proportion of the fund
6 Capital gains tax assumed to be payable at the rate of 10% of each year's growth
7 Lump sum exhausted after 23 years

J	*K*	*L*	*M*	*N*	*O*	*P*	*Q*	*R*
Interest Net of Tax £	*Professional Costs 1.00%* £	*Dealing Costs 0.25%* £	*Net Income for Plaintiff* £	*Annual Sum (Appendix 8)* £	*Added to/ (Withdrawn from) Fund of Damages* £	*Capital Growth 7%* £	*Capital Gains Tax on Capital Growth* £	*Balance of Fund of Damages* £
55,949	1,539	2,363	52,047	59,000	(6,953)	66,150	(6,615)	1,402,582
57,999	1,599	2,455	53,945	61,950	(8,005)	68,727	(6,873)	1,456,431
60,100	1,660	2,549	55,891	65,048	(9,157)	71,365	(7,137)	1,511,502
62,248	1,723	2,645	57,880	68,300	(10,420)	74,064	(7,406)	1,567,740
64,441	1,787	2,744	59,910	71,715	(11,805)	76,819	(7,682)	1,625,072
66,677	1,853	2,844	61,980	160,743	(98,763)	79,629	(7,963)	1,597,975
65,620	1,822	2,796	61,002	95,147	(34,145)	78,301	(7,830)	1,634,301
67,037	1,863	2,860	62,314	99,904	(37,590)	80,081	(8,008)	1,668,784
68,382	1,902	2,920	63,560	104,899	(41,339)	81,770	(8,177)	1,701,038
69,639	1,939	2,977	64,723	110,144	(45,421)	83,351	(8,335)	1,730,633
70,794	1,973	3,029	65,792	246,586	(180,794)	84,801	(8,480)	1,626,160
66,720	1,854	2,846	62,020	155,640	(93,620)	79,682	(7,968)	1,604,254
65,865	1,829	2,807	61,229	163,422	(102,193)	78,608	(7,861)	1,572,808
64,638	1,793	2,752	60,093	171,593	(111,500)	77,068	(7,707)	1,530,669
62,995	1,745	2,679	58,571	180,173	(121,602)	75,003	(7,500)	1,476,570
60,885	1,683	2,584	56,618	327,133	(270,515)	72,352	(7,235)	1,271,172
52,875	1,449	2,225	49,201	198,641	(149,440)	62,287	(6,229)	1,177,790
49,233	1,343	2,061	45,829	208,574	(162,745)	57,712	(5,771)	1,066,986
44,912	1,216	1,867	41,829	219,003	(177,174)	52,282	(5,228)	936,866
39,837	1,068	1,640	37,129	229,954	(192,825)	45,906	(4,591)	785,356
33,928	895	1,374	31,659	434,935	(403,276)	38,482	(3,848)	416,714
19,551	475	729	18,347	253,524	(235,177)	20,419	(2,042)	199,914
9,745	228	350	9,167	266,200	(257,033)	9,796	(980)	(48,303)

CHAPTER 19

Trial

Sir David Latham
James Badenoch QC

SUMMARY

Introduction

19.1 At the end of a long and difficult medical negligence action the trial judge observed (unfairly in the eyes of one observer), that although he had had the advantage of a clear and detailed exposition from counsel of the aetiology of the plaintiff's disease (which had been hotly contested over many weeks in court), it had not come until counsel's *closing* speech!

19.2 Given the learning process which occurs when we actually hear the respective experts in the witness box, we can all sympathise with the advocate who attains the Nirvana of complete understanding only at the very end of the case. None the less the goal is to get there beforehand, and to be able and equipped, however complex or abstruse the issues, to interest and enlighten the judge from the outset, to cross-examine economically and effectively, and to assist the expert witnesses to get their message across without the obstacle of the lawyers' (or the judge's) incomprehension.

19.3 It is to help in the achievement of these goals that this chapter is designed. Conscious of how difficult it is to take a fresh look at problems which might seem trite to many practitioners, we will consider the trial under four main headings:

(1) the documents;
(2) the order of events;
(3) the evidence; and
(4) judgment.

We shall highlight some of the pitfalls which exist, which can be spectacularly awkward in this field. If we appear to state the obvious in any respect we are glad, because what is to us self-evidently common sense does not appear, in our experience, always to find universal acceptance.

THE DOCUMENTS

19.4 Crucial to the process of enabling difficult (and to the judge possibly completely unfamiliar) issues properly and fairly to be tried, is the availability of all the necessary documentation in a *clear, uncluttered, logical* and *easily handled* format. Remember that though this may be true also of other kinds of trial, it is necessarily true of the medical negligence action, throughout which there is likely to have to be:

(a) continuous and detailed attention to the contemporaneous notes and records;
(b) repeated reference to a variety of written expert reports;
(c) the assimilation of, and frequent recourse to, a body of scientific literature, articles, and extracts from textbooks;
(d) ease and speed of access to an assemblage of diagrams, tables, illustrations, and sometimes photographs too;
(e) rapid switching of attention from one kind of document to another, and the simultaneous study or comparison of two or more different documentary sources.

19.5 With this in mind we suggest that a fresh eye be turned on the preparation of the bundles, to make them really useful, readily accessible, and an aid to clarity of exposition and thought. The bundles can and should be crucial equipment, with a vivid impact, rather than simply unwieldy repositories for every document the lawyers can put their hands on (with a dangerous propensity to enrage the judge who has to grapple with them). Their format and the arrangement of their contents ought to be seen as being as much a part of the presentation of the case in court as, for example, the opening speech. It is for this reason that in a chapter on 'the trial' we offer the following as guiding principles in the preparation of the bundles:

(1) each bundle should be marked very clearly with a legend and with a number (on the spine, if any, as well as on the face), have a clear key or index, and be paginated;
(2) each bundle should be instantly distinguishable from the others, preferably by colour (too much time is spent helping the judge to re-find a bundle, when to point him to, say, 'the red one' would have been the work of an instant);

(3) the pleadings should always form a totally separate and independent bundle;
(4) no bundle should ever be allowed to be so voluminous as to be awkward to move about, or to turn the pages over, or to find a place in (lever arch files often have a vengeful will of their own);
(5) the expert reports should be in a single bundle, with dividers to separate them according to author, and each designated clearly at the top as plaintiff's or defendant's witness;
(6) unless the whole of the notes fit into one manageable bundle, they should be divided up so far as possible into separate bundles according to species, so that you have, for example, the clinical notes in one place, the nursing notes in another, and the pathology laboratory reports in yet another;
(7) any further logical division of notes into separate bundles or sections should be made wherever it is an aid to manageability and clarity;
(8) all illustrations (which experts should be encouraged to produce) should be put together in their own bundle (unless they fit more naturally as annexes to the expert's reports);
(9) even if it makes a very slim volume the schedules relating to damages should be bundled together, but separately from the supporting documentation for special damage and further loss claims, so that there is no need to bother with the bulky material on quantum except when specifically required;
(10) the handwritten notes and records should be typed up, wherever they have more than peripheral importance, and the typed version interleaved with the handwriting so as to oppose the transcript on the left hand side (facing the handwriting it translates);
(11) if it is really necessary to have a correspondence bundle (which should only be in rare cases), all communications of the routine and mundane kind which proliferate between solicitors should be ruthlessly excluded from it;
(12) the experts should be pressed to provide all published material relied upon early enough to enable a definitive and complete bundle to be prepared well in advance of the hearing. We know that directions in this regard are probably honoured more in the breach, but it is particularly wasteful of time for lawyers and experts to have to try to absorb and deal with late additions to the literature for the first time at trial.

19.6 If bundles are prepared in accordance with these principles, the getting up of the case for trial, the identification of the live issues, the presentation of the case to the judge, and the progress of the evidence and argument are all greatly facilitated. Cases difficult enough in themselves are made longer and more complicated when the participants must battle as much with the paperwork as with the opposition. The price paid in needless loss of time, patience and concentration can be a heavy one. Judges are becoming more ready than before to question the entitlement of lawyers to costs which appear to have been wasted as a result of an undisciplined and unco-operative approach to the preparation of bundles. Lawyers may indeed find that they face orders to pay costs considered to have been wasted in this way. This is one area in our process in which co-operation between the parties – and not confrontation – is essential.

THE ORDER OF EVENTS

The rules

19.7 Order 35 of the Rules of the Supreme Court governs procedure at trial in the High Court. The general principles are set out in Order 35, rule 7. The plaintiff begins, opening his case and calls his evidence. Each defendant (in the order of title to the action) can open his case and call evidence; and at the conclusion of all the evidence, speeches follow first from the defendants (again in the order of title to the action) and finally from the plaintiff. If a defendant calls no evidence, he has no right to open his case; but he gains the advantage of the last word. There is no equivalent rule in the County Court Rules: Order 35 therefore applies to the county court by virtue of section 76 of the County Courts Act 1984.

19.8 It is one thing, of course, to know what the sequence of events should be, and another to bring about in court under the adversarial system the orderly succession and logical progression of each component of the trial. We therefore focus below on the elements which seem most frequently to give rise to problems for practitioners.

The opening speech

19.9 It is vital that the plaintiff's counsel should be able and prepared to explain in the opening, in immediately assimilable terms, what the case is about, and what the medical issues which divide the parties are. To do so in an abstruse and disputed area of medical science (as is not infrequently the position), can be very difficult. To get it right there is no substitute for a full and detailed conference with the experts shortly before trial, in addition to those that will have been essential during the preparation of pleadings and the final expert reports.

19.10 Having thoroughly understood the medical evidence counsel ought to be able in the opening to reduce the issues to be tried, both on liability and causation, to clear and relatively simple terms. He should provide the judge with a typed outline of his opening and a typed chronology. The latter should, if possible, be agreed with the defence. Although neither is yet required by Rules of Court, they are increasingly required by practice directions, for example in the Court of Appeal, and applications and appeals to the judges in chambers; and judges have begun to expect them as a matter of course in trials.

A suggested structure for the opening

19.11

(1) Describe the condition of the plaintiff today, in respect of which he/she claims damages.
(2) Explain who is said to have been to blame for the suffering complained about, and what their status and duties were at the material time, briefly setting out the basis for vicarious liability, if any.
(3) Set out how, when and why the plaintiff came to be in the care of the

allegedly negligent staff – with an account of the disease/condition if any from which he was suffering, and for which he required their attentions.

(4) Propound, with clear reasoning, what the plaintiff had a right to expect by way of outcome, if correctly treated (eg restoration to ordinary physical fitness and capability, and to his pre-treatment employment).

(5) Now advert to the pleadings. These may be, as in the modern way, very full and detailed. It is to be hoped that the judge will indicate that he has read and digested them. Subject to the extent to which the pleadings cover the ground comprehensively, go on as follows.

(6) Explain step by step the care/treatment which the plaintiff needed, and why, and which it is alleged should properly have been given to him if the duty of care had been discharged, and

(7) Detail the care/treatment in fact given to the plaintiff, which is said to have been negligent, doing this where possible by way of juxtaposition so that the alleged shortcomings are individually and tellingly highlighted, in chronological sequence.

(8) Now advert to the expert reports, and discover whether the judge has (a) read them, and (b) understood them.

Either deficiency, if identified, must now be remedied. If the reports are as yet un-read it is usually desirable for the judge to be invited, if he does not volunteer, to retire and read them all through before the opening proceeds further.

(9) Subject to the judge's indication, and/or counsel's perception of the need, now present a concise summary of the arguments between the opposing experts as they emerge from the reports, and give an explanation of the crux of the dispute or disputes which require to be judicially resolved. This is obviously the opportunity which must be taken by the plaintiff's counsel to highlight and fix in the judge's mind the merits and persuasive force of the plaintiff's case, as they are perceived to be, and to attack, undermine and diminish the defence case so far as possible. Remember that with the burden of proof on the plaintiff the opportunity provided by the right to open the case should be exploited as efficiently and effectively as possible.

(10) Beware at all times during the opening of hyperbole or exaggeration, and of emotive or excessively colourful language. The media, especially the tabloid press, have the habit of latching on to counsel's more vivid excursions and turning them into headlines ('Mother left lying in a pool of blood', or 'Patient fled in terror from the dentist's chair'). Unless what you describe is strictly accurate, and also a necessary part of the case, any excesses may return to haunt you. Even if they do not, they may cause considerable unnecessary pain to the professionals thus publicly pilloried, and/or give the impression (rightly or wrongly) to the judge that counsel is improperly playing to the gallery. This could prove extremely damaging to the plaintiff's case.

(11) Obviously, where quantum is in issue it is necessary to deal as clearly and shortly as is reasonably possible with the matters which remain to be tried. It will have been everyone's proper concern to reduce to the irreducible minimum the areas of dispute, and wherever possible to confine the triable issue to the matters of principle rather than mathematical disputation.

Getting the witness order right

19.12 Here, too, it is forward planning which is the key, as well as common sense and proper co-operation between the parties. Keep two particular aims in mind:

(1) call the factual evidence before the expert evidence; and
(2) have your own expert in attendance when the opposing witness in his field is giving evidence.

These may seem simple and obvious aims, but they are often difficult to accomplish, and the logistics need careful thought, and arrangements made well in advance. If either aim is not achieved much time and effort may be wasted, and unnecessary problems are likely to be created for the parties, their advisers, and for the judge too.

As to the factual evidence

19.13

(a) The importance of getting this out first, and preferably in the presence and hearing of all the experts is obvious. The experts must be able to give views which are based on, and proceed from, the facts as the judge has heard them. An expert without this advantage must rely on assumed facts which may differ from the reality in respects which materially affect the opinion he gives. If his assumptions have later to be discarded the cogency and relevance of his evidence may be diminished or nullified.
(b) Ideally the facts for this purpose ought to be seen as including not only the recollections of the plaintiff and any lay witnesses (together with the background history, personal and medical), but also the accounts given by the qualified personnel involved of the events alleged to have constituted negligence.
(c) Where there is an obvious dispute on facts which are likely to affect the experts' opinions, and/or where the experts' opinions may help to resolve important issues of fact, the two sides ought to give consideration to compartmentalising the trial (with the approval of the judge), in such a way that *all* the factual evidence, *on both sides* is called first, and the expert evidence for both sides follows. This is discussed in more detail under the heading 'The new approach', below.
(d) If you must interpose an expert early, to suit his commitments, make sure that he covers the different permutations of fact which seem most likely to emerge. If you do not you may find, by the time you appreciate the need to recall him, that he has gone off on that lecture tour of Australia!

As to expert cover

19.14

(a) It is certainly desirable, and ought in most cases to be regarded as essential, to have the relevant expert at hand in court when the opposing expert in his field is giving evidence; but there are situations when this is difficult to achieve. Especially in a long trial you cannot forecast with confidence the day when expert A will be in the box, and the requirement that for an indeterminate period expert B remain at court, or on call and ready to appear at short notice, may be intolerable or impracticable.

(b) If he cannot be in court at the critical time a conference should be convened with the missing expert over the adjournment, at a time or times which enable instructions and advice to be taken, and informed cross-examination prepared. If that proves impossible, the expert must be asked to make himself available at appointed times and places for telephone consultation. The medical profession is generally receptive to such requests, and less hide-bound about the need for formality of meeting or venue than the lawyers have traditionally been.

(c) Both sides are generally aware of the constraints of cost and practicability in having the experts present all the time, and equally keen to ensure that their own experts hear their opposite numbers. The utmost mutual co-operation should therefore be given, to make it happen. If this co-operation is for any reason lacking the judge's assistance should be enlisted. His task is not made any easier if he finds that the view of one expert on some crucial point has not been appropriately challenged or tested in cross-examination directed by his opposite number.

(d) It will be seen that forward planning is indeed the key to the effective deployment of the experts. In particular we commend to solicitors, when they first enlist the expert's help, that a complete picture be given of the likely pattern of events if the case goes all the way to trial, and the degree of help and commitment of time that may be required.

The new approach

19.15 We are in the throes of a procedural revolution. The current Rules of the Supreme Court make provision in many specialist actions for departure from the traditional approach to adversarial trial. The Civil Justice Review clearly envisages that these changes should eventually apply across the whole spectrum of litigation.

19.16 These changes include the exchange of witness statements (not merely expert reports) before trial, the submission of argument and material in writing to cut down time spent in court, and a flexible approach to the procedures during the course of a trial. These may well make it more difficult for a defendant to decline to call evidence: the expectation is for more open justice.

19.17 In medical negligence cases, the greatest procedural handicap to a just result is rigid adherence to the traditional requirement that each side deploys the whole of his case, factual and expert, sequentially. It has the intrinsic vice that the plaintiff's experts do not have the opportunity to comment on the full factual picture presented by the witnesses from both plaintiff and defendant, whereas the defendant's do.

19.18 The tradition is in one sense unwritten: the Rules of the Supreme Court make no overt requirement as to the order in which evidence is called. It is inherent in the general principle of the burden of proof; and it is implicit in the order of speeches set out in Order 35, rule 7. The changes will undermine this tradition.

19.19 In a recent commercial case, *Bayer v Clarkson Puckle Overseas Ltd*,[1] Saville J held that a judge was master of procedure in his own court and could require factual evidence to be called for both sides before expert evidence for either side. This was a comment on the changes in practice in commercial cases; it was based on an assertion of principle as to inherent jurisdiction of the court. Whether judges will be so bold as to follow in other types of case remains to be seen. So far, there has merely been wholehearted approval by judges of agreements between the parties which procure this result, e g by French J in *Hunt v East Dorset Health Authority*.[2]

1 [1989] NLJR 256.
2 (17 May 1989, unreported).

19.20 But the trend is clear. The courts are likely to encourage and maybe even insist on the factual evidence being heard before the expert evidence. Although this may deprive defendants of a marginal advantage, in that in some cases the element of control available to them over the evidence they choose to call at the end of the plaintiff's case is reduced, overall the quality of the comment made by their experts on the evidence of the plaintiff's experts will be more valid and the debate between the experts more satisfactory.

19.21 This division of the trial into separate compartments enables evidence as to quantum to be dealt with in a similar way. This has the advantage of separating out into a discrete part of the case all evidence relating to quantum so that it does not interfere with the evidence on liability, enables sensible timetabling of witnesses, and has the advantage that everyone concerned can concentrate properly on what is often a difficult part of the case. The temptation to adjourn quantum to a later date should be resisted. Not only will there be considerable delay, but there is, inevitably, considerable extra cost. However it may be a sensible step where there is a real prospect of agreement, or the issues are so complex that they will make a trial of liability and quantum unwieldy.

Closing submissions

19.22 By this stage of the trial, the issues should have crystallised, as should the advocates' ideas on how to deal with them. If at all possible, the judge should be provided with a written skeleton of the main submissions. There is no doubt that the advocate who has produced such a skeleton (provided always that it is clear, concise, and logical) will have an advantage over the advocate who has not. First, the discipline of producing it will have helped to structure the submission. Second, the judge has ready to hand the framework of his judgment.

19.23 In relation to quantum, it is sensible to ensure that the original schedule provided before trial is updated to take account of the evidence and any consequential change in the position of either party. This process of itself provides an opportunity to come to further agreement on matters of detail.

THE EVIDENCE

Admissibility

19.24 Medical negligence trials tend to consist of oral commentary on two distinct bodies of documentary evidence, the contemporary notes, and the expert medical reports and supporting literature. It is easy to lose sight during the course of the trial of the status as evidence of these various documents.

19.25 The notes will usually consist of the clinical notes, nursing records, laboratory reports, and correspondence. These do not prove themselves. If they are to be relied on as evidence, this must be agreed, otherwise the relevant witnesses must be called and/or the appropriate Civil Evidence Act notices must be served. This topic has been covered generally in the section on preparation for trial. But the advocate at trial must remember the basic principles relating to the proof of facts so as to ensure that he does not make unwarranted assumptions about the value of any particular document.

19.26 The usual problem arises out of a limited agreement as to the status of the medical records. For example, it may have been agreed that a document was made by the person who purports to have made it; that does not amount to an agreement that its contents are true, or accurately record what happened. The appropriate use of civil evidence notices is the proper way to overcome this sort of problem. And if, at trial, it becomes clear that such notices should have, but have not, been served, application should be made to the judge for the exercise of his discretion to hear the records as evidence to prove the facts stated in them: see Order 38, rule 29 of the RSC.

19.27 The expert reports raise different problems. Under the new practice (see *Naylor v Preston Area Health Authority*[1]), the reports of both sides will have been exchanged in advance of the trial, together with the supporting material upon which each expert intends to rely. This material commonly consists of articles in medical journals, textbook quotations, and reports of experiments of studies. This material is in itself of only limited evidential value. It can establish the state of knowledge at a particular time, and help to establish a pattern of practice and support a standard of treatment. But at the end of the day, it is only material against which to test the validity of the evidence of the expert in the witness box. If, for example, the factual basis of a study is to be proved, primary evidence of the facts has to be before the court. There is no special rule of evidence which applies to render admissible the raw material of a scientific investigation if it would otherwise be hearsay, which has not been catered for either by calling first hand evidence or by taking appropriate steps under the Civil Evidence Act.

1 [1987] 2 All ER 353, [1987] 1 WLR 958, CA. See paras **11.87** et seq.

19.28 One particular consequence of disclosure of experts' reports should be mentioned here. There is no obligation on the party disclosing a report to call the maker as a witness: but if disclosure has been by order of the court, or otherwise pursuant to the provisions of Order 38 of the RSC, the other party or parties can put that report in evidence pursuant to the provisions of Order

38, rule 42, without themselves calling that expert. The rule is silent as to the time at which such a report has to be put in evidence. The traditional approach might suggest that a plaintiff would have to make the decision as to whether or not to put a defendant's report before he closed his case. And where it is clear that such a report is favourable, it might be prudent for him to do so. But where a defendant declines to give any indication of whether or not the maker of the report is to be called, and a fortiori if he resiles from an indication that he will call such an expert, the judge will clearly have the power to permit the plaintiff to put the report in evidence at any time. The 'new approach' would certainly favour complete flexibility to ensure that all admissible material was available to the court before the judge gives his judgment.

Cogency

19.29 Never forget, and this applies to all the stages on the way to trial as well as to the calling or cross-examining of experts in court that the scientist, and the expert doctor is a scientist, has a built in tendency to extreme caution when he cannot be certain of a matter in question. The intellectual discipline or rigour of the scientist makes him reluctant to ascribe a cause to an event unless and until he can prove and demonstrate conclusively the correctness of the hypothesis which is advanced. For this reason the lawyer must take every opportunity to remind the expert of the legal standard of proof:

(a) the court is only concerned with determining facts on the balance of probabilities;
(b) the existence of 'possibilities' should not deflect the expert from providing a view on 'probabilities';
(c) above all, the expert must not confuse the scientific concept of proof with the legal concept of proof.

The greatest problem which advocates are likely to be faced with in this kind of litigation is (a) and (b). Experts on either side can be cross-examined satisfactorily by laymen on the factual basis of their views: but there is substantial scope for misunderstanding in the language used to define 'proof'.

19.30 This applies to both parties. Cross-examining medical experts is for this and many other reasons fraught with problems for any advocate. The golden rule must be: do not ask a question to which you do not know, and have a real understanding of, the answer. This rule is of general application, but is of greatest importance when cross-examining someone who, ex hypothesi, knows more about the subject than the advocate. Careful preparation is essential: there is no substitute for detailed consultation with your own experts in order to understand as precisely as possible the nature of the dispute between them and the opposing experts. It also enables the advocate to test the extent to which either side has fallen into the trap of thinking in 'scientific' as opposed to 'legal' terms in relation to proof. The value of any expert's evidence depends critically on the extent to which it is directed to solving the legal as opposed to the scientific question. This does not mean that the doctor should be required to relax or compromise his own concept of proof. But he should be prepared to give as much help as he conscientiously can to reach answers based on probabilities.

JUDGMENT

Generally

19.31 There are no unique problems relating to the form of judgment in a medical negligence action. It is an action for damages for personal injuries. As a result, the judgment if the plaintiff is successful will be for a sum of money, being the damages, and a separate sum being the interest ordered by the court either on special or general damages. The only circumstance in which judgment after trial can take any other form is where the court makes an order for provisional damages pursuant to section 32A of the Supreme Court Act 1981 (see below).

Minors

19.32 The usual order on judgment will be for the sum to be invested and accumulated in a Short Term Investment Account for the benefit of the minor pending further order. Such further order will depend on whether it is to remain in court, managed by the local District Registry, or paid out into an approved trust; see RSC Order 80, rule 12, and the notes to this rule in the Supreme Court Practice.

Patients

19.33 The usual order where the successful plaintiff is a patient will be for the judgment sum to be paid to the Court of Protection for the benefit of the plaintiff: see RSC Order 80, rule 12 and the notes to this rule in the Supreme Court Practice.

Provisional damages

19.34 These will only be awarded when the plaintiff establishes that there is a chance that at some time in the future he may develop (by reason of the defendant's negligence) some serious disease, or some serious deterioration in his physical or mental condition. Damages are assessed on the basis that neither event will take place: if the event takes place the plaintiff is entitled to a further award. The judgment itself identifies the event; and provision is made for the case file to contain not only the judgment, but the transcript of the judge's oral judgment, the pleadings, the medical reports, and a transcript of any parts of the evidence the judge considers necessary: the details of the practice to be followed are set out in RSC Order 38, rules 7–10, and the notes to these rules in the Supreme Court Practice. (See paras **17.16** ff.)

Costs

19.35 After a trial, costs will follow the event. There is no justification, save in the most exceptional circumstances, for making any other order than that costs be taxed on the standard basis. This is so even in cases involving minors or patients.

Conclusion

19.36 There is no special mystique about trials of medical negligence actions. Many are resolved as questions of fact. Many do not involve any more complex expert evidence than factory accident cases. On the other hand, many are concerned with controversial issues at the limits of scientific knowledge. There is an undeniable fascination for the lawyer in exploring such topics with the experts intimately concerned with providing solutions for human suffering. Provided everyone concerned appreciates that at the end of the day the law is a crude instrument for resolving the questions of fault and causation raised in any given case, both lawyers and medical experts can give a sensible service to their clients. If either side becomes seduced by the fascinations of exploring these questions into treating the exercise as a scientific voyage of discovery, or the opportunity to establish a scientific or other principle, the ultimate casualties are going to be the litigants, and in particular plaintiffs, be it as a result of the consequential delay while the debate is resolved, or its cost. Delay and cost are both of themselves a form of injustice.

CROSS-REFERENCES

For information related to topics in this chapter see Chapters 10, 11, 14 and 16.

CHAPTER 20

Product liability for medicinal products

Ian Dodds-Smith *Solicitor*
Michael Spencer *QC*

SUMMARY

INTRODUCTION

20.1 It was the injuries caused by thalidomide that first alerted consumers to the potential hazards of medicinal products and not only gave rise to the Medicines Act 1968 but also began the debate about the basis upon which companies that research and market products should be liable for any injury they cause. Regulatory control by subordinate legislation under the Medicines Act has been extended to virtually every aspect of the marketing of medicinal products and European initiatives to develop and harmonise controls continue at an unrelenting pace. However, a series of cases or threatened cases involving products or classes of products said to have caused injury, including hormone pregnancy tests, oral contraceptives, Debendox, Opren, Pertussis vaccine, prednisolone, intra-uterine devices, benzodiazepines, blood products, contrast media (Myodil), human insulin, human growth hormone and steroids, has kept the debate in the forefront of discussions about possible changes in the law relating to product liability generally. That debate continues with the focus switching to changes in the procedure whereby the courts may deal efficiently with multi-claimant litigation and the application of strict liability principles to claims concerning injury caused by such products.

20.2 There are no easy solutions. Liability for injuries associated with the use of medicinal products represents the type of product liability that engenders not only the most emotive and often misinformed comment but also the most complex of questions. The use of drugs is always attended by risks and one industry executive has suggested in exasperation that unrealistic patients should be advised 'If you do not like the risk of the drug, try the risk of the disease.'[1] On any view, the nature of these products and the conditions which they are used to treat would make the simplest of systems, where compensation depended only upon showing causation, difficult enough, for their adverse effects are frequently difficult to distinguish from the adverse progression or the recrudescence of the underlying condition for which the product was given. Their adverse effects are sometimes said to appear many years after use and not in the patient but in her offspring. Moreover, the difficulties are accentuated where, as is common, a person has taken many different products for separate conditions or a series of similar products from different manufacturers for one condition. Merely identifying the product used years after the event has proved impossible for some claimants.[2]

1 Widely quoted and attributed to Dr Brian Cromie previously of Hoechst on an occasion unknown to the authors.
2 In *Mann and Close v Wellcome Foundation Ltd* (20 January 1989, unreported) QBD, the claimants ultimately conceded that there was insufficient evidence to establish that the defendant's subsidiary (Calmic Ltd) had supplied the relevant neomycin spray alleged to have caused deafness and the case against the manufacturer defendants failed.

20.3 Scientists seek to perfect the architecture and performance of statistical studies that can reliably identify the adverse effects of medical products but the enormous potential for bias entering into the collection of epidemiological data and the existence of confounding factors correlating positively both with an increased likelihood of the product being prescribed and an increased incidence of the condition under consideration, make interpretation of such data very difficult, particularly where low levels of risk are under consideration.[1] Moreover, the courts have made it clear that reports of epidemiological studies are not of themselves admissible evidence of the facts on risk reported in them (see *H v Schering Chemicals Ltd*[2]), although they can be introduced into evidence through expert testimony.

1 At a conference organised by the Royal Society of Medicine on 17/19 July 1989 concerning oral contraceptives and breast cancer Professor S Shapiro commented that a relative risk of 1–2 is 'beyond the resolving power of the epidemiologic microscope'.
2 *H v Schering Chemicals Ltd* [1983] 1 All ER 849, [1983] 1 WLR 143.

20.4 Proving causation – both general and in the individual case – is therefore a major problem for claimants whether their claim is based on negligence or strict liability principles. It often dwarfs all other problems.[1] If liability is to be based upon something more than causation alone, the difficulties for the claimant increase and many argue require that product liability for medicinal products be taken completely outside the existing contractual and tortious law system so that compensation is based upon an insurance based 'no fault compensation scheme'.[2]

1 In *Loveday v Renton and Wellcome Foundation Ltd* [1990] 1 Med LR 117, the court found that the plaintiffs had failed to establish a causal relationship between the use of Pertussis vaccine and brain damage in young children. In *D and R v Schering Chemicals Ltd* (2 July 1982, unreported) QBD, the claimants sought leave to discontinue cases alleging malformations had been caused by exposure to the hormone pregnancy test Primodos in utero after exchange of extensive expert evidence, on the basis that – as their leading counsel put it – there was no real possibility of establishing that the products were teratogenic as alleged.

2 A L Diamond and D R Laurence 'Product Liability in Respect of Drugs' in P F D'Arcy and J P Griffin (eds) *Iatrogenic Diseases* (3rd edn, Oxford, Oxford University Press, 1986) pp 117–123.

20.5 All of the Commissions in the United Kingdom that during the last decade have looked at the general issue of product liability have expressed concern about the inadequacies of the traditional remedies in contract and in negligence, particularly as they concerned the position of those injured by defective drugs.[1] The basis upon which compensation could be claimed was seen to vary according to the nature of the legal relationship between the injured person and those persons in the chain of supply who had been instrumental in bringing the product to the consumer. The European Community has now embraced strict liability on the basis that 'liability without fault on the part of the producer is the sole means of adequately solving the problem – peculiar to our age of increasing technicality – of a fair apportionment of the risks inherent in modern technological production'.[2]

1 The Law Commission and the Scottish Law Commission, Liability for Defective Products, 1977 (Cmnd 6831, HMSO) and Royal Commission on Civil Liability and Compensation for Personal Injury, 1978 (Cmnd 7-54, HMSO).

2 See the preamble to EC Directive 85/374 on the approximation of the laws, regulations and administrative provisions of the member states concerning liability for defective products, OJ L210/29.

20.6 This initiative is implemented in the United Kingdom by Part I of the Consumer Protection Act 1987 ('CPA') and purports to offer more certainty that persons injured by defective products may obtain compensation. However, pending scrutiny by the courts of the Act's provisions and those of the EC Directive to which it owes its existence, that remedy remains of uncertain application in the pharmaceutical sector. In any event, strict liability is not a substitute for the existing remedies (see CPA, section 2(6)) but an addition and these remedies will continue to be relevant not least in relation to products supplied before the new Act came into effect or where the time period for advancing a case based on strict liability has expired.

20.7 Accordingly, for the present, product liability for medicinal products concerns a melange of contractual and tortious principles where the scientific uncertainties are further compounded in the United Kingdom by the absence of judicial decisions on the impact of these principles upon the activities of the industry. It is important to note that no case against a commercial manufacturer has been taken to judgment on liability in the United Kingdom.[1]

1 See para **20.2**, n 2, para **20.4**, n 1, above, and settlement of Opren litigation (NLJ 18 December 1987 at 1183). Cases concerning alleged side effects of long-term use of prednisolone in the 1960s and 1970s for juvenile rheumatoid arthritis (see Scrip no 1212, 10 June 1987, p 2) were also settled immediately prior to trial. However further claims are now under consideration (see AVMA Medical and Legal Journal, April 1992, p 2).

CONTRACTUAL CLAIMS

20.8 There is, of course, normally no contract between the pharmaceutical manufacturer and the ultimate recipient of his product (except in certain special circumstances of research where the manufacturer contracts with volunteers) and, unlike the case in some American jurisdictions, statements made in promotional material issued by the manufacturer do not, of themselves, provide the user with a quasi-contractual remedy based on an implied warranty that the statements were true.[1] However, where products are sold by a retailer to the ultimate user (as will often be the case with products whose status under the Medicines Act allows them to be made available over-the-counter) contractual claims move back up the chain of supply and ultimately the subject of a request for indemnity from the manufacturer cannot be ignored.

1 *Lambert v Lewis* [1978] 1 Lloyd's Rep 610 at 628.

20.9 The Sale of Goods Act 1979 implies certain conditions into contracts of sale which cannot be excluded in the case of consumer sales and can only be excluded in commercial sales if the exclusion is 'reasonable'. The effect of these conditions is, first, that the seller will be liable independent of fault on his part for injury suffered by the buyer if the product is not of adequate quality and, secondly, that the seller will be liable if the product was of adequate quality for some purposes but unfit for the particular purpose that the buyer made known to the seller in circumstances where the buyer was relying on the skill and judgment of the seller. Similar terms are implied by the Supply of Goods and Services Act 1982 into a contract for the performance of a service in the course of which a product is administered.

20.10 Liability for defective products under the Sale of Goods Act 1979 only arises between persons in a contractual relationship and ignores any of the persons involved with the use of the product who are not purchasers, such as a purchaser's friends or family who may use a product and be injured while doing so. However, where goods supplied under contract are 'defective', in the sense either of being of inadequate quality or unfit for purpose, it is no defence for the seller to argue that he has exercised all reasonable care in the supply of such goods.[1] Such liability has always been 'strict'. It is the existence of, and not the discoverability of or reason for, the defect in the product which renders the seller liable for the resulting damage caused. Moreover, there is no doubt that such liability may arise out of the inadequate nature of the labelling or instructions for use rather than the inherent design of the product itself.[2]

1 *Frost v Aylesbury Dairy Co Ltd* [1905] 1 KB 608, CA.
2 *Wormell v RHM Agriculture (East) Ltd* [1986] 1 All ER 769, [1986] 1 WLR 336.

20.11 Accordingly, under sale of goods legislation, the buyer of a defective medicinal product available over-the-counter (OTC) could successfully sue the pharmacist who supplied it, provided it was the buyer – and not someone to whom the buyer gave it – who was injured. Likewise, if a product supplied by the pharmacist on private prescription – and therefore in effect 'sold' – turns out to be defective, the pharmacist will be vulnerable to a claim from the buyer. However, in the latter case, the pharmacist may be able to show that the injured person relied upon the prescribing doctor rather than the pharmacist for the choice of product, making any claim based upon breach of the implied condition of fitness for purpose unrealistic. In respect of any loss he suffers the pharmacist may be entitled to bring a claim for reimbursement against the wholesaler who in turn could bring a similar claim against the manufacturer, each claimant relying on the implied conditions. Such claims for reimbursement may, however, be limited by exclusion clauses in the contract governing the supply.

20.12 In principle, contributory negligence by the buyer is not a defence to an action based in contract.[1] The law proceeds on the basis that the seller promised that he would provide a product which was of merchantable quality and fit for purpose and if he did not provide such a product he should be liable to compensate the buyer. However, contributory negligence by the consumer may have the effect of reducing the level of compensation recoverable.[2]

1 *Basildon District Council v J E Lesser (Properties) Ltd* [1985] QB 839, [1985] 1 All ER 20.
2 *Forsikringsaktieselskapet Vesta v Butcher* [1989] AC 852, [1989] 1 All ER 402.

20.13 The standard adopted for determining whether a product has achieved the benchmark of 'merchantable quality' might, however, be difficult to apply to medicinal products. Section 14(6) of the Sale of Goods Act provides the following definition:

Goods of any kind are of merchantable quality . . . if they are as fit for the purpose or purposes for which goods of that kind are bought as it is reasonable to expect having regard to any description applied to them, the price (if relevant) and all the other relevant circumstances.

20.14 The nature of some pharmaceutical products arguably makes it unreasonable for a consumer, having knowledge that they carry unavoidable risks, to expect them to be free of side-effects – even unknown but serious ones. The position of products supplied on a named-patient basis and before research is completed and a licence granted springs to mind.[1] Although it would be rare for such products to be 'sold', strict liability under the Sale of Goods Act might be found not to be so strict after all.

1 See Medicines Act 1968, ss 9 and 13.

20.15 However, the focus in product liability litigation is unlikely to be on these contractual remedies, as the courts have declared that when a medicinal product is prescribed under the National Health Service Scheme, that product is not supplied pursuant to a contract between the patient and the pharmacist at all. The pharmacist has a statutory duty to give it to the patient on presentation of a prescription and the appropriate prescription charge (if the patient is not exempt).[1]

1 *Pfizer Corpn v Ministry of Health* [1965] AC 512, [1965] 1 All ER 450, HL, and *Appleby v Sleep* [1968] 2 All ER 265, [1968] 1 WLR 948, DC.

20.16 As the medicinal products most likely to be associated with injury are those available only through the intervention of a prescribing doctor, and the majority of prescriptions are dispensed under the National Health Service, a contractual claim for injury caused by a medicinal product is likely to be comparatively rare, although the recent restrictions on sale of presentations of aspirin for children due to the purported association with Reye's syndrome, indicate that such a claim is not wholly theoretical.

20.17 In the circumstances, where a patient believes that he has been injured by a medicinal product, his only cause of action against persons involved in its supply – the manufacturer/product licence holder, wholesaler, pharmacist, or doctor – is likely to be in negligence or (as regards the manufacturer and licence holder) under strict liability. The term 'product liability' is normally used only to describe the liability of the manufacturer and is the focus of this chapter but as in practice many claims are also brought against the regulatory authorities, the position of such bodies and certain other intermediaries will also be discussed.

20.18 The manufacturer of a pharmaceutical product may not be the person holding the product licence and responsible for placing the product on the market in the United Kingdom. He will frequently be the parent company manufacturing for his distributing subsidiaries on a multi-national basis. However, for simplicity in this chapter, unless the context indicates otherwise, the term manufacturer will be used to describe a person having full responsibility for the research, manufacture and distribution of the product.

THE PRINCIPLES OF FAULT LIABILITY AND STRICT LIABILITY COMPARED

Fault liability

20.19 It is the duty of every person in the chain of supply of a product to take reasonable care to avoid causing injury to the consumer by his careless act or failure to act, i e by his negligence.[1] The degree of care involved must have regard to the seriousness of the consequences of failure.[2] On this basis those dealing in medicinal products and possibly even the Licensing Authority and its expert committees are vulnerable to claims. To succeed under fault liability the injured person must prove not only that he has been injured by the product and that the relevant person has been negligent but also that but for the negligent act, the claimant would not have suffered the injury or it would have been reduced. The burden of proving each of these ingredients of liability lies with the claimant and the standard of proof required is the 'balance of probabilities'.

1 *Donoghue v Stevenson* [1932] AC 562, HL.
2 *Paris v Stepney Borough Council* [1951] AC 367, [1951] 1 All ER 42, HL.

20.20 As regards the issue of causation, one decision previously suggested was that where a substance is known to cause the injury complained of, and the defendant negligently exposed the claimant to that substance, the burden of proof is reversed and the defendant must show that another factor was as likely or more likely to have caused the injury in the case in question. However, this reasoning, which could have assisted claimants in product liability litigation involving medicinal products, was rejected by the House of Lords and the burden of proof lies firmly on the claimant's shoulders to show that but for exposure his injury would not have occurred.[1] (See paras **16.59**ff.)

1 See *McGhee v National Coal Board* [1972] 3 All ER 1008, [1973] 1 WLR 1, and *Wilsher v Essex Area Health Authority* [1988] AC 1074, [1988] 1 All ER 871, HL.

20.21 The manufacturer of medicinal products has a most onerous obligation although, in the absence of decided cases in the UK, the application of negligence principles to his position depends considerably on extrapolation from cases arising in other industries. It is clear, however, that at every step in research and marketing he must take such care as the reasonably skilful manufacturer would take and his conduct will at all times be measured against the prevailing state of scientific and technical knowledge ('the state of the art').[1] Failure to exercise care in research and design of the product or in manufacture of it or in labelling and warning through product information of possible risks associated with normal use – and conceivably foreseeable misuse – may lead to liability in negligence.[2] Where an enterprise is inherently dangerous, liability can arise even where it may be said that it involved 'work which was both at and beyond the frontier of professional knowledge'.[3] A manufacturer's duty is not limited to assessing for safety those parts of the product that he has researched and developed himself. It may extend to raw materials supplied by others.[4]

1 *Vacwell Engineering Co Ltd v BDH Chemicals Ltd* [1971] 1 QB 88, [1969] 3 All ER 1681; and *Stokes v Guest Keen & Nettlefold (Bolts and Nuts) Ltd* [1968] 1 WLR 1776 at 1783.
2 *Cartwright v GKN Sankey Ltd* [1972] 2 Lloyd's Rep 242 at 259; *Fuller v Baxenden Chemical Co Ltd* (1 February 1985, unreported) QBD, and *Devilez v Boots Pure Drug Co Ltd* (1962) 106 Sol Jo 552.
3 *Independent Broadcasting Authority v EMI (Electronics) Ltd and BICC Construction Ltd* (1980) 14 BLR 1 at 27, HL.
4 *Taylor v Rover Co Ltd* [1966] 2 All ER 181 at 186 and *Winward v TVR Engineering Ltd* (4 March 1986, unreported) QBD.

20.22 The issue of drugs being taken by pregnant women and possibly exposing their unborn children to injury has gained much publicity in recent years and therefore it is important to note that by virtue of the Congenital Disabilities (Civil Liability) Act 1976 a manufacturer owes a duty of care to the fetus in utero and can be liable to a child for a disability suffered as a result of a pre-natal occurrence affecting the parent. The Act only applies in respect of births after 22 July 1976 but there is now considerable precedent for the principle that a duty of care exists at common law.[1]

1 *Burton v Islington Health Authority* [1993] QB 204, [1992] 3 All ER 833.

20.23 It was thought at one time that the duty of care to the ultimate consumer only applies where there is 'no reasonable possibility of intermediate examination'.[1] However, the meaning of 'intermediate examination' has been severely qualified in decisions of the courts and, as a result, it is probably correct to say that, if a product is defective, the possibility of intermediate examination will only assist the manufacturer if he could reasonably have anticipated that the examination conducted by the intermediary would be of such a type as to reveal the defect.[2] Where such an examination is anticipated a duty of care may not arise at all. The intervention of a regulatory authority, prescribing doctor or a pharmacist in the supply of a medicinal product therefore raises the question of whether that intervention could reasonably be expected to have isolated the defect. Clearly, a latent defect such as a design defect would often not be apparent and the intervention of such third parties will not automatically insulate the manufacturer from liability. In contrast, failure by an intermediary to isolate an obvious defect such as a packaging failure which has led to deterioration in the product or its sterility, could on particular facts give rise to a defence that a duty of care on the part of the manufacturer did not arise or will be sufficient to sever the causal link between the creation of the risk by the manufacturer and the injury it causes. Difficult questions of law may arise in the case of an allegation of 'failure to warn' (see paras **20.80** ff below) concerning a prescription-only product. The reasonable expectation that the prescribing physician (or specialist to whom the patient may be referred) will exercise his knowledge and skill in deciding whether and how to prescribe a product, may affect the determination of whether a duty of care is owed at all to a particular patient.

1 See *Donoghue v Stevenson*, above, at 599.
2 *Griffiths v Arch Engineering Co (Newport) Ltd* [1968] 3 All ER 217.

20.24 The exercise of reasonable care is a defence to a claim in negligence and adherence to the common practice of the industry is accordingly a useful starting point in defending an action in negligence because it is admissible evidence of what a reasonably prudent manufacturer would do under the same circumstances.[1] However, it is certainly open to the court to hold that common practice does not amount to a proper precaution to avoid foreseeable risk.[2] The type of information that must accompany an application for a marketing authorisation is now increasingly harmonised within the European Community but the requirements refer to types of research. They still leave room for some discretion both on the part of the regulatory authorities and the manufacturer as to what is appropriate for a particular type of product. Guidelines from time to time issued by regulatory authorities and the industry itself reflect and explain standard practice. The fact that a manufacturer has complied with such requests is not, therefore, to be treated as an automatic defence to a claim in negligence. The court may find that the manufacturer knew that the general requests were not directly applicable to the research into the product in question and additional research should be done. This may be particularly pertinent to the application of pre-clinical animal testing guidelines given the known physiological differences between humans and laboratory animals that make the use of particular animal species unsuitable for certain drug testing. It is safe to assume that, in the absence of a considered basis for divergence, non-compliance with common practice and guidelines aimed at promoting safety is unlikely to be held consistent with the exercise of proper care.

1 *Marshall v Lindsey County Council* [1935] 1 KB 516, CA.
2 *Morris v West Hartlepool Steam Navigation Co Ltd* [1956] AC 552, [1956] 1 All ER 385, HL.

20.25 Compliance with statutory requirements is better evidence that the duty to take proper care has been discharged. The rationale of any regulation is that it enshrines the legal standard of care at the time when the regulation is promulgated. On the other hand, compliance cannot be regarded as conclusive for the courts have consistently held that statutory regulations do not supersede the general duty to take whatever care is appropriate in the particular circumstances.[1] Accordingly, the licensing of the product is not of itself a defence to any claim. Indeed article 9 of Directive 65/65/EEC notes that a marketing authorisation under European law 'shall not affect the civil and criminal liability of the manufacturer and where applicable, of the person responsible for placing the proprietary medicinal product on the market'.[2] Even where regulations made under the Medicines Act do prescribe a detailed standard, eg in relation to certain aspects of labelling, compliance is not decisive.

1 *Bux v Slough Metals Ltd* [1974] 1 All ER 262, [1973] 1 WLR 1358, CA.
2 65/65/EEC OJ 22, 9 February, 1965, p 369.

20.26 In practice, however, the licensing of a product and a manufacturer's compliance with all applicable regulations will often be a difficult hurdle for a claimant to overcome. Where regulations in question cover precisely the circumstances which give rise to the complaint, the courts have shown themselves slow to substitute their own version of reasonableness in relation to activities which have clearly been regulated by Parliament.[1] Moreover, the control exercised by the Licensing Authority may indirectly be evidence that the manufacturer's research or prescribing information was acceptable on the grounds that an independent body, such as the Committee on Safety of Medicines or Committee on the Review of Medicines, has reviewed the same data and information and reached the same conclusion as the manufacturer on the probable safety of the product or, as the case may be, the adequacy of the prescribing information put in the data sheet.

1 *Budden v BP Oil Ltd and Shell Oil Ltd* [1980] JPL 586, CA.

20.27 Failure to meet Medicines Act requirements will place the manufacturer in a very vulnerable position because the injured person will argue that, independent of any criminal sanctions imposed because of the breach, the breach is also admissible evidence in a civil case based on negligence. However, under section 133(2) of the Medicines Act breach of the provisions of the Act or regulations made thereunder is specifically declared not to amount to negligence per se.

20.28 If a pharmaceutical company chooses to instruct another to carry out preclinical or clinical research work or to manufacture or package a product, rather than use its own resources, the question arises whether the company is liable in tort for any injury or damage caused by the negligence of the other. The general rule is that an employer is not responsible for the negligence of his independent contractor, provided reasonable care was exercised in appointing that contractor by establishing the adequacy of the facilities and reputation of the contractor for careful performance of work. There are ill-defined exceptions to this rule that seek to categorise certain duties as 'non-delegable'.[1] Some decisions[2] have appeared to elide the contractual duty to carry out work carefully – which is clearly non-delegable – with the parallel tortious duty to exercise reasonable care in relation to the performance of such work. However, where a duty in contract is not owed to the injured person it would seem contrary to other trends in the law to treat the manufacturer as owing such a non-delegable duty.

1 *Alcock v Wraith* (1991) 59 BLR 16.
2 See for instance, *Cynat Products Ltd v Landbuild (Investment and Property) Ltd* [1984] 3 All ER 513.

Strict liability

20.29 There have been various European and separate member state initiatives in recent years to establish a new approach to the problem of providing compensation for personal injury caused by defective products. The Council of Europe began work on a draft Convention on Liability for Defective Products in 1970 but by the time the so-called 'Strasbourg Convention' was open for signature the Commission of the European Communities had produced its own preliminary draft Directive on the same subject, with the result that many states, including the United Kingdom, decided to seek agreement over the Directive before taking any final steps to change their own law. Nevertheless it took ten years to finalise the Directive. Disagreement on the balance to be struck between the rights of the injured person to receive compensation and the need not to stifle innovation by producers has led to a compromise that allows member states to deviate from the basic provisions in certain limited but important respects. Thus although strict liability brings the legal position of the producer closer to the position of the person who sells a product direct to the consumer, the post Consumer Protection Act position of a manufacturer of medicinal products in the United Kingdom remains more favourable than that of the pharmacist selling a product to the patient and this remains the subject of considerable comment. Critics point out that while the thalidomide tragedy was the catalyst for proposed changes in the law, it is by no means clear that claimants would have been markedly better off had strict liability, as now implemented, applied to their claims.

20.30 The Consumer Protection Act was enacted on 15 May 1987, and Part I came into force on 1 March 1988. The Act follows the text of the Directive closely in most respects. Under CPA, section 50(7) strict liability does not apply to a product supplied to another in the course of the producer's business before 1 March 1988 and this provision refers to the actual product that caused the injury and not to the date the first product of that description was put into circulation by the producer. Strict liability may not be limited or excluded by a notice issued to consumers (see section 7).

Products affected

20.31 Not only all finished medicinal products but also any component part or raw material, fall within the definition of 'a product' subject to strict liability. Moreover, the Act will impact upon any natural product (e g herbal or blood product) which, while not strictly 'manufactured' still has 'essential characteristics' attributable to an industrial or other process. It does not affect the manufacturer's liability just because the product is given away as a sample or is a research product provided the product was supplied to another in the course of business (see CPA, section 4(1)(c)). In contrast, where a product is stolen, the producer has a defence because the manufacturer did not 'supply' the product. Equally, injury due to exposure to products or raw materials in the work place and prior to supply of the product to another will continue to be governed by existing laws.

20.32 Two provisions of the Directive (articles 1 and 4) encapsulate the central principles. The producer is liable for damage caused by a defect in his product and the injured person must prove the damage, the defect and the causal relationship between the defect and damage. Most significantly, therefore, the person allegedly injured by a defective medicinal product will still have to prove that the injury complained of was, in fact, caused by the product or the defective nature of the product contributed materially to the injury. Strict liability is therefore not to be confused with absolute liability. There is no decision of the English court that suggests judges will assist the claimant further by adopting the novel concept developed in some US jurisdictions[1] in diethylstilboestrol (DES) cases (where identifying which manufacturer's product was used can be difficult) of imposing upon each of the relevant manufacturers the burden of showing that, on the balance of probabilities, his product was not used. In the absence of such proof, in those jurisdictions damages may be apportioned on the basis of market share of the sales of the compound in question. Abrogation of the need to show causation in this respect appears to have reached its zenith in a New York case,[2] where the need for identification was dispensed with completely and the defendants were found liable for the percentage of the claimant's total damages equal to their national share for DES products, even where they could individually show that on the balance of probabilities their product had not been used. As yet DES litigation in England has merely been threatened. However, claimants in the Netherlands alleging trans-placental injury, due to exposure of their mothers on various dates between 1953 and 1967 to DES, commenced proceedings in 1986 for compensation against some of the pharmaceutical companies said to have supplied DES in the Netherlands. The claimants could neither identify all the producers of DES at the relevant time nor the producer of the specific product administered to their mothers. Nevertheless, the claimants argued that each company was in principle liable to pay any damages awarded. The case turned upon the interpretation of a provision of section 6.99 of the Civil Code relating to joint and several liability added in 1992. This provides:

> Where the damages may have resulted from two or more events for each of which a different person is liable, and if it is certain that the damage has arisen from at least one of these events, the obligation to repair the damage rests upon each of these persons, unless he proves that the damage is not the result of an event for which he himself is liable.

The reference to 'events' in this context means 'unlawful act'. The Supreme Court concluded that the section contemplated a claimant succeeding against one of a number of persons (assumed for the purposes to have acted negligently) even though that claimant was unable to show from which company the DES taken by her mother originated. Although the provision was not in existence in the relevant years (1950s) the court concluded that it reflected principles of law applicable at that time. An argument that such an interpretation conflicted with the Directive was rejected on the ground that, as the products were supplied prior to the coming into force of the Directive, its provisions could not have relevance on any view. The Supreme Court also found that a defendant could defeat a claim by showing that the injury of a specific claimant was not the result of DES marketed by him but rejected a concept of liability limited to market share because placing a limit upon the ability of a claimant to recover from a particular producer and requiring the claimant to bear the risk of insolvency or liquidation of a producer was seen as unfair to claimants. Statements of Claim have yet to be served and a hearing on the substantive issues is a long way off.[3]

1 See *Sindell v Abbott Laboratories* 26 Cal 3d 588, 607 P 2d 924, 163 Cal Rptr 132, cert denied, 449 US 912 (1980).
2 *Hymowitz v Eli Lilly & Co* 73 NY 2d 487 (1989).
3 *XX v Bayer Nederland BV* (Rechtspraak van de week 1992 No 219).

Persons liable

20.33 Strict liability is imposed on 'producers' but whereas fault liability focuses upon the conduct of manufacturer and asks whether it was reasonable, strict liability focuses upon the product, and imposes liability on the manufacturer if it was defective and no statutory defences are applicable. The manufacturer may be anyone from a major pharmaceutical company to a hospital pharmacist making up a limited amount of product from bought-in materials. It also follows that a company manufacturing under contract for the product licence holder will be subject to strict liability regardless of his lack of involvement in research and development of the product. He may therefore be more exposed than when his liability was governed only by negligence principles and he must carefully consider the terms of his supply contracts. Similar considerations apply to persons manufacturing and supplying under licence but essentially relying upon the licensor's know-how.

20.34 The manufacture of medicinal products frequently involves several different stages from preparation of the basic product to final assembly and packaging of the finished dosage form. Neither the Directive nor the CPA defines precisely what constitutes an act of manufacture but there is obviously a risk that anyone involved in preparing the finished dosage form could be joined in proceedings as a 'manufacturer'. It is less clear that a person merely packaging the product would be treated as a manufacturer as his 'product' is not comprised in another (see CPA, section 1(2)), although he might be liable in negligence for defects in the packaging he supplied that rendered the final product defective.[1]

1 For the purposes of labelling with the manufacturer's name (see note to para **20.38**, below) Directive 92/27/EEC defines manufacturer in a way that encompasses both total and partial manufacture and various processes of packaging.

20.35 Primary liability is extended beyond the manufacturer himself and embraces any person who by putting his name, trademark, or other distinguishing feature on the product (eg 'brand-naming') represents himself to be the producer. Any person who imports a product into the European Community for supply in the course of a business is also deemed to be a producer in order that the injured person does not have to commence litigation outside the European Community in order to seek compensation. Finally, where the injured person cannot identify the producer of the product, the person who supplied the product to the injured person is treated as the producer unless he is able within a reasonable time to answer the request of the injured person to identify one or more of the persons who fall within the definition of 'producer' of the product or at least the person who supplied him with the product (see CPA, section 2(2) and section 46 for the definition of a supplier).

20.36 Once in receipt of the identity of the immediate supplier, the claimant may repeat his request until he either establishes the identity of the producer or importer or finds a supplier unable to identify his immediate supplier, who may then be treated as though he was the producer. The implication is that retailers and wholesalers supplying generic products sourced from a variety of companies could be exposed to strict liability if they do not keep adequate records. Many believe that the trend towards original pack dispensing, even for generics, will considerably assist those dealing in them to avoid claims.

20.37 It follows that more than one person in the chain of supply of medicinal products may be liable strictly for the same injury. The manufacturer of the finished product, the manufacturer of any defective raw material and the product licence holder importing the product from outside the Community may all be exposed and will be liable on a joint and several basis (ie the injured person can sue any of them and recover full compensation) but that liability is without prejudice to national rights of contribution or indemnity between each person liable (see CPA, section 2(5) and article 5 of the Directive).

20.38 Many medicinal products are imported from outside the Community and arguably under fault liability the importer would only be exposed in respect of patent defects in the product but not those where special research or testing to confirm safety would be necessary. In contrast, under strict liability the importer may be obliged to pay compensation to the injured person and rely upon a right to recover indemnity from his foreign supplier through specific contractual provision or by operation of law. Such indemnities may be of equal importance to 'own-branders'. However, it is not clear whether a company procuring the manufacture of medicinal products to his own specification and applying his own brand name can avoid the implicit representation that he is the manufacturer by stating elsewhere in the labelling that the product was manufactured by another or merely 'manufactured specially for him'. Suffice it to say, this provision worried pharmacists sufficiently for the Pharmaceutical Society to seek an assurance from the Department of Health that dispensing from bulk (which under the Medicines Act labelling legislation requires the pharmacist to label the container with his name and address) would not expose the pharmacist to strict liability as if he were a producer. The Department did not believe that the Society had cause for concern but certainly this provision could be of importance to the major supermarkets and retail chemist chains whose product 'get-up' is designed to foster brand identity and where statements qualifying the inference that the product is their own are not prominent. In fact, new requirements relating to labelling of all medicinal products (including dispensed products) and package leaflets will require all products to have leaflets noting the name and address of the manufacturer (as well as the product licence-holder) unless this information appears on the outer packaging or on the immediate packaging.[1]

1 Directive 92/27/EEC OJ 30 April 1992, L113/10, see art 71(a).

Definition of defect

20.39 The cornerstone of the Directive is the definition of a defective product (see article 6(1)) which reads:

A product is defective when it does not provide the safety which a person is entitled to expect taking all circumstances into account including:

(a) the presentation of the product
(b) the use to which it could reasonably be expected that the product would be put
(c) the time when the product was put into circulation.

This is obviously not an all-embracing list of relevant considerations but equally some considerations are irrelevant and the Directive goes on to state that a product shall not be considered defective for the sole reason that a better product was subsequently put into circulation (article 6(2)). The issue of whether a particular medicinal product is defective depends, therefore, upon whether it could properly be termed defective on the date that the actual product was supplied. Storage by the consumer beyond the expiry date would be relevant under this provision. Equally a product must be judged by reference to circumstances prevailing at the date of its supply by the producer regardless of whether subsequent scientific advances have enabled others to licence and supply a product with an improved safety profile for the same indication. However, once an improved product is available, the continued supply of those older generation of products might in theory present problems for their manufacturers. In practice, of course, it may still be possible to claim advantages for the older products, either for specific groups of patients, or more generally on the basis of the greater clinical experience with them.

20.40 For the purposes of strict liability, safety in relation to a product refers to safety in the context of risk of damage to property as well as risk of death or personal injury (see article 9 of the Directive and section 3(1) and (5) of CPA). However, damage to property is only compensated if what is damaged is property of a description ordinarily intended for private use, occupation or consumption, and it was being used by the claimant for such use, occupation, or consumption. In addition there is a threshold of 500 ECU (£275) for property damage, below which strict liability does not apply. Death of the family pet caused by a defective veterinary drug might, therefore, only be compensated if the pedigree of the dog made it particularly valuable and equally injury to the animals of commercial breeders would not be compensated at all (unless under fault liability or contractual principles).

20.41 The essence of the definition of a defective product is lack of safety which is seemingly to be determined objectively by reference to a 'consumer expectations test'. For this reason perhaps the most important factor relevant to the expectation of safety in the case of medicinal products is the 'presentation of the product'. The phrase was not defined in the Directive but by CPA, section 3(2) it is treated as covering the following aspects:

The manner in which, and the purposes for which, the product has been marketed, its get-up [e g its packaging], the use of any mark in relation to the product, and any instructions for or warnings with respect to doing or refraining from doing anything with or in relation to the product.

20.42 The CPA, therefore, suggests that the consumer's expectation of safety may quite properly be qualified by contra-indications, warnings and precautions whether issued to an intermediary (such as the prescriber) or to the user himself. Although the safety of the product is tested against the expectation of persons generally rather than the particular user, it has long been recognised that a test which hinges on consumer expectations poses serious difficulties of application in the case of medicinal products. The Department of Health in the United Kingdom has emphasised this point[1] saying:

> Medicinal products by their very nature all carry a risk of adverse effects. Even over-the-counter remedies for minor ailments may produce side effects in a small number of people because of such factors as biological idiosyncracies, interaction with other medicines or food . . . etc.

1 Department of Health and Social Security, Medicines Division Consultation Paper, Product Liability: Special Features of the Medical Sector (1979).

20.43 In relation to medicinal products the risk of treatment, therefore, has to be weighed against the benefit, or more correctly the prospect of benefit, because there can be no guarantee of cure or (as the case may be) symptom relief or disease prevention. It is not thought that this familiar concept is affected by strict liability but the implications of the particular focus of such liability will be further considered in the discussion below concerning marketing defects and 'failure to warn' cases.

20.44 A defence is allowed the producer under the CPA where the defect 'is attributable to compliance with any requirement imposed by or under any enactment or with any Community obligation'. At one stage in the development of the draft Directive, it seemed as though the fact of complying with regulations or a recognised standard might provide a defence to the manufacturer but after amendment of the wording of this defence it is clear that the producer has no defence unless the defect was the *inevitable* result of compliance with a statutory requirement.

20.45 As a result the defence may be relevant where the Licensing Authority refuse to allow the licence holder to incorporate a warning in his prescribing information or where the precise form of a warning is dictated by the authorities pursuant to a statutory power, leaving the producer with no discretion as to whether it is an effective warning. Otherwise, however, licensing or compliance with regulations will not automatically protect the producer. It may, however, be possible to argue that the published or applied standard of the authorities represented the reasonable safety expectation of the time. The position is therefore not radically different to that arising under existing negligence principles.

Criminal liability

20.46 For completeness, reference should be made to the fact that certain medicinal products may also fall within the criminal law regime under Part II of the CPA. This places a general obligation on the suppliers of consumer goods to achieve an acceptable standard of safety. Consumer goods are declared to be goods ordinarily intended for private use or consumption. There are specific exclusions from the definition including licensed medicinal products on the basis that the Medicines Act provides an existing regime of control. However, *unlicensed* products, such as those supplied on a named patient basis or for clinical trials as part of research, are not excluded.

20.47 Under section 10 of the CPA the liability is imposed upon persons who possess, supply or offer to supply goods that do not comply with the 'general safety requirement'. Goods are deemed to fail to comply with the general safety requirement if they are not reasonably safe taking into account the manner and purpose for which they are marketed and the instructions or warnings provided, published standards of safety relevant to that class of goods and the existence of any means of making the goods safer.

20.48 Products are treated as satisfying the general safety requirement in respect of anything which is attributable to compliance with any requirement imposed by any statute or Community obligation. They also automatically comply if they satisfy the safety regulations imposing requirements in respect of the feature under discussion or they comply with a standard of safety approved for the purposes of Part II of the Act by regulations. It would seem therefore, that adherence to Medicines Act provisions and, as applicable, good clinical practice will go a long way to ensuring that manufacturers do not fall foul of Part II of the Act.[1] A claim under civil law for breach of statutory duty does not arise in respect of contravention of the general safety requirement.

1 The European Community has now adopted a directive on general product safety (92/59/EEC) aimed at prohibiting the supply of unsafe products and giving the Commission power to take Community-wide action if necessary (see OJ L228/24, 11 August 1992). There are no individual sectoral exclusions from this directive, and medicines come within its scope. However, to the extent that there are product safety provisions applicable to specific products (such as those in Directive 65/65/EEC) these supplant the requirements of the general product safety Directive. Thus, medicines will be subject to any of the provisions contained in the general product safety Directive which do not exist in an equivalent form elsewhere in EC rules applicable to medicinal products.

Insurance and financial limits

20.49 The rationale of strict liability has always been that the producer can include the cost of premiums for insurance against his liability in his production costs and in this way risks are spread. Unfortunately, many companies operating in the health care sector have found it difficult to obtain adequate cover recently even in respect of fault liability. The common experience of manufacturers renewing their cover has been of increased excess levels, significantly reduced aggregate limits, product exclusions and rocketing premiums. There have also been attempts by some insurers to write cover only on a 'claims made' basis. The issue of a limit for strict liability exposure was therefore discussed at length when the Directive was under discussion.

20.50 Under article 16 of the Directive member states can provide that a producer's total liability for damage resulting from death or personal injury caused by identical items with the same defect should be limited to an amount of not less than 70m ECU (£55m). This limit is so high (and will apply to each company in a group satisfying the definition of 'producer') that for all practical purposes liability is unlimited even in countries applying the limit.

In the United Kingdom the decision was taken not to limit liability because of the difficulties of deciding what is an identical product with the same defect. In addition, where it looks as though the limit might be exceeded, there is great difficulty in deciding how to apportion compensation between all claimants. It would perhaps be necessary to wait very many years before it could be established how many claims existed and therefore how the limit should be apportioned. Although Germany has incorporated a limit,[1] its implementing legislation does not describe how these issues would be tackled. Meanwhile, in the United Kingdom the liability of producers is unlimited – which mirrors the position with fault liability.

1 See s 10 of the Product Liability Act 1989 (limit DM 160m) but note that the Pharmaceutical Products Act 1976 remains in force and imposes strict liability for defective pharmaceuticals up to an aggregate limit of DM 200m.

LIABILITY OF THE MANUFACTURER IN PRACTICE

20.51 The main bases upon which product liability for manufacturers may arise can conveniently be broken down into four types of product defect: processing defects, packaging defects, design defects and marketing defects. These will be considered in more detail by reference to both fault and strict liability principles, as for some considerable time it is likely that litigation in this area will concern patients whose treatment dates will result in their claims being assessed by reference to fault liability rather than strict liability.

Processing defects

20.52 Where a product is defective because there has been some irregularity in the process of manufacture, with the result that it fails to meet the manufacturer's own specification for the product, it may be said to have a processing or manufacturing defect. Cases of contamination and mistakes of formulation and filling do occur.[1]

1 See report: 'Patients get rogue drug after mix-up' – Guardian, 29 June 1985; involved accidental filling by Organon of ampoules of hydrocortisone sodium succinate (used in shock treatment) with vecuronium bromide (used in anaesthesia).

20.53 If injury does result from such a defect, the manufacturer's position is likely to be a difficult one. Even when applying fault liability principles, this is an area where the courts have shown a particular readiness to reverse the burden of proof. In relation to negligence it is in theory open to a manufacturer to argue that he has a defence because he took reasonable care in operating a comprehensive and generally safe system of manufacture which complied with GMP Guidelines.[1] It now seems arguable that proof of a good system of quality control, even perhaps better than the general industry standard, will not be sufficient where a defect arises which does not ordinarily arise in the manufacturing process. The courts appear to recognise that the injured person is invariably faced with an impossible task in showing by reference to a complex production and delivery process, precisely where the manufacturer failed to take reasonable care. An inference of negligence arises which the manufacturer will be hard pressed to rebut.[2]

1 91/356/EEC OJ 17 July 1991 L193/30 and *Guide to Good Pharmaceutical Manufacturing Practice 1971* (as amended), Department of Health (HMSO).
2 *Hill v James Crowe (Cases) Ltd* [1978] 1 All ER 812.

20.54 Accordingly, in the case of a defectively manufactured medicinal product, provided it is clear that the defect arose while the product was under the manufacturer's control and, for instance, an intermediary did not tamper with the product, a finding of liability in negligence is fairly predictable. The position may be different, of course, if the defect was one which the pharmacist or indeed the patient should have identified. In such a case the manufacturer may properly argue that the causal link has been severed. It will also be different if the 'contamination' can be said to be wholly outside the manufacturer's ability to avoid given the prevailing state of scientific knowledge. An example might be the existence of HIV in blood products prior to the recognition of the virus or the means to screen blood or heat treat products.

20.55 As a matter of strict liability, the user is certainly entitled to expect products to be made according to specification and if a product is not properly made and causes injury strict liability will apply in respect of the defect. In its evidence of 1974 to the Royal Commission on Civil Liability and Compensation for Personal Injury the ABPI accepted that responsibility for such injuries should fall 'unequivocally on the shoulders of the manufacturer' but in practice the record of the industry on quality control is an excellent one.[1]

1 See Memorandum of Evidence of the Association of the British Pharmaceutical Industry to Pearson Commission and to Law Commission Working Paper No 64.

20.56 To reduce their exposure to such claims, it is crucial for manufacturers to maintain a proper procedure for recall. While it is a condition of the grant of a product licence that such procedures exist,[1] a claim in negligence could arise because a company did not follow it properly, even if – as might be the case with a recall based on realisation of a design defect – the initial supply of the product would not have attracted liability in negligence or strict liability.[2] In principle, the failure of a third party to act upon a properly advertised and organised recall, might allow the manufacturer to argue that the injury in any particular case was caused not by the defect in the product but by the intervening negligence of the third party but it is worth noting that, as far as strict liability is concerned, article 8(1) of the Directive provides that without prejudice to national laws governing contribution and indemnity the liability of the producer 'shall not be reduced when the damage is caused both by a defect in the product and by the act or omission of a third party'.

1 See para 6 of Pt I of Sch 1 to the Medicines (Standard Provisions for Licences and Certificates) Regulations 1971 (SI 1971/972) as amended.
2 *Walton v British Leyland (UK) Ltd* (1978) Times, 13 July. Referenced in *Products Liability Casebook* (Lloyds of London Press Ltd, 1984).

20.57 It should be noted, however, that the producer has a defence to strict liability if the defect which caused the damage did not exist at the time when the product was supplied (see article 7(b) and CPA, section 4(1)(d)). Therefore, if on the evidence it is probable that the defect arose after supply, perhaps through poor storage, the application of inapplicable labelling, or the removal of product information from the package subsequent to supply, the defence may be applicable. Inadequate labelling for specific markets and deterioration through improper storage has been a concern in relation to parallel importing and the defence could be relevant here. Equally, some doctors direct the pharmacist to remove patient leaflets from original packs and indeed some Family Planning Clinics substitute their own leaflets for those of manufacturers when prescribing contraceptive preparations and products. This could be of significance as manufacturers' leaflets tend to contain increasingly comprehensive information and warnings (see para **20.89**).

20.58 In terms of fault liability, manufacturers of raw materials or component parts must take care to see that their products do not suffer from any manufacturing defects but difficulties can arise because often such products can be used for a variety of purposes and in many different situations. The manufacturer supplying them does not always know the use to which his product will be put. His basic obligation is, therefore, to deliver a product manufactured to the correct specification. If an inappropriate use was clearly foreseeable he might be obliged under fault liability principles to issue a warning as to the limits of his product's suitability but otherwise his position is fairly secure.

20.59 Under strict liability principles if the defective nature of the finished product arises from a deficiency in a raw material or component part then the producer of the relevant material or part component will be liable jointly with the producer of the finished product. In such circumstances there would exist no liability on the part of producers of other component parts that were not defective. However, the peculiar difficulties for manufacturers of raw materials and components are recognised by the Directive in that such producers have a specific defence if they can show that the defect in their product was wholly attributable to the design of the finished product or to compliance, by the producer of the raw material or component part, with instructions given by the producer of the finished product (see article 7(f) and section 4(1)(f) of CPA). The position of such manufacturers is therefore largely protected unless they fail to meet the specification.

Packaging defects

20.60 Under fault liability principles the manufacturer must take reasonable care in developing his packaging and may be exposed to liability in respect of defects which, for instance, render the product subject to deterioration. Under strict liability, the definition of a defective product requires consideration of 'get-up' (see section 3(2)(a)) which would appear wide enough to encompass the quality of and design of packaging such as whether it is child-proof.

20.61 Interesting questions have arisen in relation to the design of tamper free – or more properly tamper evident – containers given the increased incidence of intentional tampering and blackmail of health care companies, so graphically illustrated by the Tylenol incident in the USA. The manufacturer may argue that he took reasonable care to see that the integrity of the product was not compromised prior to the time it left his control and that he has a statutory defence to strict liability because it was not defective when he supplied it. However, if such seals are technically and economically practicable to incorporate, it might be argued that the product has a design defect and does not offer reasonable safety. Clearly the issue of a causal relationship between defect and injury will arise in any event, but thus far, even in the USA, claims based on the existence of a design flaw have tended to be unsuccessful.[1]

1 See, for instance, *Elsroth v Johnson and Johnson*, US District Court, Southern New York, 700 F Supp 151, (1988) US Dist Lexis 13167.

Design defects

20.62 Clearly any product may suffer from a design defect which makes it intrinsically unsafe for the majority of foreseeable users, regardless of whether it has been manufactured correctly according to the manufacturer's specification. The concept of safety has always been difficult to apply to medicinal products where safety is more than ever relative. However, in principle under fault liability the manufacturer has to decide whether the level of risk associated with a product is acceptable, bearing in mind the benefits ('risk-utility/benefit test'). The task of the manufacturer is to take all reasonable steps to exclude the risks that are avoidable and by appropriate user/prescribing information minimise the risks that remain.

20.63 In this regard, a distinction has to be drawn between non-liability for allergic/idiosyncratic reactions and liability for extreme reactions to a medicinal product that is known to cause injury of the type suffered by the patient in question. If the adverse reaction itself was due to idiosyncrasy, which by definition is an abnormal and sporadic response and of an unpredictable nature, the manufacturer should not be exposed to liability. It is a reaction that no amount of care on his part can guard against and therefore the issue of negligence should not arise. On the other hand if the injury sustained is not due to idiosyncrasy and is of a type, given the design of the product, which the manufacturer ought reasonably to have foreseen as a real risk and therefore should have made the subject of a warning, the fact that the patient possibly suffered an extreme reaction peculiar to him would not assist the manufacturer. He may be liable for all the consequences of pain and suffering that flow from the initial injury even if such injury was exacerbated by an abnormal physical susceptibility on the patient's part.[1]

1 *Smith v Leech Brain & Co Ltd* [1962] 2 QB 405, [1961] 3 All ER 1159.

20.64 If it turns out that a medicinal product does suffer from a design defect, the outcome of an action in negligence will depend upon whether the court finds that the manufacturer ought to have foreseen that the dangerous nature of the product was a probable outcome of its design. Such an analysis raised the reasonableness of the steps that were taken to research the qualities of the product. Under English law, the conduct of the manufacturer is to be judged by reference to his actual scientific knowledge or his constructive knowledge, i e the means of knowledge available to him when the product was under development – the so-called 'state of the art'. This actual knowledge may derive from his pre-clinical work and clinical trials (and conceivably research conducted by associated companies) but he will also be treated as having constructive knowledge of the international literature relating to the compound in question or the class of compounds.

20.65 Many of the significant claims in the United Kingdom and elsewhere in the last twenty years have concerned products with design defects or alleged design defects. The incidence of phocomelia following exposure in utero to thalidomide (Distaval) is the classic example, although thalidomide continues to be used successfully in treating certain conditions such as leprosy and has been reported effective in the treatment of ulcers in HIV-sero-positive patients.[1] More recently oculomucocutaneous syndrome and other problems were experienced by patients prescribed practolol (Eraldin) and ICI set up a voluntary scheme of compensation in 1975 as a result. More recently still, litigation occurred in the late 1970s in the United Kingdom based on an alleged link between the use of hormone pregnancy tests and teratogenic effects manifest in the newborn.[2] The alleged association between use of Pertussis vaccine and brain damage[2] and between benoxaprofen (Opren) and liver damage[3] are further examples. Most recently the propensity of neomycin spray to lead to hearing defects when administered to burns was the subject of litigation.[4]

1 See Scrip no 1390, 1 March 1989, p 28.
2 See para **20.4**, n 1, above.
3 See para **20.7**, n 1, above and the personal review of the issues by Dr Ian Shedden, previously vice-president of Lilly Research Laboratories, published in Scrip no 1284, 19 February 1988, p 30.
4 *Mann and Close v Wellcome Foundation Ltd*, para **20.2**, n 2, above.

20.66 Invariably in such litigation allegations about inadequate research on the part of the manufacturer are made. There is, however, a limit in English law to liability for design defects. If a manufacturer does everything that can reasonably be expected of him, but still does not discover the existence of a defect, then under negligence principles this 'development risk' falls upon the consumer rather than the manufacturer. As a general principle, it must be emphasised that, unlike the case with manufacturing defects, a defect of design can arise quite independent of negligence. The courts made it clear long ago that if strict liability was to be imposed upon manufacturers in these circumstances, it was for Parliament so to enact[1] and in recent cases concerning deafness said to have resulted from the use of neomycin spray Waterhouse J (obiter) rejected the suggestion that pharmaceuticals belong to the category of things dangerous per se and therefore subject to strict liability principles at common law.[2]

1 *Read v J Lyons & Co Ltd* [1947] AC 156, [1946] 2 All ER 471, HL.
2 See *Mann and Close v Wellcome Foundation Ltd*, para **20.2**, n 2, above.

20.67 However, although strict liability has now been introduced through the CPA, application to design defects remains uncertain. If a product does prove to be unsafe for the majority of users it is likely to be found defective. However, liability will not automatically arise because the Directive (see article 7(e)) allows a defence for the producer where 'the state of scientific and technical knowledge at the time when [the producer] put the product into circulation was not such as to enable the existence of the defect to be discovered'. Most member states have retained this 'development risks defence'.

20.68 The implications of this defence were criticised by consumers in the United Kingdom as reintroducing concepts of negligence into strict liability, which in its purest form would not depend upon showing that the manufacturer was at fault. However, the Directive represents a compromise between the conflicting interests of consumer and producer and in any event, whereas under negligence the burden is upon the injured person to prove that the manufacturer should have been aware of the defect given the state of the art at the time he supplied the product, under strict liability the producer must prove as a defence that he could not have discovered the defect.

20.69 The burden of proof is therefore reversed and the courts will no doubt impose an exacting standard in respect of research and monitoring international literature. Courts may not take as lenient a view as Mustill J (as he then was) took in *Thompson v Smiths Shiprepairers (North Shields) Ltd*. This case concerned knowledge of the risks of noise and the means to avoid it and the judge noted that 'great pains' had been taken to comb the literature for references that the defendants should have heeded, but he added:[1]

> One must be careful when considering documents culled for the purpose of a trial, and studied by reference to a single isolated issue, not to forget that they once formed part of a flood of print on numerous aspects of industrial life, in which many items were bound to be overlooked. However conscientious the employer, he cannot read every textbook and periodical, attend every exhibition and conference, on every technical issue which might arise in the course of his business; nor can he necessarily be expected to grasp the importance of every single item which he comes across.

1 *Thompson v Smiths Shiprepairers (North Shields) Ltd* [1984] 1 All ER 881 at 894. See also *Roe v Minister of Health* [1954] 2 QB 66, [1954] 2 All ER 131, CA.

20.70 The problems of establishing, at any particular time, the limits of the state of the art in a fast developing industry will often be considerable. It has been suggested by some commentators that keeping records of technical knowledge at particular times (including the specification and product information of competitor products) may be helpful in later litigation but whether a comprehensive record tailored to litigation is really practicable must be doubtful.

20.71 At first blush, the form of words used in the Directive to describe the development risks defence omits any reference to the practicability of the measures that might enable the defect to be discovered. In contrast, under negligence principles the producer only has to show that his conduct has been reasonable and this must involve some assessment of the cost and practicability of the steps that might have enabled him to discover the 'defect' and adjust the design or incorporate a warning. It is estimated that the larger pharmaceutical companies already spend 10–15 per cent of their annual turnover on research and development.[1] Research and development is ultimately a compromise that takes account of what is scientifically and commercially practical and nowhere is the position more acute than in the research of new medicinal products.

1 See 'Rising research costs add strain', Financial Times, 22 March 1989.

20.72 Although drugs are tested in laboratory animals before being administered to humans, the extrapolation of such results to man is a difficult task, even if one is satisfied that the most suitable animal models have been found. Frequently, as the laboratory work must be in a limited number of animals, it will identify a problem only where the numerical chance of an adverse reaction occurring is high. The question quickly becomes 'What incidence of adverse effect is it reasonable to try to detect.' The same issue arises at the clinical research stage. As Professor William Asscher has remarked:[1]

> Even with the drugs used for the treatment of common disorders, clinical experience may be limited to use in 2–3,000 patients by the time a new drug receives its licence. The rationale for this policy is that the hazards of a new drug are more likely to be discovered when it is used extensively in clinical practice, rather than under the artificial circumstances of a clinical trial.

1 A W Asscher, Paper entitled 'Developments in Risk Assessment and Management' presented at a conference on Risk in Medicine, 28–29 April 1988, London.

20.73 Where a risk may be small numerically but severe in impact, it remains impracticable to detect it by clinical research – it is simply not possible to recruit to studies sufficient volunteers to give studies the statistical power to produce reliable results. Information about a product is gained from healthy volunteer studies and clinical trials but in practice no programme of testing that is feasible, commercially or practically, will enable a manufacturer to say that he has isolated all possible risks. The real test is widespread marketing.

20.74 However, after a rare side-effect becomes manifest from such marketing, a claimant might argue that, even if clinical research to identify that effect was impracticable, the defect would have been observed if the drug in question had been tested in very large numbers of primates rather than the limited numbers of rodents and other smaller laboratory animals that it is normal to test drugs upon. If the incidence of a very serious side effect would have been established if the drug had been tested on 10,000 baboons, will not the injured person argue that the state of scientific knowledge was such that the defect could technically have been discovered?

20.75 The interpretation of the wording of the development risks defence is, therefore, very important. It is worth noting that in the United States the majority of jurisdictions in effect allow a development risk defence and incorporate a concept of reasonableness or 'practical technological feasibility'. Even in California, where it seemed this might not be the case, the Court of Appeals has recently declared that under strict liability principles as applied to design defects in products such as pharmaceuticals, there is in practice no real difference between the negligence standard and the strict liability standard. Policy issues seem slowly to be coming to the surface, for the court[1] remarked:

> Perhaps a drug might be made safer if it was withheld from the market until scientific skill and knowledge advanced to the point at which additional dangerous side effects would be revealed. But in most cases such a delay in marketing new drugs – added to the delay required to obtain approval for release of the product from the Food and Drug Administration – would not serve the public welfare. Public policy favours the development and marketing of beneficial new drugs, even though some risks,

perhaps serious ones, might accompany their introduction, because drugs can save lives and reduce pain and suffering.

If drug manufacturers were subject to strict liability, they might be reluctant to undertake research programmes to develop some pharmaceuticals that would prove beneficial or to distribute others that are available to be marketed, because of the fear of large adverse monetary judgments. Further, the additional expense of insuring against such liability – assuming insurance would be available – and of research programmes to reveal possible dangers not detectable by available scientific methods could place the cost of medication beyond the reach of those who need it most.

1 *Brown v Abbott Laboratories* Supreme Court of California, 44 Cal (3d) 1049, 751 P2d 470 (1988). Compare rejection of the defence in an asbestos case – *Beshada v Johns-Manville Products Corpn* 1988 CCH Prod Liab Rep P9344, 90 NJ 191, 447 A 2d 539, 33 ALR 4th 353.

20.76 In the USA inhibitory effects on research of product liability litigation in certain therapeutic areas, notably vaccines and contraception has finally become manifest.[1] Mindful of this, HM's government made it clear in a minute of the Council of Ministers that it interprets the development risks defence as incorporating some consideration of what it is reasonable to expect the manufacturer to discover. In contrast, France minuted that in its view economics have no relevance to the scientific question of whether a defect is discoverable. Given that a purposive approach to the interpretation of Directives is required, and the narrow interpretation would rob the defence of most of its value for the innovative company, it is suggested that there is a strong case for saying discoverability must incorporate some consideration of economic feasibility.

1 See The Economist, 8 October 1988, p 59 and Scrip no 1367, 7 December 1988, p 16.

20.77 The text of the CPA (see section 4(1)(e)) reflects HM's governments approach. It states that the defence arises where:

> The state of scientific and technical knowledge at the relevant time was not such that the producer of products of the same description as the product in question might be expected to have discovered the defect if it had existed in his products while they were under his control.

20.78 During debate in the House of Lords it was decided to revise the text of the defence so that it followed the wording of the Directive more closely. However, a special committee of the House of Commons reviewing the proposed law returned the text to its original form. The debate continues, and the Consumer Association has complained to the European Commission that the United Kingdom has not implemented the Directive properly in this respect. On 22 December 1988, the Commission announced an intention to bring infringement proceedings under article 169 of the Treaty of Rome against the UK in respect of their interpretation of the defence but the proceedings have still not commenced. The matter will ultimately have to be resolved by the European Court.

20.79 It should be noted that the CPA implicitly contemplates a situation where a manufacturer has a defence to liability in circumstances where he acquired knowledge of a harmful characteristic of his product before its administration but after its date of supply by him. A claim in negligence may, however, arise for failure to use that after-acquired knowledge reasonably by issuing warnings or (depending upon the hazard in question) organising a recall. Such issues clearly were relevant to the carefully organised initiative of the Aspirin Foundation, in notifying the trade, doctors and patients of the suspicion that the use of aspirin in young children had been associated with an increased risk of developing Reye's syndrome, at the time they discontinued 'junior' formulations of that popular analgesic.[1] Interestingly, the wording of the CPA (see section 4(2)) would appear to result in a situation where a mere supplier of the product, who is nevertheless strictly liable because he cannot identify the producer or his own supplier, will not be able to claim the protection of the development risk defence where the knowledge of hazard was known at the time he supplied the product, although not known when the producer supplied it to him.

1 See Hansard 24 July 1986, pp 814–822.

Marketing defects and warnings

20.80 The absence of satisfactory product information can turn an intrinsically safe product into an unsafe product and given the nature of its products, the 'failure to warn' claim is very familiar to the pharmaceutical industry. The prevailing interest in consent issues and disclosure of risks by doctors to patients can only increase this type of litigation.[1]

1 See, for instance, *Sidaway v Board of Governors of the Bethlem Royal Hospital and the Maudsley Hospital* [1985] AC 871, [1985] 1 All ER 643, HL.

20.81 As regards fault liability, part of any duty of care found to be owed by a manufacturer to a consumer is undoubtedly to formulate and supply adequate information about the product, so that it can be used safely. The essence of a warning is that it allows the user to confront and avoid the hazard which it describes. The location and prominence of warnings, as well as their existence, may be important particularly with products promoted direct to the public. If the manufacturer supplies a proper warning in his technical information about the product and the user or intermediary ignores that warning, then the causal link between the manufacturer's action in putting the product on the market and the injury to the user is broken and no liability will result.

20.82 It is settled English law, however, that the duty to supply information may in certain circumstances be discharged by supplying the relevant information to a responsible intermediary.[1] In the field of medicinal products available on prescription, it is accepted English law that the doctor is such an intermediary, although the concept has been challenged in Canada in a case where the issue of a warning direct to patients using oral contraceptives was found to be practicable and necessary.[2] The basic rule is reflected in section 96 of the Medicines Act 1968 which provides that a licence holder may not promote a product to doctors unless those doctors have been supplied with a data sheet about the product in the prescribed form. Information to doctors is traditionally supplied by inclusion of data sheets in the compendium of products prepared by the Association of the British Pharmaceutical Industry and supplied free to all registered medical practitioners.[3] The Medicines Act does not provide that such information must be supplied by manufacturers to patients. However, if a manufacturer wishes to rely upon the right to supply information only to doctors, it is important to ensure that such information is adequate. Regulations[4] made under the Medicines Act prescribe the form that data sheets must take. A Medicines Act Leaflet[5] issued by the Department of Health describes the purpose of data sheets as being to provide 'an objective statement in a convenient form for reference, giving essential particulars about the medical product'. These particulars include '*main* side-effects and adverse reactions *likely* to be associated with the product' (emphasis added) and therefore do not contemplate an exhaustive statement about the drug or proper medical practice in its use but rather a practical guide to the nature of the product.

1 *Holmes v Ashford* [1950] 2 All ER 76, CA; and *Kubach v Hollands* [1937] 3 All ER 907.
2 *Buchan v Ortho Pharmaceutical (Canada) Ltd* (1984) 46 OR (2d) 113.
3 Reg 2(1)(b) of the Medicines (Data Sheet) Regulations 1972 (SI 1972/2076).
4 MAL 25. Department of Health (Revised May 1985).
5 The Medicines (Data Sheet) Regulations 1972 (SI 1972/2076) (as amended).

20.83 The need for and adequacy of warnings in relation to medicinal products will depend upon a number of factors but primarily upon the magnitude of the risk both in terms of the numerical chance of it occurring and the seriousness of the injury that might result. The manufacturer may justifiably take into account the knowledge he knows the reasonable prescriber will have from other sources, but that does not mean the manufacturer can justify a general failure to warn on the grounds that the industrious prescriber could have obtained the information from elsewhere, if only he had searched properly. In practice, research shows[1] that doctors in the UK obtain information from a variety of sources including established reference sources such as The British National Formulary (published by the British Medical Association and The Pharmaceutical Society of Great Britain and supplied to all NHS doctors) and MIMS – the Monthly Index of Medical Specialties (an independent monthly publication of the Haymarket Press sent free to full-time general practitioners and heads of hospital pharmacy departments). It would appear that these sources are more influential than the manufacturer's data sheet but the latter's status under the Medicines Act means that its contents are frequently the focus of litigation. In principle, however, to show a causal link between any alleged 'failure to warn' by the manufacturer and the injury sustained by the claimant, it would be necessary to show that the prescriber relied upon the manufacturer's prescribing information and his actions would have been different were it not for the postulated breach of duty in relation to the supply of adequate product information.

1 See for instance G Eaton and P Parish (1976) Journal of the Royal College of General Practitioners (Suppl no 1) 22, 64–68 and R R Miller (1974) Drug Intelligence and Clinical Pharmacology 8, 81–91.

20.84 The most difficult problem in developing prescribing information is, however, deciding the level of suspicion that is required to justify a contraindication or warning of possible adverse effects. In this regard, it may not always be appropriate for a manufacturer to wait for a risk to be proven before inserting a warning. In determining the level of suspicion that should trigger a warning the manufacturer must take into account a variety of factors including the benefit to be derived from the drug and the alternative treatment possibilities. The less serious is the illness to be treated, the greater the onus, it is argued, upon the manufacturer to advise the doctor –

and through him the patient – of the possibility of a serious adverse reaction, even if the evidence of hazard in man is only flimsy or is based on animal evidence of questionable extrapolability. A Canadian Court applying English law principles has emphasised that where medical evidence exists which indicates the possibility of a serious adverse effect, it is not reasonable for the manufacturer to ignore that information because he finds it unconvincing.[1] Equally, this does not mean that the manufacturer cannot exercise some judgment about the validity of data adverse to his product and indeed as prescribing information is developed by industry doctors for doctors, it might be argued that provided, when developing that information the manufacturer's medical staff adopt an approach that would be supported by a respectable body of scientific opinion, neither they personally nor the manufacturer will have been negligent.

1 See *Buchan v Ortho Pharmaceutical* para **20.82**, n 2, above. An immediate obligation to disclose a suspicion of hazard was found in *Wells v Ortho Pharmaceutical Corpn* 615 F Supp 262 at 294 (DC Ga 1985). See also *McColl v Strathclyde Regional Council* 1983 SLT 616 in relation to possible carcinogenic risks of fluoridation of water supply.

20.85 Even if the defect was 'unknowable' when a product was first designed and marketed, an injured person may still be able to show that at some later date the manufacturer was in a position to establish the existence of the defect, as a result perhaps of new information available in the technical literature or reports of adverse events involving that type of product. This situation was the basis of ICI's liability in *Wright v Dunlop Rubber Company*[1] where the court found that although ICI did not initially realise that a chemical they were supplying to Dunlop was a carcinogen, they later should have taken note of increasing evidence that it had this property. There is increasing importance attached by manufacturers and the regulatory authorities to systematic post-marketing surveillance, especially in the case of the products of biotechnology where traditional 'screening' methods at the research stage are inapplicable. Withdrawal from the market in the face of the results of such surveillance is now quite frequent and often controversial.[2]

1 *Wright v Dunlop Rubber Co Ltd* (1972) 13 KIR 255, CA.
2 See generally Scrip no 1303, 27 April 1988. The worldwide withdrawal by Hoechst of nomifensine in the face of a risk of drug induced immune haemolytic anaemia reported in the international literature and to regulatory authorities through the ADR system is an illustration of the importance of post-marketing surveillance. (See Lancet, 5 November 1988, p 1059.) Moreover Riker Laboratories somewhat controversially discontinued its laxative, Dorbanex (danthron/poloxamer) in the light of data derived from animal studies that danthron could have caused tumours of the liver and bowel (see Lancet, 31 January 1987, p 287). More recently Kabi Pharmacia decided in September 1991 to discontinue its product Micturin (terodiline) world-wide following concern about a possible association with rare cardiac reactions and later decided that the discontinuation should be permanent bearing in mind the methodological and other difficulties of proving the absence of a causal relationship.

20.86 Positive statements about safety made through promotional material and statements by company representatives when detailing products may affect the status of product information. An otherwise adequate warning may be judged ineffective if issued against the background of advertising copy which seeks to deny the existence of any danger that is the subject matter of the warning.[1] The 'dilution of warnings' in this way may lead to liability on the part, not only of the manufacturer, but also possibly, advertising agencies and others who have developed or approved the promotion in question.

1 See, for instance, *Love v Wolf, Parke Davies & Co* 38 Cal Reptr 183 (1964).

20.87 In relation to strict liability, the Directive makes it clear that instructions for use and warnings will have a major bearing upon whether the product is deemed to offer the safety that the public are entitled to expect. In describing the considerations relevant to the existence of a defect, section 3(2) of the CPA raises the purposes for which the product is marketed and the manner of its marketing. Equally, it is thought that the courts will look closely not only at instructions and warnings supplied with the product but also the wider activities of the producer in promoting his product which would appear to be covered by the expression 'manner of marketing'. Expectations of safety may inadvertently be created by advertising that information provided with, or in connection with, the product will be unable to qualify satisfactorily. A Directive[1] on advertising has now been adopted and both the Licensing Authority and the Association of the British Pharmaceutical Industry, through the newly formed Prescription Medicines Code of Practice Authority, are increasingly vigilant in monitoring the accuracy of advertising with a view to ensuring that the safety and efficacy of products are not 'over-sold'.[2] Advertising for products available over-the-counter requires prior approval under the Code of Practice of the Proprietary Association of Great Britain.[3]

1 92/28/EEC OJ 30 April 1992, L113/13.
2 *R v Roussel Laboratories and Good* (1988) 153 JP 298, CA, and the *Code of Practice for the Pharmaceutical Industry* (8th edn, 1 January 1993), Association of the British Pharmaceutical Industry.
3 The Proprietary Association of Great Britain Code of Standards of Advertising Practice 1994.

20.88 In relation to all these matters the CPA would not appear directly to undermine the principle that the informational activities of the manufacturer of medicinal products can properly be concentrated upon an intermediary – the prescribing doctor. More generally, it is suggested that although a high standard of product information will be required there can be no absolute standard for such information and it is difficult to see how its adequacy can be judged by anything other than the same concept of what is reasonable given the state of scientific knowledge as has been considered in the context of negligence. A decision to add a warning after reassessment of the literature will not be taken automatically as an admission of prior negligence.[1]

1 See *Hart v Lancashire and Yorkshire Rly Co* (1869) 21 LT 261 at 263.

20.89 A major issue in Europe at present is patient information. Directive 75/319/EEC[1] set out requirements for the contents of any leaflets provided with a medicinal product but there was no requirement that manufacturers provide leaflets. Directive 89/341/EEC[2] amended the Directive to make leaflets compulsory but, before implementation in Member States, Directive 92/27/EEC[3] legislated for revised and extended heads of information unless the required information appears on the container or packaging. The European Directives contemplate original pack dispensing which will be necessary if the provision of increasingly lengthy leaflets is to be practicable. Further Directives are envisaged on specific aspects of leaflets. Amending

Regulations under the Medicines Act[4] implement the latest Directive and now require a leaflet for all products first licensed after 1 January 1994 and for existing products when the product licence is first renewed after that date. The licence-holder must obtain an approval for its text from the Licensing Authority before supplying it with a product. Although the entries are required to be compatible with the Summary of Product Characteristics, there remains a lack of consensus as to how detailed such entries should be for some matters such as contra-indications and side effects. In the UK, prior to the adoption of 92/27/EEC, the Association of the British Pharmaceutical Industry[5] and the Department of Health[6] have argued that some selectivity is necessary in order to meet the principal aim of providing understandable information of practical benefit to the patient. Some commentators too have noted that

> Life would be impossible if every practitioner, let alone every patient, were to be exposed to all available data and were expected to take all postulated risks into account before prescribing or using a drug.[7]

Nevertheless, consistency in approach from Member State to Member State appears a long way off and the text and presentation of leaflets in the meantime seems likely to spawn its own rash of litigation.

1 75/319/EEC, OJ 9 June 1975, L147/13.
2 89/341/EEC, OJ 25 May 1989, L142/11; see art 2, para 2.
3 92/27/EEC, OJ 30 April 1992, L113.
4 The Medicines (Leaflet) Amendment Regulations 1992 (SI 1992/3274).
5 'Information to Patients on Medicines', Association of the British Pharmaceutical Industry 1987.
6 Evidence to the Select Committee of the House of Lords (HL Paper 77, 1990 HMSO).
7 Dukes & Swartz: *Responsibility for Drug Induced Injury* (1988, Elsevier).

20.90 In the light of strict liability, manufacturers will undoubtedly reassess the accuracy of their information to doctors (and the reasons for any inconsistency between markets) but the manufacturer's legal position will seldom be better than when he can show that the patient's safety expectations were directly qualified by supply of a patient-orientated package leaflet. On the other hand the difficulties of making inherently technical information understandable cannot be underestimated and detailed information may serve only to confuse the patient. Keeping patient information up to date and broadly consistent with the relevant data sheet poses administrative problems for the manufacturer and if the manufacturer is selective about what he tells patients in his leaflet, he may be challenged.

20.91 Misuse is another important issue. In determining whether a product is defective, the CPA states that one consideration is what might reasonably be expected to be done with or in relation to the product (see section 3(2)(b)). Typically, warnings have been related in the pharmaceutical industry to the recommended use of the products particularly if the product in question is only available through the intervention of a doctor. Although the position is somewhat unclear, it is thought that the law relating to liability for gross misuse by a patient will not change radically as a result of strict liability and indeed contributory negligence is retained (see article 8(2) of the Directive and section 6(4) of CPA) but the manufacturer will be well advised to consider issues of possible misuse particularly in relation to products available OTC.[1] Moreover, if he knows of 'misuse' by prescribers which he believes may be hazardous then there is good reason to consider the issue of a warning through the medium of a 'Dear Doctor' letter.

1 Even with products available POM, the decision of the Frankfurt Appellate Court requiring more detailed warnings with an Orciprenalin aerosol for asthma illustrates the trend. (see BGH, NJW 1989, 1542 FF).

PHARMACISTS, IMPORTERS AND OTHER INTERMEDIARIES

20.92 The retail pharmacist's liability in negligence is, in principle, the same as that of the manufacturer – to take reasonable care to avoid causing injury to others – but it is more limited in scope. He must undertake a reasonable inspection and isolate obvious defects, eg products that are obsolete or damaged in such a way as to be hazardous. He should not, therefore, be liable for manufacturing or design defects unless he could have discovered their existence by reasonably practical inspection or testing.

20.93 Pharmacists may also be exposed to claims in respect of hazards they have created or to which they have contributed, eg by failing to supply product leaflets intended by the manufacturer to be passed to the user or failing to note an obvious error by the prescribing doctor when writing a prescription.[1] Persons such as wholesalers acting merely as a conduit between manufacturer and pharmacist or other 'retailer' also owe the ultimate user a duty to exercise reasonable care but they too would not normally be expected to carry out independent inspection or testing. If their own supplier is reputable they should only be liable for obvious defects and defects they create themselves such as through improper handling.

1 *Prendergast v Sam & Dee Ltd* (1989) Times, 14 March, CA.

20.94 The courts in some countries are minded to treat all companies within a recognised group as one entity when considering liability. In the Canadian case of *Phillips v Ford Motor Co of Canada Ltd*[1] the court treated the defendant as if he had been responsible for the manufacture and design of the defective vehicle, even though, in fact, the car had been designed and manufactured by the American parent company and not the Canadian subsidiary. If justice requires it, the English court might in terms of testing and assessment impose a greater burden under fault liability upon a person importing a product from a manufacturer in the same group of companies but in principle he will not be found negligent for failing to notice a latent defect.[2]

1 *Phillips v Ford Motor Co of Canada Ltd* (1970) 12 DLR (3d) 28.
2 *Goodchild v Vaclight* [1965] CLY 2669.

20.95 Under strict liability it has been seen that importers from outside the Community are treated as producers and strictly liable for product defects. However, other intermediaries such as wholesalers will not seemingly be subject to strict liability unless they imported the defective finished product direct from outside the Community or failed to keep a proper record of who was the producer of a product supplied to them or at least the immediate supplier. In any event, identifying the producer is not going to be a common problem in the case of most branded medicinal products.

20.96 Pharmacists and doctors in the United Kingdom will not be subject to strict liability unless they manufacture their own medicines, import them direct from outside the Community or fail to keep proper records identifying the product supplied or at least their immediate supplier.

LICENSING AUTHORITY AND THE MEDICINES ACT COMMITTEES

20.97 It is a common misconception that the Licensing Authority which sanctions the manufacture and distribution of medicines is the Committee on the Safety of Medicines (CSM). In fact the Licensing Authority 'responsible for the grant, renewal, variation, suspension and revocation of licences and certificates' (see section 6(1) of the Medicines Act) is 'a body of Ministers consisting of all the Ministers specified in paragraphs (a) and (b) of section 1(1) of the Medicines Act 1968. The CSM is one of the Committees set up by the Ministers under section 4 of the Act to 'give advice with respect to safety, quality or efficacy' of medicines and to promote 'the collection and investigation of information relating to adverse reactions, for the purpose of enabling such advice to be given'.

20.98 Undoubtedly the Licensing Authority relies very heavily on the advice of the CSM in deciding which products to licence and upon what terms and subject to which conditions. This is because the Licensing Authority has placed upon the CSM the responsibility for assessing product licence applications for new products and investigating the adequacy of the data upon which such applications are based. Applicants for licences may appeal to the Medicines Commission (a body corporate established by section 2 of the Medicines Act to advise the Minister on all aspects of the Act and medicinal products) if the Licensing Authority indicates that the advice of the CSM is adverse to the grant of a licence on the terms of the application. Nonetheless the final decision about the grant etc of licences under the Act must always rest with the Licensing Authority properly so called and therefore if it is to be suggested that a licence has been negligently granted it would be incorrect merely to make allegations against the CSM or Medicines Commission.

20.99 To date the focus in litigation has been upon advice given by the CSM, although similar principles to those discussed below would apply in relation to the Commission. It would be difficult to argue that, applying the now well-established test of proximity, a duty is not owed to members of the public by the Licensing Authority to take reasonable care in or about the discharge of their statutory obligations under the Act and the regulations pursuant to which the CSM was established. Recent decisions concerned with other areas of economic activity[1] have raised questions as to whether a public body of this type owes obligations to the public as a matter of private law but on the assumption that the Licensing Authority does owe a duty of care to patients, in each case it would be necessary to consider the individual contributions of the CSM and the Licensing Authority to the decision to grant a licence. Thus if the Licensing Authority granted a licence in spite of the contrary advice of the CSM it would be difficult to see what more the CSM could have done to fulfil its obligations owed to the public. If on the other hand the Licensing Authority followed the recommendations of the

CSM, then if the CSM were negligent it is difficult to see how the Licensing Authority could be impugned unless the negligence of the CSM was so obvious that the Licensing Authority ought itself to have recognised this and acted in respect of it.

1 See, for instance, *Peabody Donation Fund (Governors) v Sir Lindsay Parkinson & Co Ltd* [1985] AC 210, [1984] 3 All ER 529, HL; *Yuen Kun Yeu v A-G of Hong Kong* [1988] AC 175, [1987] 2 All ER 705 and *Rowling v Takaro Properties Ltd* [1988] AC 473, [1988] 1 All ER 163, PC.

20.100 In addition to the CSM there are a number of other committees established under section 4 of the Act. For the purposes of this chapter the only other committee worthy of special mention would appear to be the Committee on the Review of Medicines (CRM) which is now disbanded but was charged with the task of reviewing product licences and licences of right (the latter were issued on implementation of the licensing provisions of the Act in 1971 where the product was on the market already). It would be difficult to argue that that Committee did not also owe a duty of care to the public as to the way it discharged its statutory obligations and in certain circumstances it could also be made defendant to an action in negligence at the suit of an individual or individuals who had suffered damage.

20.101 While both the CSM and the Licensing Authority have been made defendants to actions in negligence (examples are the multi-plaintiff litigation which arose out of the marketing of the drug benoxaprofen (Opren) and proceedings concerning the marketing of blood products), the extent to which the exercise of their statutory obligations can be the subject of a negligence action has yet to be determined by the courts. In the first of the Pertussis vaccine cases tried in this country the position of the Department of Health and Social Security was considered in relation to the way in which it promoted vaccination as a policy under the provisions of the National Health Service Acts. In *Kinnear v DHSS*,[1] Stuart-Smith J (as he then was) considered claims brought against the DHSS by persons who claimed that they had suffered injury as a result of a reaction to inoculation with whooping cough vaccine. He decided that those claims did not disclose any reasonable cause of action and would be struck out in so far as they were based upon the formulation and promotion by the Department of a policy which resulted from a bona fide exercise of this statutory discretion, but would not be struck out in so far as they alleged that the Department had given negligent or misleading advice to local health authorities regarding the circumstances in which such inoculations should be performed and the factors to be applied in determining whether a given individual should or should not be inoculated. The judge decided, relying on the judgment of Lord Wilberforce in *Anns v Merton London Borough Council*,[2] that actions by the Department of an 'operational' rather than of a 'policy' nature were actionable if done negligently and that it was at least arguable that advice as to immunisation provided from time to time by the Department fell within the operational scope of the Department's activities.

1 *Department of Health and Social Security v Kinnear* (1984) 134 NLJ 886.
2 *Anns v Merton London Borough Council* [1978] AC 728 at 754, HL.

20.102 While it is right that recent cases have qualified to a considerable extent the general applicability of the decision of the House of Lords in the case of *Anns*, the decision is still arguably of considerable importance with respect to its consideration of the duty owed by a public authority to the general public to avoid damage or the risk of damage to public heath and safety (as opposed to economic loss) in the performance of its statutory obligations. In this regard the decision is directly relevant to the duty owed by both the Licensing Authority and the CSM and CRM to the public in or about the performance of their statutory obligations. Alternatively, through the use of the 'proximity' test applied in *Murphy v Brentwood District Council*,[1] which effectively overruled *Anns*, a court could readily distance itself from an approach under which actions have to be allocated to either the operational or policy field, even though in applying *Murphy* and similar cases there are grounds for distinguishing circumstances where personal injury is in contemplation, as opposed merely to economic loss.

1 [1990] 2 All ER 908.

20.103 While section 133(2)(a) of the Act expressly provides that the provisions of the Act shall not be construed as conferring a right of action in any civil proceedings in respect of any contravention of the Act, subsection (c) of the same subsection expressly provides that the provisions of the Act shall not be construed as derogating from any right of action or other remedy in proceedings instituted otherwise than under the Act. It follows that there can be nothing to stop a court from considering to what extent a common law duty of care is owed by the Licensing Authority or the statutory committees to members of the public in or about the performance of their obligations and responsibilities under the statute. Nor too would there be anything to prevent a court from holding in a proper case that a negligent failure properly to perform such obligations gives rise to a claim for damages at the suit of an individual or individuals who can show that as a consequence they have suffered personal injury. In *Re HIV Haemophiliac Litigation*[1] the Court of Appeal was required to consider, in the context of a discovery application, whether an arguable case of negligence or breach of statutory duty had been pleaded against the regulatory authorities including the CSM. The court found that the plaintiffs' case on breach of statutory duty was at best of uncertain validity but that the plaintiffs appeared (per Ralph Gibson LJ) 'on their allegations of fact, to have at least a good arguable claim in law based upon common law negligence'. On this basis, and as it was not argued that the documents were relevant to only one of the causes of action, the court's decision in relation to ordering discovery was not viewed as affected by any apparent weaknesses in the plaintiffs' case. The settlement of that litigation and the dropping of the CSM and Licensing Authority as defendants in the Benzodiazepine litigation means that the issues relating to causes of action remain unresolved.

1 [1990] NLJR 1349, CA.

PROCEDURAL ASPECTS

Foreign manufacturers and parent companies

20.104 The basic approach of the English courts as to jurisdiction has been that of service of proceedings. If it is possible to serve a defendant with proceedings then the court will exercise jurisdiction in respect of the person served. In certain cases, English claimants alleging injury from pharmaceutical products have sought to have their cases heard in American courts against the parent company, on the grounds that control over warnings etc rested with that company, but the companies sued have normally been able to have the cases remitted back to the United Kingdom on the grounds of *forum non conveniens*.[1] Typically, the American court has tended to make the dismissal conditional upon the defendant agreeding to accept service in the jurisdiction where the plaintiff resides, provide documents and witnesses at the defendants' expense, and to waive limitation in so far as such a defence has arisen while the plaintiff was pursuing the case in the foreign court. However, the potential for commencing proceedings merely to gain these ancillary benefits was recently recognised in a case involving Irish plaintiffs suing in the USA in respect of injury allegedly caused by Benzodiazepines licensed in the Republic of Ireland, supplied in Ireland by a UK company and prescribed by Irish physicians to the plaintiffs in Ireland. The court[2] refused to attach conditions to the dismissal on the grounds of *forum non conveniens* saying that the purpose of conditions was to preclude the possibility of defendants being insulated from the plaintiffs claims in the foreign forum and the plaintiffs had not shown that there was any real potential for this. The court added that there was no evidence that the discovery rules in Ireland and the USA were incapable of providing adequate protection in relation to discovery and it viewed limitation issues as irrelevant to the factors in a *forum non conveniens* inquiry.

1 In relation to oral contraceptive litigation see *Harrison v Wyeth Laboratories* 676 F 2d 685 (3W Circ 1982); *Jones v Searle Laboratories* 93 Ill 2nd 366, 67 Ill Dec 118, 44 NE 157 (1982) and *Re British Oral Contraceptive Cases No* L-44473–78 (NJ Super Ct Law Div, 20 July 1981). In contrast see *Holmes v Syntex Laboratories Inc* 156 Cal App 3d 372, 202 Cal Rptr 773 (1987); now disapproved in *Stanqvik v Shiley Inc* Supreme Court of California 1993 IL Pr 173. Regarding benoxaprofen litigation see *McCracken v Eli Lilly & Co* 494 NE 2d 1289 (1986) but in contrast in relation to Dalkon Shield litigation see *Hodson v A H Robins Co Inc* 528 F Supp 809 (E D Va 1981). With regard to blood product litigation see *Dowling v Hyland Therapeutics* 767 F Supp 57 (SDNY 1991).

2 *Oxley v Wyeth Laboratories Inc* (ED Pa 1992).

20.105 Until the Civil Jurisdiction and Judgments Act of 1982 (CJJA) the power of the English courts to exercise jurisdiction over companies resident outside the jurisdiction was provided for by Order 11 of the Rules of the Supreme Court which set out the circumstances in which leave to serve proceedings outside the jurisdiction might be granted. These provisions still apply with respect to non-EC domiciled companies and are considered below. The CJJA was enacted to give effect to the 1968 Brussels Convention on Jurisdiction and Enforcement of Judgments in Civil and Commercial Matters (the Convention) signed by the six original members of the EC and acceded to by the United Kingdom after becoming a Community member.[1] The CJJA provides for a special regime relating to jurisdiction over EC domiciled companies which operates throughout the United Kingdom and replaces previous rules as to jurisdiction and service of proceedings on persons outside the jurisdiction.

1 On 10 September 1988, the 12 Member States of the European Communities and 6 Member States of the European Free Trade Association (ie Austria, Finland, Iceland, Norway, Sweden and Switzerland) adopted the Lugano Convention on Jurisdiction and Enforcement of Judgments in Civil and Commercial Matters, also known as 'the Parallel Convention' as it is closely modelled on the Brussels Convention and is intended to operate alongside it. Although there are differences between the Conventions, they are intended to have a similar

general effect, ie free movement of jurisdiction and enforcement of judgments within Europe. The Parallel Convention is due to come into force following domestic instruments of ratification. Thus far only Finland, France, Ireland, Italy, Luxembourg, the Netherlands, Norway, Portugal, Sweden, Switzerland and the UK have ratified the Convention. The relevant UK legislation is the Civil Jurisdiction and Judgments Act 1991 (amending the CJJA) which came into force in May 1992.

EC-domiciled companies

20.106 The key to the rules on jurisdiction is that a Community-domiciled defendant is, in principle, to be sued in the state where he is domiciled and any issue as to domicile is to be determined by the internal law of the state in which it is alleged he is domiciled. Section 41 of the CJJA provides that to be domiciled in the United Kingdom an individual:

(a) must be resident in the United Kingdom; and
(b) the nature and circumstances of the person's residence must indicate that he has a substantial connection with the United Kingdom.

Article 53 of the Convention requires that the place of the seat of a company is to be treated as its domicile and section 42 of the CJJA provides that a corporation has its seat in the United Kingdom if

(a) it was incorporated or formed under the law of a part of the United Kingdom and has its registered office or some other official address in the United Kingdom; or
(b) its central management and control is exercised in the United Kingdom.

20.107 However, to this basic rule there are a number of exceptions the most important of which is that contained in article 5.3 of the Convention which is relevant to negligence cases.

TORTS

20.108 Article 5.3 states that a party domiciled in a contracting state may be sued in the courts for the place where the harmful event occurred, even if not domiciled there. The European Court has given a wide interpretation to 'harmful event'. Thus in the case of *Bier v Mines des Potasse*,[1] a pollution case in which a Dutch nursery farmer had crop damage due to irrigation of his crops with water polluted by the defendants who were a French mining corporation, the European Court held that article 5.3 referred to both the place where the river was polluted (France) and the place where the damage was suffered (Holland) and that accordingly the Dutch court had jurisdiction to entertain the farmer's claim. Thus an English plaintiff damaged by a pharmaceutical product made for example by a German manufacturer would have the right to sue either in England or in Germany, choosing presumably whichever jurisdiction was most advantageous to him.

1 *Handelswekerij G J Bier BV and Stichting Reinwater v Mines des Potasse d'Alsace SA*: 21/76 [1976] ECR 1735, [1977] 1 CMLR 284, ECJ.

SUBSIDIARY COMPANIES

20.109 Many Community pharmaceutical companies have a local subsidiary company in other European jurisdictions. If the product the subject matter of the litigation was developed by the parent it is often advantageous for the claimant to seek to join the parent as a defendant to the action, if only to obtain orders for discovery of documents held only by the parent. Article 5.5 of the Convention provides that a dispute arising out of the operations of a branch, agency or other establishment within the jurisdiction is sufficient to establish the right to sue the parent even if the parent itself is not domiciled within the jurisdiction. An establishment covers a body with a separate legal personality.[1] The test applied to determine what constitutes a branch or agency turns on the question whether that branch or agency is subject to direction and control by the parent and is largely autonomous in operation but acts on behalf of and binds the parent. It must have a fixed permanent place of business in that jurisdiction. The same principles are likely to be applied in determining whether a parent can be sued in the jurisdiction of a subsidiary. Usually, however, a subsidiary will not act on behalf of its parent company.

1 See *Sar Schotte GmbH v Parfums Rothschild SARL* 218/86 [1987] ECR 4905.

CO-DEFENDANTS

20.110 Article 6 provides for the joining of a co-defendant (or third party) not domiciled in the state exercising jurisdiction in an action against other defendants properly sued within the jurisdiction. Thus if a plaintiff in this country sues the prescribing doctor he would be entitled (quite apart from article 5.3) to join a manufacturer domiciled in Europe in the action if that was thought appropriate. Alternatively the practitioner could join the manufacturer as a third party.

CONTRACT

20.111 Though unlikely to be of significance in this context, it should be noted that there are specific provisions relating to the exercise of jurisdiction over non-domiciled defendants who are parties to contracts which require performance of the contractual obligations within the jurisdiction of the court proceeded in (article 5.1). Moreover a consumer, being a person who has concluded a contract for a purpose outside his trade or profession, can elect to sue either in the country of the contracting state in which he is domiciled or that in which the defendant is domiciled (article 14).

CONFLICTS OF JURISDICTION

20.112 If, as frequently happens, more than one Community court has jurisdiction, then the court first seised of the dispute shall be the only court to try the matter (article 21).

Non-EC-domiciled defendants

20.113 In the case of non-EC domiciled defendants the court will grant leave for service of proceedings out of the jurisdiction only in specific circumstances exclusively set out in Order 11, rule 1 of the Rules of the Supreme Court. The principal circumstances relevant to this chapter are as follows:

Order 11, rule 1(1)(a)
If in the action begun by writ relief is sought against a person domiciled within the jurisdiction

This is similar in effect to the provision of article 6 of the Brussels Convention referred to above.

Order 11, rule 1(1)(c)
If in the action begun by writ the claim is brought against a person duly served within or out of the jurisdiction and a person out of the jurisdiction is a necessary or proper party thereto.

This might be used to argue for service of a foreign parent company of an English company, in circumstances in which (for example) the parent developed the pharmaceutical product in question and the defendant English company manufactured and distributed it.

Order 11, rule 1(1)(f)
If in the action begun by writ the claim is founded on a tort and the damage was sustained, or resulted from an act committed, within the jurisdiction.

This might be used to argue that joinder was appropriate where, for example, the product was developed, manufactured and distributed by a foreign corporation having no licence holding subsidiary within the jurisdiction. While instances of this would be rare, they are by no means impossible.

20.114 Before leave to serve out of the jurisdiction is granted the applicant for leave must show that there is a good arguable case that the jurisdiction under the Order has been established and that the evidence discloses that there is a serious issue to be tried.[1] While Order 11 provides for effecting service out of the jurisdiction with leave of the court it does not follow from the grant of leave itself that the court will automatically exercise jurisdiction. Thus it would be open to a defendant properly served out of the jurisdiction to apply to the court for the service to be set aside. If such application is made the court will determine which is the appropriate court or *forum conveniens* and exercise its discretion accordingly. Many different considerations go to the determination of this question and they include cost and convenience – see *MacShannon v Rockware Glass Ltd*[2] and *Spiliada Maritime Corpn v Cansulex Ltd*.[3]

1 In *Seaconsar Far East Ltd v Bank Markazi Jomhouri Islami Iran* [1993] 4 All ER 456, HL.
2 *Macshannon v Rockware Glass Ltd* [1978] AC 795, [1978] 1 All ER 625, HL.
3 *Spiliada Maritime Corpn v Cansulex Ltd* [1987] AC 460, [1986] 3 All ER 843, HL.

Multi–plaintiff litigation

20.115 Litigation arising out of adverse drug reactions usually involves a large number of plaintiffs and this poses particular problems relating to the handling of the claims for all parties. Experience initially learned from the way in which the courts dealt with these problems in the Opren and Pertussis vaccine cases has been developed in the Benzodiazepine litigation and Myodil litigation and provides some guidance as to how the courts might approach similar cases in the future.[1] However, what follows is only a brief outline of some of the difficulties and the way they were resolved and it is important to stress that any court would be free to pursue its own course in the light of circumstances prevailing before it. These might differ very markedly from cases previously before the court. However it can be said with a fair degree of confidence that any arrangements which have the effect of easing the management problems of conducting such litigation will be welcomed by the court and most particularly if such arrangements can be shown to ease the burden of costs. The desirability of bringing such cases to trial or prior disposal speedily and economically will be a major consideration and to achieve this the court will welcome flexibility and imaginative use of the Rules rather than strict insistence on adherence to their letter.

1 A Guide to Group Actions of the Supreme Court Procedure Committee (1991) also sets out various considerations for plaintiffs and defendants in such litigation.

Service of proceedings and venue

20.116 Normally service of proceedings poses no problems and can be effected either personally or by post. In many instances prior correspondence will have taken place between the parties, and solicitors acting for the proposed defendants will have been authorised to accept service of proceedings on their clients' behalf. If either the Licensing Authority or the CSM or CRM are to be parties then proceedings can be served on them through the Attorney General who is empowered to accept service of any proceedings on any government department where it is a matter of doubt as to how service should be effected (see section 17(3) of the Crown Proceedings Act 1947). Such defendants are usually represented by the Treasury Solicitors and in cases of doubt there is nothing to prevent a party enlisting their assistance as to how service should best be effected.

20.117 If government defendants are brought into the action they are entitled by reason of section 19 of the Crown Proceedings Act 1947 to insist on all such proceedings being pursued against them in the Central Office and therefore proceedings in District Registries will be transferred to London at their option and the trial must take place in the Royal Courts of Justice unless the court with the Crown's consent otherwise orders.

20.118 Quite apart from this it is obviously undesirable that in multi-plaintiff litigation cases should be pursued up and down the country. The courts will look favourably on an application to bring cases into one court centre and the Central Office is usually (but not necessarily always) the obvious venue.[1]

1 In *Re Benzodiazepine Litigation* the Practice Note (6 December 1990) of the Lord Chief Justice noted that the court had no power to order transfer save on the application of a party but delays in the disposal of summonses in the litigation caused by a failure to transfer would probably have cost consequences.

Nomination of judge and transfer of interlocutory proceedings

20.119 It has become the practice in cases of this sort for a single judge to be nominated to control the litigation and ultimately to try it.[1] This the Lord Chief Justice does of his own initiative though his practice has arisen out of approaches made to him in the past by the parties for this to be done. Such an appointment is usually accompanied by an order that all interlocutory matters relating to such cases be determined by the nominated judge. This ensures that a consistent strategy for the conduct of the litigation can be pursued, and considerable savings in time and costs can be achieved in that at all stages the interlocutory tribunal is fully acquainted with the issues in the case and the problems arising. It can be of the greatest assistance to all the parties in that ready access to the judge can often be provided for.[2]

1 However in the intra-uterine device litigation against G D Searle & Co Ltd, a Master was appointed for the pre-trial procedures.
2 In *Re Benzodiazepine Litigation* a Master was also allocated to deal with more minor interlocutory matters on appointed days each month.

20.120 The only disadvantage to this is that there is a risk that due to his management of the interlocutory proceedings the nominated judge may become disqualified from presiding over the substantive trial, for example by having to consider proposed evidence to rule on its admissibility. This risk can be avoided to some extent by the referral of that type of issue to another tribunal.

Co–ordinated arrangements

20.121 In the Opren cases the parties and the judge (Hirst J) sensibly devised special interlocutory procedures based on consensus and designed to cut down unnecessary expense and effort which strict adherence to the Rules of Court would have required. They became known as 'the co-ordinated arrangements', and they have been adopted and evolved in subsequent cases, notably by Ognall J in the blood products litigation commenced by HIV positive haemophiliacs, Steyn J in the Myodil litigation and Ian Kennedy J in the Benzodiazepine litigation.

20.122 The Guide of the Supreme Court Procedure Committee on Group Actions[1] also covers the co-ordination of cases. It envisages changes in the law and Rules of Court to provide better for the conduct of group actions, but no immediate changes are proposed. Meanwhile, the law is likely to continue to evolve through the cases.

1 See para **20.115**, n 1, above.

20.123 A detailed consideration of group litigation is given in Chapter 14. While it is outside the scope of this chapter to consider co-ordinated arrangements in detail, examples of the arrangements and how they have operated can be given to demonstrate the thinking behind them.

(a) *Master pleadings etc* In the Opren litigation, it was agreed that one 'master' set of pleadings should apply to all cases. These pleadings contained the general allegations and responses, which were common to all or a substantial number of the individual cases. Individual particulars were then provided by schedule which contained not only particulars relating to the individual case (eg in respect of specific injuries and quantum) but also additional material such as the identity of general practitioners or treating hospitals. Individual statements of claim have been further refined, although the problems of pleading such claims accurately may be impeded by the division of responsibility between 'generic' solicitors and counsel on the one hand and those responsible for individual claimants on the other hand. The latter's understanding of the generic issues and the relevance of certain parts of the Master Statement of Claim to their client's circumstances is bound to be reduced by the Legal Aid Board's natural restrictions upon them all becoming involved in the 'generic' issues.

This distinction between matters which apply to all or a substantial number of individual cases, and matters which relate to specific individual cases, has now evolved to cover matters other than pleadings. Interlocutory applications which seek directions relating to all cases are issued in the name of the litigation, without any specific reference to any individual cases: orders made on these summonses are binding on all individual parties. Where specific relief leave is sought in an individual action, then a summons naming the individual action is issued. Similarly, discovery is given on a 'general' or 'master' basis in connection with the issues raised in the master pleadings as between the Steering Committee for the plaintiffs' solicitors group and the various defendants: as well as discovery being given between the individual plaintiffs and the defendants in respect of the issues raised in the individual pleadings.

(b) *Costs* It is trite to say that the costs of multi-claimant litigation are likely to be enormous, both in respect of the investigation of the general scientific and state of the art issues and issues raised in individual pleadings such as causation. Most claimants are legally aided, and their advisers, the Legal Aid Board and the courts have developed a system of sharing the general costs which allows such costs to be pro-rated across all plaintiffs. However, even taking this arrangement into account, the costs of an individual plaintiff are likely to be great. It is clear from the rules relating to legal aid that non-legally aided plaintiffs cannot be allowed to ride on the backs of their legally aided co-plaintiffs without making at least a pro-rata contribution to the overall costs and undertaking at least a pro-rata liability for the defendants' costs. In the Opren cases Hirst J provided for this by ordering that the costs liability of the lead actions should be borne equally by all the plaintiffs and this novel solution to a problem never before considered by the courts was upheld by the Court of Appeal (see *Davies v Eli Lilly*).[1]

The Legal Aid Board are bound to refuse funding to a person if that person does not have reasonable grounds for taking or defending proceedings: and there are only reasonable grounds to proceed if 'the solicitors would advise the applicant to take or defend proceedings privately, i e if he had means which were adequate to meet the likely costs of the case or would make payment of the likely costs possible although something of a sacrifice'.[2] In particular, legal aid is likely to be refused as unreasonable if 'the proceedings are not likely to be cost effective, i e the benefit to be achieved does not justify the costs'.[3] Of course, for the position to be otherwise, an assisted person would be put into a better position than a privately funded litigant of moderate means, which is not the purpose of the legal aid legislation.[4]

As a result of these provisions, and pressure from the courts and defendants, the Legal Aid Board now looks more closely at the viability of group actions prior to committing large amounts of public funds to their prosecution. It is possible that the funding of such litigation will itself come before the courts in the form of judicial review proceedings, but it is difficult to envisage the courts requiring the Board to fund claims that are not on any view commercially viable (in terms of the balance between the potential fruits of the litigation, and the potential costs including the costs of the defendant(s) should the claim fail) and which would not on any view be pursued by privately funded claimants.

In *R v Legal Aid Area Committee (No 10), ex p McKenna* a divisional court reviewed the refusal of legal aid to one of the Opren plaintiffs in the context of the then relevant regulations and in particular Regulation 78(c) of the Legal Aid (General) Regulations 1980. This provided that the Area Director should discharge a certificate if, as a result of information which comes to his attention, he considers that it is unreasonable in the particular circumstances that the assisted person should continue to receive legal aid. The decision to refuse aid was quashed on the specific facts of the case but in the course of a concurring judgment Roch J said:[5]

> Of course, the cost of litigation against the amount which would be recovered in a successful action is one factor, and a very important factor . . . to take into account . . . But in my judgment it should not be the sole factor, or necessarily, the decisive factor. Were that to be so then all the claimants in the Opren litigation should have had their Legal Aid Certificates withdrawn as soon as the probable cost of the litigation was known, because it is quite clear that the estimated costs of pursuing the claims to judgment was many times greater than the global value placed on all the claims of the qualifying plaintiffs. If that were the correct application of Regulation 78(c) it would place multi-national corporations in a position of advantage vis-à-vis individual claimants which, in my opinion, such commercial concerns ought not to enjoy.

The precise implications of this statement were unclear in the context of the principles underlying the legal aid system and indeed, in *R v Legal Aid Area (No 8) (Northern) Appeal Committee, ex p Angell* Simon Brown J questioned its validity.[6]

> I cannot think that in that final sentence Mr Justice Roch was intending to suggest that legal aid authorities are bound to treat all claimants as if they were in the same financial position as multi-nationals, let alone that a cost/benefit ratio approach is irrelevant. That could not be so. The test is surely as suggested elsewhere in the Law Society's Notes for Guidance, namely, whether a client with sufficient but not superabundant means would in similar circumstances under competent advice decide to take proceedings.

There is little doubt, therefore, that the plaintiffs' advisers have to balance the value of the claim against the prospects of establishing liability and the costs likely to be incurred in so doing. If this produces an unpalatable conclusion, it is no doubt the same conclusion most privately funded litigants face every day: the cost of litigating has increased far faster than the rate of inflation in personal injury awards which are, themselves, the subject of much criticism when compared with the value of awards for damage to reputation in defamation cases. The legal aid legislation does not seek to remedy that imbalance for a small proportion of the population.

(c) *Lead actions and preliminary issues* In the Pertussis vaccine cases, Stuart-Smith J ordered the trial of a preliminary issue common to all the claims of 'whether Pertussis vaccine is capable of causing permanent brain damage in young children to whom it is administered'. This arose as a result of withdrawal of legal aid in the first test action (*Kinnear v*

DHSS) after parental evidence made it obvious that the claim could not succeed on its own particular facts. This occurred well into the trial and resulted in a massive waste of costs as nothing was in fact decided apart from the issue of liability in that case alone, thereby defeating the principal purpose for which a test action is embarked upon.

The attraction of a trial of preliminary issues, to all the claims in a multi-claimant case is that it appears to offer a way out from the possibility of having endless trials based on individual facts. However, it is interesting to note that trial of a preliminary issue of general causation was proposed in the hormone pregnancy test cases, but this approach was rejected by the Court of Appeal.[7] Experience has indeed shown the difficulty in identifying preliminary issues for trial, without reference to the facts of individual cases. It is rare that a preliminary issue such as that in the Pertussis vaccine cases can be identified in this type of litigation. Preliminary issues on matters of breach of duty were not seen by Ognall J as practical in the blood product litigation. Questions of breach of duty such as those raised in 'failure to warn' cases are likely to defy attempts to find discrete issues that can be efficiently tried as preliminary issues in the expectation that the result can be applied to the bulk of the cases. Most such issues would require the majority of the evidence relevant to the litigation as a whole to be heard in any event and the prospects for significant savings in time and costs will usually be poor.

As a consequence, the courts (particularly Ian Kennedy J in the Benzodiazepine litigation) have approached multiple claims by requiring there to be a cut-off date to limit the claims within the co-ordinated proceedings, and by then seeking to identify those issues raised by the individual cases, which can be illustrated by the parties and court in the selection of lead actions. The use of cut-off dates as a proper means of case management has been specifically approved by the Court of Appeal.[8] The issues to be illustrated must be sufficiently common amongst the cases in the group to warrant the costs of being pursued. The lead cases, whilst not being determinative of the balance, are carefully selected so that they will provide guidelines to the parties, to enable them to ascertain the likely result of the balance of cases if they are pursued further. It is likely that this process of lead case selection and determination will be further evolved by the courts through the pending cases.

1 *Davies v Eli Lilly & Co* [1978] 3 All ER 94, [1987] 1 WLR 1136, CA.
2 Section 15(2) of the Legal Aid Act 1988 and para 6.06 of the Legal Aid Handbook 1992.
3 Para 6.07 of the Legal Aid Handbook 1992.
4 *McColl v Strathclyde Regional Council* 1983 SLT 616.
5 [1990] 1 Med LR 375 at 384.
6 [1990] 1 Med LR 394 at 407.
7 *Hyman and Williams v Schering Chemicals Ltd* (1980) Times, 9 June, CA.
8 *AB v John Wyeth & Brother Ltd* [1993] 4 Med LR 1.

20.124 The courts have given directions to ensure that the defendants to the litigation are put into the position where they can properly investigate individual cases expeditiously. It is now common for the court to direct (usually by agreement) that a plaintiff serves a consent to inspect medical records and copies of any medical records in their possession, with either the writ/county court summons or the individual statement/particulars of claim. Further, the courts have ordered plaintiffs to waive their right of confidentiality in respect of their treating physicians, to enable the defendants to approach those treating physicians to ask questions concerning the complainant's medical history: indeed, the courts have gone further on the particular facts of a case and required the plaintiff not only to give such a consent, but also to waive any rights they may have in pursuing a treating physician, to avoid the possibility of a treating physician refusing to speak to a defendant on the grounds that he or she may be joined into the action by the plaintiff as a result of what might have been said.[1] Equally, pending an order to serve a master defence, which was viewed as premature, Ian Kennedy J, required corporate defendants to serve a 'Commentary' upon the Master Statement of Claim to give the plaintiffs an indication of the defendants' position on the so-called 'generic' issues.

1 *AB v John Wyeth & Brother Ltd* [1993] 4 Med LR 1, CA.

Limitation

20.125 English law provides that a person must bring his claim within a reasonable time ('the limitation period'). The law arises from the Limitation Acts 1939–1980. A claim in contract to recover loss cannot in general be pursued after six years from the date of the breach of contract, although if the contract in question was made 'under seal' the period is extended to twelve years. The breach normally takes place, at the latest, when the product is delivered under a contract of sale to the buyer. In cases founded on the law of tort (such as negligence) the limitation period is generally six years from the date of damage. (See generally Chapter 13.)

20.126 However, in the case of personal injuries allegedly caused by a product, where the claim is based either on a breach of duty arising by virtue of a contract or on a breach of the tortious obligation to take care, the claim will be time-barred three years after the date the claimant knew or should have known of the damage, that it was significant, that the defect in the product caused it, and the identity of the person responsible for the defect in the product. The court has power to disapply these strict time limits and frequently, in its discretion, does so. Special rules apply to persons under disability (e g children) at the date the cause of action accrues. They may wait for up to three years after their age of majority to bring the claim. In a recent case arising out of the Opren litigation, it was stated that under section 14(1)(b) of the Limitation Act that the act or omission of which the plaintiff must have knowledge is the provision of an unsafe drug capable of causing the damage complained of/or in failing to discover its defective nature so as to protect such patient. It was also said in relation to the right under section 33 to disapply the three-year rule that there is no public policy presently requiring a different approach to the exercise of discretion in group actions although this may be a matter that ought to be considered by legislation.[1]

1 *Nash v Eli Lilly & Co* [1992] 3 Med LR 353, CA.

20.127 As far as strict liability is concerned, the CPA retains the general rule – the injured person must bring a claim within three years from the date he became aware or should reasonably have become aware of the damage, the defect and the identity of the producer. More significantly, however, all rights conferred by the Directive upon the injured person are extinguished ten years from the date on which the producer supplied the actual product which caused the damage (not the date upon which the class of product was first marketed) unless the injured person has begun his legal proceedings in the meantime.

20.128 Given that the latency period for adverse effects in the case of drugs is often very great – the suggested link between the treatment of threatened abortion with stilboestrol and vaginal carcinoma in children born to treated women, is a classic example – the existence of this ten year limit may mean that many claimants will still have to sue in negligence. Likewise children, who under existing limitation rules may wait to bring their claims in negligence at any time up to the expiry of three years from their age of majority, may be prejudiced by the ten year liability life rule.

20.129 Furthermore, interesting questions may arise where repeated exposures to a product have occurred. Very often treatment is over a long period and the claimant will be unable to identify which administration(s) actually caused the injury. The courts may treat any use of the product within the ten year period as making a material contribution to the cause of the injury.

20.130 This raises the importance under strict liability of manufacturers maintaining adequate records so as to be able to show that an action is barred through lapse of time (although a claim in negligence may still be possible). Their insurers will probably wish to see that they keep proper records so that the position of the insurer is not prejudiced through the inability of the insured to show that the product at the centre of a claim was supplied more than ten years before the claim was commenced. The concept of a product having a 'liability life' is quite novel to English law, although it is common in the United States.

RESEARCH INJURIES

20.131 As regards fault liability, it is difficult for a research subject to prove fault against the manufacturer or investigator because by its very nature research involves the investigation of the unknown and adverse reactions can occur despite the exercise of reasonable care. Nevertheless, the sponsoring manufacturer may be exposed to a claim if he has failed to isolate a discoverable risk, to pass on information to the investigator or to choose a reputable research company with adequate research facilities. In each case the research subject would have to show that but for such carelessness the injury would not have been suffered.

20.132 It has been suggested by the Department of Trade that research products are excluded from the principles of strict liability.[1] This is not easy to reconcile with the CPA or the Directive but in any event the research subject faces an immediate difficulty in showing that the product was 'defective'. Clearly, a person could not reasonably expect the same level of safety from a product under research as a product that has been licensed for marketing. Even if the product was shown to be defective, the sponsoring manufacturer may be able to rely upon the 'development risks defence'.

1 Implementation of the EC Directive on Product Liability, an explanatory and consultative note, Department of Trade, November 1985, at para 56 on p 14.

20.133 Despite the formal legal position, many argue that there is an ethical obligation to compensate solely on proof that the test substance caused the injury. In practice research ethics committees reviewing protocols in the United Kingdom demand extra protection for research subjects from product injuries. Various special arrangements have been proposed in the pharmaceutical industry to compensate injured research subjects but they do not exclude the right of the subject to sue for negligence or on the basis of strict liability.

20.134 As regards healthy volunteers participating in Phase I studies, under the Association of the British Pharmaceutical Industry Guidelines of 1988[1] (amending 1970 and 1984 guidelines) the sponsoring companies are advised to enter a legally binding agreement with the volunteer to pay compensation regardless of whether the volunteer can prove that the sponsor was negligent or the product was 'defective' under the CPA, provided the injury was caused by participation in the study. The normal consent form is extended to cover the issue of compensation and an arbitration procedure is suggested where a dispute arises as to the amount of compensation payable or whether the drug actually caused the injury.

1 ABPI Guidelines for Medical Experiments in Non-Patient Human Volunteers, March 1988.

20.135 As regards clinical trials, in 1991 the ABPI issued guidelines[1] in respect of injury sustained by clinical trial patients which developed previous guidelines of 1983.[2] The sponsoring company is advised to give a non-legally binding undertaking 'to consider favourably' payment of compensation to patients injured by a medicine under trial. The undertaking is not recommended to apply to patients continued on the trial drug after the study has been completed.[3]

1 ABPI Clinical Trial Compensation Guidelines January 1991.
2 ABPI Guidelines: Clinical Trials – Compensation for Medicine-Induced Injury, August 1983.
3 ABPI Circular No 494/86 of April 1986.

BIBLIOGRAPHICAL REFERENCES

ABPI Guidelines: Clinical Trials – Compensation for Medicine-Induced Injury, August 1983.

ABPI Guidelines for Medical Experiments in Non-Patient Human Volunteers, March 1988.

ABPI Guidelines: Clinical Trial Compensation January 1991.

Asscher A W 'Developments in Risk Assessment and Management', Paper presented at a conference on Risk in Medicine, 28–29 April 1988, London.

Association of the British Pharmaceutical Industry *Code of Practice for the Pharmaceutical Industry* (8th edn, 1 Jan 1993).

Department of Health and Social Security *Guide to Good Pharmaceutical Manufacturing Practice 1971* (as amended, HMSO).

Department of Health and Social Security, Medicines Division Consultation Paper, Product Liability: Special Features of the Medical Sector, 1979.

Department of Trade, Implementation of the EC Directive on Product Liability, November 1985, p 14, para 56.

Diamond A L and Laurence D R 'Product Liability in Respect of Drugs' in D'Arcy P F and Griffin JP (eds) *Iatrogenic Diseases* (3rd edn, Oxford, Oxford University Press, 1986).

Eaton G and Parish P (1976) Journal of the Royal College of General Practitioners (Suppl no 1) 8, 64–68.

European Commission Consultation Paper, Proposals for Completion of the Internal Market (1989) III/3878/89, para 40.

The Law Commission and the Scottish Law Commission, Liability for Defective Products, 1977 (Cmnd 6831, HMSO).

Miller R R (1974) Drug Intelligence and Clinical Pharmacology 8, 81–91.

Products Liability Casebook (Lloyd's of London Press, 1984).

Proprietary Association of Great Britain, Code of Standards of Advertising Practice, 1984.

Royal Commission on Civil Liability and Compensation for Personal Injury, 1978 (Cmnd 7–54, HMSO).

Supreme Court Procedure Committee, A Guide to Group Actions, 1991.

CROSS–REFERENCES

For information related to topics in this chapter see Chapters 9, 14 and 21.

CHAPTER 21

Epidemiology

Dr Kenneth D MacRae

SUMMARY

INTRODUCTION

21.1 The word epidemiology comes from the Greek for *upon* (epi) and *people* (demos). The original field of application was that of communicable (infectious or contagious) disease, but nowadays the vast majority of epidemiological investigations are into non-communicable diseases, such as cancer and heart disease. There have been many definitions of epidemiology. For example, John M Last's definition in his *A Dictionary of Epidemiology* (1983) is 'The study of the distribution and determinants of health-related states and events in populations, and the application of this study to control of health problems.' Kleinbaum, Kupper and Morgenstern (1982) have a similar concept, viz 'the study of health and illness in human populations'. Lillienfeld and Lillienfeld (1980) state that 'Epidemiology is concerned with the patterns of disease occurrence in human populations and the factors that influence these patterns.' Dr Alvan Feinstein (1985) is somewhat more specific, by saying that 'in epidemiological studies the data refer to groups of people and the fundamental unit under observation is a person, in contrast to the animals, inanimate substances, human organs or human fragments that are the basic materials investigated in other forms of medical research'.

21.2 What all these definitions amount to is that the method employed to study disease is statistical (as opposed to biological), and the object of study is a group. The results of an epidemiological investigation are statistical, such as associations, differences, or time trends. The aim of an epidemiological study is usually to identify 'risk factors' for disease, or to study methods for the prevention or early diagnosis of disease (as opposed to evaluating the merits of different treatments for the disease – this is what 'clinical trials' are used for). The crucial issue, of course, is whether statistical studies of the sort carried out in epidemiology can by themselves establish the cause or causes of a disease – i e, to what extent is it a scientific method as well as a way of studying public health issues? The difficulty faced by epidemiology in this respect arises from the fact that true experiments are hardly ever possible – instead, epidemiological studies are almost always observational, that is, they use data generated under the uncontrolled conditions of everyday life rather than the controlled conditions of an experiment. Why the difference between observation and experiment is so important will now be considered.

A TRUE EXPERIMENT

21.3 A properly designed (and conducted) clinical trial is a true experiment. The simplest such study compares two treatments in order to see if they differ in their success rates with a particular disease. The resulting data might look like this:

	Treatments	
	A	**B**
Success	67 (82.7%)	58 (66.7%)
Failure	14	29
Totals	81	87

21.4 Under what circumstances would it be possible to conclude that the difference in the percentage of success in the two treatment groups has been caused by the superiority of treatment A over treatment B? The simple principle we use is that we can conclude that the difference reflects causation *if it is possible to exclude any other possible explanation for the difference.* Clinical trial design and analysis is based on the premise that the data in a partcular study might show a difference between the treatments for one or more of four possible reasons. These are:

Allocation, selection or group-membership bias

21.5 This means simply that the difference is between the people in the two groups, not the treatments. The standard method used in clinical research to prevent this bias is to assign individuals to the treatments randomly, so that no bias can result from selection or choice by the doctors or by the patients involved in the study. An example of the bias that can result from deliberate selection by the study subjects themselves can be seen in the results of the Coronary Drug Project (1980). An extract from the results of the study illustrates the problem:

Mortality at 5 years

Compliance	*Clofibrate*	*Placebo*
80%+	15.0% (N=708)	15.1% (N=1813)
<80%	24.6% (N=357)	28.2% (N=882)

21.6 Clofibrate is a drug that may lower cholesterol, and the data show a lower mortality at five years for those who took at least 80 per cent of the prescribed dose than in the patients who took less than 80 per cent. However, a similar difference was found between those who took at least 80 per cent and those who took less than 80 per cent of the placebo. As the placebo is pharmacologically inert, this difference is a reflection of the difference between groups of individuals with different attitudes to health – ie, those who were prepared to take the medication regularly presumably differed in other respects from those who did not do so (eg, diet, exercise, lifestyle).

Assessment, measurement or data bias

21.7 This means that 'success' and 'failure' were not assessed in an identical manner in the two groups being compared. This can arise if the assessor (the doctor or the patient describing his or her own condition) knows the identity of the treatment – knowledge that the patient has received a placebo is an obvious source of such a bias. If different doctors have been responsible for assessing the two groups of patients, or if the assessments are not contemporaneous (ie, a doctor's standards may alter over time), the difference could simply be a result of the non-comparability of the basic data. This source of bias is prevented either by having objective data, or by 'blinding' both the doctor and the patient to the treatment's identity (hence the term 'double-blind').

21.8 An example of data bias is provided by the study by Schull and Cobb (1969) on the question of whether rheumatoid arthritis clusters in families. The first part of their investigation compared patients with rheumatoid arthritis (the 'cases') with persons free from arthritis (the 'controls') and found that 84 per cent of the cases and only 45 per cent of the controls reported having a parent with arthritis. However, the second part of their study compared each case with a sibling free from arthritis (who, of course, had the same parents as the case), and still found a case-control difference (74 per cent of cases and only 50 per cent of controls reporting arthritis in a parent).

Chance

21.9 A third reason for an apparent difference between the two groups is chance, which simply means that, despite there being no 'real' difference, sampling error or random variation has resulted in a difference in the study data. Small differences from the true success rates will occur very often just because of chance variation, and occasionally a large difference will be seen. Statistical tests are used to calculate the probability that the observed result was simply a matter of chance and that there was no real difference between the treatments. In the data set in para **21.3**, a chi-square test (which is a particular statistical technique suitable for such data) can be used to calculate such a probability. The value of chi-square is 5.67, which tells us (from a suitable table of probabilities) that the probability of the difference or a larger difference occurring entirely by chance is 0.017 (or 1.7 per cent). This is normally written as P=0.017. Suppose instead that the data had been as follows:

	Treatments	
	A	**B**
Success	65 (80.2%)	69 (69.0%)
Failure	16	27
Totals	81	87

The value of chi-square is now 2.80, giving P=0.095 (or 9.5 per cent). The value of P is used as a standard to decide if chance is a plausible or reasonable explanation of the difference seen. If P is low, chance is not thought to be the likely explanation of the difference. The famous British statistician and geneticist Sir Ronald Fisher FRS proposed that the value 0.05 (or 5 per cent) should be used as the criterion for judging if a value of P was sufficiently low to reject chance as the explanation of the difference – this is called the 0.05 (5 per cent) level of statistical significance. So, the P=0.017 from the analysis of the data in para **21.3** would be sufficiently low to permit the conclusion that the difference was statistically significant – ie, chance was an implausible (but not impossible) explanation of the difference – whereas the difference in the table in this section, giving P=0.095, is sufficiently likely to occur by chance to be thought not to be statistically significant if the 0.05 criterion is used.

21.10 Three important points should be emphasised at this stage. First, the calculation of a statistical test and the obtaining of a value for P addresses only chance as the possible explanation for the difference; being statistically significant is therefore not a sufficient basis for a conclusion that the difference is real – allocation and assessment bias must also be considered. Second, it is, of course possible that the statistically significant difference has occurred by chance – improbable though that may be. Third, although the probability that a statistically significant difference will occur by chance is less than 0.05 (or 5 per cent) for any *one* statistical analysis, the probability that a statistically significant difference will be found increases if several statistical analyses are performed on the same data.

21.11 An interesting example of this phenomenon can be seen in the study by Lee et al (1980) in which 1,073 consecutive patients from the Duke University data bank who had been treated medically for coronary artery disease were randomised into two groups. Fourteen characteristics of the patients at the onset of treatment were tabulated and the groups (group 1 had N = 539 and group 2 had N = 534) were compared. P values less than 0.05 resulted for two of the characteristics. Further, although the groups as a whole had similar survival rates, a sub-group analysis of patients who had three-vessel disease and abnormal left ventricular contraction found statistically significant differences in survival (P = 0.02, or 2 per cent) – the 194 such patients from group 1 having better survival than the 203 such patients from group 2. This difference is, as it happens, simply a chance difference in that the treatment policies for the two groups were identical. This issue was succinctly encapsulated in the statement Bibby (1983) attributes to Ronald Coase, viz 'If you torture the data enough they will eventually confess'. The problem can be seen quantitatively in the following table:

Number of statistical tests	*1*	*5*	*10*	*14*	*25*	*100*
Probability of one or more P less than 0.05	0.05	0.23	0.40	0.51	0.72	0.994

If 14 or more separate and independent analyses are carried out, it is more likely than not that at least one statistically significant difference will be found just as a result of the play of chance, even if there are no real differences in truth. The problem of multiple analyses also, of course, arises when several different studies have been carried out, and a particular difficulty is that authors of articles and journal editors may prefer 'positive' findings (statistically significant) to negative ones, creating a possible bias in the literature towards positive studies.

A 'real' difference – cause

21.12 The fourth explanation for any difference seen in study is that it represents cause and effect, a real difference between the treatments in other words. When allocation bias and assessment bias have been eliminated by the design and conduct of a true experiment – for the former, as has been discussed, usually by random allocation to treatment groups and the latter by obtaining prospectively objective data or blinded subjective data – a P value less than 0.05 is sufficient to permit the conclusion that the difference in the data is real, ie, it represents a causal effect of the difference between the treatments. Since chance is still a possible, if unlikely, explanation of the difference, a single study would not by itself normally be taken as establishing a causal effect and corroboration from other independent studies would be sought. It is especially important to note that this use of a P value is appropriate only if one P value has been calculated. As has been seen in the previous section, low P values become more and more likely if several are calculated. Also, it is assumed that the P value relates to a single hypothesis explicitly set out in the study plan before the data were collected. A comparison suggested by inspection of the data after they have been tabulated is particularly dubious, because such a *post hoc* selection is just one of many possible selections that could have been made prior to inspection of the data. Therefore, such a P value is invalid. In epidemiology, however, because such control of bias is not possible, the situation is quite different. The essential difference between epidemiology and a true experiment is the fact that epidemiology is observational – it looks at the world as it is, and cannot experimentally control exposures.

STUDY DESIGNS IN EPIDEMIOLOGY

21.13 Epidemiological studies can be classified as being either descriptive or analytic. Descriptive studies include national mortality (death) or morbidity (illness) statistics, international mortality or morbidity comparisons, geographical or ecological association studies (of the association between an exposure and a disease), and secular trends of disease over time. The two sorts of analytic study are the case-control design and the cohort design. Each will be described briefly, but it is important to appreciate that all of these, whether descriptive or analytic, are observational and not true experiments.

Descriptive epidemiology

National mortality and morbidity statistics

21.14 In most countries, a register of deaths is maintained, and numbers of deaths in any year can be ascertained. In addition, cause of death is usually recorded by a medical practitioner on the death certificate, and therefore the total can be subdivided according to the certified cause. The accuracy of the certification of cause is, however, a major problem, in that autopsy or biopsy evidence is often not obtained. Estimates of error in certifying cause of death for certain causes have been as high as 30–40 per cent. Statistics regarding illness (whether or not death results from the illness) are available to a lesser extent. Cancer registries exist in many countries, but these have been set up relatively recently and the completeness of registration is very variable. As with deaths, the accuracy of diagnoses may be in doubt, especially in the absence of definitive biopsy data. The collection of data on illnesses other than cancer is relatively unusual. In the UK, for example, diagnoses for hospital in-patients are recorded, but illnesses that have not resulted in hospitalisation will not be included in the resulting statistics – whether or not medical attention has been sought. Diagnostic fashions may vary from country to country (for both deaths and illnesses) and within a country they may change over time.

International comparisons

21.15 Because international comparisons are based on nationally collected statistics, the problems outlined above obviously also apply to this type of study, but the problems tend to be greater on an international scale because greater variability of these factors usually exists. Striking differences are sometimes found, such as the much higher mortality from cancer of the stomach and the much lower mortality from cancer of the breast in Japan than in Britain and Western Europe (Doll and Peto, 1981). The differences may be so large that it is highly likely that they are 'real'. However, diagnostic errors or fashions are ever-present problems, and caution should be exercised in the interpretation of such comparisons.

Association studies

21.16 These geographical or ecological association studies are in effect an extension of simple international comparisons of mortality or morbidity statistics, in that differences in a particular 'exposure' are related to the differences in death or illness statistics. For example, Hirayama (1980) plotted the breast cancer mortality rate in various provinces of Japan against the per capita daily intake of pork, finding a direct positive relationship. St Leger et al (1979) found a negative association between ischaemic heart disease mortality in men aged 55 to 64 and the annual consumption per capita of wine. Again, the caveats about the statistics on causes of death apply, and the presence of a strong relationship does not 'prove' a causal link either on a national scale or, a fortiori, in individuals within any country. Indeed, the extrapolation of ecological associations to individuals is known as the *ecological fallacy*. There is no guarantee that the cases of the disease in the population came from the exposed individuals in that population. A further problem with such studies is migration. Since the time between exposure and the clinical manifestation of a disease such as cancer may be many years, the individual may have migrated from an area with a high level of exposure to one with a low level, or vice-versa.

Secular trends

21.17 Changes in the incidence of deaths or illness from a particular cause over time (usually within a single country) may suggest an increasing or decreasing problem. The classic study of this sort was that carried out by Lenz (1965) in West Germany in which the dramatic rise and fall in phocomelia (a limb-reduction defect) was noted and related to the increase and subsequent decrease in the use of the drug Thalidomide by pregnant women. Once again, of course, diagnostic errors and fashions must be considered in the interpretation of changes over time.

Analytic epidemiology

21.18 In analytic epidemiology the data have been collected or assembled specifically for the purpose of the study being undertaken, in contrast to descriptive epidemiology in which use is made of routinely collected information. A major difference between analytic and descriptive epidemiology is therefore that the researchers will have direct contact with the study subjects (or their relatives or medical records). Because of this, two other types of evidence that may be collected should be mentioned at this point, viz case reports and case series. A case report is simply an individual who has a certain condition and who has (usually) had a certain exposure. A case report is of no value at all in judging whether the exposure caused the effect (being an example of the logical fallacy post hoc ergo propter hoc), but may be a source of an hypothesis that can be explored in other studies. A case series is simply a number of case reports, some or all of whom have had a similar exposure. Again, causation cannot be deduced from such evidence. Indeed, even a statistical association cannot be established from a series of cases – this would require a comparison or 'control' group. For this reason, analytic epidemiology uses study designs that enable comparisons to be made, the case-control and cohort designs. In the case-control study the comparison is between cases (who have the disease) and controls (who do not have the disease); in the cohort study the comparison is between those exposed to a suspected 'risk factor' and those who are not exposed. These two types of study will now be considered in more detail.

The case-control study

21.19 A case-control study begins by specifying what disease the cases have or that resulted in their deaths. When the cases alone are studied, the result is a case-series, and statements such as '90 per cent of the cases had taken drug X in the week prior to developing heart failure' can be made. However, a case-series alone cannot establish a statistical association between exposure (to drug X) and disease (heart failure). So, controls who do not have the disease that defines the cases are also studied. The aim is to compare the exposure histories of the cases and the controls in order to determine if any exposure has occurred more or less frequently in the cases than in the controls. A case-control study is often referred to as being 'retrospective', partly because the direction of the search is from the 'effect' backwards to the possible 'causes', and partly because the data on the exposures are obtained after, perhaps long after, the exposures occurred. The resulting data from a case-control study might look like this:

	Cases	*Controls*
Drug X in last week	90	80
No drug X in last week	10	20
Totals	100	100

The case-control study is especially prone to confounding (see below) and bias, and these difficulties make the establishing even of a statistical association very problematic.

BIAS

21.20 A bias is a systematic effect in the design, conduct or analysis of a study that results in a distortion of the association between an exposure and a disease. The bias may overstate or understate the association. If the data from a case-control study are set out as a 2 × 2 table:

	Exposed	*Not exposed*
Cases	W	X
Controls	Y	Z

then a bias is any aspect of the study's design, conduct or analysis that tends to systematically distort (in either direction) any of the four numbers W, X, Y and Z.

21.21 Many biases may affect a case-control study, and several of these are unpreventable. Sackett (1979) has catalogued no fewer than 40 biases that can affect the selection of the cases and controls, the measurement of the exposures and diseases, and the data analysis of case-control studies (many of which also apply to cohort studies). For example, recall bias can arise because the cases have more reason to recall past exposures than the controls. Diagnostic suspicion bias can arise if the researchers know of a particular past exposure and are thereby more likely to suspect a particular disease is present. Exposure suspicion bias occurs if knowledge of the disease status of the cases (as opposed to the controls) leads to a suspicion that a particular exposure has occurred. Prevalence-incidence bias is possible if the disease being studied is fatal in some individuals and not in others, and if the study includes either just non-fatal or just fatal cases. Admission rate (Berkson's) bias occurs when admission to hospital is affected by exposure to a possible risk factor, and the selection of the cases or controls (or both) is made from hospital in-patients. For example, a child having a febrile convulsion may be more likely to be admitted to hospital if he or she had been recently vaccinated than if there had been no recent exposure to a vaccine.

CONFOUNDING

21.22 Confounding is derived from the Latin confundere, meaning to mix together, and means that a third variable or factor is responsible for an apparent association, or the absence of an association, between an exposure and being a case. Therefore, a confounding factor must be associated with both the exposure and with being a case. A simple example is the following (the data are, of course, fictitious):

	Cases (with liver cirrhosis)	*Controls (with no cirrhosis)*
Drinks tonic water	40	20
Does not drink tonic water	60	80
Totals	100	100

The obvious confounding factor is alcohol (in the form of gin or vodka most probably), in that the drinking of alcohol is associated both with the exposure (to tonic water) and the disease (liver cirrhosis).

21.23 If a confounder is known and information about its presence in individual cases and controls can be obtained at the time the controls are being chosen, the cases and controls can be matched on that confounder. Here, the cases and controls would be matched for the drinking of gin and vodka. The most obvious confounders in any case-control study are age and sex, in that almost all diseases and very many exposures vary according to these two factors. Thus, most case-control studies will attempt to match cases and controls on age and sex, and often also on socio-economic status, area of residence, and ethnicity.

21.24 There are, however, major difficulties in dealing with confounding factors. First, the confounders have to be known, and it is impossible to know if all the confounders have indeed been established – because if all the causes of a particular disease were understood there would be no point in using epidemiology to study it. Second, it is very difficult in practice to match cases and controls closely even on a few confounders, and virtually impossible so to do on many confounders.

21.25 Unfortunately, very close case-control matching can result in the problem of 'over-matching'. This is matching on the exposure variable itself – deliberately or inadvertently. For example, if one member of a pair of identical twins was a case, the other member would seem to be an ideal control. However, it is probable that they would have been treated almost identically by their parents, and this might make differences in exposure between the case and control to many risk factors very unlikely.

21.26 The problem of confounding can be illustrated by considering the apparently simple problem of determining if a particular colour (red, say) makes a motor car more likely to have an accident. A simple table (the data are fictitious) such as the following might be produced:

	Cases (major accident)	*Controls (no accident)*
Red	20	10
Not red	80	90
Totals	100	100

An obvious confounder is the type of motor car. Suppose, for example, that red is a particularly popular colour for high performance sports cars. Do the red cars have more accidents because they are red or because they are more likely to be sports cars? Matching the case cars and the control cars for type of car could be carried out to deal with this source of confounding. However, suppose also that car colour fashions change over time, and that red is now a less popular colour than it was five to ten years ago. The question then arises as to whether the red cars have more accidents because they are red or because they are likely to be older? In addition, as cars become older they cost less to buy, and therefore older cars are likely to be bought by younger drivers, who are more likely to have accidents. The complexity of this problem is trivial compared with the problem of studying disease in humans. Because of the problem of case-control matching for confounding factors even on those that are known (or suspected), the statistical analysis of the data may have to attempt an adjustment or correction for those known confounders on which matching was impossible. The methods used for such statistical correction are the Mantel-Haenszel method and logistic regression (Kahn and Sempos, 1989). However, once again statistical adjustment is possible only for confounders that are known and for which data have been obtained on the cases and controls – and inevitably any correction (as with matching) must be incomplete.

21.27 The presence of an association in a case-control study often occurs because there is a small excess of exposed cases (or controls). The fact that a low 'P' is obtained from the statistical analysis addresses only the possibility that the case-control difference may be due to chance. As Sir Austin Bradford Hill (1965) commented in discussing the role of significance tests, 'Such tests can, and should, remind us of the effects that the play of chance can create, and they will instruct us on the likely magnitude of these effects. Beyond that, they contribute nothing to the "proof" of our hypothesis.' Confounding and bias still remain as possible explanations of any difference between the cases and controls in response to a risk factor.

The cohort study

21.28 The most obvious difference in approach from the case-control study is that a cohort study begins before the 'effect' has occurred, and therefore the search is from the possible 'causes' forwards in time to the possible 'effects'. Information on exposures is collected and then follow-up is carried out to see what happens to the individuals in the study. For these reasons, the cohort design is often called 'prospective'. The main advantage of this approach is that the assessment, measurement or data biases that apply to exposure data are prevented, in that the future disease status of the study subjects is unknown when these data are being recorded. However, diagnostic suspicion bias is still a possibility as exposure data may be known when the diagnosis of an illness is being performed. Also, the study is still observational, in that the individuals will choose many of the exposures themselves (e g diet, smoking, drinking alcohol, exercise, occupation etc) or have them chosen for them by doctors (e g treatment for an illness), their parents or be simply a result of their social and geographical circumstances. Thus confounding and group-membership bias are fundamental problems in the analysis and interpretation of cohort studies.

21.29 The major problems with cohort studies are that they usually need to be vary large (especially if the events of interest are rare) and that they may require follow-up over a long period of time. For instance, two cohort studies were begun in 1968 to study oral contraceptives, and in the first 13 years of follow-up there were 249 deaths in the 46,000 women in the Royal College of General Practitioners' study (Royal College of General Practitioners, 1981) and 81 deaths in the 17,032 women in the Oxford study (Vessey et al, 1981) – i e only about 0.5 per cent of each cohort had died. A further difficulty is that by the time an adequate amount of data for analysis are available, the question posed by the study design may be obsolete. This is the case with these two cohorts, because the formulations of oral contraceptives at the time the studies began were completely different from those being currently produced.

EPIDEMIOLOGY AND CAUSATION

21.30 From the foregoing, it is apparent that a statistical association in an observational epidemiological study can arise for one or more of a number of reasons, viz, cause, chance, bias and confounding. Only chance can be considered in the same way as in a true experiment, and even this presents formidable problems – especially that of multiple analyses. Attempts can be made to lessen the effects of bias and confounding, but these efforts can never be completely successful. Indeed, the extent to which bias and confounding have been prevented in any study is unknowable.

The US Surgeon General's criteria

21.31 In discussing this issue, the US Surgeon General's (1982) report stated (p 16):

In practice, epidemiologic methods have been employed to study cancer in man. These studies result in observational data that may establish a statistically significant association between variables or attributes. This association may be artifactual, indirect, or direct. The possibility of an artefactual (or spurious) result can be eliminated if the design and conduct of the studies are adequate, and if studies conducted in different population groups produce the same or similar statistical associations. Once an artefactual association has been ruled out, it is then necessary to determine whether the association is an indirect or direct (causal) one.

The US Surgeon General went on to list five criteria (p 16) to be used for the evaluation of the reported associations between cigarette smoking and cancers of various sites. These were:

(1) the consistency of the association;
(2) the strength of the association;
(3) the specificity of the association;
(4) the temporal relationship of the association; and
(5) the coherence of the association.

Consistency

21.32 This criterion requires repeated observations of the association by different investigators, in different locations, at different times, and using different study methods. This is necessary to try to prevent artefacts due to bias in study methodology or subject selection, and to attempt to eliminate confounding such factors as diet, occupation or genetics.

Strength

21.33 Strength of an association in epidemiology is usually expressed by a relative risk or an odds ratio, depending on the study design. A very strong association (say 10 or more) which was either spurious or indirect would require major biases or degrees of confounding to be present – which, it is hoped, would be obvious. Of course, in judging the strength of an association, the point estimate alone is not sufficient – the confidence interval must be considered, especially its lower limit. If the lower limit of the confidence interval is not greater than 1, it cannot be concluded that there is any statistical association. The lower limit of the confidence interval is the strength of association it is 'safe' to consider to exist. Dose-response (meaning the greater the exposure, the stronger the association) is also mentioned in this context by the Surgeon General.

Specificity

21.34 At its extreme, specificity would imply that a disease is rare or unknown in the absence of an exposure, and occurs always or often in the presence of the exposure. For a number of reasons, extreme specificity would be seldom expected (eg diseases may have several causes, an exposure may produce several diseases, an exposure may really be several exposures – tobacco smoke contains several thousand constituents). So, although specificity would be a positive factor in judging causation, absence of specificity does not negate such an hypothesis.

Temporal relationship

21.35 This means that the exposure must precede the disease. This is sometimes difficult to determine, especially if the disease could have been present in latent form prior to exposure.

Coherence

21.36 This means that the epidemiological association is coherent with the known facts regarding the natural history and biology of the disease. Once more, dose-response is mentioned as being important. The final two sentences (p 20) in the Surgeon General's report regarding coherence are:

> Coherence is clearly established when the actual mechanism of disease production is defined. Coherence exists, nevertheless, although of a lesser magnitude, when there is enough evidence to support a plausible mechanism, but not a detailed understanding of each step in the chain of events by which a given etiologic agent produces disease.

Can 'criteria' determine causation?

21.37 The US Surgeon General (p 20) concludes his discussion of these criteria by stating:

> The causal significance of an association is a matter of judgment which goes beyond any statement of statistical probability.

This issue had been debated by many eminent epidemiologists, and the major issues are outlined in a book resulting from a meeting of the Society for Epidemiologic Research in June 1985 (Rothman, 1985). Various lists of criteria have been proposed (the best known being the US Surgeon General's five, and Sir Austin Bradford Hill's nine (Hill, 1965) – five of which are the Surgeon General's five). It is a considerable understatement to say that no agreed criteria for coming to a judgment regarding causation from statistical associations in observational epidemiology exist. Indeed, there is no consensus whether or not causation can be addressed at all by applying criteria to epidemiological evidence.

WHAT CAN EPIDEMIOLOGY TELL US?

21.38 Simply, epidemiology can tell us whether or not a statistical association exists between an exposure and an outcome, although it can be difficult, perhaps impossible to decide if the association is spurious (due to one or more biases) or indirect (due to confounding).

21.39 What, then, is the point of doing epidemiological studies at all? First, hypotheses can be generated that can be used to suggest research studies in other disciplines. Second, although cause in a scientific sense may not have been established, if the evidence seems substantial (perhaps meeting the criteria of constistency and strength) statistical associations may be used in pragmatic decisions on public health matters – to suggest or advise changes in exposures that are associated with serious or common diseases.

STATISTICAL MATTERS

21.40 Some basic statistical issues will be considered here, and further details on the issues discussed and on more complex matters can be found in Dawson-Saunders and Trapp (1990) and Kahn and Sempos (1989). The standard reference works on the statistical analysis of case-control and cohort studies are volumes I (1980) and II (1987) respectively of *Statistical Methods in Cancer Research* by NE Breslow and NE Day. A particularly good basic presentation on case-control studies is in JJ Schlesselman's book (1982).

Introduction

21.41 The subject 'statistics' is so called because its starting point is a sample statistic. For example, if 24 of the 40 people in a room are wearing spectacles at a certain time, the statement that 24 of the 40 people, or 60 per cent, are wearing spectacles is a statistic that describes the sample (in a very limited way, of course). The average age, the proportion wearing brown shoes, the percentages of males and females, and so on, are also sample statistics. A sample statistic is a *description* of the sample, and the topic known as 'descriptive statistics' deals with the calculation and presentation of sample statistics.

21.42 However large the group being described, it is a sample, even if it comprises all such people who exist at a given point in time. So, the population of the UK at mid-day on 1 April 1992 is still considered to be a sample, in that individuals continually leave and enter this population. As it is not possible to say how large a population might eventually be, it is assumed that populations are infinitely large – this is why they are considered to be infinite hypothetical populations. In using statistics in science, the aim is to make inferences about the population or populations that the sample or samples which have produced that statistic represent. So, if 60 per cent of the sample are wearing spectacles, what can we say about the population this sample represents? If the sample has been selected in a way that makes it representative of some population, we could *estimate* that the percentage of spectacle wearers in the population is also 60 per cent. Using a sample to estimate something about a population is an example of *inferential statistics*.

21.43 Of course, this estimate is only a guess – the true percentage could be higher or lower, but it is the best guess available if the sample is a truly representative one. Such an estimate is known as a *point estimate*. However, it is important to consider how far from the point estimate the 'true' population value might be. Consider the following three samples:

	A	*B*	*C*
Number of spectacle wearers	24	240	2400
Number of non-wearers	16	160	1600
Sample size	40	400	4000
Point estimate	60%	60%	60%

The three samples give the same point estimate, but it is intuitively obvious that the larger the sample the more precise the estimate. That is, a point estimate from a large sample is more likely to be close to the 'true' percentage than a point estimate from a small sample. This issue is dealt with by calculating the *standard error* (SE) of the estimate. For a single percentage, p, the formula is:

SE of p = $\sqrt{p(100\text{-}p)/N}$.
So, for A, SE of p = $\sqrt{(60 \times 40)/40}$ = 7.75%;
for B, SE of p = $\sqrt{(60 \times 40)/400}$ = 2.45%;
for C, SE of p = $\sqrt{(60 \times 40)/4000}$ = 0.77%.

This illustrates the fact that the SE becomes smaller as the sample size increases. Usually, the SE is used to calculate an interval within which the 'true' percentage (the percentage in the population) is likely to fall. The most widely used confidence interval is one in which the population value is 95 per cent likely to fall – i e at 95 per cent confidence interval. If the sample is at least 30, a 95 per cent confidence interval can be calculated by the expression: point estimate ± 1.96 SE, or (approximately), point estimate ± 2 SE. Thus, for A, the 95 per cent confidence interval for the estimate of the percentage of spectacle wearers is 60 per cent ± 2 × 7.75 per cent, or 60 per cent ± 15.5 per cent, or 44.5 per cent to 75.5 per cent. For B, the 95 per cent confidence interval is 60 per cent ± 2 × 2.45 per cent, or 55.1 per cent to 64.9 per cent. For C, the 95 per cent confidence interval is 60 per cent ± 2 × 0.77 per cent, or 58.46 per cent to 61.54 per cent.

21.44 Often, a scientific investigation involves two or more samples, and it is wished to make a comparison or comparisons to decide whether the data are consistent with the hypothesis that the samples come from the same population, or whether they are so different that this seems implausible. This issue was addressed in para **21.9** above. The value of 'P', the probability that two samples selected at random from the same population might differ by the amount seen in the study data, is used for this purpose. This process is known as *hypothesis testing*, and is also part of inferential statistics.

21.45 Finally, when two (or more) samples are being compared, it is often useful to *estimate* the difference between the populations the samples represent. So, the actual difference in the data gives a point estimate of the difference. In the data shown in para **21.9** above, $P=0.017$, which is sufficiently low to conclude that the difference is statistically significant. The difference in the percentage success between the two samples was 16.0 per cent (82.7 per cent − 66.7 per cent), which is a point estimate of the 'true' difference. A standard error for this difference can be calculated, the appropriate calculation giving a value of 6.57 per cent. A 95 per cent confidence interval for the estimated 'true' difference is therefore 16.0 per cent ± 2 × 6.57 per cent, or 2.86 per cent to 29.14 per cent. In contrast, the data shown in para **21.9** gave $P=0.095$, a non-significant difference. The point estimate of the difference is 11.2 per cent (80.2 per cent − 69.0 per cent), and the SE of the difference is 6.65 per cent. The 95 per cent confidence interval for the estimated 'true' difference is now 11.2 per cent ± 2 × 6.65 per cent, or −2.1 per cent to 24.5 per cent. The former confidence interval excludes the value 0 per cent, while the latter includes 0 per cent. Thus if the difference is statistically significant ($P<0.05$), the 95 per cent confidence interval will exclude zero, while if the difference is not statistically significant ($P>0.05$) the 95 per cent confidence interval will include zero as a plausible true difference.

21.46 In summary then, we use statistics first of all to *describe* one or more features of the sample or samples. Various *inferences* can then be made, such as point and interval estimates from a single sample about the population the sample can be considered to represent, a test of the hypothesis that two samples come from the same population, and point and interval estimates of the 'true' difference between the populations the two samples represent.

Study size and statistical power

21.47 'Power' is the term used in statistics to denote the probability that a study will give a statistically signifiant P value if there is a 'real' difference to find. It is customary to design studies to have a power of at least 80 per cent of detecting a 'real' difference, and often 90 per cent or 95 per cent power will be used. For any given power, the larger a study, the smaller the difference it is capable of detecting. Although this concept is important in deciding how large a study it is sensible to perform, once the study data are available, interval estimates of the likely true differences are of greater value in interpreting the results – in that the sorts of differences that could exist, and those that are unlikely to exist, can be readily seen.

MEASURES OF RISK USED IN EPIDEMIOLOGY

Absolute risk

21.48 Risk, or absolute risk, is the probability that something will happen (to an individual of a specified type in a particular population within a period of time or by a stated age). It is usually possible to estimate an absolute risk only from a prospective cohort study (or, for certain events – especially death – from routinely collected national statistics).

Relative risk

21.49 A relative risk is used to compare two absolute risks. It is the ratio of the absolute risk in a particular group of individuals to the absolute risk in another group. Commonly, it will be the ratio of the absolute risk in an exposed group to the absolute risk in an unexposed group. If the two absolute risks are the same, the relative risk will be 1. A figure greater than one means that the exposed group have a higher absolute risk than the unexposed group, and a figure less than one means the exposed group have a lower absolute risk than the unexposed group.

Odds ratio

21.50 An odds ratio is used to estimate the relative risk if the study is a case-control one. A case-control study does not give estimates of absolute risks, but it is easy to show that an odds ratio gives an accurate estimate of the relative risk without direct knowledge of the absolute risks. A cohort study can be represented as follows:

	Exposed	*Unexposed*
Cases	A	B
Non-cases	C	D

The absolute risk in the exposed group is A/(A + C) and in the unexposed group B/(B + D). The relative risk is therefore:

$$RR = \frac{A(B+D)}{B(A+C)}$$

The odds ratio on the other hand would be just

$$\frac{AD}{BC}$$

If the absolute risk is low, A will be small compared with C and B will be small compared with D. So, A + C will be almost the same as C and B + D will be almost the same as D. The relative risk and the odds ratio will therefore be very similar.

21.51 If a case-control study is constructed from the cohort, there will be A + B cases and, if one control is matched to each case, A + B controls. The proportion of exposed cases will be A/(A + B), and the proportion of exposed controls will C/(C + D). The number of exposed cases will be A, and the number of exposed controls will be (A + B)C/(C + D). If the case-control study is represented thus:

	Cases	*Controls*
Exposed	W	X
Not exposed	Y	Z

The odds ratio is

$$\frac{WZ}{XY}$$

So, W = A and X = (A + B)C/(C + D).

The number of unexposed cases will be B and the number of unexposed controls will be (A + B)D/(C + D). So, Y = B and Z = (A + B)D/(C + D).

The odds ratio is therefore

$$\frac{A(A+B)D\ (C+D)}{(C+D)\ (A+B)CB}$$

This simplifies to

$$\frac{AD}{BC}$$

Thus, the case-control study's odds ratio is an unbiased estimate of the cohort study's odds ratio, and this is very close to the relative risk.

Excess risk

21.52 The excess risk is the difference between two absolute risks, usually the difference between the absolute risks in an exposed and an unexposed group. This cannot usually be estimated from a case-control study, although the National Childhood Encephalopathy Study (Alderslade et al, 1981) did calculate an estimate of the excess risk resulting from pertussis vaccination (which they called the attributable risk).

Attributable risk

21.53 The term attributable risk is used in several ways, one of which is described above as excess risk. The two main uses are to refer either to a population (some of which are exposed and some of which are not) or to an individual who is exposed.

21.54 The population attributable risk is an estimate of the proportion of the disease in the population that can be attributed to a particular exposure. This calculation requires both the relative risk and the prevalence of exposure in the population to be known. If prevalence is denoted by P and relative risk by R, the attributable risk (or proportion) in the population is

$$AR(p) = P(R-1)/(1+P(R-1))$$

The exposed attributable risk just requires the relative risk to be known:

$$AR(e) = (R-1)/R$$

If the relative risk is 2, AR(e) is 0.5, which means that half the cases of the disease who have been exposed can be attributed to that exposure (and a half of the cases would have occurred anyway even if they had not been so exposed). Of course, this begs the question of whether the association reflects causation. It raises the problem of how accurate the estimate of the relative risk is.

ESTIMATION AND CONFIDENCE INTERVALS

21.55 Consider the four (hypothetical) case-control study results in para **21.57**.

21.56 First of all, the analyses of the four data sets have been performed with methods for unmatched data in order to make the examples simpler, although if the cases and controls had been matched in pairs (and they almost certainly would have been) methods for matched data would be more appropriate. However, it is the nature of the answers and what they mean that is important whatever the precise method used.

21.57 The chi-square test is performed to get the probability (P) of the difference in exposure between the cases and controls under the null hypothesis – ie, how often would the difference in the data occur purely by chance if the true difference really is zero. In the smallest data set (1) the P is 0.54, meaning that the difference is not unlikely. In (2) the P is 0.048, and this is less than 0.05, the level of statistical 'significance' used as the criterion for rejecting chance as a plausible explanation of the difference. In (3) and (4) the even higher chi-square values indicated that the chance probabilities of the case-control differences are very low indeed, and again chance would be rejected as a plausible explanation of the differences. So, the case-control difference in (1) is not statistically significant, while those in (2), (3) and (4) are. It is important to bear in mind that rejecting chance as the explanation of the case-control difference does not mean the difference is 'real'; bias and confounding are still possible reasons for the difference.

(1)

	Cases	*Controls*
Exposed	2	1
Not exposed	8	9

Chi-square = 0.39; P = 0.54
or = 2.25 (0.18–28.48)

(2)

	Cases	*Controls*
Exposed	20	10
Not exposed	80	90

Chi-square = 3.92; P = 0.048
or = 2.25 (1.01–5.02)

(3)

	Cases	*Controls*
Exposed	200	100
Not exposed	800	900

Chi-square = 39.2; P < 0.001
or = 2.25 (1.75–2.90)

(4)

	Cases	*Controls*
Exposed	2000	1000
Not exposed	8000	9000

Chi-square = 392.2; P < 0.001
or = 2.25 (2.08–2.43)

21.58 The odds ratio in all four data sets is 2.25. This is what the calculation gives each time, and is known as a 'point estimate' of the 'true' odds ratio. A true odds ratio of 2.25 has a higher probability of giving an odds ratio of 2.25 in a study than any other true odds ratio. However, it is possible that a true odds ratio greater or less than 2.25 could also have given a value of 2.25 in a particular data set, the difference between the value of 2.25 in the data and the true value being due to chance. In each of the four data sets the point estimate of 2.25 is followed by an interval known as a 'confidence interval', the larger the study the narrower the interval. A confidence interval is a range of possible true odds ratios that could have given the value in the data. A 95 per cent confidence interval is a range of possible true values under which the value in the data (2.25) has a probability of 0.05 (5 per cent) or more of occurring by chance. True odds ratios outside the 95 per cent confidence interval would be rejected as being a plausible true odds ratios because the value of 2.25 in the data has a probability of less than 0.05 of occurring if any of these is true. In (1) therefore, any true odds ratio in the range 0.18 to 28.48 has a probability of 0.05 or more of giving a value of 2.25 in this data set. Note that 1 (the null hypothesis value of the odds ratio) is included in the range of possibilities, and this is consistent with the hypothesis test (chi-square) giving $P = 0.54$. A simple and clear description of the calculations involved for matched and unmatched data sets is given by Kahn and Sempos (1989). In (2) the interval is 1.01 to 5.02, showing that a true odds ratio of 1 has a probability of less than 0.05, and the chi-square gave $P = 0.048$ under the null hypothesis. As the study becomes larger, the interval narrows, so that the lowest true odds ratio with a probability of 0.05 of giving the value in the data becomes larger, 1.75 in (3) and 2.08 in (4). Of course, the narrowing of the confidence interval also occurs at the top end of the range of possibilities too. In common sense terms, a large study is less subject to chance variation, and therefore gives a more precise estimate of the 'truth'.

SURVIVAL AND LIFE TABLES

21.59 Sometimes, it is necessary to estimate how long an individual can be expected to live. This is often the basis for comparing two treatments in a prospective randomised clinical trial, particularly in studies of cancer or heart disease. Or, one may wish to describe the mortality experience of a certain group – an occupational category, the population of a defined geographical area, or individuals with a specified medical condition. The basis for such calculations is the observation of an appropriate group or groups over time – a longitudinal or follow-up study. The life table is the most informative way of describing such data. Again, Kahn and Sempos (1989) provides a simple introduction to this method, and more details can be found in Dawson-Saunders and Trapp (1990), and the present discussion will concentrate just on the basic principles. The older life table method is known as the actuarial method and the newer one the Kaplan-Meier method. The basic difference between the two methods is in the length of the follow-up intervals used in the calculation and in the way that 'censored' observations are dealt with.

21.60 A censored observation is one which is incomplete. For example, a person who is being followed up but who has not died at the time of analysis of the data is an incomplete observation; we know how long the person has lived so far, but we cannot say how long the person will live in the future. In the actuarial method, the follow-up intervals are relatively long, often at least a month or even a year. If a person was alive when last seen (at the beginning of an interval), but has not yet reached the end of the interval, the actuarial method arbitrarily assumes the person has survived for half the interval. An adjustment is made to the number of persons 'at risk' of death to take account of this. In the Kaplan-Meier method, however, survival is usually measured in days, and it is assumed that a person who was alive when last seen has survived to the end of that day. Apart from that technical matter, the two life-table methods provide essentially the same information. A simple numerical example of an actuarial calculation will show how the method operates:

Interval (yrs)	N *Starting*	N *Censored*	N *At risk*	N *Dying*	P *Dying*	P *Surv*	Cumul *P Surv* (%)
0–1	80	6	77	7	0.091	0.909	90.9%
1–2	67	4	65	9	0.138	0.862	78.4%
2–3	54	5	51.5	10	0.194	0.806	63.2%
3–4	39	2	38	8	0.211	0.789	49.8%
4–5	29	3	27.5	8	0.291	0.709	35.7%

Note that the number (N) at risk is the number who start the interval less half the censored number. The probability (P) that an individual will die in an interval is, of course, just the number who die as a proportion of the number at risk (eg $7/77 = 0.091$). The probability that an individual will survive an interval is simply $1 - P$ of dying in the interval (eg $1 - 0.091 = 0.909$). The probability that an individual will survive to the end of an interval is obtained as a cumulation of the probabilities of survival of all intervals up to and including that interval (eg the probability of surviving to the end of the 2–3 year interval is $0.909 \times 0.862 \times 0.806 = 0.632$ or 63.2 per cent).

21.61 Expectation of life is a figure often quoted for a population. From age 0, it is the average number of years of life lived by a hypothetical population subject to certain assumed death rates – usually the death rates that apply to that population at around the time the calculation is performed. From any later age than 0 it is the average number of years lived from that age by such a hypothetical population.

21.62 Often, however, a more interesting survival statistic is the median survival time – the time within which 50 per cent will die and beyond which 50 per cent will live. This can be estimated before all the individuals have died. In the numerical example above, this will be just less than four years (as the proportion surviving to the end of the 3–4 year interval is just less than 50 per cent at 49.8 per cent). Of course, estimates of survival from a sample of individuals are subject to sampling error, and details of the calculation of confidence intervals for these estimates will be found in the texts referred to earlier.

LEGAL AND EPIDEMIOLOGICAL STANDARDS OF PROOF

21.63 It is often ensured that the standard of proof in science and epidemiology in particular is higher than that used in legal actions. This is sometimes put as science requiring 95 per cent certainty (because of the 0.05 level of statistical significance and the use of 95 per cent confidence intervals), whereas the law merely requires that, on the balance of probabilities, it is more likely than not that there is a causal connection – effectively requiring a degree of confidence of just greater than 50 per cent. Meeran (1992a, 1992b) put this argument in its conventional form.

21.64 There are two fundamental misconceptions with this analysis. First, it focuses merely on the P value (or the confidence interval). This addresses just chance as the possible explanation for the apparent difference or statistical association. Bias and confounding also remain as explanations of what is seen in the study data. It is because of this that Hill (1965) and the US Surgeon General (1982) proposed criteria or guidelines that might be used in judging whether or not a body of evidence amounted to a strong enough case for a causal connection to be established. The second misconception arises from an erroneous interpretation of what a P value is the probability of. A P value is the probability of what is seen in the study data if there is no real difference or association. It is exactly the same concept as saying that the probability that an unbiased coin when tossed with fall 'head' up is 0.5. If a head does occur, one could say $P = 0.5$. This does not mean that there is a 50 per cent chance that the coin is unbiased and a 50 per cent chance it is biased. If two heads in succession occur, $P = 0.25$. Again, this does not mean that there is a 25 per cent chance the coin is unbiased and a 75 per cent chance it is biased. That is, the misconception is to use the P value as the probability of the hypothesis, whereas it is the probability of the data (under the hypothesis that there is no real difference or association).

CONCLUDING REMARKS

21.65 This chapter is just an introduction to epidemiology and some of its methods. The subject has generated controversy about its methods and the conclusions that can legitimately be drawn from them. The issues dealt with are often very important, and it can be very difficult to evaluate the relevant epidemiological evidence. It is hoped that this brief outline will have clarified the subject sufficiently to enable a more detailed study of a particular matter to be carried out more easily.

BIBLIOGRAPHICAL REFERENCES

Alderslade R, Bellman M H, Rawson N S B, Ross E M, Miller D L 'The national childhood encephalopathy study' in Whooping Cough Reports from the Committee on Safety of Medicines and the Joint Committee on Vaccination and Immunisation (1981) London, HMSO, 79–169.

Bibby J Quotes, Damned Quotes, and .... (Halifax, Demast Books, 1983).

Breslow N E and Day N E *Statistical Methods in Cancer Research vol I – The Analysis of Case-Control Studies, vol II – the Design and Analysis of Cohort Studies* (Lyons, International Agency for Research on Cancer, 1980 and 1987).

Coronary Drug Project Research Group 'Influence of adherence to treatment and response of cholesterol on mortality in the Coronary Drug Project' (1980) New England Journal of Medicine 303: 1038–1941.

Dawson-Saunders B and Trapp R G *Basic and Clinical Biostatistics* (London, Prentice Hall International, 1990).
Doll R and Peto R *The Causes of Cancer* (Oxford, Oxford University Press, 1981).
Feinstein A R *Clinical Epidemiology. The Architecture of Clinical Research* (Philadelphia, WB Saunders Company, 1985).
Hill A B 'The environment and disease: association or causation?' (1965) Proceedings of the Royal Society of Medicine 58: 295–300.
Hirayama T 'Epidemiology of breast cancer with special reference to the role of diet' (1980) Preventive Medicine 17: 173–195.
Kahn H A and Sempos C T *Statistical Methods in Epidemiology* (New York, Oxford University Press, 1989).
Kleinbaum D G, Kupper L L and Morgenstern H *Epidemiologic Research. Principles and Quantitative Methods* (New York, Van Nostrand Reinhold Company, 1982).
Last J M *A Dictionary of Epidemiology* (New York, Oxford University Press, 1983).
Lee K L, McNeer F, Starmer F, Harris P J and Rosati R A 'Lessons from a simulated randomised trial in coronary artery disease' (1980) Circulation 61: 508–515.
Lenz W 'Epidemiology of congenital malformations' (1965) Annals of the New York Academy of Sciences 123: 228–236.
Lillienfeld A M and Lillienfeld D E *Foundations of Epidemiology* (2nd edn, New York, Oxford University Press, 1980).
Meeran R 'Scientific and legal standards of proof in environmental personal injury cases' (1992a) Lancet 339: 671.
Meeran R 'Problems of causation in environmental personal injury' (1992b) Solicitors Journal, 804–806, 14 August.
Rothman K J (ed) *Causal Inference* (Chestnut Hill, Epidemiology Resources Inc, 1985).
Royal College of General Practitioners 'Further analyses of mortality in oral contraceptive users' (1981) Lancet i: 541–546.
Sackett D L 'Bias in analytic research' (1979) Journal of Chronic Diseases 32: 51–63.
St Leger A S, Cochrane A L, Moore F 'Factors associated with cardiac mortality in developed countries with particular reference to the consumption of wine' (1979) Lancet i: 1017–1020.
Schlesselman J J *Case-Control Studies. Design, Conduct, Analysis* (New York, Oxford University Press, 1982).
Schull W J & Cobb S 'The intrafamilial transmission of rheumatoid arthritis' (1969) Journal of Chronic Diseases 22: 217–222.
US Surgeon General *The Health Consequences of Smoking: Cancer* (Rockville, US Department of Health and Human Sciences, 1982).
Vessey M P, McPherson K and Yeates D 'Mortality in oral contraceptive users' (1981) Lancet i: 549–550.

ACKNOWLEDGMENT

I am grateful to Dr Anthony Barton for suggesting the discussion in paras **21.63** and **21.64**.

CHAPTER 22

The position in Scotland

Robert Dickson

INTRODUCTION

22.1 It is essential to realise that the legal system in Scotland is totally different from that which prevails in England and Wales. Many laws and procedures are different and this particularly applies to the timing and conduct of court cases. The Mental Health (Scotland) Act 1984 lays down procedures and time limits which are not the same as those contained in the equivalent legislation referred to elsewhere in this book. The procedure following a sudden or unexplained death is unique to Scotland. A decision in an English case, even by the House of Lords, is not binding in Scotland.

22.2 Scotland's courts are on three levels. The district courts in which one or more JPs sit deal with minor crime. They have no civil powers and it is impossible to take an action for damages there. JPs do, however, have authority to grant search warrants including one under the Misuse of Drugs Act 1971 if the warrant is requested by an authorised person.

22.3 Most cases in Scotland are conducted in the sheriff court. The Country is divided into six sheriffdoms and they are further divided into a number of sheriff court districts where (depending on the population of the area) one or more sheriffs may be based. A sheriff is legally qualified, having been an advocate [a Scottish barrister] or a solicitor for at least ten years. The nearest equivalent in England is a crown court judge but the powers and responsibilities are different. In criminal matters the sheriff sits with a jury on more serious cases and has an upper sentencing limit of three years' imprisonment (and an unlimited fine). In civil matters he sits alone and there is no limit on the nature or value of the claim with which he can deal. Thus a medical negligence claim for £500,000 could be dealt with in a sheriff court. The procedure there is quicker, far less expensive and most cases are conducted by solicitors.

22.4 Sheriffs have all the powers of JPs in relation to the granting of search warrants. Their other miscellaneous powers include responsibility for confirming compulsive detentions under the Mental Health legislation, conducting Fatal Accident Inquiries (FAIs) (see para **22.18**) and the taking of evidence for use in foreign courts. They also take dying depositions; a procedure whereby the evidence of a dying witness can be officially recorded in writing and later presented in court.

22.5 There is a right to appeal in civil matters from the sheriff to a sheriff principal or directly to the Inner House of the Court of Session. The six sheriffs principal each have administrative and appellate responsibility for one sheriffdom. In addition, they can preside over FAIs (eg the Lockerbie Inquiry).

22.6 The Supreme Civil Court in Scotland is the Court of Session. The judges also act in the High Court of Justiciary in criminal matters. In the Court of Session, a judge usually sits alone although, unlike the sheriff court, there is still provision for civil jury trials (although these are very rare). Medical negligence claims are among those for which a civil jury trial can be sought.[1] The procedure in the Court of Session is more complex and costly and it can take longer for cases to reach a conclusion. For a pursuer (the Scottish equivalent of a plaintiff) the advantages of a Court of Session action include that the potential expense can force the defenders (the Scottish equivalent of defendants) to consider a compromise and a case is heard by a judge in Edinburgh as opposed to a sheriff in the local court. The Legal Aid authorities have power to limit the court in which legal aid will be granted if they consider the case is more appropriate to a sheriff court. Claims for £1,500 or less must be taken in the sheriff court.

1 *Barr v Tayside Health Board* 1992 SLT 989.

22.7 The Court of Session never goes on circuit, all cases are heard in Edinburgh and only advocates or advocate solicitors can appear in the court. To raise an action in the Court of Session, an Edinburgh solicitor, while no longer essential, may be required in addition to any locally based lawyer.

22.8 Appeals against a decision of a single judge lie to the Inner House of the Court of Session where three or more judges hear the arguments. A similar provision of an Appeal Court of three or more judges exists for all criminal appeals no matter in which court the case started.

22.9 There is a further limited right of appeal in civil matters only to the House of Lords. There is no right of appeal to London in a criminal case.

USEFUL INFORMATION

22.10 The High Court in Scotland deals solely with criminal matters; its civil equivalent is the Court of Session.

22.11 While, as in England and Wales, the Scottish legal profession is divided into solicitors and advocates [including QCs], certain differences are apparent north of the border.

22.12 Advocates do not work in sets of chambers; they are all independent of each other and most work from Parliament House, Edinburgh, where the Court of Session is situated. Instructions to counsel for advice or opinion should be addressed to the named advocate, c/o Advocates' Library, Parliament House, Edinburgh EH1 1RF.

22.13 While certain counsel have a greater knowledge and experience of medical negligence cases, the Scottish Bar is not divided into categories of specialisation and most advocates are able and willing to undertake work in any legal field. The Faculty of Advocates has produced a directory listing all members and the fields of law in which they are prepared to advise. Further information can be obtained from the Clerk to the Faculty of Advocates at Parliament House.

22.14 Solicitors in Scotland have a much deeper involvement in court work than elsewhere. They undertake most court appearances in the sheriff court, including the preparation and conduct of cases. The Law Society of Scotland, 26 Drumsheugh Gardens, Edinburgh EH3 7YR retains a list of all Scottish legal firms and a note of those who profess an expertise in medico-legal matters.

22.15 Most Scottish doctors and dentists (unless they are covered by Crown Indemnity) belong to the Medical and Dental Defence Union of Scotland although both the MDU and the MPS have members in Scotland. The Defence Societies, as well as providing protection from claims, also give advice and assistance to their members on all medico-legal matters including representation at inquiries and tribunals.

22.16 All the Scottish Health Boards are represented on legal matters by the Legal Adviser, Scottish Health Service Central Legal Office, Trinity Park House, South Trinity Road, Edinburgh EH5. This ensures a high and constant standard in dealing with claims against hospital staff and also results in a consistent approach to matters such as the recovery of hospital records.

22.17 The Secretary of State for Scotland is responsible for health matters dealt with elsewhere by the Health Secretary. An important difference in his obligations and potential liability was illustrated in two cases arising out of the alleged consequences of whooping cough vaccine. In *Bonthrone v Secretary of State for Scotland*[1] a Scottish court ruled that there was no legally enforceable claim available to the parents of a brain-damaged child against the relevant government minister following an advertising campaign encouraging parents to have their children vaccinated. In England, in *Kinnear* it was accepted that such a claim could arise.

1 1987 SLT 34.

FATAL ACCIDENT INQUIRIES

22.18 There is no post of coroner in Scotland and accordingly, the provisions for an inquiry into a sudden or unnatural death are totally different. These provisions are contained in the Fatal Accidents and Sudden Deaths Inquiry (Scotland) Act 1976 and the 1977 Procedure Rules, SI 1977/191.

22.19 Investigations into deaths are conducted initially by the local procurator fiscal (the public Prosecutor for the area) to whom all sudden and unexplained deaths and in particular those which occur within 24 hours of anaesthesia must be notified. The procurator fiscal works under the ultimate direction of the Lord Advocate. He will, through the police and other officials, obtain such information and reports as he requires before deciding whether he wishes to instigate an FAI. In most cases notified to him there is no public inquiry.

22.20 Only if the death occurred:

(1) in the course of the deceased's employment; or
(2) while the deceased was in legal custody; or
(3) in circumstances in which it appears to be expedient in the public interest because it was sudden, suspicious or unexplained

will a Fatal Accident Inquiry be held (section 1(1)).

22.21 Thus, unless it is considered to be in the public interest to hold an inquiry into a death (other than at work or in custody) then there will be no public hearing of the issues. While the ultimate decision whether to request an FAI lies with the Lord Advocate and his local representative, the procurator fiscal, the views of the relatives and any interested party are carefully considered. As only the Lord Advocate (through the procurator fiscal) can petition for a public inquiry, there is no right to the relatives or other interested parties to demand one.

22.22 FAIs into the victims of crimes are very rare and it is almost never considered to be in the public interest to hold a public inquiry into a suicide.

22.23 An FAI is presided over by a sheriff sitting alone. The proceedings are in public. Any interested party, including relatives and their legal representatives, are entitled to attend and ask witnesses questions. They can call witnesses and produce documents and reports. Written statements signed and affirmed by a witness may be allowed in evidence by the sheriff but only if all parties agree or if the sheriff considers it would not result in unfairness to any party represented at the inquiry.

22.24 Most witnesses are called by the procurator fiscal and are then cross-examined by the legal representatives of the relatives, doctors, Health Board etc.

22.25 After hearing all the evidence the sheriff is required to issue a determination in terms of section 6(1) of the Act, setting out as far as possible:

(a) where and when the death or any accident resulting in the death took place;
(b) the cause or causes of such death and any accident resulting in the death;
(c) the reasonable precautions, if any, whereby the death or any accident resulting in the death, might have been avoided;
(d) the defects, if any, in any system of working which contributed to the death or any accident resulting in the death; and
(e) any other facts which are relevant to the circumstances of the death (section 6(1)(a)–(e)).

22.26 No corroboration is required to establish any fact nor is any admission made in the witness box a bar to subsequent criminal proceedings. A witness is not obliged to answer any question which might incriminate him (section 5(2)).

22.27 A copy of the sheriff's determination, which can be given orally at the end of the hearing or later in a written form, is available to any party to the inquiry. A copy of the shorthand notes of the inquiry can be obtained but only if it is ordered within three months of the date of the determination (rule 14).

22.28 As the notes may be essential in deciding what evidence might be available for any subsequent claim for damages, it is essential that an application for a copy is made to the sheriff clerk at the time of the case or within the statutory time limit.

22.29 The determination of the sheriff is not admissible in evidence nor can it be founded on in any judicial proceedings of whatever nature arising out of the death (section 6(3)). In Scotland, therefore, an FAI determination can not be used or referred to in any other court case connected with the death.

22.30 As, however, the Act applies only to Scotland (section 10(6)) the GMC and GDC have ruled that disciplinary hearings which take place in London can refer to the sheriff's determination as the Act has no application in England and the restriction on its use is accordingly not effective. Presumably also if it was possible to found jurisdiction before an English court in a case where there had been an FAI the same consideration would apply.

22.31 Legal Aid is available for representation at an FAI.

LEGAL AID

22.32 The Legal Aid (Scotland) Act 1986 together with subsequent regulations governs this field of practice North of the Border. One fundamental difference between the legal aid position in Scotland and England and Wales lies in the ability of the intended defender to lodge written objections to the proposed grant of legal aid. This must be done within 14 days of the intimation of the application. The Legal Aid Board sends a copy of the application (but not the claimant's financial details) together with the applicant's memorandum stating the basis of claim to any prospective defender. There is no need to send copy precognitions or reports to the other side but the memorandum must give fair notice of the person or authority against whom the claim will be made and the nature of the claim. Vague statements such as 'medical negligence' or 'the patient died following the operation' will result in a successful objection and the refusal of the application by the Legal Aid Board.

22.33 A memorandum for legal aid is required to state the legal test which has been failed and the nature of that failure. As Scottish medical negligence law is based on Lord President Clyde's test in *Hunter v Hanley*[1] it is necessary to support an application with a medical report confirming that no doctor of similar skill and experience would have acted in this way.

1 1955 SC 200, 1955 SLT 213, Ct of Sess. Dicta of Lord President Clyde applied, *Maynard v West Midlands Regional Health Authority* [1984] 1 WLR 634.

22.34 Doctors and dentists, on receiving a copy legal aid application, must forward it immediately to their defence society or the Central Legal Office (as appropriate). Failure to do so could result in the period for objecting passing by. The Scottish legal system applies time limits far more rigorously than elsewhere and the legal aid regulations are no exception. Late objections are usually rejected as time barred and are not included in the papers when the application is considered by the Board.

22.35 If legal aid is granted for a sheriff court action then sanction will be required if it is intended to use counsel. In deciding in which court to raise an action regard must be had for the likely value of the claim. A claim for up to £1,500 must be taken in the sheriff court. The complexities involved and the anticipated time scale for reaching judgment are other relevant factors. The Court of Session is much slower and more expensive than the sheriff court but it does ensure that the case is heard by a judge (and possibly a jury). The Legal Aid Board can refuse to grant a certificate to pursue a case in the Court of Session if they feel that there is no justification for not proceeding in the local sheriff court.

22.36 A Legal Aid Certificate is effective for one year after its issue to enable an action to be commenced in court after service on the other side. The Certificate must be lodged in court within that time period; failure to do so can have two horrific consequences. Firstly, the Legal Aid authorities are entitled to consider that the Certificate has lapsed (and will refuse to pay any fees) and secondly, the court may not regard the pursuer as legally aided and therefore entitled to any modification of an adverse expenses award.

RECOVERY OF MEDICAL RECORDS

22.37 Most claims for medical negligence cannot be established without a detailed examination of the medical records. The Access to Health Records Act 1990 applies in Scotland and the arguments as to how and to whom records require to be made available are dealt with elsewhere. Because all Health Boards in Scotland use the same legal adviser (the Central Legal Office) and most doctors and dentists are members of the MDDUS who have one firm of solicitors to advise them, an acceptable practice has arisen in Scotland.

22.38 Where the patient has given written consent, a copy of the records will generally be sent to the claimant's solicitors to enable them to instruct their own expert. Where there is a good reason [such as the patient's disturbed background], there may be a restriction placed on the documents which may be shown to the patient. In the event of this leading to an impasse a court will be required to rule.

22.39 In terms of the Act, there is an obligation to respect a child's medical records where a child, having consented to a treatment or procedure, such as an abortion or the fitting of a contraceptive device, refuses to allow the doctor to reveal information to a parent. In such a case, the medical practitioner must respect that confidentiality.

22.40 There is no obligation to exchange medical reports at any stage. There is also no obligation to lodge any medical report in court unless it is intended that a witness will refer to it. Tactically, it may however be a useful move to reveal the weight of the medical authority available in the hope of forcing an early settlement.

22.41 There is no restriction (other than the limits of a Legal Aid Certificate or the expense involved) as to the number of reports sought or experts consulted. A court has no power to restrict the number of medical witnesses called nor can it force one side to reveal either the name or the possible evidence of any witness prior to that persons' appearance in the witness box.

22.42 Meetings between opposing experts never occur nor is there any question of settling experts' reports. In Scotland, oral evidence in court is normal and written reports are rarely accepted as substitutes. Where a report on the claimant's present medical condition and prognosis is prepared and both sides can agree then a joint minute (a document for the court, signed by both sides) can be lodged accepting its terms. Under no circumstances, however, will the terms of such a report be adjusted between the sides to reach an acceptable compromise.

22.43 Any application to a court for the production of medical (or other records or documents) is dealt with by a Specification of Documents. This states the nature of the documents which are sought, the person or authority believed to have them, the dates between which the relevant records relate and the treatment (or lack of it) in relation to which the documents may refer. If the application includes hospital records, the motion to the Court to authorise the recovery of the records must be intimated to the Lord Advocate, Crown Office, 5–7 Regent Road, Edinburgh EH7 5BL. Failure to intimate will result in the application being refused.

22.44 Where the court grants a specification, the records must be delivered within seven days to the court concerned who will pass them to the solicitor seeking them. If a doctor considers some or all of the records are confidential and should not be revealed he will place them in a separate sealed envelope and this can only be opened with the consent of the court.

CONSENT

22.45 As elsewhere, it is normally necessary to obtain the consent of a patient before carrying out any operation, medical procedure or examination. To fail to obtain such consent could amount to an assault. Such consent may be implied (by the patient presenting himself at the doctor's surgery for treatment). Written consent, signed by the patient, is normal before any surgical operation. In emergencies common sense and the welfare of the patient will prevail over strict legal requirements.

22.46 Subject to the terms of the Age of Legal Capacity (Scotland) Act 1991 either parent can consent on behalf of a child but where legal custody has been awarded by a court to one parent it is he/she who should give consent. Where the child is in care – then the local authority is *in loco parentis*. A parent can delegate the authority to another adult [a teacher, camp leader etc].

22.47 Consent requires informed knowledge of the nature and extent of the procedure which is to be carried out. It does not, however, involve a requirement that every possible risk in detail is specifically explained.[1]

1 *Moyes v Lothian Health Board* 1990 SLT 444.

22.48 The Scottish courts have ruled that the case of *Sidaway* has not altered the view that the appropriate test in medical negligence cases is contained in *Hunter*. The decision as to whether a patient should be warned of a particular risk and the nature and extent of any warning is a matter governed by medical criteria.

> The risk inherent in a particular operation or procedure, the manner in which the operation may affect or damage a particular patient, the medical need for the operation, and the abilility of the patient to absorb information about his situation without adding damage to his health, are all matters where the doctor, with his own clinical experience and the benefit of the experience of other practitioners is best able to form a judgment as to what the patient can safely be told in the exercise of medical care. Nor is it practical or necessary that the patient should be told of every risk.[1]

1 *Moyes v Lothian Health Board* (see para **22.47**).

Children's consent

22.49 The Children Act 1989 is largely not applicable in Scotland. The problems raised by the age at which a child can consent to his or her own medical treatment are dealt with by the Age of Legal Capacity (Scotland) Act

1991. This Act came into effect on 25 September 1991. Until then, children in Scotland had been divided into two categories: pupils (girls below 12 and boys below 14) and minors (those below 16 who were above the maximum age for pupils).

22.50 Pupils were regarded as having almost no authority to enter into any agreement including one for medical or dental treatment and parental consent was essential. Minors were regarded as having limited powers and the nature and extent of the medical procedure was an important factor in deciding whether consent could be given.

22.51 The new Act abolished the distinction between pupils and minors and in section 2(4) provides:

> A person under the age of 16 shall have the legal capacity to consent on his own behalf to any surgical or dental procedure or treatment, where, in the opinion of a qualified medical practitioner attending him, he is capable of understanding the nature and possible consequences of the procedure or treatment.

Accordingly, a child can agree to treatment provided 'a qualified medical practitioner' (not a nurse or receptionist) 'attending him' [not an official who is not directly involved with the patient] is satisfied as to the child's 'understanding of the nature and possible consequences of the procedure and treatment'. The Act does not mention dentists but common sense and the fact that *Hunter v Hanley* has been held to apply to dental practitioners, must mean that the law regards medical and dental practitioners equally. Consent obtained after a procedure has been explained by a qualified dentist will therefore be regarded as valid.

22.52 This imposes a heavy duty on such a practitioner to ensure that the patient is able to make a balanced judgment in the light of the relevant information. As in all cases where the patient does not sign a consent form, it is essential that the practitioner makes a contemporaneous note that the procedure, treatment and consequences have been explained and that the child understands and has given informed consent. Lack of such a written record, while not fatal, will make it more difficult to show years later that informed consent was obtained.

22.53 The doctor must make a professional judgment based on the age and maturity of the child, the gravity and complexities of the operation or procedure and the nature and extent of any risks involved, in deciding whether the child can give a valid consent. The Act gives no other guidelines and the matter has, as yet, not been tested in court.

22.54 The Act, in section 3, provides a procedure whereby a person, before the age of 21, can make an application to a court to have an agreement made between the ages of 16 and 18 set aside if it is 'prejudicial'.

22.55 Section 3(3)(e) specifically excludes from this loophole consent obtained to any surgical, medical or dental procedure or treatment. Accordingly, a person over the age of 16 – who gives consent to treatment – cannot later seek to challenge that consent because an adult would not have agreed or because of any substantial prejudice to him.

MEDICAL COMPLAINTS PROCEDURES

Clinical judgment complaints

22.56 While the Hospital Complaints Procedure Act 1985 applies also in Scotland there are different circulars dealing with the procedures for complaints. NHS Circular 1981 (GEN) 43 is still in force and provides for a three stage procedure for complaints relating to clinical judgment.

22.57 The first stage involves the consultant in charge of the patient looking into the clinical aspects of the complaint, endeavouring to resolve matters 'within a few days' and probably meeting the complainant to discuss the problem.

22.58 If the complainant remains dissatisfied he can renew his complaint. At the second stage the complaint should be in writing and it will be dealt with by the Chief Administrative Medical Officer (CAMO). If the CAMO is, despite any further meetings with the complainant, unable to achieve a resolution, or if he himself considers it appropriate he can set in motion the third stage.

22.59 This stage, the Independent Professional Review involves the CAMO arranging for all aspects of the case to be considered by two independent consultants in active practice in the appropriate speciality. The consultants concerned, one of whom will come from a comparable hospital in another Health Board, are nominated by the Joint Scottish Consultants Committee. They will meet with the complainant (together with a friend/relative and, if appropriate, the GP). The consultant in charge of the case will not be present unless required.

22.60 The independent consultants produce a confidential report for the CAMO who must advise both the complainant and the doctor concerned of any action which the Board has taken as the result of the complaint.

Informal procedure for other complaints

22.61 Using his powers under the National Health Service (Scotland) Act 1978, the Secretary of State for Scotland issued a Direction (The Hospital Complaints Procedure Act 1985 Direction 1991). This applies to all National Health Service hospitals and came into effect on 19 September 1991. The position of hospital trusts was clarified by a further direction in 1992 which required the two trusts then existing (Aberdeen Royal Hospitals and South Ayrshire Hospitals) *mutatis mutandis* to comply with the 1991 Direction with effect from 9 October 1992. Future trusts will presumably be treated similarly as and when they are created.

22.62 The 1991 Direction requires each Health Board to publicise the arrangements for dealing with complaints. The staff must be trained to ensure that patients, visitors, staff and any consumer organisation (including the Local Health Council) are fully informed of arrangements made by the Board for dealing with complaints. Each hospital or group of hospitals must have a nominated officer to deal with complaints and his name, address and telephone number must be adequately publicised.

22.63 The Direction defines those who are entitled to use the complaints procedure as:

(1) a person who is or has been a patient at a hospital for the management of which a Board is responsible and who makes to that Board a complaint which arises out of the person being or having been a patient at that hospital,
(2) a person acting on behalf of and with the consent of any such person referred to in (1) above, or
(3) a person who is a relative or representative of any such person referred to in (1) above where such person has died or is otherwise unable to act for him or herself.

It is therefore essential that the complaint relates to the period when the person was a patient and that if the patient himself is not making it personally, that his or her consent is obtained. The only exception to this is if the patient has died or is unable to act for himself. In that event, a relative is entitled to lodge a complaint; somebody other than a relative claiming to represent the patient would probably be required to show his entitlement to do so. A court order appointing a *curator ad litem* or a power of attorney will clearly suffice.

22.64 Following a death, an executor, once he has taken out confirmation [the Scottish equivalent to probate] has clear authority to act.

22.65 There is no restriction on the word 'relative' and theoretically anybody claiming a blood relationship with the deceased could lodge a complaint. Friends and companioins have no right to complain unless they are an authorised representative.

22.66 All complaints must be in writing. They must be lodged within three months of the date of the event giving rise to the complaint. Nominated officers do, however, have a discretion to consider complaints made outwith this time limit but only if the complainer had good cause for not having made the complaint earlier (para 3).

22.67 It is important to note that the dispensation will only apply when

(a) the person had 'good cause' for failing to comply with the three-month limit and
(b) that there was 'good cause' for not lodging the complaint 'earlier'.

Where a complaint has not been made within three months, it must therefore be sent in immediately that it is found that grounds exist.

22.68 A patient (or his relatives or representatives) who discovers four months after an event that a ground for complaining exists must send that complaint in forthwith. Failure to do so could result in a nominated officer accepting that while there was a valid reason for not complying with the three-month time scale, there is no 'good cause' for a further delay of, say six weeks, before intimation of the written complaint was made.

22.69 The direction does not allow a three-month period from the time the complainant became aware of the circumstances giving rise to the complaint; the time scale runs from the date of the event.

22.70 The nominated officer is required to investigate complaints promptly and to give both the complainer and any hospital staff involved an opportunity to put forward any information or comment which is relevant. The time scale, progress, and result of the investigations must be sent to the complainer, any staff involved and to the Board.

22.71 If the nominated officer, at any stage, considers that the complaint concerns a matter which may be the subject of separate investigative, judicial or disciplinary procedures, including:

(1) the exercise of clinical judgment by a hospital doctor or dentist (a separate procedure exists for these cases under NHS Circular 1981 (GEN)43);
(2) conduct of hospital staff, which may be the subject of disciplinary proceedings;
(3) the possibility of a criminal offence having been committed; or
(4) a serious incident involving harm to any patient;

he is required to refer the matter to the general manager of the Board and if there is a possibility of a criminal offence – to report the facts to the procurator fiscal. Thereafter, he will not proceed further with his investigation but he must in due course advise the complainer of any action taken by the Board.

GENERAL PRACTITIONERS' TERMS OF SERVICE

22.72 General practitioners [and dentists in general practice] are not employees of the Health Board. Accordingly, the Board cannot be sued as employer and any claim for damages must be directed against the named individual. The Health Board do, however, retain certain responsibilities for general practitioners and as the body responsible for the provision of all local medical and dental services under the National Health Service those responsibilities include the control and authorisation of GPs.

22.73 The National Health Service (General Medical and Pharmaceutical Services) (Scotland) Regulations 1984 have been the subject of a number of amending statutory instruments but, to date, no codifying official rewrite has taken place. The Scottish General Medical Services Committee has, however, prepared a very useful amalgam of the Rules and Schedules showing the dates and extent of the changes.

22.74 The Regulations do not provide any effective redress for a dissatisfied or damaged patient but they do define a doctor's duties and responsibility. They provide the framework for the contract between the Board as the supplier of medical services and the practitioner in the doctor's terms of service. Any breach of those terms of service may, if appropriate, be the subject of a complaint and any proven breach may assist a subsequent claim for damages if that arose. A finding of a breach of a doctor's terms of service may not be referred to in a subsequent FAI.[1]

1 Sheriff Principal RB Taylor QC in FAI Mary Band at Kirkcaldy Sheriff Court.

22.75 The paragraphs covering a doctor's terms of service are contained in Schedule I of the Regulations. Most fundamental is para 9(1), which provides (subject to certain specific restrictions):

A doctor shall render to his patients all necessary and appropriate personal medical services of the type usually provided by general medical practitioners.

This 'catch all' provision includes an obligation 'to give advice on the significance of diet, exercise, the use of tobacco and the misuse of drugs and solvents' (para 9[1A](b)) and 'giving advice, as appropriate, to enable patients to avail themselves of Social Work Services provided by a local authority' (para (9)(1A)(f)).

22.76 It clearly covers the obligation to visit and treat a patient where it is necessary but the decision as to whether a visit is appropriate and what, if any, treatment is required is a matter of medical judgment. No patient has a right to demand a doctor's visit and a failure to come when requested is not per se a breach of the terms of service.

22.77 A doctor, in exercising his professional judgment in making a decision to which his terms of service relates, is not required to exercise a higher degree of skill, knowledge or care than that which general practitioners as a class might reasonably be expected to exercise (para 3A).

22.78 A doctor is entitled to state that on the information available he made a clinical judgment not to visit. If a patient (or his relatives) complains that due to the lack of a required domiciliary visit the condition worsened or some further complication arose, then it is vital to know exactly what the doctor was told and when he was told it. Details of who made the telephone call, what symptoms they described, whom they spoke to and whether a visit was specifically requested are essential and should be recorded as soon as possible.

22.79 A doctor's obligation to a patient ends on death and no doctor is required to attend immediately to issue a death certificate.

22.80 A doctor who does attend a patient can still fall foul of his duties to provide 'all necessary medical services'. Rudeness and aggression are unacceptable and may amount to a breach of a doctor's obligations.[1]

1 *Bennet v Scottish Health Board* 1921 SC 772.

22.81 A doctor's obligations include a requirement within 28 days to invite any new patient (over the age of 5) to participate in a consultation which includes taking a full medical history and the analysis of a urine sample (para 10A), offer a similar consultation to any patient between the ages of 16 and 75 who has not attended at a consultation or clinic for three years (para 10B) and offer such a consultation every 12 months to any patient over the age of 75 (para 10C).

22.82 As the apparent aim of these provisions (brought in by SI 1989/1990) is to ensure the early detection and diagnosis of illness and disease, a doctor who fails to comply and whose patient develops a controllable or preventable illness which could have been diagnosed earlier, may be the subject of a successful claim. Such a claim would not be under the legislation or terms of service; it would arise because no doctor exercising normal skill would have ignored his terms of service obligations (*Hunter v Hanley*).

22.83 A list of people for whose treatment a doctor is responsible is contained in rule 4(1). The list has been expanded since 1974 by a series of statutory instruments. Doctors who act as Deputies are now responsible for patients in respect of whom they are acting (para 4[1](h)) if they are on the medical list of the Health Board (rule 12(2A)). Doctors who have accepted responsibility for patients during hours when the Board have relieved the patient's own doctor of responsibility are in the same position (para 4(1)(k)).

22.84 A doctor is entitled to seek to have a patient removed from his list. The removal will be effective eight days after the doctor has given written notice to the Board unless the Board have assigned the patient to another doctor's list earlier. If, however, the doctor is treating the patient at the time (other than for a chronic illness requiring less than weekly visits) such treatment must be completed before the eight-day period commences.

22.85 The doctor need give no reason for his requirement that the patient's name be removed (para 7).

Complaints

22.86 Where a patient is dissatisfied with his treatment by his general practitioner and believes that there has been a breach of the terms of service, he can complain to the Health Board. No complaint which relates to matters of clinical judgment can be considered.

22.87 Many complaints can be dealt with informally and Health Boards are encouraged, where possible, to try and resolve difficulties amicably. Where however, it is shown that a timeous valid complaint has been made and that there has been an apparent breach of the terms of service, the matter will be considered by the Local Medical Services Committee.

22.88 The MSC is presided over by a lay chairman and consists of six members, three lay and three professional. While the chairman has considerable powers to consider applications and complaints, he has no deliberative vote in any decision of the Committee. Only when the Committee is equally divided does he have a casting vote. The Committee's quorum is four.

22.89 The procedures for the making of complaints to and their investigation by Service Committees are dealt with in the National Health Service (Service Committees and Tribunal) (Scotland) Regulations 1992 which came into force on 3 April 1992. Any complaint, no matter when it arose, if made on or after that date, is covered by the Regulations.

22.90 The time for lodging a complaint is now 13 weeks (formerly six weeks) after the event giving rise to the complaint (regulation 3(2)). Only if the delay is due to illness or other reasonable cause and the doctor agrees to the late intimation can this rule be waived by the Board (regulation 6(2)(b)).

22.91 There is a right of appeal against any refusal to consider a late complaint to the Secretary of State for Scotland but such an appeal must be made within four weeks of the Board's refusal to allow the complaint to be received.

22.92 Where a complaint has been made timeously (it must be in writing unless due to physical disability) it will be considered by the Service Committee Chairman.

22.93 Any person can lodge a complaint but if one is made on behalf of the patient, the Board will require to be satisfied that the patient has consented or that the person is an authorised representative of the patient. If the patient can but does not consent then the complaint cannot proceed.

22.94 If the complaint does not allege a breach of the terms of service, then the Service Committee cannot consider it unless the Board are satisfied that the doctor's persistent conduct could affect adversely the provision of local medical services. In that event, the Board itself can refer the matter to the Committee. They have a similar power if they consider that a complaint, although not from or on behalf of a patient, raises a matter of public interest (regulation 8(1)).

22.95 Removal of the doctor's name from the Health Board list, subsequent to an alleged event, does not preclude a Service Committee investigation.

22.96 Any complaints which allege a breach of the terms of service must be considered by the Chairman of the Committee who can rule that it is trivial, vexatious or does not reveal any reasonable grounds. If the complainer fails on notification of this ruling to respond within two weeks thereafter or if any response is such that the Chairman considers a hearing is unnecessary then he can so report to the Committee and if they agree, no hearing will take place. In that event, the complaint will be disregarded.

22.97 A patient can appeal to the Secretary of State against the Committee's decision to disregard a complaint.

22.98 Where the Chairman decides that the complaint should proceed, the practitioner is sent all the relevant papers, including a copy of the complaint, and is entitled to lodge a response within four weeks. A copy of that response will be sent to the complainer, who will be given a further four weeks to make any observations on the practitioner's reply.

22.99 If the Chairman or the Committee consider it is necessary or if the practitioner has not responded, a hearing of the Committee will take place. This will be in private and the public and media will not be present.

22.100 At the hearing a patient can arrange for the presentation of his case by anybody except somebody who is legally qualified (even if that person is a relative). It does not matter whether the legally qualified person is practising or non-practising, paid or unpaid, the prohibition against presenting the case of another is absolute. A legally qualified complainer can however present his own case. Where a legally qualified person accompanies a party, he can assist but not present the case. The same rules apply to the doctor.

22.101 Witnesses and documents will be heard and considered by the Committee who will be required to rule on whether there has been a breach of the terms of service and, if so, what, if any, action should be taken.

22.102 The Committee must issue its findings in writing. There is a right of appeal (except in the case of a referral to a National Health Service Tribunal) to the Secretary of State for Scotland. Such an appeal must be lodged in writing within four weeks.

22.103 If the Committee holds that a breach has taken place, it can, if it decides to recommend any action, propose that the doctor be reprimanded, recommend withholding a specified sum of money from his remuneration or report the matter to the National Health Service Tribunal with a view to having the doctor's name removed from those allowed to practice within the NHS in the Health Board area on the grounds that the doctor's continued inclusion on the medical list is prejudicial to the efficiency of the Service. The Health Board must ratify the Committee's decision and any withholding is subject to the approval of the Secretary of State.

22.104 The Secretary of State can refuse an appeal without a formal hearing. Where one is fixed, the parties can be represented by lawyers and the proceedings before commissioners (usually an advocate and a suitably qualified doctor) are more formal. If the patient is the appellant, then he/she will be required to present the arguments and proof in support of the appeal. Where the complainer is the respondent in the appeal, while the obligation to oppose the appeal remains with that party, the Board may assist in ensuring the attendance of witnesses and documents in support of the alleged breach. Provisions exist to ensure the compulsory attendance of witnesses.

22.105 The Secretary of State has power (rarely exercised) to award expenses against the unsuccessful party to an appeal.

22.106 All findings of a Service Committee are reported to the General Medical Council by the Health Board. All recordable criminal convictions of doctors are reported to the GMC or GDC by the Scottish Criminal Records Office.

22.107 Where a patient dies before a decision has been made by the Health Board on any complaint then a relative, executor or representative can continue with the complaint. Where the practitioner dies, the complaint terminates and no further action will be taken.

22.108 Where the matter is referred to the National Health Service Tribunal for consideration, the conduct of the case is undertaken by the Health Board and the complainer is merely a witness. A Tribunal, having heard evidence, issues a Report to the Secretary of State agreeing or refusing to allow the removal of the practitioner's name from the list for the local Health Board.

22.109 The findings and decisions of the Health Board or the Tribunal are not binding on the General Medical Council who are entitled to consider the matter anew.

NEGLIGENCE

22.110 As in England the standard of proof in Scotland in any claim for medical negligence is 'balance of probability'.[1]

1 *Scott v Highland Health Board* (29 January 1981, unreported).

22.111 In Scotland the starting point for testing whether the facts and evidence amount to medical negligence is the case of *Hunter v Hanley*.[1] Despite the passage of nearly 40 years the tests laid down by Lord President Clyde remain unchallenged and have been approved in subsequent cases. The test was accepted in *Bolam v Friern Hospital Management Committee*[2] and expressly adopted by Lord Scarman in the English case of *Maynard v West Midlands Health Authority*.[3] In Scotland the case of *Gordon v Wilson*[4] reaffirmed the authority of *Hunter v Hanley* as 'central to the issue of liability in cases relating to diagnoses and patient management'.

1 1955 SC 200, 1955 SLT 213, Ct of Sess.
2 [1957] 1 WLR 582.
3 [1985] 1 All ER 635 at 638.
4 1992 SLT 849.

22.112 The tests in *Hunter v Hanley* have been held to apply to cases of alleged dental negligence also.

22.113 Lord Clyde's dictum [at 206] specifically provides that deviation from normal medical practice is not per se evidence of negligence. Even where there is 'substantial deviation' this may 'be warranted by particular circumstances.'

22.114 The legal test in *Hunter* states:

> To establish liability by a doctor when deviation from normal practice is alleged three facts require to be established. First of all it must be proved that there is a usual and normal practice; secondly, it must be proved that the defender did not adopt that practice and thirdly, [and this is of crucial importance] it must be established that the course the doctor adopted is one which no professional man of ordinary skill would have taken if he had been acting with ordinary care.

22.115 It cannot be emphasised too strongly that Lord Clyde referred to a course of action which *no professional man of ordinary skill would have taken*. Accordingly, unless the pursuer's experts are prepared to affirm that no professional colleague would have acted in that way then the claim is doomed. If the defender can produce evidence which is accepted by the court from a professional man that he would have done likewise or alternatively that while he personally would have adopted a different approach, that this is a matter of medical judgment and others might follow the defender's line, then the pursuer's case will fail.[1]

1 *Gordon v Wilson* 1992 SLT 849.

22.116 The test, as Lord Clyde pointed out, puts a heavy onus on the claimant. English cases which appeared to take a less severe line had been rejected in Scotland and had no binding legal authority in Scottish courts.[1]

1 See *Miller v Lanarkshire Health Authority* disapproving *Beswick v North Manchester Health Authority* reported 14 March 1980.

22.117 It is also important to note that the Scottish courts will require evidence from a professional witness of comparable standing and expertise. They will expect a witness to be able to speak as to how someone with the medical knowledge which existed at the time of the occurrence and with the facilities available at the time would have acted. Evidence of the state of medical knowledge at the time of the proof,[1] evidence from a surgeon attacking the actions of a radiologist[2] or evidence from a specialist with the unique facilities and equipment not available in the hospital where the claim arose[3] have all been held to be of no assistance in tackling the test in *Hunter*.

1 *Moyes v Lothian Health Board* 1990 SLT 444.
2 *Scott v Highland Health Board* (29 January 1981, unreported).
3 *Craig v Glasgow Victoria and Leverndale Hospital Board of Management* (1 December 1972 unreported).

22.118 There is no restriction on the number of experts or witnesses which either side may call and there is no duty to exchange or compare expert reports. Any document however which is to be referred to in the proof must be lodged with the court 28 days before the hearing as a production.

INITIAL MEETING TO FINAL SETTLEMENT

22.119 The time, from the moment the client first seeks advice, in relation to a possible claim for damages until the final closing of the file, the successful award and the payment of all expenses can prove to be a long one. In a field of law where the possible defenders are using legal advisers who have considerable expertise and experience in this field, it is important to avoid the most obvious pitfalls.

22.120 Legal Aid may be available to carry out initial investigations, including the taking of a precognition from the client. In certain cases the basis of claim will be obvious (eg amputation of the wrong limb) and it will only be necessary to concentrate on the value of the claim and exactly against whom the claim should be intimated.

22.121 Following the introduction of Crown Indemnity, hospital doctors are included under the usual employee cover provided by Health Boards. The result of this is that where it is impossible to specify the name of the doctor involved, a claim can still proceed against the Board as employer of all the staff concerned.

22.122 Where the basis of the claim is not obvious or where it is unclear whether there is any liability then expert medical advice is essential. Following the dicta in *Scott v Highland Health Board* the opinion should be from a doctor in the particular field of medicine concerned. He should be reminded that he is judging the standard against that of a doctor of ordinary skill, acting with ordinary care and with the expertise and qualifications of the doctor in question [*Hunter v Hanley*]. In particular, it is essential that a professor from a leading major teaching hospital with state of the art equipment does not compare his position to that of a junior house officer on duty in a cottage hospital where certain facilities do not exist. A copy of the medical records together with other relevant data should be forwarded to the expert.

22.123 The expert must consider the case on the basis of the state of medical knowledge and expertise at the time of the incident. He should have recent experience of the procedure complained about and be able to give evidence of a practical nature. The views of a pure academic or a long retired consultant carry little weight when the tests in *Hunter v Hanley* are considered. Such people may not even be accepted as 'expert' by a court.[1]

1 *Moyes v Lothian Health Board* 1990 SLT 444.

22.124 Having obtained a favourable opinion (one is sufficient as the law requiring corroboration only extends to criminal matters) the claim can now proceed. Assuming that attempts to negotiate a settlement with Central Legal Office or the defence society have proved unsuccessful, a decision as to whether to proceed to court action will need to be made.

22.125 Before taking final steps to put the matter into court certain questions should be answered.

(1) Can the client afford to proceed with a lengthy and expensive court case? If Legal Aid is not available, the cost of fighting an action, including the cost of expert witnesses, will be immense. Even if Legal Aid is forthcoming, can the client afford to pay (and possibly lose) his Legal Aid contribution?
(2) Why are the defenders refusing to settle? Is it because they have a reputable expert opinion which supports the defence? The test in *Hunter v Hanley* is 'No doctor etc' and a medical person with the appropriate qualification and skill who states that either he or colleagues would have done likewise, will, if accepted by the court as reliable, demolish any hope of a successful claim.

22.126 Informal discussions with the defence solicitors will often reveal who their experts are. An offer to exchange opinions may help to show the flaws in your case or expose the gaps in theirs. Neither side can be compelled to reveal the name or address of an expert, nor is an exchange of opinions compulsory. However, if a claim is doomed then it is as well to know as soon as possible without further expense and anxiety; if it is ultimately going to be successful the defenders will wish to avoid unnecessary expense.

22.127 As all medical legal case defences in Scotland are dealt with by the Central Legal Office or a maximum of three legal firms acting for the defence societies, it is reasonably certain that if liability is persistently denied that there is a valid reason for this line. Successful actions for medical negligence in Scotland are very rare because such cases which are indefensible are settled and only those with a seemingly valid defence are taken into court. A determined firm denial of liability from such an experienced source as the Central Legal Office is at least an amber light to check again how strong the claim is.

22.128 The question of whether the client can afford to proceed into court may also govern in which court the action is raised. For claims in excess of £1,500 the Court of Session and the sheriff court have concurrent jurisdiction but the latter is faster and considerably less expensive. The patient's life expectancy and his financial position are both factors to be weighed up as is the value of the claim. The greater the possible award, the more likely it is that the case should be in the Supreme Court. While Scottish juries and judges make smaller awards than can be obtained elsewhere, the normal rule of thumb that juries are more generous than a judge or sheriff, probably applies equally in Scotland. Only in the Court of Session can trial by jury be obtained.

22.129 The Legal Aid authorities may also dictate that the case should be heard in the sheriff court despite the wishes of the applicant.

22.130 Awards in Scotland are not specifically divided between general and special damages. Unlike England, a court writ must specify the sum of money sought. An assessment of the true value of the claim must therefore be made before any case commences.

22.131 The various heads of damage, including 'solatium' (suffering) both past and future, financial loss, including past and future loss of earnings, loss of society and support (following a death) and loss of life expectancy, must all be valued and a total reached. As the court cannot award anything larger than the sum sued for, an inflated figure to cover any under-calculations should be craved.

22.132 Interest should also be sought at a specific rate (usually 8 per cent in terms of the Interest on Damages (Scotland) Act 1971) from the date of any incident. In terms of section 1(1A) interest on solatium should be included in any award by a court unless there are special reasons for not doing so.

22.133 A crave (a written claim in the court writ) for expenses must also be made to ensure the court has authority to award them in the event of success.

22.134 Having decided on the amount to be claimed, the party or parties to be sued and the forum for the case then the initial writ or summons should be prepared. This document must set out the basis of the claim and the grounds of fault.

22.135 Scottish procedure is based on each side stating clearly, in written pleadings, the facts on which the claim or defence is based and the duties of care which are alleged. Whether the case is in the sheriff court or the Court of

Session, the position is the same; unless clear and specific grounds are contained in the pleadings, the action will be dismissed at legal debate.

22.136 Nothing which is not contained in the body of the pleadings can be referred to in any evidence. Any alleged breach of care must be stated averring who owed the duty, to whom it was owed and in what respect any alleged failure caused the pursuer to suffer loss, injury and damage.

22.137 Any averments made by the other side, which are within the knowledge of a party, must either be answered or denied. Failure to do so will result in the averment being regarded as accepted and any attempt to challenge it by evidence will be refused.

22.138 The threat that pleadings, which lack clarity or do not refer to a legally enforceable duty against specified defenders, will be dismissed is a real one. While it is possible to start again the law on prescription may prevent this.

22.139 One of the fundamental differences between Scottish and English procedure arises in the law on prescription. In Scotland, not only must the writ be warranted by the court, it must also be served successfully on the defenders within the three year time limit. There is no further period allowed for service of the writ. It is therefore essential to know the address and whereabouts of a defender if the three year time limit is approaching so that service can be effected timeously.

22.140 Section 17(2) of the Prescription and Limitation (Scotland) Act 1973 (as amended) provides that in any action which includes a claim for personal injuries:

no action shall be brought unless it is commenced within a period of 3 years after:

(a) the date on which the injuries were sustained or where the act or omission to which the injuries were attributable was a continuing one, the date or dates on which the act or omission ceased, whichever is the later, or

(b) the date (if later than any date mentioned in paragraph (a) above) on which the pursuer in the action became [or on which, in the opinion of the Court, it would have been reasonably practical for him in all the circumstances to become] aware of all the following facts –

  (1) that the injuries in question were sufficiently serious to justify his bringing an action for damages on the assumption that the person against whom the action was brought did not dispute liability and was able to satisfy a decree;

  (2) that the injuries were attributable in whole or in part to an act or omission; and

  (3) that the defender was a person to whose act or omission the injuries were attributable in whole or in part or the employer or principal of such a person.

Section 17(3) states that in calculating the three year period no regard shall be had for any time during which the person was 'under legal disability by reason of non-age or unsoundness of mind'.

22.141 The effect of the Act is that the three year period starts from the date of the incident unless the pursuer can show that it was not until a later date that he became aware that the injuries were so serious as to justify him raising an action of damages; that the injuries were attributable to an act or omission and that he had only then become aware of the person responsible for that act or omission. In that event, the three year period will run from that date.

22.142 Section 18 indicates that the three year period in the case of a death runs from the date of death or any later date when the claimant became or could reasonably have become aware of the fact that the injuries of the deceased were attributable to an act or omission and the person responsible for that act or omission.

22.143 Section 19A allows a court to override the three year limit if 'it would be equitable to do so'. The Scottish courts frequently refuse to allow a late action. If the delay in raising the action is due to professional negligence by a solicitor or other adviser then the courts frequently expect the claimant to direct the action against the professional adviser and allow the original proposed defender to escape.

22.144 In terms of section 19(4), if an action is allowed to commence late the right to a jury trial is lost.

22.145 There is no specific time limit for lodging or accepting a tender. In Scotland payments into court are made by lodging in court a document offering a specified sum in settlement. No actual money is lodged.

MENTAL HEALTH

22.146 The Mental Health (Scotland) Act 1984, as amended by the Mental Health (Detention) (Scotland) Act 1991, deals with the law on the detention and treatment of those suffering from mental disorders. The Act provides for three forms of detention in hospital. Emergency admissions under section 24 permit the detention of a patient for up to 72 hours on a doctor's certificate.

22.147 In terms of section 26, a patient can thereafter be detained for one period of 28 days (short-term detention) and, if no appeal is lodged, then the order takes effect for that period without any reference to the courts. Prior to the end of the 28-day period, if it is considered appropriate to detain the patient for a further period, then an application must be made under section 18 to a sheriff for the patient's long-term detention.

22.148 A section 18 application must be accompanied by certificates from two medical practitioners and requires the approval of the sheriff. One of the doctors must be approved for the purposes of the Act by the Health Board. One doctor should be the patient's general practitioner or somebody who has been concerned in his earlier treatment. Only one doctor should be a member of the staff of the hospital where it is proposed the patient should be detained. Only in exceptional circumstances can this be waived (section 20(2)).

22.149 The Act is rigid in its timetable and where an application is made outwith the time limits, it will be refused. No extensions other than under the 1991 Act can be granted.[1]

1 *B v Forsey* 1988 SLT 572 and *R, Petitioner* 1990 SCLR 783.

22.150 The 1991 Act deals with the situation where, due to a sudden relapse close to the end of a period of detention, a timeous application to detain cannot be made. In that event, a further three days of 'interim detention' is authorised on a report prepared by one practitioner. A full application must be lodged within that three day period as no further extensions are permitted.

22.151 Where, due to court delays, public holidays etc a hearing for a timeous application cannot take place before the expiry of a previous order, then the previous order remains in force for five working days after a section 18 application is lodged.

22.152 It should be noted that the time for lodging applications and seeking further procedure is measured strictly (ie 72 hours, 28 days etc) and no allowance is made for public holidays or weekends. Once the application is lodged then five working days (ie excluding weekends, holidays etc) is allowed for the hearing of the case by the sheriff, and during that period the order remains in force.

22.153 Procedures for the detention of patients under the criminal law are covered by the Criminal Procedure (Scotland) Act 1975 (as amended).

CHAPTER 23

General practice

Professor Brian Jarman *OBE MA PhD FRCP FRCGP*

SUMMARY

THE NATURE OF THE GENERAL PRACTITIONER CONTRACT

23.1 People are employed as servants (who can be told what to do and how to do it) or as contractors (who are told what to do but do it in their own way). General practitioners working in the NHS are, unlike hospital doctors, independent contractors. They may also be employed simultaneously as servants by, for instance, companies or other doctors. When they are included in the Medical List of a Family Health Services Authority (FHSA) (or Health Board in Scotland) they must sign a form of contract agreeing to keep to their Terms of Service. Arrangements for the provision of general practitioner services in the UK are laid down in the 1992 statutory instrument – NHS (General Medical Services) Regulations[1] that came into force on 1 April 1992, and in the Statement of Fees and Allowances for general practitioners (the 'Red Book') which is regularly updated. The details of the contract are subject to revision mainly as a result of negotiations between the government and the General Medical Services Committee of the British Medical Association.

1 The National Health Service (General Medical Services) Regulations 1992, SI 1992/635 (London, HMSO).

23.2 Paragraph 3 of Schedule 2 of the NHS (General Medical Services) Regulations 1992 – the Terms of Service for doctors – states that:

> a doctor shall not . . . be expected to exercise a higher degree of skill, knowledge and care than . . . that which general practitioners as a class may reasonably be expected to exercise.

Paragraph 12 states that 'a doctor shall render to his patients all necessary and appropriate personal medical services of the type usually provided by general medical practitioners', which include the following:

(a) giving advice, where appropriate, to a patient in connection with the patient's general health, and in particular about the significance of diet, exercise, the use of tobacco, the consumption of alcohol and the misuse of drugs or solvents;
(b) offering to patients consultations and, where appropriate, physical examinations for the purpose of identifying, or reducing the risk of, disease or injury;
(c) offering to patients, where appropriate, vaccination or immunisation against measles, mumps, rubella, pertussis, poliomyelitis, diphtheria and tetanus;
(d) arranging for the referral of patients, as appropriate, for the provision of any other services under the Act; and
(e) giving advice, as appropriate, to enable patients to avail themselves of services provided by a local social services authority.

General practitioners on the child health surveillance, obstetric or minor surgery lists are expected to exercise the relevant skills and provide the relevant services. The doctor should render these services at his practice premises, or, if the patient's condition so requires, in the patient's home (at the address when he joined the list or the address at which the doctor has informed the FHSA and patient he has agreed to visit) or at some other place in the doctor's practice area.

23.3 A doctor in private practice is considered to have a contract with a patient each time the patient consults. This is in contrast to NHS general practitioners who have no contractual relationship with their NHS patients. Their contract is with the FHSA and covers all patients registered with them as permanent or temporary registrations and any NHS patient in their practice area whom they see in an emergency who is unable to obtain treatment from their own doctor, or a deputy acting for their own doctor.

DISCIPLINARY PROCEDURES AGAINST GENERAL PRACTITIONERS

23.4 Disciplinary action may be taken against a general practitioner or a hospital doctor on the grounds of personal or professional misconduct or professional incompetence but, in addition to this, NHS general practitioners have to keep to their Terms of Service. These cover matters such as the standards of accommodation they provide, the quality of the records they keep, the use of deputising services, writing medical sickness certificates, the need to visit a patient at home or refer a patient to hospital when it is indicated and providing cover for 24 hours a day every day of the year.

23.5 Complaints may be made about general practitioners to the FHSA Medical Service Committee or to the General Medical Council (GMC): general practitioners may also be prosecuted in the criminal courts and sued in the civil courts – all for the same incident. The Patient's Charter has also made it clear that the public have the right to have a complaint investigated and to receive a full and prompt reply. A complaint may be made to the FHSA by the patient or by someone with the patient's written authority, or on behalf of an elderly or sick patient, or by anybody if the patient has died or is under 16, or by the FHSA (usually regarding prescribing, certification or clinical records). The complaint should be within 13 weeks of the event unless the delay is due to illness, bereavement or other reasonable cause. The police may report cases to the GMC, as may the Secretary of State particularly when a general practitioner has more than a small withholding of remuneration as a result of an FHSA Medical Service Committee decision against the general practitioner.

23.6 It therefore behoves a general practitioner to continue to keep well informed in order to maintain professional competence and be aware of changes in the Terms of Service and current opinion. It is not adequate for a general practitioner just to leave things to the medical defence societies to solve any problems if they arise: instead a process of continuing medical education and updating of knowledge is needed. Unfortunately Vocational Training Schemes (VTSs), which are provided for trainee general practitioners, do not feature questions of medical malpractice very strongly in their courses. This is partly because of the shortage of available information regarding the types of cases that are most likely to give rise to problems.

23.7 Complaints made about a general practitioner to the FHSA are considered by the FHSA's Medical Service Committee[1] (MSC), which consists of three lay members appointed by the FHSA, three medical members appointed by the Local Medical Committee (a body elected by and from the general practitioners in the FHSA area) and a lay chairman appointed by the FHSA (who is often legally qualified). Most complaints involve paragraphs 3, 12 or 13 of the Terms of Service that came into force on 1 April 1992 (see para **23.3**). The chairman usually decides whether a complaint to the FHSA deserves a hearing by the Committee because it relates to an alleged failure to comply with the Terms of Service. If the complaint is heard by the Committee, neither the complainant nor the doctor may have their case presented by a paid advocate, although they may be accompanied by a friend. Evidence is taken, but not on oath, and witnesses may be called but not compelled to attend. The MSC will decide whether the general practitioner has been in breach of the Terms of Service, report its findings to the FHSA and may recommend a penalty if there has been a breach. The penalties may be a caution, a withholding of remuneration, a limitation of the list size or a recommendation that a tribunal be held to consider the removal of the general practitioner from the FHSA's medical list. Appeals are allowed to the Secretary of State. If the general practitioner is not found to have broken the Terms of Service, the person bringing the complaint cannot be reprimanded or penalised in any way. Complaints to an FHSA are privileged and so a doctor cannot bring an action for slander or libel if the complaint appears to be defamatory. There are proposals to change the MSC complaints system, by introducing in-practice complaints procedures for minor incidents, giving formal training for members of the MSC, having a legally qualified chairman and for the FHSA, with which the general practitioner is in contract, to act as the patient's advocate and the patient to have only the responsibility of presenting evidence.

1 The National Health Service (Service Committees and Tribunal) Regulations 1992, SI 1992/664 (London, HMSO).

23.8 Complaints that the GMC receives cover matters of professional etiquette such as advertising, the abuse of personal relationships with patients and neglect of professional responsibilities to patients. The Professional Conduct Committee of the General Medical Council investigates complaints of serious professional misconduct: these include cases of medical negligence. There is also a GMC Health Committee in parallel with the Professional Conduct Committee for doctors who are ill, especially mentally ill or addicts. The majority of complaints investigated by the GMC regarding treatment in general refer to general practitioners.[1] The Professional Conduct Committee considers about 3 per cent of the cases received by the GMC, about a third of which concern professional responsibilities and clinical competence.[1,2] Hence the GMC does not devote much of its time to investigating incompetent doctors. This is because the GMC, under its statutory jurisdiction through the Medical Act 1983, can only restrict or remove a doctor's registration where a doctor is found guilty of 'serious professional misconduct' or has been convicted of a criminal offence in the British Isles. However, the GMC is proposing to introduce performance reviews for doctors whose 'general pattern of practice is so poor as to put patients at risk' but does not constitute serious professional misconduct – 'the biggest change in its powers since it was set up in 1858'.[3] This would cover a doctor who 'is failing to keep proper clinical records, or often prescribes inappropriately, or lacks basic professional knowledge and medical skills' . . . 'It would involve a local assessment conducted in private by a team of three: two doctors with expertise in the appropriate speciality and a third, non medical assessor'.[3] They would recommend remedial action when necessary and if this were not successful a new committee of the GMC would have the power to restrict or suspend the doctor's registration.

1 Fry J Annual Report of the General Medical Council (London, GMC, 1991).
2 DHSS *Health and Personal Social Services Statistics for England, 1992* and other editions (London, HMSO, 1993 (and other years)).
3 Kilpatrick R 'The Council's Proposals for Performance Procedures' (1992) GMC News Review 1: June.

23.9 The NHS ombudsman – the Health Service Commissioner – can investigate alleged failures in the health service or maladministration of the service, but his powers do not cover general practitioners or the FHSA complaints procedure.

THE FREQUENCY OF COMPLAINTS AGAINST GENERAL PRACTITIONERS

23.10 Although detailed information is published annually of complaints to FHSAs[1] (see Table 23.1), these data are not broken down to give the content of the complaints. However, Klein has analysed FHSA complaints against general practitioners and shown[2] that failure to visit or delay in visiting, failure to treat a patient in an emergency, failure in the provision of surgery accommodation, failure of deputising services and incorrectly demanding fees were some of the commonest causes for complaint in the early 1970s. Additional information is available from a random sample of a thousand records from the computer database of the Medical Protection Society of formal complaints about the general practitioners to FHSAs between 1982 and 1989.[3] The commonest cause for complaint was failure to visit (25 per cent), and failure to diagnose was the next commonest cause (20 per cent). Other causes were error in prescription, failure to arrange emergency admission, delay in diagnosis, failure to examine, unsatisfactory attitude and failure to refer for investigation or opinion.

1 DHSS (1992).
2 Klein R E *Complaints against Doctors* (London, Charles Knight, 1973); Ham C, Dingwall R and Harris D Medical Negligence – Compensation and Accountability, Briefing Paper 6 (London, King's Fund, 1988).
3 Owen C 'Formal complaints against general practitioners: a study of 1,000 cases' (1991) British Journal of General Practice 41: 113–115.

23.11 The number of complaints to FHSAs has been rising gradually both in absolute numbers and when expressed as complaints per 1,000 general practitioners (unrestricted principals – i e not including restricted principals, trainees or assistants), Figure 23.2, or per 100,000 of the population, Figure 23.1. These figures, which are taken from the DHSS annually published Health and Personal Social Services Statistics,[1] are shown in Table 23.1, for the years from 1972 to 1992. Because the number of general practitioners has been increasing more rapidly than the population, the complaints per 100,000 of the population has increased faster than the complaints per 1,000 general practitioners and this is shown in Figures 23.1 and 23.2.

1 See para **23.10** n 1.

23.12 It is not easy to compare the changes in general practice with what has been happening in the hospital service because little information is available. However, data extracted from figure 5 of the King's Fund Briefing Paper 6 – Medical Negligence,[1] published in 1988, shows the claims opened in two NHS Regional Health Authorities from 1977/78 to 1987/88. The regions are labelled C and E in the figure. In published DHSS statistics Trent Region is normally labelled C and North West Thames Region labelled E. These data have been plotted in Figure 23.3 to show the trends in hospital and general practice. It should be remembered that the data are not strictly comparable and can only be used to show trends. There is some indication that the increase in the rate of claims opened in the two hospital regions is increasing more rapidly than the rate of FHSA Service Committee complaints investigated.

1 Ham et al (1988).

23.13 About 6 per cent of general practitioners have a formal complaint made to the FHSA about them every year, and this figure has doubled in the last 20 years. The general practitioner is found to be in breach of his Terms of Service in about a quarter of these complaints. Correspondingly detailed data are not available about claims for medical negligence involving general practitioners but there is evidence, from the medical defence societies annual subscription rates, that these have also increased less rapidly over the years than for hospital doctors. Since 1989 the medical defence societies have offered lower rates for general practitioners than for hospital doctors.

REASONS FOR LOWER GENERAL PRACTITIONER COMPLAINT RATES

23.14 Margaret Brazier, in her book *Medicine, Patients and the Law* (1992),[1] says that 'malpractice actions against general practitioners are rare and only a handful of reported cases exist'. The reasons that she gives for a lower rate of complaints against general practitioners are, first, that the NHS arrangements for general practice and the quality of care offered by most general practitioners are such that family doctors still occupy a high measure of esteem. Second, most patients enjoy a longstanding personal relationship with their general practitioner – lasting on average for about ten years – and mistakes are more likely to be overlooked than in the less personal atmosphere of a hospital. Third, it has been suggested that negligence is more difficult to prove against general practitioners.

1 Brazier M *Medicine, Patients and the Law* (London, Pelican Books, 1992).

23.15 Another reason why there are relatively fewer cases of litigation for negligence against general practitioners may be that the FHSA complaints procedure allows patients, at no cost, to air their grievances with their general practitioners if they feel they have broken their Terms of Service. With an average patient consultation rate of about four consultations per patient per year it can be calculated that there are annually about eight formal complaints per million general practitioner consultations, in only two of which a breach of the Terms of Service is found. The FHSA Medical Services Committee is bound to investigate any written complaint which is made within the time limit (which is effectively around three months although there is an 'out of time' mechanism). These complaints procedures are available to the vast majority of the population of the UK, 98 per cent of whom are registered with an NHS general practitioner.[1] Only 1 per cent of consultations in the community are with private general practitioners.[2] Patients can change their general practitioners when they wish and, although general practitioners do not have to accept patients, there is an allocation system for patients who find difficulty getting another general practitioner. Since 1991 it has been easier for patients who have not changed their address to change their general practitioner. General practitioners also have to prepare practice booklets describing the services they offer – as part of the general thrust of the NHS White Paper[1] to give patients more choice.

1 DHSS and Secretaries of State for Health, Wales, Northern Ireland and Scotland 'Working for Patients' Cmnd 555 (London, HMSO, 1989) (the White Paper on the review of the NHS).

2 Office of Population Censuses and Surveys *General Household Survey 1982* (and other years) (London, HMSO, 1984 (and other years)) Table 8C.

23.16 In addition there is a system of referral of patients to a specialist for an opinion or admission to hospital by the general practitioner rather than allowing the patient direct access to hospital. This has been in existence since Lloyd George's National Health Insurance Act 1911 and probably fosters loyalty between patients and their general practitioners and reduces excessive use of specialist services.[1] The rule applies on all occasions except accidents and emergencies, sexually transmitted diseases and drug misuse.

1 Quam L, Fenn P and Dingwall R 'Medical Malpractice in Perspective: II – The Implications for Britain' (1987) British Medical Journal 294: 1597–1600.

MEDICAL NEGLIGENCE AND GENERAL PRACTICE

23.17 For negligence to be proved it must be shown that:

(a) the doctor owed a duty of care to the patient;
(b) the doctor was in breach of that duty; and
(c) the patient suffered damage.

Usually in NHS practice, the fact that the patient is registered (either as a temporary or permanent patient or when being treated as an emergency) with the doctor is sufficient to establish a duty of care for the patient. However it can be difficult to establish that a general practitioner's treatment, or failure to treat, was negligent and the onus of proving negligence normally rests with the patient and not the doctor.

23.18 The main question in negligence for a general practitioner is whether there was a breach of the duty to exercise reasonable skill and care – the reasonable skill and care being that of an average general practitioner. It is no defence to say that the general practitioner has just entered practice or is old and infirm.

23.19 General practitioners must use their judgment at all times in their actions to ensure that they are acting at least at the standard of skill, knowledge and care of an average general practitioner, both in the organisation of the practice in order that patients can be seen in the surgery or at home when necessary, and in examining, diagnosing, prescribing and referring patients to hospital. This does not mean, for instance, that every patient needs to be visited when they ask for a visit, but they should be visited if, with the information available to the general practitioner, it seems that a visit is necessary. If the information given by the patient suggests that a visit is necessary, then it should be done and it is no defence against negligence if the receptionist or other member of staff, a deputy or a locum was at fault for the visit not being done. It is the general practitioner who has the duty to care for the patient and, if the care given is inadequate and leads to damage to the patient as a consequence, it is the general practitioner who is responsible in law.

23.20 The damage suffered is assessed financially in terms of general damages – loss of function, loss of earnings and pain – and special damages, such as medical expenses. The degree of negligence is not necessarily related to the level of damages. A patient needs to prove that an error of judgment amounted to negligence to obtain compensation for damages.

23.21 In a general practice partnership under the Partnership Act 1890, each doctor is individually and jointly liable with their partners for acts of negligence by the partnership, and a patient can sue the partners. A general practitioner principal is responsible for the actions of an assistant and both may be sued, as can a general practitioner employed nurse. General practitioners have to be wary of tasks that are delegated to practice employed nurses and should normally be expected to diagnose and initiate treatment themselves. The general practitioner is responsible to the patient for ensuring that a nurse has been adequately trained for any procedure that is delegated to her.[1] Nurses are advised, but not compelled, to be insured against liability. However, general practitioners are vicariously liable for the negligence of their employees. There are difficulties, however, regarding locums and deputies. General practitioner principals are responsible to their FHSA for the actions of their deputies and trainees who are not in contract with that FHSA. Now that Joint Deputising Committees and Deputising Service Sub-Committees of FHSAs are no longer functioning, the general practitioner is less certain that the standards that the FHSA considers to be adequate are in operation by the deputising services.

1 General Medical Council *Professional Conduct and Discipline: Fitness to Practice* (1992).

23.22 Nearly all cases of medical negligence come under civil law, ie they are rarely criminal offences except, for instance, in the case of gross negligence leading to death that might result in a charge of manslaughter where there was 'such disregard for the life and safety of others as to amount to a crime against the State and conduct deserving punishment'. There is a general time period of three years from the accrual of the course of action (see Chapter 13).

CASES OF NEGLIGENCE CLAIMS IN GENERAL PRACTICE

23.23 Data is not available from the medical defence societies from which it is possible to list the commonest causes of negligence in general practice. However, from analysis of the reports of the medical defence societies, the GMC, and of cases that I have seen, the following are common:

(a) failure to visit a patient at home when requested (eg for meningitis or acute abdominal pain);
(b) failures of communication, for instance between hospital and general practitioner or in not acting on the results of tests (such as an abnormal cervical smear result), or not carrying out treatment suggested by specialists. It is not adequate to rely on a patient as an intermediary between doctors: the communication should be directly from one doctor to another. There can be problems in group practices, especially if they also use deputising services, when information is not passed between doctors when more than one is involved in the case;
(c) failure to examine, to refer to a specialist, or keep proper records;
(d) drug treatment, for instance known allergies or where a general practitioner may, for instance, prescribe ampicillin for a case of infectious mononucleosis (which might cause a rash) rather than giving penicillin;
(e) failures of practice management.

23.24 Drug treatments can, and do increasingly, give rise to problems of medical negligence. The number of powerful drugs available to a general practitioner increases each year, and with each the number of possible side effects and interactions also increases. Prescriptions are given in about three-quarters of all consultations[1] (ie at about 5,000 consultations per general practitioner per year) and 'repeat prescriptions', when the patient is not seen in a consultation but receives a prescription, usually handed to them by the receptionist, account for about a further 40 per cent of prescriptions.[2] The number of prescriptions given to each patient per year has increased from four and a half in 1950 to eight in 1992.[3,4]

1 Office of Population Censuses and Surveys (1984).
2 Jarman B (ed) *Primary Care* (London, Heinemann, 1988).
3 Office of Health Economics *Compendium of Health Statistics* (6th edn, London, OHE, 1987).
4 DHSS (1993).

23.25 Although a doctor may write a prescription on the advice of a consultant, it is the doctor who writes the prescription who is responsible legally for that prescription. The practice of some health authorities of encouraging hospital doctors to transfer the prescribing of drugs from the hospital budget to the general practice budget, without simultaneously transferring the clinical control of the patient, is not to be recommended. *The doctor who has clinical responsibility for the patient should undertake the prescribing*. This is doubly important if there is poor communication between the hospital doctor and the general practitioner, or if the patient is used as an intermediary in transferring information between hospital doctor and general practitioner. An example might be where a hospital doctor is treating a patient with warfarin to thin the blood after the patient has had a pulmonary embolism, and the treatment is expected to last for, say, six months during which period the prothrombin time has to be monitored carefully to avoid excessive bleeding. In this instance the hospital is clearly monitoring the clinical situation and it is important that the hospital doctor has the responsibility for prescribing the dosage of warfarin (which is a dangerous drug and one of the drugs most likely to have serious side-effects). It is a dangerous practice for a general practitioner to prescribe warfarin without having clinical control of this aspect of the patient's treatment by means of history, examination and monitoring the prothrombin time.

23.26 Drug treatment given by a general practitioner must, like any other treatment, be the correct treatment and it should be administered correctly. A general practitioner may have chosen, or have had recommended by a specialist, the correct treatment for the patient's condition, but then has to think of the potential contraindications for that particular patient, the side effects and the drug interactions. The general practitioner must also communicate with the hospital regarding the patient's allergies and idiosyncrasies in relation to drug treatment. The general practitioner should preferably write the drug prescription legibly and must advise the patient clearly regarding the dosage and method of taking the drug.

23.27 A situation arose in 1988 regarding the prescription of benzodiazepines by general practitioners. Although they were considered not to cause dependence when they were first released in the 1960s, they have, since at least 1980, been considered to cause dependence if given for more than about two or three weeks. The *British National Formulary*[1] recommends that benzodiazepine (and other) hypnotics and anxiolytics should be limited to short courses and long term use be avoided. It is possible that about a million people may be taking benzodiazepines that have been prescribed by their general practitioners for a year or more. In January 1988 the Committee on Safety of Medicines found it necessary to issue recommendations relating to benzodiazepine dependence and withdrawal symptoms. This situation is an illustration of the need for general practitioners to be constantly aware of the side-effects of drugs they prescribe and to keep up to date with the literature, particularly in areas where there are changing medical opinions.

1 BMA and the Royal Pharmaceutical Society of Great Britain *British National Formulary* Number 25 (December 1992) and earlier editions (London, BMA and RPS of GB, 1992).

23.28 Many general practitioners are now on the *minor surgery* list under the terms of the new contract. Only those who are considered to have the necessary skills should have been accepted for the list by their FHSA. Many will have had special courses run by surgeons. They will need to take care to carry out only those procedures for which they are competent, to record the patient's consent and, where appropriate, to obtain written consent, to have good sterilising equipment and sharps disposal boxes, and to arrange for the histology of excised lesions to be examined.

GENERAL RULES REGARDING MEDICAL NEGLIGENCE

23.29 In the cases on which I have been asked to give an opinion regarding the possibility of negligence in general practice there have usually been one or two critical points in the flow of events when the question had to be asked 'Would the average general practitioner have been expected to have taken this or that particular course of action?' For example:

(a) did the general practitioner record an adequate history and examination?
(b) was it reasonable to give a particular treatment?
(c) should the general practitioner have visited the patient at home?
(d) should the patient have been referred to a specialist?
(e) did poor communication between doctors lead to mismanagement?

23.30 General practitioners should not get into trouble if they use their common sense and follow the rules:

(a) listen attentively;
(b) examine;
(c) record meticulously in the notes and keep records of appointments and visit requests;
(d) if in doubt, record this doubt and do any necessary tests;
(e) ensure good communication between doctors, including deputising doctors and locums;
(f) treat and explain carefully and courteously;
(g) visit at home or refer to a specialist when necessary;
(h) keep up to date;
(i) have the patient's welfare in mind always.

23.31 A good doctor/patient relationship in general practice may avoid the patient resorting to legal action partly in order to obtain a full explanation of what really happened – something which patients need in order to resolve the events in their own minds. Dr Garth Hill, writing in the Winter 1988 edition of the Journal of the Medical Defence Union, has reiterated the MDU's view that 'the patient is entitled to a prompt, sympathetic and above all truthful account of what has occurred'. The proposed in-practice system for minor complaints may help patients to feel satisfied that they know what happened if something goes wrong.

INFORMED CONSENT IN GENERAL PRACTICE

23.32 Consent may be implied or expressed. Implied is the commonest in that the patient presents at the surgery, or asks for a home visit, implying that he or she agrees to a medical examination in a general sense. Permission should be explicitly requested for a rectal or vaginal examination or a blood test (written consent is needed for more complicated procedures, such as endoscopy). Oral or written consent is expressed consent (oral has the validity of written consent if witnessed, but written is easier to prove). Informed consent implies a reasonable explanation of a procedure to enable the patient to make an informed decision. Male doctors examining female patients, especially rectally or vaginally, should do so in the presence, or hearing, of a female relative or nurse, receptionist or other members of the practice team. The consent of a spouse to matters relevant to marriage is advisable but not legally required. Parents or the guardian of someone under the age of 16 should give consent for children, although it is possible, if the child is thought to have sufficient maturity, for them to make the decision themselves. A doctor prescribing contraception for a girl under 16 should try to persuade her to inform her parents. If this is not successful then the doctor, acting in the girl's best interests, can give contraception to a girl under 16 if she is likely otherwise to have unprotected sexual intercourse.[1] Mentally ill patients' consent depends on the status of their mental illness.

1 Department of Health Patient Consent to Examination or Treatment (HC(90)22, 1990).

23.33 When general practitioners are working with social workers, they may have difficulties about consent to reveal information, for instance in cases of suspected non-accidental injury or in connection with the Children Act 1989 (which came into force on 14 October 1991). Child care legislation has as its main consideration the protection of children and therefore places on local authority social services departments statutory duties in relation to children. The general practitioner is best advised in non-accidental injury cases to follow the 1988 DHSS guidelines for co-operation with social workers as published in *Working Together*.[1]

1 DHSS and Welsh Office *Working Together* (London, HMSO, 1988).

23.34 Consent and AIDS is a problem which arose in 1987/88. Guidelines published by the GMC on 8 August 1988 state that where blood samples are taken to detect HIV infection 'the test should be carried out only where the patient has given explicit consent' . . . 'this is not because the condition is different in kind from other infections but because of the possible serious social and financial consequences that may follow for the patient from the mere fact of having been tested for the condition'. This applies both in relation to treatment and for screening purposes. Other guidelines from the BMA state that HIV tests should not be carried out without pre- and post-test counselling. It is advisable to ask the patient to sign a form saying that they understand the issues involved (or at least for the general practitioner to record the fact in the medical notes).

23.35 Confusion had arisen in 1987 because, although the Annual Conference of Local Medical Committee representatives (who are all general practitioners) had voted in favour of explicit consent being required, the annual representatives meeting (ARM – of both general practitioners and hospital doctors) later in the year had decided that explicit consent was not necessary. The Council of the BMA sought legal advice and was told that explicit consent was always essential before testing for HIV infection. The BMA therefore reversed the advice given in the decision at the ARM. In 1988 the general practitioners at their LMC conference again voted for explicit consent but at the ARM a compromise motion was adopted advising explicit consent in all normal circumstances, but recognising that situations might arise in which it would be proper for the doctor, acting in the patient's best interests, to test without explicit consent. This did not preclude anonymous prevalence screening and the Government announced on 24 November 1988 that anonymous unlabelled blood samples taken from patients in NHS hospitals and clinics would be screened for HIV infection for epidemiological purposes (without the knowledge or consent of the patient).

23.36 A further complication arises for general practitioners who have used computers supplied by companies, usually at no cost, so that the general practitioner can provide the company with computerised records of most consultations and drugs prescribed – the so-called 'no cost' option for computers in general practice. The Joint Computing Group of the BMA and Royal College of General Practitioners have drawn up a series of guidelines[1] for the release of data from organisations external to the practice which general practitioners should follow to maintain complete confidentiality of any patient information passed outside the practice by computers. Part of the guidelines deal with the need to comply with the Data Protection Act 1984.[2]

1 General Medical Services Committee of the BMA Annual Report 1988 (London, GMSC, 1988) Appendix X, p 39.
2 See also the Access to Medical Reports Act 1988, which establishes a general right of access by individuals to reports relating to themselves provided by medical practitioners for employment and insurance purposes.

23.37 About 80 per cent of general practitioners in the UK use computers in the surgery and this percentage is increasing.[1] They are mainly used for administrative work and for repeat prescriptions. Those general practitioners who are aiming for a 'paperless office' and record most of their clinical notes on their computers have to be aware of the implications for possible medical negligence claims because the computers use coding systems for diagnoses and often do not have good facilities for free text or for diagrams, e g for recording the site of abdominal pain. Even though the coding system most used in this country, the Read Codes, has hundreds of thousands of rubrics (one subset of which is the International Classification of Diseases), it still cannot have the wealth of detail contained in written clinical notes. If computer recorded evidence is to be used there should ideally be an 'audit trail' which gives assurance that the records have not been altered. Hard copies of print-outs should be kept in the clinical notes. Long-term computer-issued repeat prescriptions for e g benzodiazepines or analgesics are difficult to justify and the computer system should have a means of reviewing all repeat prescriptions regularly.

1 Department of Health *Information for GPs on Practice Computer Systems* (London, HMSO, 1993).

WHEN CONSENT MAY NOT BE NECESSARY

23.38 In general it is necessary (as expressed in the Hippocratic Oath and the Declaration of Geneva) to keep the patient's confidence, except in the following circumstances:[1]

1 General Medical Council *Professional Conduct and Discipline: Fitness to Practice* (London, GMC, 1992).

23.39 (a) If the patient agrees to disclosure. However, there may be problems if the patient signs a form agreeing to allow the general practitioner to disclose details of his medical record, for example for an Insurance Company, because this may not be fully informed consent. The Access to Medical Reports Act 1988 (29 July 1988) establishes a right of access by individuals from 1 January 1989 to reports relating to themselves provided by medical practitioners for employment or insurance purposes and makes provision for related matters. Access to the medical report should normally be requested within three weeks of giving consent to its preparation, although it can be requested at any time within a period of six months. The Act applies only to reports prepared by a medical practitioner who is or has been responsible for the clinical care of the individual.

23.40 (b) The parents of children under 16 and relatives who need to look after a patient are told of a patient's illness, preferably in the patient's presence, and the patient thereby gives implied consent. Particular care is needed with sexually transmitted diseases, AIDS, and contraception.

23.41 (c) If there is a statutory duty, as with:

(a) infectious and industrial disease notification;
(b) birth, stillbirth, death certificates;
(c) notification of drug misuse (Misuse of Drugs Act 1971);
(d) revealing the identity of a patient treated after a road traffic accident (Road Traffic Act 1972);
(e) in Northern Ireland (Prevention of Terrorism (Temporary Provisions) Act 1984) to notify medical conditions to the police.

23.42 (d) Public duty:

(a) a doctor's conscience may make him or her report, for instance, a murder to the police and break medical confidence;

(b) for an epileptic driver;
(c) for a chronic infective disease in a food handler.

In these instances it is best first to contact one of the medical defence societies and to give the information to a doctor if possible. Patients should be recommended to pass on the information themselves to avoid breaking medical confidentiality.

23.43 (e) Court of law order: if ordered by a judge, magistrate or a coroner. Doctors who refuse are in contempt of court. They may request not to be forced to break a professional confidence (or to do so only in writing). All divulgences are absolutely privileged and there is no risk of action for breach of confidence.

23.44 The police have no more right than anyone else to disclosure of information and they should not give the impression that they have such a right. Information can only be given with the patient's written, informed, consent (or the consent of a parent/guardian). Doctors should only need to give information without consent for the public good if this is more important than the ethical duties of confidentiality.

23.45 Medical records should not be given without the patient's consent, for example to solicitors, employers, insurance companies. However courts may obtain access to a patient's notes if legal action is contemplated. The Access to Health Records Act 1990, which came into operation on 1 November 1991, gave people to whom the records relate (the patient, their representative with written authority, or any person who may have a claim after the patient's death) the right to examine the records and correct any inaccuracies. There is provision for the holder of the records to resist disclosure if in their opinion it would cause serious harm to the physical or mental health of the patient.

POSSIBLE FUTURE CHANGES

23.46 The difficulty for the patient, in all cases of medical negligence, is that he or she has the task of proving negligence by the doctor, i e that the balance of probability is more than likely that the doctor was at fault in not providing the skill and care which should, currently, be expected from an average general practitioner. The judge will weigh the balance on the basis of evidence from expert witnesses acting for and against the doctor. The principle of medical ethics that one doctor should not criticise another to the patient may be thought to weigh against the patient. However, doctors should not adopt this attitude if asked to act as an expert witness, because they would be acting for the good of society and the patient by giving a carefully considered opinion to the court to help the judge to decide upon a case. To quote the GMC,[1] 'honest comment is entirely acceptable in such circumstances [e g when called upon to express a view about a colleague's professional practice], provided that it is carefully considered and can be justified, that it is offered in good faith and that it is intended to promote the best interests of the patient'.

1 *Professional Conduct and Discipline: Fitness to Practice* (1992).

23.47 The obligation on the patient to prove his case does not arise if it is obvious that, by any normal standards, the doctor is negligent (the facts speak for themselves – *res ipsa loquitur*) but these cases are likely to be rare in general practice. The patient also has the problem, which the doctor generally does not have, of financing the cost of the claim for negligence, unless he can prove that he is poor and entitled to legal aid and can convince the Law Society that he has a case that is worth fighting with a fair chance of success. This may deter many patients who might otherwise have a case worthy of taking to court from doing so because they may fear being involved in heavy legal costs. Therefore, it is probable that some patients who should be compensated for medical injury are not. It is understandable that doctors would defend themselves against charges of negligence which might affect their whole career, but it is also unfortunate if patients are missing compensation that should be their due. At present only 30–40 per cent of medical negligence claimants receive compensation (compared with 86 per cent in other personal injury cases).[1] A study[2] of 31,429 randomly selected patients in New York State hospitals compared the patients who had made claims for medical negligence with patients who had had injuries caused by medial management (adverse events). Of the 280 patients who were judged to have had adverse events only 8 filed malpractice claims. However, in the study sample, 51 malpractice claims were identified, but most of these were not in the adverse events group. The conclusion of the study was that 'medical-malpractice litigation infrequently compensates patients injured by medical negligence and rarely identifies, and holds providers accountable for, substandard care'.

1 Quam et al (1987).
2 Localio A R, Lawthers A G, Brennan T A et al 'Relation between malpractice claims and adverse events due to negligence' (1991) New England Journal of Medicine 325: 245–251.

23.48 To overcome these difficulties the question of 'no-fault' compensation, as used in Sweden, has been discussed more in this country in recent years[1] (possibly only for expensive cases such as babies who are brain damaged at birth). NHS general practitioners have their medical defence society subscriptions reimbursed via their Basic Practice Allowance and hospital doctors working full-time for the NHS have two-thirds of their subscriptions paid by their health authority.[2] The government has introduced Crown Indemnity for doctors employed in the NHS (but not general practitioners who are self-employed contractors) by which health authorities have taken over responsibility for compensating for medical negligence from individual doctors. However, it has been suggested that 'the existing system of tortious liability is alleged to fulfil a quasi-disciplinary function' and that its corrective effect in making doctors more careful has been lost.[3] On the other hand it has been pointed out that the growth of insurance cover mitigates against this possible advantage of using legal processes to settle medical negligence claims.[4]

1 Ham et al (1988).
2 Dyer C 'Defence Societies' Price War' (1988) British Medical Journal 297: 1356.
3 Harvey I M and Roberts C J 'Clinical Guidelines, Medical Litigation and the Current Medical Defence System' (1987) Lancet 1: 145–147.
4 Rosenthal M *Dealing with Medical Malpractice* (London, Tavistock, 1987).

23.49 The ultimate aim must be to improve medical audit in order to reduce the number of mistakes which are made. The 1989 White Paper[1] 'Working for Patients' resulted in the introduction of Medical Audit Advisory Groups (MAAGs) in general practice. Medical audit was defined as 'the systematic, critical analysis of the quality of medical care . . .' All FHSAs have set up MAAGs but they are still at a relatively early stage in developing routine auditing of the work of most general practitioners. A Vocational Training Scheme course for trainee general practitioners provides an excellent forum for teaching young doctors how this should be done. One difficulty however is that most of the information on which such courses should be based regarding the types and frequency of problems is not readily available, even in a National Health Service where the cost of the medical defence societies' subscriptions is paid almost entirely by the government. In Sweden there is regular feedback to doctors regarding the types of cases that lead to medical accidents.[2] Perhaps such a scheme in this country might help to improve the standards of medical audit and to reduce the number of medical accidents.

1 DHSS et al (1989).
2 Rosenthal M *Dealing with Medical Malpractice* (London, Tavistock, 1987).

BIBLIOGRAPHICAL REFERENCES

BMA and the Royal Pharmaceutical Society of Great Britain *British National Formulary* Number 25 (December 1992) and earlier editions (London, BMA and RPS of Great Britain, 1992).

Brazier M *Medicine, Patients and the Law* (London, Pelican Books, 1992).

Department of Health Patient Consent to Examination or Treatment (HC(90)22, 1990).

Department of Health *Information for GPs on Practice Computer Systems* (London, HMSO, 1993).

DHSS *Health and Personal Social Services Statistics for England, 1992* and other editions (London, HMSO, 1993 – and other years).

DHSS and Secretaries of State for Health, Wales, Northern Ireland and Scotland 'Working for Patients' Cmnd 555 (London, HMSO, 1989) (the White Paper on the review of the NHS).

DHSS and Welsh Office *Working Together* (London, HMSO, 1988).

Dyer C 'Defence Societies' Price War' (1988) British Medical Journal of Medicine 297: 1356.

Fry J Annual Report of the General Medical Council (London, GMC, 1991).

General Medical Council *Professional Conduct and Discipline: Fitness to Practice* (London, GMC, 1992).

General Medical Services Committee of the BMA Annual Report 1988, Appendix X, p 39 (London, GMSC, 1988).

Ham C, Dingwall R and Harris D Medical Negligence – Compensation and Accountability, Briefing Paper 6 (London, King's Fund, 1988).

Harvey I M and Roberts C J 'Clinical Guidelines, Medical Litigation and the Current Medical Defence System' (1987) Lancet 1: 145–147.

Jarman B (ed) *Primary Care* (London, Heinemann, 1988).

Kilpatrick R 'The Council's Proposals for Performance Procedures' (1992) GMC News Review 1: June.

Klein R E *Complaints against Doctors* (London, Charles Knight, 1973).

Localio A R, Lawthers A G, Brennan T A et al 'Relation between malpractice claims and adverse event due to negligence' (1991) New England Journal of Medicine 325: 245–251.

Office of Health Economics *Compendium of Health Statistics* (6th edn, London, OHE, 1987).

Office of Population Censuses and Surveys *General Household Survey 1982* (and other years) (London, HMSO, 1984 – and other years) Table 8C.

Owen C 'Formal complaints against general practitioners: a study of 1000 cases' (1991) British Journal of General Practice 41: 113–115.

Quam L, Fenn P and Dingwall R 'Medical Malpractice in Perspective: II – The Implications for Britain' (1987) British Medical Journal 294: 1597–1600.

Rosenthal M *Dealing with Medical Malpractice* (London, Tavistock, 1987).

FIGURE 23.1 FHSA SERVICE COMMITTEE FORMAL COMPLAINTS

Complaints/100,000 population

FIGURE 23.2 FHSA SERVICE COMMITTEE FORMAL COMPLAINTS

Complaints/1000 general practitioners

FIGURE 23.3 RATES OF FPC COMPLAINTS or RHA CLAIMS

Complaints or claims/100,000 population

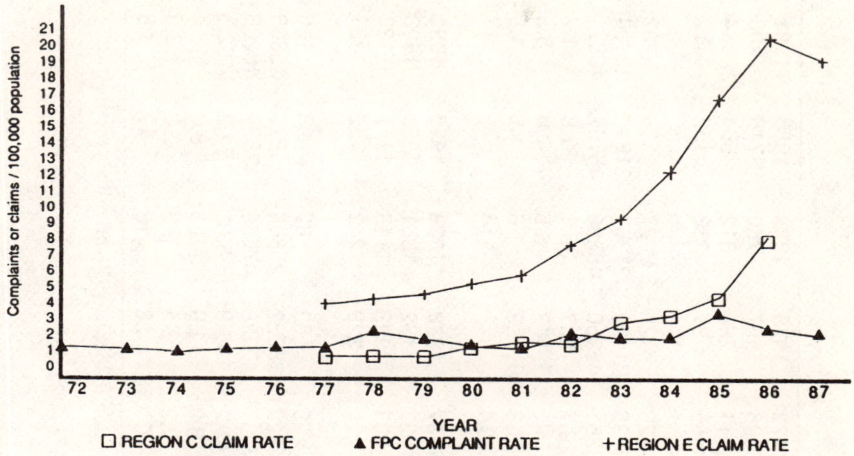

TABLE 23.1 FHSA SERVICE COMMITTEE CASES INVESTIGATED, ENGLAND, 1972–92

YEAR	**1972**	**1973**	**1974**	**1975**	**1976**	**1977**	**1978**	**1979**	**1980**	**1981**
Number of cases investigated	542	508	434	545	587	596	857	750	716	706
No breach found	445	410	369	453	506	511	766	612	564	584
Breach found	97	98	65	92	81	85	91	138	152	122
Decision to withhold remuneration	43	35	27	23	21	25	25	27	36	32
Unrestricted principals (GPs)	19775	19997	20219	20377	20551	20796	21040	21357	21812	22304
Population England (1000s)	46290	46405	46400	46391	46374	46351	46350	46396	46787	46821
Cases/1000 GPs	27.4	25.4	21.5	26.7	28.6	28.7	40.7	35.1	32.8	31.7
Breach found/1000 GPs	4.9	4.9	3.2	4.5	3.9	4.1	4.3	6.5	7.0	5.5
Cases/100,000 population	1.2	1.1	0.9	1.2	1.3	1.3	1.8	1.6	1.5	1.5
% breach found	18	19	15	17	14	14	11	18	21	17

YEAR	**1982**	**1983**	**1984**	**1985**	**1986**	**1987**	**1988**	**1989**	**1990**	**1991**	**1992**
Number of cases investigated	989	914	952	1286	1138	1027	1162	1361	1339	1608	1445
No breach found	727	744	774	995	829	807	933	1119	1117	1187	1082
Breach found	262	170	178	291	309	220	229	242	222	421	363
Decision to withhold remuneration	42	40	36	109	64	75	63	82	98	115	121
Unrestricted principals (GPs)	22786	23254	23640	24035	24460	24922	25322	25608	25622	25686	25968
Population England (1000s)	46795	46846	46958	47112	47254	47407	47536	47689	47837	48208	?
Cases/1000 GPs	43.4	39.3	40.3	53.5	46.5	41.2	45.9	53.1	52.3	62.6	55.6
Breach found/1000 GPs	11.5	7.3	7.5	12.1	12.6	8.8	11.8	9.5	8.7	16.4	14.0
Cases/100,000 population	2.1	2.0	2.0	2.7	2.4	2.2	2.4	2.9	2.8	3.3	3.0*
% breach found	26	19	19	23	27	21	26	18	17	26	25

Source: *Health & Personal Social Services Statistics for England* DHSS 1993 and other editions (London, HMSO, 1993 (and other years)).
*estimate February 1994

CHAPTER 24

Accident and emergency departments; the speciality of accident and emergency medicine

Mr Robin Touquet *RD FRCS MRCGP FFAEM DCH*
Dr Jane Fothergill *MRCP FRCS (Ed) FFAEM*
Mr Nigel H Harris *MA MB BChir FRCS*

SUMMARY

THE RAPID TURNOVER OF DOCTORS STAFFING ACCIDENT AND EMERGENCY DEPARTMENTS

24.1 Accident and emergency medicine (A & E) is a relatively newly defined speciality, the first 30 consultants being created in 1974. Prior to this date the majority of departments were under the control of orthopaedic surgeons. There are now about 270 consultants in accident and emergency medicine, and they are responsible for the standards of medical care practised in their departments. The Faculty of Accident and Emergency Medicine was inaugurated on 2 November 1993.

24.2 The British Association for Accident & Emergency Medicine (formerly The Casualty Surgeons Association) recommends that any department seeing over 25,000 new patients a year should have two consultants, a department seeing over 55,000 should have three, and over 75,000, four.[1]

1 British Association for A & E Medicine *Medical Staffing Accident and Emergency Departments* (November 1993).

24.3 Public hospital medicine has always been organised so that young doctors and nurses learn on the job. If hospitals abstained from using inexperienced people, they could not staff their departments and the junior staff could never learn. The longer-term interests of patients as a whole are best served by this present system, even if this may diminish the rights of individual patients. However, the ratio of more senior staff to junior staff does need to improve; the prime role of the former is supervision. The problem is that in the main A & E, or Casualty as it was officially known until 1978, is still largely staffed 24 hours a day by inexperienced senior house officers who change jobs every six months. It is increasingly expected by purchasers in the NHS that the quality of supervision of junior staff must improve by the provision of middle-grade staff, whether by career grade registrars or senior registrars, staff grade doctors or associate specialists. Since April 1991, like other hospital services, Accident and Emergency services have been the subject of contracts between purchasers (District Health Authorities) and providers (directly managed units or NHS trusts). The British Association for Accident & Emergency Medicine recommends that approximately one third of a staffing establishment in the junior medical ranks should be at middle-grade level. Accident and emergency departments have to cope with patients of all ages who may be suffering from many different illnesses or injuries, at any time of the day or night. In order to do so, the departments need to be appropriately staffed, well organised and managed, and fully supported by other specialities and services. See para **25.3**.[1]

1 National Audit Office *NHS Accident & Emergency Departments in England, Report by the Controller and Auditor General* (1992) HMSO 158.

SYSTEMS TO ENSURE A REASONABLE STANDARD OF CARE

24.4 A health district is offering an inferior standard of care if it does not provide specific A & E consultants to take charge of their departments.[1] The most recent report of the British Orthopaedic Association (1992) indicates that deficiencies still exist – only 38 per cent of A & E departments in

Scotland have a consultant in charge, compared with 82 per cent in England and Wales. It is disturbing to note also that some of the busiest hospitals have the least proportion of training posts and 66 per cent have no intermediate trainees. Equally, however, the consultant must set up systems to cope with the high turnover of medical staff. The following are procedures which respond to this problem, remembering that the consultant can only be in his department for a proportion of each 24 hour working day.[2, 3]

1 Royal College of Surgeons of England (1988) Report of the Working Party on the Management of Patients with Major Trauma, p 10.

2 'Recommended teaching standards in accident and emergency departments' (1991) Archives of Emergency Medicine 8: 162–163.

3 British Association for A & E Medicine *Senior House Officer Training Guide Book* (October 1993).

24.5 (1) The creation of *induction courses* for every new set of senior house officers which would cover the management of the common clinical problems that present to an A & E department, together with training in resuscitation techniques and protocols.

24.6 (2) The production of a procedure book of *medical guidance notes* easily available in the department, to which the staff can refer, and which will cover the initial management of the common clinical problems of patients whilst they are in the department. A copy should be given to every doctor who is to work in the department, before he takes up his post.

24.7 (3) The provision of an *on-going teaching programme*, which for instance could be provided by weekly meetings.

24.8 (4) The provision of *situational teaching* for some part of every day, where there is readily available in the department a middle- or senior-grade accident and emergency doctor or doctors to give advice and teaching to the senior house officers on clinical problems as they present in real time. This cannot be expected to be provided solely by consultants, who have to give time to administration and attend meetings. Hence the necessity for permanent middle grade staff, such as clinical assistants and associate specialists, together with the newly created staff doctor grade, or else regional career accident and emergency registrars, overseas district registrars and senior registrars. The support from the duty medical teams is no substitute for this, as the threshold for the senior house officers to call them is inevitably higher, and they cannot continually provide the immediacy of consultation. The revision of the numbers of junior staff[1] is increasing the need for dedicated middle grade accident and emergency medical staff (see **24.3**).

1 DHSS Hospital Medical Staffing – Achieving a Balance (1987).

24.9 (5) The provision of *review clinics*, where all patients, who need to return to the department, come to the next available review clinic and see a doctor more senior than a senior house officer. This helps cope with the problem of departments being open 24 hours a day and yet, for instance at night, there being only inexperienced SHOs in the department. Both medical management and the quality of record-keeping are informally audited in these clinics. When the A & E doctor is in doubt about the appropriate management of a patient it is necessary for him to seek guidance, either by referral to a more senior A & E doctor or specialised team, or by referral to the accident department's next review clinic.

24.10 (6) The training in, and *audit* of, medical staff record-keeping. For every consultation each doctor must record the date and time he sees the patient, an adequate history and examination, a diagnosis, any investigations which will affect the management of the patient in the department, the management and, in particular, the disposal of the patient. The history and examination may well be brief, and cover only what is strictly relevant to the presenting clinical problem. The volume of new patients demands that patients should not be 'clerked in' and have full details recorded, but only those that are necessary to determine a reasonable standard of care. Finally, the doctor must sign and print his name – a personal self-inking stamp aids clarity.

24.11 (7) The establishment of *reliable and effective referral procedures* with colleagues to ensure adequate follow-up of patients. This is particularly important with the management of fractures and dislocations. If the A & E consultant does not have accreditation in orthopaedic surgery (granted by the Specialist Advisory Committee from the appropriate – English or Scottish – College of Surgeons), and most will not, a reasonable standard of care for a common fracture, eg a Colles fracture of the wrist, is that the fracture is reduced in the A & E department by A & E doctors competent to carry out that reduction, or supervised by those who are, whether part of the A & E team or orthopaedic team. The patient should then be followed up in the orthopaedic fracture clinic. There may be different local procedures, but ultimately what must be established is that whereas the initial care is quite reasonably the responsibility of a consultant with A & E accreditation, the continuing management must be the responsibility of a consultant with an orthopaedic accreditation.

24.12 (8) *Liaison with the general practitioner*. Establish a reliable system of communication with the patient's primary care physician: the general practitioner. Ideally for every patient's visit to an accident and emergency department a letter to the general practitioner should be produced. What may appear to be a minor isolated problem to the accident department may be a much more serious one when reviewed with the patient's, and indeed their family's, medical records. Unless the patient has detailed hospital records it may be the general practitioner who is the only doctor who can pick up the seriousness of the situation, eg non-accidental injury to a child (see paras **24.96–24.97**), and unrecognised depression perhaps with underlying suicidal thoughts.

24.13 If there is some doubt about the cause of the patient's symptoms, but the patient is not ill enough to warrant admission, and follow-up is not going to be undertaken by the hospital, it is an inferior standard of care not to ensure follow-up by the general practitioner. A letter may be sent by post or given to the patient to deliver to his doctor. In the latter case the doctor should be aware that it only has approximately a 60 per cent chance of being delivered.[1] It is wise to assume that the letter will be read by the patient.

1 Sherry M, Edmunds S and Touquet R 'The Reliability of Patients in Delivering the Letter from the Hospital Accident and Emergency Department to their General Practitioner' (1985) Archives of Emergency Medicine 2, 165–169.

24.14 The junior doctor must be encouraged to telephone the general practitioner and discuss the case with him. Unless a clinical problem has been dealt with satisfactorily it is not generally acceptable to leave the patient without follow-up. If the A & E doctor instructs the patient to return if the symptoms do not improve or worsen, then he must ensure the patient understands this advice and is in a position to carry it out. He also must document advice given in the notes.

24.15 (9) *Ensure adequate staffing*. The A & E consultant is responsible for organising the doctors' rotas to ensure that, within the limitations of the staff available, as balanced as possible a staffing structure is created to cope with average work loads. Every effort must be made not to employ locum senior house officers in accident and emergency medicine because of the problems of supervision and training, together with the immediacy of an accident and emergency work practice. If a health authority fails to make such provision of staff, then the A & E consultant must make the health authority aware of this, and also of the consequences to patient care. The Royal College of Surgeons of England recommends that there should be approximately one trainee for every 5,000 new patients per annum,[1] and these have now been further enhanced by the recommendations of the British Association for Accident & Emergency Medicine (see para **24.3**). A staffing level of less inevitably means a deterioration in levels of service, because of the pressures that prolonged waiting times create: lack of supervision, teaching and audit, with doctors unable to spend the time that is necessary with each patient to ensure adequate standards of care.

1 Royal College of Surgeons of England (1987) *Guidelines for Pre-Fellowship Surgical Training Posts in A & E*.

24.16 (10) Create a *failsafe mechanism for the recall of patients* whose diagnosis has initially been missed. This is particularly so in the case of the missed fracture; it is always a problem for accident and emergency departments, because of lack of experience of senior house officers, no matter how good the training and supervision. All X-ray films taken in A & E must be reported on by a radiologist. This should be carried out within 24 hours, but certainly within three working days. The radiologist should be aware not only of the A & E doctor's clinical diagnosis, but also of his radiological diagnosis (this should have been written on the request card). The radiologist with his report should then specify 'Agree' or 'Disagree'. It is then the responsibility of the radiologist to inform the A & E consultant of any missed fractures or other pathology. The A & E consultant, or a member of his team, must then quickly recall the patient to the A & E department for definitive treatment and can also review all the 'disagrees' received from the radiologist. (It may be that the inexperienced SHO is incorrectly detecting 'fractures' on X-rays which are not there.) The patient will then be referred to the fracture clinic. Failure to pick up the fracture on the X-ray may not be negligent. Failure to recall a patient with a missed fracture, if that fracture warrants treatment other than what was initially given, is negligence. The A & E consultant must attempt to set up such a system; if lack of resources in a hospital prevents him so doing, then he must inform the health authority in writing, and make them aware of the consequences. He is then no longer negligent, because he has done everything that is in his power to ensure the patients who present to his department have a reasonable standard of care. See para **25.3**.

24.17 (11) There are a number of other *rules for A & E radiology* which must be followed especially by the inexperienced:

(1) take a history and examine the patient before requesting an X-ray. This is particulary important in patients with serious multiple injuries. Dramatic and obvious injuries must never distract the doctor from assessing the patient as a whole, systematically. Only three X-rays in general should be taken in the resuscitation room: lateral of cervical spine, chest and pelvis. The patient must be in a stable clinical condition before being moved to an X-ray department or for a CT brain scan. If, for example, signs of internal bleeding are overlooked then patients can deteriorate clinically and die whilst relatively unsupervised in an X-ray department. The doctor in the A & E department may be the only doctor to examine the patient in their entirety, and if this was not possible this omission must be recorded in the notes and the admitting team told;

(2) never look at an X-ray without seeing the patient. Hand-over time can be very dangerous in A & E. If doctor A has seen a patient and ordered an X-ray, when going off duty he must record in the notes that he has handed the patient on to doctor B. Doctor B will then view the X-rays but must also examine the patient himself in order that no pathology is missed.

The same rule applies to more senior staff than the A & E SHO. The A & E consultant is often asked for an opinion on an X-ray. Because he is primarily a clinician it is always wise for him to examine the patient: the junior may not have ordered the appropriate X-rays for that particular clinical condition;

(3) treat the patient not the X-ray. For example the fracture–dislocation of the ankle joint should be diagnosed clinically and reduced immediately as there is a risk of skin necrosis if the bones are left out of joint for any length of time. In this situation the clinical urgency overrides the usual rule of X-raying fractures or dislocations both before and after any manipulation. The reduction cannot be left to await an X-ray;

(4) re-examine the patient where there is an incongruity between the X-ray and the expected findings.

24.18 (12) An A & E department will normally run both nurse-led *dressing clinics* for those patients who can not yet be discharged back to the primary care doctor (GP), in addition to consultant-led *review clinics* detailed above (para **24.9**). The provision of other more specialist clinics, e g hand clinics, within an A & E department, run by A & E consultants, is more contentious.[1] The National Audit Office considers that all of these should be properly justified, regularly reviewed, and organised so that they do not interfere with the care of A & E patients.[2] It is good practice that all fractures and dislocations are followed up in fracture clinics run by orthopaedic consultants, as it is they who are usually accredited in Orthopaedic Surgery. To do otherwise is to create professional jealousies which usually work to the patients' disadvantage.

1 Touquet R and Fothergill J 'Putting A & E consultants in their place' (1992) British Journal of Hospital Medicine 47,625.

2 National Audit Office *NHS Accident & Emergency Departments in England, Report by the Controller and Auditor General* (1992) HMSO 158, 2.23.

24.19 (13) Key *support services on site* must provide experienced medical help at short notice at any time. Patient care may be prejudiced if this is not forthcoming.[1] These include medicine, surgery, anaesthetics, orthopaedics, paediatrics, obstetrics and gynaecology, intensive care, radiology, pathology – especially blood transfusion. If this is not possible a Provider must make due provision to ensure patient care is not put at risk. At the very least a department to be called an accident & emergency department must have 24-hour support, on the same site, living in, middle grade staff in each of the specialities of medicine, surgery and anaesthetics who preferably have an appropriate postgraduate degree and are of the minimum rank of registrar (together with a minimum of 24 hours radiology and pathology on site service).

1 National Audit Office *NHS Accident & Emergency Departments in England, Report by the Controller and Auditor General* (1992) HMSO 158, 2.46.

PATHOLOGY RESULTS

24.20 A & E consultants must ensure that their departments have systems in place so that all returning pathology results, including haematology, biochemistry, histology and bacteriology results are checked by a doctor prior to filing, and also that the general practitioner is kept informed. Abnormal results must be promptly acted upon, otherwise the original doctor that saw the patient, the A & E consultant in charge and the hospital are all guilty of medical negligence. This is much more feasible with middle-grade staff in place, but if the staffing and funding of a department are such that this checking cannot be done, then the consultant in charge must inform the hospital authorities and detail what action is necessary to remedy this deficit.

Again this is why all X-rays must be reported on by a radiologist, preferably within 24 hours. Similarly all electrocardiograms of patients discharged from the A & E department must be viewed by a doctor more senior than a SHO, and preferably checked by trained A & E staff or reported on by a cardiologist.

24.21 With these prerequisites in mind there follows a review of some specific areas of A & E work where particular diagnostic and management problems commonly occur. See also Chapters 25 (orthopaedics) and 27 (paediatrics).

MISSED FRACTURES AND DISLOCATIONS

24.22 It is mandatory for a history to be obtained first, because this will indicate the force and direction of injury, which in turn suggest likely patterns of injury. Secondly, an adequate examination must be carried out. Thirdly, if a fracture which would require specific treatment is suspected, relevant X-ray films should then be taken.

24.23 A fracture of the waist of the scaphoid, for a patient seen initially in the A & E department, is often a clinical diagnosis rather than a radiological diagnosis, because this fracture may not become apparent on an X-ray until after a period of ten days, and sometimes longer, has elapsed. Tenderness in the anatomical snuff box at the base of the dorsal aspect of the thumb, or pain produced by proximal pressure on the wrist joint in radial deviation, by comparison to the uninjured side, together with diminished power of grip, is an indication for the forearm to be put into a scaphoid plaster of Paris. The patient must have the plaster checked the following day and will need to be X-rayed again in 10 to 14 days if a fracture line was not initially visible. When a fracture of the scaphoid is suspected 'scaphoid views' are asked for. The doctor must ensure that four views have been carried out: anterior–posterior, lateral, supination oblique and pronation oblique. If there is doubt about the diagnosis or the fracture is displaced, then a more senior or orthopaedic opinion must be sought forthwith, otherwise a scaphoid plaster must be applied, and the patient referred to the next A & E review clinic or fracture clinic.[1]

1 *Modern Emergency Department Practice* ed Brooks D K and Harrold A J, ch 10, p 167.

24.25 A fracture of the neck of the femur is a common injury in the elderly, and therefore there must be a high index of suspicion when such a patient presents who has fallen on their hip and has pain on walking. The patient may be able to walk, albeit with a painful limp. The only clinical sign may be pain on gentle passive rotation of the leg.[1] The impacted subcapital fracture may be difficult to delineate on the X-ray. A lateral as well as an anterior–posterior view must be obtained. When there is a fracture of the neck of the femur the leg is usually shortened and externally rotated. If the hip is X-rayed with the leg in this position the greater trochanter may obscure the neck of the femur thereby making the fracture line indiscernable. It is therefore imperative that the leg is supported in a neutral position when X-rayed; if in doubt one side should be compared with the other not only clinically but also radiologically.[2] If the SHO is still in doubt, then both the patient and the X-rays must be referred to a more senior orthopaedic opinion. A patient who was previously mobile and now cannot walk must not be sent home without such a referral.

1 Yates D W and Redmond A D *Lecture Notes on Accident and Emergency Medicine* (1985) ch 7, p 102.
2 Williams P H, McCutcham J D S and Barrington N A 'Pitfalls in diagnosis of femoral neck fracture' (1992) Injury 23: 140–141.

24.26 Posterior dislocation of the shoulder is uncommon by comparison to anterior dislocation. It is most usually precipitated by an epileptic convulsion or an electric shock. Clinically the arm is held in medial rotation and external rotation is restricted when compared to the normal arm. It is mandatory that an axial or lateral scapular view X-ray is obtained, as well as an anterior–posterior view, because a posterior dislocation is difficult to detect solely on the latter view.[1] The diagnosis should first be suspected clinically, a cannula inserted into a vein and opiate analgesia given so that appropriate views of the possible dislocation are obtained, without pain being caused to the patient. See para **25.25**.

1 Craig O, Pitfalls in Diagnostic Radiology in *Protection Matters* The Medical Protection Society 19, 14.

24.27 It is usually mandatory to obtain X-rays of a dislocation or fracture both before and after it is reduced (but see para **24.17**(3)). This provides evidence that the dislocation actually was there (eg dislocated patella) and that it was successfully reduced. It is often the case that once a dislocation has happened, and the associated soft tissues have been stretched and torn, that redislocation easily occurs again. This is particularly the case for the shoulder, and therefore repeat axial or lateral scapular view and anterior–posterior view must be carried out to document success after attempted reduction of all types of dislocation of the shoulder.

24.28 Spinal injuries (see paras **25.26, 25.27**(7)). The inexperienced doctor in A & E must be aware of the forces that can cause injury to the spine, especially the cervical spine (ie the patterns of injury), and of the appropriate action to be taken in such cases. All patients with an altered level of consciousness who have any evidence of an injury above the level of the clavicle must be suspected of having an injury to the cervical spine and therefore, at the very least, be managed initially with a hard cervical collar. The lateral X-ray view of the cervical spine must always show the top of the first thoracic vertebra, in order to detect a possible fracture–dislocation at that level. Otherwise a 'swimmer's' lateral X-ray is called for, where one arm is fully abducted so that the cervico-thoracic vertebral junction can be delineated. Three X-ray views must be taken of the cervical spine when an injury is suspected: anterior–posterior, lateral and a through-the-mouth view to demonstrate the odontoid peg (part of the second vertebra), the axis.

The other area of the spine that is especially at risk from trauma is the thoraco-lumbar junction. A thorough 'head to toe' examination of the multiply injuried patient must be carried out and documented before the patient is allowed to leave the A & E department, unless his clinical condition dictates that this must be deferred, perhaps because he requires urgent surgery. If this is the case the omission must be recorded in the patient's notes. This examination includes a log roll which allows the doctor safely to inspect and palpate the whole length of the spine. The A & E doctor may be the only doctor to examine the patient in his totality in the accident department, although this should be carefully repeated on the ward when the patient's clinical state has stabilised.

NEUROLOGICAL AND VASCULAR COMPLICATIONS OF FRACTURES AND DISLOCATIONS

24.29 Having made the diagnosis of a fracture or dislocation, the doctor must carefully examine the patient for the associated complications. Injuries often follow a pattern, and junior doctors must have to hand a copy of the departmental guidance notes and, in addition, access at all hours to a basic library of books held in the accident department in order to look up the complications.

24.30 Injury to the axillary nerve of the posterior cord of the brachial plexus of the arm may be caused both by anterior dislocation of the shoulder and by the reduction of this dislocation. The injury to the axillary nerve is demonstrated by finding a small patch of anaesthesia over the deltoid muscle, or soon after reduction by the patient's inability to abduct the arm. This must firstly be looked for, and secondly recorded in the notes.

24.31 Humeral supracondylar fractures are common injuries of childhood, the extension-type fracture being the most frequent. This fracture is the commonest cause of Volkmann's ischaemic contracture in childhood. The clinical symptom is pain which increases in spite of immobilisation and analgesia, and which is made worse by extension of the fingers as this stretches the dying flexor muscle bellies. If the distal pulse is not present, urgent treatment by senior A & E staff together with immediate referral to the orthopaedic team is mandatory for all such displaced fractures. In addition, injury to the median nerve, damage to the radial nerve and anterior interosseous nerve must be looked for and documented.[1]

1 Alpar E K and Owen R *Paediatric Trauma* (1988) ch 12, p 163.

24.32 A & E staff must do everything reasonably expected of them to prevent the development of fracture blisters because this may well prevent definitive treatment of a fracture with internal fixation (because of the risk of infection), e g the grossly displaced fracture dislocation of the ankle must be approximately reduced at once before the patient is sent for appropriate X-rays (see para **24.17**(3)).

LACERATIONS TO THE HAND AND WRIST

24.33 Nerves and tendons in the hand and wrist are very vulnerable to partial or complete division from lacerations, especially those caused by glass. It is mandatory to exclude damage to underlying structures by careful clinical examination, and if necessary thorough exploration of the wound.

24.34 Sensory loss may be difficult to detect during the first 48 hours, even if a nerve has been completely divided, because sensation is initially not completely lost if the cut ends of the nerve are in apposition. It is necessary to compare quality of sensation between the injured and uninjured sides, in addition, there may be a decrease in two-point discrimination. This is especially important for the external aspects of the index and little fingers, because of their exposed position and their vulnerability without protective sensation. If there is any suspicion of altered sensation and nerve damage, then the patient must be referred immediately either to senior A & E staff or to the duty orthopaedic team. See para **25.18**.

24.35 Injury to flexor tendons is also easily overlooked. The doctor must exclude each specific injury by individual testing of the function of each finger. Initial inspection of the posture of the fingers may indicate the injury. Division of flexor digitorum profundus alone causes loss of active flexion at the distal interphalangeal joint. Division of the flexor digitorum superficialis tendon alone causes loss of the ability to flex the affected finger while the other fingers are held in extension.

24.36 Divided flexor tendons of the hand present problems of such severity that they must always be referred immediately to the duty orthopaedic or plastic surgery team.

24.37 Divided extensor tendons are much more straightforward to repair, and may be done in the accident department by an A & E doctor, provided that he has been trained in the procedure. However, referral may well be appropriate if there is a mallet finger deformity (where the extensor tendon is disrupted at its insertion into the dorsal surface of the proximal end of the distal phalanx) or if the extensor expansion over the proximal interphalangeal joint is damaged, because of the likelihood of a 'Boutoniere' deformity developing with consequent fixed flexion of the joint. The Boutoniere injury – rupture of the central slip of the extensor hood of the proximal inter-phalangeal joint of the four fingers – is easily missed.[1] Both these injuries require specific splintage and follow-up.

1 Elson R A 'Rupture of the Central Slip of the Extensor Hood of the Finger' (1986) Journal of Bone and Joint Surgery 68B, 229–231.

GLASS AND OTHER FOREIGN BODIES (INCLUDING OCULAR)

24.38 Virtually all glass, except certain types of fluorescent tubing, is radio-opaque. If a patient has an injury involving broken pieces of glass, it is mandatory that a radiograph is taken to exclude glass foreign bodies. Furthermore, if there is a suspicion of more than one fragment of glass, after initial removal, further films must be taken to ensure that no glass remains.

24.39 Perforating injuries of the eye, especially with high speed pieces of metal, are easily overlooked. Injuries sustained whilst using a hammer and cold chisel, or when using a drill bit which suddenly breaks, are likely to be associated with small fragments of flying metal. The history must alert the doctor to this possibility, and a careful examination be carried out.

24.40 If there is any suspicion of an intra-ocular foreign body, then lateral and PA films, with up and down eye movements, must be taken on non-screen film. An acceptable alternative is to use plates specially protected from scratches and blemishes and kept solely for such films. Even if a foreign body is not seen, the patient must be referred for a specialised opinion[1] because of the very serious consequences of any piece of metal, no matter how small, being left in the eye ball.

1 Townsend C 'Acute Ocular Emergencies' in *Modern Emergency Department Practice* ed Brooks and Harrold, ch 18, p 269.

PRETIBIAL FLAP LACERATION

24.41 This is colloquially known as the 'suitcase injury'. The anterior aspect of the lower leg has a poor blood supply compared with the posterior. The skin is especially fragile in the elderly and in those on steroid medication, e g for rheumatoid arthritis. The clinical problem is that if this type of laceration is not treated correctly in the accident department initially, the likelihood of it becoming a chronic leg ulcer (which will take a long time to heal), with resulting morbidity, is increased.

24.42 The more severe pretibial lacerations should be referred to the duty plastic surgery team.

24.43 The management of such an injury in A & E is careful cleaning and approximation of the edges of the skin with thin 'steri-strip' adhesive tapes. Sutures must not be used because they further devascularise the flap, are foreign material which acts as a nidus for infection, and cut through the edge of the flap like a cheese wire. Sutures are also not necessary, because with a flap laceration there is no potential space to be approximated as there is with a wound with more square and vertical edges. Steri-strips take the tension away from the edges of the flap.

24.44 The patient must be advised to rest and elevate the leg, and must be followed up in the A & E clinic or by the GP until the wound is healed.

24.45 Education on wound management and particularly on the management of the pretibial laceration must be given to new A & E doctors when they take up their post. All grazes and lacerations which contain grit must be cleaned meticulously, if necessary by scrubbing with a sterile brush, otherwise the grit will remain and the patient will be permanently tattooed.

CARDIOPULMONARY AND TRAUMA LIFE SUPPORT

24.46 Most of the patients in Accident and Emergency will be seen initially by inexperienced SHOs. However, it is now becoming increasingly expected that senior and middle-grade A & E doctors should be present to receive the seriously injured, and those who have had a cardiac arrest. Increasingly, A & E consultants will be expected to have gained an Advanced Trauma Life Support certification, and an Advanced Cardiac Life Support certification. Their role is not only to lead the resuscitation team when they are in the department, but to ensure that the junior A & E staff have a thorough training in both trauma and cardiopulmonary life support. It is now necessary to document the steps in any resuscitation of a patient, especially when this is unsuccessful.

24.47 Failure to follow the guidelines of the Resuscitation Council (UK) without a good reason would be an inferior standard of care (e g not using the standard sequence of drugs for the treatment of cardiac arrest). Furthermore, the relatives could quite reasonably request to see the A & E records which would have to demonstrate that the accepted procedures were adhered to.[1]

1 'Guidelines for advanced life support. A statement by the advanced life support working party of the European Resuscitation Council' (1992) Resuscitation 24, 111–121.

24.48 The resuscitation team for both medical and surgical emergencies in A & E must be led by the minimum of a Registrar (of any appropriate speciality, e g anaesthetic, A & E, medical, surgical). This of course assumes that the registrar has received appropriate training in resuscitation. This is increasingly being accepted as certification in ACLS (Advanced Cardiac Life Support), ATLS (Advanced Trauma Life Support) and the newer APLS [UK] (Advanced Paediatric Life Support – first UK course, held in Bolton in 1992). The importance of the team approach is emphasised with both doctors and nurses using standard sequences of resuscitation: ABC (Airway, Breathing, Circulation), with standard drug regimes, repeatedly reviewing the vital signs (pulse, respiratory rate, blood pressure), and carrying out appropriate procedures to stabilise the clinical state of the patient, together with calling appropriate specialists, eg surgeons. The teams may well be led by appropriately trained A & E staff – registrars and above – during the initial hour (known as the 'golden hour'). A & E staff (including consultants) must keep these skills up to date, and regularly keep in practice skills such as intubation (of the trachea) and the placement of central venous pressure lines. Otherwise such senior staff must appropriately delegate such tasks to other, in date, trained doctors.

24.49 The Royal College of Surgeons of England followed the American College of Surgeons by setting up the first United Kingdom Advanced Trauma Life Support Course – with the latter's help – in November 1988. The initial management of trauma is now standardised, as for a cardiac arrest, and the documentation of this will also have to be of a corresponding standard.[1] The serious deficiencies in the services for managing severe injury have been highlighted.[2] Increasingly, the importance of quantitative measurements of the severity of injury are being appreciated. Such scoring systems as the Revised Trauma Score and the Injury Severity Score will together enable the comparison between the predicted outcome and the actual outcome.[3] Discrepancies will in the future need to be explained, both from a medical viewpoint and also a legal viewpoint. Accurate record-keeping will therefore be even more important than it is now. At present relatively few A & E departments calculate the Revised Trauma Score of patients presenting with multiple injuries.

1 American College of Surgeons *Advanced Trauma Life Support Program for Physicians* (1993) ch 1.
2 Anderson I D, Woodford M, de Dombal F T and Irving M 'Retrospective Study of 1,000 Deaths from Injury in England and Wales' (1988) British Medical Journal 296: 1305–8.
3 Yates D W 'ABC of Major Trauma; Scoring Systems for Trauma' (1990) British Medical Journal 301: (6760) 1090–1094.

24.50 The National Audit Office concluded that provider hospitals need to identify staff for whom advanced life support courses are essential training. These staff should be required and funded to undertake such training.[1]

1 National Audit Office *NHS Accident & Emergency Departments in England, Report by the Controller and Auditor General* (1992) HMSO 158, 3.35.

24.51 Every providing District must appoint a Resuscitation Officer whose role is to provide training in, standardisation of and auditing of resuscitation.[1] Not to do so is to risk inferior standards of resuscitation in the hospitals concerned and is therefore negligent.

1 Royal College of Physicians of London *Resusciatation from Cardiopulmonary Arrest; Training and Organisation* (1988).

HEAD INJURIES

(See also para **26.20**)

24.52 The initial management of a patient with a serious head injury in the accident department is to assess the patient as a whole under the standard headings of Airway, Breathing, Circulation, Disability and Exposure.

However, the majority of head injured patients will have a minor or trivial head injury. The accident doctor has to make two decisions: whether to X-ray the skull and whether to admit to hospital.

24.53 The A & E doctor needs to follow standard guidelines, which can be easily referred to:[1]

Criteria for skull X-ray

(1) Loss of consciousness or amnesia at any time;
(2) neurological symptoms and signs;
(3) cerebrospinal fluid or blood from the nose or ear;
(4) suspected penetrating injury;
(5) marked scalp bruising or swelling;
(6) alcohol intoxication;
(7) difficulty in assessing the patient, eg epilepsy, stroke.

Indications for admission to a general hospital

(1) Confusion or any other depression of level of consciousness at time of examination;
(2) skull fracture;
(3) neurological symptoms or signs;
(4) difficulty in assessing the patient, eg alcohol, epilepsy;
(5) other medical condition, eg haemophilia;
(6) lack of responsible adult to supervise the patient; other social problems.[2]

1 'Guidelines for the Initial Management of Head Injury': suggestions from a group of neurosurgeons (1984) British Medical Journal 288: 983–985.
2 Crockard A and Garlick R 'Head Injuries' in *Current Surgical Practice* ed Hadfield J and Hobsley M vol 4, ch 16, p 273.

24.54 When assessing the conscious level of the patient, the now widely used and easily understood Glasgow Coma Scale should be defined under the terms of eye opening, best motor response, and best verbal response (minimum score 3, maximum score 15).

24.55 Head injured patients are admitted to hospital for the treatment of a condition that already exists, or for complications that may develop rapidly. However, after initial resuscitation and assessment of the severely injured patient, early consultation with the neurosurgeon should be considered under the following sets of circumstances:

(1) coma continuing after resuscitation;
(2) deterioration in level of consciousness;
(3) fractured skull with any of the following:
   - confusion or impairment of consciousness
   - one or more epileptic fits
   - any other neurological symptoms or signs;
(4) persistent confusion or other neurological signs (over six to eight hours);
(5) depressed fractured skull vault, compound skull fracture;

(6) fracture at base of skull (cerebrospinal fluid leak, bilateral periorbital haematoma), haemotympanum, weakness of facial nerve, bruising behind ear, fluid level in sphenoid sinus or air in cranial cavity;
(7) penetrating injury (spike, gun shot).

24.56 The A & E doctor must ensure that there are no other injuries to the patient, which may not be detected initially because attention is being focused on the often dramatic head injury. Precipitous referral to specialist teams may mean that the patient has had an inadequate initial assessment. Therefore it is very important that the patient is examined in an orderly and standardised manner.[1]

1 American College of Surgeons *Advanced Trauma Life Support Program for Physicians* (1993) ch 1.

24.57 Once again, the most difficult decision for the junior A & E doctor with the patient who is not severely injured, is whether to seek further advice, and whether the patient is safe to send home. Consideration should be given to this latter course of action when:

(1) there is no skull fracture;
(2) there are now no abnormal physical signs and the patient is fully conscious, alert and orientated;
(3) there is no severe headache or persistent vomiting;
(4) a responsible adult can supervise the patient.

24.58 The A & E doctor must give the patient a written set of instructions, and these should include the advice to rest at home for at least 48 hours in order to minimise the chances of developing the post-traumatic syndrome. The name of the patient and the date should be put on the advice sheet in order to alert anyone who finds such a patient with a decreased level of consciousness who has such an advice sheet in their pocket. As always the general practitioner should be notified at least by letter (see paras **24.12–24.15**).

ABDOMINAL PAIN

(See also para **33.40**)

24.59 The assessment of patients with abdominal pain is a common clinical problem in the A & E department and must follow the set pattern of history (main site, radiation, character, duration, frequency and periodicity, special times of occurrence, aggravating factors, relieving factors, associated phenomena, and in women, questions must be asked about the menstrual periods – which may indicate an ectopic pregnancy); examination (inspection, palpation, percussion, ausculation, groins and pelvis); and thirdly, appropriate special investigations. By the last is meant those investigations that will determine the management of that patient whilst they are in the A & E department; investigations that will not affect patient management in the A & E department should not be carried out there and are the responsibility of the admitting teams.

24.60 When it is possible to make a diagnosis, patients with abdominal pain of pathological consequence can be classified into one of the following pathological groups:

(1) inflammation of the peritoneum – the lining of the abdominal cavity;
(2) obstruction of a hollow viscus;
(3) interruption of the blood supply to an organ;
(4) haemorrhage, eg ectopic pregnancy;
(5) trauma;
(6) medical conditions that simulate acute abdominal emergencies.

24.61 Each of these groups has certain common features, but not uncommonly a patient may exhibit symptoms and signs which defeat neat classification. In one series it was documented that the admitting diagnosis was only correct in 44.8 per cent of patients.[1]

1 de Dombal F T 'Computers, diagnoses and patients with abdominal pain (guest editorial)' (1992) Archives of Emergency Medicine 9: 267–270.

24.62 In general, diagnoses are made by pattern recognition, but if this is not possible, the doctor employs a pay-off technique of the best odds combined with the maximum safety. For instance, because a child with abdominal pain will be more difficult to assess using the criteria mentioned above, he is more likely to be admitted for active observation.[1]

1 Glazer G 'Abdominal Emergencies' in *Modern Emergency Department Practice* ed Brooks and Harrold (1983) ch 7, p 113.

24.63 Similarly, at the other extreme of age, the A & E doctor should be aware that the elderly may not present with characteristic symptoms and signs of serious abdominal pathology.

24.64 Relatively junior doctors in the A & E department are, in the great majority of instances, able to make correct decisions about the initial management of patients presenting with acute abdominal pain.[1] If the diagnosis is uncertain then the A & E doctor has to decide if he is going to seek more senior guidance from A & E doctors or refer the patient to the duty surgical team. If he does not take this action then the key question for the accident doctor is, 'Can the patient safely go home?', by which he is really asking 'How ill is the patient, if at all?' It is because a junior doctor can only be expected to practise to the level of his training and experience, that he must manage patients in a standard way and make careful notes.

1 Gatzen C, Paterson-Brown S, Touquet R, Dudley HAF 'Management of Acute Abdominal Pain: Decision Making in the Accident and Emergency Department' (1991) Journal of the Royal College of Surgeons of Edinburgh 36: 121–123.

24.65 It is especially important in such cases of an uncertain diagnosis that the general practitioner is contacted (see above, para **24.13**), provided the patient's symptoms and signs have abated such that he can be sent home.

GYNAECOLOGICAL EMERGENCIES

24.66 There is regrettably a wide variation in the level of service offered to patients with gynaecological emergencies in A & E departments. Minimum standards of care are:

(a) improved in-service training of A & E doctors;

(b) the use of protocols relating to common gynaecological problems;
(c) explanatory leaflets for patients, e g a miscarriage advice sheet;[1]
(d) an agreed system of liaison with gynaecologists for difficult cases;
(e) privacy for patients;
(f) adequate first-line investigation and treatment facilities.[2]

1 Gilling-Smith C, Zelin J, Touquet R, Steer P 'Management of early pregnancy bleeding in the accident and emergency department' (1988) Archives of Emergency Medicine 5: 133–138.
2 Gilling-Smith C, Regan L, Touquet R 'Gynaecological Emergencies' in *Cambridge Textbook of Emergency Medicine* ed Skinner D, Peyton R, Robertson C, Swain A, Worlock P; Cambridge University Press, Cambridge, Section 111, ch 16.

Ectopic pregnancy

24.67 This is the most important gynaecological condition seen in A & E because, undiagnosed and untreated, the natural history of the ectopic pregnancy with acute rupture of the fallopian tube is death. The incidence is increasing because of the increased incidence of Pelvic Inflammatory Disease and also because of successful treatment of prior ectopics, this condition being recurrent. The acute picture is one of haemorrhagic shock. The safe rule for doctors to remember is: *lower abdominal pain in female patients of reproductive age is due to the presence of an ectopic pregnancy until proved otherwise. Doctors must not send home such patients until it is known that a pregnancy test is negative.* A simple, rapid one-step test for chorionic gonadotrophin should be available for the initial evaluation of emergency gynaecological problems.[1]

The patient may notice symptoms of early pregnancy with nausea and breast pain, her period being overdue by a few days. She then develops an ache in one or other iliac fossa with bouts of severe pain with associated syncope, followed by slight vaginal bleeding from either uterus or from the affected tube. In A & E it is important to enquire directly about any momentary feelings of faintness. The vaginal bleeding may abate temporarily. With the greatly improved accuracy of ultrasound, this investigation should be obtained (unless the patient's clinical state is such that she should be taken to the operating theatre forthwith), a vaginal examination in the A & E being omitted.

1 Kingdom J C P, Kelly T, MacLean A B, McAllister E J 'Rapid One Step Urine Test for Human Chorionic Gonadotrophin in Evaluating Suspected Complications of Early Pregnancy' (1991) British Medical Journal 302, 1308–1311.

Urinary tract infection

24.68 Consider this diagnosis not only when there are urinary symptoms and lower abdominal pain, but also when women are feeling generally unwell. Urine testing with 'Nephur-test sticks' may reveal not only protein but nitrites, indicating a urinary infection. Provided a mid-stream urine sample is sent first for definitive culture and sensitivity, antibiotic treatment should be started in the A & E department. The patient should be followed up by the general practitioner, and the A & E doctor must ensure that the patient is not only registered with a general practitioner, but also that he is fully informed of all test results and advised that a post-treatment MSU be sent to confirm that the infection is no longer present. Similarly microscopic haematuria must always be taken seriously and not assumed to be due to infection, further urine testing being carried out if necessary, e g after menstrual bleeding ceases. Failure to do this may delay the investigation of possible neoplasia of the urinary tract, with fatal consequences for that patient.

When there is more than one plus of protein in the urine on stick testing, doctors should *not* assume that this is due to infection but check the patient's blood pressure, examine for oedema, send a blood sample for creatinine and elecrolyte levels, and consider renal causes together with pre-eclampsia if the patient is pregnant.

Amoxycillin and Septrin are suitable for the pregnant patient, but not tetracyclines.

CHEST PAIN OF CARDIAC ORIGIN

Angina and unstable angina

24.69 Approximately 3 per cent of all patients attending A & E departments come for assessment of chest pain, and the majority are assessed by A & E SHOs and discharged home.[1] Angina pectoris is chest pain of cardiac origin caused by myocardial ischaemia (shortage of oxygen), which has not progressed to actual death of an area of heart muscle (myocardial infarction).

Any newly presenting chest pain must be considered to be of cardiac origin until proved otherwise. Cardiac pain is typically:

(a) described as 'tight, heavy, weight, crushing, pressure', felt over the front of the chest and/or the arms and/or the jaw and unaffected by breathing;
(b) associated with anxiety, pallor and sweating;
(c) related to exertion, although pain from unstable angina or myocardial infarction may occur early in the morning, wakening the patient from sleep;
(d) present in a patient with risk factors for heart disease, such as being male, smoking, Asian, hypertensive, diabetic, known to be hyperlipidaemic or with a positive family history.

1 Fothergill J, Hunt M, Touquet R 'Audit of patients with chest pain presenting to an A & E department over a six month period' (1993) Archives of Emergency Medicine 10, 155–160.

24.70 If the pattern of angina alters, with increasing severity and frequency, or onset at rest, it is said to be unstable. The hallmark is the unpredictability of the onset of symptoms. Failure to document the historical features of a patient's chest pain as outlined above, and, if anginal, to ascertain the frequency and predictability of episodes may be considered to be negligent, since physical examination and investigations such as an electrocardiogram (ECG) may be normal and the diagnosis of unstable angina (or acute myocardial infarction) often rests on history alone. The pain may have gone when the patient is seen.

24.71 The patient with unstable angina warrants immediate referral for treatment and hospital admission. This is because the subsequent risk of myocardial infarction is high – 40 per cent within one to three months – as is the mortality – 17 per cent within one to three months. The patient has not at this time suffered an actual infarction, but is at severe risk from doing so. Such a patient must not be allowed to go home.[1]

1 Kirby N J *Accidents and Emergencies* (1988) ch 3, p 34.

Suspected acute myocardial infarction

24.72 Patients with anginal chest pain which is not relieved quickly by glyceryl trinitrate must be seen immediately by a doctor, who should attach a cardiac monitor, gain intravenous access and take a brief history (covering all the points given in para **24.69** above) whilst examining the cardiovascular and respiratory systems.

24.73 The best widely available investigation for the early diagnosis of acute myocardial infarction is the 12-lead ECG, but this will be diagnostic in only around 50 per cent of cases and will be virtually normal in 10 per cent.[1] The ECG changes accompanying early acute myocardial infarction may be extremely subtle, and studies have shown that of all ECG abnormalities seen by SHOs in A & E, around 20 per cent are missed and these are clinically significant in around 4 per cent of cases.[2]

1 Rouan G W, Lee T H, Cook E F, Brand D A, Weisberg M C, Goldman L 'Clinical characteristics and outcome of acute myocardial infarction in patients with initially normal or nonspecific electrocardiograms [a report from the multicenter chest pain study]' (1989) American Journal of Cardiology 64: 1087–1092.

2 Morrison W G and Swann I J 'Electrocardiograph interpretation by junior doctors' (1990) Archives of Emergency Medicine 7: 108–110.

24.74 The SHO in A & E must therefore receive instruction in the interpretation of the ECG, and in cases where he has doubt over its interpretation, seek a more senior opinion from A & E or on-take medical doctors. Failsafe mechanisms should be set up by the A & E consultant so that ECGs of all patients discharged from the A & E department are reported upon urgently by senior A & E or cardiological doctors. For a doctor to misinterpret an ECG is not negligent, but failure to act on an ECG report at variance with that given by the doctor who saw the patient in the A & E department, if the ECG findings indicate that treatment or follow-up should have differed, is negligent.

24.75 Once a diagnosis of acute myocardial infarction has been made, a decision must speedily be taken on whether it is safe or appropriate to administer a thrombolytic (clot dissolving) injection, which is of proven value in reducing mortality in these patients. The 'door to needle time', which is the time-lapse between the patient arriving in the A & E department with symptoms of acute myocardial infarction to the time at which the thrombolytic agent is administered, should constantly be kept under review, ideally by regular medical audits.[1] The indications and contraindications for this treatment vary between hospitals, but a policy should exist whereby nursing staff know which doctors (eg A & E or cardiology) are responsible for prescribing thrombolysis and who therefore need to be called to see appropriate patients urgently, and also which particular drug is given, its indications and contraindications.

1 Saetta J P, Quinton D, Dacruz D and Barnes M 'Delay in thrombolytic treatment in acute myocardial infarction: the role of the accident & emergency department' (1990) Archives of Emergency Medicine 7: 206–211.

PULMONARY EMBOLISM

24.76 A pulmonary embolism (PE) is a clot lodged in the arteries supplying blood to the lungs, which has travelled from a clot in a vein elsewhere, usually from the deep veins in the legs (see paras **33.20–33.24**). Tragically, the diagnosis is often missed, and untreated with anticoagulant drugs the mortality from a large PE is 30 per cent.[1]

1 Barritt D W and Jordan S C 'Anticoagulant drugs in the treatment of pulmonary embolism' (1960) Lancet i: 1309–1312.

24.77 Although commoner in patients with risk factors, which include a history of deep vein thrombosis, taking the combined oral contraceptive pill, recent surgery (particularly to the legs) or a period of immobilisation, the diagnosis should be considered in any patient presenting with any of the following:

(a) acute breathlessness, collapse or chest pain;
(b) insidious onset of breathlessness alone;
(c) pleuritic chest pain (worse with deep breaths), particularly if accompanied by coughing up blood.

24.78 Although there may be physical signs such as tachycardia, and indications that the right side of the heart is under strain, examination may be entirely normal. There may be no clinical signs of a deep vein thrombosis in the legs even if these veins are later found to have been the source of the embolism.

24.79 When a PE is considered a possibility because of the patient's symptoms or signs, there are three investigations which must be carried out in the A & E department; although abnormalities in any of these investigations is neither sensitive nor specific for the diagnosis of PE, if all three tests are normal the diagnosis is extremely unlikely, so for the doctor working in the A & E department they are useful in excluding the diagnosis. The investigations are a chest X-ray, an ECG and arterial blood gas estimation. The last of these tests is the most sensitive for the diagnosis of PE, which is more likely if the arterial oxygen tension is less than 10.7 kPa.[1]

1 Fennerty A G, Shetty H G M, Paton D, Roberts G, Routledge P A and Campbell I A 'Clinical presentation and investigation of patients proceeding to isotope lung scanning for suspected pulmonary embolism' (1990) Postgraduate Medical Journal 66: 258–259.

24.80 If a diagnosis of possible PE is made in the A & E department, the patient should be admitted that same day by the on-take medical team, and treated whilst further investigations (usually a ventilation/perfusion lung scan) are arranged to confirm or refute the provisional diagnosis.

COLLAPSE

(See also para **24.82**)

24.81 Frequently patients attend the A & E department with the triage diagnosis 'collapse'. The first doctor to see the patient must keep an open mind about the cause of this collapse and consider all the various possibilities, listening carefully to whoever brought in the patient, especially the ambulance crew.[1]

1 Touquet R, Fothergill J and Jones R 'Resuscitation' in *Clinical Surgery in General*, ed Kirk R M, Mansfield A and Cochraine J, Royal College of Surgeons of England, ch 6.

HYPOGLYCAEMIA

24.82 Any patient who is brought into the A & E department with an altered level of consciousness, abnormal behaviour or who has developed unexplained neurological signs must have a finger prick test for the blood level of glucose.[1] This should be carried out by the nursing staff as a routine, but it is the responsibility of the senior doctor attending the patient that he knows the result. If this is 2 mmols/litre or less, a blood sample must be sent to the laboratory for definitive estimation. If the patient is unable to swallow safely he must be given intravenous glucose or intramuscular glucagon (a hormone which rapidly raises the blood sugar) without delay. In an emergency intravenous glucose is usually given as a hyperosmolar solution of 50gms in 50ml of water for injection, i e a 50 per cent solution. This must be given into a large vein (preferably at least proximal to the wrist) and flushed through with an isotonic solution otherwise there is the risk of superficial thrombophlebitis, as well as necrosis of tissue if there is a leak outside of the vein.

1 Fulde G W P *Emergency Medicine* (1988) ch 33, p 185.

24.83 A patient may be brought into the department with multiple trauma. However, the reason that the patient sustained that trauma may have been due to an alteration in the behaviour of that patient, making them less alert to surrounding dangers. Therefore, irrespective of the apparent cause of a patient's altered level of consciousness, a blood sugar test must still be carried out.

24.84 The doctor must also be aware of the association between hypoglycaemia and alcohol. A patient may appear to be drunk, but part or all of his symptoms may be due to a low blood sugar that has been precipitated by the alcohol. In alcoholic patients thiamine (B vitamin) must first be given intravenously, before glucose, to prevent the development of Wernicke's encephalopathy.

SUBARACHNOID HAEMORRHAGE

24.85 The A & E doctor must be aware that this diagnosis is rarely straightforward (see para **26.27**). Its most common presentation is of severe headache of sudden onset with neck rigidity and a positive Kernig's sign (restricted passive knee extension with a flexed hip). However, the patient may present with the complaint of migraine, or with a diminished level of consciousness. The circumstances of onset may be embarrassing, e g during coitus.[1]

1 Nieman E A 'Coma and Neurological Emergencies' in *Modern Emergency Department Practice* ed Brooks and Harrold (1983) ch 13, p 199.

24.86 There may, or may not be, other symptoms such as nausea, vomiting or photophobia, or signs of pyrexia, raised blood pressure and neurological deficit, e g a third nerve palsy. If the headache is of sudden onset and unlike other headaches that the patient has had in the past, then it is generally not acceptable to ignore the possibility of the diagnosis of subarachnoid haemorrhage, and the patient should be referred for more senior or specialist advice.

24.87 However it is realistic to appreciate that the diagnosis is unfortunately missed even by specialist neurologists and neurosurgeons.[1] It is often not appreciated that warning symptoms – the 'warning leak' – prior to a major haemorrhage occur in between 35 per cent and 60 per cent of patients. Regrettably these are often unrecognised.[2] Leblanc from Canada reported that half the patients in his series saw a physician with symptoms of a warning leak from a subarachnoid haemorrhage, but in no case was the correct diagnosis made.[3] Therefore whilst these diagnostic points must be emphasised to inexperienced junior doctors, they cannot be held negligent if the atypical case is not correctly diagnosed on the first attendance at an A & E department. Headache is a common symptom, but the warning leak of a subarachnoid haemorrhage is not. The diagnosis must, however, be considered and it must be remembered that presentations are not always classic.

1 Hauererg J, Andersen B, Eskesen V, Rosenorn J and Schmidt K 'Importance of the recognition of a warning leak as a sign of a ruptured intracranial aneurysm' (1991) Acta Neurologica Scandinavica 83: 61–64.
2 Johnston S R D, Hammond A, Griffiths L, Greenwood R and Clarke C R A 'Subarachnoid haemorrhage – can we do better?' (1989) Journal of the Royal Society of Medicine 81: 720–725.
3 Leblanc R 'The minor leak preceding Subarachnoid Haemorrhage' (1987) Journal of Neurosurgery 66: 35–39.

REPEAT ATTENDANCE OF PATIENTS WITH POTENTIALLY SERIOUS SYMPTOMS

24.88 The majority of patients who are not ill enough to be placed in the resuscitation area may be seen initially by an SHO in A & E. This doctor must take an adequate and appropriate history, and carry out an adequate and appropriate examination. Investigations relevant (but only strictly relevant) to the clinical problem must be undertaken. However there are many common non-serious reasons why a patient may have such symptoms as chest pain, headache, shortness of breath (including hyperventilation and panic attacks). There are also rarer very serious conditions which cause such symptoms, e g unstable angina, warning headache of a subarachnoid haemorrhage, small pulmonary emboli. All these conditions can herald a catastrophic later event of myocardial infarction, subarachnoid haemorrhage or massive pulmonary embolism. The problem for the doctor in A & E is that patients with such warning symptoms may look well, no longer have the symptoms that precipitated their arrival in A & E, have no abnormal physical signs (e g no neck stiffness) and no abnormal investigations (e g a normal electrocardiogram). They may also be anxious and perhaps even have a psychiatric history. The unimportant causes of such symptoms are also much more common than the serious. The A & E doctor must consider appropriate diagnoses, but on the other hand he has to be discerning since otherwise, at minimum he will over-investigate, and at worst not see enough patients. Waiting times in the A & E department are then excessively prolonged or worse, patients in a critical condition are not attended to immediately (hence paras **24.4** to **24.21**). If he does decide that in first attendance a patient with such symptoms can be discharged, he must communicate with the general practitioner (GP) and should advise the patient to make an appointment to see the GP. This advice must be written in the notes.

24.89 However, *if a patient attends the A & E department a second time with a symptom of potentially serious pathology, such a patient must be referred to a doctor more senior than a SHO, preferably whilst that patient is in the department*. It may be acceptable however to make a referral to out patients (or to the A & E review clinic) providing the due urgency is noted. It may also be acceptable to speak directly to the GP, remembering that patients may not make an appointment themselves. To do less than this is negligent, unless there are extenuating circumstances or unless the patient is accompanied by a sensible adult who can be relied upon to ensure follow up, perhaps by the GP where appropriate.

CONSENT FOR TREATMENT

24.90 For the unconscious patient, or a patient with an altered level of consciousness, emergency treatment by an A & E doctor is acceptable in the conduct of everyday life where such treatment is vital to the survival or health of a patient. If the patient's level of consciousness is impaired from the injury, consent should be obtained from a relative, providing there is time and opportunity. No delay in medical treatment should be allowed to occur by attempting to obtain consent from patient or relative if this delay is likely to affect the patient's recovery.

24.91 The categories of patient from whom written consent is obtained in the A & E department, if the patient is attending with a genuine emergency, vary to a degree from department to department. As is current accepted surgical practice written consent should be obtained for any cold elective procedure. However, for the carrying out of standard simple procedures for emergency problems where the patient's level of consciousness is unaffected, providing the procedure is explained to the patient first, then obtaining written consent is not mandatory, but verbal consent is. Ideally this should be witnessed by a disinterested third party, such as a nurse. The patient must be warned of the prospect of the scar, prior to the laceration being sutured. Therefore, it is current practice in A & E that the majority of smaller straightforward lacerations are sutured under local anaesthetic, the doctor having obtained verbal consent only.

24.92 When complications of a specific injury have been diagnosed prior to the injury being treated (eg damage to the axillary nerve due to anterior dislocation of the shoulder), this must be documented in the records and the patient's written consent should be obtained before the injury is treated so that the complication of the injury cannot be ascribed to the doctor's treatment.

24.93 For all emergency procedures that are carried out under a general or a regional anaesthetic (eg a Bier's block of the arm for the reduction of a Colles fracture but not for a standard ring block for a finger or toe), and for those procedures when sedation is given (eg intravenous diazepam for a reduction of a dislocated shoulder) then prior written consent must be obtained.

REGIONAL ANAESTHESIA

(See Chapter 32)

24.94 The problem with a Bier's block is that the Royal College of Anaesthetists has advised that a patient should first have starved for six hours. If there is then a leak of anaesthetic from the arm the patient will much more safely be resuscitated from any side effects of that anaesthetic if the stomach is empty. However, if a severely displaced Colles (or Smiths) fracture is left for up to six hours the resulting swelling from bleeding and oedema fluid will make the reduction more difficult, with possibly increased morbidity. Therefore, in the latter case a cogent argument can be made by a trained A & E doctor to proceed with a Bier's block within six hours of the patient's last oral intake.

It is reasonable medical practice for an A & E junior doctor to carry out a Bier's block, providing he is competent so to do, and carries it out using a standard technique, including: inflating a double cuff around the upper arm, placing an intravenous cannula in the opposite arm, having the facilities present for cardiopulmonary resuscitation, and having no medical responsibility for any other procedure or patient during the time that the cuff is inflated.

CHILDREN IN THE A & E DEPARTMENT

24.95 Around 20 per cent of attenders at A & E departments are children under the age of 16 years, with a disproportionately high number of patients who are under five years old. Senior House Officers may have little postgraduate experience in paediatrics, and yet they must be able to identify those few children with early, possibly extremely subtle, signs of serious illness from the majority who will have only minor complaints. It is therefore vital not only that SHOs receive formal teaching in paediatrics, but that a second opinion is readily available from middle grade and consultant A & E staff and from paediatric registrars and above.

LIAISON WITH PAEDIATRIC COMMUNITY SERVICES

24.96 A joint statement produced in 1988 by the British Paediatric Association, the British Association of Paediatric Surgeons and the Casualty Surgeons Association (now the British Association for Accident and Emergency Medicine) laid down the minimum requirements for children in A & E departments. These requirements include that a consultant paediatrician has responsibility for liaison with the consultant in A & E medicine, and that there is a liaison health visitor to facilitate communication between the A & E department and the community. The A & E consultant must ensure that there is good liaison between his/her department, the paediatricians and the community. When funding for a liaison health visitor post is not provided by the community, there is a risk of serious consequences to the care of children attending A & E departments, as an isolated problem may not assume its correct significance when viewed without all other information relating to the child's social circumstances and previous health record.

SERIOUSLY INJURED CHILDREN

24.97 Injured children account for around 60 per cent of paediatric attendances, and most injuries will be relatively minor. Trauma is, however, the leading cause of death in children over one year of age. It is perhaps even more important in children than in adults that the protocols taught in the Advanced Trauma Life Support Course and the Advanced Paediatric Life Support Course (UK) are followed, since care is likely to be given by a multidisciplinary team of A & E, paediatric, anaesthetic and surgical doctors (paras **24.48** and **24.49**). Injured children should be admitted under the care of paediatric surgeons, or when this speciality is unavailable in the hospital, under surgeons who will share the patients' care with paediatricians.[1]

1 HMSO *The Welfare of Children in Hospital* (1992) London.

CHILD ABUSE

24.98 Most minor injuries to children are accidental, but the possibility of child abuse or neglect must always be borne in mind by the SHO in A & E (para **27.126**). Recognition of child abuse can be difficult in A & E, but it is important to be clear that it is not the duty of the A & E doctor to diagnose child abuse. His or her duty is to recognise possible abuse and to refer these children for a senior paediatric opinion.[1] The A & E doctor must always document a clear history of events leading to the child's injury, examine both the injured part and if suspicious of abuse, the entire child for further signs of injury. The doctor must attempt to gain a fuller picture of the child and of the home circumstances by questioning the carers, looking at previous A & E records and if possible liaising with the child's general practitioner, health visitor etc (see para **24.96**). If there is a possibility in the mind of the A & E doctor that the child's injury is not accidental then a more senior paediatric opinion must be obtained.

1 Morton R J & Phillips B M *Accidents and Emergencies in Children* (1992) Oxford University Press, p 178.

ERRORS IN PAEDIATRIC DIAGNOSIS

(See Chapter 27)

24.99 Potentially fatal illnesses in which diagnostic errors are common are described in detail elsewhere; three in particular are bacterial meningitis, osteomyelitis and septic arthritis. It is the duty of the A & E consultant to ensure that SHOs are cognisant of the difficulties in making these diagnoses early in the course of the disease, and of the consequences of missing the diagnosis and therefore delaying initiation of treatment. It is the duty of a doctor working in the A & E department to document the history given by the parents, together with a careful examination of all febrile children in order to delineate the likely cause. Unless the cause is clearly apparent, doctors should have a low threshold for referral of febrile children to the paediatricians on call, especially in those under one year of age in whom assessment can be extremely difficult and in whom it is sensible to make a 'diagnosis until proved otherwise'.

24.100 Failure of doctors to take parents' anxieties about their children seriously is a frequent criticism in negligence cases. The A & E doctor can avoid laying himself open to this charge by being aware that the early signs of serious illness are often extremely subtle, that the parents know their own child better than any doctor can, and by always deferring to a more senior paediatrician when he is unable to convince both himself and the parents that the child is not seriously ill.

SYSTEMS FOR CALLING HELP FOR PAEDIATRIC CASES

24.101 The A & E consultant must liaise with other hospital specialists to ensure that senior help is quickly available when needed for children presenting to the A & E department with critical illness or injury, in whom management requires a high degree of skill and expertise. Serious injury is discussed above. Children with acute upper airways obstruction from epiglottis require immediate assessment and treatment from a team comprising a paediatrician, an anaesthetist and an ear, nose and throat surgeon. The A & E doctor's duty is to recognise the condition by simply looking at the child, to place the child in an area with full resuscitation facilities under constant observation from an experienced nurse, and to summon such help immediately. The A & E doctor is expected to do no more.

THE INAPPROPRIATE ATTENDER

(See also para **24.88**)

24.102 A perpetual problem for any A & E department is the so-called inappropriate attender. By this is meant the patient who has a condition which does not warrant urgency of treatment, or which could quite adequately be treated by a general practitioner. Triage by a nurse trained to prioritise patients, and redirection of inappropriate patients to their general practitioner is an acceptable procedure in the A & E department, providing that the patient is content with this direction, and providing the nurse has received training and initial supervision and is following agreed departmental protocols (agreed by the A & E consultant) for this extended role. An extension of this is the role of the nurse practitioner which has been developed at Old Church Hospital, Romford. Due procedures and protocols must be adhered to, and the District Health Authority must take responsibility for the fact that appropriately categorised patients will be treated by nurses.

24.103 However, if a patient attends an A & E department and asks or demands to see a doctor because of a medical complaint, it is prudent policy to agree. The doctor is beholden to see the patient, take a history and carry out an examination, but he is not under any obligation to treat the patient if that patient does not have a condition requiring emergency treatment. It is a perfectly reasonable standard of care to explain this to the patient, and to refer the patient back to their general practitioner for any possible treatment. The development of an A & E GP team is a more positive solution, especially pertinent to the inner city A & E department.

VIOLENCE AND VERBAL ABUSE

24.104 The situation is different if the patient puts himself in the wrong by verbally or physically threatening the staff or other members of the public. This, unfortunately, is an all too common problem in inner city A & E departments, particularly in the evening and during the night. It is the employer's responsibility to provide a safe working environment. With such patients the A & E doctor should attempt to the best of his ability to ensure that this anti-social behaviour is not being created or perpetuated by a medical condition, e g hypoglycaemia or a head injury, both of which are associated with excessive alcohol ingestion. If medical conditions have precipitated abusive behaviour, the doctor has a duty to treat, or at least observe the patient, who may have to be restrained against his own will, for that patient's own and others' safety. If the patient's behaviour is not judged by the doctor to be directly caused by a medical condition, and the behaviour is such that it is impossible to treat the condition, e g suture a laceration, then the patient should be removed from the A & E department forthwith, and dealt with by the police surgeon if the patient has committed an offence. Any patient with an altered level of consciousness must have his blood level of sugar tested (probably by a finger-prick test). Any patient who is drunk, but is concussed from a head injury, must be observed in hospital. It must be emphasised, however, that a patient's unco-operative behaviour may make it extremely difficult for the doctor to take a history and carry out an examination. Therefore his clinical judgment will be based on less accurate information, and is therefore more likely to be incorrect.

24.105 The patient with an acute pyschosis perhaps caused by drugs, including alcohol, also causes diagnostic difficulties. It may be necessary for staff to restrain and retain the patient in the department for the patient's own safety, pending obtaining a review by an approved psychiatrist and social worker (or nearest relative) for a possible section 4 (compulsory admission to hospital for 72 hours).

24.106 Therefore, the doctor in A & E often works under difficult situations, with patients who may not be co-operative. The patient may have been brought by ambulance or by the police, having been found collapsed. No history may be available because the patient is not sufficiently alert and orientated, and because there were no witnesses to the incident that precipitated that patient's arrival in the department. Unexplained anti-social behaviour may have been the reason that the police or ambulance brought the patient to the A & E department (under section 136). That same behaviour may be continued in the department. Section 136 patients must be seen in an appropriate place of safety. In general this is not the A & E department, but a secure ward in a psychiatric department.

WAITING TIMES AND STAFFING

24.107 Long waiting times result in patients being verbally abusive to staff, especially the nurses, who then put pressure on the doctors, who are often very junior, to speed up the rate with which they see patients. This not only results in the doctor having an unhappy work practice, but also increases the risk that he will, however reluctantly, take and make shortcuts which will result in medical mistakes, which may well present medico-legal problems. Unfortunately, such situations most frequently arise in the evenings and weekends when the patient may be drugged or drunk, perhaps with a concomitant head injury. This is just the situation when the junior A & E doctor needs, firstly, time to assess the clinical problem, or problems, with which the patient presents, and secondly, needs more senior medical support. This more senior medical support is often only immediately available from the on-take teams, who may well not have empathy with the A & E SHO, who has called them to a situation which is unattractive, simply because of these pressures of long waiting times and abusive patients. Hence the drive to increase the number of senior and middle grade staff in A & E. (See para **24.3**.)

24.108 The problems often exacerbate each other in that the fewer doctors there are available, the longer the waiting times and inevitably the more impatient patients become. Alcohol removes the restraints of self control, and the potential for verbal and physical abuse is greater. (See para **24.15**.)

24.109 Under these circumstances accurate record-keeping is the greatest protection for the doctor. This, however, is time consuming, and the more difficult the situation, the less is the time available. The junior doctor therefore has to balance one need against the other. Furthermore, the more unpleasant the environment, the more difficult it is to fill staff vacancies, and in addition the quality of both staff and staff training will be bound to suffer. These facts must be considered when reviewing specific cases of medical negligence, and explain why the A & E department is so vulnerable a place in which to practise medicine. A health authority has a duty to provide adequate resources of staff, space and equipment to enable the doctor to be in a position to provide a reasonable standard of medical care.

24.110 The number of patient attendances is very variable, and no authority can staff a department for peak rates of patient attendance. Therefore, it is necessary both for this and for the reasons stated above, to have specific A & E middle grade staff who can keep waiting times – the key index of quality assurance – within a reasonable maximum. The A & E consultant must continually make the health authority aware of circumstances which inevitably predispose to medical negligence. (See para **24.3**.)

SUMMARY

24.111 An A & E doctor, like any other doctor, has to provide a reasonable standard of care to the level expected of his training, qualification and grade.[1] Often, due to lack of experience, the doctor may simply judge that a clinical situation is not as it should be, but he cannot define this situation more clearly because he has not met it before. However, if he is uncertain how to proceed with a specific patient, it is to be expected of him that he will seek guidance from a more senior and experienced doctor.

1 *Bolam v Friern Hospital Management Committee* [1957] 2 All ER 118, [1957] 1 WLR 582.

24.112 The following are a list of common avoidable errors which have been discussed above:

(1) missed fractured scaphoid;
(2) missed fractured neck of femur;
(3) missed posterior dislocation of the shoulder;
(4) not recognising damage to the circumflex nerve with dislocation of the shoulder;
(5) missed vascular and nerve damage with the supracondylar fracture of the humerus;
(6) missed tendon and nerve damage to the hand and wrist from lacerations;
(7) missed glass foreign bodies, and foreign bodies in the eye, especially metal;
(8) mismanagement of the pretibial laceration;
(9) failure to follow standard guidelines of resuscitation;
(10) mismanagement of the patient with a head injury;
(11) mismanagement of the patient with abdominal pain;
(12) non-recognition of unstable angina or acute myocardial infarction;
(13) non-recognition of pulmonary embolism;
(14) non-recognition of hypoglycaemia;
(15) non-recognition of subarachnoid haemorrhage;
(16) non-recognition of the early signs of serious illness in children.

24.113 The A & E doctor has to cope with the problems of:

(1) the inappropriate attender;
(2) violence and verbal abuse;
(3) alcohol and drug abuse;
(4) the collapsed patient with no history;
(5) patients of poor social circumstances who are immobile, incontinent and demented;
(6) long waiting times and lack of staff;
(7) his own inexperience.

24.114 Therefore, the consultant in A & E medicine who is responsible for the standards of medical care in his department, has to set up systems to cope with the problems presented by the environment in which he works. These are detailed in paras **24.4–24.21** and may be summarised as:

(1) education and supervision;
(2) referral and review;
(3) records;
(4) audit;

(5) communication;
(6) rotas and staffing;
(7) recall and failsafe mechanisms.

24.115 The junior A & E doctor, for his part, has to follow the teaching and written guidelines of the department. He has to practise a reasonable standard of care, at that level which a reasonable body of medical opinion would judge to be appropriate for his level of training, qualification and grade; but when necessary he must also ask advice from those more senior.

BIBLIOGRAPHICAL REFERENCES

Alpar E K and Owen R *Paediatric Trauma* (Castle House Publications, 1988) ch 12, p 163.

American College of Surgeons *Advanced Trauma Life Support Program for Physicians* (1993) ch 1.

Anderson I D, Woodford M, de Dombal F T and Irving M 'Retrospective Study of 1,000 Deaths from Injury in England and Wales' (1988) British Medical Journal 296, 1305.

Barritt D W and Jordan S C 'Anticoagulant drugs in the treatment of pulmonary embolism' (1960) Lancet i, 1309–1312.

British Association for A & E Medicine *Medical Staffing Accident and Emergency Departments* (November 1993).

British Association for A & E Medicine *Senior House Officer Training Guide Book* (October 1993).

Brooks D K and Harrold A J ed *Modern Emergency Department Practice* (1983) Edward Arnold, ch 10, p 167.

British Orthopaedic Association *The Management of Skeletal Trauma in the United Kingdom* (1992).

Craig O 'Pitfalls in Diagnostic Radiology' in *Protection Matters* The Medical Protection Society 19, 14.

Crockard A and Garlick R 'Head Injuries' in *Current Surgical Practice* ed Hadfield and Hobsley M, Edward Arnold, vol 4, ch 16, p 273.

DHSS Hospital Medical Staffing – Achieving a Balance (1987) Report issued on behalf of the UK Health Departments, the Joint Consultants Committee and Chairman of Regional Health Authorities, DHSS.

de Dombal F T 'Computers, diagnoses and patients with abdominal pain (guest editorial)' (1992) Archives of Emergency Medicine 9, 267–270.

Elson R A 'Rupture of the Central Slip of the Extensor Hood of the Finger' (1986) Journal of Bone and Joint Surgery 68B, 229–231.

Fennerty A G, Shetty H G M, Paton D, Roberts G, Routledge P A and Campbell I A 'Clinical presentation and investigation of patients proceeding to isotope lung scanning for suspected pulmonary embolism' (1990) Postgraduate Medical Journal 66, 258–259.

Fothergill J, Hunt M, Touquet R 'Audit of Patients with Chest Pain Presenting to an A & E Department over a Six Month Period' (1993) Archives of Emergency Medicine 10, 155–160.

Fulde G W P *Emergency Medicine* (1988) Williams & Wilkins ch 33, p 185.

Gatzen C, Paterson-Brown S, Touquet R, Dudley H A F 'Management of Acute Abdominal Pain: Decision Making in the Accident and Emergency Department' (1991) Journal of the Royal College of Surgeons of Edinburgh 36, 121–123.

Gilling-Smith C, Regan L, Touquet R 'Gynaecological Emergencies' in *Cambridge Textbook of Emergency Medicine* ed Skinner D, Peyton R, Robertson C, Swain A, Worlock P; Cambridge University Press, Cambridge, Section 111, ch 16.

Gilling-Smith C, Zelin J, Touquet R, Steer P 'Management of early pregnancy bleeding in the accident and emergency department' (1988) Archives of Emergency Medicine 5: 133–138.

Glazer G 'Abdominal Emergencies' in *Modern Emergency Department Practice* (1983) ed Brooks D K and Harrold A J, ch 7, p 113.

'Guidelines for advanced life support. A statement by the advanced life support working party of the European Resuscitation Council' (1992) Resuscitation 24, 111–121.

'Guidelines for the Initial Management of Head Injury; Suggestions From a Group of Neurosurgeons' (1984) British Medical Journal 288, 983–985.

Hauererg J, Andersen B, Eskesen V, Rosenorn J and Schmidt K 'Importance of the recognition of a warning leak as a sign of a ruptured intracranial aneurysm' (1991) Acta Neurologica Scandinavica 83, 61–64.

HMSO *The Welfare of Children in Hospital* (1992) London.

Johnston S R D, Hammond A, Griffiths L, Greenwood R and Clarke C R A 'Subarachnoid haemorrhage – can we do better?' (1989) Journal of the Royal Society of Medicine 81, 720–725.

Kingdom J C P, Kelly T, MacLean A B, McAllister E J 'Rapid One Step Urine Test for Human Chorionic Gonadotrophin in Evaluating Suspected Complications of Early Pregnancy' (1991) British Medical Journal 302, 1308–1311.

Kirby N J *Accident and Emergencies* (1988) Castle House Publications ch 3, p 34.

Leblanc R 'The minor leak preceding Subarachnoid Hemorrhage' (1987) Journal of Neurosurgery 66, 35–39.

Morrison W G and Swann I J 'Electrocardiograph interpretation by junior doctors' (1990) Archives of Emergency Medicine 7, 108–110.

Morton R J, Phillips B J *Accidents and Emergencies in Children* (1992) Oxford University Press, p 3.

National Audit Office *NHS Accident & Emergency Departments in England, Report by the Controller and Auditor General* (1992) HMSO 158.

Nieman E A 'Coma and Neurological Emergencies' in *Modern Emergency Department Practice* ed Brooks D K and Harrold A J (1983) Edward Arnold ch 13, p 199.

'Recommended teaching standards in accident and emergency departments' (1991) Archives of Emergency Medicine 8: 162–163.

Rouan G W, Lee T H, Cook E F, Brand D A, Weisberg M C, Goldman L 'Clinical characteristics and outcome of acute myocardial infarction in patients with initially normal or nonspecific electrocardiograms [a report from the multicenter chest pain study]' (1989) American Journal of Cardiology 64: 1087–1092.

Royal College of Physicians of London (1988) *Resuscitation from Cardiopulmonary Arrest; Training and Organisation*.

Royal College of Surgeons of England (1987) *Guidelines for Pre-Fellowship Surgical Training Posts in A & E*.

Royal College of Surgeons of England (1988) Report of the Working Party on the Management of Patients with Major Trauma, p 10.

Saetta J P, Quinton D, Dacruz D and Barnes M 'Delay in thrombolytic treatment in acute myocardial infarction: the role of the accident & emergency department' (1990) Archives of Emergency Medicine 7 206–211.

Sherry M, Edmunds S and Touquet R 'The Reliability of Patients in Delivering the Letter from the Hospital Accident and Emergency Department to their General Practitioner' (1985) Archives of Emergency Medicine 2, 165–169.

Touquet R and Fothergill J 'Putting A & E consultants in their place' (1992) British Journal of Hospital Medicine 47, 625.

Touquet R, Fothergill J and Jones R 'Resuscitation' in *Clinical Surgery in General* ed Kirk R M, Mansfield A and Cochraine J, Royal College of Surgeons of England, ch 6.

Townsend C 'Acute Ocular Emergencies' in *Modern Emergency Department Practice* (1983) ed Brooks D K and Harrold A J, Edward Arnold ch 18, p 269.

Williams P H, McCutcham J D S and Barrington N A 'Pitfalls in diagnosis of femoral neck fracture' (1992) Injury 23, 140–141.

Yates D W 'ABC of Major Trauma; Scoring Systems for Trauma' (1990) British Medical Journal 301 (6760) 1090–1094.

Yates D W and Redmond A D *Lecture Notes on Accident and Emergency Medicine* (1985) Blackwell Scientific Publications ch 7, p 102.

APPENDIX—MINOR INJURY UNITS

It is increasingly appreciated that smaller A & E departments (certainly those seeing less than 25,000 new patients per year) in urban areas can no longer provide the necessary standards of care for patients, especially if not supported by 24 hour on site core specialities of medicine, surgery, orthopaedics, paediatrics, gynaecology, pathology, radiology, anaesthetics and intensive care. One solution that provides a daytime and evening service for a local community, that has previously been served by an A & E department, is the Minor Injuries Unit (MIU). This is for self-referred patients with minor injuries, eg falls, cuts and burns. It does not receive ambulances, nor provide advanced resuscitation skills.

As presently demonstrated by St Charles' MIU, London W10, part of St Mary's NHS Trust, which opened on 1 February 1993, Minor Injury Units are distinct entities (as opposed to units run by general practitioners). They form part of a Directorate of Nursing, are run by nurse practitioners and are answerable to a Chief Nurse. The following are necessary prerequisites:

(1) the employing authority provides vicarious liability for the nurse practitioners;
(2) protocols, which meet with the agreement of the parent A & E department and other specialities involved, eg orthopaedics and radiology, must be adhered to by the nurse practitioners;
(3) the nurse practitioners must have had specific training (eg for ordering and reading of X-rays of knee and distal leg, elbow and distal arm) to match the spectrum of work covered by the protocols;
(4) such protocols must have the agreement of the employing authority, eg the Board of an NHS Trust;
(5) the parent A & E department must agree to accept immediately any referral from their related MIU, but the consultants in A & E medicine are not responsible for the MIU;
(6) the relevant general practitioner should be notified of every patient attendance at a MIU.

CHAPTER 25

Medical negligence in trauma and orthopaedics

Mr Nigel H Harris *MA MB BChir FRCS*

SUMMARY

25.1 Most cases of medical negligence are concerned with the practice of obstetrics, anaesthetics and orthopaedics including trauma. In 1978 settled cases of negligence amounted to 1 in 1,000 and in 1988 it was 13 per 1,000. It has been estimated that an orthopaedic surgeon is 2½ times more likely to be sued than the average doctor. A possible reason was given by a well-known orthopaedic surgeon (T T Stamm):'Other people's disasters are conveniently buried under six feet of ground whereas the orthopaedic surgeon's failures are plucking at his elbow for the rest of his life.'

25.2 Concern about the explosion in orthopaedic negligence actions has been discussed by Lacombe and O'Keefe (1989), John Woodyard (1990) and Roger Vickers (1991). This chapter will discuss standards of practice and how some of the more common errors might be avoided.

25.3 There are a number of possible explanations for orthopaedic surgeons to be involved in litigation; the rapid and therapeutically beneficial advances (joint replacement for example) associated with enhanced patient expectation, and the steadily rising incidents of trauma of all types – particularly road traffic accidents, which often produce multiple injuries of great complexity. This combination has inevitably led to a considerable increase in workload of trauma in orthopaedic units and Accident and Emergency Departments, not always matched by adequate numbers and quality of medical, nursing and ancillary staff, and deficiencies in intensive care beds and equipment are also reported from time to time. This state of affairs is not offered as an excuse for inferior standards of care (and it is not a defence in law) because it is a doctor's duty to inform management in writing if he considers circumstances are dangerous for the patient; if he fails to do so and a medical accident occurs, the doctor may be liable.[1] These problems have been highlighted by a recently published British orthopaedic association booklet (BOA 1992). It deals with the management of trauma, and it estimates that 108,000 patients a year had a serious disability which could have been prevented by the elimination of the deficiencies to which the report draws attention.

1 Journal of the Medical Defence Union, 'Economics and the NHS; are doctors liable?' (1986) I, 1.

25.4 I will indicate some of the more common errors and how the risk can be reduced. They may be conveniently classified as diagnostic consent and therapeutic errors. Together they form the normal general duty of care of a doctor for his patient. Lord Diplock emphasises the point:[1]

> that general duty was not subject to dissection into a number of component parts to which different criteria of what satisfied the duty of care applied such as diagnosis, treatment and advice. In modern medicine and surgery such dissection of various things a doctor has to do in the exercise of his whole duty of care owed to his patients was neither legally meaningful nor medically practicable.

1 *Sidaway v Board of Governors of the Bethlem Royal Hospital and the Maudsley Hospital* [1985] AC 871, [1985] 1 All ER 643, HL.

25.5 Analysis of over 400 orthopaedic patients referred for an opinion on possible negligence, reveals that in a significant number avoidable errors have occurred because responsibility for decision-making and treatment (including operation), has been inappropriately delegated to junior and inexperienced doctors. A number in John Woodyard's survey was 81 out of 236 accidents. These findings are confirmed by two reports (1987,1992). The advice was that all new patients in outpatient clinics, and patients for elective operation, should be seen by senior medical staff; and major and complex conditions should be operated on or could be closely supervised by them. It needs to be emphasised that these reports are concerned with perioperative deaths; they do not reflect the much larger number of patients who sustain injuries and disability as a result in errors of medical practice.

Consent

25.6 Obtaining the patient's consent after explaining the nature of the procedure and mentioning risk and possible complications, is one of the components of the general duty held by a doctor to his patient. The problems which arise are not unique to orthopaedic surgery, and discussion here would be inappropriate. (See Chapter 12.)

COMMON ERRORS IN ORTHOPAEDIC PRACTICE

25.7 The following are the aspects of orthopaedic practice which regularly produce negligence claims: misdiagnosis or late diagnosis, nerve damage, circulatory impairement, therapeutic errors including operative technique and wound infection.

Diagnostic errors

25.8 It is important to note that failure to make a correct diagnosis is not an indication of a poor standard of care; for the doctor to become liable it must be shown that there has been a failure to exercise reasonable skill and care.

25.9 Generally these errors amount to late diagnosis; thus a patient attends a doctor with certain symptoms, is examined and may be investigated – usually an X-ray and either no or the wrong diagnosis is made. It follows that the correct primary treatment is delayed and in the meantime inappropriate or no therapy is being given. The consequences of late diagnosis can be extremely serious – irreversible changes may have occurred and only palliative treatment can be given. More complex surgery may be required than would have otherwise been the case if the diagnosis had been made earlier. In the former, a considerable permanent disability results – the patient may lose his or her job and daily living activities including sport may be significantly affected; in the latter the more complex therapy will usually result in a long period off work and even the loss of a job.

25.10 In other circumstances the late diagnosis has no material effect on the eventual outcome; thus in spite of the delayed treatment, the condition resolves spontaneously and there is no residual disability. On the other hand there are occasions when the patient presents with a condition which as far as it is possible to judge will inevitably progress to a permanent disabling condition irrespective of whether the diagnosis was early or late, or as in a recent case there is an estimated 75 per cent chance of progression.[1]

1 *Hotson v Fitzgerald* [1985] 3 All ER 167, on appeal sub nom *Hotson v East Berkshire Area Health Authority* [1987] AC 750, [1987] 1 All ER 210; revsd [1987] AC 750, [1987] 2 All ER 909, HL.

25.11 In Vickers' review of 100 allegations of negligence (1991), almost half the cases were concerned with diagnostic errors and this is in accordance with my own experience. Many of the errors occur in the Accident and Emergency Department when there is a failure to take an X-ray following trauma; this is discussed in Chapter 24.

History taking

25.12 It is undoubtedly a truism that a doctor who cannot take a good history and a patient who cannot give one are in danger of giving and receiving bad treatment. It is absolutely fundamental that unless an adequate history is taken, mistakes will occur. An inadequate history will often lead to defects in the clinical examination and inappropriate investigation. No two patients are alike – some have poor memories for dates, others will give answers that they think the doctor expects; some, fortunately a minority, are irritated by questions and expect the doctor to come to a decision rather in a way that a veterinary surgeon does.

25.13 There is no doubt that a good history will indicate the likely site of the disease and the probable diagnosis. Fractures and dislocations complicated by nerve and vascular damage require particular careful and prompt assessment by an experienced orthopaedic surgeon if serious and disabling consequences are to be avoided.

25.14 Not only must a careful history be taken – and it is not an excuse to say 'I was too busy' – but the details must be legibly recorded in the notes. Failure to do so is inexcusable. It is not good enough to say after the event that 'I asked the patient about this and that' – failure to record means the question was not asked.

Examination

25.15 When it comes to the clinical examination the doctor should have a good idea regarding the site of the disease and even the likely diagnosis. Errors in the clinical examination are often due to not listening to the patient's story or to carelessness. The following illustrate these points.

25.16 A male patient will frequently present with pain in the buttocks, thigh, calf or foot; unless it is elicited that the pain is closely related to exercise, the examining doctor will not appreciate that the pain is typical of intermittant claudication and therefore probably due to impaired arterial blood supply to the limbs. In some instances the peripheral leg pulses are not examined. The only way to avoid such mistakes is routinely to palpate the pulses in all patients while having their back or legs examined for whatever reason. Failure to record in the notes details of the pulses indicates that the examination did not take place. Failure to examine the hips when a patient complains of knee pain is a common error. A similar example is that leg pain anywhere may be referred from the lumbar spine. It is mandatory to examine the spine including a neurological and vascular examination of the legs in all cases of low back pain. The same applies to the cervical spine when the patient presents with pain and/or parasthesiae in the hand or forearm for example. With regard to patients suffering from the effects of trauma, examination of the affected part includes observing the degree of swelling and any bruising that may be present. Mistakes will be avoided if a working rule is adopted, namely that with significant swelling and bruising which has developed within hours of the injury, it must be assumed that a fracture or a complete ligament rupture has occurred until proved otherwise. In such cases an apparently negative X-ray will not prevent appropriate treatment being given. As with the history, details of the examination must be clearly and legibly recorded including the negative or normal findings. It is reasonable to record something about the patient's demeanour such as placid or nervous individual, the ability to give a clear history and the degree of co-operation. Under no circumstances should derogatory remarks about the patient be recorded however much the doctor considers he has been provoked.

25.17 At the end of the recorded note it is good clinical practice to give a suggested diagnosis – even if it is only provisional; indeed the diagnosis may be entirely obscure in which case it should be so recorded.

25.18 Failure to test for nerve and vascular damage is one of the commonest errors in patients after trauma and orthopaedic operations, usually leading to substantial settlements. Some examples are as follows:

A patient lacerates the front of the wrist or fingers on glass. In such cases important nerves and tendons are at risk. The examining doctor must always carefully examine for loss of tendon or nerve function and record the findings. A working rule must be that a deficiency of peripheral nerve function in the presence of a recent open wound including a surgical operation indicates that the nerve has been divided and urgent exploration is indicated. A child with a supracondylar fracture, or indeed any fracture or fracture dislocation in the region of the elbow joint may have the complication of nerve and/or vascular impairment on admission to hospital, and before treatment is given. Although it is not always easy to examine a distressed child for such deficiencies, every effort must be made to do so – not once, but at regular short intervals. It must never be forgotten that an obstructed arterial circulation from whatever cause will produce serious permanent damage to a limb if allowed to persist for more than an hour. Anterior dislocation of the shoulder may damage the nerve supply to the deltoid muscle. Similar changes may result from manipulation of the joint so it is extremely important to record in the notes whether or not the muscle is contracting before the manipulation takes place. A humeral shaft fracture may damage the radial nerve. Posterior dislocation or fracture dislocation of the hip may damage the sciatic nerve.

25.19 Vascular damage in the leg following long bone fractures and dislocations of the knee is a familiar complication as is a compartment syndrome following a tibial fracture. In the latter case, warning symptoms are frequently ignored (disproportionate pain requiring frequent strong analgesics, a complaint of paraesthesiae in the toes and inability to move them) and the early ischaemic signs are missed (loss of light touch sensation, loss of active toe movements, change of skin colour and dramatic increase in pain with passive toe extension) leading to permanent disability from deformities in the toe and foot often associated with neurological damage.

25.20 If diagnostic errors are to be avoided in these cases, and early diagnosis may be of critical importance when there is vascular impairment, it is imperative and indeed must be considered standard practice to have a high index of suspicion that nerve or vascular damage may have occurred and the appropriate clinical examination carried out and recorded. I will go further and suggest it is accepted good practice routinely to examine the peripheral circulation and nerves in all patients after limb trauma. In this context it is perhaps important to note that it is not acceptable practice to allow only a very junior inexperienced house officer to conduct these difficult examinations; it should be normal practice that all such examinations for possible vascular and nerve damage must be done also by a senior registrar or consultant as soon as possible after admission.

25.21 There can be little doubt that for diagnostic purposes, orthopaedic surgeons more than any other speciality depend on good quality X-rays. Lawyers may not appreciate (and there is no reason why they should) that part of an orthopaedic surgeon's training is of necessity concerned with interpretation of X-rays, and it is for this reason that they do not rely entirely on radiologist's reports of skeletal abnormalities. In this context it is relevant to point out that the vast majority of skeletal X-rays are reported on by generalist radiologists because there are so very few that specialise in joint and bone radiology. I will go so far as to say that in medico-legal cases where X-rays are relevant, a consultant orthopaedic opinion should carry at least as much weight if not more so than a general radiologist. I would, however, accept that a relatively inexperienced junior doctor must rely on the radiologist's opinion and should always consult with him when in doubt about an X-ray. There are, of course, circumstances where a radiological opinion is of paramount importance. Interpretation of CT and MRI scans is best done by radiologists with special expertise. Interpretations of scans of the spine should be done by neuroradiologists.

25.22 Failure to X-ray is not a common error – and in part this is because the threat of litigation has persuaded junior doctors in particular to X-ray more frequently than is perhaps necessary (a form of defensive medicine), and the effect has been that less reliance has been placed on careful clinical examination and judgment.

25.23 The classical errors are seen usually in trauma cases. An example is the missed scaphoid fracture; it is well known that after a fall on the outstetched hand a painful wrist may be due to such a fracture but the first X-ray is often negative. These patients must always be instructed to return 10 to 14 days later for repeat scaphoid X-rays, but unfortunately this rule is not always observed. It is simply not good enough to tell a patient to return if they are worried or if pain continues.

25.24 Another example is the failure to request a lateral projection X-ray for the hip. Two common conditions may only be capable of diagnosis from such a projection, namely a subcapital fracture of the femoral neck and a displaced proximal epiphysis. Although most clinicians would expect an antero–posterior and lateral projection to be done if a request is written on the form 'X-ray hip', this is unreliable and it is always wise to specifically request both projections. This applies to all joints and the spine, and in children it is always wise to request the opposite normal side for comparison.

25.25 Trauma to the shoulder joint gives rise to problems in diagnosis and usually it is a missed posterior dislocation. All acute dislocations to the shoulders should have an axillary or axial projection as well as the standard antero–posterior film and then serious error will be avoided. It has been said in defence of failure to take the appropriate lateral X-ray that it could not be done as the patient had too much pain. This is not an acceptable excuse because the arm can be held in the appropriate position by a doctor; it must not be left to the radiographer or the nurse; in addition the patient can of course be given analgesic medication prior to the X-ray.

25.26 Failure to X-ray the cervical spine after a head injury has led to very serious consequences, a fracture dislocation or dislocation of the cervical vertebrae may occur; it is frequently unstable. If left untreated further displacement occurs causing damage to the spinal cord and/or nerve roots resulting in a variable degree of limb and bladder paralysis which was not evident when the patient was first examined. It should be remembered also that many of these patients have been concussed and will be incapable of explaining to the doctors that their neck is painful. The only safe rule in these cases is to say that it is obligatory to examine and X-ray the cervical spine in all cases of head injury. Another important point to note is that sometimes due to poor technique the lateral X-ray of the cervical spine is inadequate and may not show the lowest one or two vertebrae thus missing the fracture or dislocation.

25.27 There follow some illustrative case reports:

Case reports (1) A middle aged woman complained of increasing severe lumbo-dorsal back pain over a period of three months and eventually she had night sweats, difficulty of walking and retention of urine. At no time was she examined by her doctor during four consultations, and was simply prescribed analgesic tablets. After two months she was sent for a lumbar spine X-ray which was normal. A week or two later she was admitted to hospital as emergency with a paraplegia caused by tuberculosis in the lumbo-dorsal region of the spine. Emergency surgery failed to prevent permanent neurological damage to the legs and she also had bladder paralysis. More careful history taking and clinical examination would have indicated that there was lower dorsal spine pathology and an appropriate X-ray would have been requested and the tragic end result avoided. This case was indefensible and the patient received a very large sum in damages.

(2) An infant's hips were routinely checked at birth and at six weeks by the general practitioner; a further check at the health centre at the age of seven months reported normal hips. At 15 months the mother was concerned the child was not walking. When walking, which started between 16 and 18 months, the mother noticed a limp. Despite the history of late walking and a limp, the general practitioner did not examine the hips. At two years the health visitor confirmed mother's continued concern about an awkward gait, and the left leg looked different from the right. This was reported to the general practitioner who did not find an abnormality. No X-ray was requested. At 2½ years an X-ray was requested and a diagnosis of a left congenital dislocation was confirmed. Subsequently, after closed reduction, a Salter innominate osteotomy was performed. At the age of nine years a significant defect of the acetabulm persists.

This case illustrates how important it is to listen to what a mother is saying about her child and to act accordingly. It also illustrates the importance of a careful clinical examination of a child's hips by an experienced doctor who has been trained in the standard techniques. It is the orthopaedic surgeon's responsibility with the health authority to ensure that satisfactory arrangements exist for the routine screening of children's hips. (See para **27.71**.)

(3) A 15-year-old boy presented to his general practitioner with a two month history of knee pain; there was no history of trauma and the general health was good. He was promptly referred to hospital as a possible hip problem. The hospital doctors thought that he may have 'Still's disease'; no X-rays were taken and one month after first presenting he was referred to a rheumatologist. A total of 19 blood investigations were done and all major joints were X-rayed; the hip had an AP projection only and these films were reported as normal; aspirin was prescribed and he was told to return in six months. He was seen again four months later, still complaining of knee pain but no examination of the hips took place. Six months after presenting the hips were examined by the rheumatologist and X-rays revealed a very severe chronic epiphyseal displacement with fusion of the growth plate.

This case illustrates the failure to understand the significance of the history leading to failure to examine the hips and request lateral hip X-rays. The general practitioner and the doctor in the Accident and Emergency Department are usually the first to see children who complain of knee pain. Even if there is no complaint of hip pain the only way that mistakes will be avoided is routinely to examine the hips in these cases and take ablunofinote X-rays, including the opposite side for comparison.

In this case the consultant rheumatologist accepted the radiological report and did not himself inspect the X-rays. It should of course be routine to take two projections for the study of joint pathology. In this case there were in fact very suspicious signs on the antero-posterior X-ray, which an orthopaedic surgeon and a bone and joint radiologist would almost certainly have spotted and requested a lateral projection.

(4) A 17-year-old man involved in a road traffic accident sustained a compound fracture of the left tibia and fibular. He complained of left hip pain but the joint was not examined or X-rayed. After 10 weeks the plaster was removed from the leg and he was told that he could put weight on it; as a result he had increasing pain. Four months after the accident a doctor noticed the limb to be short and fixed in internal rotation. An X-ray of the hips revealed a fracture dislocation of the hip. The joint needed open reduction and subsequently developed avascular necrosis and will eventually require major surgery. This case was indefensible, and illustrates the point that in all cases where there appears to be an isolated fracture of the tibia or femur it is imperative that the hip should be examined and if there is doubt an X-ray taken.

(5) A 40-year-old man who plays regular sport is one day playing squash when he suddenly feels severe pain in the back of the ankle. He said to the hospital doctor 'it feels as if a brick had been thrown at me and I fell to the ground'. This history is quite typical of a ruptured achilles tendon, and clinical examination is only necessary to confirm the diagnosis. Nevertheless, the doctor failed to make the correct diagnosis saying that he had simply strained a few muscle fibres and required no treatment. Two days later he told the general practitioner, who ordered physiotherapy without examining him. After two months he reported no improvement and was referred to an orthopaedic surgeon. The correct diagnosis was made and complicated reconstructive surgery was required. Prompt diagnosis and treatment would have prevented permanent disability. This case could not be defended and again illustrates the point that it is extremely important to listen to what the patient is saying.

(6) A 28-year-old architect injured his shoulder in a road traffic accident; he was admitted to hospital and a fracture dislocation of the joint was noted from an antero-posterior projection X-ray. After manipulation he was told that the joint was correctly aligned. He returned to the hospital two weeks later and stated he was not happy with his lack of progress and 'the joint felt displaced'. He was reassured. He reported his continued concern one week later and was referred to physiotherapy. No improvement took place and he requested a second opinion from another orthopaedic surgeon three months after the injury. The correct diagnosis was made, namely that he had an unreduced posterior dislocation of the shoulder joint. The failure to diagnose at the first hospital was due to the fact that an axillary or axial X-ray projection was not taken; it is obligatory to take such an X-ray in all suspected cases of shoulder dislocation and if done, a commonly missed posterior dislocation will be diagnosed. The error was indefensible.

(7) A 42-year-old veterinary surgeon sustained a head injury in a road traffic accident and was knocked unconscious. On admission to hospital he complained of neck pain and an X-ray of the cervical spine was reported as showing no bone injury. During the course of the next few days he complained of weakness of the arms and hands with paraesthesiae, and progressive weakness of the legs and difficulty standing. At first these symptoms were ignored by the medical staff; no records were made and no examination carried out which would have indicated gross neurological signs in the arms and legs suggesting damage to the spinal cord in the cervical region. Three weeks from injury a re-X-ray of the cervical spine showed a fracture dislocation of cervical vertebra 6 on the 7th. the error was that the first X-ray was accepted as showing no injury on the films and of course it should not have been accepted as an adequate X-ray because cervical 6 and 7 were obscured by the shadow of the shoulder. This case was indefensible. Failure of the clinician and radiologist to appreciate that the X-ray was inadequate is not uncommon and is inexcusable. In this case the error may not have had serious consequences if the patient's complaints had been taken seriously and a full clinical examination carried out.

(8) A 13-year-old boy sustained a displaced angulated distal tibial fracture, which was manipulated into a satisfactory position, and a complete plaster cast was applied; it was not split. A few hours later he complained of a lot of pain accompanied by burning sensation in the foot and toes which were swollen. At 48 hours there was evidence of reduced sensation in the toes. He was allowed home on the fifth day. The plaster was removed at two months and since then he has noticed an increasing foot deformity. Ten years after the fracture at the age of 23 he complained of burning pain in the ankle which had persisted since the injury, and inability to put the foot to the ground. He was noticed to have 45 degrees of plantaris deformity, and considerable calf atrophy, claw toes and absent instrinsic muscle function; the skin on the sole of the foot was hypersensitive. The history and clinical findings are consistent with an ischaemic episode which occurred soon after application of the plaster. He clearly had a compartment syndrome and even though it was suspected, a 'wait and see' policy was not justified. If splitting the plaster and underlying padding does not rapidly relieve the symptoms and unequivocally restore the circulation, then urgent exploration and decompression is obligatory.

Sometimes the diagnostic error is not so straightforward as illustrated by *Hotson v East Berkshire Area Health Authority*.[1] A child of 13 years fell from a tree and sustained an acute displacement of the upper left femoral epiphysis. He was taken to hospital immediately and sent home but the correct diagnosis was not made until five days later when he had an emergency operation. Subsequent avascular necrosis of the femoral head developed. Eight years later the hip was painful and deformed and the leg short. Further surgery will inevitably be necessary. The patient not unreasonably brought an action because of a delay in diagnosis, which it was contended affected the final outcome. However, all the evidence indicated that there was a 75 per cent risk that the original accident was responsible for the necrosis – in other words on the balance of probabilities it was inevitable and the late diagnosis did not affect the issue. Substantial damages were initially awarded on the basis of a 25 per cent lost chance of obtaining a better result. Eventually the House of Lords reversed the decision, principally because the patient was unable to prove on the balance of probabilities that the delayed diagnosis (and treatment) had been a material contributing cause to avascular necrosis. In this case the patient did not in fact have the chance to lose because of the inevitability of avascular necrosis. In future cases where loss of a chance of a better result is an issue it is unlikely to succeed unless the patient can establish causation on the balance of probabilities.

1 [1987] AC 750, [1987] 2 All ER 909, HL.

Vascular damage

25.28 Most cases that come to litigation are the result of trauma leading to circulatory deficiency which is not recognised until irreversible (ischaemic) changes have occurred. The supracondylar fracture in the child and the tibial fracture in adults are two common sites of vascular trauma. The compartment syndrome after trauma or an operation is a relatively common cause for litigation. The subject has been discussed under Diagnostic Errors (paras **25.8–25.27**).

Nerve damage

25.29 There are two groups of patients with neurological deficits which lead to negligence claims, namely post-traumatic, which was discussed earlier, and iatrogenic nerve injury. This subject has been reviewed by Bonney (1987) and Birch et al (1991). More recently Birch pointed out (1992) that since 1990, the peripheral nerve injury at the Royal National Orthopaedic Hospital has treated 44 patients with iatrogenic peripheral nerve injuries, 22 of which occurred during day case operation procedures; 11 of these resulted from operations on the posterior triangle of the neck, 9 from operations on the upper limb, and 2 following operations for varicose veins. It was exceptional to make an early diagnosis, and in only 4 patients was the diagnosis made by the operating surgeon who rarely saw the patient again.

25.30 The message is clear – day case surgery is not necessarily a minor procedure; operations should not be done by minor surgeons! Consultants or senior registrar surgeons and anaesthetists who should do this work must not give in to pressure from management to do more day care surgery unless they are satisfied with the arrangements for the patient's safety and that the general organisation is of an appropriate standard. (See Chapter 33.)

25.31 Direct damage to peripheral nerves occurs in the field of operation – usually by cutting, encircling with a ligature, pressure or traction. Traction or pressure may also damage nerves not in the field of operation. Nerve damage is inexcusable and is usually the result of carelessness or the operation has been delegated inappropriately to a junior doctor with inadequate experience. Direct damage may occur from the application of the tourniquet – particularly in susceptible patients (muscle atrophy and lack of subcutaneous fat as seen in some rheumatoid arthritics). Ischaemic damaged nerves result from trauma to main vessels and in the compartment syndrome.

25.32 Examples which regularly lead to litigation are damage to the musculo-cutaneous nerve in the arm during the anterior approach to the shoulder, the posterior interroseus nerve when exposing the radial head, digital nerves during operations for Dupuytren's contracture, the radial nerve in exposure of the humeral shaft, the sciatic nerve during hip replacement operations, and the accessory nerve during removal of the lymph gland from the posterior triangle of the neck.

25.33 It is surprising how often a post-operative nerve injury is treated by a 'wait and see' policy. The rule should be that loss of nerve function in the presence of an open wound (traumatic or operative) must be presumed to result from nerve division and early exploration is therefore obligatory. If the affected nerve is not in the field of operation, it may be reasonable to adopt a 'wait and see' policy in anticipation that it has been damaged by a pressure or traction and that spontaneous recovery will occur; in such cases electromyography after about two to three weeks may be helpful. Not all orthopaedic surgeons are experienced in treating peripheral nerve injuries. Patients will benefit and litigation will be reduced if these patients are promptly referred to centres with the appropriate expertise.

25.34 In cases where the operation is to remove a malignant tumour, nerves may be sacrificed if excision is to be effective; in such cases the risks must be carefully explained to the patients. It is inexcusable to damage nerves during excision of a benign tumour. A good example is excision of a Schwannoma with a portion of the nerve trunk on the assumption that it is a ganglion.

25.35 Special problems arise with regard to lumbar disc surgery because nerve roots have to be exposed and retracted. Excessive traction can be applied without the surgeon being aware of it. Operative difficulties arise sometimes – excessive bleeding, difficulty with exposure, cerebro-spinal fluid leakage are some examples. The disability from nerve damage may be signficant and is often permanent. The risk can be reduced to a mininum if a pre-operative myleogram or scan is done, the surgeon is experienced, the patient is properly positioned, and given hypertensive anaesthesia and there must be adequate exposure and gentle handling of nerve roots.

25.36 It is noteworthy that only a few years ago if a case of a nerve injury came to litigation, the Statement of Claim would have indicated the surgeon failed to explore the nerve at the optimum time, or alternatively no exploration was carried out. The defence would have been that nerve repair would be too difficult or likely to fail. Nowadays such a defence is invalid because of greatly improved nerve repair techniques, including grafting.

25.37 Some of the above points will be illustrated by case reports.

Case reports (1) A 24-year-old dentist had an operation for recurrent dislocation of the shoulder, following which he manifested signs of damage to the musculo-cutaneous nerve. A 'wait and see' policy was adopted. The clinical picture of a deep muscle paralysis and sensory loss persisted, and even at eight months no thought was given to the possibility that the nerve might have been divided. No exploration was carried out and it was not until 2½ years after the event that he was referred to the orthopaedic expert, when it was clearly too late to produce benefit from surgery.

(2) A 60-year-old man had a Charnley total hip replacement from osteoarthritis with moderate protrusio of the acetabulum, performed through a postero-lateral incision. Following the operation he had a sciatic nerve palsy. Two days later the surgeon explored the nerve and found the medial division had been cut, the proximal end of which was retracted under the gluteus maximus muscle. The surgeon also noted some unconstrained cement from the acetabulum and he attributed the nerve injury to a burn from this material. Nothing was done about the nerve injury and an opinion from an expert was not obtained. All the evidence was in favour of surgical division of the nerve, but even if cement was responsible it certainly should have been preventable.

(3) A 49-year-old man presented with a three year history of a lump on the flexor aspect of the wrist, and it was diagnosed as a probable ganglion. An inexperienced junior doctor excised the lump which was described as a neuroma arising from a branch of the ulnar nerve. In fact the tumour was excised with a portion of the motor branch of the ulnar nerve, and histologically proved to be a neurilemmona. Surprisingly a second opinion was obtained from a plastic surgeon, who advised nerve grafting would be required but was likely to fail, so he was never given the chance to obtain the opinion of a nerve repair expert. This sequence of events is unfortunately not uncommon. It illustrates the fact that minor operations require the skill of a qualified surgeon, and inappropriate delegation as in this case is to be deplored.

Therapeutic errors

25.38 There is no doubt that errors in the course of treatment – operative and non-operative – appear to be more common than diagnostic errors. The explanation may be that therapeutic errors more often lead to serious disability or death and hence are more likely to be reported and possibly followed by litigation.

25.39 A study of the Confidential Enquiry into Perioperative Deaths to which I referred earlier, although concerned with mortality, probably reflects the main causes of morbidity; these may be listed as follows and apply to all surgical specialties: the surgeon is too junior and/or inexperienced and may fail to discuss the case with the consultant, lack of supervision of junior staff by consultants, inappropriate pre and post operative management, and inappropriate operations.

The indications for operation

25.40 A decision that an operation is the treatment of choice, especially for a non-urgent condition, must be fully explained to the patient by a consultant or senior registrar. It is good practice also to explain what will happen if the operation is not performed and any alternative non-operative treatment.

25.41 To avoid misunderstanding, the surgeon should explain his reason in the notes and also the letter to the general practitioner. A further check on the operation to be performed and the patient's understanding of it should be made by the consultant or his deputy after the patient's admission for operation.

25.42 All new patients referred to orthopaedic outpatients by general practitioners are entitled to the opinion of a consultant and in his absence by a senior registrar.

25.43 There are some surgeons who have a particular interest in a certain operation and at times are over enthusiastic about advising operation when the facts suggest that there is no good indication, or alternatively adequate conservative treatment has not been given the chance to give benefit. A good example is lumbar spinal fusion. There is a recognised failure rate and complications may produce very severe disability. It is the duty of the surgeon in these circumstances to ensure that detailed clinical and investigative procedures have been done to indicate the site or level in the spine of the pathological process which is giving rise to the pain, and whether or not there is evidence of nerve root damage. There is no place for exploratory surgery in the spine in the absence of signs to indicate the pathological site, and confirmed by one or more of the standard investigations such as myelography, CT and MRI scans.

25.44 Failure to operate at the optimum time may be especially harmful in more acute conditions. The circumstances are usually that a correct diagnosis has been made but surgical treatment is not considered necessary. Examples are as follows.

25.45 A patient is admitted with increasing low back pain and sciatica over a period of seven days and it is noticed that there are bladder symptoms and some neurological signs in the legs. The diagnosis is nerve root compression from a disc prolapse. Urgent decompression of the affected nerve roots is required if permanent damage is to be avoided, and conservative (non-operative) treatment is contraindicated.

25.46 A child is admitted with a two-day history of increasing pain in the hip, and is found to have a high fever and is obviously ill. A diagnosis of septic arthritis with or without acute osteomyelitis is made. Failure to improve significantly after 24 hours antibiotics is generally an indication for surgical drainage of the abscess. Persistence of conservative treatment in such circumstances often results in permanent joint damage or chronic osteomyelitis.

25.47 A limb that has been subjected to trauma and a long bone fracture sustained is likely to be encased in a plaster cast, perhaps following a closed manipulation. The periphery may show evidence of ischaemia. If a simple measure of splitting the plaster cast and underlying woollen bandage (and the latter is obligatory) does not unequivocally restore the arterial circulation to normal within a few minutes (as tested clinically and with the aid of a doppler if necessary) then surgical exploration and decompression of the affected artery must be done as a matter of urgency.

25.48 In many of these instances the surgeon is thought to have made an error of judgment. More often than not the error occurs because the surgeon concerned is too junior in experience and the consultant is not informed of the problem.

25.49 Some surgeons may be still under the illusion that an error of clinical judgment may be put forward as an absolute defence against a claim for negligence, and it would therefore be appropriate to quote two learned authorities. According to Lord Edmund-Davis:

> To say that the surgeon committed an error of clinical judgment was wholly ambiguous, for, while some such errors might be completely consistent with the due exercise of professional skill, others might be so glaringly below proper standards as to make the finding of negligence inevitable.[1]

And in the view of Lord Scarman:

> There is seldom any one answer exclusive to all the problems of professional judgment. A doctor is unlikely to succeed by saying he was not negligent because he had made an error of clinical judgment – an error of judgment is not by itself incompatible with negligence.[2]

1 *Whitehouse v Jordan* [1981] 1 All ER 267, [1981] WLR 246, HL.
2 *Maynard v West Midlands Regional Health Authority* [1985] 1 All ER 635, [1984] 1 WLR 634, HL.

Intraoperative damage

25.50 It is clearly impossible to give an account of every possible error. Those that occur most often, and after a relatively common standard procedure will be discussed.

25.51 It would be appropriate at this point to say something about the use of the tourniquet. This device is used almost exclusively by orthopaedic surgeons in order that they may operate in a bloodless field when dealing with burns, joints, tendons and nerves. The advantages are that persistence and unavoidable bleeding during the operation are avoided. The advantages carry certain risks which can only be prevented by the diligence of the surgeon (who is entirely responsible for the application and the removal of the tourniquet). There is some damage to the tissues – particularly peripheral nerves and the skin which are susceptible to direct damage by the cuff of the tourniquet (the most likely mechanism), and ischaemia from too high a cuff pressure for too long a period.

25.52 To avoid injury from the use of a tourniquet a generally accepted protocol should be followed and the important points are listed as follows:

(1) only a pneumatic type of tourniquet should be used and the apparatus, particularly the pressure gauges, must be checked at regular intervals;
(2) a tourniquet should only be applied under direct supervision of the surgeon;
(3) a record must be made of the time of application and removal of the tourniquet;
(4) direct damage to normal nerves can be avoided by protecting them with a layer of soft material and avoiding pressure of 250 mms Hg in the adult upper limb (200 mms Hg in children) and 300 Hg in the lower limb;
(5) avoid the use of a tourniquet in those limbs with susceptible nerves and in all cases where there is evidence of peripheral vascular disease;
(6) there is no general agreement about the permissible length of time for application of a tourniquet but most orthopaedic surgeons would accept one hour.

25.53 Operating on the wrong limb or digit is clearly indefensible and if amputation is involved a major disaster. These errors can be avoided by a combination of the following: clearly written medical records, correctly labelled X-rays which must always be referred to by the operating surgeon immediately prior to the operation, clearly written operating list and the patient's skin must be marked identifying the side and where appropriate the digit concerned.

25.54 Brief mention will now be made of some other common intraoperative errors. All the examples at one time or another have been the subject of litigation and are difficult to defend.

A TOTAL HIP REPLACEMENT

25.55 An intraoperative femoral shaft fracture occurs when excessive force is used during manipulation to dislocate the joint; sometimes the risk of fracture is increased because of poor quality of the bone in which case special care is needed. In cases where it is clearly difficult to dislocate the joint (for example in a very stiff hip) it is wise to excise the head in situ and not attempt a dislocation. Occasionally a fracture occurs during insertion of the femoral component and this is inexcusable. Fractures which more commonly occur during revision operation may well be predictable (due to poor quality bone) in which case the patient must be warned of the possibility. Perforation of the femoral shaft by the femoral component is a relatively common complication. It should not occur, and it is important to recognise the error and correct it at the time of the operation.

OSTEOTOMY

25.56 Division of bone with or without excision of a wedge is a very common and standard orthopaedic procedure which is generally used to correct deformity; some form of internal fixation is common practice in order to maintain the correct position and healing of the divided bone and permit early mobilisation. Common sites for the osteotomy are proximal femur, distal femur and proximal tibia and the first metatarsal. The usual error is poor technique resulting in failure adequately to correct the deformity and poor internal fixation with loss of position. Osteotomy is an operation of great precision and errors of this kind should not occur.

ARTHRODESIS

25.57 Fusion of a joint is generally undertaken for painful arthritis in certain circumstances. It is a long established principal that the joint must be placed in optimum position for function and this will vary according to the joint affected and possibly to some extent the patient's sex and occupation. It should always be made clear to the patient that the joint will be stiffened and the final position with probable limitations must be clear to him. The usual error is failure to achieve a position of function and the final result may then be worse than before the operation. In normal circumstances such an error is inexcusable.

LUMBAR DISC SURGERY

25.58 Failure to relieve symptoms following operation for a lumbar disc prolapse is not uncommonly due to failure to operate at the correct level; it is an indication of careless technique and should not occur. The level to be explored should have been worked out before the operation from clinical and radiological examination. It is a relatively easy matter to decide the level by palpation and direct vision; if the space explored is found to be normal, this suggests that the wrong level has been exposed; the surgeon must then explore an adjacent space above or below as may be appropriate.

INTERNAL FIXATION OF FRACTURES

25.59 Operative internal fixation of fractures is principally used when closed techniques (conservative treatment) have failed to obtain a satisfactory position, or after a well reduced fracture has subsequently displaced, or when non-union has occurred some months after primary conservative treatment. In some circumstances primary operative treatment is obligatory and the following examples may be cited: certain unstable fractures of the spine, most displaced fractures of the radius and ulnar especially if accompanied by dislocation of wrist or elbow, severely displaced scaphoid fractures, most fractures of the femoral neck, unstable dislocation of the hip and ankle and when both the femur and tibia of the same limb are fractured. Displaced fractures involving the articular surface of joints are usually treated by reduction and internal fixation in order to minimise the risk of later osteoarthritis. Failure to undertake the appropriate internal fixation in these cases is an indication of a poor standard of treatment (assuming of course that the patient is fit for surgery) and will inevitably lead to serious and often permanent disability.

25.60 The usual error is to use an inappropriate form of fixation, or the fixation itself is inadequate; the consequence is loss of position of the fracture and either union with deformity or non-union. Avoiding these errors demands experience and considerable expertise and these operations should only be performed by adequately trained orthopaedic surgeons.

Case reports (1) A 36-year-old lady sustained a minimally displaced fracture of the proximal third of the ulnar; six days later internal fixation with a six-hole plate was performed by a senior house officer. Three days later the plaster was removed because of hand swelling and she had a sling for the next 11 days. A comment was made about the post-operative X-ray and referred to the poor quality of fixation; four screws passed into the proximal fragment, one through the fracture and one into the distal fragment. A further X-ray was not taken and a plaster back splint was applied. The next X-ray at six weeks showed a loss of fixation and significant angulation of the fracture. It was allowed to unite without correction of the deformity. She was left with an unsightly deformity, 40 degrees of loss of supination and 30 degrees loss of pronation. Due to technical error the internal fixation was wholly inadequate and it is likely that angulation would have occurred even in a cast.

(2) A 25-year-old man sustained a compound fracture of the tibia and fibula without complications. He had conservative treatment for a month followed by internal fixation with a plate; the surgeon was an inexperienced junior doctor. Post-operative X-rays showed a 20 to 25 degree angulation and 45 degrees of external rotation deformity. As a consequence he had a clumsy gait with an abnormal foot strike. This relatively common error of operative technique is avoidable.

Post-operative deep wound infection

25.61 This is a natural hazard of all surgical procedures, though it is more common after certain types of operation, and usually the more complex the procedure the longer the operation lasts and especially if implants are used, the more likely it is that a deep infection will occur. In orthopaedic practice under ideal conditions the overall deep infection rate should not be higher than 1 per cent though in many centres it is likely to be no higher than 0.5 per cent. It is difficult to generalise, but an infection rate of 2 per cent or higher will be considered unacceptable to most orthopaedic surgeons.

25.62 Notwithstanding the natural hazard of deep infection the surgeon has a duty to take all reasonable steps to reduce the risk. Some of them are obvious measures under the surgeon's control and are as follows: a clean operative enviroment, avoiding operations in the presence of a focus of infection, avoiding excessive time of wound exposure, handling the tissues with care, avoiding haematomas, using suction drainage and prophylactic antibiotics where appropriate. With regard to the latter there is strong evidence that use of antibiotic loaded cement significantly reduces the incidence of deep infection; it is reasonable to suggest therefore that its use is obligatory in those cases where it is used regularly, namely hip and knee replacements.

25.63 Superficial infection, often referred to as a 'stitch abscess' is of no consequence; it is of nuisance value and does not affect the result of the operation, though occasionally the operation scar presents a cosmetic problem.

25.64 Deep infections are more serious and may lead to failure of the operation. Examples are infections around a joint implant which often has to be removed, infection of a tendon repair leading to complete loss of function in the part concerned. The consequences are an increased length of stay in hospital, a longer recovery period than expected, loss of employment and sometimes a permanent disability.

25.65 Generally speaking the occurrence of deep infection is not a cause for action, and in the United Kingdom it is very rarely the subject of litigation. However as the following cases illustrate, patients seek compensation because of a failure to diagnose and treat the complication at an early stage.

Case reports (1) A young woman entered hospital for a menisectomy following which her knee remained painful and swollen. The fact that she had a septic arthritis went unrecognised (and therefore untreated) for several weeks. Infection had destroyed the articular surface of the joint by the time a diagnosis was made and after about two years a joint replacement operation was necessary.

(2) A young man sustained an achilles tendon rupture which was surgically explored. A deep wound infection occurred and a tendon was exposed in the wound which failed to heal. Treatment was given on the assumption that it was a superficial infection with the result that in quite a short time a two inch length of tendon was destroyed and permanent severe loss of calf function occurred.

In both cases the patient's claim for compensation succeeded, not because deep infection occurred, but because it was not recognised and treated in the early stages. These are examples of an error of clinical judgment of such a degree that in law it amounted to negligence.

Some other post-operative problems

A tight plaster cast

25.66 Following a limb operation, especially if a tourniquet has been used and not released before wound closure, a variable degree of bleeding into the tissues is to be expected and a significant swelling may result, and it will occur even if a drain is used. Similarly after a closed manipulation of a fracture swelling is to be expected.

25.67 The risk is that the initially satisfactory cast becomes tight causing increasingly severe pain and loss of sensation or numbness in the digits. Circulation may become rapidly impaired leaving necrosis of soft tissues, contractures and a neurological deficit; this is the typical compartment syndrome and a functionally useless limb may be the end result.

25.68 The surgeon's duty is to anticipate swelling and to make certain that the cast is adequately padded and if necessary split the cast before the patient is returned to the ward. The patient must be carefully monitored by the medical and nursing staff. If warning signs of impaired circulation appear (pain, impaired sensation, pale skin, loss of arterial pulsation and failure to fully extend the digits because of pain) – urgent action is necessary and the cast must be split so as to expose the skin. Failure to take standard precautions or to act promptly when signs of trouble first appear is indefensible under any circumstances. The primary responsibility for preventative measures, adequate monitoring and appropriate therapeutic measures is the doctor's even though the nursing staff have an important part to play.

Non-union of fractures or osteotomy

25.69 Patients sometimes institute a claim because a fracture or an osteotomy for correction of deformity fails to unite in the expected time. In most instances the primary treatment has been of a high standard, and non-union develops for no obvious reason; it can be predicted as likely in certain fractures (usually associated with significant displacement) in the tibial shaft for example. Explanation for non-union is usually impaired blood supply of the bone of the fracture or osteotomy site, inadequate immobilisation of the fracture and poor acquisition of the bone fragments – and it may be due to one or any combination of these factors. In considering whether or not a patient presents with features which make the development of a non-union more likely than not, the initial displacement of the fracture, the age and general health of the patient are other factors to consider.

25.70 In a few cases non-union is clearly the result of a poor standard of primary treatment usually due to failure to achieve an acceptable position of the bone fragment so that a gap exists at the fracture site; a failure may follow closed treatment of a fracture or as indicated earlier inappropriate or inefficient internal fixation. In most cases of established non-union of a fracture or osteotomy, after careful analysis, it is usually possible to decide upon causation.

Deep venous thrombosis and pulmonary embolism

25.71 The incidence is higher after major orthopaedic operations such as hip replacements than after other types of operations. It is now considered obligatory to give prophylactic low molecular weight heparin in high- and moderate-risk patients. (See Chapter 33.)

CONCLUSIONS

25.72 I have outlined some of the hazards faced by orthopaedic surgeons in current orthopaedic practice.

25.73 Avoidable injury to patients in orthopaedic practice can be reduced but probably never eliminated. It would be appropriate to conclude by indicating the prerequisite for so doing. I make no apology for stressing measures which simply amount to the application of common sense:

(1) improve the supervision of junior doctors who are usually the first to see and examine patients who come to hospital as an emergency;
(2) possible deficiencies in the Accident and Emergency Department are referred to in Chapter 24;
(3) only orthopaedic surgeons, some of whom will have special experience, should treat patients after trauma to bones, joints, nerves, muscles and tendons. It follows that cross cover with other specialities is to be avoided;
(4) patients referred for an opinion by a general practitioner should be seen by a consultant or senior orthopaedic registrar;
(5) no patient should have an elective operation unless seen by a consultant or senior registrar;

(6) operations must be undertaken only by those with the appropriate qualifications and experience, and this usually means a consultant senior registrar or registrar;
(7) inspection of many hundreds of medical records from a variety of hospitals indicates that recording of clinical details, probable diagnosis, suggested treatment and post-operative day to day recording of the patient's condition is not only deficient but frequently illegible and unsigned;
(8) history taking is a neglected art and needs to be improved. The nursing records generally set a standard which highlights these deficiencies;
(9) finally and most important of all more time should be spent talking to patients and listening to their complaints. If something untoward occurs it is especially important to explain the matter promptly, answer questions truthfully and give appropriate reassurance. Litigation is unlikely to arise if the normally acceptable standard of practice is maintained. The amount of litigation following errors in management is for the most part inversely proportional to the quality of communications with the patient.

BIBLIOGRAPHICAL REFERENCES

Birch R, Bonney G, Dowell J and Hollingdale, 'Iatrogenic Injuries of Peripheral Nerves' (1991) Journal of Bone and Joint Surgery 73, B 280.
Bonney G 'Iatrogenic Injuries of Nerves' (1987) Journal of Medical Defence Union, no 3, 4 and no 3, 2.
British Orthopaedic Association *The Management of Skeletal Trauma in the United Kingdom* (1992).
Buck N, Devlin H B, Lunn J N *The Confidential Enquiry into Perioperative Deaths* (1987) London.
Campling E A, Devlin M B, Hoile R W and Lunn J N 'The Report of the National Confidential Enquiry into Perioperative Deaths' (1992) London.
'Economics and the National Health Service: Are Doctors Liable?' (1986) Journal of the Medical Defence Union 1,1.
Lacombe D C, O'Keefe T J 'Legal Aspects of Medical Practice for the Orthopaedic Surgeon' (1989) Current Orthopaedics 3, 115.
Vickers R 'Risk Management in Trauma and Orthopaedics' (1991) Journal of the Medical Defence Union, 7, 3, 72.
Woodyard J 'Orthopaedic Negligence: The Tip of the Iceberg?' (1990) Journal of Hospital Medicine, 44, 163.

CHAPTER 26

Neurosurgery

Professor John Hankinson *MB BS FRCS*
Revised by M Briggs *MSc FRCS*

26.1 Accidents in neurosurgery leading to litigation rarely result from errors in surgical technique. Far more likely causes of litigation are delays in the definitive diagnosis, lack of informed consent and therefore unrealistically high expectations on the part of the patient and relatives and mistakes in the post-operative management. The neurosurgeon will certainly be involved in the second and third of these but may not be in the first.

HEAD INJURIES

26.2 It is not surprising that from the enormous numbers of patients who are seen in Accident and Emergency departments and admitted to hospital following head injuries a certain number of claims of negligence should arise. Each year between 200 and 300 per 100,000 of the population are admitted to hospital because of head injury (Anderson and McLaurin 1980; Jennett and McMillan 1981), i e something between 100,000 and 150,000. Four to five times that number of patients are seen in Accident and Emergency departments (Jennett and Teasdale 1981), a figure of about 500,000. Most of the patients admitted to hospital (85 per cent) will have suffered a mild head injury, with a short period of unconsciousness, and on admission will be talking and obeying commands (Miller and Jones 1985). A small proportion (5 per cent) have suffered a severe injury and are unconscious at the time of admission to hospital. About half of these patients will develop intracranial haematomas or acute brain swelling which will require operative decompression (Miller et al 1981). Clearly, selection of patients must be made in the Accident and Emergency Department for admission to the ward. In this large number of patients the possibility of error is increased by the relatively small number who may need specialised surgical treatment very rapidly.

26.3 In the Accident and Emergency department two important decisions must be taken regarding patients who are not unconscious on admission. These refer to (a) skull X-ray, and (b) admission to hospital. Radiologists have questioned the necessity for routine skull X-rays following head injury on the grounds of small effective return for very large expenditure. This is becoming an increasingly contentious issue following the introduction of the financial orientated Health Service reforms. Jennet and Teasdale in *Management of Head Injuries* (1981) point out:

Neurosurgeons have long preached that assessment of conscious level is more important than a skull X-ray, and this has been mistakenly taken to imply that they regard the detection of a fracture as unimportant, especially after mild injuries. In fact it is in the patient whose consciousness is unimpaired, and who might otherwise be sent home as a trivial injury, that the finding of a fracture can be most significant, because it alerts the clinician to the risk of complications such as intracranial haematoma or infection.

Also Becker et al (1977) showed that the risk of an intracranial haematoma in a patient who is drowsy with a skull fracture can be as high as 25 per cent. In a patient who is comatose with a fracture when evaluated the risk is twice as high again.

26.4 In order to assist casualty officers and other junior staff in Accident and Emergency Departments with these decisions a group of neurosurgeons met in 1984 and produced a set of guidelines (British Medical Journal 1984). These guidelines have been used as a basis for instructions given by Regional Neurosurgical Units to their colleagues in District Hospitals, in an attempt to prevent avoidable mortality and morbidity.

Criteria for skull X-ray after recent head injury

Clinical judgment is necessary but the following criteria are helpful:

(1) Loss of consciousness or amnesia at any time.
(2) Neurological symptoms or signs (including headache/vomiting).
(3) Cerebrospinal fluid or blood from the nose or ear.
(4) Suspected penetrating injury.
(5) Scalp bruising or deep laceration (to bone).
(6) Difficulty in assessing the patient (i e alcohol intoxication, epilepsy, children).

Criteria for admission of adults to hospital

(1) Confusion or any other depression of the level of consciousness at the time of examination.
(2) Skull fracture.
(3) Neurological symptoms or signs.
(4) Difficulty in assessing the patient, e g alcohol, epilepsy.
(5) Other medical conditions, e g haemophilia.

(6) Lack of a responsible adult to supervise the patient, or other social problems.

Brief amnesia after trauma with full recovery is not sufficient indication for admission.

Relatives or friends of patients sent home should receive written advice about changes that would require the patient to be returned urgently to hospital.

Criteria for consultation with the neurosurgical unit about patients with recent head injury

(1) Fractured skull with any of the following: confusion or more impairment of consciousness, one or more epileptic fits or any other neurological symptoms or signs.
(2) Coma continuing after resuscitation even if no skull fracture.
(3) Deterioration in level of consciousness.
(4) Confusion or other neurological disturbance persisting for more than eight hours, even if there is no skull fracture.
(5) Depressed fracture of the skull vault.
(6) Suspected fracture of the base of the skull (CSF rhinorrhoea or otorrhoea, bilateral orbital haematoma, mastoid haematoma or evidence of a penetrating type of injury such as a spike or gunshot).

NOTE: On transfer of patients in categories 1–3

(1) They should be transferred urgently.
(2) Initial resuscitation for extracranial injuries and complications must be completed, for example for shock, blood loss, compromised ventilation and first aid for limb fractures.
(3) Ensure precautions to reduce risks en route to Neurosurgical Unit (adequately equipped ambulance and a trained doctor or nurse as escort).
(4) Send all notes and X-ray films.

These guidelines for consultation with the neurosurgical unit are being used increasingly as the guidelines for CT scanning as more and more district hospitals obtain CT facilities; CT scanning alone however should not replace the need for neurosurgical consultation in these patients.

26.5 Errors at this stage of management occur in casualty departments with children who require additional vigilance as level of consciousness and minor limb weakness may be difficult to assess. If there is any doubt when assessing a child following head injury, the child should be admitted to the ward for observation. Discharge to the care of a responsible adult is obligatory both for children and adults. A catastrophic error may arise in dealing in a busy casualty department late at night with a drunken patient who has suffered a head injury. His companions may appear to be less under the influence of alcohol but may be equally quarrelsome. Before a patient's condition is attributed wholly to the effects of alcohol a blood specimen should be obtained and the level of alcohol assessed and acted upon.

26.6 A young man and his male companion had taken a great deal of drink during the course of an evening. While walking home he tried to jump over a wall and fell heavily on the other side striking his head and apparently losing consciousness for a short time and suffering a laceration of his scalp. He was then able to walk to the Casualty department of a nearby hospital supported by his friend. The department was busy and the friend was abusive to the sister in charge and said that if they had to wait any longer they would leave. Eventually a hard-pressed house surgeon sutured the scalp laceration and does not appear to have regarded the man's condition as being due to anything other than alcohol. His friend took him home but they were given no instructions, so he said, or any card indicating that he should be returned to the hospital if his condition deteriorated. His wife was evidently accustomed to him returning in a drunken state and put him to bed. During the night he vomited and then became unrousable and eventually towards noon of the next day he was seen by a general practitioner and returned to the hospital. Two hours later a large extradural haematoma was evacuated by the general surgeon on call for emergencies, as the hospital was a considerable distance from a neurosurgical centre. The patient never recovered consciousness and died a week later. The case was settled for a considerable amount on the grounds that no attempt had been made to persuade the patient to stay in hospital and no instructions had been given about measures to be taken if his condition deteriorated. Following the altercation with the nursing staff when they first arrived at the hospital the friend seems to have been excluded when the deceased was seen by the doctor. This was a serious error on the part of the staff as the doctor's attitude to the patient would have been quite different if he had had some details of the accident when he struck his head. As it was it appears that the doctor was under the impression that the man was drunk and had suffered only a trivial laceration of the scalp. However, it was his duty to discover all he could about the circumstances of the accident and he failed to do this.

26.7 Of the very large numbers of patients with head injuries seen in Accident and Emergency departments the great majority as previously indicated recover without treatment, although they may suffer post-traumatic syndromes of various types which are not our present interest. Of the severe head injuries between 40 and 50 per cent die, mostly within the first 24 hours. The interest in the progressive intracranial haematomas – the extradural haematomas – is that the initial brain injury may be insignificant just as the injury itself may be relatively minor. If the development of the haematoma can be recognised early the patient can make a satisfactory recovery. Delay leads to increasing cerebral compression and eventually to irreversible brain damage (Valtonen and Jennett 1977). The interval during which this latter stage is reached varies from a few hours to a few days. The progression of cerebral compression can be recognised by careful clinical observation and it is principally for this purpose that patients with this type of head injury are admitted to hospital. The importance of this is stressed by Miller in *Northfield's Surgery of the Central Nervous System* (1987):

> Observation of the head injured patient at frequent regular intervals is an essential part of care, ensuring early detection of complications. The nursing staff of the neurosurgical unit make these observations and record them promptly and legibly on an observation chart that in most UK centres incorporates the features of the Glasgow Coma Scale, the pupillary light response, the relative strength of movements of the right and left sides and the traditional chart of temperature, blood pressure, pulse rate and respiration rate. The level of intracranial pressure may in some instances be included in this chart. The interval at which observations are recorded must vary with the severity of the injury; quarter or half hourly recording is advisable for the first two or three hours in all but minor cases, progressing to hourly then two hourly, four hourly and twelve hourly observations as the patient improves.

The Glasgow Coma Scale (Teasdale and Jennett 1974) measures the level of response in which three features are independently observed, namely eye opening, motor response and verbal response to assess arousal and the capacity to respond to change in the environment which are the true features of consciousness.

26.8 The critical investigation is now CT brain scanning. Initially this form of investigation was only available in neurosurgical units but now CT scanning equipment is being installed in increasing numbers in District General hospitals. However it is rare for a General hospital to have available a surgeon capable and willing to perform emergency craniotomy. It is therefore essential if life is to be saved and brain damage limited, that patients are transferred from the General hospital to the special unit as soon as suspicion of intracranial haematoma arises, or before that event if risk factors are present. Telephone consultations with neurosurgical departments are usual and arrangements are made to transfer a patient for surgery if indicated. The criteria for these telephone consultations have already been referred to (para **26.4**).

26.9 Finally some striking statistics of these important injuries:

(1) Rose et al (1970) introduced the term 'avoidable factors' to those conditions or complications of head injury that can lead to death but which, if detected, can be treated or prevented. They reviewed 116 patients who had talked and subsequently died from their head injury and identified one or more avoidable factors in 74 per cent. By far the most common and important was delay in the detection and treatment of an intracranial haematoma. Following this the Glasgow neurosurgeons expanded the criteria for transfer to their neurosurgical unit of patients suspected of harbouring an intracranial haematoma, which doubled the number of head injury referrals, doubled the number of intracranial haematomas detected and reduced the overall head injury mortality (Teasdale et al 1982). Jeffreys and Jones (1981) reported that of 160 head injury deaths occurring in general hospitals in patients who had not been referred to the regional neurological centre, 33 per cent were due to intracranial haematoma;

(2) eighty per cent of head injured patients in a neurosurgical unit have a skull fracture, which suggests that skull X-ray is a useful index of severity of injury;

(3) a linear fracture increases the risk of intracranial haematoma 400 times; but

(4) a patient who is sober and correctly orientated with no skull fracture has less than one chance in 6,000 of a major complication from his head injury.

26.10 Meanwhile a number of complicated investigations and treatments, mostly unproven, are being introduced for the treatment of the severely brain damaged patient but these are hardly germane to the subject under consideration. Devoted nursing and intensive care are the basic supports on which such a patient depends for survival.

26.11 There remain the problems of infection and cerebrospinal fluid leakage – rhinorrhoea and otorrhoea. Scalp wounds need to be treated seriously because an underlying fracture or penetration of the skull by a sharp object may lead to dangerous intracranial infection. The sooner they are thoroughly cleaned, the traumatised edges removed and careful interrupted sutures inserted the better, although any general anaesthetic should be avoided if at all possible in dealing with these or other peripheral injuries while the patient's level of consciousness is being observed. With its profuse blood supply the scalp heals well but where indicated antibiotic cover should be used. The treatment of compound depressed fractures of the skull was described by Rowbotham in 1964, consisting of excision of the wound, location and removal of in-driven fragments of bone, foreign bodies and hair, evacuation of pulped brain and haematoma, dural repair and replacement of the larger bone fragments. Miller and Jennett (1968) analysed 400 cases of depressed skull fracture and amongst other complications encountered infection in 10 per cent of cases mostly due to failure to recognise the injury, underestimation of its severity or inadequate surgical treatment. They considered that the complications of depressed skull fracture were associated with a significant increase in mortality and morbidity and the incidence of post-traumatic epilepsy.

26.12 Fractures of the anterior cranial fossa involving the air sinuses may allow leakage of cerebrospinal fluid down the nose. Occasionally fractures of the middle fossa involving the temporal bone also lead to rhinorrhoea. Usually the leak occurs within a few days of the injury and most neurosurgeons do not operate to repair if it stops, as it usually does, in the next few days or a week. Persistent rhinorrhoea must be dealt with to prevent the very dangerous meningitis which can follow. When the pneumococcus is responsible meningitis can be fatal within 24 hours. Rhinorrhoea sometimes recurs and sometimes shows itself some time after the injury by the occurrence of meningitis. It is essential to treat the meningitis by antibiotics and to stop the rhinorrhoea as soon as possible. Very rarely cerebrospinal fluid leakage from the ear persists and attempts to repair the leakage often fail because of the difficulty in identifying the dural/bone defect. Fortunately most cases of otorrhoea cease spontaneously. While in hospital the occurence of a cerebrospinal fluid leak will be recognised and dealt with but if the onset is delayed it is likely to be missed unless the patient complains of it. I do not think that GPs make a practice of enquiring about fluid down the nose after a head injury.

26.13 While most patients make a good/moderate recovery following severe head injury provided appropriate treatment is given (81 per cent at twelve months, Jennett and Teasdale) a number (3 per cent) will survive in the persistent vegetative state (PVS). This state was defined in 1972 (Jennett and Plum) and should be confined to patients who show no psychologically meaningful response, as well as having the characteristic physical features of sleep/wake rhythms, periods of eye opening and also abnormal motor responses in all four limbs. Basic cardiorespiratory function is retained without artifical support. Patients can survive in this condition for many years. Jennett (1981) described a patient surviving for eighteen years after injury. The prolonged survival of these patients raises serious ethical and legal questions and is regarded by many as worse than death, a view held by doctors, relatives and theologians (Jennett 1977). The intensity of care given to patients in the PVS is the subject of continued debate and many would regard it as good medical practice not to intervene actively when complications develop, provided the family are in agreement. More recently the legality of withdrawal of artifical feeding has been raised,[1] and is certain to be a topic of intense legal and ethical discussion in the future.

1 'Tony Bland awaits final hearing – withdrawal of artifical feeding in patients in PVS' (1993) British Medical Journal.

26.14 The concept of brain death, like the persistent vegetative state, is a result of modern intensive care, particularly artifical cardiorespiratory support. The diagnosis of brain death and therefore the point at which artificial supportive measures can legitimately be discontinued, is important both in human terms to avoid unnecessarily prolonged grief and legally, particularly when the patient is being considered as a source of organ donation. The criteria for the diagnosis of brain death were published by the Royal Colleges in 1976. These criteria are designed to demonstrate that the brain stem has irreversibly ceased to function, and they consist of two components – pre-conditions, which insist that the apnoeic coma is the result of irretrievable brain damage and that reversible causes have been excluded, e g depressant drugs, neuromuscular blocking agents, hypothermia etc – brain stem tests to confirm that all brain stem reflexes are absent:

(a) the pupils are fixed in diameter and do not respond to sharp changes in the intensity of instant light;
(b) there is no corneal reflex;
(c) the vestibulo-occular reflexes are absent. These are absent when no eye movement occurs during or after slow injection of 20ml of ice cold water into each external auditory meatus in turn, clear access to the tympanic membrane having been established by direct inspection. This test may be contraindicated on one or other side by local trauma;
(d) no motor responses within the cranial nerve distribution can be elicited by adequate stimulation of any somatic area;
(e) there is no gag reflex or reflex response to bronchial stimulation by a suction catheter passed down the trachea;
(f) no respiratory movements occur when the patient is disconnected from the mechanical ventilator for long enough to ensure that the arterial CO_2 tension rises above the threshold for stimulating respiration, i e PCO_2 must normally reach 6.7 k.Pa.

It is customary to repeat the tests to ensure no observer error. The interval between testing must depend on the primary condition and may be as long as twenty four hours. The status of the doctor performing the tests is important as follows:

(a) the consultant in charge of the case and one other doctor;
(b) in the absence of a consultant, his deputy, who should have been registered for five years.

These criteria now form the basis for the diagnosis of brain death whether or not the patient's organs are to be used for transplantation purposes.

CEREBRAL TUMOURS

26.15 The presentation and management of intracranial tumours, which form a considerable part of neurosurgical activity, varies according to tumour type. Negligence claims relating to such tumours usually involve questions of delayed diagnosis or unrealistic expectations on the part of patients and their relatives resulting from inadequate pre-operative advice and information regarding results and possible complications of surgery.

26.16 The basis of diagnosis of cerebral tumours depends on the history and clinical examination indicating the need for further investigation by imaging techniques. CT scanning is now widely available in most large hospitals in this country and is the investigation of first choice in patients with a suspicious clinical presentation and has largely replaced older radiological techniques such as air encephalography and myodil ventriculography. Magnetic resonance imaging (MRI) is the latest important development in the imaging field, although at present of only limit availability, it is likely that it will become the investigation of choice for patients with intracranial tumours in the future. Brain tumours of all types present in a stereotyped pattern with epilepsy, raised intracranial pressure and focal neurological abnormalities either in isolation or combination. Such symptoms of a progressive nature should lead to early further investigation. Avoidance of diagnostic delay is particularly important when dealing with benign and potentially curable tumours in which the incidence of post-operative complications and neurological deficits is closely related to the size of the tumour and the ease with which it can be removed surgically.

26.17 The gliomas are true tumours of brain tissue and form nearly half of all cerebral tumours. They vary enormously in their degree of malignancy from the low grade well differentiated astrocytomas or oligodendrigliomas which may present with a history of epilepsy of many years duration, to the glioblastomas which can have a preceeding history of a few weeks or months only. Although surgical resection of these tumours is rarely curative, surgery is still of primary importance in the diagnosis and treatment of supratentorial gliomas. It provides a histological diagnosis, and can lower the intracranial pressure by reducing tumour bulk, before adjuvant treatment such as radiotherapy and/or chemotherapy is commenced. Despite the increasing accuracy of imaging techniques, the presence of a curable lesion such as meningioma or brain abscess will be missed, if a biopsy specimen of the tumour is not obtained for histological diagnosis. It is essential that patients and their relatives be given sufficient information before operation regarding the prognosis of the tumour and possible complications of surgery to enable them to make a balanced decision on informed consent, given the palliative nature of surgery for malignant gliomas.

26.18 Patients with gliomas are rarely the subject of negligence claims, when the question of delayed diagnosis is considered. The rapidly progressive history of the glioblastoma seldom causes diagnostic doubt, and investigation and treatment are rarely delayed. High-grade astrocytomas, presenting with a long history of uncomplicated epilepsy, can pose a diagnostic dilemma however and the eventual diagnosis may be delayed. When considering the matter of causation however this delay is of little importance as early diagnosis of these tumours rarely influences treatment or the long term outcome. Indeed the Brain Tumour Working Party of the MRC is at present (1992) conducting a trial of immediate versus deferred treatment for intracranial tumours presenting with epilepsy, such is the uncertainty of the best system of management. In order to avoid problems with informed consent, patients and their relatives must be made fully aware of the results of possible complications following surgery to the gliomas. There was a dramatic fall in surgical mortality with the introduction of steroid use in the early 1960s, e g a figure of 27.9 per cent for patients treated between 1945 and 1962 fell to 2.9 per cent for patients treated between 1962 and 1964 by Jelsma et al (1967). The incidence of neurological deterioration following tumour surgery, which may be secondary to haemorrhage in the tumour bed or acute brain oedema, varies according to the size of tumour resection, from 15–18 per cent in patients undergoing radical resection, to 27–45 per cent in those undergoing partial resection. Seizures in the peri-operative period can be a cause of neurological deterioration and can be largely controlled by adequate levels of anti-convulsant medication pre-operatively. The proper surgical management of patients with gliomas is well summarised by Kader et al (1993) as follows:

> Given the palliative nature of surgery for malignant astrocytomas, preventing complications is crucial, since the goal of the surgeon is to improve the survival and quality of life in these patients.

26.19 With the exception of tumours arising from cerebral tissue and metastatic tumours, the other intracranial tumours arise from tissue outside the brain and cause their effect by local pressure on surrounding structures and by increasing the volume of the intracranial contents and thereby the intracranial pressure. These tumours are usually histologically benign and include the meningiomas, neuromas – commonly acoustic – and pituitary and parapituitary tumours. Disputes arise after treatment of these intracranial tumours in connection with alleged delay in diagnosis and treatment and lack of informed consent, only rarely because of technical errors at the time of operation. Being benign lesions the history may be long and insidious, so that by the time the diagnosis is made the tumour may have reached considerable size and caused irreparable damage to surrounding neurological structures. In such cases the results of surgery both in terms of operative mortality and recovery of neurological deficits may be disappointing and lead to questions of negligent delay being raised by the patient or the surviving relative.

26.20 Meningiomas represent 13–19 per cent of intracranial tumours (Youmans 1990). Usually histologically benign, they can at times show a more aggressive clinical course and rarely are frankly malignant. The diagnosis is made by appropriate imaging techniques (CT or MRI) and treatment is by surgical removal. This treatment exposes the patients to a variety of complications which can be grouped according to those which are general to all meningiomas and those which are specific to the site of origin of the tumour. General complications include raised intracranial pressure post-operatively, which may be due to oedema or venous infarction. This is often resistant to treatment with steroids and may be more long-lasting than that which follows glioma surgery, contributing to the operative mortality rate of up to 5.9 per cent (Symonds 1984). This figure has been shown to be related to the size of tumour at the time of surgery which is therefore of importance when a claim of delayed diagnosis is made. Seizures are a common feature of meningiomas with a pre-operative incidence of 30–60 per cent. While there is a tendency for seizure frequency to decrease post-operatively a significant number of patients with no pre-operative history will develop post-operative epilepsy. Pertrusiel et al (1985) quote a figure of up to 20 per cent. Although as stated earlier meningiomas are usually histologically benign there is a recurrence rate of up to 34 per cent, the actual figure depending on the histological type and the degree of surgical resection (Melamed et al 1979). When one considers the site specific complications, those meningiomas arising in the anterior cranial fossa and the cerebello pontine angle have a particular incidence of post-operative complication derived specifically from the site of origin of the lesion. A common symptom of tumours arising in the anterior cranial fossa is visual dysfunction, which may present as monocular visual deterioration, bitemporal field loss or central scotomas. In a large series of patients with suprasellar meningiomas Rosenstein et al (1984) described a 60 per cent improvement in vision post-operatively, but no change in 12 per cent and a worsening in 24 per cent of patients with this symptom. The post-operative outcome being closely related to the degree of pre-operative visual loss, the duration of the symptom and the size of the tumour, emphasising yet again the deleterious effects of delayed diagnosis on outcome. Anosmia occurs frequently as a result of damage to the olfactory nerve, which may be the result of direct pressure from the tumour or unavoidable traction related to the surgical approach. The close anatomical relationship of these tumours to the arteries of Circle of Willis puts at risk the major branches of the internal carotid artery during the surgical removal of tumours in this site and contributes to the high surgical mortality of up to 23 per cent associated with sphenoid wing meningiomas (Fohammo et al 1986). Meningiomas arising within the posterior fossa form another group of this type of tumour with significant site specific post-operative complications. In particular tumours arising in the cerebello pontine angle carry a high post-operative morbidity because of their proximity to the brain stem, cranial nerves and the basilar artery. Yasargil (1980) described a complication rate of 35 per cent when analysing these tumours. Such figures must be considered during the pre-operative discussion with patients, if litigation is to be avoided following disappointing results.

26.21 Another tumour which arises in the cerebello pontine angle and which presents similar problems is the acoustic neuroma. This benign tumour arising as it does from the nerve of hearing is in close proximity to the facial nerve, brain stem and cerebellum, so that operative removal carries serious risk of facial paralysis and disturbance of balance. Historically early attempts at removal of these tumours carried mortality risks as high as 67–84 per cent. Over the years with improvement in anaesthetic techniques, the introduction of the operating microscope and earlier diagnosis of smaller tumours the safety with which surgery can be performed has greatly increased but nevertheless the successful safe removal of an acoustic neuroma is still a considerable challenge to the neurosurgeon. Overall mortality figures of 3.3 per cent are now quoted by Yasargil et al (1974), and their relationship to the size of the tumour at the time of surgery is well recognised, ie no deaths in patients in whom the tumour was less than 2 cm in diameter with 6.8 per cent mortality when the tumour was larger than 4 cm in diameter. The same authors noted the relationship between tumour size and preservation of facial nerve function, at least partial function being retained in 100 per cent of cases with tumours of 2 cm or less, 87 per cent in tumours between 2 and 5 cm and 70 per cent in tumours over 5 cm in diameter. These figures yet again stress the medico-legal implication of delay in diagnosis which results in tumours being larger at the time of surgery with consequent increase in mortality and morbidity.

26.22 Tumours of the pituitary gland frequently presented problems both pre- and post-operatively similar to those seen with suprasellar meningiomas, because of their proximity to the visual apparatus and the carotid arteries, and their removal via craniotomy carries the same overall risk. Surgery to these tumours via the transphenoidal route however is much safer and there are now relatively few contraindications to this approach (Onestri et al 1993). These authors point out that the majority of complications following this procedure are preventable and reflect a breakdown in operative techniques, having previously listed pre-operative and surgical essentials they state 'if these precautions are taken, transphenoidal microsurgery is one of the safest procedures in the neurosurgical armamentarium'.

CONGENITAL ABNORMALITIES

26.23 Among the congenital abnormalities of the central nervous system three can be considered of general neurosurgical interest, i e hydrocephalus, spinal dysraphism and spina bifida and the Arnold-Chiari malformation and syringomyelia.

26.24 Congenital hydrocephalus became effectively treatable with the introduction in the 1950s of the first reliable uni-directional valved shunts in the form of the Spitz-Holter valve system. Earlier surgical techniques have been extremely unpredictable in their results. As with intracranial tumours litigation regarding patients with hydrocephalus largely revolve around delay in diagnosis and treatment both of the underlying condition and of complications arising following shunt insertion. The diagnosis can be made very simply on the clinical grounds by entering repeated skull measurement figures on a centile chart and observing that a baby's head is enlarging more quickly than normal. This observation should lead to early further investigation in the form of ultrasound scanning or CT scanning, which both reveal the diagnosis. Progressive hydrocephalus must be treated by a shunting procedure usually ventriculo-atrial or ventriculo-peritoneal in site. Even with prompt and effective treatment the natural history of patients with congenital hydrocephalus is uncertain with regard to both physical and mental development and parents must be made aware of that fact. The common complications following shunt insertion are of blockage of the apparatus which will cause recurrence of the hydrocephalus and the symptoms related to it and infection which may cause meningitis, and potentially catastrophic brain damage. Both of these complications must be detected and treated early if irreparable brain damage is to be avoided. Shunt revisions to keep pace with growth are sometimes necessary but routine lengthening revision procedures are not common practice.

26.25 Over the years spinal dysraphism and spina bifida, a range of congenital spinal defects from minor to gross, have been involved in a great deal of ethical heart-searching. What efforts should be made to preserve some of these babies? What happens to those who are not treated? General agreement of such complex ethical problems has not yet been reached, but it is essential that the parents be closely involved with any decision-making. In any event problems with spinal dysraphism and congenital neurosurgical disorders in general are becoming less frequent with the advent of effective ante-natal screening and the more liberal abortion laws.

26.26 For more than 25 years some cases of the previously progressive spinal degenerative condition of syringomyelia have been treated by posterior fossa and upper cervical decompression of the associated Arnold-Chiari malformation. More recently decompression of the cyst by means of a syringo-pleural shunt has been performed. In about half of cases thus treated progression of the disease has been halted and in some early cases reversed. Some patients after initial improvement for many years begin to regress and on occasions second operations have led to further failure of spinal cord function. Claims have been made which seem to be related to inadequate information about the risk of further surgery compared to the expected natural progression of the underlying abnormality.

SUBARACHNOID HAEMORRHAGE

26.27 The incidence of subarachnoid haemorrhage is probably between 10 and 12 per 100,000 of the population per year. Two thirds of these prove to be due to the rupture of an aneurysm on a major vessel and in a further 5 per cent an arteriovenous malformation has bled. Without treatment, the prospects for survival of patients suffering a subarachnoid haemorrhage are poor; over 40 per cent die from the effects of the first haemorrhage, 16 per cent before reaching hospital (Brossman and Norlen 1963). There is a re-bleeding rate of 55 per cent of the survivors, and 76 per cent of those suffering a recurrent haemorrhage will die, giving a mortality rate of 41 per cent of those surviving the first bleed (Tappura 1962).

26.28 Once the diagnosis of subarachnoid haemorrhage has been made the treatment given is largely prophylactic, to prevent re-bleeding. Very occasionally surgery is attempted to treat complications of the initial haemorrhage such as intracerebral haematoma and acute hydrocephalus, but 'experience is that evacuation of an intracerebral haematoma rarely results in substantial and sustained clinical improvement and it may precipitate rupture of the aneurysm during operation; the forced attack on the aneurysm itself, in an attempt to stem haemorrhage, seldom leads to a good clinical result' (Jennett and Galbraith 1983).

26.29 In order to make the diagnosis of subarachnoid haemorrhage, the presence of that condition must first be suspected. A failure to diagnose a small first bleed in a patient who subsequently dies from recurrent haemorrhage, is a common subject of litigation and negligence claims. When patients suffer a large haemorrhage the occurrence of a significant intracranial vascular event is seldom in any doubt. The sudden onset of very severe head pain with vomiting and rapid loss of consciousness is a sufficiently dramatic event to leave little doubt as to the diagnosis. Smaller leaks, however, paint a less dramatic picture, severe headache is the usual complaint, which on close questioning is almost always of very sudden onset and of unusual nature to that patient. This may be followed by vomiting and later by a degree of neck stiffness. The conscious level is rarely altered following a small leak. The illness is often mild enough to be mistaken for influenza or acute torticollis. Careful questioning, however, will usually reveal the acute onset of the symptoms and raise suspicion as to the true diagnosis.

26.30 Lumbar puncture is the diagnostic test of choice when subarachnoid haemorrhage is suspected. Uniformly blood stained cerebrospinal fluid is obtained when subarachnoid haemorrhage has occurred, but this can only be distinguished from the result of a traumatic lumbar puncture by observing the presence or absence of xanthrochromia in the supernatant fluid once the red cells have settled. This is unequivocal evidence that breakdown of red blood cells has occurred and therefore that the blood was present in the CSF before the lumbar puncture. On occasions lumbar puncture is contraindicated, e g if there are signs of raised intracranial pressure, such as lowered level of consciousness or focal central nervous system signs suggesting the presence of an intracerebral haematoma. In these situations CT scanning should be performed before lumbar puncture. It should be noted however that CT scanning alone will miss the diagnosis of subarachnoid haemorrhage in 5 per cent or more of patients.

26.31 Following the diagnosis of subarachnoid haemorrhage the patient should be referred immediately to a neurosurgical unit. Following referral the management of the patient will depend on the policy of the receiving unit. The aim of surgical treatment is to identify the aneurysm, clip its neck with a suitable aneurysm clip thereby separating it from the cerebral circulation and removing the risk of re-bleeding. The surgical results of this type of operation are considerably influenced by the clinical state of the patient at the time of surgery (Hunt and Hess 1968). Because of this a significant number of neurosurgeons will investigate and operate early only on patients who are in good clinical grade, accepting that some patients will die from re-bleeding before reaching such a grade. The debate regarding the merits of early versus late aneurysm surgery is still unsettled (Briggs 1984). Once the patient has been transferred to a neurosurgical unit cerebral angiography will be performed urgently and if the source of haemorrhage proves to be treatable surgically, operation in the form of craniotomy and clipping of the aneurysm will be performed either early or late according to the policies of the individual neurosurgeon.

26.32 When considering the question of litigation it is essential that patients and their relatives are fully aware of the possible results of surgery and the reason for delay when late surgery is planned, i e the prevention of vasospasm and its attendant increased morbidity and mortality. The mortality rate in patients undergoing aneurysm surgery varies acccording to clinical grade at the time of surgery and the timing of operation, from 1 per cent in grade 1 to 30 per cent or more in grades 3 and 4. There is also a significant morbidity and no more than one third of the patients who have a subarachnoid haemorrhage ever return to their pre-morbid state (Solomon 1993).

STEREOTACTIC SURGERY

26.33 This is a method of three-dimensional placement of a surgical instrument within the brain, combining a three-dimensional Cartesian co-ordinate system and a three-dimensional positioning instrument which is firmly attached to the head. In the late 1950s and the 1960s stereotactic surgery was used to produce accurately situated lesions in the thalamus to treat the tremor of Parkinson's disease. The availability of the drug L-dopa after 1968 resulted in a precipitous drop in the number of such procedures performed and until the advent of CT scanning in the 1970s, stereotactic surgery became almost extinct in most centres. CT scanning provides a precise three-dimensional database which can easily be incorporated into a stereotactic system and this has led to a re-awakening of interest in stereotactic surgery for a range of purposes, such as lesion making, biopsy of deep-seated tumours, accurate placement of radioactive sources and more recently fetal tissue transplants for the treatment of Parkinson's disease (1992). Patients must be made aware that when used to treat movement disorders the placement of lesions carries risks, resulting from, lesion-site haemorrhage, errors in lesion placement and errors in the size of the lesion. The surgical morbidity may be considerable and includes hemiparesis, speech disorder, coma and even death. Stereotactic biopsy of deep-seated tumours carries a much lower surgical risk when compared to open biopsy; Apuzzo et al (1983) quote an overall morbidity of 4 per cent. It is likely that both ethical and medico-legal issues will become increasingly important in the future of stereotactic surgery, with the development of fetal tissue transplants for an increasing range of degenerative conditions such as Alzheimer's disease.

SPINAL SURGERY

26.34 The surgery of the spine is performed either by neurological surgeons or orthopaedic surgeons. In this chapter the surgery of tumours affecting the spinal cord, cervical spondylosis, thoracic and lumbar discs and lumbar stenosis will be dealt with. At the time of publication of the first edition of this book, myelography was still rightly considered to be the basis of radiological investigation prior to spinal surgery. The performance of this investigation involves a lumbar puncture which carries the risk of leakage from the puncture hole in the dura leading to changes in the cerebrospinal fluid dynamics and possible shifting of a tumour that is relatively mobile. This may precipitate the onset of serious neurological deterioration after myelography. If myelography is still considered necessary when the presence of a tumour is suspected it should be performed in a centre where a neurosurgical operation can be performed urgently if it becomes necessary. Failure to take heed of this risk and subsequent delay in treatment has led to disaster on a number of occasions. In order to perform the myelogram, following lumbar puncture a radio-opaque contrast material is injected in the cerebrospinal fluid. Myodil, an oily based substance, was the contrast media commonly used until the late 1970s. The association between Myodil myelography and the later development of spinal arachnoiditis was not appreciated until 1978 when figures of 74 per cent (Johnson & Burrows) and 70 per cent (Hansen et al) were quoted as its true incidence. The ongoing

Myodil arachnoiditis litigation is well recognised. One can be certain that this will not be a problem in the future for two reasons. Firstly, while the non-ionic water-soluble agents introduced to replace Myodil caused transient side-effects such as headaches, nausea and vomiting, they did not cause arachnoiditis even in the presence of subarachnoid blood (Haughton & Ho 1982). Metrizamide had the additional problem of precipitating epileptic seizures in patients prone to epilepsy, but the newer contrast media such as Iopamidol and Iohexol are largely free from such side effects. Secondly, and more importantly, although myelography still has a place in the investigation of patients with spinal disorders, magnetic resonance imaging (MRI) is steadily replacing it and as its general availability is increasing this totally risk-free imaging technique is becoming the investigation of choice for patients suspected of having spinal problems such as tumours or disc lesions.

26.35 As with so many other neurosurgical disorders, the two main sources of disagreement in the management of patients with spinal tumours are delay in arriving at the diagnosis and inadequate description of the risks of surgery. The progression of tumours affecting the spinal cord, which are often benign, can be very insidious. With the tumours pressing on the spinal cord from without, that is the extra-medullary tumours such as meningiomas and neurofibromas, the outcome depends upon treatment at a stage before complete compression and loss of cord function has occurred. With these tumours it is fortunate that even at a very late stage, but before complete paralysis, excellent recovery can occur. When an extra-medullary tumour which is almost certainly benign, can be recognised by the appropriate imaging technique, the patient can be given a good prognosis provided that the progress of the condition has not advanced as far as complete paraplegia. In contrast, the prognosis for the results of surgical treatment of the intra-medullary tumours can be very difficult and it is most unwise to give a favourable prognosis before operation and before the histological nature of the tumour has been demonstrated. This is particularly so with intra-medullary tumours in the cervical and thoracic regions of the spinal cord because of the variable and sometimes borderline nature of the blood supply of the thoracic cord. In such cases a patient with only moderate spinal cord dysfunction pre-operatively may awaken from surgery at which biopsy or partial removal of such a tumour has been undertaken, with a paraplegia extending from the spinal level of surgery downwards and involving loss of sphincter control. Almost certainly this is not due to any error of surgical technique but there will be no defence if the patient has not been warned of the possibility before operation.

CERVICAL DISCS AND STENOSIS

26.36 Cervical spondylosis is a common degenerative condition of the cervical spine in middle age and beyond. The cervical spine is highly mobile and more prone to degenerative change than other levels. Compression due to either degenerative osteophytes or a disc protrusion may be lateral to involve a nerve root or central causing spinal cord compression. Myeloradiculopathy, that is the combination of disturbance of the spinal cord and of an adjacent nerve root, is usually produced by a central hard disc which is typical of spondylosis. Over the past 40 years a great variety of surgical treatments have been practised in dealing with this problem. These have varied from posterior decompression by laminectomy extending above and below the level of the lesion to the more recent anterior discectomy and interbody fusion. Lesoin et al (1985) in a report on the results of surgical treatment of myelo-radiculopathy based on 1,000 operations, recorded six deaths. Five of these were regarded as preventable and due to air embolism occurring during operation performed with the patient in the sitting position. Other complications including wound haematomas and direct neural injury due to manipulation of the cervical cord have been recorded. Cord contusion may result in temporary or permanant tetraplegia and it has also been suggested by Hoff (1977) that patients with myelopathy who are operated on in the sitting position have poor auto-regulation because the cord is ischaemic. Thus a transient episode of hypotension may produce cord anoxia which is not apparent until the patient awakes from anaesthesia. The risks of these operations in the sitting position, although still commonly performed, should not be overlooked.

26.37 In considering the possible causes of failure after such operations it should be noted that occasionally the true diagnosis has been overlooked and the neurological deterioration due to either amyotrophic lateral sclerosis, or spinal demyelinating disease. These errors in diagnosis should become less frequent with increasing availability of magnetic resonance imaging.

26.38 Extensive laminectomy sometimes leads to cervical instability. Adams and Logue (1971) recorded the occurrence of this complication two to three years after surgery, which they attributed to excessive movement after operation and recommended the use of a collar for three months to maintain the head and neck in a neutral position to encourage appropriate ankylosis of the cervical spine.

26.39 The anterior approach to the cervical spine consists of removal of the disc and associated osteophytes and usually leads to an interbody fusion between the two adjacent vertebral bodies. These operations are very frequently performed and are associated with a great variety of complications. While large series such as the 850 cases operated upon by Cloward (1971) did not describe a single operative death, others such as Eespersen et al (1987) recorded six deaths within three months of surgery. The moment of first risk is in the performance of endo-tracheal intubation when muscle relaxation from the anaesthetic agents can permit excessive extension of the neck which may cause damage to the cord in the presence of spondylosis or can aggravate pre-existing cord dysfunction. To gain adequate exposure of the anterior part of the cervical vertebral bodies considerable retraction of the structures in the front of the neck is necessary. Damage leading to temporary or permanent dysfunction has been recorded affecting the larynx, trachea and pleura and perforation and laceration of the pharynx and oesophagus have all been documented. Hoarseness, which may last for a few months or become permanent due to damage to the recurrent laryngeal nerve, has an incidence of about 1 per cent. There have also been accounts of damage to sympathetic nerves in the neck and also to the major vessels, including the carotid and vertebral arteries.

26.40 The most devastating accident encountered in this operation, as with the posterior decompressive operation, is irreversible spinal cord damage. The cord can be damaged when removing osteophytes particularly if there is some unsuspected canal stenosis. There have also been serious accidents at operation where an unguarded drill slips and damages the spinal cord and impaction of the bony dowel has been due to excessive countersinking or due to miscalculation of thickness. However, on a number of occasions spinal cord damage has been found after these operations when no obvious cause of damage during the operation has occurred. The incidence of spinal complications in recent large series of cases appears to be between 0.1 per cent and 0.3 per cent. In such cases Sugar (1982) in 'Spinal Cord Malfunction after Anterior Cervical Discectomy', advises 'Administer intravenous dexamethasone and take a lateral cervical X-ray if a fusion has been done to determine the position of the bone implant.' Horowitz and Rizzoli, in 'Postoperative Complications of Extracranial Neurological Surgery' (1987), go on to say, 'We would add that a quick CT scan through the operative level might detect a clot and would add further information about the fate of the graft. Certainly in doubtful situations it is most expeditious to re-open the wound and remove the graft and inspect the cord. The value of myelography is less clear. Five of eight done after delayed cord dysfunction were normal.' Sugar points out that 'when laminectomies have been performed at the site of post-surgical myelographic blocks no reason for the situation has been disclosed. However, it certainly seems indicated if spinal stenosis is present.' There are a number of other complications related to infection, failure of fusion and difficulties with the donor site of the dowel. Hankinson and Wilson (1975) cast doubt on the necessity for fusion. The failure rate defined as 'unchanged or worse' after anterior discectomy and fusion for myelopathy or combined myelopathy and radiculopathy varies from 15 per cent (Guidetti and Fortuna 1969) to 60 per cent (Galera and Tovi 1968).

26.41 As can be imagined from the foregoing account spinal cord surgery, and in particular the surgery of cervical spondylosis, has frequently led to litigation. Two such cases were *Hills v Potter*[1] and *Sidaway v Board of Governors of the Bethlem Royal Hospital and the Maudsley Hospital*.[2] In this latter important case the facts briefly were as follows. The plaintiff suffered paralysis following an operation upon her cervical vertebrae. The operation carried a small risk of untoward damage, about a 2 per cent risk of damage to a nerve root. Damage to the cord would produce a far more serious result and the risk of that happening was less than 1 per cent. The surgeon warned of the risk of damage to the nerve root but not of the risk to the spinal cord. The trial judge found that the patient had not been told of all material risks so as to be able to give a fully informed consent to the operation, but was satisfied that the surgeon, in giving the limited disclosure that he did, was following a practice that had the backing of a responsible body of medical opinion at the time of operation. He applied the medical standard and therefore the plaintiff failed in her contention that the surgeon, who had in fact died before the trial, had been in breach of his duty towards her. This conclusion was not reversed on appeal. Obviously when there is the opportunity for discussion, as with elective procedures, although the patient could be provided with information on every possible complication this would clearly be most undesirable even if practicable, but he is entitled to have a fair description of the risks and probable outcome. It has also been held that when questioned specifically by a patient of apparently sound mind about risks involved in a particular treatment proposed, the doctor's duty must be to answer both truthfully and as fully as the questioner requires. But in *Lee v South West Thames Regional Health Authority*,[3] the Master of the Rolls said, although obiter, that this applied to questions asked after treatment, that is, in an effort to find out what was done and what if anything went wrong. This was said in the context of an application for pre-trial disclosure under the Supreme Court Act 1981, section 33. In connection with the surgical treatment of spinal conditions it behoves the surgeon to pay particular attention to the doctrine of informed consent.

1 [1983] 3 All ER 716, [1984] 1 WLR 641n.
2 [1985] AC 871, [1985] 1 All ER 643, HL.
3 [1985] 2 All ER 385, [1985] 1 WLR 845, CA.

HERNIATED THORACIC DISCS

26.42 A prolapse of a thoracic disc is a rare occurrence. About 10 per cent are lateral prolapses presenting with radicular pain whereas 90 per cent are the more dangerous central herniations which can lead to paraplegia either in the natural course of the disease, or not infrequently, following posterior decompressive laminectomy (Ravichandran et al 1981). The hazards of thoracic spinal operations have already been remarked upon in connection with thoracic tumours and the cause of the disastrous reputation of thoracic discs is also related to the vascular supply of this part of the cord. Because of the poor results from posterior laminectomy the surgical approach was redirected laterally and eventually antero-laterally. The first move away from the posterior approach was that of Hulme (1960) who described costo-transversectomy for this purpose, an adaption of the procedure used for tuberculosis of the spine. The lateral and antero-lateral approaches are either extra-pleural or trans-pleural, the latter method accomplishing the most anterior approach to the pathological disc. Benjamin (1983) reported on 25 cases of thoracic disc approached by the antero-lateral trans-pleural method when the disc was removed and in only 7.4 per cent was the patient unchanged and none were made worse. With all disc surgery but particularly those involving the thoracic spine it is important to re-emphasise the warning voiced by all experienced operators concerning the verification of the proper vertebral level (Horowitz and Rizzoli 1987). A number of confirmed incidences of procedures performed at the wrong level are a testimony to this avoidable mistake. Prudent pre-operative planning will avoid this. At very least a skin marker placed at the level of radiological abnormality of myelographic block is mandatory. Modern portable X-ray image intensifiers available in most operating theatres are of sufficient quality to enable a lateral view of the spine to be obtained and the appropriate vertebral level identified which can then be marked either by the injection of a small amount of methylene blue or impaling the spinous process with a needle. In the cervical area a lumbar puncture needle can be inserted into the appropriate disc space pre-operatively and the correct level identified. Carelessness in these matters may lead to unnecessary prolongation of the procedure and occasionally to overlooking the abnormality entirely.

LUMBAR DISCS AND STENOSIS

26.43 Almost all lumbar disc protrusions are in the lower two spaces, most lesions being lateral and affecting either the L5 or S1 nerve roots, but the smaller number of centrally placed lesions that occur are of great importance as they can produce paraplegia with sphincter involvement which may be the subject of claims of medical negligence.

26.44 The clinical syndrome associated with lumbar disc prolapse consists of two components occurring either separately or in combination, spinal pain probably arising from a torn annulus and radicular pain. This latter is usually associated with neurological signs such as muscle wasting or weakness in the appropriate myotomal distribution, loss of the ankle reflex if the S1 root is involved and sensory loss in the appropriate dermatome. The majority of disc lesions producing this clinical picture respond to conservative measures such as bedrest, traction, a course of anti-inflammatory drugs and occasionally manipulation. This is being practised increasingly both by medically qualified personnel and specialists in complementary techniques such as osteopathy and chiropraxy. A word of caution is necessary on the subject of manipulation, particularly when performed under general anaesthetic, as this may occasionally be followed by acute cauda equina compression with disastrous complications. Surgery should only be considered when conservative measures have failed and the main indications for operative intervention include repeated attacks of severe sciatica, an acute attack which fails to respond to conservative measures, or progressive neurological problems. Operation should be reserved for patients with unequivocal evidence of neural compression either clinically or by appropriate imaging (MRI, myelography +/− CT scanning), a view stated by Fager (1993) and held by most neurosurgeons.

26.45 About 2 per cent of lumbar disc protrusions are central in situation and cause compression of the cauda equina resulting in bilateral leg pain, bilateral neurological signs and symptoms and evidence of sphincter disturbance. Failure to diagnose this condition, resulting in delayed surgical decompression is a recurring source of potential litigation. The surgical treatment of acute cauda equina compression by a central disc prolapse is regarded by many as a surgical emergency akin to the removal of an acute extradural haematoma (Robinson 1965). Recovery of neurological function, in particular sphincter control, is felt to be closely related to the duration of nerve root compression. Recently, however, Gleave et al (1990) have challenged this view to a degree, finding little correlation between the duration of urinary incontinence and eventual outcome in 33 patients with incontinence from acute central disc prolapse. Nevertheless they felt that such a disc prolapse should be removed at the earliest opportunity, 'both from the point of view of patient morale and comfort, and because any delay in treatment can only worsen neurological recovery'.

26.46 The surgical technique employed to treat a laterally placed prolapsed lumbar disc will vary according to the training and preference of the operating surgeon and will range from the classical hemi-laminectomy to the micro-discectomy, all of which can be equally successful if preceeded by adequate thought and planning. A successful outcome is achieved in 80 per cent of suitably selected patients although there is a recurrence rate of 10 per cent after initial success, which may be due to recurrent disc material at the site of previous surgery, a new disc prolapse at a different spinal level, or the development of adhesions at the site of the original operation.

26.47 Post-operative surgical complications are unusual following lumbar disc surgery but nevertheless, because the complications which do occur may have serious sequelae, patients must be made aware of their possibility at least in general terms if not specifically. A surgeon could be excused for not specifying the remote possibility of mortality less than 0.02 per cent, cauda equina syndrome and root injury between 0.01 and 0.2 per cent, or injury to abdominal viscera 0.05 per cent, when obtaining pre-operative consent prior to lumbar disc surgery.

26.48 Lumbar spinal stenosis with facet joint arthropathy has become more of a problem in our increasing elderly population (Weinstein 1993). While this is found commonly on routine radiological investigation, surgery in the form of wide decompression should be reserved for those patients with clear evidence of nerve root or cauda equina compression both clinically and by suitable imaging techniques. In these more elderly patients the post-operative complication of a dural tear with subsequent CSF fistula is commoner than in the younger population with soft disc prolapse, occuring in up 2.7 per cent. The leak can usually be recognised and treated by dural suture during the operation but nevertheless as it can lead to prolonged hospitalisation and delayed rehabilitation patients undergoing wide decompressive laminectomy for lumbar stenosis should be warned of its possible occurrence, if potential litigation is to be avoided.

BIBLIOGRAPHICAL REFERENCES

Anderson D W and McLaurin R L (1980) J Neurosurg Suppl, s 1.
Apuzzo M and Sabstri J (1983) J Neuro Surg 12, 277.
Becker D P, Miller J D, Ward J D, Greenberg R P, Young H F and Sakalas R (1977) J Neurosurg 47, 491.
Benjamin V (1983) Clin Neurosurg 30, 577.
Briggs M *Clinical Dilemmas in the Management of the Neurological Patient* (Churchill Livingstone, 1984).
British Medical Journal 'Diagnosis of Brain Death' (1976) 2, 1187.
British Medical Journal 'Guidelines for the Initial Management After Head Injuries in Adults' (1984) 288, 983.
British Medical Journal 'Tony Bland awaiting final hearing – withdrawal of artificial feeding in patients in PVS' (1993) 11–12.
Brossman T and Norlin G (1963) Nord Med 69, 645.
Cloward R B (1971) Surgery 69, 175.
Eespersen J O, Buhl M, Eriksen E F et al (1984) Acta Neurochir (Wien) 70, 97.
Fager C A (1978) Clin Neurosurg 25, 218.
Fager C A In *Lumbar Disc Disease* (Raven Press, New York, 1993).
Fohammo D et al (1986) Adv Tech Stand Neurosurg 14, 137.
Galera R and Tovi D (1968) J Neurosurg 28, 305.
Gleave J R W and Macfarlane R (1990) Br J Neurosurg 4, 205.
Guidetti B and Fortuna A (1969) J Neurosurg 30, 714.
Hankinson H L and Wilson C B (1975) J Neurosurg 43, 452.

Hansen E B, Fahrenkrug A and Praestholm J (1978) Br J Radiology 51, 321.
Haughton V M and Ho K C (1982) Radiology 143, 699.
Hoff J T 'Discussion' in Dunsker S B (1977) Clin Neurosurg 24, 522.
Hulme A (1960) J Neurol Neurosurg Psychiat 23, 133.
Hunt W E and Hess R M (1968) J Neurosurg 28, 14.
Jeffreys R V and Jones J J (1981) Lancet 2, 459.
Jelsma R and Bucy P (1967) J Neurosurg 27, 338.
Jennett B and McMillan R (1981) British Medical Journal 282, 101.
Jennett B and Teasdale G *Management of Head Injuries* (Philadelphia, F A Davis Co, 1981).
Jennett B and Galbraith S *An Introduction to Neurosurgery* (William Heinemann Medical Books Ltd, London, 1983).
Jennett B and Teasdale G (1977) Lancet 1, 878.
Jennett B and Plum F (1972) Lancet 1, 734.
Jennett B (1977) British Medical Journal 1, 45.
Johnson A J and Burrows E M (1978) Br J Radiology 51, 196.
Kader A and Sisti M *Post-operative Complications in Intra-cranial Surgery* (Thieme Medical Publications Inc, New York, 1993).
Lesoin F, Boussakao N, Clarisse J et al (1985) Surg Neurol 23, 350.
Melamed S (1979) Acta Neurochir (Wien) 22, 47.
Miller J D in *Northfield's Surgery of the Central Nervous System* (2nd edn, Oxford, Blackwell Scientific Publications, 1987) p 18.
Miller J D and Jennett W B (1968) Lancet 2, 91.
Miller J D and Jones P A (1985) Lancet 1, 1141.
New England Journal of Medicine, Editorial on 'Fetal Tissue Transplant in Parkinson's Disease' (1992), 327.
Nugent G R and Berry B (1974) J Neurosurg 40, 517.
Onestri S et al (1993) *Post-operative complications in Intra-cranial Surgery* (Thieme Medical Publications Inc, New York, 1993).
Perot P L Jr and Munro D D (1969) J Neurosurg 31, 452.
Pertrusiel B (1985) Acta Neurochir 76, 2.
Robinson R G (1965) Brit J Surg 52, 858.
Rose J, Valtonen S and Jennett B (1977) British Medical Journal 2, 615.
Rowbotham G F *Acute Injuries of the Head* (4th edn, Edinburgh, Livingstone, 1964).
Solomon R (1993) *Post-operative Complications in Intra-cranial Surgery* (Thieme Medical Publications Inc, New York, 1993).
Sugar O (1982) Surg Neurol 15, 4.
Sweet W H and Wespic J C (1974) J Neurosurg 40, 143.
Symonds L (1984) J Neurosurg 61, 633.
Tappura T (1962) Acta Medica Scandinavica Suppl 392, 1–75.
Teasdale G, Galbraith S, Murray L, Ward P, Gentleman D and McKean M (1982) Br Med J 285, 1695.
Teasdale G and Jennett B (1974) Lancet 2, 81.
Weinstein P R in *Lumbar Disc Disease* (Raven Press, New York, 1993).
Yasargil M G et al (1980) Adv Tech Stand Neurosurg 7, 4.
Yasargil M G and Fox J L (1974) Surg Neurol 2, 393.
Youmans J R *Neurological Surgery* (W B Saunders Co, Philadelphia, 1990) p 3251.

CHAPTER 27

The paediatrician and medical negligence

A G M Campbell *MB FRCP(Ed) DCH*

INTRODUCTION

27.1 The care of infants and children is one of the most enjoyable and rewarding fields of medical practice but it can be fraught with particularly poignant tragedies when things go wrong; when children on whom parents had pinned so many hopes for the future die or are seriously disabled as a result of medical accidents or errors in diagnosis or treatment. The years of 'chronic sorrow' that follow such tragedies may be accompanied by feelings of bitterness and anger, perhaps directed against the hospital and doctors involved. A legal action claiming damages for negligence may follow, perhaps after many years. This chapter will consider some of the principal problems that occur in the care of children, will suggest ways in which they might be avoided and indicate other areas at the medical-legal interface that may be relevant to paediatricians.

When things go wrong

27.2 It is never easy to convey bad news but doing it sensitively and well is an important part of being a good doctor. Some clinical problems are extremely complex and what really happened may never be known. Occasionally, in the heat of the moment, perhaps when exhausted or affected emotionally by the stress of dealing with tragedy, junior and senior doctors make accusatory statements of culpability either about themselves or colleagues that are later seen to be unjustified when the circumstances are examined objectively and dispassionately. Doctors have a responsibility to give factual information to parents and to respond to their questions, but snap judgments about the actions or omissions of medical or nursing colleagues must be avoided. Contrary to popular belief, the medical defence organisations do not advise members to maintain a 'wall of silence' or to refuse to answer questions. Successive annual reports of the Medical Protection Society have included the following advice:

> In circumstances where complications and errors arise it is proper that objective factual information with appropriate clinical reassurance is provided. Adequate explanations, ideally from the responsible consultant or principal, assist in reducing fear and uncertainty which may give rise to complaints and claims.

27.3 Parental suspicion that the staff may be at fault will be heightened if questions are met defensively, or if doctors and nurses are brusque or seem indifferent and unsympathetic to the family's distress. Many legal actions originate simply because parents or families cannot find out what went wrong in any other way, or are offended by the attitude of the doctors and nurses in whom they had placed their trust.

Informed consent: talking to parents

27.4 Some doctors argue that while 'the truth, the whole truth, and nothing but the truth' may be all very well for courts of law it is a principle that may not always be good for patients. The stark and sometimes brutal facts about an operation or illness, no matter how sensitively presented may be counter-productive in obtaining consent for necessary and perhaps urgent procedures and may affect the patient adversely by destroying the hope that is so important to recovery. In these situations some latitude in the exercise of medical judgment should remain although there must be convincing justification for withholding information in each case. Following the *Sidaway* case,[1] decided by the House of Lords in 1985, it seems to be accepted that 'appropriate disclosure' should be judged by what might be called the 'sensible doctor' test and tied to the standard of care adopted by reasonably careful and prudent practitioners. In the United States, on the other hand, the standard is what the 'prudent patient' might consider as adequate for the purpose of giving consent.

1 *Sidaway v Board of Governors of the Bethlem Royal Hospital and the Maudsley Hospital* [1985] AC 871, [1985] 1 All ER 643, HL.

27.5 When the patient is a child, arguments for honesty and complete openness with parents are much more compelling. In obtaining parental consent for treatment of a child there should be a greater degree of disclosure of the nature and risks involved than when such advice is given directly to an adult patient (Brahams 1986a). If possible parents should be seen together, and kept fully informed on all details of diagnosis, treatment and prognosis as far as they are known at the time. Shielding one or other parent from the truth, even at one or the other's request, is a mistake and will undermine trust in the doctor or even between the parents. Erosion of trust may be the first step in the process of disillusionment and suspicion that causes families to seek legal redress. When discussing difficult decisions with single parents they should be given the opportunity to have a friend or relative with them for support.

27.6 It is important to view the obtaining of 'informed consent' not simply as a tiresome legal chore to get someone's signature on a piece of paper but as an important process in building a 'therapeutic alliance' with parents. (Gutheil et al 1984). In other words, it should not be a 'one-off' episode at the start of treatment but an on-going interactive exchange of relevant information to explore the parents' understanding of the clinical issues, the potential benefits and risks of treatment and the likely outcomes. Such a process, while time-consuming, is an important element in building a trusting relationship between the doctor and the family.

Age of consent

27.7 In *England*, anyone who has attained the age of 16 years, and is of sound mind, may give a legally valid consent to surgical, medical or dental treatment or procedures (Family Law Reform Act 1969, section 8). According to common law, anyone under the age of 16 years can give consent provided that they understand the underlying issues (accepted by the House of Lords in the *Gillick* case[1]), but as far as possible the prudent doctor should also attempt to obtain the consent of the parents.

1 *Gillick v West Norfolk and Wisbech Area Health Authority and Department of Health and Social Security* [1986] AC 112, [1985] 3 All ER 402, HL.

27.8 In *Scotland*, the legal age of consent for treatment was rather unclear though generally interpreted to be 12 years for girls and 14 years for boys. It was reviewed in the Scottish Law Commission Report of 1985 and is now consistent with that in England following the Age of Legal Capacity Act (Scotland) 1991. Under this legislation a person aged 16 and above can give effective consent to proposed treatment (and non-therapeutic medical research). Section 2(4) refers to a person under the age of 16 years who 'shall have capacity to consent on his own behalf to any surgical, medical or dental procedure or treatment where, in the opinion of a qualified medical practitioner attending him, he is capable of understanding the nature and possible consequences of the procedure or treatment.' It is important to note that it is thought sufficient for the attending doctor to *think* that the child has sufficient understanding as legislation based on actual understanding was thought to be unworkable. (See Chapter 12 for an authoritative account of the law relating to consent.)

27.9 The General Medical Council guidance on parental involvement states that 'even if a doctor thinks a child has sufficient capacity to understand and consent to proposed treatment he or she should persuade the child to involve the parents in the consultation. Where the child refuses to involve the parents the doctor has to decide whether or not to continue to offer advice and treatment.'

27.10 What information is given to a child will depend on the parents' and the doctor's assessment of the emotional maturity and level of understanding of the child. 'Telling all' to young children about serious illness and going into complex technical details will largely be incomprehensible and frightening to those already intimidated by hospital experiences. As a basis for obtaining consent, in most cases it will be sensible to withhold certain details from the child but wrong to withhold *any* information from the parents.

Special problems with consent

Children under 16 years

27.11 Paediatricians are aware of great variability in the rates of physical, psychological and emotional development in the years of late childhood and adolescence. Some children, though under the age of 16 years, are perfectly able to understand the implications of medical decisions that affect them and are legally capable of giving or refusing consent to treatment. Their consent should always be sought but it will be wise additionally to seek the assent of the parents. For those children who cannot understand and who therefore cannot give a personal consent, it will be necessary to obtain consent for treatment from the parent or legal guardian.

27.12 This issue became a matter for public debate over the controversy about providing contraceptives for under age girls without their parents' knowledge or consent. Perhaps more than any other, this vexing topic underlines how illogical and undesirable it is to use age as the only criterion for consent.The House of Lords decided (by a majority) that a doctor could advise and treat children without the consent of parents provided certain criteria were met. As enumerated by Lord Fraser of Tullybelton, these were:

(1) that the girl (although under 16 years of age) will understand his advice;
(2) that he cannot persuade her to inform her parents or to allow him to inform the parents that she is seeking contraceptive advice;
(3) that she is very likely to begin or to continue having sexual intercourse with or without contraceptive treatment;
(4) that unless she receives contraceptive advice or treatment, her physical or mental health, or both, are likely to suffer;

(5) that her best interests require him to give her contraceptive advice, treatment,or both, without parental consent.

27.13 Lord Scarman stated: 'Parental right yields to the child's right to make his own decisions when he reaches a sufficient understanding and intelligence to be capable of making up his own mind on the matter requiring decision.' He also pointed out that this view of the law places great responsibility upon the medical profession and he warned that abuse of this power would render a doctor liable to severe professional penalty (in this context it is worth noting that medical confidences, unlike legal ones, are not privileged in law). The principle of a child's right to decide in some circumstances, e g to refuse to submit to a medical examination, is central to the Children Act 1989 (see para **27.131**).

27.14 Paediatricians are strong advocates for children, the family as a social unit and parental responsibility in child rearing. Like family doctors, many paediatricians were disturbed by this judgment, but it must be acknowledged that there are many children who, for various reasons, are denied help and guidance from parents on such crucial matters as the implications of sexual relationships, contraception, pregnancy and abortion. The fact that so many young girls (and boys) remain ignorant and feel the need to consult a doctor without parental knowledge is some indication of increasing disruption of the family unit and how badly communication within some families has broken down. In each individual case there must be room for the exercise of discretion and clinical judgment but unless teenagers can trust the doctor to maintain confidentiality about the consultation they will not seek help when help is badly needed. There will be times when it will be right to try to prevent an unwanted pregnancy without telling the parents, and there will be times when *in the best interests of the child* it is right to inform parents without the agreement of the child. In these 'exceptional circumstances' the reasons for the doctor's decision should be documented.

Jehovah's Witnesses

27.15 In the exercise of autonomy a competent adult patient has the right to refuse treatment even if the consequences of such refusal could include his or her death. When the patient is a Jehovah's Witness whose faith prohibits acceptance of blood or blood products, the doctor should respect the patient's refusal of blood transfusion as to do otherwise would constitute assault. For the children of Jehovah's Witnesses the position is more complicated. Parents do not have the right to make martyrs of their children and if a blood transfusion is essential, it may be necessary for the doctor to take action in the child's interests but against the express wishes of the parents. In these circumstances it used to be the practice for the doctor, acting through the hospital or health authority, to take legal action by application to a magistrate (or Sheriff in Scotland) and for the child to be made a ward of court when the transfusion would be ordered as part of necessary treatment. While this procedure is still available, it is considered preferable by everyone, including the parents, for the doctor in charge to proceed with any treatment that is deemed necessary without involving the court. In so doing, the doctor must have due regard for all the relevant circumstances, should consult with appropriate colleagues and be satisfied that there is no suitable

alternative treatment. In other words, the decision must be justified on good grounds which should be apparent from reading the clinical record. Adequate documentation of a carefully considered decision making process will be particularly important should the aggrieved parents decide to initiate legal action against the doctor and the hospital.
Note: The Children and Young Persons Act of 1933 makes it an offence for anyone over 16 who has the custody, charge or care of a child under 16, wilfully to illtreat, neglect or abandon that child and expose him to unnecessary suffering or injury to health.

Sterilisation

27.16 There is no particular problem where sterilisation is an inevitable consequence of necessary treatment but the sterilisation of minors for social reasons, eg mental incapacity, is likely to be unlawful. In *Re D (a minor) (wardship: sterilisation)*,[1] the judge ruled that a proposed sterilisation on an 11-year-old girl with Sotos syndrome was neither medically indicated nor necessary and that it would not be in the child's best interests for it to be performed. With recent improvements in contraceptive techniques, sterilisation in these circumstances is almost always unnecessary.
Note: This judgment may be relevant to other non-therapeutic procedures on minors but it has never been tested specifically in its application to research (see below).

1 [1976] Fam 185, [1976] 1 All ER 326, Heilbron J.

Children as subjects of research

27.17 To date, no doctor has been charged with an offence because he or she used a child as a research subject without consent, yet doubts remain as to the validity of consent, particularly for *non-therapeutic research* (research where there is no direct benefit to the subject). It is self-evident that children must participate in research if there is to be progress in solving some of the problems that are unique to the developing child and for which research using adults would be inappropriate. Nevertheless, medical researchers are regularly under pressure from powerful lobbyists who argue for stricter controls, or even for outright prohibition, their emotive statements too often based on ignorance of the facts (Forfar & Campbell 1987). Paediatricians must be particularly scrupulous in the conduct of their research because of the special difficulties of proxy consent, and there is a strongly held view that parents cannot legally give consent for any research that is of no direct benefit to the child subject.

27.18 In 1963 the Medical Research Council included the following statement in their research guidelines on the advice of Sir Harvey Druitt; 'In the strict view of the law, parents and guardians of minors cannot give consent on their behalf to any procedures which are of no particular benefit to them and which may cause some risk of harm' (Medical Research Council 1963). It has been pointed out that this is just one legal opinion and not based on any statute or case law and that 'no particular benefit to them' is coupled with 'risk of harm' (Curran & Beecher 1969, Campbell 1974, Dworkin 1978). In the absence of any testing in court, paediatric investigators have taken this to mean that they have some discretion in carrying out non-therapeutic research provided that the risks to the child are negligible in relation to the expected benefits and that parental consent has been obtained.

27.19 The benefits versus risks equation has been amplified in recent authoritative guidelines. These include attempts at defining levels of benefit and risk, and the British Paediatric Association's current document contains a statement to the effect that 'a research procedure which is not intended directly to benefit the child subject is not necessarily either unethical or illegal' (British Paediatric Association 1992). The Medical Research Council (1991) has also re-examined its 1963 advice, and directly addressed the problem of non-therapeutic research:

> We do not seek to argue that a child's participation in non-therapeutic research is in his best interests. But we recognise that there are circumstances in which it is important to gain knowledge which may be of benefit to children in general and which can only be acquired as a result of research which involves children.

The working party considered that there was a strong case for including children in such research provided that 'participation places a child at no more than negligible risk of harm', and that the usual safeguards are observed, eg parental consent and the approval of a local research ethics committee.

27.20 Research Ethics Committees still tend to vary considerably in their membership and in their authority although the Department of Health's fairly prescriptive 1991 Circular should lead to some improvements in consistency and effectiveness (Department of Health 1991). Unfortunately it only increases the uncertainty as regards consent for non-therapeutic research when it states (in para 4.4):

> The local Research Ethics Committee should note that those acting for the child can only legally give their consent provided that the intervention is for the benefit of the child. If they are responsible for allowing the child to be subjected to any risk (other than one so insignificant as to be negligible) which is not for the benefit of that child it could be said they were acting illegally.

27.21 Most doctors (and lawyers) who recognise the importance of properly conducted research are cautious about creating specific legislation to set the boundaries of permissible research as,on matters of principle, the law is likely to be conservative and perhaps unnecessarily restrictive. This makes it all the more important that paediatric research continues to have the confidence of the public and that it can withstand rigorous medical, ethical and legal scrutiny.

Screening programmes

27.22 The screening of pregnant mothers and newborn infants for a wide variety of abnormality and illness is now a regular feature of perinatal care. Many mothers remain ignorant about the implications of some screening tests because the doctors, albeit with the best of intentions, do not wish to worry them with the details and perhaps raise anxiety levels unnecessarily. Problems arise when the result is abnormal or suspicious and further action is offered for which the parents were unprepared. Failure to obtain properly informed consent for screening is unethical and will also expose doctors and the health authority to the risk of litigation (Edwards & Hall 1992). Just as for treatment and research, the subject of a screening programme (or the parents in the case of young children) should know what is going on. Thus when a mother is entered into a programme, e g for the antenatal detection of Down's syndrome or spina bifida, she should be given a full explanation of the screening test and the associated risks before she has her blood taken. In these circumstances, the consequences can be serious, perhaps entailing complications of the test, further extensive investigations and perhaps even culminating in the loss of a normal infant because of a false positive result. On the other hand, a false negative may result in the birth of a severely handicapped child, or may delay the diagnosis of a potentially correctible condition because it creates a false sense of security that all is well.

THE NEWBORN INFANT

27.23 A large proportion (perhaps as many as 50 per cent, amounting to about 85 per cent of the costs) of the claims against paediatricians involve newborn infants, and about half of these relate to infants said to have been 'brain damaged' as a result of perinatal asphyxia. Most of the other claims result from errors in the intensive care nursery where 'iatrogenic disease' continues to increase in proportion to the increased use of complex and invasive treatment.

Limitation Act

27.24 Doctors should be aware that, for practical purposes, the Limitation Act 1980 has only limited relevance to infants as the 'time-clock' does not start to run until they reach the age of majority. Thus under English law the time limit for initiating litigation is such that a case may commence at any time before the plaintiff's 21st birthday and the plaintiff then has a further year in which to serve the writ. Case notes on minors should be retained until at least they have reached the age of 25 years (DHSS HC (80) 7).

27.25 However, the High Court has discretionary powers to permit litigation to take place even outside these generous time limits provided by Parliament so that it is extremely important that doctors *make* and *keep* good notes.

27.26 In Scotland the position is covered by the Prescription and Limitation (Scotland) Act 1973 (as amended) but the time limits for initiating legislation are not substantially different from those that apply in England.

The paediatrician in the delivery room

27.27 In spite of modern advances in obstetric and newborn care which have helped to reduce overall perinatal mortality and morbidity, the complications of late pregnancy, labour and delivery still contribute to a disproportionate share of infant deaths and lifelong disability for some of the survivors. It is easy to understand why the perinatal period should be such a fertile ground for medical negligence. When instead of being healthy, a baby is stillborn, is abnormal or is grieviously damaged, the triumph of birth quickly turns to tragedy. Joy at the birth of an eagerly awaited new member of the family is suddenly replaced by shock, then sadness and anger. Whilst most parents, even in the depths of their despair, recognise that 'these things happen' and that nobody is to blame, some may recall certain incidents in the pregnancy, labour or delivery which will cause them to question their care and to seek explanations about what went wrong and why. Sometimes, the doctors or nurses or both are blamed for what happened and legal action may follow, but perhaps not until many years later when the extent of the child's disabilities become all too apparent. Most accusations about a 'brain-damaged baby' are made against obstetricians and midwives, but paediatricians may also be involved in 'blanket' allegations that cover the whole perinatal period. In complex cases there may also be specific allegations against the doctor or doctors who attended to the infant at birth and in the neonatal period.

Problems in communication

27.28 The obstetric paediatric interface is often plagued by problems in communication and these will be exacerbated by the stresses imposed by difficult or abnormal birth. When something goes wrong and the outcome is bad the doctors may feel guilty, often for no particular reason, and they may express this guilt in various ways that can upset good relationships between colleagues and undermine the trust of patients. For example the obstetrician who has cared for a mother throughout her pregnancy may become difficult to contact and is defensive in answering questions. The obstetrician may also be feeling distressed at what has happened but to grieving parents this distancing will seem cold and unfeeling. Such an attitude will be particularly upsetting if labour has been prolonged and painful and may raise parental suspicions of mismanagement. The paediatrician may be in a difficult position when faced with distressed parents asking pointed questions about obstetric management. It is unlikely that he or she will have met the parents until tragedy struck, will be in no position to comment on what happened pre-natally, and may misinterpret the information given second or third hand, or obtained from the records. The paediatrician may even feel some resentment about certain aspects of the obstetric management and blame them for giving rise to difficulties with the baby.

27.29 When abnormal birth occurs the responsible consultants, obstetric *and* paediatric, should discuss and clarify their respective responsibilities for regular contact and communication with the parents and not delegate these crucial tasks to junior doctors. What exactly went wrong may never be known but, as part of ongoing clinical audit, the obstetricians, paediatricians and others involved should subject to detailed analysis all the cases that contribute to perinatal mortality and morbidity 'by regular discussions involving midwives, anaesthetists and perinatal pathologists'. It is particularly important that these discussions do not result in 'scapegoating' but concentrate on constructive review of the problems with the aim of identifying errors of management that can be avoided in future.

Perinatal asphyxia and cerebral palsy

27.30 The increasingly costly litigation which seeks to link 'brain damage' in infants (cerebral palsy) to perinatal events is a serious problem for health authorities, particularly as, since the introduction of Crown Indemnity, they must bear the cost out of their own resources. Paradoxically, the increasing tendency for parents to seek compensation in these cases coincides with a growing body of evidence that in only a small proportion of infants (perhaps less than 10 per cent) is there likely to be any causal link with perinatal events (Illingworth 1985, Nelson & Ellenberg 1986, Freeman & Nelson 1988, Hall 1989, Golden 1991, Stanley & Watson 1992).

27.31 Any child who is severely brain damaged is a personal and family tragedy. The parents of these children feel betrayed by a modern medicine that promises so many miracles yet seems to allow a natural process like childbirth to go so badly wrong. Expectations of normality and success are now so high that parents are less tolerant of imperfections in their baby, and are more aware and less forgiving of apparent mistakes in treatment, no matter how honestly or sensitively explained. What is viewed as the increasing mechanisation of childbirth has contributed to a climate of mistrust and adverse criticism about many aspects of hospital maternity care. In the worst scenario, the consistent supervision and comforting human contact during labour traditionally provided for the mother by the family doctor or midwife have largely been replaced by fleeting contact with anonymous members of a multidisciplinary team who are seen to 'interfere' in natural childbirth with various new technologies not adequately explained. If a baby is 'brain damaged', it is only natural for parents to wonder why this could not have been prevented or treated more effectively. It is difficult for them to accept that the cause of their infant's difficulties may be more fundamental and unlikely to have any relationship to problems that developed while under medical and nursing supervision. It is easy to understand why an increasing number of families seek compensation as the crippling educational and financial implications of the lifelong care of a handicapped person become increasingly apparent with age and are added to the crushing physical and emotional burdens experienced from birth.

27.32 Most of the claims against doctors and midwives focus on allegations that the baby was asphyxiated and deprived of oxygen for a time sufficient to cause brain damage. The obstetrician may be accused of failing properly to monitor a high-risk pregnancy or ignoring signs of fetal distress that should have led to an emergency Caesarean section. The paediatrician may be accused of failures in resuscitation, e g failing to intubate (Nocon & Coolman 1987). The case records will be scrutinised carefully for deficiencies in management that 'on a balance of probabilities' are claimed to be the material cause of the infant's subsequent disabilities. To establish a causal link between perinatal events and the later neurological disabilities it should be necessary to demonstrate an association between definite evidence of fetal distress during labour along with the clinical findings of hypoxic-ischaemic encephalopathy (HIE) in the early neonatal period. In the current medico-legal climate however, if there is clinical or cardiotocographic (CTG) evidence of fetal distress it may be difficult to defend various errors of omission or commission by the doctors and midwives even if the infant seems healthy at birth and only develops signs of neurological abnormality later in infancy or childhood. Paediatricians know that many severely asphyxiated infants do not develop cerebral palsy and that most infants with cerebral palsy have no history of perinatal asphyxia. 'Cerebral palsy' is an imprecise diagnosis that embraces many different forms of neurological disability and probably many aetiologies.

27.33 Doctors must be aware of the pathophysiological changes that accompany asphyxia and how the infant's behaviour and recovery pattern in the early neonatal period can give a more accurate assessment of the severity of the asphyxia and the likelihood of brain damage than can be obtained from such early and relatively crude indices as the Apgar rating. An infant should not be labelled as 'severely asphyxiated' when recovery is rapid, intubation is unnecessary and there are no early signs of neurological dysfunction. Conversely, an infant who is asphyxiated during labour to an extent sufficient to cause damage will usually require intubation and recovery will be prolonged with clinical findings consistent with HIE. For example there will usually be delay in return of reflexes such as sucking, which makes feeding difficult, abnormal and changing muscle tone, and the early onset of seizure activity, usually within 24 hours from birth. There may also be evidence of asphyxial damage to other organs such as oliguria and haematuria from tubular necrosis of the kidneys.

27.34 When doctors, acting as expert witnesses, are asked to advise on a possible causal relationship between a brain abnormality and perinatal events they must be very cautious in assuming that any link exists without satisfying themselves on the points mentioned above and making sure that there is no alternative explanation. They should analyse the family and maternal history, the pregnancy and labour, the infant's appearance and clinical progress in sufficient detail to identify factors that may be more relevant (Table 27.1) (Naeye & Peters 1987). Some important but subtle clues may point to alternative diagnoses (Dar & Jaffe 1983). In cases going back some years new knowledge and more recently developed techniques may

TABLE 27.1 FACTORS IN THE EARLY HISTORY AND EXAMINATION THAT MIGHT INDICATE AN ALTERNATIVE EXPLANATION FOR CEREBRAL PALSY

Parents	*Infant*
Family history	'Small for dates'
Congenital abnormality	Symmetric/asymmetric
Mental handicap	Head circumference
Consanguinity	Microcephaly or hydrocephaly
Infertility	Dysmorphism
Previous fetal/neonatal death	Facial abnormalities
	Hypertelorism
Obstetric history	Microphthalmia/optic atrophy
Maternal age	Micrognathia
Maternal disease	Low set/abnormal ears
First trimester bleeding	Scalp defects
Drugs	Clinodactyly/syndactyly
Alcohol	polydactyly
Hypertension/oedema	Dystrophic nails
Poor fetal growth	Dermatoglyphics
Poly/oligo hydramnios	Abnormal genitalia
Antepartum haemorrhage	Micropenis
	Cryptorchidism

identify new syndromes that were unknown at the time of the original allegations. For example it might be important to repeat the chromosome studies looking specifically for 'Fragile X' if the clinical features are consistent with this diagnosis. It may also be important to find out if the placenta was retained and examined by an experienced perinatal pathologist as it can provide important information about pre-natal events (Benirschke 1990), and if the infant dies a necropsy may give further clues to aetiology (Towbin 1986).

27.35 In May 1992, a six-year-old boy was awarded substantial damages after suing his mother for severe injuries sustained in a car accident before he was born. This case was the first brought under a section of the Congenital Disabilities (Civil Liability) Act 1976, which imposes a duty of care towards an unborn child on a pregnant woman driver. The baby was delivered soon after the accident and from analysis of both the clinical and neuroradiological evidence it was possible to time the insult to the brain and correlate it with the fetal injury.

The infant record

27.36 The paediatric notes should describe the clinical problems as they present and reflect the doctor's careful attention to the infant's needs. They should contain sufficient detail of the infant's condition and treatment to indicate that a logical approach was taken to solving the clinical problems as they developed; and to justify each action or non-action, e g if intubation was not used as part of neonatal resuscitation the reasons should be stated. In other words, it should be obvious from the clinical record, that the management was appropriate for the condition described. It is also helpful to record the main points covered in discussions with the parents. A summary of what they have been told about the infant's condition and prognosis should be part of any 'hand-over' note, a particularly important aid to continuity of care where there are frequent rotations of staff. Doctors must be careful not to criticise colleagues in the medical record as their opinions, perhaps written at a time of stress, may not be correct and are likely to reflect only one view of a complex problem.

27.37 Paediatricians have been responsible for legal action being initiated against obstetricians because of intemperate and misleading statements that were not justified when examined dispassionately. In one example, a paediatrician told parents that their infant's cerebral palsy 'must have resulted from lack of oxygen at birth' although there was no real evidence for this when the record was examined. In another, the father was told that his infant was 'flat at birth' because his wife was given pethidine. The paediatric SHO who was called to the delivery room in the middle of the night to resuscitate the baby, perhaps somewhat resentfully, wrote in the case record, 'baby asphyxiated – overdose of pethidine'. It took many thousands of pounds and several days in court to correct the unfortunate impression created by that statement and to convince the judge that the dose of pethidine was within acceptable limits and was necessary to control the mother's pain. It was also possible to argue that the dose of pethidine was irrelevant provided that the resuscitation at birth was competently performed.

Intubation: yes or no?

27.38 When allegations embrace both prenatal and postnatal care they involve obstetricians, midwives, paediatricians and sometimes anaesthetists. Junior members of the paediatric staff are usually involved if the allegations include inadequate treatment at birth. These may include a number of criticisms of resuscitation and perhaps the commonest are accusations relating to intubation.

27.39 With enough practice most doctors and nurses can become skilled in the technique of neonatal intubation but it takes longer to become experienced in judging when it is necessary. Inexperienced doctors tend to intubate more frequently, whereas those with extensive experience of normal and abnormal neonatal adaptation at birth may give a baby longer to breathe spontaneously before taking action thereby minimising the risks of injudicious intubation such as trauma or laryngospasm. Deciding to defer intubation while carefully observing spontaneous recovery, especially if combined with oro-pharyngeal suction, may sometimes be misconstrued as 'failing to intubate expeditiously' and later become the subject of medical and legal dispute. Doctors called to attend an infant at birth should document the reasons by describing the clinical condition of the infant paying particular attention to the heart rate, respiratory effort and tone.

27.40 For an asphyxiated infant the first priority is to restore oxygenation and eliminate carbon dioxide towards correcting the acidaemia invariably present. Effective respiration must be maintained until the baby can breathe spontaneously. The heart rate is the best indicator of oxygenation in an asphyxiated infant. If the bradycardia of severe hypoxia (<100 per minute but usually <60 per minute) does not quickly accelerate to over 100 within 30 seconds of birth some assistance will be necessary. Resuscitation may require only gentle upper airway suction and mild stimulation followed by bag and mask ventilation ('bagging'), but if there is no response from the heart rate or if the initial response is not maintained over 100 per minute and accompanied by other signs of recovery, eg improving peripheral perfusion (colour) and tone, intubation is indicated so that the lungs may be insufflated directly by controlled intermittent positive pressure ventilation (IPPV). Failure of the heart rate to respond to intubation and IPPV within seconds usually means that the endotracheal tube is misplaced with the tip lying in the oesophagus instead of the trachea. This is an important pitfall of intubation at any age and may occur even in experienced hands. It must be recognised quickly and corrected by immediate re-intubation.

27.41 Occasionally, neonatal intubation can be extremely difficult because of congenital abnormality, eg micrognathia, or may fail simply because of inexperience. Rather than persist with panicky and usually futile attempts at re-intubation which, apart from prolonging the hypoxia, may cause severe trauma to the airway, a junior doctor should summon help from a more experienced colleague, while reverting to bag and mask or even mouth-to-mouth respiration. These techniques may be quite effective in maintaining some oxygenation, at least temporally, until assistance arrives. For complicated labours an anaesthetist may be present in the delivery room and his or her particular expertise in intubation should be utilised. This is no time for concerns about status and 'loss of face'. Demarcation disputes about who is or is not responsible for infant intubation must be avoided. Apart from deflecting attention from the infant's urgent needs, delivery room arguments will not inspire confidence in the parents who, being anxious witnesses to these conflicts, will remember them if subsequent problems arise with their baby.

Resuscitation: yes or no?

27.42 Many infants who recover from severe asphyxia (even apparent stillbirth, Apgar 0 with loss of heart beat just prior to delivery) will be normal at follow up (Thomson et al 1977). Therefore maximum efforts at resuscitation must be started immediately for *all* severely asphyxiated infants. Subsequent decisions to continue or withdraw intensive life-prolonging treatment largely will be dependent on the response to initial treatment and should be made by the senior doctor in charge, usually the consultant, after discussion with the parents. A study of perinatal cardiac arrest indicated that if regular respirations are not established within 30 minutes of return of the heartbeat there is a very high likelihood of severe permanent brain damage (Steiner & Neligan 1975). In these and similar circumstances continued attempts at resuscitation are unjustified (Davies & Reynolds 1992).

27.43 Dilemmas about resuscitation in the delivery room are not confined to infants with severe asphyxia. Neonatal intensive care has become extremely successful in ensuring the survival of smaller and smaller infants born prematurely; and infants with major congenital abnormalities who would have died in earlier years. While most grow up to be healthy, some will be left with grievous mental and physical impairments. The prognosis for very tiny infants born at the limits of viability has altered most dramatically as has the concept of viability, now more accurately identified at about 23–24 weeks of gestation. (The Still-Birth (Definition) Act, which came into force in 1992, reduces from 28 to 24 weeks the minimum gestation age by which a stillbirth is defined. From 1 October 1992, all babies born dead after 24 weeks' gestation require stillbirth certification).

27.44 Where to 'draw the line' at resuscitation and who should draw it will continue to be controversial issues not only in paediatric practice but in ethics and in law (Campbell 1982, Campbell 1989). In practice, 'the law' seems to agree that a line has to be drawn somewhere and, to a large extent, judges will rely on medical evidence as to viability. Doctors must have good grounds for taking such fundamental decisions and these should be indicated in the clinical record. They cannot be justified on one simple criterion like weight, a poor indicator of maturity or 'viability'.

Case report In a 1987 Scottish case, a Fatal Accidents and Sudden Deaths enquiry was held into the death of an infant who was born weighing 675 g and who was 'allowed to die' (Brahams 1988). The parents were upset that apparently little effort was made to treat their daughter, e g by putting her on a respirator, and they alleged that it was 'hospital policy' not to resuscitate babies under a certain weight. The Sheriff who heard the case made a number of criticisms of the doctors' communication with the parents and of the process of decision making in general, but he accepted the decision itself on the basis that the infant was 'not viable'.

27.45 As junior doctors usually attend the delivery room for premature and abnormal births it is important that they are given clear instructions about their responsibilities regarding neonatal resuscitation. Any infant who is alive at birth has the full protection of the law. With very few exceptions infants of any gestation age, weight or apparent abnormality should be resuscitated if signs of life are present. Subsequent decisions about the wisdom of continuing life support should be the responsibility of the consultant after discussion with the parents and after taking full account of the opinions of the doctors and nurses most closely involved with the hour to hour progress of the infant. It may also be necessary to consult with specialist colleagues to ensure that the facts of diagnosis and prognosis are as accurately established as possible. Exceptions to this extended process of decision-making include those infants with gross abnormality particularly of the CNS, who, with modern techniques, are identified during the pregnancy, but for whom termination of pregnancy has not been possible. Discussions with the parents before birth should involve a paediatrician and should include consideration of the appropriate care to be given to the infant at birth. In these circumstances there is usually no justification for aggressive methods of resuscitation or for the use of life-supporting treatment, but the infant must not be abandoned to die in a corner of the labour ward. He or she should be admitted to the neonatal unit and given all normal basic nursing attention with relief of apparent distress or discomfort until death. The family should be provided with facilities and support to enable them to spend time as they wish with their dying infant (Duff & Campbell 1976).

The place of birth

27.46 The understandable wish of women to experience 'natural childbirth' and to reject interference by electronic monitors, artificial induction of labour and the use of drugs has increased demands for delivery at home or in small 'consumer friendly' cottage hospitals, a trend that is often in conflict with specialist professional advice. Obstetricians and paediatricians generally advocate the concentration of maternity and neonatal care to fully equipped maternity units that are large enough for the staff to maintain expertise which may be essential not just for those deliveries thought to be at 'high risk', but to enable them to act quickly and appropriately to the sudden emergencies that can occur during any labour. Indiscriminate intervention in labour is to be deprecated, and there is some evidence that it may actually increase risks to the baby, but occasionally intervention on behalf of the baby may be life saving or may prevent life-long disability. For example urgent action will be necessary on the discovery of a prolapsed cord, and an occasional infant born after what seemed to be an entirely normal pregnancy and labour will need skilled resuscitation, including endotracheal intubation.

27.47 In the process of selecting the place of birth and in assessing risks, the possible needs of the infant *after* birth should be given at least as much consideration as the convenience of the mother or obstetrician. Paediatricians may become embroiled in litigation over tragedies that were all too predictable but over which they had little or no control. In a medically advanced society parents are entitled to expect that there will always be someone available at their child's birth with the experience and skill to perform neonatal resuscitation efficiently and that there will be suitable facilities for any continuing care that may be necessary. This is difficult, if not impossible, to achieve except in the larger maternity units which usually have a neonatal unit almost immediately adjacent. For births at home or in small isolated rural units it is difficult for midwives or family doctors to maintain the necessary skills, especially in neonatal intubation which will only rarely be needed. Some compromise between insistence on a natural childbirth in domestic or rural surroundings on the one hand and meddling intervention on the other can be achieved by developing 'low-tech' units within or adjacent to large maternity hospitals where the 'high-tech' facilities are available when necessary. For a few mothers this must mean a few days of inconvenience and separation from family, but a small price to pay if the occasional catastrophe can be prevented.

27.48 Obstetricians sometimes create problems for themselves and their paediatric colleagues by insisting on conducting 'high risk' obstetrics in hospitals that do not have resident paediatric help. In one example, a paediatric registrar from a neighbouring hospital came under severe criticism for being late for the delivery of an asphyxiated premature baby, and for leaving the infant unattended after she had completed the resuscitation. She had been called to this maternity unit from her main base of responsibility, a special care baby unit six miles away, the nearest source of specialised neonatal help for high risk births. In my view, such a situation is indefensible, both on the part of the obstetrician who has created it and the health authority that condones it.

The intensive care nursery

27.49 Many of the problems that result in litigation are the consequences of modern medical progress. 'Iatrogenic disease', any adverse condition occurring as a result of treatment, is a growing problem in all branches of clinical medicine but it is particularly prominent in intensive therapy with its invasive and potentially damaging treatments. As the treatment of critical illness has become more complex (and successful) many more patients survive their original illness only to suffer the consequences of complications and 'medical accidents' that have arisen during their treatment. Being relatively fragile and immature, preterm infants are particularly vulnerable to iatrogenic disease. An extensive review of the problem has identified four different groups of aetiologies: conditions arising from:

(1) the result of progress in medical treatment;
(2) new or quasi-experimental treatments;
(3) unproved treatments;
(4) what has been called 'iatrogenesis imperfecta', where investigations and treatments are initiated not because of symptoms or signs of illness but because of falsely positive laboratory tests; or
(5) simple human error.

All may result in litigation (McClead & Menke 1987).

Retinopathy of prematurity (ROP)

27.50 This is perhaps the best-known example of a condition arising from medical progress. Previously known as retrolental fibroplasia (RLF), it became the commonest cause of blindness in children during the past few decades. Apart from the disastrous consequences for children's vision it also became notorious as a reason for costly medical litigation (Bettman 1985). ROP first became apparent in the United States in the early 1940s following the introduction of improved infant incubators which enabled the nursing of premature infants in an oxygen enriched environment. Many theories of aetiology were proposed and oxygen was suggested as a critical factor in 1951 (Campbell 1951). The association between ROP and oxygen was later confirmed in subsequent trials (Ashton et al 1953, Patz et al 1953). For a time it was thought that a simple cause–effect relationship existed (i e prematurity plus too much oxygen equals ROP) to the extent that many doctors found that it was impossible to defend themselves against a claim that they had been negligent in their use of oxygen because of *res ipsa loquitur* – the facts speak for themselves. It was also particularly difficult to mount a defence as the control of ambient oxygen levels was relatively crude and bedside methods for measuring arterial oxygen tension were not available. With the newer techniques for continuous monitoring of blood oxygen levels, increased understanding of neonatal physiology and as more and more very immature babies survive against all the odds, a simple cause–effect relationship between oxygen and ROP has had to be revised. Other causative factors have been proposed in individual cases and in a number of critical reviews of the literature, it is pointed out that the exact cause of the condition is not yet known (Lucey & Dangman1984, Ben Sira et al 1988). The aetiology probably is multi-factorial. It may simply not be possible to prevent ROP in some infants, particularly if they, and therefore their developing retinas are very immature. The exact role of oxygen, while undoubtedly important, remains debatable. It had been hoped that ROP would simply disappear once care was taken to ensure that the oxygen tension of the arterial blood perfusing the retina was kept within strict limits, e g below the normal oxygen tension of a healthy infant breathing air yet sufficiently high to prevent chronic hypoxaemia, also potentially damaging to infants. Unfortunately it is now apparent that ROP may occur even with the meticulous and continuous regulation of oxygen in neonatal units staffed and equipped to the highest standards. Moreover, in some affected infants there is no evidence that oxygen levels were significantly different from those measured in unaffected control infants. One might speculate that if the relative hypoxaemia of fetal life is a factor in normal retinal development as it probably is for other adaptive changes around birth, then even breathing air after birth with the inevitable increase in oxygen tension may be sufficient to affect some immature retinae adversely. Although complete prevention may not be possible, doctors must remain alert to the possible development of ROP in any premature infant as early intervention in the diagnosis and management of these infants has greatly improved their visual prognosis (Weakley & Spencer 1992).

Case report All that notwithstanding, doctors are still liable to be sued on the basis that they were careless in the use of oxygen by failing to use it only when indicated and by not monitoring blood oxygen frequently enough to prevent 'damaging hyperoxia'. The outcome for some of these cases is now rather uncertain following the judgment in a recent widely reported case. To be successful, a claim for negligence depends on proving on a balance of probabilities that the excessive oxygen caused the retinopathy and that the doctors (and nurses) were at fault in their use and monitoring of oxygen. In *Wilsher v Essex Area Health Authority*,[1] there were admitted errors in the sampling of oxygen which had misled the doctors and the judge found for the plaintiff. However, when the case was appealed and reached the House of Lords a retrial was ordered on the basis that causation had not been proved, a judgment consistent with current medical opinion that the precise cause of the condition is not yet known. In one Appeal Court judge's view (Mustill LJ): 'the plaintiff must prove, on a balance of probabilities that the defendant's negligence causes or materially contributes to his or her injury – defendant's negligence had merely added another factor to those which might have led to RLF. Which fact had caused the injury had not been established – it was for the plaintiff to show which part if any, the negligence had played' (Boon 1988). In the event, a further testing of this point did not take place as the health authority negotiated a private settlement with the family, possibly because the calculated legal and other expenses that would be necessary to continue the action were likely to exceed the sum due as compensation to the child.

1 (21 December 1984, unreported) QBD; on appeal [1987] QB 730, [1986] 3 All ER 802; revsd [1988] AC 1074, [1988] 1 All ER 871, HL.

'Inexperience' as a defence to negligence

27.51 The case described above is of potential importance to junior doctors in that the judge did not accept that the inexperience of the junior doctor responsible for the sampling error was any defence (Brahams 1986b). He considered that when a highly specialised standard of care is offered, as in a Neonatal Intensive Care Unit, then all those working within the unit will be expected to reach the standards applicable to that unit. Juniors cannot plead ignorance or junior status as excuses for falling below reasonable standards of care (see section on delegation).

The use of oxygen

27.52 Although this court ruling on causation must cast some doubt on the prospects for success by plaintiffs in other cases involving ROP, the meticulous control of oxygen in the care of premature infants remains of paramount importance. It is difficult to defend doctors in their use of oxygen if their clinical notes make no reference to the indications for its use or indicate that regular consideration was given to the benefits and risks of continuing treatment. In evidence a doctor may say that oxygen was used only when necessary but unless the indications are clearly expressed in the clinical notes, it is difficult to mount a defence when the nursing records include statements like 'looks pink, no apnoeic spells today', 'breathing normally' etc. On the other hand, doctors have a strong defence against liability if they can demonstrate, through careful documentation, that they minimised the risks to the infant by:

(1) prescribing oxygen only when indicated, e g to relieve cyanosis, dyspnoea, apnoea etc;

(2) reviewing the indications for oxygen regularly and stopping it when it was no longer necessary;
(3) keeping the arterial oxygen tension as far as possible within limits generally accepted and recommended in contemporary authoritative texts;
(4) monitoring oxygen continuously, or regularly at a frequency determined by the infant's condition but often enough to minimise exposure to hyperoxia, e g at least four to six hourly but more often if dictated by fluctuations in the infant's condition or by changes in treatment, e g alterations in ventilator settings;
(5) being alert to any discrepancies between the infant's condition and the blood gas results, e g an infant who appears unexpectedly pink yet with a low P_aO_2, or a cyanosed infant with a high P_aO_2. These 'rogue results' may indicate that a monitor requires calibration or that there is a sampling error and underline the importance of a *combined* clinical and laboratory approach to monitoring changes in a patient's condition. Relying too heavily on laboratory results without paying enough attention to the clinical condition of the patient is a common pitfall in intensive care at any age.

Practical procedures

27.53 Practical procedures that result in serious complications frequently end in claims for compensation, especially when there has been some failure in communication with the parents. This failure may merely indicate the parents' incomplete understanding of the complexities of caring for their sick premature infant and lack of appreciation that a particular procedure or treatment was an essential part of management, e g a scalp vein infusion. More seriously, it sometimes indicates that the doctor did not adequately explain the benefits and risks of the procedure, and reveals a general failure to obtain appropriately informed consent.

27.54 Procedures that are part of ordinary everyday care in intensive therapy units do not require the *written* consent of parents, consent being assumed as part of the general consent obtained for overall treatment. It is sometimes difficult to know when a procedure becomes significantly unusual (or risky) enough to warrant a separate approach to parents for specific consent whether verbal or written. Much is left to the judgment of the individual doctor and this can vary according to the circumstances, e g the urgency of the procedure and the availability of a parent. If at all feasible, the prudent doctor will take time to explain any treatment or procedure, especially ones associated with potential risks, even if formal consent is unnecessary. It is particularly important to tell parents why such a procedure is needed and to explain any complications that may occur. In considering potentially risky procedures the doctor should be satisfied that the patient's condition warrants taking these risks. In other words, the documentation should indicate that the potential benefits to the patient outweighed the risks and should show what steps were taken to prevent complications and enable their early identification, e g by providing adequate guidance to the nurses.

Case report A child lost part of a forearm and hand when ischaemic gangrene resulted from thrombo-embolic complications of an inadequately supervised radial artery catheter inserted for blood gas monitoring. This procedure carries significant risks yet it may be indicated in critically ill children. In this case, as the clinical notes made clear, the child's condition was not critical. He was showing signs of cardio-respiratory improvement with adequate capillary perfusion at the time the decision to insert the catheter was taken. Furthermore, no instructions on the care of the catheter were given to the nurses or written in the notes and it was clear that early warning signs of ischaemia such as 'blanching of fingers' were ignored. Thus although in other respects the care of the infant was exemplary, it was not possible to defend what happened as a regrettable yet, in some circumstances, unavoidable complication of intensive care.

27.55 Claims may be initiated on behalf of infants left with unsightly scars from intravenous infusions that have 'tissued' and caused ischaemic necrosis of surrounding skin. This seems a relatively common problem with the use of pressure pumps so that particular care is necessary in their use. Doctors working in neonatal units should appreciate that damage from extravasated 10 per cent dextrose, not usually considered particularly irritant, is common, and some care should be taken to avoid siting drips in areas with limited subcutaneous tissue for expansion as tissue ischaemia may result. If hyperosmolar solutions are used, the potential for serious tissue damage and scarring is greatly increased, e g injection of calcium solutions to correct hypocalcaemia. A bolus injection should only be given into a freely running infusion and stopped immediately on signs of extravasation. Consideration should also be given to choosing drip sites that minimise the cosmetic damage if leakage should occur. For example, scalp vein infusions are likely to cause problems if sited below the hair line, and if at all possible these should not be sited on the forehead or temple. Good communication with parents will minimise misunderstandings about scalp vein infusions and may prevent resentment and blame if anything goes wrong. Understandably, some mothers get very distressed when they find that their infant's head has been shaved, and it is good practice to warn them in advance that this might be necessary.

27.56 Another procedure fraught with potential difficulties is catheterisation of the umbilical artery or vein though, fortunately, recent advances in monitoring and treatment have reduced the number of circumstances when such an invasive procedure is necessary for prolonged periods. Use of these vessels for infusions or for monitoring may be justified but the indications should be clear from the clinical notes. There should also be some evidence that the risks were appreciated by the staff and that the procedure was discontinued immediately it was no longer essential.

Umbilical vein catheterisation may be necessary for brief emergency access to the circulation for infusions or drugs but it should not be considered as a convenient and temptingly easy route for prolonged infusions or for bolus injections of hyperosmolar solutions as there may be a significant risk of infection or liver damage respectively. Because of considerable risk of air embolism, an umbilical venous catheter must never be left open to the atmosphere during or after insertion.

Umbilical artery catheterisation is less risky and remains a valuable technique for arterial access in sick infants, complements non-invasive monitoring and can be used for intravenous fluid therapy and drugs with less disturbance to the infant than required for the frequent resiting of peripheral infusions. If an umbilical artery catheter is inserted, its position should be checked by X-ray, taking care to confirm that it is in the arterial and not the venous system. A lateral X-ray incorporating chest and abdomen clearly demonstrates the separation of arterial and venous access. Opinions vary as to the best location of the catheter tip but wherever sited the staff should be alerted to signs of distal spasm or emboli, e g in the lower limbs.

Any intra-vascular catheter, wherever sited should be removed immediately there is persisting evidence of interference with the circulation such as mottling of the skin or blanching of the toes. If immediate improvement is not apparent a vascular surgeon should be consulted. In several cases that have come to medico-legal dispute it was established that the damage might have been considerably reduced by earlier specialist consultation and more vigorous treatment by arteriotomy and thrombectomy.

Infection

27.57 Infection is an important cause of neonatal morbidity and mortality and a prominent source of medico-legal difficulties for doctors. Septicaemia, meningitis and infections of bones and joints have been particularly troublesome because of the difficulty in recognising the early signs of developing bacterial sepsis in infants.

27.58 Throughout infancy, serious infection may present insidiously with only slight alterations in temperature and subtle clinical signs like minor variations in colour, breathing pattern or muscle tone. A change in the infant's pattern of feeding with lack of interest and weak suck are particularly ominous signs. It is not well enough appreciated how such minor variations in an infant's condition and behaviour can herald a rapid progression to critical illness and death from fulminating infection.

27.59 In the neonate, infection is acquired either from the mother, perhaps during passage through the birth canal, or may be transmitted from the infant's attendants and surroundings after birth, particularly in hospital – nosocomial infection. Predisposing maternal factors which should lead doctors to anticipate infection include maternal pyrexia, prolonged membrane rupture with its increased risk of chorioamnionitis and the need for instrumental delivery. Neonatal infections are seen most commonly among preterm infants who have deficiencies in humoral and cellular immunity and who are more likely to require invasive procedures as part of treatment. There is reduced transplacental endowment of immunoglobulin (IgG) and the infant's ability to respond to infection by immunoglobulin production (IgM) is relatively sluggish. Cellular defences are also deficient or functionally immature, and because of inadequate chemotaxis, phagocytosis, intracellular bactericidal activity and deficient complement, bacterial invasion may occur more easily than in the older (and maturer) infant and child.

27.60 After birth a newborn infant's skin, respiratory and GI tracts rapidly become colonised with organisms lurking in the surroundings – in incubators, other items of nursery equipment and from the hands of attendants especially if techniques to limit cross-infection such as handwashing and gloves are poorly enforced. It is sometimes difficult to know why only a few infants develop serious infection when all are colonised but presumably one reason is the well-known but complex interaction between 'seed' and 'soil' with infection depending, on the one hand, on the dose and nature of colonising organisms and, on the other, on the vulnerability of the infant. Breaks in the integrity of the skin or mucous membrane barriers will increase susceptibility so special vigilance is necessary for those infants with abraded skin; or those who have been subjected to invasive procedures.

27.61 *Osteitis and septic arthritis* are particular medico-legal pitfalls. Unexplained fever, failure to feed, pallor, vomiting, especially when associated with a whimpering cry when disturbed, are warning signs of osteitis. A careful search may reveal localised swellings or 'bogginess' over bones or joints and there will be lack of movement of the affected limb or limbs and obvious resentment on handling. The favoured sites for neonatal osteitis are the head of the femur, often with involvement of the hip joint, the humerus, maxilla and the bones of the ankles and heels. If osteitis or septic arthritis is suspected, the paediatrician is advised to consult with an orthopaedic surgeon as soon as possible. Co-ordination of medical with surgical management which may include the early release of pus with drainage of an abscess or affected joint may help to minimise eventual disability.

> **Case report** An eight-day-old infant was discharged from a newborn unit without telling the general practitioner and without any arrangements for hospital follow-up although she had had a persistent mild fever and an inflamed heel thought to be due to the repeated heel stabs necessary for measuring serum bilirubin. She had had Rh haemolytic disease which was successfully treated by an exchange transfusion on the second day of life. She was brought back to hospital ten days after discharge with extensive osteitis involving both ankles. She was left with considerable disability and was awarded damages in excess of £100,000.

27.62 In preterm low birthweight infants at birth or shortly afterwards *bacterial sepsis* may present abruptly with signs of shock (peripheral circulatory failure), attacks of apnoea or rapidly progressive respiratory distress leading quickly to respiratory failure and death. This is particularly likely to happen with Group B haemolytic streptococcal (GBS) infection invading through the lungs. Infection with this organism is currently a leading cause of perinatal infection, particularly congenital pneumonia, sepsis or meningitis. It may be confused with hyaline membrane disease and even a few hours delay in starting vigorous treatment with antibiotics will result in a high mortality rate (up to 30 per cent in preterm infants). Paediatricians must maintain a very high index of suspicion of neonatal infection particularly in low birthweight infants and treat all symptomatic infants vigorously with broad spectrum antibiotics until the results of cultures are available. Some paediatricians give antibiotic prophylaxis to all low birthweight infants especially if mother has been identified as a carrier of GBS, but 'among proposed strategies, including chemoprophylaxis and immunoprophylaxis, only selective intrapartum maternal chemoprophylaxis has been evaluated for safety and efficacy' (American Academy of Pediatrics 1992).

Hypoglycaemia

27.63 Paediatricians are alert to the need to screen certain infants at increased risk from hypoglycaemia, e g infants of insulin-dependent mothers, infants with severe growth retardation and asphyxiated infants. This screening is best accomplished by using bedside reagent strips, usually on a half-hourly or hourly basis for the first 24 hours, until early feeding is established or blood glucose levels stabilise. As a result, *symptomatic* hypoglycaemia, a well-recognised 'brain damager' in infancy, is now very unusual with modern neonatal care. Nevertheless doctors may find themselves involved in litigation if they use the term 'hypoglycaemia' following a screening test result and the infant is later found to have various neurological disabilities or mental handicap, even though symptoms of hypoglycaemia were absent in the neonatal period. A basic problem is the continuing confusion and controversy over the definition of what constitutes hypoglycaemia to the extent that we need to be concerned about the risks to the developing brain. It is not possible to view this as a simple association between symptoms and damaging hypoglycaemia as we know that, in contrast to older children, newborn infants may have profound hypoglycaemia without showing any obvious clinical manifestations.

27.64 In analysing neonatal records, therefore, it is particularly difficult to know if there could be any causal connection between later neurological dysfunction and *asymptomatic* hypoglycaemia identified by some low readings on reagent strips with or without the occasional blood glucose result. In writing their clinical notes doctors should be precise in their use of the term 'hypoglycaemia' and indicate their concern to maintain adequate levels of blood glucose even in the absence of 'classical' symptoms of hypoglycaemia like tremor (jitteriness), hypotonia, attacks of apnoea and tachypnoea, irritability, feeding difficulties and frank convulsions.

27.65 In the current state of knowledge the prudent neonatologist will screen those babies at increased risk and view 2.6mmol/l as the lower limit of the normal range of glucose concentration, and the level at which more active treatment (e g background dextrose infusion) should be considered for both term and preterm infants (Lucas et al 1988). 'Small-for-dates' infants pose a particular dilemma as many remain asymptomatic at glucose concentrations considerably below 2.6mmol/l. Transient low levels are unlikely to lead to brain damage but if levels do not rise after adequate milk feeds, intravenous glucose is indicated.

27.66 Blood glucose test strips are widely used for cot-side *screening*, but for the more accurate *diagnosis* of hypoglycaemia their use should be complemented by laboratory measurements of blood glucose. Some types of these test strips perform better than others and their accuracy may be affected by the infant's haematocrit, the use of alcohol for skin cleansing, the age of the strips and minor variations in the technical performance of the test (Wilkins & Kalra 1982, Togari et al 1987).

Hyperbilirubinaemia and kernicterus

27.67 In some cases there are allegations that neurological damage has resulted from failure to control unconjugated hyperbilirubinaemia in jaundiced infants, but there is continuing uncertainty about 'safe' levels of bilirubin in both mature and preterm infants. It has been generally accepted that the unconjugated bilirubin concentration should be kept below 340 mmol/l during the first week of life in term infants, using phototherapy with exchange transfusion when necessary. For preterm infants there are no established criteria although neonatologists tend to reduce the threshold for exchange transfusion according to the degree of immaturity using weight categories as a guide eg <250 mmol/l for infants of 1500 g or less and <180 mmol/l for infants under 1000 g. However the lack of any precise and easily reproducible measure of the risk of brain damage by bilirubin at any particular concentration; at any particular maturity; or with any particular associated condition such as infection that may increase the infant's vulnerability, remains of concern to the neonatologist. With modern intensive care, kernicterus is now very unusual, and like oxygen and ROP, it is unlikely that the level of bilirubin is the sole cause of kernicterus. Some investigators have even suggested that hyperbilirubinaemia may be beneficial to the preterm neonate as a natural anti-oxidant (McDonagh 1990). As indicated in a recent extensive review of the subject, carefully conceived and executed studies are necessary before changes in the current guidelines for clinical management can be entertained (Watchko & Oski 1992).

Pitfalls in screening

27.68 The clinical and biochemical screening of all newborn infants is particularly important for conditions that may not otherwise be detectable until irreversible damage has occurred. Unfortunately screening tests are not infallible and they contain potential pitfalls for doctors and nurses. They may be omitted for one reason or another at the routine time and then forgotten, they may be carried out under unsatisfactory conditions, performed incompetently, the results ignored or there may be errors in the laboratory. There will also be false positives and false negatives that require follow-up and reappraisal. The relative responsibilities of doctors and nurses in carrying out these screening tests and in acting on the results require that clear and unambiguous policies are formulated in the hospital and community health services.

The Guthrie test

27.69 The test is a good example of an invaluable screening test that can prevent major causes of mental handicap. Originally developed to detect phenylketonuria it has been extended to include congenital hypothyroidism and several other inborn errors of metabolism. However, having such a good screening test may encourage a false sense of security to an extent that obvious clinical features of a condition are ignored until it is too late for the most effective treatment. For example, if there is clinical suspicion of hypothyroidism, it should never be dismissed as a possible diagnosis without making sure that the Guthrie test was done and that there is no possibility of a laboratory error. The test or tests should always be repeated if an infant's appearance or progress give cause for concern. The Guthrie test is normally done on the fifth or sixth day after birth, but if anything occurs to interfere with this routine, such as early discharge from hospital, admission to a special care unit or a surgical procedure, particular care is needed to ensure that the test *is* done (and recorded) by someone whenever appropriate and not omitted through some failure of communication.

> **Case report** An infant was transferred to a medical centre for the treatment of transient respiratory distress a few hours after birth. He improved quickly and was returned to the small district hospital on the fifth day still mildly jaundiced. It was assumed that the Guthrie test would be performed at the district hospital on the following day but the nurses there assumed that it would have been done at the main hospital prior to transfer. Nobody checked. The baby was seen regularly by his general practitioner who noted that the jaundice cleared after about six weeks. He measured the baby carefully and regularly but did not plot the measurements on growth centile charts and did not appreciate that although the infant's weight was increasing normally his head circumference and length were lagging behind. At the age of nine months it was obvious that the infant was severely delayed in development and when seen again by the paediatrician who had discharged him from the main hospital nine months earlier there were obvious clinical features of hypothyroidism.

27.70 There are a number of lessons to be learned from this case apart from the failure of communication that led to the omission of the Guthrie test. For example, it was clear that the general practitioner had wondered about the significance of the persistent jaundice but had assumed that it was due to breast-feeding as the Guthrie test had 'ruled out' hypothyroidism. It also underlined the importance of using centile charts to identify early any subtle variations in growth.

Congenital dislocation of the hip (CDH)

27.71 Examination of the hips is one of the important clinical screening tests performed for all newborn infants but as the validity of this test in the *early* neonatal period remains in doubt it should be repeated at every opportunity throughout infancy until normal walking is established. 'False negative' results may occur at the time of the early checks in the days after birth (as do 'false positives', but these usually result in arrangements for follow-up). It is now generally accepted that one reason for a false negative test just after birth is that late dislocation may occur in some hip joints that are easily 'dislocatable' due to lax supporting structures. It is therefore important for any doctor – family doctor, clinic doctor or paediatrician – who sees infants during the first year, for whatever reason, to take the opportunity to check the hips even if the neonatal examination was reported as normal. On a firm flat examining surface the 'set' of the infant's thighs, legs and feet should be observed for telescoping, abnormal rotation, or asymmetry (remember however that dislocation may be bilateral). Normally if the hips are flexed to 90 degrees, the legs, with the knees flexed, can be abducted easily and symmetrically. If there is any suspicion of abnormality, referral for X-ray and/or specialist opinion is important as delay will make treatment more complicated and will affect the eventual prognosis.

27.72 Most claims that allege failure to detect congenital dislocation of the hip do not implicate those responsible for the neonatal examination but, rightly, lay more blame on the doctor or sometimes a succession of doctors, nurses and health visitors who have seen the child at regular clinic visits and who have ignored the signs of dislocation, sometimes even after questions from the mother about the odd appearance of the child's legs, delay in standing or walking, or an abnormal gait. In these circumstances, failure to diagnose CDH any time after the first six months is difficult to defend. Failure to make the diagnosis until the child is walking with an abnormal gait is not only likely to be indefensible but it will be much more expensive as treatment is likely to involve repeated hospitalisation, major surgery and a rather less than satisfactory result when compared with early treatment.

27.73 In expert hands, ultrasonography seems to be a reliable method for examining the infant hip. At the present time logistics rule it out as a screening technique that can be applied to all infants, but long-term trials could indicate that it would be cost-effective though 'selective' screening failed to reduce the incidence of late cases of CDH (Clarke et al 1989). *Repeated* clinical assessment of the hips during infancy remains the crucial factor in preventing the problem of late diagnosis and subsequent disability.

THE OLDER INFANT AND CHILD: AT HOME AND IN HOSPITAL

27.74 Allegations about diagnosis and treatment occur throughout childhood but they arise less frequently with increasing age, thus emphasising the special vulnerability of infants. *Errors in diagnosis* which lead to delays in starting effective treatment are particularly prominent with failure to suspect meningitis as the commonest (and most expensive). *Errors in management* particularly involve failure to anticipate and prevent cardiorespiratory arrest and other life-threatening crises, failure to initiate and maintain basic resuscitation or to give crucial treatments in time, e g glucose in hypoglycaemia or acyclovir in suspected viral encephalitis. Other relatively common errors involve mistakes with drugs or intravenous fluids where there is less margin for error than with adults, or arise from the hazards of practical procedures, or result from the misinterpretation of X-rays and laboratory reports.

27.75 As with the neonate, infection in an infant can develop quickly and the presenting signs of meningitis may be subtle and confusing. Considerable experience and a high index of suspicion are important in the recognition and interpretation of the 'warning signs' of serious illness and in some circumstances, making a 'diagnosis until proved otherwise' coupled with vigorous treatment is the prudent approach. Like the neonate grievously damaged by asphyxia, the infant or child left with severe neurological sequelae from meningitis or following cardiac arrest may cause the family all the physical, emotional and financial burdens of years of dependent care. The modern intensive care that does so much to prevent disability in some infants may be responsible for some of these tragedies from the complications of invasive treatment or by ensuring the survival of infants who would otherwise have died from catastrophic illness involving the brain.

Errors in diagnosis

27.76 Accusations about delays in the diagnosis of serious infant illness seem to be a particular problem in general practice as it is usually the family doctor who has the first opportunity to see children in the early stages of a developing illness. From reviewing many of these cases, it is my impression that these allegations have increased with the increasing tendency to form large group practices and to employ short term locums or deputising services. Unless carefully organised this practice can affect continuity of care and upset patient/doctor relationships and trust. Doctors employed by a commercial deputising service cannot know the families concerned to the same extent nor are they likely to instill the same confidence. Rapport with anxious parents may be less satisfactory at a one-off consultation as the family will be disappointed and somewhat resentful at the appearance of a substitute doctor they do not know and may never see again. Continuity of observation, so important in assessing the significance of developing clinical symptoms and signs, becomes very difficult, especially if there is little or no communication between the doctors involved or an inadequate practice system for the transfer of information. Failure to operate an efficient system within group practices has been the basis for a number of recent claims. These may not only arise through 'doctor error' but from omissions by practice nurses or receptionists for whose actions the doctors are liable.

Bacterial meningitis

27.77 In spite of modern treatment this remains a life-threatening condition particularly for infants and, disappointingly, the mortality has remained relatively unchanged in recent years. In the newborn period the mortality varies with the organism responsible and the gestation age, but overall is about 20–25 per cent with the highest rate of over 60 per cent found in preterm infants with E. Coli meningitis. In older infants the mortality is now about 5 per cent but bacterial meningitis continues to be a major cause of morbidity. Apart from variations due to age and micro-organism, morbidity and mortality are affected adversely by delay from the onset of symptoms to the start of adequate treatment. It has been estimated that up to 50 per cent may have some sequelae of the disease, ranging from minor behavioural disorders, defects in hearing and vision to severe neurological handicap. Tuberculous meningitis, though now relatively rare, remains a particular problem for recognition, has a higher mortality and is a major cause of morbidity if the diagnosis and correct treatment are delayed (Cybulska 1988).

27.78 The problem for general practitioners is that, in infancy, the early signs and symptoms of septicaemia and meningitis are less specific than they are in older children and adults. For example, it is difficult to pick out the occasional child with early meningitis from the hundreds of children with identical clinical features who appear in the surgery every year, yet who are suffering from nothing more than a viral upper respiratory tract infection. Meningitis should be considered as a possible diagnosis if there is no obvious focus for the child's illness. It is particularly important that some arrangements are made for early follow-up which might give reassurance about spontaneous recovery, or identify the appearance of other features that indicate deterioration and the need for further investigation. The onus for arranging the follow-up of a sick infant should not be left to the parents. A common pitfall is the prescription of an antibiotic in the early stages of what is likely to be a viral illness. Such treatment may mask, at least for a time, the more obvious signs of developing meningitis and delay the correct diagnosis yet be insufficient to eliminate the meningeal infection.

27.79 If a doctor suspects meningitis the child should be referred to hospital immediately for confirmatory tests and treatment. If the child is obviously ill and could have meningococcal disease, sometimes prevalent in a community, it is recommended that the referring doctor administer benzylpenicillin (or chloramphenicol) parenterally in full anti-meningitic doses prior to transfer to hospital (Department of Health & Social Security 1988a). This action may be life-saving and should not affect the ability to make an exact bacteriological diagnosis (Begg 1992).

27.80 Clinical acumen is probably the best single factor in making this diagnosis in infants. As with a newborn infant, features that should arouse suspicion of meningitis include persistent unexplained fever, drowsiness or alternating lethargy and irritability, anorexia and vomiting. On examination there may be very little to find except a sleepy infant who is irritable when aroused and is not interested in feeds. In infants under one year, a 'boggy' or bulging fontanelle provides an obvious clue to the diagnosis, but the fontanelle is often too small to be helpful or reliable, and neck stiffness and other signs of meningeal irritation may be completely absent. A careful search should be made for a skin rash that might be a sign of developing meningococcaemia – classically a petechial rash, but it must be remembered that it will be macular in its early stages.The examining doctor may not see this rash unless the infant is seen undressed.

Case report A 15-month-old boy seemed feverish on wakening one morning and had several 'rigors'. He seemed much sleepier than usual throughout the morning and fed poorly. When his mother requested a visit this was refused by the receptionist who asked her to attend the evening surgery. The general practitioner (Dr A) diagnosed 'flu' and prescribed paracetamol and erythromycin.

On the following day the child was no better. He remained lethargic and vomited once. He took some liquid but refused food. His temperature was 103°F. That evening his mother again sought medical help and was seen by Dr B from the deputising service. He examined the infant, gave instructions on reducing body temperature, prescribed more paracetamol and a different antibiotic, and left a dose of Stemetil (prochlorperazine) for the vomiting. His diagnosis was recorded as 'gastric flu'.

On receipt of the report from the deputising service Dr A made a further home visit on the following day (day 3). He found the infant to be sleeping, did not waken him, yet later insisted that there was 'no clinical indication to change his treatment or diagnosis'.

On the evening of the following day (day 4) Dr A received an urgent request for a visit as the infant was convulsing and unconscious. He was admitted to hospital where haemophilus influenzae B meningitis was diagnosed. Recovery was slow and the infant was left severely mentally handicapped and epileptic.

Comment This case was indefensible and illustrated a number of errors that commonly lead to medico-legal difficulties for general practitioners:

(a) Dr A did not make notes of his home visits;
(b) if the mother's description of Dr A's examinations was correct they were unsatisfactory, e g he did not see the infant undressed and did not waken the infant on his second visit;
(c) there was no direct communication from Dr A to Dr B which might have helped Dr B to reach a different conclusion;
(d) a different antibiotic was prescribed on successive days for what was diagnosed as a viral infection. There was no obvious focus for the child's infection but the ears were not examined. Dr A later insisted that he had 'considered meningitis but found no evidence of neck stiffness'. Both doctors failed to consider the possible serious significance of such signs as persistent fever with no obvious cause, persistent vomiting, lethargy and refusal of feeds;
(e) Stemetil is not an appropriate drug for infants who are vomiting. If the vomiting is persistent attention should be directed towards replacing fluids and electrolytes while a cause for the vomiting is sought.

Tuberculous meningitis (TBM)

27.81 This presents particular pitfalls in diagnosis in addition to the obvious one of simply being forgotten in a society where tuberculosis is now relatively uncommon. Recent cases have mainly, but not exclusively occurred in immigrant families so that a high index of suspicion is necessary in these circumstances. One recent case involved failure of prevention as well as delay in diagnosis. The general practitioner as well as the community health doctors and nurses were aware of a strong family history of open pulmonary tuberculosis yet failed to protect a newly born infant with BCG. Furthermore, in spite of the family history, the infant's subsequent visits to the surgery with persistent fevers and 'chestiness' went unrecognised as developing tuberculosis until the onset of meningitic signs precipitated hospital admission.

27.82 In hospital practice delay in the diagnosis of TBM usually occurs through failure to take an adequate history or to consider tuberculosis in cases of meningitis when there are some puzzling inconsistencies between the provisional clinical diagnosis of bacterial or viral meningitis, and the findings in the CSF. For example, TBM should always be considered when examination of the CSF reveals lymphocytes in association with a marked reduction in CSF glucose. It should also be suspected if 'bacterial meningitis' seems resistant to the usual anti-bacterial treatment and if 'viral meningitis' is associated with focal neurological signs or continues to worsen instead of improving spontaneously after a few days.

Infection in immunologically compromised infants

27.83 An increasing proportion of serious infection now occurs in children whose susceptibility is greatly increased because the normal defence mechanisms are absent or deficient, as seen in various immuno-deficiency states, congenital or acquired. Resistance to infection may also be undermined by chronic diseases like cystic fibrosis or suppressed by cytotoxic drugs, steroids and radiation given for acute leukaemia and other malignant conditions, or following organ transplantation. Any of these conditions, especially when accompanied by neutropenia will render children vulnerable to infection. Doctors should be alert to the importance of protection for these children if exposed to infection at home or in hospital by such measures as reverse isolation, early and vigorous use of antibiotics or passive immunisation with specific immunoglobulin (Campbell 1988). Live virus vaccines such as MMR (measles-mumps-rubella) and OPV (oral polio vaccine) must not be given to children when immunosuppressed but inactive vaccines are safe, although they may not be so effective. For children who later develop secondary immunosuppression from disease or treatment these problems can be reduced by ensuring that all children are adequately protected with the recommended vaccines at the appropriate times and that their immunisation status is clearly recorded. Deaths from measles are tragic at any time but seem particularly poignant when they happen to children in remission from acute leukaemia (Gray et al 1987).

Case report A family lost their first child from overwhelming infection because of SCID (severe combined immuno-deficiency), a familial disease, but the parents did not receive genetic counselling. Three years later a second infant was born but through failures of communication within the general practice this important family history was not recorded anywhere and was forgotten when the child had repeated episodes of gastro-enteritis and other infections in the early weeks of life. He eventually died from overwhelming measles at the age of nine months.

Errors in treatment

27.84 Many claims against hospital doctors reflect parental dissatisfaction and lingering resentment about the standards of care given to their child when critically ill. Their anger may be directed against the institution and include members of staff as secondary defendants but it is often focussed on a doctor or doctors because of specific incidents that upset them and were never adequately discussed or explained. Sometimes 'accidents' or complications of treatment may be unavoidable or there may be mitigating circumstances. For example, the parents may not understand that the staff are working at considerable disadvantage. Staffing levels, facilities and equipment will vary considerably from hospital to hospital. In a small district hospital it is unrealistic to expect the same facilities as in a large teaching hospital and when tragedy occurs, such as the death of a child, it may be difficult to keep things in perspective. It should also be remembered that, in spite of all the recent advances in medical diagnosis and treatment there remain many uncertainties and unpredictabilities about the human body, and its reaction to disease. When these intangibles are interwoven with the complex technical demands of intensive therapy, there is ample room for confusion, misunderstandings, questionable clinical decisions (especially with hindsight), technical facilities and simple human error.

27.85 All that notwithstanding, whether care is provided in a small hospital or in a large medical centre certain minimal standards must be provided and maintained or children should not be admitted to that facility. Parents are entitled to expect that their children will receive correct treatment and, if not available, that arrangements will be made to ensure that it can be obtained elsewhere. Doctors have an obligation to inform parents of all factors relevant to their child's illness and treatment and deal courteously and sensitively with their questions and requests, including their wish for a second opinion or transfer to another hospital. Good communication and empathy with parents will do much to minimise resentment whatever the outcome. Recurring problems that seem particularly fraught with difficulties in providing the appropriate treatment include *upper airway obstruction* and *respiratory failure*.

Upper airway obstruction ('croup')

27.86 'Croup' is not a specific diagnosis but is descriptive of the difficult and noisy inspiration that characterises obstruction of the upper airway, in particular the laryngeal inlet and upper trachea. A general practitioner is likely to see many examples of mild croup, often beginning during the evening and improving by the following morning. This common condition is not usually associated with much constitutional upset beyond a cough and other features of a mild upper respiratory tract infection perhaps with some contribution from allergy and/or spasm. If the inspiratory stridor is noticeable only when the child is crying and upset, and absent at rest, the obstruction is relatively mild. These infants can safely be treated at home and may be helped by warm humidification of the atmosphere.

27.87 Severe croup, characterised by a distressing cough, noisy inspiratory stridor present even at rest and hoarseness is less common. It almost always results from infection with viruses notably parainfluenza, influenza, and the respiratory syncytial virus (RSV), which cause extensive inflammatory subglottic oedema involving the larynx, trachea and upper bronchi (laryngo-tracheo-bronchitis), or with the bacterium *haemophilus influenzae b* which causes an acute inflammation and swelling of the epiglottis. It is sometimes possible to distinguish viral croup from the potentially more dangerous bacterial epiglottitis by the clinical findings, but there is considerable overlap, and this distinction is less important than assessing the degree of airway obstruction to determine if the child needs immediate referral to hospital. Referral is indicated if the child appears toxic or has persistent stridor, even at rest. Hoarseness, laboured respiratory effort, refusal to drink, drooling of saliva and refusal to lie down are signs that the patency of the child's airway is severely compromised, and that urgent action is necessary to prevent complete obstruction. Epiglottitis is a particularly dangerous condition as the time course from onset to death may be measured in hours.

Case reports (a) A three-year-old boy complaining of a sore throat was taken to see his family doctor at his morning surgery in a nearby town. The doctor examined the throat and prescribed Erythromycin. The child did not seem particularly ill, an observation that was confirmed by his mother at the fatal accident enquiry, as she felt he was well enough to accompany her on a shopping expedition, before she drove the ten miles to their home before noon. During the journey the boy seemed restless and irritable and began to have noisy breathing. When they got home he was put to bed and his mother prepared lunch for the rest of the family. About an hour later when she went upstairs to see if he would like some lunch he was dead. A necropsy demonstrated a swollen epiglottis obstructing the airway and *haemophilus influenzae b* was cultured from the throat and blood.

Comment This case is unusual in its extremely rapid course. In the absence of stridor at the time of the surgery visit, the family doctor could not possibly have foreseen the tragic outcome, but this case also underlines the importance of treating all cases of stridor extremely seriously because of the potential for airway obstruction with rapidly progressive exhaustion from the greatly increased work of breathing, hypoxaemia, sudden cardio-respiratory arrest and death. Perhaps even more tragic are those children who survive after resuscitation but not before catastrophic brain damage has occurred. Litigation may arise because the risk has not been properly appreciated and there has been failure to take reasonable steps to protect the child from the disastrous consequences of complete airway obstruction. For example, if instead of being monitored under close supervision in an intensive care area the child is placed, perhaps at night, on a general paediatric ward where the hard pressed staff cannot possibly give the close attention necessary, they may miss the warning signs of impending obstruction or even if they identify them, they may not appreciate their significance or be in a position to respond immediately with the appropriate action.

(b) At 7.30 pm an inexperienced doctor, just two days into her post as an SHO in paediatrics, admitted a 15-month-old boy with the history of a few hours' fever and increasing respiratory stridor. On examination the infant was distressed with tachycardia and marked inspiratory stridor. His temperature was 39.5°C, heart rate 150 per minute and respiratory rate 50 per minute. He was admitted to the general paediatric ward with the provisional diagnosis of acute epiglottitis. The SHO deliberately (and correctly) did not examine the throat 'for fear of precipitating respiratory obstruction'. Over the next two hours she set up an intravenous infusion, started an antibiotic (ampicillin) and a cortico-steroid and placed the child in humidified air in an oxygen tent. She took an arterial blood sample and walked to the SCBU (special care baby unit) some distance away to check the blood gases. While there at approximately 9.30 pm she received a call from the ward to tell her that the child had had a cardiac arrest. Resuscitation was unsuccessful and post mortem examination confirmed epiglottitis due to infection with *haemophilus influenzae b*.

Comment In many respects, this young doctor, in spite of her inexperience, did everything right, except perhaps the most important – she did not ensure that the airway was protected. She made the correct diagnosis and she started the correct medical treatment for epiglottitis. It is easy to imagine how distressed she must have been at the tragic outcome. Anyone faced with such a difficult emergency early in a new post deserves our sympathy. Unfortunately, she did not notify her consultant about the admission of this severely ill child; she failed to recognise the potential seriousness of this type of respiratory obstruction, and she did not appreciate how quickly a child, particularly if hypoxaemic, can deteriorate to a state of exhaustion and cardiac arrest. Rather academically, she spent two hours on the initial assessment including X-rays and blood gases, instead of arranging for urgent relief of the obstruction which would have prevented such a calamity. This case also demonstrates the value of ward protocols or practice guidelines for dealing with such emergencies and indicates the necessity for consultants to give their junior doctors clear instructions about contacting them for help, especially during the early stages of an appointment.

27.88 In hospitals that admit severely ill children with airway obstruction it is prudent to devise a consistent policy that involves an agreed team approach to management whereby every child admitted with severe croup is seen in consultation with an anaesthetist and an ENT surgeon. The child's throat should not be examined in the admitting room or on the ward in attempts to see a swollen epiglottis nor should he or she be subjected to any investigations at that stage that might cause disturbance or distress such as X-rays or blood gases. Assessment of the need for early protective endotracheal intubation is the first priority, and if agreed, the child is taken immediately to the operating theatre. With a brief anaesthetic, laryngoscopy will identify the site of obstruction and intubation is performed using a non-cuffed nasotracheal tube. If because of the obstruction, intubation is not possible, the ENT surgeon is then available to proceed to immediate tracheostomy, but in practice this is rarely necessary. Relief of the obstruction brings dramatic relief to the respiratory effort and the child usually goes off to sleep. Other treatment measures before and after intubation include an antibiotic known to be effective against *haemophilus influenzae b*, increased humidification of the inspired air and adequate hydration by intravenous infusion which also provides easy access for other drugs. The inflammatory swelling of epiglottitis usually subsides quickly and extubation may be possible after 24 to 48 hours. In viral croup there may be more extensive subglottic oedema and a longer period of intubation will usually be necessary.

27.89 If the child's condition is relatively good on admission and intubation is not immediately indicated the child must be nursed where a high level of observation and frequent and consistent monitoring of the vital signs can be guaranteed. At least half-hourly observations of alertness, colour, heart and respiratory rates are necessary, associated with less frequent measurements of blood gases and pH which will indicate deterioration or improvement in the first few hours and certainly before the child becomes exhausted. Until it became standard practice to intervene early with protective intubation or tracheostomy there was a significant mortality in severe croup (18 per cent) and in those children who survived some were permanently brain damaged (Battaglia and Lockhart 1975). The mortality in infectious croup is now about 1–2 per cent and in children who reach hospital it should be zero.

27.90 Epiglottitis may occur in older children and adults and can be just as dangerous as a cause of rapidly progressive airway obstruction (McNellis 1985, Gerrish et al 1987).

27.91 Fortunately, it is likely that invasive disease from the encapsulated form of *haemophilus influenzae b* will be greatly reduced following the introduction of an effective vaccine (Hib) from 1 October 1992 (Department of Health 1992). This vaccine is administered as part of the primary course for infants at two, three and four months of age and should protect those most vulnerable (under four years).

Intensive care and assisted ventilation

27.92 A considerable proportion of the claims received by the medical defence societies on behalf of older children relate to failure of provision of intensive monitoring and treatment. Some will result from actual or perceived delays in the recognition that intensive therapy, particularly assisted ventilation, is necessary and some will result from complications that arise during treatment e g accidental ventilator disconnection.

Case report A three-year-old girl was admitted to a district hospital at approximately 6 pm with a two-day history of fever, cough and shortness of breath. On admission she was febrile (T 38.6°C), and dyspnoeic, with a respiratory rate of 60 per minute. Moist crepitations were audible over the lung fields bilaterally. She was thought to have bronchopneumonia and was placed on the children's ward where she was examined by the consultant and his registrar. She was nursed in an oxygen tent and given ampicillin through an intravenous infusion. Blood gases were estimated at approximately 9 pm – pH 6.98, P_aO_2 2.4 kPa and P_aCO_2 18.6 kPa. The medical record did not indicate if this sample was arterial, capillary or venous and there was no record of the ambient oxygen concentration. At about the same time the nursing notes included the statement 'very pale and cyanosed and very distressed with grunting respirations'. The consultant 'did not believe the blood gases', but did not ask for them to be repeated.

The child was visited again by the consultant just after midnight and was noted to be 'restless, cyanosed in oxygen, respiratory rate 80 per minute with intercostal and sternal recessions, heart rate 220 per minute'. No further action was taken. At 7.45 am she had a cardiac arrest, was resuscitated by an anaesthetist and at 9 am she was placed on a respirator. Blood gases were repeated several times throughout the day. The ambient oxygen, times of sampling and sources of sampling were never recorded. At no time did the pH (? of venous blood) rise above 7.00. There was a doctor's clinical note which stated 'the baby remains cyanosed despite being on ventilator', and the nursing notes recorded that 'bradycardia attacks occurred 6 times this afternoon usually coinciding with oxygen cylinder running out or ventilator machine playing up'. At 10 pm, i e approximately 28 hours after admission, she was transferred to a regional paediatric intensive care unit. When she recovered several weeks later it became obvious that she was severely handicapped.

Comment These doctors working in a busy and probably understaffed district hospital simply were out of their depths.They failed to provide adequate care for a child in respiratory failure. This child was in urgent need of assisted ventilation probably from the time of admission but did not get it until she collapsed and was seen by the anaesthetist who responded to the cardiac arrest call. Even after IPPV was introduced she was never adequately ventilated as was clear from the descriptions of her condition in the nursing record. The interpretation of blood gases as an aid to clinical management betrayed considerable ignorance of respiratory patho-physiology. Throughout the child's hospital course the doctors' clinical notes were extremely poor, but the nurses' notes provided ample testimony to the inadequacy of the whole medical performance, the poor state of the hospital's equipment and its unsuitability for caring for children who require intensive care.

27.93 If doctors are unable to provide an appropriate standard of care for a desperately ill child for whatever reason, once the initial resuscitative measures have been taken and the child's condition is reasonably stable, they should make arrangements for transfer to the nearest paediatric facility that can cope with the demands of intensive care.

27.94 In any setting the above case would be indefensible but many do seem to occur against a background of overstressed doctors and nurses working in unsatisfactory conditions and with poor equipment. Whether such problems reflect unacceptable standards of medical care, shortage of resources, simple human error or technical failure they usually lead to catastrophe for the patient with death or grievous disability a frequent outcome. Patients have great expectations of what modern intensive treatment can accomplish and these have been heightened by media exposure and often by over-optimistic predictions by doctors themselves. The reality may be very different.

27.95 When a child dies or is damaged parents may feel betrayed and wonder what went wrong and why. Even in the best hospitals the potential for electronic and mechanical failure and for human errors of judgment by the large numbers of people involved must not be underestimated. In the atmosphere of frenetic activity that characterises an intensive therapy unit, some misunderstandings are almost bound to occur. Occasionally, because they were present, parents will know or suspect that mistakes were made. It is usual for parents to be encouraged to spend as much time as possible at their child's bedside and to become involved in some practical aspects of the care.They may maintain an anxious vigil for hours on end while shifts of nurses come and go. They will become experts on respirators, monitors, drips and tubes and will become sensitive to all the subtle nuances of success or failure. They will develop feelings of ambivalence towards their child and towards the staff, and go through stages of hopefulness and euphoria alternating with helplessness and bleak despair often triggered by the actions and attitudes of the staff. Their feelings of total dependency towards the intensive care unit and the staff, particularly to individual members, will include expressions of gratitude at the one extreme and intense bitterness and anger at the other that may be wrongly focussed and without foundation. The close proximity of anxious parents and their scrutiny of every move can make life extremely difficult for the doctors and nurses involved. They can help themselves and the parents by recognising that support in coping with these stresses is necessary and by encouraging the involvement of others more skilled in counselling, e g the unit social worker or a member of the clergy. The staff of these units also need help and support from time to time. For example, staff 'burnout' is a well-recognised problem in neonatal units (Marshall and Kasman 1980).

27.96 Paying attention to the needs of parents is not only an essential part of being a good paediatrician but may avoid some of the misunderstandings that lead to litigation. Parents particularly appreciate:

(a) *regular contact* with a senior doctor who can provide team leadership, co-ordinate information and be readily available. Parents particularly value a doctor who shows that he cares and who will allow parents the time and the opportunity to express their own feelings;
(b) *consistent information* given frequently in a form that can be readily understood. According to individual circumstances a middle ground should be sought between giving patronising over-simplifications and excessive and confusing details. Parents should be warned of planned changes in treatments and the likely outcomes. Surveys have consistently shown that parents prefer more information than doctors tend to provide (Sharp et al 1992);
(c) *honesty and frankness* at all times. Parents should know all the facts about their child's illness and care and be given realistic expectations about outcome. Doctors must avoid the excessive optimism that raises false expectations or the excessive pessimism that destroys all hope;
(d) *opportunities to ask questions* especially about any misunderstandings that have occurred during the course of treatment.

MEDICO-LEGAL HAZARDS AT ANY AGE

Pharmacological tests

27.97 For years, growth specialists have recognised that insulin-induced hypoglycaemia as a pharmacological test of growth hormone secretion is potentially dangerous especially if carried out by inexperienced staff. Some specialists have given up using this test as safer alternatives are available. Litigation is likely to follow if death or disability results from such a test usually from the profound hypoglycaemia itself or from the complications of cerebral oedema that may occur with the over-energetic use of hyperosmolar glucose solutions. Paediatricians are urged to be more selective in their use of this test and ensure that junior doctors know the course of action to take in the management of severe hypoglycaemia (Shah et al 1992).

Drug disasters

27.98 'The adult may be safely treated as a child, the converse can lead to disaster': William E Ladd.

Children, particularly young infants, are vulnerable to errors in the calculation of drug doses as the complex mechanisms involved in the absorption, distribution, metabolism and excretion of drugs may be relatively immature. Paradoxically, over the age of about four to five months, children metabolise most drugs at greater rates than adults and often require a larger dose per unit weight or surface area. Dosages must be determined precisely and may need to be modified according to the clinical response and blood concentration to avoid the problem of inadequate treatment on the one hand and adverse reactions on the other.

27.99 A number of rules have been devised to help doctors to calculate doses for children but it is far better to learn the correct dose of each drug per unit weight or surface area. If not well known through regular usage or the drug is unfamiliar, the doctor should always check the dose carefully by looking it up either in a current British National Formulary (BNF) or in one of the numerous books on paediatric doses (Insley 1990, Fleming et al 1991).

27.100 Unfortunately, knowing about drugs and having the correct references to hand do not prevent all medication errors. The most serious often result from simple human error or sheer carelessness and may have tragic consequences (Perlstein et al 1979, Koren et al 1986). The most dangerous errors occur in hospital practice where particularly potent drugs are used to treat life-threatening illness. In a series of medication errors reviewed for the first edition of this book, 39 per cent resulted in death and a further 29 per cent caused permanent disability.

27.101 A number of factors contribute to serious drug errors. They include:

(1) the increasing complexity and potency of modern treatments especially for such diseases as acute leukaemia and solid tumours;
(2) staffing patterns that interfere with continuity and consistency of care for both doctors and nurses, e g short-term rotations through specialist units or the necessity for inexperienced doctors to cross-cover for colleagues either because of staff shortages from leave, illness or from the required reduction in junior doctor hours without a commensurate increase in staff;
(3) inappropriate delegation of specialised treatment procedures to relatively junior and inexperienced staff;
(4) physical and emotional exhaustion from working long periods without sleep;
(5) an inadequate or non-existent system of cross-checking of potent drug doses between doctors, between nurses or between doctors and nurses;
(6) persistence in the use of decimals in the calculation of drug doses;
(7) failure to identify certain drugs or substances as particularly dangerous by distinctive labelling and safe storage;
(8) use of the intrathecal route of administration, especially by the inexperienced.

Case reports (a) A SHO was covering an unfamiliar baby ward when a premature infant just recently discharged from the local neonatal unit was admitted in the early hours of the morning in congestive heart failure. The SHO had been on duty continuously for 18 hours. He ordered intramuscular digoxin and calculated (by mental arithmetic) that the first dose for a 3 kg infant should be 0.6 mg. As he crawled into bed exhausted, a nurse from the ward telephoned and asked if he really meant 0.6 mg as she had had to open 3 ampoules and the volume to be given seemed unusually large. Angrily he replied, 'Give it as I ordered'. One hour later he was called to the ward as the baby had suffered a cardiac arrest.

Note This case illustrates the danger of trying to calculate doses using the decimal point when tired. Misplacing the decimal point meant that the infant was given ten times the correct dose of 0.06 mg.

(b) A doctor participating in a GP vocational training scheme was asked to give vincristine to a three-year-old child with acute leukaemia who was attending the outpatient clinic. The doctor had previously been involved with similar children on the paediatric ward when 'lumbar puncture with drugs' was ordered. Without checking the prescription card where the drug had been prescribed correctly she gave vincristine intrathecally instead of intravenously. The child died one week later.

(c) A paediatric registrar asked a nurse to prepare a tray for adding a regular dose of amoxycillin to an intravenous infusion for a six-year-old child with pneumonia. Having checked the label he dissolved the amoxycillin at the bedside using the diluent fluid provided which he assumed to be water for injection. During the infusion the child suddenly collapsed with cardio-respiratory arrest and it was discovered that the 'diluent' was potassium chloride 15 per cent.

(d) A pre-registration house officer on a surgical ward was asked to give penicillin intrathecally to a 15-month-old infant with meningitis. He had no previous experience of meningitis in children but was familiar with the usual doses of penicillin. Accordingly, he gave 300,000 units of benzyl penicillin by intrathecal injection. Almost immediately afterwards the child suffered the first of a series of convulsions, became deeply comatose and, in spite of intensive treatment, died several days later. There was a medical paediatric unit in the same hospital but advice from a paediatrician was not sought until after the intrathecal injection.

Note Giving excessive intrathecal penicillin is an all too common medication error. It is doubtful if this route of administration confers much benefit and *is no longer recommended*. (BNF).

Comment These four cases are typical of the tragic accidents that occur every year. They are usually the result of momentary lapses in due care by otherwise competent doctors. They illustrate some of the problems of inappropriate delegation to inexperienced staff; of doctors working out of their usual field of practice and out of their depths, and emphasise the importance of double-checking all drug orders.

27.102 In November 1991, two junior doctors at a district hospital who gave intrathecal vincristine in error to a 16-year-old-boy were convicted of manslaughter, a verdict which 'confirms the existence of a new and, for doctors, worrying trend – namely, the criminalising of death unintentionally caused by serious medical negligence' (Brahams 1991). Although the prosecution accepted that the two SHOs had not intended to cause harm the charge was that they had acted with criminal recklessness (albeit momentarily). The doctors had been in post only four weeks and could not have been very experienced in the specialised treatments required for acute leukaemia, but the court apparently accepted that they had been given but had ignored warnings about how the drug should be injected. Nevertheless the judge (Owen J) said: 'It seems to me that you could have been helped much more than you were helped. This could have ensured that this particular tragedy never happened.' This case again emphasises the importance of appropriate delegation, especially when specialised treatments are given in a general paediatric ward or outpatient clinic.

27.103 The above case is not very different from the others described except that the doctors involved in the earlier cases were not prosecuted in a criminal court. The 'criminal' case followed one in 1990 in which the conviction on manslaughter charges of two locum anaesthetists 'made English legal history'. If these two cases represent a trend, no doubt others will follow. It is difficult to know when lack of due care or negligence is considered sufficiently heinous to constitute *criminal* negligence, and what mitigating factors might alter the point at which this line is drawn. Brahams recalls the words of Lord Denning uttered nearly forty years ago:

It would be in the highest degree unjust that the hospital board, by getting inexperienced doctors to perform their duties for them, without adequate supervision, should be able to throw all the responsibility on to those doctors as if they were fully experienced practitioners.

27.104 Drug errors in general practice usually occur through careless prescribing. Recent examples include the misreading of badly written and illegible prescriptions when drugs with similar proprietary names but very different actions become confused e g Inderal for Intal or Chlorpromazine for Chloramphenicol; or the prescription of adult strength tablets instead of those designed for children, e g Stemetil 25 mg instead of 5 mg.

27.105 *Writing a prescription* for a child requires particular care:

(a) it should always contain the child's age, a legal requirement under 12 years, and in certain circumstances should also contain the weight and/or surface area;
(b) it should be written in capital letters and in English. Old fashioned symbols, abbreviations and Latin should be avoided;
(c) particular care is necessary with the decimal point. The safest policy is to avoid it altogether. Quantities less than 1 g should be written in milligrams and quantities less than 1 mg should be written in micrograms. 'Micrograms' and 'units' should not be abbreviated (BNF). When decimals are unavoidable, a zero should be written in front of the decimal point when there is no other figure;
(d) the exact dose and the volume required for administration should be stated. If small quantities are prescribed for oral use the preparation is usually diluted by the pharmacist to allow the dose to be delivered in 5 ml, which is relatively easily measured. For infants, smaller volumes may be necessary, e g digoxin elixir can be measured accurately by the mother if she is provided with the appropriate measuring dropper or a 1 ml syringe;
(e) telephoned orders for potent drugs should not be given or accepted.

27.106 The misplaced decimal point is a regular cause of tragic accidents involving drugs. Particularly notorious are digoxin and vincristine, often prescribed as fractions of a milligram. Care should be taken to prescribe these drugs in micrograms, e g 50 micrograms not 0.05 mg. All calculations involving decimals should be done on paper and checked by someone else.

Communication about drugs

27.107 It will be to the doctor's as well as to the child's advantage to inform parents about the drugs prescribed. This information should both reassure and forewarn about possible side-effects. Parents should know the name of the drug and the reason for using it. The doctor should be satisfied that the parents know how to measure the drug and give it safely and how to identify adverse reactions. It is particularly important to warn them about side-effects that will be distressing to the child, eg alopecia. Writing down the drug name with the important points about its use is particularly helpful to parents who may find it difficult to retain these details after their visit.

27.108 A few further guidelines for the safe prescription and administration of drugs for children may be helpful:

(1) develop your own restricted formulary containing perhaps the 50 drugs used most frequently and with which you can become familiar. Only rarely will you need to prescribe other drugs;
(2) wherever possible, only *paediatric* preparations should be issued or kept on nurseries and children's units. Particularly potent and potentially dangerous drugs should be clearly identified and stored separately. For example, potassium chloride should not be stored with infusing fluids and diluents for injection;
(3) if a nurse or pharmacist questions one of your drug orders or prescriptions always check it carefully and accept the query graciously as a sensible precaution in your own as well as your patient's interests (Folli et al 1987). Nurses should question the correctness of doses that require the utilisation of unusually large volumes for injection;
(4) no matter how much you trust a colleague, doctor or nurse, always insist on checking all drugs, including diluent fluids, before injecting or adding to an infusion;
(5) the ordering of complicated drug regimens or the administration of potent drugs should not be delegated to inexperienced staff or student locums without adequate explanation and close supervision;
(6) before injecting penicillins or preparations derived from foreign proteins always exclude a history of drug sensitivity or anaphylaxis;
(7) take special care with intrathecal drugs, especially cytotoxics. Check that your instructions are accurate. Always check the *correct intrathecal dose* carefully and enquire if there is a special preparation for intrathecal use;
(8) remember that some topical preparations eg neomycin spray, may cause severe toxicity (eg deafness) from absorption through raw areas such as burns or if they are used for extended periods. Nursing staff should be issued with clear instructions on when to stop such treatment;
(9) it may be helpful to post warning notices in treatment areas where drugs are prepared and administered – they may just remind the doctor or nurse to think carefully and help to prevent a tragedy (Figure 27.1).

Sudden death

27.109 The death of a child at any time is a tragedy for the family but when it occurs suddenly and totally unexpectedly in a child who seemed perfectly healthy, it is a particularly shattering blow. In addition to the grieving process that follows all such loss, parents, grandparents and sometimes general practitioners and hospital doctors who have had contact with the child may have feelings of guilt and ask themselves if it might have been avoided 'if only' this or that had been done to prevent it.

FIGURE 27.1 EXAMPLE OF A DRUG WARNING NOTICE FOR A TREATMENT AREA

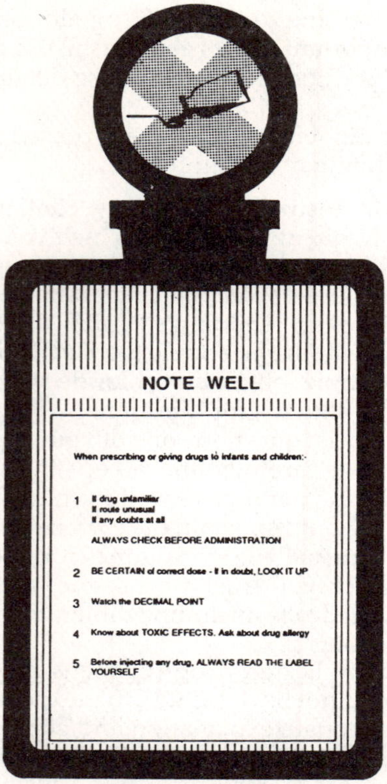

27.110 In older children and young adults death may strike suddenly in those known to have heart abnormalities like aortic valve stenosis, or from previously 'silent' conditions like hypertrophic cardiomyopathy. The doctor may be accused of not providing more information such as giving clear warnings about the risks of physical exercise. For example, it is customary to recommend avoidance of competitive sports for children with severe aortic stenosis, but sudden death may sometimes occur unpredictably, even at rest. It is difficult to steer a middle course between warning parents about potential disasters and thus changing their attitudes to child rearing, perhaps drastically, with detrimental effects on the whole family life, and accepting some risks to ensure that the child's growing up is as normal as possible. Warnings in the form of practical recommendations to parents are reasonable, indeed essential if, as a result, they are made alert to symptoms and signs of impending trouble and will be able to take effective action. It is unreasonable, and even meddlesome to warn parents about the risk of sudden death if little or nothing can be done to prevent it and the warnings are given merely to protect the interests of the doctors.

27.111 Sudden unexpected death in hospital where children are supposed to be under particularly close medical and nursing supervision will almost always raise questions about predictability or prevention. Such deaths can sometimes lead to legal action against the hospital, doctors, or nurses who may be blamed for various failures in allowing such an 'avoidable' death to happen. The death may be an unexpected but possible sequel to the condition for which the child was admitted to hospital or it may be completely unconnected.

Case report A three-month-old boy was being treated in hospital for a mild upper respiratory tract infection with nasal congestion. He had been helped by nasal suction before feeds but at 6 am he seemed normal, was able to suck vigorously and finished his feed within 15 minutes. He was afebrile and it had been planned to send him home later in the day. On passing his cubicle about half an hour after the feed a nurse thought he looked pale and when she investigated she found that he had no respiratory effort and no heart beat. There was a patch of mucousy vomitus on the sheet and some mucous around the nose and mouth. The SHO on the ward immediately started resuscitation by cardiac massage, intubation and IPPV while the cardiac arrest team was summoned. After 20 minutes heart action was restored but it became obvious that he had suffered severe brain damage and he died some hours later. The pathologist found evidence of milk in the infant's lungs and concluded that death was due to 'aspiration of stomach contents'. Subsequently the parents initiated legal action against the hospital for failure to prevent such a disastrous complication.

27.112 The most likely cause of this infant's death was the Sudden Infant Death Syndrome (SIDS), a condition that has become well known to the general public as the usual cause of 'cot death'. It usually occurs at home, during sleep and often at night. Members of the public have every sympathy for shocked and bereaved parents who experience the tragedy of finding their child dead although seeming perfectly well only a short time before, but they do not usually associate such deaths with hospital care where staff are on duty 24 hours a day. It is easy to jump to the conclusion that someone must be at fault, but as SIDS is the commonest cause of death between one month and one year of age (1–2 per 1,000 live births) it is inevitable statistically that it will occur occasionally in hospital and in infants who have been admitted for trivial illness or minor surgical procedures.

27.113 The exact cause (or causes) of SIDS is unknown but there is evidence that the incidence has fallen during the past two years by at least 30 per cent. The reason for this fall is uncertain but, as with SIDS itself, is probably multi-factorial. In part, at least, the fall has been attributed to the recent recommendation that babies should be nursed supine rather than prone. A number of risk factors for SIDS have been identified eg social disadvantage, young mother, smoking mother, low birthweight, need for special care, bottle feeding, etc, and these form the basis for several scoring systems in attempts to predict those babies at greatest risk (Carpenter et al 1977). The value of apnoea monitors in preventing SIDS at home remains uncertain but when infants identified as being at increased risk are admitted to hospital during the first year of life, consideration should be given to the electronic monitoring of heart rate and/or respirations during the hospital stay.

27.114 For all deaths in childhood, but especially for sudden and unexpected deaths, a necropsy is essential and will usually be required by the coroner or fiscal to whom all such deaths must be reported. Not only may a detailed examination remove uncertainty about the exact cause of death but it can provide vital evidence to either side in any legal action that may follow. It may also provide important information for genetic counselling. Ideally, the post mortem examination should be carried out by a pathologist experienced in paediatric pathology. This is particularly important in infant necropsies and the case reported above illustrates one frequent pitfall for inexperienced pathologists, i e attributing deaths to the finding of stomach contents in the infant's lungs. Many infants vomit copiously and often but it is very rare for an otherwise healthy infant with a normal gag reflex to aspirate sufficient to cause death. Aspiration almost always occurs agonally as part of dying when the reflexes are disappearing or absent and is the *result* rather than the cause of death (Knight 1975).

Immunisation

27.115 The control of childhood infectious disease by immunisation is one of the success stories of modern medicine. Enthusiasm for immunisation among doctors and nurses and its ready acceptance by the public is perhaps higher now than for many years yet it remains vulnerable to claims about adverse reactions that tend to get much wider media publicity than any of the success in preventing morbidity and mortality in the childhood population.

27.116 In 1974 a report was published which suggested that pertussis vaccine was responsible for causing brain damage in a number of infants (Kulenkampff et al 1974). Although only pertussis vaccine was thought to be particularly reactogenic there was a severe loss of confidence in immunisation in general. Doctors and nurses felt under considerable pressure to postpone or avoid immunising many infants because of concern about the possible legal consequences of a vaccine reaction, and not surprisingly, the prevalence of whooping cough increased and the uptake of newer vaccines like measles was extremely disappointing (Campbell 1983).

27.117 One problem with primary immunisation is its timing during the early months of infancy, a period of rapid change when the earliest inklings of abnormal development become apparent. It also spans the time of peak incidence of the Sudden Infant Death Syndrome (SIDS), and may coincide with the earliest presentation of various neurological conditions associated with deterioration in development, e g infantile spasms (West's syndrome). Thus many events that will be temporally linked to immunisation are merely unfortunate coincidences.

27.118 With the climate of concern about immunisation that existed in the 1970s it was perhaps inevitable that a number of legal actions were initiated against doctors, usually general practitioners or clinic doctors, because they had administered pertussis vaccine to children who subsequently developed a serious neurological illness. Causation was alleged on the basis of a temporal relationship between the giving of the vaccine and an illness preceding 'brain damage', or apparent delay or deterioration in development. Some of these legal actions were encouraged by success in obtaining limited compensation (up to £20,000) from the vaccine damage compensation scheme. These infants and their families deserve help though it must be said that some of these payments were made on a fairly arbitrary basis and more out of sympathy with the family than from any evidence that immunisation had anything to do with the child's disability. Because of the continuing debate about pertussis vaccine, the National Child Encephalopathy Study (NCES) examined 1,182 children with serious acute neurological illness between 1976 and 1979. (Miller et al 1981). Only 39 had recently been given pertussis vaccine and in many of these, the association between the neurological illness and immunisation could have occurred by chance. Analysis and re-analysis of the results have suggested that the vaccine may very rarely be associated with an acute neurological illness in previously apparently normal children but that most of these children suffered no long-term harm. However, even in this extensive study, the number of cases was too small to show conclusively whether or not the vaccine can cause permanent brain damage.

27.119 These findings are also consistent with two American studies. In one, children who had convulsions or hypotonic/hyporesponsive episodes within 48 hours following DTP (diphtheria-tetanus-pertussis vaccine) did not show any neurological damage or intellectual impairment when reviewed six to seven years later (Barraff et al 1988). In the other, while an association was present between the first febrile convulsion and the scheduled age of giving pertussis vaccine, no relationship could be demonstrated between immunisation and the age of onset of epilepsy (Shields et al 1988).

27.120 Pending litigation in a number of UK cases came to a halt in 1988 when the High Court agreed that there was insufficient evidence to prove that the vaccine can cause brain damage. However, in 1992 the Irish Supreme Court held that Wellcome, the vaccine's manufacturer was liable for the damage suffered in infancy by an infant now 23 years of age and severely handicapped. This judgment may stimulate further moves by lawyers in the UK to mount a new series of cases in the courts. In the last few years public and professional confidence in immunisation has largely been restored and it will be a tragedy if further litigation about pertussis vaccine leads to the kind of emotive and distorted reporting that can lead to many infants remaining unprotected not just from pertussis but from other potentially serious childhood infections.

27.121 Effective new vaccines have been introduced into the routine national programme and the regular surveillance of uptake and adverse reactions has been greatly improved. More positive guidelines from the Department of Health, updated every two years and issued to every doctor have also improved education and communication about immunisation practice (Department of Health 1992). Doctors who are uncertain about the immunisation of children with special problems are also encouraged to seek advice and practical help from special clinics or through a system of local immunisation co-ordinators. The emphasis is on protecting all infants except those with genuine contra indications (probably less than 1 per cent).

When a doctor's immunisation practice is in accordance with the published guidelines and the exercise of reasonable medical judgment, there should be no risk of medico-legal liability if a rare but serious adverse event is associated with immunisation. On the other hand, it is difficult to defend a doctor who immunises a child in the face of a *definite* contra indication and, in my view, a doctor is just as culpable, if he fails, on spurious grounds, to protect a child who subsequently dies or is damaged from the disease that the vaccine is designed to prevent.

27.122 If a serious reaction or illness follows immunisation and could possibly be related to the vaccine it must be thoroughly investigated. The immuniser should have details of the vaccine batch and if the child requires admission to hospital, a detailed record should be kept of the clinical progress. For any infant admitted to hospital, details of any immunisation, particularly in the previous month, should be included in the history, and if a connection to a vaccine is suspected, the immunisation co-ordinator and local laboratory should be contacted to determine the appropriate specimens for confirmation. Suspected adverse reactions must be reported through the 'yellow card' system to the Committee on Safety of Medicines (CSM).

27.123 Vaccines are not inert. They are potent agents that have been thoroughly tested for efficacy and safety before being licensed for routine use. On a balance of benefits and risks, an informed decision about immunisation is taken about the introduction of a vaccine into the national programme. For individual children doctors and parents must take similar informed decisions according to such variables as age, vulnerability to infection, living conditions, current disease patterns, and according to current national guidelines.

27.124 Whether written consent should be required for immunisation is a difficult question to resolve. Some doctors and local authorities have allowed their anxiety about liability and possible legal repercussions to outweigh their primary responsibility to ensure that as many children as possible are protected. They have evolved elaborate consent forms for mothers to sign before each immunisation session. Some of these detail almost all the known hazards of immunisation and are major disincentives to the success of any programme that tries to promote a positive attitude to protection. On reading such forms it is not surprising that many mothers will demur and perhaps think again. The Joint Committee on Vaccination and Immunisation (JCVI), responsible for advising the government on immunisation strategy, does not believe that *written* consent is essential for immunisation and the wording of its guidelines is sensibly flexible (Department of Health 1992):

(i) Consent must always be obtained before immunisation.
(ii) Written consent provides a permanent record, but consent – either written or verbal – is required at the time of each immunisation after the child's fitness and suitability have been established.
(iii) Consent obtained before the occasion upon which a child is brought for immunisation is only an agreement for the child to be included in the immunisation programme.
(iv) The bringing of a child for immunisation after an invitation to attend for this

purpose may be viewed as acceptance that the child may be immunised. When a child is brought for this purpose and fitness and suitability have been established, consent to that immunisation may be implied in the absence of any expressed reservation to the immunisation proceeding at that stage.

(v) Similarly, the attendance of a child at school on the day that the parent/guardian has been advised that the child will be immunised may also be viewed as acceptance that the child may be immunised, in the absence of any reservation expressed to the contrary. However, because of the parent/guardian's legal responsibilities in respect of the child's attendance at school, the possibility that immunisation will be offered should be made clear to the parent/guardian.

(vi) A child under 16 years of age may give consent for immunisation, provided he or she understands fully the benefits and risks involved. However the child should be encouraged to involve a parent/guardian if possible, in the decision.

(vii) Where a child under 16 who fully understands the benefits and risks of the proposed immunisation wishes to refuse the immunisation, that wish should be respected.

(viii) If a child's fitness and suitability cannot be established, immunisation should be deferred.

27.125 The most dangerous (and immediate) adverse event is *anaphylaxis* but, fortunately, this is extremely rare following immunisation. Furthermore, during the period 1978–89, no deaths from this cause were reported. Nevertheless, such events can occur without warning. At each immunisation session, the prudent doctor or nurse will have adrenaline immediately available, and as emphasised in the Department of Health's guidelines: 'All doctors and nurses responsible for immunisation must be familiar with the practical steps necessary to save life following an anaphylactic reaction.'

Child abuse

27.126 Cases involving child abuse have not been frequent sources of medico-legal difficulties for paediatricians. However the incidents in Cleveland, Rochdale and the latest furore in Orkney have brought to public attention some of the problems faced by professionals in attempting to strike a balance between protecting the interests of children and infringing their rights or those of their parents.

27.127 The physical abuse of children has been a well recognised problem for several decades but the Cleveland experience emphasised the need for greater awareness of sexual abuse. Rochdale and Orkney included allegations about other forms of abuse involving black magic and other rituals but these remain unproven and somewhat speculative. In all these unfortunate episodes the media response and the publicity generated by subsequent enquiries can well be counter-productive if they cause paediatricians to be excessively careful in protecting their own positions rather than making their primary responsibility the protection of the child. More usefully, the Cleveland cases also indicated the importance of keeping some of the suspicious physical signs of sexual abuse, such as the notorious anal dilatation test, in their proper perspective and relating them to a detailed history, the child's general health and the views of the many other agencies involved in child care and protection. In other words, it is important to keep an open mind to the evidence until a reasonably complete picture emerges and to be be certain that removing children from their homes is in their interests or for their protection. After Cleveland 28 families sued the health authority and the two paediatricians involved, but these actions were settled out of court.

27.128 In any form of child abuse and neglect whether it be the more obvious non-accidental injury, the difficult areas of neglect and failure to thrive or the always troubling and at times appalling sexual exploitation of children in all its forms, paediatricians must act in close communication and constructive collaboration with the many other individuals and agencies involved including the family doctor, class teacher, social work department, the police and perhaps the NSPCC (or RSSPCC). The child or children's interests must take precedence even if this means occasional threats of legal action and exposure to accusations of professional arrogance and the over-zealous persecution of 'innocent' parents. However the Orkney cases demonstrated that many of the lessons of Cleveland are still being ignored with individual agencies working independently and failing to communicate; with professional workers using flawed interviewing techniques, refusing to keep an open mind to conflicting evidence and taking drastic action without sufficient thought about the consequences for the children or their parents. On the other hand, social workers and doctors are still liable to be blamed if they fail to act speedily enough to remove from their parents' custody children who are then killed or seriously injured. In Cleveland and Orkney basic deficiencies in the methods of handling these difficult problems were cruelly exposed, but until more time and money is invested in adequate training programmes for all kinds of staff, it seems likely that such experiences will be repeated and children will continue to be abused by a system that was designed to protect them (see para **27.131**).

27.129 Like most doctors, paediatricians lack adequate training in forensic skills and it is particularly important that they co-operate with police doctors in the special aspects of the examination and collection of specimens that require corroboration and may provide crucial evidence for court purposes. In July 1987, the British Paediatric Association and the Association of Police Surgeons of Great Britain issued a joint statement on child sexual abuse (British Paediatric Association 1988) which, inter alia, stated:

> As part of the initial full assessment of the child, where there is a need for a forensic examination, there should only be one such examination. It may be appropriate to delay this examination until further information is obtained and the child interviewed. It should be carried out in a paediatric environment by an appropriately trained doctor. There are advantages in a joint consultation being carried out, eg between a paediatrician and an experienced police surgeon.'

27.130 A number of official guidelines on the diagnosis and management of child sexual abuse have been issued (Department of Health and Social Security 1988b). Most Regional Health Authorities or Districts in England and Health Boards in Scotland also expect their staff to conform to local guidelines drawn up by their standing committees on child abuse.

The Children Act 1989

27.131 Called 'the biggest reform of law relating to children in living memory', this Act was implemented from October 1991. It aims to promote and protect the welfare of children and make child law easier to understand. How well it will be implemented remains uncertain as considerable resources, particularly for training, will be necessary to do justice to its laudable aims. While most of its provisions are outside the scope of this chapter, several have relevance to paediatricians who should be aware of the broad principles of the Act particularly as it affects their shared responsibilities with parents, social services and the law in matters affecting child welfare (Cretney 1991, Miles 1991).

27.132 'The principal theme of the Act is partnership – partnership with parents to provide support, care, and services to benefit children' (Tuke 1991). Within the Act child protection is viewed broadly with consideration given not only to child abuse in all its forms, but also to children who are homeless and in the care of local authorities. It is also supposed to protect children from 'professional' or 'agency' abuse, with local authorities having to convince courts that what they have to offer in the way of residential homes or fostering is better than what children would have received had they remained at home. Paediatricians should have a broad understanding of the principles of parental responsibility, a new concept which implies that 'the legal role of parents will change from being based on guardianship – with its proprietorial rights and duties – to being based on responsibility for the child's benefit'.

27.133 There will be an increased need for medical (and psychiatric) assessments to assist the court in deciding about a child's welfare. It is unlikely that a court will reach a decision about what constitutes 'significant harm' to a child without proper expert evaluation. To ensure that the 'whole child' is considered a checklist of factors that a court must take into consideration when making a decision is provided, e g:

(a) the ascertainable wishes and feelings of the child concerned, considered in the light of his or her age and understanding;
(b) the child's physical, emotional and educational needs;
(c) the likely effect of any change in his circumstances;
(d) the child's age, sex and background and any characteristics that the court considers to be relevant;
(e) any harm suffered or at risk of suffering;
(f) how capable is each of his parents, and any other person in relation to whom the court considers the question to be relevant, in meeting the child's needs;
(g) the range of powers available to the court under this Act in the proceedings in question.

27.134 A child is considered to be *in need* if:

(a) he or she is unlikely to achieve or maintain, or to have the opportunity of achieving or maintaining, a reasonable standard of health or development without the provision of services by a local authority;

(b) health or development is likely to be significantly impaired, or furthe: impaired, without the provision of such services;
(c) he or she is disabled.

27.135 In care proceedings a 'guardian ad litem' is to be appointed tc represent the interests of the child unless the court is satisfied that such ε step is not necessary to safeguard the child's interests. In many cases the guardian will also require medical assistance to decide what recommendations should be made to the court.

27.136 *Care orders*: The Act states that compulsory intervention must be fully justified with the demonstration of 'significant harm', essentially a deficit in or detriment to the standard of health, development and well being that can reasonably be expected for the *child in question*.

27.137 The Children Act introduces new protection orders that also have implications for paediatricians. An *emergency protection order* will last for eight days and can be extended only once for a further seven days. It replaces the place of safety order and will be taken out when there is reasonable cause to believe that the child is likely to suffer significant harm if not made 'safe'. There is also a *child assessment order*, which lasts for seven days, under which a court can authorise a health or developmental assessment.

Social Work (Scotland) Act 1968

27.138 The Children Act 1989 does not apply to Scotland, where the legal context of child care is quite distinct from other parts of the UK. The statutory responsibilities for child care derive from the Social Work (Scotland) Act of 1968 under which Local Authority Social Work Departments are charged with enquiring into reports suggesting that a child may be in need of compulsory measures of care and with taking appropriate action to protect the child and promote his or her welfare. This primary responsibility of the Social Work Department does not diminish the role of other agencies (including the health services) and emphasises the need for inter-agency co-operation in the planning and provision of services for a child and family (Scottish Office 1989). Not all cases require compulsory measures of care, but those that do are dealt with by the Reporter to the Children's Panel who occupies a key position within the Children's Hearing system which increasingly deals with children who are the victims of physical or sexual abuse. The reporter, usually a lawyer, examines the case and evaluates the evidence impartially before deciding whether or not to refer the case to a Children's Hearing. At the hearing the child and the parents are able to discuss the issues in question with members of a lay panel which then can decide on appropriate measures of care, subject to the child's and parents' rights of appeal to the Sheriff on either the referral or the decision. In some cases the reporter may place great reliance on the views of a paediatrician. The paediatric assessment may be of fundamental importance in protecting the future welfare of the child so it is essential that reports are accurate, carefully prepared and as complete as possible. Attendance at case conferences, while time-consuming are also an essential feature of inter-agency co-operation. The children's hearing system has the advantage over the courts of handling children's problems in a relatively open, informal, and non-threatening atmosphere but there are flaws, some of which were exposed by the events in Orkney. In a recent report, a series of changes to strengthen the system have been recommended, notably to improve consistency and the training of reporters (Scottish Office 1992).

POINTERS TO PREVENTION OF MEDICAL NEGLIGENCE

27.139

(1) Show by your actions that you care about your patients. Listen carefully and courteously to parents' views and questions, and give them adequate time to express their feelings. Develop 'long antennae' for misunderstandings and unspoken anxieties.

(2) If a *general practitioner*, accede to parents' reasonable requests for a home visit to a sick child particularly an infant, whose condition can deteriorate so quickly. Make your examination as complete as circumstances allow, *and record your findings* – it is difficult to mount a defence if there is no record of a home visit. An infant who is asleep and fully dressed cannot be adequately assessed. Beware of the dangers of telephone diagnoses. All telephone calls from anxious parents should be 'logged'. Receptionists and practice nurses should have guidelines to ensure effective communication between parents and doctor and minimise delays in providing appropriate help.

(3) If a *hospital doctor* make sure that you see a parent or parents at regular intervals during critical illness. Keep them informed about progress. Give explanations and reassurances where due – paediatricians have a duty to share relevant information with the parents. If you do not know the answer to a question, admit it, but take steps to find out. Try not to appear rushed – if you do not have time to listen to parents because of pressing problems elsewhere, say so, but find time later.

(4) If a child is critically ill be as realistic as possible. Avoid raising false hopes on the one hand or destroying all hope on the other – the outcome may surprise you. Explain complicated investigations, procedures and laboratory tests especially if there is a risk of complications. Encourage second opinions and specialist consultations where appropriate – the parents should be confident that everything possible is being done for their child. At any level of seniority do not stray out of your own field of expertise – if anything goes wrong you will not have the support of colleagues.

(5) With your colleagues consider drawing up agreed guidelines to indicate good clinical practice and review them regularly in the light of experience, new scientific knowledge and outcome ('clinical audit'). These guidelines should be robust enough to withstand scrutiny as a competent standard yet not so inflexible as to inhibit reasonable clinical freedom to act in the interests of individual patients. Where scientific uncertainty exists, this should be made clear. Innovative, untried or eccentric treatments should not be used on the basis of clinical 'hunches' but subjected to properly designed and authorised clinical trials.

(6) It is only through delegation with responsibility that junior doctors will grow in experience and judgment. They must be given opportunities to learn but *do not delegate inappropriately to inexperienced staff.* Without adequate explanation and instruction they must not be asked to undertake tasks outwith their experience and competence and they must be supervised until their ability to carry them out is assured. Before a senior doctor delegates a task such as a practical procedure to a junior he or she must be satisfied that the junior doctor is competent to undertake it. Equally a junior doctor should only accept a task if she or he feels able to handle it.

If delegation is inappropriate, the consultant in charge will be considered at least partly liable for any claim for negligence arising out of the actions of the junior staff. Junior doctors must be adequately supported in their work. They should feel that they can call on senior doctors for help easily and without being criticised. Consultants who are difficult to contact or who get upset (and even abusive) when called by a junior have only themselves to blame if they become involved in resulting litigation. When a junior doctor asks a consultant for advice in difficult cases the time and substance of the discussion should be recorded in the clinical notes.

(6) Pay particular heed to a mother's feelings about her child and to the views of the nurses who have more consistent contact with the patient on the ward. They are in a much better position to notice subtle but important changes in the child's condition. In hospital, make a habit of reading the regular reports by the nursing staff.

(7) If a casualty or emergency room doctor, do not be dismissive of a GP's referral diagnosis. The family doctor is likely to know the child and family better than you do so take it seriously until proved otherwise. If admission is requested, but you disagree, check with a more senior colleague and if possible notify the GP before sending the child home.

(8) Take particular care with your clinical notes. They may be taken as a reflection of your style and standards of practice. Remember that the quality of a doctor's defence against allegations of negligence may only be as good as the quality of the *recorded* information. The notes should be written contemporaneously and if it is necessary to add a retrospective clarifying note or addition to the record it should be explained and signed giving time and date. An original entry must not be obliterated. On no account succumb to the temptation to change the record by 'doctoring' it with the benefit of hindsight. Altered records are an increasing problem in medico-legal work (Prosser 1992). They are usually obvious, will raise suspicions of deceit and may be damning not only to your defence but to that of other doctors who are blameless. Changing the record may also get you into difficulties with the General Medical Council:

> A doctor who with intent to deceive, makes an entry in a patient's medical records, knowing it to be false or misleading, or amends an entry by adding or subtracting false information or by deleting genuine information, is deliberately falsifying the case notes. This is unethical and a doctor so doing will be liable, if the matter is reported to the council, to disciplinary proceedings.

(9) *In hospital,* make a point of writing regular progress notes. If a child is seriously ill a clinical note should be written at least once a day and often much more frequently as changes in the child's condition or treatment dictate. Take time to include the important points discussed in conversations with the parents. If going off service and handing over to a colleague, a brief transfer note containing the essential details of management to date and further plans will not only be helpful to your successor but may avoid wasteful duplication and prevent important errors of omission.

(10) *In general practice*, record details of all home visits to a child, otherwise your defence may be compromised and it will be your word against the mother's in court.

(11) Above all, have the right *attitude*. Do not:

(a) treat anxious parents with irritation and condescension;
(b) refuse to visit an acutely ill child at home or in a hospital ward when called by an anxious parent or experienced nurse;
(c) be defensive in response to questions and criticisms;
(d) refuse to talk to parents if a problem or complication is encountered. Face up to it, obtain appropriate consultations and take corrective steps immediately. Tell the truth about what happened without admitting blame or blaming others. It is necessary to admit that there is a problem and to explain what is being done about it. Maintain a caring and supportive attitude even in the face of parental hostility and threats of legal action. Parents recognise that doctors, like other human beings, are imperfect and like anyone else can make mistakes, but they will not forgive attempts to conceal what happened. They may have no wish to bring a law suit unless they sense that this is the only way they are going to discover the truth.

BIBLIOGRAPHICAL REFERENCES

American Academy of Pediatrics, Committee on Infectious Diseases 'Guidelines for prevention of Group B streptococcal (GBS) infection by chemoprophylaxis' (1992) Paediatrics, 90, 775–778.

Ashton N, Ward B, Serpell G 'The role of oxygen in the genesis of retrolental fibroplasia' (1953) British Journal of Ophthalmology 37, 513–520.

Barraff L J, Shields W D 'Infants and children with convulsions and hypotonic/hyporesponsive episodes following DTP immunization: follow-up evaluation' (1988) Paediatrics, 81, 789–794.

Battaglia J D, Lockhart C H 'Management of acute epiglottitis by naso-tracheal intubation' (1975) American Journal of Diseases of Children 129, 334–336.

Begg N 'Reducing mortality from meningococcal disease' (1992) British Medical Journal, 305, 133–134.

Benirschke K 'The placenta in the litigation process' (1990) American Journal of Obstetrics & Gynaecology 162, 1445–1450.

Ben Sira I, Nissenkorn I, Kremer I 'Retinopathy of prematurity' (1988) Surveys of Ophthalmology 33, 1–16.

Bettman J W 'The retinopathy of prematurity: medico-legal aspects' (1985) Survey of Ophthalmology, 29, 371–373.

Boon A 'Medical negligence: a suitable case for treatment' (1988) Lancet, 1, 718–719.

Brahams D 'Explanation and disclosure of risks in the treatment of children' (1986a) Lancet, 1, 925–926.

Brahams D 'A doctor's inexperience is no defence to a claim for negligence' (1986b) Lancet, 1, 1346–1347.

Brahams D 'No obligation to resuscitate a non-viable infant' (1988) Lancet 1, 1176.

Brahams D 'Manslaughter and reckless medical treatment' (1991) Lancet 2, 338, 1198–1199.

British Paediatric Association *Joint statement with working party of the Association of Police Surgeons of Great Britain* (London, British Paediatric Association, 1988).

British Paediatric Association *Guidelines for the ethical conduct of medical research involving children* (London, British Paediatric Association, 1992).

Campbell AGM 'Infants, children and informed consent' (1974) British Medical Journal, 3, 334–338.

Campbell AGM 'Which infants should not receive intensive care?' (1982) Archives of Disease in Childhood, 57, 569–571.

Campbell AGM 'Measles immunisation: Why have we failed?' (1983) Archives of Disease in Childhood, 58, 3–5.

Campbell AGM 'Immunisation for the immunosuppressed child' (1988) Archives of Disease in Childhood, 63, 113–114.

Campbell AGM 'Some ethical issues in neonatal care' In Dunstan G R, Shinebourne E A (eds) *Doctors' Decisions: Ethical conflicts in medical practice* (Oxford, Oxford University Press, 1989).

Campbell K 'Intensive oxygen therapy as a possible cause of retrolental fibroplasia: a clinical approach' (1951) Medical Journal of Australia 2, 48–50.

Carpenter R G, Gardner A, McWeeny P M, Emery J L 'A multistage scoring system for identification of infants at risk of unexpected death' (1977) Archives of Disease in Childhood, 52, 606–612.

Clarke N M P, Clegg J, Al-Chalabi A N 'Ultrasound screening of hips at risk for CDH: failure to reduce the incidence of late cases' (1989) Journal of Bone & Joint Surgery (Br), 71, 9–12.

Cretney S M 'Implications of the Children Act 1989 for paediatric practice' (1991) Archives of Disease in Childhood, 66, 536–541.

Curran W J, Beecher H K 'Experimentation in children: a re-examination of legal ethical principles' (1969) Journal of the American Medical Association 210, 77–83.

Cybulska E 'Tuberculous meningitis' (1988) British Journal of Hospital Medicine, 39, 63–66.

Dar H, Jaffe M 'Dermatoglyphics and palmar crease alterations as indicators of early intrauterine insult in mental retardation' (1983) Developmental Medicine and Child Neurology, 25, 53–59.

Davies J M, Reynolds B M 'The ethics of cardiopulmonary resuscitation II. Medical logistics and the potential for good response' (1992) Archives of Disease in Childhood, 67, 1502–1505

Department of Health & Social Security *Meningococcal infection: meningitis and septicaemia* (London, DHSS, 1988a PL/CMO (88) 2).

Department of Health and Social Security *Diagnosis of child sexual abuse: guidance for doctors* (London, HMSO, 1988b).

Department of Health *Local Research Ethics Committees* (London, DOH, 1991, HSG (91) 5).

Department of Health *Immunisation against Infectious Disease* (London, HMSO, 1992).

Duff R S, Campbell A G M 'On deciding the care of severely handicapped and dying persons: with particular reference to infants' (1976) Paediatrics, 57, 487–493.

Dworkin G 'Legality of consent to non–therapeutic medical research on infants and young children' (1978) Archives of Disease in Childhood, 53, 443–446.

Edwards P J, Hall D M B 'Screening, ethics and the law' (1992) British Medical Journal 305, 267–268.

Fleming P, Speidel B D, Marlow N, Dunn P M *A neonatal vademecum (2nd edn)* (London, Edward Arnold, 1991).

Folli H L, Poole R L, Benitz W E, Russo J C 'Medication error prevention by clinical pharmacists in two children's hospitals' (1987) Paediatrics, 79, 718–722.

Forfar J O, Campbell A G M 'Medicine and the media' (1987) British Medical Journal 295, 659–660.

Freeman J M, Nelson K B 'Intrapartum asphyxia and cerebral palsy' (1988) Paediatrics, 82, 240–249.

Gerrish S P, Jones A S, Watson D M, Wight R G 'Adult epiglottitis' (1987) British Medical Journal, 295, 1183–1184.

Golden G S 'Medico-legal aspects of neurologic problems' (1991) Current Problems in Paediatrics 21, (6), 259–281.

Gray M M, Hann I M, Glass S, Eden O B, Morris Jones P, Stevens R F 'Mortality and morbidity caused by measles in children with malignant disease attending four major treatment centres: a retrospective review' (1987) British Medical Journal, 295, 19–22.

Gutheil T G, Bursztajn H, Brodsky A 'Malpractice prevention through the sharing of uncertainty: informed consent and the therapeutic alliance' (1984) New England Journal of Medicine 311, 49–51.

Hall D M B 'Birth asphyxia and cerebral palsy: Birth asphyxia is hard to define and measure but is rarely the cause of cerebral palsy' (1989) British Medical Journal 299, 279–282.

Illingworth R S 'A paediatrician asks – why is it called birth injury?' (1985) British Journal of Obstetrics and Gynaecology 92, 122–130.

Insley J (ed) *A paediatric vademecum* (London, 12th edn, Edward Arnold, 1990).

Knight B H 'The significance of the postmortem discovery of gastric contents in the air passages' (1975) Forensic Science 6, 229–234.

Koren G, Barzilay Z, Greenwald M 'Ten-fold errors in administration of drug doses: a neglected iatrogenic disease in pediatrics' (1986) Paediatrics, 77, 848–849.

Kulenkampff M, Schwartzman J S, Wilson J 'Neurological complications of pertussis inoculation' (1974) Archives of Disease in Childhood, 49, 46–49.

Lucas A, Morley R, Cole T F 'Adverse neurodevelopmental outcome of moderate neonatal hypoglycaemia' (1988) British Medical Journal 297, 1304–1308.

Lucey J F, Dangman B 'A re-examination of the role of oxygen in retrolental fibroplasia' (1984) Paediatrics 73, 82–96.

McClead R E Jr, Menke J A 'Neonatal iatrogenesis' (1987) Advances in Paediatrics 34, 335–356.

McDonagh A F 'Is bilirubin good for you? (1990) Clinics in Perinatology, 17, 359–369.

McNellis F L 'Medical and legal management of acute adult epiglottitis' (1985) Laryngoscope 95, 125–127.

Marshall R E, Kasman C 'Burnout in the neonatal intensive care unit' (1980) Paediatrics 65, 1161–1165.

Medical Research Council *Responsibility in investigations on human subjects* (London, Medical Research Council, 1963).

Medical Research Council *The ethical conduct of research on children* (London, Medical Research Council, 1991).

Miles M 'Implications of the Children Act for paediatricians' (1991) Archives of Disease in Childhood, 66, 457–458.

Miller D L, Ross E M, Alderslade R, Bellman M H, Rawson N S B 'Pertussis immunisation and serious neurological illness in children' (1981) British Medical Journal, 282, 1595–1599.

Naeye R L, Peters E C 'Antenatal hypoxia and low IQ values' (1987) American Journal of Diseases of Children 141, 50–54.

Nelson K B, Ellenberg J H 'Antecedents of cerebral palsy' (1986) New England Journal of Medicine 315, 81–86.

Nocon J J, Coolman D A 'Perinatal malpractice: risks and prevention' (1987) The Journal of Reproductive Medicine 32, 83–90.

Patz A, Eastman A, Higginbotham D H, Kleh T 'Oxygen studies in retrolental fibroplasia II: the production of microscopic changes of retrolental fibroplasia in experimental animals' (1953) American Journal of Ophthalmology 36, 1511–1522.

Perlstein P H, Callison C, White M, Barnes B, Edwards N K 'Errors in drug computations during newborn intensive care' (1979) American Journal of Diseases of Children 133, 376–379.

Prosser R L 'Alteration of medical records submitted to medico-legal review' (1992) Journal of the American Medical Association, 267, 2630–2631.

Scottish Law Commission *Legal Capacity and Responsibility of Minors and Pupils. A Consultation Document* (Edinburgh, 1985).

Scottish Office *Effective Intervention: child abuse. Guidance on co-operation in Scotland* (HMSO, 1989).

Scottish Office *Reporters to Children's Panels: Their role, function and accountability* (HMSO, 1992).

Shah A, Stanhope R 'Hazards of pharmacological tests of growth hormone secretion in childhood' (1992) British Medical Journal, 304, 173–174.

Sharp M C, Strauss R P, Lorch S C 'Communicating medical bad news: parents' experiences and preferences' (1992) Journal of Paediatrics, 121, 539–546.

Shields W D, Nielson C 'Relationship of pertussis immunization to the onset of neurological disorders: a retrospective epidemiological study' (1988) Journal of Paediatrics 81, 801–805.

Stanley F J, Watson L 'Trends in perinatal mortality and cerebral palsy in Western Australia, 1967 to 1985' (1992) British Medical Journal, 304, 1658–1662.

Steiner H, Neligan G 'Perinatal cardiac arrest: quality of the survivors' (1975) Archives of Disease in Childhood 50, 696–702.

Thomson A, Searle M, Russell G 'Quality of survival after severe birth asphyxia' (1977) Archives of Disease in Childhood 52, 620–626.

Togari H, Oda M, Wada Y 'Mechanism of erroneous Dextrostix readings' (1987) Archives of Disease in Childhood, 62, 408–409.

Towbin A 'Obstetric malpractice litigation: the pathologist's view' (1986) American Journal of Obstetrics & Gynaecology 155, 927–935.

Tuke J 'Doctors and the Children Act' (1991) British Medical Journal, 303, 868–869.

Watchko J F, Oski F A 'Kernicterus in pre-term newborns: past, present and future' (1992) Paediatrics, 90, 707–715.
Weakley D R Jr, Spencer R 'Current concepts in retinopathy of prematurity' (1992) Early Human Development, 30, 121–138.
Wilkins B H, Kalra D 'Comparison of blood glucose test strips in the detection of neonatal hypoglycaemia' (1982) Archives of Disease in Childhood 57, 948–950.

CHAPTER 28

Paediatric neurology

Dr Lewis Rosenbloom *MB FRCP DCH*

SUMMARY

28.1 Paediatric neurology is concerned with the prevention, identification, alleviation and treatment of acute and chronic nervous system disorders throughout infancy, childhood and adolescence. Children's brains are vulnerable to permanent damage and resulting dysfunction as a result of a variety of disease processes that can operate before conception, through pregnancy, around the time of birth and subsequently. The clinical features that result are, alone or in combination and in varying degrees of severity, mental handicap, physical disability, impairment of vision, hearing or other sensory functions, epilepsy and behavioural or emotional disturbance.

28.2 Given the wide range of complex issues related to the definition, recognition and appropriate management of the very large number of medical problems in childhood that comprise paediatric neurology, a degree of selection of relevant material for this chapter is inevitable. When reviewing medico-legal referrals, the most numerous and contentious are those that are concerned with the following issues:

(a) brain damage acquired around the time of birth;
(b) meningitis;
(c) traumatic head injury;
(d) the management of epilepsy;
(e) immunisation procedures;
(f) life expectation.

28.3 Following a general overview of the causes, time of onset and pathologies of childhood neurological disorders therefore, each of these six areas of practice will be examined in some detail.

GENERAL CONSIDERATIONS

28.4 Anatomically, the structures that can be affected in paediatric neurological disease are the brain and its surrounding membranes, ie the meninges, the spinal cord, peripheral nerves and conventionally skeletal muscles. Being in physical continuity they all can be disordered alone or in combination. The time-honoured commitment of the medical profession to distorted Greek and Latin as well as to obscure eponyms is perhaps seen particularly in neurology. As a result terms such as encephalopathy, myelopathy, neuropathy and myopathy whilst strictly speaking meaning no more than disorders of brain, spinal cord, nerve or muscle respectively, frequently also carry implications of a specific disease process in terms of causation, symptoms, cause or outlook. As an example, 'myopathy' when applied to a child implies that he has a mild and non-progressive muscular disorder causing moderate weakness and physical disability. It follows that lawyers cannot assume that Greek and Latin terms can ever be literally translated into English and explanations of their precise meanings should always be requested.

GENETIC TRANSMISSION

28.5 Like all other disease processes, neurological disorders can either be genetically determined or acquired subsequent to conception. There are a number of possible genetic mechanisms including inheritance in dominant, recessive, sex-linked recessive and polygenic fashions by which nervous system disorders can be transmitted and from time to time their recognition is important in medico-legal practice. Moreover, what is described as the new genetics which involves the detailed mapping of genes on their particular chromosomes, identification of the particular protein constituents of individual genes and the likelihood that these can be synthesised leading to the concept of genetic engineering, is not only adding an increasing dimension to our understanding of genetic disorders but has implications also for the qualities of advice and practice offered by specialist clinical genetic services. Dominant inheritance implies that one parent is affected with the disorder possibly in mild or asymptomatic form but can then statistically pass it on conceivably more severely to 50 per cent of his or her offspring. Examples of such neurological conditions are Huntington's chorea, which causes dementia in late adult life, tuberous sclerosis and neurofibromatosis. These latter two are examples of neurocutaneous syndromes in which the common features are skin lesions, epilepsy and mental handicap and more rarely brain and other tumours. It is not infrequent, especially in neurofibromatosis, also called Von Recklinghausen's disease, for the affected parent to have the characteristic skin abnormalities of which the commonest are a number of brown or café-au-lait spots, for the existence of these to be known to the individual doctor but for appropriate warnings and genetic advice not to have been given, with offspring subsequently being more severely affected. This failure to advise could well be considered as constituting an inappropriate standard of practice in some circumstances.

28.6 Recessive inheritance implies that both parents are carriers and that statistically they have a one in four chance of passing the full-blown condition on to their children and a one in two chance of their children also becoming carriers. These genetic defects are usually chemically mediated, for example by deficiency of vital enzymes. Tay-sachs disease is a good historical and current example of a recessive disorder in which affected children rapidly become profoundly handicapped and die in infancy. It is commonest in Ashkenazi Jews and the specific enzyme defect which is that of hexosaminidase A is known. Carriers, who are asymptomatic can be identified and counselled pre-conceptually. It is reasonable to speculate therefore that an appropriate standard of care would be for a doctor with significant numbers of Jewish patients to make this information available to them.

28.7 Conditions inherited in sex-linked recessive fashion are exhibited in males but transmitted and carried by females. Examples are the commonest form of muscular dystrophy eponymously termed Duchenne and haemophilia. Current research is very close to identifying the site of the genetic abnormality in muscular dystrophy and hence the identification of carriers. When this occurs it could reasonably be argued that the failure to identify and counsel female carriers of this condition, thus giving them the option of whether or not to become pregnant, could in particular circumstances again amount to an inappropriate level of care.

28.8 The inheritance of many other conditions is polygenic with a genetic component interacting with environmental factors. In child neurology neural tube defects resulting in the condition commonly known as spina bifida are a good example of this type of disorder and it has recently been demonstrated that the administration of folic acid to women prior to and around the time of conception is a significant prophylactic factor. However, the relevant screening tests for neural tube defects, viz the estimation of alphafetoprotein levels in serum and amniotic fluid and ultrasound studies of the developing fetus, can only be performed after conception. It follows that once a neural tube defect is detected antenatally, therapeutic abortion should be considered and failure to do this on the part of the doctor can rightly be criticised.

28.9 Within this context there is of course the additional and major consideration that the handicapped child or indeed any other individual cannot bring an action in law for having been allowed to be born alive because of the failure of doctors to predict or diagnose that he may have a genetically determined disabling disorder. However, the parents can bring an action in their own right for the financial and emotional consequences of having a child who for whatever reason is unwanted and where appropriate preconceptual or post-conceptual advice has not been given.

ACQUIRED DISORDERS

28.10 Herein lie the vast majority of neurological problems in childhood. Aetiological, i e causative issues, and the clinical features that are produced are usually complex. The nature of the insult to the nervous system, its timing in relation to the patient's age, the regions of the brain that are affected and the limiting effects of treatment on the symptoms all have to be borne in mind when patients present for diagnosis, or in medical negligence cases, for consideration of causation. To make matters worse, more aetiological and clinical issues in neurology are unknown, assumed or just plain guessed at in ignorance than are definitely known or established, given that our understanding of the microstructure and even more so of the chemistry of the brain is in its very earliest stages. It is incumbent upon lawyers therefore to ensure that doctors clarify their degree of certainty when addressing these issues in individual cases.

Intra–uterine causes of neurological disorder

28.11 Following conception and assuming a normal genetic endowment the fetus nevertheless remains vulnerable to a variety of problems. In the first trimester these range from conditions whose nature have been studied in detail, notably rubella (German measles) and cytomegalovirus and the effects of various medications to devastating maldevelopment of unidentified cause. In practice, unless an intra-uterine cause for a child's problem is clearly attributable, there has to be the greatest caution in assuming causation. The Thalidomide saga illustrates this well. Here not only was there in due course ample confirmation of a time relationship between the maternal ingestion of Thalidomide and limb reduction and other deformities in the child, but confirmation came also in due course from animal experiments that the drug was toxic in this way.

28.12 It does not follow, however, that all children born with limb reduction deformities have been affected by Thalidomide or any other drug. One sees in clinical practice one or two children each year born without one or more limbs for which no possible cause can be found in full enquiry. Similarly, while it is a wise precaution in general for women to avoid medication in early pregnancy, the scientific evidence that some incriminated drugs, for example Debendox, actually cause fetal malformations is simply not available.

28.13 While it is good practice therefore to search diligently for the cause of a child's neurological problems which appear to have arisen after conception but before the end of pregnancy, it would be much more common than not for such a cause not to be found and potentially litigious parents are therefore likely to be disappointed.

28.14 Even when a cause is found, for example rubella, intra-uterine treatment of the affected fetus is not normally possible and therapeutic abortion because the fetus is likely to have multiple handicaps becomes the only available option to allowing the pregnancy to proceed. This raises a number of diagnostic, treatment and legal issues. Firstly, immunisation against rubella is possible and indeed with the advent in 1988 of the combined measles, mumps and rubella immunisation procedure (MMR) it is hoped that the whole child population in infancy, rather than only prepubertal girls, will be offered protection against having German measles. The pros and cons of immunisation procedures are discussed presently but the specific point meriting consideration with rubella is the possible assignation of blame if an unprotected woman transmits the condition to her child. What contribution has been made to this tragedy by her parents, she herself, the Department of Health, the local health authority and individual personnel including her doctor and health visitor?

28.15 Again, pregnant women are all screened by blood testing to check their immunity against German measles. Assuming each presents sufficiently early in pregnancy, that the test is taken, is promptly processed and reported, and that note is taken of the result (rather than as has occasionally happened it is filed or misfiled), then if it proves positive appropriate advice, counselling and treatment can be offered. Given the current trend to limit abortion to 20 weeks of gestation or so, major difficulties can arise if for any reason the definitive result of the test is delayed. Whilst such an eventuality is unlikely for rubella testing, it is very much more on the cards for complex testing (involving perhaps an examination of the amniotic fluid) when, for example, chromosomal disorders such as that producing Down's syndrome (mongolism) are being performed. If delay in confirming an abnormal result leads to therapeutic abortion not being available then both the quality of service provision given by the health authority as well as the practice of the individual doctors merit examination.

28.16 Finally, on this issue however, and as has been referred to above, it has to be recalled that a neurologically handicapped child cannot currently bring an action for being born alive, i e for not having been aborted. Should, however, there be future legislation to allow this, it is interesting to speculate on the width of these potential legal flood gates.

The perinatal period

28.17 Indices of national health and of the efficacy of local services include such statistics as the perinatal mortality rate currently in the region of 10 per 1,000 births in the United Kingdom but with significant national and regional variations. Perinatal mortality includes stillbirths and deaths in the first week of neonatal life for whatever reason, and clearly is a very crude statistic. Slightly more refined is perinatal morbidity and within this grouping are included children who have sustained brain damage. There has been much research and even more speculation on the numbers of children who acquire brain damage in the perinatal period, the mechanisms by which they do so, the clinical features that they demonstrate before and immediately after they are born and their long-term symptoms and outlook. All of these have to be seen against a background, firstly, that perinatal morbidity and mortality figures include far more children than those with neurological impairment, for example those with congenital heart disease, and also that neurological abnormalities seen in the perinatal period or later by no means necessarily imply that the underlying brain damage is perinatally determined. This whole area of practice is comprehensively reviewed in Baillière's Clinical Obstetrics and Gynaecology of March 1988.[1] This discusses in detail the literature on antenatal and perinatal causes of handicap.

1 Patel N (ed) 'Antenatal and Perinatal Causes of Handicap' (March 1988) Baillière's Clinical Obstetrics & Gynaecology, 2, 1.

28.18 The hazards for children's immature brains during the later part of pregnancy and the birth period are premature birth, deprivation of oxygen, deprivation of nutrients and trauma. All of these are potentially capable of causing damage to nerve cells directly or by interfering with their blood supply.

Deprivation of nutrients

28.19 This applies particularly during the last trimester of pregnancy. An unsuitable uterine environment due for example to pre-eclampsia (toxaemia of pregnancy) can cause failure of the baby to grow satisfactorily and to be light for his gestational age (LGA). LGA infants have a statistically increased likelihood of having a variety of neurological dysfunctions including cerebral palsy and mental retardation. The evaluation of the cause and possibly prevention of these features in individual cases requires careful consideration by obstetricians and neonatal paediatricians. In general, however, when failure to thrive in utero occurs due to inadequate placental function the development of future function of the brain is largely spared, the evidence for this being preservation of a normal rate of head growth in utero. This is termed asymmetrical intra-uterine growth retardation and can be contrasted with conditions where there is symmetrical intra-uterine growth retardation with restriction of both somatic and head growth. This is frequently a consequence of there having been an adverse intra-uterine environment for whatever reason from very early on in the pregnancy. From the medico-legal view point it is often difficult when there has been intra-uterine growth retardation of whatever degree leading to an infant who is LGA to establish that different obstetric and neonatal management would necessarily have led to a better outcome.

28.20 LGA babies post-natally run the further risk of having symptomatic hypoglycaemia, ie a low blood glucose because they have inadequate liver reserves of glycogen. In such circumstances symptoms such as irritability and convulsions can occur and hypoglycaemia can cause irreversible and profound brain damage. The appropriate neonatal management of an LGA baby includes preventing and if necessary detecting and treating hypoglycaemia at a pre-symptomatic stage. Not to do so amounts to an inappropriate standard of care.

Trauma during pregnancy

28.21 It is generally held that trauma to the mother during pregnancy if sufficiently severe will produce abortion and death of the fetus rather than long-term neurological handicap. This subject has been well reviewed by Crosby as long ago as 1974.[1] Exceptions occur from time to time, however. In such circumstances the trauma will normally produce some degree of placental separation or other damage. It is usual but not invariable in such circumstances for the mother to be symptomatic with abdominal bruising and tenderness and vaginal bleeding and possibly also to be hypotensive. Premature delivery often follows. Alternatively the infant may survive but fail to thrive in utero and although apparently in good condition when eventually born may subsequently show clinical and radiological features consistent with having sustained brain damage at the time of the original injury. Within this context appropriate radiological evidence (see para **28.37**) supporting the timing of the injury needs to be sought.

1 Crosby W M 'Trauma during Pregnancy: Maternal and Fetal Injury' (1974) Obstetrical and Gynaecological Survey 29, 10 (The William & Wilkins Co).

Trauma during delivery

28.22 This has been discussed in detail in the chapters on obstetrics (Chapter 35) and on neonatal paediatrics (Chapter 27). There is no doubt that normal force exercised during delivery can from time to time cause children's brains to be damaged. There is even less doubt that inappropriate force can do the same. In such circumstances, either by causing bleeding in the brain or by direct injury to the brain or nerves, clinical features referable to the area of damage are usually seen immediately if they are sought. A particular example is damage to the brachial plexus, the complex of nerves in the axilla that supplies the arm and hand. When force has to be used to deliver the baby's shoulders, stretching or avulsion injuries can occur leading to a permanent upper limb weakness known as Erb's palsy. It has of course to be an obstetric opinion with regard to whether the force used in delivery was appropriate or otherwise while it is up to the paediatric neurologist or paediatrician to then describe the extent of the damage and give a view on the appropriateness of treatment and the outlook. It has to be borne in mind of course that curative treatment for neurological damage is physiologically impossible. The best that can be hoped for is limitation of resulting disability and methods of accomplishing this are frequently unproven or controversial. Management of Erb's palsy once it has been recognised falls within this category in that although splinting followed by a period of physiotherapy and sometimes orthopaedic surgery are prescribed, the efficacy of these therapeutic approaches has never been established. A less common example of birth trauma is spinal cord damage. This has a clinical association with difficult breech deliveries leading to the birth of a totally flaccid infant. Death or profound disability are the commonest sequelae.

Prematurity

28.23 The risks to babies' brains of being born prematurely increase more or less in exponential fashion in inverse ratio to their maturity. Whilst children can survive from as early as 24 weeks gestation or thereabouts, the immature structure and function of many of their vital organs, for example those concerned with circulation and respiration, produces a cerebral vulnerability that can be manifested by bleeding either into the cerebral ventricles or into the brain substance or both. Many of the complications of prematurity are best managed following good liaison between obstetric and neonatal services and by the infant being nursed in appropriately staffed and resourced special care baby units. Clearly written operational protocols and a high standard of record keeping are common in these specialised units but when brain damage occurs it may nevertheless be extraordinarily difficult to demonstrate, either legally or clinically, that different management would have produced a better result given our limited understanding of the pathogenesis of brain damage and the known vulnerability of the very premature infant. Retinopathy of prematurity (ROP) (see para **27.50** on neonatology) is a good example. Is this caused or contributed to by relative oxygen overdose, if so how much and for how long, and how would the infant have been without oxygen? The simplistic approach that this condition is purely due to oxygen toxicity following a monitored over dosage does not correlate with its continuing infrequent occurrence in premature infants managed and monitored intensively today. The twist in this tale is that all premature infants of around 32–33 weeks post-conceptual age should now be screened by ophthalmologists using the technique known as indirect ophthalmoscopy for the early stages of retinopathy of prematurity as the condition is now very largely treatable at that time.

Hypoxia

28.24 Over and above all other potential causes of brain damage in medical and legal practice, fetal cerebral hypoxia occurring during pregnancy or labour figures most prominently. Obstetric and neonatal aspects of this problem are elsewhere described in detail (see paras **35.16** and **27.30**), but in terms of resulting neurological abnormality need to be summarised at this stage.

28.25 Hypoxia before labour can occur. In such circumstances, deprivation of oxygen supplied to the fetal brain in late pregnancy is likely to be secondary to placental malfunction from whatever cause. When this happens, there is likely to be a relative failure of the infant to have grown normally before birth. In addition it is likely that the infant's head and its enclosed brain will also have failed to grow normally and there is the possibility of established radiological changes of damage in the brain being demonstrable at birth or shortly afterwards. It is also quite likely that the infant will not demonstrate significant neurological or other symptoms at the time of birth, although later a pattern of neurological disability which may be indistinguishable from damage acquired during labour and delivery will be seen.

Hypoxia during labour and delivery

28.26 When this occurs for whatever reason the infant usually will show evidence of this before delivery, around the time of birth and if brain damage has ensued, continuously from then on.[1]

1 Freeman J M and Nelson K B 'Intrapartum Asphyxia and Cerebral Palsy' (1988) Paediatrics 82, 240–249.

28.27 During labour, as described in Chapter 35, evidence of fetal cerebral hypoxia may be adduced by abnormalities of the fetal heart rate, the passage of meconium into the amniotic fluid and by fetal scalp blood sampling which may show both hypoxia and an associated acidosis. It needs to be emphasised most strongly, however, that the likelihood of hypoxia occurring during labour as identified by an obstetrician does not inevitably lead either to neonatal symptoms or to evidence of later damage. Some children's brains undoubtedly have the ability to cope satisfactorily with intra partum hypoxic stress whilst others do not. Given that the methods of recognising, measuring and recording this stress are both indirect and empirical, it should not be surprising that they are of limited predictive value. This subject has been fully reviewed by Gibb and Arulkumaran.[1]

1 Gibb D and Arulkumaran S *Fetal Monitoring in Practice* (Oxford, Butterworth Heinemann, 1992).

28.28 At the time of birth the infant who has suffered intra partum hypoxia is likely to be asphyxiated and hence to have difficulty in establishing independent respiration and circulatory functions. The more prolonged the pre-natal hypoxia and the nearer in time it continues to the moment of birth, the more profound the neonatal asphyxia is likely to be. The conventional method of assessing neonatal status is by means of the Apgar score (see para **27.33**) and there are significant correlations between very low Apgar scores of less than 3 at birth and moderately low Apgar scores of less than 8 continuing beyond the first 20 minutes of life and later neurological dysfunction. There is however far more to the care of asphyxiated newborn infants than merely assessing their status and inappropriate management of respiratory, circulatory or neurological abnormalities in the neonatal period can contribute to or exacerbate brain damage acquired during labour and delivery. It follows that in medical and legal enquiries it is always appropriate to evaluate the standard of neonatal paediatric care even when it is thought that obstetric or midwifery care is primarily at fault.

28.29 Just as the presence of asphyxia in the newborn can strongly support the likelihood of there having been intra partum hypoxia, so also the converse tends to hold true. This is that the absence of significant neonatal asphyxia as evidenced by the Apgar scores and other clinical criteria is a strong pointer against intra partum hypoxia having adversely affected the infant's brain to such degree as to inhibit neurological functioning. In such circumstances, brain damage is not totally excluded but its occurrence is significantly less likely.

28.30 Should deprivation of oxygen prior to birth have caused brain damage then the next series of symptoms are seen in the hours and days following birth. These range in potential severity and are included in the umbrella term of hypoxic ischaemic encephalopathy (HIE). At the extreme end of the spectrum, brain swelling termed cerebral oedema, and bleeding producing intra cerebral or intraventricular haemorrhage can cause coma and convulsions. Floppiness also termed hypotonia, asymmetries or other abnormalities of movement, apathy, irritability, sleep disorders, poor sucking and other feeding difficulties may also be seen. It has to be stressed, however, that the range of symptoms that the infant can demonstrate in the first week or two of life is limited and can be produced by a variety of causes, for example, inborn metabolic errors or congenital malformations in addition to hypoxic brain damage. Their significance therefore is greatest when pre-existing intrapartum hypoxia and neonatal asphyxia have been recognised.

28.31 The next step in the chronological sequence is for affected children to show a variety of neurological abnormalities in infancy and later childhood. The most characteristic finding is that of the spastic quadriplegic form of cerebral palsy. The term cerebral palsy implies that the affected individual has an evolving movement disorder secondary to there being non-progressive damage to the immature brain. 'Spastic' indicates increase in muscle tone so that the limbs appear stiff and quadriplegia signifies involvement of all four limbs. The anatomical basis of spastic cerebral palsy is damage to the motor areas of the cerebral cortex and the pyramidal tracts that lead from them. It would appear that these parts of the brain are particularly vulnerable to perinatal hypoxia and in the absence of spasticity there needs to be considerable caution in linking oxygen deprivation with later neurological symptoms. It needs to be pointed out also that in association with spastic cerebral palsy caused in this way, there are frequently other neurological abnormalities, notably some degree of mental handicap, epilepsy and visual impairment.

28.32 More rarely, however, other abnormalities can occur. These include firstly the dyskinetic or athetoid forms of cerebral palsy in which unwanted or involuntary movements of the head, trunk and limbs producing very poor postural control, dominate the picture. The anatomical basis here is damage to the brain's basal ganglia and extrapyramidal motor system and is more commonly associated with severe jaundice in the neonatal period or a very acute and profound degree of hypoxia late during the course of labour, e g after prolapse of the umbilical cord. Secondly the hemiplegic variety of cerebral palsy can occur as a consequence of intrapartum hypoxia although it is more usually seen when localised cerebral infarction (areas of cell death) occurs in response to a variety of pre-natal and perinatal stresses. Also uncommonly a syndrome of very severe epilepsy associated with severe retardation can follow profound perinatal hypoxia. Affected children also have a spastic quadriplegia although this is not the most obvious finding and has to be elicited on examination.

28.33 By contrast many neurological and developmental abnormalities in children are highly unlikely to be sequelae of perinatal hypoxia. These include isolated mental retardation of mild or severe degree which is not associated with cerebral palsy, epilepsy when it is not associated with mental retardation and cerebral palsy and infantile autism. All of these are nevertheless sometimes associated with minor birth abnormalities, for example, meconium in the amniotic fluid or neonatal feeding difficulties, so that they may be linked in the eyes of parents or lawyers as effect and cause. It is more logical, however, to see affected children having prenatally determined cerebral problems whose first symptoms are manifest around the time of birth.

28.34 It has also to be said that children with spastic quadriplegia, dyskinetic cerebral palsy and severe mental retardation with epilepsy can have their problems for many reasons other than having sustained perinatal hypoxic brain damage. More than just these abnormalities alone is therefore needed before causation can be assumed. Hagberg and Hagberg[1] have recently reviewed the current information that is available in the causes of cerebral palsy based upon their experience in Western Sweden.

1 Hagberg B and Hagberg G in T J David (ed) *Recent Advances in Paediatrics II* (London, Churchill Livingstone, 1993).

28.35 In summary then, hypoxia during labour and delivery can:

(a) be recognised by fetal symptoms, notably cardiac rate abnormalities, meconium in the amniotic fluid and acidaemia;
(b) cause neonatal asphyxia recognised most easily by inadequate respiratory and circulatory function immediately after birth;
(c) cause neonatal neurological symptoms, termed hypoxic ischaemic encephalopathy associated with disturbance of function of other organs and systems;
(d) be responsible for the brain damage that causes cerebral palsy usually in association with other neuro-developmental problems.

28.36 When all four of these stages can be recognised, and when also there can be confidence that other causes of neurological disease, be they genetic, chemical or another, can be excluded, then causation in a medico-legal sense can be reasonably assumed. Difficulties arise when there are missing or contradictory links in the chain of events; in such cases careful evaluation of individual circumstances is essential and they should if necessary, be combined with appropriate chemical, radiological and genetic investigations. So far as radiological investigations are concerned, there is now the ready and increasing availability of cerebral ultrasound, computerised tomographic (CT) scanning and magnetic resonance (MR) scanning. When some or all of these studies have been performed during the neonatal period, they can be particularly helpful in determining the cause of an individual child's brain disorder. Magnetic resonance imaging (and CT scanning to a much lesser degree) can also be helpful when performed in older children in an attempt to look at the cause of neurological dysfunction retrospectively. This subject has been well reviewed by Barkovich and Truwit.[1] Essentially abnormalities of myelination (white matter formation) can be timed to within 2–4 weeks of gestation from approximately 24 weeks of post-conceptual age, until some weeks after term. These radiological abnormalities correlate well with a variety of pathological processes including pre-natal and intrapartum hypoxia. In consequence appropriate brain imaging can either add support to the concept of an infant's brain having been damaged around the time of birth or alternatively, if for example, a subtle brain malformation is demonstrated, or there is an abnormality not consistent with such timing, the possibility can be refuted. Lawyers need to be aware of the availability of these investigations and request that they should be performed if necessary.

1 Barkovich and Truwit C L 'Brain damage from perinatal asphyxia: correlation of MR findings with gestational age' (1990) American Journal of Neuroradiology 11, 1087–1096.

MENINGITIS

28.37 The meninges are the membranous coverings of the brain. Although infections which may be bacterial or viral can primarily affect the brain substance and are then most appropriately termed 'cerebritis', 'cerebral abscess' or 'encephalitis', it is commoner for the primary site of the central nervous system infection to be within the meninges, hence 'meningitis'. The pattern of the resulting disease processes is well described by Volpe.[1]

1 Volpe J J *Bacterial and Fungal Intracranial Infections, Neurology of the Newborn* (2nd edn, Saunders, 1987) pp 596–623.

28.38 Infection causes the meninges to be swollen and to impair their ability to contribute effectively to cerebrospinal fluid (CSF) and blood circulation within the nervous system. Brain function can also be compromised in meningitis by direct spread of the infection from the meninges.

28.39 In general, viral infections causing meningitis have less significance in both the short and long term, than do bacterial ones. This is just as well given the virtual absence of useful antiviral chemotherapeutic agents. It is, however, worth a mention in passing that early recognition of the viral brain infection herpes simplex encephalitis in children is important both because of its mortality and morbidity and also because early treatment with an antiviral agent, Acyclovir, is likely to improve the prognosis.

28.40 By contrast bacterial meningitis is highly likely, not only to cause children to be very seriously ill in the short term and to carry an appreciable risk of death, but also to cause brain damage and long-term neurological sequelae. It follows that its early identification and prompt and appropriate treatment are crucial. Even when these are ideal, however, the nature of the infection is such that there continues to be an appreciable morbidity. Medico-legal evaluation has to take this into account; death or neurological handicap does not necessarily equate with a child having received inappropriate standards of medical care.

28.41 From the clinical viewpoint it is helpful to pay specific attention to the age of the child and to a slightly lesser degree to the nature of the infecting micro-organisms.

The neonatal period and early infancy

28.42 The commonest infecting organisms are E-coli and group B streptococci. Beyond these the same range of pathogenic bacteria that affects older children can also cause illness in the early weeks of postnatal life.

Meningitis in this age group is always preceded or accompanied by septicaemia, ie generalised systemic infection via the circulation. Symptoms initially are usually non-specific. Indeed they may be so dramatic as to be overwhelming in even their earliest stages and this seems to hold true particularly for group B streptococcal infection in small and otherwise vulnerable infants, for example, premature infants who acquire the infection from their mothers' genital tract. It follows that in this age group medical attendants must have an exceedingly low threshold of suspicion and any symptoms at all need careful evaluation. These symptoms include poor feeding, undue sleepiness, irritability and jaundice. Not only are none of these neurological but moreover they are not even typical of infection as seen in the older child. Appropriate medical care at this stage, whether the infant is at home or in hospital consists of a preparedness to visit the child promptly, a full and careful clinical history and examination, a decision whether the child is ill or not, and the request for a more experienced opinion if the child is ill or if there is doubt.

28.43 It cannot be stressed too strongly that to await the development of meningitic or other neurological symptoms in children of this age group is to wait too long; the affected child's best chance of escaping unscathed is for his condition to be confirmed and then treated at the earliest possible moment. It follows therefore that once referred to a hospital paediatric service, if prompt and full examination confirms a cause for anxiety, investigations including taking blood for bacterial culture and lumbar puncture to obtain CSF need to be undertaken equally promptly and if the condition of the child is worrying, immediate antibiotic treatment whilst awaiting the investigation results needs to be commenced.

28.44 What is not known are the specific or statistical chances of a neonate with septicaemia and meningitis surviving with or without residual symptoms. Published series inevitably lump together children treated early and those treated late, nor do they necessarily distinguish between different treatment approaches. All that can be said of the general principle, therefore, is that the more promptly a child receives effective treatment the better his chances and that conversely, once neurological symptoms are demonstrable long-term sequelae are likely even if treatment is then appropriate. The worrying neonates medico-legally are those who, with hindsight, were undoubtedly seriously ill on presentation, but whose symptoms were missed and were ignored by doctors for some hours. A defence might justifiably argue in these circumstances that even though the child received an inappropriate standard of care, that this did not contribute materially to the eventual outcome, the brain damage having occurred by the time the first symptoms were seen.

Older children

28.45 Beyond the early weeks of life, the commonest organisms causing bacterial meningitis are the meningococcus, the pneumococcus and haemophilus influenzae. Others occur but more rarely. As for newborn infants, the most important principle of medical care is that the best chances for full recovery are obtained by early diagnosis and prompt treatment.

28.46 Meningococcal infection carries the additional risk of septicaemia as well as meningitis and the two can co-exist or occur separately. Meningococcal septicaemia is frequently accompanied by extensive and damaging bleeding into the skin and internal organs. It is absolutely vital that when this sign occurs, it is recognised at as early a developing stage as possible; even then it carries a high risk but the mortality rate increases rapidly the longer the infection is established and the bleeding continues. Recommended practice now when a child presents with suspected meningococcal septicaemia is for intravenous antibiotics to be given on presentation.

28.47 With this exception, however, the general rule holds true that the diagnosis of meningitis should always be considered when a doctor is faced with an older infant or young child who is non-specifically unwell, febrile and in whom there are no other abnormal signs to explain the symptoms. This applies particularly when the child appears to be more ill than the symptoms would lead the doctor to expect. The failure to visit or examine a young child in these circumstances is among the commonest reasons why the parents of children who later turn out to have meningitis have recourse to litigation in the first place; only when the child has been promptly examined, when competent notes have been made and when a feasible plan based upon these findings has been decided upon is the doctor likely to have an adequate defence if it turns out that he was mistaken and the child had meningitis after all.

28.48 It follows from this argument that the time to diagnose meningitis in children is before the symptoms become established and localised to the meninges and nervous system. The classical symptoms of a stiff neck which is painful on flexion and due to meningeal irritation, severe headache and vomiting which are due to cerebral oedema causing raised intracranial pressure, drowsiness or other disturbance of consciousness and convulsions which are due either to the raised temperature or extension of the infection from meninges to brain are late in coming. It is not an adequate defence, therefore, for the claim to be made that the typical features of meningitis were sought and not found, and that therefore the diagnosis was excluded in an otherwise ill child. No reasonable body of paediatric opinion would support this approach.

28.49 When these signs are present, however, and they must always be sought, urgent investigations including lumbar puncture and blood cultures are needed. Even whilst awaiting the immediate results of these, and especially if the CSF obtained at lumbar puncture is cloudy, prompt intravenous antibiotic treatment should be commenced. The details of treatment including which antibiotics are used and for how long, vary from case to case but when litigation is involved must always be examined. Difficulties arise medico-legally when neurological sequelae follow acute bacterial meningitis in children. These are common even given prompt and optimal treatment and can range from devastating mental handicap with epilepsy and spasticity to include hydrocephalus with its need for neuro-surgical treatment and to deafness.

28.50 As with newborn infants and those within the first few weeks of life it is both conventional medical wisdom and accepted in litigation that for older children also, early diagnosis and vigorous treatment reduce the risk of late brain damage. Although this probability does indeed hold statistically there can be no doubt that there are individual children who have received irreparable damage before diagnosis and treatment could reasonably have been expected. This appears to happen for example, when severe hearing loss occurs as a complication of pneumococcal meningitis. It is postulated that in such cases a bacterial toxin produced by the infecting organism causes the deafness and it may well not be preventable even by prompt and appropriate treatment.

28.51 Two other issues concerning meningitis merit discussion. The first are the specific problems of tuberculous meningitis (TBM). Although currently uncommon this has never totally disappeared from clinical practice and in numerical terms seems to be over-represented in medical negligence litigation. If unrecognised and untreated, TBM inevitably causes death or severe disability but it differs from acute bacterial meningitis in that the symptoms are frequently insidious and subtle in their early stages being those of unexplained general ill health, with malaise, anorexia and weight loss, rather than being specifically neurological or meningitic. Whether in general or hospital practice it is essential that doctors looking after children keep this condition in mind, ask about any possible history of or contact with tuberculosis, perform the appropriate intradermal screening test for tuberculous infection, arrange for chest X-ray and if need be for lumbar puncture and CSF examination. Failure to consider and exclude this diagnosis can continue for days or even weeks and has no adequate legal defence.

28.52 A more contentious issue relates to the appropriateness or otherwise of the treatment given for children with meningitis and whether the treatment itself contributes to neurological sequelae. Some drugs have recognised side effects, for example streptomycin used historically in tuberculosis meningitis and gentamycin are ototoxic and cause hearing loss. Even when this has occurred, however, these drugs might have been life saving. The fundamental issue in these circumstances is the judgment of the doctor with regard to the suitability of the medication, its dosage and whether all appropriate precautions have been taken; for example, the monitoring of gentamycin blood levels is an essential part of treatment with this antibiotic. One specifically controversial problem is the giving of antibiotics intrathecally, that is, direct into the cerebrospinal fluid at lumbar puncture. The benefits of doing this routinely are uncertain and the dose which must be very small needs careful calculation. Overdosage has been alleged on a number of occasions to have exacerbated a child's long-term neurological problem and it is difficult to defend.

HEAD INJURY

28.53 Trauma to children's brains does not usually occur as a result of medical negligence although children being dropped or falling from their cots onto hard hospital floors and suffering head injuries as a result are not rare. Similarly, and in spite of publicity to the contrary, direct assaults on children by their parents or caretakers is a relatively uncommon cause of brain damage. Instead society most frequently injures the brains of children by involving them either as passengers or as pedestrians in motor vehicle accidents.

28.54 Nevertheless, the relevance of head injury to discussion on medical negligence issues lies in a consideration of the evolution of symptoms in children following cerebral trauma, and in their resulting degree of disability, and is therefore of clear importance for lawyers when considering quantum. The argument can be similarly applied to other causes of brain damage and the range of possible residual symptoms is therefore fully described presently. Given, however, that children who have sustained head injuries are likely to have had a period of normal development previously, evaluation of the functional losses they have sustained is marginally easier than for those who have never been normal.

28.55 Children who receive accidental head injuries and brain damage are not a representative sample of the population. Boys are over-represented, particularly in the age ranges two years to five years, and older than ten years. Similarly, children who are either subject to less supervision than is ideal because of their socio-economic circumstances, or who are inherently more disinhibited and active, are particularly vulnerable. When questions of litigation or compensation arise, it is important to obtain as detailed a picture as possible of the individual's premorbid functioning and of whether this or the parental care he has received has contributed to his disability.

28.56 The immediate effects of the injury next have to be taken into account. Trauma that does not cause unconsciousness or evidence of localised cerebral damage, for example weakness down one side or convulsions, is most unlikely to leave long-term sequelae. Conversely, prolonged unconsciousness, especially when accompanied by the necessity for assisted ventilation, evidence of focal pathology for example as a result of bleeding or a depressed skull fracture, and recurrent convulsions, all carry a more ominous prognosis. Present practice dictates that children who have sustained a significant head injury should not only be intensively managed with general supportive treatment including maintenance of respiration and with specific neuro-surgical procedures where these are indicated, but also that appropriate investigations including CT brain scanning and electroencephalography (EEG) should be performed. Any abnormalities found on these investigations contribute to the assessment of the likely long-term outlook; in essence, a history of coma lasting more than 24 hours and documented brain damage are likely to lead to long-term deficits.

28.57 After recovering consciousness, children pass through a distressing stage of disorientation and disinhibition which generally lasts some days and then more often than not, a period of relatively rapid recovery. During this stage, both parents and medical staff may be unduly optimistic as to the degree of recovery that will be finally obtained as movement, understanding, self-care, speech and emotional reactions all progressively improve. There is evidence that at this stage an integrated rehabilitation programme with teaching, physiotherapy, occupational therapy and speech therapy all contributing is the most effective way of promoting recovery. By contrast there is no evidence, unless the child is actually suffering from epileptic convulsions, that anticonvulsant medication either prevents the emergence of these, or helps in any other way.

28.58 It is in the longer term, however that, more often than not, neurological, learning and emotional difficulties are seen after severe head injury. There is firstly a significant risk of epilepsy which, following penetrating brain injuries, is at least of the order of 5 per cent compared with 1 per cent in the general population. This is a continuing risk, lessening only marginally the longer is the fit-free period after the trauma. Its occurrence cannot be predicted by EEG studies which are likely to be abnormal anyway, nor is prophylaxis with anticonvulsant drugs necessarily effective. In litigation, therefore, the argument could very reasonably be made that there should be a contingency element for the possibility of epilepsy developing when calculating damages.

28.59 Secondly, difficulties with control and speed of movement may occur. These may range from there being frank features of cerebral palsy to more subtle deficits producing clumsiness of gait, mild unsteadiness, asymmetry of performance, or impairment of manipulation. In addition to a formal neurological examination which might not show abnormalities, children should also receive a functional motor evaluation, preferably by an appropriately experienced physiotherapist in order to demonstrate these problems. Their importance is nevertheless self-evident, not only in sports and pastimes but also in speed of performance in writing at school and in later employment opportunities.

28.60 Thirdly, disorders of sensation may be seen. These include a variety of visual problems including unsuspected poor vision, especially if it affects only one eye, and visual field defects which may not have been recognised as such by the child or by his parents. Less commonly there may be defects in sensory appreciation of the limbs so that there can be, for example, a lack of appreciation of body awareness or difficulty in discrimination between different sensations. These abnormalities all have to be deliberately sought by an examiner. Post-traumatic headache is also frequent. Whether its origins lie in a disorganised cerebral vasculature or are psychological is unclear, but the symptom can be long-term and disabling.

28.61 Learning difficulties can also occur. Whilst there may be a general lessening of intellectual capacity, it is more characteristic to find a patchy and uneven cognitive performance which is said to be characteristic of acquired brain damage. Typically there is preservation of a number of previously acquired skills, for example with reading and number work, but with difficulty in acquiring new concepts and with abstract and symbolic thought processes. Serial detailed intellectual and educational assessments of children who have sustained head injuries are essential for educational planning and remediation as well as for evaluating disability for legal reasons. A psychologist with relevant expertise is usually the appropriate professional to undertake this task and he should if need be supplement his findings with details of past and present school reports. The 1981 Education Act, which has included amongst its provisions the obligation of local Education Authorities to prepare statements of children's special educational needs when these exist, may need to be invoked as part of the assessment and remediation provisions. It may be as long as five years before the injured child's pattern of learning and associated range of disabilities can be clarified.

28.62 Emotionally a disconcerting lack of inhibition and social judgment is sometimes seen as a long-time sequel to head injury. So also are labile and unstable emotional reactions, often to relatively trivial incidents. When, as frequently occurs, these behavioural changes are combined with the uneven cognitive profile described above, it is clear that long-term adjustment and achievement are in danger of compromise.

28.63 The variability and to a degree the unpredictability of post traumatic sequelae demonstrated by brain injured children are such that it is really not possible to produce an initial assessment of their nature in individual cases for some two years and the earliest that confident predictions for the longer term can be made is around five years from the time of the original injury. Attempts to come to earlier conclusions tend to underestimate the problems that the children face.

EPILEPSY

28.64 Epilepsy can be defined as recurrent convulsions (synonyms: fits, seizures). Defining convulsions is more difficult but most usefully these can be regarded as paroxysmal and recoverable disturbances of cerebral function, usually but not invariably marked clinically by a temporary disturbance of consciousness or arousal, often with accompanying motor phenomena, and electrically by a disturbance of the electroencephalogram (EEG). The diagnosis of epilepsy is clinical and is not always easy. Management involves accurate diagnosis including where possible, defining why the child is epileptic, i e elucidating the underlying cause or where this cannot be achieved, by identifying the variety of epilepsy affecting the child, i e the specific epileptic syndrome. Within the context of overall management of the epileptic child, careful judgment is required with regard to the pros and cons of anti-convulsant therapy and then of which anti-epileptic drugs (AEDs) to use. Difficulties which may lead to medico-legal evaluation arise when the diagnosis of epilepsy is not made when it should be, or wrongly made when it is not present, when AEDs are used inappropriately producing damaging side effects or poorly controlled epilepsy and when recurrent fits including status epilepticus are held to have produced avoidable brain damage in individual children.

28.65 The nuances of a diagnosis of epilepsy have been fully discussed by Stephenson[1] and up to 20 per cent of children referred as epileptic to specialised clinics are found not to have the diagnosis, sometimes after years of treatment. The potentially disastrous educational and social disadvantages of such incorrect labelling do not require emphasis and in some specific circumstances legal redress may be sought. Conversely situations can arise where unusual attacks which are later demonstrated to be epileptic may be regarded as having other causes, e g simple faints or hysteria and in consequence appropriate investigations and treatment may not be undertaken with deleterious effects upon the child. A related problem occurs on the infrequent occasions when a child's epilepsy is symptomatic of a treatable or progressive brain disorder, eg a brain tumour. Careful clinical judgment is required by paediatricians on how far to investigate recurrent convulsions in order to ensure that such diagnoses are not missed.

1 Stephenson J B P *Fits and Faints, Clinics in Developmental Medicine* (London, MacKeith Press with Blackwell, 1990).

28.66 The range of AEDs available for treating epilepsy is extensive and increasing. All have potential side effects and may interact with one another. The relevant section of the *British National Formulary*[1] is mandatory reading for all prescribers. Nevertheless difficulties have arisen if side effects are not recognised or ignored and if appropriate dosages and drug levels are not maintained especially when drug combinations are being used. Certain AEDs, eg Valproate and Phenytoin are also potentially teratogenic, ie can cause fetal malformations and this needs to be kept in mind when older epileptic girls are being treated.

1 *British National Formulary* (London, British Medical Association, 1992).

28.67 During the course of epileptic convulsions, especially when these are prolonged or continuous (status epilepticus) brain damage can occur due to a variety of factors including hypoxia, impaired cerebral perfusion and changes in brain chemistry. Management involves not only the use of appropriate AEDs but also attention to maintaining the airway, circulation and fluid balance. Paediatric units that treat acutely ill children should have protocols for the management of a variety of life-threatening disorders including status epilepticus. When protocols are not available or not rigorously observed, liability for resulting harm may well lie with those undertaking the treatment.

IMMUNISATION

28.68 Immunisation to promote an individual's immunity against an infectious disease has an honourable history going back to Jenner's use of cowpox as smallpox prophylaxis. We now have mass and, in general, acceptable and successful programmes against diphtheria, tetanus, poliomyelitis, whooping cough, measles, mumps, German measles and tuberculosis. All of these conditions have a significant propensity to kill or cause severe illness and their eradication is an appropriate aim of health policy. It is noteworthy that smallpox has been eradicated in this way.

28.69 Some side-effects to immunisation procedures undoubtedly occur. Most are trivial, consisting of local pain and swelling or a self-limiting febrile episode with malaise and irritability lasting little more than 24 hours. More seriously fatal generalised and encephalopathic reactions to smallpox vaccination are historically documented, so that extrapolation to the possibility of these occurring with other immunisations is understandable. Whether they do so or have done so with pertussis immunisation will be examined presently.

28.70 Prior to that, however, two specific points with regard to whooping cough immunisation require consideration. Firstly, does this immunisation work satisfactorily? In spite of views to the contrary, the clinical and epidemiological evidence produced by the Health Departments' experts on immunisation and vaccination is that it does and that significant protection against contracting the infection is offered. This protection is not complete, however, as some individual children contract the disease even after immunisation and in addition there appear to be organisms other than bacillus pertussis capable of producing a whooping cough variant.

28.71 Secondly, it is relevant that although whooping cough is a serious and prolonged disorder in older infants and children, it is in general only a killing disease and that infrequently in babies of less than six months of age. However, available immunisation procedures do not directly protect this group! Immunisation is commenced at two or three months of age and concludes some months later which is when protection is fully established. The only way to protect the most vulnerable younger infants, therefore, is not to immunise them directly but is to raise the level of immunisation in the community, probably to a level of greater than 90 per cent, so that the reservoirs of children capable of transmitting the infection is reduced to epidemiologically negligible proportions. In other words, protection of the most vulnerable sector of the population can only be accomplished by a satisfactory degree of 'herd immunity' bearing in mind that at the age when most members of the herd are immunised they are unlikely to have been fatally affected by the disease should it be contracted. Reducing the argument to simplistic personal terms 'should parents allow their older infants to be protected against a non-fatal condition when the procedure has an alleged risk of producing permanent brain damage in order to primarily but ultimately protect other parents' younger and more vulnerable children?'

28.72 Clearly this scientific argument can only be advanced if the alleged risk of brain damage can be sustained and quantified and if moreover it can be placed within the context of being lower than the risk of whooping cough itself producing brain damage as an anoxic complication. All that can be said on this last point is that such complications do occur but extremely rarely.

28.73 What then are the risks of whooping cough immunisation producing brain damage? Since the procedure was first commenced in the 1940s there have been very worrying but anecdotal reports of catastrophic and permanent neurological sequelae. The evidence of these has, however, purely been one of time coincidence and a number of typical scenarios can be described. Firstly, many – perhaps the majority – of infants do have a brief systemic reaction to pertussis immunisation with screaming, malaise and fever. This lasts no more than 24 hours. Secondly, in association with the raised temperature some children have brief generalised epileptic convulsions. Again full recovery with no sequelae occurs.

28.74 Thirdly, and more worryingly, within a few hours or days of immunisation a few children have more serious neurological symptoms which are termed encephalopathic and include convulsions, coma, and a particular pattern of childhood epilepsy termed infantile spasms or West's syndrome. Some seem to recover but many never do and become severely handicapped. It has to be said, however, that in spite of all claims to the contrary, no pathological connection has ever been made between whooping cough immunisation and encephalopathy; toxic, allergic and immunological mechanisms have all been postulated but have never been demonstrated either in animal studies or the few children's brains that have been examined. Moreover, epidemiological studies, notably the National Childhood Encephalopathy Study,[1] have not produced compelling evidence that encephalopathies in childhood occur more frequently after immunisation than at other times. Again, and in spite of claims to the contrary, the encephalopathic symptoms that occur in chronological association with immunisation are no different in their pattern or intensity than those which are not.

1 Bellman M H, Ross E M, Miller D L 'Infantile Spasms and Pertussis Immunisation' (1983) Lancet 1031–1034.

28.75 All that can justifiably be claimed therefore is that there is a weight of anecdotal support for immunisation and encephalopathy to be linked in some children. It is particularly unfortunate, however, that this link has been enshrined both in legislation and in current Department of Health guidelines.[1] The relevant legislation is that which currently allows for payments of £20,000 for children who are considered by a Vaccine Damage Board to have been severely brain damaged by immunisation procedures. It would seem that this Board and its advisers accept the principle that a close time association between immunisation and the development of neurological features equals causation, which is a very uncomfortable scientific precedent and proposition.

1 DHSS 'Immunisation against Infectious Disease', Joint Committee on Vaccination and Immunisation (HMSO, 1988).

28.76 Based on this acceptance that immunisation encephalopathies can and do occur, the British Departments of Health have then gone on to postulate that certain pre-existing conditions in children make a brain-damaging reaction to whooping cough immunisation more likely. The most important of these pre-existing conditions are alleged to be overt brain dysfunction manifesting itself as epilepsy or covert brain dysfunction, such as a family history of epilepsy which may show itself eventually in the child. There is no scientific evidence whatsoever to justify this approach[1] and indeed United States' health policy is not to regard pre-existing brain problems as a contraindication to immunisation. Nevertheless, as a result of UK policy many thousands of children each year were denied pertussis prophylaxis until recently when UK guidelines were changed.

1 Miles R N and Hosking G P 'Pertussis: Should We Immunise Neurologically Disabled and Developmentally Delayed Children?' (1983) British Medical Journal 287, 318–319.

28.77 Two clinical questions remain outstanding. Firstly, it cannot be excluded that occasionally and quite idiosyncratically and by some mechanism as yet undetermined, pertussis immunisation can produce a catastrophic encephalopathy. Negative scientific evidence cannot rule out this possibility. Secondly, a situation appears to arise from time to time in which a child reacts adversely and with increasing severity to successive immunisation procedures. For example, immediately after the first whooping cough immunisation there may be a brief episode of fever, irritability and possibly a convulsion followed by full recovery. Then after the second immunisation there may be further convulsions and after the third evidence of irreparable brain damage. In these very rare situations it would be difficult to argue against an unidentified causal connection.

28.78 This then is the present state of the argument. Whooping cough can kill very young infants prior to the age when they are immunised. Their best protection is offered by immunising a very high proportion of older children in the community. No specific brain damage complications with immunisation have ever been convincingly demonstrated but occasionally such idiosyncratic reactions may occur and it just may be that occasional warning of these is obtained by previous reversible reaction to earlier immunisation procedures.

28.79 In these circumstances it would probably be reasonable to take the view that so long as informed consent is given by parents neither the vaccine manufacturers, nor the Department of Health nor local health authorities, nor individual doctors could be held to be liable for any adverse reactions that might occur after immunisation. This should hold true even for infants who have evidence of pre-existing brain damage but possibly not if the individual child had a previous history of an adverse immunisation reaction. Whilst this viewpoint will offer little comfort to the parents of many brain damaged children who blame immunisation, or to their supporting legal and political lobbies, it appears now to have increasing credibility and may signify the forthcoming end of this particular medico-legal issue.

28.80 Other immunisation procedures are occasionally the subject of medico-legal enquiry. This can occur if an immunisation has been omitted following incorrect or inappropriate medical advice with the child not only developing the condition, e g measles, but also a damaging complication, e g measles encephalitis. Latterly too some evidence has accrued that a mild meningitis like disorder can rarely follow measles, mumps and rubella (MMR) immunisation. The specificity, significance and implications of this complication of immunisation have yet to be evaluated.

LIFE EXPECTATION

28.81 Nobody knows how long any individual whether brain damaged or not is going to live. Moreover, although there are actuarial tables for the life expectation of men and women at different ages who are assumed to be healthy, no corresponding estimates are available for those who are brain damaged or ill, although not necessarily suffering from any lethal or progressive condition.

28.82 The vast majority of plaintiffs in paediatric neurological practice fall into this category. Their brain-damaging conditions are usually not remorselessly progressive or lethal in their own right, but are usually regarded as placing the affected individual at some greater or lesser risk of a shortened life span. In determining quantum in individual cases an agreement on how long the child may live is the major determinant of the multiplier to be used and within the limitations that these multipliers produce may therefore be the major factor in calculating the total amount of damages. This holds true even when structured settlements are negotiated.

28.83 Given the absence of relevant life tables, and it would not be possible in any case to have identical or similar tables for children with differing neurological problems, reliance has to be placed firstly on a general consideration of what might be termed the constraining factors on survival in individual children and secondly on survival information available from a variety of research studies.

28.84 The constraining factors on survival of severely handicapped individuals are:

(1) lack of awareness of common dangers;
(2) immobility;
(3) vulnerability to illness;
(4) inability to indicate illness;
(5) respiratory infection;
(6) spinal curvature;
(7) chewing and swallowing difficulties;
(8) epilepsy;
(9) availability of caring adults.

28.85 Many of these are not only self-explanatory but also overlap with one another. Risks are run by the handicapped by a lack of awareness of danger leading to the likelihood of accidents, for example burns. Immobility both leads to an inability of the handicapped person to remove himself from danger and also predisposes to respiratory, renal and skin infections secondary to circulatory stasis. Infections are generally debilitating as well as possibly being life threatening in themselves. This enhanced vulnerability to illness is often exacerbated by dietary inadequacy. Many handicapped children also fail to thrive physically and are anaemic as a result of not having enough calories, protein and iron. Moreover the most handicapped may well be unable to indicate that they are unwell and symptoms may not therefore be recognised until infections and other disease states are well advanced.

28.86 Respiratory infections pose a particular problem. There may well be an inherent difficulty in clearing bronchial secretions as part of the motor handicap of cerebral palsy. Compounding this, especially in older children and adults, there can be a major degree of spinal curvature affecting the thoracic region and reducing ventilatory capacity. If in addition there are significant chewing and swallowing difficulties due to pharyngeal incoordination with the accompanying risk of aspirating food into the trachea and bronchial tree, the risk of dangerous or fatal respiratory infections becomes a continuing hazard. The unsatisfactory diet of the severely handicapped which in these circumstances has to be mashed or blended contributes to their vulnerability.

28.87 Epilepsy, with the risk of death in an isolated convulsion, for example secondary to aspiration or due to status epilepticus, is a continuing hazard also. The incidence of epilepsy in the general population is in the order of 1 per cent but is significantly greater when there is other evidence of brain damage. Even in individuals who have cerebral palsy but are of normal intelligence, or those who have sustained head injury but have had long fit-free periods, there is a continuing risk with about a 5 per cent chance of developing convulsions. This risk increases rapidly for those with a combination of severe mental and physical handicap and there are a few children in this grouping who have many fits each day. Whilst it is generally thought that a fit-free period of five years in people who are not otherwise handicapped signifies a remission of their epilepsy, much caution is needed in applying this figure to those with brain damage. It is wiser to regard them as being at continuous risk and whilst this is likely to be lessened by using anticonvulsant medication it is by no means abolished. Children and adults die from epilepsy even when this is appropriately treated. The risk is low but needs to be taken into account when estimating life expectation.

28.88 Survival in general for children depends on the capacity and competence of their parents to care for them. If a handicapped individual cannot care for himself, then in this respect he is childlike indefinitely. In looking into the future of the brain-damaged child, it is crucial therefore to take a realistic view of whether he or she can live independently as an adult. Parents and many doctors, teachers and therapists frequently have unduly high expectations on this score, especially during the first ten years of life, and medical reports that take a cautious or adverse view on the likelihood of eventual independent living may be the first indication to some parents of this aspect of their child's outlook. Whilst the lack of mobility, blindness, deafness or occasional convulsions are not in themselves a bar to independence, a major impairment of manipulation, serious mental retardation or multiple handicaps usually are. It has to be emphasised also that whilst the brain function of handicapped individuals is limited, their bodies continue to grow. Whilst some remain small and light, the majority attain normal physical size and weight and go through the normal physiological stages of puberty. They are therefore heavier to lift and move and these difficulties are frequently compounded by the development of limb contractures or spinal curvature. At the same time, their parents are getting older and in due course less physically able. It is inevitable that eventually they will be unable to care for their handicapped child. Statistically, in addition, the stress of caring makes parents more likely to have debilitating illnesses or die early. It would seem reasonable therefore to postulate that by the time parents reach around the age of 60 years, either the will or the capacity or both to continue caring for their handicapped offspring will have diminished. This lack of continuity of parental care is likely to be a very major constraint on survival, if only because alternatives are few and far between and because historically survival of the profoundly handicapped in institutions has been for much shorter periods than if they had lived at home.

28.89 Even though careful thought is inevitably given in these circumstances as to where, how and by whom a brain damaged individual will be cared for, it has to be recognised that there is a paucity of provision, that most institutions are now closed and that community care is a euphemism encompassing an inconsistent range of provision needing scrupulous definition in individual cases. It is likely to follow, therefore, that even currently it remains likely that the most profoundly handicapped will remain vulnerable if their parents cannot look after them.

28.90 More research evidence on survival rates is rapidly becoming available.[1,2,3] These studies not only emphasise the very high risk of the order of 10–20 per cent that the most profoundly handicapped and brain damaged have of dying in the first two years of their lives but also lead to the conclusion that the survivors then have an excellent chance of living at least until the age of 20 with a small minority of the population dying each year between the ages of 2 and 21. These studies confirm that immobility, profound mental handicap and a requirement for feeding by tube or gastrostomy very adversely affect the prognosis for survival. These studies do not support the likelihood that epilepsy per se limits life expectation but the British study[3] that makes this point hypothesised that this would not be borne out in more extensive studies.

1 Hunt G M 'Open spina bifida: outcome for a complete cohort treated unselectively into adulthood' (1990) Developmental Medicine and Child Neurology 32, 108–118.
2 Eyman R K et al (1990) 'The life expectancy of profoundly handicapped people with mental retardation' (1990) New England Journal of Medicine 323, 584–589.
3 Evans P M, Evans S J W, Alberman E 'Cerebral palsy: why we must plan for survival' (1990) Archives of Disease in Childhood 65, 1329–1333.

28.91 It would be reasonable to postulate that at the very least there would be very similar figures for the less severely handicapped and this appears to be borne out when individuals with Down's syndrome are studied.[1] These suggest that the majority of affected people survive well into middle age and it would be reasonable to infer similar figures for others with a similar degree of handicap.[2]

1 Baird P A and Sadovnick A E 'Life Expectancy in Down's Syndrome Adults' (1988) Lancet 2, 1354–1356.
2 Balakrishnan T R and Wolf L C 'Life Expectancy of Mentally Retarded Persons in Canadian Institutions' (1976) American Journal of Mental Deficiency 80, 6, 650–662.

28.92 It is against this theoretical background that it would seem reasonable in current practice to offer the following estimates:

(1) for those individuals who are handicapped but mobile and communicating a life expectation of 50–70 years in all can be expected;
(2) for those who have moderate disabilities, ie minimal or limited mobility and some but limited self-care skills so that they are dependent, but nevertheless living with their families, a life expectation of 35–55 years seems reasonable;
(3) for the most profoundly handicapped and dependent who are nevertheless living with their families and reasonably free of life-threatening illness, especially respiratory infections, a life expectation of 20–40 years once the first two years have been survived would again seem likely;
(4) further limitations must be recognised for those profoundly handicapped individuals who are either living in institutional care or require very frequent hospital admissions or other treatment for respiratory infections or status epilepticus or who have physically failed to thrive because of feeding or nutritional difficulties. In these circumstances death is likely to occur in childhood even if the first two years are survived and it is reasonable to estimate a total life expectation of 10–25 years in all.

BIBLIOGRAPHICAL REFERENCES

Baird P A and Sadovnick A E 'Life Expectancy in Down's Syndrome Adults' (1988) Lancet 2, 1354–1356.

Balakrishnan T R and Wolf L C 'Life Expectancy of Mentally Retarded Persons in Canadian Institutions' (1976) American Journal of Mental Deficiency 80, 6, 650–662.

Barkovich and Truwit C L 'Brain damage from perinatal asphyxia: correlation of MR findings with gestational age' (1990) American Journal of Neuroradiology 11, 1087–1096.

Bellman M H, Ross E M, Miller D L 'Infantile Spasms and Pertussis Immunisation' (1983) Lancet 1031–1034.

British National Formulary (London, British Medical Association, 1992).

Crosby W M 'Trauma during pregnancy: Maternal and Fetal Injury' (1974) Obstetrical and Gynaecological Survey 29, 10 (The William & Wilkins Co).

DHSS 'Immunisation against Infectious Disease', Joint Committee on Vaccination and Immunisation (HMSO, 1988).

Evans P M, Evans S J W, Alberman E 'Cerebral palsy: why we must plan for survival' (1990) Archives of Disease in Childhood 65, 1329–1333.

Eyman R K et al (1990) 'The life expectancy of profoundly handicapped people with mental retardation' (1990) New England Journal of Medicine 323, 584–589.

Freeman J M and Nelson K B 'Intrapartum Asphyxia and Cerebral Palsy' (1988) Paediatrics 82, 240–249.

Gibb D and Arulkumaran S *Fetal Monitoring in Practice* (Oxford, Butterworth and Heinemann, 1992).

Hagberg B and Hagberg G in T J David (ed) *Recent Advances in Paediatrics II* (London, Churchill Livingstone, 1993).

Hunt G M 'Open spina bifida: outcome for a complete cohort treated unselectively into adulthood' (1990) Developmental Medicine and Clinical Neurology 32, 108–118.

Miles R N and Hosking G P 'Pertussis: Should We Immunise Neurologically Disabled and Developmentally Delayed Children?' (1983) British Medical Journal 287, 318–319.

Patel N (ed) 'Antenatal and Perinatal Causes of Handicap' (March 1988) Baillière's Clinical Obstetrics & Gynaecology, 2, 1.

Stephenson J B P *Fits and Faints, Clinics in Developmental Medicine* (London, MacKeith Press with Blackwell, 1990).

Volpe J J *Bacterial and Fungal Intracranial Infections, Neurology of the Newborn* (2nd edn, Saunders, 1987) pp 596–623.

CHAPTER 29

Neurology

Dr F B Gibberd *MD FRCP(Lond) FRCP(Ed)*

SUMMARY

INTRODUCTION

29.1 The nervous system and especially the brain is particularly liable to suffer permanent damage even from transient insults. The sensitivity to damage means that neurological problems are frequently encountered in medico-legal practice. However, the insult is often administered through the cardiovascular or respiratory system so that the consequent neurological lesion is a result of a misadventure while the patient was under the care of a doctor other than a neurologist.

29.2 Sumner (1988) found that of 203 medico-legal claims involving neurological damage only 72 were associated with primary neurological disease, the remainder were consequential neurological lesions, usually following anaesthesia or surgery and resulting in diffuse brain damage. This chapter does not consider problems secondary to non-neurological antecedents.

Details of the 72 medico-legal cases with primary neurological disease are shown in Table 29.1 on p 784.

29.3 This chapter is primarily concerned with the roles of the neurologist, neurosurgeon and the general physician. A general practitioner would be expected to refer a patient for specialist advice if he had any doubt about the correct management. However, the division of work between the general physician and the neurologist is not clear in the United Kingdom. Only a proportion of patients with neurological disease can be seen by a neurologist. A consultant trained in general medicine would have passed the examination for the membership of the Royal Colleges of Physicians of the United Kingdom which would indicate a level of knowledge of common neurological problems such that he would be expected to be able to manage the initial care of a patient with neurological disease. If in the judgment of the general physician more specialised help was required then he would refer the patient appropriately. In this chapter it is considered that the patient is under the care of a neurologist or of a general physician who feels that further help from a neurologist is unnecessary.

29.4 A large number of patients are managed by junior medical staff and are rarely seen by the consultant neurologist or physician. It is interesting that Sumner (1988) found, that amongst patients managed in neurological clinics or departments, the vast majority of problems arose in patients who had seen a consultant neurologist. This implies that when junior staff on neurological firms were confronted with difficulties they sought help from their consultant. However, the situation was very different in the general medical clinics when half the problems arose in patients who had not been seen by the consultant. It is therefore clear that in general medical firms the consultant has a responsibility to supervise his junior staff more closely and to impress upon them the importance of seeking help from more senior doctors whenever there is doubt about the diagnosis or management. Neurologists frequently receive referrals from other consultants, usually general physicians. The neurologist has a greater responsibility to ensure that his advice is correct in these circumstances because the referring consultant has indicated his difficulty with the management of the particular patient. In these circumstances the neurologist should investigate more thoroughly than usual especially if he is going to return the patient's care back to the referring consultant.

CONSENT

29.5 In Chapter 12 there is a discussion on the medico-legal aspects of consent. It is important that patients are informed of the risks inherent in an operation even though this may frighten the patient so much that consent is withheld. Obtaining consent from patients with diseases of the brain and cranial nerves needs particular care. Clearly special problems arise if the patient is unconscious. In these circumstances the doctor must do what he feels is best for the patient, if necessary immediately, but he should attempt to obtain consent from the nearest available relative as soon as he can.

29.6 If the patient is conscious and able to communicate but has a disease which could affect brain function and judgment, care must be taken in the process of obtaining consent. It is particularly helpful if a comment is written in the medical notes at the time of obtaining consent saying exactly how the consent was obtained and with whom the discussions occurred so that the consent form alone does not become the only written evidence. When relatives, especially the next-of-kin, can attend the hospital the procedure should be explained to both the relatives and the patient, preferably together, so that they come to a consensus agreement amongst themselves to accept or refuse the procedure. If there is disagreement between the relatives of the patient, or no relatives are available it becomes more necessary for the doctor to decide to what degree the patient's brain disease is affecting his judgment. If there is doubt in the opinion of the consultant then it is necessary to get further advice, usually from a psychiatrist. If a patient is unable to make rational judgments and his illness is so detrimental to his health that a procedure must be carried out for his benefit then the circumstances may be covered by relevant portions of the Mental Health Act and a psychiatric opinion is mandatory. If the patient is covered by the Mental Health Act the psychiatrist can take the necessary action. If the psychiatrist feels that the use of the Mental Health Act is not appropriate and the patient refuses consent after the doctors have on more than one occasion explained the situation then the doctor should accept the patient's decision but feel that he has been through a process which would protect him from an accusation of negligence. This should all be recorded in the notes with the names of all concerned and any relevant witnesses.

CHRONIC NEUROLOGICAL CONDITIONS

29.7 Chronic neurological conditions which affect brain function and judgment can have medico-legal implications which occur independently of the immediate medical management. For example, it may be necessary for a doctor to give an opinion in a divorce case concerning the difficulties the patient may have looking after a child without the help of a spouse. A patient's competence to make a valid will may be challenged in court after the patient's death and the doctor asked for an opinion about the patient's health when the will was made even though the doctor was unaware that the patient was making a will. A doctor must keep careful records so that if medico-legal queries arise he has available evidence which will help the court to accept the doctor's opinion.

INVASIVE PROCEDURES

29.8 An invasive procedure is one in which something is done to the patient which may alter his health status, whether this is intended or not. An operation is obviously invasive, but so is putting in a needle to take blood as complications might just occur. Putting pads on the chest to record an electrocardiogram would not be invasive. However the distinction between a very mildly invasive procedure and a complex non-invasive procedure is not always clear.

29.9 Invasive procedures can be therapeutic or diagnostic. Therapeutic procedures are performed because the procedure itself could help the patient and therefore the possible advantages can be judged against the potential risks. Diagnostic procedures give no direct benefit and therefore the risks are relatively more important. The benefits to the patient are indirect and will only materialise if the procedure reveals a disorder which can be treated subsequently. Angiography and myelography have been associated with medico-legal consequences. Therefore in assessing diagnostic procedures one should consider the subsequent possible therapeutic management. Given the risks involved it would be difficult to justify any diagnostic invasive procedure if no possible therapeutic advantage is foreseen. When deciding to do diagnostic invasive procedures one should consider the later management of the illness. This would include considering the management if the test was normal. For example, if a low spinal canal lesion is suspected but not certain it may be inadequate just to ask for a radiculogram because if the radiologist did only that and the result was normal the neurologist might then wish that the injected contrast had been screened to a higher level. Therefore the neurologist should consider asking for the contrast to be screened to the foramen magnum if there is the possibility of a lesion above the area thought to be the most likely site. Of course the neurologist would have to consider whether the general condition of the patient warranted the increased discomfort and problems that a wider screening would entail.

29.10 Before an invasive diagnostic procedure, the possible findings and subsequent treatments should be explained to the patient and relatives. The possible future treatment should be taken into account when the decision to perform a procedure is made. If the patient signified that he would not wish to undertake any of the possible treatments that would be a reason for not doing the diagnostic procedure. It would not be an absolute contra-indication because one never knows exactly what the test will show and the patient may change his mind. It would be wrong to hold a patient to his opinion given before all the evidence was available.

29.11 Occasionally one does invasive diagnostic procedures not because they could lead to treatment but in order to confirm a diagnosis, give a prognosis and advise the patient about the future. This is particularly true for chronic life-long illnesses when further information about the illness could help the patient plan his future life more rationally.

29.12 Invasive diagnostic procedures in neurology are becoming safer and less necessary and unfortunate complications are likely to be less frequent in the future. Air encephalography is almost obsolete since the introduction of Computerised Tomographic (CT) Scanning and Nuclear Magnetic Resonance (NMR) also called Magnetic Resonance Imaging (MRI).

29.13 Angiograms have become safer with the use of Digital Subtraction Angiography (DSA). First because intravenous injections which have a much lower morbidity can often be used, rather than intra-arterial injections. Second because the amount of contrast needed for each run of images is less than with the older methods of angiography. Myelography has also improved with the introduction of safer contrast media and the use of concomitant CT scanning.

29.14 Unfortunately all these procedures are not universally and quickly available and therefore a possible medico-legal problem would arise if the doctor is accused of not doing a test, the availability of which presents difficulties. It is the duty of the doctor to decide if the test is indicated whether or not it is available. If it is not available to him that would be a reason to refer the patient to a unit where the test could be done. This solution is not always practicable as the services of the local specialist unit could become overloaded if the demand exceeded the service capacity. The consultant then has the responsibility to bring to the notice of management either in his hospital, district or region the inadequacy of the facilities available to him. The availability of tests is not the only criterion as some may be more quickly available; for example, a doctor may advise a myelogram this week rather than a NMR next month.

29.15 In the future it is more likely that a doctor will be accused of not having done a 'necessary' diagnostic procedure rather than that he will be accused of inducing patient morbidity by performing a test – the reverse of what was happening in the past.

EPILEPSY

29.16 Epilepsy has very important social and legal consequences and is a frequent source of problems to neurologists.

29.17 Epilepsy can be manifest in so many ways and is so relatively common that it is surprising that it does not lead to even more medico-legal problems. Very often general physicians and cardiologists refer patients to neurologists because of some transient phenomenon. The neurologist needs to consider the possibility that the symptoms which may suggest neurological disease could be evidence of heart, vascular, psychiatric or other disease. It is important that the consultant neurologist has good communications with his colleagues.

Diagnosis

29.18 The diagnosis of epilepsy can be considered in two ways. First the episode itself; was it epileptic? Second has the patient got a continuing tendency to epilepsy and what is the underlying cause?

29.19 There is no difficulty in diagnosing epilepsy when the patient has had many typical grand mal fits but the diagnosis of a single episode or few episodes not obviously epileptic can be difficult. Epileptic attacks need to be distinguished from other causes of loss of consciousness or changed awareness and from psychiatric disorders. The neurologist cannot be expected to make a diagnosis if the evidence is inadequate but he does have a duty to seek out the evidence. Clearly if he or a trained observer has witnessed an attack then the diagnosis is easier, but may still be difficult. The doctor could be accused of negligence if he does not take all the information which the patient can remember about the episode including its immediate antecedents and subsequent situation. The doctor should never accept from the patient: 'I can remember nothing.' A careful history of what the patient remembers prior to the 'I can remember nothing' will often help to distinguish epilepsy from hysterical hyperventilation, syncope, hypoglycaemia etc. If the patient's attacks continue the patient should be told to write down what is remembered as soon as possible after the attack. Also the patient should ask witnesses to record the attack. It is important to stress to the patient that diagnosing an event which occurred in the past and which has left no obvious sequelae depends to a major extent on the evidence that the patient produces. It is the responsibility of the patient to help produce that evidence and not to feel the doctor should be able to produce the diagnosis without any help.

29.20 An Electroencephalogram (EEG) may be helpful but if it is done when the patient is not having an attack, a negative result does not exclude epilepsy. Similarly an EEG with epileptic features does not prove epilepsy but will make the diagnosis more likely. Several normal prolonged EEGs make the diagnosis increasingly unlikely, especially if the patient has had several attacks and the EEG was taken under circumstances similar to those when previous attacks had occurred (eg fasting). A normal EEG during a major attack demonstrates that the attack during the EEG was not epileptic but does not prove that all the previous attacks were not epileptic. Careful EEG assessment is helpful and the neurologist should seek help of a neurophysiologist when necessary. The neurologist may receive a report from an EEG technician and although this can be very helpful the neurologist should realise that he, not the technician, will take responsibility for any action which follows that opinion. If the neurologist wants a professional opinion a neurophysiologist's report should be requested.

29.21 The diagnosis of epilepsy can be confused with psychiatric disease. Hysteria may be wrongly diagnosed. Epilepsy should be considered as a differential diagnosis if the psychiatric abnormality is paroxysmal (Plesner, Munk-Andersen & Luhdorf 1987).

29.22 Diagnosing a previous attack as epileptic does not mean that there is a continuing tendency to epilepsy. The cause of the epilepsy must be found in order to give the best advice. Epilepsy of late onset may be due to an underlying lesion but a doctor's duty to diagnose such a cause does not end if he carries out all the tests and they are negative at the time of the first epileptic fit; an underlying lesion may be so small that it is not seen on a CT scan. Therefore a doctor should ensure an adequate follow-up of the patient either by seeing the patient at intervals or by asking the general practitioner to be responsible.

Management

29.23 The commonest complaint by patients with epilepsy is that their epilepsy has been improperly managed. None of the anti-epileptic treatments can be guaranteed to be successful and all of the treatments have unwanted effects. Compliance by the patient in taking his medication correctly is often poor. The neurologist has a duty not only to prescribe the treatment but also to monitor its effect and help the patient to achieve maximum benefit. Confusion often arises because both the hospital doctors and the general practitioner may independently and at different times prescribe treatment. It is therefore advisable for the medication always to come from one source and for that source to be responsible for monitoring. If the attacks are well controlled and there are no problems this can be done by a general practitioner, especially if he has access to a laboratory where blood levels of the anticonvulsant can be measured. However for more difficult situations a neurological clinic, preferably one specialising in epilepsy, would be better. There are insufficient facilities and it is unnecessary for all patients with epilepsy to attend a clinic specialising in epilepsy.

Information for the patient

29.24 The problems associated with epilepsy and its management go beyond the narrow medical care of the patient. A doctor has a duty to inform the patient of the diagnosis and its implications. This is important for many reasons, in particular:

Social

29.25 The doctor should help and advise the patient to overcome any prejudice associated with the diagnosis of epilepsy. A patient will often need information or advice about the relationship between his epilepsy and his work and his social life.

Fetal abnormalities

29.26 The incidence of fetal abnormality is greater when the mother has epilepsy and is on anticonvulsants than when the mother is healthy. The various anticonvulsants probably have different risks of inducing fetal abnormalities. Although the role of the anticonvulsant drugs may be small and fetal abnormalities relatively uncommon, if a fetal abnormality does occur in a baby whose mother was taking anticonvulsants the anticonvulsants may be blamed. It is therefore necessary to inform women of childbearing age of this risk and for the doctor to make a judgment as to whether anticonvulsant drugs should be continued before conception and during pregnancy and if so which ones.

29.27 Some other neurological diseases are directly due to genetic abnormalities and many have a genetic component in their aetiology. For epilepsy genetic factors are only partially responsible but the doctor still has a duty to inform his patients of this especially when the patient may become a parent. If genetic counselling may be required the neurologist should seek further advice, sooner rather than later.

Contraceptives

29.28 Anticonvulsant drugs can reduce the efficacy of the contraceptive pill and the patient should be advised not to take a 'low dose' pill and to get advice from the doctor supervising her contraceptive regime.

Driving

29.29 Patients who have had an attack of epilepsy should never drive unless the Driver and Vehicle Licensing Agency (DVLA) having considered the circumstances grants a licence or allows a valid driving licence to continue. It is possible that the laws for driving licences will be changed in order to achieve a more uniform policy throughout the EC, but at the present time the exact wording of the regulations used by the DVLA is:

Epilepsy is prescribed for the purpose of section 87(3)(b) of the 1972 Act (Road Traffic Act) [Section 92(4)(b) of the 1988 Road Traffic Act] and an applicant for a licence suffering from epilepsy shall satisfy the conditions that

(a) he shall have been free from any epileptic attack during the period of two years immediately preceding the date when the licence is to have effect; or
(b) in the case of an applicant who has had such attacks whilst asleep during that period, he shall have had such attacks only whilst asleep during a period of at least three years immediately preceding the date when the licence is to have effect; and
(c) the driving of a vehicle by him in pursuance of the licence is not likely to be a source of danger to the public.

As the regulations are liable to be changed a neurologist should make himself conversant with the current regulations. The regulations for a heavy goods vehicle licence or a public service vehicle licence are stricter.

29.30 If the doctor believes that it is unsafe for the patient to drive he should inform the patient so. Quite apart from the medical opinion about the fitness to drive there are legal aspects.

29.31 On the older United Kingdom driving licence there is written: 'You are required by law to inform the DVLA Swansea SA99 1AT at once if you have any disability which is or may become likely to affect your fitness as a driver unless you do not expect it to last for more than 3 months.'

29.32 On the newer licences the wording is slightly different: 'Drivers Medical Branch, Swansea SA99 1TU must be told at once if you now have any physical or mental disability or condition which affects your fitness as a driver or which might do so in the future (you need not tell the DVLA if the effect of the disability or condition is not expected to last more than 3 months) or you come to know in the future that you have such a disability or condition.'

29.33 This is a requirement laid on all drivers whatever a doctor may say or advise. The doctor does have a responsibility to tell the patient that his epilepsy is something which may affect his fitness to drive. If more than one attack has occurred then the caveat 'more than 3 months' cannot be reasonably used as a reason for not informing the DVLA. Whether the attacks were definitely epileptic is not really relevant as the patient should inform the DVLA of 'any disability', not just epilepsy. The patient has the entire responsibility to inform the DVLA, but the doctor does have a duty to draw the patient's attention to his responsibility. A problem arises if the patient does not inform the DVLA. The DVLA had a form, CLE678, which did make it easier for the patient. The form was simple and said – 'I wish to notify the Driver and Vehicle Licensing Agency that I have a medical condition', followed by the patient's signature, name and address and driver number (if known) or date of birth. Unfortunately this form is no longer available but a patient could write a similar letter himself without using a form. The decision as to whether the licence should be withdrawn is not the doctor's as he can only advise the patient but in many instances he will advise the patient not to drive whilst awaiting the DVLA decision. When the patient has informed the DVLA the patient will be sent a form asking for more details including the names of doctors, who will then be approached by the DVLA. The doctor's report should state the facts and evidence he knows.

29.34 Although the patient will have given signed consent for the doctor to write to the DVLA it is usually helpful for the doctor to show the patient the report.

29.35 The procedure of informing the DVLA should be followed even if the patient stops driving because the requirement to inform the DVLA is independent of whether the patient is actually driving.

29.36 Problems occur when the patient refuses to inform the DVLA and continues driving and the doctor considers he should not be driving. Although the doctor has a duty of confidentiality he still has a duty to the patient to encourage and persuade him to comply with the law. In these circumstances the doctor should protect himself from subsequently being told by the patient that he had not discussed the matter with him. He should make a clear note in the patient's notes about the discussion and write to the general practitioner asking him to try and persuade the patient to stop driving and to tell the DVLA. There is no reason why a relative should not write to the DVLA telling them the patient has an illness that might affect driving. If one considers that the patient's behaviour is psychotic a psychiatric referral is necessary. It has been argued by some that doctors have a duty to inform the authorities, especially when a Public Service Vehicle licence, train driving or flying is concerned, but the correct action in individual cases can be difficult.

29.37 It is essential that the doctor reiterates his advice at every opportunity and records it each time. Only by doing this can the doctor easily justify his position if there is a subsequent accident with serious consequences.

SPACE OCCUPYING LESION

29.38 The commonest medico-legal problem in this category results from delay in diagnosis; the subsequent management is rarely a problem. Early cases of subdural haematoma or a glioma can be very difficult to diagnose and it is not negligent to be unable to reach a diagnosis at the initial consultation. However it is important to consider this diagnosis even if it is only a remote possibility as it might be in the case of a patient with a single attack of epilepsy. With modern CT scanning a moderate sized tumour or subdural haematoma will be demonstrated but this does not follow for small lesions which can be missed. The injection of contrast material during the radiology increases the sensitivity of the test but does not make it fully reliable. In the absence of definite focal signs a normal CT scan may occur in the early stages of a lesion and therefore follow-up is important (Bouchez, Assaker, Hautefeuille, Combelles, Arnott 1986). CT scans may not be quickly available and it can be important to judge the best time to do the scan. A deterioration in the patient's condition is probably the most important indication to do a scan or to repeat it and it would be negligent not to investigate fully a patient who was getting worse.

MULTIPLE SCLEROSIS AND SPINAL CORD DISEASE

29.39 Patients with spinal problems may be referred to a neurologist by many types of specialist. Each consultant should consider the patient's needs not only in relationship to his own speciality but in relation to others.

29.40 Of the cases involving the diagnosis of multiple sclerosis seven out of the eight cases in the table were related to making the wrong diagnosis. Of the seven, five had been diagnosed as having multiple sclerosis but subsequently were found to have spinal cord compression. Hence it is clear that multiple sclerosis itself rarely leads to a doctor being accused of mismanagement; the problem is missing other types of spinal cord or related disease. Multiple sclerosis may be diagnosed incorrectly if the initial presentation of the illness is not typical (Rudick, Schiffer, Schwetz & Herndon 1986). In the seven cases of spinal cord disease all the medico-legal problems were associated with a failure to diagnose the illness correctly.

29.41 In the past it was accepted that making a definite diagnosis of multiple sclerosis in the early stages was often not possible and therefore that the allegation of being negligently slow in making a diagnosis was rarely sustained. However, attitudes could change because the available investigations have improved and therefore more evidence is available to confirm or cast doubt on the diagnosis of multiple sclerosis. A neurologist who did not use the newer techniques makes himself liable to an allegation of negligence. Clearly the clinical situation is the most important aspect of assessment and this has not changed. However the use of evoked potentials has developed from the initial use of visually evoked potentials to a wide range of methods of assessing nerve conduction in the central nervous system. These tests are helpful in making the diagnosis of multiple sclerosis but an abnormal evoked potential does not exclude other diagnoses such as a tumour. Evoked Potential testing is available at regional neurological centres and at some district general hospitals. They should be used when a doctor is in doubt about the diagnosis, especially if he is going to make a clinical diagnosis of multiple sclerosis and tell the general practitioner and the patient. However, in early cases, especially when there has been complete recovery, knowing the diagnosis could have no effect on the management and voicing fears about the possible diagnosis could cause the patient distress which would be difficult to justify especially if subsequently the diagnosis was found to be different. Whatever course of action is decided the doctor should make a clear statement in the notes about how he reached his conclusion so that if asked later to justify his policy he can produce evidence to show that his decision at that time was reached after proper consideration and was therefore not negligent.

29.42 Nuclear Magnetic Resonance (NMR) scanning can show plaques of demyelination within the brain. The presence of characteristic lesions on the

NMR scan is strong, but not unequivocal, evidence of multiple sclerosis. The reasons for doing or not doing the test are similar to those for and against doing Evoked Potentials. Due to the lack of resources it is not possible to do NMR scans on all the patients for whom it might be helpful. If the doctor feels that a NMR scan would be helpful he should attempt to have it done but if this is not possible he should make a note of his desire to obtain it. The doctor should also inform the relevant managers that he is unable to perform the test which he feels is necessary. The managers and not the doctor must then take the responsibility for not making the test available.

29.43 The commonest neurological medico-legal problems arising from spinal cord lesions are due to the failure to recognise the lesion early. Spinal cord trauma is more often encountered by orthopaedic or general surgeons. Neck trauma is particularly difficult to detect quickly. Trauma at the level of C6/C7 may be missed easily and later a patient develop rapidly progressive disability. Lesions can progress slowly within the spinal canal with only minimal symptoms and perhaps no signs, until suddenly there is a rapid progression of the symptoms and signs with irreversible changes. A central disc lesion may cause bladder symptoms without much else and it can be possible to miss such a diagnosis. An operation or treatment carried out too late for a condition which if it had been treated earlier was remediable has important medico-legal implications. It is therefore essential for doctors to take seriously relatively minor symptoms in the limbs, bowel or urinary systems if they could remotely be associated with spinal cord disease. It is impractical and unreasonable to investigate all the minor symptoms which may present but it is necessary for the doctor to include in his advice to the patient: 'Come and see me again at once if the condition worsens or alters.' A neurologist should include this advice in his letter to a general practitioner otherwise the general practitioner may be lulled into a sense of false security concluding that because the patient had seen a consultant neurologist there was no more need for him to remain concerned. Suspected spinal cord disease should be investigated early. The investigations available for study of the spinal canal are improving. A straight X-ray of the spine may reveal a possible pathology but a normal X-ray does not exclude a lesion within the spinal canal. The NMR scan is improving our ability to investigate the spinal canal with non-invasive techniques. The problem of obtaining a NMR scan has been considered earlier in this section, but there is an alternative available for spinal cord lesions; CT myelography and scanning – a combination of the two at the same time being the more comprehensive. However myelography is an invasive procedure and the risks and discomfort although relatively small have to be considered. Before embarking on a myelogram the neurologist must anticipate the various possibilities that may be encountered and prepare for them. The neurologist should work closely with the radiologist, preferably a neuroradiologist, so that the maximum information can be obtained from the test. Without this close co-operation a radiologist cannot be expected to understand all the possible clinical aspects which need to be considered. If a lesion is found that is causing cord compression there is a strong indication to operate at once as spinal cord damage can progress rapidly and be irreversible. Therefore the appropriate surgeon or surgical team must be consulted and prepared to act if necessary before the myelogram is begun. The surgeon may feel he should see the patient before the myelogram so that he would be better able to assess any subsequent change or he may feel that the investigation should be performed in such a way that he gets maximum information not only about the possible diagnosis but about the factors which might influence his surgical technique. Unfortunately it is not uncommon for a surgeon to wish to repeat a myelogram ordered by a physician who had not adequately consulted a neuroradiologist and a surgeon prior to the procedure. By consulting the surgeon soon rather than late one decreases the possibility of delays following the procedure. The result of any myelogram should be made known at once by the radiologist to the referring doctor especially if the radiologist finds a lesion which might progress within the following few days. It is essential for the doctor or his colleagues to observe the patient closely during the following hours and days. It is wrong to do a myelogram on a Friday and await the result on the following Monday.

29.44 A doctor must be concerned that he might miss a spinal cord compression in his patient.

HEADACHES

29.45 Headaches are very common and are rarely due to serious progressive disease. For this reason the few serious causes of headaches may be missed. It would be unreasonable and give rise to a lot of unnecessary worry for all patients with headaches to be investigated to exclude serious disease. A careful medical, psychiatric and social history will make the management easier. The doctor's assessment is easier if abnormal physical signs are present. However the absence of physical signs does not exclude a serious cause. Headaches in children are more likely to be due to organic disease and the first symptom of a tumour may be a headache. If the patient is a young child additional care must be taken to exclude such conditions as meningitis which can easily be missed in the very early stages. The length of the history of headaches of a similar nature is a helpful indicator. A patient who has been having similar headaches for several years without the development of any abnormal physical signs is unlikely to have serious progressive disease. However, if the headaches are of recent onset or getting worse or have changed in character there is an increased indication to investigate more fully. The difficulty of diagnosing the few serious cases can be decreased by follow-up appointments without necessarily having to submit the patient to investigations. The problem of diagnosing subarachnoid haemorrhage is unlikely to arise when it is of such severity that the patient has been admitted to hospital but if the initial haemorrhage is not severe or the patient did not seek immediate medical help and has some spontaneous improvement before he seeks help, the diagnosis is more difficult. In mild cases the headache may diminish in an hour or two if the patient rests and therefore the cessation of a headache while a patient waits in an Accident and Emergency Department does not exclude a subarachnoid haemorrhage. A warning leak of a small haemorrhage is not uncommon (Ostergaard 1989) and can occur in as many as 60 per cent of all patients who later have a major haemorrhage due to an aneurysm. The warning leak is often accompanied by nausea, visual disturbance due to a third nerve lesion, and transient motor or sensory symptoms. However the absence of other symptoms or signs does not exclude a subarachnoid haemorrhage. The prognosis for a major haemorrhage after a warning leak is worse than for a single haemorrhage. Doctors should be particularly careful not to exclude a small subarachnoid haemorrhage when the diagnosis is unclear.

29.46 Migraine causes a large proportion of severe headaches seen. The headaches tend to be recurrent, are not life-threatening but can cause severe disability. Because of the tendency of headaches to recur over a long period of time it is important that a policy for the management is made and the medication monitored. The drugs used can have unwanted effects which in a chronic situation should, if possible, be avoided.

NEUROLOGY AND PSYCHIATRY

29.47 The borderline between psychiatry and neurology is often unclear so a neurologist may be referred patients who suffer from psychological or psychiatric disorders. Often the neurological consultations and assessment are themselves psychotherapeutic and nothing further needs to be done. In other cases psychotropic medication given as a simple prescription is enough. However, if the neurologist feels that the patient has a psychological or psychiatric problem which he cannot relieve he has a duty to consider a policy for management. He could refer the patient back to his general practitioner asking the general practitioner to take any necessary steps. Alternatively he may decide, usually with the general practitioner's acceptance, to refer the patient to a psychiatrist. Although telling the patient about the referral may be embarrassing or difficult, it is important for the patient to understand the reason for the referral. It is much harder for the psychiatrist to help the patient if the patient only discovers that he is being referred to a psychiatrist after he has left the neurologist's consulting room. If the patient says that he does not wish to see a psychiatrist, the neurologist can explain that it is he, the neurologist, who is advising the psychiatric opinion because he, the neurologist, needs help in fulfilling his duty to the patient and that without the psychiatric advice he would be unable to advise appropriate management.

29.48 Although the interface between psychiatry and neurology rarely leads to serious medico-legal problems it is often the cause of complaints and misunderstandings which require a considerable amount of time by doctors, hospital managers and administrators to sort out. Most neurologists and psychiatrists will know of cases with long drawn out correspondence and threats of legal action which have helped neither the patient, the relatives or the hospital. Many of these could have been avoided if at an early stage the problem had been much more openly discussed.

DRUG THERAPY

29.49 Many neurological conditions are chronic and drug therapy is not entirely satisfactory. The long-term use of therapy does increase the chances of inducing toxicity which may come on so slowly that it is not easily recognised. Several medico-legal cases have occurred in which an accusation of wrong treatment has been made. A doctor who prescribes treatment does have a continuing responsibility to monitor that treatment. This is relatively easy if the same doctor continues to see the patient at intervals but if another doctor, say a junior doctor in the clinic or the general practitioner, is involved they may not be fully aware of the implications of the treatment prescribed by someone else. Therefore when prescribing treatment the situation should be carefully recorded and the general practitioner or other doctors involved should be fully informed of the circumstances.

29.50 Drug therapy instituted by others may result in neurological syndromes (Weiden, Mann, Haas, Mattson, Frances 1987). For example, extrapyramidal disease can be induced by drugs used in psychiatry. It is important that drugs are monitored and patients warned of possible long-term unwanted effects such as tardive dyskinesia (Tancredi 1988). Also there are many drugs with vascular effects which may be important in inducing cerebrovascular symptoms. Frequently patients do not associate their neurological problems with other diseases or medications and therefore the neurologist must enquire about all other diseases and medications. If the patient cannot be precise the doctor might need to pursue the matter with other doctors and ask the patient to bring all medications at the next consultation.

Acknowledgement

I should like to thank Dr D Sumner for his help and advice and in particular for providing the information in the table and Dr C J Earl who provided helpful suggestions.

BIBLIOGRAPHICAL REFERENCES

Brahams D 'Informed consent and 25% risk of paralysis' (1989) Lancet ii, 57–58.

Bouchez B, Assaker R, Hautefeuille P, Combelles G, Arnott G 'False Positive – False Negative CT Scan in late epileptic seizure; a meningioma-glioblastoma association' (1986) J Neurol 233, 218–220.

Ostergaard J R 'Warning leak in subarachnoid haemorrhage' (1989) British Medical Journal 301, 190–191.

Plesner A M, Munk-Andersen E, Luhdorf K 'Epileptic aphasia and dysphasia interpreted as endogenous depression' (1987) Acta Neurologica Scandinavica 76, 215–218.

Rudick R A, Schiffer R B, Schwetz K M, Herndon R M 'Multiple Sclerosis: The problem of incorrect diagnosis' (1986) Arch Neurol 43, 578–583.

Sumner D *Personal communication* (1988).

Tancredi L R 'Malpractice and Tardive Dyskinesia. A conceptual dilemma' (1988) J of Clinical Psychopharmacology 8, 71S–76S.

Weiden P J, Mann J J, Haas G, Mattson H, Frances A 'Clinical Nonrecognition of Neuroleptic-Induced Movement Disorders: A Cautionary Study' (1987) Am J Psych 144, 1148–1153.

TABLE 29.1 SEVENTY-TWO MEDICO-LEGAL CASES WITH PRIMARY NEUROLOGICAL DISEASE

Information supplied by Dr Sumner (1988)

The Problem	
Failure to diagnose	40
Wrong treatment	14
Wrong management	12
Problem of consent	4
Wrong advice	2
TOTAL	72
The Clinical Problem	
Invasive investigation	10
Epilepsy	10
Intracranial space occupying lesion	9
Multiple sclerosis	8
Spinal cord disease	7
Subarachnoid haemorrhage	5
Migraine	4
Meningitis	4
Others (3 or less each)	15
TOTAL	72

CHAPTER 30

Medico-legal problems in the non-surgical management of cancer

Dr A M Jelliffe *MD FRCP FRCR DCH*

SUMMARY

30.1 It is not possible to appreciate fully the special legal aspects of the treatment of cancer patients by non-surgical methods without some knowledge of the natural history of cancers and of the general principles underlying the most commonly used treatment techniques.

THE NATURAL HISTORY OF CANCER

30.2 'Cancer' covers a very large number of disease processes which vary enormously in their natural history. At one extreme there is a type of skin cancer (rodent ulcer), which usually never spreads away from its original site, which extends locally very slowly over many years and which in older people may never require treatment. At the other extreme are some types of acute leukaemia which present with generalised disease initially and which before the development of effective chemotherapy could kill the patient in two or three weeks.

30.3 With most cancers it is assumed that the initiating change develops in a single cell. Growth then occurs logarithmically with the single cell dividing repeatedly until eventually it produces a detectable local mass. A cell mass that can be felt or visualised with modern equipment such as a CT scanner has usually reached a sphere of about 1 cm in diameter. For a single cell to grow to a mass of this size requires 30 cell divisions (doubling time). The doubling time rate varies considerably with both different normal tissues and different tumours. In the case of tumours, measured doubling times have been recorded between 10–14 days up to many weeks. A doubling time of 10–12 weeks would mean that a cancer would have to be present for about six years before it could be first detected clinically.

30.4 In addition to local growth an uncontrolled cancer usually spreads eventually throughout the body. Spread may occur through the lymph vessels draining that part of the body to invade the regional lymph nodes. For example a cancer arising in the mouth may spread to the lymph nodes in the neck. Spread may also occur via the blood stream. The veins draining blood from the growing cancer are eventually invaded by malignant cells which can then be carried by the blood through the arteries to involve any known structure in the body. It is important to realise that both types of spread may occur either very early in the natural history of the cancer or very late. Obviously in general the longer a cancer has been present, the larger it will become and the more chance there is of more distant spread having occurred. However, widespread metastases sometimes occur from a very small primary cancer which may be so small that it may be very difficult or even impossible to detect. This behaviour of some cancers is well known and explains why the national breast cancer screening programme does not pretend that screening and early diagnosis can prevent all deaths from breast cancer although many cancers only a few millimetres in diameter will be detected by screening. It aims to reduce the death rate from breast cancer overall by 25 per cent. Appreciation of the variable natural history of cancer is important if a sense of perspective is to be maintained in the assessment of some plaintiffs' claims.

30.5 Other aspects of the natural history of cancer which may lead to medico-legal confusion involve the enormous variations which may occur in the presentation of cancers and the extreme rarity of some types of cancer. For example, the presenting symptom of lung cancer may not be related to the lungs but may be due to lymph node involvment pressing on nerves in the neck, or invasion of almost any part of the body by blood borne spread including bones, brain and liver, hormone producing gland destruction with hormone changes and so on. The lung primary may be very small and may be positioned so that the shadow normally seen on the chest X-ray is hidden by the heart shadow. If the cancer is of a very rare type it may easily be overlooked by a general practitioner or a general physician. For example in the UK, Hodgkins disease affected about 1,400 persons in 1988 in a total population of more than 56 million. The average GP will see not more than one or two cases in a lifetime of practice and understandably an early diagnosis is extremely unlikely.

DELAYS IN ESTABLISHING THE DIAGNOSIS AND TREATMENT OF CANCER

30.6 The Patient's Charter and the Health of the Nation published by HM Government in 1992 include targets for cancer prevention, early diagnosis and treatment waiting times. A recent report on 'Reducing delays in cancer treatment' (Joint Council for Clinical Oncology 1993) emphasises that unnecessary delay in treating cancer is unacceptable. The report refers to difficulties in quantifying the effects of delay because of the marked variations in the biological behaviour of cancer, referred to above, but confirms the well known fact that the cure rate of almost all cancers is related to their stage of advancement when first discovered. In many cases of cancer a delay of a few weeks and sometimes even a few months before commencing treatment will not affect the prognosis, but there is no doubt that delay can have a very serious psychological impact on some patients. In general every effort should be made to diagnose and treat cancers quickly.

Delay due to the patient

30.7 Some cancers progress very insidiously in which case there is a real possibility of patients failing to notice any obvious change in their well-being. In the past, delay in the diagnosis of cancer has often been due to the patient's ignorance of the possible significance of his or her presenting symptoms. With an increasingly knowledgeable public this is very much less likely and nowadays patient-attributable delay is more often due to a fear of cancer and of its treatment.

Delay due to the medical profession

30.8 Some delay on the part of the general practitioner may be expected if the cancer is uncommon or its presentation is unusual. For example a young patient may present with a sore throat, intermittently large lymph nodes in the neck and a fluctuating temperature. (See case report below.) A general practitioner would not necessarily be expected to think first of a leukaemia or lymphoma but if the patient's symptoms persisted for perhaps eight weeks or more he should certainly refer the patient for a second opinion not because he suspected a form of cancer but simply because failure to establish a diagnosis of any condition within a reasonable period of time should always be considered a possible indication for seeking further advice.

30.9 An even more difficult situation arises when a patient presents with a symptom which is extremely common and which is very rarely due to cancer. For example, a woman may present with a minor episode of vaginal bleeding after the menopause. There may have been a past history of irregular periods which have varied considerably over the years and the onset of the menopause has been dilatory with gradually increasing intervals between unpredictable periods. After a longer than usual interval, when it is assumed that the change has taken place, there is a further episode of bleeding. This is almost certainly of no serious significance. However, there is a tiny possibility that this may be the initial symptom for cancer arising in the uterus. If all such patients are referred immediately for a gynaecological opinion, hospital clinics would be inundated and in almost every case a biopsy would show no significant abnormality. In practice such a situation would probably be managed most reasonably by a period of observation and the patient referred only if the symptom reoccurred. The opposite of this situation would be the discovery of a small palpable lump in the breast of an intelligent previously asymptomatic patient. This should be accepted immediately without hesitation as a possible cancer and referred urgently to an appropriate specialist for further management. Fortunately the majority of such lumps will prove to be non-malignant but nevertheless delays should not be countenanced.

Delay on behalf of the specialist

30.10 It should be assumed with some justification that referral to a specialist should be followed by no further unreasonable delay in the instigation of further investigations, establishment of the correct diagnosis and the inauguration of whatever treatment is necessary. However, further delay may occur because the cancer itself is extremely uncommon or the presentation is particularly unusual. Chance may play a large part in the management of the disease. The specialist to whom the patient has been referred may have spent many months training as a junior hospital doctor in a busy oncology department during which time he may have seen several very similar cases and the correct diagnosis is immediately established. If he has never encountered this particular problem before, there may be a considerable lapse of time before the diagnosis is finally established and treatment inaugurated. In general a competent specialist would be expected either to carry out generally acceptable investigations which are necessary to establish the correct diagnosis and inaugurate treatment. Alternatively if the problem is not in his field of medicine he or she would be expected to refer the patient to a colleague for further study.

Administrative delays

30.11 Delays because of administrative complications do occur and are highly regrettable. In the case of suspected cancer they should be circumnavigated. A patient suspected by a general practitioner of possibly having a cancer should be regarded as urgent and seen in the relevant specialist clinic within ten to fourteen days. Urgent appointments should be made by telephone, preferably by direct contact with the specialist or his senior assistant. When the diagnosis of cancer is established many patients are referred to an oncological specialist. Most oncological out-patient clinics have no waiting time for this type of problem and are prepared to see patients with established cancer within a few days.

30.12 In the past, unacceptable delays often occurred because the waiting time for radiotherapy may have been as long as eight to twelve weeks. After the patient has been seen by the clinical oncologist further investigation may be required to determine the extent of the tumour. Treatment is then planned using a simulator. It may be necessary to prepare a mould, for example, of the head and neck. The dose distribution has to be calculated in the physics department and when all activities have been completed the patient will finally commence treatment. At each stage there may be a wait because of the enormous pressure of work due to inadequate resources in manpower and specialised equipment and facilities for radiotherapy and for chemotherapy which is unfortunately still encountered in many departments. The extremely reasonable recommendations of the Joint Council for Clinical Oncology (1993) will not then be achievable and many patients will continue to suffer unnecessarily because of prolonged delays.

Case report A 32-year-old man presented with enlarged glands in the neck which varied in size over a period of four months. During this time the patient was investigated and found to have a normal blood count and a normal chest X-ray. At times he had flu-like symptoms. The general practitioner concerned felt that he had a viral infection which was taking a long time to settle down. Eventually, the patient was referred to hospital and fully investigated. He was found to have Hodgkin's disease and the investigations demonstrated enormous gland masses in the abdomen which had produced no symptoms. The plaintiff's case was that the delay in diagnosis had made a serious difference to the prognosis and to the later management of his case.

The size of the gland mass in the abdomen inidcated that it has been present for a long period of time. Assuming the normal doubling time for the average type of Hodgkin's disease, abdominal glands had probably been present for between four and six years and the glands which presented in the neck represented spread from the abdominal disease. A delay of four months is unlikely to affect a disease which has already been present for several years and the delay made no difference to his treatment. It is also worth noting that he had a disease which is extremely rare and the presentation was unusual. Practising clinical oncologists are well aware of the fact that some tumours, particularly those akin to Hodgkin's disease, may show remarkable spontaneous variation. Tumour masses may decrease in size without treatment and then enlarge again. As the masses come and go the patient may have flu-like symptoms. In this case, not only was the delay probably of no significance but the practitioner concerned was faced with a disease which is extremely rare and which presented with manifestations which were uncommon and misleading.

RADIOTHERAPY

30.13 Because of its characteristics, the practice of radiotherapy is particularly liable to litigation. Many of the damaging effects which may follow the exposure of normal tissues to ionising radiation present themselves many years after the event and therefore long after the patient received treatment which has successfully destroyed the original life-threatening cancer. This situation is of course totally different from that commonly encountered when malignant diseases are treated with surgery or with cytotoxic drugs. A major operation such as the radical removal of the pancreas carries with it a recognised immediate morbidity and mortality, as does the attempted radical treatment of cancer with some cytotoxic drugs, but these major complications or fatalities occur at a time when the family and patient are all acutely aware of the unpleasant nature of the original disease and its possible prognosis. Mishaps at this time are more acceptable emotionally. The development of complications which may proceed to a fatal termination occurring many years after radiotherapy has successfully eradicated a malignant tumour, may be deeply resented by all those immediately concerned and litigation becomes more possible. Partly because of the sequence of events and the time intervals involved, the legal implications differ considerably from those involved in treatment by surgery. These differences are best considered after discussing the main principles of radiotherapy and cancer chemotherapy in the management of malignant disease.

PRINCIPLES OF RADIOTHERAPY

30.14 Radiotherapy is the practice of medical treatment using ionising irradiations. These include the electro-magnetic irradiations which are produced by X-ray machines and the gamma rays which are emitted from naturally occurring radium, and from artificially produced radioactive cobalt and other radioactive isotopes. They also incorporate the particulate irradiations which include electrons, alpha particles, beta particles and neutrons. Radiotherapy was often used in the management of benign conditions in the early days. This was partly because there were no other methods available. For example, antibiotics were non-existent at the turn of the century and pneumonia was a very dangerous disease. Pneumonia was apparently successfully treated by radiotherapy. Obviously this is no longer the normal procedure. A small number of benign conditions, most commonly arising in the skin, are still occasionally treated with ionising irradiation.

30.15 Nowadays radiotherapy is used almost entirely in the treatment of cancer. Its use has evolved steadily since the original discovery of X-rays by

Roentgen and of radium by the Curies. Soon after the turn of the century it was discovered that superficial cancers could disappear after exposure to X-rays or radium and sometimes the control was very long standing and occasionally permanent. Treatment remained largely empirical until reliable methods of dosage measurement were introduced in the late 1930s. Fortunately, it was appreciated early on that long-term follow-up was essential in the accurate evaluation of cancer treatment methods. Many radiotherapy centres throughout the world have maintained meticulous records since they started to function and therefore we now have voluminous records going back for up to 50 years which include reliable treatment and follow-up details. In many centres there is still pathological material available from some of the original tumours treated.

External irradiation

30.16 In the early days of radiotherapy, the ionising irradiation from the most powerful machines available, operating at 100–200 kv, did not penetrate very deeply into the body. The skin always received a relatively large dose which led inevitably to severe acute reactions and long-term sequelae. Over the years, increasingly powerful X-ray generating machines have been developed, and the standard machines nowadays available operate at 6–10 million volts. At the turn of the century, the only radioactive material available was radium and this was very expensive and in short supply. If a quantity such as 10 grams could be collected, the rays emanating from such a source could be used for the external treatment of patients. As artificially produced radioactive isotopes, such as radio-cobalt, have become freely available, it has been possible to prepare radioactive sources which emit enormous amounts of gamma rays which are exactly equivalent to the X-rays generated by X-ray machines functioning at one or more million volts. This has led to a complete change in radiotherapy. For technical reasons, X-rays and gamma rays generated at these very high energy levels of over 1 Mev penetrate very deeply and it is now possible to treat deep-seated tumours in any part of the body. In addition the dose build-up is not maximum at the level of the skin as was the case with X-rays generated at the lower energy levels. The maximum build-up occurs at a centimetre or more deep to the skin, the depth of this build-up depending upon the energy of the treatment beam. Serious skin reactions are therefore no longer one of the common complications encountered in the treatment of cancer, unless it is necessary deliberately to include the skin in the high dose volume because it is thought that it is involved by the malignancy (see Figure 30.1).

30.17 X-rays and gamma rays damage tissues indirectly. The atoms in irradiated cells are activated by energy absorbed from the electromagnetic irradiations and from these energised activated atoms, secondary electrons are ejected. These minute negatively charged particles travel for short distances but produce dramatic changes in the neighbouring cells. In particular, chromosomes are very likely to be damaged and this damage may be irreparable. Direct irradiation with beams of electrons or with other radioactive particles of a similar type, particularly beta particles which are emitted from radioactive isotopes, produce a direct effect on cells which is identical with that produced by electrons which are emitted by the atoms which have been energised by X-rays and gamma rays. However the distribution of this ionisation is totally different. Electrons have a finite range in tissue, the maximum range being dependent upon their initial energy and on the type of tissue into which they penetrate. Primary electron beams or beams of beta particles from radioactive sources can therefore be used to treat superficial structures to a very high dose while sparing the deeper tissues to which there is no penetration. In the case of X and gamma rays, the primary beam is absorbed in the tissues exponentially. As the beam is absorbed, secondary electrons are ejected and tissue effects occur. This means in effect that some irradiation is always transmitted to deeper tissues. At lower energy levels (10–100 kv) there is very great absorption in the superficial layers of tissue and very little irradiation is passed on to deeper layers. Thus with X-rays generated at 8 Mev, 50 per cent of the entrance beam reaches 20 cm in soft tissue. At 4 Mev, 50 per cent penetrates to about 10 cm and at 250 kv, 50 per cent penetrates 5 cm. If 'superficial' X-rays are used generated at about 50 kv, 50 per cent is absorbed in the first centimetre of soft tissue and with this type of irradiation it is therefore possible to treat a skin cancer of about 0.5 cm in thickness very satisfactorily without serious damage to underlying tissue. The 'quality' of electromagnetic irradiation which is defined by the energy at which it is generated, is obviously of very great importance when considering treatment planning and also the possibility of long-term complications (see Figure 30.2).

30.18 Very heavy particle irradiation has been used in the treatment of patients with cancer. Neutrons are some 1,800 times as heavy as electron particles but carry no electric charge. They react vigorously with tissues because of their mass, but because they carry no electric charge are not stopped easily and therefore may penetrate to great depths. Alpha particles are four times as heavy as neutrons and carry a strong positive charge. Because of their very heavy mass and charge, they react so intensely with tissues that all their energy is absorbed in the first few layers of cells. Deep effects do not occur unless the alpha particle emitter is absorbed into the body and distributed through the blood to various organs. These very heavy particles are at present used mainly experimentally in the management of cancer.

Internal irradiation

30.19 Soon after the discovery of radium it was found that the application of a container of radium salts to the surface of a cancerous skin growth could produce a dramatic regression and apparent cure of some tumours. Irradiation from such a superficial radioactive source will fall off very rapidly at distances away from the source. This is advantageous if the tumour is strictly localised in depth but clearly its value is limited to those malignant tumours which have no deep extension. The logical extension of this approach was to devise needles or tubes containing radium salts or other radioactive materials which could be inserted into the whole volume likely to be occupied by a tumour. For example, in a primary cancer of the mouth or tongue, the accepted practice for many years has been the insertion of radioactive needles into the tumour itself. Similarly if an organ contains a cavity (eg uterus) then it would be possible to place containers inside the cavity and irradiate it to a high dose with little effect on neighbouring organs. The interstitial and intracavity use of radium was studied extensively throughout Europe and particularly in Manchester in Great Britain where a highly sophisticated mathematical distribution system was developed by Ralston Patterson and colleagues. Before modern skin-sparing supervoltage irradiation became available, adequate irradiation of cancers arising in the mouth and pharynx were always associated with appallingly severe skin reactions. It was generally accepted at that time that many of these tumours were better treated by the implantation of radioactive needles using the method introduced in Manchester. Since the development of supervoltage external radiotherapy there has been a move away from this treatment approach with many tumours but intracavity irradiation still plays a very important part in the treatment of uterine cancer. Some tumours are still better treated by interstitial irradiation, but radium needles are no longer used. Artificially radioactive substances such as iridium are incorporated in wires.

30.20 Treatment with interstitial and intracavitary irradiation developed at first empirically. The scientific approach, introduced particularly in Manchester, has enabled the logical extension of this treatment but it has always been a totally different approach from that used with external irradiation. Because the dose was so localised it was possible to treat cancers to a very high level, in a short space of time. For example, using an implant, a tongue tumour might be given a dose of 6,000 cGy over four to five days. Using external irradiation a tumour in a similar site would receive a dose of 6,000 cGy in five to six weeks.

The effects of radiotherapy

30.21 All living cells can be damaged by ionising irradiations. It was discovered in the early days of radiotherapy that radiosensitivity appeared to be related to the morphology and functional differentiation of cells. The more primitive a cell, the more sensitive it appeared to be to irradiation. It was noted also that there was considerable variation in sensitivity to irradiation depending on the tissue of origin. Some of the most sensitive tissues are the gonads, the bone marrow, and the lining of the intestine. The clinical effects of irradiation will depend upon the normal behaviour of the cells which have been irradiated. As was indicated earlier, radiation damages cells and in particular the chromosome. If this damage is very severe, immediate cell death may occur. If the damage is minimal then normal cells may be completely repaired. In between these two extremes, many cells will receive damage to the chromosome which may not become apparent until the cell attempts to divide. Successful cell division is extremely complicated and the most important part of this cell division is replication of the chromosome. The damaging effects of previous irradiation on a chromosome is evidenced by abnormal cell division which is followed by cell death.

30.22 Rapidly dividing cells arising in organs such as the bone marrow and lining of the intestine will obviously appear to be highly radiosensitive because of the rapid rate of cell division which is normally found in these cells (see Table 30.1). The irradiation of slowly dividing cells, such as those of the normal thyroid gland, is usually followed by no immediate obvious damage. Normal thyroid function continues. Subsequently, over a period of years, progressive under-activity of the thyroid gland will develop as more and more cells attempt to divide and die. Because of the low rate of cell division of normal thyroid cells, effects of previous irradiation are thus masked until sufficient impaired cell divisions and subsequent cell deaths have accumulated over a period of sometimes many years (see Table 30.2).

30.23 The successful treatment of malignant disease with ionising irradiation is dependent upon a selective destruction of cancerous cells to a greater extent than normal tissues and this is referred to as a satisfactory therapeutic ratio.

Repair of normal and cancerous cells

30.24 It is now appreciated that a successful therapeutic ratio is dependent on the fact that cancer cells are no longer controlled by normal tissue growth restraint factors and are also not susceptible to the normal control repair mechanisms that affect normal cells. This explains why fractionating radiotherapy into small doses is beneficial. During the intervals between treatments the normal tissues are repaired but the cancerous cells do not recover to the same extent. Similar effects are recognised in cancer chemotherapy.

30.25 When considering radiotherapy a total dose is very often referred to. It is very important indeed that more information is available apart from the total dose when considering the effectiveness of any course of radiotherapy. Normally a course of radiotherapy is given in divided doses spread over a period of time. It is quite clear that a similar biological effect may be obtained by giving a smaller number of larger individual doses over the same period of time and there are many other variations which can be considered. Ellis (1969) analysed the various factors concerned in the relation between total dose fractionation and overall time and presented a clinical hypothesis on the subject which has been generally accepted and is used in practice.

30.26 For example, it is known that five daily doses of 200 cGy (rads) each week over a six week period will give a total of 6,000 cGy which produces an identical radiobiological effect with a dose of 300 cGy given three times a week over a similar six week period. In the second case the total dose is only 5,400 cGy and yet the radiobiological effect is identical in most normal tissues. The statement that a patient received a dose of 4,000 cGy means nothing. A single dose of 4,000 cGy would probably in many cases be fatal. If it was spread over 12 weeks it would probably do very little to many tumours. Using the factors quoted by Ellis it is possible to determine whether a quoted dose given in a number of fractions over a certain period of time falls within reasonable levels from the point of view of normal tissue tolerance and possible cancer destruction.

30.27 Other factors that have to be taken into consideration include the volume of normal tissue which is included in the irradiation field. For example when treating the abdomen with wide field radiotherapy not more than about 3,000 cGy can be given. Treating a small lesion in the pelvis it is possible to go up to a dose of about 7,000 cGy with few serious bowel effects (Roswit, 1974). The figure demonstrates this point diagrammatically (see Figure 30.3). The larger the volume the more likelihood that normal tissue tolerance will be exceeded and this must be taken into consideration when planning a course of radiotherapy.

30.28 The successful destruction of some cancers may sometimes be followed by quite serious damage to neighbouring normal tissues. This is partly because many cancers are treated at a very advanced stage. Very early cancers which are irradiated can be destroyed with minimal normal tissue destruction. The irradiation and successful destruction of a large cancerous tumour will lead to an area of death in a large volume of cells. This dead tissue cannot be replaced and repaired with normal tissues. Repair is associated with scarring which is the laying down of fibrous tissue. If the original tumour was very large, there will be extensive scarring. Radiation also produces thickening in the lining of small blood vessels. This may be progressive, leading to increasing damage to the blood supply of organs over many years. If this damage is minor and it develops slowly, other blood vessels will grow in from neighbouring areas and no serious damage will occur. If it was necessary to irradiate a large volume of normal tissue to cure the original cancer then it is possible that progressive reduction of the blood supply to normal tissues will lead to late complications.

30.29 The administration of a higher than average biological dose of irradiation may increase the chance of destruction of the cancer, but will also increase the possibility of late damage to normal tissues. This situation is encountered quite commonly in clinical practice. If a tumour is known to be relatively radio-resistant and therefore requires a very high dose of irradiation if it is to be destroyed, inevitably there will be a greater risk of complications and the situation should be discussed in detail either with the patient or with close relatives so that at least somebody in the family is fully aware of the situation. The extreme of this type of situation is seen in the management of some malignant tumours arising in the central nervous system. Vigorous irradiation to a small volume of tissue in the brain stem or spinal cord may be followed at a later date by very serious complications. This leads to a difficult paradoxical situation. If a patient has a malignant tumour arising in the midbrain or spinal cord, surgical excision is often quite impossible as it will lead to destruction of the nervous system in that region. Some of these tumours are radiosensitive and may respond to treatment by irradiation. Unfortunately, many of them require a dose of more than 4,000 cGy in four weeks, if they are to be successfully cured. This dose is regarded as the normal tissue tolerance dose for the central nervous system and successful cure of a tumour arising in this region by radiotherapy may be followed, sometimes after many years, by progressive neurological complications due to scarring from this treatment.

30.30 This very difficult situation can be solved satisfactorily only after discussion with patients and relatives. Most intelligent patients knowing that they have a malignant tumour arising in a situation which must inevitably lead to severe neurological complications in the near future, will prefer to accept radiotherapy with the chance of cure now, but the possibility of late complications perhaps many years afterwards.

Specific tissue radiosensitivity

30.31 Different tissues appear to have different inherent radiosensitivities (see Tables 30.1 and 30.2). Some of these differences are apparent and not real. Apparent differences have been referred to already when comparing the effects of irradiation on whole bone marrow with irradiation on the whole thyroid gland (para **30.22**). From a clinical viewpoint there may be other factors which might be considered. A seriously damaged bone marrow may require complicated remedial measures including a bone marrow transplant from a suitable donor, if such a donor is available. Thyroid failure not only occurs slowly but its effects are completely and inexpensively reversed with daily Thyroxin tablets.

30.32 When discussing the relative radiosensitivity of different organs, it is important to consider from the clinical point of view the effects of irradiation not only to the whole of an organ but also to different parts of it. In some cases, radiation damage to small parts of an organ can have very serious effects on the function of the whole body. For example, in the central nervous system, moderate radiation damage to a small part of the midbrain or cervical spinal cord (para **30.29**) may be followed by severe functional abnormalities which can include paralysis below the irradiated level. By contrast, the large frontal lobes of the brain may be irradiated to a high dose which will produce visible changes in that part of the brain, but which will not necessarily produce any clinical effects which are obvious to the patient or to the doctor.

30.33 The possibility of very late changes, long after irradiation has been used to cure the cancer successfully, is probably the most important single factor in the legal aspects of the management of cancer by radiotherapy as opposed to surgery. Many patients developing long-term complications years after they have been cured of the original cancer have completely forgotten about their original trouble. Some patients claim that they were never even aware that they had had a cancer, and it is possible that many were actually told that they did not have cancer, because it was felt at the time that they would be so frightened that they might not accept possibly curative treatment. Under these circumstances the onset of complications 30 years after treatment will obviously find the patient and the family in a very different mood from that encountered by surgeons immediately after an operation for cancer.

Carcinogenic effects of ionising irradiations

30.34 The carcinogenic effects of ionising irradiations were first reported a few years after the discovery of X-rays and radium. The risks of exposure to these rays were not at first appreciated and workers therefore made no efforts to protect themselves during their early experimentation and later during the clinical application of these rays to clinical diagnosis and therapy. Many early workers received whole body irradiation using relatively soft

X-rays over a period of many years. The organs that were most usually damaged and in which malignancies were induced, were the skin and the bone marrow (leukaemia). The late carcinogenic effects of irradiation are now well recognised, documented and protected against wherever possible. It is known that the latent period before their appearance varies between three and forty years and most commonly is in the middle of this time span. There will always be a risk of irradiation-induced cancer following radical irradiation for a primary malignant tumour, but this risk is small. The majority of patients faced with a choice of either dying in the near future from an unirradiated, inoperable cancer, or the small chance of developing a second radiation-induced cancer 20 years later, will accept the second rather than the first choice. It is a small risk and a second cancer developing in an irradiated site may still respond very well to further treatment.

Tissue radiosensitivity in the child and adolescent

30.35 The developing growing tissues of children and adolescents are in general much more sensitive to irradiation than the mature organs of adults. This is seen very dramatically with the effects of irradiation on growing bones. The growing points of the long bones are at the end of the bones. A moderate dose of irradiation (2,000 cGy) given to the growing end of a bone will lead to cessation of growth. The degree of malformation will depend upon the age at which the irradiation was administered. A 5-year-old child receiving irradiation to the end of one thigh bone will develop into an adult with one leg much shorter than the other. Similar irradiation given to a 16-year-old may be followed by minimal shortening with no serious handicap. In addition, the growth of soft tissue supporting structures and muscles may also be prevented by irradiation, which will increase the deformity due to stunting of bone growth. Another structure in the child which is particularly prone to radiation damage is the immature prepubertal female breast. A small dose of irradiation given to the undeveloped breast will lead to failure of that breast to develop normally at puberty.

30.36 Because of the longer life expectancy of young people, long-term complications due to scarring or to the development of a second malignancy occur more commonly. Special efforts must always be made to protect the young when using irradiation.

THE PRACTICE OF RADIOTHERAPY

Confirmation of malignancy

30.38 Because of the length of treatment, the possibility of acute and chronic side effects and complications, and the emotional trauma involved, the malignant nature of a presumed cancer must be confirmed by microscopical examination in every case. This examination must be carried out by a reputable pathologist. Radiotherapists in many radiotherapy centres insist that their own pathologist should see material from all tumours in patients referred to that centre so that the diagnosis of cancer can be confirmed before treatment. If a radiotherapist is to proceed without histological proof the clinical picture must be totally compatible with the suggested diagnosis and there must be absolute contraindications to a biopsy being carried out, usually because it is thought that such a procedure would endanger life. Under these circumstances it is reasonable to proceed with radiotherapy without histological confirmation, but all the evidence in favour of the tumour being malignant should be written into the notes with the reason why a biopsy was not possible. It would also be preferable to discuss the situation with the patient or with close relatives.

Tumour localisation

30.39 The next step taken in the management of the cancer by radiotherapy is the determination of the extent of that tumour and the immediate environment that must be included in the irradiated volume. In the early days of radiotherapy, diagnostic X-rays were relatively primitive and decisions were sometimes based on little more than inspired guess work. The surgical findings at an operation could provide useful information, but the radiotherapist often relied heavily on his extensive knowledge of the normal spread of tumours in deciding on the exact volume that was to be included in the treatment.

30.40 Over the last few years there have been rapid advances in radiodiagnosis, ultrasound and nuclear medicine which nowadays can provide detailed information regarding the spread of a tumour. The exact investigations which should be undertaken in any particular case will vary with the type of the cancer. The most generally useful modern investigation is the Computerised Tomographic scan (CT) which may be replaced in importance in the future by the Magnetic Resonance scan (MR). A whole body scan carried out by one of these sophisticated techniques may not only determine the local extent of many malignant growths, but may also demonstrate distant metastases at a very early stage, the discovery of which will modify treatment.

30.41 Certain investigations are accepted as part of the routine pre-treatment assessment of certain tumours. With time, these investigations will change as newer methods outdate older ones and routine investigations will differ with the particular experience of radiodiagnosticians and radiotherapists in particular centres. It is common to find differences in the investigation of patients in different parts of the world.

Treatment planning

30.42 Having determined as accurately as possible the extent of the cancer and the most likely sites of spread, treatment is planned. Most patients will be examined using a simulator. This modern machine allows the tumour site to be visualised by the therapist using a beam of diagnostic X-rays which closely simulates the beam of ionising irradiation which will later be used in the treatment of the patient. The use of this machine has increased the accuracy of modern planning and therefore modern treatment. The tumour volume as demonstrated by the simulator is then marked on an outline of the patient. The outline will also include within its volume any especially radiosensitive structures such as the spinal cord or eye, which must be protected from an excessive dose of irradiation. The body outline with the target volume and other areas of special interest is then passed to the physicist, who determines the ideal arrangement of treatment fields which will deliver the optimum dose to the tumour, while protecting sensitive tissues against excessive irradiation. The proposed plan will then be examined by the radiotherapist for his approval and confirmation before treatment starts.

Patient set-up and fixation

30.43 In order to achieve a high tumour dose and the maximum protection of normal tissues the treatment is always given with the patient in the same position. Sometimes this is achieved by simple means, for example, lying flat with the same (recorded) head support. In the head and neck region the eyes and nervous system must be carefully protected and it is customary in many cases to construct a plastic shell which fits over the patient's head. This is fixed posteriorly to a flat plastic sheet, the whole ensuring that movement is impossible during treatment which greatly improves the accuracy of treatment.

30.44 The output of many modern supervoltage machines has become very high and it is possible to give the daily dose in a minute or so. The 'patient set-up' has become the most time-consuming part of treatment. There is naturally a great desire to accelerate this process so that the through-put of patients can be increased. It would be possible to reduce the delay of set-up time by having at least two entrances to a treatment room. It is possible to visualise a system whereby patients would be fixed into their plastic moulds in one room and then pushed into the treatment room as the preceding patient leaves by the other entrance. Time could be saved in this way but this approach would reduce the contact between radiographers and patients which is so important in radiotherapy, maintaining patients' morale in what can be a harassing situation.

Machine servicing and checking

30.45 The efficiency of a machine capable of delivering powerful irradiation to patients is clearly of the greatest importance, particularly so because many patients will be treated in the course of one day. An undetected machine failure to deliver a correct dose can affect a large number of individuals and if the error is not discovered, over a period of time its accumulative effects may reach potentially dangerous levels in many patients.

30.46 Under-dosage is unlikely to feature as a medico-legal problem. Unfortunately not all patients have radio-curable tumours and when a tumour fails to respond to what is thought to have been a reasonable course of radiotherapy this is usually acceptable as a treatment failure in that particular individual. However, under-dosage of a large number of patients due to a failure in dose calculation has been recently recorded (Baldwin et al 1992). This error followed the introduction of a new computerised planning system in 1982. With earlier simpler planning techniques it had always been customary to utilise a certain correction factor if the difference between the source of the X-ray beam and the patient's body surface was other than the standard 100 cms. Using the newer technique known as 'isocentric', the same correction factor was introduced manually into the planning without it being appreciated that with this isocentric technique the computer had already corrected automatically for differences in the distance from the machine to the surface of the patient.

30.47 Overdosage as a result of machine error is much more likely to produce severe immediate or late effects which precipitate medico-legal action. However, because of invidivual variations in tissue sensitivity these errors may not be immediately apparent in individual cases. The most important incident related to multiple overdosage was that occurring in Exeter (Thwaites 1988) following installation of a new radio cobalt source. The activity of the source was calibrated to determine its output of radiation. The calculation omitted a certain factor which lead to over 200 patients receiving an excessive dose. Though the root cause of the whole incident was the single calculation error by the physicist it was recommended in the incident report that the responsible authority must review its staffing levels. Staffing levels remain dangerously low in most radiotherapy centres throughout the country and it is surprising that in general authorities have not apparently responded to the Medical Manpower recommendations of the Royal College of Radiologists (1991).

30.48 Machine servicing and the checking of output is the direct responsibility of the medical physicist working in the radiotherapy department. With a machine producing X-rays such as a Linear Accelerator, the output of the machine should be checked at the beginning of each treatment day. The treatment time to give a specific dose is calculated by the radiotherapy technicians in charge of the machine and with modern machines the output of ionising irradiation is automatically measured, confirming these calculations. With radio-cobalt machines, there is less need for repeated measurements. Radio-cobalt decays at an absolutely regular rate emitting γ rays which are the equivalent of X-rays generated at between 1 and 2 million volts. Once the output of a radio-cobalt source has been comfirmed, its radioactive output can be calculated with certainty, so much so that it is possible to estimate when the output of that source will have fallen to such a low level that it will become necessary to replace the old source with a new one. Special care must be taken when installing new machines, and when repairs or alterations have been undertaken. It is always advisable to have the local physicist's calculations checked by a second person. These and many other important precautionary measures are detailed in 'Quality Assurance in Radiotherapy' published by the Department of Health (1991). In this way incorrect dosage will be largely avoided. However, the reactions of patients during the course of radiotherapy should also be watched very closely by the clinician in charge and if the reactions are incompatible with the dose thought to have been given, the whole situation should be immediately reviewed. It should be noted that in the Exeter affair (Thwaites 1988) the first indication of excessive dosage was the clinical observation of abnormally slow healing of skin reactions.

Observations during treatment

30.49 It is customary for the patient to be greeted and set up by radiographers who are highly experienced. Each machine is managed by two or more radiographers. The largest machines, known as linear accelerators, may have four radiographers supervising their use. The daily dose given to the patient and the accumulated doses are recorded on charts by the radiographer in charge. To reduce the possibility of human error in simple addition and fact recording these charts are usually checked by an independent radiographer who is not involved in the day-to-day management of those particular patients.

30.50 During a course of treatment the patient may volunteer or reply to direct questions from the radiographers regarding any symptoms he or she may have. If these are thought to be significant they should be reported to the clinician in charge, who in any case will normally see the patient at regualar intervals during treatment. If the tumour is accessible, as in the mouth or on the skin, the sites will be examined directly on these visits to the clinician. With internal tumours, such as cancer of the oesophagus or prostate, a record will be made regularly as to the presence of symptoms suggesting a radiation reaction. If the reaction is thought to be disproportionate to the recorded dose, there is a clear indication for checking the treatment plan, all the calculations, and in some cases, the output of the machine concerned.

30.51 After completing a course of radiotherapy the patient is normally reviewed in two to four weeks time to assess any residual reaction and its recovery as well as recording the tumour response. Follow-up examinations are normally carried out subsequentially either by the radiotherapist or by his specialist colleagues and in some cases by both in a combined clinic. For example, a bladder cancer is followed up more effectively by a urologist than a radiotherapist because the urologist has the facilities for direct observation of the tumour using a cystoscope.

30.52 Depending on the type of cancer, regular investigations will be carried out to assess progress. These may include special X-rays and scans, ultrasound examinations and sometimes further biopsies to allow microscopical confirmation of the response to treatment. The interval between follow-up visits and examinations extends gradually as time goes by and the possibility of relapse diminishes. However, even when the patient is being followed up at long intervals, it is normal practice for the radiotherapist to maintain close contact with the patient's general practitioner and with all other specialists involved in the patient's management. The patient is also encouraged to consult his practitioner or the specialist concerned at any time in the future if any problems arise.

Is treatment curative, palliative or adjuvant?

30.53 When assessing the possible value of radiotherapy and also evaluating its effects on normal tissue, it is important to determine the original intention of the treatment. There are three possible general treatment categories into which radiotherapy and also surgery and chemotherapy may be placed.

Attempted cure

30.54 The general description of the practice of radiotherapy given above applies in particular to attempted curative irradiation. Curative radiotherapy is attempted when there is a reasonable chance of the complete destruction of the cancer which appears to be limited in extent to the irradiated volume. In general this involves giving a large total dose to the target volume over a long period of time with the production of variable side effects. Immediate reactions may be distressing but they are usually acceptable because the patient knows that the aim of the treatment is cancer eradication. If cure, and therefore longevity, is the aim, reasonable precautions must be taken to prevent late damage to normal tissues, but complete protection may not be compatible with cure of the tumour. For example, with cancer of the upper maxillary bone (antrum) with involvement of the lower half of the orbit, radical irradiation is impossible without including the eye in the irradiated volume. The eye may therefore receive a high and potentially dangerous dose of irradiation. Should subsequent complications develop, they are acceptable as the original treatment was aimed at curing a life-threatening tumour. Patients should be fully in the picture about possible side effects of this type and most intelligent people will accept risks which are necessary if they are to be cured. Every case must be treated according to its merits with cure as the ultimate goal.

Attempted palliation

30.55 In this situation cure is regarded as impossible, either because of the enormous local extent of the tumour, or because the tumour is known to be relatively very radio-resistant, or because the disease has already spread widely to other sites. Radiotherapy is unlikely to prolong life. However, a patient may be suffering symptoms because of the local malignant process. Palliation is the mitigation or relief of pain or other symptoms and by definition should be considered only when the patient has symptoms. Palliative treatment should produce no more symptoms than those originally complained of by the patient and it should relieve the symptoms present initially. If it is felt that the effects of the irradiation will be more distressing than the symptoms of the malignant tumour, alternative treatment methods should be considered. Because the dose given is usually much smaller than with attempted curative treatment, there is less need for complicated planning. Treatment is also given over a shorter period of time than with attempted curative treatment. If a patient with severe symptoms has only a few months to live it is unreasonable to prescribe many weeks of treatment which may occupy perhaps a third of that person's active life. Palliative radiotherapy is given if possible over a period of not more than seven to ten days, but occasionally, as in the case of an incurable bladder cancer, adequate symptom relief can be obtained only with several weeks' treatment.

Adjuvant treatment

30.56 Adjuvant treatment has been practised for many years by surgeons and radiotherapists but its use has increased over the last few years as chemotherapy has become increasingly effective. An adjuvant may be defined as an ingredient to help the main ingredient. For example, if a patient is found to have a certain type of cancer arising from one side of the mouth, it may be decided that surgical removal of all the lymph nodes on that side of the neck should be carried out, even though there is no clinical evidence that the cancer has already spread to these lymph nodes. In this situation, the decision to operate is based on the high probability that microscopic spread of the cancer to the nodes has already occurred, and that the removal of nodes which are probably involved with microscopic cancer, is a much more satisfactory operation than an attempted removal of large, obviously invaded nodes at a later date. A similar approach is often used with irradiation which is extended around macroscopic tumours to include those sites to which it is considered there is a high risk of microscopic spread. With intravenous chemotherapy, it is possible to extend the adjuvant concept to include the whole body.

30.57 The place of adjuvant treatment is dependent upon the opinion of the specialist and his personal experiences in the management of that particular tumour. With attempted cure and attempted palliation the clinician is concerned with certainties but with adjuvant treatment he is involved with probabilities. Many of the indications accepted in the past for adjuvant treatment were based on personal experiences and prejudices. Recently the place for adjuvant treatment has been increasingly investigated by Randomised Prospective Trials which compare two allegedly identical groups of patients. For example, one group will be treated with a standard 'curative' form of treatment and the other may receive the accepted 'curative' treatment and also some form of adjuvant therapy. This adjuvant therapy may involve irradiation of lymph node regions draining that site or the administration of combinations of chemotherapeutic drugs. Long-term follow-up of these two groups allows a scientific evaluation of the suggested adjuvant technique but its use introduces psychological complications. Patients must be informed that they will receive one of two types of treatment and the choice will be made by random allocation. This may introduce doubts into the patient's mind as to the efficiency of the medical personnel and the centre at which he is having his treatment. If the patient is very intelligent and is put fully in the picture, all may be well. If he is a worrier, such an explanation may increase his anxieties. There is no way of accurately evaluating adjuvant treatment other than by the use of randomised prospective trials. They have become widely accepted and have provided a great deal of very useful information in the treatment of cancer. Legal aspects of clinical trials in the United Kingdom are reviewed by Tunkel (1992).

Communicating with patients and relatives

30.58 One of the most important aspects of medical care is communication with the patient and family. When managing patients with malignant disease, this is often emotionally demanding and time consuming. Because of this, communication may be limited and in some cases sadly neglected. From the medico-legal point of view, this is of vital importance for two reasons. Firstly, time spent on communication establishes a close, caring relationship which is the best possible protection against future litigation which is often precipitated initially by emotional stress engendering dissatisfaction. Secondly, it is important that the majority of patients or one or more close members of the family are fully in the picture as regards the nature of the illness and the rationale, practice and possible complications of any recommended treatment modalities. With some diseases, such as diabetes mellitus, the prognosis is closely related to the intelligence of the patient and to his understanding of the illness and its management. With most types of cancer the situation is not so clear cut. The long-term control, which can be equated with cure, is usually not influenced by the patient's detailed knowledge of the disease. If the patient has a type of cancer in which only a small percentage of cures can be obtained by treatment, detailed knowledge of the condition may have an adverse effect on the patient's management. It is therefore very difficult to strike a balance when communicating with patients suffering from cancer. Clearly, if they are to be asked to undergo potentially unpleasant treatment, they must be fully aware of the seriousness of their underlying disease, but if they are to be given every possible chance of surviving, their hopes must not be dashed to the ground. The psychological attitude of a patient to his illness is of the greatest possible importance.

30.59 Thirty years ago, patients with cancer were in general told far too little. Many patients were cured of cancer without ever appreciating the true nature of their illness, which helped to perpetuate the myth of the incurability of all cancers. In some patients, reticence on the part of medical staff to discuss the situation fully would cause frustration and resentment, particularly in the more intelligent who wished to know more about themselves. But many other patients were happy to continue in blissful ignorance of the true nature of their disease. At that time the diagnosis of 'cancer' meant only three things to many patients. They had a disease which was totally uncontrollable, agonisingly painful and inevitably fatal. When asked by a patient in this frame of mind 'Doctor, do I have cancer?' the simple unqualified answer 'Yes' would condemn that patient as being beyond hope. Even with the most malignant tumours, unexpected cures do occur and the fatalistic acceptance of such a death sentence may destroy all morale and hope, and prove to be a self-fulfilling prophecy.

30.60 A doctor has two important duties to his patient. He must always comfort and whenever possible he must cure. In the past, the experienced doctor knew when to say little and when to speak frankly. This was because he was acutely aware of the importance that a patient attaches to everything told to him by his particular adviser, and of the need to get to know a patient before deciding on the amount of information that the patient is able to accept and digest. Today there seems to be a desire on behalf of almost everybody in the medical profession – consultants, registrars, practitioners, house officers, nursing and ancillary staff and even medical students to 'speak frankly', often about subjects of which they have little experience or knowledge. This practice demonstrates a total lack of the compassion which should be a built-in feature of the so-called 'caring' professions.

30.61 The medico-legal implications of the possible long-term complications of radiotherapy apply tremendous pressure on the radiotherapist to adopt a practice that has been accepted in many parts of the world in particular in the USA. There, almost all patients are told the exact nature of all their illness and of its possible consequences, and also the precise implications of any course of treatment that is advised with all its even remotely possible complications. All this information is presented to the patient on a detailed printed form which is signed by the patient when he or she accepts treatment. There are many patients who undoubtedly welcome all this information but there are many others who would still prefer to remain relatively uninformed as to the details of their illness. It should be emphasised that in those countries adopting this policy, patients are given and asked to sign forms containing this information, not for humanitarian reasons, but simply to protect the medical profession against medico-legal actions at a later date.

30.62 It is extremely likely that this practice will become established in Britain. The pressures on the medical profession are increasing and there is no doubt that the completion of forms of this type would confirm that the patient has given informed consent. It would also remove a great deal of strain from members of the medical profession as the full burden of knowledge of the nature of the illness and its complications would rest upon the patient. However, this may well impose an intolerable burden upon some patients from which they are at present partially protected by their medical advisers.

30.63 Written confirmation of conversations with patients and with relatives is extremely important. Important discussions with relatives and with patients should be undertaken in the presence of junior members of staff who can, if necessary, confirm the conversation at a later date. Written details need not be verbatim but they should indicate that, for example, the patient was or was not told the exact nature of his illness etc. It is a very well-known fact that unpleasant news is often not accepted by patients and relatives who may later deny that they have ever been given any information regarding the nature of the illness. This happens so frequently that every effort should be made to ensure that at least one responsible relative is fully in the picture regarding the nature of the illness and its possible sequelae. This can be best achieved by seeing and discussing the situation with the responsible relative on at least two occasions. Ideally this could be done at the establishment of the initial diagnosis and again on completion of the course of treatment.

30.64 In this country at present, communicating with the patient is frequently left to a member of the nursing staff or a relatively junior member of the medical staff. This may often be satisfactory but care should be taken to record what was said during this conversation and it is also advisable to discuss the situation with the consultant in charge so that all concerned will know exactly what patient and relatives have been told. It is very distressing for a patient to be given differing views of his or her illness.

THE MOST FREQUENT CAUSES OF MEDICO-LEGAL ACTION FOLLOWING THERAPEUTIC IRRADIATION

Long-term complications following the cure of a cancer

30.65

Case report A 35-year-old woman presented in 1951 with an advanced (Stage 3) cancer of the uterine cervix. Treatment was given with intrauterine applications of radium and with external irradiation. After the first radium insertion, the patient's late husband was reported to have been told that the radium was placed too near the right kidney and in consequence kidney damage had been caused. Subsequently the patient developed intermittent urinary symptoms. A few years after treatment she developed skin burns which have since required intermittent treatment. In 1982 the patient took proceedings for personal injury and medical negligence as a result of the treatment given in 1951.

The very detailed hospital notes made at the time were reviewed. The original tumour was extensive and the chance of cure was well under 20 per cent. The external irradiation was given with a 200 kv machine because modern supervoltage equipment (which spares the skin from irradiation damage) was not available in 1951. The recorded skin dose was high but acceptable, if an adequate dose was to be given to the centre of the pelvis. Late skin changes were always possible if the tumour was to be cured by irradiation. The patient was seen on several occasions by an experienced plastic surgeon who preferred not to attempt a plastic repair because of the known difficulties and because the patient appeared to have a fairly reasonable life over many years, in spite of the skin trouble.

Careful examination of the notes indicated a reasonable explanation for the patient's late husband's belief that misplaced radium had damaged her right kidney. The original decision was made to insert radium on three occasions. After the first insertion the radium was removed one hour later at which time comments were made to the husband. The records indicated that a routine check X-ray taken to demonstrate the position of the radium after insertion, indicated that it was badly positioned and the sources were therefore removed immediately. The husband was almost certainly told, quite correctly, that this was done in order to avoid damaging the lower end of the ureter (not the kidney) and this information was later misinterpreted by him. The patient had three subsequent radium insertions which were confirmed radiologically as being correctly placed. The husband was under the impression that too much treatment was given because four and not the originally prescribed three were given. He also misinterpreted the information given to him as indicating that a kidney had been damaged. All conversations with patients and relatives should be carefully recorded.

The cure of such an advanced cancer using the primitive radiotherapy equipment available at that time was remarkable. To achieve cure, it was necessary to give a relatively higher dose to the skin than would be necessary nowadays and this led to the subsequent skin damage. With modern supervoltage apparatus this damage would have been avoided completely, but the production of the skin complications following treatment in 1951 could not be regarded as evidence of negligence, as better equipment was not at that time available.

Comment Without very detailed notes, it would have been extremely difficult to disprove the claims of this unfortunate patient. The interval of more than 20 years between treatment and a claim for personal injury is not uncommon and emphasises the importance of exact and detailed records in the practice of radiotherapy.

By modern criteria a claim might have been considered on the grounds that there was no written evidence of informed consent, referring to the possibility that skin complications might occur if the cancer was cured. But 30 years ago the need for such informed consent was not considered.

Complications following accidental 'medical' error

30.66

Case report A 28-year-old man was referred for radiotherapy following removal of a left testicular cancer. The normal treatment for such a case involves irradiation to the lymph nodes on the posterior abdominal wall to which region cancer cells are most likely to metastasise from the testicle.

The patient arrived in the outpatient department late in the afternoon and it was decided to start treatment immediately, bypassing the normal planning routine. In this particular radiotherapy department, it was the common practice to give treatment for this tumour via one anterior abdominal field. However, because the patient had a very thick abdomen, it was decided to treat with two opposing fields. At the time of marking the treatment fields on the patient, the intended applied dose was not marked in the usual space on the treatment sheet, as it would have been if the patient had been marked-up in the planning room.

The patient arrived at the supervoltage machine after treatments had been completed for the day. The radiographers had no prior warning of his arrival. The senior radiographer calculated the applied dose from the machine data sheets but the calculations were made for a single field only and the contributions from the posterior (opposed) field were inadvertently overlooked. The figures were checked by the second radiographer on the machine, who failed to notice the error on the treatment sheet.

Treatment continued daily using the originally marked fields. On each occasion the patient received twice the intended dose. Each week the radiographers working on the machine checked the addition of the figures but no further check was made of the original tumour-dose calculations and no check was made by an independent radiographer. During treatment it was recorded that the patient suffered from nausea but was otherwise well. Regular blood counts failed to show an excessive depression of the white cells or platelets. On completion of treatment the details were summarised and the assumed midline abdominal dose was recorded. Because he had in fact received a midline abdominal dose of 6,000 cGy in 26 days, severe late complications developed to which the patient finally succumbed.

Comments Accidents are rarely due to a single error on the part of one person. They almost always follow a succession of errors made by two or more individuals. This case illustrates several very important points:

(1) There must be no deviation from an established planning routine except for the very rare acute emergency. Patients commencing treatment as an acute emergency must then be reviewed in the Planning Department and treatment plans checked. The modern Planning Department provides the best possible protection for the patient including, as it does, the opportunity for open discussion of each case amongst the doctors, senior radiographers and physicists.

(2) Checking of treatment sheets by a senior radiographer who is not normally involved in the day-to-day management of that particular

patient will reduce the chances of an error in the calculation being perpetuated. In this case the initial calculations were incorrect but the incorrectly calculated dose was then correctly administered. Occasionally, radiographers, being human, may make errors in the individual dose administered and this error could then be perpetuated unless the treatment sheets are reviewed independently. The recent introduction of computerised dosage monitoring should help to reduce this possible human error in future.

(3) The possibility of error would have been reduced if staff had been working under less pressure. The increasingly severe staff shortage developing in radiotherapy departments has been referred to already, and this must lead to a greater risk of error and overdosage. The author has been personally acquainted with eight similar cases during the last decade, all of which could probably have been prevented by accurate checking, by independent observers and by a reduction in the pressure in which these departments work. The potential cost of litigation in such cases is so enormous that it would be thought that the administration would be prepared to provide adequate staffing to ensure that such litigation does not happen. Unfortunately, this is not so. Throughout the country radiotherapy departments continue to struggle on, grossly overloaded and understaffed, despite the strongest possible staffing recommendations of the Royal College of Radiologists and Physicians and the Royal College of Radiographers (Royal College of Radiologists, 1991).

Complications following accidental 'technical' error

30.67

Case report In 1961 a 31-year-old woman received superficial X-ray treatment to the dorsum of both hands and fingers for chronic eczema, a benign condition. The prescribed dose was 100r, using 10 kv X-rays (Grenz rays) which was a conventional dose often used at that time for benign conditions of this type. Within a few days of receiving treatment, the skin became reddened, painful and eventually intensely inflamed and oedematous. Eventually there was complete loss of the epithelial surface, the appearance resembling a thermal burn, with the destruction of the full thickness of the skin. Healing was extremely slow but occurred eventually with the aid of plastic surgery. Twenty years later the patient remained crippled by severe hand deformities which had led to fixation and almost total loss of all hand and finger movements due to the gross scarring.

The X-ray unit which had delivered the dose was capable of functioning at several different voltage levels from 10 kv up to 50 kv. It is normal practice with X-ray therapy equipment to filter out very soft (relatively long wave) irradiation by inserting a suitable layer of material, or filter, between the target emitting the ionising radiation and the machine shutter aperture. The filter for 10 kv X-rays is very thin and that for 50 kv X-rays is much thicker. This particular machine had been serviced during the weekend and it had not been returned to its normal state prior to giving the treatment to the patient. The patient therefore received 50 kv X-rays, rather than 10 kv X-rays. In addition, the treatment was given through a filter which was normally used for 10 kv X-rays which resulted in an enormous overdosage of 6,500 rads.

Comment Ten more patients also received an overdosage of this order and all were severely damaged. An accident of this type is no longer possible because modern machines which are capable of working at several energy levels always have built in safety locks which prevent treatment unless the correct filter is used for the correct energy level. However, this accident emphasises what is potentially the most serious source of multiple overdosage in radiotherapy. It is necessary to service X-ray machines regularly and sometimes to carry out procedures such as the replacement of parts which are no longer functioning correctly. After any such manipulation, the machine must be rechecked with the greatest possible care and the checks should be repeated by an independent individual. In the case of a cobalt unit, the quality of the irradiation cannot alter appreciably and the output of the unit will decrease at a known rate as the radioactive source decays. The only major change in output will follow the replacement of an old, low-output source, with a new replacement cobalt source. Such a replacement must always be followed by careful checking of the unit's output, the checks being repeated by an independent person.

30.68 A complete check of this type is mandatory following the installation of a new radiotherapy machine before it is allowed into clinical service, but any change, however slight, in the possible functioning of the machine must also be accepted as an absolute indication for a recheck. Unfortunately, because of the work load in many radiotherapy departments, there is always great pressure on the physics staff to return a machine to clinical use at the earliest opportunity. This pressure is not helped by the antiquity of much of National Health Service radiotherapy equipment which necessitates frequent servicing and repair work if it is to be kept functioning correctly.

Complications following inadequate communication with the patient

30.69 It may be difficult to determine how much a 'lack of understanding' by a patient is genuine and how much is engendered by a desire for financial profit at a later date.

30.70

Case report A 57-year-old woman presented in 1976 with an early left-sided breast cancer. Local excision was followed by radiotherapy to the breast and lymph node regions. The following year, the patient complained of feeling generally unwell and, in addition, referred to a severe pain over the centre of the back. Radiographs of this region demonstrated a collapsed vertebral body which was assumed to be due to a metastatic deposit from the breast cancer. The painful bone was treated with local radiotherapy in conventional doses, and treatment was also started with injections of 'Decadurabolin' which is an accepted drug for hormone manipulation of breast cancer, widely used in the 1970s. The immediate response to treatment was very satisfactory but later the patient had other symptoms including multiple aches and pains. Some of these were proven not to be due to metastatic deposits and eventually she moved away to a different part of the country.

In 1981 a complaint was lodged against the Regional Health Authority claiming negligence on the part of the health authority and the radiotherapist concerned, as a consequence of which the plaintiff claimed that she had suffered injury and financial loss. The plaintiff complained that treatment for metastatic disease was incorrect because she was still alive, that she had suffered because she had been told that she would become paralysed and live for only six months, and that she had lost her job because of a letter written by the radiotherapist to her employers which was followed by her dismissal. In addition she stated that she had had a severe accident at work about six weeks before consulting the radiotherapist and that no attention was paid to this accident as a possible cause of her pain.

Very full and detailed notes were available. From an examination of these notes it was possible to deny all these points. Retrospectively, the five year interval without further deposits certainly reduced the chances that she had had a metastatic deposit in 1977 for which she had received irradiation. At that time the pain was apparently very severe and X-rays revealed a partially collapsed vertebral body in the mid thoracic spine. Retrospectively it could be argued that further investigations should have been carried out to determine the cause of the collapse. However, the only definitive way of establishing the presence of a malignant deposit in a vertebral body is by performing a needle biopsy of the affected bone and confirming the presence of malignant cells under a microscope. Unfortunately a negative biopsy does not exclude malignancy and because this patient was at that time in great pain, it was felt that radiotherapy would have been recommended anyway whatever the result of the biopsy. The patient's improvement after radiotherapy and hormone injections appeared to justify the initial diagnosis and treatment.

The radiotherapist's letter referred to by the plaintiff was sent on receipt of a request for information from her employers which was accompanied by a signed letter of consent by the patient herself. Both these letters had been kept in the hospital notes and were available. The reply sent by the radiotherapist was thought to be eminently reasonable, referring to 'severe pain, most probably due to metastases' and stating 'it seems that the disease is probably progressing gradually . . . She may not be fit to return to work again.' There was no evidence from the notes that the patient had ever been told that she only had six months to live and that she would become paralysed. Breast cancer is very unpredictable in its behaviour and many patients with widespread disease live normal active lives for many years. It is also uncommon for a patient with metastases from breast cancer to become paralysed. The letter to her employers conveyed a more accurate idea of the radiotherapist's views on her outlook. 'Progressing gradually' does not equate with only six months of life.

Finally, the detailed notes made when she first saw the radiotherapist with her back pain contained no reference to an accident. It was inconceivable that a severe accident taking place only six weeks before the interview with the radiotherapist would not have been referred to by the patient and recorded in the notes.

Comment The defence of this case is totally dependent on the adequacy of the notes. Fortunately they were very detailed and fully supported the radiotherapist's actions. Whether or not one should biopsy a presumed early metastasis is often a difficult decision. In general, treatment of malignant disease must always be preceded by histological proof. Even when there is a past history of a primary malignant tumour, a biopsy from an apparent metastatic deposit should always be considered when the overall history is long and when there are atypical features present. However, a bone biopsy may be painful and, depending upon the site of the bone, sometimes dangerous. In addition it also usually requires seven to ten days preparation before it can be examined under the microscope. If a patient is in severe pain, it is not uncommon to carry out a biopsy and then commence irradiation quickly before the results are available. This is reasonable because the conventional dose given for a metastatic deposit is small and does not entail any complications at a later date. Obviously, each case must be determined on its own merits.

30.71

Case report A 16-year-old girl presented with an ugly, irritating, painful keloid scar following an appendicectomy. It was decided that her symptoms justified the use of irradiation to the scar and a single dose of 500 cGy was given. The pain and irritation disappeared over the following four weeks and when seen, one year later, the scar was no longer raised and red. Nineteen years later, a letter was received from a solicitor requesting full details of the treatment which was held to be responsible for her persistent infertility after six years of marriage.

Examination of the original notes showed that the scar had been treated with beta rays from a radioactive plaque. It was also clearly recorded in the notes that this irradiation technique had been chosen deliberately in order to ensure that no ionising radiation could reach the ovaries deep in the pelvis. As described previously, beta rays are a form of particulate irradiation. The particles have a finite range in soft tissue and penetrate for only a few millimetres. A photocopy of the records was sent to the solicitor, who immediately dropped the matter.

Comment Although it was thought that an adequate explanation had been given to the patient at the time of her original treatment, clearly the passage of time had dulled her memory. It is probable that even if the original notes had not been obtainable, she would have been able to recall that treatment had not been given with an X-ray machine. Under these circumstances, it would be difficult to be sure of the actual type of irradiation without having access to good clinical records.

SUMMARY

30.72 Medico-legal problems which are associated with the practice of radiotherapy fall into three main categories:

(1) *Paradoxical* Cure of a cancer may be associated with a long life expectancy, particularly in the young, during which time long effects of irradiation on normal tissues may develop. There is a real need for full discussion between the radiotherapist and patient or a responsible member of the family before commencing treatment. Details of such a

conversation should be recorded in the notes. In future, it may be necessary to ask patients or relatives to sign detailed consent forms which include a full account of the underlying cancer and all possible complications of the suggested radiotherapy. With many patients this will be acceptable but there are others who will undoubtedly be terrified and who may perhaps be unable to accept potentially curative treatment.

(2) *Human error* 'Medical' and 'technical' accidents are largely avoidable by adopting routines which always involve double checks at all levels. Routine procedures must be rigidly adhered to except when dealing with emergencies and as soon as possible, after an emergency situation has been managed, all steps taken should be carefully checked. Any procedure involving alteration to the function of a radiotherapy machine must always be followed by very careful checking which should be confirmed independently.

(3) *Emotional* Very close contact between the patient and the treatment team reduces the possibility of stress engendering dissatisfaction which may precipitate litigation at a subsequent date.

CHEMOTHERAPY

30.73 The use of cytotoxic drugs in the attempted control of cancer is much less liable to litigation than radiotherapy. Most of the side-effects associated with the use of these drugs are relatively acute. There is therefore much less chance of a patient developing late complications many years afterwards due to the drugs which cured the cancer. However, there are certain situations where the use of cytotoxic drugs may be followed by litigation.

Principles of chemotherapy

30.74 Many drugs affect growing cells. A wide range of drugs has been developed which affect the growing cancer cell more than the average growing cell in normal tissue. The first drug to be used successfully was mustine. Early publications in 1946 indicated that this drug could have an effect on many types of cancer including lung cancer and particularly some of the lymphomas. Mustine is a direct derivative of mustard gas and its beneficial effects were discovered after noting that mustard gas, used in the First World War, produced very severe falls in the blood count as well as damage to the lining of the mucosal surfaces and in particular the lungs. Mustine must be administered by intravenous injection. It is a very reactive drug, interacting vigorously with many tissues. It is prepared by dissolving a dried powder in water. The solution must be given immediately, intravenously. It is so irritating that it may produce phlebitis in the vein into which it is injected, an effect which is very rarely seen with modern cytotoxic drugs. Each injection is followed by severe vomiting about half an hour to one hour later, and is also followed by measurable bone marrow depression, which usually recovers spontaneously. When this drug was used as a single agent, it was found that its effect on tumours was transient and no more than a temporary improvement could be produced.

30.75 Since the introduction of mustine, hundreds of other agents have been investigated of which a small number remain in current use. Some of these cytotoxic drugs are indicated in Table 30.3 in which their main toxic effects are summarised. It should be emphasised that there are many special toxicities associated with the various drugs and they should be used only by specialists who are well acquainted with all their side effects and the correct precautions that must be taken with their administration. Although phlebitis is very rarely seen now with most modern drugs given by intravenous injection, most cytotoxic drugs are very reactive. If there is leakage (extravasation) outside a vein during injection, there may be a development of an acute inflammatory reaction which can be very painful. This may be followed by dense induration with subsequent skin ulceration, which fails to heal. The best treatment following severe extravasation may be urgent exicision and skin grafting. Extravasation is a possible cause for litigation if normal precautions are not taken. It is usually recommended that all the more irritating cytotoxic drugs must be given into an established fast running intravenous infusion. In patients where there are considerable difficulties in giving intravenous injections because of the small size of the peripheral veins, it may be preferable for an indwelling intravenous cannula (Hickman line) to be inserted by a surgical colleague, which can be used over a period of many months. In general, once the line is estabished, the most important precautions include strict asepsis and the flushing though of a dilute solution of heparin at regular intervals to prevent blood clotting in the line.

30.76 Before using any cytotoxic drugs it is important to calculate the correct dose that should be used. This is normally based on the weight and height of the patient which are combined to give the surface area. Normally, before commencing chemotherapy, all patients have kidney and liver functions performed as well as full blood investigation to assess bone marrow function. For drugs which are excreted through the kidney (methotrexate, cisplatinum) it is particularly important to measure renal function. If kidney function is impaired then dangerously high blood levels of the drug may be obtained following administration of a standard intravenous injection. Depression of the bone marrow with cytotoxic drugs is the most common side effect, but this is not seen after bleomycin and is very uncommon with vincristine. It is customary for all patients receiving cytotoxic drugs to have a full blood count carried out before each new course of treatment is commenced, in order to avoid cumulative suppression of the bone marrow.

The practice of chemotherapy

30.77 Patients commencing chemotherapy are normally measured very carefully to estimate the correct doses of the drugs to be used. The regime that is to be used is decided by the clinician in charge who must be fully aware of all possible side effects of the drugs. If there are any specific toxicities associated with any of the drugs that are to be used, then special tests may be necessary. For example, before the use of doxorubicin, cardiac studies should be carried out including an electrocardiogram. It is well known that the prolonged use of doxorubicin may damage the heart if certain dose levels are exceeded. If the patient already has a damaged heart before treatment, then the risks are greater. Similarly, with cisplatin and vincristine, peripheral neuritis may develop and in the case of cisplatin, damage to the eighth (auditory) nerve may lead to progressive deafness. It is customary to examine the eighth nerve and the nervous system in cases receiving these drugs in order to detect the development of any of these complications. Reference has already been made to the need for kidney function studies during the use of methotrexate and cisplatin. If a patient is found to have impaired renal function before starting treatment with these drugs, it may be necessary to review the whole case and reconsider alternative treatment methods.

30.78 Having investigated the patient completely before treatment commences, arrangements are made to start either as an out-patient or as an in-patient depending on the severity of the treatment, the possibility of side-effects and the need to give antidotes for any acute side effects which may occur. For example, if a patient is to be treated with high-dose Ifosfamide, very severe vomiting may follow and it may be advisable to admit the patient so that high-dose antiemetic treatment can be given during the acute phase. Because Ifosfamide also has a severe effect on the bladder when given in large doses, it may be necessary to counteract this toxicity by giving the drug Mesna, which can be best accomplished by maintaining the patient as an in-patient.

30.79 When using chemotherapeutic drugs which are likely to produce vomiting, in the past it was customary to cover their period of administration with large loses of antiemetic drugs, and if necessary, to treat the patient as an in-patient. Recent advances in the control of vomiting have lead to the development of new highly effective $5HT_3$ antagonist antiemetics such as Odansitron. These drugs allow many patients to tolerate even some of the most emetogenic cytotoxic drugs as an out-patient. Unfortunately these new drugs are very expensive. Many drugs used in chemotherapy do not produce severe vomiting and these have always been used for out-patient treatment.

30.80 Provided patients are aware of the nature of their disease and the treatment that is being advised for them, there are rarely any legal complications during the acute treatment of cancer with cytotoxic agents. The clinician concerned in the management must have specialised knowledge to appreciate and avoid all the side effects that have been referred to above and records will normally be kept indicating the blood counts and the function of any other relevant organs during the course of treatment which may extend over 6–12 months. It is essential that all patients are warned beforehand regarding any toxicity which may occur, including hair fall.

Chronic side-effects

30.81 As indicated above, dissatisfaction leading to subsequent litigation is most likely to occur when a patient has been cured of a cancer and later develops chronic complications associated with the treatment. Dissatisfaction of this type is best avoided by very careful explanation beforehand of any possible long-term effects. When dealing with children, it is important that possible long-term effects are discussed with the parents. A written record must be made of the discussion so that there is ample evidence available in the future should it be needed. The following are the most common long-term possible effects which might precipitate legal complications.

Bone marrow suppression

30.82 Permanent bone marrow suppression is very uncommon when drugs are given in reasonably large doses intermittently. Between the injections, the bone marrow recovers and it is normal practice to re-examine the blood count before commencing the next course of treatment. More recently, a more vigorous form of treatment has been introduced in the management of malignancies. This involves the use of bone marrow aspiration from the patient, and storage in a deep freezer, followed by massive doses of chemotherapeutic agents. The dosage of drugs is such that destruction of the patient's remaining bone marrow is inevitable. Following such treatment, the blood count will plummet and the patient will be prone to all types of serious infections. During this period of time, the patient must be nursed in hospital under sterile conditions. At the correct moment after this treatment, the patient's own marrow, which was removed and stored before treatment commenced, will be reconstituted and given back intravenously. Under normal circumstances, after a period of considerable illness due to the low blood count, the blood count recovers as the patient's own bone marrow cells repopulate the patient and commence functioning normally. There are risks associated with this type of treatment and clearly these risks must be discussed with the patient beforehand. However, it is extremely unlikely that any serious complications following this type of treatment will be associated with litigation because the whole procedure is carried out at a time when the patient and relatives are fully aware of the unpleasant nature of the patient's disease. Even fatal complications can be accepted in this situation.

30.83 The long-term administration of drugs such as chlorambucil, without regular blood counts can lead to severe depression of the bone marrow and is a situation where litigation might occur.

Renal and peripheral nerve damage

30.84 These complications have been referred to already, particularly with cisplatin. This complication should certainly be referred to before using drugs of this type and very careful measurements should be carried out. Should there be indications that these complications are developing then the situation should be discussed with the patient. For example, if the patient has a highly malignant ovarian tumour which was responding well to cisplatin, then it may be preferable to continue with a different platinum derivative because without continued treatment relapse of the malignancy is possible. However, this must be carefully considered with the patient and relatives. Alternative treatment methods may be possible.

Gonadal suppression

30.85 This is extremely common with all alkylating agents but many of the other drugs can also produce testicular atrophy and amenorrhoea. It is less common for hormone production to be affected although the menopause may be induced earlier than normal in the case of women. However, again, there should be no serious complications from this point of view if the possibility is discussed carefully with patients beforehand. Most patients who are fully in the picture regarding their disease will accept the risk of sterility in exchange for life. In the male, sperm storage before commencing chemotherapy should be considered. The possibility of sterility has to be discussed in great detail with parents, most of whom would prefer to have their children alive but sterile, rather than dead.

Second malignancies

30.86 An uncommon late complication of cytotoxic drug therapy is the development of a second malignancy due specifically to the cytotoxic drugs that were administered. This occurrence is being recorded with increasing frequency as patients live for longer and longer periods of time. It is seen most commonly after diseases such as Hodgkin's disease which can be cured so successfully with radiotherapy or with chemotherapy. After chemotherapy, there is a definite risk of a development of acute leukaemia or non-Hodgkin's lymphoma at a later date. If a patient needs repeated treatment courses over many years, then the risks are very considerable, rising to 20 per cent. However, once again the alternative is earlier death from the Hodgkin's disease and the planned treatment is therefore acceptable to most intelligent people. Should a leukaemia develop at a later date in this type of patient, the leukaemia can be treated and in some cases controlled.

Prevention of litigation

30.87 Litigation in the practice of cytotoxic management of cancer is less likely to occur than in the practice of radiotherapy. The reasons for this are given above. Litigation can be avoided almost completely by careful explanation, by close co-operation between the patient and medical staff, by control of the patient by an expert who is fully aware of all possible complications and takes every possible precaution to avoid or reduce the chance of these complications and by very careful recording.

BIBLIOGRAPHICAL REFERENCES

Baldwin, Sir P, Joslin C A F and Williams P C 'Report of independent inquiry into the conduct of Isocentric Radiotherapy at the North Staffordshire Royal Infirmary between 1982 and 1991' (1992) West Midlands Regional Health Authority.

Ellis F 'Dose, time and fractionation: a clinical hypothesis' (1969) Clinical Radiology 20, 1–7.

Joint Council for Clinical Oncology 'Reducing delays in Cancer Treatment. Improving quality control. Some treatment targets' (1992) Royal College of Radiologists and Royal College of Physicians.

Roswit B 'Complications of Radiation Therapy: The Alimentary Tract' (1974) Seminars in Roentgenology 9, 51–63.

Royal College of Radiologists *Medical Manpower and Workload in Clinical Oncology in the United Kingdom* (Royal College of Radiologists, 1991).

Secretary of State for Health *The Health of the Nation. A Strategy for Health in England* (HMSO, 1992a).
Secretary of State for Health *The Patient's Charter* (Department of Health, 1992b).
Standing Subcommittee on Cancer *Quality Assurance in Radiotherapy* (Department of Health, 1991).
Thwaites Sir B, Burlin T and Joslin C A F Incident in Radiotherapy Department. The report of the committee of enquiry (Exeter Health Authority, 1988).
Tunkel V 'Legal aspects of clinical trials in the United Kingdom' in Williams C J (Ed) *Introducing new Treatments for Cancer: Practical, Ethical and Legal Problems* (John Wiley & Sons, 1992) pp 9–24.

CROSS-REFERENCE

For information related to topics in this chapter see Chapter 41.

FIGURE 30.1 TYPICAL BUILD-UP OF INTENSITY OF IONISATION USING SUPERVOLTAGE RADIATION (>1 meV)

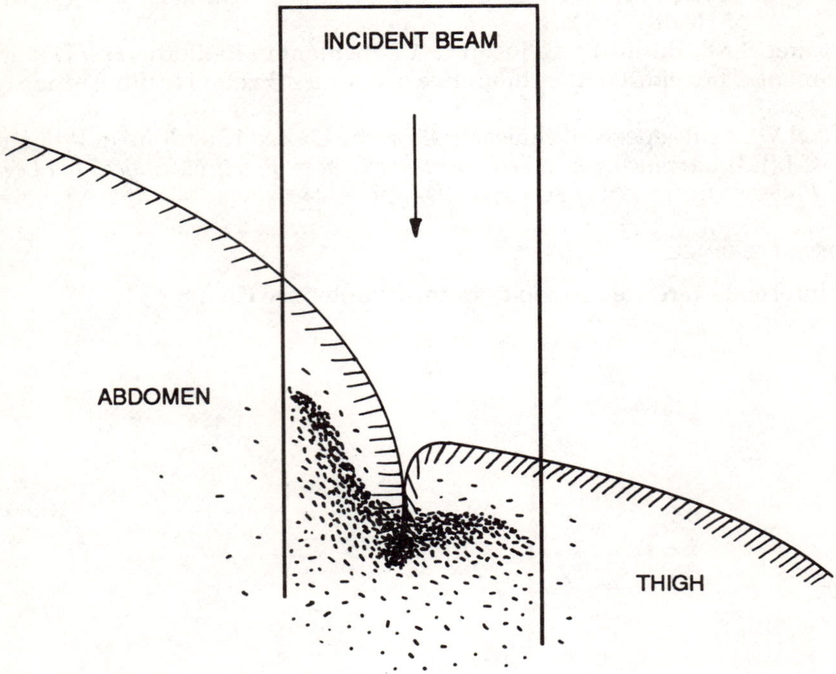

For technical reasons the maximum radiation effect occurs not in the skin (as with 200 kv 'Deep' X-rays) but below the skin. The depth of this maximum effect is related directly to the energy of the irradiating beam. Maximum skin sparing is only seen when the beam is vertical to the skin surface. Protection is less if the skin surface is angled to the incident beam. There is no protection in skin creases and folds, as is seen in this diagram of a supervoltage beam used for the treatment of malignant lymph nodes in the groin. Skin reactions of this type may be unavoidable and are not an indication of bad treatment.

FIGURE 30.2 THE RELATIONSHIP BETWEEN RADIATION DOSE AND FREQUENCY AND SEVERITY OF PATHOLOGICAL EFFECTS ON NORMAL TISSUES

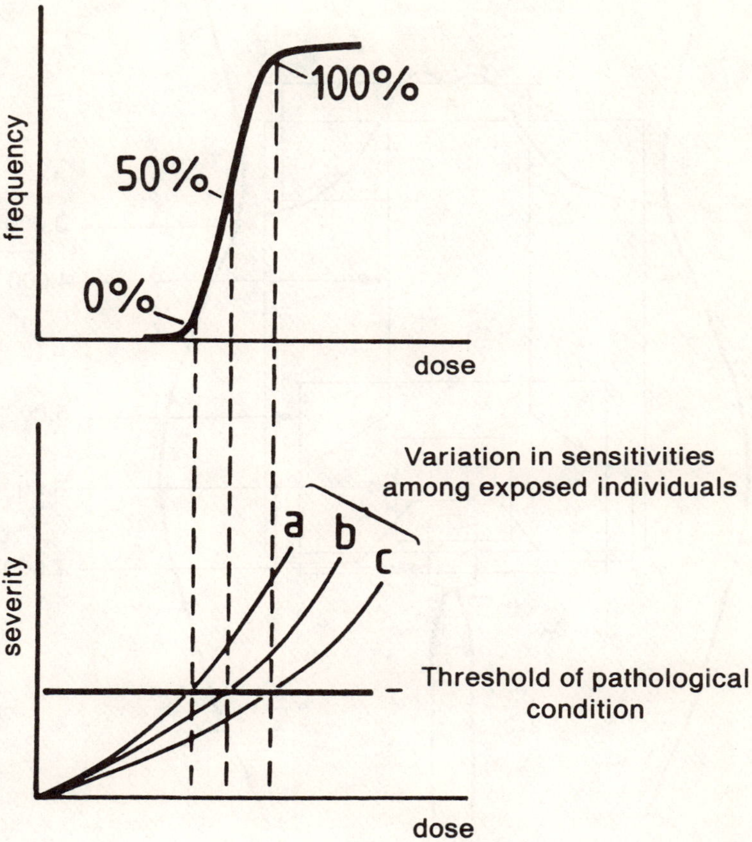

These two figures demonstrate that both the severity and frequency of these effects increase as a function of dose in a population of varying susceptibilities. The severity of the effect increases most steeply in individuals of greatest susceptibility (curve a) and becomes clinically apparent at a lower dose than in subgroups of less susceptible individuals (curves b, c). The range of doses over which the different subgroups cross the same threshold of severity is reflected in the upper curve.

(Figure 30.2 with grateful acknowledgments to S B Field and A C Acton and the Editor, International Journal of Radiation Biology.)

FIGURE 30.3 GRAPHIC PRESENTATION OF REASONABLE 'MAXIMUM' DOSE LEVELS IN RELATION TO TREATMENT VOLUME AND ANATOMIC ZONE

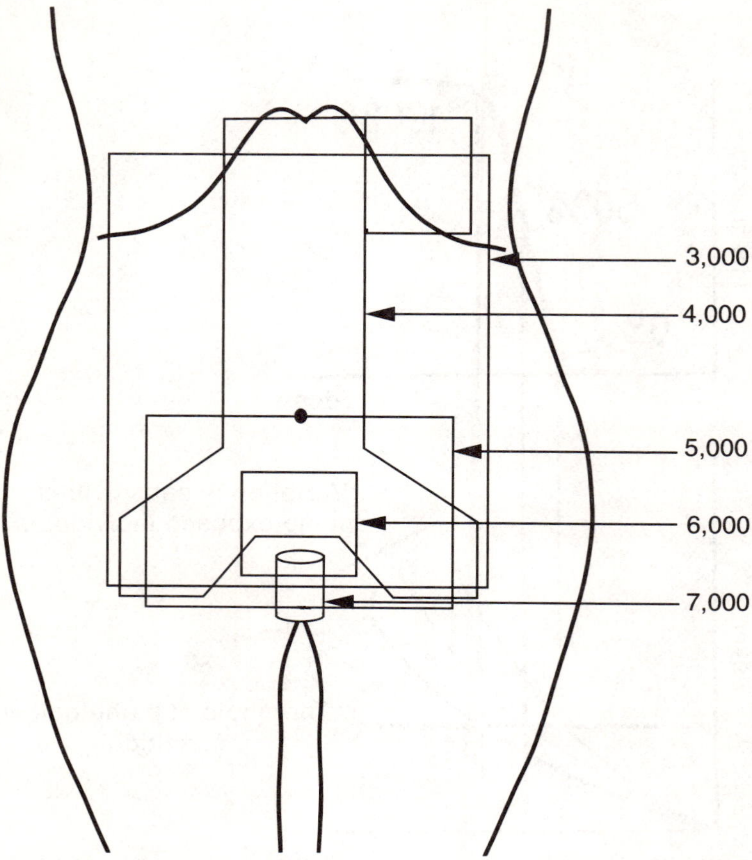

For total abdomen, 3,000 rads (eg for advanced ovarian cancer); inverted 'Y', 4,000 rads (eg for malignant lymphoma); total pelvis, 5,000 rads (eg for advanced cervical cancer); limited pelvis, 6,000 rads (eg for bladder cancer); and local perineal, 7,000 rads with rotation (eg for prostatic cancer).

(Figure 30.3 from Roswit B 'Complications of Radiation Therapy: The Alimentary Tract' (1974) Seminars in Roentgenology, 9, 51–63, with grateful acknowledgments to the Author and the Editor.)

TABLE 30.1 THE RADIOSENSITIVITY OF HIGHLY RADIOSENSITIVE ORGANS WHICH MAY REQUIRE SPECIAL PROTECTION DURING CONVENTIONAL RADIOTHERAPY

Relative radiosensitivity of highly radiosensitive organs receiving conventionally fractionated irradiation (after S B Field and A C Upton)

Organ	*Average threshold dose*
Haemopoietic system	Highly sensitive
Whole body	250–500 cGy L.D. 50
Eye	
Lens (cataract)	550–600 cGy
Testicle	500 cGy
Ovary (age dependent)	400–800 cGy

TABLE 30.2 THE RELATIVE RADIOSENSITIVITIES OF NORMAL ORGANS, WHICH MAY BE INCLUDED IN TREATMENT VOLUMES RECEIVING THERAPEUTIC IRRADIATION

The clinical manifestations produced may be greatly reduced if only part of an organ is irradiated (eg lung, kidney)

Relative radiosensitivity of various tissues and organs receiving conventionally fractionated irradiation (after S B Field and A C Upton)

Organ	*Average threshold dose*
Skin	5,000 cGy
Digestion system	
Whole liver	2,000–2,500 cGy
Gastrointestinal tract	4,500 cGy
Salivary gland, pancreas	5,000 cGy
Cardiovascular system	
Whole heart	4,000 cGy
Nervous system	
Brain, spinal cord	4,000 cGy
Urinary tract	
Both kidneys	2,000 cGy
Respiratory system	
Both lungs	2,000 cGy
Endocrine	
Thyroid	2,500 cGy
Infantile breast	1,000 cGy

TABLE 30.3 SOME CYTOTOXIC DRUGS COMMONLY USED IN CANCER THERAPY

	*Administration**	*Toxicity*
Alkylating agents		
Mustine	iv +	Vomiting, phlebitis, marrow
Chlorambucil	po	(Chronic) marrow
Cyclophosphamide	iv/po +	Hair, vomiting, marrow
Ifosfamide	iv +	Hair, vomiting, marrow
Melphalan	po	Vomiting, marrow
Busulphan	po	Marrow
Thiotepa	im/iv	Vomiting, marrow
Cytotoxic antibiotics		
Doxorubicin	iv +	Hair, vomiting, marrow, mucositis, cardiac
Actinomycin D	iv +	Hair, vomiting, marrow, mucositis
Bleomycin	iv +	Hair, mucositis, hypersensitivity, pneumonitis
Antimetabolitis		
Methotrexate	iv/po (intrathecal)	Hair, mucositis, marrow (Kidney)
5 Fluorouracil	iv/po	Mucositis, marrow
Vinca alkaloids		
Vinblastine	iv +	Neuritis, marrow
Vincristine	iv +	Neuritis (marrow)
Etoposide	iv/po +	Hair, marrow, vomiting
Cisplatin	iv +	Vomiting, kidney, 8th nerve, neuritis, marrow

* *Route of administration:* iv – intravenous injection; po – by mouth; im – intramuscular injection.

There is great variation in the effects of cytotoxic drugs, which are summarised briefly in this table. A serious side effect common to many of these drugs given intravenously is that accidental extravasation outside the vein may be followed by severe tissue damage (+). Many drugs may produce nausea and vomiting, hair loss and marrow depression. Some have special toxicities affecting the peripheral nerves (Vincristine) or the kidneys (Cisplatin). Interference with gonadal function has not been referred to in the table; it is seen most commonly with the alkylating agents but almost any of these drugs may produce permanent damage if high doses have to be used.

CHAPTER 31

Psychiatry

Professor Robert Bluglass *MD FRCPsych MRCP DPM*

SUMMARY

31.1 Until a decade or more ago there were relatively few allegations of medical negligence directed towards psychiatrists and there are several possible explanations for this. Firstly, the expectations of patients were probably ill defined; diagnosis and treatment lacked precision, and psychiatric patients not only often lacked the capacity to formulate a complaint, but were also frequently constrained by the circumstances of compulsory detention. The fear of frivolous complaints or of allegations arising without foundation resulted in special protection for the staff of psychiatric hospitals under the Mental Health Act 1959, so that leave of the court had to be obtained before proceedings could be initiated. Psychiatric patients are more likely than others to misinterpret what is said to them, to be impulsive, irrational, paranoid, to have a faulty recollection or to be driven unreasonably by delusional beliefs or by hallucinatory instruction. They are also more vulnerable to exploitation, to misinterpretation of their competency and to suffer inadequacies in their treatment without protest. Because of their vulnerability, particularly when severely mentally ill or mentally handicapped, and because sometimes the liberty of such patients may be lawfully restricted, they are provided with a range of protective measures by statute which are not so far available to other, non-psychiatric patients.

31.2 That is not to say, however, that psychiatric patients are necessarily incompetent to take responsibility for their own decisions or are inevitably to have their credibility doubted. In criminal proceedings the ability to understand the proceedings and give a valid plea must be tested by the court if it is in doubt (Criminal Procedure (Insanity and Unfitness to Plead) Act 1991). In the Ashworth Inquiry (1992), detained patients in a maximum security hospital were considered capable of giving witness evidence to a tribunal, and the consent provisions in legislation imply that detained patients may be competent to give or refuse consent to treatment.

31.3 There are two principal categories of litigation which concern psychiatrists:

(1) cases relating to psychiatric diagnosis, treatment or management;
(2) other medical cases which include a psychiatric element or claim.

STANDARDS OF PRACTICE

Training

31.4 Psychiatrists are qualified registered medical practitioners who have undertaken a programme of general psychiatric training of three or four years duration in schemes approved by the Royal College of Psychiatrists leading to the higher registered qualification of Membership of the Royal College of Psychiatrists (MRCPsych). This is followed by three or four years higher professional training at senior registrar level in the fields of general adult psychiatry or in mental handicap (now also known as developmental psychiatry or mental disability), child and adolescent psychiatry, psychotherapy, the mental disorders of the elderly, substance and alcohol abuse or forensic psychiatry. Completion of training qualifies for appointment as a consultant.

31.5 Forensic psychiatry is a fast-growing speciality; in 1966 there were five full-time specialists in this field in England and Wales and now there are more than eighty. Forensic psychiatrists specialise in the medico-legal aspects of psychiatry. Although the main focus of their work is with offenders who also suffer from psychiatric disorder many also have a specialist knowledge and experience of civil litigation. Training includes working in forensic psychiatric hospitals and units, the management and treatment of mentally disordered offenders, knowledge of the law, the preparation of court reports and giving evidence as an expert witness in criminal or civil cases.

31.6 Child and adolescent psychiatrists have also extended their field of activity to include a growing experience of medico-legal work in recent years as a result of new child care legislation and consequent litigation.

THE FIELD OF PRACTICE

31.7 Fewer psychiatrists now work in large mental hospitals. As a result of current policies these are steadily being closed and psychiatric care and treatment is provided in small district general hospital psychiatric units and, increasingly, in the community in day hospitals, out-patient clinics, general practices and at the patient's home. Most psychiatric treatment is provided by family doctors who refer about ten per cent of patients with psychiatric problems to specialists; mostly those with more severe and serious conditions.

31.8 Child psychiatrists are based in local authority NHS clinics; mental handicap specialists in community clinics and in a few remaining hospitals, and forensic psychiatrists are mostly based in regional medium secure psychiatric hospitals and clinics, in the three large high-security hospitals, in prisons and remand centres. Psychotherapists provide specialised forms of treatment based upon a personal dialogue and therapeutic interaction with the patient who is seen in an out-patient clinic or private rooms. The private sector is generally growing in importance although it still provides a relatively small amount of the total psychiatric care.

31.9 Psychiatrists now work in multi-disciplinary teams which they usually lead, together with community psychiatric nurses, psychologists, occupational therapists and social workers. However, grave shortages of staff of all kinds often lead to deficiencies at the present time and this can sometimes lead to mishap in the care of patients. Decision-making is frequently shared by these professionals although the doctor often, although not always, has a statutory responsibility.

31.10 The special requirements of mental health legislation also define specific obligations and confer powers and responsibilities upon the consultant psychiatrist, over and above those inherent in the requirements of the common law, with the complication of possible pitfalls which are confined to psychiatry.

31.11 The Secretary of State for Health is also required by legislation to make provision for the care of psychiatric patients including aftercare.

31.12 The rights of patients when they are detained in hospital as permitted by sections of the Mental Health Act 1983 are monitored by the Mental Health Act Commission, a special health authority appointed by the Secretary of State. The Commission is required to undertake the following:

(1) to protect the interests of detained patients by
   (a) visiting and interviewing patients in hospitals and mental nursing homes;
   (b) investigating complaints by, and about, detained patients;
   (c) keeping under review the way in which the powers and duties under the Act are carried out (so far as they relate to detained patients);

(2) (a) the provision of a second opinion by doctors appointed by the Commission on behalf of the Secretary of State (and in special cases also other commissioners) where the Mental Health Act 1983 requires such opinions to be obtained before treatment is given to detained patients (or in special cases to informal patients as well);
   (b) the carrying out of reviews of such treatments at later stages when second opinions have previously been given;

(3) on behalf of the Secretary of State, drafting a code of practice periodically;

(4) reviewing any decision made at a special hospital to withhold a postal packet or its contents if a review is applied for.

31.13 The quality of care given in psychiatric hospitals is influenced by regular visits by the Mental Health Act Commission who comment with increasing confidence upon weaknesses which indirectly affect the civil rights of patients. The Health Advisory Service, appointed by the Secretary of State also carries out periodic intensive inspections of psychiatric hospitals to monitor the standards of care and to disseminate good practices. The Royal College of Psychiatrists and the Joint Committee for Higher Psychiatric Training regularly inspects training posts in hospitals to ensure they meet prescribed standards. Hospitals which detain patients are also subject to the scrutiny of the European Committee on Torture and Inhuman or Degrading Treatment which may visit, without immediate notice, any institution in the European Community which subjects patients to involuntary confinement.

31.14 In 1984 the Council of Europe established the following principles which are binding upon all member states:

(1) a wide definition of 'unsoundness of mind' is accepted and includes personality disorders as well as mental illness. Diagnosis must however be based on an 'objective medical assessment' and the seriousness of the disorder must be sufficient to justify detention;
(2) the detention of a mental patient can only be lawful (unless other motives for detention recognised by the convention exist) if the detention takes place in a hospital, a clinic, or a special institution for the mentally disordered;
(3) the detained mental patient must have easy access to a court, which need not be a regular criminal court, but must have the following features; independence from the government and administration, procedural guarantees, and the right for the patient to be heard and represented. The decision of the court must not be subject to confirmation by a government or administrative official or body. The patient has the right to a periodic review since the conditions concerning the detention (notably the mental state) may change;
(4) the conditions for detention must correspond to therapeutic standards. Solitary confinement must be accompanied by adequate supervision and appropriate psychiatric treatment and must be linked strictly according to objectively established security needs.

31.15 The rights and freedoms accorded to persons who may be subject to psychiatric care are protected by the European Convention of Human Rights.[1]

1 See also chapters by Harding T and Bowden P in Bluglass R and Bowden P (eds) *The Principles and Practice of Forensic Psychiatry* (Churchill Livingstone, 1990).

THE CARE AND MANAGEMENT OF PSYCHIATRIC PATIENTS

Informal patients in hospital

31.16 Informal psychiatric patients are patients under treatment in hospital without formality. They have freely consented to accept admission. They cannot be subject to any restraint, be locked up, secluded or treated without their informed consent. To do so would invite the possibility of an allegation of false imprisonment or of assault or battery. An informal patient should be free to leave subject to reasonable arrangements if he wishes to do so. Bearing in mind the possibility of irrational judgment in some patients, consent should be freely given and the exchange between doctor and patient recorded or witnessed. Consent forms for ECT or medication are often inadequate and in any case are simply a record that a proper explanation has been given and that it has been understood.

INVOLUNTARY HOSPITALISATION

31.17 The power to detain a patient in hospital compulsorily is an authority given by the Mental Health Act 1983, which should always be used with restraint and caution. In England and Wales compulsory committal does not involve a judicial authority but relies upon the medical recommendations of doctors, the application of a social worker or relative, and the acceptance of a patient by the hospital managers. The patient should always be admitted informally if this is possible. Compulsory admission implies a deprivation of liberty and restriction of individual rights, although there are many safeguards to protect the patient.

31.18 Sections 2 and 4 (admission for assessment) and 3 (admission for treatment) of the Mental Health Act 1983 require recommendations from two registered medical practitioners, one of whom must be approved by the Secretary of State in terms of section 12 of the Act as having special experience in the diagnosis or treatment of mental disorder ('an approved doctor'). The two doctors should ideally be the patient's family doctor and the consultant psychiatrist receiving the patient, but often they are two other doctors, such as a deputising general practitioner and an 'approved' doctor who is not on the staff of the receiving hospital, neither of whom knows the patient; this has of course potential risks.

31.19 The independence of the two doctors making medical recommendations is of special importance to protect the patient from any possibility of collusion, improper influence or interference with independent clinical judgment. The two doctors are required to examine the patient personally, which means interviewing him before signing any documents.

31.20 The Mental Health Act 1983 requires that the two doctors must each sign the documents on or before the date of application to the hospital managers and that they will have examined the patient personally, either together or separately. In the latter case, not more than five days must have elapsed between the day on which the separate examinations took place. Only one of the two medical recommendations may be given by a doctor on the staff of the receiving hospital in normal circumstances (see section 12(4)).

31.21 A medical recommendation shall not be given by:

(a) the applicant;
(b) a partner of the applicant or of a practitioner by whom another medical recommendation is given for the purposes of the same application;
(c) a person employed as an assistant by the applicant or by any such practitioner;
(d) a person who receives or has an interest in the receipt of any payments made on account of the maintenance of a patient; or
(e) a practitioner on the staff of the hospital to which the patient is to be admitted (with certain exceptions).

31.22 A general practitioner who is employed part-time in a hospital shall not, for the purpose of providing medical recommendations, be regarded as a practitioner on the staff of the hospital. The medical recommendations for the purpose of compulsory admission for treatment (section 3) or for guardianship (section 7) will have no effect unless they both describe the patient as suffering from the same form of mental disorder, whether or not he is also described as suffering from another form.

HAZARDS AND PITFALLS

31.23 It is essential that all the procedures described above are properly followed, the correct forms completed, as required, and that the doctors involved qualify appropriately and act in good faith and with reasonable care.[1] Errors frequently occur and usually take the form of badly completed forms, failing to give the grounds for the diagnosis, failing to state why detention is necessary, or omitting the necessary technical details. Unsatisfactory documents can mean that the patient is unlawfully detained.

1 See *Winch v Jones* [1986] QB 296, [1985] 3 All ER 97, CA.

31.24 It has also happened that two doctors who had close knowledge of a patient did not carry out a specific personal examination for the purpose of a medical recommendation but simply signed the form. The patient succeeded in an action against a psychiatrist and a general practitioner.[1]

1 Brahams D 'Proceedings for False Imprisonment and Negligence under 1959 Mental Health Act' (1983) Lancet 2, 466.

31.25 In another recent case, the visiting consultant was refused an interview with the patient at her home. She was resentful and hostile, appeared briefly and then locked herself in her room. The psychiatrist had extensive previous knowledge of the patient and was able to interview a relative who provided convincing evidence of psychotic relapse. The psychiatrist signed a form to detain the patient under section 2 but was subsequently challenged on the grounds that the order was invalid as he had not examined the patient and she had, therefore, been falsely imprisoned. The doctor's actions were upheld.

31.26 It is rare, in the author's experience, for doctors to be involved who did not qualify in terms of the Act. It is, however, not unknown for both of the doctors not to be approved under the Act (where one must be) thereby invalidating the procedures.

SAFEGUARDS

Duties of managers to give information

31.27 The managers of a hospital or nursing home are required by the Mental Health Act 1983, section 132 to take such steps as are practicable to ensure that the patient understands:

(a) under which provisions of the Act he is detained and its effects;
(b) his rights to apply for a Mental Health Review Tribunal hearing to have his case reviewed.

Information should be given in language the patient can understand and leaflets are available in appropriate languages.

31.28 The managers must also ensure that the patient understands the effect of the consent to treatment procedures, the requirements of the Act with regard to correspondence (where relevant), and must furnish relatives with a copy of information given to the patient, unless the patient requests that it is not done. The managers must inform the nearest relative when the patient is to be discharged; within seven days of discharge if practicable (unless the patient or nearest relative requests otherwise).

Managers appeals

31.29 Since the managers are the detaining authority they may also discharge the patient who has a right to apply to the managers if he believes he is wrongly detained. The role of the managers in giving consideration to applications for discharge is not clear in the Act. District Health Authorities directly managing hospitals may delegate this function to a sub-committee of individuals to act on their behalf. Managers of Trust hospitals cannot delegate and must hear applications themselves. Increasingly formalised procedures for this purpose have been devised by managers and the revised Code of Practice (1993) gives guidance to managers on this subject. The patient cannot receive legal aid or be legally represented but may be accompanied by a friend or relative. If the managers decide to discharge the patient against the advice of the responsible medical officer, they must be careful to consider all the implications. Unlike a Mental Health Review Tribunal, the managers do not have an independent medical member to assist them in making a decision.

Mental Health Review Tribunals

31.30 The function of Mental Health Review Tribunals is to provide detained patients with the right to apply to an independent body (not the detaining authority) to have their detention reviewed and to be discharged. The Tribunal is appointed by the Lord Chancellor and consists of a legal chairman, a psychiatrist and a lay member. The Tribunal operates under rules (SI 1983/942) and the patient is entitled to legal aid in the form of Assistance by Way of Representation. A substantial number of solicitors now have experience in representing such patients. Evidence is heard in a relatively informal way from the patient, relatives, responsible medical officer, nurse, social worker and any other appropriate person. The Tribunal may discharge the patient or refuse discharge. For restricted patients the Tribunal may discharge or conditionally discharge. The Home Secretary's objection to discharge may be overruled except for certain cases such as prisoners transferred to hospital who are serving life imprisonment.

31.31 A conditional discharge may be given to a restricted patient even though the Tribunal does not consider that the patient suffers from mental disorder if the Mental Health Review Tribunal believes that he should still be liable to recall. The conditions can include virtually any reasonable requirement considered necessary by the Tribunal. Conditionally discharged patients can be recalled to hospital by the Home Secretary, who is not required to obtain medical advice before so doing.[1]

1 *R v Secretary of State for the Home Department, ex p K* [1990] 3 All ER 562.

31.32 The Home Secretary's actions have been upheld but are the subject of proceedings before the European Court of Human Rights. It should be noted that the responsible medical officer may not recall the patient under these provisions, although he may invite the patient to return to hospital informally or may detain the patient under sections 2, 3 or 4.

31.33 A consultant who wrongly recalled a patient was the defendant in an action alleging false imprisonment when the recalled patient discovered after a year that the doctor had no powers to detain him on this basis. The allegation was upheld and damages awarded.

Complaints

31.34 The patient may register complaints to the managers and to the Mental Health Act Commission which is empowered to investigate them. Only rarely are complaints unresolved when the patient may resort to the Health Service Commissioner or to litigation. Before a detained patient may sue a doctor or other person in connection with a claim arising out of his detention, he or she must first obtain the leave of the High Court (Mental Health Act 1983, section 139). The court must be satisfied that the claim justifies investigation and raises a prima facie case that the person acted without reasonable care or in bad faith. There remains a tendency not to take seriously the actions of those suffering from mental disorder who may be disadvantaged by the section 139 test, which is designed to protect staff from frivolous complaints influenced by the patient's mental illness.

CARE OF THE DETAINED PATIENT IN HOSPITAL

Responsible medical officer

31.35 In relation to patients liable to be detained under an application for assessment (and necessary treatment) (section 2 or section 4) or for treatment (section 3) the responsible medical officer (RMO) is the registered medical practitioner in charge of the patient's treatment (sections 34(1) and 55(1)).

31.36 The responsible medical officer is the person who has the ultimate clinical responsibility but it has no meaning in relation to informal patients (with one exception under the Act, section 47(1)). In relation to guardianship the RMO is the medical officer authorised by the social services authority to act as the RMO (section 34(1)).

31.37 The RMO has specific powers and duties, including the power to grant or revoke leave, make statutory reports for the renewal of detention or guardianship, bar the discharge of certain patients by the nearest relative, and to discharge certain patients. He is the 'doctor in charge of the patient's treatment' and 'medical treatment' is defined as including 'care, habilitation and rehabilitation', 'under medical supervision'. The consultant, as RMO, has ultimate responsibility, even though a multidisciplinary team may agree that a patient should, for example, be given leave of absence or parole in the grounds of the hospital. He is responsible for approving the involvement of another professional, a psychologist for instance, but can assume that such a professional is properly qualified if appointed by a health authority. He may decide to terminate the arrangement if he has good reason to believe the patient may not be benefiting from the treatment (or may be harmed).

31.38 The term RMO has a similar meaning in relation to the consent to treatment provisions under the Act.

FURTHER HAZARDS AND PITFALLS

31.39 The consultant, as RMO, must remember that he will be held finally responsible for decisions which the Act specifically delegates to him (over and above any common law or good-practice obligations). It is therefore important to ensure that his team are aware of his responsibility and to prevent any decisions being made which he could not accept. Should a detained psychotic patient leave the hospital and attack a member of the public, for instance, the RMO would need to demonstrate that he had agreed with leave of absence and had taken into account the opinions of his team, in demonstrating that he has measured up to an acceptable standard.

31.40 The RMO must delegate his responsibilities to a colleague during periods of prolonged absence who becomes the acting RMO. The RMO is also responsible for nominating a doctor to act as his deputy for the purposes of section 5(2) of the Act. Only one doctor at a time may be nominated.

31.41 Health authorities should scrutinise the qualifications of those appointed to locum consultant psychiatrist posts. The Royal College of Psychiatrists recommends that only doctors trained to consultant level should be appointed as a locum; others, such as registrars, who are often appointed because of manpower shortages, are vulnerable in the event of a mishap. A hospital authority may be held to be negligent in failing to employ competent staff.[1] Vacancies should be filled by doctors in an alternative grade who are supervised if fully trained practitioners cannot be found.

1 *Wilsher v Essex Area Health Authority* [1986] 3 All ER 801.

DUTY OF CARE

Medical recommendations

31.42 According to Gostin[1] a doctor signing a medical recommendation under the Act has a duty of care towards the patient and it follows that an action in negligence may be sustained where the standards used in making the recommendations are not those that would be used by others of comparable qualifications and skill.

1 Gostin L *Mental Health Services – Law and Practice* (London, Sweet and Maxwell, 1986).

PREVENTING DANGEROUS ACTS BY DETAINED PATIENTS

31.43 A person responsible for detained psychiatric patients must take reasonable care to prevent their unauthorised escape without leave. If leave of absence is granted, with due consideration, when the patient is at the appropriate stage of his treatment and with the support of other professionals, the RMO is unlikely to be regarded as negligent even though the patient behaves in a dangerous way towards a member of the public. The RMO is not liable for mere errors of judgment (Gostin 1986, above) and the House of Lords said[1] that the release of a mental patient could result in liability only if it was authorised so carelessly that there had been no exercise of real discretion.

> **Case report** A mentally handicapped patient was detained on a hospital order (section 60 of the Mental Health Act 1959). The RMO had awarded him increasing freedom so that he now worked in a garden party in the grounds of the hospital. He saved the pocket money that he earned from this during a period of months, then left the hospital, became drunk, and set fire to the portakabin offices of a construction company, also damaging a half built building. The company held the consultant and health authority liable for a failure in their duty to care for the patient. The court held that the doctor had measured up to the required standard and it could not be foreseen that the patient would leave and behave as he did. The action failed.

1 *Holgate v Lancashire Mental Hospitals Board, Gill and Robertson* [1937] 4 All ER 19.

31.44 The consultant has a duty to prevent fellow patients being harmed by his patient, but there must be power to control the patient who caused the injury. The occurrence of harm to one patient from another can lead to liability with respect to the doctor, only if he is negligent (Gostin 1986, above).

31.45 It is probable that the RMO will be held to have a duty to prevent his patients from coming to any reasonably foreseeable harm. However, if an obviously suicidal patient was allowed to leave and, indeed, committed suicide, there could be liability.

31.46 Gostin (1986, above) also refers to the case of a detained patient discharged by an RMO who, immediately upon leaving hospital, commits suicide or murder. The RMO could be liable if he acted with gross negligence meaning, presumably, that any reasonably competent RMO would have foreseen the risk from his knowledge of the patient and his behaviour.

RISK OF SUICIDE

31.47 As is the case for all doctors, psychiatrists have a duty of care to their patients and the *Bolam* test will apply. *Bolam*, the plaintiff, was in fact a psychiatric patient.[1]

1 *Bolam v Friern Hospital Management Committee* [1957] 2 All ER 118.

31.48 A psychiatrist has a duty to take reasonable steps to ensure that a patient who has attempted suicide and is known to be at risk of suicide is protected from doing so. The hospital should have an established policy on the management of such cases and, when necessary, sufficient staffing levels to ensure close and continuous observation of the patient. The ward or room used should be suitable so that the patient cannot leave unsupervised or get out of the windows, as failure to consider these matters has frequently resulted in a finding of negligence by hospital authorities. Staff shortages or insufficient nursing manpower levels are often found to be the cause of failure.

31.49 A doctor cannot always foresee the risk of suicide and would only be at risk of an action if he had not carried out a proper examination, reviewed his patient regularly or otherwise taken those reasonable clinical routines that others would regard as necessary and which would have revealed a risk.

31.50 It is now considered good practice to review a patient's progress regularly with all members of the clinical team and to discuss with them important decisions, such as granting leave of absence, parole or discharge. The support of the team, representing a range of professional expertise strengthens the doctor's hand. A decision which is not supported by the team should be made with caution, although it may not necessarily be inappropriate.

RESTRAINT AND SECLUSION

31.51 With respect to detained psychiatric patients, compulsory detention necessarily involves control and 'discipline', but this must be reasonably related to health, safety, care and treatment. The use of seclusion for any other purpose, for instance, as a consequence of a shortage of staff, or a nurses' strike, could be regarded as unlawful imprisonment, even within the confines of a hospital (and even a secure hospital). Strict policies for the use of seclusion must be followed and these have been prepared in many hospitals. The use of force in the control of patients should only be sanctioned on similar principles to follow good practice and avoid liability.

31.52 Hospitals should have clearly written policies for the use of seclusion and its monitoring which are known to all staff. It should rarely be used and many medical authorities believe that it should be phased out entirely (see the Report of the Committee of Inquiry into Complaints about Ashworth Hospital 1992).

31.53 The Mental Health Act does not grant any power to restrain individuals until an application for admission is completed. The person cannot be restrained for the purposes of interview or examination. If he refuses access to his home an approved social worker must obtain a warrant to search for and remove him. After an application is completed the Act provides authority for the patient's conveyance to hospital and when the patient is actually admitted and accepted by the managers, there is a power to detain him.

31.54 Restraint may be justified in other circumstances to prevent harm, to remove an unauthorised offensive weapon and in self-defence.

STANDARDS OF HOSPITAL CARE

31.55 During the 24 years of operation of the Mental Health Act 1959 there were a series of major scandals involving allegations of maltreatment of patients in psychiatric hospitals with at least ten major inquiries of national significance.[1] The Mental Health Act 1983 created the Mental Health Act Commission, which was intended to prevent such malpractice occurring again by regular inspection of hospitals. This has been partially successful but has not eliminated these problems. The Ashworth Hospital inquiry is an example and the report revealed serious inadequacies in this special hospital providing conditions of high security for patients suffering from severe mental disorder who exhibit dangerous, violent or criminal tendencies.[2] As a consequence of the report major changes are occurring in the management and organisation of these hospitals. As psychiatric care moves to the community future malpractice is likely to be found in the community care or exploitation of psychiatric patients.

1 Martin J P *Hospitals in Trouble* (Basil Blackwell, 1984).
2 Report of the Committee of Inquiry into Complaints about Ashworth Hospital (Chairman Sir Louis Blom-Cooper QC) (London, HMSO, Cm 2028) 1992.

AFTERCARE

31.56 Section 117 of the Mental Health Act 1983 places a duty on the District Health Authority and the local social services authority to provide, in co-operation with relevant voluntary agencies, aftercare services for patients discharged under section 3, section 37, or sections 47 or 48. This duty is mandatory[1] and the arrangements must be made irrespective of prevailing resources.

1 *R v Ealing District Health Authority, ex p Fox* [1993] 3 All ER 170, QBD.

FALSE IMPRISONMENT

31.57 The restraint of a patient can only be authorised by implementing an appropriate section of the Mental Health Act 1983 and then, only if the patient's condition justifies it and no less restrictive alternative is available.

31.58 It is not lawful to admit a patient compulsorily simply to activate the sections of the Act allowing compulsory treatment, with the intention of then discharging the patient back into the community. Detention is lawful only with the intention of treating the patient as an in-patient.[1]

1 *R v Hallstrom, ex p W; R v Gardner, ex p L* [1986] QB 1090, [1986] 2 All ER 306.

31.59 A conditionally discharged patient (a patient discharged by a Mental Health Review Tribunal) who was previously detained by virtue of a hospital order (MHA 1983, section 37), with a restriction on discharge (MHA 1983, section 41) may only be recalled to hospital by the Home Secretary. In a recent case a consultant was seeing such a patient as an out-patient and was concerned that his mental state was deteriorating. He readmitted the patient to hospital without obtaining the Home Secretary's order of recall. Later the patient commenced an action against the consultant complaining of his unlawful imprisonment.

31.60 Section 136 of the Mental Health Act 1983 authorises a police constable who finds a person who appears to be suffering from mental disorder, in a place to which the public have access, to remove him to a place of safety. He may do so if the person appears to be in immediate need of care and control and if he thinks it necessary to do so in the person's interests or for the protection of other persons. The person may be detained in a place of safety for a period not exceeding 72 hours for the purpose of enabling the patient to be examined by a registered medical practitioner and to be interviewed by an approved social worker, and for the purpose of making any necessary arrangements for his care and treatment. Once the patient has been seen, and this should be at the earliest opportunity, he should be released or detained under an appropriate section.

31.61 It has been suggested that this section has sometimes been used improperly to detain patients for three days and in place of other sections with more stringent requirements. Such a practice may place a doctor in a hazardous position.

CONSENT TO TREATMENT

31.62 Psychiatric treatment may only be administered to a patient with his real and informed consent. Compulsorily detained patients are not necessarily less competent to give consent. Although the severity of the mental disorder from which the patient is suffering may have warranted compulsory admission, it cannot be assumed that the patient is unable to understand the nature, purpose and likely effects of a proposed treatment and to give or withhold his consent to its administration. Some patients, because of the nature and severity of their condition, clearly cannot assess or understand the need for treatment rationally and a refusal (or an agreement) may be the result of a distorted judgment as a consequence of disordered mental functioning. Parliament has agreed that in some of these cases it may be justified to treat the patient, despite his inability to provide real consent, and has given statutory authority to do so in the Mental Health Act 1983. Apart from this legislation relating to mental disorder and detained patients, the common law alone protects the right of the individual to give or withhold his consent to medical treatment.

Consent to treatment and compulsorily detained patients

31.63 The requirements of the Mental Health Act 1983 apply to any patient liable to be detained under the Act for medical treatment for mental disorder, with the exception of certain treatments (discussed below) the arrangements for which apply both to detained and non-detained patients (any patient). However, there are several categories of patient to which the arrangements *do not* apply, as follows:

(a) patient detained in an emergency (section 4) for 72 hours;
(b) informal patients detained for 72 hours under section 5 of the Act, to prevent them leaving hospital;
(c) patients detained in a place of safety for up to 28 days awaiting transfer to hospital (section 37);
(d) patients removed to a place of safety under section 135;
(e) patients detained in a place of safety by a police constable (section 136);
(f) patients who are conditionally discharged (sections 42(2), 73 and 74); and
(g) patients remanded by a court to hospital for a report to be made (section 35).

31.64 The consent to treatment arrangements *do apply* to the following categories:

(a) patients detained for assessment and treatment (sections 2 and 3);
(b) patients detained on a hospital order (section 37) or an interim hospital order (section 38);
(c) patients detained on a hospital order with restrictions on discharge (section 41);
(d) convicted prisoners transferred to hospital (section 47);
(e) other prisoners transferred to hospital (section 48);
(f) patients detained under the provisions of the Criminal Procedure (Insanity and Unfitness to Plead) Act 1991 (not guilty by reason of insanity and unfit to plead); and
(g) patients remanded for treatment by a court.

Treatments of 'special concern'

31.65 Some specified treatments may be given only with the patient's true consent, the endorsement of the validity of that consent by an independent panel, together with the clinical approval of an independent psychiatrist, after he has consulted members of the clinical team. The consent of the patient for these treatments is an absolute requirement and an inability to consent invalidates the treatment.

Treatments requiring consent and a second opinion (MHA 1983, section 57)

31.66 This section applies to:

(a) any surgical operation for destroying brain tissue or for destroying the function of brain tissue;
(b) such other forms of treatment as may be specified by the Secretary of State in regulations (initially the surgical implantation of hormones to reduce male sexual drive, is the only treatment specified).

No patient (detained or informal, in-patient or out-patient) may be given a treatment specified here, for the treatment of mental disorder unless:

(a) he has consented to it; and
(b) an independent doctor and two other persons appointed by the Secretary of State (the latter two not being doctors) have certified in writing that the patient is capable of understanding the nature, purpose and likely effects of the proposed treatment and has consented to it; and
(c) the independent doctor has certified in writing that, having regard to the likelihood of the treatment alleviating or preventing a deterioration of the patient's condition, the treatment should be given;
(d) before giving his clinical opinion the independent doctor is required to consult two other persons who have been professionally concerned with the patient's medical treatment. One of these persons must be a nurse and the other neither a nurse nor a doctor.

31.67 The above arrangements apply normally to stereotactic surgical procedures to relieve unremitting severe depressive illness and, more rarely, severe obsessional disorders. The Mental Health Act Commission nominates the independent doctor and non-medical assessors to provide opinions in these cases, usually from among its own members. It also defines the procedures and arrangements for the assessments. Fifty-four cases were considered for a proposed psychosurgical procedure between 1 July 1985 and 30 June 1987, 52 in 1987–1989 and 65 between 1989 and 1991.[1]

1 Mental Health Act Commission, Fourth Biennial Report, 1989–1991 (London, HMSO, 1991).

31.68 A proposal to treat a mentally disordered patient with hormones by surgical implantation to reduce male sexual drive is very rarely requested because this is not normally a treatment for mental disorder as defined in the Act. Such treatment is given very infrequently in any case, but in a few instances may be recommended in cases of sexual deviation which is not classified as a 'mental disorder' in law. A doctor prescribing the surgical implantation of hormones would therefore not be required to obtain the second opinion indicated in section 57 of the Act. During the period 1985–87 (as above) only one case was considered by the Mental Health Act Commission.[1]

1 Mental Health Act Commission, Second Biennial Report, 1985–1987 (London, HMSO, 1987).

31.69 In 1988 a Dr Silverman proposed to treat a patient (W) with goserelin (Zoladex ICI) a drug normally prescribed for the treatment of prostate carcinoma which radically reduces levels of circulating testosterone. His patient had a history of sexual offending and had not responded well to other treatments. Although it is not clear whether or not the patient also suffered from mental disorder, as defined in the Act, Dr Silverman referred the case to the Mental Health Act Commission for an independent approval for the treatment to be given. The Commission refused on the grounds that the patient had not fully understood the nature, purpose or likely effects of the treatment which was untried as a treatment for sexual problems. The patient applied successfully for a judicial review, claiming that the Commission was preventing him from receiving a treatment recommended by his doctor which would benefit him. The court agreed that the treatment could be given. Although the drug was given by a form of injection it was not given by way of surgical implantation. Goserelin is a synthetic hormone analogue but is not a hormone, so that the Act did not apply. Further, the Commission had applied a test with respect to the patient's ability to consent which was too stringent.[1]

1 Brahams D 'Voluntary Chemical Castration of a Mental Patient' (1988) Lancet 1, 1291–1292; *R v Mental Health Commission, ex p W* (1988) Times, 27 May.

Other treatments requiring consent or a second opinion

Medication

31.70 Compulsorily detained patients have the right to accept or refuse medication for the treatment of mental disorder if they have the capacity to do so. A patient who is incompetent to give real consent may be treated by his consultant (RMO) without his consent for three months of his continuous detention (under one or more sections of the Act) without formalities. The consultant must continue to respect his common law rights however, although his position during this three month period is not entirely clear in law and there are no reported cases which help in providing clarification. If there is any uncertainty about the patient's capacity it would be good practice for the consultant to obtain an independent clinical opinion and, in all cases, to consult his multidisciplinary team before taking the decision to treat the patient, despite his inability to consent.

31.71 After three months treatment the detained patient may only be treated with medicine by any means for the treatment of mental disorder, if he has given his competent consent, or an independent doctor has given approval as required by the Act.

Electro-convulsive therapy

31.72 Electro-convulsive therapy (ECT) is normally given for the treatment of severe depressive illness. It may only be given to a compulsorily detained patient for the treatment of mental disorder with the patient's informed consent or with the approval of an independent doctor. This applies at any time during which the patient is compulsorily detained.

Treatments requiring consent or a second opinion (section 58)

31.73 This section applies to:

(a) such forms of treatment as may be specified by the Secretary of State in regulations (ECT is, so far, the only specified treatment);

(b) the administration of medicine by any means (not included in section 57) if three months have elapsed since the first occasion during the period of detention that medicine was first administered to the patient. No patient may be treated as above (being a treatment for mental disorder) unless:

  (i) he has consented to it and either a responsible medical officer, or an independent doctor (appointed by the Mental Health Act Commission on behalf of the Secretary of State) has certified in writing that the patient is capable of understanding the nature, purpose and likely effects of the proposed treatment and has given consent; or

(ii) an independent doctor has certified in writing that the patient is not capable of understanding the nature, purpose and likely effects of the treatment, or, has not given consent, but that having regard to the likelihood of it alleviating or preventing deterioration of his condition the treatment should be given;

(iii) before giving his clinical opinion the independent doctor is required to consult two other persons who have been professionally concerned with the patient's medical treatment. One of these should be a nurse and the other neither a nurse nor a doctor.

31.74 The consent or certificate may be for a plan of treatment for a defined period of time. The consent properly given by a patient may be withdrawn at any time when the doctor may request an independent opinion. Periodic reviews of treatment are required by the Act.

Urgent treatment (section 62)

31.75 The consent of the patient and/or an independent second medical opinion is *not* required as above in certain situations as follows:

(a) when the treatment is immediately necessary to save the patient's life; or

(b) which (not being an irreversible treatment) is immediately necessary to prevent a serious deterioration of the patient's condition; or

(c) which (not being irreversible or hazardous) is immediately necessary to alleviate serious suffering by the patient;

(d) which (not being irreversible or hazardous) is immediately necessary and represents the minimum interference necessary to prevent the patient from behaving violently or being a danger to himself or others.

Irreversible treatment refers to a treatment which has unfavourable, irreversible, physical or psychological consequences.

Hazardous treatment refers to a treatment which entails significant physical hazard.

31.76 Doctors must use their own knowledge and judgment in deciding whether or not a treatment is irreversible or hazardous.

31.77 For any other treatment the consent of the patient should be obtained although section 63 of the Act provides that consent or a second opinion is required only for the treatments specified above. It is unlikely in practice that other treatments such as psychological treatments or occupational therapy could be given in practice without the patient's co-operation, even though he had not given his consent.

31.78 It was at one time the practice of psychiatrists to grant leave of absence to some detained patients and to recall them to hospital before the order detaining them expired in order that it could be renewed. The patient would then be given further leave of absence but remained on the order. The purpose of this practice was to retain control of the treatment of the patient. If he defaulted in taking medication, for instance, his leave could be revoked and he could be easily and lawfully returned to hospital.

31.79 The Mental Health Act provides that an order (section 3) detaining a patient for treatment expires at the end of six months. If at this time the patient is on leave of absence his order cannot then be renewed (since he is not a patient in hospital). This was made clear in a judicial review in the cases of *R v Hallstrom, ex p W; R v Gardner, ex p L.*[1] This case also confirmed that there is no authority under the Act which allows a doctor compulsorily to treat a patient outside hospital. Should a patient fail to take his treatment and deteriorate a new compulsory detention order would be necessary to return him to hospital and the condition of the patient would have to justify it. The possibility of new legislation which would allow a 'supervised discharge order' is under consideration at the present time.

1 [1986] QB 1090, [1986] 2 All ER 306.

Physical treatment for detained psychiatric patients

31.80 The Act only provides for the administration of certain treatments, even though the patient cannot, or does not, consent, for the treatment of mental disorder. Other treatments, including surgical or medical treatments, require the patient's consent. This has led to considerable difficulty in providing physical treatment for mentally ill or handicapped patients unable to consent, but the position of doctors has been clarified by the House of Lords in a recent case.[1] In this case Lord Brandon said:

> The common law would be seriously defective if it failed to provide a solution to the problem created by . . . inability to consent. However, the common law did not so fail.
>
> The solution to the problem which the common law provided was that a doctor could lawfully operate on or give other treatment to, adult patients incapable of consenting, provided that the operation or other treatment was in the best interests of such patients. It would only be in their best interests if, but only if, it was carried out in order to save their lives or prevent deterioration in their physical or mental health.
>
> When persons lacked the capacity, for whatever reason, to take decisions about operations or other medical treatment on them, it was necessary that others with the appropriate qualifications should make decisions for them. Otherwise they would be deprived of medical care which they needed and to which they were entitled.
>
> In many cases it would be not only lawful for doctors, on the grounds of necessity to operate on, or give other medical treatment to, adult patients disabled from giving consent; it would be their common law duty to do so.

1 *F v West Berkshire Health Authority* [1989] 2 All ER 545, [1989] 2 WLR 1025, HL.

31.81 The decision in such cases is to be taken by doctors, with proper safeguards (such as second opinions, consulting relatives and others) in the patient's 'best interests'. It is not a matter which requires the approval of a court unless there is doubt about the actions proposed.

Sterilisation

31.82 The case of *F* (see para **31.80**) involved a mentally handicapped woman and sterilisation. The court decided that although in law it was not strictly necessary for doctors to seek the court's approval before carrying out the operation, it was in the interests of the woman because of the nature of the operation to do so. There might be cases of other special operations to which secondary considerations applied (as arose in this case) and each would be examined as and when they arose.

Consent to treatment and prisoners

31.83 Prisoners are not subject to the Mental Health Act and any treatment required is subject to the normal rules of consent to treatment. There are other factors to bear in mind in the prison setting. A prisoner is in custody and a doctor is in a position to influence a prisoner's situation and prospects so that a real consent may be open to question. It is therefore important to be doubly certain that consent is freely given and that there is no possibility of an allegation that any pressure has been used to persuade the prisoner. These issues were discussed in detail in the case of *Freeman v Home Office (No 2)*.[1]

1 [1984] QB 524, [1984] 1 All ER 1036, CA; see Brahams D 'Is a Prisoner Capable of Giving Informal Consent to Treatment?' (1984) Lancet 1, 746.

Legal proceedings by detained patients (section 139)

31.84 Section 139 of the Mental Health Act 1983 provides a protection from litigation in respect of any act done in pursuance of the Act or any regulations or rules arising from it. No person is liable to any civil or criminal proceedings in carrying out duties under the Act unless the action was done in bad faith or without reasonable care. No civil proceedings may be brought against any person in any court in respect of such an act without leave of the High Court. No criminal proceedings may be brought against any person in any court in respect of any such act except by or with the consent of the Director of Public Prosecutions. These arrangements and safeguards do not apply in respect of any offence under any provision of the Act which provides that the proceedings can *only* be instituted by, or with the consent of, the Director of Public Prosecutions.

General note

31.85 The Act consists of a very wide variety of powers and duties any of which could be brought into question. Here, the most significant have been discussed but, for accuracy, the original statute, regulations and orders must be consulted. More detailed guidance may be found in Gostin[1] and Bluglass.[2]

1 Gostin L *Mental Health Services – Law and Practice* (London, Sweet and Maxwell, 1986).
2 Bluglass R *A Guide to the Mental Health Act 1983* (Edinburgh and London, Churchill Livingstone, 1983).

Children

31.86 The parent or guardian of a child under the age of 16 may consent to treatment on the child's behalf and other rules of explanation apply as for consent to treatment in the adult.

CONFIDENTIALITY AND PSYCHIATRY

31.87 Psychiatrists have the same duty of confidence with respect to information received from and about their patients as other doctors. They need to keep this in mind in sharing confidential information with other professionals with whom they work, such as psychologists and social workers. In the past concern was raised in the case of a member of Birmingham Social Services Committee who obtained access to confidential material obtained by social workers. Doctors were advised by the GMC not to share information with social worker colleagues unless they were satisfied it would remain confidential.

31.88 An exception to the general duty of confidence applying to psychiatrists may exist in the case of detained patients where it has been said that the duty was less extensive.[1] In this case a psychiatrist retained on behalf of a detained patient revealed to the Home Office information obtained at interview without permission. The patient brought an action against the doctor which was dismissed by the judge at first instance and this decision was upheld on appeal.

1 *W v Egdell* [1989] 1 All ER 1089, [1989] 2 WLR 689.

INTERPERSONAL THERAPIES

31.89 Psychiatrists are particularly vulnerable to allegations of misconduct or assault from patients who become emotionally involved or dependent upon them in individual therapeutic settings, such as psychotherapy and sex therapy. They are usually well aware of this and an understanding of the risks and psychological problems involved are emphasised in training. The judicious use of assistants or chaperones, where necessary, should be considered.

MEDICAL CARE AND PSYCHIATRIC ILLNESS

31.90 Increasingly claims of medical negligence arising from a medical, surgical or obstetric procedure or episode of care are accompanied by an element relating to psychological damage, mental illness, 'nervous shock' or post-traumatic stress disorder resulting from the injury. The assessment of each case must be thorough in order to distinguish mental illness which was present before the incident from abnormality clearly arising from it. Comprehensive records must be scrutinised including previous hospital records, general practitioner notes and other relevant information. The relatives or others close to the patient should be seen and a detailed interview and examination carried out. It may be necessary to see the patient several times. Cases in this category may involve claims based upon one of the following resulting from the injury or experience:

(1) mental illness;
(2) 'nervous shock';
(3) post-traumatic stress disorder.

Mental illness

31.91 The disorder must result from the incident or, if pre-existing, be exacerbated by it. Mental illness implies the existence of a recognisable psychiatric disorder such as depression, or dementia resulting from brain damage.

Nervous shock

31.92 This is a legal term which incorporates mental illness and implies the existence of a positive psychiatric illness which goes beyond the grief, distress or other normal emotion which normal people experience following loss or injury. It must be pathological or abnormal in extent and duration.[1]

1 *McCloughlin v O'Brian* [1983] 1 AC 410, 421.

Post-traumatic stress disorder (PTSD)

31.93 The essential feature of this condition is the development of characteristic symptoms, categorised in the *American Diagnostic and Statistical Manual of Mental Disorders* (3rd edn, revised) 1987, following a psychologically distressing event that is outside the range of usual human experience and would be severely distressing to most people. The traumatic event is persistently re-experienced by recurrent and intrusive flashbacks, or intense distress at exposure to events resembling an aspect of the traumatic event. There are other symptoms such as numbing of general responsiveness, sleep difficulties and outbursts of anger. Sometimes individuals suffer from pathological grief; an excessive grief reaction continuing beyond the time grief is experienced normally. PTSD and pathological grief were recognised in the claimants following the Zeebrugge ferry disaster.[1]

1 *A v P & O Ferries (Dover) Ltd* (*Herald of Free Enterprise* arbitration) (1989) Independent, 5 May.

BIBLIOGRAPHICAL REFERENCES

American Diagnostic and Statistical Manual of Mental Disorders (3rd edn, revised, 1987) American Psychiatric Association.

Bluglass R *A Guide to the Mental Health Act 1983* (Edinburgh and London, Churchill Livingstone, 1983).

Bluglass R and Bowden P (eds) *The Principles and Practice of Forensic Psychiatry* (Edinburgh and London, Churchill Livingstone, 1990).

Brahams D 'Proceedings for False Imprisonment and Negligence under 1959 Mental Health Act' (1983) Lancet 2, 466.

'Voluntary Chemical Castration of a Mental Patient' (1988) Lancet 1, 1291–1292.

'Is a Prisoner Capable of Giving Informal Consent to Treatment?' (1984) Lancet 1, 746.

Gostin L *Mental Health Services – Law and Practice* (London, Sweet and Maxwell, 1986).

Martin J P *Hospitals in Trouble* (Basil Blackwell, 1984).

Mental Health Act Commission, Second Biennial Report, 1985–1987 (London, HMSO, 1987).

Mental Health Act Commission, Fourth Biennial Report, 1989–1991 (London, HMSO, 1991).

Report of the Committee of Inquiry into Complaints about Ashworth Hospital, (Chairman Sir Louis Blom-Cooper QC) (London, HMSO, Cm 2028).

CHAPTER 32

Anaesthesia

Professor M Rosen *CBE MB ChB FRCA FRCOG*
Dr J N Horton *MB BS DA FRCA*

SUMMARY

32.1 Claims arising from untoward incidents during anaesthesia form a substantial proportion of those handled by health authorities and the defence organisations in the NHS and the private sector. This is partly because the anaesthetist uses a large armamentarium of potent drugs and complex and invasive equipment, and because a lapse in judgment or concentration during the administration of an anaesthetic can have, with a small margin for error – virtually seconds – lethal or damaging consequences for the patient. It is also because patients are less willing to suffer even the so-called minor mishaps of anaesthesia such as the cracked tooth or the thrombosed superficial vein, and the speciality unlike most others is faced with high expectations from its patients.

32.2 The marked increase in the number of complaints received by hospital managers may be more related to a heightened awareness by the public of their rights as stated in the Patients' Charter than by a fall in standards of clinical practice, and in fact standards of practice now expected by the profession as a whole are higher than ever before. In medico-legal work it is often necessary to take the advice of a 'responsible body' on professional standards. In anaesthesia this would be one of the two major professional organisations, the Royal College of Anaesthetists and the Association of Anaesthetists of Great Britain and Ireland. Additionally there are many academic leaders and practitioners with special expertise who have published work in peer-reviewed journals. In anaesthesia as in any other speciality, however, experts can express opinions on rare conditions based only on a very limited personal experience and a review of the literature which may be made up of only a few cases throughout the world.

32.3 An area of contention may be in the type of hospital in which the event leading to an allegation of negligence took place. In the regional centre the anaesthetist may have access to very sophisticated means of pre-operative investigation and equipment for management and monitoring during anaesthesia and intensive care. In a District Hospital these may be unavailable. The anaesthetist should have access to, and use, all reasonable pre-operative investigations; there should be guidelines for the minimum level of pre-operative investigations of patients before elective surgery. The anaesthetist cannot be criticised for the unavailability of facilities which reasonably could not be provided in his type of hospital. This is not to say that facilities in a District General Hospital should be substandard; monitoring of patients in the operating theatre must be at least at the level recommended by the Association of Anaesthetists.

32.4 In the National Health Service, vicarious responsibility for the actions of its employees has been assumed by health authorities through NHS Indemnity. This covers the normal clinical work of anaesthetists but most will retain membership of one of the traditional defence organisations because of the advice and support to be obtained from an independent organisation as well as indemnity for actions taken in the course of private practice and for 'Samaritan' actions. This dual responsibility may lead to complexities as both the health authority and the defence organisations have limitations to their range of cover.

32.5 There can be very few aspects of anaesthetic practice which, at some time or another, have not led to allegations of negligence (Gray 1985) and this chapter concentrates on the more common mishaps. Not all untoward incidents result in litigation, of course, but it should be the aim of the profession to work towards near perfection. Early publications identified aspiration of gastric contents and hypovolaemia as the most frequent causes of death, and these still remain as significant factors today. The National Confidential Enquiry into Perioperative Deaths (Campling, Devlin, Hoyle, & Lunn 1992) has repeatedly identified areas for improvement in clinical practice. Their Report did not quote an incidence of mortality because of lack of information on the number of surgical procedures carried out in the UK. It is likely to be very low but appears to have remained unchanged, despite improvements in drugs, monitoring and the training of anaesthetists. This apparently unsatisfactory situation is partly because of changing attitudes to fitness for surgery and anaesthesia; today few patients would be turned down for essential surgery because of an uncorrectable medical condition, yet a few years ago patients were denied surgery on age alone. Lunn and Mushin's survey did reveal, however, that of the 280 deaths represented by this incidence, no fewer than 125 included avoidable factors, with errors of judgment being present in 70 per cent of cases.

32.6 Fifty-two per cent of cases referred to the Medical Defence Union involving anaesthetists described damage to the teeth. More serious claims requiring expert assessment are shown in Table 32.1.

DIFFICULTIES IN INTUBATION

32.7 Intubation of the trachea is carried out in a high proportion of patients under general anaesthesia. The indications are well defined and confer a high degree of safety on the anaesthetic procedure – indeed in some circumstances not to intubate would be to court disaster. The commoner indications for intubation are listed in Table 32.2.

32.8 Nevertheless, intubation carries its own risks.

32.9 (1) The soft tissues of the lips, mouth and tongue, pharynx and the larynx itself may be damaged by careless manipulation of the laryngoscope. Commonly these injuries are caused by trapping of tissues between the laryngoscope blade and the teeth, or by forcing the tube blindly into the pharyngeal wall. A particular injury may occur if a nasal tube impacts against the posterior wall of the nasopharynx. The mucosa may be stripped and the tube forced into a false passage between the mucosa of the pharynx and the anterior surface of the cervical vertebrae. Again, this injury is preventable by careful and gentle manipulation of the tracheal tube. Most experienced anaesthetists have encountered this complication and while the complication might be regarded as careless where the anaesthetist is suitably experienced, the situation is less clear in the case of a trainee, especially in emergency circumstances.

32.10 (2) The teeth, particularly the upper incisors and canines, may be chipped, broken or dislodged by the laryngoscope blade (Hargrove 1986). It is essential that during laryngoscopy the head is correctly positioned and the correct manoeuvre is carried out when visualising the larynx, avoiding using the upper teeth as a fulcrum for the laryngoscope blade (Figure 32.1).

32.11 Damage to, and displacement of, teeth accounts for a large number of claims against anaesthetists and in most cases is preventable by correct and careful use of the laryngoscope, and therefore it is difficult to defend a claim of negligence in most cases. However, where the anaesthetist has to perform an emergency intubation to save a patient's life and the dentition is especially difficult, a reasonable defence may be presented. In normal circumstances, though, inspection of the patient's dentition is an essential part of the pre-operative assessment, and particular note must be made of loose teeth, crowns, and bridgework, and missing teeth which may make intubation difficult. The use of a plastic protector over the upper anterior teeth may be advisable especially if difficulty could be anticipated.

32.12 A particular problem is the displaced tooth which cannot be found. It is essential to carry out an immediate search which must, if necessary, include bronchoscopy. Teeth are notoriously difficult to see on a chest radiograph so an apparently clear film does not exclude aspiration of the tooth. Whatever the circumstances, whereas displacement of a tooth may be defensible in certain circumstances, failure to look for and retrieve a missing tooth will usually be indefensible.

32.13 It may be possible for an oral surgeon to reimplant a displaced tooth, and it is worthwhile attempting to contact an oral surgeon at the time of the accident to see if such a procedure is feasible.

32.14 (3) Failure to achieve tracheal intubation is a hazard which can be encountered by the most experienced anaesthetist from time to time, and in itself is not negligent. There are a number of well-documented circumstances in which difficulty in intubation may be anticipated (Table 32.3). Avoidance of problems with a potentially difficult intubation starts with the assessment of these factors beforehand. It goes without saying that the potentially difficult intubation should be attempted only by an anaesthetist of sufficient experience, and failure to obtain assistance, or failure by those responsible for the provision of the anaesthetic service to provide adequate senior cover, could be regarded as negligence on the part of the anaesthetist and his employer respectively.

32.15 Difficult intubation may result in serious hypoxia if the airway is compromised as a result, or if intubation being carried out to gain control of an obstructed airway is unsuccessful. It is mandatory for all anaesthetic units, particularly those involved in obstetric anaesthesia, to have a clear policy ('failed intubation drill') for the management of unexpected failure (Figure 32.3). Failure to provide a policy, or not to follow it might, in view of the well established need for such a policy, be indefensible.

32.16 Whether the difficult intubation is anticipated or is unexpected, special equipment will be required to deal with the problem. Many cases of minor difficulty can be managed by threading the endotracheal tube over a gum-elastic bougie or malleable introducer, although it should be noted that the use of the latter may cause damage to the pharyngeal tissues if it is used blindly and without due care. Simple equipment for the difficult intubation (straight and extra-long laryngoscope blades, introducers, equipment for retrograde intubation (Latto 1985), and a percutaneous cricothyrotomy with a wide-bore cannula or a disposable cricothyrotomy set) should be immediately available at all intubations, and more advanced equipment such as the fibreoptic laryngoscope should be available to each operating theatre from a reasonably accessible central 'depot'. At present wide training in the use of the fibreoptic instrument is available and should be undertaken by all anaesthetists as it requires considerable practice on elective cases before the technique can be successfully employed in difficult circumstances.

32.17 (4) Misplacement of the endotracheal tube, usually in the oesophagus is, like difficult intubation, an occasional event in the hands of even an experienced anaesthetist. In itself therefore it cannot constitute negligence. However, failure to recognise that the tube is misplaced before hypoxic damage occurs is undoubtedly so. Serious hypoxic brain damage has resulted from failure to recognise oesophageal intubation and several large settlements have been made as a result of such cases. It is mandatory for verification of the correct placement of the tube to be obtained as a part of every intubation procedure. There are several accepted means of doing this. Probably the most reliable sign of correct placement is the clear sight of the tube in position between the vocal cords of the larynx, although this reassuring observation does not preclude subsequent displacement of the tube into the pharynx or the oesophagus. Other means include observation of chest movement with artificial ventilation and auscultation over the chest. These precautions are essential following intubation and should be accompanied by auscultation over the trachea to verify the sound of gas passing through the airway, and over the epigastrium to exclude the sound of gas entering the stomach in the case of oesophageal intubation. These signs are not totally reliable, however, and false 'breath sounds' as gas passes down the oesophagus have been noted on occasions. Nevertheless, failure to carry out auscultation after every intubation would probably be regarded as negligent, particularly if not accompanied by other means of checking for correct placement. A valuable, though again not totally reliable, method involves identifying the passage through the airway of end-tidal carbon dioxide with each ventilation. This requires an infra-red carbon dioxide analyser and is one of several justifications for the wide availability of this useful piece of equipment. Other methods include the rapid withdrawal of 50 ml of gas or air from the tracheal tube. In the event of the patient becoming cyanosed or a fall in haemoglobin saturation being detected with the pulse oximeter at any time, misplacement of the tube should be one of the diagnoses considered. The presence of gas in the stomach is an unreliable indication of oesophageal intubation as there are other causes for gaseous distension of the stomach and bowel.

32.18 In summary, although there is no universal agreement on the most reliable method of verifying correct tube placement, it is essential to carry out some means of post-intubation check (repeated after events likely to cause displacement such as repositioning of the patient on the operating table) and to take steps to test for misplacement if a fall in haemoglobin saturation is detected.

32.19 (5) Inadvertent endobronchial intubation may occur if the endotracheal tube is too long and passes beyond the carina into (usually) the right main bronchus. The effect of this is that only blood in the pulmonary artery of the side being ventilated is oxygenated, and severe hypoxemia results.

Again endobronchial intubation is always possible and if immediately identified can be corrected by the simple process of withdrawing the tube into the trachea. It is essential that a check is always made by auscultation of both sides of the chest, well away from the midline and including the apices as well as the bases, to verify the equal inflation of the lungs. It is possible for a previously correctly positioned tube to slip into a bronchus in the course of the operation, and unexplained hypoxia during an endotracheal anaesthetic should immediately alert the anaesthetist to the possibility of this complication. The presence of a pulse oximeter throughout the procedure would give early warning of this problem.

BRAIN DAMAGE

32.20 The human brain is a dynamic system of neurones performing in a way far superior to the most advanced computer yet devised by mankind. Brain size has, despite previous notorious and largely discredited work, no relation to intellect. This almost unimaginable performance is not achieved without cost, however. The consumption of oxygen (the basic energy source for every organ in the animal body) is, even with a basal level of cerebral activity, extremely high compared with most organs in the body (3.3 ml O_2 per min per 100 ml tissue, 46 ml per min for the average adult human brain). In states of intense cerebral activity, such as epileptiform seizures, the consumption is much higher. The blood supply to the adult brain is approximately 750 ml/min at rest, and since even blood with haemoglobin fully saturated with oxygen will supply only 150 ml/min it can be understood that the extraction of oxygen from the cerebral blood is considerable and hence the reserve for emergencies is small. The potential for disaster of rapid onset is made the more serious by the inability of the brain to recover from a hypoxic insult to the same extent as other organs. As Haldane put it many years ago, 'hypoxia not only stops the machine, but wrecks the machinery'. As a result, any deprivation of the brain of oxygen will have a profound effect. At the very least this will produce an impairment of intellect, perhaps detectable only by those closely acquainted with the patient, and at worst death or a severely handicapped patient who will be almost totally dependent on the community for his existence.

32.21 The severity of any particular lesion will depend on a number of factors; for example, there is evidence that incomplete ischaemia paradoxically leads to more severe damage than total ischaemia, and that the combination of ischaemia and hyperglycaemia results in more severe damage than a similar degree of ischaemia with normo- or slight hypoglycaemia (Weir and Jones 1987). Assessment of the likely extent of damage from a particular anoxic insult is therefore extremely difficult.

32.22 Hypoxic brain damage associated with anaesthesia can arise for a variety of reasons. The factors which are responsible for the supply of oxygen to an individual cell are enumerated in Figure 32.2.

32.23 The commonest cause of failure of oxygen supply to brain tissue is a fall in alveolar O_2 tension with possibly cessation of cardiac output (cardiac arrest). There are numerous causes for the former, but most relate either to delivery of an abnormally low oxygen tension to the breathing system or to blockage of the airway, which in this context can be anywhere between the oxygen source and the alveoli. The causes of an abnormally low oxygen tension are protean, ranging from failure of the central oxygen supply to the operating theatre; an empty oxygen cylinder on an anaesthetic machine; cross-connection of the oxygen and nitrous oxide pipelines (Adams and Henville 1979); wrong setting of the oxygen flowmeter or leakage of oxygen from a damaged rotameter. Failure of artificial ventilation will result in hypoxia; the ventilator may cease to function or may become disconnected from the patient – both these have formed the basis of a number of actions for substantial damages. Errors of endotracheal intubation have been mentioned above; these too are a potent source of litigation as a result of death or brain damage.

32.24 Failure of oxygen delivery to the brain may also result from circulatory failure. Although the pulmonary circulation receives oxygen from the alveoli the failure of the 'pump' prevents delivery to the tissues. Again, there are numerous reasons for this in anaesthetic practice, mainly associated with myocardial depression by drugs or circulatory failure due to hypovolaemia. Cerebral hypotension may occur in a normovolaemic patient if the vascular space is increased deliberately in the course of induced hypotension or epidural or spinal block. A particularly dangerous situation may occur during epidural block for pain relief in labour or during Caesarean section if the gravid uterus is allowed to compress the inferior vena cava and aorta (aortocaval compression). Severe hypotension may result in damage to both mother and child if the comparatively simple measures required to prevent and treat this condition are not carried out.

32.25 In view of the serious consequences of cerebral hypoxia the question of negligence is clearly of the utmost importance. It has been established that it is the responsibility of the anaesthetist to ensure that his equipment is functioning correctly throughout the time that the patient is dependent on it. He is not, at least within the British National Health Service, responsible for the supply of the correct gas to the operating theatre; this is the responsibility of the health authority. Thus, if the anaesthetist allowed the ventilator to become disconnected from the patient, he would reasonably be held to be at fault; if the piped oxygen were inadvertently connected at its source to a supply of pure nitrous oxide, it would be the responsibility of the health authority to have carried out the appropriate test procedures. The establishment of Trusts, with their own legal responsibility, makes this position unclear.

32.26 An anaesthetist in modern practice would be expected by his peers to take the following precautions to avoid accidents resulting in cerebral hypoxia:

(1) a pre-operative check routine of his anaesthetic machine and equipment at the start of the operating list. There is no universally accepted routine but a typical sequence of checks is shown in Table 32.4;
(2) precautions to detect inadvertent oesophageal or endobronchial intubation as outlined in paras **32.7** ff;

(3) a level of monitoring at least that of the accepted 'minimum monitoring'. The Association of Anaesthetists of Great Britain and Ireland has made recommendations which have wide acceptance (Table 32.5). Although most untoward incidents which give rise to claims of negligence occur during the maintenance of anaesthesia, the induction of anaesthesia is often accompanied by major and potentially hazardous physiological changes, and it is essential that these are detected by observation of the full range of minimum monitoring equipment which should be attached to the patient and in working order before the induction of anaesthesia. Health authorities and health Trusts should be prepared to accept vicarious liability when they are unable to provide monitoring equipment which is, on the advice of the Department of Anaesthetics, considered necessary for essential surgery;

(4) it is accepted that an anaesthetist should at all times be in close contact with his patient and in a position to maintain continuous observation of the patient and the monitoring equipment. It is difficult to achieve this throughout a case lasting for many hours by a lone anaesthetist without a medically qualified assistant. A supportive Department of Anaesthetics should provide occasional relief when needed. Anaesthetists who do not have this support have a personal responsibility to ensure that they are in a state to work effectively, and their employers have a responsibility to ensure that they can work efficiently at all times. The recently agreed 'Heads of Agreement' (NHS Management Executive, 1991) on the hours of work of junior doctors, while having a considerable impact on the provision of medical services in hospitals, has reduced the likelihood of errors due to fatigue. Junior anaesthetists may perceive pressure to breach the agreed hours of work to maintain the clinical service and feel that their professional obligations conflict with their contractual requirements. However, they should not work beyond their contractual requirements. There will be occasions where a clinical episode inescapably detains the doctor beyond his hours of work. In these circumstances there is apparently extended cover of his legal indemnity. Anaesthetists may encounter this when an operation lasts longer than anticipated (para **32.88**).

NERVE INJURIES

32.27 The unconscious patient is particularly susceptible to damage to peripheral nerves where these are placed superficially and therefore at risk from damage through pressure or stretching. The incidence of nerve damage associated with anaesthesia has been found in a large series to be approximately 1 in 1,000 anaesthetics (Parks 1973). Additionally anaesthesia may be associated with nerve damage in a number of other circumstances.

32.28 Nerves are more likely to be damaged if the patient is thin and underweight as the superficially placed nerve is more exposed. Additionally it appears that pre-existing peripheral nerve lesions, either single or as part of a generalised polyneuropathy, are more likely to produce signs of neurological damage if subjected to trauma.

Specific nerves liable to damage during anaesthesia

Upper limb

BRACHIAL PLEXUS

32.29 This is most commonly damaged by stretching, particularly with the arm in extreme abduction with external rotation and the elbow extended and forearm supinated. The effect has been described by Sunderland (1978) as follows:

(a) the humeral head is displaced inferiorly out of the glenoid fossa of the scapula, and the cords of the brachial plexus are bow-strung across it;
(b) the trunks of the plexus are entrapped between the clavicle and the first rib;
(c) if the arm is forced posteriorly this entrapment will be more severe. The same effect will result from the arm falling from the operating table to hang downwards and posteriorly.

32.30 The brachial plexus is also at risk if the patient is in the Trendelenberg position and is prevented from slipping down the table either by wrist restraints, which exert traction on the brachial plexus, or by shoulder supports. These, if placed too medially, compress the plexus between clavicle and first rib; if too lateral, depression of the shoulder tip causes stretching of the plexus. The brachial plexus may also be damaged if the head is turned sharply away from the side of the abducted arm.

32.31 The whole or part of the plexus may be damaged. The degree of recovery cannot be assessed initially and does not bear a relationship to the magnitude of the damage. Trojaborg (1977) found that complete recovery occurred in less than five months in 58 per cent of cases, in more than five months in 28 per cent, and remained incomplete in 6 per cent. It is possible that predisposing factors may exist, including a cervical rib or fibrous band from the seventh cervical vertebra to the first rib, and assessment of a brachial plexus injury should include examination for such an abnormality.

32.32 Prevention of brachial plexus injury during anaesthesia should include the following precautions:

(a) avoidance of restraints to the arms or shoulders to prevent slipping in the Trendelenberg position. Instead, a non-slip mattress should be used;
(b) the arm should not be abducted beyond a right angle, particularly when the patient is in the Trendelenberg position. An arm-board with a secure clamping mechanism should be used. Preferably the arm should not be abducted at all; if access is required the arm should be flexed across the chest;
(c) when the patient is prone the arms should not be placed above the head;
(d) when the patient is in the lateral position the head should be supported to prevent excessive lateral traction (Payan 1987).

ULNAR NERVE

32.33 This is vulnerable to injury as it winds round the medial epicondyle, and in its superficial position may be compressed between bone and the operating table and its fitments. Experience has shown that as little as 30 minutes' compression may cause clinically detectable damage. Ulnar nerve lesions are frequently slow to recover and the incidence of permanent damage is high. Prevention is therefore important. During surgery the arm should be protected from pressure on the extensor surface of the elbow by suitable padding. The author has seen an ulnar nerve lesion caused by the prolonged application of an arm splint applied to the back of the forearm which migrated upwards in a semi-conscious patient to cause pressure on the nerve at the back of the elbow. The anaesthetist has a responsibility to ensure that the arm is protected during surgery.

RADIAL NERVE

32.34 This is most frequently damaged as it winds round the shaft of the humerus. It lies in close apposition to the bone and can therefore be injured by compression between this and hard surfaces such as the edge of the operating table pressing on the middle of the upper arm, particularly in thin subjects. The effect is usually a wrist-drop though a wide variety of sensory and motor losses within the distribution of the nerve can occur. Unlike the ulnar nerve, recovery of function is almost invariable, although this may take time.

Lower limb

SCIATIC NERVE

32.35 This nerve supplies most of the lower limb below the knee and injury has a profound effect. It is likely to be damaged by compression of the buttock over a long period of time, especially in a thin patient, and very rarely by intramuscular injections into the buttock rather than the thigh. A sciatic nerve lesion is unlikely to be due to faulty positioning provided the anaesthetist is aware of the risk of compression in an individual patient, but intramuscular injections into the buttock cannot readily be defended (Hoyte 1987).

LATERAL CUTANEOUS NERVE OF THIGH (COMMON PERONEAL NERVE)

32.36 This nerve is particularly liable to damage as it lies superficial to the neck of the fibula below the knee. It is commonly injured by compression on the lateral side of the leg, usually by a lithotomy pole or stirrup, or by a projection of the operating table if the patient is lying flat or prone. The result is a foot-drop which is slow to resolve but nearly full recovery is usual. It would be difficult to justify this lesion as the causes are well known.

Nerve lesions elsewhere in the body

32.37 It should also be noted that the tibial nerve may rarely be damaged by compression in the popliteal fossa behind the knee. This may occur in patients whose legs have been placed in the lithotomy stirrups but is rare and not necessarily related to malposition, especially in obese subjects. In these circumstances the unfortunate result could not be regarded as the result of negligent practice.

SUPRAORBITAL NERVE

32.38 This may be damaged by compression by connections to the endotracheal tube and is sufficiently well known to be regarded as negligent if it occurs as a result of this (Barron 1955).

FACIAL NERVE

32.39 This may rarely be compressed by the anaesthetist's hand holding a facemask over a period of time or by a mask-holding strap (Conway 1984). The result is loss of motor power of the facial muscles in the lower part of the face. The lesion is well known but the risks of intubation are such that the anaesthetist may well decide that the use of a supported facemask is preferable in certain cases. Under these circumstances allegations of negligence could be defended.

Nerve injuries due to needle injections

32.40 These may result from attempts at a nerve block or as a result of an intramuscular injection. It is accepted practice that when paraesthesiae are obtained during the initial localisation of the nerve to be blocked, the needle should be very slightly withdrawn to avoid injection of the local anaesthetic directly into the nerve itself. The use of a nerve stimulator to locate the nerve will help to prevent damage; the instrument is widely available and an anaesthetist who carries out a block 'blind' may be judged to be acting below an acceptable standard of practice.

32.41 Intramuscular injections are by long-established practice not given into the buttock for fear of damaging the sciatic nerve, nor into the upper arm because of the risk to the radial and circumflex nerves. The correct site is the lateral aspect of the thigh, slightly anterior to the coronal plane, and to use other sites would almost certainly be regarded as negligent.

Nerve lesions due to anaesthetic agents

32.42 The whole subject of nerve injuries in association with anaesthesia is covered in detail by Payan (1987).

Prognosis after nerve injury

32.43 The early course of a nerve lesion is of little help in determining the eventual outcome and in most cases only time will tell. Nevertheless valuable information can be gained by electromyography carried out after about ten days. The advice of an expert neurologist is essential in interpretation, but in general if the lesion is shown to be a block of conduction rather than neuronal degeneration, recovery can be confidently expected. In most cases of nerve lesions sustained under anaesthesia, recovery occurs within six to eight weeks (Payan 1987).

INTRAVENOUS REGIONAL ANAESTHESIA

32.44 This block has in recent years acquired a reputation for causing severe systemic toxicity if the local anaesthetic agent used is allowed to escape in large quantities into the circulation. This may result in convulsions, cardiac depression and even death. It is noteworthy that in every case where complications of this type have been reported, there has been a departure from accepted practice and, correctly carried out, the block is safe, effective and useful (Atkinson, Rushman, and Davies 1993). The following guidelines are currently accepted as mandatory in the conduct of the block:

(1) an indwelling venous access should be established in another limb to enable emergency drugs to be given in the event of a complication;

(2) after exsanguination of the limb the cuff should be applied over a gamgee pad to the middle of the upper arm or the thigh, as appropriate. The cuff itself should be wide and should have been thoroughly tested to ensure that leaks will not occur when inflated. It is essential to use a special cuff with an attached gas source and a bleed valve which will automatically introduce more gas into the cuff in the event of leakage. A double cuff is also desirable for patient comfort but is not essential for the safety of the procedure. The pressure to which the cuff is inflated is very important and an accurate pressure gauge is therefore necessary. This should be open to the cuff throughout the procedure and not clamped off. It is generally accepted that the cuff should be inflated to 100 mm Hg above the systolic arterial pressure in the limb;

(3) the local anaesthetic should be as non-toxic as possible. Bupivacaine (Marcain) was at one time popular but the margin of toxicity is so small that it is not now recommended. This is very well recognised and the use of bupivacaine would almost certainly be regarded as negligent. The agent least likely to cause complications is prilocaine but the use of lignocaine could be defended (Wildsmith, Scott and Brown 1979). Prilocaine 0.5 per cent is the drug of choice in most cases;

(4) the cuff must remain inflated for at least 15 minutes. Premature release will allow local anaesthetic to flood the circulation, giving rise to blood levels above the threshold level for toxic reactions (Thorn-Alquist 1969). When the cuff is released it must be deflated slowly and the patient warned about slight dizziness which is not uncommon at this stage.

32.45 The potential dangers of this block are sufficiently well known to make departure from any of the above precautions difficult to defend. It must be stressed, though, that the block, carried out in the manner described is a useful and widely used procedure and claims of negligence based on its correct use can readily be defended.

SPINAL AND EPIDURAL BLOCK

32.46 These blocks have been in widespread use for many years, both for analgesia during surgery and for pain relief in labour. The use of spinal anaesthesia fell into disfavour after the famous *Wooley and Roe* case (Cope 1954) when long-lasting paralysis followed the administration of spinal anaesthetics to two patients on the same operating list. The cause was said to be contamination of the local anaesthetic with the solution used to preserve the sterility of the ampoules but this has subsequently been questioned. Spinal anaesthesia has had a revival of popularity among anaesthetists in recent years and is now an acceptable form of regional anaesthesia. Complications are rare, but not non-existent. Headache may occur and more so when a large-bore needle is used; nevertheless the use of the recommended 25 gauge needle is difficult in some patients and the use of a needle of 21 gauge or smaller can be readily defended if the anaesthetist anticipates difficulty, can justify his use of spinal anaesthesia in the case, and has explained to the patient the possibility of post-operative headache. It should be noted at this stage that post-operative 'spinal' headache, although severe, is always self-limiting after about six days, and allegations of continuing headache require careful evaluation by an expert neurologist. Some experts would consider that the performance of a regional block while the patient is anaesthetised is unacceptable because the patient is unable to complain of pain which might draw the attention of the anaesthetist to damaging intraneural injection. Similarly, if the anaesthetist performs a block while the patient is asleep without obtaining the consent of the patient beforehand, it could be difficult to defend any sequelae from the block such as prolonged paralysis or headache.

32.47 Epidural block is favoured by many anaesthetists because it does not breach the spinal subarachnoid space with the risk of introducing infection, and for its facility for continuing analgesia by means of an indwelling catheter through which supplementary doses of local anaesthetic or opioid drug can be given. It is widely used for pain relief in labour and the informed mother in the UK expects that this facility will be available to her. Unfortunately the provision of epidural analgesia is extremely labour-intensive and some units cannot provide an 'on-demand' service. There is no question that to provide epidural analgesia without the appropriate on-call and backup services, including, according to Trust or health authority policy, the availability of a midwife trained to carry out 'top-ups' and deal with ensuing complications, or alternatively the immediate availability of an anaesthetist, would fall short of acceptable practice. The Royal College of Anaesthetists considers that obstetric anaesthesia and analgesia (including epidural blocks for pain relief) should be provided by an anaesthetist of at least one year's experience. In the same way that awareness can occur in inappropriately managed general anaesthesia, regional analgesia occasionally provides inadequate pain relief. Inadequate analgesia after a regional block should receive immediate attention, which might include 'top-up' of the anaesthetic agent; a new block; or conversion to an alternative method of pain relief such as general anaesthesia. To persist with a block in the face of clear lack of analgesia is clinically unacceptable.

32.48 There are certain well-defined contraindications to both spinal anaesthesia and epidural anaesthesia and analgesia. These are well known and divergence from them would be hard to defend.

HAEMORRHAGIC DISEASE

32.49 Pre-existing conditions and full anti-coagulation are clear contraindications but the use of this type of regional analgesia with low dose heparin or dextran used for prophylaxis against deep vein thrombosis is controversial (Odoom 1984).

INFECTION AT OR NEAR THE SITE OF BLOCK

32.50 The risk of introducing infection into the epidural or subarachnoid space clearly is bad practice.

PATIENT RELUCTANCE

32.51 The British public expects to be asleep during surgery and does not readily accept that there can be analgesia without the obtunding of consciousness. Explanation and careful discussion will usually persuade the patient but there remains a small group who are totally opposed to a regional technique. The wise anaesthetist does not attempt further persuasion as the incidence of allegations of negligence, justified or not, is higher in this group.

NEUROLOGICAL DISEASE

32.52 This is a difficult problem as a regional block is frequently appropriate for patients with paralyses because their respiratory function may be impaired. There is no evidence that epidural or spinal block aggravates a neurological condition. Nevertheless conditions such as multiple sclerosis are prone to spontaneous exacerbations and remissions and a coincidental relapse at the time of the block might be interpreted as an effect of the block on the disease. Most anaesthetists would therefore avoid regional blocks of all types in patients with neurological disease unless there were a very strong indication. However, in view of the lack of evidence of association between relapse and the carrying out of a regional block, an allegation of negligence could, with some difficulty, be defensible.

32.53 Deafness after spinal anaesthesia is a well-recognised though rare event and may be related to the type and size of needle used for the block. Although it is regarded as good practice to use the finest diameter needle possible, the occurrence of deafness after spinal block would not necessarily imply unacceptable practice by the anaesthetist. The use of indwelling catheters in the subarachnoid space is more contentious, however, and it is of interest to note that the American Food and Drugs Agency has recently withdrawn the licence for some subarachnoid spinal catheters because of an unacceptably high incidence of cauda equina syndrome.

AWARENESS DURING ANAESTHESIA

32.54 It is axiomatic that general anaesthesia produces unconsciousness and relief of pain, and the anaesthetist regards it as his prime duty to produce this state safely and reliably. There are, unfortunately, many recorded instances where this is not achieved, and the patient is aware and can subsequently recall events occurring during the operation. It should be stressed that this is not always accompanied by pain as might be expected, and the degree of recall varies from brief episodes when a single remark or sensation is experienced to serious disasters when the patient lies awake and in extreme pain throughout the procedure.

32.55 The incidence of awareness is variously quoted as up to 10 per cent (Scott 1972). Dreaming, unrelated to actual events, is much more common and an incidence of 44 per cent has been reported by Brice et al (1970).

32.56 There is a great deal of uncertainty about the actual nature of anaesthesia itself. Most patients experience total oblivion for the duration of the anaesthetic, awakening with no perception of the passage of time. Nevertheless, several investigators have found that patients appear to retain auditory stimuli in the subconscious mind even during deep anaesthesia, and are capable of recall under appropriate conditions (Jones 1986). There is a difference between some retained memory and suffering arising from feelings of pain.

32.57 There are a number of causes of excessively light anaesthesia.

INADEQUATE DOSES OF ANAESTHETIC DRUGS

32.58 This may be due to misjudgment or miscalculation by the anaesthetist, or a deliberate need to keep the dose minimal in a very sick patient. The dose of thiopentone may be inadequate to obtund totally consciousness at the induction of anaesthesia, so that the patient is aware of the passage of the endotracheal tube into his trachea. This is a very frequent cause of awareness and the patient may well be asleep for the rest of the operation when the drugs used for maintenance are subsequently given. A particular cause of awareness due to inadequate dosage occurs during Caesarean section although it is interesting to note that this constitutes only 28 per cent of cases of awareness handled by the Medical Defence Union (Hargrove 1987). The anaesthetist may have used the lightest level of anaesthesia possible, usually nitrous oxide without supplementation with volatile agents or narcotics, in an attempt to prevent depression of the infant at the moment of birth. This technique was widely used until recently but is no longer acceptable; the infant is no more likely to be depressed as a result of a low concentration of a volatile agent added to the nitrous oxide than if the mother had been breathing the same volatile agent from a fixed-concentration self-administration vaporiser during normal labour – a widespread and effective practice. Indeed the raised level of catecholamines in the maternal circulation as a result of the light level of anaesthesia may have a positively disadvantageous effect on the placental blood flow which is essential for fetal welfare before delivery. Under these circumstances a claim for negligence from awareness during Caesarean section would normally be difficult to defend.

32.59 Most cases of awareness due to inadequate drug dosage or concentration arise in patients who have had a neuromuscular blocking agent to produce muscular paralysis as well as anaesthetic agents. This is a widespread practice as excellent surgical conditions are produced with a light level of anaesthesia. Unfortunately it is possible for the patient to be fully paralysed and yet aware, and this is the cause of most true cases of awareness. The unavailability of neuromuscular blocking drugs before the early 1940s was presumably the reason for the almost non-existence of claims of negligence due to awareness before that time.

INADVERTENT DILUTION OF NITROUS OXIDE WITH OXYGEN

32.60 The commonest reason for this is the oxygen bypass being inadvertently switched on during the course of an anaesthetic. The bypass delivers at least 35 l/min and, with a fresh gas flow of 6 l/min and 66 per cent nitrous oxide set on the flowmeters the gas mixture delivered to the patient will actually contain at least 9.8 per cent nitrous oxide – barely enough to provide detectable analgesia.

ENTRAINMENT OF AIR INTO THE GAS MIXTURE

32.61 It is possible for air to be admitted to the breathing system if the fresh gas flow is insufficient. This will dilute the gas mixture and lower the concentrations of the anaesthetic gases and vapour. The same result may occur if the ventilator becomes disconnected from a patient who is nevertheless capable of breathing spontaneously.

ABNORMAL RESISTANCE TO ANAESTHETIC AGENTS

32.62 Some patients require more anaesthetic drugs than others. Although there are published figures for the MAC (minimal alveolar concentration which will obtund reflex movement in response to a surgical stimulus for a given agent in 50 per cent (MAC_{50}) or 95 per cent (MAC_{95}) of patients), there is a wide variation in the dosages required. It can be anticipated that certain patients, e g those with a large muscle mass or with a high alcohol consumption, will require higher dosages, but there will always be the patient who for no apparent reason other than biological variation requires more than most to produce reliable surgical anaesthesia.

32.63 Despite the difficulty in predicting the anaesthetic requirements in every patient there are reasonably reliable clinical signs of light anaesthesia:

(a) a rise in pulse or blood pressure which cannot be accounted for by any other physiological event;
(b) the appearance of sweating and lacrimation;
(c) a reaction to light of the pupil of the eye;
(d) an abnormally high dosage of neuromuscular blocking drug to maintain adequate muscular relaxation.

32.64 This requires constant vigilance on the part of the anaesthetist as these are clinical observations which are not readily amenable to instrumental monitoring.

32.65 Evoked potentials may be of value in a few cases. Stimulation of a peripheral nerve or an appropriate sensory cranial nerve (ear or eye) can be detected in the awake patient by electrical activity over the cerebral cortex.

The voltages involved are minute, and the technique is fraught with difficulty. It has been used for this purpose but is not of proven reliability.

32.66 The question of negligence in cases of awareness is a difficult one and would, in the view of the author, depend on the circumstances. The opinions of lawyers on this subject have been given by Powers (1987) and Puxon (1987).

32.67 A clear episode of awareness during a routine operation, with accurate recall of incidents which occurred and remarks made by those present at the time, would be difficult to defend. The defence might be even more difficult if it were shown to be due to an error of technique such as leaving the oxygen bypass on, rather than the result of an error of judgment made by a less experienced trainee attempting to produce the safest conditions with the minimum of anaesthetic agents. Some might insist that an oxygen monitor be used for this reason. The physical signs of awareness in the course of an anaesthetic using light anaesthesia and neuromuscular blocking agents are sufficiently well known by anaesthetists of all degrees of experience, and sufficiently easy to interpret provided the level of vigilance is adequate.

32.68 There will be many cases of less certainty. An emergency such as a sudden massive haemorrhage causing profound hypotension would be treated by measures that would include the administration of 100 per cent oxygen. In a patient already lightly anaesthetised, this withdrawal of anaesthetic agents could readily lead to transient awareness, yet would be a correct and essential aspect of the management of the emergency to preserve the patient's life.

32.69 The interpretation of the alleged episode as awareness must be made with caution. Dreaming is not uncommon during anaesthesia and is not necessarily due to incorrect anaesthetic technique, since the content of the dream does not relate to any actual events taking place at the time. There is also evidence that some anaesthetic drugs, even when appropriately used, can induce subconscious responses which may result in allegations of impropriety by the anaesthetist. Propofol and fentanyl have been implicated (Boheimer & Thomas 1990). Ketamine in subanaesthetic doses produces vivid hallucinations which may be of a sexual nature. The male anaesthetist should always have a female chaperone when administering anaesthetic or sedative drugs to a female patient (General Medical Council 1989). Theatre managers, faced with staff shortages and a changing skillmix, may place pressure on male anaesthetists to release female staff from the anaesthetic room for other duties. This is unacceptable and the chaperone must remain in the anaesthetic room until the patient is transferred into the operating theatre. Whether the reverse situation applies, in the case of the female anaesthetist dealing with the male patient, remains untried.

32.70 It is important to attempt to establish the timing of the episode of awareness. Patients will sometimes allege that they were aware during the operation, yet careful enquiry determines that they are recalling their recovery, which is frequently preceded by return of hearing rather than full awareness of their surroundings. The author was involved in a complaint against an experienced trainee anaesthetist by a patient alleging that she had been aware during a thyroidectomy. Detailed discussion with her revealed that she had known that she was awake because she saw the unmasked face of the surgeon looking down at her. When it was pointed out that the surgeon would have been wearing a mask during the operation, and furthermore that the procedure involves placing a sterile towel around the head in such a way that her eyes would have been covered, and that the comments of the surgeon were confirmed by him as having been made in the recovery room as she was waking up, she was satisfied that awareness had not occurred during the operation.

32.71 The view of the Medical Protection Society on the defensibility of allegations of awareness is noteworthy (Medical Protection Society 1986). The Society considers that defence of the anaesthetist is not possible in the majority of cases in three circumstances:

(1) where there was a failure to adhere to generally accepted clinical practice in the choice of anaesthetic technique;
(2) where there was a failure to keep an adequate record of the anaesthetic procedure.
(3) where there was faulty equipment.

32.72 The Society emphasises the importance of the pre-operative check of equipment before the procedure which could avert awareness. Where awareness has apparently occurred they recommend that a full explanation by a senior anaesthetist be made to the patient at an early stage, since frank and sympathetic handling of a patient's complaint may reduce the likelihood of litigation.

32.73 Recommendations for the avoidance of overt awareness which would be regarded as reasonable by most experienced anaesthetists have been made by Vickers (1987) (Table 32.6).

MINIMUM MONITORING

32.74 Considerable discussion has taken place in recent years about the standards of monitoring which should be practised during routine anaesthesia. The development of a wide range of accurate instruments capable of monitoring most aspects of physiological change in the anaesthetised patient has led to widely differing standards of practice among anaesthetists. In some cases these differences have been based on ignorance of the availability of the technology, unwillingness to change the habits of a lifetime, or a feeling that clinical assessment of the patient gives as much information as a range of expensive and complex instruments. These factors have led to the development of protocols by British professional organisations and individual Departments of Anaesthesia. The purpose of these is twofold. The first is to set a standard of intra-operative patient monitoring less than which, for ordinary purposes, would be regarded as unacceptable by peers, and hence to force anaesthetists to practise monitoring to at least this standard (and to instruct trainees in the minimum standard which is acceptable). The second reason is to make it clear to employers that a certain amount of equipment is necessary to enable this basic standard to be achieved.

32.75 The drawing up of standards for minimum monitoring does, of course, introduce the question of whether a practitioner who falls below the standards is negligent. The answer to this must be in the affirmative, although it should be said that the protocols have been so recently introduced that cases of alleged negligence through failure to conform to a minimum standard protocol are rare. Nevertheless, the standard published by the Association of Anaesthetists (1988) (Table 32.5) is widely accepted in the UK and claims of negligence would be difficult to defend if the standard was not observed. There will inevitably be conflict between an anaesthetist and his employer if the necessary equipment is not made available, but nevertheless the anaesthetist would be expected, under normal circumstances, to maintain the standard, and in some cases this might require him to decline to give an anaesthetic if the appropriate equipment was not forthcoming. The professional defence organisations advise that, where monitoring equipment considered necessary by the anaesthetist is not available because of failure to provide or maintain it by the employing authority, and the anaesthetist considers that, on balance, it is nevertheless necessary to proceed with the anaesthetic, the employing authority should be required to carry vicarious liability for the action of the anaesthetist in so proceeding.

MISCELLANEOUS MATTERS WHICH MAY GIVE RISE TO ALLEGATIONS OF NEGLIGENCE

Assistance for the anaesthetist

32.76 Modern anaesthesia is essentially safe, and morbidity and mortality ascribable solely to anaesthesia are rare. Nevertheless, serious complications can develop at any time and the ability of the anaesthetist to cope with the situation will depend in some measure on the skill and anticipation of the assistant he has at his side at the time. It is generally acknowledged that a fully trained assistant is essential for the safety of the patient, regardless of the severity or urgency of the surgery. It is the responsibility of the anaesthetist to ensure that his assistant is competent to provide adequate assistance in all reasonable circumstances, and generally anaesthetists insist on their employing authorities providing the necessary level of assistance. It is therefore only in the most extreme urgency that the anaesthetist is justified in proceeding with the anaesthetic when a fully trained assistant is not immediately available. To induce anaesthesia without adequate assistance would be regarded in most circumstances as sub-standard practice.

32.77 The definition of 'adequate assistance' is more difficult. Anaesthetists have assistance from two sources:

(1) Operating Department Assistants or Operating Department Practitioners who, when fully trained have obtained a City and Guilds diploma or National Vocational Qualification which certifies their ability to assist the anaesthetist;
(2) Registered General Nurses (formerly State Registered Nurses) or State

Enrolled Nurses who have undergone special training in the care of the anaesthetised patient, including assisting the anaesthetist. It should be emphasised that the possession of a RGN or SEN diploma per se does not certify the nurse as competent in this specialised and difficult field, despite the view of many employing authorities. Although one cannot be dogmatic about this matter, an adequate level of assistance could be defined as the undivided attention of an assistant who has had additional training in this field and who has gained one of the diplomas (ENB 182 or 176 or equivalent) which certify competence in this field. Despite this, there are undoubtedly many nurses who assist the anaesthetist very adequately without formal qualifications of the type mentioned, particularly where only a limited range of anaesthesia is carried out and therefore the skills required, although taxing, are limited. Nevertheless the anaesthetist must satisfy himself that the level of assistance available at the time is, in his view, adequate; to embark on an anaesthetic with assistance less than this would be difficult to defend.

Dental out-patient anaesthesia

32.78 Until quite recently it was common to give general anaesthesia in the dental surgery for extraction of teeth and other procedures. The difficult conditions of the ill-equipped surgery and the lack of back-up facilities in the event of an emergency, together with the occasional lack of preparation of the patient, sometimes led to serious complications and even death. This problem was addressed by a Government Working Party (Department of Health 1991) which recommended that general anaesthesia should only be given in clinics which were equipped to standards which they outlined, and that those involved should be trained to defined levels in anaesthesia and resuscitation. It is now widely regarded that to give general anaesthesia or sedation in an environment less ideal than defined in the Report would fall below an acceptable level of practice.

Identification of patients and operations

32.79 The pressures of a busy operating theatre are such that the potential for operating on the wrong patient, or performing an operation on the wrong limb or the wrong side of the body is very real. Patients are incredibly compliant when it is suggested, for instance, that it is necessary to place their legs in the lithotomy stirrups before excising a mole from the face (an event which the author has actually witnessed) and the influence of sedative premedicant drugs will further dull the patient's ability to call attention to an attempt to carry out inappropriate procedures on his body. It is therefore necessary to have rigorous procedures for checking that the correct patient is being operated on and that the correct procedure is being carried out. A set of guidelines has been produced jointly by the Medical Defence Societies, the Royal College of Nursing, and the National Association of Theatre Nurses (Anonymous 1986). The anaesthetist is responsible for ensuring that the correct patient is anaesthetised. The reasonable measures he can take to confirm this are as follows.

32.80 (1) At a pre-operative visit, confirm verbally the identity of the patient and ensure that an approved identification band is attached to either wrist or ankle (in many cases there will be bands on both limbs). Where the patient, by the nature of his condition, cannot confirm his identity, the anaesthetist must take every reasonable step to ascertain the identity of the patient. *The essential information is the allocated hospital number for that patient.* The name is not sufficient; the author knows of a situation where two members of a family, father and son, involved in a road accident, had the same forenames and surnames (not uncommon in areas such as Wales). Both required surgery and blood transfusion. Unfortunately they were of different blood groups and one patient died as a result of a confusion of identities and the ensuing incompatible transfusion.

32.81 (2) On arrival in the anaesthetic room both the surgeon and the anaesthetist (or their competent and medically-qualified deputies) should check by reference only to the identification band that the correct patient is about to undergo surgery. *It is not sufficient to check the patient's identity against the accompanying case notes, since if the wrong patient has arrived in the anaesthetic room, his notes will have accompanied him and will therefore be of no value in the verification process.* Asking a patient under the influence of a premedicant drug for important medico-legal details such as his name and the site of the operation is equally unsatisfactory. In the author's opinion the only accurate verification of identity is obtained by comparison of the identification number on the operation list with that on the patient's band. It is therefore important to ensure *in advance* that the published operating list contains accurate and complete details of the patient and his operation. Unfortunately this is a task often delegated to the newly qualified house surgeon with the minimum of experience and supervision.

32.82 It is essential that the surgeon verifies the site of operation by a similar procedure, using limb marking, but the prudent anaesthetist, although not legally responsible for this aspect of the procedure, will check this information again before the patient is anaesthetised.

32.83 It is common practice for the theatre nurse to check various aspects of the patient's preparation on arrival in the theatre; this is an important practical procedure but does not in any way absolve the anaesthetist from confirming that the correct patient is to be anaesthetised as it is not the legal responsibility of the nurse to confirm details of identity or operation. Anaesthesia of the wrong patient, even if the mistake is realised before surgery is carried out, would be indefensible.

ALLERGY AND ANAPHYLAXIS

32.84 A very high proportion of the population display an intolerance to certain foods and drugs. In most cases this consists of a skin rash or other reaction which is not a threat to life. Drugs used in anaesthesia can on very rare occasions produce a potentially life-threatening emergency because of an adverse anaphylactoid reaction. Anaesthetists therefore have a double responsibility:

(1) pre-operative assessment should include:
   (a) a note of substances to which the patient has had a previous adverse reaction, and measures to avoid further exposure. To administer a drug to which a patient has a proven allergy is unacceptable practice; this has occurred when anaesthetists have administered antibiotics on behalf of surgeons before operation. Nevertheless the responsibility remains with the doctor administering the drug (the anaesthetist) to ascertain that the patient is not allergic to the drug;
   (b) identification of individuals who are particularly susceptible ('atopic') to external agents and avoidance of anaesthetic drugs which may provoke an adverse reaction;

(2) they should have a clear plan of action for the management of severe anaphylactoid reaction (the life-threatening adverse response to a drug in a susceptible individual). This should include immediate diagnosis; administration of adrenaline by intravenous injection (though this might be challenged by some authorities in favour of the intramuscular or subcutaneous route); oxygen; colloid infusion; and airway control. All anaesthetists working without direct supervision should be able to deal promptly with a severe anaphylactoid reaction. Failure to do so would represent an unacceptable level of practice.

DELEGATION OF DUTIES

32.85 The speciality of anaesthesia is peculiar in that the traditional system of 'firms' is not, on the whole, observed. As a result, doctors of varying experience often work alone without direct supervision. This is clearly labour-effective; whether it is appropriate for training is a matter outside the scope of this chapter. The question of responsibility is, however, of great importance.

32.86 All qualified doctors are personally responsible for their own individual clinical actions. They are expected, though, to seek advice about problems outside their experience and their employer is expected to provide this senior assistance as the need arises. It is therefore incumbent on a Department of Anaesthetics so to arrange its cover that there is immediate availability of senior help when the need arises. This has led to problems in the past, the interpretation of which has not been helped recently by a judgment by the Court of Appeal that inexperience is not a defence, so that the most junior doctor is expected to follow accepted principles (Law Report 1986). The best advice that can be offered at the moment is that junior doctors should be asked to undertake only what is within their own declared range of responsibility; that they should have access at all times to senior help; and that they should realise that they act on their own responsibility if they do not seek advice for matters outside their experience. In these circumstances, reasonable peers would take the view that there was no corporate or vicarious lowering of standards if delegation of duties was appropriate and advice was readily available.

VIGILANCE BY THE ANAESTHETIST

32.87 The study of Lunn and Mushin (1982) drew attention to the fact that there was an avoidable factor in over half the deaths ascribable to anaesthesia alone. An examination of 150 anaesthetic mishaps which led to claims against members of the Medical Protection Society suggested that increased vigilance would have prevented a significant number of incidents. In 3 per cent of the cases, the patient was unattended by the anaesthetist when the incident occurred. The anaesthetist is expected to maintain constant vigilance and *it is not acceptable for the anaesthetist to leave his patient for even the briefest time*. To do so would undoubtedly be regarded by the courts as negligence, even if the anaesthetist had left the patient in the charge of someone other than another anaesthetist who was sufficiently experienced to provide adequate care.

32.88 Although Lunn and Mushin (1982) did not find that fatigue was a factor in anaesthetic mishaps, it is common for anaesthetists, particularly juniors, to work long hours and sometimes to put in a full day's work after a night on emergency duty. Unfortunately a plea of fatigue is no defence against an allegation of negligence, although it may be regarded by a court as mitigation and place some liability on the health authority if the level of staffing and the workload resulted in the overtired state of the anaesthetist. Nevertheless if an anaesthetist accepts responsibility for the care of a patient he must be satisfied with his own physical and mental state to deal with the clinical problems and it is his responsibility to inform his employer or superior if he has any doubts about this.

RECORDS USED IN ANAESTHESIA

32.89 Clear and accurate records are as necessary in anaesthesia as in any other speciality. Patients coming under the care of the anaesthetist in the operating theatre or intensive therapy unit have usually been examined and treated elsewhere in the hospital, and an early task of the anaesthetist is to appraise fully all relevant aspects of previous management. Pharmacological interactions between powerful anaesthetic drugs and previous therapy are not uncommon and must be avoided by careful prescription. The records most commonly encountered in anaesthetic practice, and of importance in medico-legal cases, are the anaesthetic record (Figure 32.4) and the ITU chart (Figure 32.5). Anaesthetists frequently request pathological investigations, most commonly involving the acid-base status of the patient. This is an essential component of the management of the patient on artificial ventilation in the intensive therapy unit. An example of a 'blood-gas' report is given in Figure 32.6. It is essential that health authorities accept written records of anaesthetics administered as being documents of vital importance and take steps to ensure that they are subsequently readily available in the case notes.

32.90 The availability of systems which take real-time physiological data from monitors attached to the patient, together with entries by the anaesthetist on actions taken, drugs given, and clinical observations made, will in the foreseeable future provide true records of events during anaesthesia. The capital expenditure required is considerable and the technology is not yet perfected. Most anaesthetic departments will not have access to such systems at present. An automated record will, however, be of considerable assistance in the assessment of an incident which leads to a claim of negligence.

MEDICAL AUDIT

32.91 Departments of Anaesthetics are rightly encouraged to conduct formal discussion and resolution of clinical problems within their field of practice. Even when litigation is possible, clinical cases should be presented with identifying data removed, for peer discussion aimed at evaluating the causes of the problems and, if necessary, actions to be taken to avoid similar problems in the future. It is the view of the profession that discussion of individual cases will not jeopardise impending litigation. It is essential that audit meetings are properly convened and conducted and that minutes are taken and made available as required.

CROSS-INFECTION BETWEEN PATIENT AND ANAESTHETIST

32.92 The escalating incidence of viral diseases in the community, particularly HIV and hepatitis infective viruses, places both anaesthetist and patient at risk. Reasonable measures which should be taken to avoid cross-infection are:

(1) all anaesthetists should have immunisation against Hepatitis B;
(2) there should be a policy for the theatre management of high-risk patients, including personal protection and disposal of contaminated waste. All staff should be made aware of the policy and should abide by its provisions;
(3) gloves should be worn whenever there is a risk of blood spillage or contamination by infected material. Anaesthetists should therefore wear gloves in every case, particularly at induction and extubation. The excuse that gloves make the introduction of cannulae difficult is untenable as these procedures can readily be carried out wearing gloves, with a little practice.

The anaesthetist who is HIV- or HBV-positive presents a particular problem. The view of the Association of Anaesthetists is that HIV-positive anaesthetists should be allowed to continue in practice, under medical supervision, provided they do not place their patient at risk by cross-contamination. What this entails is at present undefined.

GENERAL CONCLUSIONS

32.93 Anaesthesia is a potent source of allegations of negligence. The anaesthetist is, like any other doctor, expected to practise with a level of skill and care which is reasonable to expect from those of comparable training and experience. A large part of his work involves vigilance and meticulous care, and to disregard these basic tenets is to act in a negligent manner. What is perceived as negligent may also change with time, and the anaesthetist has a duty to keep himself abreast of important developments in the speciality. As Lunn (1986) has aptly put it:

> It is important . . . not only for anaesthetists individually to keep up to date, but also to be seen to do so. The relevance of peer review, or self assessment of performance against agreed criteria (our American friends call this Quality Assurance) should be viewed in this light . . . Standards of contemporary practice are thus established and no-one need fear litigation so long as his standards match those of his peers.

BIBLIOGRAPHICAL REFERENCES

Adams A P and Henville J D in Hewer C Langton and Atkinson R S *Recent Advances in Anaesthesia and Analgesia* vol 13 (Edinburgh, Churchill Livingstone, 1979) p 47.

Aitkenhead A R 'Risk Management in Anaesthesia' (1991) Journal of the Medical Defence Union (4) 86.

Anonymous *Theatre Safeguards* (Medical Defence Union, Medical Protection Society, Medical Defence Union of Scotland, National Association of Theatre Nurses, Royal College of Nursing of the United Kingdom, 1986).

Association of Anaesthetists of Great Britain and Ireland *Recommendations for Standards of Monitoring during Anaesthesia and Recovery* (London, The Association of Anaesthetists of Great Britain and Ireland, 1988).

Atkinson R S, Rushman G B and Davies N J H *A Synopsis of Anaesthesia* (11th edn, Bristol, Wright, 1993) p 648.

Barron D W 'Supraorbital Neurapraxia' (1955) Anaesthesia 10, 374.

Boheimer N O, Thomas J S 'Amorous Behaviour and Sexual Fantasy following Anaesthesia and Sedation' (1990) Anaesthesia 45, 699.

Bonney G 'Iatrogenic Injuries to Nerves' (1987) Journal of the Medical Defence Union 3(2), 4–6.

Brice D D, Hetherington R R and Utting J E 'A Simple Study of Awareness and Dreaming During Anaesthesia' (1970) British Journal of Anaesthesia 42, 535–542.

Campling E A, Devlin H B, Hoyle R W, Lunn J N 'The Report of the National Confidential Enquiry into Perioperative Deaths' (1992) London, National Confidential Enquiry into Perioperative Deaths.

Conway C 'Neurological and Ophthalmic Complications of Anaesthesia' in Churchill-Davidson H C (ed) *A Practice of Anaesthesia* (5th edn, London, Lloyd-Luke, 1984).

Cope R W 'The Wooley and Roe Case – Wooley and Roe versus Ministry of Health and others' (1954) Anaesthesia 9, 249–270.

Department of Health 'Report of an Expert Working Party on General Anaesthesia, Sedation, and Resuscitation' (London, Department of Health, 1991).

Fletcher I R, Healy T E J 'The Arterial Tourniquet' (1983) Annals of the Royal College of Surgeons 65, 409–417.

General Medical Council Annual Report for 1988 (London, General Medical Council, 1989).

Gray T C 'Thoughts on Some Serious Anaesthetic Errors' (1985) Journal of the Medical Defence Union 1(3), 9–10.

Hargrove R L 'Dental Damage during Anaesthesia' (1986) Journal of the Medical Defence Union 2(1), 19–20.

'Awareness under Anaesthesia' (1987) Journal of the Medical Defence Union 3(1), 9–11.

Hoyte P 'Hazards of Injections' (1987) Journal of the Medical Defence Union 3(2), 9.

Jones J G 'Hearing and Memory in Anaesthetised Patients' (1986) British Medical Journal 292, 1291–1293.

Latto I P and Rosen M (eds) *Difficulties in Tracheal Intubation* (Eastbourne, Baillière Tindall, 1985).

Law Report 'Doctor's Inexperience No Defence to Negligence' The Times, 6 August 1986, p 3.

Lunn J N and Mushin W W *Mortality Associated with Anaesthesia* (London, Nuffield Provincial Hospitals Trust, 1982).

'The Law and the Practice of Anaesthesia' (1986) Anaesthesia 41, 1085–1086.

Medical Protection Society Annual Reports and Accounts (1986) no 94, p 33.

NHS Management Executive *Junior Doctors – the New Deal* (London, NHS Management Executive, 1991).

Odoom J A 'Epidural Analgesia and Anticoagulant Therapy – A Reply' (1984) Anaesthesia 39, 602–603.

Parks B J'Postoperative Peripheral Neuropathies' (1973) Surgery 74, 348–357.

Payan J 'Nerve Injury' in Taylor T H and Major E (eds) *Hazards and Complications of Anaesthesia* (Edinburgh, Churchill Livingstone, 1987).

Powers M J 'A Lawyer's View of the Problem' in Rosen M and Lunn J N *Consciousness, Awareness, and Pain in General Anaesthesia* (Butterworths, 1987) pp 155–160.

Puxon M 'Awareness under Anaesthesia: A QC's View' in Rosen M and Lunn J N *Consciousness, Awareness, and Pain in General Anaesthesia* (Butterworths, 1987) pp 161–164.

Scott D L 'Awareness during General Anaesthesia' (1972) Canadian Anaesthetists' Society Journal 19, 173–183.

Sunderland S *Nerves and Nerve Injuries* (2nd edn, Edinburgh, Churchill Livingstone, 1978).

Thorn-Alquist A-M 'Blood Concentrations of Local Anaesthetics after Intravenous Regional Anaesthesia' (1969) Acta Anaesthesiologica Scandinavica 13, 229–240.

Trojaborg W 'Electrophysiological Findings in Pressure Palsy of the Brachial Plexus' (1977) Journal of Neurology, Neurosurgery, and Psychiatry 40, 1160–1167.

Vickers M D 'Avoidance of "Real" Awareness' in Rosen M and Lunn J N *Consciousness, Awareness, and Pain in General Anaesthesia* (Butterworths, 1987) p 180.

Weir D L and Jones J G 'Cerebral Ischaemia: Pathophysiology and Treatment' in Kaufman L *Anaesthesia Review* (Edinburgh, Longman Group, 1987) vol 5.

Wildsmith J A W, Scott D H T and Brown D T 'Intravenous Regional Analgesia using Bupivacaine' (1979) Anaesthesia 34, 919–920.

FURTHER READING

Orkin F K and Cooperman L H (eds) *Complications in Anaesthesiology* (Philadelphia, Lippincott, 1983).

Pierce E C and Cooper J B (eds) *Analysis of Anaesthetic Mishaps* (Boston, Little, Brown and Company, 1984).

Rosen M and Lunn J N (eds) *Consciousness, Awareness, and Pain in General Anaesthesia* (Butterworths, 1987).
Taylor J Leahy *The Doctor and Negligence* (London, Pitman, 1971).
Taylor T H and Major E (eds) *Hazards and Complications of Anaesthesia* (Edinburgh, Churchill Livingstone, 1987).

CROSS-REFERENCE

For information related to topics in this chapter see Chapter 33.

FIGURE 32.1 DIAGRAM TO SHOW THE FINAL POSITION OF THE CURVED LARYNGOSCOPE BLADE

Note: The arrows denote the direction of traction on the handle.

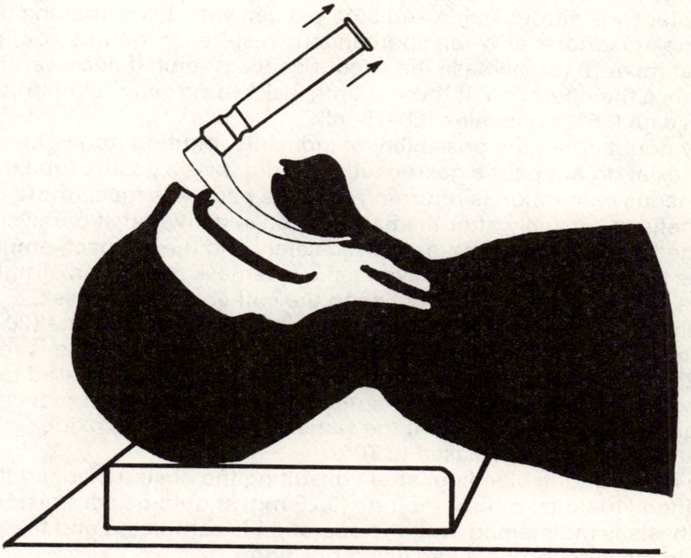

Source: K R Murrin 'Intubation Procedures and Causes of Difficult Intubation' in I P Latto and M Rosen (eds) *Difficulties in Tracheal Intubation* (Eastbourne, Baillière Tindall, 1985).

FIGURE 32.2 OXYGEN FLUX

O_2 flux = arterial O_2 content × cardiac output

(arterial O_2 content = O_2 carried by haemoglobin (haemoglobin concentration × percentage saturation × 1.39) + O_2 dissolved in plasma (3 ml/l at 37 degrees Celsius and 13 kPa))

FIGURE 32.3 FAILED INTUBATION DRILL

---

1 Maintain the patient's position (semi-lateral to prevent aortocaval compression).
2 Ventilate if the patient is not breathing and maintain cricoid pressure (at least while artificial ventilation is being used).
3 Administer 50% nitrous oxide and 50% oxygen with 1% halothane or 2% enflurane or isoflurane. When spontaneous respiration returns continue with that mixture (or increase the vapour concentration if necessary).
4 Commence the operation. If there is time, ask the surgeon to infiltrate the incision with 0.5% lignocaine (50–75 ml).
5 If in any doubt about the possibility of inducing vomiting (too light anaesthesia) do not pass a gastric tube. Do not pass a gastric tube if spontaneous respiration is returning until the patient is much more deeply anaesthetised – usually after the baby has been delivered. If paralysis is prolonged a gastric tube can be passed safely and the stomach emptied. Remove the gastric tube if it prevents the facemask making an airtight seal with the face even after partly deflating the cuff around the mask.
6 When the baby has been delivered, administer diluted pethidine (20 mg iv) over 1 min, repeated at 5 min intervals until the respiratory rate is reduced to 15–25 per min. The inspired concentration can then be lowered to halothane 0.5%, enflurane 1% or isoflurane 1% which would reduce any effect on uterine contractility. At the same time the nitrous oxide concentration can be increased to 70%.
7 If there is still undue bleeding, after consulting the obstetrician, additional syntocinon (10 units) or ergometrine (0.25 mg) should be administered.
8 Anaesthesia is maintained until the operation is completed and the patient placed in the semi-prone, head down position.

(*Note:* The author quotes an alternative published drill; the point here is that a pre-arranged drill, whatever its content, should be known by those working in the unit. It is not implied that the drill reproduced above is the only acceptable one.)

Source: M Rosen 'Difficult and Failed Intubation in Obstetrics' in I P Latto and M Rosen (eds) *Difficulties in Tracheal Intubation* (Eastbourne, Baillière Tindall, 1985) pp 153–154 (with permission).

FIGURE 32.4 ANAESTHETIC RECORD

Source: M Vater 'Monitoring' in G Smith and A R Aitkenhead (eds) *Textbook of Anaesthesia* (Edinburgh, Churchill Livingstone, 1985) (with permission).

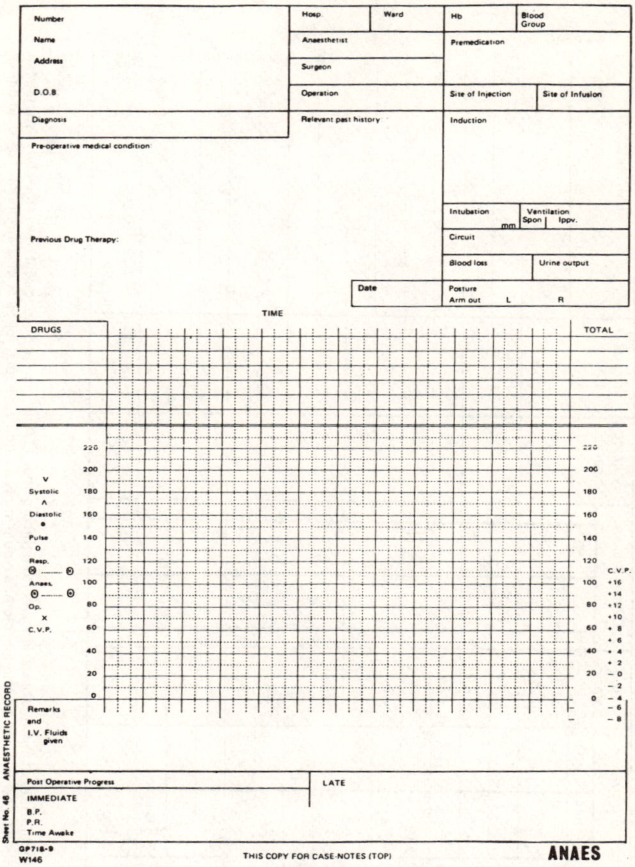
Number
Name
Address
D.O.B
Hosp.
Ward
Hb
Blood Group
Anaesthetist
Premedication
Surgeon
Operation
Site of Injection
Site of Infusion
Diagnosis
Relevant past history
Induction
Pre-operative medical condition
Intubation
mm
Ventilation
Spon
Ippv.
Previous Drug Therapy:
Circuit
Blood loss
Urine output
Date
Posture
Arm out L R
TIME
DRUGS
TOTAL
V Systolic
Λ Diastolic
• Pulse
O Resp.
Anaes.
Op.
x C.V.P.
220 200 180 160 140 120 100 80 60 40 20 0
C.V.P. +16 +14 +12 +10 +8 +6 +4 +2 −0 −2 −4 −6 −8
Remarks and I.V. Fluids given
Post Operative Progress
LATE
IMMEDIATE
B.P.
P.R.
Time Awake
Sheet No. 46 ANAESTHETIC RECORD
GP718-9
W146
THIS COPY FOR CASE-NOTES (TOP)
ANAES

Notes

It is mandatory to keep a permanent record of every anaesthetic administered. The format varies considerably. In this example there are spaces for details of the patient, surgeon, anaesthetist, and operation performed. A written summary of relevant medical problems (pre-operative medical condition) shows an appreciation by the anaesthetist of the patient's past and present health, including drugs that may interact with, or modify the action of, anaesthetic drugs. A record of injection or infusion sites is important in case of allegations of tissue damage by extravasated drugs. Details of equipment used, including the size of endotracheal tube, the type of ventilator or breathing system, and details of sizes and settings, should be noted on the record. The record should also show, in graph form, observations taken at time intervals no longer than 5 minutes of pulse, blood pressure, ventilation, and central venous pressure if measured. Additionally there should be full details of doses and timings of all drugs and intravenous fluids given during the anaesthetic. It is preferable that batch numbers are included, and this is particularly important when crystalloid fluids, blood, and blood products and substitutes are given. It is also important to note details of all monitors used and the frequency of all monitoring observations. The anaesthetic record is an essential part of the record of the patient's treatment and should be filed in the appropriate part of the notes, preferably next to the operation record. It is convenient to use the same record sheet for observations and treatment in the recovery room. Many record systems have facilities for computer storage and retrieval, permitting further analysis of data. Direct-entry electronic record systems, taking and storing data directly from the monitors and permitting keyboard or light-pen entry of drugs used, etc, are available but are expensive and not yet in widespread use.

FIGURE 32.5 SIMPLIFIED INTENSIVE THERAPY CHART

Nonameshire Health Authority LDH Hospital

Intensive Therapy Chart Sheet no.......

	Fluid intake		*Fluid output*			*Fluid balance*	*Observations*	*Nursing care*	*Drugs given*	REMARKS
	Oral	*iv*	*Urine*	*Drains*	*Other*					
PREVIOUS TOTALS	0	1200	1070		0	+130				
1200		100	150			−50				
1300		100	100	20		−20				
1400		100	50			+50				
1500		50	20	10		+20				
1600		150	110	50		−10				
1700		50	100	25		−75				
1800		100	150			−50				
1900		50	50			0				
2000		100	50	20		+30				
2100		75	100			−25				
2200		100	75	25		0				
2300		75	100			−25				
2400		50	50	50		−50				
TOTALS FORWARD	0	2300	2175	200	0	−75				

Notes

The first horizonal row shows the totals of fluid output and intake carried over from the previous 12 hour period. Subsequent rows show hourly totals; in practice, entries would be made at 15 minute intervals and additional columns would show a cumulative total for each measurement. The fluid intake columns show the amount of fluid taken by mouth and given intravenously by drip infusion. The fluid balance column is the total intake less the total output. The calculation of this balance is a frequent source of error. For the patient to be in correct fluid balance the total intake should exceed the output by about 500 ml for an adult as about this amount is lost in each 24 hour period by insensible perspiration and through the humidified expirations. In this case the patient has a measured fluid deficit of 75 ml to which must be added at least 500 ml for insensible losses. Note that other sources of fluid loss may exist, eg through fistulae – separate columns for these would probably be provided on the chart. Other columns allow the recording of observations on the patient (in this case of the circulation of an injured foot and of the level of consciousness by the Glasgow Coma Scale), nursing care, drugs administered according to the prescription chart, and for notes of other observations, actions taken, etc. Results of investigations, eg blood gases, are usually recorded separately although the taking of a sample would be noted in the Remarks column.

FIGURE 32.6 EXAMPLE OF REPORT ON BLOOD GAS ESTIMATION

Medical Biochemistry – UHW

CRN: Consultant/GP
Sex Name and Address
M EXAMPLE 2 ITU

DOB: Date/time analysed: 09-MAR-89 (12:07)

Art/Ven: arterial Lab no 00/0000

Blood gas:			Co-oximetry:			ODC data:		
pH	7.38		THb	13.9	g/dL	$PaeO_2$	47	mmHg
pCO_2	46	mmHg	SaO_2	82.8	%	P_{50}	27	mmHg
pO_2	47	mmHg	CaO_2	16.1	ml/dL	P_{95}	75	mmHg
HCO_3	26.2	mmol/L				C (a-20) O_2	10.0	ml/dL
Base	2.3	mmol/L				C (a-30) O_2	5.2	ml/dL
Temp	37.0	degC				C (a-40) O_2	1.8	ml/dL

The THb reported here is for the interpretation of blood gas analysis only.

Notes
'Blood gases', estimated from a sample taken from an accessible artery, are very frequently performed on patients in the intensive therapy unit. It is a mandatory investigation on any patient on an automatic ventilator and would be performed at least every four hours. The pH is the degree of acidity or alkalinity of the blood. The normal range is 7.36–7.44 (44 to 36 nmol/l). A low pH result would indicate an acidity of respiratory or metabolic origin. The pCO_2 is an indication of CO_2 retention for a variety of causes including underventilation, excessive deadspace in the breathing system, or disproportionate CO_2 production in the body. The pO_2 indicates the tension of oxygen in the blood; normal range 70–100 mmHg (9.31–13.3 kPa). Wide variations are possible, depending on the age of the patient and the inspired concentration of oxygen. Nevertheless a low pO_2 results in damage to tissues, and in the case of the brain may result in serious and lasting impairment of function. The bicarbonate (HCO_3) gives an indication of the metabolic state (normal range 22–32 mmol/l). This is supplemented by the base excess-deficit estimation ('base', normal −5 to 5 mmol/l) which enables calculation of the amount of acid/alkali needed to restore the physiological pH. The body compensates for a disturbance of acid-base status by altering the pCO_2 or the bicarbonate level in metabolic or respiratory abnormality respectively. Thus a low pCO_2 may be found in corrected metabolic acidosis, or a low bicarbonate and a negative base excess as physiological compensation for respiratory alkalosis, restoring the pH to normal. The co-oximetry data provide calculated (ie not directly measured) values for haemoglobin quantity (THb) degree of saturation with oxygen (SaO_2) and concentration of oxygen (CaO_2) in the blood. For the relationship between tension, concentration, and degree of haemoglobin O_2 saturation the reader is referred to a standard textbook of physiology. The ODC data provides P_{50} and P_{95} (depending on the shape of the haemoglobin O_2 curve), and a selection of theoretical arteriovenous O_2 contents. It should be noted that most blood gas estimations do not provide co-oximetry or ODC data. In the example shown, the pH, pCO_2 and bicarbonate are within normal limits, but there is extreme hypoxia (pO_2 47 mmHg, 6.25 kPa). This is reflected in a low SaO_2 and CaO_2.

TABLE 32.1 MAJOR CAUSES OF COMPLAINTS REFERRED TO THE MEDICAL DEFENCE SOCIETY 1989–90

Alleged injury	% of claims
CNS damage	23.8
Death in post-operative period	17.0
Awareness during general anaesthesia	12.2
Death during general anaesthesia	11.6
Pain during regional anaesthesia	7.5
Peripheral nerve damage	4.1
Fetal death	1.4
Suxamethonium pains	1.4
Miscellaneous injuries	21.0

Source: Aitkenhead, A R 'Risk Management in Anaesthesia' (1991) Journal of the Medical Defence Union **7**(4) 86.

TABLE 32.2 INDICATIONS FOR ENDOTRACHEAL INTUBATION IN GENERAL ANAESTHESIA

1 To preserve a clear airway in cases of airway difficulty.

2 In patients where the lungs need to be protected from aspiration of gastric contents or other foreign matter.

3 To control ventilation in special circumstances such as intrathoracic operations.

4 Where artificial ventilation is necessary to ensure adequate ventilation, eg in the prone position.

5 Where artificial ventilation is used in association with neuromuscular blocking drugs for muscle paralysis, eg in intra-abdominal surgery.

6 Where access to the head for the anaesthetist is difficult, eg head and neck surgery.

TABLE 32.3 CAUSES OF DIFFICULTY IN INTUBATION

1 Anatomical difficulties

(a) short neck (including a reduction in the distance between the occiput and the spinous process of C1 or of the C1–C2 space
(b) receding mandible
(c) prominent upper incisors
(d) narrow mouth with high arched palate
(e) limited movement of mandible
(f) increased distance between the mental symphysis and the lower alveolar margin
(g) large breasts, limited movement of the laryngoscope handle.

2 Pathological conditions

(a) rheumatoid arthritis, including hypoplasia of the mandible
(b) cervical spine instability or fixation
(c) temporomandibular fixation
(d) glottic stenosis or tumour
(e) acromegaly
(f) trauma.

TABLE 32.4 SPECIMEN EXAMPLE OF PRE-OPERATIVE CHECKS OF THE ANAESTHETIC MACHINE

Division of Anaesthetics – Cardiff – 1988 Anaesthetic Machine – Pipeline Model – Check Procedure **Guidance notes**

Procedure	*Observation*	*Conclusion*
1 Connect pipeline probes to wall outlets and close cylinder valves	Pipeline pressure dials register approximately 4 bar (if fitted)	Cylinder key available Pipeline pressures OK
2 Set O_2 and N_2O flows to 4 L/min each	O_2 and N_2O bobbins rotate	Flowmeters OK
3 Obstruct patient system gas outlet with hand and then release	Over-pressure relief valve opens with a hissing sound	Leak Test OK Over-pressure relief valve OK
4 Disconnect O_2 pipeline probe from wall outlet	Warning whistle sounds (short duration). O_2 bobbin falls. Gas flow from outlet ceases. N_2O may bleed through an audible whistle	O_2 pressure warning fitted and OK O_2 pipeline continuity OK O_2 failsafe fitted and operating
5 Disconnect N_2O pipeline probe from wall outlet	N_2O bobbin falls Warning whistle sounds (short duration)	N_2O pressure continuity OK N_2O pressure warning failure fitted & OK
6 Open N_2O cylinder valve	N_2O bobbin rises to 4 L/min	N_2O cylinder regulator OK N_2O cylinder continuity OK
7 Open O_2 cylinder valve	O_2 bobbin rises to 4 L/min Gas flows from outlet	O_2 cylinder regulator OK O_2 cylinder continuity OK O_2 failsafe OK
8 Check that appropriate vaporiser, filled, is installed with gas-tight connectors and that the control knob is free to rotate		Vaporiser OK
9 Operate emergency oxygen release	Audible hiss	Emergency oxygen OK
10 Open CO_2 cylinder & flow meter valves & then close both	CO_2 bobbin rises, rotates then falls to zero	CO_2 system OK
11 Check patient system	Component sequence, pressure test & valve function	Patient system OK
12 Close cylinders & reconnect pipelines	Pipeline pressure dials register pressure	Machine ready © P L Jones

Note: Pre-operative anaesthetic machine check as used at the University Hospital of Wales, Cardiff.

Source: Dr P L Jones. Reproduced with permission of Dr P L Jones.

TABLE 32.5 SUMMARY OF RECOMMENDATIONS FOR STANDARDS OF MONITORING DURING ANAESTHESIA AND RECOVERY
(Published by the Association of Anaesthetists of Great Britain and Ireland)

a The anaesthetist should be present throughout the conduct of the whole anaesthetic and should ensure that an adequate record of the procedure is made.

b Monitoring should be commenced before induction of anaesthesia and continued until the patient has recovered from the anaesthetic.

c Monitoring of anaesthetic machine function should include an oxygen analyser (with alarms) and devices which enable leaks, disconnections, rebreathing or overpressure of the breathing system to be detected.

d *Continuous* monitoring of ventilation and circulation is essential. This may be performed by use of the human senses augmented, where appropriate, by the use of monitoring equipment. *Clinical observations* include the patient's colour, responses to the surgical stimulus, movements of the chest wall and reservoir bag, palpation of the pulse and auscultation of the breath and heart sounds. *Continuous* monitoring devices include the pulse plethysmograph, the pulse oximeter, the electrocardiograph, the capnograph, and devices for measuring vascular pressures and body temperature.

e When intermittent non-invasive methods are used to measure arterial pressure and heart rate the frequency of measurement should be appropriate to the clinical state of the patient.

f A peripheral nerve stimulator should be readily available when neuromuscular blocking drugs are employed.

g Additional monitoring may be required for long or complicated operations and for patients with co-existing medical disease.

h Adequate monitoring is needed during brief anaesthetics or when using local anaesthetic or sedation techniques which may lead to loss of consciousness or to cardiovascular or respiratory complications.

i Appropriate monitoring should also be used during transport of the patient.

j Anaesthetists should issue clear instructions concerning monitoring of postoperative care when handing over the patient to recovery ward staff. Appropriate monitoring facilities should be available in the recovery ward.

Source: Reproduced with permission of the Association of Anaesthetists of Great Britain and Ireland.

TABLE 32.6 AVOIDANCE OF 'REAL' AWARENESS

• Premedicate with sedative or amnesia-inducing drugs.
• Give more than a 'sleep' dose of induction agent if undertaking an immediate intubation under suxamethonium, particularly if using a short-acting induction agent.
• Do not totally paralyse the patient.
• Use adequate doses of analgesics: 'pure' analgesics may be less satisfactory from this point of view than those with euphoriant effects.
• Do not rely solely on nitrous oxide as the only inhalational agent to maintain unconsciousness when giving narcotics, unless there is a very good indication to do so.
• If supplementing with a volatile, maintain the end-tidal value of the volatile at least at 0.6 MAC when using 60% nitrous oxide or more.
• Monitor the composition of the fresh gas mixture.
• Always use a breathing system disconnection (low pressure) alarm, *which cannot be turned off.*
• Make sure that the inlet of fresh anaesthetic gases cannot be disconnected from a ventilator.

Source: M D Vickers 'Avoidance of "Real" Awareness' in M Rosen and J N Lunn (eds) *Consciousness, Awareness, and Pain* (Butterworths, 1987) p 180.

CHAPTER 33

General surgery

Professor Michael Hobsley *TD MA MChir PhD*
Mr John Scurr *BSc MB FRCS*

SUMMARY

INTRODUCTION

33.1 General surgery is a changing speciality, at present encompassing gastroenterology, vascular, breast, endocrine, head and neck, and hernia surgery. An alternative way of identifying general surgery is as those aspects of surgery which remain after specialists have taken their areas. Yet another way is to define general surgeons as those who are prepared to act in the front line. They cope with the problems of patients admitted as emergencies with surgical conditions, dealing with initial assessment, resuscitation and early investigations. Some patients will then be transferred to specialist surgeons. The areas of surgery undertaken by a general surgeon will vary, with some surgeons developing a special interest within general surgery. This is important for some very complex operations performed relatively infrequently, for example, pancreatectomy, which are better done by surgeons with an interest, in a centre. The results of surgery by specialists within the sphere of general surgery are clearly better, with a lower morbidity and lower mortality (Buck, Devlin and Lunn 1987). It should be understood that the term *general surgeon* covers a vast spectrum of individuals of different interests, experience and skills. Much depends on the type of hospital in which the surgeon works. In a district general hospital the number of general surgeons is two or three, occasionally four. While each surgeon develops an area of particular interest, none can afford to become too specialised because of the extra load of work outside that speciality that he would leave for his colleagues. In teaching hospitals there are usually a larger number of surgeons and a greater degree of specialisation is feasible. The mistakes of a teaching hospital surgeon with special experience in the field concerned must be viewed in a more critical light than the same mistake by his opposite number in a district general hospital. On the other hand, was it reasonable for the latter to embark on a very complicated case, or should he have referred it to the more specialised surgeon in the teaching hospital?

33.2 The delegation of a surgical procedure to another doctor, often a doctor in training, is now seen as a major factor in many cases which are settled. A surgeon becomes trained when he receives general surgical accreditation from the Royal College of Surgeons. This occurs after a period of in excess of three years in a senior registrar grade. Surgical training starts following pre-registration house jobs, a period of time spent as a senior house officer, a period of time spent as a career registrar, and a year or more doing research, before becoming a senior registrar. The period of time spent in the junior grades will range from seven to ten years. During this period of time, a surgeon may gain experience in many surgical procedures. It remains the consultant's responsibility to delegate cases, to assist junior staff and to make sure that the standard of treatment provided conforms to that which would be considered acceptable by his colleagues.

33.3 Every doctor must remain responsible for his actions, but any consultant who permits a trainee surgeon to perform an elective operation for which he is manifestly inadequately trained is at least irresponsible, although we do not presume to comment on his legal liability for negligence.

33.4 Emergency surgery, or unplanned admissions, are different from planned, routine or elective surgery. In an emergency situation a relatively junior doctor in training may start a surgical procedure which, under normal circumstances, would be done by a more senior surgeon. Where there is an immediate threat to life, any attempt to save the patient would be considered good medical practice. Where there is no threat to life, appropriate assistance should be summoned. In most emergency situations there is time to take an adequate history, arrange appropriate investigations and prepare the patient properly, with an emphasis on appropriate pre-operative resuscitation; and only then comes the surgical treatment, performed by a surgeon competent to do this. Appropriate investigations are those which can be done without delaying the patient's management, and which add significantly to, or may alter the course of, treatment. Adequate resuscitation means placing the patient in a stable cardiovascular state so as to enable him to withstand an anaesthetic. This is done by the administration of liquids that have been lost from the circulating system by haemorrhage, the exudation from damaged or inflamed tissues (occurs in burns or peritonitis), and the loss of salts and water (excessive vomiting or diarrhoea). Administering an anaesthetic to a 'shocked' patient has been shown to be one of the commonest causes of death in patients admitted as a surgical emergency (Ellis and Calne).

33.5 The ability of the surgeon undertaking the emergency surgery is not simply a matter of his rank on the training ladder. One would not expect a houseman to undertake major abdominal surgery; however, a registrar who can show he is experienced in the management of a particular problem can achieve a perfect surgical result. It may be perfectly reasonable to let him perform quite complicated procedures provided the consultant is available.

GENERAL PRINCIPLES

33.6 With elective surgery there are general principles which affect all operations. We can identify three areas; firstly, the investigation and diagnosis; secondly, informed consent; and thirdly, complications which are common to all surgical procedures.

INVESTIGATIONS AND DIAGNOSIS

33.7 Investigations and diagnosis of a medical condition relate to the specific nature of the problem. In some situations it is not possible to make a diagnosis other than by surgical means, ie an exploratory operation or a biopsy. In the majority of surgical problems one can, having taken an adequate history and examined the patient, arrive at a working diagnosis. This diagnosis is then confirmed or refuted by appropriate investigations. Over-investigating a patient may delay the treatment and is expensive, but would not in itself constitute negligence, unless inappropriate in an urgent situation. To perform an investigation and then either not to wait for the answer, or fail to look at the answer, would represent negligence if it resulted in an error.

33.8 We do not wish to imply that the result of every investigation must be accepted by the surgeon at face value. Any single investigation is just an item of evidence which the surgeon has to evaluate in the light of many other items of evidence. A chemical investigation occasionally gives a wrong answer, and a radiological one is just a set of shadows rather than the substance. Recently, fear of litigation has led to defensive reporting of radiographs, eg 'I cannot on the basis of this mammogram exclude the possibility of carcinoma', rather than 'there is no evidence of carcinoma'. This sort of reporting does not make the surgeon's job any easier!

33.9 Before proceeding with any surgical procedure the indications for the operation must exist and adequate steps must be taken to investigate the patient properly, both in terms of the surgical procedure and in terms of assessing the patient's fitness to undergo the surgical procedure. Generalised abdominal pain is a common general surgical presentation. Whilst a laparotomy may be the most appropriate investigation, both to make the diagnosis and to effect surgical treatment, a number of steps should be taken first. On presenting, a full history and general examination is undertaken. On the basis of this information, a working diagnosis is made. Steps should be taken to confirm or refute this diagnosis. The investigations undertaken will depend on the circumstances and the urgency of the problem. Clearly, somebody with a perforated ulcer will require urgent surgery, whilst somebody with vague upper abdominal pain, possibly related to gallstones or to a peptic ulcer, will require further investigations. The extent of these investigations, again, will vary depending on the presenting symptoms, but should never be less than the specific investigations designed to refine the working diagnosis to the stage at which definitive treatment can be undertaken.

INFORMED CONSENT

33.10 Before embarking on any surgical procedure, the aims of the operation and the expected chances of success or failure should be fully explained to the patient. It is not adequate just to explain the procedure to the patient in medical terminology. It is important to explain to the patient in terms which he or she can readily understand, exactly what the purpose of the operation is, what it involves, what the outcome will be and whether there are any specific complications. In obtaining consent from a patient for a parotidectomy, a common and often unavoidable complication is weakness of the facial nerve; all patients should be prepared for this outcome (see also para **33.62**). Following any skin incision, numbness may result in the area surrounding the wound. This is unavoidable, but may cause patients some distress if they have not been warned in advance. All surgical procedures are associated with some bleeding, and wound haematomas (collections of blood deep to the skin in the operation site) may occur. A patient properly prepared is more likely to accept these problems than a patient who has been given no pre-operative information.

33.11 The question of withholding information in general surgical patients presents a number of problems. Clearly, a surgeon might elect not to tell a patient about a specific problem or complication because he feels that this course is in the patient's best interests; or the surgeon may deliberately decide not to inform the patient that he has, for example, very extensive malignant disease. These problems raise considerable ethical questions which are beyond the scope of this chapter. We believe that only very rarely is this limitation of information justified and in our own practice we fully inform the patient, or on occasions take advice from a close relative. However, we would have to accept that not all surgeons agree with us.

COMPLICATIONS OF ALL SURGICAL OPERATIONS

33.12 Complications following general surgery can be divided into two groups: those specifically related to the operation itself, and those related to any operation. Specific complications are discussed later (para **33.28**). Sometimes following a surgical procedure there is a recognised associated condition which may occur in all patients, or may occur selectively. Operations on the stomach may result in alterations in digestion, leading to the dumping syndrome. This is a well-recognised complication of gastric surgery, is not always predictable and can in some situations be quite incapacitating. The development of this syndrome is not negligent, but can be very distressing to the patient who has not been adequately informed.

GENERAL COMPLICATIONS ASSOCIATED WITH ANY SURGICAL OPERATION

Wound infection, wound haematoma

33.13 One cannot cut tissues without dividing blood vessels and causing bleeding; one cannot cut skin or the mucosa lining the alimentary tract without incurring the risk that the micro-organisms from the environment gain access to the tissues. Following general surgical procedures wound infection and wound haematomas (collections of shed blood) are quite common. The development of a haematoma or a wound infection does not in itself constitute negligence, unless it can be shown that some predisposing condition was present which was not recognised, and which clearly should have been recognised in the pre-operative period, or that there was a relevant problem during the operation, or in the immediate post-operative period which was similarly unrecognised or ignored. Some surgical procedures, eg operations on the gastrointestinal tract, carry a significantly greater wound infection rate unless appropriate precautions are taken. These precautions may include a full bowel preparation by washouts, with or without intestinal (non-absorbable) antibiotics, and the use of prophylactic systemic antibiotics. Operating on the large bowel without prophylactic antibiotics in a patient who subsequently developed a wound infection could be considered negligent. Failure to prepare the skin adequately or to sterilise the instruments could also be considered negligent. Skin preparation involves removing hair and painting the skin with an antiseptic solution. The skin is never sterile and the possibility of an infection always remains. The most common source of infection in a wound is the patient himself; his own organisms being transferred from the nasal sinuses, or other parts of the respiratory tract, or from his skin, into the wound at the time of operation. No wound can be considered immune from the possibility of infection, but incisions made into uncontaminated tissues in good operating theatres have only a 1–3 per cent chance of showing any infection. It is generally agreed that there is no indication for using prophylactic antibiotics in 'clean' cases, ie where gut or other infected body cavities are not being breached, and where there is no pre-existing infection in the tissues. However, if prostheses are being inserted it is very important to use prophylactic antibiotics, because foreign materials strongly predispose to infection, and once infection occurs, it cannot be controlled until the foreign material has been removed. There are situations, particularly in the presence of devitalised tissue which also encourages growth of micro-organisms, where failure to use prophylactic antibiotics might be considered negligent. Above knee amputation for ischaemic disease is an example where prophylactic antibiotics are required.

33.14 Wounds seldom become infected in the post-operative period, although the signs of infection manifest themselves from the second post-operative day onwards. Some wounds are nursed with no cover, and others are covered with a dressing. There is really little evidence that either makes any difference, and certainly either method is equally acceptable.

Bleeding

33.15 Bleeding occurs during all surgical procedures. The bleeding stops as a result of vessel contraction and the formation of haemostatic plugs formed from the body's own clotting system. Abnormalities in the clotting system should be recognised pre-operatively from a history of excessive bleeding tendencies, and appropriate investigations undertaken. Patients with a history of excessive bruising or bleeding at a previous surgical procedure clearly require pre-operative investigations. The minimum investigations required include a full blood count, platelet count and prothrombin time. Additional investigations may be indicated to exclude haemophilia and other congenital or acquired clotting deficiencies. Some patients may be undergoing long-term treatment with anticoagulants, but still require surgical procedures. It may be appropriate to reverse the anticoagulation before the operation, or to take steps to counter the anticoagulant during the surgical procedure. It is important to have available adequate supplies of blood and of the relevant clotting factors if appropriate. To embark upon a surgical procedure, unaware of the coagulation problem, despite a definite history, and therefore, without adequate blood stores readily available for replacing losses, would constitute negligence.

33.16 In patients where bleeding is likely to occur, drainage should be employed. The haematoma initially solidifies by clotting and then liquefies. It may become infected, leading to local or sometimes generalised sepsis. The formation of a haematoma, assuming adequate steps have been taken to prevent it, cannot be considered negligent. Failure to diagnose and treat a haematoma appropriately could constitute negligence. A small haematoma or extensive bruising around a wound will resolve with no treatment. An extensive haematoma may require formal drainage and certainly, if it becomes infected, it will undoubtedly require drainage. This should be undertaken as soon as the diagnosis is made.

33.17 In an effort to reduce perioperative blood loss when the operation involves territory with a particularly abundant blood supply, e g the face and the neck, the surgeon often asks the anaesthetist to administer drugs that lower the blood pressure during the operation. When the procedure is completed, and before the surgeon closes the wound, it is important that the surgeon asks the anaesthetist to raise the blood pressure back to normal; in the absence of this precaution a later rise in blood pressure might precipitate bleeding from imperfectly sealed blood vessels. Evidence that this precaution was not taken might well be considered negligence.

Wound dehiscence/incisional hernia

33.18 Following the repair of any surgical wound there is a chance that it will fail to heal and the tissues will part or 'break down'. In some patients it is known that there is impaired healing, and it may be necessary to take special precautions in suturing the wound. These precautions may include additional sutures, and the leaving of the skin sutures in place for a longer period of time. True wound dehiscence is now relatively uncommon because there have been improvements in surgical technique. When a wound does break down it is often the result of complicating sepsis. It is important to recognise wound dehiscence and to take appropriate action. Sometimes a minor dehiscence will occur which is not immediately apparent, and this phenomena is probably responsible for the development of an incisional hernia, a weakness in the wound, up to one or two years later. The development of an incisional hernia may require further surgery to correct it. It is not in itself evidence of negligence. If the predisposing factor was a wound infection, the surgeon would only have been negligent if it could be shown that he did not take adequate precautions, either in terms of preparing the patient, or in terms of obtaining adequate sterility during the surgical procedure. If the predisposing factor were a wound haematoma, that, similarly, would only constitute negligence if it could be shown that the surgeon knowingly operated on a patient with an increased risk without initially seeking his consent, or explaining the increased risk to him, or taking adequate precautions to prevent bleeding after the wound has been closed. A wound dehiscence occurring without any obvious predisposing causes is much more difficult to predict, and usually only occurs in a patient who is slow to heal. Surgeons tend to remove sutures as early as possible, because this is the way to obtain the best cosmetic result. Occasionally this may result in superficial wound break down, the net result being a slightly wider and uglier scar. This can be revised by excising the scar and resuturing and would not constitute negligence.

33.19 Failure to recognise the development of an incisional hernia and to give advice or explanation may prove negligent. An incisional hernia is associated with the same complications as any other hernia, including strangulation and intestinal obstruction. Having recognised the presence of an incisional hernia, appropriate treatment should be instituted. This may involve fitting the patient with a support, or suggesting surgical repair. As with any hernia, following the repair of an incisional hernia there is a small chance that it will recur. The patient should be warned that there is no guarantee of success when it comes to repairing herniae.

Deep vein thrombosis/pulmonary embolism

33.20 Deep vein thrombosis is thrombosis occurring within the deep veins. Thrombosis involves blood clotting, ie setting. A thrombus is a laminated clot involving platelets, fibrin and red cells. Blood remains fluid within the circulation because of a balance between factors causing it to clot and factors causing the clot to dissolve. Many things are known to upset this balance, and upsetting the balance can lead to excessive bleeding or excessive clotting.

33.21 The deep veins are those veins in the centre of the limbs and the pelvis; they are surrounded by muscles and lie deep to a non-elastic sleeve of fascia extending up the limb.

33.22 An embolus is a piece of solid material which migrates. An embolus can be made of any material but commonly involves clotted material or preformed thrombus, which then breaks off and travels centrally, becoming trapped in the lungs. This can occur in any patient, both medical and surgical.

33.23 The risks of deep vein thrombosis are now clearly recognised. Up to 30 per cent of patients over the age of 40 years undergoing major surgical procedures will develop an isotopically detectable deep vein thrombosis (this is a thrombosis detected by labelling one of the constituents of a clot, fibrinogen, with a radioisotope, which allows an accumulation to be readily detected). The incidence of clinical deep vein thrombosis, ie thrombosis which is apparent on clinical examination alone, is considerably lower than this, and the incidence of the two serious complications, namely the post-phlebitic limb (swollen, pigmented or ulcerated) and pulmonary embolism, are difficult to quantify. The incidence of fatal pulmonary embolism is 0.8 per cent; the incidence of large non-fatal pulmonary emboli in patients undergoing major general surgical procedures is apparently between 1 per cent and 2 per cent. A consensus conference, organised by the National Institutes of Health (NIH) of the USA, in 1986, drew attention to this problem, recognised that the diagnosis of deep vein thrombosis and pulmonary embolism could be made and that by the application of prophylactic measures, the incidence in general surgical patients could be reduced. A European Consensus Conference, held in 1991, confirmed the findings of the NIH conference and made specific recommendations. These recommendations suggest that all patients undergoing surgical procedures should be assessed for the risk of developing deep vein thrombosis and its possible sequelae. Certain patients were recognised to be at increased risk, and these included patients over the age of 40 undergoing major surgical procedures. The risks were increased still further if these patients had malignant disease, a past history of venous thromboembolic disease and obesity. It was suggested that patients should be assessed as low risk, moderate risk and high risk. Prophylactic modalities which have been shown to be effective, include: perioperative administration of subcutaneous Heparin, the use of low molecular weight Heparin, the wearing of graduated compression elastic stockings and the use of intermittent pneumatic sequential compression sleeves. These devices used singly, or in combination, significantly reduce the incidence of isotopically detectable deep vein thrombosis.

Studies looking at the incidence of pulmonary embolism are more difficult to interpret. One major multicentre study has shown a reduction from 0.8 per cent to 0.4 per cent in the incidence of fatal pulmonary embolism by the administration of subcutaneous perioperative Heparin. Further, more recent studies using low molecular weight Heparin confirm the efficacy of low molecular weight Heparin in reducing the incidence of deep vein thrombosis, but as yet, the numbers are insufficient to make a confident prediction about pulmonary embolism. It is now considered essential that all patients should be considered for the risk of deep vein thrombosis; in those patients with a moderate risk or a high risk of developing a deep vein thrombosis, DVT prophylaxis should be employed. If this prophylaxis is not employed and the patient develops a significant complication, namely, a pulmonary embolism, or a post-thrombotic limb, even many years later, the doctors could be considered negligent for failing to take steps to reduce these risks.

33.24 Early diagnosis of deep vein thrombosis with adequate treatment may be an alternative to prophylaxis. The use of new, non-invasive techniques for diagnosing deep vein thrombosis employing ultrasound are very effective, but time consuming. Once the diagnosis of deep vein thrombosis has been made and confirmed, treatment should be instituted. The treatment may involve monitoring, or may involve the use of anticoagulation. Failure to make the diagnosis and to provide reasonable treatment would constitute negligence.

Post-operative chest

33.25 Following any major surgical procedure, particularly those procedures associated with abdominal incision, partial collapse of the lungs (pulmonary atelectasis) is extremely common. The condition may manifest itself by a slight rise in temperature on the first day in the post-operative period. This is not associated with any infective process and is entirely a mechanical problem with a number of alveoli (air sacs) collapsing. These may secondarily become infected to produce a productive cough. This is a common post-operative condition, and responds very well to physiotherapy, supplemented later by antibiotics if infection becomes established. This complication does not constitute evidence of negligence. It might, however, be considered negligent to operate on a patient with a pre-existing chest infection without taking steps to reduce the risks to the patient. In a patient with acute respiratory disease an elective operation should be postponed for at least three weeks. Patients with chronic respiratory problems, for example, a productive cough, or undergoing an operation in which the risk of a 'post-operative chest' are increased (eg renal surgery) should be fully assessed before operation and, if appropriate, given antibiotics and physiotherapy. Failure to recognise these risks and to attempt to correct them could be considered negligent.

FLUID BALANCE

33.26 Patients undergoing major surgical procedures suffer considerable disturbances in their fluid balance. These disturbances may be brought about by blood loss, by excessive exudates, as for example in burned patients or in patients with pancreatitis or peritonitis, or by excessive water and electrolyte loss, as may occur from the gastrointestinal tract in the form of diarrhoea or vomiting. Additionally, in the post-operative period, fluid collects in the gut and is therefore essentially lost to the body. All patients require adequate fluid replacement, and the ideal fluid to replace the losses is the same as the fluid lost. Patients losing blood should receive blood transfusions; patients losing water and electrolytes into the gut, or with excessive vomiting and diarrhoea, should receive isotonic normal saline, while patients exuding a plasma-like material as the result of inflammation or burns should receive plasma or a plasma substitute. The amount of fluid required is enough to cope with the patient's daily requirements plus the quantity needed to replace any excess loss. Too little fluid leads to fluid depletion and the patient becomes dry and the urine output falls. Excessive fluid replacement overloads the patient, producing symptoms of cardiac failure. In patients losing or gaining considerable quantities of fluid, care must be taken to monitor their electrolyte balance and add additional electrolytes to the solution as and when required. Clearly, it is important to monitor the patient carefully in the post-operative period to assess that enough, but not too much, in the way of fluid replacement is being given. The standard fluid replacement in an adult patient is 3 litres per day, plus replacement for any additional losses. On occasions these losses can be very considerable and the volumes required to replace them equally considerable. Negligence in this field includes failure to chart intake and output, errors in such charting, and gross errors in the decisions about the volumes and nature of the liquids given.

POST-OPERATIVE MONITORING

33.27 Following any surgical procedure it is necessary to perform repeated observations on the patient. The purpose is to check for abnormalities in the pulse, blood pressure, respiration and conscious level. Following major operations, observations including the central venous pressure, the blood pressure measured by an intra-arterial line, urine output and temperature may also be recorded. The frequency of these observations will be determined by the nature of the operation and the patient's general condition. Observations are usually recorded quarter-hourly, half-hourly, hourly or four-hourly. Quarter-hourly observations, involving the blood pressure, pulse, respiration and temperature, imply that the patient is being observed almost continually. Following a general anaesthetic for a general surgical procedure, these observations would initially be on a quarter-hourly basis. If the blood pressure, pulse, temperature and respiration remain stable, the frequency of the observations is reduced. Once the patient is fully alert, then the frequency can be reduced still further. Failure to monitor a patient post-operatively is a frequent claim in medical negligence cases. The frequency of monitoring clearly depends on the clinical situation and the recordings on the chart represent the frequency with which the nurse has gone back to see the patient. Trends in measurements are more important than single observations and a declining blood pressure with a rising pulse indicates bleeding. Negligence in this field may be a failure to carry out monitoring of a nature and at a frequency required by the patient's condition, or it may be a failure to respond appropriately to the evidence produced by the monitoring. For example, in the case of a patient with a falling blood pressure and a rising pulse rate, if, despite this evidence, the frequency of post-operative monitoring is decreased still further, then this is likely to constitute negligence.

SPECIFIC OPERATIONS

Principles

33.28 In any individual operation, certain anatomical structures are known to be at risk. The basic principle is that all anatomical structures should be preserved, or if damaged, then repaired, unless the disease process necessitates their removal. Should the surgeon anticipate that it may be necessary to destroy an anatomical feature, prior consent must be obtained. The likely consequences of the damage, in regard particularly to function as well as to form, must be explained. Operating in the neck may involve dissecting nerves, such as the accessory, phrenic, vagus and recurrent laryngeal nerves. Operating in the abdomen may involve operating close to the common bile duct, which again, should be preserved unless there is a good indication for removing it.

33.29 During the course of a surgical procedure, surrounding structures that are not usually part of the field of that particular operation may be injured. For example, operating on the stomach of a patient who has had a previous abdominal operation, or in whom, for other reasons, there are adhesions present, may necessitate dividing adhesions to neighbouring loops of bowel. In the course of this dissection, it may not be possible to avoid damaging the bowel. This in itself does not constitute negligence, but failure to recognise a hole in the bowel following such mobilisation, clearly is. The hole must be repaired, or the damaged segment resected and continuity of the bowel restored by anastomosis. Removal of the spleen at the time of upper abdominal surgery is sometimes necessary. This may be due to damage inflicted on the spleen during the surgical procedure, and such damage, again usually due to adhesions, may be unavoidable. Recognising damage to the spleen and taking the appropriate action of repair or excision of the organ is not negligent. Failure to recognise the injury may then result in severe post-operative bleeding when the haematoma ruptures. In a correctly observed patient, the signs of shock will be detected early, laparotomy undertaken and splenectomy performed. Failure to observe the patient in the post-operative period may result in these early complications being missed, and this is negligent.

33.30 In the case of the spleen, it is not unusual for the surgeon to miss an injury during the operation. This is because the damage may have been produced by tension on ligaments or adhesions at some considerable distance from the spleen. A little bleeding occurs to form a subcapsular haematoma, and it is only when this ruptures that a problem occurs.

Laparoscopic surgical procedures

33.31 Laparoscopy is not a new technique. It has been widely used by gynaecologists for the diagnosis of intra-abdominal conditions. More recently, it has become possible to perform operative techniques using the laparoscope. The technique, initially pioneered by gynaecologists, has been widely adopted by general surgeons. To perform a laparoscopic surgical procedure it is necessary to introduce the laparoscope and two or three operating ports. The complications of laparoscopy are not unique to general surgery. The complications experienced may relate to laparoscopy itself, or to the specific complications of the surgical procedure being undertaken.

33.32 In general surgery, laparoscopic surgery is new and should be considered experimental. Patients should be warned that it is a new procedure, that it is associated with some risks and these risks fully explained. The introduction of laparoscopic surgery probably represents the single biggest change in surgical practice this century. The majority of surgeons performing these procedures have had little experience in laparoscopic techniques; some have attended courses; many have started the procedure having read a single account. When a surgeon experiences a complication with laparoscopic surgery, it is important to establish, firstly, the experience of the surgeon, his familiarity with the technique, and in particular, the advice and information that he had given to the patient before starting.

33.33 It is now common practice to remove the gall bladder via a laparoscopic technique. Complications may arise. These complications include: bowel perforation, perforation of vessels and other hollow organs, bleeding complications and a failure to complete the operation. The complications themselves are not necessarily negligent, but the management of these complications may be. No competent and responsible surgeon will undertake these procedures without first establishing that they are safe, that he has sufficient experience to undertake them, and that he has a full understanding and working knowledge of how to manage any complications which may arise. Any surgeon embarking upon these procedures without these qualifications would be considered negligent if complications arose.

Inguinal hernia

33.34 Repair of an inguinal hernia is one of the more common general surgical procedures, often being undertaken by surgeons in training. The hernia may be repaired electively, or as an emergency if the contents become strangulated, ie if the neck of the hernia becomes so tight that drainage of blood from the hernia through the veins is impeded. Strangulated herniae may contain gut, and herniae remain the second most common cause of intestinal obstruction; early diagnosis and adequate treatment are clearly essential. If a hernia becomes strangulated, the contents are dying. Immediate surgical treatment is required, often with resection of the contents, which in itself may necessitate removing a portion of bowel. With dead contents, the chances of local infection occurring increase considerably. Undue delay in repairing a hernia which has become strangulated increases the chance of having to resect bowel, and the liability to wound infection. The diagnosis of strangulated inguinal hernia is a clinical one and the patient should be taken to theatre straight away, delaying only long enough for adequate resuscitation (see para **33.4**). Undue delay could constitute negligence.

33.35 The repair of an inguinal hernia involves making an incision in the groin. During the making of this incision, cutaneous nerves will be divided and an area of numbness following this operation is not unusual. When these nerves regenerate, an area of over-sensitivity may occur, and with time this too will settle. Damage to deeper nerves and other structures during the course of a hernia repair may occur. One nerve which runs with the hernial sac, the ilio-inguinal nerve, may be divided, or it may become incorporated in the contracting scar of the healing tissue. If the nerve is divided it results in an area of anaesthesia over the inguinal region and the scrotum. If the nerve becomes incorporated in healing scar tissue, this can cause pain in and around the site of the hernia repair. During the course of the repair of the hernia, it is necessary to mobilise the vessels supplying the testicle. Sometimes damage to these vessels will result in atrophy of the testicles, with subsequent disappearance. This might be interpreted as negligence, depending on whether there was evidence of a particularly difficult operative field. The most common complication following a hernia repair must be recurrence. Recurrence following the repair of an inguinal hernia is expected. The recurrence rate following an indirect hernia is lower than that following a direct inguinal. An incidence of recurrence between 1 per cent and 10 per cent has been reported (*Grant's Atlas of Anatomy*). It is impossible to guarantee freedom from recurrence and recurrence does not imply negligence.

33.36 The inguinal canal, the point of weakness in the abdominal wall through which an inguinal hernia emerges, is a channel which carries the spermatic cord in the male. This consists of the vas deferens – the duct along which sperm travels, after manufacture in the testis, along with the nerves and blood vessels supplying the testis. The analogous structures in the female have no important function and can be divided; the inguinal canal can then be closed and a reasonably secure effect achieved. In male patients in whom it is thought likely that repair will be difficult, because of size, or of repeated recurrence, it may be deemed advisable to ask the patient beforehand for permission to remove the testis and cord, increasing the chances of achieving a permanent repair.

33.37 Infections and haematomas following hernia repairs can occur. Infection following a hernia repair may not settle unless any non-absorbable suture material used for the repair, such as nylon, is removed. Both infection and haematomas are recognised complications and are in themselves not negligent. Failure to recognise these complications and provide appropriate treatment, or else delay in treatment, may constitute negligence.

Stomach and duodenum

33.38 Operations on the stomach and duodenum are now much less common than they were. Operations are performed for peptic ulceration, hiatus hernia and carcinoma. The introduction of medical methods of treatment of duodenal ulcers have reduced the number of surgical procedures. Operations for duodenal ulcers are now only performed for the complications of duodenal ulcers, or for intractable disease. The complications include perforation and bleeding. A small perforation may be silent, but may require a formal laparotomy to remove the intra-peritoneal contents and close the defect. These operations are associated with an increased incidence of wound infection. Prophylactic antibiotics should be employed.

33.39 Operations on carcinoma of the stomach may be palliative or curative. The cure rate for carcinoma of the stomach is between 5 per cent and 20 per cent. Palliative procedures involve bypassing the stomach in order to allow swallowing to continue or debulking the tumour. Curative operations tend to be extensive and involve the removal of surrounding structures, including the omentum, the spleen and surrounding lymph nodes. Although these operations are undertaken (because the patient has no other hope of a cure), the five-year survival rate is extremely low; the cancers have an aggressive nature and are rarely controlled by operation. These operations may be complicated by failure to heal, breakdown of the anastomosis and alteration in digestion. The patient will notice when the majority of the stomach has been removed that he feels full, and may also have an alteration in bowel habit. These are recognised problems associated with surgery on the stomach and duodenum and should be explained to the patient beforehand.

The acute abdomen

33.40 The acute abdomen presents a difficult surgical diagnostic challenge. The list of possible diagnoses is enormous, and the crucial decision is whether to operate on the patient, or whether to treat conservatively. This decision will be based on clinical experience, the availability of any additional investigations, and a knowledge of the past history of the patient. The two common errors are failure to operate when the indications are clearly present and operating when it turns out to have been unnecessary. The latter can usually be justified. Obviously, opening an abdomen and finding nothing wrong is a relatively safe procedure, and assuming that there was a clinical indication for performing the laparotomy, this would be considered good clinical practice. Failure to operate in the presence of a clear indication may, however, be negligent. Young girls seen early in an attack of acute appendicitis which is not operated on, may go on to develop a ruptured appendix and pelvic sepsis and consequently may experience fertility problems due to obstruction of the fallopian tubes by post-inflammatory adhesions. Failure to make the diagnosis of appendicitis in the face of suggestive symptoms and signs, and failure to operate in this situation is negligent. Perforation of the bowel may occur spontaneously, or as a result of instrumentation. Failure to recognise this and to plan appropriate treatment is negligent. The appropriate treatment for most cases of appendicitis, especially in a young, fit, healthy adult, is a laparotomy followed by surgical closure and adequate peritoneal lavage. There may rarely be indications for treating patients conservatively even in the presence of obvious perforation, but the mortality in this group is very high. Conservative management can really only be justified if the patient's chances of surviving a surgical procedure are even less than his chances with conservative treatment.

Adhesions

33.41 Adhesions can be congenital, but much more commonly occur following previous intra-abdominal operations. Either kind of adhesion can result in bands which, in themselves, can cause intestinal obstruction. We still do not fully understand why some patients form numerous adhesions and others none at all. A number of factors which increase the chances of adhesion formation are known. Ischaemic pieces of tissue left within the abdominal cavity may precipitate adhesion formation. The use of starch or starch-containing gloves is also a further known precipitating cause of adhesions. Whilst nobody can prevent adhesion formation, excessive adhesion formation might make one think of some specific cause, such as starch on gloves. The operative division of adhesions is almost always followed by the formation of further adhesions. The use of a glove powder containing starch would be likely to be considered negligent if problems with adhesions subsequently arose.

Radiation enteritis

33.42 Radiotherapy is widely used in the treatment of malignant disease. In the past it has been used for a number of other conditions, and so in very elderly patients, radiation changes may be seen despite an absence of a history of malignant disease. Radiation enteritis and radiation strictures occur as a result of the bowel receiving too much radiation. Occasionally, loops of bowel are firmly adherent within the pelvis, and pelvic irradiation may then result in a slight overdose to the loops of bowel. (In the normal way loops of bowel are mobile so that no one loop gets a repeated dose in several treatments.) This is an unpreventable complication and does not constitute negligence. Excessive doses of radiation to the lower abdomen or ill-planned radiotherapy may result in extensive radiation enteritis or stricture formation, sometimes with necrosis and tissue destruction.

Vascular surgery

33.43 Peripheral vascular surgery is undertaken by general surgeons with a vascular interest. The majority of this surgery is involved in limb salvage, or attempts at improving the vasculature of the limbs. Patients presenting with vascular disease almost always have coronary artery, renal artery and cerebrovascular disease. They are inevitably a high risk group of patients and require careful pre-operative assessment. The performance of vascular surgery requires an adequate vascular laboratory for pre-operative assessment and access to good quality diagnostic radiology for the imaging of blood vessels (angiography). It is now recognised that many limbs can be saved by vascular reconstruction, and amputation without pre-operative assessment, either invasive or non-invasive, is seldom indicated. Nevertheless, in a patient presenting with a gangrenous limb, amputation is urgently indicated. All patients with pain in the lower limb at rest, or with intermittent claudication (limb pain brought on by exercise and relieved by rest) warrant further investigation. Arteriography is invasive and is itself associated with a number of complications. Arteriography, the injection of radio-opaque material into an artery, should not be undertaken lightly, and is only indicated when a decision has been made that the patient is suitable to undergo a major surgical operation and all that remains to be assessed is whether the anatomy of the arterial obstruction is amenable to surgery. The complications of arteriography include local damage to the artery, which may in itself necessitate immediate surgical treatment. Angioplasty, a technique which involves inserting a balloon into an artery and inflating the balloon to dilate the vessel, is a common surgical procedure. It must be recognised by the patient beforehand that this procedure is not always successful and may be associated with complications necessitating immediate vascular reconstruction. The complications of this procedure include failure to improve the circulation, failure to dilate the segment, and failure to deflate and remove the catheter. Rupture of the artery is a very rare complication. This is a technique, again, best performed in a special centre and not a procedure that can be undertaken on a casual one-off basis.

Vascular reconstruction

33.44 No guarantee of outcome can ever be given in vascular reconstructive surgery. There is a significant risk that the patient will in fact be made worse by a surgical procedure and that amputation of the limb may be the end result. In performing peripheral vascular surgery it is sometimes necessary to divide cutaneous nerves, and extensive areas of numbness and hyperaesthesia may result. Damage to nerves surrounding vessels should be avoided. Surgical management of carotid artery disease is in itself associated with a number of serious complications. These complications should be explained to the patient beforehand; they include: transient strokes, a dense hemiplegia, and cranial nerve palsies, involving almost all the cranial nerves (Greenhalgh). Again, these procedures should be performed in centres doing them regularly, because it has been shown that the mortality is much lower.

Aneurysm surgery

33.45 The mortality following elective aneurysm surgery is low – 1 per cent, but the mortality of emergency intervention following a ruptured aortic aneurysm can be as high as 60 per cent. A number of complications are recognised with these surgical procedures, including renal, cardiovascular and – one of the more distressing complications, particularly in younger patients – impotence. A further complication seen occasionally, and unpredictably, is paraplegia.

Venous surgery

33.46 The majority of operations performed on the veins are for varicose veins and usually consist of destruction of the veins by ligation and/or avulsion. However, attempts at surgical reconstruction and repairs of the valves within the veins are now being undertaken. This reconstructive surgery is very much an experimental area, and the likely outcomes are unknown. Before embarking on this surgery the surgeon must ensure that patients are fully informed of this beforehand.

33.47 The two major areas for negligence in varicose vein surgery involve damage to the femoral vein and femoral artery, and failure to perform an adequate operation. Damage to the femoral vein usually occurs as a result of poor surgical practice, especially failure to demonstrate the relevant anatomy in the groin. The operation is intended to divide the junction between the superficial and deep veins. This can be clearly identified and the saphenous (superficial) vein is ligated and divided. Failure to identify the saphenous vein is the usual cause of problems. Passing strippers up the long saphenous vein from below and blindly cutting down upon it at the groin is not only poor surgical technique, but also extremely dangerous, as the guidewire may pass into the deep veins at a lower level in the leg. Damage to the femoral artery is relatively uncommon, but almost always involves negligent dissection.

33.48 The most common complaint from a patient is an unsatisfactory outcome following varicose vein surgery. This may be associated with some peripheral nerve damage, pain or hyperaesthesia. Nerves commonly damaged include the saphenous nerve, which runs in close proximity to the vein below the knee and may be avulsed with the vein when a stripper is used. Careful dissection around the ankle should prevent this, and in any case, the majority of surgeons now no longer strip the veins below the knee. Some form of venous assessment prior to surgery is now becoming essential, although this is still not widely practised. Operating on patients with varicose veins who have gross underlying deep venous insufficiency may yield a poor cosmetic result.

33.49 Some patients with varicose veins are treated by sclerotherapy, the injection of chemical solutions which excite an intense inflammation in the inner wall of the veins, resulting in fibrosis, blood clotting and obliteration of the lumen. Most superficial veins can be treated by sclerotherapy, although the results are less satisfactory the higher up the leg one proceeds. One of the complications of sclerotherapy is extravasation of the sclerosant into the skin and subcutaneous tissues, resulting in persistent pigmentation and ulceration. Even in the best hands, and with the greatest care, this can occur. Problems may be encountered with bandaging the limb. The bandages may be applied too tightly, and the net result may be ischaemic changes within the limb. These changes may also include damage to the peripheral nerves, in particular, the lateral popliteal nerve, resulting in foot drop.

Compartment syndrome

See Chapter 25.

Inadvertent damage to intra-abdominal structures

33.50 During intra-abdominal surgery a number of structures may be injured, including the spleen, the bile duct, the ureter and the bowel. Damage to the spleen may necessitate splenectomy. The injury to the spleen may be produced as a result of direct damage, or due to traction on structures attached to the spleen. Removal of the spleen in older patients is less serious than in children in whom it is associated with an increased incidence of pneumococcal infections. Following splenectomy, whether elective or inadvertent, in a child, pneumococcal vaccination is indicated.

33.51 Damage to the bile duct may occur during cholecystectomy. Careful operative dissection should avoid direct injury to the bile duct. Occasionally, stricture formation may occur in the bile duct as a result of local ischaemic changes. Extensive mobilisation of the bile duct is not indicated. Exploration of a narrow common bile duct is also probably contraindicated. Exploration of a narrow bile duct and excessive mobilisation are two factors known to increase the chances of stricture formation. If an injury to the bile duct does take place, prompt recognition and appropriate treatment by somebody competent to do this is the best line of management. The majority of bile duct injuries occur as the result of inappropriate surgical treatment, i e operating on patients with acute cholecystitis at too late a stage of the acute attack, or junior surgeons inadequately assisted. Nevertheless consultant surgeons can also be responsible for dividing bile ducts, and failure to identify the structures adequately is probably the commonest cause.

33.52 The ureter may be divided in the pelvis. It is commonly injured during pelvic surgical procedures, and careful attempts at identifying the ureter and preserving it should be undertaken. Occasionally it is necessary to divide the ureter for pelvic clearances, particularly in colorectal or pelvic cancer, and under these circumstances it may be necessary to exteriorise the ureter or to reimplant it. A deliberate decision to resect the ureter does not constitute negligence. Damage to the ureter and failure to recognise this, clearly does.

Retained objects

33.53 Leaving a foreign object unintentionally in the peritoneal cavity represents negligence. Such objects range from retractors and surgical instruments through to needles and swabs. Sometimes it is necessary to leave a pack within the abdominal cavity temporarily, and subsequently remove it. The intentional retention of a pack is not negligent. Retention of instruments and foreign bodies within the abdominal cavity excites a reaction which invariably involves additional adhesion formation and requires recurrent surgical procedures to deal with the problem caused by such adhesions.

The breast

33.54 Perhaps the greatest controversies in general surgery exist within this area. The results of treating cancer of the breast have really not improved over the last half-century in terms of overall survival. Fashions, often driven by popular opinion, dictate surgical treatment because there is little evidence that any one strategy of treatment is better than others. Informed consent and careful patient management is perhaps more important in this area of surgery than in any other. Breast cancer can be managed very effectively, as far as the primary disease in the breast itself is concerned by mastectomy with or without radiotherapy and adjuvant chemotherapy. More recently there has been a tendency towards conservative treatment, with local excision of the lump with a margin of normal tissue, followed by radiotherapy and adjuvant therapy, rather than by the removal of the whole breast. The roles of adjuvant therapy and hormone therapy have become much clearer and guidelines now cover most situations. When treating patients with breast disease it is clearly important to establish a diagnosis. Cyto-diagnosis using fine needle aspiration to obtain material for cytology may be very helpful, but cannot be relied on 100 per cent to give a definite histological diagnosis. In particular a negative report on a cytological examination can never be acceptable as proof that cancer is not present. It is also necessary to have a true tissue diagnosis before proceeding to mastectomy.

33.55 Cosmetic operations on the breast, including reductions and augmentations, are fraught with problems. The outcome following augmentation or reduction can never be guaranteed. It is vital that the woman understands that the scarring may be extensive, the shape may not be predictable and surgical revision of a reconstruction may be necessary. Silicon implants may become encapsulated and hard, necessitating further operations.

Breast screening

33.56 Breast screening has now been introduced on a wide scale. The interpretation of mammograms is extremely difficult, but evidence is now becoming available that mammography screening leads to an increase in the number of early breast cancers detected. In some situations it may not be possible to make the diagnosis on a mammogram until a further film is taken a year or two later. Once the diagnosis is made, changes on the film, in retrospect, may become apparent. We would not consider it negligent to delay the diagnosis of breast cancer in debatable cases. Clearly it would be considered negligent repeatedly to reassure somebody with a large, indurated, palpable lump, with all the features of breast cancer, and make no attempt to reach a true tissue diagnosis. Failure to examine a patient must be the commonest cause of missing a breast cancer. Anyone presenting with a lump in the breast should be examined, and depending on the examination findings, appropriate investigations undertaken. These investigations may include aspiration cytology, mammography, ultrasound or Tru-cut needle biopsies. On the basis of these investigations, a decision would then be taken whether or not to remove the lump.

Head and neck injuries

33.57 The chapter on Otorhinolaryngology (Chapter 38) includes a section on the head and neck, written from the viewpoint, mainly, of the surgeon who specialises in this field. However, few district general hospitals in the United Kingdom have a specialist head and neck surgeon, and while complicated problems arising in this field are relatively uncommon and can be transferred to the care of the nearest specialist, the general surgeon has to provide a service to deal with a large number of minor and intermediate procedures necessitating an operation in this territory, for example, the excision of a lymph node for histological examination (Hobsley 1991).

33.58 It is remarkable how many important anatomical structures in the neck are damaged during minor operations. They are usually nerves, and the one most at risk seems to be the accessory nerve; destruction of this nerve leads to a dropped shoulder on the same side with consequent complaints of weakening and pain in the shoulder region. The anatomy of the accessory nerve is very well described; the two important landmarks are that, during its course downwards and slightly lateralwards in the neck, it reaches the anterior border of the sternomastoid muscle at the junction of the upper and middle thirds of that muscle, and the posterior border at the junction of the middle and lower thirds. In each of these situations there are important groups of lymph nodes that often require to be biopsied, and at both sites, the nerve is at risk. There are some circumstances, e g the obliteration of tissue planes by inflammation or gross deformity produced by tumour, in which it may be argued that damage to the nerve did not amount to negligence. However, the anatomy is so well known and the dangers so strongly emphasised in the average curriculum of the medical student, that even the most junior surgeon must be expected to be aware of the danger, and must perform his dissection with extreme caution so that he can visualise the nerve and avoid cutting it.

33.59 Another well-known trap arises in dissection above the lateral half of the clavicle. There are a number of superficial nerves in this region, called the supraclavicular nerves, that run downwards and laterally towards the point of the shoulder – they supply sensation to the skin of the shoulder and the outer aspect of the upper arm. However, this function seems relatively unimportant – their division rarely gives rise to any disability, and the nerves are frequently sacrificed during a dissection in order to gain better access to a lesion. The snag is, that on what is not always a much deeper plane, and running in much the same direction are the uppermost elements of the brachial plexus, and injury to those nerves can have severe and permanent consequences to the movements and sensation of the upper limb. Fortunately, surgical injuries of the brachial plexus are far less common than to the accessory nerve.

Major operations endangering nerves

33.60 There are two major operations undertaken by general surgeons in which important nerves are at risk because of their intimate anatomical relationship to structures that are being excised. During thyroidectomy, the recurrent laryngeal nerve may be damaged, resulting in weakness of the vocal cord on that side; while in parotidectomy, the facial nerve may be injured, with a resulting paralysis or weakness of the muscles of facial expression.

33.61 Before any operation to remove thyroid tissue, the surgeon should take two precautions. Firstly, the vocal cords should be inspected to check whether they move normally because unsuspected congenital or acquired paralysis of a vocal cord is not unknown – if this step is not taken, inspection of the cords after the operation may wrongly lead the paralysis to be ascribed to damage to the nerve during the operation. The cords should also be inspected after the operation and the result clearly documented. Some surgeons ask the anaesthetist to inspect the cords at the time that the endotracheal tube is removed, but it is probably best to make the definitive inspection a few days later, when any trauma directly to the cords by the intubation has had a chance to settle. If the cord appears paralysed at this inspection, there is still a chance that the lesion is simply a bruising of the recurrent nerve, and that this will settle down in the next few weeks or months, with return of function of the cord. It is also true that the voice can be normal even though the cord is permanently paralysed – the possibilities of local adaptive modifications of the anatomy of the voice-producing apparatus are considerable. With regard to precautions during the operation to avoid damaging the nerve, there are still two schools of thought (provided that the surgeon is aiming at only a sub-total removal of the lobe of the thyroid on the side under consideration): some feel it is best to expose the nerve and keep it under vision during the excision, whereas others feel that the exposure of the nerve may itself damage it and that it is better preserved by leaving behind a few grams of thyroid tissue at the back of the gland, in the region in which it is directly overlapping the nerve. Full exposure of the nerve is, of course, necessary if the disease demands that the whole of the lobe be removed.

33.62 In the case of the parotid gland, the facial nerve and its six (or more) named branches actually traverse the substance of the gland and are therefore at considerable risk. Before operation, which is usually carried out to remove a lump in the region of the gland, the patient should receive a full explanation along the following lines. The lump is very likely to be a benign tumour, in which case it should be possible to remove it without cutting any named facial nerve branches. Weakness due to bruising of the nerve will only be temporary. However, if during the operation the lump is found to be growing into the nerve or a branch or branches, the involved nerves must be sacrificed so as to maintain a margin of normal tissue around the lump and increase the chance of cure. It might be possible to repair the damage by various procedures, but the chances of complete recovery of nerve function are reduced. Some surgeons adopt a different approach to the problem and perform a limited excision of the lump without exposing the facial nerve, relying on later radiotherapy to prevent recurrence of the tumour, but it is more difficult to defend cutting of the nerve in these circumstances.

DAY SURGERY

33.63 Day surgery is a surgical event completed in one day, the patient arriving in the unit and being discharged later in the day. Some operations are carried out using full anaesthesia, others using local anaesthesia. Patient preference and economic considerations have made day surgery extremely attractive.

33.64 It is important that all patients undergoing day surgery are properly assessed. The patients have to be assessed regarding the suitability of the surgery and their fitness to undergo local or general anaesthesia. There is a wide range of procedures suitable for day care surgery, ranging from simple lumps and bumps through to hernias and more recently laparoscopic procedures. Patients that require more than a few hours post-operative observations would not be suitable for day care surgery.

33.65 When assessing a patient for suitability, age, home circumstances and co-existing medical illnesses should be considered. Diabetes, epilepsy and a number of other medical conditions are contraindications to day care surgery.

33.66 Before discharging a patient from the Surgical Day Unit, the patient must be assessed to check they have fully recovered from the anaesthesia, that they are aware of the surgical procedure that they have undergone and informed about any potential problems that might arise and how to deal with them. A contact telephone number should be provided and suitable arrangements made to follow the patient up. Many Surgical Day Units provide written instruction sheets to provide the patient with additional information. The patient should be given a letter for the GP indicating the treatment provided.

33.67 Day surgery is extremely effective and very efficient. It is important that all patients are properly assessed, the surgery carried out by experienced surgeons with a full working knowledge of day surgical procedures and that the patients are adequately followed up.

BIBLIOGRAPHICAL REFERENCES

Buck, Devlin & Lunn 'Confidential Enquiry into Perioperative Deaths', Report of the Royal College of Surgeons of England (Nuffield Provincial Hospital Trust Kings Fund, 1987).
Ellis & Calne *Lecture Notes on General Surgery* (Blackwell).
Forrester, Carter & Macleod *Principles and Practice of Surgery* (Churchill Livingstone).
Grant's Atlas of Anatomy (Williams & Wilkins).
Greenhalgh *Indications in Vascular Surgery* (Saunders).
Hobsley M 'Head and Neck' in Pollock A V, Evans M (eds) *Postoperative Complications in Surgery* (London, Blackwell Scientific Publications, 1991).
Macfarlane & Thomas *Textbook of Surgery* (5th edn, Churchill Livingstone, 1984).
McNair T J (ed) *Hamilton Bailey's Emergency Surgery* (Bristol, Wright).
Pegington J *Clinical Anatomy in Action* (Churchill Livingstone).
'Prevention of Venous Thrombosis and Pulmonary Embolism', National Institute of Health Consensus Development Conference Statement, vol 6, no 2.
Rains & Ritchie *Bailey and Love's Short Practice of Surgery* (London, Lewis).
Schwartz, Lillehei, Shires, Spencer & Storer *Principles of Surgery* (McGraw-Hill).

CHAPTER 34

Urological surgery

Mr Peter R Riddle *MS FRCS*

SUMMARY

VASECTOMY

34.1 When one considers the whole field of urological surgery, encompassing many and varied procedures, it is perhaps surprising that one small social operation accounts for a not inconsiderable number of cases coming to litigation. Vasectomy, an operation which is in no way essential for medical reasons but done for the social convenience of the couple or man concerned, is the one procedure fraught with so many hazards and problems that it accounts for a considerable percentage of the cases in urology coming through the Defence Unions.

34.2 It is very clear that the majority of these would never come to litigation had the common complications and pitfalls been adequately explained to the couple concerned. Counselling is the keyword used nowadays and I believe that in this case counselling is an essential feature of the doctor/patient relationship.

34.3 It is well known to every surgeon whether general or urological that any operation on the scrotum is prone to haematoma formation and infection. Bruising and haematoma (collection of blood in the tissues) formation is very variable but can, in some cases, be so severe as to necessitate admission to hospital and evacuation of the haematoma. The physical extent of the bruising as seen by the patient can be alarming; reassurance that this bruising is not harmful and may take anything up to six to eight weeks to resolve should be given. This is a rare event. However, it must be incumbent on the advising practitioner during the counselling to state quite clearly that there is a risk of such complications and certainly to state that the scrotum is an organ liable to swell and become infected. This will, of course, mean that the patient may well suffer variable pain. It is not sufficient to say that there may be a bit of pain and swelling.

34.4 Residual pain after a vasectomy is another common problem and may occur up to several years later. Sperm granulomas are the common cause for this. An explanation that some of the sperm may escape after the vas has been cut causing tissue reaction and a small painful lump is all that is necessary to avoid this pitfall. Other cases of testicular and/or scrotal pain are difficult to explain but should be warned about.

34.5 Failure to achieve sterility or, more commonly, late failure, where the procedure initially caused sterility but subsequent events proved that recanalisation had occurred, was at one time a very common cause for litigation.

34.6 It should be clearly stated that sterility is not achieved immediately, that normal contraception should continue until two consecutive negative seminal counts are achieved. Clearance of sperms from the ejaculate is variable and the generally accepted practice is to have the first analysis at three months post-vasectomy and the second a month later. It is amazing how often only one count is asked for and, incredibly, seminal analyses are not asked for at all by some surgeons. Should completely negative counts not be achieved in the first three and four months it is wise to be cautious about sterility and a further count in a month's time should be undertaken. If again this shows evidence of sperms or, indeed, had sperms disappeared and then come back on the second or third count it is safer to offer re-exploration than the chance of the patient causing a further pregnancy. If there is any doubt one must err on the side of caution. Some surgeons rely on an interval of one to two weeks between counts; this, although not so reliable, appears to be acceptable to the courts.

34.7 It nowadays has to be accepted that late recanalisation is a reality and couples must be warned. However I cannot see that it should be unduly stressed or else the fear of failure may detract from what is otherwise a very safe contraceptive procedure. Figures of less than one in a thousand cases can be quoted if necessary.[1]

1 T Philp, J Guillebaud and D Budd (1984) British Medical Journal 289, 77.

34.8 There is no doubt that this minute risk of late recanalisation was not relayed to patients in the past, leading to a large number of cases coming to litigation. In the light of such cases it is incumbent today to warn of such a risk. Strict adherence to this policy has significantly reduced the number of cases coming to litigation.

34.9 These are the problems that can easily in a reasonably short time be relayed to the couple and should be incorporated in the consent form or, preferably, added to the case record or notes so that the operating surgeon, who may not be the counsellor, is aware that the patient is cognisant of such risks.

34.10 Occasionally surgical disasters occur which may lead to the loss of a testicle or more serious damage. There can be no forewarning of these catastrophies which are usually indefensible – as negligence is usually the cause of such catastrophe.

34.11 Provided the problems outlined above are discussed with the patient, accepted surgical techniques carried out and the seminal analyses undertaken correctly, then the majority of vasectomy problems should not lead to litigation.

OPERATIONS ON THE SCROTUM (OTHER THAN VASECTOMY)

34.12 Operations on the scrotum are always liable to result in haematoma formation and the possibility of infection. This can, in extreme cases, lead to prolonged hospitalisation and even re-exploration. Very rarely a testicle may be irreparably damaged and may be lost. Of similar rarity is severe infection leading to skin necrosis and skin loss which may need subsequent operations for repair. The latter two events are fortunately exceedingly rare and are difficult to defend. The former events are natural hazards of operating on the scrotum. They are uncommon but when advising any operation on the scrotum it is necessary to point out the distensible nature of the scrotum and therefore its proneness to swell post-operatively, also because of the difficulty in applying firm dressings it is liable to bruise and develop haematomas. As it is in a potentially infected area of the body it is wise to point out that wound and scrotal infection is not uncommon. Patients will usually ask about length of hospital stay and time off work. Although these are both usually short it is as well to point out the rare possibility of delayed discharge and return to employment.

EXPLORATION FOR SUSPECTED TESTICULAR TUMOUR

34.13 This is a situation where a full and frank explanation must be given to the patient and, if necessary, the immediate family. With the recent publicity given to this condition the public are more generally aware and are also hopefully aware that it is usually a potentially curable condition. This latter aspect makes the doctor/patient relationship so much easier.

34.14 Where there is a high possibility of the swelling being a tumour this must be said, coupled with the statement that prompt operation is essential.

Some of the very aggressive testicular tumours can, in fact, spread and metastasise alarmingly.

34.15 It is essential to state categorically that the testicle should be removed with an explanation that anything less is dangerous (in our present state of knowledge). Again it should be emphasised that distinguishing a testicular tumour from some benign conditions can be very difficult and it is far safer to remove what may indeed occasionally prove to be a benign lesion than to temporise with a malignant one. On the only two occasions when I have removed a benign granulomatous orchitis testicle neither the patient nor the relatives have shown the least disquiet.

34.16 I have, however, had cases sent to me for advice where patients are endeavouring to sue for removal of a benign lesion in spite of the full warning having been given to them. Usually these cases are triggered by a chance remark overheard, inferring that such a testicle should not have been removed. With a full explanation these cases have not proceeded.

TESTICULAR TRAUMA

34.17 Occasionally during contact sports young men will suffer sufficient genital trauma to split the tunica albuginea (tough skin) of the testicle. This may lead to immediate haematoma formation with an acutely swollen and painful testicle necessitating admission to hospital. On the other hand, the pain and swelling may come on some hours later and can lead to a mistaken diagnosis of acute epididymitis or even torsion. Acute epididymitis does indeed come on from time to time after violent exercise and so this diagnosis can just be condoned.

34.18 An acutely swollen exquisitely tender scrotum following trauma should always be explored. The pain and swelling may be due to an acute increasingly tense collection of blood between the tunica albuginea and tunica vaginalis. This must be evacuated not only to relieve pain but to prevent compression and occasional atrophy of the testis.

34.19 A more usual finding is a partial or complete disruption of the testis. Having evacuated the haematoma, the bleeding will usually have stopped and the testis can often be salvaged by loosely tacking the tunica together and draining the scrotum. Sadly, a lot of these testes are removed when they could have been saved. There must, however, be occasions when the disruption is so great that salvage is not possible. Junior doctors are usually involved in these explorations and, not having met this condition before, are more inclined to remove the damaged testicle than not.

TORSION OF THE TESTICLE

34.20 If the standard guidelines taught for many decades are followed there should be no question of litigation.

34.21 It is unfortunate that the patients themselves, usually young children, hide the painful swollen testicle from their parents or teachers because of embarrassment. On account of this, a large proportion of testes are not salvageable, even if immediately referred to the surgeon. Practitioners will often procrastinate, particularly in the slightly older age group, ie post-puberty, mistakenly diagnosing acute epididymitis. Of course, the pain and swelling eventually go but the testis goes too, with atrophy. Whether or not this could have been saved depends entirely on the time factor and it could well be argued that by the time the practitioner was called the situation was past recall. However this does not excuse procrastination in this situation. Immediate, and by this I mean at the very earliest possible time, exploration is essential in order to avoid the possible loss of a testicle. At the same time, fixation of the opposite side is mandatory, as it is a potentially bilateral condition. An acutely swollen painful testicle occurring in the late teens or early twenties can indeed be epididymitis; if there is any doubt, however, immediate referral to hospital is necessary.

Torsion following trauma

34.22 This is a very difficult situation about which to be categorical. Torsion can occur at any time of the day. It follows that a large number will occur during sleep and equally the rest will occur during the daylight hours. For this reason, it is reasonable to argue that some will occur during the games period at school and equally well during contact sports.

34.23 The problem arises when torsion follows a so-called assault or actual assault. It is difficult to argue for or against such cases. Should the assault immediately be followed by a torsion and both events proven, it is difficult to argue against.

34.24 A particular case came to court when the so-called assault occurred some days before the torsion. The master temporarily left the classroom and the child claimed to have been assaulted by his peers. There was no record of this assault and it was not reported to the school or parents. Some days later he developed a swollen testicle in the night and again failed to report this. It eventually came to light and the testis explored and removed. He sued the school and local authority through his parents. The judge concurred and he was awarded damages. This was manifestly unjust as such a claim could in no way be substantiated by any real medical evidence. It is clear from this that great care should be taken in recording all the facts and findings in so-called assault cases.

ORCHIDOPEXY

34.25 Undescended testes whether true undescent or ectopic should be brought down at an early age. It is generally accepted that before the age of five is correct, as this will probably give the highest chance of fertility. Fertility cannot be guaranteed, particularly in true undescent and even more so with bilateral undescent. This should be made known to the parents.

34.26 It is questionable whether it safeguards against subsequent malignant change but it should be pointed out to the parents that a testicle in the normal situation is easier to palpate and, therefore, any change easier to detect.

34.27 Some authorities go to great lengths to search for grossly undescended testes, exploring high up on the posterior abdominal wall. Such explorations should only be undertaken in specialised centres.

34.28 From time to time in true undescent exploration and mobilisation produce a cord of insufficient length to bring the testis adequately into the scrotum without jeopardising the blood supply. If the operator unwisely, under tension, brings the testis down then subsequent atrophy may result. Whether leaving the testis in an abnormally high position, bringing it down with subsequent atrophy or simply removing it, makes any material difference provided the contralateral one is normal, is arguable. Nonetheless, cases come to court following atrophy. If the surgeon is in doubt about the viability of the testis it is wise to point this out to the parents, so that they know that every attempt was made to bring it down short of its removal. If the situation is bilateral the wise surgeon should desist after the first side, realising the second side will be equally as difficult and refer the child on to a specialist centre. Parents will grumble but when it is explained that it is in the child's best interests they will usually agree. Atrophy following orchidopexy is at times unavoidable and the generally accepted incidence of this is approximately 5 per cent.

PROSTATECTOMY AND ALLIED PROCEDURES

34.29 Prostatectomy, in the hands of a urologist, is an exceedingly safe and satisfactory procedure for the patient. Complications after the operation leading to any permanent disability are so rare that they need not be discussed with the patient pre-operatively, unless the patient specifically requests it. These permanent problems are incontinence and stricture formation. Incontinence is by far the worst disability that can affect the patient but it is so rare that I do not believe it should be brought up in the discussion. However, should the patient ask for this information it lies between 0.2 per cent and 3.0 per cent.[1] Similar figures can be quoted for stricture formation but it is difficult to find these in the literature.[2]

1 J J Kaufman and S Raz *Campbell's Urology* (1977) ch 74, pp 22–59; W K Mebust, J B Foret and W L Valk *Campbell's Urology* (1977) ch 79, pp 23–61.
2 Mebust et al, above.

34.30 Sexual function following prostatectomy is a different situation and with the general public's awareness of what their sexual function might be and the even higher expectations of the ageing population, both for their sexual prowess and of the results of surgery, these should be discussed pre-operatively.

34.31 It is true to say that if a patient is sexually very active before prostatectomy he will, in all probability, remain so afterwards. If, however, he is inactive before he will remain so afterwards. It is those patients where sexual prowess is rapidly waning before who may well find themselves impotent subsequently. One should be guarded about the future of these latter cases. The sexually very active man in my experience remains so but a warning that there is a 5 per cent chance of impaired potency after a transurethral resection and a 15 per cent chance after open procedures should be given.[1] Impotence of a psychological nature does occur after any surgery, particularly in anxious patients undergoing major surgery. Again the incidence is fairly similar to that following prostatic surgery.

1 A Finkle and D Prian (1966) JAMA 196, 125.

34.32 Retrograde ejaculation is another factor which has come into prominence over the last decade. I am sure it is right to warn all patients that retrograde ejaculation will probably occur whatever the type of prostatectomy, or with bladder neck incision. I find it is very unpredictable and, indeed, some patients volunteer a heightened sexual desire and function following prostatectomy. I find the terms most readily understood by patients for retrograde ejaculation are either 'a dry ejaculate' or 'firing blanks'. If the patient volunteers on first enquiry that he is sexually inactive then no further discussion need ensue.

34.33 It has never ceased to amaze me how little patients in fact take in even when the fullest explanation has been given to them. This applies to even the most intelligent, and it is wise to record in the notes that warning of these possible sexual dysfunctions has been given. My feelings about the inability of patients to comprehend has been borne out by an article entitled 'How Informed is Signed Consent?'[1]

1 D J Byrne, A Napier and A Cushieri (1988) Lancet 296, 839.

34.34 A word of warning must be made about prostatectomy performed by general surgeons. There is little doubt that procedures performed in specialist units carry a far less risk in mortality and therefore almost certainly in morbidity when compared to prostatectomy carried out in non-specialist units, mortality in non-specialised units being ten times that of the specialist ones.[1]

1 J S A Ashley, A Howlet and J M Morris (1971) Lancet 2, 1308.

34.35 When patients have no access to a specialist unit this probably has to be accepted. However, where there is a specialist unit available it cannot be acceptable for prostatectomy to be performed in general units.

34.36 In the USA and other countries, patients travel to the unit for their particular operation, often many hundreds or even thousands of miles. The English public, health authorities and practitioners need to consider this aspect of medicine, particularly in the area of health care purchasing: the cheapest is by no means the best.

34.37 The future management of retrograde ejaculation is usually unnecessary as the vast majority will have no wish for further children.

34.38 The management of post-prostatectomy incontinence presents more of a challenge. In my mind there is no doubt that these cases should be referred to a specialist centre which has the expertise in dealing with them.

34.39 A patient with a degree of stress incontinence may well get better with the appropriate exercises over the ensuing months. It is worth procrastinating. Patients, however, who are totally incontinent when the catheter is removed rarely if ever recover. There are a lot of urological myths in their management. There is a commonly held belief that a further period of catheterisation will cure them. This is clearly nonsense. Another widely held misconception is that urethral dilatation will help as will further resection of any remaining prostatic tissue. If the patient was in chronic retention with overflow with detrusor failure (inability of the bladder muscle to contract) there may be some merit in these procedures but this is an entirely different clinical entity and the rule for this latter situation cannot be applied elsewhere. There is no substitute for the early recognition of this disaster and therefore early referral for future expert management.

34.40 There is a minute incidence of incontinence even in the most expert urological hands and this should, under these circumstances, be defended.

34.41 If such a situation does occur I would urge that any such case be referred as soon as possible for specialist advice. However, one can no longer condone the not infrequent referrals of incontinence from general units who will insist on performing prostatectomy where a specialist urological unit is available. These I do not think can be defended in the future.

POST-HYSTERECTOMY PROBLEMS

34.42 By far the commonest major gynaecological procedure is hysterectomy. It is not my brief to discuss the indications or merits for hysterectomy but an alarming number of these cases end up in specialist urological departments. One of the commonest complaints is that the symptoms which brought the patient to the gynaecologist is that of bladder dysfunction, usually frequency, and these symptoms will often persist or, indeed, occasionally get worse following hysterectomy.

34.43 There are, of course, cases where the uterus is grossly enlarged and I have known instances where impaction has caused acute retention. It is, however, a commonly but erroneously held belief that the uterus can press on the bladder so causing frequency. These symptoms will clearly exist afterwards.

34.44 Sadly hysterectomy will, in itself, lead to a certain degree of bladder dysfunction. This is often due to failure of the bladder to empty properly afterwards. The reason for this is almost always a degree of bladder denervation. It has been estimated that up to 30 per cent of cases will suffer some impairment of the nerve supply to the bladder, leading to permanent bladder problems. Fortunately the great majority will overcome them and lead normal lives with only a modest degree of urinary symptoms. However, not infrequently, repeated bladder infections result and these are difficult to control. At the far extreme I have known cases of complete denervation and in a number the ensuing problems have finally led to some form of urinary skin diversion.

34.45 In radical (Wertheim's) hysterectomy for malignant disease it is probable that 100 per cent of cases suffer permanent nerve damage and up to 50 per cent will have continuing urological problems.[1] This must be relayed to the patient pre-operatively as problems may lead to severe disability and require artificial sphincter surgery or even skin urinary diversion.

1 L Carenza, F Lobeli and S Giacobili (1982) Gynaecol Oncol 13, 213; R J Scott, A Bergman, N N Dhatia and D R Ostergard (1986) Obstet Gynaecol 68, 111.

34.46 I am sure it is incumbent on the gynaecologist to be very sure that the hysterectomy is necessary and a warning should be given that bladder function may be impaired. As I have stressed, by far the majority with abdominal and vaginal hysterectomy have no problem from this, so that the point need not be laboured greatly.

34.47 Sadly, however, hysterectomy is followed by other urological accidents and it never ceases to amaze me that this is accepted in practice and law as a natural hazard, however careful the gynaecologist may be. There seems to be an inbred acceptance that urological injuries are acceptable. In our legal system it is the doctors who decide what is acceptable and not the courts.

34.48 How long this state of affairs will be allowed to continue I am in no way able to judge. In my own practice there are some gynaecologists who never produce these injuries and others where they are all too common. I have known one locum in a period of one month produce five such injuries, so clearly in my mind this is due entirely to technique. There must, of course, be some occasions where the operative field is so compromised with extensive malignant disease, endometriosis, inflammatory disease, or severe bleeding in the emergency situation, that the ureters or bladder are in jeopardy, but these cases must be rare, and in general such damage should not occur.

34.49 This is a topic which must be taken in hand by the gynaecologists themselves. We, as urologists, are called in to sort it out afterwards!

URETERIC INJURIES

34.50 If the injury is recognised at the time then it should be dealt with immediately. It is wise for the operating gynaecologist to call in a urologist if one is immediately available. The usual injury to be recognised at the time is a divided ureter. These are sometimes mistakenly cut and tied as part of the ovarian vessels or divided freely and left loose to drain into the pelvis. Injuries lower down in the pelvis are often unrecognised until a few days later when urinary leakage is noticed or back pain may bring to light a partial or even complete ligation. A persistently elevated temperature with no obvious cause should lead the practitioner to suspect an obstructed kidney. It is usually very obvious what is happening and prompt referral to a urologist is mandatory.

34.51 It is in this situation that patient exploration is absolutely necessary. Ureteric injuries if unilateral will almost invariably need intervention and some form of procedure; likewise bilateral injuries will certainly need intervention. The nature of the procedure depends entirely on the injury and the surgeon concerned. In ureteric injuries delaying re-exploration, unless the operative field is going to be prohibitive, is unnecessary in almost every case. Sadly, so many of these cases are not referred on for several weeks, even so, I really cannot see the reason for delay.

VESICOVAGINAL FISTULAE

34.52 There is more confusion and mismanagement of these than any other injury during hysterectomy. The majority do not immediately manifest themselves and it may be a few days to one to two weeks before urine escapes through the vagina. The diagnosis is usually very obvious and unless there is a concomitant ureteric injury they are best left until all the tissue reaction has settled before attempting repair. Some patients complain of urinary leakage very early on. Sadly the majority of these are told it is to be expected and is due to bruising and weakness of the muscles! Such advice is clearly nonsense and any loss of control of urine must be viewed with the utmost suspicion.

34.53 There is a mythical belief that prolonged catheter drainage will enable these to heal spontaneously. This will only happen in the most exceptional cases and once a vesicovaginal fistula has established itself it will have to be surgically repaired. Prolonged catheter drainage will lead to mucosal oedema and thickening and subsequent difficulty in identifying the ureteric orifices if these are near the fistula, and lower urinary tract infection is again the rule with prolonged drainage as is bladder contracture. For this reason I do not recommend catheter drainage in this situation. In the very rare circumstance that damage to the bladder is recognised at the time of surgery, in the majority it is still safer to leave this alone and repair at a later stage rather than attempt immediate repair. I say this for two reasons: the first is that the situation leading to such an injury will almost certainly have resulted from the field being obscured, usually by bleeding. The second is that to recognise a hole in the bladder usually means that it is a large hole and will probably be very adjacent to the ureteric orifices. In this situation repair would be more hazardous than conservatism and late repair. Also one cannot be sure in the immediate and often emergency situation whether the ureters themselves are intact.

34.54 There are two possible exceptions to this rule. The first is when a tiny nick is inadvertently made in the bladder, well away from the ureters. This may manifest itself by the appearance of a small drop of urine in the operative field, although the bladder is usually drained with a catheter there is always some urine remaining. This field must, of necessity, be a clear one in order to recognise it. It is justifiable under these circumstances to treat it conservatively with prolonged (ten-day) catheter drainage either after carefully closing over the defect or leaving it. This, however, is a rare eventuality. If there is any obscuring of the field or the orifices are not identifiable it is safer to proceed with conservative management and late repair.

34.55 I have only experienced this immediate situation once in my life when a patient had to be re-explored for torrential haemorrhage following a hysterectomy and a large hole was found in the bladder. Delayed repair was successful and, indeed, the left ureteric orifice was incorporated in the vesicovaginal fistula and had to be re-implanted at the time of repair. I am certain that immediate attempts to repair this fistula in the grossly obscured field would have led to further disaster.

34.56 Who does the repair? There are some specialist gynaecological centres who have a special expertise in repairing fistulae and these are absolutely first class. However, for a gynaecologist with no special training in this field to attempt to close these would be unwise and they are certainly best referred to a urologist.

34.57 In all these injuries it is correct that the consultant or possibly a very experienced senior registrar should deal with them. In my own experience they are usually referred direct from consultant gynaecologists to consultant urologists and as such should be dealt with by the consultant.

34.58 The patient should be put carefully and fully in the picture, particularly as they are going to remain in a wet condition until the repair is undertaken. It should also be explained that although the success rate is high there is always a possibility that a second or even third attempt may have to be made before success is achieved. This is a very rare event but can happen and it is better for the patient to be forewarned. I had one patient where not only were both ureters damaged, one cut and the other tied, but the bladder also was involved. I repaired this in two stages successfully. The patient still sued, fortunately not myself.

34.59 The main factors leading to possible litigation in these cases are fairly obvious but need stating.

34.60 Of prime importance is to make a rapid and correct diagnosis. This is not difficult. A ureteric injury is nearly always accompanied to a greater or lesser degree with ureteric hold-up ranging from the most minor to total non-opacification on the intravenous urogram. Another sign on the intravenous urogram is extravasation of the dye into the pelvic tissue. There is no reason why an intravenous urogram should not be performed as soon as suspicion arises. Should this be absolutely normal, it would point to a bladder rather than a ureteric injury. Any evidence of extravasation would indicate a ureteric leak. Early discovery of a ureteric injury can possibly lead to its correction without immediate re-exploration by means of endoscopy and the insertion of a 'J J' stent. Occasionally such immediate action can recover the whole situation.

34.61 It is, however, mandatory to follow the patient most carefully as removal of a ureteric stent some four to six weeks later may be followed by obstruction, which can be early or late.

34.62 Early endoscopy will often help in the diagnosis of a vesicovaginal fistula although this is not absolutely necessary as other techniques are equally satisfactory.

34.63 By making an early diagnosis the situation can be explained frankly to the patient and her family so that no misunderstanding follows.

34.64 There are various techniques for the urologist to follow. Each will depend on the particular case. Pre-operative radiotherapy will clearly have a bearing and should be borne in mind. Complex fistula in previously irradiated cases may well need extensive surgery with omental grafting to repair. I well remember one referred case where the gynaecologist asked me to see a vesicovaginal fistula informing me he was proposing to give the patient a course of post-operative radiotherapy before asking me to repair it. Clearly, of course, in such situations the fistula must be repaired before any contemplation is given to post-operative radiotherapy.

ERRORS OF DIAGNOSIS AND MANAGEMENT

34.65 Those of us who have spent most of our working lives dealing with malignant disease can be appalled at some of the cases finally referred to our specialist centres. If there had to be a good reason for the existence of centres of expertise in different sub-specialities, such as the St Peter's Hospitals and Institute of Urology, it is just that. There must always be a 'court of final appeal' where patients can be referred. Management of cases is, of necessity, a matter of opinion but overlooking and misdiagnosing is entirely different. Some of the cases grossly misdiagnosed and mismanaged coming through our doors is staggering. It is, however, virtually never that such cases come to litigation. Again I never cease to be amazed by this fact.

34.66 There are three common errors frequently seen. The first is the acceptance by the practitioner and not infrequently by surgeons of one episode of haematuria, the patient almost invariably being prescribed antibiotics and told to report should it happen again. This may not be for some months and, sadly, some patients are allowed to bleed on and off for over a year before referral. The second common error is to assume that because prostatic symptoms are present that the prostate is the cause of the haematuria and so to perform prostatectomy, whereas the diagnosis is a bladder neoplasm all the time. One of my referring centres produced more than one such case each year. The third serious error is for female patients to be referred to a gynaecologist on account of haematuria. This I will never understand, neither will I understand gynaecologists undertaking their investigation including endoscopy. In one year I was referred two cases of inoperable bladder cancer who had been cystoscoped a year previously by a gynaecologist. One of these involved a woman in her early 40s who rapidly died of her disease. The husband came to me afterwards questioning me about the earlier cystoscopy and asking if an early referral to my department would have made any difference.

34.67 The rule must be that anyone passing a cystoscope should be able to cope with anything found in the bladder. Of course, it goes without saying that it is essential to recognise any pathology within the bladder before being able to cope with it. If this is not the case then they should not be using such instruments. Ever increasingly, one sees gynaecological lists containing patients for cystoscopy and examination under anaesthesia. One wonders what the value of cystoscopy is in such cases.

34.68 Prostatectomy should not be undertaken lightly for bleeding unless one is absolutely sure there is not an underlying tumour. If the prostate is so greatly enlarged that endoscopy is inadequate the least one can do is urinary cytology and bladder ultrasound. There is an incidence of post-TUR haematuria, usually initial (at the start of the stream) bleeding. The first episode of bleeding post-TUR should be investigated, but judgment must be used in cases that recur year in year out as to whether each episode should be fully investigated.

34.69 It must be emphasised that all cases of significant haematuria, that is, total and painless haematuria, must be referred as soon as possible. All urologists will usually see such cases on their next out-patient list. There is no excuse for delay, indeed, some centres have specific Haematuria Clinics for immediate referral.

ERRORS OF JUDGMENT

34.70 Errors of judgment do not, in themselves, necessarily constitute negligence.

34.71 Bladder neck incision is a means of relieving outflow obstruction in some cases and it will, of necessity, leave the prostate *in situ*. Incidental carcinoma of the prostate can, of course, be overlooked in such circumstances as a specimen for histology is not obtained.

34.72 It is wise to obtain a transrectal ultrasound and prostatic specific antigen estimation to overcome this shortcoming, particularly in the older patient.

34.73 One case has come to litigation recently where a young man with outflow obstruction was treated with a bladder neck incision. Throughout his notes comments had been made about the suspicious feel of his prostate, even going so far as to describe a firm nodule within the prostate. No biopsy was taken. No transrectal ultrasound was obtained and no serum acid phosphatase or prostatic specific antigen estimation done (blood estimations which give an indication of possible malignancy). This patient developed advanced carcinoma of the prostate and has since died.

34.74 Another not uncommon error is making a firm diagnosis and then being unable to alter it, so going down the road of misconception. This error is often perpetuated through other departments. Because a patient has been labelled with a specific diagnosis, often a malignant one in the past, it does not automatically follow that all subsequent problems with that patient will, of necessity, be associated with the original diagnosis.

34.75 I will illustrate this point with a case referred some years ago to my department. A patient, a male, originally presented elsewhere with haematuria. Intravenous urography showed a 'stone' at the lower end of his left ureter. This was accepted as the cause of his haematuria, an attempt was made to remove the stone with a Dormia extractor which failed and, subsequently, the ureter was explored but no stone was found. The patient recovered and two months later was referred to our Cardiac Department with gross lower abdominal and limb oedema. Ultrasound showed a grossly disorganised right kidney and a completely blocked inferior vena cava due to tumour extension from the right kidney into the inferior vena cava. Following removal of this tumour he made an uneventful recovery and is alive and well nearly five years later. The original intravenous urogram from the referring hospital has never come to light! Fortunately the patient did not sue.

INSTRUMENT FAILURE AND DAMAGE

34.76 With the trend towards more and more endoscopic procedures and 'minimally invasive' techniques being undertaken there is an undoubted danger of injury to the urinary tract during the operator learning curve. There is also a greater danger of instrument failure where parts of these instruments break off and fragment whilst *in situ*.

34.77 There have been many reported cases of 'J J' stents fragmenting within the patient, having been left *in situ* too long. How long is too long? The general consensus nowadays is that three months is the maximum for long-term splintage before they are replaced. From time to time such stents are inadvertently overlooked and it may be many months or even years before they are discovered. I personally feel it wise to have shared responsibility and I tell the patient that if they do not hear from us within three months, to contact my department. This is very often the technique practised with private patients and I see no good reason why it should not be so within the National Health Service. One must, however, insist that they contact the secretary and not leave a message with the ward orderly and hope for the best.

34.78 Although earlier studies indicated a 5 per cent ureteric injury rate from ureteroscopy,[1] I would suspect that it was, in fact, much higher. I have encountered several such injuries referred to my department. Sadly, with the advent of modern urology the young enthusiast will persist far too long trying to pass these potentially very dangerous instruments, so causing damage. With the newer finer and more flexible instruments now available, injury is far less common. Of even greater concern is that future surgeons may never have explored a ureter in the whole of their training.

1 M J Coptcoat, M J Kellett and J E A Wickham 'The Complications of Ureteroscopy: Management and Prevention' (1988) Brit J Urol.

34.79 I am sure with these ureteroscopic procedures which may, indeed, save the patient an open operation and subsequent convalescent period in a large number of cases, warning should be given of a small risk of injury and of a subsequent open operation and prolonged hospital stay. In expert hands they are safe, in inexpert hands they, in fact, can prove lethal.

34.80 Percutaneous stone removal can be one of the simplest 24–48 hour stay procedures, with almost immediate return to work. However, bleeding can occur so rendering easy stone extraction impossible and turning the event into a multistage procedure. Bleeding can, in fact, be so serious as to necessitate kidney exploration or embolisation (blocking off) of the affected artery. Occasionally loss of the kidney, if not life, is the result. It is, however, a safer procedure than open stone surgery but I feel strongly that warning should be given that very occasionally it may not be a simple straightforward procedure and may well lead to prolonged hospital stay. However, percutaneous stone surgery, which had virtually replaced open stone surgery, has itself been replaced by extracorporeal shock-wave lithotripsy (ESWL) of which the second generation requires only out-patient treatments with no anaesthesia.

34.81 New techniques must carry an unknown risk and patients must be made aware of what is going on before consenting to such procedures.

34.82 Occasionally a resectoscope beak will break off during resection as can a resectoscope loop. These can usually be retrieved endoscopically but, if not, an open cystotomy will be necessary. This does not, in fact, usually prolong the patient's convalescence and so a full explanation is usually accepted. This does not constitute negligence.

34.83 Similarly, an internal urethrotomy knifeblade can break from time to time and, provided it is not buried from view, is easily retrieved endoscopically. Should the blade end become so embedded as to prevent immediate extraction the patient should be told. No immediate or even long-term harm may ensue. An open retrieval may, however, be necessary and it is better for the patient to be forewarned.

BIBLIOGRAPHICAL REFERENCES

Ashley J S A, Howlet A and Morris J M (1971) Lancet 2, 1308.
Byrne D J, Napier A and Cushieri A (1988) Lancet 296, 839.
Carenza L, Lobeli F and Giacobili S (1982) Gynaecol Oncol 13, 213.
Coptcoat M J, Kellett M J and Wickham J E A 'The Complications of Ureteroscopy: Management and Prevention' (1988) Brit J Urol.
Finkle A and Prian D (1966) JAMA 196, 125.
Kaufman J J and Raz S *Campbell's Urology* (1977) ch 74, pp 22–59.
Mebust W K, Foret J B and Valk W L *Campbell's Urology* (1977) ch 79, pp 23–61.
Philp T, Guillebaud J and Budd D (1984) British Medical Journal 289, 77.
Scott R J, Bergman A, Dhatia N N and Ostergard D R (1986) Obstet Gynaecol 68, 111.

CROSS-REFERENCE

For information related to topics in this chapter see Chapter 33.

CHAPTER 35

Obstetrics and gynaecology

Roger V Clements *FRCS (Ed) FRCOG*

SUMMARY

INTRODUCTION

35.1 Nowhere is the escalation in the number of medical negligence actions and the size of damages awarded more apparent than in the speciality of obstetrics and gynaecology. An analysis by the Medical Defence Union of United Kingdom indemnity payments made in 1989 shows that a quarter of all claims arose from obstetrics and gynaecology, accounting for nearly one third of the damages paid.[1]

1 James C E 'Risk Management in Obstetrics and Gynaecology' (1991) Journal of The Medical Defence Union 2.

35.2 In the United Kingdom a distinction between obstetrics and gynaecology is somewhat artificial; in spite of the emergence of sub-specialisation, most consultants practise in both disciplines. Claims arising in obstetrics outnumber those in gynaecology by almost two to one. Some 80 per cent of obstetric claims are brought on behalf of the baby, most alleging brain damage. In almost all the mother will have a subsidiary claim; in the remaining 20 per cent the claim is for maternal physical injury or death. The commonest source of gynaecology claims is failed sterilisation, accounting for a third of the total. Most of the remainder deal with surgical accidents.

35.3 Most women consulting an obstetrician and gynaecologist are essentially healthy and seek care for the oversight and correction of their normal physiological functions during childbearing and the control of their fertility. Such matters are widely discussed in the media and as a consequence a well-informed generation has high expectations of their medical attendants and are more likely to complain of their treatment when they feel that it has not fulfilled their expectations. These expectations are reinforced by doctors who themselves promote undue dependence on their skills by premature and over-enthusiastic public presentation of the results of research work. Further, childbearing and associated hazards such as miscarriage, ectopic pregnancy, unwanted pregnancies and the desire to limit the number of children, affect practically every woman and her partner.

35.4 The obstetrician is also concerned not just with the health and welfare of one person but with two; he has, as part of his duty of care, the management of birth. Jeffcoate[1] observed:

> In these days of high death and injury rates from traffic accidents, it still remains true that the most dangerous journey made by any individual is through the 4 inches of the birth canal.

Thirty years on this statement is still true; there is a greater chance that a baby will die during the perinatal period than during the whole of the next 50 years of its life. Just less than one out of every hundred babies born will die around the time of birth whilst a larger, but not precisely known, number will suffer some permanent damage and at least 20 of them will require special skills and assistance at the time of birth.

1 Jeffcoate T N A 'Prolonged Labour' (1961) Lancet ii, 67.

35.5 The obstetrician deals with a large number of women, most of whom are normal, in circumstances that demand special vigilance and attention to detail just because an unexpected complication can arise suddenly without warning. The obstetrician is dependent on a greater number of colleagues for the proper care of women than in many other medical circumstances. He shares antenatal care with general practitioners and midwives, as well as with his junior medical staff.

35.6 Obstetricians in particular delegate care more often than most physicians and surgeons: in labour and at the time of delivery, the obstetrician relies on the skill of midwives, who are recognised as independent practitioners, able to make diagnoses, exercise clinical judgment and prescribe treatment. Responsibility is shared more diffusely. As a consequence the obstetrician has a duty to ensure that not only the doctors, but also the midwives with whom he shares this responsibility, are properly trained and supervised. This duty is all the more onerous because the team concerned is bigger, less coherent and more heterogeneous than the medical and surgical teams responsible for the care of people in hospital. In day-to-day practice delegation does not, as it should, always begin from above. Referral for advice is a responsibility often left to the junior to decide whether or not it is necessary and/or desirable. Such a situation is fraught with potential hazard both for the medical and nursing staff and for the women for whom they have to care. Delegation should by definition be made from above, and should take place in practice.

35.7 Consultant obstetricians and gynaecologists, whatever their attitude towards delegation of care, have a duty to provide a reasonable standard of treatment for the women for whom they have accepted responsibility. Despite the standard and accepted practice of delegation outlined above, implicit delegation of responsibility on the appointment of junior staff does not absolve the responsible consultants from the duty to ensure that their staff is capable of managing appropriate situations without consultation or direct supervision, and to ensure that they do know when consultation with a senior must take place. These duties can be listed and summarised as follows:

(1) to satisfy themselves that the person to whom they delegate a particular task or responsibility is competent to carry it out safely and properly, having directly observed the abilities and skills of their junior medical staff. Generally, it would be wrong to assume by reference to their past anecdotal experience, the recommendation of others, or the mere possession of paper qualifications that the person concerned is either sufficiently skilled or competent to carry out the duty assigned;
(2) to provide guidelines in principle for their junior staff, including nurses, midwives and doctors;
(3) to leave explicit instructions in individual cases to warn of foreseeable difficulties, to call for advice, and to ask for more experienced skill;
(4) to ensure that nurses and midwives know that they can obtain consultant advice direct and to override the decision of junior medical staff;
(5) to be ready to attend in person, or know that there is a named deputy of equivalent rank experience, who can be called in their stead, whenever complications demanding their presence arise.

35.8 Given the essential normality of childbearing in a well-informed population who are more ready and able to question the decisions and skills of doctors, good communication between obstetricians and the women under their care is of particular importance. Unfortunately it is apparent from the nature of the complaints that a breakdown in communication is all too often the cause of dissatisfaction, suspicion, anxiety and unnecessary suffering. Mistakes in judgment will often be accepted if they are freely admitted, frankly explained and sincere regrets are expressed in a timely way. Frequently, such opportunities to provide information are denied, avoided, hurried or given with bad grace and/or the matter of concern to the parents is avoided.

35.9 Sometimes, the familiarity of the obstetrician with the common occurrence of reproductive accident leaves him or her to regard replacement of a lost child as easy. As a result of this attitude the feeling, not necessarily justified, of indifference, carelessness and even callousness is conveyed. This may inflame the natural anger associated with the grieving process that follows bereavement, not only for children who die after birth, but also those that are stillborn or miscarried early in pregnancy.

35.10 Obstetricians are quite often ignorant of the emergence of permanent injury and handicap caused during birth. Because they do not carry responsibility for the medical care of children once they have been born, they have little real appreciation of the enormity of the burden of caring for a handicapped child. Death and handicap cause feelings of guilt and grief in almost all of those who are associated with the event, including the professional attendants, even when no mistakes were made. The grief is often smothered and the feeling of guilt reduced by trying to forget the mistake as soon as possible, leading to avoidance of the parents. Such behaviour leads to further suspicion and resentment and may provoke the need to investigate matters by recourse to litigation.

35.11 Because more than any other specialists obstetricians are called to deal with emergencies at night and at weekends, they are particularly vulnerable to physical and emotional fatigue, rendering them more liable to make errors of judgment, cut corners, ignore detail and avoid the need to inform and explain.

35.12 The gynaecologist deals with few patients who are seriously ill. The majority seek advice about fertility, the control of family size or the correction of menstrual problems. Since none of these conditions is perceived as an illness, adverse outcome is more than usually difficult to accept.

OBSTETRICS

35.13 The main causes for complaint are summarised in Table 35.1.

35.14 Brain damage or 'cerebral palsy', thought to have arisen from injury around the time of birth, is the commonest condition leading to litigation. In most of these cases the child is severely handicapped, both mentally and physically. It is the most costly injury if liability is admitted or found by the courts. Because of the large sums of money involved, such cases are usually vigorously defended and often come to trial.

35.15 Between 1 per cent and 2 per cent of babies are born with some defect or handicap, varying from a slight blemish, such as an extra digit, to conditions causing total life-long dependence because of physical and mental handicap. The term 'cerebral palsy' is applied to a group of babies whose motor function is both delayed and deviant. The abnormality affects both posture and movement, is non-progressive and is usually acquired at a time of rapid brain development. It may be associated with other neurological impairments such as mental retardation. It is not a diagnosis, nor does it imply an aetiology. Cerebral palsy affects 1–4 per thousand of the population; in most no satisfactory causative explanation can be found. Known causes are traditionally divided into prenatal, perinatal and post-natal. Prenatal causes include inherited (genetic or chromosomal) defects, preterm delivery and intra-uterine infection. The majority of other associated conditions have as their common theme a shortage of oxygen to the baby's brain.

35.16 Hypoxia means a relative deficiency in the oxygen supply to the baby, whilst anoxia means that it is completely cut off. Asphyxia is an older term and refers to a total obstruction to the exchange of respiratory gases, including the elimination of carbon dioxide. In acute conditions it is reduction in the oxygen supply that is the crucial factor. In some chronic conditions affecting placental function the supply of nutrients to the fetus may also be reduced so that its growth and development are impaired – in addition to the exchange of respiratory gases.

35.17 The hypoxic associations with cerebral palsy include the chronic prepartum hypoxia often associated with maternal disease (such as hypertension or diabetes) and intra-uterine growth retardation (IUGR); acute prepartum hypoxia may be caused by placental separation (abruptio placentae) or intracranial haemorrhage; acute intrapartum hypoxia may be associated with an obstruction to the flow of blood through the umbilical cord (through prolapse or entanglement) with placental abruption or the entrapment of the baby in the birth canal at a time when the umbilical cord is no longer functional and the baby cannot breathe (as in delayed breech delivery or shoulder dystocia). Postpartum hypoxia may arise in a previously normal child and be caused by aspiration of meconium, depression of the neonatal respiratory centre by narcotic analgesics or by inadequate resuscitation of the baby at birth. Most often postpartum hypoxia is a continuation of a situation that began in utero.

35.18 There is a variety of types of cerebral palsy. In the mature infant, severe oxygen deprivation may later be associated with the spastic quadriplegic form of cerebral palsy; there may or may not be involuntary muscular activity of the diskynetic or athetoid type; there may or may not be mental retardation. The athetoid type of cerebral palsy is characteristic, but not exclusively, of damage to the basal ganglia of the brain (kernicterus), caused by the deposition of bile pigments released into the blood stream as a consequence of the abnormal breakdown of red blood cells in babies suffering from severe haemolytic disease, whereas spastic diplegia is typical of severe prematurity. Nevertheless the identification of a specific type does not usually allow the unequivocal identification of a cause. It is now generally accepted that only in one in ten instances can cerebral palsy be attributed to events around the time of birth. In most cases claims are made on the basis of the balance of probability concerning the cause usually with the positive exclusion of other non-negligent causes. The burden of proof of causation must depend on expert opinions from paediatricians as must evidence concerning the present condition and prognosis for the child.

35.19 The obstetrician has the right to express an opinion and will probably be expected to do so in respect of the cause of cerebral palsy when he is of the opinion that the management of pregnancy and labour was not of an acceptable standard. The essential requirements necessary to link peripartum events with cerebral palsy have been spelled out by Freeman and Nelson[1] in the form of four questions which must be answered in the affirmative:

(1) was there evidence of marked and prolonged intrapartum asphyxia?
(2) did the infant, as a newborn, exhibit signs of moderate or severe

hypoxic-ischaemic encephalopathy during the newborn period, with evidence also of asphyxial injury to other organ systems?

(3) is the child's neurologic condition one that intrapartum asphyxia could explain?

(4) has the workup been sufficient to rule out other conditions?

1 Freeman J M and Nelson K B 'Intrapartum Asphyxia and Cerebral Palsy (1988) Paediatrics 82, 2, August: 240–249.

35.20 The causes, diagnoses, types and prognosis of cerebral palsy are dealt with in Chapters 27 and 28. Table 35.2 summarises some of the errors of management associated with brain damage and cerebral palsy.

35.21 Other physical and usually less severe injuries to the baby range from paralysis of an arm to a scar on the face, buttocks or limb of a baby inflicted whilst incising the uterus at Caesarean section.

35.22 *Stillbirth* is numerically an important cause of litigation but such actions are relatively more frequently settled out of court since the amount of compensation is low and persuades the defendant health authority or trust to admit liability more readily.

35.23 The commonest reason for a woman to seek compensation on her own behalf because of injury during childbirth is for disability that limits sexual intercourse, resulting from damage to the perineum and vagina, usually because of an episiotomy and/or tear and/or its improper repair. Less often control of bladder and bowel function is lost because of more extensive damage to the sphincters and supports of these organs. The majority of these cases settle out of court.

35.24 The more serious, but less common, causes for complaint by the mother include the loss of future childbearing capacity as the result of puerperal infection that occludes the Fallopian tubes and of the need to carry out hysterectomy for uterine rupture and/or to control bleeding, damage to the bladder or ureters, the failure to remove swabs from the vagina or abdominal cavity and failure to relieve pain adequately in a variety of procedures such as Caesarean section, forceps delivery, breech delivery, twin delivery and manual removal of the placenta.

35.25 *Analgesia and anaesthesia* used to relieve pain in labour and during operative deliveries may be associated with accidents that are cause for complaint. They range from the comparatively trivial effects of inexpertly given injections, through awareness during Caesarean section, to total physical and mental handicap and sometimes death as a result of airway obstruction, the administration of wrong anaesthetic gases or total spinal anaesthesia from an epidural block.

35.26 *Maternal deaths* are uncommon and occur less than once in every 10,000 maternities. They are the subject of a special confidential inquiry by regional health authorities, as well as by the coroner. A proportion of them occur suddenly and unexpectedly in circumstances that sometimes give rise to litigation, such as during anaesthesia, as a result of uncontrollable haemorrhage or as a result of eclampsia.

35.27 Adverse outcome of labour is often followed by the break-up of parents' relationships. Where the woman has received soft tissue injuries to the vagina making intercourse painful, or has to endure a period of faecal or urinary incontinence, a period of rehabilitation and readjustment may prove too long and too difficult for both her and her partner. The damage to her self-esteem may be such that the relationship never recovers. Even without physical injury, it is common for women who have had bad experiences in labour or who have given birth to a handicapped child to lose interest in sexual relations, even to develop an aversion to sexual activity. Mothers of handicapped children frequently divert all of their physical and emotional energies into caring for the handicapped child to the exclusion of their partner. The partner, who is usually the baby's father, may have been present at the delivery, powerless to intervene and may himself suffer severe psychological sequelae. Often his perception of his own exclusion from the special relationship between mother and handicapped child may lead to estrangement.

35.28 New important areas giving rise to claims for compensation are those associated with the increasing ability to diagnose and treat some abnormalities in the fetus. Successful claims have been brought for failure to detect congenital or inherited defects leading to the wrongful birth of a handicapped child – and also in cases where an apparently healthy baby has been aborted on medical advice, because tests had, in the event wrongly, suggested that it would be born with a serious handicap or could not survive.

ANTENATAL CARE

35.29 The Maternity Services Advisory Committee (1982)[1] defines the primary aim of antenatal care as: 'to ensure as far as possible the health and wellbeing of the woman and unborn child'.

More specifically the aims may be categorised as:

(1) the detection and treatment of previously unrecognised maternal disease;
(2) the prediction, prevention, early detection and management of complications of pregnancy;
(3) the amelioration of the discomforts and minor complaints of pregnancy;
(4) formulation of a plan for delivery which takes into account, as far as possible, the individual wishes of the woman and her partner;
(5) preparation of the mother and her partner for the experience of childbirth and the responsibilities of bringing up a child; and
(6) the provision of appropriate health screening and health education.

1 Maternity Services Advisory Committee *Maternity Care in Action I: Antenatal Care* (London, HMSO, 1982).

35.30 Antenatal care is about preventive medicine, aimed to detect and, as far as possible, prevent abnormalities in the mother and fetus. It also looks forward to labour and provides an opportunity for the consultant to formulate a plan for the management of labour which can be executed even in his absence.

35.31 A review of patterns of hospital medical staffing conducted by the British Postgraduate Medical Federation[1] drew attention to the rarity of consultant sessions allocated to labour ward and delivery suites. Nearly 70 per cent of the emergency workload in the labour ward occurs outside the hours of 9 and 5 when consultants are rarely on the premises and management is left to midwives and junior hospital doctors. Some form of risk assessment in the antenatal clinic is therefore essential if accidents are to be avoided.

1 Dowie R *Patterns of Hospital Medical Staffing: Obstetrics and Gynaecology* (British Postgraduate Medical Federation) (London, HMSO, 1991: 98).

35.32 Antenatal care is all about management and planning; its most important function is risk assessment. Many women now express a preference for their pregnancies to be managed by general practitioners or midwives. A system of triage in the antenatal period is essential if the minority of women, for whom such a system is not appropriate, are to be directed towards a safer system of care.

The booking visit

35.33 The first opportunity for triage is on the occasion of antenatal booking. The diagnosis of pregnancy is often made by the woman herself or by the general practitioner. When she registers for antenatal care the first question to be determined is the place of delivery and, secondarily, the pattern of antenatal care. In the United Kingdom the vast majority of women deliver in consultant units but there is an increasing demand for home confinement or general practitioner unit delivery. The first request for such low-tech care is often made to a general practitioner or a midwife; it is essential that the practitioner who assesses that request should take into account all of the risk factors present at the beginning of pregnancy. Even for patients booking in consultant units, a system of shared antenatal care is commonly provided so that even in high risk cases the patient is seen partly by the hospital antenatal clinic and partly by her family doctor and his midwives. To facilitate this system an antenatal co-operation card (Figures 35.1, 35.2) is provided. The card, when completed, can be kept by the mother as a permanent record of her pregnancy. Alternatively, patients are increasingly encouraged to carry their own obstetric notes throughout the pregnancy. A short glossary of common terms and abbreviations should be provided to aid the patient's understanding of the entries made by the doctors and midwives.

35.34 At the booking visit a series of routine blood tests are normally taken. Whilst some of the tests are innocuous (haemoglobin, blood group, Rhesus antibodies etc) others may have potentially serious repercussions for the woman and her baby. It is routine practice to screen for previous exposure to rubella and sometimes for cytomegalovirus and toxoplasma. Whilst these require little explanation, it may be more difficult to explain to a woman the significance of positive testing for hepatitis B and syphilis.

Under no circumstances should an HIV test be requested without counselling as to the potential of either a negative or a positive result.

35.35 The booking clinic provides an opportunity to assess the medical and surgical history of the mother and, most importantly, her previous obstetric history and any difficulties she may have experienced in conceiving. Perinatal mortality and morbidity are affected statistically more often in certain groups of women who can be identified in advance, because they show one or more so-called high-risk factors (Table 35.3). There may be an accumulation of further risks as complications arise during pregnancy and labour. It is against such a known background of risk that obstetricians and midwives have to modify their management of the woman and particularly increase their vigilance.

35.36 Ethnicity and country of origin are important, principally because of the occurrence of certain inherited anaemias (haemoglobinopathies) in Afro-Caribbean women and in patients from the Mediterranean littoral. Where abnormal haemoglobin is detected it is essential to offer screening to the father of the baby; successful litigation has followed the failure properly to assess the risk to the fetus of an inherited defect of haemoglobin.

Screening for fetal abnormality

35.37 Increasingly, errors in counselling or screening for fetal abnormality are emerging as causes of litigation. Any woman with a previous history (or family history) of a child born with a congenital abnormality should be referred for genetic counselling, preferably *before* the pregnancy begins. For the remainder, certain universal screening tests are now available. Adequate counselling is essential *before* screening tests are undertaken.

35.38 Apart from haemoglobinopathies, the first widely employed test was screening for maternal serum alpha fetoprotein (MSAFP). Although its function is unknown, alpha fetoprotein is normally produced by the fetal liver; it is not produced by healthy adults. It was discovered in 1956 and by the early 1970s there were reports of raised levels of this protein in maternal serum in babies with neural tube defects (spina bifida and anencephaly). In these conditions (and in others such as exomphalos and gastroschisis) where the integument of the baby is compromised, this (normal) protein leaks into the maternal circulation. Its detection may alert the obstetrician to the fetal abnormality. The protein will also leak from a dead fetus or in circumstances where the maternal-placental barrier is breached, for instance where there had been an episode of bleeding in early pregnancy. The demonstration of raised maternal serum alpha fetoprotein is a useful screening technique for fetal abnormalities, particularly those affecting the spinal cord.

35.39 Since the late 1970s MSAFP has been in general use in the United Kingdom as a screening test for spina bifida. Initially women with raised MSAFP were further investigated by amniocentesis (sampling of the liquor) to confirm that there was an excessive leak of alpha fetoprotein into the amniotic fluid. This test, however, is not diagnostic and has gradually been replaced by careful ultrasound examination to detect the precise reason for the leak.

Down syndrome

35.40 Down syndrome (Trisomy 21) is a chromosomal abnormality associated with the reduplication of the 21st chromosome, finally detectable only by amniocentesis. Since amniocentesis carries a small risk of abortion of a (probably) normal fetus of about 0.5 per cent, amniocentesis has been reluctantly used on patients for whom the risk of Down syndrome or other chromosomal abnormality was slight. Although one form of the condition occurs sporadically throughout the population, the association with maternal age has long been established. The risk rises from 1:1,500 in teenage to 1:28 by the age of 45. Other chromosomal abnormalities are also increased with age. The overall incidence for all chromosomal abnormalities is 1 in 12 at the age of 45. This led to the screening of mothers by amniocentesis on the grounds of maternal age alone. Some departments offered screening over the age of 35 (overall risk of 1 in 250), others to later age groups up to 38 (overall risk 1 in 111). However, only 40 per cent of Down syndrome babies are detected by this means because of the relatively few babies born to women in the older age groups.

35.41 Anecdotal reporting in the late 1970s of unusually low levels of MSAFP led to the development of a screening method involving both age and MSAFP. This in turn led to the search for other markers for Down syndrome; and association with raised levels of human chorionic gonadotraphin (HCG) and reduced levels of serum oestradiol has led to the current practice of offering a 'triple test' to all mothers. Serum screening for Down syndrome, by this technique, relies on the use of four principal markers – maternal age, serum AFP, serum oestriol and serum HCG – to determine the risk of Down syndrome. These variables, together with the gestation are fed into a computer program, which produces a risk assessment. Women are screen-positive if their risk lies above a specified cut-off level, or screen-negative if they do not. The cut-off level is somewhat arbitrary and, at least in the NHS, depends on the resources available for the next step in investigation – the amniocentesis. This system is capable of identifying more than 60 per cent of Down syndrome in the population since it includes women of all ages; it also reduces the need for older women to be subjected to amniocentesis if their computer-assisted risk is low. The earliest time at which the computer can interpret results is 15 weeks and since the test takes about a week to turn round this allows amniocentesis to be performed between 16 and 17 weeks for women above the cut-off level. The search continues for other markers of Down syndrome to avoid unnecessary amniocentesis. It is essential that before embarking upon such a screening programme the parents are fully informed of the significance of an 'abnormal' result.

35.42 It should not be assumed that just because the test is positive the woman will necessarily elect for amniocentesis; many do not. Neither should it be assumed that if, following amniocentesis, a chromosomal abnormality is demonstrated, the woman will necessarily choose abortion. For some women abortion is not an option but they are greatly helped in dealing with their handicapped baby by the opportunity for counselling and support during the antenatal period.

Ultrasound

35.43 Ultrasound of the baby in the uterus has now been almost universally available throughout the United Kingdom since the 1980s. By its use pregnancies can be dated with accuracy, the placental site can be determined, the number of babies present ascertained and a search for fetal abnormalities made. Most units offer, in addition to an early pregnancy scan, a detailed examination of the baby between 18 and 20 weeks. At this stage there is optimal visualisation of the fetal skull, brain, face, spine, heart, lungs, kidneys, bladder, gut, abdominal wall and limbs. This is the optimum time for diagnosing abnormalities of the nervous system but it is essential that the training of the doctor (or more often the ultrasonographer) is adequate to recognise the important markers, such as ventricular dilatation, in cases where the defect may be small and difficult to visualise.

35.44 In addition to a search for abnormality early ultrasound is vital in confirmation of the dating of pregnancy. The usual measurement made to estimate fetal size at this gestation is a biparietal diameter of the fetal skull (BPD). This measurement is then plotted on the appropriate chart so that in later pregnancy the progress of the baby may be compared with the standard curves (Figure 35.3).

Subsequent antenatal visits

35.45 Whether with the general practitioner, his midwife or with the hospital antenatal clinic, these visits are conducted at traditional intervals (Figure 35.1) and provide further opportunities to re-evaluate the risk status of the mother. The standard observations are shown in Figure 35.2, aimed at the detection of the commoner complications of pregnancy:

(a) pre-eclampsia;
(b) anaemia;
(c) abnormal/unstable presentation of the baby;
(d) abnormalities of fetal growth;
(e) disproportion.

35.46 *Pre-eclampsia*, toxaemia and pregnancy-induced-hypertension are all terms to describe the *temporary* hypertension of pregnancy. Terminology is confused; the cause of the condition is unknown. Further confusion occurs because women already suffering from high blood pressure may have superimposed pre-eclampsia in the later weeks of pregnancy. All of these conditions may affect the growth of the baby, particularly when complicated by the presence of protein in the urine. Rarely the blood pressure may be so high as to threaten the mother either with the development of fits (eclampsia) or stroke. A blood pressure of 140/90 in a previously normotensive patient, or a significant deterioration in previous hypertension calls for admission to hospital. The condition of both mother and baby are intensively monitored. If rest in hospital does not improve the hypertension, or if there is concern for the baby's condition the only treatment available is delivery. This presents no problem if the pregnancy is near term but the early development of hypertension requires a careful risk/benefit analysis of continuing the pregnancy or alternatively delivering a premature baby.

35.47 *Anaemia* may be prevented or corrected by the administration of iron and folic acid; some prescribe routine dietary supplements; others prescribe selectively. The aim is to keep the haemoglobin above 11 grams. If it falls below 9 grams careful consideration must be given to transfusion.

35.48 *Abnormal presentation and unstable lie.* The commonest form of abnormal presentation is *breech*, which accounts for about 3 per cent of deliveries at term. Efforts to correct the malpresentation during pregnancy by turning the baby (external cephalic version – ECV) has recently enjoyed a return to favour; there are now strong advocates of attempts to turn the baby in late pregnancy, or even in early labour with the help of drugs to relax the uterus (tocolytics). This is because vaginal breech delivery carries with it an increased perinatal mortality and morbidity. Some obstetricians prefer to deliver all breeches by Caesarean section. Others allow vaginal breech delivery, but only after careful selection. The proper decision in the antenatal clinic *by the consultant* is essential. A proper antenatal assessment must include:

(1) the assessment of fetal weight (babies weighing more than 3.5 kilos do badly when delivered vaginally as a breech);
(2) an assessment of the size of the mother's pelvis, usually by X-ray pelvimetry; and
(3) the exclusion of all other pregnancy complications.

35.49 *Transverse, oblique and unstable lie.* When the baby's spine is parallel with the maternal spine, the lie is described as longitudinal. Either the head or the breech may be the presenting part. Otherwise, the lie of the baby may be transverse or oblique. The lie changes frequently in early pregnancy but a variable presentation (unstable lie) is uncommon and dangerous in the last month. In such circumstances, if the woman goes into labour when the lie is not longitudinal there is an increased likelihood that the umbilical cord will prolapse when, as is likely to occur early, the membranes rupture. A further danger is that the woman particularly if she is multiparous, will go into strong labour with a transverse lie; labour will then become obstructed and there is a real danger that the uterus may rupture. For these reasons, it is customary to admit the woman to hospital for observation from 36 weeks onwards and for immediate treatment if either complication should occur. The condition is commoner in women with a lax uterus and abdominal wall because of repeated childbearing; other causes include placenta praevia, contracted pelvis, pelvic tumours such as uterine fibroids and ovarian cysts, an excess of amniotic fluid and an abnormal fetus.

35.50 *Multiple pregnancy* is usually diagnosed by ultrasound. Occasionally twins are discovered on an early pregnancy scan but on later examinations only one baby is found because the second twin has died. The situation requires no intervention; there is usually no sign of the dead twin at the time of delivery. Special problems arise when, as the result of antenatal screening, one twin is found to be abnormal. The parents are then faced with difficult decisions. Although the abnormal twin may selectively be destroyed, the procedure requires considerable skill and inevitably puts the normal twin at risk. The Abortion Act 1967 (as amended by the Human Fertilisation and Embryology Act 1990) allows the obstetrician to reduce the number of fetuses in a multiple pregnancy, provided that grounds for abortion exist. There is no difficulty in interpreting the law if the fetus to be destroyed is severely abnormal. However if all the fetuses are apparently normal, the reduction is legal either because triplets or higher multiple pregnancies result in a greater risk to maternal health than twin or single pregnancies – or if there would be a significant stress to mental health if all the fetuses were lost as a consequence of preterm labour.

35.51 Even with ultrasound the number of fetuses may be underestimated. Occasionally twins are reported when in fact a third fetus has been missed; even twins may be missed if one fetus lies directly in front of the other. Whenever the size of the uterus exceeds expectation, it is wise to repeat ultrasound examination in late pregnancy for there may be serious consequences to the undetected second (or third) baby.

35.52 *Fetal growth.* It has been traditional (Figure 35.2) to record maternal weight at every visit. There has recently been much debate in the literature about the usefulness of this observation. Excessive weight gain, due to fluid retention, may be the first important warning sign of impending pre-eclampsia. Gross deviation from the normal pattern of weight gain (10 kilos for a woman of average weight throughout pregnancy) may also be the first warning of abnormal fetal growth. Attention has been focused mainly on the baby whose growth is reduced, IUGR, but the fetus of excessive weight (macrosomia) may also be at increased risk.

35.53 *Serial ultrasound* is the only effective means of assessing fetal weight. Clinical observations are notoriously unreliable. The growth charts (Figure 35.3) can be used to demonstrate an abnormal pattern of weight gain and to draw attention to a fetus at risk. There are two patterns of IUGR which have very different significance and prognosis.

35.54 In *symmetrical IUGR* all parameters of fetal growth are below expectation. In late pregnancy the BPD is an unreliable guide to fetal growth because of individual variations in the shape of the head but both head circumference and abdominal circumference will show similar patterns of delayed growth. The most common explanation for symmetrical IUGR is that the baby is genetically small – a small person born to small parents. There is no increased risk. In other circumstances the baby of average genetic potential may be globally retarded either because of some early pregnancy insult or because the baby has a severe inherited abnormality. In these rare cases of symmetrical growth retardation, further investigations are indicated.

35.55 *Asymmetric IUGR* is the problem which more commonly confronts the obstetrician. The growth of the baby's soft tissues is selectively reduced because the baby's nutrients are restricted. This is commonly attributed to *placental insufficiency*. The baby is effectively starved; its body fat is reduced so that its abdominal circumference lags behind its head circumference.

Even in severe malnutrition the blood supply to the brain is preserved so that the baby's head continues to grow. This head-sparing effect can only be demonstrated by comparing abdominal and head circumference. When there are grounds for suspecting chronic malnourishment of the baby a combination of ultrasound measurements should be made including the BPD, head circumference, abdominal circumference and femur length. With this combination of measurements fetal weight can be predicted. A relative diminution in amniotic fluid volume is also usual with IUGR. Nowadays every district general hospital has the ability to carry out such examinations.

35.56 More sophisticated ultrasound assessments are also possible with the production of a 'biophysical profile' of the baby. This includes not only measurements of its size and liquor volume but its movements and breathing activities in utero. Increasingly, Doppler blood flow studies of the placental, umbilical and fetal vessels are becoming available in district general hospitals and can provide vital information about fetal well-being. Where a fetus is demonstrably malnourished and particularly where there is Doppler evidence of reduced placental and umbilical blood flows, a decision must be made concerning the time and mode of delivery. An already malnourished baby is unlikely to withstand the rigours of labour without becoming still more distressed, or to remain much longer in the uterus without the risk of intrauterine death or permanent damage. These are matters of fine clinical judgment but there is general acceptance that when IUGR is established the baby should be delivered with as little further stress as possible and this usually means by planned (elective) Caesarean section. The timing of delivery, the most finely balanced decision, will depend on the maturity of the pregnancy. Generally, babies born after 36 weeks are at no disadvantage, babies born betweeen 32 and 36 weeks may require special care but the majority will survive without handicap; babies born before 32 weeks may require neonatal intensive care including oxygen ventilation with a relatively high frequency of morbidity and mortality.

35.57 *Biophysical monitoring* includes not only ultrasound but antenatal cardiotocography (CTG) and the recording of fetal movements. The 'count-to-ten' fetal activity chart (Figure 35.4) is the cheapest and least intrusive means of measuring fetal activity. The mother is asked to report a deterioration in fetal activity with the aid of a simple chart. Antenatal, non-stressed, CTGs, (vide infra) provide the most immediate indication of fetal well-being.

35.58 *Cephalo-pelvic disproportion* (CPD) means that the baby's head is too big to pass safely through the maternal pelvis. In an absolute sense the baby may be too big or the pelvis too small. More commonly it is the *attitude* of the baby which determines success or failure. The fetal head is normally completely flexed so that the chin rests on the chest. In this attitude the smallest diameter of the head presents to negotiate its passage through the bony pelvis. If the head becomes deflexed a wider diameter is presented to the pelvis; there is then *relative* disproportion. Deflexion of the fetal head is common when the back of the fetal head (the occiput) is directed towards the maternal spine instead of to the pubis – the so-called occipito-posterior position.

35.59 During the antenatal period the obstetrician may be put on notice that disproportion is likely by:

(a) previous obstetric history of difficult delivery;
(b) mother of small stature (less than 5 feet or 1.52 m);
(c) exceptionally large baby;
(d) failure of the head to engage in the pelvis in a first pregnancy.

35.60 *Engagement of the fetal head* is a critical concept for the understanding of labour. The fetal head (Figure 35.5) is not a sphere but an ovoid. The well flexed head presents its narrowest diameters to the fetal pelvis; its broadest point is always the distance between the two parietal eminences (BPD). The narrowest strait of the maternal pelvis is the entrance or inlet. Once the greatest diameter of the fetal head (BPD) has passed the narrow strait (the inlet) of the maternal pelvis, disproportion is unlikely to occur. All of this can be detected by abdominal examination of the pregnant woman to determine whether the biparietal diameter of the fetal head is still *palpable* in the abdomen. If it is, the fetal head is *not* engaged. Engagement implies that this widest diameter has passed the narrow strait and is no longer accessible to examination. To make the examination easier, the fetal head is notionally divided into fifths (Figure 35.6). If ³⁄₅ths are palpable in the abdomen the head is not engaged; ²⁄₅ths or less of the head palpable indicates engagement. The progress of the descent of the head becomes of vital importance in labour.

35.61 In a first pregnancy it is usual for the head to be engaged before the onset of labour. Engagement usually occurs sometime in the last three weeks of the pregnancy. If it does not, it behoves the obstetrician to question whether there may be some obstruction or *disproportion* preventing engagement.

35.62 If CPD is suspected digital examination of the shape and size of the bony pelvic cavity (clinical pelvimetry) through the vagina may provide a rough guide to its shape and dimensions. Most obstetricians would concede that this is not reliable and many have abandoned it. Measurement of the pelvic diameters by X-ray does provide accurate information but correlates poorly with the outcome of labour. It is not possible to forecast the diameters of the fetal head that will have to pass through the pelvis, for this depends on the degree of flexion; this in turn depends on the efficiency of the uterus and can only be tested by labour. In circumstances of clinical doubt, the consultant will determine upon a *trial of labour* in appropriate cases.

35.63 *Consultant decisions* and the proper plans for labour are essential, not only in suspected cephalo-pelvic disproportion but in certain other potentially dangerous circumstances summarised in Table 35.4.

35.64 *Serious maternal disease*, coincident with the pregnancy needs special antenatal provision. Diabetic patients should be managed in co-operation with a diabetic physician and major haemoglobinopathies with a consultant haematologist. Ideally the patient should be seen in a joint clinic but if that is not possible, at least the patient should be offered appointments on the same day and in the same hospital to see both specialists.

35.65 *Ante-partum haemorrhage* is now defined as bleeding from the genital tract after the *24th* week of pregnancy. It may be due to an abnormally situated placenta (placenta praevia) or to a premature separation of a diseased placenta (abruptio placentae or accidental haemorrhage). In either case immediate admission to hospital and further investigations are required.

35.66 *Placenta praevia* may threaten the life of both mother and baby. The placenta lies low in the uterus, in its lower segment and may cover all or part of the cervix so that as the cervix dilates the placenta separates giving rise to fresh painless bleeding. The bleeding may first occur early in the pregnancy and recur intermittently in greater or lesser amounts. The diagnosis is confirmed by ultrasound. If the amount of bleeding permits, conservative management is continued until the baby is mature, at which time it may be delivered safely by Caesarean section. Occasionally catastrophic haemorrhage may demand earlier delivery with the risk to the baby of prematurity.

35.67 *Abruptio placentae* presents a much more immediate threat to the baby – as well as to the mother. It may be unheralded and catastrophic, with total separation of the placenta and massive concealed intra-uterine bleeding, causing the death of the baby before it can be delivered. Alternatively the process of placental separation may be more gradual and partial so that the baby can be extracted from the uterus alive, but nevertheless only to survive with hypoxic brain damage. Placental abruption can also cause serious maternal complications including disseminated intravascular coagulation (leading to uncontrollable haemorrhage), renal failure and sometimes death. In lesser degrees the process may begin with repeated painful revealed losses of blood, often in association with hypertension, and with ultrasound evidence of retroplacental bleeding. In such cases, it may be possible to deliver the baby before catastrophe strikes. The balance has to be nicely judged on the clinical picture and the maturity of the pregnancy. When signs of major placental abruption occur with a mature live baby the situation is one of the greatest urgency. If the baby is to be salvaged, delivery must be achieved within minutes of the diagnosis.

35.68 *Antenatal admission* may thus be required for a variety of conditions, most commonly:

(1) hypertension;
(2) ante-partum haemorrhage; and
(3) suspected IUGR and fetal malnutrition.

Since the management of all these conditions is conservative (until the moment of delivery) mothers are constantly frustrated by the need to remain in hospital for long periods when nothing is apparently been done. Constant counselling, explanation and reassurance are essential to obtain patient compliance, particularly for the mother who has small children at home.

INDUCTION OF LABOUR

35.69 Where the continuation of the pregnancy poses a threat to mother or baby, labour may be induced. Fashions change; the high induction rates of the 1960s and 1970s are no longer considered acceptable. The main controversy centres on prolonged pregnancies. The rationale for delivery at or soon after term is that perinatal mortality and morbidity increase significantly after the completion of the 42nd week of pregnancy, attributed to placental ageing and insufficiency. Some obstetricians set an arbitrary time limit when they induce labour if it does not occur spontaneously. This varies from 41 to 42 weeks and often with sub-variables, such as maternal age, twins or a breech presentation. There is a minority view that pregnancy may be allowed to continue indefinitely in the absence of other complications provided only that the condition of the fetus is carefully monitored. There is no consensus view. Inextricably interwoven with this indication is pressure often brought on the obstetrician by the woman and her family to induce labour either because of understandable social reasons or simply because she is fed up and uncomfortable.

35.70 The second commonest indication for induction of labour is hypertension. Most obstetricians would induce labour when the diastolic blood pressure persistently exceeds 90 mmHg after 38 weeks.

35.71 Suspected IUGR is an indication for induction of labour, frequently linked to hypertension or repeated small ante-partum haemorrhage of undetermined origin.

35.72 Other less common indications include established intra-uterine death, breech presentation, twins, rhesus incompatibility, maternal diabetes and fetal abnormality.

35.73 There is now wide agreement for the preferred method of induction of labour. If there is no immediate urgency, the sweeping of membranes (digital separation of the membranes through the partially dilated cervix) is often sufficient. If the cervix is tightly closed (unfavourable) the intravaginal administration of prostaglandin (either by pessary or gel) is often sufficient to provoke uterine contractions or at least to dilate the cervix sufficently to allow the artificial rupture of the membranes. The treatment may be repeated after a few hours if labour is not established. A period of electronic (CTG) monitoring is essential after each application of prostaglandins.

35.74 The most effective method of induction is *artificial rupture of the membranes*. Once the membranes are ruptured and if labour is not well established it may be augmented by giving intravenous oxytocin (Syntocinon), usually according to a prescribed regime, standard for the unit.

35.75 *Premature rupture of the membranes* is loosely defined as spontaneous rupture of membranes, *not* followed within a few hours by the spontaneous onset of labour. There is no consensus as to the time limits to be set for the onset of labour but most obstetricians would intervene by the augmentation of labour with Syntocinon if membranes had been ruptured, close to term, for more than 24 hours. In extreme prematurity the decision to wait or to intervene is more complex; the dangers of prematurity must be weighed against the risk of intra-uterine infection which occasionally follows prolonged membrane rupture.

35.76 The complications of inducing labour include:

(a) failure to achieve the desired objective;
(b) intra-uterine infection;
(c) prolapse of the umbilical cord;

and rarely,

(d) haemorrhage from an unsuspected placenta praevia or vasa praevia.

35.76 *Vasa praevia* is a rare condition in which the insertion of the cord into the placenta is abnormal (Figure 35.7). If there is a succenturiate lobe or a velamentous insertion of the placenta the unsupported vessels may overlie the cervix. If one of those vessels is torn as the membranes rupture haemorrhage may result. Unlike other forms of ante-partum or intra-partum haemorrhage it is the baby who bleeds in this condition. There will be bright red vaginal bleeding; the baby's heart rate will be increased, sometimes with a characteristic (sinusoidal) CTG pattern. Unless the diagnosis is made quickly, the baby may be exsanguinated before delivery. Bedside tests are available for the detection of *fetal* blood, which rapidly distinguishes from maternal bleeding.

INTRA-PARTUM CARE

35.77 Admission of the mother in labour provides another critical opportunity for the reassessment of risk. Here antenatal records should be reviewed and the consultant decisions for labour appropriately implemented. If new risk factors have emerged a senior doctor must immediately be informed.

35.78 The mother's own views on the conduct of her labour should be recorded and, if there are no contraindications, implemented. Many women greatly benefit from the support of their partner during labour and are increasingly requesting management which involves the minimum of interference and the maximum of independence for the mother. Hospitals are increasingly seeking to provide a 'home from home' environment in which the mother may have some of the advantages associated with home delivery, but within a hospital where emergency help is available should things go wrong. Water baths are now commonplace. Midwives and obstetricians are still learning the rules of safe practice. In the great majority of women with no special risk factors there seems no reason to resist the request for the management of the first or even the second stage of labour in a water bath. There are, however, some concerns about the management of the third stage and most units request the mother to leave the bath before the placenta is delivered. For all patients, however, there is the distinct advantage in a period of electronic fetal monitoral (EFM) with a CTG immediately upon admission. With the reassurance of a normal *admission trace*, appropriate patients may be managed by intermittent auscultation.

35.79 The cardiotocograph (Figure 35.8) produces two recordings. The upper trace (the cardiograph) represents the fetal heart; the lower (tocograph) records contractions of the uterus. The cardiograph may be recorded by an ultrasound signal through the mother's abdominal wall or by an electrode attached to the baby's scalp (FSE). The tocograph is produced either by an external 'guard-ring' tocodynomometer or by an intra-uterine pressure catheter.

35.80 Modern machines electronically date and time the recording (provided that the clock is properly set). The record should be identified by writing on the name and registration number of the woman and by the date and time, if it is not automatically recorded. Doctors and midwives may also annotate the document with important events of the labour. The recording produced is often crucial to expert consideration of the standards of care in labour. They do not fit comfortably into record folders and are more often lost or damaged than any other part of the clinical records. They are often supplied, in the context of litigation, in unsuitable A4 fragments, impossible to interpret. A full and continuous copy must be properly assessed; such copies can be made by feeding the original through a domestic fax machine; professional copies can be made by the Times Drawing Office, 11 Pollen Street, London W1 (tel: 071–629 5661/5565). Interpretations of CTGs is a complex subject about which experts frequently differ. There has been a recent flood of textbooks on the subject. Every author has his own classification of fetal heart rate pattern; some attempt to distinguish between patterns suggestive of stress (a healthy fetus using compensatory mechanisms in response to hypoxia or other stresses) and *fetal distress*, implying a degree of fetal compromise. In practice, although fetal distress is a term which defies definition, it is used to describe all circumstances in which the baby's response is *potentially* indicative of stress. This includes not only a wide spectrum of abnormalities on the CTG but also the passage of meconium in the liquor amni.

35.81 Table 35.5 is a much simplified CTG classification.

Baseline variability is classified as:

Silent = 0.5 bpm
Reduced = 6–10 bpm
Normal = 10–25 bpm
Saltatory = >25 bpm

35.82 A *sinusoidal* pattern, sometimes seen with fetal anaemia, oscillates smoothly 2–5 times per minute with an amplitude of 5–10 bpm. There is controversy concerning its diagnosis and implications.

35.83 *Accelerations* (Figure 35.8) from a normal baseline are the hallmark of fetal health.

35.84 *Decelerations* are generally ominous and are classified:

(1) early (type I) when they are coincident with and make a mirror image of the uterine contraction;
(2) late (type II) when there is a significant lag time (Figure 35.8) between the peak of the contraction and the nadir of the deceleration; and
(3) variable when there is no fixed relationship between contraction and deceleration.

35.85 A normal CTG on admission is *reassuring*; if there are no high-risk factors, the management of labour may be according to the patient's wishes. Many patients do not wish long periods of EFM and there is no good evidence that if the mother is keen for mobilisation and natural labour she need be electronically monitored. As an alternative, the fetal heart is auscultated regularly with a Pinard's stethoscope or Sonicaid machine.

35.86 This should be done for at least one minute every fifteen minutes when labour is established; in the second stage of labour after every contraction. If such monitoring reveals abnormalities or if new risk factors emerge during labour, the need for electronic fetal monitoring should be reassessed. It is important to emphasise that variability cannot be detected by the unaided ear. Not every abnormality of the CTG requires immediate delivery. Unless the tracing is diagnostic further information about the baby is desirable if unnecessary operative intervention is to be avoided. Such information can be obtained by carrying out blood gas analysis of a fetal blood sample taken by puncturing the baby's scalp through the dilating cervix to suck up a sample of its blood. Such an analysis gives evidence of the state of exchange of respiratory gases (oxygen and carbon dioxide) and whether or not the baby is suffering from impairment of this exchange and showing acidosis. With prolonged hypoxia carbon dioxide accumulates to give a respiratory acidosis. In the continued deficiency of oxygen anaerobic metabolism results in the production of lactic acid and a metabolic acidosis.

35.87 Although *fetal blood sampling* (FBS) is described in all the textbooks it is not used in the majority of district general hospitals. Failure to use it cannot therefore be regarded as an unacceptable practice. FBS has on occasion led to litigation either because (when it was available) it was not used, the sample was improperly taken, contaminated so as to give an abnormal result, misinterpreted or wrongly relied upon. The sample is only relevant at the time it is taken and, if CTG abnormalities persist, a further blood sample should be taken to reassess the baby's condition.

35.88 Progress in labour is recorded on a partogram (Figure 35.9). Strictly only the central part of Figure 35.9 is a partograph, consisting of two plotted lines of progress. The remainder of the chart records additional information such as the quality of the uterine contraction, intravenous fluids, urinalysis etc. Critria of progress are *cervical dilatation* and *descent of the presenting part*. Cervical dilatation is measured in centimetres; there are ten points on the scale because ten centimetres equals full dilatation. Progress of labour can thus be compared with the average pattern for both first (primigravid) and subsequent (multipara) labours (Figure 35.10). Only the five bottom lines are available for the monitoring of head descent and the fifths palpable (Figure 35.6) are here recorded. It is important to emphasise that the recording of head level is by *abdominal examination*, whilst the assessment of cervical dilatation requires *vaginal examination*. In some units descent is *wrongly* charted by indicating the level of the presenting part on vaginal examination by reference to the ischial spines (Figure 35.11).

35.89 The requirements for the documentation of vaginal examination in labour are set out clearly in the standard textbooks of midwifery but scant attention is paid to proper documentation of certain critical facts such as moulding, caput and position of the fetal head.

35.90 *Moulding* describes the overlapping of the separate and mobile bones of the fetal skull (Figure 35.5B) as the result of uterine activity compressing the head into the pelvis and changing its shape so that it may be accommodated.

35.91 *Caput succedaneum* is the soft tissue swelling which forms, also as the result of pressure, further distorting the shape of the head. The examiner who relies entirely on the vaginal findings for head descent may be seriously misled (Figure 35.11). *Trial of labour* is the management of labour in the presence of suspected CPD. It is a term of art and its management is described in all the standard textbooks. Given the suspicion of disproportion, the labour is conducted under the direct supervision of a senior doctor so that if the suspicion is confirmed labour may be terminated safely by Caesarean section. In practice, such trials are often terminated for fetal distress rather than for lack of progress.

35.92 Slow progress in primigravid labour is often due to poor uterine action; this may be a response to CPD. The *active management of labour* (O'Driscoll and Meagher 1986) is the means used to distinguish the two.

35.93 Active management includes artificial rupture of the membranes and the intravenous exhibition of the hormone oxytocin (Syntocinon). The improved uterine action increases head flexion, promotes moulding and restores the progress of labour to normal (1 cm dilatation of the cervix per hour). If acceleration or augmentation of labour with oxytocin fails to achieve normal progress, the trial is deemed to have failed and the baby delivered by Caesarean section.

35.94 The length of labour is often a matter of dispute. Labour is said to be in the *active* phase when the cervix is more than 3 cms dilated. Until then the woman is said to be in the *latent* phase of labour, a phase which may without harm last for many hours (Figure 35.10). Sometimes a woman may be conscious of uterine contractions over a period of several days or even one or two weeks at a time when the cervix is not dilating, a period of *false* labour.

35.95 Generally women who have had a previous vaginal delivery do not suffer uterine inertia; they react to disproportion by an increase in uterine activity. If the obstruction is not relieved the uterus may rupture. It follows that acceleration of labour with oxytocin in the multiparous patient must be undertaken with much greater caution than in the primigravida. Her uterus may be more sensitive to oxytocin; the baby she is carrying may be much larger than any she has previously borne.

35.96 *A trial of scar* describes the management of labour in the presence of a scar on the uterus, usually from previous Caesarean section. Provided the indication for the previous Caesarean section was non recurrent, most obstetricians will allow a trial of scar under strict supervision. A scar represents a weakness in the uterus which is particularly prone to rupture. The use of oxytocin in such labour is controversial particularly if used in conjunction with an epidural analgesic block. Those who permit it must be scrupulous in their monitoring of labour.

35.97 *Rupture of the uterus* is rare but often results in fetal death, frequently causes grave maternal injury and occasionally maternal death. Whilst rupture of a previous Caesarean scar is the commonest antecedent, the intact uterus may also be ruptured by the injudicious use of oxytocin. Rarely an intact uterus may rupture spontaneously. The occurrence may be dramatic and obvious with severe internal haemorrhage or, particularly in the case of ruptured scar, may be silent and only discovered after delivery. Warning signs are unreliable but there is often a rise in maternal pulse rate and there *may be* fetal distress before rupture. The sudden loss of the fetal heart, the abrupt cessation of uterine contractions and the appearances of blood in the urine are all suggestive that the uterus has already ruptured.

35.98 *Breech labour* demands constant risk reassessment. In spite of the antenatal selection, the discovery of unfavourable presentation, such as a footling, at the beginning of labour, should lead to Caesarean section. Great care must be taken when the membranes rupture because there is an increased risk of prolapse of the umbilical cord. The membranes should not be ruptured when the breech is high or in an unfavourable position. The labour demands careful monitoring. Slow progress, in spite of careful antenatal selection, may be an indication that the baby is bigger than anticipated – and a warning of problems to come. The use of oxytocin in breech labour is controversial.

35.99 *Twin labour* demands the monitoring of both fetal hearts, effectively only possible with EFM.

35.100 *Umbilical cord complications* are frequently unpredictable, may be undetected and can cause death of the infant or cerebral palsy. Cord entanglements are common and usually of no consequence. They may be associated with signs of fetal distress of mild degree, especially late in the first stage of labour. The commonest problem is cord around the neck; the baby is not strangled by the cord but if it is tight the circulation of blood through it may be restricted causing hypoxia. Similarly, there may be a true knot in the cord which may be unnoticed by all concerned including the baby until the placenta is delivered. This is because the pulsating blood flow through the cord prevents the knot from being drawn tight.

35.101 If a loop of umbilical cord lies beside or below the presenting part of the baby – particularly likely with preterm babies, when the lie is unstable or transverse, breech presentation and twins – and is detected by its synchronous pulsation with the baby's heart on vaginal examination when the membranes are still intact, this is called *presentation of the cord*. The baby is in no immediate danger. However, the baby should be delivered as quickly as possible by Caesarean section, because the membranes may rupture at any time converting cord presentation into *cord prolapse*, a serious threat to the baby. The circulation through the cord may be occluded by the compression of the cord between the presenting part and the cervix during uterine contractions. The blood circulation through the cord may also be impaired because its blood vessels go into spasm following the drop in temperature between the mother's body and the outside air. Spasm of the cord vessels will also be encouraged when the cord is handled. The treatment for this condition is delivery of the baby as soon as possible by Caesarean section, if the cervix is not fully dilated. Whilst preparations are made for this, every precaution is taken to relieve the umbilical cord from compression, by digital elevation of the presenting part through the vagina.

35.102 *Epidural analgesia* is now frequently employed as an alternative to systemic pain relief and has its own special problems, requiring scrupulous supervision and monitoring. Whilst midwives may be trained to give subsequent 'top-up' doses the siting of the block and its subsequent supervision should be in the hands of a specially trained obstetric anaesthetist. In the event of Caesarean section or other operative delivery, the block may be continued, with suitable adjustments, to provide pain relief at delivery.

35.103 *The second stage of labour* begins from full dilatation of the cervix, ending with the delivery of the baby. The baby is at much greater risk once maternal expulsive efforts begin and a much higher standard of monitoring is required. Strict time limits should be applied if fetal compromise is to be avoided.

35.104 The length of the second stage of labour has been much complicated by the introduction of epidural analgesia. With an effective block, the mother, even with the cervix fully dilated, may have no desire to push. In those circumstances the second stage may be treated as an extension of the first and requires no different management. However, once maternal effort begins, broad time limits should be applied to the duration of pushing. The mean duration for the normal spontaneous second stage in a first labour is about 40 minutes; 15 minutes for a subsequent delivery. Provided progress is being maintained (as judged by the visible descent of the head) and provided that there is no fetal distress it is reasonable to allow a primigravida to push for about 45 minutes; after this time she will become exhausted and careful consideration should be given to operative delivery. The CTG in the second stage of labour is notoriously difficult to assess and frequently a subject of controversy between experts.

OPERATIVE DELIVERY

35.105 *Forceps delivery* is a common source of litigation. The common errors are:

(1) attempting vaginal delivery when:
 - (a) mechanical warning signs are ignored or misinterpreted;
 - (b) basic rules are disregarded;
 - (c) fetal compromise is already present; or
 - (d) head position or head level are wrongly assessed or not assessed at all;

(2) delivery is undertaken by doctors too junior or inexperienced;
(3) repeated attempts at delivery by junior doctors;
(4) delay in the decision – delivery interval.

35.106 *Trial of forceps* may be undertaken if there is doubt in the mind of the operator concerning the outcome. Such a trial is only permissible if the cervix is fully dilated, the head engaged (and no more than ⅕th palpable) and the pelvis adequate. It should be closely supervised by an experienced obstetrician, in an operating theatre with full preparations for *immediate* Caesarean section should it fail. There is no place for a trial of forceps if the baby is already showing signs of distress. The procedure frequently involves *rotation* of the baby from an occipito-posterior or occipito-transverse position with the specially designed *Kjelland's* forceps. Such an operation requires considerable skill and judgment, only acquired by extensive experience.

35.107 The *ventouse* is no longer used extensively in this country. The instrument is an alternative to the forceps and is often employed by the less experienced obstetrician whose skill is insufficient for anything other than a very simple forceps delivery. Particularly if the ventouse is applied to a malrotated head, maternal and fetal damage may follow its injudicious use and the same safeguards should be applied and caution exercised as with the application of forceps. The ventouse takes much longer in its execution and is inappropriate in the circumstances of fetal distress.

35.108 *Shoulder dystocia* is the most frightening of all obstetric emergencies. It may follow spontaneous delivery of the head but is more commonly seen after forceps or ventouse delivery; the chin fails to clear the perineum. Unless the baby's shoulders can be released within a very few minutes, disaster will surely follow. Excessive traction with lateral flexion of the neck may produce injury to the nerve roots in the neck (brachial plexus) leaving the baby with a paralysed arm (either Erb's or Klumpke's paralysis); worse, the baby may suffer asphyxia because the chest cannot be expanded. If the baby is known to be large (>4 kilos), if the mother has gained excessive weight, the pregnancy is postdates, the labour has been dysfunctional and operative delivery necessary from the midpelvis the problem can (and should) be anticipated. With such little time, it is essential that a senior doctor is present at delivery. The appropriate manoeuvres are poorly described in the textbooks which at present provide a multiplicity of confusing (and often inappropriate) advice. The combination of the McRobert's manoeuvre (extreme hip flexion), generous episiotomy and suprapubic pressure will often free the impacted anterior shoulder. If not, the shoulders must be rotatated within the pelvis (Wood's screw) to bring the erstwhile posterior shoulder under the symphysis pubis and into the pelvis.

35.109 *Breech delivery* gives rise to few problems provided only that there has been proper antenatal selection and good intra-partum monitoring to eliminate, by Caesarean section, those babies that are either too large or insufficiently robust. The common problems in the second stage of breech delivery are:

(1) incorrect diagnosis of full dilatation (leading to premature pushing and entrapment of the head);
(2) failure to appreciate the significance of delay in the descent of the baby; and
(3) difficult delivery of the aftercoming head.

35.110 *Twin delivery* demands the presence of a senior obstetrician, an anaesthetist and at least one paediatrician. Provided that the presentation of the first twin is cephalic, labour may proceed normally until after the first baby is born. It is the delivery of the second baby which poses hazards. Rarely its presence may have been missed. It is common practice to give an oxytocic drug to promote uterine contractions during the birth of the child. If this is done in the case of the first twin, the uterus contracts tightly around the second baby, seriously impairing its oxygen supply. Cerebral palsy caused by such an oversight has been the subject of large settlements. Even without such an accident, the second twin is at increased risk. The placenta may be compromised by the events of the first delivery, there is a greater likelihood of prolapse of the umbilical cord and an increased incidence of malpresentation. In practice the presentation of the second twin cannot be determined until after the first baby is delivered, for it frequently changes. The obstetrician should immediately determine the lie of the second twin. Every effort should be made to preserve the membranes intact until the lie is longitudinal; correction by external version is usually easy, provided that the membranes are intact. Should the membranes rupture with an abnormal lie, swift intervention will be necessary to save the second twin.

35.111 *Caesarean section* may be planned (elective) or become necessary during labour (emergency). It may be carried out under epidural analgesic block or general anaesthesia. With general anaesthesia a fine balance has to be struck between keeping it as light as possible in the interests of the baby and yet eliminating maternal awareness. If the mother is not actually unconscious she cannot object, because she will have been totally paralysed in order to achieve relaxation of the abdominal muscles. Several claims have been settled on the finding that the woman was aware during a Caesarean section, because the anaesthetic was inadequate.

35.112 Almost without exception the type of operation in use today is a lower segment Caesarean section (LSCS) through a transverse suprapubic (Pfannenstiel) incision. Very rarely the upper segment (classical) approach may be chosen to overcome particular problems such as a transverse lie with a prolapsed arm or uterine fibroids which totally obscure the lower uterine segment.

35.113 The most frequent complaint concerning Caesarean section is that it is performed too late. There has been considerable recent debate on the appropriate decision-delivery interval. In conditions of extreme emergency (such as prolapsed cord) it should be possible in most units to deliver the baby in 15–20 minutes. In the presence of fetal distress intervals up to 30 minutes are common; it would be difficult to justify delay beyond 40 minutes.

35.114 The commonest complications of Caesarean section are:

(1) difficulty in delivering a head from deep in the pelvis;
(2) haemorrhage; and
(3) damage to the bladder (which lies immediately in front of the lower segment).

35.115 *Hysterectomy* is sometimes necessary in order to control haemorrhage at Caesarean section, particularly in the context of a ruptured uterus. Rarely surgery in such difficult circumstances may be associated with injury to the ureter or bowel.

35.116 *Labour ward organisation* is critical to safe practice. Nowhere is communication between the various levels of staff more important. The chain of command is often difficult. The judgment of the senior midwife is often superior to that of the inexperienced SHO (or even the registrar). In every labour ward, the senior midwife should have the authority to go over the head of the junior doctor if she feels that decisions are not being taken appropriately (Figure 35.12). Labour ward protocols dealing with emergencies such as haemorrhage, ruptured uterus, prolapsed cord and shoulder dystocia are not only good practice but clearly recommended in department of health guidelines.[1] A *paediatrician* should always be present at delivery in the circumstances of operative delivery or where fetal distress suggests the need for skilled resuscitation.

1 Maternity Services Advisory Committee *Maternity Care in Action II: Intrapartum Care* (London, HMSO, 1984).

Care after delivery

35.117 The third stage of labour may be complicated by *post-partum haemorrhage* (arbitrarily defined as more than 500 mls) with or without difficulty in deliverying the placenta. The (almost) universal practice of administering oxytocic drugs during the second stage of labour has greatly reduced the incidence of haemorrhage but it still presents an occasional life-threatening emergency. The causes include:

(1) damage to the cervix and vagina (often by instrumental delivery);
(2) failure of the uterus to contract; and
(3) unsuspected rupture of the uterus.

Every unit must have a clearly defined protocol for the management of this emergency for swift intervention is essential. Senior staff are unlikely to be available and junior medical staff and midwives should be in no doubt as to the proper management. Uncross-matched O Negative blood should be available in the labour ward for use in dire emergencies.

35.118 *Episiotomies* and vaginal tears are common subjects of complaint. Failure to recognise a *third degree tear* (involving the anal sphincter) will result in loss of continence. Timely recognition and effective repair by a senior doctor with appropriate anaesthesia usually gives excellent results. Claims are commonly settled when the injury is missed or incompetently repaired.

35.119 Surprisingly it is still not universal practice to count swabs before and after the repair of the perineum; a retained vaginal swab, discovered many days or weeks after delivery will result in an indefensible action. Damages may be compounded by the breakdown of the repair, resulting from the associated infection.

35.120 Complaints arising from *secondary post-partum haemorrhage* (any excessive blood loss after the first 24 hours) associated with small pieces of retained placenta and membrane are common. They are seldom successful since it is, in practice, very difficult to be certain that the placenta has been completely delivered.

Stillbirth

35.121 A baby is stillborn when it is born without signs of life after 24 completed weeks of pregnancy, counting from the first day of the last menstrual period. The commonest causes are congenital defects, placental abruption, maternal hypertension and diabetes, intra-uterine and intra-partum hypoxia.

35.122 Intra-uterine death of the baby usually leads sooner rather than later to the onset of labour and delivery. Sometimes the birth of the baby may be delayed for many days or even weeks after it has died. When such delay occurs, post-mortem changes may be so advanced that the skin peels off (maceration), the skull collapses and vital internal organs liquify, especially the brain. This process may render post-mortem examination unhelpful as to the cause. Even with a fresh stillbirth there may be little evidence as to why it happened except for the ante-mortem changes of asphyxia. Evidence as to cause may have to be sought from chromosome analysis of parents and, if it is possible, of the baby's tissues. Examination of the mother may reveal evidence of possible causes, such as hypertension, diabetes, auto-immune disease, blood group incompatibility and unsuspected infection. More often than not, no cause is found.

35.123 A group of stillbirths that cause particular frustration to both medical attendants and the parents occur suddenly in otherwise apparently normal mature infants (38–42 weeks), even after post-mortem examination, often without any preceding evidence of serious abnormality. It is because of this that many obstetricians apply working rules and say, for example, that all women with diastolic blood pressure of 90 or more should have labour induced, and similarly in women whose pregnancy is prolonged past full term by an arbitrary number of days. Despite such rules, which can be associated with their own problems, babies nevertheless still die suddenly and unexpectedly in utero. It is from this group of women that complaints about the standard of care may arise, particularly if communication between the medical staff and the parents was not of the best before and after the event.

35.124 The mother who has suffered bereavement or whose baby is seriously ill in the first few days of life requires special attention in the puerperium. Explanations as to why the baby died or is unwell may need to be repeated many times for such news is poorly absorbed in circumstances of great distress. Where errors have occurred during pregnancy and delivery there should be a clear policy of honest explanation, given by the most senior obstetrician, supported by a consultant paediatrician. Sharing with the patient the realisation of error, admitting that it has occurred and facing squarely the responsibility for it requires considerable courage. When parents perceive that there is something covered up, they are more likely to become hostile; information imparted thereafter may not be believed.

35.125 Support and explanation to the parents in such circumstances is a basic requirement of good practice.

35.126 Failure to provide adequate counselling may exacerbate damages suffered (and subsequently claimed for) by the parents.

Consent in obstetrics

35.127 Many maternity units ask women to sign for any anaesthetic or operative procedure required for the delivery of their child when they book into hospital for antenatal care and confinement. It is difficult to understand what protection such a document offers to either the woman or her attendants. There is no possible way such a document could reasonably be regarded as providing evidence that real consent to any particular procedure was obtained.

35.128 At the other extreme women are asked to give their consent to a procedure on behalf of themselves and their baby at the height of labour when they are distressed by pain, often physically and emotionally exhausted, and under the influence of narcotic drugs. No one is likely to complain that a life-saving operation carried out under these circumstances was done without consent, but if in addition a non-essential procedure such as sterilisation is added at such a time then the woman may have just cause for complaint.

35.129 A tightrope has to be walked by the obstetrician to obtain meaningful consent appropriate to the situation. Anticipation of difficulties that can be foreseen is the key to the solution to this problem, so that the woman is adequately informed as the story unfolds. Avoidance of the problem does not help the woman's understanding of what is required for her proper management, neither does the untimely and exaggerated expression of complications that may, but are unlikely, to occur.

35.130 It is not generally accepted practice to obtain written consent for some obstetric procedures, which nevertheless may carry with them profound consequences, such as induction of labour, artificial rupture of the membranes, the acceleration of labour, the use of forceps, breech delivery and twin delivery under general anaesthesia. There should be no problems so long as the woman is properly informed and implicitly gives her consent. Further anomalies exist, particularly in respect of procedures that primarily affect the baby. For example, written consent is not usually obtained for antenatal blood tests, screening procedures, amniocentesis or CVS. Written consent is however usually obtained for HIV antibody testing.

35.131 The solution is not the profusion of yet more consent forms; rather the problem can be dealt with by providing written information to reinforce oral explanations and to be used by the woman for future reference. For example, a brief written explanation of antenatal blood tests and ultrasound examination given at the first visit to the antenatal clinic to provide information saves time for the staff and may prompt the mother to ask further questions if she needs the answer. Similarly, those contemplating the use of epidural analgesia or seeking sterilisation after delivery can be given a written summary of the issues involved.

GYNAECOLOGY

35.132 The main causes for complaint are summarised in Table 35.6.

Sterilisation

35.133 Female sterilisation is responsible for more litigation than any other single surgical procedure, either because of defective consent or because the operation was unsuccessful. There is no consensus about the most reliable technique although increasingly laparoscopic methods are employed in place of open surgery (laparotomy) largely for reasons of cost and convenience.

35.134 The most popular method at open surgery is the Pomeroy technique (Bishop and Nelms 1930), in which the tube is drawn up into a loop, ligated at its base with catgut and the redundant loop excised. Provided that the technique is followed scrupulously, the operation is highly effective. The key to success is the use of an absorbable suture, allowing the cut ends of the tube to retract; it is the gap which sterilises the patient. Failure usually results from some attempt to modify and 'improve' the original technique.

35.135 Laparoscopic methods involve either diathermy coagulation of part of the tube or the application of silastic (Falope) rings or clips (Hulka-Clemens or Filshie). When clips are applied it is particularly important for the operator to ensure that the clip is applied to the appropriate part of the Fallopian tube where it is narrow so that the clip may completely occlude the lumen; application of clips to the wider ampulla is more likely to leave a channel open. In an endeavour to reduce the failure rate many surgeons now apply two clips to each uterine tube. Diathermy coagulation has been abandoned by the majority of gynaecologists not only because of the higher failure rate, but also because of the inherent risk of causing serious damage to neighbouring organs, even if the tubes are coagulated with the safer technique using bipolar (rather than unipolar) diathermy.

35.136 Surgical mistakes are much more likely to occur with the closed laparoscopic methods than when the abdomen is open at laparotomy, particularly if the surgeon is inexperienced and unsupervised. Instead of coagulating, or applying rings or clips to the tubes, the neighbouring round ligaments are mistaken for them.

35.137 Whatever method of sterilisation is employed, a properly performed operation may still fail in its purpose. There are two principal mechanisms; the two halves of the divided Fallopian tube may come together and rejoin ('recanalisation') or a tubo-peritoneal fistula may form in the proximal segment. When natural regeneration of the uterine tube occurs, macroscopic inspection may show no evidence of previous surgery. On microscopic examination the join will usually be evident to the pathologist for whilst the inner and outer epithelium of the tube renews itself, the muscle in between is incapable of regeneration and heals by the formation of scar tissue (collagen). Fistula formation is particularly likely following diathermy coagulation of the tubes and when non-absorbable materials are used to occlude the tubes.

35.138 An advantage of sterilisation carried out at open operation is that the portion of the tubes removed may be subjected to histological examination. Following the failure of a sterilisation such an operation takes on a particular forensic significance. The operator has an opportunity and a duty to inspect carefully the site of previous surgery and to send the entire Fallopian tube en-bloc to the pathologist with a specific request to search for the reason of failure. If the second operation is undertaken by laparoscopy, the operator has only the gross appearances of the tube upon which to rely and often cannot properly advance an explanation for the failure.

35.139 Failure rates for female sterilisation are usually quoted as in the range of 3–5 per thousand women. There is no agreement that any particular technique is to be preferred; the choice is usually determined by the patient's convenience and the surgeon's skills. It follows that the failure to use a particular technique is unlikely to succeed as an allegation of negligence save only that the use of diathermy coagulation through the laparoscope is no longer acceptable.

35.140 Controversy still surrounds the performance of sterilisation during pregnancy, either at the time of Caesarean section, in the puerperium or in combination with abortion. Some reported series have shown higher failure rates at this time – but there is no agreement. Whilst planned Caesarean section may be an opportune moment to perform simultaneous sterilisation, consent for sterilisation cannot properly be obtained in the context of an emergency section. Where a decision for sterilisation is combined with a request for the termination of a pregnancy there is undoubtedly a much higher incidence of regret. There is also a significant increase in morbidity and mortality, which led the authors of the 1982–1984 report on Confidential Inquiries into Maternal Deaths to express reservations about the combined procedure.

35.141 *Abortion* is defined as the expulsion of the products of conception before 24 weeks of pregnancy. In fact there is no difference between an abortion and a miscarriage, but in the public mind the word abortion carries with it overtones that it was the result of a deliberate act, either criminal or therapeutic. Natural or spontaneous abortion is described in several stages of threatened, inevitable, incomplete and complete. The meaning of these terms is literal.

35.142 Medically induced abortions should be carried out under the terms and regulations of the Abortion Act 1967 (as amended by the Human Fertilisation and Embryology Act 1991). The techniques used to achieve it vary in accordance with the duration of pregnancy and with the skill and expertise of the surgeon. The medical errors occurring in connection with the operation include:

(1) failure to terminate the pregnancy;
(2) damage to the uterus by perforation leading to haemorrhage; and
(3) sometimes damage to neighbouring organs, particularly the bowel and bladder.

35.143 *Laparoscopy* is increasingly employed not only for diagnosis, the investigation of infertility, and for sterilisation but for much more extensive pelvic surgery including the removal of ovarian tumours and even hysterectomy. The operation involves the passage, blind, of the Veress' needle into the peritoneal cavity, in order to create a pneumoperitoneum. The procedure, in skilled and experienced hands, is simple; it has become one of the commonest of all gynaecological operations. It is essential for safe practice that junior staff are properly trained and the operation is only delegated to them when they have demonstrated a sound and meticulous technique. An increasing number of claims are being brought (and many have already been settled) for the occasionally fatal complication of posterior abdominal wall vessel injury (Figure 35.13). This particular injury can only happen if the operator choses the umbilical site for the insertion of the Veress' needle and furthermore directs the needle backwards to the posterior abdominal wall. The resulting injury to the aorta and its main branches or to the inferior vena cava and its major tributaries produces an immediately life-threatening crisis. Several deaths have been reported. With proper care this type of injury to fixed structures within the abdominal cavity whose anatomy and surface markings are well known is always avoidable. The bowel however is ubiquitous within the abdomen and even in skilled hands, the occasional bowel injury may not be avoidable. Provided the injury is recognised and the bowel repaired, long term sequelae are uncommon.

35.144 *Hysterectomy* may also result in damage to surrounding structures particularly when, as in endometriosis or cancer, the anatomy is grossly distorted. The structures most at risk are the rectum, the bladder and the ureters. Several successful actions have been brought for damage to the ureter whose intimate relations with the gynaecological organs are, or should be, well known to the gynaecologist. In conditions of *normal* anatomy, there is seldom an excuse for damage to the ureter. In circumstances of difficult surgery the damage may not be avoidable but should *always* be recognised:

The venial sin is injury to the ureter, but the mortal sin is failure of recognition.[1]

1 Higgins C H 'Ureteral Injuries' (1962) Journal of the American Medical Association 182, 3 (October 20): 225.

Consent for gynaecological procedures

35.145 The general principles for consent to surgery are explained in Chapter 12. Gynaecological surgery not only involves issues common to all forms of surgery, namely the risks of the procedure itself but also those relating to future childbearing capacity and sexual enjoyment.

35.146 For consent to be real, the woman must have a clear understanding of what is intended, the possible alternatives to the procedure and the common sequelae. The patient's signature on a form does not provide evidence that she has been properly counselled. The evidence for this must be derived from her recollection, which usually is a matter of credibility between her and the doctor concerned. Correspondence between the surgeon and the general practitioner may provide evidence that proper information was or was not given. Rarely, a surgeon may note some of the details of his discussion with the woman in advising her and obtaining her consent. If the advice is given in a true spirit of providing her with information adequate to make her choice, it is unlikely that a well-informed woman will complain that she was not properly advised. Consent is a matter of trust between the patient and the doctor; proper fulfilment of that trust should be the most important factor in reducing complaints leading to litigation, rather than a form of words agreed to by signature of the woman in terms which are non-specific, not easily understood and designed for the defence of the doctor.

35.147 Recently the Department of Health has issued guidance[1] and recommended an improved format for consent forms.

1 NHS Management Executive *A Guide to Consent for Examination or Treatment* (1990) (Department of Health, HC (90) 22).

35.148 A form of consent should fairly provide protection in the form of a contract for both the patient and the doctor. It should not require either a bespoke specification of the procedure to be carried out, or a detailed catalogue of the possible complications. It should only need to record the understanding of the woman of the intentions of the surgeon in general terms. The details should be matters of trust. Such mutual trust cannot be fostered, if the task of obtaining consent is delegated to a junior doctor with little experience either with human relationships or the operation concerned. The duty of obtaining real consent for the operation, rather than a signature to a form of words, must be the duty of the surgeon who is to carry out the operation.

35.149 Doctors exhibit paradoxical attitudes in respect of obtaining written consent to procedures concerning birth control. Some doctors, especially those who specialise in family planning, but not usually consultant gynaecologists or general practitioners, require written consent before they insert an intra-uterine contraceptive device, but not before they prescribe an oral contraceptive pill. Nevertheless, it is accepted practice that women should be informed of certain risks and warning symptoms of complications associated with the use of steroidal contraceptives and IUCDs.

35.150 Most doctors believe that it is right and important to warn women who wish to use oral contraceptives of the symptoms that may herald possible thrombo-embolic complications, such as headaches, visual disturbances, chest pain and pain in the legs. Most women are also provided with this and additional information, including a list of the contraindications of the use of oral contraceptives, in information leaflets inserted into the packet by the manufacturers.

35.151 Women who are given long-term injectable steroidal contraceptives, such as Depo-Provera, are usually warned of the incidence of menstrual disturbance, but less often of the possible delay in return of fertility and of other side effects, which may be unpleasant.

35.152 It is accepted that women should be told of the pain and menstrual upsets sometimes associated with wearing an IUCD. Less often and less explicitly are they told of the risk of infection and the relative increase in ectopic pregnancy.

35.153 Written consent is usually obtained for surgical termination of pregnancy under general anaesthesia but rarely when pregnancy is terminated, usually for fetal abnormality, by 'medical means' in a waking woman. The practice differs widely in the amount and quality of the information given to a woman who is to have a pregnancy terminated and there is no consensus in respect of standard practice. Two issues have been contested.

35.154 First, whether or not there is a duty to warn that despite carrying out an operation to terminate a pregnancy, it may nevertheless continue. This problem most often arises with attempts to terminate pregnancy early – before 9 weeks. The possibility of this happening is about 1 in 1,000; such accidents usually also involve allegations of delay in diagnosing continuation of the pregnancy so that a further attempt to terminate the pregnancy is no longer possible or acceptable to the woman. Secondly complaints have been made in respect of failure to warn (as distinct from its actual occurrence) that during the course of an abortion damage may be done to the uterus and/or other intra-abdominal organs, or that the operation may result in subsequent subfertility. However, because of the relative safety of early abortion, up to 14 weeks, in comparison with the risks of the pregnancy continuing, it is not accepted practice to warn of the risks of inadvertent damage caused by operation.

35.155 The signature of a Jehovah's Witness that she does not wish to have a blood transfusion under any circumstance is usually sought (Figure 35.14) whereas the risk inherent in blood transfusion is not acknowledged by obtaining consent from a patient who is to receive transfusion.

35.156 *Consent for sterilisation* places peculiar responsibilities upon the surgeon. It has been accepted for 25 years that women seeking sterilisation should be warned that the operation should be regarded as irreversible. It should not be contemplated or undertaken therefore, unless childbearing is complete. This warning is given almost without exception. However, emphasis on the irreversibility of sterilisation has led many women in the past to believe that this also means it cannot fail. But failure of sterilisation is a relatively common occurrence, in no way related to the concept of irreversibility. Since the early 1980s expert opinion has generally been to the effect that warnings of failure were not only appropriate but necessary. Since that time most hospitals have developed special written forms of consent for sterilisation, spelling out the appropriate risks (Figure 35.15), a practice endorsed by the Department of Health in the Red Book.

35.157 No other warnings in respect of sterilisation are issued as a matter of standard practice. However, practice is changing and it is now more common for the woman to be warned about the less common sequelae of ectopic pregnancy (associated with failure of and attempts to reverse sterilisation) and menstrual disturbance, as well as the explanation of all the alternative methods available to her – including vasectomy.

COMMON RECURRING THEMES

35.158 In my personal practice of some 400 medico-legal reports there are three powerful recurring themes. First, most successful litigants have suffered not from one single error of management but a whole cascade of deficiencies. This is particularly true in obstetric injury to the fetus where errors in the antenatal clinic, lack of consultant supervision and poor preparation for labour are exacerbated by poor systems of control in the labour ward, substandard management, often by poorly supervised junior staff leading to critical errors in the interpretation of vaginal examinations and CTG traces, culminating in a disastrous operative delivery of an already compromised baby. Matters are often made much worse by negative attitudes by obstetric and midwifery staff, particularly *after* the accident has occurred.

35.159 The second theme is delay. Delay is ubiquitous in obstetric malpractice. Care of the obstetric patient is all about the timely recognition of abnormalities and swift intervention. Delay in recognition of fetal distress and dysfunctional labour commonly ends in disaster. Even when problems are recognised, delay in implementation may exacerbate them. The same theme runs through gynaecology with delay in responding to the abnormal cervical smear, delay in recognising the ectopic pregnancy and post-operative delay in recognising complications resulting from surgical error.

35.160 The third theme is communication. Communication is the key to avoiding litigation. While good practice may provide a reasonable defence to litigation, good communication will often obviate it. The great majority of plaintiffs referred to me for expert opinions have as their main complaint that no one told them why the accident occurred. Often, an innocent explanation is available but is not given; that explanation surfaces only during the litigation process. Even when the explanation is not innocent, the adult patient may refrain from litigation if given an early and frank explanation of the accident.

BIBLIOGRAPHICAL REFERENCES

A list of references has been compiled on the assumption that generally speaking an expert has to rely on the opinions and advice given by his peers in the current textbooks. Seldom is it that a plaintiff's expert will be able to make a case by relying upon learned articles. Such articles from recent journals are of more use to a defendant to show that there is in fact doubt about the accepted learning and that there is a spectrum of opinion in respect of the matter at issue. Specialist journals are likely to be quoted only in the defence of care given in academic centres of excellence. The list, therefore, mainly comprises the standard textbooks in their various editions published in Great Britain:

Baillière's Clinical Obstetrics and Gynaecology: International Practice and Research (Baillière Tindall). Four issues are published every year since 1987, each devoted to an up-to-date review of current learning in specific subjects.
Balen A H and Smith J H *The CTG in Practice* (Churchill Livingstone, 1992).
Bishop E and Nelms W F 'A Simple Method of Tubal Sterilization' (1930) NY State JM 30 (Feb 15): 4 214–216.
Bonney's Gynaecological Surgery (10th edn, revised by J M Monaghan, Baillière Tindall; 1st edn, 1911).
Brock D J H, Rodeck C H and Ferguson-Smith M A (eds) *Prenatal Diagnosis and Screening* (Churchill Livingstone, 1992).
Cardozo L D, Gibb D M F, Studd J W W and Cooper D J 'Should we Abandon Kjelland's Forceps?' (1983) British Medical Journal, 287: 315–317.
Chamberlain G (ed) *Modern Antenatal Care of the Fetus* (Blackwell Scientific Publications, 1990).
Crichton D 'A Reliable Method of Establishing the Level of the Fetal Head in Obstetrics' (1974) South African Medical Journal 12, 784–787.
De Swiet M *Medical Disorders in Obstetric Practice* (2nd edn, Blackwell Scientific Publications, 1989; 1st edn, 1984).
Dewhurst's *Textbook of Obstetrics and Gynaecology for Postgraduates* (4th edn, ed C R Whitfield, Blackwell Scientific Publications, 1986; 1st edn, 1972).
Donald I *Practical Obstetric Problems* (5th edn, Lloyd-Luke, 1979; 1st edn, 1955).
Gibb D and Arulkumaran S *Fetal Monitoring in Practice* (Butterworth Heinemann, 1992).
Haines and Taylor *Obstetrical and Gynaecological Pathology* (3rd edn, ed H Fox, Churchill Livingstone, 1987; 1st edn, 1962).
Hawkins D F *Drugs and Pregnancy* (2nd edn, Churchill Livingstone, 1987; 1st edn, 1983).
Hibbard B M *Principles of Obstetrics* (Butterworths, 1988).
Hodgson J E *Abortion and Sterilisation: Medical and Social Aspects* (Academic Press, Grune & Stratton, 1981).
Huisjes H J and Lind T *Early Pregnancy Failure* (Churchill Livingstone, 1990).
Jeffcoate's Principles of Gynaecology (5th edn, ed V R Tindall, Butterworths, 1987; 1st edn, 1957).
Llewellyn-Jones D *Fundamentals of Obstetrics and Gynaecology*, vol 1 *Obstetrics*, vol 2 *Gynaecology* (5th edn, Faber and Faber, 1990; 1st edn, 1969).
Maye's Midwifery (11th edn, ed B R Sweet, Baillière Tindall, 1988; 1st edn, 1937).
Moir D D *Obstetric Anaesthesia and Analgesia* (3rd edn, Baillière Tindall, 1986; 1st edn, 1976).
Munro Kerr's Operative Obstetrics (10th edn, ed P R Myerscough, Baillière Tindall, 1982; 1st edn, 1908).
Myles' Textbook for Midwives (11th edn, ed V R Bennett and L K Brown, Churchill Livingstone, 1989; 1st edn, 1953).
O'Driscoll K and Meagher D *Active Management of Labour* (2nd edn, Baillière Tindall, 1986; 1st edn, 1980).
O'Grady J P *Modern Instrumental Delivery* (Williams and Wilkins, 1988).
Pearce J M and Steele S A *A Manual of Labour Ward Practice* (John Wiley & Sons, 1987).
Philipp E and Setchell M *Scientific Foundations of Obstetrics and Gynaecology* (4th edn, Butterworth Heinemann, 1991; 1st edn, 1970).
Progress in Obstetrics and Gynaecology (vol 1 (1981) – vol 9 (1992), ed J Studd, Churchill Livingstone).

Recent Advances in Obstetrics and Gynaecology (17th edn, ed J Bonnar, Churchill Livingstone, 1992; 1st edn, 1926).

Report on Confidential Inquiries into Maternal Deaths in the United Kingdom (1988–1990) (HMSO, 1994). The latest in a series of triennial reports beginning in 1952–1954.

Robb and Smith's Operative Surgery: Gynaecology and Obstetrics (4th edn, ed J M Monaghan, Butterworths, 1987; 1st edn, 1956–1958).

Royal College of Obstetricians and Gynaecologists *Litigation and Obstetrics and Gynaecology* (Proceedings of the 14th Study Group, 1985). This is one of a series of published proceedings of RCOG study groups edited by various experts and dealing with specific topics, including laparoscopy, ultrasound, genetic defects, perinatal surveillance, oncology, etc).

Shepherd J H and Monaghan J M *Clinical Gynaecological Oncology* (2nd edn, Blackwell Scientific Publications, 1990; 1st edn, 1985).

Shaw R W, Soutter W P and Stanton S L *Gynaecology* (Churchill Livingstone, 1992).

Shaw's Textbook of Operative Gynaecology (5th edn, ed J Howkins and C N Hudson, Churchill Livingstone, 1985; 1st edn, 1954).

Steer P J *Fetal Heart Rate Patterns and Their Clinical Interpretation: Sonicaid Handbook* (Sonicaid Ltd, 1982).

Studd J *The Management of Labour* (Blackwell Scientific Publications, 1985).

Turnbull A and Chamberlain G V P *Obstetrics* (Churchill Livingstone, 1989).

Vacca A *Handbook of Vacuum Extraction in Obstetric Practice* (Edward Arnold, 1992).

FIGURE 35.1 ANTENATAL CO-OPERATION CARD

THIS CARD CONTAINS THE FACTS THAT YOUR DOCTOR AND MIDWIFE NEED TO KNOW ABOUT YOUR PREGNANCY.

Please take it with you on every visit to your doctor, clinic or hospital and ask whoever sees you to fill it in.

SHARED CARE
If you are having shared care between your family doctor and your hospital, you will normally be asked to visit each one at alternate appointments.

Here is a plan to help you

When First Pregnant	GP	Referral to Hospital
At 12-16 Wk.	Hospital	Booked Blood Tests Ultra Sound Exam Introductory Parentcraft
At 16-18 Wk.	GP	Blood Tests at Hospital
At 20-28 Wk.	GP	
At 28 Wk.	Hospital	Blood Tests. 'Kick Chart' Cert. of Confinement Parentcraft Classes
At 30 Wk.	GP/or Midwives Clinic	
At 32 Wk.	Hospital	
At 34 Wk.	GP/or Midwives Clinic	
At 36 Wk.	Hospital Consultant	Blood Tests Plans for Labour
At 37 Wk.	GP/or Midwives Clinic	
At 38 Wk.	Hospital	
At 39 Wk.	GP/or Midwives Clinic	
40 Wk.	Hospital	

POST NATAL EXAMINATION 6 WEEKS AFTER THE BIRTH, SHOULD BE DONE EITHER BY YOUR GP OR AT THE HOSPITAL.

THIS VISIT IS VERY IMPORTANT

TERMS/WORDS THAT YOUR DOCTOR OR MIDWIFE MAY USE

If there are some that are not here, please ask your doctor or midwife.

Fetus	– Baby before birth
Fundal height	– Size of the womb
Uterine size	– Size of the womb
B.P.	– Blood Pressure
Presentation	– End of the baby pointing down
C.Ceph Cephalic	– Head pointing down
Vx Vertex	– Head pointing down
T Tr Transverse	– Baby lying sideways
B Br Breech	– Bottom pointing down
Relation to brim	– Whether head is in the pelvis
E Eng Engaged	– Baby's head in pelvis
FH H	– Baby's heart heard
FM (N) F	– Fetal movements (not) felt
Oedema	– Swelling
Hb Haemaglobin	– Iron Level in Blood (Anaemia)
NAD	– No abnormality discovered
VE	– Vaginal examination
Cx Cervix	– Opening to the Womb
VD	– Routine tests for syphilis
Rubella	– German measles
AF/P alpha feto protein	– Routine test for spina bifida
MSU	– Urine test
U/S	– Ultrasound scan test to look at the size of your baby

If you have any questions or do not understand something, please ask your doctor, midwife or health visitor.

PERSONAL, MATERNITY RECORD CARD

BOOKED AT **NORTH MIDDLESEX HOSPITAL**

TEL. **807 3071 EXT. 500**

IN EMERGENCY ONLY 884 1898
LABOUR WARD 'CRISIS' PHONE

FOR AMBULANCE – 999

NAME DOB

ADDRESS

CONSULTANT

HOSPITAL NUMBER

GENERAL PRACTITIONER

ADDRESS Phone No.

PREVIOUS PREGNANCIES

PRESENT PREGNANCY LMP EDD

RELEVANT MEDICAL HISTORY

FAMILY HISTORY

PARENTCRAFT

DMD
PED
FULL STAY

Form 581

FIGURE 35.2 ANTENATAL CO-OPERATION CARD (STANDARD OBSERVATIONS)

GENERAL EXAMINATION

MEDICINES

ALLERGIES

DATE OF QUICKENING

INVESTIGATIONS

BLOOD GROUP

SEROLOGY

AFP

SICKLE

RUBELLA

THALASSAEMIA

MSU

CYTOLOGY

AMNIOCENTESIS

ULTRASOUND

ANTE-NATAL EXAMINATIONS

Date	Mat in wks	Size of Uterus	Press & Pos.	Relation P/P-Brim	FH	B/P	Urine	Oedema	Hb	Wgt	Comments	Signature

ANTE NATAL ADMISSIONS

1) Admitted Reason Discharged

2) Admitted Reason Discharged

3) Admitted Reason Discharged

LABOUR/DELIVERY

DURATION OF LABOUR

TIME/DATE OF DELIVERY

TYPE OF DELIVERY

3rd STAGE

BLOOD LOSS

PERINEUM

ANY PROBLEMS / SPECIAL NOTES

INFANT MALE/FEMALE

APGAR 1' 5' B.Wt.

ADMITTED TO S.C.B.U. YES/NO

TRANSFERRED ELSEWHERE? YES/NO

IF YES – SPECIFY

DISCHARGED WITH MOTHER? YES/NO

IF NO, WHERE IS BABY?

IF YES, WEIGHT ON DISCHARGE Gm. DAY

HIPS NORMAL RIGHT YES/NO LEFT YES/NO

TESTES DESC. RIGHT YES/NO LEFT YES/NO

FEEDING

PROBLEMS:

FOLLOW UP AT HOSPITAL YES/NO

GUTHRIE TEST: DATE

PUERPERIUM

CONTRACEPTIVE ADVICE

HB ANTI. D. RUBELLA VACCINE

POST-NATAL (CLINIC) EXAMINATION

GENERAL CONDITION

VAGINAL EXAMINATION

BREASTS URINE

B/P HB

CONTRACEPTION

INFANT

FIGURE 35.3 ULTRASOUND MEASUREMENTS OF FETAL GROWTH

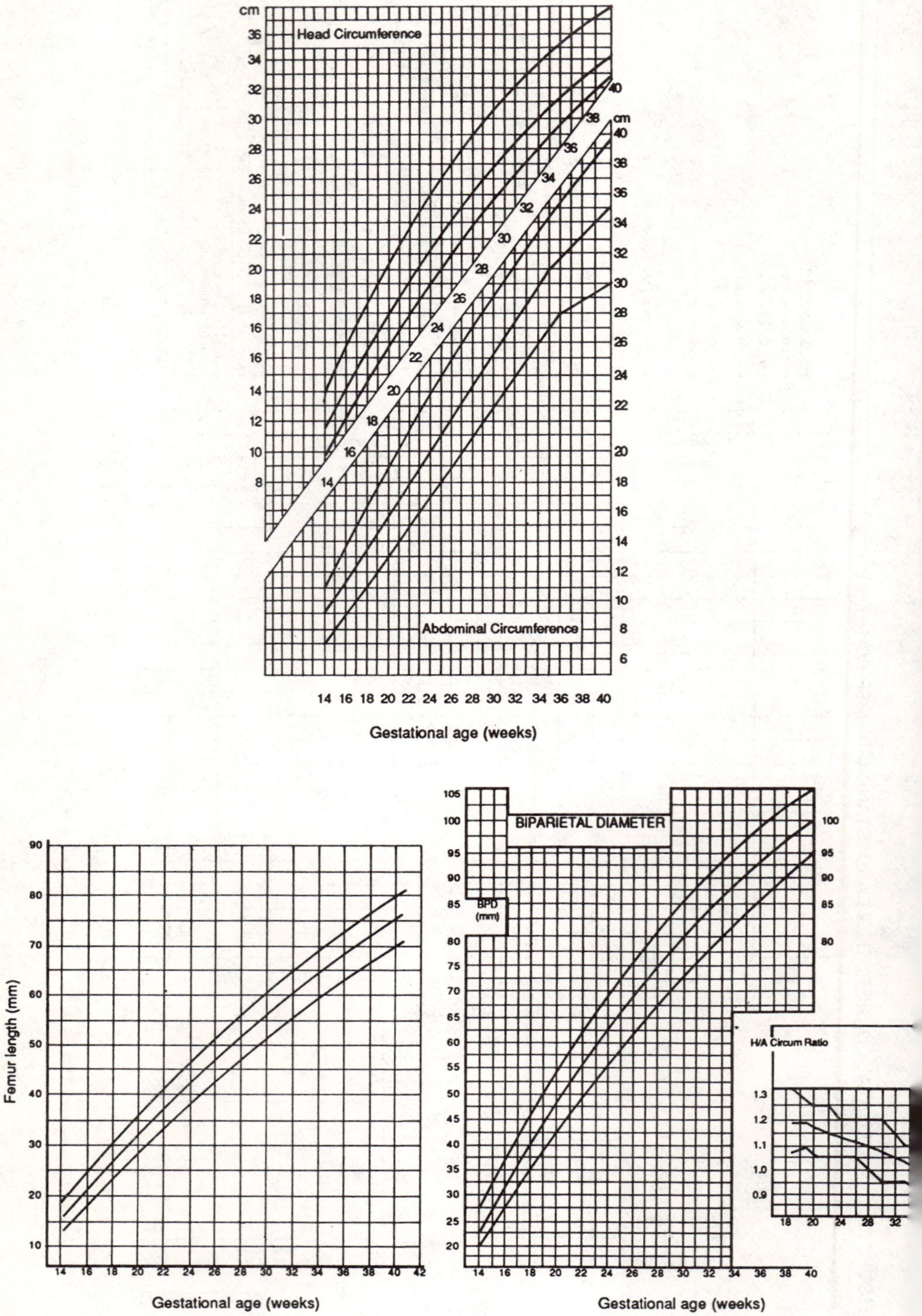

FIGURE 35.4 THE 'COUNT TO TEN' FETAL ACTIVITY CHART

The Cardiff 'count-to-ten' fetal activity chart

Name

Address

No.

Start date: 19

Duration of pregnancy

at start date:....................weeks ....days

Remember!
be HONEST
be ACCURATE

'Counting-to-ten'

This is a new and simple method by which the mother herself plays an important part in checking the health of her own baby. It involves counting the number of movements made by the baby during the day.

Starting at 9 o'clock in the morning, count the number of movements until the total equals 10. Then record the time taken to count-to-ten on the graph.

For example, if you start on say, Monday 7th July, 1988, and count to ten by 10 minutes past 2, block out the whole square between 2 p.m. and 2.30 p.m. (see 'A' in illustration). That is, rather than filling in the exact time, you must fill in the whole ½ hour period in which the 10th movement falls. It is not necessary to do any more counting until the following day when you start again at 9 a.m. and so on.

If by 9 p.m. your total is less than 10, fill in the actual number in the correct space below the thick line.

IMPORTANT

If you feel less than 10 movements for 2 days in a row (see 'B' in illustration)

Contact:

....

....

the following morning, and an appointment will be made for you to be seen by a Doctor straightaway.

But

If you feel no movements for 1 day (see 'C' in illustration) contact us immediately.

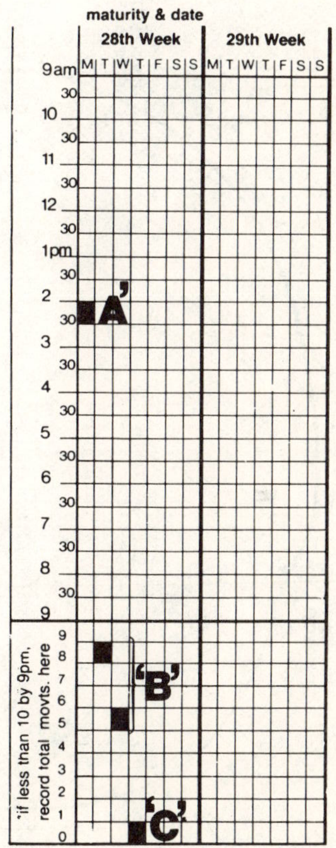

FIGURE 35.5 THE FETAL HEAD

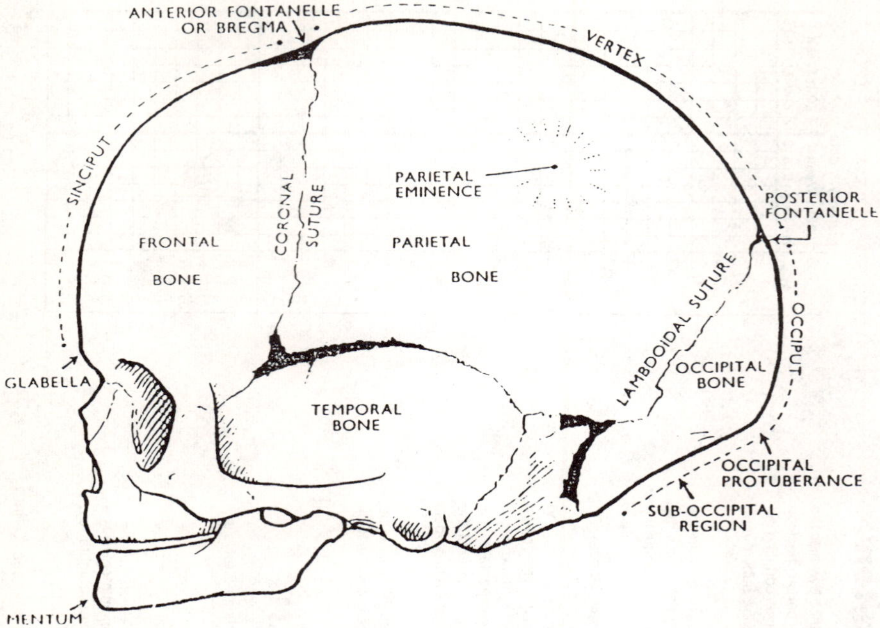

Figure 35.5A Fetal skull showing regions and landmarks of obstetrical importance

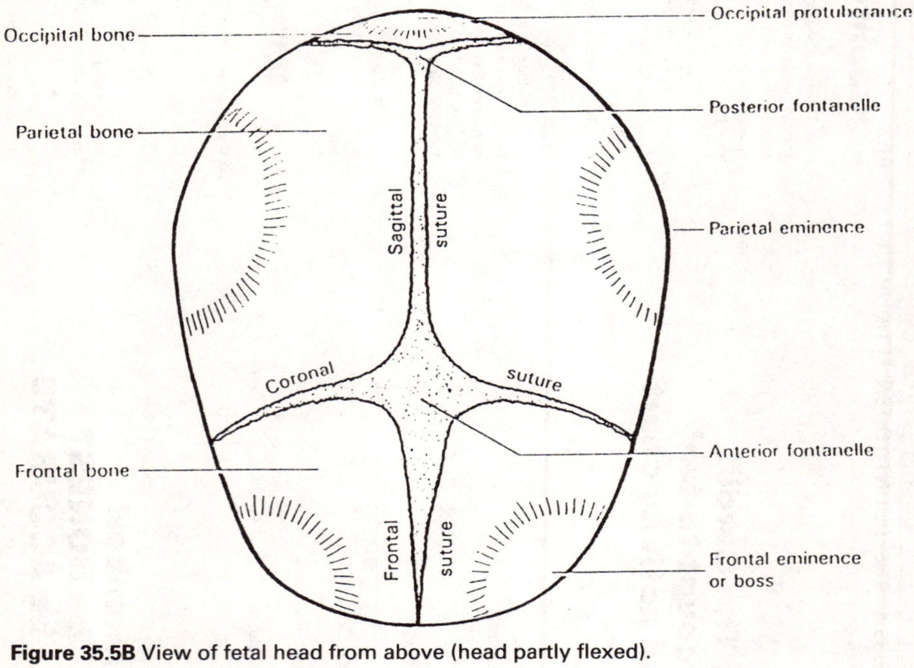

Figure 35.5B View of fetal head from above (head partly flexed).

Reproduced from *Myles' Textbook for Midwives*, Churchill Livingstone, 1989.

FIGURE 35.6 PROGRESSIVE DESCENT OF THE HEAD, ASSESSED IN FIFTHS STILL PALPABLE ABOVE THE PELVIC BRIM (AFTER CRICHTON, MODIFIED BY LASBREY)

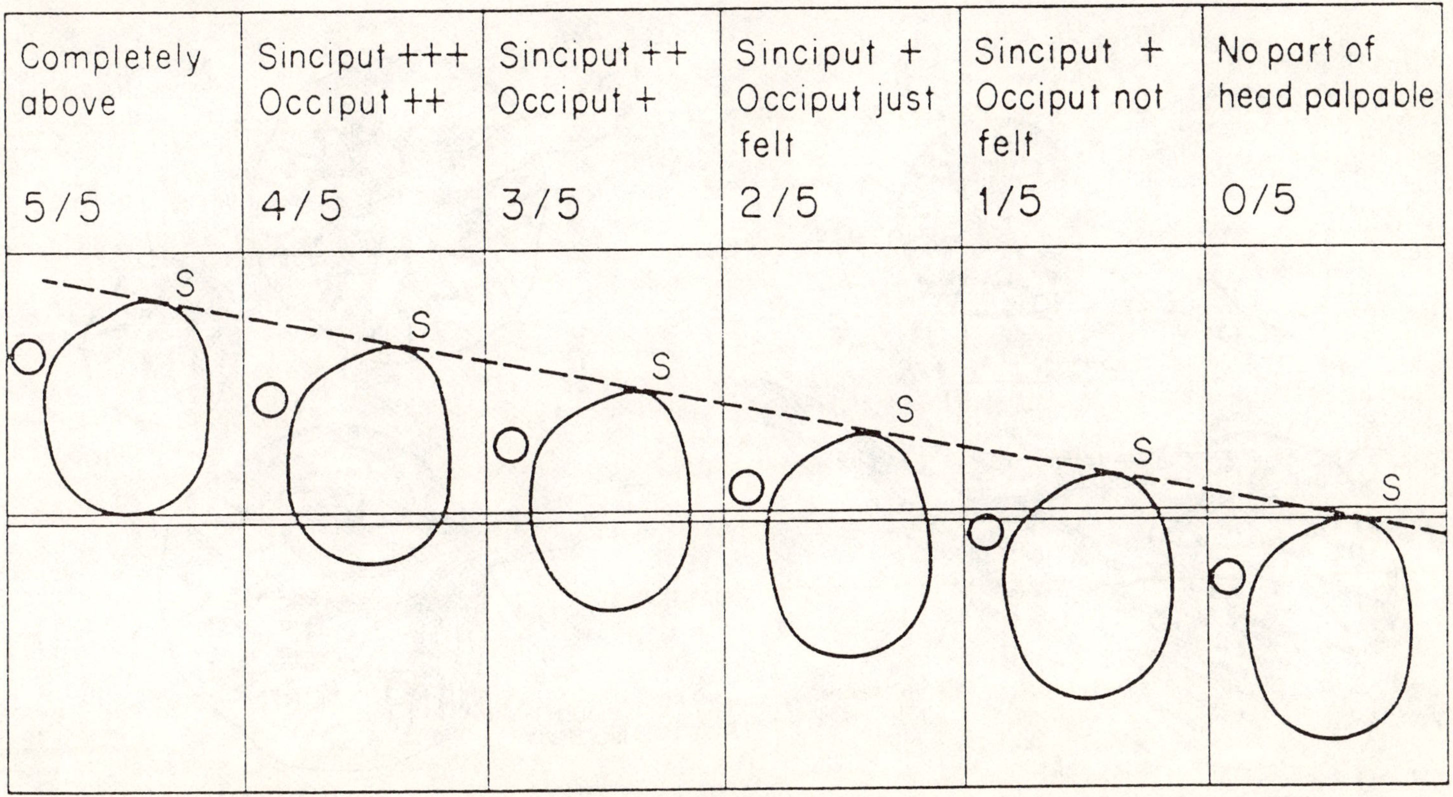

Reproduced from *Munro Kerr's Operative Obstetrics*, Baillière Tindall, 1982.

FIGURE 35.7 THE FOUR MOST COMMON ABNORMAL PLACENTAL FORMS

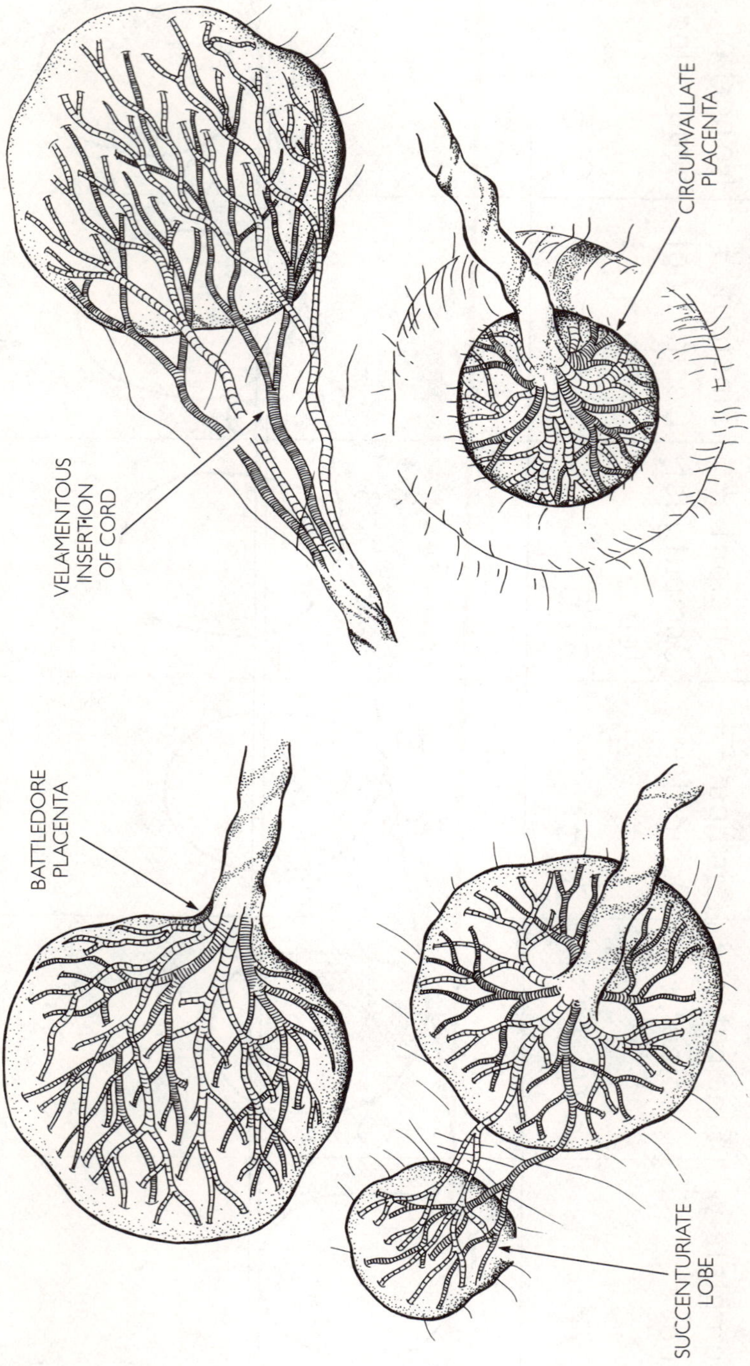

Reproduced from *Obstetrics*, Llewellyn Jones, Faber and Faber, 1990.

FIGURE 35.8 THE TWO RECORDINGS PRODUCED BY THE CARDIOTOCOGRAPH

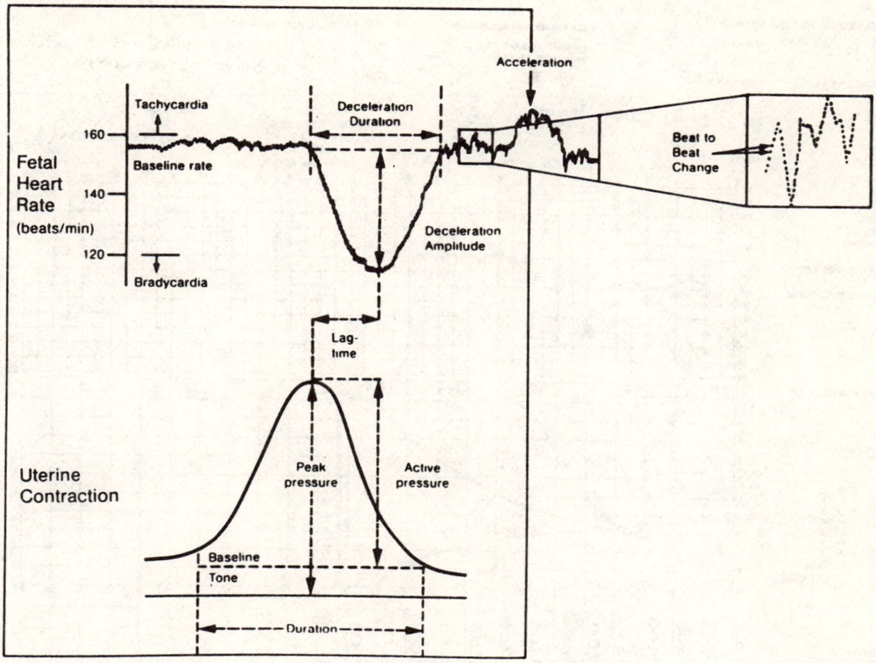

Reproduced from *Sonicaid Handbook*, 1982.

FIGURE 35.9 PROGRESS IN LABOUR RECORDED ON A PARTOGRAM

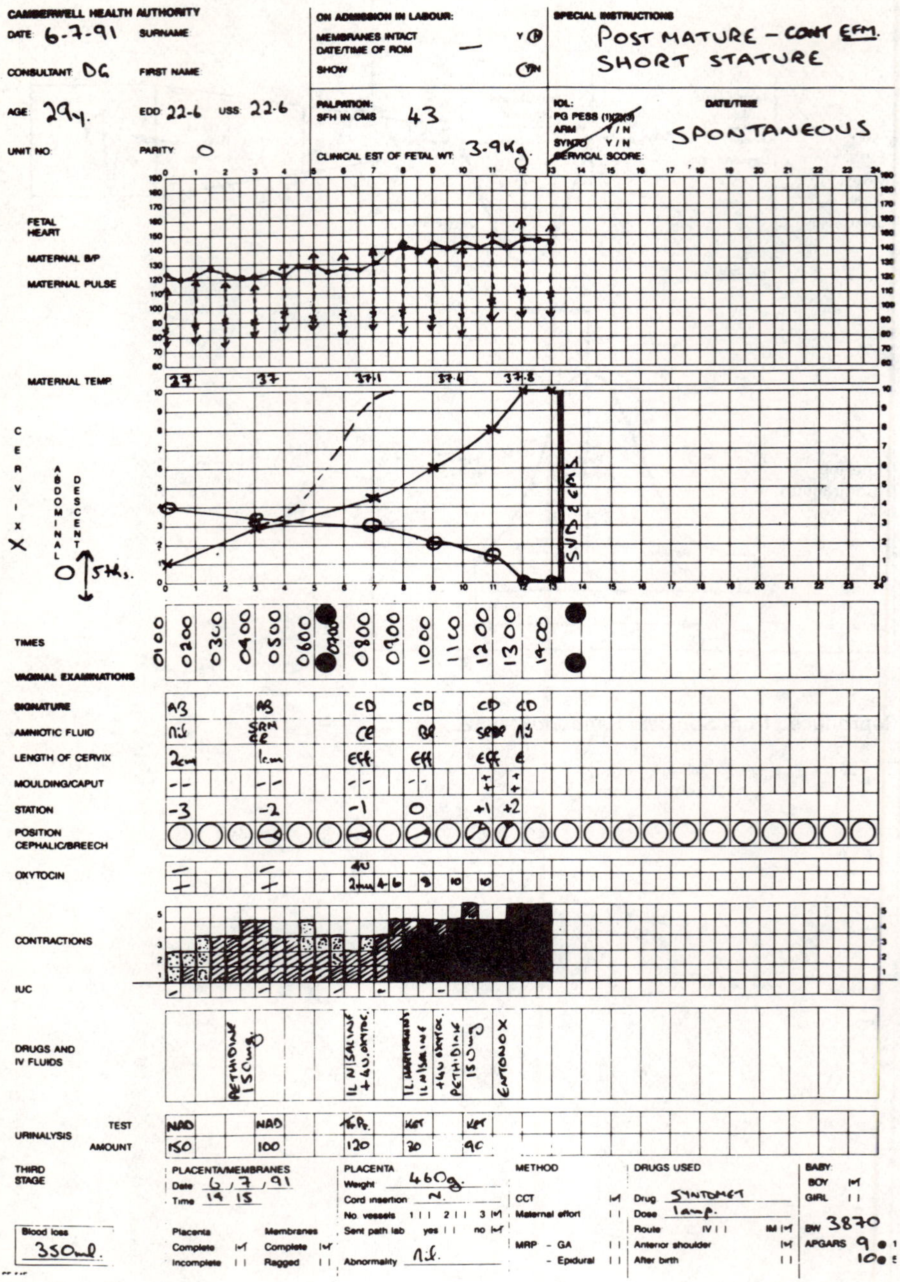

Reproduced from *Fetal Monitoring in Practice*, Gibb and Arulkumaran, Butterworth Heinemann, 1992.

FIGURE 35.10 PROGRESS OF LABOUR COMPARED WITH FIRST (PRIMIGRAVID) AND SUBSEQUENT (MULTIPARA) LABOURS

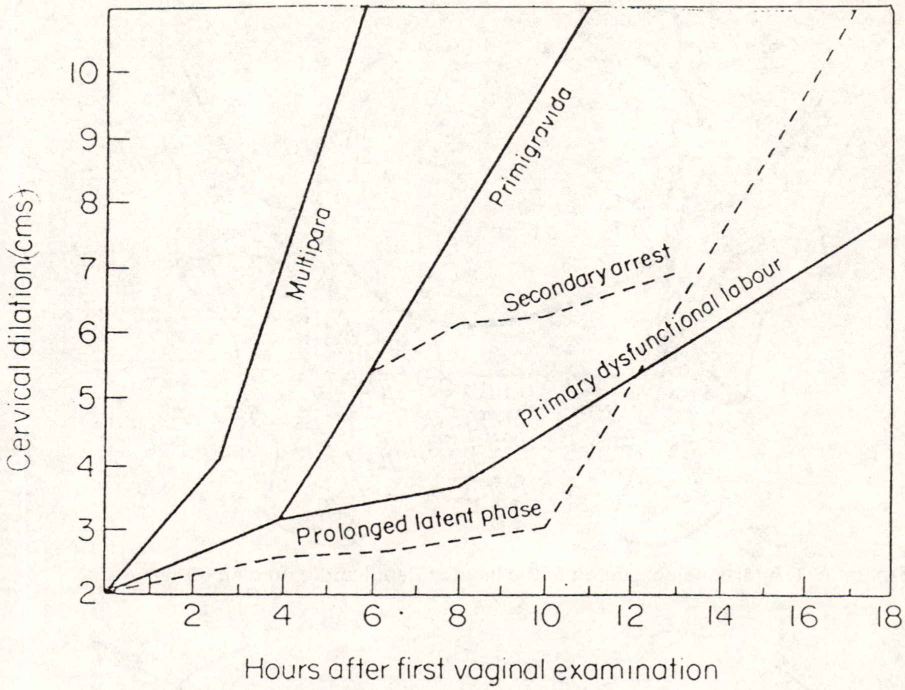

Reproduced from Dewhurst's *Integrated Obstetrics and Gynaecology for Postgraduates*, Blackwell, 1986.

FIGURE 35.11 STATION OF HEAD AND MOULDING AND CAPUT (a) DESTROYING RELIABILITY OF ASSESSING HEAD LEVEL BY STATION (b)

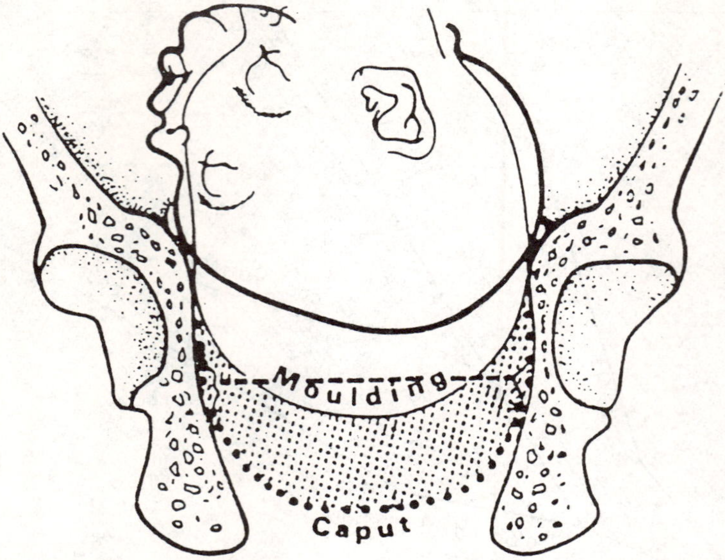

Figure 35.11A Misleading 'station of the head' if Caput and moulding exist

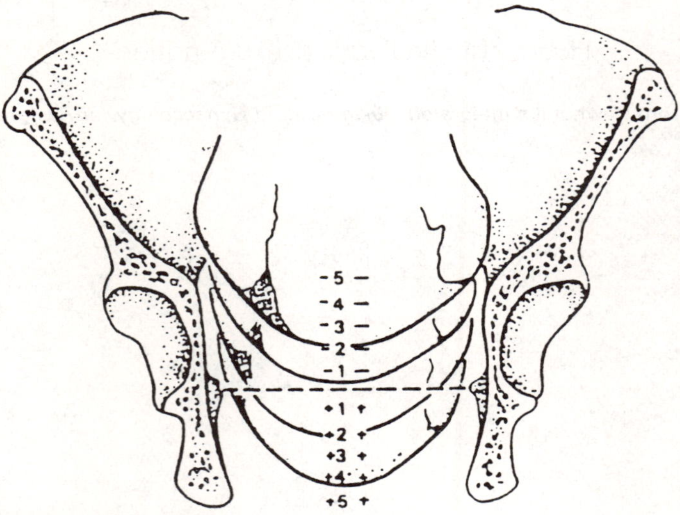

Figure 35.11B Station of the head

Reproduced with permission of the South African Medical Journal.

FIGURE 35.12 COMMUNICATION PROBLEMS IN THE LABOUR WARD

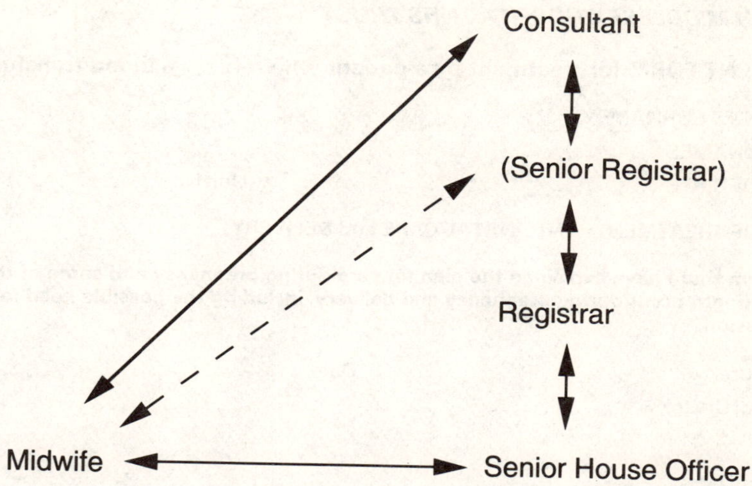

FIGURE 35.13 POSTERIOR ABDOMINAL WALL VESSEL INJURY

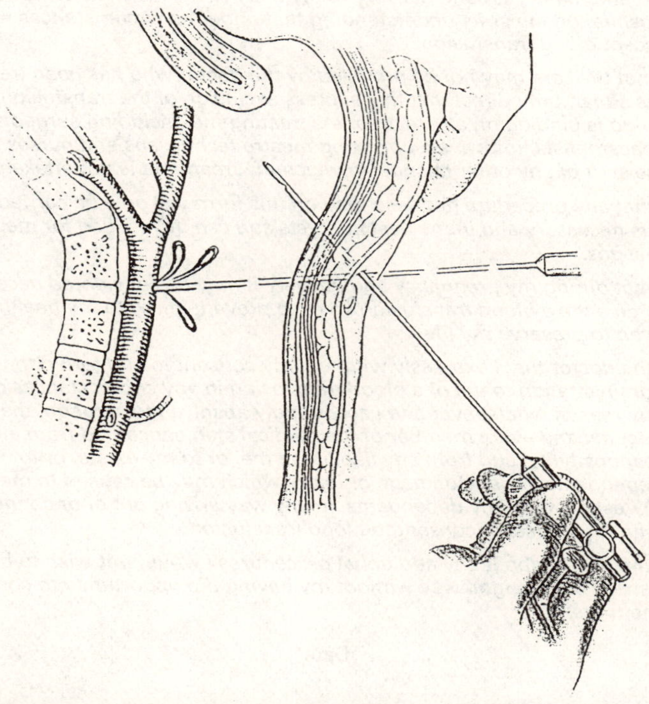

Reproduced from *Robb and Smith's Operative Surgery*, Butterworths, 1987.

FIGURE 35.14 CONSENT FORM FOR TREATMENT OF A PATIENT WHO REFUSES A BLOOD TRANSFUSION

NORTH MIDDLESEX HOSPITAL NHS TRUST

CONSENT FORM for treatment by a patient who refuses a blood transfusion

PATIENT'S SURNAME ....

OTHER NAMES ....

DATE OF BIRTH .... Unit No ....

TYPE OF TREATMENT: ANTE-NATAL CARE and DELIVERY

I confirm that I have explained the plan for care during pregnancy and some of the risks which might occur during pregnancy and delivery, including the possible need for blood transfusion.

Signature .... Date ....

Name of Doctor ....

PATIENT

1. *Please read this form very carefully.*
2. *If there is anything that you do not understand about the explanation, or if you want more information, you should ask the doctor.*
3. *Please check that all the information on this form is correct. If it is, and you understand the explanation, then sign the form.*

I agree	**to ante-natal care and delivery of my baby at the North Middlesex Hospital on the strict understanding that under no circumstances would I accept blood transfusion.*
I understand	**that the care may not be provided by the doctor who has been treating me so far, but I direct that this express exclusion of the transfusion of blood is binding on all practitioners treating me, including surgeons, anaesthetists, midwives, operating theatre technicians and nurses and on the staff of any other hospital in which my treatment is undertaken.*
	**that any procedure not described on this form will only be carried out if it is necessary and in my best interests and can be justified for medical reasons.*
	**that during my pregnancy and delivery it may be considered necessary to give me a blood transfusion so as to prevent injury to my health or even to preserve my life.*
I have told	**the doctor that I expressly withhold my consent to and forbid the administration to me of a blood transfusion in any circumstances or for any reason whatsoever and I accordingly absolve the surgeon, the hospital and every member of the medical staff concerned from all responsibility, and from any liability to me, or to my estate, or to my dependants, for any damage or injury which may be caused to me, or to my estate, or to my dependants, in any way arising out of or connected with my refusal to consent to blood transfusion.*
	the doctor about any additional procedures I would* ***not* *wish to be carried out straightaway without my having the opportunity to consider them first.*

Signature .... Date ....

Address ....

FIGURE 35.15 CONSENT FORM FOR STERILISATION

NORTH MIDDLESEX HOSPITAL NHS TRUST

CONSENT FORM for sterilisation

PATIENT'S SURNAME ....

OTHER NAMES ....

DATE OF BIRTH ....Unit No ....

TYPE OF OPERATION: STERILISATION

This operation will normally be conducted by the laparoscopy method and the Fallopian tubes closed by clips or rings. If the sterilisation cannot be performed in this way I have discussed the necessity of an abdominal incision which will involve extra days in hospital.

I confirm that I have explained the procedure and any anaesthetic (general/regional) required, to the patient in terms which in my judgement are suited to her understanding.

Signature .... Date ....

Name of Doctor ....

PATIENT

1. *Please read this form carefully.*
2. *If there is anything you do not understand about the explanation, or if you want more information, you should ask the doctor.*
3. *Please check that all the information on this form is correct. If it is, and you understand the explanation, then sign the form.*

I agree	**to have this operation, which has been explained to me by the doctor named on this form.*
	**to have the type of anaesthetic that I have been told about.*
I understand	**that the operation may not be done by the doctor who has been treating me so far.*
	**that the aim of the operation is to stop me having any children and it might not be possible to reverse the effects of the operation.*
	**that sterilisation can sometimes fail, and that there is a very small chance that I may become fertile again after some time.*
	**that any procedure in addition to the investigation or treatment described on this form will only be carried out if it is necessary and in my best interests and can be justified for medical reasons.*
I have told	**the doctor about any additional procedures I would* **not** *wish to be carried out straightaway without my having the opportunity to consider them first.*

Signature .... Date ....

Address ....

....

TABLE 35.1 OBSTETRIC CAUSES FOR COMPLAINT

(a) *Injuries to the baby*

Cerebral palsy
Stillbirth and early neonatal death
Brachial plexus injury (Erb's and Klumpke's paralysis of the arm)
Facial scars and other soft tissue injuries
Fractures of the skull and limbs
Failure to prevent Rhesus sensitisation.

(b) Wrongful abortion – termination of an otherwise viable pregnancy

(c) Wrongful birth of a handicapped child, because of failure to detect and/or prevent an inborn abnormality, e g neural tube defect, rubella syndrome, Down syndrome, haemoglobinopathy.

(d) *Maternal injuries*

Scars of the perineum and vagina causing difficult sexual intercourse
Loss of urinary control – stress incontinence, ureteric and vesico-vaginal fistula
Faecal incontinence and recto-vaginal fistula
Rupture of the uterus
Failure to remove vaginal or abdominal swabs
Anaesthetic awareness and/or failure adequately to relieve pain
Loss of future childbearing capacity from infection or the need for hysterectomy
Death or permanent brain damage due to eclampsia, anaesthesia, undetected and/or uncontrolled haemorrhage.

TABLE 35.2 ERRORS OF MEDICAL MANAGEMENT ASSOCIATED WITH CEREBRAL PALSY

Antenatal

Failure to detect or to take account of:

- high-risk factors*
- appropriate notes to draw attention to the need for special care
- fetal abnormality
- intra-uterine infection, eg rubella, toxoplasmosis, herpes
- abnormalities by making regular and appropriate clinical observations and ordering other special investigations (including ultrasound scans) throughout pregnancy and as often as the situation demands
- intra-uterine growth retardation
- symptoms and signs of impending eclampsia
- twins
- abnormal and/or unstable presentations
- cephalo-pelvic disproportion caused by a contracted pelvis and/or a large baby especially in a breech position
- risk of placental abruption
- placenta praevia
- the need to monitor fetal well-being
- premature labour

Labour

Failure to detect or to take account of:

- the need to monitor properly the dosage of oxytocin and fetal and maternal well-being, when it is used intravenously for the induction and acceleration of labour
- malpresentation
- disproportion
- umbilical cord complications, eg entanglement, presentation, prolapse and ruptured vasa praevia
- changes in the fetal heart rate
- the need to take an adequate fetal blood sample, if facilities are available, when it is indicated and to repeat the examination as indicted by the circumstances
- dysfunctional labour and the secondary arrest of labour
- the need to avoid difficult vaginal delivery especially in the presence of fetal distress
- the need to conduct an adequate trial of labour
- previous injury to the uterus (trial of scar)
- the need to conduct a proper trial of forceps
- the need to use the vacuum extractor properly
- the need to have adequate experience and expertise to carry out Caesarean section when difficulties could be anticipated
- the need to conduct delivery in an appropriate environment
- the need to have the necessary paediatric and anaesthetic assistance available.

Postnatal

Failure to detect or to take account of:

- the need to reverse the effect of narcotic drugs given to the mother
- the need to have the necessary paediatric assistance available
- the need to intubate and provide proper respiratory support for the baby
- the appropriate surroundings and expertise required and necessary for the further care of the baby.

*See Table 35.3

TABLE 35.3 HIGH-RISK FACTORS – OBSTETRICS

Pregnancy

First baby
Fourth or subsequent baby
Aged 30 years or more expecting first baby
Aged 35 years or more expecting subsequent baby
Previous subfertility
Repeated miscarriage
Previous stillbirth, neonatal death, abnormal baby, premature labour, or other obstetric abnormality in pregnancy or labour
Maternal disease:

- anaemia
- haemoglobinopathy
- hypertension (diastolic pressure 90 or more)
- renal infection
- diabetes
- auto-immune disease
- syphilis
- gonorrhoea etc
- HIV and AIDS

Rhesus negative with antibodies
Addictions:

- tobacco
- alcohol
- other drugs

Height less than 5 feet 2 inches and/or suspected cephalo-pelvic disproportion
High alpha fetoprotein
Antepartum haemorrhage
Excessive or abnormally reduced amniotic fluid volume
Excessive weight gain
Static weight
Decreased fetal movements
Postmature (over 42 weeks)

Labour

Premature (before 37 weeks)
Prolonged rupture of membranes (more than 24 hours)
Induced
Twins
Breech
Long latent phase
Secondary arrest
Meconium-stained amniotic fluid
CTG – late decelerations
– decreased variability
– complicated tachycardia
Failure of presenting part to descend
Maternal distress:

- keto-acidosis (dehydration)
- rise in maternal temperature
- rise in maternal blood pressure
- emotional

TABLE 35.4 CIRCUMSTANCES IN WHICH PERSONAL INVOLVEMENT BY A CONSULTANT IS ESSENTIAL IF ERRORS IN LABOUR MANAGEMENT ARE TO BE AVOIDED

1. **Breech labour**
2. **Suspected cephalopelvic disproportion**
   trial of labour
3. **Previous Caesarean section**
   trial of scar
   particularly the potentially dangerous use of Syntocinon (oxytocin) with a previous scar
4. **Twin labour**
   particularly where the first baby presents as a breech
5. **Diabetic pregnancy**
6. **Major haemoglobinopathy**

TABLE 35.5 CLASSIFICATION OF CTGs

Normal

Baseline rate of 120–160 bpm
Baseline variability 10–25 bpm
2 accelerations in 20 minutes and no decelerations

Suspicious

Absence of accelerations and any one of the following:

- Abnormal baseline rate (<110 >160)
- Reduced baseline variability or greatly increased variability
- Persistent early decelerations
- Variable decelerations

Abnormal

Abnormal baseline rate and abnormal variability
Late decelerations
Severe variable decelerations
Marked sinusoidal pattern

TABLE 35.6 CAUSES FOR COMPLAINT IN GYNAECOLOGY

(a) Failure of sterilisation sometimes leading to abortion or wrongful birth

(b) Complications of abortion, including:

- failure and sometimes wrongful birth
- perforation of the uterus and/or damage to other organs
- loss of future childbearing capacity due to infection or the need for hysterectomy

(c) Contraception

- failure to prevent pregnancy
- oral contraception and cardio-vascular accidents including death
- the side-effects of injectable steroidal contraceptives
- perforation of the uterus and infection following the introduction of intra-uterine contraceptive devices

(d) Failure to interpret or act appropriately upon cervical cytology

(e) Gynaecological surgery (including diagnostic and operative laparoscopy)

- defective consent
- posterior abdominal wall vessel injury at laparoscopy
- failure to detect internal haemorrhage
- injury to the gastro-intestinal tract
- injury to the bladder and/or ureters
- delay in the diagnosis of pregnancy, ectopic pregnancy and genital cancer
- inadvertent sterilisation by the introduction of infection or hysterectomy
- failure to remove swabs and other artefacts
- unnecessary operations

CHAPTER 36

Cardiothoracic surgery

Professor G H Smith *MB FRCS*

36.1 Cardiothoracic surgery is part of surgery in general and the standards of acceptable practice are identical to those of other branches of surgery. Therefore the criteria of care and proficiency have areas of overlap with the general points made elsewhere in this book and many points will not be repeated here. Only those features unique to the speciality will be discussed in this chapter.

36.2 Cardiothoracic surgery has imperatives which distinguish it from other surgical specialities. First, the diseases being managed are more immediately life threatening than in most other branches of surgery, since the efficient functioning of the heart and lungs is constantly necessary for life and failure will lead to death within a few seconds. Secondly, the choice between medical and surgical treatment is often not clear and each course of action has its own advantages and disadvantages. Finally, the margin between total success and failure is much narrower than in most branches of surgery and at times the result of surgery may be immediately determined by the placement of one stitch during the operation.

36.3 The combination of high risk disease and the complex and precise nature of the operations creates a situation where the risk of a patient dying is higher than in many other types of surgery and the possibility of major morbidity is also increased.

COMMON NEGLIGENT ERRORS IN OBTAINING CONSENT

36.4 The rapid growth in demand for cardiac surgery has led to several undesirable consequences. Surgeons have been forced to spend more and more time in the operating room and consequently less time has been spent in the clinical management before and after surgery. In particular, the time-consuming task of talking to those patients who are being prepared for operation has come to be seen as a diversion from the work for which a surgeon is uniquely qualified. *The widely accepted practice in cardiothoracic surgery is to inform patients of the risks and benefits of any procedure so that the patient may give truly informed consent*[1] *but this ideal is under pressure because of an emphasis on 'surgical productivity' by hospital managers and by some surgeons.*

1 J Glover 'The MRC and Informed Consent' (1986) British Medical Journal 293, 157–158.

36.5 In some centres the patient may not be spoken to by the operating surgeon at all but by a different doctor who may even not be surgically qualified. Patients' expectations of cardiac surgery have been increased to levels which are sometimes unrealistic as a result of very favourable experiences in friends and relatives who have had heart surgery. As a consequence of all these factors, the opportunities for inadequate pre-operative preparation of patients have increased and yet the need for such preparation has never been greater.

36.6 Units practising cardiothoracic surgery should therefore be aware of the general difficulties of obtaining consent which is truly informed and, having identified the problem, should have organised a system which will reduce the possibility of providing insufficient or poor information. The details of such an organisation will vary from unit to unit but certain broad patterns can be discerned. First, there can be no acceptable alternative to the surgeon who is going to perform the operation to be responsible for obtaining the patient's understanding and written consent to the proposed operation. If that surgeon is not the consultant in charge of the patient then the consultant must make the opportunity to talk to the patient as well. Secondly, another member of the team should also talk to the patient, probably at more leisure. This individual may be a suitably experienced nurse or the physiotherapist in charge of that patient. Patients usually talk more freely with these members of staff and many gaps in understanding can be dealt with. All objective evidence shows that the recall of patients about a consultation is very poor unless some system of this sort is in place. Although the strict legal requirements for information are met by the operating surgeon obtaining consent to the operation, a system such as the one described will help to avoid misunderstandings and therefore reduce the chances of litigation should any complications occur. An additional medical bonus on top of the legal requirement is that this is often the time at which the patient begins the process of rehabilitation which will lead to a better functional result to surgery than might otherwise be expected.

36.7 Most surgeons find that the ideal time to obtain consent to the operation is in the out-patient department on the patient's first visit after investigation. At that time it is very useful to have the next of kin present in order to inform them of the medical and surgical options and risks and to provide another source of information to the patient subsequently. Difficulties can arise in those families where an irregular relationship has been established.

36.8 The surgeon must make every effort to ensure that he is being understood by the patient and accommodate to differing levels of intelligence and emotional stability. This task may on occasion be very difficult and sometimes there will be a failure to obtain consent which is adequately informed. Nevertheless the onus is on the surgeon to try and usually this means spending some time in the process. It is useful in cases where the surgeon feels that there is a gap of understanding to record in the notes the length of the consultation and the concerns which remain afterwards.

36.9 An essential part of the consent procedure is to inform the patient of the diagnosis and the risks of the disease if untreated. Subsequently the risks and benefits of the operation are outlined. It must remain a matter of judgment how precise this information is and how it is presented to the patient.

36.10 If a patient has difficulty reaching a decision about accepting advice on treatment, the surgeon is obliged to provide more clarification or to give the patient time to consider the matter further. It is not permissible to overpersuade any patient to undergo a course of treatment against the patient's better judgment.

36.11 A cardinal part of obtaining consent must be for the operating surgeon to outline those hazards and complications of treatment which attend the procedure and these will clearly vary with each operation. Certain hazards and complications are specifically associated with cardiothoracic and oesophageal surgery.

SPECIFIC PROBLEMS OF CONSENT IN CARDIOTHORACIC SURGERY

Cardiac surgery

36.12 With the exception of some congenital heart lesions and rare acquired diseases, operations for heart disease are palliative and not curative. Patients need to be made aware of the need for continuing medical treatment after surgery and also of the fact that a further operation may become necessary at some time in the future.

36.13 Operations on the heart may be carried out as 'closed' or 'open' procedures. A closed cardiac operation is performed whilst the heart continues to beat and support the circulation of the blood. Such operations are limited in their scope and number and are confined to the treatment of easily correctable problems. The majority of cardiac operations are performed as open procedures in which the heart is stopped temporarily and the circulation is supported artificially by means of cardiopulmonary bypass using a heart-lung machine.

36.14 Certain hazards and complications arise from cardiopulmonary bypass and from emptying the heart of blood and these are sufficiently common to need outlining to every patient contemplating cardiac surgery. Cardiopulmonary bypass is an inadequate mimic of the natural circulation and only allows maintenance of the body for a limited period. During this time all the organs of the body are perfused and oxygenated in an unphysiological manner causing increasing but reversible functional failure. After a certain time that failure becomes more severe and irreversible. Prolonged periods of cardiopulmonary bypass lead to death but before that various organs in the body begin to show signs of damage. The brain is the most sensitive organ to such damage and cerebral damage is a specific hazard to cardiopulmonary bypass.[1]

1 P J Shaw, D Bates and N E F Cartlidge 'Neurological Complications of Coronary Artery Bypass Surgery: Six Month Follow up Study' (1986) British Medical Journal 293, 165–167.

36.15 Cerebral damage may occur in another way. During open heart surgery, the heart is emptied of its blood in order to perform the operation. Before the heart is capable of pumping and restoring the natural circulation, all the air which it contains must be removed because bubbles of air in the blood have the same effects as solid particles of the same size in being capable of blocking small arteries thus leading to damage of the tissues ('air embolism'). The volume of air needed to create a damaging embolism is very small and bubbles of 30 micrometres will cause serious tissue damage. Again the brain is an extremely vulnerable tissue.

36.16 Brain damage is the most significant hazard and complication of open heart surgery for these reasons and although some factors such as the removal of air are to a degree under the control of the surgeon, the remainder are not and arise as a consequence of the nature of the operations as they are presently performed. Shaw and her colleagues have shown that up to 40 per cent of patients show some temporary damage to the brain after open heart surgery and that 2 per cent will have permanent damage to a greater or lesser degree, sometimes leading to death. A recent (1986) conference held by the Society of Cardiothoracic Surgeons of Great Britain and Ireland expressed the view that any patient about to undergo open heart surgery should be informed of the possibility of brain damage.

36.17 Damage to other organ systems such as the kidneys, liver and the process of blood clotting are not specifically mentioned to patients but loosely grouped together as complications of the heart-lung machine and artificial circulation.[1]

1 M I Ionescu *Techniques in Extracorporeal Circulation* (2nd edn, Butterworths, 1981) p 730.

36.18 Every patient should also know that any cardiac operation whether open or closed carries a risk of serious bleeding and that there are rare occasions when this will become uncontrollable.

36.19 It is not the common practice of the speciality in the United Kingdom to detail every possible hazard of cardiopulmonary bypass.

Congenital cardiac surgery

36.20 A distressing feature of many life-threatening congenital cardiac diseases is that the patient and the parents may feel that the child is normal and healthy. The need for and the benefits and complications of surgery have to be very carefully explained under these circumstances and often more than one consultation is required.

Valvular cardiac surgery

36.21 Valvular cardiac surgery is almost always palliative. The benefits to the patient include a longer life span in most cases and this means that most patients undergoing valvular heart surgery will eventually require a further operation.

36.22 Replacement of cardiac valves by prostheses is common but every prosthesis which is available at the present time carries the risk of complications arising which may be lethal or affect the patient's health. There are several varieties of valve prosthesis and each has its own pattern of complications.

36.23 The choice of prosthesis depends on several factors. First, the experience, skill and judgment of the surgeon is very important. Secondly, it is now the common practice in most cardiothoracic units to inform the patient of the hazards and benefits of the available prostheses and to give the patient the final choice of the valve type. Clearly there will be occasions when the surgical and technical considerations will be paramount in determining the choice but on most occasions the patient's choice can be solicited and respected. Any patient who is about to undergo valve replacement surgery should also be told that all artificial valves eventually wear out and have to be replaced and that the rate at which any particular prosthesis will wear is essentially unpredictable.[1]

1 L I Bonchek 'Selection of a Prosthetic Valve' (1977) Chest 71, 2–3.

Ischaemic heart surgery

36.24 This category of cardiac surgery is the largest at the moment and is likely to become even greater in the future. Again it is important that the patient should understand the palliative nature of the operation and the risks and benefits of the procedure. Specifically, the progressive nature of the disease must be explained and also the fact that the conduits used to construct the bypass grafts are liable to degeneration over the years that follow operation.[1] Many grafts will be fashioned from veins taken from the legs and the incision in the leg is an important cause of post-operative pain and discomfort. The expanding use of the internal mammary artery as a conduit avoids many of these problems of degeneration and also pain in the leg and many surgeons now consider that this artery should be used in most ischaemic heart operations.[2]

1 M G Bourassa, L Campeau, J Lesperance et al 'Changes in Grafts and Coronary Arteries after Saphenous Vein Aortocoronary Bypass: Results at Repeat Angiography' (1982) Circulation (Suppl II) 65, II–90–7.

2 A Cameron, K B Davis, G E Green et al 'Clinical Implications of Internal Mammary Artery Bypass Grafts: the Coronary Artery Surgery Study Experience' (1988) Circulation 77, no 4, 815–819.

Surgery of the thoracic aorta

36.25 Diseases of the thoracic aorta are common and surgical operations are frequently advised. A distressing common complication of surgery on the descending part of the thoracic aorta is paraplegia resulting from damage to the spinal cord as a result of interruption of its blood supply during the course of the operation. Many of the reasons for this damage are understood and avoidable but any patient about to have such an operation must understand that there is a risk of paraplegia arising which in the state of our knowledge at the moment is unavoidable. Most large surgical series indicate that this complication will occur in about 2 per cent of operated cases but certain cases will carry a much higher risk.[1]

1 L Brewer, Fosberg et al 'Spinal Cord Complications following Surgery for Coarctation of the Aorta – A Study of 66 Cases' (1972) J Thorac Cardiovasc Surg 368, 64; E S Crawford, E M Mizrahi, K R Hess et al 'The Impact of Distal Aortic Perfusion and Somatosensory Evoked Potentials Monitoring in Prevention of Paraplegia after Aortic Resection' (1988) J Thorac Cardiovasc Surg 95, 357–377.

Surgery of the lungs and oesophagus

36.26 There are no specific problems which must be identified in obtaining the consent of the patient to operation.

DIAGNOSIS

Normally accepted practice

36.27 The diagnosis of cardiothoracic disease is usually a complex process and involves the usual clinical tools of history-taking, physical examination and the use of special investigations, the performance of which is a highly skilled and time-consuming task. In most cardiothoracic units this essential work is performed by specially trained cardiologists often working in collaboration with specialised radiologists. The scope of this chapter is insufficient to cover this aspect of the management of the cardiothoracic patient.

36.28 However the fact that the patient usually presents to the surgeon by referral after the diagnosis has been made and validated does not release the surgeon from the responsibility of satisfying himself that the diagnosis is correct and that considerations which might affect the risk and outcome of the operation have been evaluated and given appropriate weight.

36.29 The accepted standard of practice, therefore, is for the surgeon to see the patient as referral from cardiological colleagues and then to review the history, make a clinical examination of his own, albeit in a rather limited form, and to peruse the results of the investigations. In cases of difficulty and doubt this will be done in consultation with his medical colleague. Merely to accept the word of a medical colleague without a critical appraisal is unacceptable. A wider discussion of the role of the 'surgeon' as opposed to the 'operator' is found in Yates's chapter in *Surgery of Ischaemic Heart Disease*.[1]

1 D J Wheatley (ed) *Surgery of Ischaemic Heart Disease* (London, Chapman and Hall, 1986) p 676.

36.30 The surgical history should include those features which not only validate the diagnosis but which are relevant to the risks and outcome of surgery. Major systemic diseases such as diabetes mellitus or requiring long-term medication should be enquired for and allergies to drugs must be specifically identified. The drug history of the patient is particularly important as many commonly used drugs have serious complications if continued into the period of the operation. In particular, those drugs which interfere with blood clotting such as anticoagulants and aspirin must be stopped before open heart surgery.

36.31 A history of the patient's smoking habits is usually obtained and many surgeons are reluctant to perform surgery if the patient is smoking up to the time of the operation. However, there is no unanimity amongst the speciality about this and it cannot be regarded as negligent to operate on the patient who continues to smoke.

Clinical examination

36.32 The clinical examination of the cardiothoracic patient by the surgeon is also directed towards the goals of validating a diagnosis made by a physician and detecting those features which will have a bearing on the outcome and risks of an operation. The nature of the underlying condition will determine the nature and extent of the examination of the particular system involved.

36.33 Those patients with cardiac conditions should have a screening examination of other body systems such as the central nervous, alimentary and respiratory systems. Each of these may be damaged in the subsequent operation and it is important in the management of the patient to know exactly the level of normality beforehand.

36.34 Evidence of infection should be sought: to replace a cardiac valve with a prosthesis except under the most desperate circumstances if infection were present in, say, a tooth cavity, must be regarded as a negligent act. It would be against usual practice to incise a chest wall if the skin at the site of the cut was infected.

36.35 Those patients about to undergo operations for ischaemic heart disease which involve the use of the long saphenous vein from the leg must also be examined to exclude any possibility of varicosity since the operation will be made more risky if plans are not made to overcome this problem before surgery.

36.36 In the group of patients with pulmonary disease the clinical examination usually includes an assessment of the patient's respiratory function. Although such data are fallible, nevertheless some important information may be obtained and the situation of performing a lung resection on an individual with compromised respiratory function avoided since this is highly dangerous. It is also normal practice to assess whether the risks of pulmonary surgery could be reduced by a few more days of preparation including physiotherapy. Patients with oesophageal disease should be examined with reference to nutrition as this may be impaired by the disease. Poor nutritional status leads to a much higher rate of post-operative complications and the usual practice is to make some attempt to reverse malnutrition before operation.

Review of the investigations

36.37 This is the next important and obligatory step in the lead up to surgery. The accepted best practice is for the surgeon not to rely only on written reports of the investigations but also to look at the evidence from which those reports were made. It is therefore an accepted standard of practice that the surgeon should be capable of interpreting all but the most arcane of tests and in cases of difficulty discussing the problem with an expert in the field.

36.38 In cardiac disease this means that the surgeon will be expected to be able to interpret the plain chest X-ray, the resting and exercise electrocardiogram, the angiograms and the findings of the cardiac catheterisation. The interpretation of the results of echocardiography and of isotope studies is more usually performed in collaboration with the relevant specialist. It is unusual for the surgeon to perform any further tests himself.

36.39 The pulmonary surgeon must be capable of judging the chest X-ray, the electrocardiogram, the respiratory function tests and the flexible bronchoscopy which has been performed by the referring physician. In addition, the surgeon must make all reasonable efforts to make a diagnosis of malignancy, if that is the problem, by the most secure way possible. This will usually mean that a sample of the lesion has been obtained by biopsy and examined by microscopy and staining (histological diagnosis). The tissue sample may be obtained by a variety of invasive methods all of which carry a degree of risk. Unless the nature of the lung problem is such that the nature of the operation would be unaltered by the knowledge of malignancy any effort which is not dangerous to the patient's life must be made to substantiate the diagnosis of malignancy before performing major lung surgery. The nature of operations for lung malignancy all involve resection and loss of lung tissue and this always has an adverse effect on the patient's life and chances of early death. Such side effects are unacceptable if the reason for the resection was a non-malignant condition.

36.40 It is usual practice for the operating surgeon to perform a further bronchoscopy using the rigid instrument before performing a lung resection for pulmonary malignancy. Such an examination is necessary in order that the surgeon can determine precisely the extent of surgery needed for that particular patient and such information is not obtainable by the use of a flexible instrument especially if used by an individual who is not going to proceed to perform the major surgery.

36.41 Before oesophageal surgery, however, the flexible oesophagoscope will yield all the information the surgeon needs and also be somewhat safer to the patient. The requirement for the surgeon to obtain a histological diagnosis remains in the surgery of the oesophagus.

36.42 Any patient about to have cardiothoracic surgery needs a series of further laboratory investigations. A series of biochemical tests are performed to give information about the function of various organ systems. These are usually normal and act as a reference point should any derangement occur later. In this group are (a) haemoglobin, white cell and platelet counts in the peripheral blood; (b) serum, urea and electrolyte tests; (c) a new chest X-ray and electrocardiogram.

36.43 A further series of tests are required if there is any chance of haemorrhage occurring as a result of deranged clotting. This phenomenon is particularly common after cardiopulmonary bypass and may cause fatal blood loss. It is an agreed standard of practice that any patient who is to undergo open heart surgery using cardiopulmonary bypass, or who has a history of abnormal bleeding, should have a full battery of clotting studies performed before surgery and that any abnormalities are corrected. Furthermore, any patient undergoing major cardiothoracic surgery should have the blood group determined and at least four units of blood readily available. In addition, the services of a blood bank must be immediately at hand.

36.44 Acquisition of all the germane information about a patient takes a variable time depending on the nature of the disease and on the patient. The surgeon must then assess the risks to the life and health of the patient of the procedure which is indicated and balance those against the risks to the patient of the disease remaining untreated. This is clearly not a simple process and will depend on a mixture of facts of varying degrees of certainty. Two major general points must be made, however. First, the risks and benefits are those of the surgeon and the circumstances in which the operation is to be performed and they are not the risks which might be indicated from a study of the published literature which might be better or worse. The surgeon must consider whether his skills, the personnel or the resources available will have any impact on the risks and results of surgery.

36.45 Secondly, there is no uniform standard of philosophy about the risks and benefits of surgery and two broad streams may be identified. The first takes the attitude that cardiothoracic surgery is only acceptable if of a low risk, especially since so many people require it, and that it is not justifiable to perform operations if the risks to this particular patient are greater than those which are experienced in the broader group of patients with the same disorder having the same operation. A second group considers that the risks and needs of an individual need to be considered primarily, and if the risks of surgery are less than the risks of non-operative treatment, then surgical operation is indicated, even if the ultimate result will impair the overall results of the unit. Providing that the patient and relatives understand the basis on which the ultimate decision is made then neither attitude can be described as negligent.

Treatment

36.46 In offering surgical operation to a patient the surgeon has an obligation to ensure that the circumstances in which that procedure will occur are of a standard which are sufficient to ensure safety. In cardiothoracic operations that responsibility is made more difficult by the complexity of the procedures, the large number of personnel involved and the need for quite complex electronic and mechanical devices. In the post-operative phase the demands of good patient care may introduce complexities greater than those of the operation itself. If it were necessary to check on all these factors before each surgical procedure then very few operations would ever be performed. However it is an accepted practice that the surgeon should be involved in the setting up of the systems of care and that he should be confident that the facilities are adequate at that time and that he makes efforts to be aware of any changes which may occur.

ACCEPTABLE STANDARDS OF PRACTICE IN THE PERFORMANCE OF SURGICAL OPERATIONS

36.47 Because of the different demands of the procedures it is convenient to divide the operative procedures into minor and major.

Minor procedures[1]

36.48 This category includes all operations which do not involve opening of the chest wall by a surgical incision and includes such procedures as bronchoscopy, oesophagoscopy and insertion of a chest drain. The operations may be carried out under local or general anaesthesia.

1 Chapter by G H Smith in J Kyle (ed) *Pyes Surgical Handcraft* (Bristol, John Wright, 1984).

36.49 Before starting the procedure the surgeon must be certain that all instruments and apparatus are in working order. This is particularly important with regard to the oxygenation of the patient. Although this is an anaesthetic responsibility, the needs of the surgeon and anaesthetist are often in conflict, particularly during bronchoscopy when the patient may easily become short of oxygen during the procedure. With this in mind, a source of oxygen, a means of delivering it and a system of efficient suction to clear the respiratory tract are essential. A recent chest X-ray should be mounted on a viewing box to allow the surgeon to see it during the course of the operation.

Bronchoscopy

36.50 With the above provisos this procedure is safe and complications rarely arise. Haemorrhage may occur after a biopsy of a bronchial lesion and it is at this time that a large bore sucker and an efficient suction apparatus are essential to stop the blood drowning the patient's lungs. Certain places in the bronchial tree are known to overlie major blood vessels and in general these areas are at secondary carinae and around the orifice of the right middle lobe. Bronchial biopsy in these areas should be avoided or performed with great caution.

36.51 In the event of uncontrollable bleeding then the chest will have to be opened on the affected side and the bleeding point controlled, usually by lung resection. Even if all the above precautions are observed then there will always be a danger of bleeding during the procedure.

Possible negligent errors during bronchoscopy

36.52

Error	*Remedy*
Inadequate means of oxygenation	Preplan-discuss
Inadequate means of suction	Preplan and test
Inadequate light source	Pre-operative test
Trauma to lips and cheeks	Technique/care
Damage to teeth	Technique
Exsanguination	Thoracotomy

Oesophagoscopy with or without oesophageal dilatation

36.53 The major complication of this procedure is perforation of the oesophagus and this occurs in any hands. The incidence is greater if the patient has a rigid neck or a pronounced thoracic kyphosis. The standard practice in this procedure is to assume that any patient may suffer this complication and that steps should be taken to facilitate its early diagnosis and treatment should it happen.

36.54 Any patient having oesophagoscopy should stay in hospital overnight. During that time any pain or discomfort should be regarded as an indication that perforation might have occurred. Clinical examination of the neck may detect air in the tissues in a few cases. Should a patient suffer pain then an immediate chest X-ray and contrast swallow should be performed. If a leak is required immediately then the prognosis is good. Delay is usually fatal.

Possible negligent errors during oesophagoscopy

36.55

Error	*Remedy*
Trauma to lips and cheeks	Technique/care
Damage to teeth	Technique
Damage to pharynx	Technique + ? stiff neck
Perforation detection	Early closure

Insertion of chest drains

36.56 This procedure is performed under local anaesthesia except in children when a general anaesthetic is used. The objective of insertion is to remove air or fluid from the pleural space and allow the underlying lung to expand. The procedure is performed using a trocar and cannula inserted between the ribs. A major risk is the chance of perforating not just an intra-thoracic organ but the possibility of damaging an intra-abdominal organ also.

36.57 The accepted practice in the management of chest drains is to ensure that the chest drain is being inserted for problems which can only be treated in such a manner and to ensure that the procedure can be carried out without causing any damage.

36.58 The first objective depends on an accurate diagnosis being made and this is done by clinical and radiological examination using a chest X-ray. Under all but the most desperate of circumstances a pre-operative chest X-ray must be regarded as essential as clinical examination of the chest alone is not sufficiently reliable. Ideally the chest X-ray should be taken immediately before the procedure and should be available for the surgeon to see during the operation. It is also accepted practice to take another chest X-ray after the procedure as a check that the operation has been performed properly and has been effective in achieving its objectives.

36.59 Damage to the lung is very rare if the reason for inserting the chest drain is to remove air or fluid which is compressing the lung within the chest cavity. However, damage to the structures lying between the two lungs (the mediastinum) and to the diaphragm and the structures that lie below it is a real danger and strategies are needed to minimise this risk. The safest area of the chest wall through which to insert a cannula is laterally between the mid and anterior axillary lines and above the level of the fourth rib space. This area is also the most convenient and comfortable site for the patient and is the most commonly used site by thoracic surgeons. Non-specialists often use an area just below the clavicle on the anterior chest wall but this site carries significant dangers and should be abandoned although its use is described in many non-specialist textbooks.

36.60 Once inserted a chest drain must be attached to an underwater seal drain in order to prevent collapse of the underlying lung.

36.61 Removal of the drain should be performed only when the underlying lung has expanded to fill the chest cavity. The removal of chest drains is another procedure which is carried out with chest X-rays before and afterwards.

Possible negligent errors during insertion of chest drain

36.62

Error	*Remedy*
Damage to lung	Check indications with chest X-ray
Damage to other structures	Correct site of insertion
Pneumothorax	Underwater seal and suction

Chest aspiration and thoracoscopy

36.63 These procedures have the same dangers as the insertion of chest drains and the precautions listed above are commonly accepted standards of practice.

Major operations

General

36.64 All cardiothoracic major operations carry the risk that life-threatening complications will occur during the intra and post-operative period. A large number of these will be satisfactorily resolved if treated expeditiously by trained medical and nursing staff. To a greater extent than other specialities, therefore, the surgeon's duty is to ensure that medical and appropriately trained nursing staff are available to care for the cardiothoracic patient at all times. This is a standard which is accepted by all National Health Service institutions but should apply equally to hospitals in the private sector. Similarly, the equipment used during cardiothoracic operations is usually vital to life and it is accepted that some duplication of equipment is necessary to avoid the fatal consequences of failure of any one piece of apparatus.

Prevention of infection

36.65 Bacterial contamination during cardiothoracic operations is almost inevitable and in some cases infection will follow. Such an event usually has catastrophic results. It is therefore an accepted level of competence to reduce the chances of infection by a number of means. Such measures are particularly important in cardiac surgery because a prosthesis is often inserted.

36.66 First, no patient should receive an operation if there is known to be a source of sepsis elsewhere in the body excluding, of course, septic conditions which merit an operation within the chest.

36.67 Secondly, attempts should be made to remove as many organisms from the skin as possible. To this end it is common practice for the patient about to have surgery to be given at least one whole body bath with a dilute antiseptic solution.

36.68 Finally, since their advent in the 1940s, antibiotics have been given prophylactically during the operative period. Although no truly scientific basis for this has been established, there is evidence that such a practice is necessary, particularly in cardiac surgery. Not to give antibiotic prophylaxis during cardiac surgery would be regarded as negligent and the same rule applies to most non-cardiac thoracic operations. The nature and extent of such treatment will, however, vary according to the circumstances of each unit.[1]

1 W A Reed 'Antibiotics and Cardiac Surgery' (1965) J Thorac Cardiovasc Surg 50: 888–892.

36.69 All major cardiothoracic operations may involve the sudden loss of a large amount of blood. All patients must have cross-matched blood available before surgery and the hospital blood bank must be able to meet extra demands promptly. A large bore intravenous cannula is inserted into every patient before the operation begins so that large volumes of blood can be rapidly infused if necessary.

36.70 Perioperative monitoring of vital signs in the circulatory and respiratory functions is standard practice but the degree of this will vary according to the severity of the operation. The minimal monitoring permissible is the continuous display of the electrocardiogram and this is used in most thoracic cases. Cardiac operations should be accompanied by electronic monitoring of the arterial and central venous pressures, electrocardiograph, urinary output and body temperatures. All cardiothoracic operations should be conducted in circumstances in which measurements of the blood chemistry and gases can be performed readily.

Cardiac surgery[1]

NORMALLY ACCEPTED STANDARDS OF OPERATIVE PRACTICE

36.71 At the beginning of the operation, the chest is usually opened by a midline incision which passes through the sternum although some surgeons may on occasion use a lateral incision in difficult repeat operations. A power-driven saw is used to open the bone as this is safer than techniques where the bone is cut using devices which have to be passed blindly behind the sternum with the danger of damage to the underlying tissues. Assiduous haemostasis is required at this stage in order to prevent heavy bleeding when the patient is on cardiopulmonary bypass. After the pericardium has been opened the surgeon must make a final check on the pre-operative diagnosis and identify the cardiac structures. The surgeon is expected to identify any abnormalities and adjust his technique appropriately.

1 'Cardiac Surgery' in S W Jamieson and N E Shumway (eds) *Rob and Smith's Operative Surgery* (4th edn, Butterworths) p 622.

36.72 Cardiopulmonary bypass is used in most cardiac operations. In order that the blood can circulate through the extra corporeal circuit, heparin must be given to prevent its clotting. This drug is given intravenously and it is the responsibility of the surgeon to ensure that the drug is administered and given a few minutes to work before proceeding to insert the cannulae into the great vessels which will allow the blood to leave and subsequently return to the patient's circulation. The blood is extracted from the venous circulation by cannulae placed in the right atrium or venae cavae on most occasions although some operations may demand cannulation of another great vein such as the femoral. Having passed through the heart-lung machine the blood is returned to the patient by a cannula inserted into some part of the arterial circulation. Most surgeons use the ascending aorta as the preferred site of cannulation but it is acceptable to use the femoral artery for this purpose.

36.73 The extra corporeal circuit consists of sterile plastic tubing connecting artificial devices for oxygenating, pumping, warming and filtering the blood. All of the devices are disposable and are available in a sterile form as commercial products. The manufacturers of these devices provide full documentation of the product and, in the United Kingdom, the devices will have passed stringent safety and efficiency tests.

36.74 The heart-lung machine is run by an appropriately trained technician under the delegated authority of the surgeon and it is important that the surgeon should satisfy himself or herself that the technician is capable of fulfilling the task delegated to him. Before the operation the surgeon should inform the technician of the flows and temperatures which will be required at various stages of the operation.

36.75 The purpose of cardiopulmonary bypass is to maintain the viability of the various organs in the body whilst the heart is stopped during the operation. The most sensitive organ to damage is the brain and the artificial circulation is adjusted to allow adequate perfusion of the brain and of other vital organs such as the kidneys and liver. The flow from the pump and its pressure are both important in this respect. The flow is calculated according to the body size of the patient and the pressure is maintained at 50–60 mm mercury pressure during the procedure by the use of vasoconstricting drugs if necessary. The adequacy of cerebral perfusion is assessed with some difficulty during bypass. The usual clinical signs are masked by the anaesthetic and the only readily available indication of adequate perfusion of the brain is normally sized pupils of the eyes. Some centres use a simplified electro-encephalogram as an indication of adequate brain perfusion but difficulties in obtaining a good signal and of interpretation have led to its adoption in only a few centres.

36.76 Apart from the requirement to perform an operation on the heart the surgeon has the duty of ensuring that as little damage as possible occurs to the muscle of the heart (the myocardium). In order to perform the operation the heart must be isolated from the artificial circulation and the heart is as vulnerable to lack of perfusion as any other body tissue. If damage to the myocardium does occur then a wide spectrum of events may follow. The heart may at one extreme fail immediately after the artificial circulation is stopped and lead to the death of the patient. At the other extreme the damage may be very slight and either recover very quickly or merely lead to a heart with moderate impairment of its pumping ability.

36.77 It is therefore the duty of the operating surgeon to practise some form of myocardial protection during the period of cardiopulmonary bypass. Two statements need making immediately. First, there will always be a degree of failure in that, irrespective of the method of protection, there will always be some diminution of cardiac performance after cardiopulmonary bypass. Secondly, although most surgeons use hypothermic cardioplegia as the preferred form of protection, a minority of surgeons use other methods with perfectly acceptable results. Thus there is no single method of protection which commands universal agreement. However, it is necessary for each surgeon to have a strategy of myocardial protection for each patient on whom he is performing surgery.

36.78 Before the patient's heart can resume supporting the circulation at the end of the operation, all air must be removed from its chambers. Failure to do so will lead to the formation of bubbles of air in the arterial circulation and these act as if they were solid particles in their ability to block small arteries. Such arterial obstructions will lead to damage of the tissues and the brain is especially vulnerable to this form of injury. The available evidence suggests that it is unusual to be able to remove *all* the air from the cardiac chambers in spite of the most careful and meticulous techniques and some minor degree of air embolism occurs in every patient having open heart surgery. Nevertheless, careful and patient attempts at air removal will remove the bulk of the air and lead to a greatly reduced risk of cerebral damage.

36.79 Each surgeon has individual techniques to remove air from the heart and there is no standard procedure. The effectiveness of any technique is probably related to the length of time it is used – the longer the application the more air will be removed. The most used way to remove air depends on repeated needle aspiration of individual cardiac chambers and allowing the heart to resume support of the circulation with the patient in a head down position and with a small hole in the ascending aorta to allow the egress of any remaining bubbles.

36.80 At the end of bypass, the surgeon must satisfy himself that the heart is maintaining an adequate circulation and that all the incisions in the heart are soundly secured. If not, then additional sutures are placed at this stage. The venous cannulae for the bypass procedure are then removed and protamine sulphate, a drug which reverses the action of heparin, is given. Apart from its primary action, protamine causes an unpredictable degree of cardiac depression for a few minutes and also causes an expansion of the volume of the vascular system. It is standard practice to have at least one cannula in place at this time (usually the arterial cannula) so that in the event of cardiovascular collapse the cardiopulmonary bypass can rapidly be restarted. It follows that the machine and the perfusion technician should be at hand at this stage.

36.81 Once there is demonstrable evidence of clot formation, the remaining cannula is removed and an assiduous search made for bleeding vessels in all areas of the open chest. Only when there is evidence that no bleeding points are left should the surgeon begin to close the chest. All surgeons close the chest with one or more drainage tubes in place so that any residual bleeding will not accumulate in the chest cavity and compress the heart.

36.82 There is no standard practice with regard to closure of the pericardium: surgical opinion is evenly divided about the desirability of closing this tissue.

36.83 Most surgeons routinely place a right ventricular pacing wire at this time and bring it out through the skin at the side of the incision. A minority of cases develop a very slow heart rate after return to the intensive care ward and pacing is life-saving. Most patients do not develop this complication and have the wire removed by traction on the sixth or seventh day after the operation.

Valvular heart surgery

36.84 The normally accepted standard of practice during valvular heart surgery is as follows:

(1) the diseased valve should be assessed to determine if there is the possibility of repair. This decision will apply mainly to mitral and tricuspid valve disease: aortic valve lesions are rarely amenable to conserving procedures;
(2) if a repair is performed then the surgeon must ensure that the valve is working satisfactorily afterwards. This may be difficult and involve assessment of the valve whilst the heart is supporting the circulation with a finger inserted into the relevant chamber. Intra-operative pressure recordings are also indicated;
(3) should the valve be so diseased that replacement is necessary, the surgeon must ensure that the diseased valve is excised without damage to the surrounding cardiac tissues and without leaving any debris in the heart. This can be a time-consuming and tedious procedure but if incompletely performed then cerebral or visceral damage due to embolisation is likely. In the case of the mitral valve there is commonly extensive calcification of the posterior cusp and removal of this may create a rupture of the heart at this point. This complication is usually fatal and can only be avoided in many cases by leaving diseased tissue behind;
(4) the valve prosthesis should be inserted the right way up and it is required of the surgeon to check that its function is satisfactory when it is in place and that residual valve tissue does not impede its opening and closing. The insertion of a valvular prosthesis may be accomplished by interrupted or continuous suturing techniques depending on the nature of the native valve ring and the preference of the surgeon, always providing that there is no leak around the valve when it is in place.

36.85 The choice of the type of valve prosthesis is usually a matter of judgment on the part of the surgeon and preference of the patient. There is, however, broad agreement that certain categories of valve should not be used in certain circumstances:

(a) porcine heterograft valves should not normally be inserted into individuals with an over-active calcium metabolism, i e those patients with chronic renal failure or children;
(b) porcine heterograft valves in the aortic area should normally only be used if a size greater than 23 mm diameter can be inserted since smaller valves are significantly obstructive;
(c) mechanical valves which always require long-term treatment with anti-coagulants usually should not be used in those patients who would be at risk from bleeding complications such as haemorrhage from a duodenal ulcer.

Ischaemic heart surgery

36.86 Success and safety in the surgery of ischaemic heart disease depends on a number of generally accepted factors. First, grafts must be applied to all diseased coronary arteries distally to the obstructions. This means that it is necessary for the surgeon to review the coronary arteriograms immediately before the operation. At surgery the surgeon must identify each diseased vessel on the heart as indicated by the angiogram and this may be a difficult and lengthy process.

36.87 Secondly, the grafts should be attached to the coronary artery in such a way that the surgeon is absolutely confident that the patency of the native vessel, the graft and the anastomosis is assured. This may be done by probing each anastomosis before completion and by the surgeon wearing optical aids to vision such as magnifying spectacles.

36.88 Thirdly, the preparation of the grafts is cardinal to the long-term patency of these structures. Vein grafts should be handled carefully and not over distended. Great care is needed when mobilising the internal mammary artery to ensure its patency and this should always be checked before the graft is placed by observing the flow of blood through it.

36.89 Finally, the surgeon must ensure that the eventual position of each graft is satisfactory and that when the heart is full and supporting the circulation there is no kinking of the grafts, no graft is too tight and that no graft is twisted. All of these problems should always be searched for and, if found, remedied. At this search the possibility of bleeding tributaries and branches on the grafts should be considered.

Congenital heart surgery

36.90 The surgery of congenital heart defects is perhaps the most demanding of all the types of cardiac surgery. Each patient should be assumed to have a unique pattern of disorder and it is necessary for the surgeon to make considerable efforts to identify the precise nature of the patient's disorder, perhaps with constant reference to the pre-operative investigations. Only when the operating surgeon is totally sure that he has fully appraised the problem should correction be performed.

36.91 The correction of the defect must clearly be as complete as possible. The surgeon must ensure that no abnormal unwanted shunts are left in the heart and in particular that there is no possibility of intracardiac obstruction being left or created during the course of the repair.

Pulmonary surgery[1]

36.92 Normally accepted standards of operative practice are valid. Before the patient is anaesthetised, the chest X-ray and the results of the pre-operative tests, including respiratory function, are reassessed. The patient is anaesthetised and placed with the affected side uppermost. The chest is opened by a posterolateral incision through the fifth interspace. Extra access may be obtained by removal of the sixth rib.

1 D C Sabiston and F C Spencer (eds) *Gibbons Surgery of the Chest* (Philadelphia, W B Saunders Co, 1983) vol 1; 'Thoracic Surgery' in J W Jackson and D K C Cooper (eds) *Rob and Smith's Operative Surgery* (4th edn, Butterworths, 1986) p 380.

36.93 Most pulmonary operations involve the resection of diseased tissue and the extent of the resection will vary according to the disease and its extent. Sometimes it is possible to remove a lesion of the lung by simple excision but usually the resection will be along anatomical lines and involve the removal of a segment, a lobe or the whole lung (pneumonectomy). In each of these cases the operation involves the dissection, control and division of the arteries and veins supplying the part to be resected and then the division of the relevant bronchus or air tube. Afterwards the bronchus is repaired. Unless a pneumonectomy has been performed the rest of the lung is then allowed to expand and fill the chest cavity. If there has been a pneumonectomy then that side of the chest remains empty until such time as the accumulation of fluid and blood becomes organised into fibrous tissue.

36.94 The chest is then closed and if any lung has been left in the operated side then chest drainage is performed with large bore tubes. Should no lung tissue remain, however, many surgeons would not use chest drains but then special precautions have to be observed so that the function of the remaining lung is not compromised.

36.95 The hazards of lung resection are those of any operation involving major vessels and of disruption of the repaired bronchus.

36.96 The vessels in the lung are very thin and carry a very high blood flow. In performing a lung resection the first requirement is to dissect free the relevant blood supply and to mobilise sufficient length of vessels to be able to ligate the vessels and divide them whilst leaving an adequate cuff of tissue beyond the ligatures to prevent them falling off. Sometimes extensive disease will make the dissection impossible but usually the inadequate cuff is due to imperfect technique.

36.97 The repair of the divided bronchus needs great attention. The bronchus has a poor blood supply and heals poorly. Great delicacy is needed in handling the bronchus in order to avoid damaging the blood supply and the repair has to be meticulously accurate in order that healing may occur and that the repair should be air tight. Some repairs will break down in spite of excellent surgical technique but the chances of such an event may be greatly increased if the bronchus is roughly handled or if the sutures are imperfectly placed.

36.98 If the repair does break down then a communication will be created between the bronchial tree and the pleural space (bronchopleural fistula). If there is lung remaining in the hemithorax and if this lung can be expanded to fill the pleural space then the fistula will eventually heal. After a pneumonectomy, however, the fistula will lead to possible compression of the remaining good lung and infection of the empty hemithorax, usually with serious morbidity.

36.99 Following pulmonary surgery haemorrhage may occur from vessels in the chest wall and from the bronchial arteries which run alongside and parallel to the bronchial tree. If these arteries cause trouble during surgery they should be individually ligated and attempts at control with diathermy cautery should not be performed.

The most common negligent errors in pulmonary surgery

36.100

Error	*Remedy*
Operating on the wrong side	Care and chest X-ray in theatre
Haemorrhage	Control of major vessels Ligature of bronchial and intercostal arteries
Resection of the wrong part of the lung	Proper dissection and identification
Bronchopleural fistula	Care of the bronchus (no clamps, no stripping of peribronchial tissues), meticulous suturing

Oesophageal surgery

36.101 Normally accepted standards of operative practice are valid. Operations of the oesophagus are not the exclusive province of the thoracic surgeon and probably most oesophageal surgery is performed by suitably trained general surgeons. The familiarity of the surgeon with the surgical physiology and anatomy of the chest is very important as complications affecting every intrathoracic organ can occur and it is important that the operating surgeon *and his staff* should have familiarity and skills to deal with them rapidly and effectively. Almost all of the hazards and opportunities for negligent error are those which arise from opening the chest and are covered above. The major problem of oesophageal surgery, whether minor or major, is leakage into the mediastinum, either from a laceration or a result of a breach in an anastomosis. Such events are only rarely the result of negligence. However, the opportunities for negligent action lie in the failure to detect early and to treat expeditiously.

36.102 Any patient who has undergone oesophageal endoscopy should be considered as a candidate for a laceration causing a leak from the oesophagus. *Any* untoward symptom in the 24 hour period following the investigation should lead to a chest X-ray being taken and if symptoms persist, even if that test is normal, a contrast swallow should be ordered.

36.103 Early detection of such leaks enables the surgeon to repair the problem before extensive mediastinal contamination occurs and allows a safer and quicker recovery. Delay beyond six hours makes a repair impossible and the mortality and morbidity greatly increase.

36.104 Leaks from oesophageal anastomoses following resection may cause similar problems but are much more difficult to deal with as the opportunity for direct repair is usually absent. However, prompt drainage of the chest and mediastinum provides the best background for recovery.

Delegation of care

36.105 Cardiothoracic surgery is a speciality in which most of the care of patients and performance of operations is done by consultants directly or under their very close supervision. However, young surgeons still have to be trained for the future and certain tasks such as the care and running of the heart-lung machine are delegated to non-medical staff.

36.106 Trainees in the speciality only begin serious training after a full training in general surgery. They start therefore with a broad range of basic surgical skills and a wide knowledge of applied surgical anatomy and physiology. In the United Kingdom a requirement for starting is the possession of a Fellowship of one of the Royal Colleges of Surgeons.

36.107 In spite of the close supervision and the relative seniority of the trainees, severe problems present during the training period. Most of the complications of cardiothoracic operations are irreversible when they occur and many of these are life threatening. The same is true of decisions taken on the surgical intensive care ward. Yet the capacity to operate and to take decisions are essential parts of the training period. Experience dictates that training should be offered only to those individuals who are committed to the speciality in the long term and who in the opinion of the trainer of are sufficient calibre to become successful independent cardiothoracic surgeons.

36.108 The position of the non-medically qualified person on the cardiothoracic team is more difficult. In most cases the posts were created a long time ago and the responsibilities and demands have grown since then. Certainly many of these individuals perform tasks which, if being proposed today, would require the recruitment of a medical doctor because of the awesome nature of the responsibilities. However the system under which these people work under the delegated responsibility of the consultant surgeon seems to work well and there seems little point in changing it. In the future the pattern of junior medical staffing in British hospitals may mean that more tasks which are done by doctors at the moment may have to be delegated to appropriately trained non-medical staff.

BIBLIOGRAPHICAL REFERENCES

Bonchek L I 'Selection of a Prosthetic Valve' (1977) Chest 71, 2–3.

Bourassa M G, Campeau L, Lesperance J et al 'Changes in Grafts and Coronary Arteries after Saphenous Vein Aortocoronary Bypass: Results at Repeat Angiography' (1982) Circulation (Suppl II) 65, II-90-7.

Brewer L, Fosberg et al 'Spinal Cord Complications following Surgery for Coarctation of the Aorta – A Study of 66 Cases' (1972) J Thorac Cardiovasc Surg 368, 64.

Cameron A, Davis K B, Green G E et al 'Clinical Implications of Internal Mammary Artery Bypass Grafts: the Coronary Artery Surgery Study Experience' (1988) Circulation 77, no 4, 815–819.

Crawford E S, Mizrahi E M, Hess K R et al 'The Impact of Distal Aortic Perfusion and Somatosensory Evoked Potentials Monitoring in Prevention of Paraplegia after Aortic Resection' (1988) J Thorac Cardiovasc Surg 95, 357–377.

Glover J 'The MRC and Informed Consent' (1986) British Medical Journal 293, 157–158.

Ionescu M I *Techniques in Extracorporeal Circulation* (2nd edn, Butterworths, 1981) p 730.

Jackson J W and Cooper D K C (eds) *Rob and Smith's Operative Surgery* (4th edn, Butterworths, 1986) ch on 'Thoracic Surgery' p 380.

Jamieson S W and Shumway N E (eds) *Rob and Smith's Operative Surgery* (4th edn, Butterworths) ch on 'Cardiac Surgery' p 622.

Kyle J (ed) ch in *Pyes Surgical Handcraft* (Bristol, John Wright, 1984).

Reed W A 'Antibiotics and Cardiac Surgery' (1965) J Thorac Cardiovasc Surg 50, 888–892.

Sabiston D C and Spencer F C (eds) *Gibbons Surgery of the Chest* (Philadelphia, W B Saunders Co, 1983) vol 1.

Shaw P J, Bates D and Cartlidge N E F 'Neurological Complications of Coronary Artery Bypass Surgery: Six Month Follow up Study' (1986) British Medical Journal 293, 165–167.

Wheatley D J(ed) *Surgery of Ischaemic Heart Disease* (London, Chapman and Hall, 1986) p 676.

CROSS-REFERENCE

For information related to topics in this chapter see Chapter 33.

CHAPTER 37

Medical negligence in plastic surgery

Mr John R Cobbett *MB FRCS*

SUMMARY

INTRODUCTION

37.1 It is difficult for one who is not a plastic surgeon to understand the scope of a plastic surgeon's work and more difficult to grasp the thread which connects the multiferous operations on different tissues, in different parts of the body, often on the borders of specialist territories, which the plastic surgeon performs. It is a commonplace event for a patient who has undergone multi-staged reconstructive procedures to ask his surgeon, 'When am I having this plastic surgery then, doctor?' Except on rare occasions plastic surgery is not concerned with polythene, nylon, silicone or any of the other artificial substances that the word 'plastic' brings to mind. Rather it is 'plastic' in the sense of plasticine – capable of being moulded – it is basically the surgery of moulding tissue.

37.2 Historically Sir Harold Gillies, the first plastic surgeon in the United Kingdom, started by repairing the deformities and deficiencies of the mutilated faces of soldiers from the trenches of the First World War. To repair cheeks, noses and lips that had been totally or partially blown away, it was necessary to bring skin and usually other tissues such as subcutaneous fat, bone or muscle from another site to fill the defects caused by the mortar bomb, shell or sniper's bullet.

37.3 All living tissue in the body requires nourishment and nearly all of the body's tissue receives this nourishment from the blood which passes through the tissues in small blood vessels. If the blood supply is reduced the tissues will die if the amount of nourishment available is below certain levels; if a lesser degree of ischaemia is caused then the tissues will survive but are more vulnerable to infection and to minor injury. Hence the rough handling of such a partially devitalised piece of tissue with heavy instruments, or allowing the tissue partially to dry out during surgery, may well lead directly to the death of that tissue or at the very least reduce its already lowered resistance to infection.

37.4 For Gillies to advance a piece of cheek skin – where there was some to spare – forwards to fill a gap where skin had been shot away, necessitated at least undermining the skin to be advanced, detaching it from the underlying tethering tissues to allow it to stretch across the gap. This undermining would have cut all the blood vessels running to that piece of skin from its deep surface, leaving only those entering its periphery. Thus the 'advancement flap' of skin would have been deprived of the majority of its blood supply. If not enough skin was available locally a free skin graft might have been used – a piece of full thickness or partial thickness skin taken from another part of the body and transferred, free from all attachments, to the recipient raw area. At first, such a 'free' skin graft lives by perfusion of nourishment between itself and the raw surface upon which it is placed, but after a few days fine blood vessels grow from the recipient area into the graft and revascularise it. Obviously such a free graft is also extremely vulnerable to trauma or infection because of its vastly reduced supply of nourishment.

37.5 It is the necessary techniques of handling such vulnerable tissue that is the key to understanding the plastic surgeon's work. A fine, sharp hook does much less damage when holding a piece of tissue than does a pair of gripping forceps that crush and kill cells. A fine stitch tied not too tightly causes less damage than a heavy one. Exposed tissue is kept moist with saline swabs. None of these – and many other – minor details makes a great difference on their own but the accumulative effect of all of them is to allow a partly devitalised piece of tissue to survive which, without such techniques, would have been lost.

37.6 Scar tissue is the cement that joins together divided skin, fat, muscle or other tissue. Many factors influence the quantity and quality of the scar following any particular traumatic event – including surgery – but certainly the more the local tissue trauma the more the local scarring. Hence plastic surgery techniques are used to produce minimal scarring – not only in the skin but also in deeper tissues. In the hand there are many important structures running in close proximity to each other. Many of these need to slide against neighbouring tissues. Any injury or operation in the hand will produce subsequent scarring deep in the hand tissues and this scarring can tether the tendons or joint structures that need to be mobile for the hand to maintain its function. Plastic surgery techniques will minimise the amount of scar formed in the hand and hence help to produce an optimal result.

37.7 To many the term 'plastic surgery' is synonymous with 'cosmetic surgery'. Cosmetic surgery is only one facet of a plastic surgeon's repertoire and it belongs there because of the need for minimal scarring on areas exposed to public gaze and in many instances the need for dealing with tissues that have been partially devitalised.

37.8 To summarise then, the plastic surgeon is the expert in reducing or totally cutting off the blood supply to a piece of tissue without actually killing it. From a practical aspect plastic surgery skills are used in filling defects of skin or other tissue, in minimising cutaneous scarring, in hand surgery and in cosmetic surgery. These four aspects will be considered individually from the point of view of surgical negligence.

GENERAL CONSIDERATIONS

At consultation

37.9 Having to deal with conditions that overlap the territories of other specialities plastic surgeons are often referred patients whose conditions fall somewhere on the boundary between two disciplines. A radial nerve compression at the elbow; a low vaginal stricture; a recurrent breast tumour invading ribs; a cranial vault osteoma with intracranial extension – these all may be referred to a plastic surgeon but he must say, 'Should a plastic surgeon be dealing with this?' Naturally the answer must depend on the interests and experience of the individual, but to operate, say, on the vaginal stricture associated with painful intercourse without prior consultation with a gynaecologist would certainly be unwise, and perhaps actually negligent. It may be that in any of these conditions a combined operation between the plastic surgeon and the consultant from the other speciality is the best solution.

37.10 Secondly, the plastic surgeon must ask himself, 'Am I the right plastic surgeon to be dealing with this?' In many plastic surgery units a degree of super-specialisation exists so that when faced with a particularly difficult problem in an area where someone with special expertise is practising within the same unit, it might be negligent not to refer the case onwards.

37.11 Similarly there are conditions – such as major congenital cranio-facial defects – for which a few special centres exist in the country where all the necessary experience and facilities exist. Certainly no average plastic surgeon without the special experience required should attempt to treat these patients outside such units.

37.12 The above comments should not deter a surgeon from attempting a new technique of which he has no personal experience; either new to him, in which case he would be advised to visit surgeons expert in the particular area, or totally new, in which case appropriate pre-operative work up, perhaps with cadaver dissection, would be appropriate. Surgery must not become static but the surgeon must be doubly sure that he has taken every reasonable step to ensure successful outcome, if an operation is breaking new ground.

37.13 Surgical clinics are normally full of bustle and haste. One has to accept that it is usually not possible to give a thorough medical check-up in a plastic surgery clinic, and that any medical condition other than the problem for which the patient is referred will be picked up on admission. Nevertheless it saves at least the inconvenience to a patient of being admitted only to have the operation cancelled or postponed on medical grounds, if a brief check on his general condition can be made at the first appointment, if only by a history. The author's experience is that a referral letter from a general practitioner usually mentions intercurrent disease but that some of one's colleagues from other specialities have a rather more restricted vision and may refer for surgery an elderly patient in congestive heart failure with uncontrolled fibrillation whose basal cell carcinoma could be dealt with at least equally as well by irradiation! Combined clinics between plastic surgeons and other related disciplines can often eliminate many such problems.

Counselling

37.14 English patients tend to be much more acquiescent than their foreign counterparts, and are reluctant to question a surgeon's pronouncements. Surgical clinics (as noted above) are busy. Plastic surgeons are few and far between and so develop something of a scarcity value, to be held in even greater awe than their other surgical colleagues. Patients only hear what they want to hear. These five facts form a recipe for disaster. The sauce to add to the recipe is that most patients have unreasonable expectations. A middle-aged lady was seen in the Out Patient Clinic with a malignant facial tumour. She was admitted and the evening before operation was seen by the senior registrar to whom she said that she had been assured there would be no scar left on her face. He attempted to disabuse her of this idea, explaining what scars there would be and next morning told his consultant of the interview. The consultant interviewed the patient in the ward (before pre-medication) in the presence of the ward sister and explained exactly what scarring would result and where. After discharge the patient wrote several complaining letters to the hospital authorities complaining that her face was scarred when she had been told that it would not be!

37.15 It is desirable but not essential for the consultant to visit the patient in the ward before surgery, providing that adequate counselling is done by a junior surgeon whose knowledge is adequate for the task.

Operation

37.16 The surgeon must satisfy himself – particularly when working at a strange hospital, as tends to happen to plastic surgeons rather more often than those in other disciplines – that facilities for the care of his patient during (and after) the operation are satisfactory. Is blood available? Will frozen sections of excised material be needed? Facilities must be known to be optimal before starting surgery.

37.17 Having said 'Yes' to the two questions – is this a plastic surgery case and – am I the right plastic surgeon to deal with it – the surgeon must ask himself, 'Am I physically fit to do this?' We all know and can perhaps sympathise with the 'flu-ridden surgeon who is only controlling his fever and shivering by liberal doses of aspirin – perhaps we sometimes see him in the changing room mirror – but is not operating in such a state (which requires a positive deliberate decision to do so) even more negligent than by simple carelessness leaving a swab in the wound?

37.18 Allergies would have been enquired about pre-operatively. The use of a surgical cleansing solution to which the patient is sensitive produces a much more dramatic problem on the facial skin than anything elsewhere, so particular care is needed to avoid this.

37.19 Many plastic surgery operations take place on or about the face. If the eyes are in the operation field they must be protected. If covered by a swab, a careless forearm rested upon the face can cause corneal abrasions. Best to leave the eyes uncovered where everyone can see what is happening to them. Instruments must be passed around the face, not across it. If the eyes are close to but not actually in the operation field, the eyelids should be stuck down with adhesive tape.

37.20 Operating on the wrong patient, the wrong side, or even doing the wrong operation is much more difficult to achieve in plastic surgery than other specialities because the vast majority of lesions to be dealt with are immediately obvious even in the unconscious patient. This fact tends to breed carelessness in failing to mark the site of operation in such patients. The classic exception to the rule – which has caused problems in the past – is the patient with facial palsy. Once anaesthetised the paralysed side cannot be determined, and these patients, particularly, warrant careful pre-operative marking and recording.

Post-operative care

37.21 Prophylactive antibiotics are not required for the usual 'cold' surgical case with a surgically clean operation site. Where a large wound is open for a prolonged period, or where an implant of foreign material is used, most surgeons would use a prophylactic antibiotic but a sufficiently large number would not do so in such a situation, for failure to use them is not to be considered negligent.

37.22 Where an already open wound is being dealt with at operation, local measures with or without systemic antibiotics should have been used to clear significant pathogenes from the area if possible. If pathogenic bacteria are known to be present at the time of surgery it is difficult to justify withholding antibiotic cover.

37.23 It is the responsibility of the surgeon to ensure that the nursing staff undertaking the post-operative care of the patient understand what is required of them, and preferably written instructions should be given.

37.24 Failure to alert the surgeon if a hand surgery patient, or one who has had a blepharoplasty complains of severe pain, or if a free flap loses its colour return may only result in total failure of the operation as in the last instance; in the other two, a hand severely crippled for life or permanent blindness may result.

37.25 Plastic surgery is an inexact art. Haematoma, infection and skin necrosis are all bound to occur (often in partnership) sooner or later. Their occurrence does not represent negligent surgery, but their management once diagnosed is as important as the original surgery. When a skin flap has died, a graft has failed or a wound broken down it is a natural reaction of the surgeon to keep his mind on happier things and it is only too easy to visit the patient less often than if things had gone well. This temptation must be firmly resisted and the frequency of visits increased rather than diminished. At the end of it all when eventually the wound has healed, one is, in fact, left with a patient much more grateful for all the care than one whose surgery has been an uncomplicated success. Reduction in the frequency of visiting compounds the problem in the patient's eyes which may then turn to visions of litigation.

Burns

37.26 Patients with acute major burns are acutely ill, often for many weeks. Their management may be extremely difficult from a metabolic or bacteriological point of view but there are only a few areas where the treating plastic surgeon may be negligent. Resuscitation in the acute stage requires some experience – the commonest mistake is for the extent of the burn to be under or over-estimated with consequential administration of too much or too little intravenous fluid – usually the latter.

37.27 Metabolic problems – including acute renal failure – are not uncommon and a wise plastic surgeon invites the assistance of the physician expert in these fields, rather than trying to manage them himself.

37.28 It is easy when preoccupied with the sick patient's overall condition to overlook other important measures such as splinting to prevent foot drop or the search for other injuries. A 12-year-old boy survived an air crash with 65 per cent burns. It was only eight weeks later, after controlling his gas-gangrene infection, and very many other problems, that the fracture of his femoral neck was found.

TISSUE TRANSFER

Major problem areas

37.29

(1) Failure to diagnose the defect;
(2) unreasonable expectations by the patient;
(3) failure to deal energetically with post-operative problems.

Pre-operative

Diagnosis

37.30 Two diagnoses are necessary – the diagnosis of the condition and that of the defect. The condition may be obvious – a cleft lip or a decubitus ulcer, for example.

37.31 Commonly plastic surgeons are called upon to remove cutaneous and other head and neck tumours and subsequently repair the defect. If a lesion can be confidently diagnosed as benign, then surgery can be planned straight away. If the diagnosis is in doubt, then a biopsy of a small part of the lesion may be taken for histological examination.

37.32 The histological differentiation between a keratoacanthoma and a squamous cell carcinoma is often impossible to make on a small biopsy specimen and it is unwise to rely on a benign pathology report in such circumstances.

37.33 Basal cell carcinomata occurring at the inner canthus, the alar base and the region of the external auditory meatus, all have the tendency to spread inwards to the ethmoid area, maxillary sinus and the depths of the meatus respectively. It would be wrong to operate on an advanced lesion at these sites without pre-operative investigations to determine the degree of spread of the tumour.

37.34 The diagnosis of the defect, if correct, will prevent many problems during the operation, and will ensure that the right operation is done. The plastic surgeon is nearly always asked to provide skin cover for a defect, often padding or support as well, and sometimes sensation or movement. He must diagnose the deficit and arrange to replace what is needed – not necessarily what is missing. A bed sore occurring during a period of acute illness in an otherwise fit young individual who is returning to full mobility can be managed after his recovery quite adequately by a free split skin graft, in spite of its known poor wear and tear characteristics. A paraplegic with a similar ulcer needs good skin cover, padding over the underlying bony prominence and, if possible, sensation too. A free skin graft to provide permanent cover in such similar circumstances would be negligence in diagnosis of the defect.

37.35 Removal of a skin lesion from the face will leave a defect often capable of being healed by a simple free split skin graft. The patient deserves the best looking and functioning repair and certainly this will not be provided by such a graft. A trained plastic surgeon will have two or three pedicle flaps planned in his mind and at the time will use the most appropriate of them to fill the defect, with skin giving the best colour and texture match to the immediate surrounding skin, with the necessary scars lying as far as is possible in situations and at angles that ensure they are not too obvious. For another practitioner to deal with such a case with a simple split skin graft, where plastic surgery facilities were available, might well be negligent management.

Counselling

37.36 It is easy for both patient and surgeon to feel that if the life has been saved by removal of the cancer then the post-operative appearance is of secondary importance. Conversely, many patients knowing that a plastic surgeon can – for example – do a face lift, or cosmetic nasal surgery 'without leaving scars' expect their faces to be unmarked after removal of a cutaneous neoplasm. Often the precise mode of repair cannot be predicted pre-operatively, but where possible the extent and appearance of the necessary scarring should be explained. Many patients expect to have a 'skin graft' by which they mean a free split skin graft. If asked if they have ever seen such a graft the answer is invariably 'No' and it is often helpful to have a photograph of a skin grafted area to show the patient what an unsatisfactory result such a graft gives.

37.37 If a free skin graft is to be used it is important to discuss the donor site with the patient so that secondary defect leaves scarring no more obvious than necessary. In spite of all this, however, it is not infrequent that the repair planned pre-operatively has to be abandoned for one that at surgery appears to give a better result, and this fact should be explained.

37.38 Grafts can fail; haematoma and infection can kill pedicle flaps, and the possibility of such failures – and the subsequent management of the problem should be mentioned. This is particularly important in the case of free flaps – composite pieces of skin and other tissues such as fat or bone, which are brought free from another site, and then given a new blood supply by surgically joining the small blood vessels serving the graft to similar blood vessels at the recipient site. These blood vessel anastomoses require delicate and difficult microsurgical techniques which can fail. The big difference is that in such a failure the whole of the transferred tissue is lost, whereas if there is a problem in the case of a free skin graft or pedicle flap, a good proportion of the transferred tissue usually survives, often allowing healing to take place without further surgery. As in other branches of surgery, a patient who has been well informed is far more co-operative (and less litigious) than one who is struggling in the dark.

37.39 The comparatively new technique of tissue expansion requires special mention. In this, a deflated balloon is inserted under the skin, and gradually inflated with saline by periodical injections into an exteriorised or buried valve system. As a result the overlying skin is gradually stretched so that more local skin is available to cover a defect following subsequent excision of a lesion in the area. Unfortunately, infection of the area and extrusion or deflation of the balloon are not infrequent complications and these problems should certainly be explained to the patient as the incidence can rise as high as 30 per cent or more (Antonyshyn et al 1988).

37.40 More recent work is establishing clearer indications and contra-indications for tissue expansion (Meland et al 1992) and the complication rate can be expected to fall.

Operation

37.41 If one assumes that the usual plastic surgery techniques are used, and that normal theatre practice is observed, an accusation of negligence for events during the operation is unlikely. Nevertheless, one or two points still arise.

37.42 Haematoma spells damage to pedicle flaps. In many plastic surgery operations wide areas of skin are undermined and consequently in those areas are many bleeding points. These should all be controlled by the least traumatic technique available. A bipolar diathermy probably produces minimal tissue damage. A monopolar machine, if used, should be at a comparatively high setting and used only for very short periods to limit the spread of heat to tissues surrounding the bleeding point. Ligatures should be fine; if a blood vessel is tied, as little extraneous tissue as possible should be included in the ligature and if a long length of vessel is tied, the end beyond the ligature should be removed close to it to avoid leaving devitalised tissue in the wound. It is often a wise precaution to leave in a drain where there has been a large area of undermining.

37.43 The order of procedure of the operation needs prior planning. If an open and potentially infected wound is being skin grafted it is important that the skin graft be cut and the donor site dressed before the ulcer is touched, so as to avoid possible infection of the donor site. Were the donor site to become infected, with consequent delayed healing and excessive scarring, where such an order of precedence had not been followed, a claim for negligence might well succeed.

37.44 Overall function of mechanical surgical instruments may not be the responsibility of the surgeon but their adjustment often is. In particular, care should be taken with the various unpowered skin graft knives – a badly fitting or ill adjusted disposable blade can do considerable damage.

37.45 The wound dressing is the responsibility of the surgeon, and often an important part of the operation as it is used to maintain rest of the part concerned and to exert gentle pressure to control capillary oozing as well as to absorb any exudate from the wound. Care must be taken that a bandage does not exert undue pressure on a pedicle flap – and particular care must be taken to prevent pressure on a 'dog-ear' where the skin flap is folded on itself – by placing appropriately folded gauze either side of the 'dog-ear' to take the pressure of the bandage off the skin flap. At the same time it is helpful for post-operative management if a portion of the skin flap can be left on show so that early warning is given of any reduction in the circulation through it and of the formation of a haematoma deep to it.

37.46 A haematoma under the flap, if not removed, will often cause necrosis of part of the flap and once diagnosed must be actively removed by taking out some sutures expression and, if necessary, return to the operating theatre for its evacuation under a general anaesthetic. Failure so to treat a haematoma would be considered negligent by most plastic surgeons.

SCARS AND SCARRING

Major problem areas

37.47

(1) Unreasonable expectations by the patient;
(2) operating when surgery is unlikely to succeed.

37.48 'This girl is unhappy about the scar on her face following a road accident last year. Please will you remove it for her.' Such a letter, frequently received by a plastic surgeon from a general practitioner, implies that even qualified doctors believe that plastic surgeons can 'remove scars' – and certainly many lay people believe this (Beare 1973). This totally erroneous impression probably arises from the plastic surgeon's ability, in many cases, to place his scar where it is not seen – intranasally for a cosmetic nose operation – or largely in the scalp for a face lift procedure. In truth, if the whole thickness of the skin is cut through, a scar will result which will be permanent. The first duty of the plastic surgeon towards the patient who presents complaining of the appearance of a scar, is to explain this fact – and to go on explaining it in the face of disbelief by a patient who has been led to expect a miracle by the use of a skin graft, some form of invisible 'plastic surgery' or even the use of 'plastic skin'.

Pre-operative diagnosis

37.49 A fine flat, pale scar probably cannot be improved. More obvious scars may be improvable, but a diagnosis must be sought to explain the unsatisfactory nature of the scar. Factors influencing the eventual appearance of the scar are intrinsic or extrinsic. Intrinsic factors include the site of the scar, and its direction, the age and racial characteristics of the patient. The area of shoulder skin over the deltoid, and the skin over the sternal area are very prone to produce large, thick, itching scars, even on minor trauma. These hypertrophic or keloid scars will recur, probably even larger and more florid, if surgically removed and should not be subjected to surgery. A classic example is the excision of the keloid scar over the shoulder area resulting from a BCG injection which nearly always seems to produce a bigger and better keloid. Scars that run longitudinally over the front or back of a joint so that they are continually subject to longitudinal stretching and relaxation, tend to hypertrophy, and simple excision of such scars is unlikely to produce an improvement, though a Z-plasty procedure to break the line of the scar can often produce a better result.

37.50 Scars that run at right-angles to the line of a joint are continually subject to transverse stretching and surgery is unlikely to lessen the width of these areas of wide, shiny, atrophic scarring.

37.51 The direction of a scar in relation to the natural lines of skin tension – which on the whole follow the lines of skin wrinkles – also influences its appearance. Those that cross these lines tend to be broader and thicker than those that run parallel to the lines of tension. The latter are also less obvious in the older face as they blend with the natural ageing lines of the face. The overall direction of a scar cannot be changed but an improvement can sometimes be achieved by breaking the lines of a scar by a Z-plasty or W-plasty, producing an irregular, flat, zig-zag line which may be less obvious than a straight one.

37.52 Caucasian children from three months of age to early adulthood tend to produce rather thicker, more florid scars than their seniors. Adults of African races tend to produce large keloid scars – which can grow to horrific size. Treatment of both these types of scar is difficult but simple excisional surgery alone is unlikely to help and may make matters worse.

37.53 Extrinsic factors include the surgical management of the original wound and its subsequent progress in healing. Where a patient has an associated major injury it is reasonable that repair of the facial laceration takes second place and 'first aid' suturing is acceptable, assuming that secondary revision of the scars will be available when the patient is fit. Otherwise careful removal of devitalised tissue, meticulous haemostasis, fine non-absorbable sutures taken out early (three to five days usually), the avoidance of tension on the skin edges, if necessary using deeper absorbable sutures, and keeping infection at bay, should result in as perfect a scar as is possible. Wound breakdown after suture removal, or wound infection delaying healing will lead to poor scarring.

Counselling

37.54 So the surgeon made the diagnosis – and often multiple factors are at work. Was healing uneventful? If not, secondary surgery has a chance of improving the situation. If so, then what intrinsic factors are operating to make this a less than perfect scar, and is it possible to counter these intrinsic factors? If not, the surgeon must tell the patient that this is the sort of scar his body makes at this site and this age and surgical revision of the scar will not be helpful.

37.55 Scar tissue contracts, therefore a linear scar on a convex surface makes a groove, on a concave surface it makes a web. These deformities are correctable by Z-plasties, but it is important that the patient realises that only the contour defect will be improved, the surface discolouration and irregularity will remain.

37.56 If unsatisfactory scarring is being caused by such an intrinsic factor as race or site then it is certainly verging on negligence to operate on these relying only on simple excision to cure the problem. If excision is undertaken other measures such as local steroids by injection or other means, local pressure, or superficial radiotherapy, should follow to try and prevent recurrence of the keloid. Patients only too often come expecting elimination of a scar and it is vital that they understand the limitations of what surgery has to offer. Even patients with extensive burn scars will seek more and more surgery in attempting to obtain the impossible goal of a return to normal appearance.

Operation

37.57 Assuming that standard plastic surgery techniques are followed the commonest mistake is to operate where no surgery can be expected to improve matters. The second commonest is to do the wrong operation. The extensions of a scar necessary to perform a Z or W-plasty on a 40-year-old adult will blend into the normal facial lines, often to become unnoticeable. The same Z-plasty on a child, or even a young adult, will leave a 'streak of lightning' (Rank 1973) across the cheek as the scars refuse to fade and blend. Local skin flaps or Z-plasties on the face in the young are best avoided, however satisfactory they may be in the more mature facial skin.

37.58 A Z-plasty will release a linear pull from a contracted facial scar but where skin has been lost it must be replaced from elsewhere, and a simple Z-plasty that looks so attractive will not supply the missing skin to fill the defect.

Post-operative care

37.59 It is standard technique to maintain a dry wound and to remove sutures early – if necessary using supportive adhesive tape on the skin surface to protect the wound from early dehiscence. The patient should be warned to avoid excessive exposure of the scar to sunlight.

37.60 If the surgery had been for a keloid scar, then superficial irradiation, if that is considered advisable, is usually started, with the co-operation of the radiotherapist, as soon as the sutures are removed.

37.61 The first signs of scar hypertrophy usually start at about one month after surgery. The patient should be seen at this time and if the wound is showing signs of hypertrophic scarring, local treatment with steroid ointment begun. Further treatment, such as local pressure and steroid tape or injection, may be required but the one month appointment ensures the treatment is started in good time.

37.62 Where scar revision on a face has been undertaken in circumstances where the surgeon feels significant improvement is unlikely, so long as he has informed the patient of his opinion, the latter is often a consoled and happier person to know that at least he has done everything possible to minimise his scarring and will find it easier to accept his disfigurement thereafter.

HAND SURGERY

Major problem areas

37.63

(1) Missing the divided nerve or tendon;
(2) missing the foreign body;
(3) operating on difficult cases by inexperienced surgeons;
(4) operating on difficult cases in unsuitable conditions.

37.64 By far the commonest cause of an action for negligence in hand surgery is the failure to diagnose an injury to an important deep structure when the patient first attends the Accident & Emergency Department (see paras **24.33–24.40**). A complete division of a finger tendon may be obvious merely from the posture of the digit, without asking the patient to attempt movement, which may be limited by pain. A nerve division must be sought for, and is very easily diagnosed once suspected. A high level of suspicion is the key to avoiding these mistakes. Any wound over a tendon or nerve, or an oblique one at a distance, must raise the suspicion of damage to the deeper structures and the proper diagnosis pursued.

37.65 Problems can arise with partial division of a tendon. Posture and movement may be normal – allowing for the restriction caused by pain – and yet the tendon may be functioning on only a few fibres of uncut tissue which spontaneously rupture a few days later, apparently giving the impression of a missed diagnosis. If in doubt the wound must be explored under proper conditions with facilities for dealing with the tendon injury rather than with local infiltration anaesthetic in the Accident & Emergency Department. Particular problems arise in young children with suspected nerve or tendon injuries. They may be unco-operative during examination because of their fear and pain. They will naturally revolt against any doctor who approaches the injured hand with a gleaming sharp needle to test their sensation! Here again, it is safest to explore the hand under general anaesthesia for purposes of diagnosis as well as possible treatment.

37.66 Foreign bodies in the depths of the hand may be missed if, again, a high level of suspicion is not maintained. An accurate history will often give a clue and X-rays of the part may reveal the suspected fragment of glass – though it is important to remember that not all glass is radio-opaque. If the presence of a foreign body is suspected from the history, again, it is important that the surgery is undertaken under proper conditions with adequate anaesthesia – not merely local anaesthetic infiltration.

Counselling

37.67 Unfortunately for the surgeon, the motivation of the patient is at least as important to the final result as the skill of the surgeon. An unhappy 35 year-old woman attempted to kill herself by dividing all the blood vessels, tendons and nerves on the flexor aspect of the wrist. A skilled surgeon undertook the repair and the wound healed well. The patient continued to be apathetic and passively unco-operative and the hand finished as little more than a paper-weight. A man of the same age received an identical injury on broken glass and, again, the structures were carefully repaired by a skilled surgeon. Healing was uncomplicated. Shortly after discharge from hospital the consultant noted, 'Mr X seems to be a difficult and aggressive patient; hopefully he will be able to channel this aggression into mobilising his hand.' Shortly after this he was arrested by the police and held in various remand centres. Six months after his injury he was seen again by the consultant (the patient still being in police custody) when he had regained a totally full range of movement of all his digits, having had only one physiotherapy session in the period.

37.68 The importance of motivation makes counselling extremely difficult when it comes to giving a prognosis. The patient should be told about what will be done and why, but an accurate forecast as to the future is not possible. The delay in recovery of sensation, and its inevitable imperfection, after nerve repair or grafting should be explained. The possibility or, in some patients, probability of recurrence or extension of Dupuytren's contracture, particularly in the small finger, should be emphasised.

Operation

37.69 Most hand surgery is done with the use of a tourniquet. Care must be taken that the tourniquet is not left on at the end of the operation (not a common mistake now that large sources of compressed gas are usually attached to the cuff), that the cuff pressure is not excessive, that the cuff width is adequate and that the tourniquet is not left on for too long. In practice the most likely source of trouble is the inaccurate dial on the pneumatic tourniquet, allowing the true pressure of the cuff to be much greater than that appearing on the dial. Such gauges should be frequently tested against a mercury manometer. An uninformed theatre attendant may apply a tourniquet with too narrow a cuff, resulting in nerve damage underneath the cuff in spite of the pressure being at a reasonable level.

37.70 As mentioned above, acute surgery to the flexor tendons and nerves in the hand can require special skills, and good operating conditions and anaesthesia. Such operations are not to be done by a junior doctor in the casualty theatre. It is tempting for a trainee with some experience to undertake nerve or flexor tendon surgery in a wound which may be somewhat crushed or contaminated, in order to 'get the practice'. The results of such surgery will not be a credit to the surgeon and the temptation must be avoided. In such a situation, secondary surgery undertaken formally once the wound is healed is far more likely to produce a satisfactory outcome.

37.71 The recurrence or extension of the disease process in the hands of a patient with Dupuytren's contracture is common. It has been shown that the likelihood of recurrence at any one site can be reduced by replacing the overlying skin with a free full thickness skin graft. Such a procedure adds noticeably to the length of the operation and if the graft does not take satisfactorily (always a possibility), will delay healing and, indeed, may cause early recurrent contracture by the excessive scar formed. Therefore, it should not be used as a routine procedure for all cases but the surgeon who does not use a free full thickness graft when operating on an area of recurrent disease needs to have a good reason for his decision.

Post-operative care

37.72 A tight bandage can cause ischaemia and subsequent scarring of the small muscles in the hand, even when the finger tips protruding from the bandage have a good circulation. A less tight bandage may allow the development of a haematoma in the palm, with subsequent incapacitating deep scarring and, perhaps, overlying skin loss. Both these conditions cause severe post-operative pain and failure to remove the dressing and inspect the hand in a patient who complains of unusually severe pain might well lead to a claim for damages.

37.73 Most patients need help with mobilisation of their hands after surgery. Physiotherapy and occupational therapy – with splinting if necessary – will all help, but it must be explained to the patient that it is largely by his or her own efforts that a satisfactory result will ensue.

COSMETIC SURGERY

Major problem areas

37.74

(1) Failure of communication between patient and surgeon;
(2) operating on wrongly motivated patients;
(3) operating on patients who need psychiatric care.

37.75 It is in the field of cosmetic surgery that the plastic surgeon most commonly meets the complaining or litigious patient. There are various reasons for this but the most frequent is financial. If he thinks about it the patient knows that he is paying for his other medical or surgical treatment by his taxes or his insurance premiums, but at the time of service his treatment appears free to him. For cosmetic surgery, which is not covered by medical insurance, he must dig fairly deeply into his own pocket, and this hurts. Not unnaturally he wants to ensure he has value for his money, and a wise plastic surgeon also wishes to ensure this. As a corollary, the majority of patients who complain about the results of their treatment, do so because, for one reason or another, they wish to avoid paying the surgeon's fee. One American surgeon writes that the number of patients' complaints fell dramatically when he adopted the practice of collecting his fee before surgery (Webster 1972).

37.76 Secondly, the patient may be conventionally ugly or old-looking but is essentially 'normal'. If he is not satisfied with the result of surgery he may feel that the surgeon has made 'normal' into 'abnormal'.

37.77 Many patients have feelings of guilt about having cosmetic surgery believing that it is somehow wrong to change the appearance they have been given and wrong to take up the time of the surgeon and hospital facilities for reasons of vanity, when they could be used for 'more important' cases. If things should go wrong so that healing is delayed or scarring excessive, they feel they are being punished for their vanity and their feelings of guilt increase. As a way of dealing with these feelings of guilt they may try to transfer them to the surgeon – who may be totally blameless – becoming aggressive, demanding and litigious. It helps the surgeon to deal with the situation if he understands the roots of the aggression directed at him. There is no easy cure for the situation but frequent visiting, extra attention and a great deal of reassurance will usually result in a happy outcome at the price of some extra stress to the surgeon.

37.78 Thirdly, patients often have unreasonable expectations as to the outcome – both their post-operative physical appearance and the outcome as concerns their social or business lives. A bad actress applies for a part. The casting director knows she is a poor actress but is too kind to say so. Instead, he says, 'Your nose is too big – go and have it fixed'. So the patient has a technically satisfactory rhinoplasty and returns to the casting director. She is still a bad actress, so she is not given the part and the director may even make derogatory remarks about the result of the surgery to give himself a satisfactory excuse. Not unnaturally the patient will blame the surgeon for her not getting the desired part.

37.79 A face lift on a middle-aged woman will not bring back to the fold an errant husband who prefers his younger secretary. The wife, of course, will blame the surgeon for her 'unsatisfactory operation'.

37.80 It is vital, then, to establish the motivation behind the request for cosmetic surgery, if one is to avoid a result which may be technically perfect yet which has not produced the desired effect on a patient's life. At the initial consultation patients are usually apprehensive and worried that the surgeon may consider the request for cosmetic surgery as vain or frivolous. Usually quite a lot of information needs to be given to the patient who tends to remember only those parts that sound optimistic. It is thus good practice to have some sort of 'fact sheet' for those patients undergoing the more common cosmetic surgery procedures, for the patient to take away and read at leisure, at home. It is also good practice to see a patient more than once (perhaps without a fee) before their admission to hospital when the problems can be rediscussed and any advice or caveats reinforced. It is also helpful to have appropriate photographs taken at the first visit and these can be discussed at the following appointment. It is often easier to demonstrate points on a photograph than it is by trying to sort them out using a mirror. The commonest cause for dissatisfaction following surgery is inadequate communication between patient and surgeon in the pre-operative stage.

37.81 When advising the patient about complications of cosmetic surgery, it is the author's usual practice to ignore those that occur with the frequency of less than one per cent. If the patient actually asks what complications can occur, then a fuller explanation, including rare eventualities, is given.

37.82 It would be helpful to consider the more commonly performed cosmetic surgery procedures individually.

Face lift (rhytidectomy)

Pre-operative

37.83 The most important points are in patient selection and, as far as is possible, obtaining consent that is truly informed. As stated above, a patient who hopes to regain an errant or divorcing husband is unlikely to be helped. One who needs to look good for fear of losing her job – selling clothes in a fashion store, for example – is usually excellently motivated. One who has just survived a divorce or a bereavement (not necessarily the death of a husband) and has recovered from her grief and wants to pick up the pieces and start her life again, also is usually well motivated. So long as the patient's motivation is aimed at a reasonably achievable goal she is likely to be happy with the result of well performed surgery.

37.84 A patient who loses weight post-operatively will regain some of the folds and wrinkles that the surgery has eliminated. Therefore, patients should be advised to take off any weight they wish before the operation. The patient should be warned about the siting and probable appearance of the scars resulting from the surgery. If the anterior incision curves forwards within the scalp at the temple it will not be seen but each successive face lift (in females) will lift the hair line in the pre-auricular region so that after three operations the bald cheek skin is situated high in the temple above the normal sideburn. Many patients only intend to have a single face lift, but those in the public eye may have more, and for these patients the advantages and disadvantages of an incision placed lower, actually at the hair line, should be discussed. It may well be helpful to inspect any other operation scars to assess the quality of scar made by the patient. Those with red or auburn hair do have a tendency to make thicker, more florid scars than their colleagues, and the scar-forming quality of those races subject to keloid scars should be investigated – if necessary by making a small 'test' incision before undertaking surgery.

37.85 The patient should be told about the post-operative bruising and the anaesthesia of the cheek skin. It is the author's practice to mention post-auricular skin loss (or slow healing), minute subcutaneous self-resolving haematomata and the possibility of a major haematoma requiring return to the operating theatre. Patients are not told about permanent anaesthesia of the ear, or partial facial paralysis from damage to the greater auricular or facial nerve bundles respectively, unless they specifically ask about complications. Patients receiving the 'SMAS' more radical face lift procedure (uncommon in the author's practice) perhaps need more detailed counselling.

Operation

37.86 The surgery is comparatively standardised and provided very careful haemostasis is carried out, any reasonably trained and competent surgeon is unlikely to be accused of negligence occurring during the surgery. Should the greater auricular nerve be inadvertently damaged it should be repaired at the time.

Post-operative care

37.87 A watch must be kept for haematoma formation and any such haematoma evacuated as a matter of urgency.

37.88 The pre-auricular incision is the only one permanently on show – it has been sutured under virtually no tension so that the sutures can be removed after a few days to avoid visible stitch marks. Infection – even without antibiotic cover – is extremely uncommon, but a little marginal necrosis of the post-auricular skin flap may occur and requires merely cleanliness and a little antibiotic cream.

37.89 A few patients having standard face lift procedures, whilst looking excellent in the few months immediately after surgery, rapidly regress so that six months after their operation little improvement remains. This seems to be confined to a few individual patients, cannot be forecast pre-operatively, and responds to minor 'mini lift' procedure. The necessity for such secondary surgery would not be considered as indicating negligent surgery in the first instance.

Protruding ear correction

Pre-operative

37.90 This 'bat ear' operation is probably the commonest cosmetic surgery procedure performed. The patient and parents should be informed of the site of the scarring and the necessity of wearing a night bandage for a month post-operatively.

Operation

37.91 Many operative procedures are available – each one has its own protagonist. All produce a satisfactory looking ear, and equally, all have a definite recurrence rate. Recurrent deformity, therefore, is not evidence of negligence.

Post-operative care

37.92 Haematoma can cause necrosis and subsequent infection and death of the cartilagenous support of the ear, potentially resulting in considerable deformity. As in other situations, severe pain in the wound demands investigation, and evacuation of the haematoma, if it exists.

Eyelid reduction (blepharoplasty)

Pre-operative

DIAGNOSIS

37.93 Excess skin in the upper eyelid – causing a 'hooded' effect – is common with advancing age, and may be associated with minor fatty herniae causing bulging, particularly near the inner canthus. These cases are uncomplicated and amenable to simple, if exact, surgery. Very occasionally a patient with a heavy brow would be helped more by the excision of a crescent of forehead skin to raise the lowered eyebrow.

37.94 The lower eyelid presents more problems and it is important to be absolutely clear what it is that is troubling the patient. In most people there exists a smooth curved groove (often darkly pigmented) running downwards and outwards from the inner canthus, with its concavity upwards lying at the junction of the thin eyelid and thick cheek skin. This groove may be made slightly more shallow but cannot be eliminated nor can the pigmentation be removed. Above the groove the skin may be wrinkled and may be bulged by herniating orbital fat, or occasionally by oedema associated with renal disease, which should be excluded. The wrinkling and bulging at this site can be improved or eliminated. Many patients complain of bulging below the groove over the upper part of the prominence of the malar bone. This bulging is not amenable to surgery and it is, hence, vital to be sure precisely of what 'bulginess' the patient is complaining. If careful diagnosis is not made the wrong operation may ensue with, naturally, a dissatisfied patient.

37.95 After the surgery most practitioners use some type of blindfold bandage. When this is removed, the first thing a patient does is to test his own eyesight, to make sure it has not suffered. A small number of people have unrecognised visual defects and it is important to do some simple test of visual acuity pre-operatively to avoid a charge of damaging the sight in an eye which, in fact, was previously flawed. It is, of course, important also to ask about the wearing of contact lenses and ensure they are removed before surgery.

COUNSELLING

37.96 The patient should be warned of the scarring, of the almost inevitable bruising and of the likelihood of some watering of the eye in the first week post-operatively. It is the author's practice to mention the possibility of permanent loss of vision but to emphasise its extreme rarity.

Operation

37.97 Excess skin excision on the upper eyelid will lead to an eye not closing, and so drying and becoming subject to ulceration of the cornea. There is, however, a small margin of tolerance and careful surgery should avoid this problem. In the lower eyelid the margin of tolerance is extremely small between a successful operation and one that causes permanent lowering of the eyelid margin and, perhaps, permanent watering. There is a special danger, and even more than usual care necessary, when the patient has had the same operation previously. Again, awareness of the problem and meticulously accurate surgery will avoid trouble.

Post-operative care

37.98 Severe pain should be treated not with analgesia but by calling the surgeon and removing the dressings. A large orbital haematoma can cause blindness, and needs urgent evacuation. The surgeon should ensure that the nursing staff are aware of the danger.

Cosmetic rhinoplasty

Counselling

37.99 As has been emphasised previously, the patients' motivation should be explored. The nose seems to be the commonest organ for dissatisfaction in mentally imbalanced or ill patients. Surgery on such patients will never produce a satisfied patient as his abnormality is in his brain rather than in his nose. It is easy to pick out such patients when they complain about what is obviously a good-looking, normal nose; it is much more difficult to do so when the nose has a genuine cosmetic deformity. Such patients classically are unable to describe in detail what they feel is wrong with the nose, but keep on talking about 'a bad shape' or 'an ugly nose'. A mentally normal patient does not usually know exactly what changes are needed, but will say that they dislike the hump on the nose; that the tip is too broad, and so on. Often a question about how other people react to the patient's nose will produce evidence of paranoid delusions – 'They talk about my nose behind my back'; 'People on the bus are always looking at my nose'; 'They won't give me a better job at the office because of my nose'. If in doubt, psychiatric referral will help in selecting those patients unlikely to be helped by surgery, and indeed, those who genuinely are in need of psychiatric help.

37.100 Many patients expect the surgeon to advise them what sort and shape of nose would best suit them. This is dangerous as tastes in noses vary. The author's practice is to explain the details of the surgery and take appropriate photographs at the first visit, and ask the patient to return for more detailed discussions when more thought has been given by the patient to the exact change required. The eyelid bruising, the post-operative nasal tip anaesthesia, must be mentioned and the three or more months necessary for the result to become apparent also explained.

37.101 The possibilities and impossibilities of the patient's wishes must be discussed. A broad nose tip, with thick skin, is extremely difficult to narrow – especially in the older patient. A nasal tip that is too high is difficult to lower. The patient must have a clear idea of what can and cannot be done.

Operation

37.102 Provided adequate counselling has taken place there are few openings for a charge of negligence during the surgery, given normal care. It is important to ensure that every piece of tissue – bone, cartilage or other – that is detached from the nose is actually removed from the nasal cavity, to avoid later inhalation of such a loose body, with possible lung abscess formation. A missing fragment in the operation site often is brought out on a dry swab packed gently into the field. If this manoeuvre is not successful and no fragment can be seen, thorough suction of the post-nasal area is undertaken and the anaesthetist informed so that he may search for any such fragment at the end of the operation whilst sucking out the pharynx. If a saw has been used for the lateral osteotomy, it is important to remove all sawdust to avoid the possibility of a post-operative abscess at the inner canthus. Such an abscess may occur even if normal dust-removing procedures have been carried out, but should it arise when such precautions have not been taken, a claim for negligence might well succeed.

Post-operative care

37.103 Firm instructions must be given as to the avoidance of nose blowing, lowering the head and heavy physical exertion. Patients often need constant reassurance that all is well and that they must wait several months for the final result. During this period continued visits to the surgeon are helpful in making the patients feel they have not been neglected and in giving reassurance about minor problems.

Breast augmentation

37.104 Although successful breast augmentation produces some of the most grateful patients of any receiving cosmetic surgery, the procedure is beset with potential problems. An excellent overview of the present situation (Dunn et al 1992) is highly recommended for surgeons or lawyers becoming involved in litigation following such surgery.

Breast augmentation and breast cancer

37.105 There is no evidence whatever to suggest that augmentation with the normally used implant of a silicone elastomer bag containing silicone gel can cause breast cancer. Indeed in the largest study published (Deapen et al 1986), of over 3,000 patients having had augmentation showed this group slightly less likely to develop breast cancer than their peers who had not had augmentation.

Human adjuvant disease

37.106 There is an uncommon and mixed group of diseases known as 'Auto Immune Disease' in which the body mobilises its defences normally used against infecting organisms, against one of its own tissues. This group of disease is widespread amongst the general population and can affect many different tissues – joints – skin – thyroid gland and so on.

37.107 It has been suggested that breast augmentation with silicone bag implants may cause a similar condition – termed 'Human Adjuvant Disease' or 'Connective Tissue Disease'. The patients originally described had received injections of paraffin wax or liquid silicone (often not of medical grade), into their breasts, rather than gel filled silicone implants and are not relevant to the issue. In the United Kingdom the Department of Health commissioned a report from the Medical Devices Directorate (Tinkler et al MDD report 1993) which reviewed the literature and reported that at least as far as the commonest disease (scleroderma), suspected of being associated with augmentation mammoplasty was concerned 'there is no indication that the incidence of scleroderma in US women with breast implants is any higher than in the general population'.

37.108 A central monitoring body for breast implant patients has been set up to gather and process the imformation about this subject in the United Kingdom.

37.109 In spite of the MDD report, it might be as well for any surgeon contemplating performing augmentation mammoplasty, to explain the situation to his patient. Silicone implants have not been found guilty of causing 'connective tissue disease'; but neither have they been satisfactorily acquitted. More information is required and is being sought.

Capsule formation

37.110 After implantation of the breast prosthesis, the body forms a layer of scar tissue around them. This capsule can shrink, squeezing the implants and making them feel unduly firm or hard, and on occasions look abnormal. The type of implant with a smooth exterior normally used in the 1980s and early 1990s, produced this reaction in 30–50 per cent of patients. New prostheses with a 'textured' surface seem less likely to produce this undesirable effect (Coleman et al 1991), at least in the short term. Nevertheless, the possibility of undue firmness should be explained to the patient together with the difficulty of relieving it.

Operation

37.111 The surgical approach may be in the sub-mammary area, the axilla or the periareola position. The implant may be inserted superficial or deep to the pectoralis major muscle. Any of these techniques are acceptable, and the failure to use one or another is not negligent.

37.112 Haemostasis is important – a small haematoma contributes to scar formation. Some surgeons use drainage, others fear the introduction of infection around the foreign body and feel it wiser not to drain.

Post-operative care

37.113 If a haematoma develops it must be evacuated, probably under a second anaesthetic. If capsular contracture occurs it may be treated by open operation to remove or divide the capsule, or by 'closed capsulotomy' where a very firm squeeze is used to split the scar tissue. Recurrence after each of these procedures is not uncommon.

Breast reduction and mastopexy

Pre-operative

COUNSELLING

37.114 The operation is not a small one and patients should be advised of this and of the necessity of having help at home after their discharge from hospital. The extent and nature of the scarring should be explained – if possible with photographs of a typical case, and the patient warned also of the possibility of nipple anaesthesia and inability to suckle. It may also be advisable to warn the patient of the small possibility of skin necrosis with associated delayed healing.

Operation

37.115 If induced hypotension is not available, blood loss will be significant and transfusion often required. Many surgical techniques are described – that which normally produces the best result in any individual's hands is the best for the patient.

Post-operative care

37.116 As far as possible sutures should be removed early, but to prevent wound dehiscence in a situation where there is some tension on the wound edges, some may need to be left ten to fourteen days. The use of absorbable sutures in the dermis may help to avoid this.

Abdominoplasty

Pre-operative

COUNSELLING

37.117 Excess skin and fat can be removed from the abdominal area (with or with without the use of liposuction), but the bulging abdomen due to poor muscle tone will not be improved, and it is important that the patient realises this. If there is divarication of the rectus abdominus muscles then this can be repaired at the same time, which will help some patients. The nature and siting of the scar should be explained, together with the temporary anaesthesia of the suprapubic skin.

Operation

37.118 Technique is reasonably standardised and provided standard plastic surgery custom is carefully adhered to, a claim for negligence occurring during surgery is unlikely.

Post-operative care

37.119 As in other instances, haematomata should be evacuated as soon as diagnosed. There is often some oedema of the skin above the transverse suprapubic incision, giving an apparent overlap of the upper or lower edge of the scar, but this is temporary and not evidence of negligent suturing.

Other procedures

37.120 Reduction of pendulous upper arms, buttocks and thighs is occasionally performed. Excess fat from many sites can be removed by liposuction. Various types of hair-bearing skin transplantation may be used to treat baldness. As in other areas of plastic surgery, provided the patient knows the limitations of what can be done and reasonable surgical care is employed – particularly in respect of haematoma formation – claims for negligence are unlikely.

SUMMARY FOR THE SURGEON

37.121

(1) Trespassers may be prosecuted. Be extra careful when working close to or over the borders of other specialities;

(2) 'jaw-jaw is better than war-war' (W S Churchill). Pay extra attention to the patient whose treatment is not proceeding smoothly, and see such patients frequently;

(3) (a) diagnosis before treatment – diagnosis of the defect and of the patient;

(b) diagnosis before treatment – of severe post-operative pain;

(4) 'open all hours'. Do not make it difficult for your patients to contact and consult you – 'He wouldn't see me' is a common and often justified complaint of dissatisfied and litigious patients.

BIBLIOGRAPHICAL REFERENCES

Antonyshyn, Gruss, Zuker and MacKinnon 'Tissue Expansion in Head and Neck Reconstruction' (1988) Plastic and Reconstructive Surgery 82, 59.

Beare R L B in Hall-Smith, Cairns and Beare *Dermatology* (London, Crosby, Lockwood and Staples, 1973) p 327.

Coleman D J, Fuo I T H and Sharpe D T 'Texture or smooth implants for breast augmentation? A prospective controlled trial' (1991) British Journal of Plastic Surgery, 44, 444.

Deapen D M, Pike P H M C, Casagrande J T, and Brody G S 'The relationship between breast cancer and augmentation mammoplasty: an epidemiology study' (1986) Plastic and Reconstructive Surgery, 77, 361.

Dunn K W, Hall P N and Khoo C T K 'Breast Implant Materials; sense and safety' (1992) British Journal of Plastic Surgery, 45,315.

Meland N B, Loessin S J, Thimsen D and Jackson I T 'Tissue expansion in the extremities using external reservoirs' (1992) Annual of Plastic Surgery, 29, 36–39.

Rank Sir B K '9th Gillies Memorial Lecture' (RCS, 1973).

Shenouda N A and England J P S 'Ultrasound in the diagnosis of scaphoid fracture' (1987) The Journal of Hand Surgery, 126, 43.

Tinkler J J B, Campbell H J, Senior J M and Ludgate S M 'Evidence for an Association between the Implementation of Silicones and Corrective

Tissue Disease' (1993) Medical Devices Directorate (MDD/92/42), UK Department of Health, Her Majesty's Stationery Office.

Webster R C in Goldwyn R M (ed) *The Unfavourable Result in Plastic Surgery – Avoidance and Treatment* (Boston, Little, Brown & Co, 1972) pp 563, 564.

CROSS-REFERENCES

For information related to topics in this chapter see Chapters 31 and 33.

CHAPTER 38

Otorhinolaryngology

Professor A G D Maran *MD FRCS FRCS (Ed) FRCP (Ed) FACS*

SUMMARY

BACKGROUND

38.1 The scope of otorhinolaryngology has traditionally been confined to the original three anatomical areas of the ear, the nose and the throat. In the last 20 years, however, otorhinolaryngologists have taken a very high profile in head and neck cancer surgery and the otologists are interfacing with the neurosurgeons in the new subject of neurotology. Finally there is a group who practise facial plastic surgery. In the United States several subspecialities within otorhinolaryngology have been singled out and surcharged by the professional liability insurance industry. Surgeons practising facial plastic surgery are surcharged by most insurance companies and recently head and neck surgeons were threatened with a surcharge in several states, again without proven cause. Otologists on the other hand, are still grouped with general otorhinolaryngologists and thus pay the same premium. At the advent of neurotology there was some movement within the insurance industry to break neurotology out of general otology but fortunately this did not happen.

38.2 In the United States in past the ear was an equal partner with the nose and throat concerning the frequency and cost of claims and suits. Costly suits and acoustic neuroma surgery, plus a larger number of claims involving facial nerve paralysis, were the cause. Since the morbidity associated with the acoustic neuroma surgery has lessened and defence tactics in facial nerve surgery have strengthened, the claims against otology have dropped. In the period 1980 to 1985 otology was responsible for 16.8 per cent of all claims but received only 6.3 per cent of the money paid in settlement of the claims. In recent years however the advent of endoscopic sinus surgery has doubled the number of claims in rhinology. There is fortunately very little in the way of litigation in the field of head and neck cancer surgery.

38.3 The ten claims that cost the most to settle in the United States in the period 1980 to 1985 were as follows:

(1) tonsil and adenoid bleeding resulting in blindness;
(2) tympanoplasty and cardiac arrest;
(3) mastoidectomy with facial paralysis;
(4) failure to diagnose tuberculosis;
(5) intranasal ethmoidectomy causing blindness;
(6) injections causing foot drop;
(7) failure to diagnose cancer;
(8) failure to diagnose cause for facial paralysis;
(9) failure to diagnose ear cancer;
(10) problems from removing a lip tumour.

38.4 In the United Kingdom as in other specialities the number of claims rises yearly. There has been little difference in this rise since 1980 and it stands at 15 per cent increase per annum. The number of claims rise at this rate but what is more important is that the size of settlement of claims rises far more. The Medical Protection Society paid out £2.5 million in 1972 in settlements and in 1987 the figure was £24 million. Forty-one per cent of the Protection Society income goes in claims and 15 per cent on legal expenses.

38.5 Now that more accessible complaints procedures have been established in the NHS reforms these are rising. Last year there were three complaints per thousand in patients in Lothian. Of these, 20 per cent were of a clinical nature. Under the present mechanism the complaint is received by the hospital manager and transferred to the clinical director, who receives the report from the consultant concerned. It is very often useful to see the patient if only to show sympathy and be apologetic if appropriate. This often defuses claims at an early stage.

38.6 The Medical Defence Union gets two to three cases a week related to otorhinolaryngology. It seems that the same mistakes are made over and over again and the majority (60 per cent) are indefensible and a minority are spurious. Ninety-eight per cent of claims come from the National Health Service and claims from private practice are rare. This probably has a relation to the availability of Legal Aid. When expert reports were exchanged many claims disappeared because one of the experts had not examined all of the facts. Seventy per cent of claims are withdrawn or abandoned at this point.

38.7 The number of claims varies according to the senior/junior ratio. Following are the ratios in the UK:

(a) *High senior-to-junior ratio*
Radiology 5.6 to 1
Dermatology 3.1 to 1
(b) *The average group*
Orthopaedics 0.8 to 1
Medicine 0.9 to 1
General surgery 0.9 to 1
Otorhinolaryngology 1.07 to 1
Anaesthesia 1.41 to 1
(c) *Low ratios*
Paediatrics 0.6 to 1
Obstetrics 0.5 to 1
Cardiology 0.2 to 1
A and E 0.1 to 1

38.8 Limited resources prejudice standards. Where a consultant feels that he is working in a dangerous environment it would be necessary for him to show evidence of a complaint to the chief executive of the Trust in the way of letter that clearly identifies environmental or staff deficiencies that might lead to a claim. If this was refused by the Trust then it would be difficult for them to devolve the responsibility from any claim arising out of these deficiencies.

38.9 Three factors relate to errors:

(1) *Unsupervised junior staff*
As many junior doctors as senior doctors are sued in otorhinolaryngology. It is difficult to avoid lack of supervision on junior staff in otorhinolaryngology because the clinical load is high. Much of it involves surgery that is apparently simple and clinical decisions that are apparently straightforward. For a quarter of a million people there will usually be two consultants, two SHOs and a clinical assistant. This group can expect to see 9,000 cases a year in out-patients and do more than 1,500 operations. A consultant with six to seven fixed sessions and an SHO will therefore deal with in excess of 80 patients a week and 15 operations a week. The junior has to be left on his own for much of his time. The emergencies are dealt with by juniors who may be inexperienced. In some areas, eg the nose, a consultant training a junior will not know what he is actually doing with the end of the instrument. This is possible with television facilities but these are not widely available. The problem is that everyone has to do nasal polypectomies and these very often carry risks. Some of these risks could be lethal even with the consultant standing there. This trend may increase as trusts make more staff grades or appoint consultants whose training may not

have been adequate. In *Wilsher v Essex Area Health Authority*[1] Mustill LJ said 'if a doctor is put into a position in which he or she is insufficiently experienced to meet the demands for the job, then whilst the doctor's degree of competence may be sufficient to enable him or her personally to defend the claim in negligence, a patient may seek redress against that doctor's employer alleging negligence in allocating an inexperienced doctor to a post in which a patient is entitled to expect greater competence in treatment'.

(2) *Inexperienced seniors*

One man units are now uncommon. As mentioned earlier modern otorhinolaryngology has a very wide range of required skills from fine middle-ear surgery to major resections for head and neck cancer. The cross boundary referral is now more difficult due to the Health Service reforms. It is unusual for even two consultants to have the required skill mix to perform the entire repertoire of otorhinolaryngology. This means that operations may not be done and if they are done some may be done badly. Cross-referral between consultants has now become so common that it might be a matter for criticism if it does not happen. Things like personal incompatibility and private practice rivalries may not be kept as covert as formerly if a case arises related to experience.

(3) *Poor training*

Before 1974 and the advent of higher surgical training there was great scope for error. It was possible to be appointed to a consultant job in otorhinolaryngology with little in the way of surgical background. Some consultants were appointed with only six months' experience of general surgery and then were expected to do operations such as laryngectomy, radical neck dissection, mastoidectomy etc. Sub-optimal treatment was not uncommon but since there was a low level of litigation and a low expectation for the treatment for head and neck cancer, problems did not arise.

Some of this cohort may still be in practice. For example someone who was made a consultant at 31, which was not unusual in 1965, would now be 60 and not yet retired. Problems arise with only a few, however.

Since 1974 higher surgical training has improved otorhinolaryngology very much more than other specialities. A consultant now should be able to do the whole range but needs many cases to keep in practice. No bodies concerned with training have yet laid down a minimum number of cases that are required to maintain competence.

1 [1987] QB 730, [1986] 3 All ER 801, CA; revsd [1988] AC 1074, [1988] 1 All ER 871, HL.

38.10 It is likely that the completion of training will now be recognised by the award of a certificate of completion of specialist training (CCST). This means that a specialist will be judged capable of independent practice. With a shorter training period and a 72-hour week, standards must drop and the repertoire of the specialist will therefore have to be smaller. Under the old training scheme which will be abandoned by the end of 1995 at the latest, there were areas of otorhinolaryngology that carried great risks e g stapedectomy. Here the operative error is made in millimetres and an error could cause facial nerve damage or complete loss of hearing. There will be about 25 stapedectomies per million population and this means that each consultant will have about five a year in his service. This is little enough for a consultant to keep in practice. If the SAC requires a senior registrar to be trained in it, there is a possibility of a consultant having to let a senior registrar do an operation so as not to hold back his creditation even though he felt that he should do it himself. If the syllabus becomes shorter then it is not yet clear who will be trained to do the operations that are not in the training syllabus. This has not been addressed yet but it has obvious implications. Colleges are not immune from litigation as has been shown in the past two years and SACs and the JCHST may have to field some responsibility unless this problem is addressed.

POSSIBLE EFFECTS OF LITIGATION IN OTORHINOLARYNGOLOGY

38.11 Risk avoidance could result in the avoidance of litigious patients. This applies especially to operations that improve quality of life rather than those that are more directly related to health such as cancer surgery. Such operations may relate to cosmetic surgery or intranasal procedures.

38.12 Risk reduction leads to more diagnostic tests being done. This is particularly true of unilateral hearing loss. The test array for this common clinical situation is expensive and must include evoked response audiometry and MRI scanning. We are almost at the stage of requesting CT scans before any sinus operation including nasal polypectomy. This is of course going to become more difficult in a time of clinical directors budgets and contractual targets.

38.13 Quality assurance will also be damaged. If surgeons feel that information will be a source of litigation then enthusiasm to report results may wane. Although confidentiality is assured in department audit meetings it is certainly not assured on the information that gets to unit level and above.

38.14 There will be decreased availability of health care as more time is spent talking to patients in the clinic and ensuring that informed consent has been given. Fewer patients will be seen and inevitably out-patients' waiting time will increase. In the United States it is estimated that three to seven days a year are spent on legal activity.

INFORMED CONSENT IN OTORHINOLARYNGOLOGY

38.15 Informed consent as we should practice it today comes under four headings:

(a) you must tell the patient of your recommendation for treatment and the alternatives;
(b) you must tell them of all the likely effects of not taking your advice;
(c) you must tell them of the specific risks attached to the operation or treatment you plan;
(d) you must make them aware of the risk of surgery in general.

In former times it was usual for somebody practising head and neck cancer treatment to have figures from other centres to pass on to patients in the discussion of the choice between radiotherapy and surgery. Nowadays with audit it would be important for the surgeon to have his own data so the patient would be better able to take part in the decision-making.

38.16 With regard to specific risks it is not enough merely to give the name of complications, e g facial nerve damage. You must tell the patient what this entails and what the consequences of that complication might be.

38.17 Material risks must be disclosed. These are risks to which a reasonable person in the patient's position would be likely to attach significance as to risk. If the risk is very low, say at the 1 per cent level and obviously is so vital to inform choice, e g death, paralysis and blindness, then it would be essential to explain this.

38.18 There have been many papers relating to what patients understand and what they wish to know. Robinson and Merav[1] found that patients undergoing heart surgery generally had poor retention in all categories of informed consent. Alfidi[2] attempted to assess this in patients who were about to undergo arteriography. Twenty-seven per cent of this group said that the knowledge made them less comfortable about undergoing the procedure. The assurance that patients fully understand the information given to them before they sign consent forms for operations has never been validated.[3]

1 'Informed consent recalled by patients tested postoperatively' (1976) Am Thoracic Surg 22: 210–214.
2 'Controversy, alternatives and discussions in complying with informed consent' (1975) Radiology 14: 231–234.
3 Byrne D, Napier A and Cushieri A 'How informed is informed consent' (1988) British Medical Journal 296: 839–840.

38.19 In otorhinolaryngology informed consent is not implemented well. In a survey of the North of England Otorhinolaryngological Society and the Scottish Otorhinolaryngological Society only 1 per cent informed patients of blindness and CFS leak after a nasal polypectomy, under 10 per cent warned of the risks of orbital complications, blindness and anosmia from intranasal ethmoidectomy, and 26 per cent informed patients of the risk of perforation from oesophagoscopy.

DELAY IN DIAGNOSIS

38.20 This is more likely to happen in general practice than in hospital practice and probably reflects the poor standards of training in otorhinolaryngology in the undergraduate curriculum. Anyone can miss a diagnosis and so causation is the important factor. In other words, did the delay in diagnosis materially affect the outcome? The following examples from the author's own experience give some idea of the problem.

38.21 A 21-year-old girl was having a meal in a Chinese restaurant with her fiancé when she thought she swallowed a bone. She went to hospital that evening but a radiograph did not show any evidence of a bone. They told her to come back the next morning but she was going on holiday that day and even though the symptoms persisted she went on holiday. Four days later she was unable to eat or drink anything and went to the local Accident and

Emergency department. They told her to go back to her local hospital at the end of her holiday. She went home the next day and bled to death in her home when the foreign body eroded the oesophagus and penetrated the innominate artery. The claim was successful.

38.22 A 35-year-old male visited his general practitioner on frequent occasions with a complaint of unilateral nasal obstruction. He was treated with antihistamines and a steroid nasal spray. The condition became more painful and he started to get proptosis. The GP persisted in conservative treatment and referred him to a dentist. The dentist found no abnormality in the teeth and referred him back to the general practitioner. Some weeks later he referred him to hospital where an inoperable cancer of the maxillary antrum was diagnosed. The GP was disciplined by the Family Practice Committee.

38.23 A 17-year-old boy started having difficulty eating and speaking and had a sore throat. The general practitioner was called and diagnosed mumps. The symptoms worsened and the patient began to have difficulty breathing. In spite of three further visits by the general practitioner the diagnosis of mumps was not altered. The parents took the patient into the local hospital where he succumbed from respiratory obstruction due to a parapharyngeal abscess which blocked the larynx. The claim was successful.

38.24 A 40-year-old male had been attending hospital for the previous ten years with chronic sinusitis. He had had several minor surgical procedures performed and a previous biopsy which had confirmed chronic sinusitis. His symptoms of sinusitis recurred and his sinus was painful. He also had some bleeding from one side of his nose and tearing from his eye. A biopsy was done by a junior doctor in draining the sinus but the specimen did not go to pathology. A year later a diagnosis of cancer of the maxilla was made and he was subsequently treated by radiotherapy. There was a recurrence and salvage surgery was performed but to no avail. It was judged that the delay in diagnosis had not materially altered the prognosis. Also the original presentation of chronic sinusitis had masked the possibility of the development of a cancer which in itself was unusual.

38.25 A 35-year-old female began attending a neurologist with facial pain. She attended for five years and had various referrals to physiologists and dentists. The neurologist unfortunately wrote flippant letters to the general practitioner and when it transpired that the cause of the pain was adenoid cystic carcinoma of the parotid gland a claim for delay in diagnosis was successful.

38.26 Deafness occurs in 50 per cent of cases of Pneumococcal meningitis. After 48 hours the risk of disability increases dramatically.[1]

1 Vernon M 'Meningitis and deafness' (1967) Laryngoscope 77: 1856–1874.

38.27 A child, aged three, who was in all other respects normal, started complaining of feeling unwell with a fever. The general practitioner prescribed antibiotics by telephone. Over the next five days requests for visits were continually turned down and a visit by a district nurse confirmed the diagnosis as a respiratory tract infection and tonsillitis. The child was then admitted to hospital as an emergency taken there by the parents and a diagnosis of pneumococcal meningitis was made. The child became profoundly deaf and a claim was successful.

38.28 The author has not dealt personally with any cases of delay in diagnosis of acoustic neuroma but is informed by the adviser to a medical defence society that many cases are pending.

FACIAL NERVE INJURY

38.29 It is thought negligent to damage the facial nerve in ear surgery in the following circumstances:

(a) lack of informed consent;
(b) inadequate training;
(c) operating while unfit or in an unsatisfactory theatre without proper instruments;
(d) where surgery is not indicated;
(e) using unusual and unnecessary force;
(f) operating too close to the nerve;
(g) failure to interpret anatomy correctly;
(h) trying to find the antrum in too low a position;
(i) damaging the nerve with the drill, hooks, chisels or laser; and
(j) failure to carry out proper post-operative treatment.

38.30 The large number of claims relating to facial nerve paralysis in itself made an obvious case that facial paralysis was a bad result and not negligent. More recently surgeons are following stricter informed consent protocols which also lessen the exposure to these claims. However, even if there is no medical negligence and a bad result there may be legal negligence if informed consent is not properly obtained and explained. The best strategy is well crafted informed consent.

38.31 Damage to the facial nerve in benign parotid disease is probably not allowable. No one should be an 'occasional' parotidectomist.

38.32 A woman of 42 was seen at a district general hospital with a mass at the angle of the jaw. It was biopsied by a registrar but the pathology report showed only normal parotid tissue. The mass was then explored by the consultant. The parotid gland was removed but in removing the mass the facial nerve was divided. The mass was shown to be a neuroma of the facial nerve which is exceedingly rare. The fact that the surgeon could show that he had considerable experience of parotid surgery was an important fact in the settlement.

RECURRENT LARYNGEAL NERVE INJURY

38.33 The same principles apply to this injury. The nerve can be damaged in thyroid surgery, pharyngeal pouch removal, cricopharyngeal myotomy, radical neck dissection and partial laryngotomy. The interpretation of whether nerve damage was a bad result or negligence would be made in the light of the surgeon's experience. Fitness to perform the procedure, adequacy of the operation note and the level of pre-operative discussion with the patient are also important.

38.34 A word of caution should be inserted at this point however. There seems to be an acceptance of the fact that if the cord is seen to be moving by the anaesthetist during extubation then this means that no damage has occurred. This is not correct. It is very unlikely that the cord movement would be normal at the time of extubation if the nerve had been damaged. It is more likely that the anesthetist would see mass action of the larynx rather than true cord movement. It is, however, prudent to have the cord looked at before any thyroid surgery because it is quite possible for anyone to have a unilateral cord paralysis from a previous infection such as glandular fever and not know anything about it.

38.35 Voice and cough appreciation are of little use in the post-operative period. The cords would be swollen from the endotracheal tube and a vocal cord paralysis may be masked in the early stages. Unless the nerve was transected and the cord was in the abducted position then it is likely that a vocal cord paralysis would not be recognised for several weeks after the operation.

38.36 Another cause of damage to the recurrent laryngeal nerve apart from surgical trauma is anaesthetic trauma. There have been a number of papers[1] that suggest the nerve can be paralysed with an endotracheal tube. The nature of this injury is nearly always a type one injury and nearly all recover spontaneously.

1 Cavo J W 'True vocal cord paralysis following intubation' (1985) Laryngoscope 85: 1352–1359; Mehta S 'Safer endotracheal intubation' (1986) Lancet 74: 1148.

38.37 Grafting of the recurrent laryngeal nerve is not as successful as grafting the facial nerve. Rehabilitation therefore is by medialising the paralysed vocal cord rather than by grafting the nerve. The cord can be medialised by the injection of teflon or collagen or repositioned with a thyroplasty operation. Results of these operations in terms of voice production are good.

38.38 A consultant surgeon of high repute performed a routine thyroidectomy for a patient with Hashimoto's disease. There was some doubt about the voice afterwards but on the second post-operative evening the patient started to get swelling of the neck. The house officer thought that this was the collection of serum and undid some of the clips. The patient was in discomfort all night and by the morning the swelling was marked and all the clips had been removed by this time. The consultant saw the patient and put her on the end of his list that morning. He evacuated the haematoma and cauterised several bleeding points. In the immediate post-operative period from the second operation the patient noticed a change in the quality of voice and cough. It was confirmed that there was a vocal cord paralysis and an action was raised, not on the basis of damage to the recurrent laryngeal nerve because this had been explained and all the correct operative steps had been taken and noted, but the action related to the delay in management of the seroma. It was suggested that this had caused pressure on the nerve with the subsequent vocal cord paralysis. The plaintiff was, however, unable to obtain expert testimony on the effects of pressure on a nerve and the claim failed.

ACCESSORY NERVE INJURY

38.39 The accessory nerve may be damaged in the posterior triangle of the neck in a small local operation (eg gland biopsy) or in a radical neck dissection. It is routinely transected in a radical neck dissection and this presents no problem of litigation. Transection during a gland biopsy of the posterior triangle however does lead to problems. It is certainly the view of at least one of the defence societies that this is indefensible.

38.40 One of the main problems is that open operation is very seldom needed in this part of the neck. Indeed identification of the accessory nerve is not easy and it may be injured during the identification procedure. It is difficult to distinguish the nerve from the fat in the posterior triangle and damage to the nerve is not infrequent. The important thing is to make sure that an operation is really necessary and that a fine needle aspiration biopsy cannot be substituted. If an operation has to be done the patient should be warned of the risk to the nerve and told that rehabilitation by grafting the nerve is likely be unsuccessful.

38.41 A 42-year-old barmaid had long continued to complain of pain on the side of the neck and the side of the head. The cause of this had defied diagnosis but somebody had found a small gland in the posterior triangle. An otorhinolaryngologist biopsied this gland and transected the nerve. The results were serious because the patient could no longer draw a pint of beer and had to give up her job as a barmaid. A claim was made against the surgeon and was successful largely on the grounds that the operation was not indicated in the first place.

OTHER NERVE INJURY

38.42 A number of nerves are at risk of damage during the operation of radical neck dissection, which is performed for the eradication of metastatic nodes in the neck. It is a common operation and if a neck node is more than 3 cms or if there is more than one node then radical neck dissection is preferred to radiation therapy. Brachial plexus injuries are uncommon, but if they do occur the effect is of course devastating. The author has only had experience of one brachial plexus injury but the patient succumbed to his metastatic disease before any claim could arise.

38.43 The phrenic nerve should be identified during a radical neck dissection. It may be damaged during the course of the operation when the cutaneous branches of the cervical plexus are ligated. It is unlikely that damage to this nerve would lead to a claim.

38.44 The vagus nerve runs through the neck and if it is damaged in the removal of a metastatic node that is in the vicinity then this is not negligent, but it is negligent to damage the vagus nerve during this operation if there are no nodes in the vicinity.

38.45 The recurrent laryngeal nerve may be damaged during the surgical removal of a pharyngeal pouch. Part of this operation includes dividing the cricopharyngeus muscle; as this myotomy is made posteriorly then the nerve which lies in the groove between the oesophagus and the trachea may be damaged. The author does not however know of any successful claims from this injury which is not uncommon.

38.46 The performance of a cricopharyngeal myotomy for the globus syndrome can be regarded as an eccentric operation. It is, however, practised by a number of surgeons and in the same way as the recurrent nerve can be damaged in pouch surgery it can be damaged here. The author knows of one successful claim because of recurrent laryngeal nerve damage in a cricopharyngeal myotomy which was successful largely on the grounds that the operation was not indicated for the syndrome.

38.47 The mandibular branch of the facial nerve runs across the fascia covering the submandibular gland. It is essential that the fascia is elevated from the submandibular gland so that this nerve can be preserved during an operation to remove the gland. Failure to do so and subsequent damage to the nerve results in an unsightly cosmetic deformity. Like parotid surgery, submandibular gland surgery should not be an occasional pursuit. The author knows of one successful action arising because of damage to the mandibular branch of the facial nerve by a registrar who was deemed to be too junior to do the operation.

38.48 Damage to other neck nerves is uncommon. A middle-aged patient presented to a general surgeon with a mass in the neck. The surgeon worked in a part of the country where there was no local ENT Department. He explored the neck and found a large mass that was in close proximity to the vagus nerve. He quite correctly only took a biopsy of the mass and closed the neck. The biopsy showed that the mass was a schwannoma and he referred the patient to a regional centre. As a result of the biopsy the vagus nerve was damaged and the patient had a vocal cord paralysis. In spite of the fact that the schwannoma was subsequently removed an action was raised against the original surgeon in relation to the vocal cord paralysis. It was alleged that there had been no informed consent and that the risk of vocal cord paralysis was not discussed prior to the operation. The case did in fact go to a court hearing but the claim was unsuccessful.

ORBITAL INJURIES

38.49 The advent of endoscopic sinus surgery has lead to a dramatic increase in claims for both orbital injuries and intracranial complications. There is a steep learning curve for endoscopic surgery, as in other areas, e g laparoscopic cholecystectomy. Colleges have produced guidelines relating to training and conditions required for performance of the surgery. Failure to follow these guidelines could lead to claims being successful.

38.50 The overall incidence of complications of 'blind' intranasal ethmoidectomy is 2.8 per cent. In endoscopic sinus surgery, it has been reported that the complications rate is 29 per cent in the first 90 and decreased to 2 per cent in the second 90.[1]

1 Stankiewicz J A 'Complications of Endoscopic Nasal Surgery' (1987) Am J Rhinol 1:a 45–49.

38.51 The two problem areas are the optic nerve and the medial wall of the orbit. The optic nerve lies in close proximity to the posterior ethmoid cells. Sometimes the bone in this area is dehiscent and an exposed nerve may be damaged. This is unlikely with an experienced operator.

38.52 One of the important steps of endoscopic ethmoidectomy is to identify the bone of the medial wall of the orbit. Failure to identify this bone or perforation of this bone leads to a herniation of orbital fat. If this fat is not recognised as fat and is removed under the impression that it is thickened mucosa then bleeding can result in the orbit and damage can occur to the medial rectus muscle with subsequent diplopia which is very difficult to rehabilitate.

38.53 One of the commonest nasal problems is polyposis. The aetiology of nasal polyps is not known. Very often the removal is left to a junior doctor and damage to the medial orbital wall, etc may occur at this point without any clinical signs. It is only when these polyps recur (recurrence rate 40 per cent) that complications happen. It is important therefore that unsupervised juniors do not operate on recurrent polyposis.

38.54 The following case may illustrate this point. A serving army officer was admitted with recurrent polyposis, the previous operation having been done 12 years previously. No operation notes were available on the second occasion and the operation was delegated to a junior. As a result of the operation the patient lost the sight of both eyes. At first it was thought that this was due to direct trauma to the optic nerve but subsequent investigation showed that the patient had complained of eye pain in the recovery room and had also complained of double vision. It is likely therefore that the injury was pulling polyps of a previously exposed orbital periosteum resulting in damage to orbital vessels with subsequent bleeding into the orbit and spasm of the retinal artery. Since the end result to the patient did matter more than the reason a large settlement was made.

38.55 Damage to the orbit can also result from surgery on the turbinate. Reduction in size of the turbinate can be performed by the excision of the turbinate itself or sub-mucus diathermy where an electric current is run through the substance of the turbinate. There have been four cases of blindness reported to the defence societies in the last six years from sub-mucus diathermy. It is difficult to establish the mechanism for this injury but the connection is so well recognised that many surgeons do not perform this particular method of turbinate reduction. Blindness has also been reported from injection of steroids into the turbinate and this is a practice which is no longer acceptable.

38.56 The condition of vasomotor rhinitis was formerly treated by division of the vidian nerve in the pterygo maxillary fossa. The approach was through the maxilliary antrum and the vidian nerve was destroyed by putting a diathermy into the vidian canal and diathermising the nerve. There were, however, so many cases of blindness from this procedure that it is now seldom performed.

INTRACRANIAL COMPLICATIONS

38.57 Again these have risen dramatically with the introduction of endoscopic sinus surgery. The superior boundary of the ethmoid and sphenoid is the cribriform plate and anterior cranial fossa. The bone in parts of this is very thin and it is quite possible to perforate the area during the performance of an endoscopic ethmoidectomy. Once again it is important that the College guidelines on this procedure are followed and that the operator can demonstrate sufficient training and practice on cadavery and attendance on courses, etc.

38.58 The most common complication is CSF leak. This very often settles in the first post-operative week but if it does not settle with lumbar drainage then a craniotomy will be required to repair it. This of course results in complete and irreparable loss of the sense of smell. More seriously it could lead to meningitis and brain abscess. If these are lethal or if there is any residual neurological handicap then the claim is likely to be successful unless the operator is very experienced.

38.59 Meningitis and CSF leak can also occur after an ordinary nasal polypectomy. It would be unlikely that this could result in a successful claim unless there was evidence of undue and unnecessary roughness in the performance of the procedure. Meningitis can come on very quickly after nasal polypectomy.

38.60 The author recalls a patient who had an uncomplicated polypectomy and went home the day after surgery. At the first post-operative visit after six days he complained of a little headache. He went home and telephoned the surgeon in the afternoon saying the headache had become worse. He was told to come into hospital immediately which he did and within an hour he was deeply unconscious with pneumococcal meningitis from which he fortunately recovered. There was no claim.

38.61 The author has also been given the radiographs in relation to a successful claim that occurred in the United States. In the early days of endoscopic sinus surgery a surgeon in private practice had gone to a weekend course and had returned to perform one. He had gone through the sphenoid and the anterior fossa and had gone between the cerebral hemispheres almost as far as the occipital bone. The radiograph which was taken at the time shows the tip of the endoscope about an inch from the occiput. This means that the eyepiece of the endoscope would be at the nostril. Fortunately the patient had nothing worse than a CSF leak that was repaired with a craniotomy but not surprisingly a claim for considerable damages was successful.

FOREIGN BODIES

38.62 The problem with foreign bodies is that many patients have symptoms after the foreign body has passed on or been coughed up. Furthermore not all foreign bodies are radio-opaque and a barium swallow does not always show a foreign body. If a foreign body in the oesophagus is not recognised then it can impact in the wall, perforate it and perforate a major vessel in the mediastinum.

38.63 A 47-year-old man attended the Accident and Emergency department of a major teaching hospital complaining of dysphagia following swallowing a large piece of meat the preceding day. The meat had been part of a lamb stew which also contained pieces of bone but since a lateral X-ray of the neck showed no foreign body the patient was sent home and told to see his general practitioner. Symptoms worsened and 24 hours later he returned to the Accident and Emergency department and after a wait of several hours he was told to return home. The following morning in great distress he was seen by the ENT house surgeon and admitted immediately for oesophagoscopy. An impacted infected lamb bone was found in the lower end of the oesophagus. Removal was difficult and the oesophagus torn requiring a thoracotomy. The plaintiff's complaint was successful at court with an award of considerable damages.

38.64 Perforation of the oesophagus is not uncommon. It occurs in 1–2 per cent of oesophagoscopies. It is usually not considered negligent to perforate an oesophagus if there are technical difficulties. It is quite common to damage the lip and the teeth in oesophagoscopy and again reparation would be small. It is the management of the perforation that is important. It is usual in injuries of the cervical oesophagus to treat them conservatively, but perforation of the thoracic oesophagus requires thoracotomy.

TYMPANIC MEMBRANE INJURIES

38.65 It is difficult to damage an intact drum with syringing but it is by no means impossible. The more likely situation is that there was a pre-existing perforation or that a pre-existing perforation was healed with a very thin membrane which would not stand the impact of syringing. Most traumatic injuries heal within two weeks and it is unlikely that there would be any claims. It is also possible to damage a thin scar on a drum by using wax solvent drops.

38.66 A 50-year-old man asked a general practitioner to syringe wax from his ear. This was carried out causing some pain and was followed by permanent discharge. Examination by an otologist revealed the central perforation of the ear drum which healed quickly with antibiotics. The patient did however admit to an ear discharge in childhood and it was considered that the present defect was secondary to rupture of an old healed perforation. Following full explanation the patient was satisfied.

38.67 The author has been involved in two cases where there has been severe damage to the drum from removal – in one instance a foreign body and in another instance hard wax. In removing a foreign body or hard wax which is stuck on to the ear canal bleeding is usual. If the operator continues to attempt the removal in the presence of blood in a confined space then he will quickly become disorientated. Damage to the drum is then very likely. In the cases dealt with by the author not only was the drum removed but also the malleus and the incus. Rehabilitation from this sort of damage is very unlikely. Each case was settled out of court with considerable damages.

STAPES SURGERY

38.68 In former times stapedectomy for otosclerosis was a common operation. Great expertise was acquired by a generation of otologists but the backlog has now disappeared. In a region it is likely that only 20 to 25 stapedectomies would be done in one year. In an area where millimetres are vital this is insufficient for a number of consultants to keep in practice. It is also a very difficult area in which to train a senior registrar and it is possible that the SAC in otorhinolaryngology will not make this a requirement of training in future years. The present preferred method is only to do a stapedectomy in one ear because of late problems and in fact many patients are treated with hearing aids.

38.69 It is important that informed consent is gained. The patient must understand that complete loss of hearing is possible and that permanent vertigo and permanent tinnitus may occur. Damage to the facial nerve and loss of sense of taste must also be explained.

38.70 A 22-year-old girl with a diagnosis of bilateral otosclerosis had a right stapedectomy carried out by a first year senior registrar. This was only his second operation of this type and he chose to operate on the better ear. He did not warn the patient of any likely complication except slight vertigo nor did he discuss the possibility of a hearing aid. The operation notes recorded only an uncomplicated stapedectomy although in fact the foot plate was very thick and a fragment was displaced into the oval window and 'lost'. The patient lost her hearing completely and successfully sued the surgeon for medical negligence. At trial it was suggested that although inexperience alone is not a defect, lack of relevant information put the patient at a serious disadvantage. The absence of detailed operation notes handicapped the defence considerably.

38.71 A surgeon wished to apply laser technology to otosclerosis. Techniques had been described in the journals of merely perforating the foot plate of the stapes with a laser beam and inserting a prosthesis. The surgeon asked a laser company to bring a machine to his operating theatre. It was not clear whether or not tests were carried out on the output of the laser but what transpired was when the laser beam was fired onto the foot plate of the stapes the facial nerve was paralysed, the inner ear damaged with subsequent vertigo and tinnitus and all hearing was lost. Unfortunately there was also a post-operative infection with a subsequent perforation of the drum. The claim not surprisingly was successful on the grounds that the patient had not been warned sufficiently and that there was no previous experience with a laser and no evidence to show that the output had been tested.

SENSORY NEURAL DEAFNESS

38.72 Ototoxicity is usually defined as damage by drugs to the inner ear. It has reached prominence largely because of the permanent ototoxic effects of the aminoglycoside antibiotics. These include kanamycin, neomycin, vancomycin, gentamycin and streptomycin.

38.73 A young girl aged 14 developed a life-threatening pyocyaneus infection requiring gentamycin therapy. Treatment was started in a small peripheral hospital with serious staffing problems and only one weekly visit from an ENT surgeon. There was a delay of two days before a blood level estimation was obtained and the patient was not seen by the otologist until five days post therapy. Although she recovered from the infection there was a severe permanent bilateral hearing loss. Despite the success of treatment litigation was successful based upon inadequate monitoring.

38.74 A 66-year-old man complained to an otorhinolaryngologist of some ear discomfort after swimming. He had recently retired and had taken to going to a health club on a daily basis. The otologist found that he had a long standing simple perforation in one ear and advised the use of gentamycin drops as a phophylaxis against further infection if he intended to swim on a daily basis. He used these drops for three weeks and reported to the otorhinolaryngologist that he was now totally deaf in that ear. This was confirmed and a claim was avoided by explanation.

38.75 Anyone working in the vicinity of noise since 1963 has the right to put in a claim for noise induced hearing loss. Nearly all otologists in this country are involved in the assessment of such claims. Very few come to court but if they do it is incumbent on the examining otologist to show that he has some expertise in this field and in audiometry.

TRACHEOSTOMY AND INTUBATION INJURIES

38.76 The place of tracheostomy and intubation in ventilating patients has now been largely clarified. It is usual to intubate the patient for about a week before performing a tracheostomy if continued ventilation is required. Tracheostomy carries with it the early complication of displacement of the tube with the possible subsequent erosion of the innominate artery and the longer term complications of granulations and stenosis of the trachea. If the tracheostomy is made between the trachea and cricoid as is the case with minitracheostomies and percutaneous tracheostomies, then part of the cricoid may undergo absorption. The cricoid is the only complete ring in the respiratory tract and if it narrows then the effect on the air flow decreases according to the fourth power of the radius. It is a defect that is very hard to repair.

38.77 A tracheostomy is an operation of moderate difficulty which cannot be performed quickly in an emergency other than by someone who has done dozens. The alternatives are a percutaneous tracheostomy or a minitracheostomy. Even easier in a gross emergency is to pass a wide bore needle through the cricothyroid membrane to allow a little extra time to do one of the tracheostomies.

38.78 A junior doctor would not be expected to perform a formal tracheostomy but he would be expected to attempt the insertion of a widebore needle into the cricothyroid membrane.

38.79 The damage caused by endotracheal tubes is also well documented. If the tube is too large then the mucosa over the cartilage in the front of the larynx (anterior commisure) or the posterior part of the larynx (vocal process) can result in the baring of cartilage. If this becomes infected as is usually the case then granuloma formation ensues. This granuloma is very difficult to treat adequately because of underlying diseased cartilage and it may recur many times.

38.80 An endotracheal tube can also, as has previously been mentioned, cause temporary paresis of the recurrent laryngeal nerve.

38.81 A rough intubation can tear a vocal cord which can result in loss of vocal cord muscle and subsequent long term hoarseness and it may even dislocate an arytenoid again with serious effects on the voice.

38.82 A grossly overweight 52-year-old lawyer had an uncomplicated removal of a thyroglossal cyst in a private hospital. For no obvious reasons he developed severe laryngeal oedema several hours later and the resident medical officer attempted intubation without success. He admitted he had never seen a tracheostomy and on opening the emergency set found several essential items of equipment were absent. Several attempts to find the trachea failed but a successful operation was carried out by the original consultant who had been sent for urgently. Cardiac arrest occurred and the patient died several days later. Absence of adequate emergency equipment together with the inexperience of the only doctor available for emergency cover resulted in out of court settlement for a large sum in view of the age and expectations of the plaintiff.

38.83 A 20-year-old serviceman was admitted to hospital with epiglottitis. He began to get respiratory obstruction and a tracheostomy was performed. This was completed without any difficulty and the patient was observed in the high dependency unit. After 72 hours there was some bleeding from the tracheostomy site but no very good reason could be discovered. This continued the next day and the opinion of a thoracic surgeon was sought. There was no action taken at that point. On the fifth post-operative day there was a massive haemorrhage. General anaesthetic was administered with difficulty and the sternum was split. The bleeding was seen to be coming from the innominate artery but it was impossible to stop and the patient expired. The post-mortem showed that the tracheostomy tube had been inserted too low and while it was still in the trachea the external part of it had eroded the innominate artery. In view of the site of the tracheostomy (between the fifth and sixth rings) an out of court settlement was made.

FACIAL PLASTIC SURGERY

38.84 Although an attempt was made in the United Kingdom to limit the practice of facial aesthetic surgery to members of the British Association of

Aesthetic Plastic Surgeons this was vetoed by the Colleges. Other SACs who have an interest in regional plastic surgery (otorhinolaryngology, ophthalmology, oral and maxillo facial surgery) now require the performance of some of these regional operations during higher surgical training and candidates for the inter-collegiate examination are liable to be tested in this area. It is thus quite in order for an otorhinolaryngologist to perform rhinoplasty for aesthetic reasons.

38.85 The form of contract in this type of surgery is different. It is under contract law. The surgeon offers to do an act and the patient accepts the offer. Consideration in the way of payment is then made. There is no written agreement and it depends on oral statements. It is very important therefore to record everything that has been said. The doctor is responsible to see that the contract is carried out and he is liable even if the operation was done well if the patient is very dissatisfied. The court does take into account that there is no certainty of a good result if it depends on the healing of human tissue.

38.86 If an otorhinolaryngologist performs blepharoplasty or face lift and he is faced with a complaint by a patient for an unsatisfactory result then it would be very important for him to show that he had had training in these areas together with adequate experience.

MISCELLANEOUS PROBLEMS

38.87 There are very few problems associated with adeno-tonsillectomy. Patients should be warned of the risk of post-operative bleeding even though it is only around 1 per cent. As many of these operations are performed nowadays in private hospitals it is essential that nurses with paediatric experience are used and are available in the event of post-operative collapse. There are many minor problems such as diathermy burns, broken teeth, lip injuries etc, but these are usually settled on a local basis with expenses being paid for the damage. More serious is leaving a swab in the post-nasal space after adenoidectomy. There have been a number of cases created by this oversight.

38.88 Because of the numbers of adeno-tonsillectomies that are undertaken it is inevitable that a surgeon will be faced with the problems of a child of a Jehovah's Witness. It is essential in this instance to get a written support of opinion from a colleague and to get written agreement by the parent that the danger has been explained to them. Either parent can give consent for this.

38.89 A patient with a long history of sinusitis was having a sinus washout. In the washout there appeared a small piece of polythene tube. Many years previously the patient had been in hospital with in-dwelling polythene tubes which were used for twice daily irrigation. This practice is no longer in vogue but the patient claimed that the persistence of the polythene tube in the antrum (even though it had been in excess of ten years) had caused a long spell of ill health and a settlement was made.

38.90 Epistaxis is usually dealt with successfully either by cautery or anterior packing. If this does not succeed then the next step is posterior packing and if this is not successful then a vessel needs to be tied, either the anterior ethmoid, the maxillary or the external carotid.

38.91 The author has given opinion on an instance where a surgeon attempted to tie the external carotid artery but with inexperience in neck surgery inadvertently tied the common carotid artery. The patient did not recover from the anaesthetic and a large settlement was agreed on.

38.92 The excision of a pharyngeal pouch sounds a simple procedure. It is a procedure which has a very high complication rate. The author has been involved in cases of pharyngeal stenosis and recurrent laryngeal nerve paralysis.

38.93 The case that had the highest settlement, however, was a 52-year-old woman who had an attempted excision of the pharyngeal pouch. The surgeon obviously got lost and did in fact excise the whole pharynx. He could not identify the ends but somehow managed to get a naso-gastric tube from the base of the tongue into the remaining end of the oesophagus and into the stomach. The patient was hospitalised for two months requiring a gastrostomy. There was a considerable delay in re-exploring the neck because of the misinterpretation of the barium X-rays and eventually a skin flap reconstruction of the pharynx had to be undertaken.

38.94 The new laws with regard to product liability make it very dangerous for a surgeon to alter any prosthetic device. If the prosthetic device is altered in any way then any damage that occurs as a result of the insertion of that device is the responsibility of the surgeon and not of the product owners. It is very difficult for a patient to prove this, however. Firstly, they must prove injury but if they are successful the company must then disprove negligence.

BIBLIOGRAPHICAL REFERENCES

Alfidi R J 'Controversy, alternatives and discussions in complying with informed consent' (1975) Radiology 14: 231–234.

Byrne D, Napier A and Cuschieri A 'How informed is informed consent' (1988) British Medical Journal 296: 839–40.

Cavo J W 'True vocal cord paralysis following intubation' (1985) Laryngoscope 85: 1352–1359.

Maran A G D 'Informed consent in head and neck surgery' (1990) Clin Otolaryngol 15: 293–298.

Mehta S 'Safer endotracheal intubation' (1986) Lancet, 74: 1148.

Robinson G and Merav A 'Informed consent recalled by patients tested postoperatively' (1976) Am Thoracic Surg 22: 210–214.

Schuring A G 'Claims and suits against otology' (1989) Amer J Otol 10: 327–328.

Stankiewicz J A 'Complications of Endoscopic Nasal Surgery' (1987) Am J Rhinol 1: 45–49.

Vernon M 'Meningitis and deafness' (1967) Laryngoscope 77 :1856–1874.

CHAPTER 39

Ophthalmology

Mr Patrick J Holmes Sellors *LVO MA BM BCh FRCS FRCOphth*

SUMMARY

INTRODUCTION

39.1 Many people value their sight beyond the other senses. The loss of vision in one eye may seriously affect the lifestyle and earnings of someone dependent on having binocular vision. However, the loss of vision in both eyes is a disaster for anyone – causing loss of independence, restriction of mobility and frequently inability to earn a living. It is, therefore, not surprising that medico-legal cases involving vision give rise to large settlements.

39.2 In this chapter ophthalmic problems have been arbitrarily divided up into those which come within the sphere of the family practitioner, those which concern Accident and Emergency departments and finally those which involve the hospital doctors, including ophthalmologists.

39.3 In each section the most common causes giving rise to claims have been mentioned and this is based on a review of all the cases reported on and a summary of the computer records of one of the defence organisations over the past decade. However, the introduction of Crown Indemnity has led to a change and most of the new cases tend to be related to general practitioner practice rather than cases from hospital work. As the majority of hospital cases are dealt with by the hospital's own lawyers this means that it is much more difficult to spot alteration or new changes in the pattern of cases being brought.

39.4 In each section there is a comment which is designed to show where the 'danger area' lies and hopefully appreciation of this will spare the patient from being damaged and save the doctor from the anxieties induced by having a claim made against him.

FAMILY PRACTITIONER

39.5 There are three ophthalmic conditions in which the family practitioner is commonly involved.

39.6 Herpetic keratitis is one of the important conditions to think of in the differential diagnosis of the painful red eye. Although the risk of local steroids is widely known, inappropriate use of these drugs remain in common practice.

39.7 In recent years regular checks on children's vision have resulted in most cases being seen promptly. However, the family doctor may be the first person consulted in this matter. Children with a suspected squint should be referred for ophthalmic assessment – they do not 'grow' out of them.

39.8 Several cases involving giant cell arteritis have been brought against family doctors – it is an uncommon disease but failure to appreciate the diagnosis may cause the patient the loss of vision in both eyes.

39.9 A new group of cases is becoming apparent with general practitioners being criticised for not referring patients with retinal detachment.

Herpetic keratitis

39.10 Herpes simplex infection of the eye may cause a dendritic ulcer affecting the corneal epithelium which can recover without leaving any visual disturbance, but it can progress to cause a chronic, relapsing inflammation of the corneal epithelium and stroma resulting in corneal scarring and severe loss of vision.

39.11 A dendritic ulcer is one of the causes of an uncomfortable red eye and the diagnosis is easily missed unless the corneal reflex is inspected for irregularities or fluorescein dye is used to demonstrate the lesion. Unfortunately the correct diagnosis is seldom made by the family practitioner. If the condition is treated with topical antibiotics then no harm will result but the clinical features will remain unchanged. If, however, local steroids are prescribed the eye will whiten and become more comfortable but the ulcer will extend both in width and depth. Moreover, the risk of precipitating stromal disease with its attendant morbidity is greatly increased and the chance of relapse also enhanced.

39.12 If a patient who presents with an uncomfortable red eye does not improve with simple antibiotics within a few days immediate referral to the 'casualty department' of the local eye hospital is recommended. This applies particularly to children who can be very difficult to examine.

39.13 It is recommended that local steroids with or without antibiotics should never be used for the treatment of a red eye. Perhaps the only exception is in a patient who has had recurrent attacks of anterior uveitis (iritis) in the past. A delay in treatment seldom matters but an eye with herpetic keratitis compromised by local steroids may leave the patient with a recurrent and tiresome disease resulting in loss of vision and repeated hospital attendances.

Squint

39.14 The problems with squint usually revolve around a missed diagnosis or surgical complications arising from their treatment.

39.15 Children do not 'grow' out of squints and any child with a suspected deviation of the eye should be sent for an early examination in an ophthalmic department. However, in addition to general practitioners seeing such cases, children are examined in clinics and at school by nurses and orthoptists. Whilst much of this 'screening' is offering a valuable service some of it is done in adverse conditions with primitive equipment in difficult surroundings.

39.16 In consequence the diagnosis of squint is missed and a claim is then made that the associated amblyopia of the squinting eye has not been diagnosed until too late for any effective treatment.

39.17 Another problem arising is an infection which may follow squint surgery. This uncommon complication results from organisms introduced into the eye by the sutures used to attach the muscles to the globe. It is very difficult to establish whether the surgery was performed negligently and any claim which is brought is usually related to whether the infection was diagnosed in reasonable time and treated energetically.

39.18 These are very difficult cases. The loss of an eye in a child is distressing. It affects both employment prospects and recreational pleasures as well as being a serious cosmetic blemish.

Giant cell arteritis

39.19 This auto-immune condition causes occlusive inflammation of medium-sized arteries. The disease seldom occurs under the age of 60 and in 20 per cent of cases may involve the short ciliary arteries supplying the head of the optic nerve. If these vessels are affected the nerve head becomes swollen with splinter haemorrhages (ischaemic optic neuropathy), and there is a profound loss of vision. The most sinister feature of the condition is that both eyes may be involved in rapid succession and if the diagnosis is delayed the patient may end up completely blind. High doses of systemic steroids given in time may not restore the vision in the first affected eye but stand an excellent chance of saving the vision in the other eye.

39.20 This condition is not common and the average family practitioner will probably not see more than one or two in his career. The patient usually presents with headache which is frequently misdiagnosed as tension headaches or cervical spondylitis. However, the pain often radiates into the lower jaw and down the throat. There is also an association with polymyalgia rheumatica and the patient may already be under treatment for this. In addition, there is often malaise, temporal headache with tenderness over the artery and occasionally transient loss of vision.

39.21 Any patient over 60 who presents with headache as a new symptom should be considered as a possible case of giant cell arteritis, especially if there is associated polymyalgia rheumatica and also if the pain radiates into the jaw and throat. An urgent ESR is indicated though it has to be admitted that many people in this age group will have elevated levels from other causes. Equally important is urgent referral to any eye department which would always treat such a case as a serious emergency.

Retinal detachment

39.22 In recent years there has been a great increase in cases relating to detachment of the retina. It is hard for a GP to diagnose this condition, particularly as ophthalmoscopy is a difficult technique and because of this there is frequently a delay in referring patients for treatment. However, there are certain patterns to these cases. They particularly occur in myopic patients, which is easily recognised by looking at the patient's glasses. Often the patients complain of a decline in vision or on occasions a shadow. The visual acuity can easily be measured, although usually it is not done, and a simple confrontation test of the visual field may reveal a defect and, again, this is not usually done. Patients notice flashes and floaters which are sometimes the first signs of tearing of the retina or its detachment. There is no way in which the average GP could identify a retinal hole and most would find it very difficult even when the retina is detached.

39.23 Thus, it is perhaps wiser to put equal emphasis on examining the retina and in taking a full history and conducting a simple examination of the vision and eye. New symptoms in a myopic patient should alert the GP to the possibility of a retinal detachment. In practice, although some patients get lost in the system, the majority find their way for appropriate treatment in time, either via their GP, an optician or by self-referral. However, in some departments with huge waiting lists it may be difficult to get patients seen in reasonable time whatever priority system is used.

39.24 Finally, it is important to appreciate that, although retinal detachment is an uncommon condition, it is *bilateral* in about 20 per cent of cases.

ACCIDENT AND EMERGENCY UNITS

39.25 By far the commonest claims related to ophthalmology result from the failure to diagnose penetrating wounds which present to 'casualty departments'. These claims are expensive, usually reflecting the loss of vision or the eye itself and a consequent loss of binocular vision which may affect the patient's employment and leisure activities.

39.26 During the last two decades there have been enormous improvements in the services provided by Accident and Emergency units but the continuing incidence of missed diagnoses of perforating eye injuries suggests the need for better and continuing education of casualty officers, in a subject which receives scant attention in the undergraduate medical syllabus.

Perforating wounds of the eye with or without retained foreign bodies

39.27 A steady stream of expensive claims results from a failure to diagnose perforating wounds of the eye. The majority of the patients present to Accident and Emergency units and the circumstances of each case are monotonously similar.

39.28 The patient's symptoms are that 'something has gone into my eye'. Frequently the exact nature and circumstances of the injury are not appreciated. It is essential to ascertain the nature of the activity which the patient was indulging in at the time. Often some sort of percussive work was being performed, such as using a hammer and chisel to break up concrete or stone. The patient believes that a piece of grit has gone into the eye but in reality it is usually a flake of metal from the tool. Similarly work involving high-speed drilling, grinding, cutting wire or any injury involving broken glass should alert the doctor to the possibility of a penetrating wound. It is important to realise that an accurate history may not be forthcoming from young boys who have been 'larking about' and will not reveal that they have been playing with darts, air guns or other missiles. In many cases of penetrating wounds it is embarrassing for the doctor that a history taken by the casualty nurse is more informative than his own.

39.29 Examination of the eye in many of these cases is unremarkable. The absence of a corneal foreign body may be interpreted as evidence that the foreign body has 'bounced out'. Similarly, a sub-conjunctival haemorrhage is dismissed as a 'mere bruise' without consideration of the penetrating wound which lies deep in it. It is important to appreciate that the entry site is often very small and difficult to see without magnification and that the pain suffered by the patient may be trivial. If there is a suggestive history with no signs of a foreign body, the doctor must consider the possibility that it is inside the eye until proved otherwise. In these circumstances an X-ray examination is essential and failure to undertake this will usually be considered as negligent.

39.30 When claims arise the circumstances are very similar. An inadequate history is taken, the examination reveals either nothing significant or what appears to be a corneal abrasion or trivial wound, no X-ray examination is requested and the patient given antibiotic ointment and discharged. The patient then returns in two to three days' time complaining of blurred vision and pain and the true nature of the injury is then appreciated and specialist ophthalmic care instituted. It is often too late to save the vision and one of the most difficult points in arranging a settlement is trying to assess what effect the delay between the injury and treatment has on the final outcome.

39.31 Most of the claims related to these injuries are settled and in the majority this reflects the total or near complete loss of vision in one eye. However, special damages may be claimed for time off work related to the injury and its subsequent treatment, the late risks particularly those of cataract, retinal detachment and sympathetic ophthalmitis and also for the loss of binocular vision which will affect activities such as employment, driving and sports. Added to all this are the risks of infection, inflammation and the toxic effects of retained foreign bodies (siderosis) from particles containing ferrous compounds. These factors lead to a great deal of debate between the plaintiff's and defendant's advisers. Unfortunately the discussion is often on an anecdotal level as reliable clinical data is very scarce. For example, when an intra-ocular foreign body enters the eye it may be contaminated with bacteria. Sometimes a severe endophthalmitis develops in the eye and it may be very difficult to establish whether this is truly infective or inflammatory. What difference would it make if the foreign body were removed immediately, one day later, three days later and so on? A penetrating wound may cause a cataract and later a retinal detachment may develop – a delay in repairing the wound will have no effect on the cataract but has it rendered the eye more liable to develop retinal detachment and if so by how much? Lawyers like percentage figures and, indeed, the settlement of a case may be critically dependent on this. Doctors are very loathed to be tied down owing to the infinite variables between individual cases and advising on them is the most difficult task in medico-legal work related to ophthalmology.

39.32 Following the introduction of seat belt regulations the incidence of severe facial and eye injuries from windscreen breakages has been dramatically reduced. However, they still occur and frequently the eye injury is missed. The reason for this is that a deep wound in either lid, but particularly the upper one, produces immediate and severe oedema. It is, thus, difficult and often uncomfortable to inspect the underlying eye. Frequently the casualty doctor on duty performs a lengthy repair of the facial wounds under local anaesthesia and a day or so later the eye injury is discovered which requires a second operation under general anaesthesia for satisfactory repair.

39.33 Before undertaking repair of facial lacerations, especially those of the lid, the underlying eye must be examined. If there is any suspicion of an ocular injury or the eye cannot be visualised, do not proceed without asking for an ophthalmic examination. If an eye injury is found both it and the facial wound can be sutured under general anaesthesia.

HOSPITAL DOCTORS

39.34 The conditions considered here may involve ophthalmologists but may come within the sphere of doctors specialising in ENT, paediatrics, chest diseases and dermatology. There is some deliberate repetition particularly when considering the use of local steroids.

Cataract surgery

39.35 Modern cataract surgery produces excellent results and is a safe operation. However, complications do arise, especially from post-operative inflammation or infection and sometimes the vision does not match expectations. Many cases are reported to the defence organisations by worried surgeons but very few proceed to claims. Considering that this is by far the commonest eye operation performed it is an encouraging situation and contrasts dramatically to that in the United States of America.

39.36 With the increase in the ageing population more and more cataract operations are being performed, many under local anaesthetic. Moreover, the very success of the operation raises expectations about the results and a belief among the patients that this is a 'minor' operation. However, despite this it still remains an area where very few claims are brought.

39.37 However, a few cases have arisen where, as a result of a cataract extraction, the refraction of the two eyes becomes very different (anisometropia). The usual reason is that the strength of the implanted lens has been 'guesstimated' not assessed with the aid of ultrasound. Thus, a 'standard' power lens is inserted but an unexpected degree of anisometropia occurs (the seven dioptre surprise). This may lead to real problems and severe symptoms requiring either a second operation to change the implant or a contact lens to balance the refraction.

39.38 It is difficult to defend a case when an ultrasound examination has not been performed prior to surgery.

Drug-induced diseases

Chloroquine group

39.39 It is well known that this group of drugs can cause a serious retinopathy but this effect is dose-related. In consequence of this there has been an encouraging drop in claims over the last few years.

39.40 There is no reported case of visual loss in people using these drugs for malaria prophylaxis. Most of the cases reported in the past were those who had received more than 300 g for the treatment of rheumatoid arthritis or lupus erythematosis. A total dose of less than 100 g within a year carries no risk of retinopathy and ophthalmic supervision during the treatment period is not necessary. As with all drugs which can affect vision it is desirable to have a base-line ophthalmic assessment, although it should be stated that the measurement of visual acuity and examination of the eyes is not the exclusive preserve of ophthalmologists. In addition the patient should be warned.

39.41 It is also recognised that there are no reliable clinical features or tests which can detect the retinopathy at a reversible stage. The drug or its metabolic products accumulate in the pigment epithelium and once vision is affected and retinal signs appear it is too late, and cessation of medication will not result in any improvement on what can be a serious loss of acuity.

39.42 Chloroquine drugs can also cause corneal deposits but these are unrelated to the retinopathy, and disappear when treatment is stopped. They seldom affect vision unless they are confluent where haloes have been reported.

Ethambutol

39.43 The toxic effect of this anti-tuberculosis drug continues to be the cause of many claims. Since the introduction of the d-isomer the incidence of optic neuropathy has fallen dramatically but even if the correct drug schedules are used (15 mg per kg per day) this complication still occurs in about 1 per cent of cases.

39.44 Thus, if this drug is used it is essential that the patient is warned that his vision might be affected. Many of the patients receiving this treatment have a poor command of English and this warning should be given with the aid of an interpreter, preferably another member of the patient's family. In the present climate of medico-legal practice the prescribing doctor is advised to record the fact that he has warned the patient – a dispute in court concerning the warnings is usually resolved in favour of the patient.

39.45 When the patient is on treatment the question arises of who should monitor the patient's vision and this must be a matter of local agreement between the prescribing physician and ophthalmologist. It is probably wise to measure the vision and have the eyes examined before treatment is commenced, if for no other reason than to have a base-line from which any symptoms can be assessed. Following this, asking direct questions of the patient and measuring the visual acuity at regular intervals should be sufficient. The problem arises in that all ophthalmic out-patient departments are extremely busy with lengthy waiting times for new patients and there is an understandable reluctance to add to the burden, especially when the measurement of vision is not the sole prerogative of ophthalmologists. Moreover there is no reliable test which can be performed by ophthalmologists to detect which patients will suffer optic nerve damage. Apart from a loss of acuity and altered colour vision the clinical features are minimal.

39.46 However, if the patient does notice change in his vision he must be given the proper channels to report this. This means that the family practitioner should know that he is taking a drug which may affect his vision and that the patient should be allowed easy access to either the prescribing physician or ophthalmologist. The responsibility for stopping medication must be agreed amongst the doctors involved as timely cessation will lead to a full recovery of vision.

39.47 The problem usually arises when the patient is not aware of the risks, either because he has not been told or has not understood. The family practitioner may not be aware that the drug being used contains ethambutol with an inherent risk to the vision. The ophthalmic department is too busy to see him and weeks pass by before the treatment is stopped. The loss of vision has advanced to such an extent that no or only partial recovery of vision may occur.

39.48 These cases are very expensive as both eyes are involved and the patient may have been rendered blind.

Amiodorone

39.49 All patients treated with this cardiac drug will exhibit corneal deposits which will resolve over a year if medication is stopped. The deposits take the form of whirls of pigment cells seen best with a slit-lamp. They do not affect vision. However, the vague similarity to chloroquine deposits gives rise to anxiety that retinopathy could result. No convincing case of retinopathy has been reported and, thus, ophthalmic supervision is not required.

Steroids

39.50 The dangers of steroids are well known to all doctors. The risks involved with systemic therapy are cataract and a small risk of glaucoma. In many cases high doses have been prescribed to contain a condition and it is a balancing act between the risks of the disease versus the risks of the complications.

39.51 However, the use of local steroids continues to give rise to serious problems and resultant claims. Local steroids used for undiagnosed 'red eye' has been likened to the use of morphia in a case of undiagnosed acute abdomen. The use of steroids alone or in combination with antibiotics is best avoided except in cases of known recurrent anterior uveitis (iritis) when the patient is usually aware of the onset of an attack. A painful or uncomfortable red eye that does not improve after two or three days of treatment with local antibiotics is best referred for specialist assessment at the local ophthalmic clinic. The main danger is the use of steroids in aggravating herpetic disease of the cornea. A few days of antibiotic treatment will do no harm. A few days of local steroid treatment can be disastrous.

39.52 Uncomfortable irritable eyes are especially common in the elderly. Local steroids have been used for treatment but are best avoided. Frequently the patient will benefit from simple lubricant drops now available without prescription. If treated with local steroids they may continue to receive repeated prescriptions for years, leading to the development of glaucoma and cataract. These cases cannot be defended and are very expensive to settle as both eyes are generally affected.

39.53 In other circumstances local steroids are properly used but their side-effects, especially the elevation of intra-ocular pressure, is not monitored. It is important to use the weakest steroid preparation which is effective and to monitor the patient continually. The most distressing cases reported concern children with vernal conjunctivitis and several have ended in blindness owing to poor supervision. The cost in personal as well as financial terms is enormous, considering that the patient's employment prospects may be severely reduced.

Photocoagulation

39.54 Photocoagulation of the retina by lasers is widely used in the treatment of diabetic retinopathy, and in selected cases of senile macular degeneration.

39.55 Several cases of accidental burns to the foveal area have been reported in diabetic patients. The operator has usually 'got lost' when performing extensive pan-photocoagulation and strays into the macular area damaging the fovea and central vision. These cases cannot be defended and are very costly as the vision is already affected by the disease and such an injury may tip the patient into the blind registration category.

39.56 The beneficial effect of widespread photocoagulation in early proliferative diabetic retinopathy is well established. Some cases have arisen where the initial treatment is totally inadequate leading to the development of severe fibrotic and often untreatable retinal changes when the vision might have been saved by more energetic measures in the beginning. Such cases have usually been settled.

39.57 Where treatment is used for macular degeneration the laser burns are delicately placed near, but not on, the fovea. In the few cases which have been reported the treatment is completely inappropriate and the original diagnosis suspect. There is no defence to these cases which can be expensive if both eyes are mistreated.

Chiasmal compression

39.58 The loss of visual acuity and the bitemporal field defects caused by chiasmal compression are well known to all ophthalmologists. However, two groups of patients still give rise to expensive claims.

39.59 Meningiomas in the chiasmal region often present with unilateral visual loss. The acuity is diminished and optic atrophy is seen on examination. Skull X-rays are ordered but are reported on as normal. The patient is then diagnosed as having 'low tension' glaucoma or ischaemic optic neuropathy and no further action is taken. Although the visual fields are frequently performed, the temporal nature of the loss may not be apparent, particularly as the other eye may be normal in the early stages. These tumours are easily detected by CT scanning and this investigation should be requested for any patient who develops optic atrophy without an obvious local cause. Unfortunately, although CT scanning was developed in this country, it has not been widely available until recently but hopefully this should lead to a reduction in these tumours being missed.

39.60 The other group concerns failure to examine the visual fields. Bitemporal field loss from chiasmal compression occurs very slowly and many patients are unaware of the nature of their visual problems or are unable to express it. Some patients may complain that they bump into things or that people suddenly appear in their vision. Others complain of difficulty doing close work, such as in cutting fingernails or doubling of letters when reading. This is due to the visual difficulties arising when the temporal field defects of each eye meet at fixation. But for all these clues visual problems are commonly put down to refractive errors and delayed diagnosis is very common. Frequently the visual fields are not examined because the need for it is not apparent. However, when they are tested the bitemporal nature of the loss is usually obvious and X-ray studies will confirm the diagnosis. Claims are seldom made because of minor delays but are usually brought when the delayed diagnosis has led to profound visual loss. In this regard children with craniopharyngiomas are particularly vulnerable as they are considered too young to co-operate with visual field testing. However, simple confrontational methods are easy and quick to perform and will demonstrate gross defects. One child who was almost stone blind was considered 'hysterical'.

Delayed diagnosis of glaucoma

39.61 Several claims have been made over the last few years and broadly fall into two groups.

39.62 Some of these claims have arisen from examinations conducted under the general ophthalmic services. Frequently the facilities available for complete eye examination are lacking and the ophthalmic medical practitioner does not suspect that the patient's declining vision is due to glaucoma. Often the decline is attributed to cataract which is common in this age group of patients. Indeed, the brown colour of nuclear sclerosis may impart a better colour to the optic nerve head than actually exists. In almost all cases the visual fields have not been assessed or the intra-ocular pressure measured until late on, and these cases are usually not defensible. The difficulty in arriving at a settlement is related to what effect, if any, the delay has made to the patient's current condition. These cases are becoming more common, especially in areas with long waiting lists.

39.63 The other group of patients are those who have been on long-term steroids, usually in the form of eye drops. In some cases the use of steroids was not appropriate and the patients get lost in the system, receiving repeat prescriptions from either the family doctor or ophthalmic department. In others, the use of local steroids is appropriate (vernal conjunctivitis, uveitis, etc) but the intra-ocular pressure is not monitored. This occurs frequently when the patients are children. Most of the cases cannot be defended – often the intra-ocular pressures have not been recorded at all or at very long intervals. These cases can be expensive as both eyes are occasionally involved. The use of long-term local steroids should only be considered for appropriate conditions. The 'weakest' steroid (to produce a clinical effect) should be used and the intra-ocular pressures should be regularly measured.

Delayed diagnosis of retinal detachment

39.64 A steady flow of claims are brought because the delay in making the diagnosis has compromised the chances of subsequent surgery.

39.65 There are several patterns of presentation. Children, especially boys, around the age of ten may present with reduced vision in one eye. Examination through an undilated pupil reveals no abnormality and a past history of trauma may not be forthcoming. A diagnosis of amblyopia is made in error. These retinal detachments, normally caused by retinal dialysis, are slowly progressive and the shallow detachment makes diagnosis difficult unless the pupil is dilated and the eye properly examined. As these cases have an excellent prognosis if treated in time the failure to diagnose is usually negligent and the settlement is that for the loss of an eye.

39.66 Another situation is when the patient presents with premonitory signs such as flashes and floaters and is usually seen by the junior doctors staffing the Accident and Emergency department. They may not have the experience or skill to diagnose an open retinal tear, which can be sealed with photocoagulation or cryotherapy, thus preventing a retinal detachment. It is not negligent to look for a retinal tear and not see it but if a retinal detachment develops very soon after the initial visit it may be difficult to resist a claim that a patient has had to undergo a major operation instead of simple prophylactic treatment.

39.67 The most common situation is that either opacities in the vitreous or lens obscure the view of the retina. In some cases the presence of cataract is sufficient to suggest a cause for the loss of vision but more usually it is blood in the vitreous which makes examination difficult. The blood may result from a retinal tear, the consequence of previous retinal surgery, or from neovascularisation of the retinal vessels such as those found in diabetes mellitus. In each case the delay may lead to fibrotic changes on the retinal surface, which can only be dealt with through sophisticated retinal surgery or may, indeed, be too advanced to make further surgery worthwhile. With the advent of B scan ultra-sonography, which is widely available, a delay in diagnosis need not occur.

39.68 The establishment of several specialised retinal units makes timely referral advisable and a poor result after multiple surgery may be difficult to defend if the final referral to such units has been too late. The success rates of these special units is better than for a general unit and this applies particularly to complex cases. It is not expected or anticipated that every routine retinal detachment will be treated in special units but complicated cases and those which have not done well with standard procedures require urgent referral. Failure to arrange this is now considered negligent.

39.69 Recently a few cases have presented where the plaintiff, presumably with the aid of an ophthalmic expert, sued for negligence on the grounds of highly technical reasons as to why a particular operation had been selected or been done in a particular way. In my opinion even the most expert advisers combing through the notes will never be able to arrive at the same conclusion as the man on the spot. Fortunately one of these cases has been withdrawn and two others remain on the files but in ophthalmology they have heralded the day of the super specialist in every branch of the subject.

Basal cell carcinoma

39.70 These tumours are very common in the lid area and usually present no problem in diagnosis. However, a small number masquerade as infective lesions of the lid and are diagnosed as a meibomian cyst or chronic blepharitis.

39.71 If a supposed inflammatory lesion does not resolve within a reasonable period or does not respond to local medication a neoplastic process should be suspected. It is not good practice just to 'nip off' the lump, it should be properly excised or treated where appropriate with radiotherapy.

Dermolipoma

39.72 These uncommon lesions are unsightly and their removal is requested for cosmetic reasons. However, their surgical removal is fraught with hazard unless a partial removal of the lesion near the cornea is undertaken. A radical removal involves deep dissection in the orbit resulting in possible damage to the extra-ocular muscles (causing squint and/or ptosis), or injury to the lacrimal gland or ducts (causing a severe dry eye).

39.73 Surgical treatment should be confined to local excision of tissue avoiding deep dissection. Major surgery should be performed by those with training in orbital surgery.

Orbital cellulitis

39.74 Orbital cellulitis is usually the result of acute sinusitis and the inflammatory process within the orbit builds up considerable pressure, which can compromise the circulation to the eye.

39.75 The front of the orbit is closed by the orbital septum which in young people is both strong and intact – it is in this group in which the vision can be affected. These patients usually present to paediatricians or more commonly to ENT surgeons who are not always aware of the risks to vision. The risk is made less easy to avoid as the lids may be so tense as to make examination of the eye or vision very difficult. It is important in these cases to ask for ophthalmic advice at an early stage and it is equally important for ophthalmologists to seek assistance in the diagnosis and treatment of cellulitis. Patients with this condition should be admitted, have a CT scan and be treated with intensive antibiotics and appropriate drainage surgery.

CHAPTER 40

Dental surgery

Professor K V Mortimer *BDS PhD LDSRCS*

INTRODUCTION

40.1 Dentistry is a discipline within medicine and as such many of the areas of negligence discussed elsewhere can be applied to the dental situation. There are, however, some aspects of treatment peculiar to the teeth and their supporting structures and diseases which occur only within the mouth. Hence situations can occur which are unique to dentistry. In the main it is these areas which will be discussed within this chapter. The other aspects of medical negligence covering such errors as, for example burns, failure to diagnose fractures, incorrect surgery or misuse of drugs can equally be applied to dentistry.

40.2 It is generally understood that negligence is the failure to exercise reasonable skill and care, or omitting to do something which a reasonable man would do, or undertaking a procedure which a prudent man would not do. Hence any dentist should possess a degree of skill which, when exercised, should produce a standard of work comparable with that of his colleagues, and enable him to undertake only such work as he is capable of completing to such a standard. He should be especially careful not to undertake work beyond the limit of his capabilities to produce a satisfactory result.

40.3 Not all accidents which occur during dental procedures are due to negligence. There are inevitable accidents which are not avoidable by any such precautions as a reasonable man, doing such an act then and there, could be expected to take. There are no degrees of negligence, an accident is either negligent or it is not. However, there are many examples in the dental literature of contributory negligence, where the patient at least in part is to blame for the complications which have resulted. In particular, the patient may make a sudden movement during an operation, which results in the dental surgeon causing damage to the tissues, similarly a failure to follow post-operative instructions may lead to complications. In such cases it may still be possible to claim for damages due to the fault of the operator but the claim would be proportionally reduced. It is the legal duty of any dental surgeon to use reasonable skill and care and a failure to fulfil this would be a breach of that duty. Anyone can claim compensation for negligence, but to succeed the patient must show that the dentist owed a 'duty of care' to the patient in the existing circumstances and that this duty was breached and damage was sustained as a result.

40.4 The dental surgeon is responsible not only for his own actions but can be held liable for any action or omissions by his staff. The patient can claim against the dental surgeon or his staff or both. This situation can also occur with partners in a practice when both could be responsible for any breach of care.

40.5 The skill expected of a general dental practitioner is that of an average general dental practitioner. However, once a dental surgeon accepts referrals from colleagues for specific aspects of treatment he is offering a higher standard of care. A consultant would usually be expected to offer a high level of skill and in consequence is expected to avoid the majority of pitfalls in planning and treatment.

40.6 It is not a defence to a failure of treatment to say 'it is the way I always do it', particularly where the method used is not generally accepted.

40.7 It is also essential to inform the patient of the treatment to be undertaken before commencing work and to gain the agreement of the patient to the procedure. This is especially important when general anaesthesia or sedation are being used. Failure to do this could result in a charge of assault. There are many areas of dental treatment where negligence can occur, and it will be appropriate to consider the commoner areas of dispute within the following pages.

40.8 After any course of dental treatment it is reasonable for the patient to expect that he/she will be better off than before. It is expected that reasonable skill and care will be exercised and this will result in an improvement of the state of dental health and aesthetics where appropriate. Dental treatment is not free from risk to the patient and sometimes this results in damage despite skill and care being exercised. Certain well established risks are known and provided that they are explained to the patient in advance of the treatment then such resultant damage cannot be considered as negligent, if reasonable care has been taken.

40.9 There are five main areas of complaint by the patient related to dental treatment:

(a) appearance – aesthetics related especially to colour and form;
(b) comfort – elimination of pain and awareness of teeth;
(c) function – ability to chew, bite and eat;
(d) failure to recognise or treat adequately dental disease and giving inadequate advice;
(e) iatrogenic damage.

APPEARANCE

40.10 The expectations of an individual patient may exceed what it is possible to attain, particularly with respect to aesthetics, and these expectations should not be promised by a dentist and then not achieved. It is a reasonable maxim to expect an improvement in appearance if this has been promised and failure to achieve this may constitute negligence.

40.11 Dental treatment specifically aimed at improving aesthetics must of course not create problems under (b)–(e). Several areas of dental treatment are mainly, although not entirely, concerned with the appearance of the teeth.

Restoration of missing tooth tissue or teeth

Tooth-coloured restorations in anterior teeth

40.12 For these restorations to be satisfactory they should match the colour of the remaining natural teeth – either adjacent or opposing. Teeth are not a uniform colour but are usually darker where they meet the gum and translucent towards the incisal edge; furthermore, not all teeth in a given mouth are the same colour. In general, from the canine backwards they are darker than the incisors and all teeth tend to darken with age.

40.13 These points are of considerable importance when disputes occur over the colour of restorations, crowns and dentures. A dentist would normally aim to simulate the 'correct natural' colour when replacing teeth and should be especially careful not to be persuaded to give a patient 'white teeth' without very carefully discussing with the patient the problems with appearance such 'white teeth' would create. If a patient has insisted on 'white teeth', then negligence cannot be attributed to the dentist for the subsequent poor aesthetics of such teeth. A failure to match colour correctly usually results in poor aesthetics and frequently leads to legal disputes. The colour of the teeth is of importance in all areas of dentistry including restorations, crowns, bridges and dentures. In all, excepting the case of complete dentures, where no natural teeth are present, the colour should be matched to the natural teeth. With full dentures the choice of shade is a guess but should correspond in general to hair and skin tones with an element of modification for age. In all such cases and where crowns, veneers or bridges are to be constructed, the patient should be consulted over the colour, and before restorations are finally cemented agreement as to the appearance should be obtained.

Form

40.14 As important as colour is the shape of the replacement teeth and failure to recreate a matching shape where possible also leads to a poor appearance and consequent disputes.

40.15 It is important for the patient to realise that to avoid stagnation and food trapping, particularly under bridgework, it is essential to create spaces between pontics (replacement teeth) and natural teeth at the necks of crowns. This may not give exactly the appearance that would occur with natural teeth, but is much healthier for the gingival tissues. The amount of space available where teeth are missing may have a major effect on the shape and size of the replacement teeth and this should be taken into account and explained to the patient before treatment in order to avoid subsequent dissatisfaction. In addition to such explanation it is often desirable to have a diagnostic 'wax-up' of the intended restoration on a model for the patient to assess. This technique is particularly necessary when major changes in the shape or size of teeth is contemplated by irreversible techniques (e g preparation of intact teeth for crowns). Careful construction of the temporary restorations is also of considerable importance particularly when they are intended to be present for a long period of time.

Arrangement

40.16 The alignment of the teeth also markedly affects appearance. It is frequently not possible to create a 'film star smile' by restorations despite the patient expecting this with crowns and bridges; failure to obtain such a result is not negligent unless exaggerated claims have been made in advance.

40.17 If the natural teeth are in an irregular arrangement it is probable that without orthodontic treatment or appreciable grinding of adjacent or opposing teeth that restorations, crowns or replacement teeth will resemble the previous natural teeth.

Placement of metal or tooth-coloured restorations in posterior teeth

40.18 The large majority of restorations inserted behind the canines are metallic and are silver or gold in colour. Even where crowns of tooth-coloured porcelain are used it is normal to strengthen these by using metal cores and in some instances by metal biting surfaces. If the use of metal is necessary for strength the patient cannot reasonably complain about the appearance of such metal in the appropriate areas, although it would be prudent for the dental surgeon to explain the need in advance.

40.19 If entirely tooth-coloured restorations are placed in posterior teeth the possible shortcomings of such restorations should be considered by the dentist and explained to the patient, eg all porcelain restorations may chip or break under the forces of the occlusion and hence have a limited life. Tooth-coloured 'plastic' restorations frequently wear away more rapidly than metal and hence need fairly regular replacement or repair. These occurrences will all involve the patient in additional costs, and could not be considered negligent provided the dental surgeon has explained the limitations of such restorations to the patient. However, failure to explain such limitations to the patient may be construed as negligent if restorations fail after a short period of time when longevity has been promised. Improvements in the tooth-coloured 'plastic' materials are occurring all the time and there are claims for some of them to have similar life expectancy to amalgam.

40.20 Any restoration can fail within a very short period after placement but under such circumstances the operator should accept responsibility and replace the restoration without charge to the patient. Failure to accept responsibility for such a situation is often a cause of dispute and litigation.

40.21 The duties of the dental surgeon in placing restorations are not limited to appearance and long life but also to maintaining normal function and avoiding iatrogenic disease. The restoration should not result in further damage to the teeth or supporting structures – this will be dealt with later.

Orthodontic treatment

40.22 Although the dentist in carrying out such treatment is mainly concerned with improving occlusion, the patient associates this aspect of treatment with improvement in appearance. Their expectations are that with realignment of the teeth the aesthetics will improve. Frequently this is the case but the results are not always a perfect alignment of the teeth or a superb appearance. Success depends on patient co-operation and if this is not forthcoming the end result may be a deterioration in appearance. In many cases orthodontic treatment is aimed at improving occlusion or appearance but seldom sets out to create a perfect occlusion, since this could be impossible due to underlying skeletal abnormalities. In some cases, without additional jaw surgery, the end result of orthodontic treatment can only produce a very limited improvement and this should be explained before treatment is commenced. If there are risks of a relapse after treatment these risks should be explained before commencement. Similarly missing teeth should be checked for by radiographs to assess if they are unerupted or impacted or actually missing. For negligence to be demonstrated, an incorrect diagnosis in the treatment plan, a failure to carry out the treatment correctly, or a failure to advise the patient adequately of the scope of the treatment, the likely end result and the risks of failure, would have to be proven.

COMFORT

40.23 One of the main reasons for patients attending the dentist is pain or discomfort in teeth, gums, jaws, face or temporomandibular joints. These pains vary in distribution, origin, intensity, frequency and duration but because of a patient's heightened perception of their mouth and face such pains or discomfort are particularly of concern. The level of awareness varies greatly from patient to patient with some threshold levels being extremely low resulting in quite minor discomfort being considered as severe pain.

40.24 Pain can be present before or after treatment or a combination of both. The most likely areas of negligence are in cases where the pain arises after, and as a result of, treatment or persists and worsens after treatment.

40.25 The majority of cases of pain arise from damage to the pulp of the tooth which can be reversible or irreversible leading to pulp death and possible abscess formation. The enamel of a tooth has no innervation but the dentine and pulp have a nerve supply and hence pain within the tooth must arise from stimuli to dentine or pulp.

40.26 Dental caries is the usual cause of pain in these tissues and failure to recognise *obvious* lesions and to treat them could be considered negligent. However, the diagnosis of dental caries under or at the margins of restorations is not always easy. There are, of course, an enormous range of causes of pain in the mouth and it is clearly inappropriate to discuss in detail each possible reason. Nevertheless there are certain groups of pains which any reasonable dentist should be able to categorise and investigate. Failure to investigate discomfort and take appropriate radiographs could be considered negligent.

Temperature changes and pain

40.27 Pain associated with temperature changes is invariably associated with pulp reaction, and can be related to damage to the dentine or pulp associated with dental caries, trauma, loss of protective enamel or failure to insulate restorations by lining from the underlying dentine. This type of pain should be readily recognised and treated since there is rarely any other cause for these symptoms.

Pain on biting

40.28 Pain in the jaws or teeth associated with biting or chewing is again almost always related to disease or trauma to the periodontium which supports the teeth and is almost always due to periodontal inflammation or abscess formation and can be related to causes which any reasonable dentist should be able to identify and treat. If the cause is difficult to identify then in such a case a second opinion should be sought. Discomfort with biting can sometimes be associated with damage to the temporomandibular joint (see later).

Other pains

40.29 Other pains are less easily categorised and in fact some facial pain is of psychogenic origin. Any symptom which persists and whose cause cannot be identified should be referred for further advice, since trigeminal neuralgia or an underlying sinister cause such as a neoplasm in, for instance, the maxillary sinus, could be the origin. Hence any pain or discomfort which continues or worsens despite treatment and appropriate investigations should be referred for consultant advice. Failure to do so within a reasonable period of time could justifiably lead the patient to consider litigation. There are of course some cases where no cause can be diagnosed and then only treatment of the symptoms can be given.

FUNCTION

40.30 The ability to chew and eat is taken for granted by people with a healthy, full dentition, while others with no teeth at all can eat and chew to their own satisfaction. The extent of the occlusion and the ability to masticate adequately is extremely variable within the population, some patients claiming that the loss of a single tooth seriously affects the process, while others can cope with very few or even no teeth at all. Hence not all patients require replacement of missing teeth for adequate masticatory ability.

40.31 The provision or maintenance of adequate function depends therefore on the needs of the individual patient and it is difficult to lay down the needs in a general manner to cover all patients. There are, however, certain requirements for any satisfactory treatment to restore function where teeth have been lost or wear has occurred. Firstly, any replacement of missing teeth or tooth substance should result in a balanced occlusion on both sides of the mouth at a level of occlusion which is acceptable to the patient and can be tolerated by the temporomandibular joints. In general the occlusal level should be that which pertained when the natural teeth were present. However, if wear has occurred and significantly reduced the occlusal level it may be necessary to re-establish the occlusal plane to near its former level. Any alteration to the occlusal level, with which the patient presents, should be undertaken initially on a temporary and easily reversible basis. This should then be shown to be tolerated by the patient over a period without adverse signs or symptoms before any attempt to create a permanent occlusal level is undertaken. If this type of procedure is not followed and the patient subsequently develops symptoms due to alterations of the occlusal height, then the procedure may be considered as undertaken negligently. Secondly, the replacement of missing teeth should result in normal jaw movements being maintained and not create parafunctional activity to compensate for incorrect contours of the occlusal surfaces. The occlusion resulting from treatment should be balanced on both sides and avoid an undue loading on any individual teeth. The chewing ability of replacement teeth or crowns should attempt at least to maintain and preferably improve that which was present before treatment. It is not possible always to recreate the original incising ability with anterior crowns, nor the chewing ability of a young dentition in an older patient.

40.32 Finally, replacement by dentures of natural teeth can never recreate all the chewing and incising ability of the patient's own teeth and this should be explained by the dentist and understood by the patient, so that although improvement over the previously edentulous spaces will occur, former chewing ability will not be fully achieved. The ability to cope with dentures depends as much on the patient's perseverance and dedication to wearing them as to the dentist's skill in their construction. Faults with dentures which may be considered as negligence by the operator are discussed later.

FAILURE TO RECOGNISE OR TREAT DENTAL DISEASE

Judgment and forethought

40.33 Before any treatment is undertaken, the patient must be assessed as to their suitability for the procedures in the light of their medical history, oral hygiene, attitude and age. The practitioner should be careful not to guarantee results but should undertake to achieve the best result of which he is capable. In planning and carrying out any item of treatment the operator should, in the light of his experience and knowledge, assess the alternative procedures and undertake those which are least likely to cause complications whilst fulfilling the treatment requirements satisfactorily. The treatment provided for a very old patient for a given condition may vary considerably from that offered to a young patient with a similar complaint.

40.34 The frequency of taking radiographs or other investigations and of recall appointments will differ from patient to patient as a result of activity of dental disease in the individual. This clinical judgment comes with experience and it is difficult, if not impossible, to draw a dividing line between what is just acceptable and what is just unreasonable. The extremes are much easier to identify. Errors in judgment can result in serious problems which could lead to claims for compensation.

Clinical and radiographic assessment

40.35 All new patients should have a careful clinical, and where appropriate, radiographic assessment before treatment is undertaken. This would include a medical history check, extra-oral and intra-oral examination involving the teeth and supporting structures. Wherever there are contacts between adjacent teeth, where dental decay could have started, radiographs should be taken and all teeth with doubtful vitality responses or showing clinically significant bone loss should also be assessed radiographically. Missing teeth, which the patient considers have not been extracted, should also be checked by radiographs to see if they are unerupted or impacted. This establishes the base line for future assessments of the activity or progress of dental disease. At future visits and recall appointments, it may be necessary to take further radiographs, but this initial set should be carefully maintained for comparison purposes. Failure to make a satisfactory initial assessment, and to record the position for the future, could lead to a charge of negligence if incipient dental disease is neither treated nor monitored.

Restorative problems

40.36 All restorations should be examined for faults, defects and recurrent caries. Some may need repairs or replacements, but records of faults which are not to be treated at this stage should be made and followed by clinical or radiographic examination at subsequent visits. The oral hygiene should be assessed and instructions given to the patient on dental care to reduce the risk of future problems.

40.37 The main faults which must be treated are positive ledges and major deficiencies at the margins of restorations, recurrent caries, inadequate contact points, traumatic occlusion and non vital teeth. Failure to recognise and deal with these faults could be negligent.

Periodontal deterioration

40.38 The main area of problems within this discipline are failure to recognise disease and to provide adequate advice and treatment to prevent a progressive deterioration of the periodontal tissues. Basically, periodontal disease arises from the accumulation of plaque and debris at the junction between the soft tissues of the gum and the neck of the tooth. It is a progressive condition unless the cause is eliminated by a thorough cleaning of the teeth by the hygienist or dental surgeon and followed by instructions to the patient how to avoid further deposits occurring. This depends on patient co-operation and monitoring by the dental practice. If the disease is advanced when first recognised by the operator then root planing and possible gingival surgery will be necessary. It is failure to undertake an adequate periodontal assessment and follow a correct regime of treatment which leads to claims for negligence, since the disease will progress continually over a long period and result in a considerable loss of support of the teeth and ultimately in their complete loss. In a patient who attends regularly, it is reasonable to expect an average dental practitioner to recognise and treat this disease before it progresses to a significant extent. There are a few situations where despite adequate care and patient co-operation a form of periodontal disease is rapidly progressive and mainly untreatable.

Prosthetic

40.39 Ill fitting or badly constructed dentures should be easily rectified and if causing the patient a problem must be dealt with. The main problems are associated with dentures constructed to an incorrect occlusion – this is usually reasonably easy to recognise both from clinical examination and from the history given by the patient. Ill fitting dentures again are easy to recognise but do not always need urgent replacement especially if they are long-standing, as the patient may be perfectly happy with them and have adapted to their fit. Although there are often complaints about denture faults they seldom cause permanent damage to the patient. In some cases, patients cannot wear satisfactorily any dentures however well they are constructed, and in fact patient tolerance of dentures is the most important factor in many instances.

Soft tissue lesions

40.40 Any ulcers, swellings or other lesions of the soft tissues of the mouth should be carefully examined and if they have been present for more than a couple of weeks or appear in any way unusual should be referred for a consultant assessment. Many of these lesions are quite innocent but others are much more serious and need early treatment. Failure to refer these could certainly be construed as negligent. As a general rule any condition which persists and for which a diagnosis cannot be made should be referred for a consultant opinion. Even where a diagnosis is made and the symptoms persist despite treatment, it would be prudent to seek a second opinion.

Surgical treatment

40.41 Any lesions requiring surgical treatment should be identified and treatment instigated or arranged by referral to a hospital. Delaying such treatment unnecessarily can cause pain and suffering or result in the final treatment being more extensive and would be unjustified. In this field in particular care should be exercised to undertake only such treatment as can be completed satisfactorily by the operator to prevent complications arising, or failure to achieve the desired result, e g attempted extraction of impacted wisdom teeth (third molars) which are too difficult to be completed under local anaesthetic in the dental chair. After any surgical procedure the patient should be carefully instructed on after care, particularly with respect to haemorrhage, and pain control and similar complications. This would be a requirement and expected from any reasonable dentist.

Orthodontic care

40.42 While many practitioners do not carry out their own orthodontic treatment it is reasonable to expect them to recognise a problem with occlusion or alignment and aesthetics and to seek advice. Failure to do so while probably not negligent could lead to more extensive and difficult treatment later which may result in a complaint from the patient.

40.43 It is the duty of a dental surgeon to recognise dental disease and abnormalities and to act on them either by treatment, referral, advice or monitoring. Failure to undertake any of these would be negligent.

IATROGENIC PROBLEMS

40.44 The majority of cases which are successful in litigation claims are those where patient complaints result directly from the treatment they have received. These claims can arise from many different causes and as explained earlier have a similar basis in law to those described elsewhere, e g burns, scalds, incorrect drug dosage, retention of foreign bodies in the tissues or carrying out the wrong operation. Only those which are specific to the teeth and supporting structures will be covered in this section.

Surgical

Extracting the wrong tooth

40.45 This occasionally occurs and is more frequent where the operator is not the same person as the one who has charted the treatment or where the charting of the extraction has occurred at a previous visit. The usual reasons are recording the wrong side or using the numerical system of recording the teeth incorrectly, so as to give the wrong number for the tooth. When an orthodontist requests the extractions, the dental surgeon must be especially careful as frequently the teeth to be extracted are sound and are less obvious as the appropriate teeth for extraction.

Problems of fractures during extraction of teeth

40.46 Among those which can be considered negligent are fracturing the teeth or jaws and not diagnosing and informing the patient that such an accident has occurred. The breaking of a root during an extraction is a relatively common complication but it is the duty of the dentist either to remove the root or arrange for its removal, if it is considered that this is necessary. If it is decided that greater damage to the patient would occur by removing the root than the risks of any complication in leaving it, then the patient must be informed of the decision. It is usual to leave and monitor small apical fragments especially when they are close to other important structures which might be damaged during their removal. Small pieces of bone are sometimes fractured during extraction and are normally removed to minimise infection. This is not of any significance. However, major fractures of the mandible, maxilla or alveolar process may be negligent especially where adequate pre-operative radiographs were not taken and where such a complication was not anticipated and advised to the patient in advance.

Other sequelae

40.47 Further complications are the loss of the whole or part of the tooth or instruments into the soft tissue spaces of the neck, lungs, gut or antrum during extraction. These are often unjustified and hence negligent. However, where such complications are considered a possibility all necessary precautions to prevent them should be taken, eg the packing of the throat during any general anaesthetic involving work on the teeth and jaws, to prevent inhalation or ingestion of foreign bodies.

40.48 Dislocation of the jaw is a complication which can occur during extraction or as a result of the use of gags and may result in a charge of negligence if excessive force was applied.

Paraesthesia

40.49 An occasional complication of an extraction is damage to the sensory nerve supply to the soft tissues. This is almost always confined to the lower lip, tongue and cheek related to the lower teeth. It should be a relatively rare occurrence in general dental practice to obtain a numb lip, as teeth which are closely related to the nerve trunk should be identified by radiographs and it would be prudent to refer these for treatment in a hospital. Paraesthesia of the tongue should again be rare in a general practice but both the lip and tongue are at risk, with the more difficult extractions of the type of third molars (wisdom teeth) encountered in specialist practice. In these cases it would be normal to warn the patient in advance of such risks.

40.50 Resultant paraesthesia following dental procedures is not necessarily negligent and certainly cannot always be avoided. It frequently resolves over a period of up to two years but is sometimes permanent. Each case will need expert assessment before negligence can be proved.

Complication associated with underlying medical conditions

40.51 Clearly failure of the operator to obtain a satisfactory medical history and record of drug therapy before commencing treatment is unsatisfactory. If subsequently there are complications due to the treatment, which would have been unlikely to have occurred if precautions had been taken, then failure to obtain a satisfactory medical history and act upon it would be negligent. If complications occur when the correct precautions are undertaken, no blame can be attached to the operator.

40.52 In particular patients with heart valve defects or a history of rheumatic fever must have prophylactic antibiotic cover before any procedure which would involve cutting or damaging the mucous membranes. The other major group of conditions of great importance to the dental surgeon are any with underlying clotting or bleeding problems where dental treatment could lead to prolonged haemorrhage. Failure to heed such conditions would be to take unjustified risks.

40.53 Patients who are receiving or have recently received steroid therapy, anticoagulant therapy or anti-rejection drugs for transplants need special precautions to be taken. These and similar conditions involving prolonged drug therapy need careful assessment and advice before carrying out invasive dental treatment. Similarly administration of drugs must be carefully considered when there may be interaction with pre-existing therapy. Failure to follow such procedures would be considered negligent.

Traumas to soft tissues

40.54 During any dental procedure there is the possibility of instruments slipping and traumatising the tongue, cheeks or lips. If there is no contributory factor by the patient then this is likely to be due to negligence by the dental surgeon.

40.55 There are, of course, other possible complications or errors in surgery of a nature similar to those elsewhere in the body which can be considered to be negligent but this covers the commonest mistakes which may be encountered in normal dental practice.

Local anaesthetic complications

Fractured needles or instruments

40.56 If a needle or other instrument is fractured during use, an immediate attempt to recover the piece should be carried out. If this proves impossible, then the patient should be referred for consultant assessment. The use of very thin needles or inserting them right up to the hub are the most likely causes of fracture. It is likely that such an accident would result in a case of negligence being enacted, although it could arise from sudden patient movement or a flaw in the metal of the needle which would mitigate against negligence. The fragments should be kept for metallurgical examination as this would be of importance if a flaw is present and would be an example of an inevitable accident.

Adverse reaction to local anaesthetic

40.57 Reactions to local anaesthetics and the vasoconstrictor are reasonably common and certainly unpredictable. Unless there is a previous history of such reactions or an underlying medical condition these complications cannot be considered negligent. If the patient faints or feels unwell after a local anaesthetic they should be placed supine and treated appropriately and when recovered they should be allowed to rest for a period under supervision before leaving the surgery. Failure in making certain they are fully recovered and allowing them to leave prematurely could result in a subsequent collapse and an injury to the patient. This situation clearly also applies to patients who have received a general anaesthetic or intravenous sedation. However, depositing the local anaesthetic at the wrong site and causing damage as a result, eg anaesthetising the facial nerve during an inferior dental injection causing unilateral facial paralysis (Bells Palsy), could certainly be considered as negligent. The deposition of a local anaesthetic in a blood vessel can cause complications and may be avoided by the use of an aspirating syringe although at present these are not in general use.

Needle track infection

40.58 Nowadays with presterilised disposable needles and sterile anaesthetics in cartridges this complication should not occur. If this problem does arise, then it would be indefensible.

Incorrect solution

40.59 The injection of a solution other than a local anaesthetic in error occasionally occurs and is again clearly negligent if injury results from the mistake.

Restorative procedures

Endodontics errors

OVERFILLING CANALS

40.60 During root canal therapy the object of the treatment is to remove the pulp from within the tooth and eliminate infection, both within the root canal and adjacent periapical tissues, and to seal the canal to prevent any further risk of infection. The preparation of the canal should be carried out carefully and instrumentation must be within the confines of the root canal. The material obtunding the canal should not extend beyond the root of the tooth into the bone of the jaw.

40.61 The majority of the materials now used to seal and fill root canals are relatively bland. However there are some materials in use which are quite toxic to living tissues. These materials must be kept within the root canal as they can cause serious damage if they enter the periapical tissues, especially in the molar region of the mandible, where the nerve trunk runs, and here it can result in permanent anaesthesia of the nerve producing a numb lip. This has been the cause of a number of successful negligence claims. The extrusion of material apically from the root canal while nearly always undesirable is certainly not always negligent. Occasionally, particularly with calcium hydroxide materials, they are deliberately extruded apically to assist healing. It is when the more toxic materials (eg Spad, N_2 and Endomethasone) are used that extrusion must be avoided. This requires accurate preparation of the canals and a careful radiographic assessment during and after the treatment. In the event of extrusion under these circumstances, the patient should be immediately referred to a consultant for removal of excess material from the tissues especially in the lower molar region.

UNDERFILLING CANALS

40.62 As mentioned above, a successful root filling should seal the canal to within about 1mm of the apex. It is not always possible to fulfil this criterion due to the anatomy of the canals. Nevertheless, the canal should be instrumented as close as possible to the ideal and completely sealed at the level of the instrumentation.

40.63 Failure to place an adequate root filling which seals the cavity of the root canal can lead to periapical infection or cystic formation. This can be considered negligent especially where it results in the failure of crowns and bridges placed on a tooth with such a defective root filling. Failure to place any root filling in a non-vital root canal (except where sclerosed) and subsequently to restore the tooth permanently would normally be unacceptable.

INCORRECT PREPARATION OF CANAL

40.64 Under-preparation is undesirable but can usually be put right and often results in little if any permanent damage to the patient, but could result in the restoration (eg crowns) needing replacement when at a later stage an adequate root filling is placed. Over-preparation and perforations of the root are much more serious. These usually result from the use of rotating engine driven drills or instruments. In general it is recommended that root canals should be prepared only by hand instruments or non-rotating (ie oscillating) engine-driven instruments. Most perforations must be considered as probably negligent and certainly so if they are not recognised and treatment of the perforation, by sealing, attempted. If the root is intact before preparation of the root canal, perforations, except at the apex, should not occur using careful techniques. The closer any perforations are to the cervical half of the tooth the poorer the prognosis. The region of the cervix or apex is not so serious for perforations as these can usually be treated surgically. If teeth have root fractures due to previous trauma then it may not be possible to avoid perforations. Similarly with teeth where full development of the root has not occurred apical perforations are difficult to avoid. It is necessary for an expert opinion to be given on the cause of a perforation before litigation proceeds as there may be reasons why a perforation has occurred which are not negligent.

BROKEN INSTRUMENTS

40.65 This is a hazard of root canal therapy which can occur despite all reasonable care by the operator. It can of course happen due to lack of care or incorrect use of an instrument. The instrument (normally a reamer, file or spiral filler) should be removed from the canal where possible. However it is frequently jammed and not possible to retrieve. An attempt should then be made to bypass the fractured instrument and root fill the canal apical to it or to remove it surgically from the root end. The breaking of the instrument is not usually grounds for a claim of negligence but failure to inform the patient, and if possible effect a satisfactory root filling, would be negligent.

Care of the pulp

40.66 During cavity preparation the most important requirement is to avoid damage to the pulp wherever possible. Sometimes the pulp is already involved or compromised by dental disease or the existing restoration and hence it is already damaged. There are several ways in which a previously healthy pulp can be damaged:

(1) overheating due to vigorous cutting of dentine or inadequate cooling of the bur;
(2) over-preparation of the tooth which can result in large areas of freshly cut dentine which lead to irritation of the pulp or actual direct exposure of the pulp due to removal of too much dentine;
(3) failure to protect the pulp during the restorative stage. It is necessary with any cavity extending into fresh dentine, which is of anything but minimal depth, to place a sedative and insulating lining between the dentine and the restoration. If this lining is not placed, the pulp may be affected by temperature changes in the mouth or by chemicals in the filling material and become irritated. This can result in pulpal pain which can be transient, intermittent or continual and can lead to pulp death. These sequelae can be considered as caused by negligence in some instances, although this requires expert assessment since even when all precautions are taken pulp irritation or death can still occur, particularly in young teeth with large pulps. If expensive restorations are to be placed on teeth showing symptoms of pulpal irritation they should be placed with temporary sedative cements and permanent cementation delayed until symptoms have resolved or, if they persist or the teeth die, then root canal therapy is undertaken. It would be a case for potential litigation if bridges or crowns were cemented permanently on teeth displaying symptoms of pulp damage.

Fit for restorations

40.67 All restorations placed on or in the teeth should adapt to the cavity margins and follow the correct contours of the teeth. This should result in no gaps or overhangs at the periphery of restorations and the contours should prevent food and debris accumulating around the teeth. Clearly there are many restorations which have minor defects in these respects which are not detrimental to the health of the teeth or the patient. However, the larger the defect in general the more serious the possible damage which may occur to the teeth and supporting tissues. If there are significant deficiencies or excesses on restorations at the time of placement, these must be corrected forthwith and failure to correct these faults would be negligent, since such deficiencies can result in new caries occurring due to the ingress into the gaps of food debris and bacteria. Excess filling, particularly at the cervical margin, can result in accumulation of plaque and physical damage to the gingival tissues which can progress to periodontal destruction and bone loss.

Incorrect occlusion

40.68 The placement of restorations or prostheses to an incorrect occlusion can result in damage to the periodontal membrane of the teeth or to the temporomandibular joint and muscles of mastication. Occasionally hearing problems and tinnitus or persistent headaches have resulted from occlusal discrepancies. If these problems are not corrected they can lead to persistent symptoms or permanent damage and would be negligent. Occlusal problems are one of the main complaints concerning dentures and bridge work and expert assessment is essential before a claim for negligence is justified. This is an area where there are many views on what is correct for a given situation and the significance of minor occlusal discrepancies. For a case of negligence to succeed a fairly major discrepancy would probably be necessary as minor faults are very much a matter of opinion and frequently do not result in any symptoms or damage to the tissues.

Instability of dentures

40.69 This is a frequent complaint, particularly with full dentures, and is usually associated with incorrect marginal adaptation to the tissues or occlusal faults (discussed elsewhere). Under-extension of the periphery can lead to instability and be unsatisfactory but is unlikely to cause permanent damage. Over-extension will irritate the tissues and can lead to hyperplastic tissue forming, which is undesirable and might cause other problems. The problem with assessing this as potentially negligent is that it can arise from other causes, in particular ridge resorption producing over-extension of initially accurately constructed dentures. Badly designed and ill-fitting partial dentures can lead to damage to the remaining natural teeth or their periodontal support and this could be the basis of a claim.

Periodontal

40.70 There are few causes of iatrogenic disease associated with periodontal procedures. Most periodontal treatment does not create other disease. However, over-vigorous use of electrosurgery, particularly very close to the bone and cementum, can lead to necrosis of the tissue and in turn create pain and further deterioration of the support for the teeth worsening the problem. It should probably be explained that where root planing is to be carried out recession of gingivae and post-operative sensitivity may occur.

Orthodontic failures

INCORRECT TREATMENT

40.71 This usually results from an original error in diagnosis and treatment planning and a course of treatment entered upon which cannot succeed. Such examples are the use of a removable appliance where a fixed appliance is necessary, the creation of an unstable relationship which will relapse or the tilting of crowns into position rather than bodily movements of the whole tooth. This will lead to failure of the treatment and may result in damage to the teeth and supporting tissues and occlusion.

REPEATED OR EXCESSIVE MOVEMENTS

40.72 All orthodontic movements of teeth should be gentle and sustained. Failure to carry this out can result in damage to the periodontal membrane, cause resorption of the roots or loosening of the tooth or cause tooth death and loss of the tooth. Depending on the precise details of the treatment and the damage resulting, such actions can be negligent. There are many cases where the results of orthodontic treatment do not attain everything that would be desirable. This may be due to lack of patient co-operation, tissue response to the forces of movement being unfavourable, or where to obtain the ideal occlusion would entail so much treatment as to be unacceptable to both patient and operator, or in fact be impossible.

Radiological damage

40.73 The dosage involved in dental radiography is very low and reasonable usage with adequate apparatus is of no danger to the normal patient. Great care should be taken with any patient who has received radiotherapy to the head and neck. The number of radiographs taken should be kept as low as possible and care should always be taken to protect patients, who may be pregnant, by the use of a protective apron. It is probably wise to protect all patients in this way especially when a number of radiographs are to be taken. It is also essential that all staff are positioned away from the X-ray tube by about two metres at all times. No member of staff or patient should ever be in the direction of the beam except for the recipient. This is of particular importance with respect to waiting and reception areas with thin partition walls. The X-ray machine must be regularly serviced and checked to avoid any risk of exposure due to radiation escaping. Failure to follow these guidelines could lead to claims for negligence.

Sedation and general anaesthetic accidents

40.74 Most of these will have been covered in the appropriate chapter and throughout any of these procedures nursing staff should be present. However there are certain special factors relating to dental procedures carried out under general anaesthetic. The anaesthetic should not be given by the operator, this dual procedure by a single operator would be considered as negligent in almost all instances. Other specific dental risks are associated with maintenance of the equipment in a fully functioning condition, adequate packing of the throat to prevent anything in the mouth from passing down into the lungs or gut, the immediate availability of a full resuscitation kit with appropriate drugs always at hand and the provision of adequate recovery facilities. Failure of any of these could be negligent. It is of the utmost importance that no patient should ever be given a general anaesthetic or sedation in the dental chair when unaccompanied by a responsible adult. Recovery should be complete before allowing the patient to leave. Specific advice to dental surgeons on general anaesthesia and sedation sets out requirements which if ignored would constitute negligence. The anaesthetist should be adequately trained at a postgraduate level in the appropriate procedures, and should be supported by a specifically trained assistant. Monitoring equipment and a defibrillator should be available along with suction and oxygen inflation equipment. Sedation may be undertaken by a single operator but a second trained person should be present throughout the treatment. Sedation is a widely used technique and results in a depression of the central nervous system by drugs but the patient will respond to command throughout the period of treatment. Written pre- and post-operative instructions must be provided and written consent obtained. Throughout all general anaesthetics and recovery periods, assistance in the surgery should be available.

Drug therapy and interaction

40.75 Care must be taken to establish any drug therapy which the patient is receiving as adverse reactions can occur with drugs or anaesthetics which the dentist may administer. There are instances where the treatment may need to be modified or special care taken because of the effect of the drugs – this is especially the case where the patient is receiving anticoagulant or immunosuppressive therapy or where steroids are being taken or have been taken recently. If the dentist is in doubt over the relevance of any drug therapy and the precautions which are necessary with respect to dental treatment, then the medical practitioner should be approached for advice. Care in avoiding these situations is essential as the resultant complications can be very dangerous and even be a threat to life.

Cross-infection

40.76 The risk of cross-infection from patient to patient, or patient to staff, or staff to patient is to be avoided at all costs. Blood is the most serious way of transferring diseases such as AIDS or hepatitis in the dental surgery and it is often shed by the patient during routine procedures. Adequate precautions are essential to avoid blood contact with the skin of staff and transference to other patients. Sterilising of instruments and disinfection of all working surfaces must be carefully carried out to adequate standards to prevent cross-infection. Failure to follow an adequate regime would be negligent. Great care must be taken in the handling of clinical waste in particular with needles and scalpel blades. These must always be disposed of in a satisfactory 'sharps' container and arrangements made for the subsequent disposal by incineration. This is essential to prevent risk of injury to staff, waste disposal personnel and the general public.

Over-prescription

40.77 The extent or need for dental treatment is a matter of clinical judgement but should be kept to the minimum required to make the patient dentally fit and provide adequate aesthetics. Excessive treatment is never justified but the parameters for deciding what is justified are impossible to define for a group of patients. This assessment must be made for an individual case. The general move today is to reduce the amount of operative treatment carried out and to monitor the progress of lesions over a period. This is resulting in a preventive approach to the incipient lesion rather than the more radical approach of yesteryear. Occasionally the patient will request treatment which is not clinically necessary, e g a gold crown, where no restoration is required, purely for aesthetics. This should in general be resisted by the dentist due to the unnecessary risks involved.

Temporomandibular joint disorders

40.78 These can result from errors in the occlusion produced by restorative or orthodontic procedures. Patients, however, are more likely to attend complaining of pain in the joints from causes not arising from dental procedures. They are dealt with in a variety of ways and sometimes do not respond to any treatment. If normally accepted procedures are not successful within a reasonable period then it would be wise to seek a second opinion as the distress resulting from this condition may have a serious effect on the patient psychologically.

ACTIONS REQUIRED BY A REASONABLE DENTAL SURGEON

40.79 Any unorthodox procedure carried out by the operator should be explained to the patient and agreement obtained. Accurate notes should be recorded in such cases or else a charge of negligence could be levied.

40.80 Consent to any procedure should be obtained from the patient or, if under age, by the parent or guardian after explanation of the treatment. The age of consent is 16 years but where complex or extensive treatment is required it is wise to discuss this with the parent or guardian up to 18 years.

40.81 Written consent should be obtained for procedures under a general anaesthetic. Procedures under local anaesthesia can proceed by verbal agreement with the patient. The dental surgeon must give adequate pre- and post-operative advice and provide an after treatment service at all reasonable times. Failure to provide such advice and aftercare is negligent. If the patient does not follow the advice which has been given, then he/she has contributed to their own complications. Contributory negligence is quite common in dental accidents where the patient suddenly moves while the drill or other instruments are in the mouth producing an injury to the soft tissues. A similarly induced injury may occur when the patient grabs hold of the operator's hand or arm. This is especially a problem with children and it would be unwise for any operator to proceed with an operation where a difficult child is indulging in any of these sudden movements. Care must be taken with restraint of the patient who is acting in this manner as a claim of assault may ensue if significant force is used. Much dentistry is today carried out in a supine position which requires special care to prevent damage to the patient's eyes by dropping instruments, medicaments or other materials. It is advisable to have a nurse present during all dental treatment to minimise the risk of accusations of improper conduct.

40.82 Throughout and following all treatment the dental surgeon has a continuing responsibility of care for his actions. Any treatment which fails, or where a complication arises within a short period of time, should be put right by the operator. There should be no charge except where the patient has caused the damage by an unreasonable action.

40.83 When something goes wrong the patient should be informed and the practitioner should do all he can to reassure and help the patient including referring the case, where appropriate, to a consultant or other specialist. Lack of care by the dental surgeon and failure to provide satisfactory subsequent treatment is likely to result in a legal dispute.

40.84 Throughout all dental procedures any force should be kept to a minimum to avoid the risks of damage to the tissues. Failure to follow this maxim can result in damage which should have been avoided. Despite all reasonable care, inevitably accidents will occur. If these were not avoidable by any such precautions as a reasonable operator doing such an act would have been expected to have taken, then the charge of negligence is not justified.

40.85 The dental surgeon must keep accurate contemporary dental records of all treatment undertaken. All incidents and accidents must be accurately recorded and any witnesses to such occurrences noted and their written report obtained. The operator should inform the defence organisation with a full report of anything untoward that occurs and should pass any communications from the patient or their solicitor to this organisation for advice and reply.

40.86 Any dental surgeon may be asked to act as an expert witness on dental matters and should be careful to accept such requests only if he feels capable of giving expert advice and providing a written report. The report should be presented in a completely unbiased, factual way and should have any sections which are opinions clearly indicated. Once having given a report it must be supported in court if the need arises. Since negligence is a 'civil tort' the case is decided by a judge in the county court or High Court depending on the level of the claim.

40.87 As developments occur in dentistry new areas of possible negligence can arise. The most recent major development is the use of implants which, although known about for many years, have until recently been considered of doubtful justification. New techniques have been developed which scientifically are much sounder than previous methods. Inevitably errors in their placement will result in damage to adjacent structures or localised necrosis due to incorrect preparation of the bone to receive the implant. It is a technique which at present requires meticulous care in preparation and placement and a level of expertise obtained from postgraduate training. The failure of implants which are very expensive to place will inevitably result in disputes over the costs of correcting the failure and the area of responsibility for this, as usually more than one operator is involved.

40.88 The damage which can result from failures may be quite serious and if the operation is carried out by an inexperienced dental surgeon who does not follow all the correct procedures and avoid the risk of complications, then a claim for negligence may result. It should however be realised that there will always be a few failures with any technique of this kind and these are certainly not always due to negligence.

CHAPTER 41

Litigation concerning clinical radiology

J O M C Craig *FRCR FRCS FRCGP MRCP FRCSI FFR RCSI(Hon)*

SUMMARY

INTRODUCTION

41.1 In the United Kingdom there is a 'league table' for the specialities most involved in litigation. This is headed by obstetrics and gynaecology, followed by general surgery, orthopaedics and accident and emergency services. Radiologists are not high on the list of doctors sued in the United Kingdom at the present time. However, in the United States of America, although obstetrics and gynaecology and surgery head the list, radiology lies in third place. This trend may appear in the United Kingdom, especially since radiologists have become more involved in complex vascular and interventional procedures, which carry a high risk, and since radiologists have become more central to the overall management of the patient including both diagnosis and treatment.

DETAILS OF RADIOLOGICAL LITIGATION

41.2 An analysis of 360 cases of litigation involving radiology was reported by the author in the Knox Lecture in 1989.[1] This analysis showed that 78 per cent of litigation in radiology concerned accident and emergency cases. The most commonly missed fractures were those of the spine, neck of the femur and scaphoid and the most commonly missed dislocations were posterior dislocation of the shoulder and dislocations of the carpus and tarsus. By far the most serious cases were fractures of the spine, of which there were eight in this series, three of whom became paraplegic. Particular care is needed in cervical spine lesions, and the doctor examining the radiographs must make sure that all seven cervical vertebrae are seen clearly and especially the C7/D1 level where lesions are common. Repeat radiographs must be taken where there is doubt. Missed scaphoid fractures continue to cost the profession dearly. It is taught clearly that all suspected scaphoid fractures should be treated as fractures, and if no fracture is seen on the radiograph, then a further radiograph should be taken in 10–14 days. Scaphoid views are essential in all suspected cases. These basic rules are frequently overlooked.

1 J O M C Craig The Knox Lecture 'Radiology and the Law' (1989) Clinical Radiology 40, 343–346.

41.3 In this traumatic group of cases were some where glass foreign bodies were missed. Glass is radio-opaque and any injury involving glass warrants a radiograph. There were also some cases of failure to radiograph the eye for suspected foreign bodies, even though the history suggested something 'flying into the eye'.

41.4 One of the major problems in these accident and emergency cases is that in the 278 traumatic cases investigated, there was no radiological report in 32 per cent. The interpretation of the radiography was by doctors not trained in diagnostic radiology. This state of affairs may persist due to the sizeable shortage of posts in clinical radiology and the enormous increase in the workload performed by radiologists including many 'hands-on' clinical procedures. A paper by Vincent et al in the Archives of Emergency Medicine in 1988[1] examined the ability of junior doctors in Accident and Emergency departments to detect radiographic abnormalities. The assessment of a radiograph by a senior house officer was compared with the assessment by a radiologist of senior registrar or consultant status. The error rate was 39 per cent for accident and emergency doctors, for abnormalities with clinically significant consequences. No improvement was found in the accuracy of the senior house officers over the six months' tenure of the post. The paper makes the valid point that it is unrealistic to expect senior house officers working in the Accident and Emergency departments to acquire the difficult skills of image interpretation simply through experience in that time. Despite the manpower problem in radiology and the increasing workload, radiologists should give priority to the reporting of accident and emergency radiographs. It would also be beneficial if radiological instruction could be given to accident and emergency doctors, but this would add yet another burden to the overstretched departments of clinical radiology.

1 C F Vincent, P A Driscoll et al 'Accuracy of Detection of Radiographic Abnormalities by Junior Doctors' (1988) Archives of Emergency Medicine 5, 101–109.

41.5 Of the 360 litigation cases analysed, 22 per cent were not related to trauma. These cases included contrast reactions, barium examinations, myelography, computed tomography, angiography and ultrasound errors.

41.6 The contrast reactions included two deaths, two arrests, more minor reactions and one contrast extravasation. The barium mishaps included five falls from the radiographic table and four barium extravasations during barium enemas. Myeolgraphy claims related to fits, missed tumours and negligent injections. Since 1988 other claims have appeared relating to the use of Myodil for myelography. These claims related to the development of arachnoiditis secondary to the use of Myodil. There have been remarkably few claims in this series regarding angiography. There was a claim for failed angioplasty, for post-procedure haemorrhage, post-procedure embolus and one case of injection of surgical spirit in error.

41.7 Claims referring to CT and ultrasound examinations concerned missed diagnoses, but there was one death from haemorrhage following biopsy under ultrasound control.

LITIGATON CONCERNING MYODIL

41.8 In recent years there has been increasing litigation related to Myodil (Pantopaque) myelography. The plaintiffs claim the onset of arachnoiditis due to the past use of Myodil and its incomplete removal following the procedure. The vogue that arose for this legal action posed a sizeable threat to many radiologists and also a costly threat to defence organisations, health authorities and trusts. The impending number of cases was such that the Royal College of Radiologists and the British Society of Neuroradiologists issued a joint statement in December 1991[1] giving a consensus view on the use of Myodil. Before detailing the situation in the United Kingdom, it should be appreciated that in the United Kingdom, the average volume of Myodil injected was 6 mls, whereas much larger quantities, even 100 mls, were used routinely in the United States of America. The following points were covered in the statement:

(1) was the use of any contrast medium for myelography justified?
(2) was the use of Myodil justified in the light of other contrast media available?
(3) should Myodil have been aspirated after the examination had been completed?
(4) what was the relevance of informed consent in the Myodil era?

The statement was detailed and covered the relevant history and facts relating to each of these questions. There were 33 literature references providing evidence for the opinions stated. It would be appropriate to quote the conclusions that were reached.

1 Royal College of Radiologists 'Statement on Myodil' (December 1991).

Conclusions

41.9

(1) We consider that where clinical features of possible spinal pathology indicated the need for a definitive diagnosis and precise localisation of a lesion, radiculography or myelography was essential;
(2) we consider it correct that in 1944–1972 Myodil was the contrast medium of choice for radiculography and full myelography;
(3) during the Conray/Dimer X era, the use of Myodil was still acceptable for radiculography and it remained the medium of choice for run-up myelography;
(4) following the introduction of Metrizamide, despite its advantages, a decision had to be made balancing the quality of the images against the potential severity of immediate complications. It became widely accepted as a contrast medium for myelography in the early 1980s;
(5) despite the recommendations in the data sheet that Myodil should be removed after the examination, unless it was required for a further study, it was common practice in the United Kingdom not to aspirate the relatively small volumes used here. This practice is supported by work which showed that aspiration failed to prevent the development of arachnoiditis, and we consider non-aspiration of the contrast medium to have been an acceptable practice;
(6) current practice regarding 'informed consent' did not apply in the Myodil era, and, in any case, there are reports indicating that the rate of symptomatic post-Myodil arachnoiditis was not greater than 1 per cent.

IONISING RADIATION REGULATIONS

'Protection of persons undergoing medical examination or treatment'

41.10 These regulations (POPUMET) dated 1988[1] related to 'clinically directing' and 'physically directing' a radiological examination. 'Clinically directing' is the clinical responsibility for the decision to effect the medical exposure. This decision is invariably taken by the radiologist, who should satisfy himself that the examination is clinically indicated and that the choice of a particular examination is the correct choice. 'Physically directing' is the act of effecting the exposure. This is invariably the act of the radiographer. There can be occasions when the radiologist may be both clinically and physically directing, e g during fluoroscopic procedures. There can be occasions when a physician or surgeon is clinically or physically directing, e g screening a cardiac catheter or pinning a hip. The POPUMET regulations require that those persons clinically directing medical exposures should have received 'adequate training'. This requires instruction in the 'core of knowledge' regarding competence in radiation protection. The regulations also state that the smallest possible irradiation dose should be used to obtain a satisfactory medical result. The regulations are not related to the request for an examination, but to the decision to perform it and to effect the exposure. Failure to observe these regulations can lead to criminal prosecution enforceable under section 15 of the Health and Safety at Work Act 1974.

1 'Protection of Persons Undergoing Medical Examination or Treatment' (POPUMET) 1988 EC (88) 29.

LOW OSMOLAR CONTRAST

41.11 Guidelines were published in a letter to Clinical Radiology by Professor R Grainger in 1984[1] regarding the use of low osmolar contrast, on the assumption that 'low osmolality' agents, which may be ionic (Hexabrix-Ioxaglate) or non-ionic, are safer than the conventional agents, but much more expensive. It was felt that their use was justified in particular patients. Since 1984 some anxiety persists among radiologists about their medico-legal position if a mishap occurs using conventional contrast medium. Because of this, the Royal College of Radiologists consulted Professor Grainger and Dr Peter Dawson and new guidelines were issued (1991).[2] However it was accepted opinion that the ultimate objective was to replace high osmolar contrast media by low osmolar media when the financial climate was satisfactory. The following indications for the use of low osmolar contrast are taken directly from the Royal College of Radiologists guidelines:

(1) Hexabrix (Ioxaglate) may be used to best advantage in arteriography as the agent of lowest osmolality. Low osmolality agents, ionic or non-ionic, should be used in all arteriography which is expected to be painful;
(2) non-ionic agents should be used in intravenous applications in all patients thought to be at higher risk of an anaphylactoid reaction, i e previous reactors, asthmatics, atopic patients and those allergic to other drugs or agents;
(3) non-ionic agents should be used generally in all procedures anticipated to be, in either absolute or relative terms, high dose procedures. Patients unable to tolerate a high osmolic load such as those in oliguric and anuric renal failure, especially if complicated by poor cardiac reserve, should be given a low osmolality agent, ionic or non-ionic;
(4) infants and babies should be given the benefit of non-ionic agents because of the risk of 'overdose';
(5) non-ionic agents should be used if there is difficulty in directly monitoring the patient or when machinery makes vomiting a particular hazard. This is the case with CT scanning;
(6) patients with known haemodynamic instability or limited cardiac reserve merit the use of an agent associated with the least cardiovascular stress. Either a non-ionic or, in arteriography, ioxaglate should be used;
(7) there is no convincing evidence that elderly patients are at significantly increased risk. However, the use of less stressful low osmolality agents is advisable;
(8) either type of low osmolality agent should be used in patients with sickle cell disease or trait. Ideally, they should be delivered diluted approximately 1 in 2 to render them virtually iso-osmolar with respect to plasma;
(9) in angioplasty low osmolality agents should be used in order to minimise the pain of the concomitant angiography;

(10) there is no evidence that clinically manifest contrast agent-associated nephrotoxicity is reduced or increased with any type of agent in current use. An argument may be made that, in patients with pre-existing renal impairment, the most inert agent should be used, namely a non-ionic, in the smallest possible dose. Dehydration should be corrected and never actively encouraged;

(11) recent concern about a possible increase in the incidence of thromboembolic phenomena in clinical angiography with non-ionic agents has probably been exaggerated. They do have less marked anticoagulant properties than ionic agents, conventional or ioxaglate, but the consequent increase in risk appears to be small in practice;

(12) adverse reactions usually begin within 10–15 minutes of contrast medium administration and patients should not be left unattended during that period. Major drug reactions may occasionally have a later onset;

(13) no contrast agent is completely safe and full resuscitation equipment should always be close at hand whenever one is administered.

1 R G Grainger 'The Clinical and Financial Implications of Low Osmolar Media' (1984) Clinical Radiology 35, 251–252.

2 R G Grainger, P Dawson Editorial 'Low Osmolar Contrast Media: An Appraisal' (1991) Clinical Radiology 42, 1–5.

UNREPORTED FILMS

41.12 It is mainly due to the manpower shortage and the alarming increase in radiological work load that there is a need on occasions to send unreported films to our clinical colleagues. This regrettable habit would cease if immediate reporting became possible. In some European countries films never leave the department of radiology, and clinical colleagues view them, preferably along with a radiologist, in the department. This practice, however, also requires adequate radiological staff and adequate space, but has much to recommend it. In certain circumstances, the decision to release a film unreported, when a radiologist is not available, must be correct, if it acts in the best interests of the patient. However, when this is necessary certain principles should be made clear. If a film is to be released without a report then there should be a clear patient need. When films are released on a regular basis to serve a particular clinic, this should only be following an agreement between the clinician and the radiologist, and there should be a full understanding of the medico-legal implications. The hospital management should be informed of the agreed practice, and the need for it. If the clinician agrees to this system and interprets a radiograph, then he undertakes the medico-legal consequences of that interpretation. It is also advisable that a record of his interpretation should be entered into the patient's notes. It is essential that the Department of Radiology has a record of to whom the film was sent, and there should be an agreement that the film is returned for a radiological report as soon as possible. That report should then be sent to the clinician.

41.13 The agreement to release unreported films does not absolve the radiologist's responsibility for 'clinically directing' the examination, even though he may not be present, e g a chest radiograph. The method of examination and the views taken are the radiologist's responsibility, which the radiographer 'physically directs' according to the department standing orders.

STANDING ORDERS

41.14 The consultant in charge of a department of radiology is responsible for the standing orders of that department. These should cover the course of action to be taken for any emergency from a departmental fire to dealing with the radiography of casualties from a major accident. Standing orders include the radiography that is necessary for routine examinations, eg cervical spine, skull, chest. All radiological and radiographic staff should be aware of these standing orders. If these are not followed and litigation resulted, the defendant would be required to justify such a digression. Standing orders should include after-care in vascular and interventional cases, and medical, radiographic and nursing staff should be aware of these, as should the staff on the ward to which the patient may be returned.

MEDICO-LEGAL ASPECTS OF DELEGATION

41.15 Delegation of tasks is necessary in the management of a department of radiology, and in the training of medical, nursing and radiographic staff. Delegation is an issue with significant legal implications and must be undertaken with the utmost care and responsibility.

41.16 It must be appreciated in reading this section, that although there are legal probabilities, each case varies according to the circumstances pertaining to it. The Royal College of Radiologists, appreciating the importance of this topic, are issuing guidelines[1] on which this section is based.

1 'Medico-Legal Aspects of Delegation' (Pamphlet, 1993).

41.17 To delegate is to trust or empower a colleague medically or non-medically trained to perform a task. A senior colleague may delegate a task to a junior, trained or training in the same speciality; to a colleague not trained in that speciality, or a mecially trained practitioner may delegate a task to a non-medically qualified colleague.

41.18 Medico-legal responsibilities lie both with the delegator and the delegatee. The delegator must be certain that the task to be performed by the delegatee is within his/her training, experience and skill. If this is so, then a 'proper delegation' has been performed; if not then an 'improper delegation' has been effected. If a mishap were to occur, and a 'proper delegation' had been made, then it is likely (depending on the varying circumstances of each case), that the medico-legal responsibility would rest with the delegatee. If a mishap were to occur and an 'improper delegation' had been made, it is likely (again depending on the varying circumstances of each case) that the medico-legal responsibility would rest with the delegator. In a personal communication with Dr Roy Palmer of the Medical Protection Society, he pointed out that if a death resulted from an improper delegation, it is possible (no more than that) that not only may there be a negligence action, but there could also be the possibility of a charge of manslaughter. Dr Palmer continued 'that whilst one did not wish to alarm unnecessarily, it is well that practitioners appreciate the full extent of their potential liability. In recent years we have seen increasing numbers of manslaughter charges brought against practitioners whereas even a decade ago no such criminal prosecution would have been brought.'

41.19 It is necessary that the delegator is aware of the ease or difficulty of a particular case, and the need for supervision and contactability. The delegatee should declare if he/she thinks that the task delegated is beyond his/her competence.

41.20 In radiological practice a task may be delegated to a non-radiologically trained medical colleague, such as the interpretation of a radiograph. This can occur when releasing non-reported radiographs. Most often the radiologist is satisfied that this is within the competence of the colleague, e g a chest physician interpreting a chest radiograph, but there are medico-legal consequences arising from this, which have been outlined elsewhere in this chapter.

41.21 Increasingly, tasks are being delegated to non-medically qualified nursing and radiographic staff. The need to delegate tasks to non-medically qualified personnel is acknowledged by the General Medical Council,[1] but it is considered serious professional misconduct to delegate to persons not medically qualified tasks requiring the knowledge and skill of a medical practitioner. The delegator must be satisfied that the delegatee has received sufficient training to perform the delegated task. An essential point is that a medical opinion cannot be given by a non-medically qualified practitioner.

1 'Professional Conduct and Discipline: Fitness to Practise' (Pamphlet, 1985).

41.22 The ionising radiation regulations, with regard to clinically and physically directing a radiological examination, apply to all to whom a task is delegated and these must also be observed.

INFORMED CONSENT

41.23 The lack of informed consent has been an increasing cause for litigation in recent years. In an article by Lord Scarman, published in 1986[1] he said 'Medical paternalism is no longer acceptable as a matter of English law, that has gone. The sovereignty of the patient has been re-instated.'

1 'Consent, Communication and Responsibility' (1986) Journal of Royal Society of Medicine 79, 697–700.

41.24 Radiologists have been concerned for some time as to when they should obtain written consent from the patient. It is clearly not logistically possible to obtain written consent for every examination, such as intravenous urography, barium examinations and the like, but it is necessary in all these investigations that a full explanation is given to the patient about the need for the examination, the method of the examination, the complications and what the examination hopes to achieve. The radiologist must be sensitive to the patient's anxiety and be prepared to answer any questions that the patient might raise. This approach to the patient is not only good medical practice, but creates a good doctor/patient relationship which is the best adversary to litigation. More complex procedures, certainly all vascular and interventional procedures, warrant written consent. In obtaining this consent, the procedure and its complications, alternative methods and the reasons for a particular choice should be explained. A recurring question is how detailed should the discussion be on complications, and should all the complications be listed, however rare they may be. This does require careful thought and judgment. Lord Scarman's opinion was 'Information of risk which the doctor judges to be significant must be given to the patient.' What is significant can be a point of legal argument. It is said that a complication occurring in more than 1–2 per cent of cases should be told to the patient. However, it may be that a complication that occurs less often, but is of a serious nature, needs to be disclosed. The difficulty is to inform the patient as fully as possible, without causing undue alarm or precipitating a refusal to undergo a procedure, and by so doing, act against the patient's best interests. Some patients do not wish to be told of complications or alternative methods. The responsibility of obtaining consent is a heavy one with no clear cut guidance to cover every possibility and so the doctor's professional judgment must be exercised carefully, appreciating that the wishes, the mental and physical well being of the patient, take prior consideration. It is advisable that as well as having written consent, a record of what was told to the patient and presumably understood by the patient, should be kept in the patient's notes. This is especially important when the patient does not wish to be fully informed. The doctor's memory of what took place may be very vague, some years later.

41.25 Consent should be obtained in sufficient time before the procedure so that the patient can come to a reasoned decision, and certainly not just prior to the procedure in the department, or when pre-medication has been given.

41.26 The obtaining of consent is often delegated to a junior or to the colleague referring the case. This is not recommended, but it may be necessary from time to time. Such a delegation must be a 'proper' one, ie the delegatee must be familiar with the procedure to be performed, the alternatives and the complications and be able to answer any relevant questions asked by the patient. The delegatee must also record in the patient's notes the details of the consent.

ULTRASOUND

41.27 There has been anxiety among radiologists regarding their medico-legal responsibilities in departments of ultrasound. In modern practice ultrasound examinations are performed by radiologists, obstetricians, radiographers, nurses, midwives and physicists; doppler examinations are often performed by surgeons or cardiologists. It is clear also that delegation is an important aspect of every ultrasound department. If a legal case were to arise an important issue would rest on the appropriate training and experience of the ultrasonographer, and whether or not the conduct of the procedure was considered to be accepted practice.

41.28 The radiologist has obligations and responsibilities when he/she is in charge of an ultrasound service. This includes providing the appropriate instruction and supervision of radiographers and other paramedical staff. When delegating, the consultant in charge must decide to whom to give responsibility for conducting examinations and also the protocol for such examinations. The radiologist may issue a report on an examination performed to his satisfaction by a radiographer or other paramedical colleague. In these cases, it is essential that the name and status of the ultrasonographer should also appear on the report. Radiographers and other paramedical personnel may make observations on an ultrasound examination conducted by them, and if so their name and status should appear on the report. The consultant in charge bears the final clinical responsibility to the patient.

GUIDELINES

41.29 The number of radiological examinations and their complexity have been increasing substantially over the past two decades. This has caused some anxiety related to medical manpower, cost, clinical efficacy and patient irradiation dose. The National Radiological Protection Board and the Royal College of Radiologists published a report in 1990[1] on 'Patient Dose Reduction in Diagnostic Radiology' and pointed out that 20 per cent of radiological examinations had no clinical justification. The Royal College of Radiologists published a booklet 'Making the Best Use of a Department of Radiology' in 1989 and again in 1993.[2] This booklet gives guidelines covering the requests for the 12 most frequently performed radiological examinations in national health service hospitals. These covered 95 per cent of radiological practice in these hospitals and in the later edition included guidelines for CT and ultrasound examinations. These guidelines when followed reduce appreciably the number of radiological examinations performed.

1 'Patient Dose Reduction in Diagnostic Radiology' (1990) 1, 3.
2 'Making the Best Use of a Department of Radiology' Guidelines for Doctors (1989, 1990, 1991, 1993).

41.30 Radiological examinations must be based firmly on clinical need and clinical justification. In clinical practice today, to irradiate a patient without clinical justification would be difficult to defend. To have followed the guidelines issued by the Royal College of Radiologists would be a sound point in any legal case.

41.31 Radiology has changed immensely over the last two or three decades, with the advances in technology and the introduction of interventional radiology. Radiologists are now central to the diagnosis and management of patients and closer to the bedside. Radiological practice can only be conducted satisfactorily in close co-operation with colleagues of other disciplines and personal prejudice and ambitions must not cloud good clinical interaction. Conferences encourage good clinical practice and make litigation less likely. However, with the changing role of the radiologist will come an increased exposure to litigation. How sad it is that this is the price to pay for increased clinical involvement, but it must be accepted and confronted. In the final analysis, the most important antagonists to litigation are a good doctor-patient relationship founded on good communication, and clinical decisions founded on the patient's best interests.

BIBLIOGRAPHICAL REFERENCES

Craig J O M C The Knox Lecture 'Radiology and the Law' (1989) Clinical Radiology 40, 343–346.

General Medical Council 'Professional Conduct and Discipline: Fitness to Practise' (Pamphlet, 1985).

Grainger R G 'The Clinical and Financial Implications of Low Osmolar Media' (1984) Clinical Radiology 35, 251–252.

Grainger R G, Dawson P Editorial 'Low Osmolar Contrast Media: An Appraisal' (1991) Clinical Radiology 42, 1–5.

National Radiological Protection Board and Royal College of Radiologists 'Patient Dose Reduction in Diagnostic Radiology' (1990) 1, 3.

'Protection of Persons Undergoing Medical Examination or Treatment' (POPUMET) 1988 EC(88)29.

Royal College of Radiologists 'Making the Best Use of a Department of Radiology' Guidelines for Doctors (1989, 1990, 1991, 1993).

Royal College of Radiologists 'Statement on Myodil' (December 1991).

Royal College of Radiologists 'Medico-Legal Aspects of Delegation' (Pamphlet, 1993).

Scarman (Lord) 'Consent, Communication and Responsibility' (1986) Journal of Royal Society of Medicine 79, 697–700.

Vincent C F, Driscoll P A et al 'Accuracy of Detection of Radiographic Abnormalities by Junior Doctors' (1988) Archives of Emergency Medicine 5, 101–109.

APPENDIX

National Health Service circulars

HM (54) 32

LEGAL PROCEEDINGS

Summary: The present policy of taking legal action to secure contributions from doctors in respect of whose negligence successful claims may be brought against hospital authorities is to be modified. In future, where any doctor who may be liable is a member of a Defence Society and that body accepts responsibility for him, any payment made to the plaintiff is to be apportioned between the doctor(s) and the hospital authority as agreed privately between them or, in default of agreement, in equal shares.

1. As Boards and Committees are aware, it has been the Minister's policy (see paragraph 6 of RHB(49)128/HMC(49)108/BG(49)113) that where proceedings are brought against a hospital authority and/or a doctor employed by them for alleged negligence by the doctor the authority should not undertake the defence of the doctor and that if it is sought to make them liable for negligent acts of a doctor employed by them, they should normally take such steps as are open to them under the Law Reform (Married Women and Tortfeasors) Act, 1935, to obtain a contribution from him in respect of damages which may be recovered. It has been represented to the Minister that this policy may tend to prejudice that successful conduct of the defence which is in the interest of doctor and hospital authority alike. The Minister has therefore reviewed the position in consultation with representatives of the profession and the Defence Societies and has agreed with them the revised procedure set out in this memorandum.

2. Actions may be brought against the hospital authority alone, or against one or more members of their medical staff alone, or against the hospital authority and a member or members of the medical staff jointly. The arrangements set out in the two succeeding paragraphs will apply to all three classes of action so far as regards medical practitioners who are to be defended by the Medical Defence Union or the Medical Protection Society or the Medical and Dental Defence Union of Scotland. As regards medical practitioners not so defended the arrangements hitherto in force should continue even in actions in which the new arrangements are being applied to other parties defended as above.

3. Where both the hospital authority and one or more hospital doctors are cited by the plaintiff as defendants, the following arrangements will apply:

(1) Any defendant may, on notifying the other(s), decide to settle the case out of Court at any stage in the proceedings, but if he does so, he must accept sole liability for payment of the whole sum for which the case is settled; but each defendant shall pay his own costs.

(2) If the defendants decide to explore the possibility of settlement out of Court (and a settlement is ultimately effected), the payment made to the plaintiff shall be borne between the defendants agreed to be liable in such proportion as they may agree between themselves or, in default of agreement on the proportions, in equal shares.

(3) If the defendants agree to defend the action in Court the procedure should be as follows:

(a) the defendants should try to agree before the action comes to Court on the proportion in which any damages and costs which may be awarded to the plaintiff shall be borne between them;
(b) if this proves impossible, the defendants should try to reach such agreement after the trial of the action;
(c) failing agreement under (a) or (b) the damages and costs awarded to the plaintiff shall be borne in equal shares between such defendants as are held liable.

(4) In exceptional circumstances where some important legal or professional principle is involved, any defendant may give notice to the other before delivery of defence by either party that sub-paragraphs (1)–(3) above shall not apply; and the normal legal processes will then be open to all defendants.

4. Where either the hospital authority alone or a hospital doctor alone is cited as defendant in the action, the defendant will have complete discretion whether to fight the action or to attempt to settle it out of Court. The hospital or the doctor solely cited shall not take legal action to obtain a contribution from the other, nor cite the other unless requested so to do when the request shall be conceded forthwith. The Defence Societies recognise, however, that there will be cases where, although one of their members has not been cited, they might properly be asked to make a contribution towards any payment made by the hospital authority to the plaintiff, because the action or inaction of the practitioner in question was a material factor in the negligence complained of. Conversely, in actions in which a hospital doctor alone is cited, there may be circumstances in which the Defence Society asks the hospital authority to make a similar contribution. In either case the procedure should follow the principles set out in paragraph 3(2) and (3) above, as if the party not cited were a defendant.

5. The success of the new arrangements set out above clearly depends on mutual confidence between the defendants and a fully co-operative attitude on the part of both parties from the beginning, and hospital authorities are urged to bear this in mind. There should be full consultation at the request of either party in the formulation of the defence. In any case where, in accordance with paragraph 4, there is a possibility of a contribution being requested from a hospital authority or a doctor who has not been cited, full information about the incident and the possibility of such a request should be exchanged at the earliest opportunity, which normally should be as soon as the Statement of Claim has been delivered, and in any event not later than delivery of Defence.

6. The principles of paragraph 5 of RHB(49)128/HMC(49)108/BG(49)113 (which require hospital authorities to obtain the Minister's prior authority to settling any

case out of Court for a sum exceeding £500 plus costs and also to consult the Minister on cases raising certain major legal issues) continue to apply. Where, however, in a case to be settled out of Court, the sum to be paid is apportioned between a hospital authority and one or more members of its medical staff, the Minister's authority need be obtained only where the sum apportioned to the hospital authority (not the total sum) exceeds £500.

7. It has been the normal practice of the Defence Societies to claim the protection of section 21 of the Limitation Act, 1939, where action is not commenced within one year of the occurrence of the cause of action. Hospital authorities should, as hitherto, not plead this section except with the Minister's prior approval. No liability under paragraphs 3 or 4 for any damages or costs, other than his own costs, should be regarded as falling on any doctor where the hospital authority or the Minister is satisfied that exemption from liability could be successfully claimed under section 21.

8. The provisions of this circular should be applied to all proceeding which are commenced on or after the 1st day of April, 1954, and also if it is agreed by, or on behalf of, the hospital authority and the doctor or doctors concerned, to any proceedings which are pending on that date and in which judgment has not been given.

MINISTRY OF HEALTH
SAVILE ROW
LONDON W1

29 March 1954
94111/3/66

To: Regional Hospital Boards,
Hospital Management Committees,
Boards of Governors.

Appendix

HC (82) 16

To: *Regional Health Authorities* *District Health Authorities* *Special Health Authorities for London Postgraduate Teaching Hospitals* *Boards of Governors*	for action
Family Practitioner Committees *Community Health Councils*	for information

September 1982

HEALTH SERVICES MANAGEMENT

SUPPLY OF INFORMATION ABOUT HOSPITAL PATIENTS IN THE CONTEXT OF CIVIL LEGAL PROCEEDINGS

Summary

This Circular draws attention to recent legislation concerning the powers of the High Court to order disclosure of documents before and in proceedings for personal injury or death and sets it in the context of existing guidance on voluntary disclosure of information about hospital patients contemplating or engaged in civil legal proceedings.

Existing guidance and practice

1. Guidance on the voluntary release of information about patients contemplating or engaged in civil legal proceedings is contained in HM (59) 88.* Paragraphs 3 and 4 (the texts of which are reproduced at Annex A) advise on the action to be taken by health authorities when a request for case notes** or information from them is received from the patient concerned or his representative. This advice remains applicable, in particular that authorities should not stand on their strict rights in these circumstances and that the doctor concerned must always be consulted where medical matters are in any way involved.

2. It has since become a widely accepted practice for disclosure in these circumstances to be made to the applicant's medical adviser. This practice is commended as a means of ensuring that case notes are correctly interpreted for the applicant's benefit.

Powers of High Court to order disclosure in advance of proceedings

3. In addition to the inherent power to order disclosure between parties to proceedings which have been commenced the High Court has for some years had powers to order disclosure of relevant documents where the applicant and the person ordered to make disclosure are both likely to be parties to proceedings in cases of personal injury or death (and to order disclosure to a party to such proceedings which have

* HM (61) 110, paras 1–3, gives guidance on the special considerations which apply to the release of information about psychiatric patients. This guidance remains in force.

** This Circular is concerned primarily with hospital patients' case notes, including records and information contained therein which have been compiled by non-medical staff, because most requests and orders for disclosure will be for such records. The advice, adapted as necessary to fit the particular circumstances of each case, is also applicable to records held outside hospitals (other than those held by family practitioners or Family Practitioner Committees), for example by clinical medical officers in the community health services, by district nurses, health visitors, midwives or community psychiatric nurses.

commenced from someone who is not a party to them). Such powers were first conferred in the Administration of Justice Act 1970. A decision of the House of Lords in 1978 in a Northern Ireland case (*McIvor v Southern Health and Social Services Board*) established that under that Act, if the court did make an order, the documents would have to be made available to the applicant and that there was no power to restrict disclosure, as had earlier been the practice, to a medical or other adviser of the applicant. HN (78) 95, which is cancelled by this Circular, drew the attention of authorities to this decision.

4. Since then, there have been further changes in the law and the relevant powers of the High Court, as amended, are now contained in sections 33(2) and 34(1) and (2) of the Supreme Court Act 1981. The text of these sections is reproduced in Annex B, together with that of section 35 which contains supplementary provisions. Under the new law, which came into operation on 1 January 1982, the court has power to order production to the applicant or, on such conditions as may be specified in the order, to

(a) the applicant's legal advisers, or
(b) the applicant's legal advisers and any medical or other professional adviser of the applicant, or
(c) if the applicant has no legal adviser, to any medical or other professional adviser of the applicant.

Requests for information from patients

5. In considering requests from patients or their authorised representatives* for disclosure of case notes or information from them in connection with actual or possible litigation, authorities should continue to observe the spirit of HM (59) 88. In cases of doubt account should be taken of the powers of the High Court to order disclosure in advance of proceedings. It would not be appropriate for health authorities to adopt a more stringent test than would be likely to be applied by the court when considering an application under section 33(2) or 34(2) of that Act since this could have the effect of forcing the applicant to resort to court action when there was no real doubt as to the outcome. Authorities are reminded that for the purpose of an order under section 33(2) of the Act the applicant would not need to convince the court of the merits of his claim against the authority, but he would, under the Rules of the Supreme Court, be required to state the grounds on which he was likely to be a party to subsequent proceedings.

Requests from third parties for information about patients

6. Where a request (as opposed to a subpoena or court order) for information is received not from the patient himself or his authorised representative but from some other party engaged in or contemplating legal proceedings with him, the information requested should not be supplied without the written consent of the patient concerned and of the doctor concerned where medical matters are in any way involved. This replaces the advice in paragraph 5 of HM (59) 88 which is withdrawn.

Action on receiving an order or subpoena

7. Any health authority officer (for example, a hospital medical records officer) who is served with a court order or subpoena for the production of case notes or the giving of evidence based on them should immediately notify the District Administrator. The District Administrator should notify the doctor concerned (normally the consultant in charge of the case, or his successor) and should consider whether the

* 'Authorised representative' in this context means anyone who the authority is satisfied is acting on behalf of the patient with the patient's consent in the actual or proposed litigation or, where the patient is deceased or incapable of giving consent, is legally entitled to act on behalf of him or his estate.

authority's legal advisers and any other members of staff concerned should be informed. While there should be no delay in acting on the order, in cases of doubt the authority's and the doctor's legal advisers may need to advise on whether an appeal should be entered against it. In complying with an order for the production of documents care should be taken to ensure that the documents are made available only to the person or persons to whom the court has ordered the production, and that any conditions specified in the order are observed.

Fees for supplying information

8. The circumstances in which a member of the medical staff of the hospital may charge a fee for supplying information are covered in the Schedules of Category I and II work set out in the Handbook of Terms and Conditions of Service for Hospital Medical and Dental Staff. Paragraph 6 of HM (59) 88 is withdrawn.

Cancellation of earlier guidance

9. The following are cancelled:

HM (59) 88, paragraphs 5 and 6 (paragraph 8 was cancelled by HM (61) 110; HN (78) 95; HN (80) 32.

Action

10. Health authorities are asked to bring the contents of this Circular to the attention of all staff who may be involved with orders or requests for disclosure of information about patients.

From:

Children's Division D
Alexander Fleming House
Elephant and Castle
London SE1 6BY
Tel 01-407 5522 Ext 6381 CFD/35

ANNEX A

SUPPLY OF INFORMATION ABOUT HOSPITAL PATIENTS ENGAGED IN LEGAL PROCEEDINGS (EXTRACT FROM HM (59) 88)

3. Where a request for records or reports is made on what are manifestly insubstantial grounds, the hospital cannot be expected to grant it, but where information is being sought in pursuance of a claim of prima facie substance against the Board or Committee or a member of their staff or both, the decision is more difficult and each request must be examined on its own merits, in the light of legal advice, and of course in consultation with any member of their medical or dental staff directly concerned in the outcome of the claim (in this connection see HM (54) 32). The production of case notes and similar documents is not obligatory before the stage of discovery in the actual proceedings is reached,* but the Minister does not feel that boards and committees, especially as they are public authorities, would either wish or be well advised to maintain their strict rights in this connection except for some good reason bearing on the defence to the particular claim or on the ground that the request is made without substantial justification.

* There is now an exception to this, namely where a court order is made under the Supreme Court Act 1981 (see paragraph 4 of the main body of this Circular).

4. Where the information is required in a matter which has nothing to do with the hospital or any member of its staff, for example in litigation between the patient and a third party, hospital authorities should be prepared to help by providing, as far as possible, the information asked for subject always to the consent of the patient.** Sometimes the information sought may be entirely unrelated to medical matters – for example the date of the patient's admission or discharge; whether he was a private patient and signed the appropriate form of undertaking; and if so, the amount paid by way of hospital charges. Such information may properly be given by the Secretary of the Board or Committee, without reference to the medical staff. But in all cases – and they will undoubtedly be the majority – where medical matters are in any way involved (for example where information is wanted about the diagnosis made on admission, details of treatment, conditions on discharge, or prognosis) the doctor or dentist who was in charge of the patient's treatment at the hospital, or his successor, should be consulted. It is self-evident that this must be done when a medical or dental report is being asked for. But the principle is equally important when the request is only for extracts from the case notes, since it is necessary for the doctor or dentist to ensure that any extracts which are made are not misleading, and also that their disclosure to the patient cannot in any way be harmful medically to him – it would no doubt often be undesirable to let the patient himself have so detailed a report or such full extracts from the medical records as it would be proper to give to his general practitioner. This decision is one which can be made only by a professionally qualified person. At the same time it is imperative that no material information which can in any way be relevant to the matter should be withheld in such a way as to convey a wrong picture.

ANNEX B

SUPREME COURT ACT 1981

33.–(2) On the application, in accordance with rules of court, a person who appears to the High Court to be likely to be a party to subsequent proceedings in that court in which a claim in respect of personal injuries to a person, or in respect of a person's death, is likely to be made, the High Court shall, in such circumstances as may be specified in the rules, have power to order a person who appears to the court to be likely to be a party to the proceedings and to be likely to have or to have had in his possession, custody or power any documents which are relevant to an issue arising or likely to arise out of that claim –

(a) to disclose whether those documents are in his possession, custody or power; and
(b) to produce such of those documents as are in his possession, custody or power to the applicant or, on such conditions as may be specified in that order –
  (i) to the applicant's legal advisers; or
  (ii) to the applicant's legal advisers and any medical or other professional adviser of the applicant; or
  (iii) if the applicant has no legal adviser, to any medical or other professional adviser of the applicant.

34.–(1) This section applies to any proceedings in the High Court in which a claim is made in respect of personal injuries to a person, or in respect of a person's death.

(2) On the application, in accordance with rules of court, of a party to any proceedings to which this section applies, the High Court shall, in such circumstances

** Where the request for information is not from the patient himself or his authorised representative see paragraph 6 of the main body of the Circular.

as may be specified in the rules, have power to order a person who is not a party to the proceedings and who appears to the court to be likely to have in his possession, custody or power any documents which are relevant to an issue arising out of the said claim –

(a) to disclose whether those documents are in his possession, custody or power; and
(b) to produce such of those documents as are in his possession, custody or power to the applicant or, on such conditions as may be specified in the order –
 (i) to the applicant's legal advisers; or
 (ii) to the applicant's legal advisers and any medical or other professional adviser of the applicant; or
 (iii) if the applicant has no legal adviser, to any medical or other professional adviser of the applicant.

(3) On the application, in accordance with rules of court, of a party to any proceedings to which this section applies, the High Court shall, in such circumstances as may be specified in the rules, have power to make an order providing for any one or more of the following matters, that is to say –

(a) the inspection, photographing, preservation, custody and detention of property which is not the property of, or in the possession of, any party to the proceedings but which is the subject-matter of the proceedings or as to which any question arises in the proceedings;
(b) the taking of samples of any such property as is mentioned in paragraph (a) and the carrying out of any experiment on or with any such property.

(4) The preceding provisions of this section are without prejudice to the exercise by the High Court of any power to make orders which is exercisable apart from those provisions.

35.–(1) The High Court shall not make an order under section 33 or 34 if it considers that compliance with the order, if made, would be likely to be injurious to the public interest.

(2) Rules of court may make provision as to the circumstances in which an order under section 33 or 34 can be made; and any rules making such provision may include such incidental, supplementary and consequential provisions as the rule-making authority may consider necessary or expedient.

(3) Without prejudice to the generality of subsection (2), rules of court shall be made for the purpose of ensuring that the costs of and incidental to proceedings for an order under section 33(2) or 34 incurred by the person against whom the order is sought shall be awarded to that person unless the court otherwise directs.

(4) Sections 33(2) and 34 and this section bind the Crown; and section 33(1) binds the Crown so far as it relates to property as to which it appears to the court that it may become the subject-matter of subsequent proceedings involving a claim in respect of personal injuries to a person or in respect of a person's death.

In this subsection references to the Crown do not include references to Her Majesty in Her private capacity or to Her Majesty in right of Her Duchy of Lancaster or to the Duke of Cornwall.

(5) In sections 33 and 34 and this section –

'property' includes any land, chattel or other corporeal property of any description;

'personal injuries' includes any disease and any impairment to a person's physical or mental condition.

HN (88) 3, HN (FP) (88) 5

To: Regional Health Authorities *District Health Authorities* *Special Health Authorities for the London Post-Graduate Teaching Hospitals* *Family Practitioner Committees* *Public Health Laboratory Services Board* *Disablement Services Authority* *The Health Education Authority* *Community Health Councils* *Special Hospitals (England & Wales)*	For information

March 1988

PROCUREMENT PRODUCT LIABILITY

This Notice will be cancelled and deleted from the current communication index on 28 February 1993 unless notified separately.

Summary

This Notice draws attention to the main implications for health authorities of Part I of the Consumer Protection Act 1987 and offers guidance to help minimise NHS liability for defective products.

Background

1. The Consumer Protection Act 1987 covers three main consumer issues:

Part I Implementation of the EC Product Liability Directive which creates a regime of strict civil liability for damage caused by defective products.
Part II The introduction of a general safety requirement which makes it an offence to supply unsafe consumer goods.
Part III Provisions concerning misleading price indication which make it an offence to give such an indication.

The general safety provisions came into effect on 1 October 1987; those relating to product liability are effective from 1 March 1988. There is no element of retrospection.

The National Health Service is affected by Part I of the Act and the applicability of this Part to the Crown is specifically mentioned in the Act.

2. The essence of the product liability provisions is that where any damage is caused by a defect in a product, the producer or, where the producer is outside the European Community, the original EC importer shall be liable for the damage. If the producer or importer cannot be identified, then the supplier of the product shall be liable. The person suffering damage has to prove that the damage was caused by the defect but does not have to prove negligence on the part of the producer.

Implications for the NHS

3. The NHS appears to be affected by these provisions in three circumstances:

a. *As a supplier*
Where a patient is supplied a product which is later shown to have been defective and to have caused injury or damage, the supplying health authority may incur liability for that defective product unless either the producer or the authority's supplier can be identified. This will require the keeping of records to show clearly

from whom and when a product was obtained and to whom and when it was supplied. For this purpose it would seem necessary to record such detail as the supplier, serial or batch number and the date of issue of the product to wards, clinics, etc for clinician/patient use and to be able to show that any instructions or warnings in relation to use, maintenance, storage, expiry dates, etc are observed and/or passed on to the user. There will be practical limitations to such record keeping but in the field of medical products health authorities should review their record systems to determine the extent to which products can be linked to potential claimants.

b. *As a keeper*
If any person suffers damage as a result of the use of any equipment owned by the NHS, or from defects in products which it has purchased for its use, it is the producer or supplier who would be liable. However, the producer or supplier of equipment may seek to escape liability on the grounds that the equipment has not been maintained, calibrated or used in accordance with his instructions. If the producer succeeds in avoiding liability in this way it may still be open to the plaintiff to pursue a claim for negligence on the part of the health authority. All equipment in use in the NHS should be properly maintained and calibrated and records of such operations should be kept to demonstrate that this is the case (see Health Equipment Information No 98 – January 1982). Such maintenance is also a general requirement under the Health and Safety at Work etc Act 1974.

c. *As a producer*
NHS manufacture covers a wide range of products including medicinal preparations, blood products, diagnostic reagents and kits, disablement aids and appliances, sterile dressing and ward packs. This list is by no means exhaustive and within a general heading of NHS manufacturing activities there will, for example, be a variety of medical products which spring from experimental and development work as well as other products made in hospital workshops and some food products made in hospital kitchens for distribution outside the NHS. Whether or not all such operations constitute 'manufacture' of 'other process' within the meaning of the Act will need to be determined in individual cases, particularly where the activity relates to the modification, adaptation, processing or packaging of products obtained from another source. The attached Guide to the Act issued by the Department of Trade and Industry gives broad guidance on this point. In all manufacturing activities it is important that every effort be made to avoid producing defective products. This means that products should conform to any relevant standards which exist and that records are kept to demonstrate conformity. It is also important that products should be manufactured correctly with traceability of constituents or components; where appropriate compliance with Guides to Good Manufacturing Practice should be demonstrated. This will not provide a defence under the Act but will reduce the likelihood of claims and will increase the confidence level of in-house manufacturing activities.

Record keeping

4. It will be apparent from the above guidance that in most instances the capacity to avoid liability or defend an action brought under Part I of the Act will depend substantially on the maintenance of clear, accurate and comprehensive records relating to the procurement, use, modification and supply of products. And, since an obligation arising from liability is extinguished only after a period of 10 years and up to 1 year is allowed for the serving of a writ, such records should be retained for a period of 11 years. Record keeping procedures will necessarily vary from one authority to another but an authority considering the modification of an existing system or the introduction of a computerised system may wish to explore the feasibility of recording information as suggested in paragraph 3. The Department does, however, recognise that local circumstances may make it very difficult or impracticable to record in equal or sufficient detail all products/actions to link a

potentially defective product with a potential claimant. If the introduction and maintenance of new or more sophisticated systems will add substantially to an authority's costs, or disrupt patient service, the authority may wish to make its own judgment in balancing the effects of additional record keeping against the likelihood of claims. In this respect authorities should note that any increase in costs arising from a tightening up of procedures to minimise the possibility of litigation, will need to be met by health authorities from existing resources. The price of any affected product marketed for sale by the NHS should allow for recovery of an appropriate proportion of these costs. The general rule that the Crown bears its own risks precludes the option of insurance cover against the increased risk of claims for damages. The cost of successful claims would be a direct health authority liability.

Medicinal products

5. It is recognised that particular problems may arise from the supply of medicinal preparations by hospital pharmacies as a result of the sheer volume of transactions and the extended chain by which a medicine can pass from producer to patient. In addition hospital pharmacies which make up preparations from ingredients will be regarded as producers for purposes of the Act. Liability for a defective product arising from the functions of a hospital pharmacy would, however, rest with the health authority and not the member of staff concerned. This liability could of course be avoided if the authority was not the producer within the meaning of the Act and either the authority's own supplier or the producer could be identified. This would require records to be kept along the lines indicated in paragraph 3. No detailed central guidance can be given to provide traceability of medicines along the supply chain but Regional Pharmaceutical Officers should consider the extent to which existing record keeping needs to be altered to meet the essential requirements of a system to link unambiguously the producer of the product, or its ingredients, with the end user. Such a system would need to take account of the special problems relating to the variety of sources, the breaking/repacking of bulk supplies, the re-constitution of preparations, the number of outlets for hospital-dispensed medicines and the considerations in paragraph 4.

Other products

6. The guidance in this Notice relates principally to medical supplies. However, very few products are excluded from the provisions of the Act and authorities should recognise that they may be affected as suppliers, keepers and producers of non-medical items which may give rise to claims. The Department considers that observance of the implications for medical products should generally suffice in the wider context of non-medical supplies.

7. It is impossible to forecast the extent to which the Act may impact on health authorities, or the ways in which its effects may be felt. This may become more apparent as case law evolves; the increased level of producer/supplier risk may only become evident in the longer term. Authorities may therefore wish to view the potential implications against the background of their existing liability in tort in the event of claims for damages.

Enquiries

8. Enquiries on the content of this Notice should be addressed, as appropriate, to the following points in DHSS:

a. *Medicinal products*
Pharmaceutical Division, Eileen House, 80 Newington Causeway, London SE1 6EF. Tel 01 703 6380 Ext 3355.

b. *Other products*
NHS Procurement Directorate, 14 Russell Square, London WC1B 5EP. Tel 01 636 6811 Ext 3248.

c. *Interpretation of the Consumer Protection Act and the liability of health authorities and their employees*
Solicitors Office, Alexander Fleming House, Elephant and Castle, London SE1 6BY. Tel 01 497 5522 Ext 6670.

From:

NHS Procurement Directorate
AD2
14 Russell Square
London WC1B 5EP
Tel 01 636 6811 Ext 3248

HC (88) 37, HN (FP) (88) 18

To:	*Regional Health Authorities* *District Health Authorities* *Special Health Authorities*	for action
	Community Health Councils *Family Practitioner Committees*	for information

June 1988

HEALTH SERVICES MANAGEMENT

HOSPITAL COMPLAINTS PROCEDURE ACT 1985

Unless otherwise notified, this Circular but not the directions to which it refers will cease to be valid on 31 May 1993 [extended until further notice].

Summary

1. This Circular encloses at Annex A a copy of the directions required by s 1 of the Hospital Complaints Procedure Act 1985 and advises on the procedure to be operated in respect of complaints by hospital patients.

Background

2. The Hospital Complaints Procedure Act received the Royal Assent in July 1985. The Act requires the Secretary of State to issue directions on the complaints procedure to be operated in respect of hospital patients and the steps to publicise the procedure.

3. Health Authorities were invited in 1986 to comment on proposals for handling complaints. The consultation exercise offered the opportunity to re-examine existing complaints procedures. Many authorities confirmed either that their local practices corresponded already to the proposed procedures or that arrangements were being made to align their procedures accordingly.

4. The directions enclosed at Annex A confirm the arrangements which health authorities are obliged to make for dealing with complaints and for publicising these. The remainder of this circular advises how authorities may interpret the requirements of the directions.

The need for a complaints procedure

5. Patients are entitled to bring to the attention of health authorities aspects of their care and treatment about which they are unhappy. The Department recognises that suggestions, constructive criticism and complaints can be valuable aids to management in maintaining and developing better standards of health care. It is important that no one (staff or patients) should be inhibited from making valid complaints and that there is full confidence that these will be given full, proper and speedy consideration. Many matters that trouble patients can be dealt with as they arise. Staff should be encouraged to be aware of and to deal with these in a way which reassures the patient and to bring the complaint to the attention of management when this is appropriate.

Procedural requirements

6. The basis of any complaints procedure is good communication. Problems of communication between patients and staff can generate misunderstandings which

can result in complaints. Good communications may help defuse awkward situations. However, not all complaints can be dealt with on the spot and in this informal way. Some complaints will be of such concern to the patient that they warrant consideration and a formal response by a senior officer of the authority or it may be that the complaint is comparatively trivial but the patient feels unwilling or unable to discuss the matter with the staff who are directly involved. Again, good communications will be necessary to ensure that the complainant can give full expression to his concerns and that the full facts about the complaint are obtained.

7. The directions outline the mandatory requirements which health authorities must adopt in establishing complaints procedures. They involve

i. *A designated officer*. Each Health Authority must designate a senior officer for each hospital or group of hospitals for which it is responsible. The designated officer should be located in the hospital for which he is responsible and his whereabouts made known to facilitate contact by patients or those acting on a patient's behalf. The Unit General Manager might be the appropriate person for this task. The designated officer will be the recipient of formal complaints made by or on behalf of patients and will be accountable for the investigation of complaints other than those involving clinical judgement, serious untoward incidents, disciplinary proceedings, physical abuse of patients or criminal offences. Where the designated officer is also the Unit General Manager he may well be directly involved in these particular complaints. But investigation of these may also involve other senior officers, eg the Regional Medical Officer (RMO) or the equivalent or the District General Manager (DGM), or members of the Authority (see sub paragraph iv below). The designated officer should not be denied access to relevant records which are essential for the investigation of a complaint. The designated officer should normally be available to assist in cases of minor grievances which the patient feels unable to discuss with eg ward staff.

ii. *Who may complain*. Any person who is or has been a patient at the hospital (either as an inpatient or outpatient) is eligible to make a complaint. If the person concerned has died or is otherwise unable to act for himself the complaint should be accepted from a close relative, or friend, or a body or individual suitable to represent him. The designated officer must be satisfied that where the patient is capable, the complaint is being made with his knowledge and consent.

iii. *Investigating the complaint*. In investigating the complaint, the designated officer must ensure that he has a full picture from the complainant of the events complained about. This may involve a preliminary interview to clarify the nature of the complaint or to obtain further information. It may be possible at this stage to resolve the issue to the complainant's satisfaction without taking the matter further. Care must be taken not to prejudice the outcome of any further investigation.

The designated officer, in liaison with other appropriate senior officers, should circulate details of the complaint to the staff concerned for their comments and seek to agree a reply. General complaints about, for example, the hospital services would be sent to the Head of the Department concerned for advice on a reply. Care must be taken not to introduce delays into the system by allowing excessive periods for comment. The aim should be to process the complaint speedily and thoroughly at all stages. The complainant must be kept informed of progress and where appropriate interim replies or holding letters must be sent.

Where the designated officer considers that a complaint carries a threat of litigation he should seek legal advice on whether and in what form an investigation might proceed to minimise the risk of prejudicing any civil proceedings. The possibility of legal proceedings should not prevent the officer undertaking the investigations necessary to uncover faults in procedures and/or prevent a recurrence.

iv. *Further action to certain complaints*. Where the complaint concerns:

(a) the exercise of *Clinical Judgement* which cannot be resolved by discussion with the consultant concerned;
(b) what the Authority is satisfied constitutes *a serious untoward incident* involving harm to a patient;
(c) the conduct of hospital medical or dental staff which the Authority considers ought to be the subject of *disciplinary proceedings*;
(d) the alleged *physical abuse of patients*;
(e) a possible *criminal offence*;

the designated officer should bring the matter to his senior officers' attention (or if appropriate the RMO) without delay so that appropriate action can be taken to ensure that the complaint is dealt with promptly in accordance with the Department's guidelines and local procedures.

v. *Conclusion of an investigation*. When an investigation into a complaint has been completed the designated officer must complete a report and send a letter detailing the results of the investigation to the person who made the complaint, to any person who is involved in the complaint and where appropriate to the manager of any Department or service concerned. The letter should be informative both as to the reasons for any failure in service and any steps taken to prevent a recurrence and should contain an apology where appropriate. If the complainant remains dissatisfied he should be advised to refer the matter to the Health Service Commissioner unless the complaint is clearly outside the Health Service Commissioner's jurisdiction or the complainant proposes to take further action through the courts.

vi. *Monitoring complaints*. Health Authorities must monitor the arrangements. The purpose of this requirement is to ensure that health authorities monitor trends in complaints and can direct that appropriate action is taken. The designated officer should therefore provide summaries of complaints for the health authority. These summaries should be anonymised to preserve confidentiality of patients. The monitoring role must be undertaken by the authority itself, a committee of the authority or specified authority members. Progress in dealing with complaints should be kept under review by the District General Manager who should report to the Authority at quarterly intervals about any cases outstanding.

vii. *Publicity*. Publicity must be given to the procedure. This is an essential part of improving the public perception of the complaints procedure. Health authorities should consider giving publicity to the procedures using:

(a) *Admission booklets*. Information about making a complaint should be given in the hospital booklet issued to patients on or prior to admission to hospital and available in hospital outpatient departments. It is essential for the location of the designated officer to be included.
(b) *Leaflets*. A leaflet explaining the complaints procedure and including a reference to the Health Service Commissioner's role in investigating complaints should be available for all patients. In addition to explaining the procedure in straightforward terms, the leaflet should give the location of the designated officer. Authorities should consider the need to make leaflets available in ethnic minority languages.
(c) *Notices*. These should be displayed in health authority premises including reception areas. Notices should give the location of the designated officer to whom appropriate comments, suggestions and complaints should be addressed.
(d) *CHCs*. Publicity material should be available to CHCs for information and issue to the public.
(e) *Staff Training*. All staff will need to be made aware of the complaints procedure and to know the name and location of the designated officer to enable them to refer patients. Training will be needed to ensure that staff attitudes are positive and do not deter legitimate complaints.

Additional procedures

8. In considering their procedures health authorities are asked to take the following elements, which are not requirements under the directions, into account.

i. *Form of complaint*. It is not a requirement that a complaint should be in writing. But it is important that a note be made in cases where the complaint is not readily settled and where a dispute as to the precise nature of the complaint might arise. This is particularly so when a formal investigation is likely. Where the complainant is unable to put the formal complaint in writing the designated officer should ensure that a record of the complaint is made and ask the complainant to sign it. A refusal to sign by the complainant should not delay investigation of the complaint.

ii. *Time limits*. Complaints should be made and dealt with as quickly as possible. The longer the delay the more memories fade and less fruitful the investigation of the complaint. It is reasonable to expect that complaints should be made within three months of the incident giving rise to the complaint and publicity should encourage this. However there may be circumstances in which this recommended time limit may not be appropriate and the directions provide the designated officer with the discretion to extend the period if it is considered that the complainant has good reason for delay.

iii. *Complaints about the Community Health Services*. Complaints about the Community Health Services do not come within the scope of the procedures to be laid down in the directions under the Hospital Complaints Procedure Act 1985. Health Authorities are asked to consider that the procedure directed for the handling of general complaints about hospital services should also be adopted in respect of the community health services.

Investigation by statutory authorities

The Health Service Commissioner

9. Section 1(2) of the Hospital Complaints Procedure Act provides that nothing in the procedure promulgated in the directions shall preclude investigation by the Health Service Commissioner. The Health Service Commissioner may therefore investigate a complaint about health authority services or maladministration if a complainant is not satisfied with the conduct or outcome of the health authority's own investigations. The Health Service Commissioner cannot investigate complaints relating to actions taken solely in consequence of the exercise of clinical judgement. Whether the action is taken solely in consequence of the exercise of clinical judgement will be determined by the Health Service Commissioner.

The Mental Health Act Commission

10. Section 120(1) of the Mental Health Act empowers the Mental Health Act Commission to investigate any complaint which a detained patient thinks has not been dealt with satisfactorily by the hospital managers. Nothing in the directions preclude such investigation by the Mental Health Act Commission.

The Police

11. The District General Manager must be consulted where it appears that a criminal offence may have been committed. Where the allegation is serious and substantial the police must be notified immediately.

Complaints about clinical judgement

12. The current procedures for dealing with complaints relating to the exercise of clinical judgement by hospital medical and dental staff are subject to an agreement with the medical profession. The procedures were outlined in circular HC (81) 5 Annex Part III (a copy is attached as Annex B).

13. The procedures provide for the complainant to be accompanied by a relative or personal friend. It is for the complainant to decide who the friend is. Such a person is there to help and support the complainant and not to act as an advocate nor in a way which detracts from the clinical nature of the consultation. The friend may sometimes help a less articulate complainant explain their concerns but this should not be allowed to create an adversarial situation.

Cancellation of circulars

14. The guidance contained in HN (78) 39, HC (81) 5, HN (83) 31 and DA (86) 14 is hereby withdrawn and those circulars should be regarded as cancelled.

Action

15. Health Authorities are asked to consider this guidance and to ensure that the directions enclosed with this circular are complied with. Regional Health Authorities are asked to confirm by 26 August 1988 to the address below that the required procedures are in place.

From:

Health Services Division (HS1C)
Alexander Fleming House
Elephant and Castle
London SE1 6BY

Tel 01-407 5522 Ext 6682 CPL 31

ANNEX A

DIRECTIONS ON HOSPITAL COMPLAINTS PROCEDURES

The Secretary of State for Social Services, in exercise of the powers conferred on him by section 17 of the National Health Service Act 1977, hereby directs:–

(i) each district health authority in England or Wales;

and each of the following special health authorities:–

Each of the Authorities for the London Postgraduate Teaching Hospitals;
The Board of Governors of the Eastman Dental Hospital;
Broadmoor Hospital Board;
Moss Side and Park Lane Hospitals Board;
Rampton Hospital Board;

to make arrangements, as specified or described in the following paragraphs of these directions, for dealing with complaints made by, or on behalf of, persons who are or have been patients at any hospital for the management of which that authority is responsible and for monitoring the effectiveness of, and for publicising, the arrangements made for dealing with such complaints; and

(ii) that such arrangements should be made and brought into force not later than 29th July 1988.

1. In these Directions:–

'authority' means any district health authority or special health authority to whom these directions are given;

'complainant' means a person who is or who has been a patient at a hospital or the person acting on behalf of any such patient in making a complaint in relation to such hospital;

'designated officer' means a person who has been designated by a health authority as having responsibility for dealing with complaints made in relation to that hospital or group of hospitals.

2. (1) For each hospital or group of hospitals for which an authority has responsibility, there must be an officer designated by the authority as having responsibility for dealing with complaints made in relation to that hospital or group of hospitals.

(2) The duties of a designated officer must include responsibility for receiving, and seeing that action is taken upon, any formal complaint made at the hospital or hospitals for which he is given responsibility and, where the complainant had indicated a wish for him so to do, assisting in dealing with a complaint that is likely to be able to be dealt with informally.

(3) Except to the extent that the subject matter of a complaint falls within any of the categories specified in the next sub-paragraph of these directions the duties of the designated officer must include responsibility for investigating and reporting on the investigation of any formal complaint to the complainant, to any person involved in the complaint, and to such other persons as the authority may require.

(4) To the extent that the subject matter of any complaint made at a hospital or group of hospitals for which a designated officer is responsible:–

(a) concerns the exercise of clinical judgement by a hospital doctor or dentist and cannot be resolved by discussion with the consultant concerned; or
(b) relates to what the authority is satisfied constitutes a serious untoward incident involving harm to a patient; or
(c) relates to the conduct of hospital medical or dental staff which the authority considers ought to be the subject of disciplinary proceedings; or
(d) gives reasonable grounds for inviting a police investigation as to whether a criminal offence may have been committed;

the duties of the designated officer in accordance with arrangements made pursuant to these directions shall not involve responsibility for investigating the complaint but the designated officer shall be required to bring the matter to the attention of his authority who shall, in the case of a matter specified in (a), (b) or (c) of this sub-paragraph, secure that the matter is promptly dealt with in accordance with the appropriate procedure laid down in guidance issued to authorities by the Department of Health and Social Security in respect of England and by the Welsh Office in respect of Wales.

(5) Arrangements made may include provision for a designated officer to have the assistance of other officers of the authority in carrying out his duties under those arrangements and, with the agreement of the designated officer, such other officers may act on his behalf in the performance of those duties.

3. Each authority shall secure that arrangements are made for staff at any hospital for which that authority is responsible to seek to deal informally to the satisfaction of the complainant with any complaint made at that hospital and to advise any complainant, whose complaint cannot be so dealt with to his satisfaction, to make a formal complaint to the designated officer for that hospital.

4. Arrangements for making formal complaints should secure that such complaints are made or recorded in writing. Such complaints should normally be made within three months of the matter complained of arising although the designated officer ought to have a discretion to allow a longer period if satisfied that the complainant had good cause for not having made the complaint earlier. Arrangements made should secure that formal complaints are investigated promptly and that both the complainant and any hospital staff involved are afforded an opportunity to bring to

the attention of the designated officer any information or comments they wish to make that are relevant to his investigation of the complaint.

5. Each authority must monitor arrangements made for dealing with complaints at hospitals for which it is responsible. Arrangements must be made for reports to be prepared at quarterly intervals for use by the authority in monitoring progress on the procedure for dealing with complaints, for considering trends in complaints and for taking remedial action on complaints as appropriate.

6. Each authority shall take such steps as are necessary to ensure that any patients at, or visitors to, any hospital for which the authority is responsible, as well as the staff working at the hospital, and any Community Health Council covering an area served by that hospital, are fully informed of the arrangements for dealing with complaints made at the hospital and are informed of the identity and location of the designated officer for such hospital.

ANNEX B

MEMORANDUM OF AN AGREEMENT FOR DEALING WITH COMPLAINTS RELATING TO THE EXERCISE OF CLINICAL JUDGMENT BY HOSPITAL MEDICAL AND DENTAL STAFF (FIRST ISSUED AS PART OF CIRCULAR HC (81) 5)

First stage

18. As explained in Paragraph 5 of Part I, a complaint may initially be made, and dealt with, orally or in writing. Complaints concerning clinical matters may be made direct to the consultant concerned, or to a health authority or one of its officers. In either case it is the responsibility of the consultant in charge of the patient to look into the clinical aspects of the complaint. This must be the first step in handling the complaint at the *first stage*.

19. If another member of the medical[1] staff is involved, the consultant should discuss the complaint with the doctor concerned at the outset and at all later stages in this procedure. It may be helpful to discuss the complaint with the patient's general practitioner. The consultant should try to resolve the complaint within a few days preferably by offering to see the complainant[2] to discuss the matter and seek to resolve his anxieties. If there is any delay, he should get in touch with the complainant and explain the reason. When the consultant sees the complainant, he should make a brief, strictly factual, record in the hospital notes.

20. Where a complaint is made which involves hospital medical staff other than consultants, the consultant in charge of the patient and the doctor concerned should both be involved in the handling of the complaint at all stages.

21. If the consultant feels the risk of legal action is significant, he should at once bring the matter to the notice of the district administrator.* Where there are non-clinical

1 In this Memorandum the terms 'medical' and 'doctor' include 'dentist' in appropriate cases.

2 The doctor's first responsibility is to the patient, hence this Memorandum is concerned with complaints made by patients. It applies also to complaints made by parents or guardians of minors, and relatives of those patients with physical or mental disability limiting their competence to deal with the matter themselves, and of deceased patients. The term 'complainant' is used to cover all such cases.

* References made to 'district administrator' should be substituted with the words 'district general manager'.

aspects to a complaint made direct to a consultant, the consultant should inform the district administrator, who will arrange for these aspects of the complaint to be considered by an appropriate member of staff.

22. Where a complaint which has a clinical element is made to the authority or one of its officers, the district administrator should show the complaint to the consultant concerned and refer the clinical aspects to him.

23. The normal practice will be for the district administrator to send a written reply to the complainant on behalf of the authority. Any reference to clinical matters in the reply, whether interim or final, should be agreed by the consultant concerned. Sometimes it may be appropriate to confine this to mentioning that the clinical aspects had been discussed between the consultant and the complainant. On occasion, the consultant may wish to send the complainant a written reply direct covering the clinical aspects.

Second stage

24. Where a complainant is dissatisfied with the reply he has received at the first stage, he may renew his complaint either to the authority, one of its administrators or to the consultant. In any case, if he has not so far put his complaint in writing, he should now be asked to do so before his complaint is considered further. The next step, *in this second stage*, is for the Regional Medical Officer (RMO) to be at once informed; this should be done by the consultant, informing the district administrator that he has done so. The RMO will discuss the matter with the consultant.

25. At this point, the consultant may indicate to the RMO that he also wishes to discuss the matter with his professional colleagues. After these discussions, he may consider that a further talk with the complainant might resolve the complaint. If this fails, or if the consultant feels that such a meeting would serve no useful purpose, the RMO should discuss with the consultant the value of offering to the complainant the procedure – outlined more fully below – whereby the RMO would arrange for two independent consultants to see the complainant jointly to discuss the problem. If in the light of his discussion with the consultant and – where necessary – the complainant, the RMO considers it appropriate, the procedure of the *third stage* should be set in motion.

Third stage, independent professional review

26. The procedure at the third stage is intended to deal with complaints which are of a substantial nature, but which are not prima facie (and in the light of legal advice where appropriate) likely to be the subject of more formal action either by the health authority or through the courts. The procedure is intended for use in suitable instances as an alternative to the inquiry procedures provided in HM (66) 15, though these will remain available for use when necessary. It would not be appropriate if legal powers such as subpoena seem likely to be required. Nor is it intended that the new procedure should be invoked for complaints of a trivial nature.

27. Arrangements should be made by the RMO for all aspects of the case to be considered by two independent consultants in active practice in the appropriate speciality or specialities. They should be nominated by the Joint Consultants Committee. At least one should be a doctor working in a comparable hospital in another Region. These 'second opinions' should have the opportunity to read all the clinical records. They should discuss the case with the consultant concerned and any other member of the medical staff involved as well as with the complainant. The meeting between the two independent consultants and the complainant should be in the nature of a medical consultation. The consultant who had been in charge of the patient at the time of the event giving rise to the complaint should not be present at

the meeting, but should be available if required. The complainant should, if he wishes, be accompanied by a relative or personal friend and might wish to ask the general practitioner to be present.

28. 'Second opinions' should discuss the clinical aspects of the problem fully with the complainant. In cases in which it is their view that the clinical judgment of the medical staff concerned has been exercised responsibly, they should endeavour to resolve the complainant's anxieties. The view they have reached and the outcome of the discussion with the complainant should be reported to the RMO on a confidential basis.

29. In other cases the 'second opinions' might feel that discussion with the medical staff concerned would avoid similar problems arising in the future. When they had held such a discussion they would inform the complainant and would explain to him, as far as appropriate, how it was hoped to overcome the problems which had been identified. They should not provide a detailed report for the complainant but they should report the action they had taken to the RMO. The 'second opinions' would also consider whether there were any other circumstances which had contributed to the problems in the case and on which they could usefully make recommendations, which they would include in their report to the RMO. These might include matters requiring action by the health authority, for example the workload carried by the medical or nursing staff.

30. In exceptional cases it may appear to the 'second opinions', at any stage of an investigation, that the particular case is not appropriate to the second opinions procedure and that the complaint would be best pursued by alternative means. In this event they should report to the RMO accordingly.

Concluding action by the health authority

31. The district administrator will, on completion of the review by the 'second opinions', write formally to the complainant on behalf of the authority, with a copy to the consultant. The district administrator will, where appropriate, explain any action the authority has taken as a result of the complaint but, where clinical matters are concerned, he will follow the RMO's advice regarding the comment which would be appropriate. So far as the authority is concerned the matter will remain confidential unless previous or subsequent publicity makes it essential for the authority to reply publicly, in which case comment on clinical matters will be confined to the terms of the district administrator's letter.

The Health Service Commissioner

32. Complaints relating to clinical judgment remain outside the responsibility of the Health Service Commissioner. However, it will be possible for him to advise complainants whose complaints contain elements of clinical judgment of the availability of the procedure described in this part of the Memorandum.

Appendix

HC (89) 20

<table>
<tr><td>To:</td><td>Regional Health Authorities
District Health Authorities
Special Health Authorities</td><td>for action</td></tr>
<tr><td></td><td>Family Practitioner Committees
Community Health Councils</td><td>for information</td></tr>
</table>

August 1989

HEALTH SERVICES MANAGEMENT

PRESERVATION, RETENTION, AND DESTRUCTION OF RECORDS

RESPONSIBILITIES OF HEALTH AUTHORITIES UNDER THE PUBLIC RECORDS ACTS

The guidance in this circular will be cancelled and deleted from the current communication Index on 31 July 1994 unless notified separately.

Summary

National Health Service records are public records for the purpose of the Public Records Acts 1958 and 1967. This circular advises on the requirements of the Public Records Acts and the main periods of retention for administrative, financial and medical purposes of authorities, including possible use in litigation.

It does not apply to the records of Family Practitioner Committees, for which minimum periods for retention are set out in ECL 2/68, nor to those of Community Health Councils.

Action

Each health authority should designate an officer to make appropriate arrangements for the selection and permanent preservation of public records and to liaise as necessary with the Public Record Office and confirm to Regional Liaison Division no later than November 1989 that this action has been taken.

Background

1. In its White Paper *Modern Public Records* (Cmnd 8531, March 1982) the Government accepted the need for revised guidance to NHS authorities on the selection of records for preservation under the Public Records Acts. The guidance in this circular had been prepared with the two objectives stated in the White Paper, namely to reduce to a manageable level the categories of records whose preservation is required and in particular to remove clinical records of individual patients from those categories.

2. The circular draws on advice and comments from the National Health Service, particularly the National Association of Health Authorities, (NAHA) and the Association of Health Care Information and Medical Records Officers (AMRO) and from the Public Record Office.

3. Advice on the application of this guidance to the records of individual authorities, including the selection of records for preservation under the Public Records Acts, is available from the Liaison Officer, Public Record Office, Kew, Richmond, Surrey, TW9 4DU (Tel: 01-876 3444).

4. Advice on good practice in medical record keeping can be obtained from the

Association of Health Care Information and Medical Records Officers, Whitecroft, Wilmore Hill Lane, Hopton, Stafford, ST18 0AW.

Guidelines

5. Guidelines are enclosed

Appendix A: Requirements of the Public Records Acts.
Appendix B: Criteria for selection of NHS records for permanent preservation.
Appendix C: Minimum retention periods for records which are not for permanent preservation.
Appendix D: Summary of destruction periods for records which are not for permanent preservation.

Cancellation of earlier guidance

6. Circulars HM (61) 73, HN (76) 48 and HC (80) 7 are cancelled. HM (63) 71 amended.

From:

Health Services Division (HS1C)
Eileen House
80-94 Newington Causeway
London SE1 6EF
Tel. 01-972 2000 Ext 22729

HMR 32

ANNEX A

REQUIREMENTS OF THE PUBLIC RECORDS ACTS

1. The following is a summary of the requirements of the Acts as they affect health authorities:

(i) All NHS records with minor exceptions (see paragraph 10 below) are public records within the meaning of the Acts and must be retained, preserved or destroyed according to the provisions of those Acts;
(ii) Health Authorities have a duty under section 3 of the Public Records Act 1958 to make appropriate arrangements for the selection for permanent preservation of public records within their control, under the guidance of the Keeper of Public Records, and for their transfer before they are 30 years old to the Public Record Office or other place of deposit appointed by the Lord Chancellor (see paragraphs 3–9 below);
(iii) Under section 5(1) of the 1958 Act as amended public records in the Public Record Office or in places of deposit are closed to the public until they have been in existence for 30 years.* However if health authorities give access to records before transfer and records have been open to inspection, they remain so after transfer. The Lord Chancellor may, at the request of health authorities, prescribe longer or shorter periods of closure for particular classes of records (see paragraphs 5 and 6 below).
(iv) Under section 3(4) of the Public Records Act 1958 health authorities may retain records for a period longer than 30 years after their creation, for administrative or other special reasons, provided that the Lord Chancellor has been informed of the facts and given his approval.

* This may generally be interpreted as 31 years after the year of the last entry in a record.

Old records

2. In no circumstances may a record older than 1660 be destroyed. The local record office should be consulted before records more than 60 years old are destroyed.

Selection of records for permanent preservation

3. Appendix B sets out criteria by which records should be selected for permanent preservation under the Acts. *If material is in a category selected for permanent preservation, the original documents must be preserved*. Microfilm and other photocopies are rarely an acceptable alternative. When no longer required for use by the authority material not selected should be destroyed in accordance with local destruction procedures.

4. Clinical records of individual patients will not normally be preserved permanently under the Public Records Act 1958, other than by way of samples. That is best done by hospitals who are prepared to select and deposit samples in agreement with local record offices which have suitable facilities and are prepared to house such records.

Extended closure

5. Section 5 of the Public Records Act 1958 as amended makes provision for the Lord Chancellor to prescribe periods of closure in excess of 30 years. A 100 year closure period was prescribed in 1961* for medical records of individual patients; it applies only to records then in existence. Health authorities are reminded that other sensitive material may exist among records selected for permanent preservation and that they are responsible for identifying such material and for applying to the Lord Chancellor, through the Keeper of Public Records, for an extension of closure beyond 30 years. The criteria for extended closure are:

(i) Exceptionally sensitive papers, the disclosure of which would be contrary to the public interest whether on security or other grounds (including the need to safeguard the Revenue);
(ii) Documents containing information supplied in confidence the disclosure of which would or might constitute a breach of good faith; and
(iii) Documents containing information about individuals, the disclosure of which would cause distress to, or endanger, living persons or their immediate descendants.

6. Under section 5(4) of the 1958 Act records of health authorities which are not yet open to public inspection may not be examined without the express permission of those authorities or their successors. In exercising such discretion, health authorities should observe the following conditions:

(i) Permission should be restricted to the specific applicant;
(ii) For medical records, the consent of the patient or his next of kin and the agreement of the appropriate health professional should be sought, [if practicable];
(iii) A signed undertaking must be obtained from the applicant not to identify any patient or member of staff in any work resulting from his research;
(iv) Any text concerning transcripts from or reference to material not open to public inspection should accordingly be submitted to the health authority before publication, to verify that the undertaking has been kept.

Place of deposit

7. Public records selected for permanent preservation are normally transferred to the Public Record Office. However, under section 4 of the 1958 Act public records may be held locally in a place of deposit appointed by the Lord Chancellor, if the authority responsible for records deposited in that place so agrees. In general, NHS

* By Lord Chancellor's Instrument No 3 of 7 January 1961.

records are appropriate for local deposit. Records created or inherited by district and regional health authorities should usually be deposited in the approved place of deposit nearest to their administrative headquarters. Those places of deposit are normally local authority record offices maintained by county and district councils. In a very few instances individual hospitals have made suitable arrangements for care of their own records and have been appointed as places of deposit to hold them; certain libraries of medical institutions have also been appointed as places of deposit for records of hospitals, particularly personal health records.

8. The storage accommodation provided for the records must conform as nearly as possible to the British Standards Institution's *Recommendations for the storage and exhibition of archival documents* (BS 5454: 1989). In particular the accommodation must be secure, with proper environmental controls and adequate protection against fire and flood. Members of the public wishing to consult those records which are open to inspection must be able to do so in a properly supervised search room, where finding aids to the records must be available. There should be a guarantee of continued existence and commitment on the part of the authority maintaining a place of deposit. Ideally, the records there should be in the care of a professionally qualified archivist.

9. Whether records are held in the Public Record Office or a Place of Deposit, the transferring authority has the right, under section 4(6) of the 1958 Act, to have its records temporarily returned to it.

Exempt records

10. The following records, although technically exempt from the provisions of the Public Records Acts, contain information which meets the criteria for retention for the purposes of statutory audit or civil proceedings.

(i) Records of non-Exchequer funds.
(ii) Records of private patients admitted under section 58 of the National Health Service Act 1977 or section 5 of the National Health Service Act 1946.

Authorities should consider treating such records as if they were not so exempt. Advice on this point may be obtained from the Liaison Officer.

Retention of records: general

11. Permission to retain records for a period longer than 30 years, under section 3(4) of the 1958 Act, must be sought in respect of *all* records which are so retained, whether or not they have been selected for permanent preservation. Health authorities are responsible for identifying records which are already or within the next ten years will become 30 years old and for applying to the Lord Chancellor, through the Keeper of Public Records, if they need to be retained by the authority rather than transferred to a place of deposit or destroyed.

Administrative retentions

12. Administrative records may, with the approval of the Lord Chancellor, be retained by health authorities for more than 30 years if they are required for the day-to-day conduct of business. It should however be rare for administrative records in which the last entry was made 31 years previously to be still required for the day to day conduct of business. Before giving that approval, the Lord Chancellor will require to be informed whether arrangements can be made for members of the public to have access to the retained material. No approval of this kind will be given for a period in excess of 5 years.

Retention of records for other reasons

13. Health authorities may need to retain administrative records and personal health records for other purposes after these are no longer required for administrative or

operational use, e g for research or for use as evidence in litigation. The minimum period for retention of personal health records (other than FPC records) no longer required for clinical purposes should take account of the provision of the Limitation Act 1975 and the Congenital Disabilities (Civil Liability) Act 1976 and the Consumer Protection Act 1987. In the event of their retention for a period longer than 30 years, the same considerations apply as with retention for administrative purposes (see paragraph 12 above). Recommendations for minimum retention periods are contained in Annex C.

ANNEX B

CRITERIA FOR SELECTION OF NHS RECORDS FOR PERMANENT PRESERVATION

General

1. The destruction of records worthy of permanent preservation is an irreversible act, while the cost of preserving records worthy of permanent preservation is high and continuing. The criteria which follow are intended to give guidance on the identification, with relative ease, of records of permanent value, avoiding both ill-considered destruction and excessive selection.

2. The officer responsible for public records matters must ensure that records no longer required for local use are reviewed as soon as practicable under the criteria in paragraph 6 below. Those records selected for permanent preservation should be transferred to a place of deposit appointed by the Lord Chancellor for that purpose. The remainder should *either* be destroyed *or* be retained by the health authority for its research or litigation purposes.

Guidelines for selection under the Public Records Acts

3. The nominated officer should prepare local guidelines supplementing and adapting the criteria in paragraph 6 below in conjunction with the local record office.

4. In preparing guidelines the nominated officer should bear in mind that selected records are used rarely in isolation but are liable to be used in conjunction with records from other sources and be used for research unconnected with the purpose for which they were created.

5. In deciding whether particular records contain information in sufficient quantity or of such quality that they should be preserved, account should be taken of any informed opinion available, whether from inside or outside the authority. In cases of doubt the advice of the Liaison Officer must be sought.

Records for preservation

6. Record sets of major reports and publications and of the minutes of the authority and its predecessors, together with those of major committees and sub-committees should be selected for permanent preservation.

7. Records which seem likely to provide material for research should be scrutinised with a view to permanent preservation particularly those relating to:

- (i) the history of the authority (including that of its predecessors) its organisations and procedures;
- (ii) the history of individual hospitals under the control of the authority, including

matters relating to their history before the NHS and under predecessor authorities;

(iii) notable events or persons where the records add significantly to what is already known;

(iv) major events (whether in national, regional or purely local terms) or trends in political, social and economic events;

(v) scientific, technological and medical research and development;

(vi) major plans and projects, including projects which have been abandoned or deferred;

(vii) industrial relations (not routine staff matters);

(viii) records of benefactions in addition to those included in records of non-Exchequer funds (see para 10 of Annex A).

Financial records

8. Key financial records are of great importance and may merit permanent preservation. Nevertheless in the course of everyday financial business large masses of documentation are generated which serve no purpose after comparatively short periods of time. They should be retained only for the periods set out in Annex C. The following must be selected for permanent preservation:

(i) one set of the annual accounts and statements submitted to the Secretary of State each year in accordance with the requirements of the National Health Service Acts;

(ii) documents relating to the terms of any trusts administered by health authorities whether or not they are included in records of non-Exchequer funds;

(iii) key records, in addition to final accounts, relating to building and engineering works such as surveys, site plans, drawings, bills of quantities, contract documents, including those relating to major projects which have been abandoned or deferred.

Property records

9. Records which are evidence of title must never be destroyed. Examples of documents of title are: title deeds and correspondence relating to the transfer of hospital property to the Secretary of State, to the apportionment and vesting in the Secretary of State of interests in premises used partly for hospital and partly for other purposes; to the purchase, disposal and leasing of property by or to the Secretary of State; and to the transfer and discharge of mortgages. If documents of title have been lost the administrative files relating to the ownership of the land must be retained for as long as the documents of title would have been kept.

Personal health records

10. Although personal health records of patients will not normally be preserved permanently, arrangements may be made for samples to be taken (see paragraph 4 of the Annex A).

ANNEX C

MINIMUM RETENTION PERIODS FOR RECORDS WHICH ARE NOT FOR PERMANENT PRESERVATION

1. The recommendations which follow are intended to give guidance to health authorities on the destruction, at the earliest possible date, of all records, which have not been identified as suitable for permanent preservation (see Annex B) or which are no longer required for their original purpose. A list of classes of such documents, indicating the periods after which they may be destroyed is given at Annex D.

Financial records

2. Financial records which have not been selected for preservation should be retained for varying periods having regard to the following requirements:

(i) Audit–all original documents such as invoices, payroll documents, stores issue noted, etc must be retained for inspection and examination by the auditors appointed by the Secretary of State and the staff of the National Audit Office for at least eighteen months after the end of the financial year to which they relate.

(ii) Possible litigation – an authority may need, for example, to defend itself against an action for payment of an invoice which has already been settled or to take legal action against a debtor who has failed to pay the authority. The retention period will represent the length of time which has to elapse before such a claim is statute barred, i e six years. In this connection the Department is advised that properly certified microfilm records of original documents are acceptable in evidence;

(iii) Superannuation purposes – pay and service records must be retained for a substantial period to safeguard the superannuation rights of staff. While destruction may be considered *after 10 years* some authorities may wish to retain such records until the subject reaches benefit age.

3. With these considerations in mind the records listed in Annex D should be retained for the periods shown therein. Once the period of retention for audit purposes is complete, however, the original documents except for forms SD55 (ADP) and SD55J, may be destroyed provided a properly compiled microfilm record is retained for the remainder of the prescribed period, embodying a suitable certificate by the Treasurer as to its accuracy and completeness.

Each authority should however weigh the cost of microfilming (including buying, borrowing or sharing the basic equipment) against the cost of storage space and staffing involved in keeping original documents.

4. With regard to the retention of records produced by computers the normal consideration will apply where printed statements and records are produced. Where the records are held only on microfilm, microfiche or original magnetic data files, they should be retained, using the same criteria governing the retention of more conventional records, but extra care will be necessary to prevent corruption or deterioration of the data. For computerised records it will also be necessary to provide a prompt print out facility and printed end of year statements for audit purposes and the question of re-recording may have to be considered as equipment becomes obsolete.

Records of legal value

5. The nominated officer must ensure that records of legal value to the health authority, the Crown and other public bodies, survive for as long as laid down in paragraphs 6 to 9 below.

Building and engineering works records

6. Records of building and engineering works must be considered not only in the light of the Public Records Acts and of their usefulness for reference (e g in cases of maintenance, repair or alteration) but also in the light of the law relating to litigation in cases of negligence in design or construction involving latent defects. The general principles to be followed in regard to these records are, therefore, that they should be preserved for the life of the buildings and installations to which they refer or permanently if they merit it (see para 8(iii) of Annex B).

7. In accordance with these principles, records to be preserved should include as well as town and country planning matters all formal contract documents for

building and engineering works (eg executed agreements, conditions of contract, drawings, bills of quantities and specifications) and other documents required by the conditions of contract to be prepared, together with site plans, surveys, 'as built' record drawings and documents on the appointment and conditions of engagement of private buildings and engineering consultants. In addition, records of decisions leading to the adoption, abandonment or deferment of major works projects should be preserved.

8. Notwithstanding the above, documents for contracts purely for the routine maintenance, repair or servicing of buildings and engineering installations, not involving significant amounts of design work or alterations may be destroyed six years after the end of the financial year in which the work was completed if the contract was executed under hand, or twelve years after if the contract was executed under seal. Engineers' inspection reports on boilers, lifts and the like should be preserved for the life of the installations to which they refer.

Legal actions or complaints about hospital or community health services

9. Any documents (other than personal health records – see para 12) relating to legal actions or to complaint, including accident reports, should be kept for a minimum of ten years after the incident or matter complained of, or, when an action has been commenced, as legally advised.

Product records

10. The Consumer Protection Act 1987 covering the liability of producers for defective products came into force on 1 March 1988. Health authorities are affected by those provisions as producers of products and equipment. They may also be liable in certain circumstances as suppliers and users of products. Full details are contained in health notice HN (88) 3.

11. A health authority's capacity to avoid liability or defend an action brought under the Act for damages resulting from a defect in a product depends upon its keeping comprehensive records relating to the procurement, use, modification and supply of products. An obligation arising from liability lasts for ten years after the product was supplied by the producer and up to one year is allowed for serving a writ. Those records must therefore be kept for 11 years.

Personal health records

12. Personal health records need to be retained for minimum periods to take account of the Limitation Act 1975 and the Congenital Disabilities (Civil Liability) Act 1976. The Limitation Act 1975 amends the law on the time limits within which actions for personal injuries, or arising from death, may be brought. The Congenital Disabilities (Civil Liability) Act 1976, clarifies the right of a child born disabled, as distinct from the right of his mother, to bring a civil action for damages in respect of that disability. The limitation period for bringing such actions remains 3 years, but this now runs from when it is first realised that a person has suffered a significant injury that may be attributable to the negligence of a third party. The lapse between the 'injury' and 'knowledge' of it is without limit of time. For a minor the limitation period runs from the time he attains the age of 18 years and may be extended where material facts are not known.

13. A person of 'unsound mind'* can, as long as he remains under the disability in question, bring an action without limit of time through his 'next friend'. After the

* The definition of 'unsound mind' is not at present prescribed in law but the Department's advice is that a Court would be likely to find that a person suffering from any of the forms of a mental disorder within the meaning of section 2 of the Mental Health Act 1983 (which includes mental handicap and mental illness) would be treated as being under a disability for the purpose of the Limitation Acts.

person's death, the period of limitation will run against his personal representative(s). Authorities will appreciate that, in the context of current practices in the care and treatment of mentally disordered persons, discharge from hospital can no longer be regarded as implying that the person has ceased to suffer from the disability.

14. The limitation period of three years applies only to actions which include a claim for damages in respect of personal injuries. In the case of other claims, e g a claim by a mentally disordered patient that he has been falsely imprisoned, the appropriate limitation period prescribed by Section 2(1) of the Limitation Act 1939 is six years from the date when the patient ceases to be under a disability or dies.

15. Personal health records may now be required as evidence in legal actions for considerably longer than hitherto. The Department's advice is that the minimum periods proposed are likely to be regarded as acceptable by the Courts. It is not necessary however to keep every single piece of paper received in connection with patients. Health Authorities should determine in consultation with their health professionals their policy with regard to the elements which should be regarded as a permanent constituent of the record and those elements of a transitory nature which may be discarded as their value ceases.

16. Special considerations apply to records relating to children, young people and mentally disordered people. In most other cases a person or his representatives might be expected to know whether he has a cause of action within five years of the alleged negligence, from which time the limitation period should be taken to run. It is recommended that the following minimum retention periods should be observed:

(i) Obstetric records: 25 years.
(ii) Records relating to children and young people (including paediatric, vaccination and community child health service records): until the patient's 25th or 26th birthday if an entry was made when the young person was 17.
(iii) Records relating to mentally disordered persons within the meaning of the Mental Health Act 1983: 20 years from the date at which, in the opinion of the doctor concerned, the disorder has ceased or diminished to the point where no further care or treatment is considered necessary.

Except that such records need only be retained for a minimum of 8 years after the death of a patient (or, in the case of obstetric records, death of the child – but not of the mother). Obstetric records of stillbirths need to be kept only for 8 years.

(iv) All other personal health records: 8 years after the conclusion of treatment.

17. After the appropriate minimum period has expired the need to retain them further for local use should be carefully and if necessary periodically, reviewed. Because of the sensitive and confidential nature of such records and the need to ensure that decisions on retention balance the interests of professional staff, including any research in which they are or may be engaged, and the resources available for storage, some health authorities have established committees to oversee the procedures for the retention and destruction of these records. Others may wish to consider if it would be helpful to do so.

18. As records could be required in litigation virtually without limit of time, the Department recognises that some records may be destroyed that might otherwise subsequently have been required for litigation. The Department's view, however, is that the cost of indefinite retention of records would greatly exceed the liabilities likely to be incurred in the occasional case where defence to an action for damages is handicapped by the absence of records. If a hospital doctor involved in litigation claims that prior disposal of relevant medical records has prejudiced the outcome, this should be considered by the health authority along with all other factors when

the apportionment of any liability as between the doctor and health authority is being contemplated.

Destruction of confidential records

19. The methods used for the destruction of confidential records should ensure that their confidentiality is fully maintained. Normally destruction should be by incineration or shredding. Where this service is provided by a contractor it is the responsibility of the health authority to satisfy itself that the methods used throughout all stages including transport to the destruction site provide satisfactory safeguards against accidental loss or disclosure.

ANNEX D

SUMMARY OF DESTRUCTION PERIODS FOR RECORDS WHICH ARE NOT FOR PERMANENT PRESERVATION

Number and Class of Documents	Period after which documents may be destroyed
Part I – Financial	
1. Salaries and wages records, ie employees' pay cards and personal pay records (except those for part-time doctors and dentists employed by RHA's and HA's which should not be destroyed).	Ten years after the end of the financial year to which they relate.
2. Copies of forms SD55 (ADP) and SD55J (Originals are sent to Health Services Superannuation Branch of the Department).	Ten years after the end of the financial year to which they relate.
3. Principal Ledger Records: including such documents as cash books, ledgers, income and expenditure journals, etc.	Six years after the end of the financial year to which they relate.
4. Bills, receipts and cleared cheques.	Six years after the end of the financial year to which they relate.
5. Documents, other than those of permanent relevance in relation to trust funds and the terms of any trusts administered by health authorities.	Six years after the end of the financial year in which the trust moneys became finally spent, or the gift in kind was accepted.
6. Major Establishment Records: including personal files, letters of appointment, contracts references and related correspondence and records of sick leave (except those for part-time doctors and dentists employed by RHA's and HA's which should not be destroyed).	Six years after the officer leaves the service of the hospital or on the date on which the officer would reach the age of 70, whichever is the later, provided that if an adequate summary of the personal and health record is kept for this period the main records may be destroyed six years after the officer leaves the service of the hospital.
7. Pay Sheets and Records of unpaid salaries and wages.	Six years after the end of the financial year to which they relate.
8. Estimates: including supporting calculations and statistics.	Three years after the end of the financial year to which they relate.

Number and Class of Documents	Period after which documents may be destroyed
9. Cost accounts prepared in accordance with the directions of the Secretary of State or at the request of the Department.	Three years after the end of the financial year to which they relate.
Audit reports . . .	Two years after formal clearance by Statutory Auditor.
11. Minor Accounting Records:	
a. Pass-books, bank statements of accounts, paying-in slips, cheque counterfoils and cancelled and discharged cheques other than cheques bearing printed receipts; accounts of petty cash expenditure; travelling and subsistence accounts; minor vouchers, including duplicate receipt books; income records; laundry lists and receipts; forms AP1, 2, 3 and 4 (used in connection with the supply of surgical appliances), etc.	Eighteen months after the end of the financial year to which they relate.
b. Debtors' record . . .	Eighteen months after the end of the financial year in which the accounts are paid or are written off, but at least six years in respect of any unpaid account which has not been written off.
Part II – Stores, Equipment and Buildings	
12. Engineers' inspection reports on boilers, lifts etc.	When the plant to which they relate goes finally out of use.
13. Agreements and simple contracts (and documents subsidiary to these) which are only of temporary or minor importance, i e short-term agreements and minor contracts; papers preliminary or subsidiary to contracts; documents relating to contracts for the supply of goods.	Six years after the end of the financial year in which the agreement or contract expires.*
14. Major Stores Records: stores ledgers and equivalents.	Six years after the end of the financial year to which they relate.*
15. Minor Stores Records: requisitions, issue notes, transfer vouchers, goods received books, etc.	Eighteen months after the end of the financial year to which they relate.*
16. Minor Supplies Records: including invitations to tender and unaccepted tenders, routine papers relating to catering and demands for furniture, equipment, stationery and other supplies.	Eighteen months after the end of the financial year to which they relate.*
17. Records (other than those of permanent value see Appendix B paras 6 and 7) relating to capital and other building works or improvements; including plans and specifications prepared for temporary purposes and papers relating to them.	Eighteen months after the end of the financial year in which they ceased to be effective.

Number and Class of Documents	Period after which documents may be destroyed
18. Inventories not in current use of utensils, instruments, bedding, etc not held on store charge, having a life of less than five years.	Eighteen months after the end of the financial year in which the inventories were in use.
Part III – Personal Health	
1. Obstetric records.	Twenty five years; or 8 years after stillbirth or death of child (but not mother) if sooner.
2. Records relating to children and young people.	Until patient's 25th birthday or 26th if entry made when young person was 17; or 8 years after death of patient if sooner.
3. Records relating to mentally disordered people within meaning of Mental Health Act 1983.	Twenty years after no further treatment considered necessary; or 8 years after patient's death if sooner.
4. All other personal health records.	Eight years after end of treatment.

Destruction of personal health records is subject to consultation with the appropriate health professional.

* But see Annex C, paras 10 and 11.

Appendix

HC (89) 34, HC (FP) (89) 22

To: *Regional Health Authorities*
District Health Authorities
Special Health Authorities

Family Practitioner Committees
Community Health Councils } For information

December 1989

CLAIMS OF MEDICAL NEGLIGENCE AGAINST NHS HOSPITAL AND COMMUNITY DOCTORS AND DENTISTS

This circular will be cancelled and deleted from the current communications index on 1 December 1993 unless notified separately.

Summary

This circular describes the arrangements to apply from 1 January 1990 to the handling of claims of negligence against medical and dental staff employed in the hospital and community health services. General practitioners are not directly affected by these new arrangements, unless they have a contract of employment (for example, as a hospital practitioner) with a health authority.

Action required

Health authorities are asked, with effect from 1 January 1990, to:

(i) assume responsibility for new and existing claims of medical negligence;
(ii) ensure a named officer has sufficient authority to make decisions on the conduct of cases on the authority's behalf;
(iii) cease to require their medical and dental staff to subscribe to a recognised professional defence organisation and cease to reimburse two-thirds of medical defence subscriptions;
(iv) encourage their medical and dental staff to ensure they have adequate defence cover as appropriate;
(v) distribute urgently to all their medical and dental staff, including those with honorary NHS contracts, copies of a leaflet explaining the new arrangements (which will be sent separately).

Handling claims of medical negligence

Claims lodged on or after 1 January 1990

1. Health authorities, as corporate bodies, are legally liable for the negligent acts of their employees in the course of their NHS employment. From 1 January 1990 health authorities will also be formally responsible for the handling and financing of claims of negligence against their medical and dental staff. With regard to claims lodged on or after 1 January 1990, it is for each health authority to determine how it wishes claims against its medical or dental staff to be handled. Health authorities may wish to make use of the services of the medical defence organisations (at rates to be agreed), but they may also put the work out to other advisers or deal with it in-house, provided they have the necessary expertise.

Claims notified to an MDO before 1 January 1990

2. Subject to final agreement with the medical defence organisations (MDOs) on the detailed financial arrangements, health authorities will take over financial

responsibility for cases outstanding at 1 January 1990. The medical defence organisations have been asked to inform health authorities of the cases in which they may have a substantial liability.

3. Health authorities are entitled to take over the management of any cases outstanding, since they will become liable for the costs and damages arising. However, they are strongly advised to employ the MDOs to continue to handle such claims, in consultation with them and on their behalf, until completion. This is essential not only because of the amount of work in progress, but mainly because the re-insurance cover of the MDOs for claims initiated before 1990 would remain valid only if the MDO currently handling the case continued to do so. If required, health authorities should co-operate with an MDO's re-insurers in the conduct of a claim. Since some of the cover is on an aggregate basis the advice in this paragraph applies to both large and small claims. Health authorities are asked to give prior notice to the Department (finance contact point at paragraph 17) where they wish to adopt a different approach in the handling of claims notified before 1 January 1990.

General handling principles

4. Health authorities should take the essential decisions on the handling of claims of medical negligence against their staff, using MDOs or other bodies as their agents and advisers. Authorities should particularly ensure that authority is appropriately delegated to enable decisions to be made promptly, especially where representatives are negotiating a settlement, and are asked to give such authority to a named officer.

5. In deciding how a case should be handled, and in particular whether to resist a claim or seek an out-of-court settlement, health authorities and those advising them should pay particular attention to any view expressed by the practitioner(s) concerned and to any potentially damaging effect on the professional reputation of the practitioner(s) concerned. They should also have clear regard to:

(i) any point of principle or of wider application raised by the case; and
(ii) the costs involved.

6. Where a case involves both a health authority and a general medical practitioner (or any other medical or dental practitioner in relation to work for which a health authority is not responsible), the health authority should consult with the practitioner(s) cited or their representative to seek agreement on how the claim should be handled. Where a health authority (or its employees) alone is cited, but there is reason to believe that the action or inaction of a practitioner outside the health authority's responsibility was a material factor in the negligence concerned, the health authority should similarly consult with a view to obtaining a contribution to the eventual costs and damages. Conversely, in cases where such a practitioner alone is cited, there may be circumstances in which an MDO asks the health authority to make a similar contribution, as if it were a defendant. In any such circumstances, health authorities should co-operate fully in the formulation of the defence and should seek to reach agreement out of court on the proportion in which any costs and damages awarded to the plaintiff should be borne.

7. It is open to the practitioner concerned to employ at his or her expense an expert adviser, but the practitioner can be represented separately in court only with the agreement of the Court. The plaintiff and the health authority may agree to separate representation for the practitioner, but under normal circumstances the health authority should not do so if it considers that this would lead to additional costs or damages falling on the health authority.

Coverage of the scheme and practical arrangements

8. The Health Departments' views on some of the questions that have arisen about the coverage and practical operation of the new arrangements are at Annex A. The indemnity scheme applies to all staff in the course of their HCHS employment, including those engaged through private agencies. The Annex is to be reproduced as a leaflet, which the Health Departments will shortly be making available to health authorities who should distribute them to all their medical and dental staff, including those with honorary NHS contracts.

9. Since authorities will be taking financial responsibility in cases of medical negligence it will no longer be necessary for them to require employed staff to subscribe to a recognised professional defence organisation, for example, as in the recommended form of consultant contract at Annex D of PM (79) 11. Authorities should inform their medical and dental staff that the provision no longer applies, but they should encourage such staff to ensure that they have adequate defence cover as appropriate.

Financial arrangements

Pooling arrangements for major settlements

10. Where they have not already done so RHAs are strongly recommended to introduce arrangements (for both medical and non-medical negligence) so as to share with Districts the legal costs and damages of individual large settlements or awards, whose incidence can be quite random. The Department will be making arrangements for Authorities without an RHA, for example the London SHAs, to limit the financial effects on them of substantial settlements.

Funding of claims

11. Subject to final agreement with the MDOs, the public sector will have access to a share of the MDOs' reserves in respect of the hospital and community health services. It is expected that the MDOs will each establish a fund to be drawn on according to criteria set by the Health Departments. The Health Departments will be introducing a transitional scheme under which these reserves will be made available to assist health authorities to meet the costs of particularly large settlements. These will usually, but not necessarily, be cases which arose from incidents before 1 January 1990. The Departments propose to set a threshold, initially £300,000 in England and Wales; 80 per cent of the costs of a settlement above this threshold, including the legal costs, would be met from this source, until the identified funds are exhausted. Detailed information on the means of access to the funds will be given in the December 1989 edition of 'Financial Matters'.

NHS Trusts

12. NHS Trusts will be responsible for claims of negligence against their medical and dental staff. The Departments are considering what arrangements will apply to NHS Trusts and further guidance will be issued in due course.

Monitoring resource consequences

13. To enable the Departments of Health to assess the resource consequences of these changes, health authorities will be required to submit a return (in the form set out at Annex B) shortly after the end of each financial year, starting with the period 1 January–31 March 1990 in order to obtain an early indication of the costs of the scheme.

Review

14. The Health Departments plan to review the operation of these arrangements in 1992, including the effects on individual practitioners.

Cancellation of existing guidance

15. Circulars HM (54) 32 and HM (54) 43 will be cancelled from 1 January 1990. Paragraph 4(iii) of Annex 1 of EL (89) P/148 (Hospital medical and dental staff: Locum tenens engaged through private agencies) will be cancelled from 1 January 1990.

16. Paragraph 310 of the Terms and Conditions of Service for Hospital Medical and Dental Staff, and paragraph 289 of the Terms and Conditions of Service for Doctors in Community Medicine and the Community Health Service, (the two-thirds reimbursement scheme) shall not have effect after 31 December 1989.

17. Enquiries which cannot be dealt with by RHAs should be addressed as follows:

General
Mr A Doole
FPS1A2
Room 426 Portland Court
158–176 Great Portland Street
London W1N 5TB

Tel: 01–872–9302
Ext 48306

Finance
Mr M Horah
FA2
Room 629 Friars House
157–168 Blackfriars Road
London SE1 8EU

Tel: 01–972–2000
Ext 23024

ANNEX A

MEDICAL NEGLIGENCE: NEW NHS ARRANGEMENTS

Introduction

1. New arrangements for dealing with medical negligence claims in the hospital and community health services are being introduced from 1 January 1990. Subject to final agreement with the medical defence organisations on the financial arrangements, health authorities will take direct financial responsibility for cases initiated before that date, as well as for new claims. In future, medical and dental staff employed by health authorities (health boards in Scotland and Northern Ireland) will no longer be required under the terms of their contracts to subscribe to a medical defence organisation. However, the health authority indemnity will cover only health authority responsibilities. The Health Departments advise practitioners to maintain their defence body membership in order to ensure they are covered for any work which does not fall within the scope of the indemnity scheme.

Set out below are the Health Departments' replies to some of the questions most commonly asked about the operation of the new arrangements.

2. *Why is this change necessary?*

Medical defence subscriptions rose rapidly in the 1980s, because of growth both in the number of medical negligence cases and in the size of the awards made by the courts. Subscriptions tripled between 1986 and 1988, and the Doctors' and Dentists' Review Body concluded that to take account of the increase in subscriptions through practitioners' pay would lead to distortions in pay and pensions. The pressure to relate subscription rates to the practitioner's speciality underlined the difficulty of maintaining the system. The Health Departments issued in March 1989 a proposal for a health authority indemnity. The new arrangements follow discussions with the medical defence organisations, the medical profession, health authority management and other interested bodies.

Coverage

3. *Who is covered by the health authority indemnity scheme?*

Health authorities as employers are liable at law for the negligence (acts or omissions) of their staff in the course of their NHS employment. The legal position is the same for medical and dental staff as for other NHS employees, but for many years doctors and dentists have themselves taken out medical defence cover through the three medical defence organisations (MDOs). Under the indemnity scheme, health authorities will take direct responsibility for costs and damages arising from medical negligence where they (as employers) are vicariously liable for the acts and omissions of their medical and dental staff.

4. *Does this include clinical academics and research workers?*

Health authorities are vicariously liable for the work done by university medical staff and other research workers under their honorary contracts in the course of their NHS duties, but not for pre-clinical or other work in the university.

5. *Is private work in NHS hospitals covered by the indemnity scheme?*

Health authorities will not be responsible for a consultant's private practice, even in an NHS hospital. However, where junior medical staff are involved in the care of private patients in NHS hospitals, they would normally be doing so as part of their contract with the health authority. It remains advisable that any junior doctor who might be involved in any work outside the scope of his or her employment should have medical defence (or insurance) cover.

6. *Is Category 2 work covered?*

Category 2 work (e g reports for insurance companies) is by definition not undertaken for the employing health authority, and will therefore not be covered by the indemnity scheme; medical defence cover would be appropriate.

7. *Are GMC disciplinary proceedings covered?*

Health authorities should not be financially responsible for the defence of medical staff involved in GMC disciplinary proceedings. It is the responsibility of the practitioner concerned to take out medical defence cover against such an eventuality.

8. *Is a hospital doctor doing a GP locum covered?*

This would not be the responsibility of the health authority, since it would be general practice. The hospital doctor and the general practitioners concerned should ensure that there is appropriate medical defence cover.

9. *Is a GP seeing his own patient in hospital covered?*

A GP providing medical care to patients in hospital under a contractual arrangement, e g where the GP was employed as a clinical assistant, will be covered by the health authority indemnity. On the other hand, if the health authority is essentially providing only hotel services and the patient(s) remain in the care of the GP, the GP would be responsible and medical defence cover would be appropriate.

10. *Are GP trainees working in general practice covered?*

In general practice the responsibility for training and for paying the salary of a GP trainee rests with the trainer (with funds from the FPC). Where the trainee's medical defence subscription is higher than the subscription of an SHO in the hospital service, he or she may apply through the trainer for the difference in subscription to be reimbursed. While the trainee is receiving a salary in general practice it is advisable that both the trainee and the trainer, and indeed other members of the practice, should have medical defence cover.

11. *Are clinical trials covered?*

The new arrangements do not alter the current legal position. If the health authority was responsible for a clinical trial authorised under the Medicines Act 1968 or its subordinate legislation and that trial was carried out by or on behalf of a doctor involving NHS patients of his, such a doctor would be covered by the indemnity scheme. Similarly, for a trial not involving medicines, the health authority would take financial responsibility unless the trial were covered by such other indemnity as may have been agreed between the health authority and those responsible for the trial. In any case, health authorities should take steps to make sure that they are informed of clinical trials in which their staff are taking part in their NHS employment and that these trials have the required Research Ethics Committee approval.

12. *Would a doctor be covered if he was working other than in accordance with the duties of his post?*

Such a doctor would be covered by the health authority indemnity for actions in the course of NHS employment, and this should be interpreted liberally. For work not covered in this way the doctor may have a civil, or even in extreme circumstances criminal, liability for his actions.

13. *Are doctors attending accident victims ('Good Samaritan' acts) covered?*

By definition, 'Good Samaritan' acts are not part of the doctor's work for the employing authority. Medical defence organisations are willing to provide low-cost cover against the (unusual) event of a doctor performing such an act being sued for negligence.

14. *Are doctors in public health medicine or in community health services doing work for local authorities covered? Are occupational physicians covered?*

Doctors in public health medicine, or clinical medical officers, carrying out local authority functions under their health authority contract would be acting in the course of their NHS employment. They will therefore be covered by the health authority indemnity. The same principle applies to occupational physicians employed by health authorities.

15. *Will NHS hospital doctors working for other agencies, e g the Prison Service, be covered?*

In general, health authorities will not be financially responsible for the acts of NHS staff when they are working on a contractual basis for other agencies. (Conversely, they will be responsible where, for example, a Ministry of Defence doctor works in an NHS hospital.) Either the agency commissioning the work would be responsible, or the doctor should have medical defence cover. However, health authorities' indemnity should cover work for which they pay a fee, such as domiciliary visits and family planning services.

16. *Are retired doctors covered?*

The health authority indemnity will apply to acts or omissions in the course of NHS employment, regardless of when the claim was notified. Health authorities will thus cover doctors who have subsequently left the Service, but they may seek their co-operation in statements in the defence of a case.

17. *Are doctors offering services to voluntary bodies such as the Red Cross or hospices covered?*

The health authority would be responsible for the doctor's actions only if the health authority were responsible for the medical staffing of the voluntary body. If not, the doctors concerned may wish to ensure that they have medical defence cover, as they do at present.

18. *Will a health authority provide cover for a locum hospital doctor?*

A health authority will take financial responsibility for the acts and omissions of a locum doctor, whether 'internal' or provided by an external agency.

19. *Are private sector rotations for hospital staff covered?*

The medical staff of independent hospitals are responsible for their own medical defence cover, subject to the requirements of the hospital managers. If NHS staff in the training grades work in independent hospitals as part of their NHS training, they would be covered by the health authority indemnity, provided that such work was covered by an NHS contract.

20. *Will academic General Practice be covered?*

The Health Departments have no plans to extend the health authority indemnity to academic departments of general practice. In respect of general medical services FPCs will be making payments by fees and allowances which include an element for expenses, of which medical defence subscriptions are a part.

Practical arrangements

21. *On what basis will medical defence organisations handle claims for health authorities?*

MDOs, in advising on claims for health authorities, will act as their agents; the charging arrangements for such services are for agreement between the MDO and the authority concerned.

22. *Will doctors be reimbursed by MDOs for the 'unexpired' portion of their subscriptions?*

This is a matter between each MDO and its members.

23. *Will membership of a medical defence organisation continue to be a contractual obligation?*

On an individual basis doctors and dentists may wish to continue their membership in order to receive the cover referred to in paragraphs 5–20 above, as well as the other legal and advisory services provided by the MDOs. The Health Departments are advising health authorities that they should no longer require their medical and dental staff to subscribe to an MDO, but a health authority could require a doctor to be a member of an MDO if the doctor were to be carrying out private work on NHS premises. The two-thirds reimbursement of subscriptions will cease at the end of 1989.

24. *Will medical defence subscriptions be tax-allowable in future?*

The Health Departments understand that medical defence subscriptions will continue to be allowable under income tax rules.

25. *What happens if a doctor wishes to contest a claim which the health authority would prefer to settle out of court, eg where a point of principle or a doctor's reputation is at stake?*

While the final decision in a case rests with the health authority since it will bear the financial consequences, it should take careful note of the practitioner's view. Health authorities may seek the advice of the relevant MDO on whether a case should be contested, and they should not settle cases without good cause.

26. *If a doctor wishes to have separate representation in a case, what would be the extent of his liability?*

Since it is the health authority which is sued for the medical negligence of its staff and which will in future be solely financially liable, then it must have the ultimate right to decide how the defence of a case is to be handled. Subject to this, a health authority may welcome a practitioner being separately advised in a case without cost to the health authority. However, if a practitioner claims that his interests in any case are distinct from those of the health authority and wishes to be separately represented in the proceedings, he will need the agreement of the plaintiff, the health authority and the court. If liability is established, he would have to pay not only his own legal expenses but also any further costs incurred as a result of his being separately represented. The health authority would remain liable for the full award of damages to the plaintiff.

27. *Will health authorities put restrictions on the clinical autonomy of doctors?*

Health authorities have a responsibility to organise services in a manner which is in the best interests of patients. In the past, medical defence organisations have advised doctors and dentists on patterns of practice carrying unacceptable dangers to patients. However, there is no question of health authorities barring certain services which carry risks but are a high priority for patients.

28. *Will health authorities be able to secure statements from doctors for the defence of a case of medical negligence?*

Health authorities will need co-operation from medical and dental staff if they are to defend cases. As part of this, practitioners should supply such statements or documents as the health authority or its solicitors may reasonably require in investigating or defending any claim. A doctor's refusal without good reason to provide a statement could result in the health authority being unable to defend itself properly and so incurring additional costs.

29. *Will health authorities be able to trace doctors who formerly worked for them?*

It is accepted that health authorities may have difficulty in tracing the doctors responsible, especially if they were junior medical staff at the time, and in securing statements from them; they may find the MDOs helpful in this respect. Often, however, good medical records kept at the time will be of more value than statements made some years after the event.

30. *Will the new arrangements apply to NHS Trust hospitals (self-governing units)?*

As employers, NHS Trusts will be vicariously liable for the acts of their employed medical and dental staff, and will take the financial responsibility for negligence. Further guidance will be issued in due course.

Financial effects

31. *How can District Health Authorities meet damages which could be as much as £1m for a single case?*

RHAs have been asked to make arrangements under which they will provide an element of cost-sharing with Districts for medical negligence costs above a certain level, as most RHAs do for non-medical negligence actions at present. And for a transitional period health authorities will have access (under certain criteria) to some of the reserves of the MDOs.

32. *The incidence of medical negligence damages may be uneven as between Regions; how will that be met?*

It is quite likely that some Regions will have to pay out more under the new arrangements than they would in reimbursing two-thirds of medical defence subscriptions. The funds from the MDOs will be of some help in the short term, but in the longer run the incidence of medical negligence costs and damages will fall on the Regions where they arise.

UK Health Departments
December 1989

ANNEX B

INFORMATION TO BE RETURNED ANNUALLY, NO LATER THAN 31 MAY (STARTING 31/5/90)

1. The following information should be supplied for the previous financial year:
   i. The number of claims of medical negligence against the health authority and/or its employees, including the number of cases brought forward from an earlier period;
   ii. The number of such cases settled during the period with the health authority's costs, including damages payable, in the following cost bands:

	Number of cases	£	£
(a)			0–100,000
(b)			100,000–200,000
(c)			200,000–300,000
(d)			over £300,000

   iii. The total cost of the settlements reached or awards made; distinguishing
      (a) the Authority's costs from the payment of the plaintiff's costs and damages; and
      (b) an estimate of costs and damages attributable to medical negligence, as distinct from negligence of other staff.
2. Returns to be sent to: FPS1A2
   Room 426 Portland Court
   158–176 Great Portland Street
   London W1N 5TB

HC (90) 9

To: *Regional Health Authorities*
District Health Authorities
Special Health Authorities } for action

Regional and District Directors of Public Health } for information

March 1990

DISCIPLINARY PROCEDURES FOR HOSPITAL AND COMMUNITY MEDICAL AND DENTAL STAFF

This circular will be reviewed on 1 March 1994 unless notified separately.

Summary

This circular consolidates previous guidance following the recommendations (Annex A) of the Joint Working Party on Disciplinary Procedures. It replaces HM (61) 112 and sets out changes to Paragraph 190 of the Terms and Conditions of Service for Hospital Medical and Dental Staff and Doctors in Community Medicine and the Community Health Service (England and Wales). It also introduces two new procedures:

(i) Professional Review Machinery; whereby a professional panel reviews the conduct of hospital consultants who are alleged to have failed repeatedly to honour their contractual commitments;

(ii) Intermediate Procedure: A new procedure for dealing with cases of professional misconduct and professional incompetence which warrant disciplinary action short of dismissal.

Action

With effect from 19 March 1990 Authorities are asked to introduce the changes detailed in the annexes as follows:

HM (61) 112: Annex B of this circular supersedes HM (61) 112. Particular changes have been sidelined in the annex.

PARAGRAPH 190: Annex C details changes to Paragraph 190 of the Terms and Conditions of Service for Hospital Medical and Dental Staff and Doctors in Community Medicine and The Community Health Service (England and Wales). These changes have been approved by the Secretary of State for Health under Regulation 3 of the National Health Service (Remuneration and Conditions of Service) Regulations 1974. The new procedure will apply to appeals lodged with the Secretary of State after 19 March 1990. Replacement pages for the respective handbooks will be issued in due course. Particular changes have been sidelined in the annex.

PROFESSIONAL REVIEW MACHINERY: Annex D introduces informal 'pre-disciplinary' machinery for reviewing the conduct of hospital consultants who are alleged to have failed repeatedly to honour their contractual commitments. The procedure is in addition to, and does not replace, either Health Authorities' existing powers to take disciplinary action or the arrangements for dealing with sick doctors outlined in HC (82) 13. This procedure shall apply from the date of this circular and may include the investigation of acts or omissions which have occurred before this date.

INTERMEDIATE PROCEDURE: Annex E introduces a new procedure for dealing with cases of professional misconduct and professional incompetence which warrant disciplinary action short of dismissal. This procedure shall apply from the date of this circular and may include the investigation of acts or omissions which have occurred before this date.

Application

1. The grades to which each procedure will apply are included in the appropriate annex. Discussions are continuing on the application of these procedures to other grades.

2. In this circular, where the circumstances are applicable to Wales, for Regional Director of Public Health, read Chief Medical Officer (or DCMO) and for District Director of Public Health, read Chief Administrative Medical Officer (CAMO).

Definitions

3. The procedure(s) to be followed following allegations of misconduct will depend on the nature of the allegation. It is recognised that authorities sometimes have great difficulty defining the nature of the conduct which is the subject of an allegation, and the following definitions have been agreed between the Departments and the professions:

PERSONAL CONDUCT – Performance or behaviour of practitioners due to factors other than those associated with the exercise of medical or dental skills.

PROFESSIONAL CONDUCT – Performance or behaviour of practitioners arising from the exercise of medical or dental skills.

PROFESSIONAL COMPETENCE – Adequacy of performance of practitioners related to the exercise of their medical or dental skills and professional judgment.

General

4. In respect of the Working Party's other recommendations, authorities should note that, in cases involving personal conduct, the position of doctors and dentists is no different from that of other NHS staff. As envisaged by recommendation 2 of the WP report, health authorities should review their disciplinary procedures in respect of personal misconduct to ensure that they include doctors and dentists adequately and may need to revise them following local consultation. Authorities should in particular take account of the provisions of Section 40 of the General Whitley Terms and Conditions of Service and, where appropriate, of the composition of the appeal panel proposed at paragraph 8 of Annex E for cases involving medical and dental staff.

5. The attached Annexes B–E will, in due course, be reproduced in the form of a booklet which will be issued to Authorities for use by staff involved in the administration of these procedures.

6. Recommendation 14 provided for a review of these procedures within a period of three years and in the light of this authorities are also asked to maintain records of the number of cases brought under the new procedures, together with details of the nature of the allegation, the procedure followed in each case, the stage reached in the procedure, and the outcome. These records are for monitoring purposes only, and anonymised returns only will be required. Authorities will be asked, in due course, by the Departments for this information, and in addition, for views on the effectiveness of the procedures.

Circular cancelled

7. Circular HM (61) 112 is cancelled from the date of this circular except where Authorities have started proceedings on the basis of HM (61) 112 before this date.

8. Enquiries which cannot be dealt with by RHAs should be addressed as follows:

Mr M Evans
FPS1A2
Room 430 Portland Court
158–176 Great Portland Street
London W1N 5TB

From:

Family Practitioner Services Division 1A
Portland Court
158–176 Great Portland Street
London W1N 5TB

ANNEX A

SUMMARY OF WORKING PARTY RECOMMENDATIONS

Recommendation 1: The introduction of Professional Review Machinery in all health authorities.

Recommendation 2: Health authorities should review their disciplinary procedures in respect of personal misconduct to ensure that they include doctors and dentists adequately.

Recommendation 3: The intermediate procedure should be introduced subject to detailed negotiation between the parties.

Recommendation 4: There should be improved guidance designed to make the HM (61) 112 procedure less cumbersome and ensure that it is applied more uniformly.

Recommendation 5:* Legal representation at HM (61) 112 hearings should be amended, so that both the practitioner and the health authority concerned employ solicitors rather than barristers.

Recommendation 6: Indicative time limits for HM (61) 112 enquiries should be introduced.

Recommendation 7: There should be a central standing panel of lawyers acceptable to both sides and readily available – perhaps including those recently retired – to chair investigating panels in HM (61) 112 cases.

Recommendation 8: Paragraph 190 rights should not apply to dismissal on grounds of personal misconduct.

Recommendation 9: Professional committees (in Paragraph 190 cases) should in future be assisted by a legal assessor or adviser.

Recommendation 10: The professional committee in Paragraph 190 cases to test the acceptability of a third solution with both parties to try to ensure that a decision is not delayed by the Secretary of State suggesting a third solution when it is unlikely to be feasible.

Recommendation 11: It is inappropriate for certain practitioners with a limited work commitment with health authorities and with a significant alternative source of medical or dental income, to retain rights under Paragraph 190.

* Following further consideration it has been agreed that this recommendation would not be implemented at this time. Authorities and practitioners are asked, however, to make efforts generally to reduce the formality of the proceedings and the time they take as a consequence.

Recommendation 12: Time limits should be introduced for the Paragraph 190 procedure.

Recommendation 13:* The possibility of arrangements for voluntary early retirement in the interests of the service should be considered in the appropriate negotiating forum.

Recommendation 14: Arrangements for monitoring the new procedures, including the regular collection of data, should be introduced and that the effectiveness of the procedures should be reviewed after a period of three years from the date of implementation.

ANNEX B

DISCIPLINARY PROCEEDINGS IN CASES RELATING TO HOSPITAL AND COMMUNITY MEDICAL AND DENTAL STAFF AND DOCTORS IN PUBLIC HEALTH MEDICINE AND THE COMMUNITY HEALTH SERVICE

Summary

Guidance is given on the procedure to be followed in serious disciplinary cases involving hospital, public health and community health doctors or dentists.

General

1. This Annex replaces HM (61) 112 and outlines the procedures which Health Authorities should use when handling serious disciplinary charges, for example, where the outcome of disciplinary action could be the dismissal of the medical or dental practitioner concerned. For such cases Authorities should also apply the guidance contained in section 40 of the General Whitley Council Terms and Conditions. The lines of procedure proposed are designed to ensure that justice is done and seen to be done and injustice avoided in respect of all the parties concerned (patient, practitioner and employer).

2. The arrangements described below are without prejudice to the right of the Authority to take immediate action (e g suspension from duty) where this is required in cases of a very serious nature.

3. There are broadly three types of case which may involve medical or dental staff:

(a) cases involving personal conduct;
(b) cases involving professional conduct;
(c) cases involving professional competence.

It is for the Authority to decide under which category a case falls. Guidance on the definition of each category is given in paragraph 3 of the Circular.

Cases involving personal conduct

4. In cases involving personal conduct, the position of a doctor or dentist is no different from that of other health service staff. Accordingly, provisions from time to time applicable to health service staff generally (at present those set out in section 40 of the General Whitley Council Terms and Conditions) also apply in such cases.

* Discussions on this recommendation are to take place soon between the Departments and the Profession. Details will be issued when these discussions are concluded.

Cases involving professional conduct and professional competence

i. *Preliminary investigation – establishment of prima facie case*

5. The first step when an incident occurs or a complaint is made involving the professional conduct or competence of a medical or dental officer should be for the Chairman of the Health Authority to decide whether there is a prima facie case which, if well founded, could result in serious disciplinary action such as dismissal. Such preliminary inquiries if any as are necessary before this decision is reached should be in the hands of the Regional or District Director of Public Health (DPH) on behalf of the Regional or District Health Authority, whichever is the appointing authority. In appropriate cases, the legal adviser or solicitor to the Authority should be called in to assist. Where the matter arises from an incident for which an accident report has been made in accordance with HM (55) 66, the Chairman, before reaching his decision, should have regard to the accident report, but normally no subsequent use should be made of the report in the proceedings, except insofar as it is used by the appointing authority's solicitors in preparing the case to be presented to the investigating panel (see paragraph 8 below).

6. Unless the Chairman decides forthwith that there is no prima facie case, the doctor or dentist should be warned in writing immediately of the nature of the incident which has been alleged, or of the complaint which has been made and that the question of an inquiry, which might lead to serious disciplinary action, is under consideration. Copies of all relevant correspondence should be sent to the practitioner, and he should be informed that any comments made by him will be placed before the Chairman and any investigating panel which may be appointed. The practitioner should be given reasonable time to make representations and to seek advice if he so wishes before any final decision is taken on whether an inquiry is necessary.

7. If, on considering the allegation or complaint made and the practitioner's comments, if any, in reply to the written warning given in accordance with paragraph 6, the Chairman decides that a prima facie case exists, and that there is a dispute as to the facts, the Authority should proceed to an inquiry, as in paragraphs 8–15. If the Chairman decides that a prima facie case exists, but there is no substantial dispute as to the facts, any subsequent disciplinary action which the Authority may take should comply with the guidance contained in GWC section 40. An inquiry on the lines laid down in paragraphs 8–15 below would normally be unnecessary also where, in a matter affecting the practitioner's professional conduct or competence, the facts in question have been the subject of a criminal charge on which he has been found guilty in a court of law or have been established by a public inquiry set up by the Government. Where the facts have been established by a public inquiry and there is a dispute as to whether further facts need to be established or as to the conclusion to be drawn from the facts, an investigating panel set up in accordance with paragraphs 8 and 9 below will consider if a further inquiry is required (in which case they will proceed in accordance with paragraphs 10–15 below). Where the panel consider that no further inquiry is required they will proceed in accordance with paragraphs 14–18 below.

ii. *Inquiry*

8. An investigating panel, the composition of which should differ with the type of inquiry, should be set up by the Authority responsible for apppointing the practitioner. No member of the panel should be associated with the hospital(s) in which he works, or, in the case of a doctor in Public Health Medicine or the Community Health Service, in the Authority in which the practitioner concerned works. In all cases the panel should be small, normally of three persons, including a legally qualified Chairman, not being either an officer of the Department of Health or a

member or officer of the Authority concerned, who will be nominated in each case which arises by the Secretary of State from a panel appointed by the Lord Chancellor. In cases involving professional conduct, the members other than the Chairman should contain an equal proportion of professional and lay persons, unless the charges relate only to relationships between a doctor or a dentist and his professional colleagues, when it would clearly be appropriate to have a panel wholly or predominantly of professional members, apart from the Chairman. In cases involving solely professional competence, all the other members should be professionally qualified, and it will probably be appropriate that at least one of their number should be in the same speciality as the practitioner whose professional competence has been called in question; it may also be appropriate that one of them should be a practitioner from another hospital in the same grade. Before the professional members are chosen, there should be consultation with the Joint Consultants Committee (JCC) or Community Medicine Consultative Committee (CMCC) as appropriate. In the case of a dental officer, the appointment of the professional member should be made after consultation with the appropriate group of the British Dental Association.

9. Payment should be made by the Authority to the Chairman and members of the panel at a rate determined from time to time. This fee covers any preparatory work required and any time spent on preparation of reports. Travelling and subsistence expenses of both the Chairman and members of the panel should be payable in accordance with the National Health Service and English and Welsh National Boards for Nursing, Midwifery and Health Visiting (Travelling) Allowances etc. Determination 1983.

10. The terms of reference of the panel should include the nature of the incident or complaint against the practitioner, who should be informed of the setting up of the panel and its terms of reference and given not less than 21 days' notice in order to prepare his case. He should be provided as soon as possible with any copies of correspondence or written statements made. A copy of the list of witnesses referred to in paragraph 11, and the main points on which they can give evidence, should be furnished to the practitioner as long as possible before the hearing if he so requests, unless for any exceptional reason the Chairman of the panel gives authority for the names of the witnesses not to be provided in advance of the hearing.

11. The investigating panel should be held in private, and should establish all the relevant facts of the case. To that end, the panel should ensure, as far as possible, that colleagues of the practitioner should be asked to give factual evidence, rather than personal impressions or opinions. A list of witnesses should be drawn up with the main points on which they are to give evidence; in the case of a Regional Health Authority, this task might with advantage be undertaken by the legal adviser or solicitor to the Authority, assisted by the Regional Director of Public Health. Subsequently at the hearing, the case should be presented by the legal adviser or solicitor, who should conduct an examination of the witnesses before the investigating panel. In the case of other Authorities, these tasks would no doubt be undertaken by the Authority's solicitor acting on the instructions of the Authority. The Authority and/or the practitioner may be represented before the panel by a lawyer, although both sides should make efforts to reduce the formality of the proceedings and the consequent time they take.

12. The practitioner should have the right to appear personally before the investigating panel and to be represented (either by a lawyer in accordance with paragraph 11 above, or otherwise), and to hear all the evidence presented to the panel. He should have the right to cross-examine all witnesses and to produce his own witnesses, and they and he may also be subjected to cross-examination. The question of what is to happen upon any application for adjournment in the event of the illness

or unavoidable absence of the practitioner, or any witness, should be a matter for the Chairman to decide in accordance with the normal procedures for similar inquiries.

13. The procedure and rules as regards the admission of evidence before the investigating panel should be determined by the Chairman who may,if he wishes, hold a preliminary hearing with the parties (or their representatives) for the purpose.

14. The report of the investigating panel should be presented in 2 parts. The first part should set out the committee's findings and all the relevant facts of the case, but contain no recommendations as to action. The second part should contain a view as to whether the practitioner is at fault, and may, at the request of the Authority appointing the panel, contain recommendations as to disciplinary action. In no circumstances should the investigating panel itself be given disciplinary powers.

15. The panel should send the practitioner a copy of the first part of their report, and should allow a period of 4 weeks for the submission to them of any proposals for corrections of fact, or for setting out in greater detail the facts on any particular matter which has arisen. It would be for the panel to decide whether to accept any proposed amendments and whether any further hearing was necessary to enable them thus to decide. Subject to this procedure, the facts as set out in the panel's report should be accepted as established in any subsequent consideration of the matter.

16. The Authority should then receive the full report of the investigating panel and decide what action to take. In the event of the investigating panel finding that the practitioner is at fault, the substance of their views on the case and recommendations in the second part of their report should be made available to him in good time before the meeting of the Authority, and he should be given the opportunity to put to them any plea which he may wish to make in mitigation before they reach any conclusion as to action.

17. The Departments and the professions are concerned at the length of time some hearings take before conclusion. In all cases, it has been agreed with the professions that the following time limits will apply to each stage, and in all cases, the time taken from the decision that there is a prima facie case to referral to the Health Authority should not exceed 32 weeks:

(a) Chairman decides that there is a prima facie case and informs the practitioner.	
(b) Practitioner comments on the case	– within 4 weeks.
(c) After receipt of comments, Health Authority decide to follow this procedure	– within 2 weeks.
(d) Health Authority appoints Chairman and rest of inquiry panels and panel meets	– within 3 months.
(e) Hearing is concluded	– within 1 week.
(f) Report is produced and factual part sent to practitioner	– within 4 weeks.
(g) Practitioner makes comments	– within 4 weeks.
(h) Report goes to Health Authority	– within 4 weeks.

18. These provisions are without prejudice to the provisions of Paragraph 190 of the Terms and Conditions of Service of Hospital Medical and Dental Staff and Doctors in Community Medicine and the Community Health Service (England and Wales).

ANNEX E

INTERMEDIATE PROCEDURE

Introduction

This new procedure involves the use of independent professional assessors, nominated by the JCC, who would be invited by the Director of Public Health (DPH*) (on behalf of the employing authority) to investigate and advise him on matters involving professional conduct or competence. The assessors themselves would have no disciplinary powers. The procedure could be used both in cases where there is a specific disciplinary allegation against a consultant or consultants and where there are problems arising from differing professional views within a department.

The following procedure will require commitment from the profession in that the JCC would have to find suitable assessors speedily and there would have to be sufficient volunteers to act as assessors; there will also need to be commitment from health authorities in releasing assessors, including perhaps by allowing locum cover. Travelling and subsistence expenses of the assessors are payable in accordance with the NHS and English and Welsh National Boards for Nursing, Midwifery and Health Visiting (Travelling) Allowances etc. Determination 1983.

Procedure

1. On receiving an allegation from any source the DPH* will need to make some preliminary enquiries in order to determine whether:

(a) there was no substance in the allegations and therefore no further action was necessary.
(b) the case was a minor one which the DPH* thought suitable to deal with on an informal basis.
(c) it was a case appropriate to Professional Review Machinery.
(d) the procedure set out in HC (82) 13 might be appropriate, or the DPH* wished to advise that it was a suitable case to refer to the sick doctors' scheme.
(e) it was personal misconduct, in which case the disciplinary code drawn up in accordance with section 40 of the GWC Handbook would be followed.
(f) it involved serious allegations about professional conduct or competence and, if so, whether or not it was serious enough to warrant procedures under Annex B of this circular.
(g) it involved less serious allegations about professional conduct or competence, and was suitable for the intermediate procedure.

During these preliminary enquiries, the DPH* will normally wish to have a discussion with the doctor involved.

2. If the DPH* decides that the case(s) falls into category 1(g), he will normally write to the JCC with details of the practitioner's speciality and the District(s) and the hospital(s) where he/she works, together with a very brief indication of the problem (eg whether there are doubts about a consultant's clinical practice or a clash of professional views). At the same time, the DPH* will inform the doctor(s) involved and others he thinks appropriate that he has taken this action.

3. The JCC will nominate impartial assessors from another Region† (normally two, with at least one from the same speciality as the consultant concerned), and agree their appointment with the DPH*. The JCC will aim to provide the names of assessors within one month.

* Reference to the DPH where asterisked includes a reference to CAMO in Wales and the equivalent medical officer in other employing authorities.

† This will not, of course, apply to Wales and Scotland, but the JCC Secretariat and the CMO/CAMO will aim to find assessors who are not from the immediate locality.

4. When the DPH* receives notification of the assessors and agrees their appointment, he will provide them with a detailed statement of the case within one month, copying it at the same time to the doctor(s) involved. The assessors will examine the statement and first consider whether or not it is appropriate to this procedure.

5. i. The assessors may wish to meet the DPH* at this stage for a preliminary discussion of if they need further background information.

ii. If they consider that it falls into categories 1(c), (d) or (e) or is so serious that Annex B procedure is clearly appropriate, they will discuss with the DPH* how best to proceed.

iii. Otherwise, the assessors will determine whom they wish to interview: through the DPH* they will provide the doctor(s) involved with the list of those to be interviewed and ask the doctor(s) whether he/she/they would like anybody to be interviewed by the assessors.

iv. The assessors will visit the District and undertake the necessary investigations. They will not be able to compel anybody – including the doctor(s) involved – to meet them, and refusal to do so should not frustrate the enquiry. Anybody who is interviewed should be informed that they will be expected to provide a written statement or to sign an agreed record of the interview, and that copies of these records and statements will be passed to the doctor(s) involved.

v. The doctor(s) involved will be invited to meet the assessors and may do so either alone or accompanied by a representative of their professional organisation or a friend.

vi. During the period of the investigation and preparation of the report, the DPH* will arrange for the provision of secretarial and administrative assistance for the assessors.

6. As far as possible, the investigation will be completed within three months of the assessors receiving the statement of the case from the DPH*. The assessors will prepare a report, which shall be divided into two parts. The first part shall set out the assessors' findings on all the relevant facts of the case, but contain no recommendations as to action. The second part shall contain a view as to whether and to what degree the doctor(s) involved is/are at fault and may also contain recommendations regarding, e g organisational matters within the Department or advice to be given to the consultant. In no circumstances should the assessors themselves be given disciplinary powers.

7. The assessors will send the doctor(s) involved and the DPH* a copy of the first part of their report and should allow a period of 14 days for the submission to them of the doctor(s) comments on its factual accuracy. The assessors will then submit the full report to the DPH*.

8. The DPH* will then decide what further action is necessary, and will inform the doctor(s) involved accordingly. If he decides that disciplinary action is necessary e g a warning is appropriate, the local procedures based on paragraphs 12(a) and 12(b) of the ACAS Code of Practice would be followed. If the doctor(s) involved wishes to appeal against any disciplinary action, the appeals procedure based on the principle of Section 40 of the GWC Handbook, suitably adapted for medical staff, should be used. It is suggested that the Appeal Committee might be made up of the Chairman of the Authority (or a deputy), a doctor who is a member of the Authority, and another doctor in the same or associated speciality as the doctor involved. The

* Reference to the DPH where asterisked includes a reference to CAMO in Wales and the equivalent medical officer in other employing authorities.

appointment of the latter would normally be made from outside the Region but, in appropriate cases, could be made from within the Region.

9. This procedure shall also apply to Directors of Public Health and other consultants in public health medicine. The references to 'JCC' shall be read as 'CMCC' and where the subject of the allegation is the Regional Director of Public Health, a reference to 'DPH' shall be to 'Regional General Manager' who will seek appropriate professional advice.

GEN (1992) 27

To: *General Managers, Health Boards*
General Manager, State Hospital
Chief Executives, NHS Trusts
} for action

General Manager,
Common Services Agency
General Manager,
Health Education Board for Scotland
Chief Executives Designate,
NHS Trusts
Chief Officers of Local Health Councils
Health Service Commissioner for Scotland
} for information

October 1992

NATIONAL HEALTH SERVICE IN SCOTLAND MANAGEMENT EXECUTIVE

HANDLING AND MONITORING OF COMPLAINTS

Summary

1. This Circular applies to NHS Trusts the terms of the Hospital Complaints Procedure Act 1985 Direction 1991 (the 1991 Direction); gives guidance on monitoring of complaints and requires Health Boards and NHS Trusts to provide statistical information on the handling of complaints.

Action

1. NHS Trusts should ensure that the complaints procedures operated by them comply with the terms of the 1991 Direction. This is required in terms of the Direction attached as Annex A.

2. The establishment of NHS Trusts and the introduction of the purchaser/provider split requires a different approach to the monitoring of complaints. Health Boards should review their procedures in the light of the guidance given in Annex B.

3. The Patient's Charter and the 1991 Direction emphasise the importance of monitoring complaints to see what lessons can be learnt. No information is at present collected centrally on this and Health Boards and NHS Trusts are now being asked to provide statistical information on the handling of complaints as set out in Annex B.

4. Health Boards and NHS Trusts should bring this Circular to the notice of those persons identified as nominated recipients for the handling of complaints, to Chief Administrative Medical Officers, Primary Care Administrators and any other persons who have a role in the investigation and monitoring of complaints.

ANNEX A

NATIONAL HEALTH SERVICE HOSPITAL COMPLAINTS PROCEDURE ACT 1985 DIRECTION 1992

The Secretary of State for Scotland, in exercise of the powers conferred on him by section 2(5) of the National Health Service (Scotland) Act 1978 as read with sections 1(1) and 1A of the Hospital Complaints Procedure Act 1985 hereby directs the

Appendix

Aberdeen Royal Hospitals National Health Service Trusts and the South Ayrshire Hospitals National Health Service Trust ('the Trusts') as follows:

1. The Trusts shall, *mutatis mutandis* comply with the Hospital Complaints Procedure Act 1985 Direction dated 19 September 1991.

2. This Direction comes into force on 9 October 1992.

From:

Director of Health Care
Management Executive Division 5
Room 55
St Andrew's House
Edinburgh EH1 3DE

ANNEX B

HANDLING AND MONITORING OF COMPLAINTS

Patient's Charter

1. The Patient's Charter encourages members of the public to say what they think about the services they receive from the National Health Service. Where complaints are received, they should be dealt with efficiently and sympathetically; but replying to and resolving complaints should not be considered the only objective. Complaints can serve to draw attention to shortcomings in practice or procedures. Those persons charged with investigating or monitoring complaints should use them to identify areas which may be in need of improvement.

2. This Circular deals with some aspects of handling of complaints, emphasises the operational benefits to be gained from monitoring of complaints and sets up a system to collect information on a Scotland basis.

Hospital Complaints Directions

3. The terms of the Hospital Complaints Procedure Act 1985 Direction 1991 (the 1991 Direction) applied only to Health Boards. The 1992 Direction attached as Annex A to this Circular applies the terms of the 1991 Direction to the 2 NHS Trusts which came into being on 1 April 1992. Directions similar to the 1992 Direction will be issued in subsequent years as necessary.

4. Most complaints will fall to be dealt with under the 1991 Direction (in respect of Health Boards) and the 1992 Direction (in respect of NHS Trusts). The Directions are, to all intent and purposes, the same and very little change should be required in the event of a Directly Managed Unit becoming an NHS Trust. Although the terms of the Hospital Complaints Procedure Act 1985 do not allow for the Directions to be applied to Community Health Services, the Secretary of State has asked Health Boards to apply similar procedures to such services. NHS Trusts are asked to adopt a similar approach.

5. Directly Managed Units and NHS Trusts, as providers, should ensure that complaints procedures are in operation in their hospitals in accordance with the terms of the appropriate Direction. This should include a review of the time taken to reply to complaints in relation to the target set in the letter accompanying the 1991 Direction i e 50 per cent of complaints being dealt with within 4 weeks. In some Units this target may be easily achieved and, if so, a more challenging target should be introduced.

6. Providers should produce a complaints summary and make use of it as a means of monitoring the services they provide. The subject matter of the complaint may point to areas where procedures should be examined or improvements to services are required. In some cases this may be obvious from the terms of an individual complaint but in other cases the possible need for changes or improvements may become apparent only when figures are analysed over a longer period and trends are established.

7. Health Boards as purchasers also have a role in monitoring complaints. In terms of the Hospital Complaints Procedure Act 1985 Direction 1991, they require to ensure that complaints procedures are in operation in hospitals under their control and that regular summaries of complaints dealt with are submitted to and considered by Health Board members. Health Boards should include in contracts with private hospitals a requirement that they operate procedures for handling complaints. For both NHS Trusts and private hospitals, Health Boards will wish to ensure that they receive summaries of complaints made by patients treated under their contracts with the Trusts or private hospitals. This feedback from providers will be one measure of the standard of care provided. Summaries of complaints may point to a need to review contracts with a particular provider or to review the overall provision made by the Board in respect of a particular service.

8. Letters of complaint received in the Management Executive are passed to the Chairman or General Manager of the appropriate Health Board for reply. Such letters should continue to receive replies from the Chairman or General Manager as appropriate. Complaints relating to NHS Trusts are similarly sent to the appropriate Trust for investigation and reply.

9. The Hospital Complaints Directions do not place any requirements on GP Fundholders as purchasers of services. However, GP Fundholders will wish to satisfy themselves that the providers of services operate a complaints procedure and inform them of complaints made by their patients. In the same way as for Health Boards this feedback from providers will be a measure of the standard of services provided. GP Fundholders can assume that Directly Managed Units and NHS Trusts will be operating a complaints procedure in accordance with the appropriate Direction but no such assumption can be made in respect of private hospitals. A specific reference to this would require to be included in contracts which GP Fundholders enter into with private hospitals and other private providers.

Clinical complaints procedures

10. The clinical complaints procedure is set out in a Memorandum enclosed with NHS Circular No 1981 (GEN) 43 issued on 30 November 1981. This procedure was drawn up on a UK basis and any changes to it have to be made in consultation with our colleagues in the Department of Health and with the medical profession. In the application of this Memorandum to NHS Trusts, the first stage of the process should be dealt with within the trust as is done at the present time in Directly Managed Units. We have considered what to do about the role of the Chief Administrative Medical Officer (CAMO) in relation to the second and third stages. Given the small number of cases which proceed to the second stage and the possibility of the whole procedure being looked at afresh it has been decided for the time being to maintain the status quo i e NHS Trusts should continue to use the CAMO in the second and third stages as at present.

Service Committee complaints procedures

11. These procedures have been extensively revised and new Regulations (The National Health Service (Service Committees and Tribunal) (Scotland) Regulations 1992) came into force in April of this year. Guidance on the operation of the

Regulations was given in separate guidance notes issued to Health Boards at that time. Boards are now expected to operate an informal complaints procedure to deal with minor grievances which may have arisen from misunderstandings and also issues which do not relate to terms of service.

12. Following comments received from the Scottish Committee of the Council of Tribunals at the consultation stage, it had been intended to amend the draft Service Committee Regulations to give the Council member the right to be present at the deliberative stage of hearings. Due to an oversight, this change was not made and the Regulations (paragraph 20 of Schedule 1) allow the member to be present only if the service committee and parties agree. The Regulations will be amended when an appropriate occasion arises. Meantime, Health Boards are asked to make their service committees aware of this proposed change and ask them to allow any Council member to remain for this stage of the proceedings if the parties are agreeable.

Role of the Mental Welfare Commission for Scotland

13. The Commission has a statutory duty generally to protect persons who may, by reason of mental disorder, be incapable of adequately protecting themselves or their interests. This duty extends to all people whether in hospital or in the community. The Commission is specifically required to enquire into any case where it appears that there may be ill-treatment, deficiency in care or treatment, improper detention of any person who may be suffering from mental disorder or where the property of any such person may be exposed to loss or damage because of his or her mental disorder.

Role of the Health Service Commissioner

14. If a complaint has been made to the Health Board or NHS Trust and the complainant is not satisifed with the reply recieved, he or she can complain to the Health Service Commissioner. The Commissioner cannot investigate certain types of complaints such as matters relating to commercial or contractual dealings, personnel matters, complaints dealt with under the service committee procedures and complaints concerned solely with the exercise of clinical judgement. However the Commissioner can decide to look into some matters which touch on these issues such as the handling of a complaint under the clinical complaints procedure and any action taken before a complaint is considered formally under the Service Committee Regulations.

15. The Commissioner publishes reports twice a year of a selection of those cases (in anonymised form) which have been investigated and reported on in a 6 month period. These are distributed to Health Boards and NHS Trusts along with shortened versions of the cases (epitomes) so that lessons learnt from these cases can be given a wider application across the whole of the National Health Service. Two of the recurring problems identified by the Health Service Commissioner are poor communications with patients and their relatives and poor record keeping. People who complain to the Commissioner are often as concerned about the way in which their complaint was dealt with as about the subject matter of the complaint itself.

16. The Commissioner has produced a leaflet entitled 'How the Health Service Ombudsman Can Help You' which can be obtained from his offices free of charge. The address is – The Health Service Commissioner for Scotland, Second Floor, 11 Melville Crescent, Edinburgh EH3 7LU. Tel: 031–225 7465. If a complaint has been dealt with under the Hospital Complaints Directions and the complainant is clearly dissatisfied with the response from the Health Board or Trust, his or her attention should be drawn to the service provided by the Health Service Commissioner for Scotland.

17. It is possible that a complaint may be made to the Commissioner relating to services provided by a hospital which has subsequently become part of an NHS Trust.

If a complaint relates to services before the NHS Trust was established the Health Board will be responsible for liaising with the Health Service Commissioner in any investigation. If the matters complained of span the period before and after the establishment of a Trust, the Trust should take the lead in liaising with the Commissioner, keeping the Health Board informed of the progress with the investigation and any action taken.

Role of local health councils

18. Local health councils have a direct role to play in advising members of the public on their concerns about the health service including the procedures which exist for investigating complaints. As part of this role they can assist complainants and accompany them or represent them at meetings or hearings. With this direct involvement in complaints and more generally as the statutory representatives of consumers, local health councils are well placed to offer views on the operation of complaints procedures and on the issues which are of most concern to the public. As a matter of routine, Health Boards and NHS Trusts should send copies of their regular monitoring reports to the local health council or councils concerned. However, it would not be appropriate to include information about the names of the complainants in the information sent to local health councils. Health Boards and NHS Trusts will also wish to consult local health councils on other issues and procedures relating to complaints.

Monitoring of complaints by the Management Executive

19. The Hospital Complaints Directions place an obligation on Health Boards and NHS Trusts to monitor the handling of complaints made in relation to hospitals for which they are responsible. Although not formally required to do so, most Health Boards will have had some system for monitoring complaints before the 1991 Direction came into force. No attempt has been made in the past to collect statistical data from Health Boards (with the exception of complaints dealt with under the clinical complaints procedure). At present, unlike the Management Executive in England, we are unable to say how many complaints there have been in Scotland and whether the numbers are increasing or decreasing – in actual terms or expressed in terms of the number of patients treated.

20. To enable us to compile such statistics and compare trends in different areas, Health Boards and NHS Trusts are now required to provide some details of the number and type of complaints which they have dealt with on a quarterly basis. For completeness, we are seeking information not only about complaints dealt with under the Hospital Complaints Directions but also those dealt with under the Clinical Complaints Procedures and the Service Committee Procedures. It is appreciated that complaints can often be made orally and can be satisfactorily resolved at the time. Although some record of oral complaints might be made, it would be impossible to produce accurate and consistent figures and the returns should relate only to complaints in writing.

21. It is recognised that statistics on complaints have to be treated with caution. An increase in the number of complaints does not necessarily mean that there has been a reduction in the standards of service. It may have been prompted by a greater awareness of complaints procedures among the public eg following a publicity campaign. It would be helpful if Health Boards and NHS Trusts would draw attention to any such factors which may have influenced the statistics.

22. Health Boards are required to publish details of handling of complaints in their annual reports. It is intended that the figures supplied by Health Boards to the Management Executive should also be published by the Information and Statistics Division and be included in the Management Information System.

23. Health Boards and NHS Trusts will be asked to make returns in the form sent out in Form 1 attached to this Annex which relates to complaints dealt with under the Hospital Complaints Directions and Form 2 which relates to complaints dealt with under the clinical complaints procedures. Health Boards will also be asked to complete Form 3 which relates to service committee complaints procedures. These returns will be called for on a quarterly basis by the Information and Statistics Division of the Common Services Agency.

24. It is appreciated that Health Boards and NHS Trusts will require time to adjust their statistical returns to correspond to the attached forms. It is intended, therefore, that the first returns to be made in terms of the Circular will be for the period January–March 1993. ISD will provide their own versions of the attached forms within the course of the next few weeks with further guidance on the completion of the forms. Health Boards and NHS Trusts are asked to nominate an officer who will be responsible for liaising with ISD on the submissions of the returns. The name of the officer should be notified to Mr Peter Knight in ISD as soon as possible.

FORM 1
Quarter Ending ______

WRITTEN COMPLAINTS REPLIED TO

______ Board/Trust

	COMMUNITY SERVICES	OUT-PATIENTS	DAY-PATIENTS	DAY CASES	IN-PATIENTS	TOTAL
ISSUES RAISED (Note 1) *Staff* Attitudes/ Behaviour } Medical Attitudes/ Behaviour } Nursing Other Shortage/Availability *Waiting Times for* Date for admission Date for appointment Results of tests *Delays* In Admission/Discharge Procedures At Out-patient and other Clinics *Environment/Domestic* Laundry Catering Cleanliness Privacy Other *Treatment* *Shortage of Beds* *Transport Arrangements* *Other* TOTAL NO OF COMPLAINTS DEALT WITH (Note 2) OF WHICH NO DEALT WITHIN 4 WEEKS AVERAGE TIME IN DAYS TAKEN TO DEAL WITH COMPLAINTS *OUTCOME* Complaint upheld Complaint upheld in part Complaint not upheld						

CHANGES TO PROCEDURE
(Please provide a note of any changes made to practices or procedures as a result of investigation and monitoring of complaints.)

GENERAL COMMENTS
(Eg any unusual circumstances which have affected numbers of complaints or response times.)

Notes
1. A complaint which raises more than one issue should be included under all appropriate headings.
2. The number here is the total number of complaints – not the total number of issues raised.

FORM 2

CLINICAL COMPLAINTS DEALT WITH

Quarter Ending ____________

Board/Trust ____________

STAGES	1	2	3
Number dealt with during period			
Average time (in days) taken to complete that stage			
Outcome			
Complaint resolved			
Complaint partially resolved			
Complaint not resolved			

Comments

Notes

Each stage of the process should be considered a separate entity. If a complaint is dealt with under stage 1 of the procedure it should be entered under '1' even though it is subsequently dealt with under stage 2. It should also be recorded under '2' when that stage has been completed which may be during the same quarter or a later one.

FORM 3

Quarter Ending ____________

SERVICE COMMITTEE COMPLAINTS DECIDED

____________ Board

	Medical	Dental	Optical	Pharmaceutical	Joint	Total
ISSUES RAISED (Note 1)						
Inadequate examination						
Incorrect diagnosis						
Delay in referral to hospital						
Attitude/behaviour of Practitioner						
Inadequate treatment (dental)						
Defective treatment (dental)						
Denture not acceptable (dental)						
Failed to make home visit						
Wrong drug dispensed						
Incorrect quantity or strength of drug dispensed						
Wrong prescription issued (optical)						
TOTAL NUMBER OF DECISIONS ISSUED (Note 2)						
AVERAGE TIME (IN DAYS) TAKEN TO DEAL WITH COMPLAINT						
Outcome						
Practitioner in breach (in whole or in part)						
Practitioner not in breach						
NUMBER OF CASES WHERE LATE COMPLAINTS PROCEDURE WAS FOLLOWED						
NUMBER OF CASES WHERE HEARING WAS HELD						
NUMBER OF CASES CONSIDERED UNDER INFORMAL PROCEDURE						

Comments

Notes
1. A complaint which raises more than one issue should be included under all appropriate headings.
2. The number here is the number of decisions issued – not the number of issues raised.

Appendix

HSG (92) 32

To: Regional Health Authorities *District Health Authorities* *Special Health Authorities for the London Postgraduate Teaching Hospitals* *Special Hospitals Service Authority* *Family Health Services Authorities* *NHS Trusts*	for action
Community Health Councils	for information

July 1992

NHS MANAGEMENT EXECUTIVE

PATIENT CONSENT TO EXAMINATION OR TREATMENT

Summary

The handbook 'A guide to consent for examination or treatment' which accompanied HC (90) 22 introduced new model forms for obtaining a patient's written consent to examination or treatment.

Following discussion with representatives of the medical profession, the Department has revised the model consent forms at Appendix A and Appendix B of the handbook. This should remove some of the misunderstandings that have arisen since HC (90) 22 was introduced.

Action

NHS Authorities should:

- bring this circular and its enclosures to the attention of all their health professionals;
- introduce revised documentation based on the revised model consent forms enclosed.

Cancellation of circulars

Appendices 1 and 2 of the handbook 'A Guide to Consent for Examination or Treatment' which accompanied HC (90) 22 are cancelled.

ANNEX A(1)

CONSENT FORM

For medical or dental investigation, treatment or operation

Health Authority	Patient's Surname ....
Hospital	Other Names ....
Unit Number	Date of Birth ....
	Sex: *(please tick)* Male ___ Female ___

Doctors or dentists *(This part to be completed by doctor or dentist.)*

Type of operation, investigation or treatment for which written evidence of consent is considered appropriate

I confirm that I have explained the operation, investigation or treatment, and such appropriate options as are available and the type of anaesthetic, if any (general/local/sedation) proposed, to the patient in terms which in my judgement are suited to the understanding of the patient and/or to one of the parents or guardians of the patient.

Signature .... Date ..../..../....

Name of doctor or dentist ....

Patient/parent/guardian

1. Please read this form and the notes overleaf very carefully.
2. If there is anything that you don't understand about the explanation, or if you want more information, you should ask the doctor or dentist.
3. Please check that all the information on the form is correct. If it is, and you understand the explanation, then sign the form.

I am the patient/parent/guardian *(delete as necessary)*

I agree
- to what is proposed which has been explained to me by the doctor/dentist named on this form.
- to the use of the type of anaesthetic that I have been told about.

I understand
- that the procedure may not be done by the doctor/dentist who has been treating me so far.
- that any procedure in addition to the investigation or treatment described on this form will only be carried out if it is necessary and in my best interests and can be justified for medical reasons.

I have told
- the doctor or dentist about the procedures listed below I would *not* wish to be carried out without my having the opportunity to consider them first.

....

....

....

Signature ....

Name ....

Address ....

(if not the patient) ....

....

Notes to:

Doctors, dentists

A patient has a legal right to grant or withhold consent prior to examination or treatment. Patients should be given sufficient information, in a way they can understand, about the proposed treatment and the possible alternatives. Patients must be allowed to decide whether they will agree to the treatment and they may refuse or withdraw consent to treatment at any time. The patient's consent to treatment should be recorded on this form (further guidance is given in HC (90) 22: A Guide to Consent for Examination or Treatment).

Patients

- The doctor or dentist is here to help you. He or she will explain the proposed treatment and what the alternatives are. You can ask any questions and seek further information. You can refuse the treatment.
- You may ask for a relative, or friend, or a nurse to be present.
- Training doctors and dentists and other health professionals is essential to the continuation of the health service and improving the quality of care. Your treatment may provide an important opportunity for such training, where necessary under the careful supervision of a senior doctor or dentist.
- You may, however, decline to be involved in the formal training of medical, dental and other students without this adversely affecting your care and treatment.

ANNEX A(2)

CONSENT FORM

For sterilisation or vasectomy

Health Authority .... Patient's Surname ....

Hospital .... Other Names ....

Unit Number .... Date of Birth ....

Sex: *(please tick)* Male ___ Female ___

Doctors *(This part to be completed by doctor.)*

Type of operation: sterilisation or vasectomy

Complete this part of the form

I confirm that I have explained the procedure and any anaesthetic (general/local) required, to the patient in terms which in my judgement are suited to his/her understanding.

Signature .... Date ..../..../....

Name of doctor ....

Patient

1. Please read this form very carefully.
2. If there is anything that you don't understand about the explanation, or if you want more information, you should ask the doctor.
3. Please check that all the information on the form is correct. If it is, and you understand the explanation, then sign the form.

I am the patient

I agree
- to have this operation, which has been explained to me by the doctor named on this form.
- to have the type of anaesthetic that I have been told about.

I understand
- that the operation may not be done by the doctor who has been treating me.
- that the aim of the operation is to stop me having any children and it might not be possible to reverse the effects of the operation.
- that sterilisation/vasectomy can sometimes fail, and that there is a very small chance that I may become fertile again after some time.
- that any procedure in addition to the investigation or treatment described on this form will only be carried out if it is necessary and in my best interests and can be justified for medical reasons.

I have told
- the doctor about the procedures listed below I would *not* wish to be carried out straightaway without my having the opportunity to consider them first.

....

....

....

For vasectomy
I understand
- that I may remain fertile or become fertile again after some time.
- that I will have to use some other contraceptive method until 2 tests in a row show that I am not producing sperm, if I do not want to father any children.

Signature ....

Notes to:

Doctors

A patient has a legal right to grant or withhold consent prior to examination or treatment. Patients should be given sufficient information, in a way they can understand, about the proposed treatment and the possible alternatives. Patients must be allowed to decide whether they will agree to the treatment and they may refuse or withdraw consent to treatment at any time. The patient's consent to treatment should be recorded on this form (further guidance is given in HC (90) 22: A Guide to Consent for Examination or Treatment).

Patients

- The doctor is here to help you. He or she will explain the proposed procedure, which you are entitled to refuse. You can ask any questions and seek further information.
- You may ask for a relative, or friend, or a nurse to be present.
- Training doctors and other health professionals is essential to the continuation of the health service and improving the quality of care. Your treatment may provide an important opportunity for such training, where necessary under the careful supervision of a senior doctor.
- You may, however, decline to be involved in the formal training of medical and other students without this adversely affecting your care and treatment.

ANNEX A(3)

CONSENT FORM

For treatment by a health professional other than doctors or dentists

Health Authority .... Patient's Surname ....

Hospital .... Other Names ....

Unit Number .... Date of Birth ....

Sex: *(please tick)* Male ___ Female ___

Health professional *(This part to be completed by health professional.)*

Type of treatment proposed for which written evidence of consent is considered appropriate

Complete this part of the form

I confirm that I have explained the treatment proposed and such appropriate options as are available to the patient in terms which in my judgement are suited to the understanding of the patient and/or to one of the parents or guardians of the patient.

Signature .... Date . . . ./. . . ./. . . .

Name of health professional ....

Job title of health professional ....

Patient/parent/guardian

1. Please read this form and the notes overleaf very carefully.
2. If there is anything that you don't understand about the explanation, or if you want more information, you should ask the health professional who has explained the treatment proposed.
3. Please check that all the information on the form is correct. If it is, and you understand the treatment proposed, then sign the form.

I am the patient/parent/guardian *(delete as necessary)*

I agree
- to what is proposed which has been explained to me by the health professional named on this form.

Signature ....

Name ....

Address ....

(if not the patient) ....

....

Notes to:

Health professionals, other than doctors or dentists

A patient has a legal right to grant or withhold consent prior to examination or treatment. Patients should be given sufficient information, in a way they can understand, about the proposed treatment and the possible alternatives. Patients must be allowed to decide whether they will agree to the treatment and they may refuse or withdraw consent to treatment at any time. The patient's consent to treatment should be recorded on this form (further guidance is given in HC (90) 22: A Guide to Consent for Examination or Treatment).

Patients

- The health professional named on this form is here to help you. He or she will explain the proposed treatment and what the alternatives are. You can ask any questions and seek further information. You can refuse the treatment.
- You may ask for a relative, or friend, or another member of staff to be present.
- Training doctors, and dentists and other health professionals is essential to the continuation of the health service and improving the quality of care. Your treatment may provide an important opportunity for such training, where necessary under the careful supervision of a fully qualified health professional.
- You may however decline to be involved in the formal training of medical, dental and other students without this adversely affecting your care and treatment.

ANNEX B

Medical or dental treatment of a patient who is unable to consent because of mental disorder

Health Authority .... Patient's Surname ....

Hospital .... Other Names ....

Unit Number .... Date of Birth ....

Sex: *(please tick)* Male ___ Female ___

Note:

It is the personal responsibility of any doctor or dentist proposing to treat a patient to determine whether the patient has capacity to give a valid consent.

It is good practice to consult relatives and others who are concerned with the care of the patient. Sometimes consultation with a specialist or specialists will be required.

The form should be signed by the doctor or dentist who carries out the treatment.

Doctors/dentists

Describe investigation, operation or treatment proposed.

(Complete this part of the form)

In my opinion .... is not capable of giving consent to treatment. In my opinion the treatment proposed is in his/her best interests and should be given.

The patient's next of kin have/have not been so informed. *(delete as necessary)*

Date: ....

Signature: ....

Name of doctor or dentist who is providing treatment:

....

Index

References are to paragraph numbers. The precedents at the end of Chapters 8 and 9 are indicated by the number of the last paragraph, followed by Pr. for precedent, e.g. 8.100.Pr.B or 9.101.Pr.2.

The glossaries of common hieroglyphs and abbreviations (9.101.Gloss.) occur in Chapter 9 between the precedents and the figures, starting on page 206.

The appendices at the end of Chapter 18 are indicated by the number of the last paragraph, followed by App. for appendix, e.g. 18.173.App.1

Index